Human Resource Management Highlights...

ETHICAL PERSPECTIVES

- How Organizations Encourage Ethical Behavior (Ch. 1)
- Privacy and Accuracy of Computerized Employee Records (Ch. 3)
- Anti-Nepotism Rules—Fair or Unfair? (Ch. 5)
- Ethics in Recruiting and Job Search (Ch. 6)
- Developing a Procedurally Just Performance Appraisal Process (Ch. 10)
- Reward Systems and Inappropriate Behavior (Ch. 12)
- Universal Human Rights in Employment (Ch. 15)
- Permanent Replacement of Strikers (Ch. 15)
- Firing for Off-Duty Behavior—Legal? Ethical? (Ch. 16)
- Ethical Relativity Versus Ethical Absolutism: HR Decision Making in Overseas Operations (Ch. 17)

INTERNATIONAL PERSPECTIVES

- Manufacturing Overseas (Ch. 3)
- Sexual Harassment—Or Is It? (Ch. 5)
- Job Ads—A Window on the National Soul (Ch. 6)
- Selection Techniques Around the World (Ch. 8)
- Intercultural Issues in Training (Ch. 9)
- Performance Appraisal and Performance-Based Rewards in China (Ch. 10)
- International Compensation Comparisons (Ch. 11)
- International Benefits: Comparisons and Complications (Ch. 13)
- Decent Work—Safe Work: The International Picture (Ch. 14)

FLEXIBILITY IN THE WORKPLACE

- Family Friendly Policies Attract Applicants (Ch. 6)
- Flexibility and Industrial Relations (Ch. 15)
- Are You Flexible Enough for Today's Employees? (Ch. 16)

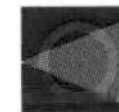

DIFFERENT POINT OF VIEW

- Blow the Sucker Up (Ch. 1)
- Pitfalls on the Road to Measurement (Ch. 2)
- Do We Really Need Job Descriptions, or Even Jobs? (Ch. 4)
- There's More to Utility Than Meets the Eye (Ch. 7)
- Fixing Weaknesses of Building Strengths? (Ch. 9)
- Does the Downside of Performance Appraisal Outweigh the Benefits? (Ch. 10)
- Some Myths About Pay (Ch. 11)
- Do Rewards Motivate Performance? (Ch. 12)

PARTNERSHIPS FOR STRATEGIC SUCCESS

- Building New HR Leaders: The Case of United Technologies (Ch. 2)
- Strategic Recruitment in the Bookstore Industry (Ch. 6)
- Improving the Selection of Prison Correction Officer Trainees in Pennsylvania (Ch. 7)
- The Office of Personnel Management and the U.S. Border Patrol (Ch. 8)
- The Learning Revolution at Rockwell Collins (Ch. 9)
- Benefits Match the Culture at Patagonia (Ch. 13)
- Safety at NexTech is *SHARP* (Ch. 14)

Human Resource Management

Sixth Edition

Cynthia D. Fisher
Bond University

Lyle F. Schoenfeldt
Appalachian State University

James B. Shaw
Bond University

Houghton Mifflin Company
Boston New York

Publisher: Charles Hartford
Editor in Chief: George T. Hoffman
Senior Sponsoring Editor: Lisé Johnson
Associate Development Editor: Suzanna Smith
Editorial Assistant: Amy Galvin
Project Editor: Kerry Doyle
Executive Marketing Manager: Steven Mikels
Marketing Associate: Lisa Boden

Cover image: © Getty Images

Printed in the U.S.A.

Library of Congress Control Number: 2005925781

ISBN: 0-618-527869

23456789-DOW-09 08 07 06 05

Brief Contents

Contents

PART 4 Building and Motivating Performance 373

14 *Safety and Health: A Proactive Approach* 605

15 *Labor Relations and Collective Bargaining* 648

16 *Employment Transitions* *686*

PART 6 Multinational Human Resource Management 731

17 *Managing Human Resources in Multinational Organizations* *732*

Preface

The Sixth Edition of *Human Resource Management* offers students a comprehensive, current, and research-based introduction to the human resource management function. The book is designed for a survey course in human resource management at the junior, senior, or graduate level, but it also serves as a useful reference for practicing managers and HR professionals in search of sound advice on human resource issues. Drawing from more than eighty years of combined teaching experience and the results of the most recent literature, we have produced a text that is logically organized, clearly presented, fully substantive, and interesting.

Important Themes

Several themes have guided our discussion of the subject matter. The first theme is strategic human resource management. Chapter 2 is devoted entirely to strategic issues and their impact on the choices rooted in human resource practices. Subsequent chapters include further discussion of how the organization's strategy should affect choices with respect to the activities described in that chapter. A new boxed feature, *Partnerships for Strategic Success*, gives detailed examples of how specific companies are using state-of-the-art practices to maximize performance.

The second theme is the international dimension of human resource management. Human resource management in multinational organizations is introduced in the first chapter and discussed extensively in Chapter 17, which is devoted entirely to multinational human resource management. Further, nine *International Perspective* boxes provide comparative information on how other nations and cultures deal with human resource management issues. The authors are well qualified to discuss international HRM, as all three have led study-abroad tours related to human resource management. In addition, Drs. Fisher and Shaw have held teaching posts in Singapore and Australia, as well as in the United States.

The third theme focuses on the human resource manager's responsibilities for facilitating ethical behavior among employees and for dealing ethically with employees. This theme is introduced in the first chapter and reinforced throughout the book via ten *Ethical Perspective* boxes. Topics include employee rights, procedural and distributive justice in reward systems, ethics in recruiting, privacy, and other ethical dilemmas confronting practitioners.

A fourth theme is utility or cost-benefit analysis. Human resource programs can produce quantifiable returns for organizations, but the results of programs are seldom evaluated carefully in monetary terms. Utility is discussed in connection with recruiting, selection, training, performance appraisal, and employee-assistance programs.

A new theme, *flexibility in the workplace*, is incorporated in three new boxes which highlight the increasing extent to which employers are customizing relationships with employees and working to accommodate off-the-job responsibilities.

A final theme is represented in the *Point of View* boxes that appear throughout the text. These reflect our opinion that the world is a complex place; there are a variety of potentially useful ways to look at any given problem. These boxes point out inherent contradictions or alternative or potentially controversial positions on aspects of human resource management. As the text is designed for more advanced students, we think there is value in presenting alternative points of view that may start students questioning various messages they receive.

Content and Organization

The book is organized into six parts and seventeen chapters that logically follow the progression of individuals into, through, and out of the organization.

The first part, Overview and Introduction, defines human resource management and outlines the plan of the book. Here we introduce the themes described above, consider trends and challenges that have been affecting the practice of human resource management, and explore career tracks and preparation for the human resource profession.

The second part, Planning for Organizations, Jobs, and People, is comprised of three chapters. Chapter 2, in addition to introducing strategic issues in human resource management, is intended to capture the interest of the general business student by demonstrating that appropriate human resource management practices are critical for successful strategy implementation. It also shows that the human resource manager is a vital part of any management team. Some instructors may prefer to use Chapter 2 as a final capstone chapter, putting together what students have learned throughout the course. We have placed this chapter early in the book because it sets the stage for all the material to come. It clearly demonstrates how effective management of the human resource function can make a significant difference to the success of the organization as a whole.

Chapter 3 discusses forecasting the demand for and the supply of human resources, planning programs to deal with anticipated shortfalls or surpluses, and planning managerial succession. The increasing level of diversity in the American workforce is also described. Chapter 4 contains a thorough discussion of job analysis techniques and the practical and legal issues involved in planning and conducting job analysis projects. Strategic considerations in job analysis are also presented.

The third part of the book, Acquiring Human Resources, is devoted to organizational entry. It begins with Chapter 5, which provides a thorough presentation of the latest Equal Employment Opportunity legislation, court decisions, and enforcement procedures. Chapter 6 presents internal and external recruitment techniques, describes how to plan and evaluate recruiting efforts, and cites the latest research on how job applicants respond to recruiters and make decisions about job offers. Chapter 7 discusses procedures for validating selection devices. Decision-making in selection and evaluating the utility of a selection system round out the chapter.

Chapter 8 begins with a discussion of the relationship of strategy to staffing, then describes a number of specific selection tools. The interview is thoroughly discussed, including particularly effective techniques of behavior description and situational interviewing. A number of methods for managerial selection are also described, and the chapter closes with a discussion of criteria that must be considered in choosing selection devices.

The fourth part of this text, Building and Motivating Performance, consists of four chapters. Chapter 9 provides a complete discussion of human resource development, from needs assessment through training design through evaluation. It includes recent research on trainee motivation and adult learning, provides extensive information on transfer of training, explores high-tech training delivery, and discusses the utility of training programs. Chapter 10, Performance Assessment and Management, provides in-depth coverage of performance appraisal methods, issues, and uses. Chapter 11 outlines the basics of developing a compensation system, beginning with the concepts of internal and external equity and motivation. The chapter goes on to describe job evaluation methods, wage surveys, creating wage grades, the trend toward broadbanding, and the laws that regulate compensation. Chapter 12 explores individual and group pay-for-performance systems and includes expanded coverage of executive compensation. It also discusses strategic issues and new variable pay approaches.

The fifth part, Maintaining Human Resources, includes four chapters. Chapter 13 is devoted entirely to a consideration of employee benefits and related issues. Chapter 14 addresses safety and health including occupational safety and health laws, standards, and enforcement procedures. Chapter 15 addresses the role of unions and the human resource manager's activities in dealing with organized employees. It also clearly describes the legal environment of labor relations, the process of certification, preparation for and the conduct of collective bargaining, strikes and other dispute resolution procedures, and the grievance process. A substantial new case has been added to the end of this chapter. Chapter 16 is now called Employment Transitions. This chapter begins by considering career paths and career planning within an organization, culminating in a decision to retire. The chapter then turns to the issue of employee turnover. An extensive section considers the causes and costs and benefits of voluntary employee turnover. Retention management programs are discussed, including consideration of exit interviewing and knowledge retention mechanisms. We then turn to involuntary turnover, including issues such as employment-at-will, discipline systems, discharge for cause, and managing layoffs effectively.

The sixth part of this textbook, Multinational Human Resource Management, raises issues particular to multinational corporations. A good portion of Chapter 17 focuses on the special problems of managing expatriate employees—their selection, training, compensation, and repatriation. The remainder of the chapter considers culture and related issues in selecting, appraising, and compensating host-country nationals when conducting business abroad.

New in the Sixth Edition

- All chapters have been thoroughly updated with the most recent developments in law, practice, and research.
- A previous single chapter on incentives and benefits has been split into two chapters to provide more information on these two distinct topics.
- A chapter on human resource approaches to improving competitiveness that appeared in previous editions has been dropped.
- A new boxed feature, Partnerships for Strategic Success, highlights how real organizations adopt and implement innovative practices consistent with their strategy.
- Three Flexibility in the Workplace boxes point to the changing relationship between employer and employee.

- There are several new chapter-opening HR Perspectives and a number of new end-of-chapter exercises and cases.

Pedagogical Features

A number of pedagogical features enhance the learning experience:

- The chapter outline introduces students to text material and provides an overview of important concepts and topics.
- Each chapter opens with an HR Challenge vignette. These brief case scenarios pose a realistic question or problem related to chapter content and serve to stimulate student interest.
- Numerous figures and tables highlight important points and expand upon text discussion to aid in the understanding of key concepts.
- A complete chapter summary reviews the major topics discussed.
- Questions for Discussion encourage recollection of information as well as the application of concepts to real-world situations and problems.
- End-of-chapter cases and exercises help students develop skills and integrate human resource management concepts with their own knowledge and work experience. Internet exercises appear in most chapters.
- A Manager's Vocabulary list appears at the end of each text chapter to encourage students to check their mastery of terms presented in the chapter.
- An extensive subject and author index facilitates many uses of the book.

Support Materials

For the Students: A web site for students provides study aids such as chapter learning objectives and chapter outlines. The ACE self-assessment quizzes have been completely updated to reflect the changes throughout the text. All these resources encourage students to take a hands-on approach to solving HR problems and making HR decisions.

For the Instructors: The teaching package for the Sixth Edition includes the electronic *Instructor's Resource Manual with Test Bank* available on the instructor's website, a computerized test bank, PowerPoint slides, and an updated video program with the video guide.

- The *Instructor's Resource Manual with Test Questions* contains instructional resources as well as a complete test bank of questions. For each chapter in the textbook, the resource manual includes a chapter synopsis, chapter objectives, an overview of the HR Challenge, an extensive lecture outline, suggested answers to the end-of-chapter discussion questions, teaching notes for the end-of-chapter cases and exercises, summaries of the boxed text features, additional lecture topics, sources for further reading, and suggested research paper topics. For users of previous editions, the *Instructor's Resource Manual* also includes a detailed transition guide describing changes in the text.
- *Test Bank and Computerized Test Bank* includes a pre-lecture quiz as well as true/false, multiple choice, and essay questions for each chapter. An electronic version of the printed *Test Bank* allows instructors to edit or add questions, select questions, or generate randomly selected tests. The program also includes an Online Testing System, which allows instructors to administer

tests via a network system, modem, or personal computer, and a grading function that lets instructors set up a new class, record grades from tests or assignments, and analyze grades to produce class and individual statistics.

- *Videos.* A video package highlights real companies and key themes in human resources management. It includes a video guide that summarizes the segments and proposes questions to encourage class discussion.
- The *PowerPoint program* for this edition has been professionally prepared for instructors who wish to use computer projection and/or customize our slides to fit their own lectures.
- *Instructor web site.* This password-protected site features the electronic Instructor's Manual and lecture outlines that can be downloaded for customization. PowerPoint slides are available for previewing and downloading.

Acknowledgments

We would like to thank everyone who adopted the first five editions of this text, and we trust that you will find this sixth edition equally satisfying.

A number of individuals provided reviews and suggestions that helped in improving this text. We appreciate their time and effort.

Yohannan Abraham
Southwest Missouri State University

Peggy Anderson
University of Wisconsin—Whitewater

Jeff Bailey
University of Idaho

Susan Burroughs
Washington State University—Vancouver

Alan Cabelly
Portland State University

Sheri Caldwell
University of Toledo

Anne C. Cowden
California State University—Sacramento

Joseph Culver
University of Texas—Austin

Thomas Daymont
Temple University

Cynthia Devers
Texas A&M University

Mildred Doering
Syracuse University

James Dulebohn
Michigan State University

Walter O. Einstein
Southeastern Massachusetts University

David M. Hegedus
University of Wisconsin—Oshkosh

Brenda Johnson
St. Mary's University of Minnesota

Bruce H. Johnson
Gustavus Adolphus College

Brian Klaas
University of South Carolina

Michael Koshuta
Purdue University, North Central

Dianne R. Layden
University of Redlands

Nancy McDaniel
Hocking College

Jeff Mello
Golden Gate University

Marsha P. Miceli
Ohio State University

Elaine King Miller
Colorado State University

R. LaVelle Mills
Tarleton State University

Karen Minchella
Baker College

Jonathan S. Monat
California State University—Long Beach

William M. Moore
Drake University

Earl C. Nance
Brewton-Parker College, emeritus

Robert Paul
Kansas State University

Gary C. Raffaele
University of Texas—San Antonio

Hyman Sardy
Brooklyn College

Dale Scharinger
University of Wisconsin—Whitewater

Joseph G. Smith
Hawaii Pacific University

Charles N. Toftoy
George Washington University

Thomas R. Tudor
University of Arkansas—Little Rock

Steve Werner
University of Houston

Paul L. Wilkens
Florida State University

Laura Wolfe
Louisiana State University

Arthur Yeung
University of Michigan
Brewton Parker College

We would also like to thank the following individuals for special contributions.

Hugh Hindman of the Appalachian State University, for updating the Labor Relations chapter.

Hugh's student, Josh Livesey, for a draft of the new *Flexibility in the Workplace* box in chapter 15.

Bob Goddard of Appalachian State University for updating the *Instructor's Resource Manual* and the *Test Bank.*

Peter Howes of HRM Consulting Ltd., Brisbane, for permission to modify and reprint the Jumbuck Enterprises case at the end of Chapter 2.

Lyle would like to thank his family—Wanda, Beth, Todd, and Sarah—for their special support during the writing of this book.

All of the authors express their appreciation to Maggie Kearney of Houghton Mifflin Company for her support during this revision.

PART 1

Overview and Introduction

CHAPTER 1

An Introduction to Human Resource Management

- The Critical Importance of Human Resources in the Twenty-First Century
- Human Resource Management: Definition and Functions
- Recurring Themes in Human Resource Management
- Current and Future Challenges to Human Resource Management
- Jobs and Careers in Human Resource Management

HR Challenge

How does a company become top ranked on Fortune *magazine's list of the "100 Best Companies to Work For?"[1] How does a company become one of the "100 Best Companies to Work For" in each of the seven years of the survey, 1998 to 2004? The best company for 2004 and a top 100 company in each year of the survey is not a glitzy high-tech company but J. M. Smucker, the 108-year-old company known for its jellies and preserves. According to the co-CEOs of this family-controlled business, Tim and Richard Smucker, the secret recipe is a culture and management style as straightforward and likable as strawberry jam.[2]*

Many of the 100 Best Companies have nice perks and killer benefits: Such things as on-site day care, concierge services, fully paid sabbaticals. The approximately 3,000 Smucker employees don't get unusual perks but a gimmick-free approach indicative of a simpler time. The Smucker brothers adhere to an extremely simple code set forth by their father, Paul Smucker, "Listen with your full attention, look for the good in others, have a sense of humor, and say thank you for a job well done."[3] The result, according to co-CEO Richard Smucker, "Employees are really energized."[4]

The "thanks" part of the equation is evidenced by celebratory barbecues after hitting new records, lunches and gift certificates for teams, and annual commemorative events. All of this is part of the culture of Smuckers, a culture that has been tested as it absorbed the acquisitions of Jif peanut butter and Crisco shortening brands from Procter & Gamble.[5]

At the same time, the acquisition nearly doubled the company's revenues and tripled profits in fiscal 2003. In fact, the results of that acquisition were so positive that Smuckers will try it again with the $500 million *purchase of Pillsbury and Hungry Jack brands from International Multifoods.[6] Companies on the 100 Best list tend to outperform companies in general as well as industry competitors.[7]*

Does it surprise you that J. M. Smuckers' straightforward approach to human resource practices are credited with the major role in its success? Did you expect that a company like J. M. Smucker would be one of just twenty-four companies to be one of the 100 Best Companies to Work For in each of the seven years of the survey? How can other organizations be human resource champions and join J. M. Smuckers as among America's Best Companies to Work For?

THE CRITICAL IMPORTANCE OF HUMAN RESOURCES IN THE TWENTY-FIRST CENTURY

These are exciting times for organizations and, as a result, for human resource (HR) professionals. Hardly a day goes by when organizational and HR issues are not in the news. A small sampling of recent issues includes the following:

- Loss of manufacturing, service, and technical jobs, either through global outsourcing,[8] productivity gains,[9] or shifts in the economy[10]
- Organizational restructuring and redirection[11]
- Ethics of corporate leaders and corporate employees[12]
- Pay, including that of workers and executives[13]
- Benefits, particularly Social Security[14] and health care[15]
- Corporate mergers[16]

All of this suggests that world-class HR is both interesting and complex. One purpose of this text is to convey those aspects of HR that make a difference to the success of organizations.

The HR goal is to support organizations in gaining a competitive advantage. Organizations can be thought of as entities that require a number of things to be competitive:

1. Physical resources, including the manufacturing facilities and equipment to produce a product or service
2. Financial resources, including equity, leverage (debt), and retained earnings
3. Marketing capability to connect whatever products or services are created with customers
4. Human resources, including the experience, skills, knowledge, judgment, and creativity belonging to the organization, along with the means of organizing, structuring, and rewarding these capabilities

These are all important to organizational effectiveness, but the factor most likely to provide potential competitive advantage is human resources and how these resources are managed. Production technology, financing, and customer connections (marketing) can all be copied. The basics of managing people can also be copied, but the most effective organizations find unique ways to attract, retain, and motivate employees—a strategy that is more difficult to imitate.[17]

In *The Human Equation: Building Profits by Putting People First,* Jeffrey Pfeffer outlined his blueprint for organizational success (profitability).[18] Front and center is Pfeffer's belief that organizational success is based not on conventional factors such as large size, a unique image, the right market niche, dominant market share, being in the right industry (e.g., high tech), and so forth, but on how employees are treated. Pfeffer believes that these seven human resource practices, taken together, lead to organizational success, profitability, and survival:[19]

- Employment security as a way of building commitment to employees[20]
- Selective hiring to recruit the right people for the organization
- Self-managed teams and decentralization as basic elements of organizational design
- Higher compensation contingent on organizational performance
- Extensive training so employees can use their skills and initiative to identify and resolve problems
- Reduced distinctions based on status
- Extensive sharing of information

Consider Southwest Airlines, one of many companies committed to the practices described by Pfeffer. Most think of Southwest Airlines as a small, low-fare carrier. However, according to Herb Kelleher, Southwest's CEO (now retired), "Southwest has been kind of like a little puppy that gets fat off the table scraps of other airlines."[21] Today Southwest, the often overlooked airline, rules the skies in many respects:

- Southwest is the nation's most valuable airline, with a market capitalization of $11.7 billion—more than American, United, and Delta combined.
- In 2003 Southwest earned $442 million, more than all the other U.S. airlines combined.
- Southwest has the lowest expenses in the industry, 7.6 cents cost per available seat mile (CASM) versus between 9 cents and 13 cents for the big carriers.
- While the rest of the industry laid off thousands of people and lost more than $22 billion in the months and years following 9/11, Southwest did not furlough a single employee and remained in the black every quarter.
- Southwest is the most profitable airline in the industry, showing annual profits in each of the thirty-one years since its inception in 1971.
- Southwest has been ranked in the top ten of *Fortune's* Most Admired Companies in each of the six years of such ratings—a distinction shared with only three other companies (Berkshire Hathaway, General Electric, and Microsoft).[22]

Southwest's success has nothing to do with competitive advantage in the traditional sense. It has the same access to capital, the same planes (Boeing 737s), and the same technology as all other airlines. It sells what is essentially a commodity product—low-cost, low-frills airline service at prices its competitors have difficulty matching. Most of Southwest's success comes from its very productive, very motivated work force. For example, in its thirty years of operation, Southwest has never laid off an employee.[23] Southwest is extremely selective in who it hires. They receive 140,000 applications a year for 4,000 to 5,000 positions.[24]

Smuckers and Southwest Airlines provide vivid examples of the role that people—human resources—play in determining the competitiveness and effectiveness of organizations in meeting the challenges of the twenty-first century. The success of both organizations comes from managing people effectively, a combination of a number of important but less visible aspects of operations. From these examples it is clear that many of the changes and challenges facing organizations have to do with their employees. In organizations as diverse as *Fortune* 500 corporations, nonprofit universities, NFL football teams, and local restaurants, CEOs are seeing the results of employee involvement, of having the right people to do the job, and of getting managers to care about their people. The successful organizations of the recent past have adopted a professional approach to human resource management that will ensure continued success in the twenty first century.

What are the HR challenges facing organizations? The five HR challenges shown in Table 1.1 resulted from a survey of more than 7,000 individuals from 241 diverse, global companies representing a variety of industries.[25] Data were

TABLE 1.1

Top Challenges for Organizations and the HR Profession

Challenge	Notable Characteristics
HR professionals as strategic business partners	Identify the culture required to make the business strategy a reality. Make change happen fast. Identify problems central to business strategy and forecasting potential obstacles to success. Identify critical business information and move it across the organization so people can act.
Personal credibility	Establish effective relationships with key people inside and outside the organization. Establish a reliable track record for delivery of results.
HR delivery	HR functional competencies, including: • Staffing • Development • Organizational structure • HR measurement • Legal compliance • Performance management
Business knowledge	Understand the organization and the industry. Use business and industry knowledge to drive strategy.
HR technology	Leverage technology in the delivery of HR services to employees. Use technology to track applicants' and employees' skills and experiences. Allow technology to handle administrative aspects of HR so that HR professionals can devote time to other aspects of their organizational role.

Sources: Adapted from "More on What CEOs Want from HR," *HRFocus,* Vol. 80 (4), 2003, pp. 5–6; "New Study Identifies Key Competencies Necessary for HR," *Society for Human Resource Management,* June 22, 2003. (Available at: http://www.shrm.org/press_published/1CMS_004834.asp#P28_180)

gathered from three sources: HR professionals evaluating themselves, HR colleagues evaluating the HR professional participating in the study, and line executives. Survey participants came up with the five challenges shown in Table 1.1. The challenges seen by human resource professionals and line managers include acting strategically, personal credibility, delivery of HR capabilities, business knowledge, and keeping up with changing technology.[26]

It is one thing to look at the challenges in Table 1.1 and another to more fully visualize how these challenges might be met by a top-level HR executive. A recent article entitled "Kodak to Cut Staff up to 21% Amid Digital Push" outlined changes under way at Kodak.[27] The changes were as follows:

- No more big investments in traditional film, including films, darkroom agents (chemicals), and light-sensitive papers.
- Acquisitions and expansion to broaden Kodak into three imaging businesses: consumer, commercial, and health.
- Closing operations associated with film and film-cameras including the elimination of 12,000 to 15,000 jobs.
- Elimination of corporate staff commensurate with downsizing and changing operations.

Although on the surface the article seems to be about the elimination of roughly 15,000 jobs, or 21 percent of the work force, it is about business challenges facing a major global organization.[28] The article is about the efforts of a company that invented popular photography more than 115 years ago, and came to dominate the business for over a century, to drastically alter their business model. There were few smiles at Kodak as three major credit-rating agencies downgraded its debt to a notch above junk status and the stock slid to twenty-year lows in 2003 (a negative 23.8 percent return), leading the *Wall Street Journal* to designate Kodak as the worst performer of 2003.[29] Thus, this is no idle exercise; Kodak needed to reinvent itself and quickly. The business moves along with some of the major HR moves are described in Table 1.2. As can be seen, HR professionals need many skills as part of Kodak's vast strategic moves.

Ultimately, organizations that are most successful over an extended period of time are those that are both innovative—as places to work and in the products and services they offer—and profitable. Yet, as seen from the Kodak example, innovation does not just happen but requires continual vigilance, flexibility, change, and leadership. Of course, not all human resource management is cutting edge. See A Different Point of View (p. 8) for an alternative view of human resource management.

The general purpose of this text is to explore the range of practices that defines human resource management and its relationship to other organizational objectives, such as quality of the product or service and financial success. This chapter examines some of the general issues related to human resource management, including the following:

- The scope of human resource management
- Recurring themes that appear in human resource management
- Challenges facing human resource management
- Professional opportunities in human resource management

TABLE 1.2

Business and HR Challenges Facing Kodak

Business Challenge	A Sample of Key Activities Associated with the HR Challenge
Phase out of film business	• Be a strategic partner in planning for closing. • Use familiarity with laws and regulations to manage the severance process. • Determine whether key employees associated with the film business should be placed elsewhere in Kodak.
Acquisitions and expansion to broaden Kodak's imaging presence	• Be a strategic partner in planning for the acquisitions. • Identify duplicated positions in the two organizations and set in place a process to determine to whom the position will be offered. • Use familiarity with laws and regulations to manage the merger process. • Determine whether excess employees should be placed elsewhere in Kodak.
Job loss due the elimination of business units	• Identify units and positions to be eliminated. • Use familiarity with laws and regulations to manage severance. • Work to bolster the morale of employees being retained.
Elimination of corporate staff commensurate with changes in Kodak's direction	• Be familiar with staff responsibilities and the positions to be eliminated. • Determine whether excess staff should be placed elsewhere in Kodak. • Use familiarity with laws and regulations to manage severance. • Work to bolster the morale of employees being retained.

Sources: Adapted from James Bandler, "Kodak to Cut Staff up to 21%, Amid Digital Push," *Wall Street Journal*, January 22, 2004, p. A1; "Has Kodak Missed the Moment?" *The Economist*, January 3, 2004, p. 46.

HUMAN RESOURCE MANAGEMENT DEFINITION AND FUNCTIONS

Human resource management (HRM) involves all management decisions and practices that directly affect or influence the people, or **human resources,** who work for the organization. In recent years increased attention has been devoted to how organizations manage human resources. This increased attention comes from the realization that an organization's employees enable an organization to achieve its goals and the management of these human resources is critical to an organization's success.[30] Table 1.3 shows how the emphasis in HR has shifted over the years as the environment of business has changed.

The number of activities involved in human resource management is potentially large, depending on the size of the organization and its needs. For the purposes of the present discussion, human resource activities are organized into six general areas that constitute the sections of this text. Those general areas, along with related topics that constitute the chapters of this text, are shown in Table 1.4.

Figure 1.1 is a human resource management model that illustrates how HRM activities come to bear on an organization's environment, employees, jobs, job outcomes, and organizational outcomes. All these forces are in turn affected by the organization's external environment. Note that the HRM activities in the model represent the sections and chapters of this text as listed in Table 1.4, and are discussed in more detail later in the chapter.

A DIFFERENT POINT OF VIEW

Blow the Sucker Up

Clearly, this text takes the stance that HR is a necessary function with the capacity to add greatly to an organization's competitive position. Although this is the dominant view, it is not universally accepted. In a much-discussed article entitled "Taking on the Last Bureaucracy," Thomas Stewart suggested that most HR departments are 80 percent routine administration with little value added. Here is Stewart's vivid suggestion for HR:

> Why not blow the sucker up? I don't mean improve HR. Improvement's for wimps. I mean abolish it. Deep-six it. Rub it out; eliminate, toss, obliterate, nuke it; give it the old heave-ho, force it to walk the plank, turn it into road kill.

Stewart's characterization, although accurate for many companies, is the HR department of the past. Consider the situation of a new HR professional. As a first job assignment, she was asked to meet with department managers to gain their perspective on the role of HR. In one of those meetings she is told:

> In this organization, HR does nothing more than churn paper. I call them "the boulder in the road to progress." All we hear from HR is what we cannot do. Somebody from HR is always rattling the old saber about going to jail or getting sued for something. We never hear constructive ideas from them about how to help us better manage our people, develop our talent, build our bench strength, achieve business results, or deal realistically with the people-oriented problems we face on a minute-to-minute basis. It would certainly be refreshing if we had someone in HR who would help us drain the swamp of problems while we fight off the alligators.

To be sure, Smucker's HR department (see the HR Challenge) is a value-adding partnership that contributes to Smucker's at each step of the business cycle, product development, marketing/sales, and customer support. At Smucker's, HR is not a "boulder in the road to progress"; it is a bridge connecting major sections of the business highway. The value-added paradigm for HR includes the following:

- Focusing on deliverables, such as customer (employee) understanding, operational excellence, and profitability
- Understanding *why* things work in the particular organization instead of just copying what works for others
- Mastering HR competencies, some of which are not yet defined
- Extending boundaries, such as involving suppliers and customers in the design and delivery of HR services
- Measuring the impact of HR practices on the market value, the intellectual capital, or the maneuverability of the firm

The excitement and challenge of an HRM career in the twenty-first century is one of understanding business, understanding what it takes to maximize the contributions of employees at all levels, and bringing the two together. The new HRM paradigm is a true partnership between top corporate officers and senior HR executives to meet the exciting challenges facing the nation's organizations. There is no excuse for the HR alluded to by Stewart in a progressive organization; in its place is the new HR partnership paradigm.

Sources: Thomas A. Stewart, "Taking on the Last Bureaucracy," *Fortune,* January 15, 1996, pp. 105–108; Jac Fitz-enz and Jack J. Phillips, *A New Vision for Human Resources* (Menlo Park, CA.: Crisp Publications, 1998); Dave Ulrich, *Human Resource Management,* Vol. 36 (1), Spring 1997, pp. 5–8; W. Warner Burke, "What Human Resource Practitioners Need to Know for the Twenty-First Century," *Human Resource Management,* Vol. 36 (1), Spring 1997, pp. 71–79; and William J. Rothwell, Robert K. Prescott, and Maria W. Taylor, *Strategic Human Resource Leader: How to Prepare Your Organization for the Six Key Trends Shaping the Future* (Palo Alto, Calif.: Davies-Black Publishing, 1998).

TABLE 1.3

Evolution of HR Management

Time Period	HR Focus	HR Activity	Example Event
Before 1890	Industrial technologies	Disciplinary systems	
1900–1910	Employee well-being	Health and safety programs	National Cash Register (NCR) forms first personnel department to handle employee issues
1920s	Task design, efficiency, and impact of work groups on individual workers	Time and motion studies Employee counseling and testing	Period of scientific management
1930s	Unionization of workplace Passage of major labor laws	Communication programs Anti-union campaigns Personnel becomes staff support to operational line units	Major labor relations legislation: Norris–LaGuardia Act National Labor Relations Act (Wagner Act)
1940s	Employee benefits and compensation	Wage increases Cost-of-living adjustments Pension, health, and other benefit plans	General Motors and the United Auto Workers sign first contract with "escalator" clause
1950s	Employee relations Specialized personnel functions	Training and development Separate divisions within personnel established: recruitment, labor relations, training, benefits, etc.	The Hawthorne studies from the human relations movement find widespread applicability.
1960s	Employee participation	Employee involvement Management by objectives, quality circles, sensitivity training	Peter Drucker's encyclopedic *The Practice of Management* (1954) finds widespread applicability.
1970s	Government intervention	Employee rights issues now regulated in areas of discrimination, equal opportunity, safety and health, and various benefit reforms	*Griggs v. Duke Power* is the first U.S. Supreme Court employment discrimination case.
1980s	Employee recognition Displacement	Enrichment of employee knowledge, skills, and abilities through: job rotation, formation of integrated task teams, and outplacement	William Ouchi's *Theory Z* examines the applicability of Japanese employment practices to Western companies.
1990s	Changing demographics of work force Technology	Diversity programs Employees rights issues Global perspective Information technology	About 70 percent of married women are employed, more than double the 1960 rate.
2000 and beyond	Strategic HR planning	Transition from service and support to consultative and leadership role	Exemplified by David Ulrich's book *Human Resource Champions,* which examines the role of HRM in the twenty-first century.

Source: Adapted from William J. Rothwell, Robert K. Prescott, and Maria W. Taylor, *Strategic Human Resource Leader: How to Prepare Your Organization for the Six Key Trends Shaping the Future* (Palo Alto, CA: Davies-Black Publishing, 1998) and Michael Losey, "HR Comes of Age," *HR Magazine,* Vol. 43 (3), 1998, 40–52.

TABLE 1.4

Human Resource Management: Major Areas and Related Topics

Major Areas	Related Topics
Planning for Organizations, Jobs, and People	
Strategic management of human resources	Human resource management practices for a retrenchment strategy
Human resource planning	Strategic compensation
Job analysis: Procedures and choices	Forecasting the demand for labor Career and succession planning Methods of job analysis Purposes of job analysis
Acquiring Human Resources	
Equal employment opportunity: The legal environment	Title VII of the Civil Rights Act
Recruiting and job search	Affirmative action
Measurement and decision-making issues in selection	Evaluating recruiting sources
Assessing job candidates: Tools for selection	Realistic job previews
	Determining the validity of a selection device Interviews Selection tests
Building and Motivating Performance	
Human resource development	Principles of learning
Performance assessment and management	Methods of appraisal Providing feedback to employees
Compensation system development	Evaluating the worth of jobs
Incentive compensation	Gain-sharing programs
Maintaining Human Resources	
Benefits	Controlling benefit costs
Safety and health	Occupational Safety and Health Act Stress at work
Labor relations and collective bargaining	How unions are formed Collective bargaining Employment-at-will
Employment transitions: Managing careers, retention, and termination	Reductions in force Career management Retention programs
Multinational Human Resource Management	
Managing human resources in multinational organizations	Staffing of foreign plants Selection and training of expatriates

FIGURE 1.1
Human Resource Management Model

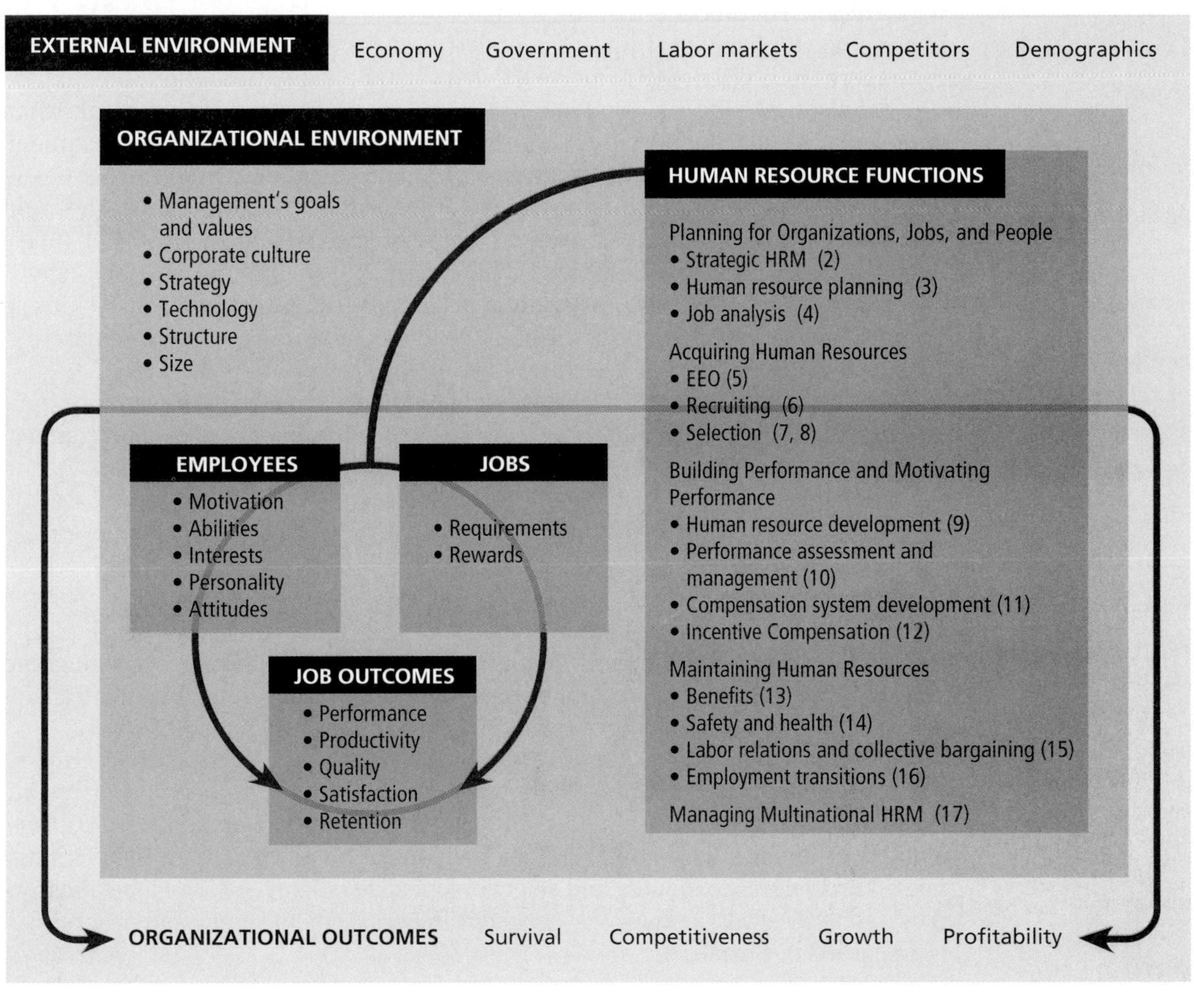

Within each functional area of human resource management, many activities must be accomplished so that the organization's human resources can make an optimal contribution to the organization's success.

Planning for Organizations, Jobs, and People

Associated with the increased attention HRM is receiving is top management's realization that HR needs to be closely integrated with managerial planning and decision making. Increasingly, top management is aware that the time to consider organizational HR strengths or limitations is when strategic business decisions are being formulated, not after critical policies have been decided. For instance, a decision to open a new facility should be made only after considering the availability of labor at the new location and the availability of experienced managers to run the facility. Furthermore, closer integration can result in HR practices that help to elicit and reward the types of behavior necessary for the organization's strategy. Suppose an organization is planning to become known for its high-quality products. Ideally, HR practitioners will design appraisal and reward systems that emphasize quality to support this competitive strategy. **Strategic human resource management** is discussed in more detail in Chapter 2 and throughout the text.

The planning process is essential to meet the staffing needs that result when complex and changing organizations encounter a dynamic business environment. The planning process involves forecasting HR needs and developing programs to ensure that the right numbers and types of individuals are available at the right time and place. Organizations depend on what-if scenarios that look at future needs in the context of work force demographics, economic projections, anticipated technological changes, recruitment success, retention goals, and shifts in organizational strategy. Specific **human resource planning** procedures are discussed in Chapter 3.

Careful descriptions and analyses of current jobs are needed to plan for future selection systems and training programs and to ensure that appraisal and compensation systems are rationally based on job demands. The development and use of job analysis information are the topics of Chapter 4.

Acquiring Human Resources

Once HR needs are determined, the next step is filling positions, or acquiring human resources. Staffing activities include recruiting applicants, screening and selecting the most qualified candidates, and filling some positions through transfer or promotion.

Staffing is a far more complex activity than in previous times when employment managers could rely on a "help wanted" sign in front of the plant or recommendations from current employees. Equal employment opportunity (EEO) laws, along with the increased complexity of positions to be filled, require more sophisticated procedures to identify and select prospective employees. The legal environment—specifically EEO laws—associated with organizational entry and progression is discussed in Chapter 5.

The selection process includes several important steps. The first is carefully defining the open position and determining which skills are needed to hold the job successfully. Having determined the specific skills and competencies, employment managers go to great lengths to increase applicant flow through a variety of recruitment strategies. These activities are the subject of Chapter 6.

The employment manager must then use carefully developed and validated procedures in screening and evaluating job candidates. These may include application blanks, interviews, ability tests, and reference checks, to name a few of the possibilities. Information from several of these procedures is then combined into a judgment of the potential of the applicant as an employee. These activities constitute the measurement and decision-making process in selection, the topics addressed in Chapters 7 and 8.

Building Individual and Organizational Performance

Human resources are unique in their potential to grow and develop to meet new challenges. Many individuals look at the chance to develop and move up as important in where they will seek employment. To facilitate employee progression, many organizations choose to spend substantial sums to train and develop their employees.

Employee training and development may be implemented by formal or informal procedures. Formal training is often associated with the introduction to a new job; it is also a means of keeping up with technological or procedural changes. Formal training can be coordinated and taught by HR or technical professionals in the organization, or employees may be sent to training programs offered by professional associations or universities.

Informal training occurs on the job and is administered by superiors and peers. The HR department may provide train-the-trainer courses and coordinate on the job-training (OJT) opportunities with employee career plans and the organization's forecast of HR needs. Procedures for determining training needs and then constructing, delivering, and evaluating HR development programs to meet these needs are the topics of Chapter 9.

Performance assessment and management are a crucial link in the HRM process: They are the means by which organizations assess how well employees are performing and determine appropriate rewards or remedial actions. The HRM role in performance assessment and management is one of working with line managers to establish performance standards, the performance dimensions to be measured, as well as the appraisal procedures to ensure accuracy. Also included in performance assessment and management are the requirements for the use of results to coach and develop employees. Performance assessment is not a favorite managerial activity, yet it is important that it be undertaken in a timely manner and be done as accurately as possible. Issues relating to performance assessment and management are discussed in Chapter 10.

A logical result of the performance assessment process is determining which employees most deserve rewards. Allocating rewards is a complex and specialized activity. Intuition would suggest that the higher the compensation an employee receives, the greater that employee's satisfaction would be. Indeed, this tends to be the case although the relationship is not a strong one.[31] In addition to the level of pay, a successful compensation system is based on fairness: the perceived equity of pay differentials for different jobs within the organization, the perceived equality of pay for similar jobs either within the organization or in competitor companies, and the perceived fairness of the differences in pay between employees who are in the very same job. Employees bring a variety of perspectives to bear in deciding whether they are satisfied with the compensation they receive, thus making the management of compensation a particularly challenging HR activity.[32]

As if this were not enough of a challenge, compensation practices are also affected by legal requirements of equal pay for equal work, minimum wage, and overtime provisions. Finally, compensation systems do not exist in a vacuum. They need to be designed to mesh with the strategic objectives of the organization. They also need to integrate the realities of prevailing pay levels in the labor market with an organization's profitability and ability to pay. The general issues related to developing reward systems are the subject of Chapter 11, and specific concerns associated with performance-based reward systems are covered in Chapter 12.

Maintaining Human Resources

The job of the HR manager does not stop once employees are hired, trained, and paid. Additional issues relate to retaining and maintaining a healthy, willing work force—maintaining human resources. The fifth major section of this book focuses on employee benefits, health and safety, industrial or labor relations, and the management of employment transitions.

These days such things as health insurance, pension plans, and vacation are important considerations among employees. They are so important that employees have been known to engage in lengthy job actions (strikes) over proposed cuts in benefits.[33] Mandatory and optional benefits are discussed in Chapter 13.

An important source of workplace change has been the desire to promote a safer and more healthful work environment. Part of the concern for health and safety is a result of the Occupational Safety and Health Act of 1970. A second source of such change has been societal concern about exposure to hazardous substances, stress, and even violence in the workplace. These issues are discussed in Chapter 14.

A part of the HRM function is establishing and maintaining effective relationships with employees. The process of **collective bargaining** requires unionized companies to negotiate with employee representatives on wages (e.g., base pay, increases, overtime), benefits (e.g., vacations, holidays, pensions), hours (e.g., breaks, cleanup time), and other conditions of work, such as seniority, discipline, and discharge procedures. A unionized work force can be an asset, as evidenced by Southwest Airlines, or a liability, as is the case of Northwest, Delta, American, and United (at the present time).[34] Companies with nonunionized employees generally find it necessary to display equal concern for these issues to maintain a positive nonunion relationship with their employees.

For organizations with unions certified to represent employees, the union contract is an important document. Those involved in human resource management must be intimately familiar with the contract and the issues it covers. This familiarity is important both for the contract negotiation process and for using the contract to guide day-to-day HR activities. The topics of labor relations and collective bargaining are covered in Chapter 15.

Another issue of importance to HR managers is managing employee transitions. This includes career structures and career planning systems for managing internal promotions and transfers as well as transitions at the boundary of the organization in the form of exits. Most employees desire some form of career planning or career progression, but patterns of growth and movement over a career have been changing as organizations adopt leaner, flatter structures. In terms of exit, individuals and organizations part company for a number of reasons. Nonvoluntary terminations may occur in the case of underperforming individuals. Acquisitions, mergers, divestitures, or other economic circumstances may require reductions in force, in which surplus employees are retrenched and remaining employees optimally redeployed.

In recent years there has been greater emphasis on the right of individuals to due process, dignity, and self-expression in the workplace. This trend is especially apparent in the case of **employment-at-will,** a legal theory that states that either the employee or the employer can terminate the employment relationship at any time for any reason. Recent state laws and court decisions have limited an employer's right to terminate an employee at will.

Voluntary turnover of staff is also an important concern for many employers. Employee turnover skyrocketed during the boom of the late 1990s, with many retail and fast-food organizations having turnover rates in excess of 100 percent per year. When valued, scarce, and skilled employees quit, work is disrupted, growth plans may be derailed, and extensive costs are incurred in locating and training replacements. Leading employers are now seeking to actively manage the retention process by understanding why employees might leave and acting to prevent or reduce turnover of valuable staff. Career planning, employee retention, reductions in force, discharge for cause, and the associated HR challenges are the topics of Chapter 16.

Multinational Human Resource Management

Chapter 17 extends the concerns of the previous chapters to an international arena through a discussion of multinational human resource management. More than ever before, U.S. companies are drawing on and contributing to a global economy. Foreign firms are establishing operations in the United States, and increasing numbers of both large and small U.S. firms are establishing plants and operations outside the borders of the United States. In conjunction with the 1992 formation of the European Union (EU), many U.S. firms entered joint ventures or built production facilities in Europe. Eastern Europe, the Commonwealth of Independent States (formerly the Soviet Union), and Russia are being dramatically reshaped and represent potential international opportunities for firms of other nations, including those of the United States. China's entry into the World Trade Organization (WTO) in 2001 offers additional opportunities for investment by U.S. firms in that economy.[35] North America is fast becoming an open trade region, as evidenced by the North American Free Trade Agreement enacted in 1993. Other global expansions are also taking place, including new opportunities in the Pacific Rim and South America, to name a few.

Examples of internationalized corporate operations and their impact on human resource management abound. Many of the foreign automobiles on U.S. highways were manufactured in this country. The challenge to organizations such as Nissan Motor Company is in selecting and training a U.S. labor force to fit the standards and procedures preferred by the foreign parent company. To what extent can or should Japanese HR practices be imported and applied at plants in the United States? To what extent can or should HR practices of the United States be exported and applied to plants in China?

On the other side of the coin, with more than 30,000 restaurants in 119 countries, McDonald's is growing far faster outside the United States than within its borders. For example, McDonald's went from a single location to more than 130 restaurants in Beijing in just three years, and at the end of 2002 McDonald's had 540 restaurants in 23 Chinese provinces.[36] McDonald's has 103 restaurants in Moscow and surrounding areas, with the Pushkin Square location having the distinction of being the busiest McDonald's in the world.[37] In both countries—the People's Republic of China and Russia—the McDonald's operations are joint ventures with local partners. From an HRM perspective, the objectives of these and other international joint ventures are the following:

- To develop U.S. managers who are ready and willing to work effectively abroad
- To select foreign nationals as employees for these overseas sites
- To develop foreign nationals with broad training and background to assume management responsibility in the overseas locations
- To develop and implement HR policies and practices that optimally merge the concerns of both the home country and the host country

HR and the Implementation of Business Decisions

Many organizational decisions are not seen as affecting employees, but, in fact, they have a critical impact on them. Every functional area of HR may be important in implementing a business decision successfully. Examples of business decisions made by operating managers and their impact on human resources are shown in Figure 1.2. It is clear that various HR functions would be needed to fully implement the intended action. As an example, the top management decision of a major airline to purchase new jumbo jets will be discussed in detail. The airline has flown the more than 6,000-mile intercontinental route, nonstop from the United States to Asia, for a number of years. To serve this route, the airline has used a fleet of Boeing 747–400s, a class of airplane with long range and a capacity of approximately 375 passengers. Business has been good, and projections are for even more passenger traffic in the future. As a result of the importance of Asia as a destination and the business prospects, the airline has decided to purchase four of the new

FIGURE 1.2

Strategic Decisions and Their Implications for Human Resource Management

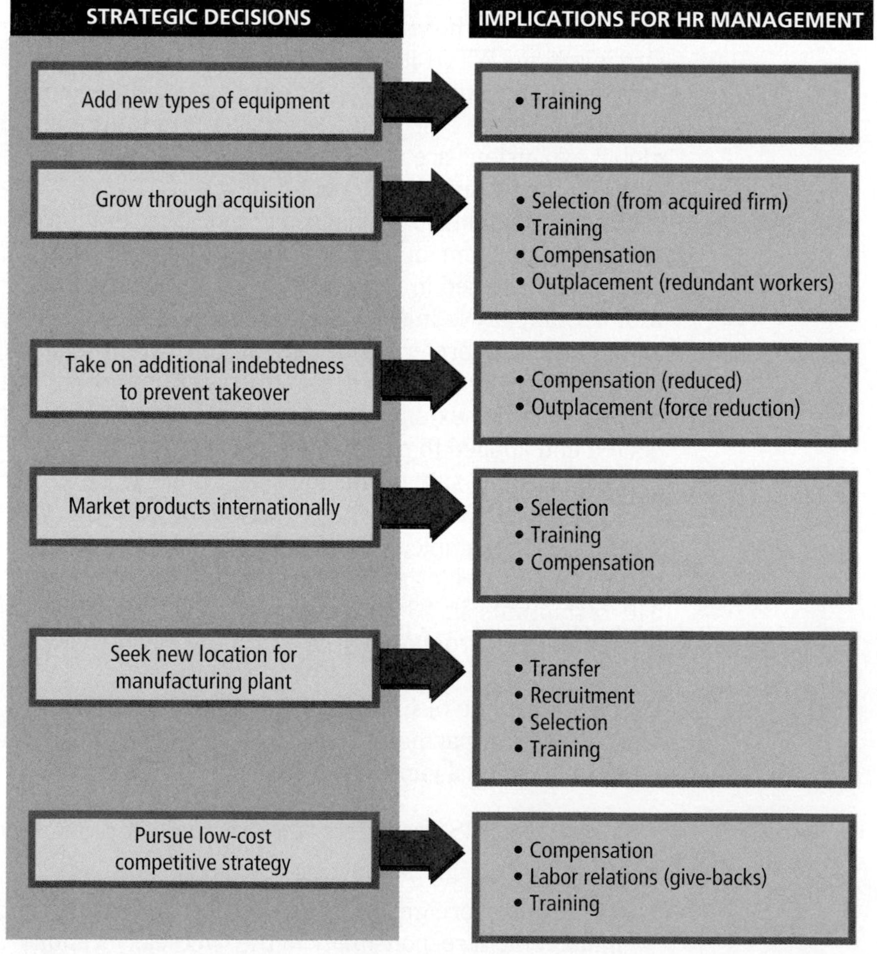

Airbus A380s, the 555-seat "superjumbo" aircraft recognized as the largest commercial craft. The $240-million-plus flying palace will be spacious enough to feature sleeping quarters, shops, and exercise rooms.[38]

Such a decision has major HR implications that will ripple throughout the organization. To begin with, pilots chosen to fly the new class of equipment, generally the most experienced captains with the airline, will need extensive training on the new aircraft. Of course, this will create training needs throughout the cockpit ranks as other captains move up to more sophisticated equipment, first officers (copilots) qualify as captains, and flight engineers move up to first officer. Cabin attendants will need training in service and in the safety features of the airplane. Ground crews will need to be trained in any new procedures for loading and unloading the airplane. Maintenance mechanics will need training in routine and special servicing requirements of planes previously unfamiliar to them. For purchasing agents, different parts and supplies will need to be ordered to support the equipment. Construction will need to be undertaken to alter the airport gates from which passengers will enter and leave the plane. Marketing representatives will need to be taught about the airplane's special features to promote travel on it. This seemingly straightforward decision to purchase the new class of aircraft, a sound decision in light of business projections, has set in motion a vast series of HR activities that affect many parts of the organization.

The manner in which HR decisions are made and carried out will have a profound effect on the employees. At the same time, these decisions will affect the long-range evaluation of the decision to fly the routes, the decision on the purchase of aircraft, and the success of the organization. A sound business decision will not be successful if HR difficulties make implementation problematic. The airline will be borrowing approximately $220 million for each plane and will have monthly payments of approximately $20 million per plane. If the plane remains idle as a result of failure in the HR chain outlined previously—for example, because maintenance mechanics have not yet completed their certification or too few cockpit crew members have been trained—the cost to the airline is a whopping $670,000 for one day, with no offsetting income. Furthermore, the passengers scheduled to fly that day, the more than 500 of them, must make other arrangements and may be reluctant to return to travel on an airline that previously disappointed them.

In summary, there is increased realization of the critical importance of human resource management in organizational effectiveness. Simply put, HRM is the set of functions and activities designed to bring the employee and the organization together so that the goals of both are met.

RECURRING THEMES IN HUMAN RESOURCE MANAGEMENT

Four general concerns span all functions of human resource management in organizations: the strategic approach; the increasing globalization of HR activities; maintaining ethical policies and behavior within the organization; and the need to benchmark, measure, and evaluate the **cost-benefit utility** of HR endeavors. These themes are addressed throughout this book in a variety of ways.

Strategic Approach

Business organizations use the resources available to compete with other companies. These include physical resources (e.g., plant, equipment, technology), organizational advantages (e.g., structure, coordinating systems), and human resources. The human resources include the experience, skill, training, and commitment of the employees. It is the allocation and integration of these resources that provides a company with a competitive advantage.

Human resources are directly or indirectly related to all organizational processes and thus are important in allowing an organization to gain and sustain a competitive advantage. To be maximally effective, the human resource management function must be integrally involved in any company's strategic management process. This means that people-related issues should be a primary concern in any organizational decision. Further, an accumulation of important research now demonstrates that when strategically linked, HR practices have an economically significant impact on both employee outcomes (turnover and productivity) and short- and long-term measures of corporate financial performance.[39]

Some of the most interesting aspects of human resource management are not just acquiring human resources, building performance, rewarding employees, and maintaining human resources, but the fusion of these elements with the strategic goals of the organization. In any organization, the challenge is managing the interplay of resources, including human resources, to gain and sustain a competitive advantage.[40]

Chapter 2 examines the process by which organizations respond to business pressures and opportunities and the role of human resource management in this process. Subsequent chapters examine the link between various HR functions and the successful implementation of organizational strategies.

International Human Resource Management

The impact of the dynamic international economy has become a major force in business in general and in human resource management in particular. Much of this book describes state-of-the-art HR practice in North America; however, other nations have sometimes chosen different approaches to dealing with the human side of organizations. For instance, in some countries a condition of doing business is a government mandate on the number of individuals who must be employed. Obviously, this alters many HR practices, including HR planning, selection, compensation, and job design, to name a few. Although interesting in their own right, these varied practices are also important realities faced by multinational firms doing business overseas. Thus many chapters of this text include an International Perspective box comparing HRM practices in the United States with those in other countries. The specific issues of managing human resources in multinational organizations are the focus of Chapter 17.

Maintaining Ethical Policies and Behavior

It has long been recognized that managers have a duty to serve the interests of the business and its owners (shareholders). In the last two decades, however, there has been an increasing realization that profit cannot be the only goal—that managers and corporations have a duty to behave in a responsible fashion toward a set of **stakeholders,** which goes well beyond owners. These stakeholders include customers, the community in which the business is located, employees, and even nonhuman entities such as the environment.

The HR manager has a special role in ensuring that the organization deals fairly and ethically with its employees and that employees deal fairly with one another, the organization, and clients. Some theories of ethics list the duties that human beings owe to one another in general. Although organizations are not necessarily subject to all the **ethical duties** to which people are, at least some of these duties might be applied to businesses to guide their dealings with employees and applicants.[41] These duties include the following:

- Respecting people and not using them solely as means to one's own ends
- Not doing any harm
- Telling the truth
- Keeping promises
- Treating people fairly and without discrimination
- Not depriving people of basic rights, such as the right to free speech and association

In organizational terms, fulfilling these duties may translate into the following:

- Instituting careful health and safety practices, informing employees of potentially hazardous working conditions, and taking responsibility for occupational disease and stress-related illnesses traceable to working conditions (see Chapter 14)
- Being truthful in recruiting (see Chapter 6)
- Avoiding the use of invalid and discriminatory selection, appraisal, and advancement systems (see Chapters 5, 7, 8, and 10)
- Providing equal pay for work of comparable worth (see Chapter 11)
- Providing ways for employees to voice their concerns and not illegally constraining employees from exercising their right to form a union (see Chapter 15)
- Following fair policies with regard to discipline, termination for cause, and reductions in force (see Chapters 3, 15, and 16)

Clearly, as an intermediary between the organization and the employee, the HR professional has a large role to play in ensuring fair treatment. In fact, the Society for Human Resource Management (SHRM) has recognized this role by adopting a Code of Ethics to guide the activities of HR professionals. This code, originally adopted in 1972 and most recently revised in 2001, is summarized in Figure 1.3. Each of the six principles is defined with a statement of the intent of the principle and guidelines for adhering to it.[42]

The HR function is also charged with protecting the organization from potentially unethical employees. According to the "bad apple" perspective, some individuals are simply predisposed to behave unethically and should be weeded out by the selection process. Applicants who are likely to steal from their employer, take bribes, demand kickbacks, violate the law, or work under the influence of drugs sometimes may be identified by careful background investigation, reference checks, or paper-and-pencil honesty testing (see Chapter 8). More recently, after

FIGURE 1.3
Code of Ethics of the Society for Human Resource Management
Source: Adapted from Society for Human Resource Management. (Available at: http://shrm.org/ethics/code-of-ethics.asp)

Professional Responsibility

As HR professionals, we are responsible for adding value to the organizations we serve and contributing to the ethical success of those organizations. We accept professional responsibility for our individual decisions and actions. We are also advocates for the profession by engaging in activities that enhance its credibility and value.

Professional Development

As professionals we must strive to meet the highest standards of competence and commit to strengthen our competencies on a continuous basis.

Ethical Leadership

HR professionals are expected to exhibit individual leadership as a role model for maintaining the highest standards of ethical conduct.

Fairness and Justice

As human resource professionals, we are ethically responsible for promoting and fostering fairness and justice for all employees and their organizations.

Conflicts of Interest

As HR professionals, we must maintain a high level of trust with our stakeholders. We must protect the interests of our stakeholders as well as our professional integrity and should not engage in activities that create actual, apparent, or potential conflicts of interest.

Use of Information

HR professionals consider and protect the rights of individuals, especially in the acquisition and dissemination of information while ensuring truthful communications and facilitating informed decision making.

several horrific incidents, there is ever-increasing concern with violence in the workplace.[43]

Although there is some merit to the "bad apple" perspective, it is far from the whole story. Employees do not make ethical choices in a vacuum or entirely on the basis of their preexisting values and ethical upbringing. Instead, they behave within a context that includes organizational training, role models, formal rules and policies, and appraisal and reward systems. The unethical and illegal behavior at Enron is exemplary of widespread practices that even involved complicity by their accounting firm, the former Arthur Andersen, investment banks, and law firms.[44] It is the responsibility of the HR manager to ensure that these influences are positive and consistent with the ethical values desired by the top managers of the organization. The Ethical Perspective box lists some ways in which HR staff can help to elicit and maintain ethical behavior among employees. Ethical Perspective boxes in subsequent chapters will raise additional issues of concern to the responsible HR practitioner.

Benchmarking, Measuring, and Evaluating Human Resource Results

Another ever-present reality in today's organizations is the need to strive for the best practices (i.e., **benchmarks**) and to then substantiate the cost-effectiveness of programs, approaches, and policies. HR benchmarking is the process of comparing one's HR practices with those of another firm, particularly a competitor, as a way to outperform the competition.[45]

Top management wants to know in bottom-line (i.e., dollar) terms the extent to which the benefits of a policy or program outweigh the costs. Although HR programs can have a significant impact on profits, little has been done thus far to evaluate HR programs in these terms. The benchmarking perspective is basically a method that allows a manager to strive for the best practices and then compare the costs associated with selecting, training, and rewarding employees to the dollar benefits resulting from these efforts. For example, many training programs are proposed and undertaken without examining the extent of increased productivity (benefit) as opposed to the costs of training material, time away from the job for those being trained, salary of the trainer, and so forth.

There is an ever-increasing need for HR managers to speak the language of business and, in so doing, to justify the economic value of existing or proposed programs. The key question decision makers must answer with respect to all programs is this: How can we best allocate our limited resources in the most cost-effective way? As with international considerations, the concept of cost-benefit utility spans all areas of human resource management and thus is considered in many chapters of this text.

CURRENT AND FUTURE CHALLENGES TO HUMAN RESOURCE MANAGEMENT

There can be little doubt that in the twenty-first century human resource management faces some of the greatest challenges since its definition as a separate staff function almost a century ago. This renewed vigor stems from numerous influences, such as the changing nature of the economy and governmental-legal influences, new organizational forms, global competition, changing employee expectations, and the increased feeling that organizations are vehicles for fulfilling societal goals. Some of the major factors that have forced human resource management to be transformed from a narrowly defined specialty to a more strategic function are discussed in the sections that follow.

Corporate Reorganizations

The last two decades have been characterized by acquisitions and mergers of almost unbelievable proportions as well as other forms of corporate reorganization. In many industries it is all about market share. Hardly a week goes by without one or more instances of one corporation purchasing another, two corporations joining forces, or companies undergoing massive reorganizations. America Online's purchase of Time Warner in 2001 set a record.[46] The purchase was with AOL stock, which made the value of the deal $181.9 billion when announced, but it was closer to $100 billion (still a large amount) when the acquisition was finally consummated in early 2001.[47] In virtually every major industry, the number of major players is shrinking. The reorganizations continue in an effort to improve competitiveness, either by cutting layers of managers and restructuring the work forces or by gaining economies through combining efforts.

As can be seen from Table 1.5, many of the megamergers of recent years involve related companies seeking to gain an advantage by entering new markets. For example, AOL's $100 billion purchase of Time Warner is a way for both companies to

ETHICAL PERSPECTIVE

How Organizations Encourage Ethical Behavior

Ethical or unethical behavior is not entirely a matter of the character of individual employees; it is determined at least in part by factors in the organization. People are influenced by the forces surrounding them—their peers, their superiors, the reward system, group norms, and organizational policies and values. Ethical behavior in organizations can be encouraged in a number of ways, many of which involve the HRM department through its roles in training, employee communication, and discipline. In some organizations the HR department is assigned primary responsibility for managing and monitoring ethical behavior. In others a separate ethics office takes the lead in this endeavor.

When a number of defense industry scandals were exposed in the 1980s, organizations became more sensitive to ethical issues, and many implemented corporate ethics programs. The scandals of the early 2000s suggest that further, and more effective, attention to ethics in organizations is required. Federal guidelines require smaller fines for corporate ethics violations when a company has a program in place to encourage ethical behavior and the reporting of violations. A comprehensive corporate ethics program might include six components:

1. A formal code of ethics or code of conduct.
2. Ethics committees to develop ethical policy and investigate alleged violations.
3. Ethics communication systems to allow employees to make queries, get advice, or report wrongdoing. Ideally, several means of inquiry will be available (telephone hotlines, e-mail, suggestion boxes, ethical ombudsman, etc.), and at least one of them should permit anonymous contact.
4. Ethics officer(s) and an ethics office to oversee the process and help communicate policy to employees. Ethics Officer has become a recognized job title, and there is now a professional association for such individuals (www.eoa.org).
5. Ethics training programs to help employees understand the ethical issues likely to arise in their work and how to deal with these issues.
6. A disciplinary system to promptly and decisively investigate and deal with violations. Employees ex-

achieve much greater penetration in the growth markets of telecommunications and entertainment. Other large mergers involved overlapping companies, such as Hewlett-Packard and Compaq or the more recent Cingular and AT&T Wireless, seeking economies of scale through combined efforts.

It is difficult to imagine circumstances that pose a greater challenge for human resource management than the reorganizations that have characterized the last twenty years. Such reorganizations inevitably affect many organizational levels and employees. Furthermore, given the complexities of the situation, decisions may be slow in coming. In the meantime, employees are left wondering what, if any, role they will play in the "new organization."[48] As a result of reorganizations, employees may face these potential changes:

- Loss of job, pay, and benefits
- Job changes, including new roles and assignments
- Transfer to a new geographic location
- Changes in compensation and benefits
- Changes in career possibilities

pect inappropriate behavior to be disciplined. Failure to respond to unethical behavior may lead to feelings of inequity on the part of ethical employees and threaten the entire social system that supports ethical behavior in the organization.

It is important that codes of ethics be customized to each organization. The company's values and the types of ethical issues likely to arise in its industry should be reflected in the code and in the associated training for employees. For instance, Lockheed Martin's ethics training is based on thirty-four case scenarios representing real problems that have arisen in their organization. When managers conduct the training for their own employees, they choose the scenarios most relevant to their particular work setting.

The vast majority of companies with codes of ethics report that these codes are conveyed to new hires during orientation training. Some companies, such as Raytheon and Lockheed Martin, require an annual one-hour refresher program on ethics for all employees, from the CEO on down. Lockheed Martin reinforces its code with a self-study CD-ROM, an ethics calendar, and a screen saver featuring the company's twelve important values—their "building blocks of trust." Texas Instruments provides employees with ethics training, a booklet, and a wallet card containing a mini-ethics test. The card instructs employees to review the following points before taking an action:

- Is it legal?
- Does it comply with our values?
- If you do it, will you feel bad?
- How will it look in the newspaper?
- If you know it's wrong, DON'T DO IT!
- If you're not sure, ask.

In sum, ethics has become an important issue in many corporations, and HR managers are often at the forefront of efforts to instill and enforce ethically appropriate behavior among employees.

Sources: J. T. Delaney and D. Sockell, "Do Company Ethics Training Programs Make a Difference? An Empirical Analysis," *Journal of Business Ethics,* Vol. 11, 1992, pp. 719–727; G. R. Weaver, L. K. Treveno, and P. L. Cochran, "Corporate Ethics Programs as Control Systems: Influences of Executive Commitment and Environmental Factors," *Academy of Management Journal,* Vol. 42, 1999, pp. 41–57; S. J. Wells, "Turn Employees into Saints?" *HR Magazine,* December 1999, pp. 48–58; D. Fandray, "The Ethical Company," *Workforce*, December 2000, Vol. 79, No. 12, pp. 74–77; and A. Meisler, "Doing Right and Doing Well," *Workforce Management*, March 2004, Vol. 83, No. 3, pp. 50–51.

- Changes in organizational power, status, and prestige
- Staff changes, including new colleagues, bosses, and subordinates
- Change in corporate culture and loss of identity with the company

There is little indication that the pace of corporate reorganizations will slacken in the near future. To a greater extent than ever before, corporations consider reorganizations (acquisitions, mergers, divestitures, downsizing) to be routine business transactions. Yet an important key to the success of almost any reorganization is the management of human resources.

Global Competition

A long-term trend with profound and far-reaching implications for HR professionals is that of a global economy. International competition in goods and services is forcing major economies into a global affiliation. Rather than being the dominant economic force, the United States is one of a small (and changing) group of

TABLE 1.5
Megamergers of Recent Years

Acquirer	Target	Date Announced	Transaction Value When Announced ($ billions)	Comment
American Online	Time Warner	January 2000	$181.9	Worth approximately $100 billion when consummated
MCI WorldCom	Sprint	October 1999	$127.3	Blocked because of regulatory concerns
Pfizer Inc.	Warner-Lambert	November 1999	$87.9	
Exxon	Mobil	December 1998	$86.4	
American Home Products	Warner-Lambert	November 1999	$76.1	
Travelers Group	Citicorp	April 1998	$72.6	
SBC Communications	Ameritech	May 1998	$72.4	
Bell Atlantic	GTE	July 1998	$71.3	
AT&T	Tele-Communications	June 1998	$69.9	
Comcast Corp.	Walt Disney Co.	February 2004	$66.7	
Sanofi-Synthelabo SA	Aventis SA	January 2004	$60.7	
JP Morgan Chase	Bank One Corp	January 2004	$58.7	
Bank of America	FleetBoston Financial	October 2003	$49.3	
Cingular Wireless	AT&T Wireless	January 2004	$41	
Hewlett-Packard	Compaq	September 2001	$25	

Source: Adapted from "25 Largest Deals" CNN.COM (Available at: http://money.cnn.com/news/deals/mergers/biggest.html); Andres Ross Sorkin, "Merger Renaissance a Good Possibility in the Coming Year," *New York Times*, January 1, 2004, p. C-1.

economically strong countries. In addition, the United States is no longer an isolated national economy but part of a world economic community.

The transition has not been an easy one for U.S. industry. For example, even in recent times, the United States had strong textile and apparel industries. U.S. companies supplied many parts of the world with finished cloth products. As competition with developing countries increased, U.S. manufacturers insisted that their products were superior to the less expensive imports. Consumers soon realized, however, that imported textile and apparel products were as good as the domestic counterparts and also cheaper. Examine the labels of the apparel in your wardrobe or of other finished textile products and you will see that the reach of the U.S. textile industry is much diminished.

What has transpired in the textile industry is an example of a trend toward a global economy. From an HR perspective, this trend has represented a monumental challenge. Relationships between employees and employers have been shaken in industries that have been reduced dramatically in the United States, such as the shoe, automobile, steel, and electronics industries. The readjustment for workers in these industries has usually involved switching from the declining manufacturing sector of the economy to the service sector.[49] All of this led Carly Fiorina, Chairman of Palo Alto technology giant Hewlett Packard, to proclaim, "There is no job that is America's God-given right anymore."[50] Talk about a reality check—such a comment engendered considerable debate.

More and more, HR professionals are becoming primarily responsible for helping to make the efforts at business globalization effective. The need to identify and place U.S. employees, mainly managerial and professional personnel, in foreign subsidiaries or joint ventures is one of the important challenges of the global economy. The problems associated with the selection, training, and compensation of expatriate managers is discussed in Chapter 17.

Cyclical Growth

Cyclical organizational growth as a result of both market shifts and competitive factors has resulted in a redefinition of the workplace. In the past, people entered an organization and then progressed as they gained new skills and as expanded business created opportunities for advancement. Now employees are being asked to prepare for a radical new condition of permanent insecurity—a future full of endless efforts to upgrade job skills, perpetual recombining of work teams, and, when business wanes, sporadic layoffs. The approximately 15,000 layoffs by Kodak is a good example.[51] Those Kodak employees who remain are experiencing the feeling of permanent insecurity as they seek to continually upgrade job skills just to stay in place.

At the same time, this is not a saga about rampant unemployment but one about an emerging redefinition of employment. The movement to cyclical growth is a long-term trend that is driven by some of the following changes:

- Continued automation and information technology to increase productivity, requiring fewer workers[52]
- Flatter organizations, with fewer layers between top and bottom, thus cutting out unneeded managers[53]
- Plant closings to bring production capacity in line with business realities
- Redesigning the work force to be more flexible, such as by using temporary workers

Clearly, managing human resources in times of slower or negative growth will be a significant challenge for the HR professional throughout the twenty-first century. Likewise, periods of strong growth, such as those in the late 1990s, impose demands to effectively recruit and retain large numbers of employees who have many other employment options from which to choose.

Increasing Diversity in the Work Force

Another major challenge for human resource management is the changing nature of the work force. Figure 1.4 illustrates the dimensions of **diversity,** with six primary elements at the core surrounded by secondary dimensions. Taken together, the increased diversity of the work force has caused organizations to reexamine policies, practices, and values.

FIGURE 1.4

Primary and Secondary Dimensions of Diversity

Source: Marilyn Loden and Judy B. Rosener, *Workforce America: Managing Employee Diversity as a Vital Resource,* p. 20. © 1991 by Business One Irwin. All rights reserved. Reproduced with permission of The McGraw-Hill Companies.

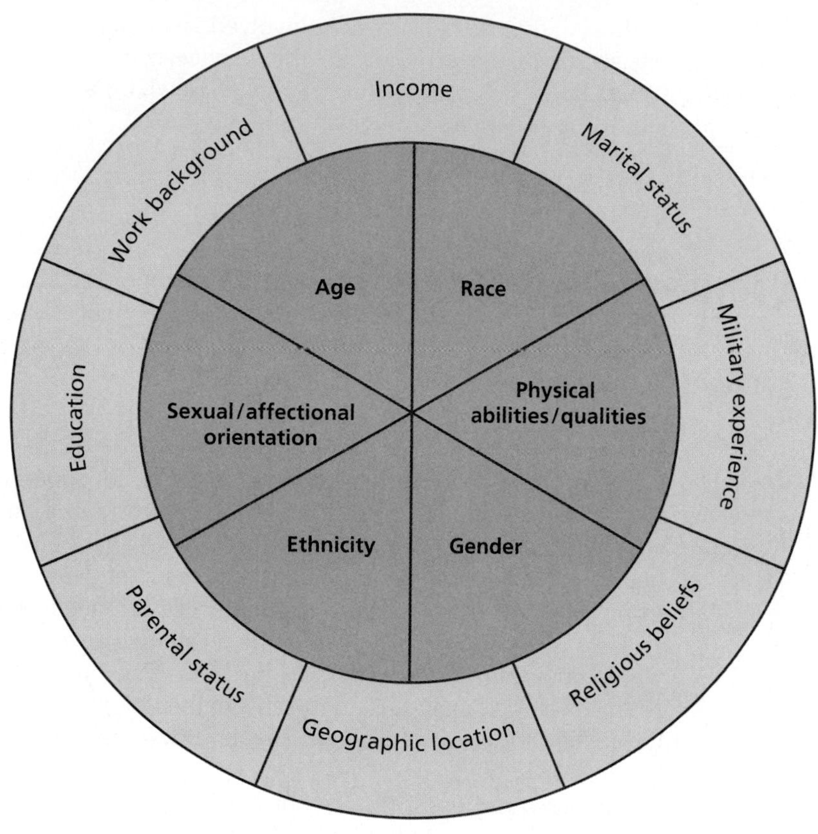

The percentage of American women who participate in the work force has increased significantly over time, with the figure now approximately 61 percent. This is almost double the rate of participation in 1950.[54] Women now account for about 47 percent of the work force and will approach parity with men in the near future.[55] This shift has led to fundamental changes toward family-friendly working conditions and benefits, changes discussed in Chapter 13.

The minority (Black, Asian, Hispanic) share of the population, and therefore the work force, will continue to grow from 29 percent in 2000 to approximately 35 percent by the year 2020, 38 percent in 2025, and 47 percent in 2050 (see Figure 1.5).[56]

Progress in accommodating gender and racial diversity has already been dramatic, and many readers will think that most organizations have climbed the learning curve with respect to opportunities for the diverse groups that now make up the work force. However, lasting improvements have been slow in coming. How many organizations have women and minorities in executive roles? Even organizations with a substantial record of progress do not have them in significant numbers at higher levels. An example of this situation is the recent concern with the underrepresentation of minorities in managerial roles in professional sports.

Another aspect of diversity is related to the topic of affirmative action (see Chapter 5). The notion that employers must commit to equal employment opportunity through positive, affirmative steps (action) has a history of more than thirty

FIGURE 1.5

The Ethnic Composition of the American Work Force

Source: "National Population Projections," U.S. Census Bureau (Available at: http://www.census.gov/population/www/projections/natsum-T3.html).

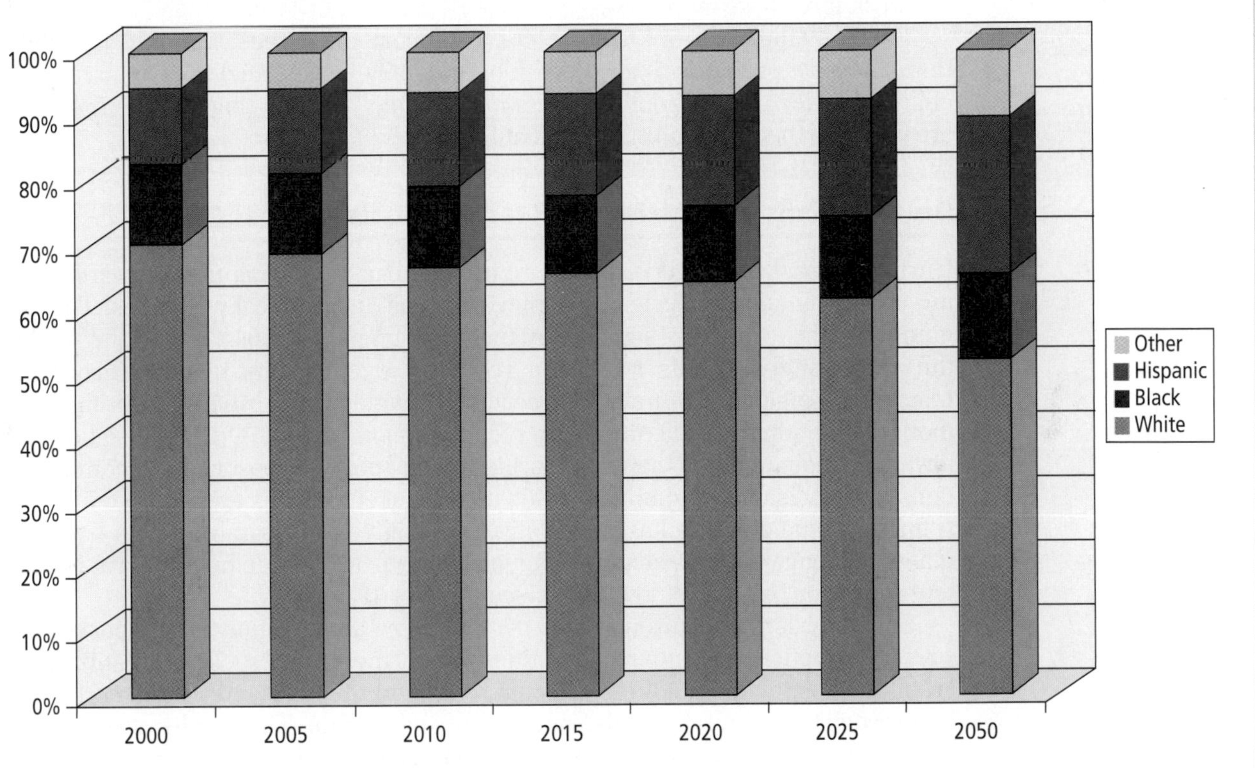

years. Despite this long-standing policy, the idea that employers (and educational institutions) can (and in some cases, must) adopt a specific set of results-oriented procedures to achieve equal employment is a continual topic of public debate.

Still another trend that is posing a challenge for human resource management relates to the increasing average age of the work force. The average age of the work force and the population are increasing. By 2025 the proportion of all Americans who are elderly will be the same as the proportion in Florida today. The United States, in effect, will become a nation of Floridas. In the twenty-year period from 2010 to 2030, the proportion of the U.S. population over age 65 is expected to grow by as much as it had grown in the previous eighty years.[57]

Trends in work force diversity pose many challenges to HR managers and are reshaping organizations and how they relate to the work force.

Employee Expectations

As levels of education have increased among the population, values and expectations among employees have shifted. At present, fully one-quarter of the work force has a college degree. The result has been an emphasis on increased participation by employees at all levels. Previous notions about managerial authority are giving way to employee influence and involvement, along with mechanisms for upward communication and due process.

With more working women and dual career couples, employees' desires for flexible working arrangements and means of varying their level of involvement in the work force have increased.

Further, employers are taking steps to support employees' family responsibilities. They are paying increased attention to family issues, such as day care, sick children, elder care, schooling, and so forth. One result is that more employees are enjoying the opportunity to work at home.

Organizations as Vehicles for Reaching Societal Goals

During the past several decades, there has been an increasing trend toward viewing organizations as vehicles for achieving social and political objectives. The beginning of this trend was signaled by the adoption of the 1964 Civil Rights Act by the U.S. Congress. This legislation required organizations to deal fairly with minorities—including women and racial and religious minorities—in hiring, promotion, and other aspects of human resource management. Other legislation followed, including requirements that organizations provide reasonable accommodations for the disabled and not discriminate against employees over the age of forty. A further issue discussed as a legislative possibility is comparable worth—that is, mandating equal pay for women doing jobs equivalent in value but different in content from jobs typically held by men (see Chapter 12).

Such legislative requirements generally follow a realization that important issues need national attention. As entities within the larger society, organizations are influenced by the ideology and culture around them. As changes occur in the larger society, organizations also must adapt and change. The results of social and legislative changes are added pressures on organizations. HR practices are not formed in a vacuum but must represent the societal ideology in which they are embedded.

All this adds up to extensive economic, social, political, and technological changes that affect what organizations do and the expectations of their employees. Procedures used in the past to handle the human side of business are no longer effective. The net result is a tremendous challenge for HR managers.

JOBS AND CAREERS IN HUMAN RESOURCE MANAGEMENT

Jobs and careers in human resource management can be both challenging and rewarding. In this section we examine HRM jobs, typical compensation, and future HRM career opportunities.

What competencies are required if one is to be an effective HR professional? A recent report has suggested that in the twenty-first century HR professionals will be expected to contribute to the strategic direction of the organizations that employ them by helping to create and sustain the competitive advantage of the firm.[58] The following competencies are considered critical to this expanded role:

Business capabilities—having knowledge of financial, strategic, and technological aspects of business marketing and sales, computer information systems, customer relations, and production capabilities

Human resource practices—attracting and promoting appropriate people, designing development programs, developing effective appraisal programs and feedback processes, communicating organizational and HR policies, and providing a mechanism for integrating different business units

Managing the change process—establishing trust, providing vision, putting problems in the context of larger systems, clarifying roles and responsibilities, encouraging creativity, and being proactive in bringing about change

These competencies represent a mix of skills that can be acquired through education (e.g., general business knowledge, functional HR expertise) and experience. The HR professional of the twenty-first century is viewed as a strategic partner in running the business.

Types of Jobs

Opportunities vary across organizations, and they vary within organizations depending on the level at which one is working. Professional positions can be divided into three categories: HR specialist, HR manager, and HR executive. In addition, there are numerous support positions (e.g., clerical personnel and computer programmers).

Human Resource Specialist **Human resource specialist** jobs are usually the entry-level positions for an HRM career. Included would be such roles as interviewer, compensation analyst, benefits coordinator, job analyst, and trainer. In larger organizations, there may be promotional opportunities within the specialized functions. For example, a new specialist might begin as an interviewer, move up to coordinating college recruiting in a region, and progress to supervising all college recruiting.

Alternatively, an entry-level specialist might work in a smaller company or plant as one of two or three professionals providing HR services. In this case, the specialist might do a little of everything. For example, on any given day the specialist might run an orientation program for new employees, interview applicants, develop information for contract negotiations, or check with other companies in the area regarding hourly wages.

HR specialists typically have formal college training in human resource management or a related area, such as industrial-organizational psychology, adult education, or industrial relations. Some organizations hire business or liberal arts graduates with excellent interpersonal skills to start in a specialist role while continuing their education in an HR program at the master's degree level.

Human Resource Manager The **human resource manager** is a generalist who administers and coordinates programs spanning several functional areas. The HR manager is usually a top-ranked person at a plant or facility and, as such, is expected to be knowledgeable about all areas of human resource management, to oversee the implementation of organizational human resource policies at the facility, and to advise line managers on human resource issues.

Another role for the HR manager would be to head a functional personnel activity at the corporate level. Many large organizations are organized into relatively autonomous divisions. Typically, such organizations have functional specialists at the corporate level to translate corporate strategy into HR policy and to coordinate this policy throughout all divisions. For example, the corporate headquarters may have a manager of affirmative action develop a comprehensive plan based on corporate objectives and commitments. The manager would then coordinate with divisional HR managers to make sure that plans at the local level are consistent with corporate objectives.

The HR manager is an experienced professional, usually someone who has served in several specialist positions. The individual in such a position will have obtained knowledge and skills through experience but may or may not have a degree in human resource management.

Human Resource Executive The top-level **human resource executive,** usually a vice president of the organization, has the responsibility of linking corporate policy and strategy with human resource management. The top HR executive would also be expected to have input into organizational goals, especially as these goals affect or are affected by personnel activities. It is important to consider HR opportunities and limitations in establishing overall organizational directions.

Compensation for HR Professionals

The Society for Human Resource Management conducts an annual survey of compensation for HR professionals. The 2003 survey included approximately 1,300 public and private organizations of all sizes, with a combined total of more than 10 million employees.[59] In Table 1.6, average base pay for top HR positions in the respective areas is given. On average, top HR executives for large companies earn just over $200,000 (before incentive compensation). Top managers in specialty areas had average earnings of between $124,400 (human resource director) and $70,800 (payroll manager), depending on the specialty.[60] Specialist pay ranged from $71,800 (Senior HR generalist) to $44,800 (general recruiter). About two-thirds of HR executives are eligible for long-term incentives in the form of stock

TABLE 1.6

Pay Levels for Common HR Positions (Total Cash Compensation)

Positions	2003 Median Total Cash Compensation
Top HR Management Executive	$204,900
HR Director	$124,400
Compensation Manager	$97,800
HR Manager	$91,400
Employment and Recruiting Manager	$87,500
Benefits Manager	$85,500
Senior HR Generalist	$71,800
Payroll Manager	$70,800
Senior Compensation Analyst	$64,700
HRIS Specialist	$53,500
Trainer	$46,900
General Recruiter	$44,800

Source: Joe Vocino, "Accelerating Compensation Reflects the Changing World of HR and Increased Emphasis on Variable Pay," *HR Magazine*, November 2003, pp. 75–84.

options. In addition, nine out of ten HR executives are eligible for short-term incentives, such as annual bonuses. Actual awards were as high as 50 percent of mean base pay for the top HR executives but were typically in the range of 25 to 30 percent for the other executive positions.

Obviously HR pay varies by size of company (number of employees) and industry. For example, although top HR executives average $204,900, pay varies from $147,300 in companies with less than 1,000 employees to $285,400 in companies with 10,000 or more employees.[61] Interestingly, specialist positions do not necessarily vary with the size of the company. For example, remuneration for senior compensation analysts varies little as a function of company size. The reason for this is that the job is probably pretty much the same in terms of scope and responsibility.

Career Opportunities

The career outlook for HR professionals is reasonably strong. The external factors discussed previously—events related to corporate reorganizations, global competition, and changes in work force demographics—represent long-term trends that have transformed the way organizations interact with employees. HR professionals are in a pivotal position in terms of these challenges.

An even more promising trend is the strategic role played by HR professionals. More and more, organizational effectiveness is being determined by the degree to which strategic objectives are formulated in light of HR considerations. This means that HR professionals must look ahead with respect to corporate objectives—whether they involve a new line of business, a possible acquisition, or a new corporate emphasis—and make sure that the HR policy is consistent with the overall objectives.

The increased status of human resource management can be illustrated by tracking HR reporting relationships over the past several years. Ten to fifteen years ago, senior HR executives typically reported to the third level of management—for example, to an administrative vice president. Now senior HR managers often report to first- or second-level managers—for example, to the president or executive vice president. Today many senior HR executives are officers of the corporation and represent the HR point of view as members of the board of directors.

Career Progression

- **Entry** The HR competencies discussed earlier in this section outline how one can build a career in this area. Technical knowledge is essential. For most, the career entry point with a college degree is the position of **HR specialist.** Many business schools have a specialization in human resource management, including courses in most of the major areas addressed as topics in this text. One also can major in the social sciences—for example, in psychology, sociology, or economics, perhaps with a minor in business—and then gain further learning on the job as a technical specialist. The Society for Human Resource Management (formerly called the American Society for Personnel Administration) has student chapters at many colleges and universities. Campus chapters of SHRM provide speakers, field trips, and internship opportunities for participating students.

Many institutions of higher education have graduate programs in human resource management. Such a program normally would lead to a master's degree in business, with a specialization in human resource management. A typical curriculum would include courses in business (accounting, finance, marketing, organizational sciences) and graduate-level study in major HRM areas. Frequently, students would be encouraged to hold an internship as an HR assistant for a semester.

A final entry route is as a line employee who transfers into human resource management. After gaining experience as a supervisor, for instance, it may be possible to switch areas and become an HR specialist.[62]

The competition for entry-level HRM jobs is often quite stiff. These jobs attract new graduates, internal candidates, and would-be career changers from other human service areas, such as teaching and social work. The key to getting interviews and landing the first job is experience: Students who have completed one or more HR internships have much greater success in the HRM job market.

Advancement Career advancement is earned by gaining experience in the major areas of human resource management and at different levels within the organization. Hypothetical organizational structures within typical HR departments are shown in Figure 1.6. Table 1.7 illustrates how one might progress. These department structures show the different specialist, managerial, and executive roles that might exist in a large corporate environment.

It is not necessary to rotate through all major areas and levels of an organization when pursuing a career in human resource management, although it is important to gain experience in most areas. Progression is not always stepwise, from plant to division to corporate headquarters. It is possible to start at the plant, move to the division or headquarters, and then move back for further experience at the plant.

Certification as an HR Professional

The Human Resource Certification Institute (HRCI), an affiliate of the Society for Human Resource Management, is a nonprofit corporation that recognizes and accredits individuals who have met experience requirements and have demonstrated a mastery of the HR body of knowledge. The levels of **human resource certification** offered by the institute and the requirements for each level are as follows:

Professional in Human Resources (PHR): (a) Four years of professional HRM experience or (b) two years of HRM experience and a related bachelor's degree or (c) one year of HRM experience and a related graduate degree

Senior Professional in Human Resources (SPHR): (a) Eight years of professional HRM experience or (b) six years of HRM experience and a related bachelor's degree or (c) five years of HRM experience and a related graduate degree; the most recent three years of experience must include policy-developing responsibility

In addition to meeting the educational and experience requirements, applicants must pass a 225-question multiple-choice, four-hour examination to demonstrate mastery of the various types of knowledge. The exam is administered by computer (at Prometric testing centers) and covers the six areas shown in Table 1.8. As indicated, the greatest weight goes to general management and HR practices, followed by compensation, selection, and employee/labor relations. PHR questions tend to be at an operation/technical level. SPHR questions tend to be more at the strategic or policy level. Approximately 65 percent taking the PHR exam pass, and approximately 55 percent of those taking the SPHR exam pass.[63]

FIGURE 1.6

Organization Charts for Typical Human Resource Departments

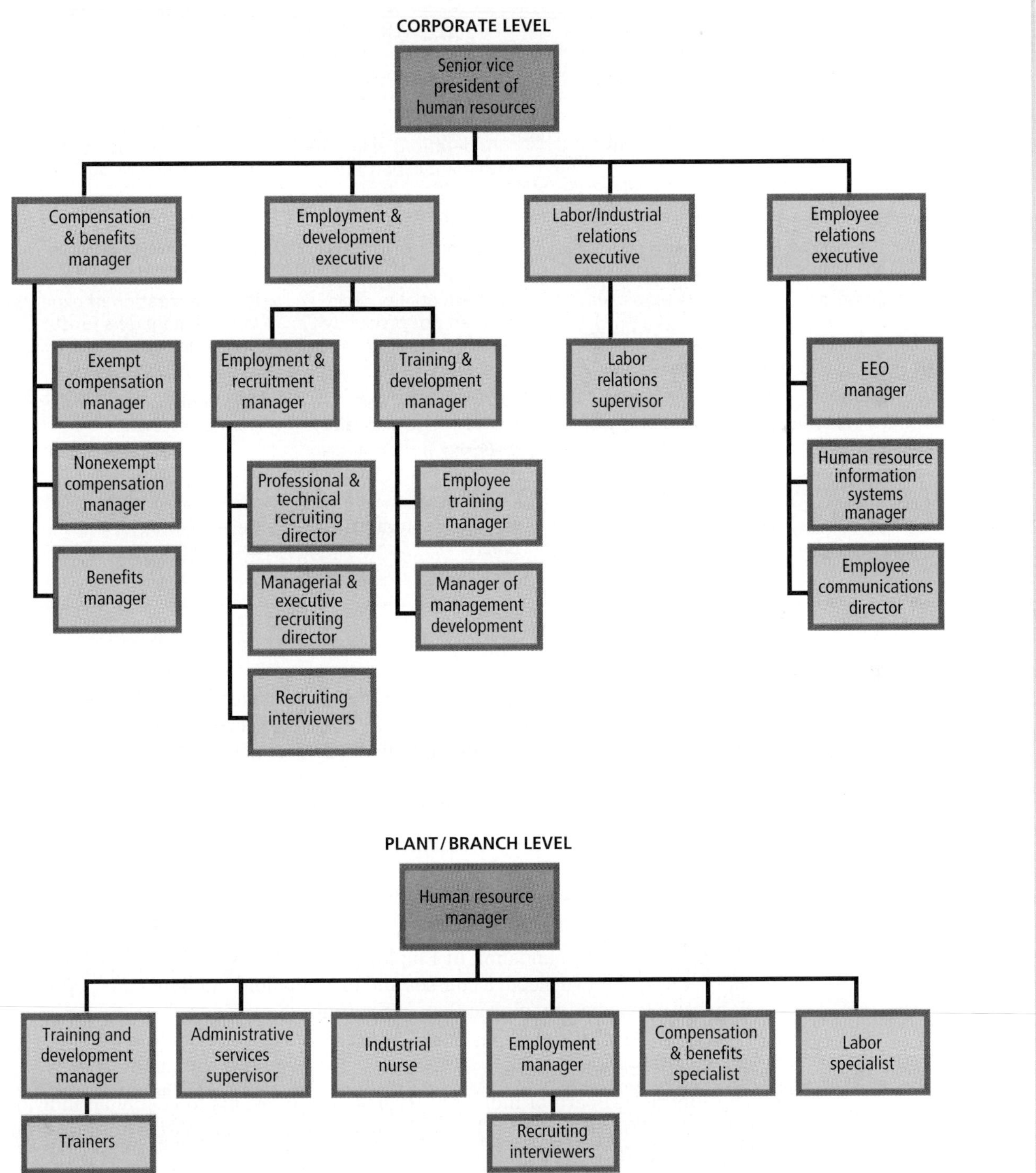

TABLE 1.7

Typical Job Activities in Human Resource Management

	Possible Job Activity		
Experience Area	**Plant**	**Division**	**Corporation**
Planning	Analyze jobs for compensation decisions	Analyze human resource considerations associated with plant expansion	Analyze human resource considerations associated with new line of business
Organizational entry	Visit technical schools to recruit hourly workers Test applicants for hourly positions	Visit colleges to recruit graduates Develop affirmative action goals	Develop company-wide EEO plan Develop succession plan for key executives
Developing employees	Orient new employees Monitor plant-wide suggestion system for productivity improvement	Establish quality circle program for productivity improvement	Plan job rotation of experienced managers for further training
Performance, evaluation, and reward systems	Apply job evaluation procedure to new job titles Supervise performance evaluation	Develop policy for annual wage and salary increases	Plan bonus system for corporate executives
Maintaining human resources	Resolve employee grievances Conduct exit interviews	Negotiate contract with union	Develop plans for organizational retrenchment

The certifications serve largely to indicate the qualifications of the recipients and to ensure the professionalism of the HR field. The certification exam has become popular among professionals, and by mid-2003 almost 70,000 HR professionals had been certified.[64]

Other types of specialist certification are possible:

- The World at Work (the professional association for compensation, benefits, and total rewards, formerly know as the American Compensation Association), through a series of six required and three elective examinations, allows a qualified professional to be designated as a Certified Compensation Professional.[65]
- The International Foundation of Employee Benefit Plans, through a series of six required and two elective courses and examinations, authenticates a professional as a Certified Employee Benefit Specialist.[66]
- The Board of Certified Safety Professionals certifies an individual as a Certified Safety Professional.[67]
- The American Board of Industrial Hygiene offers exams to certify an individual as a Certified Industrial Hygienist (CIH) or Certified Associate Industrial Hygienist (CAIH).[68]
- The Human Resource Certification Institute launched (2004) the Global Professional in Human Resources (GPHR) exam as a companion to the PHR and SPHR certifications. The GPHR is for HR professionals who develop and implement global HR strategies or manage HR operations overseas.[69]

TABLE 1.8

Content Areas Covered for HR Certification

Chapter 1 Content Area	Example Topics*
Strategic Management (12%, 26%)**	• Lawmaking and administrative regulatory processes • Environmental scanning techniques • Strategic planning process and implementation • Organizational social responsibility • Management functions
Work Force Planning and Employment (26%, 16%)	• Legal and regulatory factors • Quantitative techniques in HR • Recruiting and staffing • Selection methods • International HR
Human Resource Development (15%, 13%)	• HR training and organizational development theories and applications • Training methods, programs, and techniques • Employee involvement strategies • Performance appraisal and performance management methods • Instructional methods, program delivery, and program effectiveness
Compensation and Benefits (20%, 16%)	• Tax and accounting treatment • Economic factors affecting compensation • Compensation philosophy, strategy, and policy • Compensation and benefit programs • Executive compensation
Employee and Labor Relations (21%, 24%)	• Union representation of employees • Employer unfair labor practices • Union unfair labor practices, strikes, and boycotts • Collective bargaining • Individual employment rights issues and practices
Occupational Health, Safety, and Security (6%, 5%)	• Health • Safety • Security

*Topics listed in descending order of coverage within the section.
**Percentage weighting PHR and SPHR exams, respectively.
Source: Certification Information Handbook, 1998 edition. Copyright © 1997 by Assessment Systems, Inc. Reprinted by permission of the HR Certification Institute, Society for Human Resource Management, Alexandria, VA.

Summary of Key Points

Human resource managers perform an identifiable set of activities that affect and influence the people who work in an organization. These activities include HR planning, job analysis, recruitment, selection, placement, career management, training, designing performance assessment and compensation systems, and labor relations.

The current challenge of human resource management is to integrate programs involving human resources with strategic organizational objectives. More and more, organizations are under tremendous competitive pressure worldwide. HR managers must find ways to develop effective international programs to meet this challenge. Another important aspect of human resource management is the need to ensure the cost-effectiveness of programs and policies through the optimal utilization of human resources.

Since the HR department plays a support role within the organization, it interacts with a variety of constituencies. It is important to note that the needs of these constituencies are likely to vary. Research offers a useful framework for understanding the conflicting demands on HR professionals.

The challenges to human resource management in the twenty-first century involve setting directions and formulating policies to address current and future business trends. The challenges of corporate reorganizations, global competition, competitive markets, increasing diversity in the work force, employee expectations, and legal and governmental requirements will allow HR managers to play a dynamic and pivotal role in meeting organizational goals.

Career opportunities are many and varied. The entry-level position is often that of technical specialist. In this role, one would assume responsibility for handling and coordinating well-defined HR programs in a single area. Progression would be to HR manager, a generalist responsible for administering programs across activity areas. The final step would be that of HR executive. In this role, one assumes responsibility for overseeing major areas of activity and for integrating organizational and HR objectives.

The Manager's Vocabulary

benchmarks
collective bargaining
cost-benefit utility
diversity
employment-at-will
ethical duties
HR specialist
human resource certification
human resource executive
human resource management (HRM)
human resource manager
human resource planning
human resource specialist
human resources
stakeholders
strategic human resource management

Questions for Discussion

1. What are some of the HRM characteristics that have enabled J. M. Smucker to be consistently regarded as one of the "Best Companies to Work For" in America?
2. Of Pfeffer's seven human resource practices indicative of organizational success, which do you think is most important? Why?
3. What is it about Southwest Airlines' success that is so difficult to duplicate? Why?
4. Think of the jobs you have had in the past or expect to seek in the future. What two features of employment did you (or will you) value most? How can HRM activities contribute to the presence and success of these employment features?
5. If you were the executive in charge of HR at Kodak, what are the first five steps you would take toward the goal of cutting up to 15,000 jobs? Describe each step and the reason for taking it.
6. Describe the major types of HRM activities.
7. How does the HR function become involved with business ethics concerns in the organization?
8. Should HRM programs have to be justified on a cost-benefit basis? Why or why not? What problems does the need to justify activities from a cost-benefit perspective pose for HRM?
9. A medium-sized manufacturing company is considering a major business decision to upgrade its technology by purchasing computer-driven equipment. What HR considerations need to be factored into the decision?
10. In what ways has increased international competition influenced human resource management? What types of organizational changes have resulted from increased international competition, and how has the field of human resource management helped achieve these changes?
11. Identify three ways in which HR can add value to an organization.
12. What are some of the factors that have increased the organizational status of the HR function?
13. What do you think will be the two most important challenges to HR managers in the next five years? Why did you pick these two?
14. What types of careers are available in human resource management? What kinds of entry-level positions are available? What should an individual do to prepare for a career in HRM?
15. What are some of the things that make a career in human resources attractive? What are some of the drawbacks? How would a career in HR fit your abilities, interests, and personality?
16. On the basis of your own part-time or full-time work experiences, how do you think the HR function could be improved?

Case 1.1
Human Resources at Leah's Bakery

While out shopping, you decide to stop in at a friend's business, Leah's Bakery. Leah recognizes you and invites you into her office. She is eager to talk about her work, and in the conversation that follows she tells you she is about to mark the second anniversary of what has turned out to be a remarkable business. In terms of the breads, pastries, and other baked goods, customers cannot seem to get enough. On the other hand, Leah has the feeling that she is working harder than is ideal and that the bakery is less profitable than expected. Being a people-oriented person yourself, you pick up on Leah's comment on her difficulty in finding good employees. The following aspects of Leah's Bakery emerge:

1. It takes fifteen employees to staff the bakery for a full week.
2. Leah defines six different positions: two bakers (pastries and breads), one cake decorator, a retail clerk, and a shift supervisor who also works behind the counter.
3. Leah has employed 240 people in the two years of operation. The shortest tenure was two hours and the longest was twelve weeks.
4. Pay for the employees ranges from $6.50 per hour (retail clerk) to $9.50 per hour (shift supervisor). There are no benefits.

Having 240 employees within a two-year period seems to you extraordinary; it represents an 800 percent turnover—equivalent to a new set of employees every six weeks. Yet the information Leah has provided jibes with your observations. Even though you visit the bakery at least once a week, you seldom see familiar faces. The "help wanted" sign is a permanent fixture in the front window. On several occasions, you have even seen the shift supervisor interviewing applicants at the end of the counter. As a frequent customer, you have noticed that the employees are pleasant and are obviously trying their best. At the same time, they frequently do not appear to understand certain common aspects of their jobs—for example, the functions of the cash register, how to enter special orders, the schedule for baking, ingredients of special items, and so forth.

1. What are some possible causes of the high turnover Leah's Bakery is experiencing?
2. If you were asked to help put human resources on a more even footing, on what HR activities would you concentrate?
3. What are three or four human resource programs Leah could implement to reduce the high turnover?

Exercise 1.1
Human Resource Management in the News

Divide the class into groups of three or four students each. Assign one of the following types of publications to each group:

- **Business magazines** *Business Week* (last three months), *Fortune* (last three months), *Harvard Business Review* (last six issues)
- **Newspapers** (last two weeks) *Wall Street Journal, New York Times,* or other major daily newspaper
- **News magazines** (last three months) *Time, U.S. News & World Report, Newsweek*

Each group is to go to the library and search the assigned sources for the following:

1. Articles directly relevant to HRM, such as layoffs, union activities, recruiting and selection practices, employment law developments, compensation practices, training and development programs, productivity improvement techniques, turnover, performance appraisal, discipline and discharge, and so forth.
2. Articles about aspects of the environment that have indirect implications for HRM, such as changing social values, demographics, technological change, trends in the economy, and so on.

Each group of students should then organize its materials and prepare an oral summary of what it has found. (Presentation materials, such as PowerPoint, flip chart pads, or blank overhead transparencies and markers, should be made available to students in each group as they prepare their presentation.)

International Option Additional groups may be assigned to search recent English-language publications from a specific country or geographic region. Their task would be to look for articles related to human resource management that might be of interest to a multinational organization with operations in the target country or region. The following are examples of regions and sources:

- **Europe** *London Times, International Herald Tribune;* major English-language dailies in France, Germany, Spain, and other countries
- **Pacific Rim** *Asian Wall Street Journal, Asian Business Week, Far Eastern Economic Review;* major English-language dailies in Tokyo, Hong Kong, Taiwan, Singapore, and Seoul
- **Australia** *The Australian* (newspaper), *Business Review Weekly*

Presentation Option 1: Time permitting, each group will make a five- to seven-minute presentation of its findings to the entire class.

Presentation Option 2: Combine groups into triads (quartets if international groups were formed), each triad consisting of a newspaper group, a business magazine group, and a news magazine group (and an international group). Each triad (quartet) should move to a separate room (or corner of the classroom) and present its summary to the other groups in the triad (quartet).

Exercise 1.2
Jobs in Human Resource Management

Form the class into groups of four to five students each. Read the brief descriptions of different human resource management jobs provided here. In groups, discuss the following questions:

1. Which job does each of you prefer, and why?
2. What do you see as the advantages and disadvantages of each job?
3. What skills, experience, and formal education would be needed to do each job well?
4. How do you suppose each job has changed in the past thirty years? How might each change further between now and 2015?

Manager, Human Resources Plans and carries out policies relating to all phases of HR activity: Recruits, interviews, and selects employees to fill vacant positions. Plans and conducts new employee orientation to foster a positive attitude toward company goals. Keeps record of insurance coverage, pension plan, and personnel transactions, such as hires, promotions, transfers, and terminations. Investigates accidents and prepares reports for insurance carrier. Conducts wage survey within labor market to determine competitive wage rate. Prepares budget of HR operations. Meets with shop stewards and supervisors to resolve grievances. Writes separation notices for employees separating with cause. Conducts exit interviews to determine reasons behind voluntary separations. Prepares reports and recommends procedures to reduce absenteeism and turnover. Represents company at HR-related hearings and investigations. Contracts with outside suppliers to provide employee services, such as canteen, transportation, or relocation service. May prepare budget of HR operations using computer terminal. May administer manual and dexterity tests to applicants. May supervise clerical workers. May keep records of hired employee characteristics for governmental reporting purposes. May negotiate collective-bargaining agreements with business representatives, labor union.

Manager, Compensation (Alternate Title: Wage and Salary Administrator) Manages compensation program in establishment: Directs development and application of techniques of job analysis, job descriptions, evaluations, grading, and pricing to determine and record job factors and to determine and convert relative job worth into monetary values to be administered according to pay-scale guidelines and policy. Analyzes company compensation policies, government regulations concerning payment of minimum wages and overtime pay, prevailing rates in similar organizations and industries, and agreements with labor unions to comply with legal requirements and to establish competitive rates designed to attract, retain, and motivate employees. Recommends compensation adjustments according to findings, utilizing knowledge of prevailing rates of straight-time pay, types of wage incentive systems, and special compensation programs for professional, technical, sales, supervisory, managerial, and executive personnel. Approves merit increases permitted within budgetary limits and according to pay policies. Duties may also include administration of employee benefits program.

Manager, Employment (Alternate Title: Employment Supervisor) Manages employment activities of establishment: Plans and directs activities of staff workers concerned with such functions as developing sources of qualified applicants, conducting screening interviews, administering tests, checking references and background, evaluating applicants' qualifications, and arranging for preliminary indoctrination and training for newly hired employees. Keeps records and compiles statistical reports concerning recruitment, interviews, hires, transfers, promotions, terminations, and performance appraisals, utilizing knowledge of job requirements, valid selection processes, and legislation concerning equal employment practices. Coordinates employment activities, such as those concerned with preparing job requisitions; interviewing, selecting, and hiring candidates; conducting on-the-job indoctrination and additional training; providing supervisory follow-up, development, and rating of employees; and conducting exit interviews. Analyzes statistical data and other reports concerning all aspects of employment function to identify and determine causes of personnel problems and to develop and present recommendations for improvement of establishment's employment policies, processes, and practices.

Manager, Labor Relations (Alternate Title: Labor Relations Representative) Manages labor relations program of organization: Analyzes collective-bargaining agreement to develop interpretation of intent, spirit, and terms of contract. Advises management and union officials in development, application, and interpretation of labor relations policies and practices according to policy formulated by the industrial relations director. Arranges and schedules meetings between workers with grievances, supervisory and managerial personnel, and the labor union's business representative to investigate and resolve grievances. Prepares statistical reports using records of actions taken concerning grievances, arbitration and mediation cases, and related labor relations activities to identify problem areas. Monitors implementation of policies concerning wages, hours, and working conditions to ensure compliance with terms of labor contract. Furnishes information, such as reference documents and statistical data concerning labor legislation, labor-market conditions, prevailing union and management practices, wage and salary surveys, and employee benefits programs, for use in review of current contract provisions and proposed changes. May represent management in labor contract negotiations. May supervise employees and be known as Labor Relations Supervisor. May be employed by firm offering labor relations advisory services to either management or labor and be known as Labor Relations Consultant. May be employed by governmental agency to study, interpret, and report on relations between management and labor and be known as Industrial Relations Representative.

Training Representative (Alternate Title: Training Instructor) Develops and conducts training programs for employees of industrial, commercial, service, or government establishment. Confers with management to gain knowledge of work situations requiring training for employees to better understand changes in policies, procedures, regulations, and technologies. Formulates teaching outline and determines instructional methods, utilizing knowledge of specific training needs and effectiveness of such methods as individual training, group instruction, lectures, demonstrations, conferences, meetings, and workshops. Selects or develops teaching aids, such as training handbooks, demonstration models, multimedia visual aids, computer tutorials, and reference works. Conducts training sessions covering specified areas such as those concerned with new employee orientation, on-the-job training, use of computers and software, apprenticeship programs, sales techniques, health and safety practices, public relations, refresher training, promotional development, upgrading, retraining of displaced workers, and leadership development. Tests trainees to measure progress and to evaluate effectiveness of training. May specialize in developing instructional software.

Employment Interviewer (Alternate Title: Placement Interviewer) Interviews job applicants to select people meeting employer qualifications. Reviews employment applications and evaluates work history, education and training, job skills, compensation needs, and other qualifications of applicants. Records additional knowledge, skills, abilities, interests, test results, and other data pertinent to selection and referral of applicants. Reviews job orders and matches applicants with job requirements, utilizing manual or computerized file search. Informs applicants of job duties and responsibilities, compensation and benefits, work schedules and working conditions, company and union policies, promotional opportunities, and other related information. Refers selected applicants to person placing job order, according to policy of organization. Keeps records of applicants not selected for employment. May perform reference and background checks on applicants. May refer applicants to vocational counseling services. May conduct or arrange for skills, intelligence, or psychological testing of applicants. May evaluate selection and placement techniques by conducting research or follow-up activities and conferring with management and supervisory personnel. May specialize in interviewing and referring certain types of personnel, such as professional, technical, managerial, clerical, and other types of skilled or unskilled workers. May search for and recruit applicants for open positions. May contact employers in writing, in person, or by telephone to solicit orders for job vacancies for clientele or for specified applicants and record information about job openings on job order forms to describe duties, hiring requirements, and related data.

Job Analyst (Alternate Title: Personnel Analyst) Collects, analyzes, and prepares occupational information to facilitate personnel, administration, and management functions of organization. Consults with management to determine type, scope, and purpose of study. Studies current organizational occupational data and compiles distribution reports, organization and flow charts, and other background information required for study. Observes jobs and interviews workers and supervisory personnel to determine job and worker requirements. Analyzes occupational data, such as physical, mental, and training requirements of jobs and workers, and develops written summaries, such as job descriptions, job specifications, and lines of career movement. Utilizes developed occupational data to evaluate or improve methods and techniques for recruiting, selecting, promoting, evaluating, and training workers and administration of related personnel programs. May specialize in classifying positions according to regulated guidelines to meet job classification requirements of civil service system and be known as Position Classifier.

Exercise 1.3
Professional Ethics

Figure 1.3 gives the Code of Ethics of the Society for Human Resource Management. Using an Internet browser (e.g., Netscape or Internet Explorer), examine the codes of ethics of two of the three professions listed here that also serve business or nonprofit organizations.

Profession	**Internet Address for Code of Ethics**
Environmental professionals	*http://www.customcpu.com/professionalscommercial/aaep/code.htm*
Industrial hygienists	*http://www.aiha.org/ethics.html*
International Webmaster Association	*http://www.iwanet.org/about/ethics.html*

After examining the SHRM Code of Ethics and those of two of the professions listed, answer the following questions:

1. What are the similarities in these codes to that of the SHRM?
2. What are the differences?
3. Using the codes of other professionals, what changes would you suggest for the SHRM?

Notes and References

1. Robert Levering and Milton Moskowitz, "100 Best Companies to Work For," *Fortune,* January 12, 2004, pp. 56–80.

2. Ibid., pp. 58–59.

3. Ibid.

4. Robert Baker, "No Suckers, Those Smuckers," *Business Week,* March 4, 2002, p. 112.

5. Ibid.

6. Janet Adamy, "Smucker Agrees to Acquire Maker of Pillsbury Mixes," *Wall Street Journal*, March 9, 2004, p. A3.
7. Ingrid Smithey Fulmer, Barry Gerhart, and Kimberly S. Scott, "Are the 100 Best Better? An Empirical Investigation of the Relationship Between Being a 'Great Place to Work' and Firm Performance." *Personnel Psychology*, 2003, pp. 965–993.
8. Michael J. Mandel, "Commentary: Outsourcing Jobs: Is It Bad?" *Business Week*, August 25, 2003, pp. 36–38.
9. James C. Cooper, "The Price of Efficiency," *Business Week*, March 22, 2004, pp. 38–42.
10. Peter Coy, "Where the Recovery Won't Reach," *Business Week*, May 13, 2002, p. 92; "The Great Hollowing-Out Myth," *The Economist*, February 21, 2004, p. 48.
11. James Bandler, "Kodak to Cut Staff up to 21%, Amid Digital Push," *Wall Street Journal*, January 22, 2004, p. A1.
12. Mike France, Wendy Zellner, and Mike McNamee, "The Case Against Jeff Skilling," *Business Week*, March 1, 2004, pp. 32–35.
13. Louis Lavelle and Michael Arndt, "Living Large in the Corner Office," *Business Week*, February 23, 2004, p. 47; Naween A. Mangi, "Do 'Living Wages' Kill Business?" *Business Week*, October 29, 2001. (Available at: http://www.businessweek.com/smallbiz/content/oct2001/sb20011029_228.htm)
14. David Wessel, "Debate on Social Security Looks Promising," *Wall Street Journal*, March 4, 2004, p. A2.
15. Catherine Arnst, "Health-Care Hikes: Slowing, Sort Of," *Business Week*, December 30, 2003. (Available at: http://www.businessweek.com/bwdaily/dnflash/dec2003/nf20031230_9187_db038.htm)
16. "Cingular Wins the Bidding for AT&T Wireless," *CNN.com,* February 17, 2004. (Available at: http://nn.com/2004/US/02/17/cingular.att/)
17. Jay B. Barney and Patrick M. Wright, "On Becoming a Strategic Partner: The Role of Human Resources in Gaining Competitive Advantage," *Human Resource Management*, Vol. 37 (1), 1998, pp. 31–46.
18. Jeffrey Pfeffer, *The Human Equation: Building Profits by Putting People First* (Boston: Harvard Business School Press, 1998).
19. Jeffrey Pfeffer and John F. Veiga, "Putting People First for Organizational Success," *Academy of Management Executive*, Vol. 13 (2), 1999, pp. 37–48.
20. See also, Fred Reichheld, *Loyalty Rules! How Today's Leaders Build Lasting Relationships* (Boston: Harvard Business School Press, 2001).
21. Cited in "The Southwest Train," *USA Today*, December 12, 2000, pp. 9–10.
22. Andy Serwer, "Southwest Airlines: The Hottest Thing in the Sky," *Fortune*, March 8, 2004, pp. 86–90.
23. H. Kelleher, "A Culture of Commitment," *Leader to Leader*, Vol. 1, 1997, p. 23.
24. Joanne Cole, "Flying High at Southwest," *HR Focus*, Vol. 75 (5), May 1998, p. 8.
25. "More on What CEOs Want from HR," *HR Focus,* Vol. 80 (4), 2003, pp. 5–6.
26. "New Study Identifies Key Competencies Necessary for HR," *Society for Human Resource Management,* June 22, 2003. (Available at: http://www.shrm.org/press_published/1CMS_004834.asp#P28_180)
27. Bandler, "Kodak to Cut Staff up to 21%."
28 "Has Kodak Missed the Moment?" *The Economist*, January 3, 2004, p. 46.
29. James Bandler, "Worst 1-Year Performer: Eastman Kodak," *Wall Street Journal*, March 8, 2004, p. R1.
30. Dave Ulrich, "Judge Me More by My Future Than by My Past," *Human Resource Management*, Vol. 36 (1), Spring 1997, pp. 5–8.
31. H. G. Heneman III, "Pay Satisfaction," in *Research in Personnel and Human Resources Management*, Vol. 3, ed. K. Rowland and J. Ferris (Greenwich, Conn.: JAI Press, 1985).
32. R. W. Scholl, E. A. Cooper, and J. F. McKenna, "Referent Selection in Determining Equity Perceptions: Differential Effects on Behavioral and Attitudinal Outcomes," *Personnel Psychology*, Vol. 40, 1987, pp. 113–124.
33. "Health Care is Making Labor Sick," *Business Week*, November 13, 2003. (Available at http://www.businessweek.com/bwdaily/dnflash/nov2003/nf20031113_4031_db038.htm) 34 George Edmonson, "Bush's Weight Felt in Airline Affairs Unprecedented Vow: His Determination to Keep 'Strikes from Happening' Loomed Large in Talks with Delta Pilots," *The Atlanta Journal-Constitution,* April 24, 2001, p. D–4.
35. "China's Economic Power," *The Economist,* March 10, 2001, pp. 23–25.
36. McDonald's 2002 Summary Annual Report. (Available at: http://www.mcdonalds.com/corp/invest/pub/printable.html)
37. McDonald's Worldwide Corporate Site. (Available at: http://www.mcdonalds.com/countries/russia/index.html)
38. John Rossant, "Airbus: Birth of a Giant," *Business Week* (International Edition), July 10, 2000. (Available at: http:/www.businessweek.com:/2000/00_28/b3689015.htm)

39. Mark A. Huselid, "The Impact of Human Resource Management Practices on Turnover, Productivity, and Corporate Financial Performance," *Academy of Management Journal*, Vol. 38 (3), 1995, pp. 635–672; John T. Delaney and Mark A. Huselid, "The Impact of Human Resource Management Practices on Perceptions of Organizational Performance," *Academy of Management Journal*, Vol. 39 (4), 1996, pp. 649–696; and Mark A. Huselid, Susan E. Jackson, and Randall S. Schuler, "Technical and Strategic Human Resource Management Effectiveness as Determinants of Firm Performance," *Academy of Management Journal*, Vol. 40 (1), 1997, pp. 171–188.
40. Pfeffer, *The Human Equation;* Reichheld, *Loyalty Rules!*
41. Kenneth Goodpaster and John B. Matthews Sr., "Can a Corporation Have a Conscience?" *Harvard Business Review*, January–February 1982, pp. 132–141.
42. The complete document is available on the Web site. SHRM Code of Ethical and Professional Standards in Human Resource Management. (Available at: http://www.shrm.org/ethics/code-of-ethics.asp)
43. Mary Williams Walsh, "Lessons from the Battle to End Workplace Violence," *New York Times*, December 31, 2000. (Available at: http://www.nytimes.com/2000/12/31/business/31FIVE.html)
44. Mimi Swartz and Sherron Watkins, *Power Failure: The Inside Story of the Collapse of Enron* (New York: Random House, 2003)
45. Dave Ulrich, "Benchmarking and Competitor Analysis," in *The Blackwell Encyclopedic Dictionary of Human Resource Management* (Oxford, U.K.: Blackwell, 1997).
46. "The Net Gets Real," *The Economist*, January 13, 2000, pp. 22–24.
47. "The Great Merger Wave Breaks," *The Economist*, January 25, 2001, pp. 59–60.
48. Matthew Boyle, "Gearing Down: The Not-So-Fine Art of the Layoff," *Fortune*, March 19, 2001, pp. 209–210.
49. As of early 2004, the U.S. nonfarm work force consisted of 130 million. Of these 17 percent were classified as manufacturing (including construction) and 83 percent as service. "The Employment Situation: February 2004," U.S. Department of Labor, Bureau of Labor Statistics. (Available at: http://stats.bls.gov/news.release/pdf/empsit.pdf)
50. Carolyn Lochead, "Tech Bosses Defend Overseas Hiring," *San Francisco Chronicle,* January 8, 2004. (Available at: http://sfgate.com/cgi-bin/article.cgi?file=/chronicle/archive/2004/01/08/MNGDI45PV01.DTL)
51. Bandler, "Kodak to Cut Staff up to 21%."
52. Pamela L. Moore, "Jack the Job-Killer Strikes Again," *Business Week*, February 12, 2001, p. 12.
53. Andrew Balls, "The Flattening of Corporate Management," National Bureau of Economic Research, October 2003. (Available at: http://www.nber.org/digest/oct03/w9633.html)
54. "The Employment Situation: February 2004," U.S. Department of Labor, Bureau of Labor Statistics. (Available at: http://stats.bls.gov/news.release/pdf/empsit.pdf)
55. Ibid.
56. "National Population Projections," U.S. Census Bureau. (Available at: http://www.census.gov/population/www/projections/natsum-T3.html) Note: "Other" ethnic groups include Asian and Pacific Islanders along with American Indians.
57. Watson Wyatt Worldwide, *A Nation of Floridas.* (Available at: http://www.watsonwyatt.com/research/resrender.asp?id=W-233&page=3)
58. Susan Meisinger, "Assessing HR: The View from the C-Suites," *HR Magazine*, January 2004, p. 10; Rich Vosburgh, "The State of the Human Resources Profession in 2003: An Interview with Dave Ulrich," *Human Resource Planning*, 2003, vol. 26 (1), pp. 18–23.
59. Joe Vocino, "Accelerating Compensation Reflects the Changing World of HR and Increased Emphasis on Variable Pay," *HR Magazine*, November 2003, pp. 74–84.
60. Ibid.
61. Ibid.
62. Steve Bates, "No Experience Necessary?" *HR Magazine*, November 2001, pp. 34–41.
63. Human Resource Certification Institute. (Available at: http://www.hrci.org/certification/passrate.html)
64. Human Resource Certification Institute. (Available at: http://www.hrci.org/directory/stats.html)
65. World at Work Society of Certified Professionals. (Available at: http://www.worldatworksociety.org/)
66. International Foundation of Employee Benefit Plans. (Available at: http://www.ifebp.org/cebs/overview.asp)
67. Board of Certified Safety Professionals. (Available at: http://www.bcsp.org/cspspecialty_fr.html)
68. American Board of Industrial Hygiene. (Available at: http://www.abih.org/Exam/homepage.htm)
69. Human Resource Certification Institute. (Available at: http://www.hrci.org/gphr/)

PART 2

Planning for Organizations, Jobs, and People

CHAPTER 2

Strategic Human Resource Management

- Why Is Managing Human Resources So Important?
- What Is Strategic Human Resource Management (SHRM)?
- Transforming HR Staff and Structure
- Enhancing Administrative Efficiency
- Integrating HR into Strategic Planning
- Fitting HR Practices to Business Strategy and to One Another
- Partnership
- Measuring HRM
- Is Strategic HRM Really Worth All the Trouble?

HR Challenge

In 2003 Xilinx was one of the fastest growing companies in the semiconductor industry. Xilinx is a publicly traded company headquartered in San Jose, California, with a work force of approximately 2,600 employees. Xilinx was a pioneer in the development of the field programmable array (FPGA), and in 2003 Xilinx filled more than 50 percent of the worldwide demand for this product. FPGAs are computer logic chips that can be produced as a standard product then customized by clients to meet the client's particular needs. This is in contrast to the earlier approach of chips having to be manufactured to customized specifications. In addition to FPGAs, Xilinx designs, manufactures, and markets computer hardware and software products used in a broad range of digital electronic products. In 2003 Xilinx had more than 7,500 customers worldwide including such global leaders as Cisco Systems, Ericsson, Fujitsu, Hewlett-Packard, IBM, Lucent Technologies, Nokia, Samsung, Siemens, and Toshiba. A 2003 market research report by Gartner Dataquest ranked Xilinx as the fourth largest ASIC (application specific integrated circuit) company in the world, up from being fifth the previous year.

Thanks to these performance figures, in 2003 Xilinx was ranked seventeenth among Business Week's *fifty best-performing companies in the Standard & Poors 500 and was also named as one of the 400 best big com-*

panies by Forbes *magazine. Two of its customers, Cisco Systems and Lucent Technologies, named Xilinx their supplier of the year. In addition to this very positive financial and customer performance, Xilinx was also noted as one of the best firms to work for in the United States. It was ranked fourth among* Fortune *magazine's "Best 100 Companies to Work For" and the* San Francisco Chronicle *named Xilinx among its top fifty companies to work for in the Silicon Valley.*

So, with financial and human resource performance like this, why is Xilinx being presented as an "HR Challenge?" The answer—in 2001 Xilinx faced a far less positive financial outlook and needed to make some very difficult business and HR decisions. Market demand for Xilinx's products plummeted. For the quarter ending June 30, sales were down 21 percent with operating profits of $30.3 million, down from $121.3 million the year before. In the next quarter of 2001, sales were down 48.6 percent compared to the year before, and the previous year's $147.1 million operating profit was replaced by an operating loss of $115 million. This negative financial performance was made more problematic because it came after a period of extensive growth in sales revenue, profits, and the size of Xilinx's work force.

Xilinx had been proud of its ability to recruit the very best employees. In an article published in Design News *in 2003, CEO Wim Roelandts noted that a major problem he faced in 2001 was that much of the labor force at Xilinx was made up of intelligent, motivated, and well-educated engineers. Much of the intellectual property and know-how in the company was found in the heads of these employees. If they were lost, so was valuable company and product knowledge. This intellectually gifted and innovative human resource had, since the company's founding, proven to be a significant element in Xilinx's competitive success.*[1]

How did Xilinx deal with this difficult situation? What information was critical in helping Mr. Roelandts and his executive team make the right decisions? What human resource initiatives were taken to protect the financial viability of Xilinx during tough economic times, yet protect the firm's long-term competitive position? This was truly an HR challenge![2]

The problems faced by Xilinx are not unlike those faced by many firms that have undergone major changes in the nature of their business environments. The idea that constant change is a fact of organizational life has become widely accepted among practicing managers, organizational consultants, and business academics. Since September 11, 2001, managers worldwide have had to recognize that, in addition to "normal" changes in business conditions, their market environments may shift dramatically and with a suddenness unheard of only a short time before. In these new worldwide business conditions, a common theme is the important role that human resource management plays in the success or failure of firms. Xilinx's business challenge in 2001 was, to a large extent, focused around the need to protect their human capital under tough market conditions. The view that human resource managers are simply "paper pushers" is rapidly disappearing, to be replaced by the notion that they play a key role in determining the competitive success of firms in a dynamic and unpredictable business world.

In a generic sense, the new view of human resource management has been referred to as **strategic human resource management (SHRM).** This chapter takes a look at this concept. Specifically, the business factors that contribute to the increased importance of human resources as a source of a firm's strategic competitive advantage are discussed. Several theoretical perspectives on what strategic human resource management actually involves are described. Then the key elements needed to develop strategic human resource management practices within an organization are discussed in detail. Examples are given of how these aspects of SHRM have been operationalized by firms that have undergone or are currently undergoing the transformation from a traditional to a more strategic view of human resource management. The chapter also examines the question of whether strategic HRM practices actually enhance firm performance. Is the move from traditional to strategic HRM really worth all the effort required? Evidence supporting the value-adding effects of strategic HR practices is discussed.

This chapter plays a critical role in establishing the context for all subsequent chapters. Following Chapter 2, the text explores a variety of HR functional areas and issues and introduces a large number of sophisticated HR techniques. Some believe that practicing good HRM requires a firm to use the most advanced and sophisticated HR methodologies. As shown in this chapter, however, simply using the most advanced techniques may not necessarily add the greatest value to a firm's operations or ensure its long-term success. Within the framework of strategic human resource management, effectively managing human assets in a firm requires a far broader view of what is good or bad, efficient or inefficient. What is required is an understanding of the complex interactions among the unique characteristics of the firm, its customers, the business environment in which it operates, its products or services, and the nature of its employees. This chapter provides a broader, more strategic and complex view of managing human resources for long-term competitive success. It is from this expanded perspective that the reader must view the methodologies and techniques discussed throughout the remainder of the text.

WHY IS MANAGING HUMAN RESOURCES SO IMPORTANT?

In the past decade, increasing attention has been paid to the importance of human resource management in determining a firm's competitive advantage. Wayne Brockbank suggests that an increasing attention to strategic HR issues is evidenced in several ways.[3] First, in an increasing number of firms, the chief HR executive reports directly to the organization's CEO, indicating higher HR status within the organization. Second, CEOs in major companies such as Sears, General Electric, Ford, and Allied Signal are encouraging a greater focus on HR issues as part of programs to enhance competitive advantage. Finally, HR contributions are increasingly given credit for playing a critical role in improving the performance of major firms (e.g., Baxter International, Harley Davidson, Quantum, Unilever, Arco).

Why is this so? What factors have caused businesses to focus increased attention on HRM? Randall Schuler identifies several changes in the basic business environment that place increased importance on human resources. Among these are:

- Rapid change
- High levels of uncertainty about basic business conditions
- Rising costs
- Rapid technological change

- Changing demographics
- More limited supplies of highly trained labor
- Rapidly changing government legislation and regulations
- Increased globalization of industries[4]

Recent analyses of future trends in HRM support the importance of these factors, with particular emphasis on the HR implications of an aging work force in many developed countries and advances in technology that will result in an increased use of Web-based HR systems and the interaction of employees within a "virtual office."[5]

In his 1997 book, *Human Resource Champions,* Dave Ulrich argued that these factors place additional pressure on firms to be innovative and to create new ways of doing business with new technologies, new products, and new services to meet an increasingly diverse and demanding customer base.[6] The enhanced value of innovation in determining competitive advantage requires firms to attract, train, and retain employees of the highest quality. Firms have to move from a situation where financial capital was the key to strategic success to an era where human talent and adaptability determine strategic goal achievement.[7] From this realization has come the approach to managing human resources referred to as SHRM.

WHAT IS STRATEGIC HUMAN RESOURCE MANAGEMENT?

Before one can understand what strategic human resource management (SHRM) is, it is essential to have a clear picture of the "traditional" view of HR because it is still the prevalent form of HR activity in many organizations. Traditional HR activities include the following:

- Human resource planning
- Recruitment
- Job analysis
- Establishing performance review systems
- Wage, salary, and benefits administration
- Employee training
- Personnel record keeping
- Legislative compliance (affirmative action, EEO, etc.)
- Labor relations

Much of the time of HR units within firms is still focused on these traditional activities as compared to more strategic "business partner" functions. In 2000 HR leaders in more than 100 large firms indicated that they spent 80 percent of their time on traditional HR activities such as (a) collecting, tracking, and maintaining data on employees; (b) ensuring compliance with internal operational procedures, legal and other external regulations, and union requirements; (c) assisting with the implementation and administration of traditional HR practices; and (d) developing new HR systems and practices. The HR leaders reported that only 20 percent of their time was spent as a "strategic business partner," involved in executive management team activities related to strategic planning, organizational design, and strategic change. A good example of this was found in another survey of 447 senior HR executives. Only 20 percent of them indicated that they were part of the pre-deal phase of mergers and acquisitions, a major strategic action taken by any firm.[8]

The traditional personnel department still exists in many firms and is often both physically and psychologically separated from the "real work" of the organization. A visual representation of the traditional role of the personnel department in organizations is shown in Figure 2.1a. The key points represented in Figure 2.1a are that the traditional personnel orientation involves a limited number of functional tasks and that personnel activities and staff are relatively isolated from the "profit-making heart" of the organization.

FIGURE 2.1
Traditional and Strategic Views of HRM

(a) Personnel—The traditional view

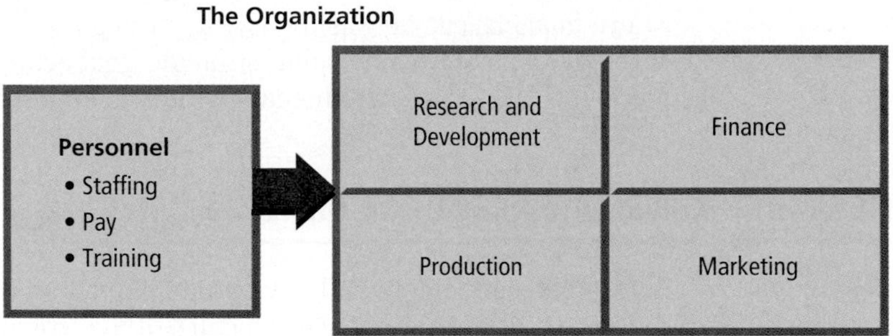

(b) HRM—The strategic view

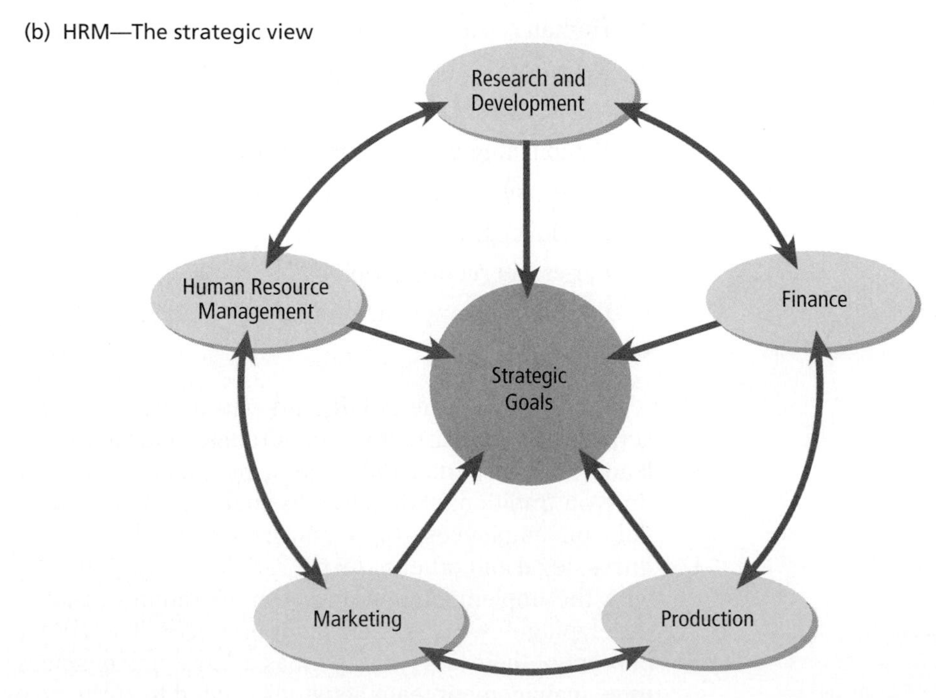

Strategic HRM: Some Theoretical Perspectives

In the strategic view of HRM, the functional duties described earlier remain important. Certainly hiring, training, and providing pay and benefits to employees are essential tasks that must be accomplished in any organization. However, given the changes in the business environment discussed earlier, many organizations are developing new structural and cultural patterns to meet the competitive demands of their dynamic and international marketplace, and the role of HR in these organizations has had to change to meet these challenges as well.

As a result, a new strategic view of HR has tended to emerge (see Figure 2.1b). In these firms, HR is integrated fully and plays a central role in helping the organization reach its strategic objectives, interacting with other functional areas within the firm.

The new role of HR can be described most simply as one of helping managers maximize the contribution of employees in achieving **competitive advantage.** Strategic HRM is "concerned with the promotion of efficiency and profitability. . . . Strategic HRM centers on how organizations can improve their competitive performance by considering and utilizing their human resources more effectively."[9] These definitions seem straightforward, but there is considerable debate about what "helping managers maximize the contribution of employees" or "utilizing their human resources more effectively" really involves. A number of theoretical models have been developed to explain exactly what SHRM requires in an organization and the processes by which SHRM contributes to the bottom-line success of a firm. A summary of these theoretical perspectives is given in Table 2.1.

In his book, *The Human Equation,* Jeffrey Pfeffer notes strong evidence for a set of HR practices that have a positive effect on organizational performance, regardless of a firm's particular business environment and strategy.[10] This set of HR practices include the following:

- High levels of employment security
- Selective hiring practices
- A focus on teams and decentralized decision making

TABLE 2.1

Theoretical Perspectives on SHRM

Perspective	Description
Universalistic	There is one best way to manage human resources. Strategic HRM is the process of transforming traditional HR practices into a limited set of "correct" HR procedures and policies.
Strategic best-fit	Strategic HRM involves matching specific HR practices to the firm's overall business strategy.
Configurational	Various configurations, or "bundles," of HR practices go together and, collectively, can improve business performance. Certain bundles are effective in certain industries or in certain business conditions; other bundles should be used in other industries or under different business circumstances.
Resource-based	SHRM engenders organizational success by enhancing a firm's ability to acquire, develop, utilize, and retain employees with high competence levels relevant to firm activities.

- High pay levels
- Extensive employee training
- Practices that reduce status distinctions among employees
- High levels of information sharing

The basic assumptions behind this **universalistic approach** to SHRM is that these best practices are universally applicable and are directly related to firm performance, which can be measured in financial terms.[11]

Contrary to the universalistic view, the **best-fit perspective** of SHRM suggests that "firm performance will be enhanced to the degree that firms adopt human resource management practices that complement and support both other HR policies and practices and the other elements of the organization's strategic plan."[12] Although Pfeffer's practices fit with one another, they may or may not fit an organization's strategic approach. There are actually three aspects of "fit" within this best-fit approach to SHRM. *Horizontal fit* refers to the consistency among various HR practices within a firm. Thus, if a firm's selection procedures seek to hire highly innovative, risk-taking employees, the firm's performance appraisal and reward systems also should assess and reward innovation and risk taking. *Vertical fit* is the degree to which HR practices are consistent with the firm's overall business strategy. For example, suppose that a firm has decided to enhance its competitive standing relative to other firms in its industry by becoming highly "customer focused." HR training programs that help employees develop better customer relations skills would be consistent with this overall business philosophy. If training programs in the firm concentrated solely on upgrading technical skills unrelated to employee–customer interactions, the training system would be inconsistent with the customer-oriented business strategy. *External fit* refers to how well HR practices align with specific aspects of the external environment. For example, in the United States and Australia, demographic changes are occurring, creating a work force that is far more multicultural in nature. Diversity management training, remedial language training, or new approaches to selection of employees from nonmajority cultures may be required as part of the overall HR system to fit this new external environment and enhance the competitive value of employees.

The **configurational approach** to SHRM proposes that the strategic effectiveness of HRM depends on a set, or bundle, of HR practices rather than on any single HR program or policy. The idea here is "that employment practices often complement each other, so that the adoption of one employment practice is only effective when it is adopted in combination with one or more supporting work practices."[13] Over the years, programs such as "quality circles" have been heralded as a cure-all for many organizational ills. Few of these single-program approaches have resulted in the kind of improvements in organizational performance that were promised by their proponents. The configurational view of HR focuses on implementing **HR bundles** rather than single, "magic bullet" programs. The configurational approach to SHRM is consistent with the long-held view that employee performance is determined by a number of factors, such as motivation and ability. Thus, to increase employee performance, HR programs are needed that enhance both motivation (e.g., reward systems) and ability (e.g., hiring or training systems). One could argue that the configurational view is simply an extension of the universalistic approach described previously; that is, that some single bundle of HR practices have universally positive effects on employee performance. However, recent research on HR practices in Germany, Italy, the United

States, and Japan found that although bundles of HR practices had a greater positive effect on organizational performance than did single practices alone, the nature of those bundles varied from one country to the next.[14] So the universalistic and configurational views are not the same after all. One of the major contributions of the configurational approach is that research associated with it has identified a number of different "bundles" of HR practices that contain individual HR elements that are internally consistent with one another. Some of these different types of HR systems are described in Table 2.2.

TABLE 2.2
Types of HR Systems

Source	Types of HR Systems		
Dyer and Reeves (1995)	*Control systems:* • Centralization of decision making • Low employee involvement • Tight controls through rules, policies, appraisal	*Commitment systems:* • Decentralized decision making • High employee involvement • High levels of autonomy and empowerment	
Snell and Youndt (1995)	*Behavior control systems:* • Standardized responsibilities set by management • Employee accountability for actions regardless of results • Supervisor-conducted behavior-based appraisals • Use of feedback to fix problems	*Output control systems:* • Mutually set performance targets • Results-based appraisals • Monetary rewards for achieving results	*Input control systems:* • Rigorous selection and training; ensuring of requisite skills • Systems to ensure that employees understand and internalize firm's values
Delery and Doty (1996)	*Market-type systems:* • Hiring from outside • Little training • Evaluation of performance through the use of results measures • Little employment security • Little voice • Narrowly defined jobs	*Internal systems:* • Internal labor market • Extensive socialization and training • Performance assessment through behavior • Appraisal feedback for developmental purposes • High degree of employment security • Great deal of voice • Employees as excellent sources of information • Broadly defined jobs	

(continued)

TABLE 2.2
Continued

Source	Types of HR Systems			
Lepak and Snell (1999)	*Developing human capital:* Commitment system • Internal development • Loosely defined jobs • Training to develop unique skills • Career development and mentoring systems • Development appraisal • Extensive information sharing	*Acquiring human capital:* Market-based system • Acquisition of human capital from the market • Development of symbiotic relationship between firm and employees • Selection for skills with immediate use • Not a lot of training • Externally equitable wages	*Contracting human capital:* • Compliance system • Contract with external suppliers • Development of transactional relationship between firm and employees • Focus on terms and conditions of employment to ensure compliance • Lots of rules and procedures • Reliance on good selection procedures • Little training	*Creating human capital:* • Collaborative system • Use of both internal and external selection • Development of partnership relationship between firm and employees • Encouragement of and reward cooperation • Lots of information sharing • Little training • Possible use of exchange programs and job rotation

Sources: Adapted from information in Lee Dyer and Todd Reeves, "Human Resource Strategies and Firm Performance: What Do We Know and Where Do We Need to Go?" *The International Journal of Human Resource Management,* Vol. 6 (3), 1995, pp. 656–670; Scott Snell and Mark Youndt, "Human Resource Management and Firm Performance: Testing a Contingency Model of Executive Controls," *Journal of Management,* Vol. 21 (4), 1995, pp. 711–737; John Delery and Harold Doty, "Modes of Theorizing in Strategic Human Resource Management: Tests of Universalistic, Contingency, and Configurational Performance Predictions," *Academy of Management Journal,* Vol. 39 (4), 1996, pp. 802–835; David Lepak and Scott Snell, "The Human Resource Architecture: Toward a Theory of Human Capital Allocation and Development," *Academy of Management Review,* Vol. 24 (1), 1999, pp. 31–48.

In a 1995 article Jay Barney discussed a **resource-based model** of strategic HRM. This model is based on the idea that organizations gain competitive advantage when they possess resources that are valuable, rare, difficult for competitors to imitate, and organized in such a way as to maximize their overall value to the firm.[15] Subsequent work on this perspective concluded that strategic HRM involves HR managers solving four basic questions about human resources. These four questions are:[16]

1. How can the HR function aid in either decreasing costs or increasing revenues in the firm; that is, adding value?
2. How can the HR function identify and take advantage of the rare skills and characteristics of employees?
3. How can the HR function help create a labor force that is very difficult for other competitors to imitate?
4. How can the HR function help structure the firm so that it can best exploit its **human capital advantage**?

A recent analysis of research on the resource-based view identified three major implications of this SHRM perspective about which there is significant consensus.[17] First, HR managers must focus on the **human capital pool** within their firm, which consists of the skills, abilities, and knowledge that exist among employees at any one particular time. To gain competitive advantage, HR managers must (a) help the organization develop a human capital pool that has a higher overall level of skills, abilities, and knowledge than competitors; and (b) ensure that the skills, abilities, and knowledge within the human capital pool are more closely aligned with the strategic objectives of the firm than is typical among competitors. The resource-based approach to SHRM also requires constant monitoring of the characteristics of the human capital pool within the firm because the nature of this pool will change over time.

Experts point out that "employee behavior is an important independent component of SHRM. . . . employee behavior recognizes individuals as cognitive and emotional beings who possess free will. . . . Firms may have access to valuable human capital, but either through the poor design of work or the mismanagement of people, may not adequately deploy it to achieve strategic impact."[18] HR managers must develop systems within the firm to ensure that employees' discretionary behavior is actually directed toward activities that are strategically beneficial to the firm.

Finally, the resource-based view encourages HR managers to focus on the development of multiple rather than single practices to affect employees. This aspect of the resource-based view is similar to that of the configurational approach to HR. However, the resource-based view suggests that these systems of multiple practices need not be made up solely of traditional HR activities (e.g., recruiting, selection, performance appraisal) but must extend to activities related to the development of organizational culture, leadership, and other strategically critical aspects of the organization's life.

There are many examples of how firms have attempted to enhance their human capital pool.[19] Federal Express increased revenues by using employee attitude surveys to identify managers with poor employee relations skills. FedEx then used the survey information to improve managerial skills through training and performance management systems, which eventually led to improved customer service by employees. FedEx improved the overall competitive level of the skills, knowledge, and abilities of managers within its human capital pool. Southwest Airlines' extensive selection procedures identify flight attendants who contribute to the "fun" atmosphere of the airline. Top management empowers employees to "be inconsistent" and create new, fun, and interesting ways to satisfy customers. These selection and empowerment systems engender employee behavior that is highly consistent with the firm's overall business strategy. Importantly, these systems are also difficult for other firms to imitate. Nordstrom uses selection and compensation systems that select highly customer-oriented employees and then reward excellent customer service behavior. Through these systems, Nordstrom ensures that its highly capable employees actually contribute their discretionary effort to enhance firm performance. For all three of these firms, multiple HR practices have been used to enhance the firms' human capital advantage, which is consistent with the resource-based perspective.

Theoretical Perspectives: Conclusions About SHRM

As is often the case with theories about human behavior in organizations, the question for HR practitioners is this: "Which theoretical approach is correct, and from a practical perspective, what does it suggest are the important aspects for creating a strategically oriented HR function?" Unfortunately, the answer to this question is not simple. Like many other theories about organizations, none is completely correct. Rather than being right or wrong, each approach points to different aspects of the process needed for developing an effective strategic HR function. Taken collectively, the research conducted to test these different perspectives identifies six key elements required in developing SHRM within a firm:

1. Internally transforming HR staff and structure
2. Enhancing administrative efficiency
3. Integrating HR into the strategic planning process
4. Linking HR practices to the business strategy and to one another
5. Developing a partnership with line management
6. Focusing on the value of the human capital pool within the firm so as to have a direct business impact (and being able to measure that impact in a meaningful way)

Although these essential processes are listed as if they were independent of one another, there is obvious overlap among the concepts as there are overlaps among the theoretical perspectives from which they are derived.

Because traditional HR remains a dominant perspective in many organizations, creating a SHRM perspective requires the internal transformation of existing staff who perform HR duties and the structure within which they operate. It is these individuals who must champion and enact the change to SHRM. New skills are usually needed, as are new perspectives about the structure and processes of HRM. Within an SHRM perspective, traditional administrative tasks remain important. Employees must receive their pay and benefits, safety programs must be developed and administered, and EEO laws must be obeyed. However, the focus becomes one of performing these administrative tasks in as efficient and cost-effective a manner as possible.

In terms of the remaining elements of SHRM, the integration of HR into the strategic planning process is critical. Only by being part of the strategic planning process can HR practitioners link business strategy and HR practices to one another. Borrowing concepts from the configurational perspective, the focus of SHRM is not on linking single HR programs to business strategy. Rather, to enhance a firm's strategic effectiveness, SHRM must develop bundles of internally consistent HR activities that contribute to the achievement of the firm's strategic goals and objectives. This can only be accomplished once an effective partnership between line managers and HR staff is established. Otherwise, HR's ability to contribute to strategic planning and to develop useful bundles of HR practices will be limited. Finally, all theoretical perspectives of SHRM point to the need for a direct business impact of HR practices. The competitive business environment that most firms face today precludes the luxury of engaging in HR practices that simply "feel good" or "look good" or happen to be the latest HR fad. Human resource management activities must add value to the firm. In the following pages, each of these elements of SHRM is discussed, along with examples of how firms have operationalized them in their own transformation to a strategic approach to human resource management. However, before moving to a detailed discussion of the six elements for HR transformation, a brief discussion of a critical "pretransformation" activity is needed.

One key barrier to effective HR transformation is the attitude of many senior executives who still see HR as primarily an administrative function. For example, the results of a survey on how Chief Financial Officers (CFOs) in firms viewed HR showed that only 39 percent of CFOs viewed HR as mainly or somewhat as a strategic partner, while 33 percent viewed HR as an equal combination of "cost center" and strategic partner, and 28 percent viewed HR as somewhat or mainly a cost center. Thus, before any true transformation of HR can occur, top management must be brought "on board."[20] A number of authors have examined this issue, and several consistent themes have developed about how best to achieve top management "buy-in" to an HR transformation.[21]

First, the leader of any HR change effort must be a highly competent and credible leader within the organization. Second, a compelling business reason for change must be built with which the top managers can easily identify. To create a **compelling business case,** HR managers must "create an awareness of potential 'gain or pain' for a specific business. Human resource initiatives are successful when they resolve an issue—they make the issue 'go away.' Without clearly defined issues, human resource strategies are rhetoric and action plans lose connection with purpose."[22] For maximum impact, HR initiatives should be backed by compelling data and should focus on a few critical issues rather than on a huge range of problems.[23] Third, those leading the HR change process must be able to articulate a clearly defined "end-state vision" for HR and the major steps that will be needed to achieve that vision. This should involve an interactive process between HR and other top managers who help HR define that end state. The involvement of top managers will help ensure their commitment to the HR change process. Finally, measures must be developed to monitor the progress of the changes. These measures should be focused on the value added by HR. Such measures will not only help *get* the CEO and top management team "on board" the HR transformation train but will help *keep* them on board as the train weaves through what will likely be a difficult, challenging landscape.

TRANSFORMING HR STAFF AND STRUCTURE

To create a strategic HRM philosophy within a firm, attention must be paid to the transformation of HR staff and the organizational structure in which these people carry out their HR activities. There are two aspects of this transformation: (1) transforming the people and (2) transforming the structure.

Transforming HR People

There are significant differences in the skills needed by HR staff to function effectively in a strategic versus traditional HR role. A traditional HR role required a staff member to be a highly skilled specialist in a particular HR functional area, such as training or recruitment interviewing. Traditional HR staff, including the senior HR manager, needed relatively little financial or marketing skills. They were not particularly concerned with global or cross-cultural factors that could affect HR practices. Traditional HR staff members "stayed within their box" and interacted only rarely and in a fairly limited way with line managers and top executives of the firm.

Contrast this with the information in Table 2.3, which summarizes the characteristics of HR leaders found in a survey of 490 HR leaders and 2,463 other individuals (mostly middle managers) who were the direct clients of those HR leaders.[24] The skills, abilities, knowledge, and behavioral capabilities required of a strategic HRM staff member are clearly much greater and more far reaching than those required by the traditional HR function.

The information in Table 2.3 presents a "universalistic view" of HR skills; that is, all HR staff will need these skills to enhance HR's strategic role in the organization. This may not be the case. In her 1997 article on "Training HR Pros to Fit Your Culture," Connie Freeman suggests that the competencies HR professionals need will vary (as for other employees) depending on the strategy of the firm.[25] Freeman's view represents a strategic-fit approach to the specific issue of HR competencies. For example, Freeman suggests that in firms whose strategy is focused on delivering highly reliable, low-cost products and services, HR professionals need particular skill in procedural knowledge, self-control, and attention to detail. On the other hand, for HR professionals in customer service-oriented firms, critical competencies include service orientation, team building, achieving consensus, and communication. However, regardless of whether strategic HR competencies are universal in nature or require a strategic best-fit approach, most HR units will face a significant transformation when adopting a new strategic view.

The processes by which firms have attempted to transform HR staff from traditional specialists to strategic generalists are quite varied. The University of Nebraska Medical Center (UNMC) went to extremes to transform its HR function.[26] Following a series of focus groups, along with surveys of 300 managers, the nine-member HR redesign team identified a number of aspects of HR practices and HR staff that were in need of transformation. In a somewhat radical move, UNMC essentially "fired" all current HR staff and then allowed them to reapply for their positions. Behavioral interviews were conducted on these "reapplicants," with each being assessed against a new set of strategic HR skills criteria.

Extensive groundwork must occur prior to establishing programs for transforming the skills and abilities of HR staff within a firm. A good example of the efforts required can be found in a program to identify, coach, develop, and foster high-level professional skills in AT&T's HR staff.[27] The objective of the program was to enhance the skills of HR professionals so that they could contribute to strategic business success. The process began with extensive research conducted on what line managers needed from HR, using surveys and focus groups to collect the data.

Literature reviews were done, and a survey of 150 HR people was conducted to zero in on the behavioral skills that helped differentiate the top-performing HR staff members in AT&T from more average performers. The skills and behaviors identified from this process are presented in Table 2.4. Once the new HR skills and behaviors were identified, a program for marketing the vision of HR Professionalism was implemented using videos, brochures, and a talk by the CEO. In addition, a Professional Development Profile (PDP) procedure was developed. In the PDP process, HR staff self-assessed against the new professional standards. Then each HR professional was asked to distribute an assessment survey to five of his or her customers. The customers assessed the individual against the new professional standards, and an individual feedback report comparing the manager's self-assessment with that of his or her customers was provided. This feedback was backed up by Professional Development Workshops to help individuals close any

TABLE 2.3

Core Capabilities of HR Leaders

Business Knowledge: The HR leader must understand . . .

- market, industry, competitive, and other external forces that affect the firm's business
- the firm's mission, vision, values, objectives, and organizational capabilities
- financial, production and operations, and marketing aspects of the firm

HR Functional Knowledge: The HR leader must understand . . .

- strategic staffing
- performance management
- development and learning
- rewards and recognition
- organizational design and change
- employee relations

Mindset: The HR leader must . . .

- focus on quality
- think globally
- think analytically
- think strategically
- adapt quickly, flexibly
- cope with ambiguity
- challenge the status quo

Interacting with Others: The HR leader must . . .

- communicate effectively orally and in writing
- listen actively
- influence acceptance of ideas
- be caring, sensitive, and relate well to others
- establish networks to get things done

Individual Performance: The HR leader must . . .

- focus on results
- make decisions effectively
- act with integrity
- initiate change, innovate, and think creatively
- manage information and technology
- manage personal time and organization
- develop his or her personal capabilities

Shapes Business Strategy: The HR leader . . .

- understands the business context and develops plans to achieve competitive advantage
- assesses market, industry, competitive, and other external forces that affect the firm
- conducts financial analysis and planning
- helps develop the business mission, vision, and values
- helps develop company objectives and action plans

Develops HR Strategy: The HR leader . . .

- identifies people-related business issues
- formulates human resource strategy/action plans
- assesses the current and defines the further organization/situation
- integrates HR plans with business plans
- defines required changes in the human resource function

Leading Change: The HR leader . . .

- builds a shared urgency for and promotes needed change
- empowers, motivates, and involves stakeholders
- integrates change initiatives and where necessary operates across borders
- measures the success of change and communicates that impact

Aligning HR Processes: The HR leader . . .

- changes roles, activities, and systems to achieve desired outcomes in HR functions, including:
- strategic staffing
- performance management
- development and learning
- rewards and recognition
- organizational design and change
- employee relations
- leadership succession and development

Achieving Results: The HR leader . . .

- organizes work
- builds partnerships
- manages conflict
- builds team effectiveness
- coaches others
- evaluates results

Source: Adapted from Exhibits 1 and 2 in James W. Walker and William E. Reif, "Human Resource Leaders: Capability Strengths and Gaps," *Human Resource Planning*, Vol. 22 (4), 1999, pp. 21–32, at 23–24.

TABLE 2.4

Skills and Behaviors of Top-Performing HR Staff at AT&T

Accountability for Business Results	Self-Image	Managing Interpersonal Relationships
Is results oriented	Sees self as catalyst for change	Builds information networks
Engages in strategic thinking	Sees self as member of a leadership team	Is effective at influencing others
Develops a business partnership with line managers	Demonstrates self-confidence	Exhibits interpersonal flexibility
Is customer-focused		Is effective at building and managing teams
Uses HR expertise		Energizes and empowers others

Source: Adapted from information in Jill Conner and Jeana Wirtenberg, "Managing the Transformation of Human Resources Work," *Human Resource Planning,* Vol. 16 (2), 1993, pp. 17–34.

gaps between the new professional standards and their self-assessed or customer-rated performance. The final step in the development of AT&T's HR Professionalism program involved a one-day meeting of HR leaders, followed by half-day training sessions to ensure that HR leaders could use the PDP process in their own locations.

The AT&T program for transforming HR is by no means the only effective approach. A more recent example of how United Technologies Corporation (UTC) went about transforming the skills of its HR staff can be found in the Partnerships for Strategic Success box.

What AT&T's and UTC's efforts indicate, however, is the complexity of transforming HR skills within a large organization. Time, effort, money, and patience are needed. Although the large size of AT&T's and UTC's HR staffs increase the overall magnitude of the transformation process, some essential elements of their processes are applicable to medium-sized and small firms. First, an HR transformation should be part of and directly linked to the strategic orientation of the organization involved. This helps to enhance motivation, provide direction, and give a real sense of importance to the transformation process. Second, active participation of HR personnel in the transformation must occur, and individuals must take on the role of "champion" of the program's objectives. Third, critical emphasis must be placed on getting line managers involved in defining the skills and behaviors needed in HR staff. Fourth, the transformation must be viewed as a major change effort. In the case of UNMC, rather drastic action (forcing everyone to reapply for their positions) was taken to overcome the resistance and inertia associated with the change effort. Finally, UTC's ongoing process of grooming HR staff through job rotations and extensive personal development and training indicates the patience needed in bringing about a true transformation of HR.

Transforming HR Structure

In conducting the transformation of traditional personnel to SHRM, it is quite common for the structure of the HR unit to be transformed as well. At Northern Telecom, all HR staff members were consolidated into a single corporate unit under a

PARTNERSHIPS FOR STRATEGIC SUCCESS

Building New HR Leaders: The Case of United Technologies

United Technologies Corporation (UTC) is a $25 billion global, high-tech company, which includes business groups such as Otis Elevator, Pratt & Whitney, Sikorsky Aircraft, and Carrier. To make a difference within the organization, UTC understands that its HR employees need new skills to effectively link HR practices to business objectives.

Each year the senior HR executives from the business units meet and review the HR talent within their operations. They use this information to develop job rotations and targeted job assignments for high-talent HR staff. Over time, these high-potential individuals are typically moved among two or three businesses as well as into international assignments. HR staff are also moved into line positions, and some line staff are moved into HR. All of these movements of personnel are integrated within the annual HR strategic plan.

In addition to these rotations and targeted job assignments, there are a wide range of developmental opportunities for HR professionals. All HR staff must establish a personal development plan as part of a company-wide process. Among training programs provided by UTC to help HR staff develop their talent are:

- Scholars Program: Encourages employees to take coursework leading to a degree. UTC reimburses the cost of courses and rewards the employee with 200 shares of stock upon successful completion of the degree.
- Company-sponsored workshops: These focus on functional knowledge updates, internal consulting skills, and various current HR topics.
- Human Resource Business School: HR leaders and candidates for HR leadership positions attend a week-long program focusing on capabilities needed to meet the needs of the changing role of HR. The program focuses on UTC's own business strategies and the role that HR must play in achieving business objectives. The participants are introduced to "best practice" methods in formulating HR strategies, leading change, and measuring the business impact of HR initiatives. The program also provides participants with feedback from multiple sources as to their own capabilities and skills. The program includes time for participants to examine their personal development plans and provides guidance and support for that process.

Source: Information taken from statements made by Lee Dailey, Director, Education and Development of United Technologies Corporation, in James Walker and William Stopper, "Developing Human Resource Leaders," *Human Resource Planning,* Vol. 23 (1), 2000, pp. 38–44, at 41.

senior vice president of HR. At Benetton in Italy, various recruiting and development activities were centralized. In the case of Siemens Rolm, a team-based structure was implemented.[28]

As with many other forms of organizational restructuring, a key issue in designing a new strategic HRM unit is to determine which activities should be centralized and which should be decentralized or outsourced. During the 1990s, new roles were created around partnering approaches for HR. Companies such as Warner-Lambert, Motorola, Coca-Cola, and Whirlpool have created new HR-organization structures to realign roles to separate transaction fulfillment work (administrative role) and consultative, business-partnering work (strategic role). These and other companies have reported significant improvements in delivering strategic results when traditional roles are replaced with more consultative organization-effectiveness roles, supported by small centralized staffs of HR experts. These companies have also directly assigned HR partners to front-line business units while aggressively consolidating delivery of employee services.[29] If we look at how firms have gone about restructuring HR, three common structures often result. These are (a) **centralized centers of expertise,** (b) **business partner teams** assigned to specific business units (and sometimes regional or country-specific units), and (c) **central administrative service units.** The basic functions of these three HR structures are listed in Table 2.5. The task of a centralized center of expertise is *effective strategy formulation and provision of highly specialized technical expertise.* Business partner teams provide *effective and efficient strategy implementation at the business-unit (or regional/country) level,* although they may occasionally also have to formulate HR strategies specifically for their own business units. The task of a central administrative service unit is *efficient delivery of administrative transactions* such as payroll, responses to benefit inquiries, and so forth.[30]

Obviously, the appropriate structure for the HR function will depend on the nature of the firm's business activity, its size, and its overall business strategy. In some organizations, a more centralized structure for HRM may be appropriate to ensure quality of HR products and gain economies of scale in their development and delivery. In other situations, highly decentralized HR units may be necessary.

TABLE 2.5

Three Roles in the New HR Organization

Centers of Expertise	Business Partner Teams	Central Administrative Service Center

• Work with top management on policy and strategy issues
• Create regional policies, processes, and products
• Provide expert technical advice to HR business partners within specific units
• Ensure global or regional consistency where needed
• Search for new thinking and best practice
• Manage specific development projects
• Benchmark HR practices against best practice
• Develop HR competencies in HR and non-HR staff
• Assure alignment of total HR system with company strategy
• Support rollout of programs:
  • Teach others how
  • Support external consultants with "best practices"
  • Exchange best practices throughout the firm
	• Work with line managers to deliver business objectives
	• Incorporate HR elements into unit business plans
	• Help develop business unit and individual capabilities
	• Manage client expectations about HR activities
	• Develop people strategies for their operating units—with line leaders
	• Become decentralized, business unit-aligned "generalists"
	• Tailor and implement new practices/programs to fit business unit needs
	• Identify new applications for current programs
	• Manage specific client projects
	• Ensure linkage between business units issues and problems with people issues
		• Meet all current service obligations
		• Manage all "transactional" support processes
		• Manage rules and exceptions to rules
		• Drive the consolidation of activities to increase productivity
		• Manage specific projects to eliminate unnecessary work
		• Enable work force access to information
		• Apply information systems to automate all necessary services
		• Consult in systems design and information requirements

Source: Adapted from Gregory Kesler, "Four Steps to Building an HR Agenda for Growth: HR Strategy Revisited," *Human Resource Planning,* Vol. 23 (3), 2000, p. 35; and Neil McEwen, "Transforming HR: The Practitioner's Perspective," *HR Review,* Vol. 2 (1) 2002, pp. 18–23.

Regardless of which particular structure is used, the key element in successfully transforming traditional HR functions into SHRM units is to find a structure that meets the pressing needs of the business strategy of the organization and allows the HR unit to provide services designed to help the firm achieve strategic objectives. The newly acquired strategic focus of HR does not mean that the function can afford to relegate administrative efficiency to the background. On the contrary, given the focus on cost savings in today's competitive environment, there is increasing pressure on HR to become even more efficient. The next section deals with this issue.

ENHANCING ADMINISTRATIVE EFFICIENCY

Dave Ulrich has suggested that one of the key roles of HR staff is to be "administrative experts." As administrative experts, HR staff members must take an active role in reengineering administrative and other processes within the firm and in finding ways to share services more effectively throughout the organization.[31] The objectives here are to increase HR service efficiency and to save money. For example, a survey to identify characteristics of "best" versus "typical" HR units found that the average cost per employee of HR services in the best firms was around $800, whereas the per-employee cost in typical firms was $1,675. One possible factor contributing to the lower HR costs in the best firms was that their HR administrative services (payroll, benefits, etc.) tended to be highly integrated and shared, whereas these services were more often rather fragmented and duplicated in typical firms.[32]

Several processes are needed to enhance the administrative expertise of HR units. One of these is to focus on improving **administrative efficiency** by targeting *current* processes for improvement. The role of the HR unit is to examine the gaps between the "as is" process and what the system "should be." Once these gaps are identified, programs can be developed to close them. This could involve dropping a traditional HR program. For example, Alcatel Network Systems in Richardson, Texas, got rid of its managerial performance appraisal system because there was clear evidence that the system did not improve managerial performance.[33] In implementing new programs, the HR unit must measure whether efficiency has indeed been enhanced. For example, Air France USA made considerable use of search firms in its recruiting efforts. In 2002 the company moved to an Internet-based approach, using such Web-based recruitment sites as Monster.com. The company found that it could reach a larger number of applicants in a shorter amount of time using the Internet. The costs were substantially lower than more traditional recruiting methods, and the Internet approach was also found to have some unexpected advantages.[34]

Administrative efficiency can also be enhanced through the development of **centralized HR services** that are shared throughout an organization. For example, University of Nebraska Medical Center (UNMC) developed a **"one-stop shop"** for all its payroll, benefits, and other HR administrative services.[35] Another process involved HR staff members' becoming "administrative experts," completely rethinking how they create value for the firm through their administrative activities. The HR unit must create programs that give value as perceived by the customers of the program, not as perceived by the provider of the program (HR).

For example, the tasks performed by HR units often involve maintaining information about employees, such as benefits and home addresses. Many organizations have developed a "self-service" concept to HR in which employees become responsible for their own information input and retrieval. The HR unit at Colwell Industries Inc. (Minneapolis) found it difficult to deliver a variety of HR services to many Colwell employees because three-fourths of the employees worked on rotating shifts. The HR unit implemented a self-service HR information system with PCs located on the factory floor so that employees without PCs at home could use the system. The new system was greeted favorably by employees, particularly as those who participated in the system were entered into a drawing for cash prizes. Significant cost savings have been realized through the reduction in the number of employee handbooks and other policy materials that have to be printed.[36]

As both the Air France and Colwell Industries examples suggest, another means of enhancing HR administrative efficiency is through the use of information technology systems including Web-based technology. A survey of more than 200 executives in 2001 revealed that almost two-thirds of the companies represented in the survey were planning to either increase or accelerate investments in HR related technologies in the immediate future. In a 2002 survey on Web-based HR self-service systems, more than 90 percent of salaried employees at the companies surveyed had access to their organization's HR intranet. Access was not limited to professional and managerial personnel, with 72 percent of hourly employees having such access. Hourly employee intranet access was even higher in the health care and financial services industries, with access at 94 percent and 86 percent, respectively. A 2002 survey of 649 firms discovered that nearly every organization in the survey had made significant investments in HR technology including Enterprise Resource Planning (ERP) systems, high-tech HR service centers, Interactive Voice Response (IVR) or Voice Recognition Systems (VRS) systems, and various Web-based HR applications. These high-tech systems have substantial benefits to the firms involved. Seventy-four percent of the firms that had implemented Web-based employee self-service HR systems reported significant improvement in the data accuracy, and 80 percent of the firms indicated improvement in the timeliness of HR data. Sixty percent of the firms indicated an overall reduction in the workload of their HR units. A workload reduction of 30 percent was not uncommon in those areas where self-service systems had been implemented.[37]

A final method for enhancing HR efficiency is through outsourcing. **Outsourcing** involves firms contracting various HR administrative duties to external firms. There are a variety of operational and strategic reasons firms have decided to outsource some of their HR functions. Among the operational reasons are the need for specialized HR expertise, the demands of increasingly complicated HR technology, time pressures and workloads that in-house HR units have difficulty meeting, and the reduction of liability and risk in some areas of HR. Perhaps the most important strategic reason for HR outsourcing is to provide in-house HR units with additional time to focus on strategic rather than purely operational issues.[38] Regardless of the initial reasons for outsourcing, companies have found that HR outsourcing can have significant efficiency and cost benefits. A 2002 survey in the U.K. indicated that over the previous five years 28 percent of the organizations had increased their use of HR outsourcing. In 2002 American Express expanded its HR outsourcing contracts to Mellon HR Solutions. HR administration and record keeping, learning services administration, compensation planning, and payroll operations for 50,000 U.S.-based and 30,000 overseas employees were provided via

Mellon's Web-based HR systems.[39] Some firms have become engaged in "end-to-end" outsourcing. British Petroleum contracted its entire global human resources function to Exult for £430,000,000. Another British firm, BAE, entered a joint venture agreement with Xchanging worth more than £1 billion to manage procurement and a variety of administrative functions including HR.[40] Although some reports indicate that as many as 90 percent of firms surveyed indicate that they are satisfied with their outsourcing experiences, other outsourcing ventures (including the one between BP and Exult) have met with more limited success. Nevertheless, the use of HR outsourcing for at least some HR functions is a widely used method of reducing HR costs, increasing HR efficiency, and allowing HR professionals to concentrate more of their time on strategic rather than purely administrative aspects of managing human resources.[41]

INTEGRATING HR INTO STRATEGIC PLANNING

Strategic integration of HR requires (1) that a strategic planning process occur in the organization and (2) that HR managers play an important role in that process. The requirement that a strategic planning process occurs before strategic HRM can develop is often not met in small and medium-sized firms. In an HRM course taught at Bond University in Australia, students are required to analyze several different aspects of HR activities within a local firm. The students try to determine whether the firm is engaged in strategic HRM and then make suggestions as to how the firm can become more strategic in its HR approach. The first part of this assignment asks students to describe the strategic plan of the firm, including its mission, values, and strategic objectives. In the majority of cases, students find that the firms they have chosen to analyze have no written strategic plan and have a mission and set of strategic objectives that state simply "to make money and not go bankrupt." The next section of this chapter presents a brief description of the strategic planning process. Following that, examples of how HR, specifically, can be integrated into the strategic planning process are provided.

The Strategic Planning Process

The development of a strategic plan typically involves top management, sometimes with the aid of outside consultants, sitting down to analyze the current and future state of the organization. The process involves answering basic questions such as "Where do we want to be as an organization in the next five years? What are our strengths and weaknesses? What opportunities exist in the business environment? and What challenges are we likely to face?"

Mission, Goals, and Values Statements The **mission statement** delineates the organization's reason for existing. It is important to operationalize a mission and ensure buy-in if a mission statement is not to degenerate into mere rhetoric. The leadership center of General Electric, for example, trained its managers to operationalize a mission or an initiative by frequent use of visualization, backward imaging, and "starting with the end in mind." Managers were asked to imagine themselves at a party six months or a year hence, the purpose of which is to celebrate the achievement of some mission or corporate initiative. They were then asked to describe, in very specific terms, how their leaders', peers', and subordinates' behavior had changed—what they were actually doing more of and less of—in the future compared to in the present. This process was used to ensure that GE's vision and mission statements were operational rather than being merely sweet words or numerical.[42]

In terms of General Electric's most current mission statement, the GE Web site states that "GE does not have a mission statement, per se, but its operating philosophy and business objectives are clearly articulated each year in the *Letter to Stakeholders* in the GE Annual Report."[43] If one examines the *Letter to Stakeholders,* the essential nature of GE's mission can be readily identified. The essential elements of this "mission statement" are shown in Figure 2.2 From Figure 2.2 we can gain an understanding of the basic approach that GE takes to running its business through a focus on diverse business enterprises, operating efficiency and quality, and its employees and organizational culture. In its "strategies for growth," GE describes the methods it uses to maintain a competitive advantage over other firms.

Also in GE's 2002 Annual Report there is a statement about the overriding values of the firm. GE is a place where "people are committed to the greater good of the company, to our customers' success and to each other." (p. 14) These are reflected in the "Our Commitment" section of Figure 2.2 There are at least two benefits to be gained from the articulation of a **values statement.** First, a statement of fundamental beliefs can guide strategic change. Second, just as individual behavior is shaped by a personal value system, organizational behavior and success are influenced by employee perceptions of corporate beliefs. The degree to which values create desired organizational outcomes is a function of the extent to which such beliefs are clearly articulated, successfully communicated, and integrated into the way of doing business.[44]

Environmental Threats and Opportunities Another integral step in the development of a strategic plan is the analysis of environmental factors that influence organizational objectives. **Environmental threats** are features of the external surroundings that may prevent the organization from achieving its strategic goals. For example, it is obvious from reading the HR Challenge that Xilinx faced new threats from worldwide terrorism and its impact on the global economy. **Environmental opportunities** are aspects of the surroundings that may help the organization to achieve its goals. Xilinx's base of large and successful customers worldwide provided it with a strong foundation on which to rebuild its financial success after the economic downturn of 2001. For any firm preparing a strategic plan, an environmental scan should include an analysis of technology, economic factors, the legal/political environment, international markets, competitors, the labor supply, and its customers. Some features of the environment will have more influence on the organization than others. In any case, a strategic planning process should help managers develop as complete an understanding as possible of all the features of the organization's environment and how they come together to affect the enterprise.

Organizational Strengths and Weaknesses *Organizational strengths* are positive internal characteristics on which an organization can draw to achieve its strategic goals. *Organizational weaknesses* are characteristics that may stand in the way of particular accomplishments. The analysis of strengths and weaknesses typically focuses on specific functions such as marketing, finance, production, and re-

FIGURE 2.2

Excerpts from General Electric's 2002 Annual Report and Web Site

Source: Direct quotes are in italics and taken from the *General Electric 2002 Annual Report,* "Letter to Stakeholders," February 14, 2003, pp. 5–15. Available at: http://www.ge.com/ar2002/editorial/ltr5.jsp (accessed October 28, 2003); Information for "Our Commitment" section was obtained from http://www.ge.com/en/commitment/ (accessed October 28, 2003).

Overall Mission:

As managers, it is our principal job to make and sell great products and services that people need and thereby increase earnings. (p. 6)

Our Goal:

To grow earnings 10%-plus annually with 20%-plus return on total capital . . . reliably, sustainably, through the cycles. (p. 6)

The GE Business Model:

A Diverse Set of Leading Businesses Driving Performance:
GE has great businesses, most of which we've been in for decades, some for 80 years or more. In addition to leading in their markets, these businesses have many traits in common: an unparalleled technical foundation; direct customer interfaces; multiple ways to make money through products, services and financing; global scale; and low capital intensity. (p. 6)

Operating Rigor with a Focus on Cash Generation:
Strong processes are the foundation of our operating rigor. We are in the ninth year of Six Sigma at GE, and it has become a permanent initiative . . . focused primarily in three areas: working with our customers on their issues; improving our internal processes to improve our customer interfaces and generate cash; and improving the flow of high-technology products and services to the marketplace. (p. 8)

People and Culture:
The CEO of GE outlined a number of important people issues including:

- *to attract and keep talented and loyal people who work together as a team.*
- *to build a culture based on performance, compliance and teamwork.*
- *to enhance a culture of Imagination at Work with a daily rallying cry of "what we imagine, we can make happen."*
- *to make GE a meritocracy, where the best-performing people get the best rewards. But everyone must operate in a system where the company comes first. (p. 9)*

Our Strategy for Growth:

- *Technical Leadership that expands margins and grows the installed base.*
- *Services Acceleration that improves returns, competitiveness and customer satisfaction.*
- *Enduring Customer Relationships that are unbreakable because we win together over the long term.*
- *Globalization as a way to grow faster and be more competitive.*
- *Resource Reallocation to build positions in new markets where we can achieve superior growth and returns. (p. 9)*

Our Commitment:

GE is committed to serve the communities where we do business, to provide our customers with innovative, high-quality products and services and to protect the health of our workers and our environment.

Integrity
We are a company of integrity. We are a company of standards. Our worldwide reputation for honest and reliable business conduct, built by so many people over so many years, is tested and proven in each business transaction we make. We invite you to read our company's integrity policy that all employees sign upon joining the company.

Corporate Governance
The changes in our corporate governance are designed to strengthen the board of directors' oversight of management and to serve the long-term interests of shareowners, employees and other stakeholders.

Social Performance
Demonstrating corporate responsibility for more than 100 years, we are proud of the GE team and its dedication. Just as GE business operations are managed for the long-term, our commitment to social performance is lived and improved on every day.

Environment, Health and Safety
We are committed to keeping workers safe on the job, ensuring that we are good neighbors to the communities in which we do business by complying with environmental laws and regulations; addressing historical contamination issues cooperatively and completely; and incorporating this commitment into our processes and products.

Quality
GE success with Six Sigma has exceeded our most optimistic predictions. Across the Company, GE associates embrace Six Sigma's customer-focused, data-driven philosophy and apply it to everything we do.

Innovation
The company's limitless future is seen in an array of innovative, technically advanced products and services developed by its businesses—after extensive interviews with customers—to meet Six Sigma standards of invariable quality and performance.

search and development (R&D). Management philosophy and human resources are areas that also may be considered in an analysis. Returning to our HR Challenge example, Xilinx has several notable strengths, including its innovative technology and dominant market position in field programmable arrays, an excellent relationship with its customers, and its human resources (highly educated and committed employees). Xilinx's most notable weakness was market vulnerability to dramatic international events such as the terrorist attack on September 11, 2001, and to general downturns in the world economy.

Goals and Objectives After an organization has defined its mission and analyzed both external opportunities and threats and internal strengths and weaknesses, it can realistically establish goals and objectives that will further its mission. As seen in Figure 2.2, one of GE's major goals is to "grow earnings 10%-plus annually with 20%-plus return on total capital . . . reliably, sustainably, through the cycles." General goals such as this have specific implications for all aspects of human resources as these goals are translated into actions that individual work units and employees must take. The definition of goals has several important benefits to an organization and its employees. First, goals are a source of motivation. They describe the purpose of the organization to all involved. Second, goals also provide the basis for decisions. Managers and employees must make many decisions in their day-to-day activities. Knowing the goals, they can make decisions with the desired outcome in mind. Finally, goals become the basis for performance measurement. Comparing performance and goals helps managers guide their future actions.

Formulation of Strategies Only after the mission has been defined, environmental threats and opportunities analyzed, organizational strengths and weaknesses considered, and goals established can management undertake **strategy formulation.** In Figure 2.2, GE's "strategies for growth" represent such a formulation. For any organization, the task is to select the most effective game plan or course of action to achieve the organization's goals and objectives. Strategy may be formulated and implemented at the corporate level and for individual business units and functions. Regardless, the HRM function will likely be a critical element in the overall success of any strategy formulation and implementation process. To ensure the success of the overall strategic planning process, HRM will have to be completely integrated and a full partner in the strategic planning team.

How to Strategically Integrate HRM: Some Ideas and Examples

Integration does not simply mean that HR managers are allowed to provide HR-related information to those making strategic decisions. To achieve full integration, HR managers must have the ability to influence the development and selection of information used in making a decision, as well as the ability to make or strongly influence the decision itself. The process of integrating HR into the strategic decision-making process can occur through a variety of actions.

For example, IBM incorporated human resource issues into all of its business planning processes by including HR functional staff on management decision-making teams throughout the organization. The Vice President for Talent served as a member on the top management team that was in charge of all strategic business planning. A similar approach was taken by Marriott International, which integrated human resource issues into their strategic planning processes at both the corporate and operational levels in the firm. Two HR executives were placed on the CEO's senior executive team. Their role was to ensure that human resource issues were taken into account in all discussions of the firm's strategic plan. At the operational level, managers were required to incorporate HR implementation issues in all proposals for business expansion, thus ensuring that HR issues were integrated into the strategic planning processes throughout the firm.[45] Getting HR managers on strategic planning teams is a good first step in HR strategic integration, but a number of other things are required. First, there must be strong CEO support for the new role of HR in the strategic planning process. Second, as noted earlier, HR personnel placed on strategic planning teams must have the skills needed to function as strategic business partners with other managers. Finally, when placed in a strategic planning role, HR personnel must be able to bring to the decision-making process information and data that is important and compelling to managers from other functional areas.[46]

FITTING HR PRACTICES TO BUSINESS STRATEGY AND TO ONE ANOTHER

The issue of *fitting* HR practices to business strategy has become increasingly relevant in modern business and is perhaps the most important HR issue for HR staff and line managers.[47] HR fit involves making sure HR activities "make sense" and help the organization achieve its goals and objectives. As noted earlier in this chapter, there are three aspects of HR fit. The first aspect, **vertical fit,** concerns the match between HR practices and overall business strategy. The second aspect, **horizontal fit,** relates to the interrelationship among HR activities; that is, the extent to which they are mutually consistent. Consistency ensures that HR practices reinforce one another. HR consistency means that all programs send a common message to all employees, which makes it easy for workers to understand what behaviors are required of them. There are also technical advantages of HR practice consistency; for example, a firm that invests heavily in training programs will likely benefit from also having a good selection system that reduces the likelihood of employee turnover.[48] The third aspect is **external fit,** which concerns how well HR activities match the demands of the external environment. If vertical fit occurs, then horizontal fit should follow. However, it seems useful to think of these two aspects of fit separately to ensure that both are managed effectively within the organization. To achieve external, horizontal, and vertical fit, HR staff members, working closely with line managers, must make correct choices about the nature and specific types of HR programs used in an organization.

Human Resource Practice Choices

The process of ensuring external, vertical, and horizontal fit requires that HR systems adapt to an often highly dynamic external business environment by implementing HR practices that mutually reinforce behaviors needed to achieve both short- and long-term organizational objectives. This can often prove very difficult to do. The situation faced by Xilinx in the HR Challenge presented HR managers with a set of very difficult choices. Both the external environment and short-term financial goals of the firm were placing pressure on HR to enact rather drastic HR measures, including mass layoffs. Balancing that pressure was the knowledge that long-term strategic success rested heavily on the skills, knowledge, and abilities of the research and product development staff at Xilinx. Difficult HR choices had to be made. As shown in Figure 2.2, General Electric's globalization focus as part of its "strategies for growth" requires the development of a wide range of HR initiatives to ensure that employees can effectively manage, market, and produce in an increasingly complex, multicultural business environment. As with Xilinx, many critical HR choices must be made to succeed. So what are the common "choices" HR staff face?

Figure 2.3 organizes **HR practice choices** into six categories and defines opposite ends of each practice continuum, such as promoting entirely from within versus filling all openings from the external labor market. Clearly, an intermediate choice is also possible for most practices. Furthermore, for large organizations different units could use different practices, or the practices might vary by level or job category.[49] The challenge is to develop internally consistent configurations of HR practice choices that help implement the organization's strategy and advance its competitiveness. To accomplish this successfully, a clear understanding of the nature of the HR choices available is needed.

Staffing Many staffing decisions have implications for strategy implementation. Perhaps one of the most basic choices is whether the firm hires from external sources or relies primarily on promoting people from within the organization to fill vacant positions. A related issue is whether recruitment and career decisions will be open or closed. In some organizations, notices of job opportunities are posted, resulting in an extremely open process. In others, decisions are made by a relatively small group of upper-level managers and are simply announced.

Appraising Performance appraisal is a linchpin in strategic management. Once strategic goals are established, it is important that the performance appraisal system be adjusted to evaluate the behaviors needed to achieve these objectives. Methods of appraisal should vary with the organization's strategy. For example, firms following an "operational excellence" strategy (low-cost producer) should have performance measures focused on such things as total cost of production, errors, waste, net sales, and so forth. On the other hand, firms following a "customer-intimacy" strategy (unique solutions and high levels of product customization) will need to assess performance in terms of things like customer retention rates and number of referrals from current customers.[50]

Compensating Perhaps more than any other area of human resource management, the reward structure communicates the overall philosophy and strategy of the organization. Furthermore, choices with respect to rewards overlap many other areas of human resource management. As with performance appraisal systems, different reward systems are needed for different strategies. For example, some experts suggest that operational-excellence firms should focus on team productivity, profit sharing, and skills-based pay to enhance the ability and motivation of employees to increase efficiency. On the other hand, customer-intimacy firms should focus on individual rewards, nonfinancial rewards, and service award programs to focus them on better face-to-face, highly personal customer service.[51]

FIGURE 2.3

HR Practice Choices

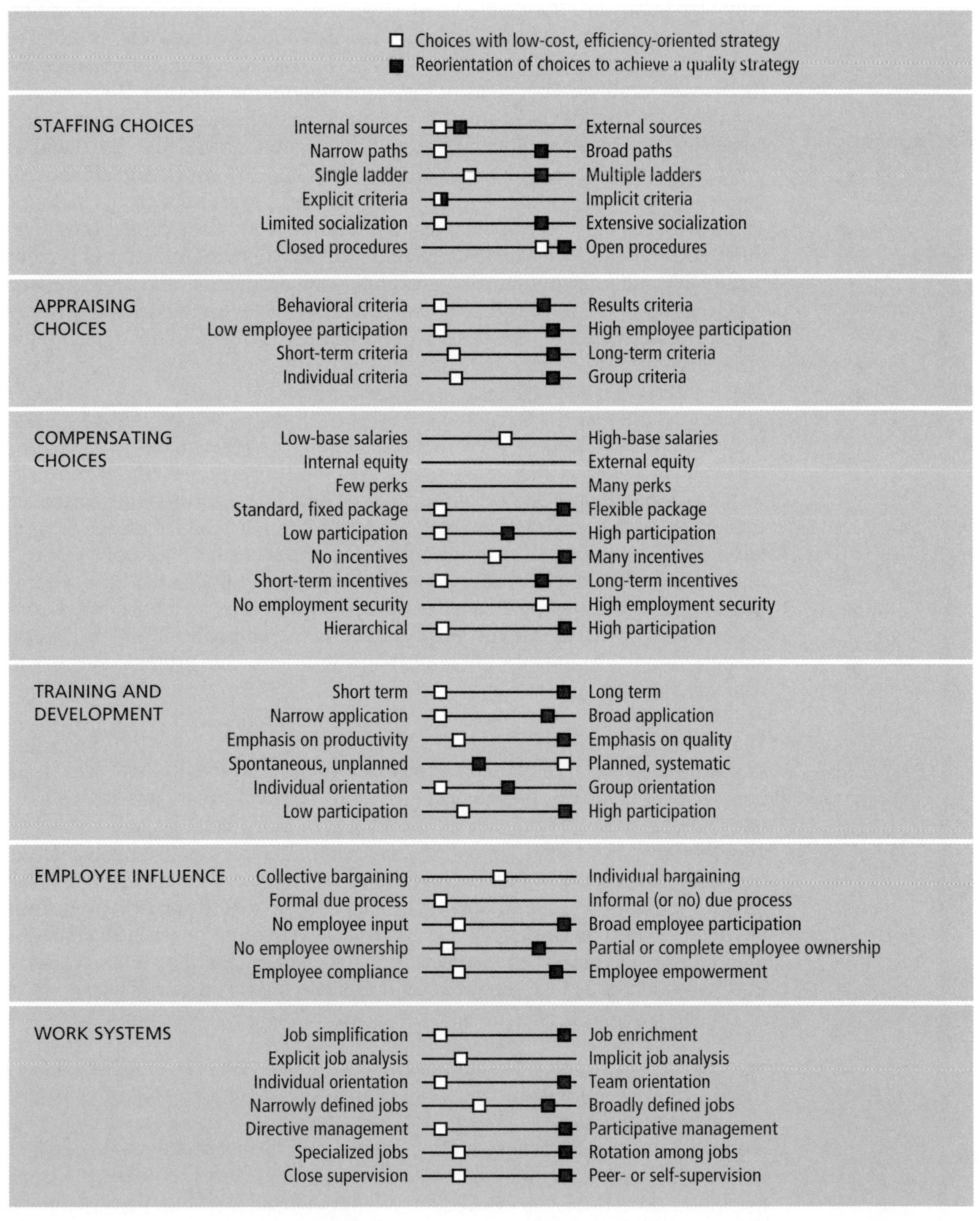

Choices with low-cost, efficiency-oriented strategy
Reorientation of choices to achieve a quality strategy
STAFFING CHOICES
Internal sources — External sources
Narrow paths — Broad paths
Single ladder — Multiple ladders
Explicit criteria — Implicit criteria
Limited socialization — Extensive socialization
Closed procedures — Open procedures
APPRAISING CHOICES
Behavioral criteria — Results criteria
Low employee participation — High employee participation
Short-term criteria — Long-term criteria
Individual criteria — Group criteria
COMPENSATING CHOICES
Low-base salaries — High-base salaries
Internal equity — External equity
Few perks — Many perks
Standard, fixed package — Flexible package
Low participation — High participation
No incentives — Many incentives
Short-term incentives — Long-term incentives
No employment security — High employment security
Hierarchical — High participation
TRAINING AND DEVELOPMENT
Short term — Long term
Narrow application — Broad application
Emphasis on productivity — Emphasis on quality
Spontaneous, unplanned — Planned, systematic
Individual orientation — Group orientation
Low participation — High participation
EMPLOYEE INFLUENCE
Collective bargaining — Individual bargaining
Formal due process — Informal (or no) due process
No employee input — Broad employee participation
No employee ownership — Partial or complete employee ownership
Employee compliance — Employee empowerment
WORK SYSTEMS
Job simplification — Job enrichment
Explicit job analysis — Implicit job analysis
Individual orientation — Team orientation
Narrowly defined jobs — Broadly defined jobs
Directive management — Participative management
Specialized jobs — Rotation among jobs
Close supervision — Peer- or self-supervision

Training and Development Some organizations do not train and develop their work force but instead seek to hire skilled employees from the outside. At times, as a result of either fast growth or rapidly changing technology, this is the only way to acquire the needed expertise. Other organizations prefer to develop expertise in-house, although training and developing employees is both costly and time consuming. To be effective, training and development must be tied to the overall strategic objectives of the organization and to other HR systems. For example, due to tight labor-market conditions and the need to keep its costs low as part of a cost-leadership strategy, an organization may need to develop its non-managerial workers for managerial jobs. One step toward this goal would be to have them work with and learn from current managers. However, if existing managers are not rewarded for helping to develop others, they probably will devote little time and energy to the task. In addition, development efforts will be counter-productive unless promotional opportunities are available for those who complete the program. If employees cannot use what they have learned in-house or are not rewarded for doing so, the best of them will tend to depart for opportunities in other organizations.

Employee Influence The concept of employee influence has evolved from superficial participation (e.g., suggestion systems) to responsibility for direct input into the decision process, accountability for outcomes, and sharing in the wealth created by these outcomes. As a result, one of the HR practice issues that continues to be prominent is the amount of influence accorded to employees in such matters as organizational goals, rewards, working conditions, and the work itself. Organizations are finding that **empowered employees** are more able to have a "line-of-sight"—that is, see the link between their own behavior and organizational success. Employee line-of-sight contributes to the overall strategic success of the firm via employee motivation.[52]

Work Systems Another factor in individual productivity and organizational effectiveness is the design of work. Research over many years has shown that jobs have greater motivational value when they give individuals greater responsibility and control of their work as opposed to being simplified or overspecialized. The use of **work systems** to influence productivity has also been manifested in an emphasis on teams. The team approach is consistent with **delayering**—that is, the trend for fewer management levels and fewer managers. As a result, more authority and responsibility are delegated to self-managed teams or autonomous work groups to plan, organize, supervise, and evaluate their own work.[53]

Changes in Strategy, Changes in Choices Figure 2.3 presents graphically how the HR choices that a firm makes can change as a result of a shift in firm strategy. The example in Figure 2.3 represents a change from a low-cost, efficiency-driven strategy to one focused more on the quality of the firm's products. As can be seen in Figure 2.3, some HR practices remain essentially the same under the two business strategies (e.g., both strategies rely on internal staffing) whereas other HR practices are at almost opposite ends of the continuum (e.g., employee compliance versus employee empowerment).

HR Practices and Strategic Fit: Putting It All Together

One of the times when organizations have an opportunity to successfully achieve vertical, horizontal, and external fit in their human resource practices occurs when the organization is brand new. A good example of this is Agilent Technologies,[54] which was created as the result of a split-up of Hewlett-Packard (HP). In late 1999 CEO Ned Barnholt set out to transform a former part of HP into an independent, dynamic, and successful company with its own cultural identity. The culture that Barnholt set out to establish contained values leftover from the HP days (innovation and contribution, trust and respect for the individual and team, and integrity) as well as new values focused on speed, customer-focus, and accountability. Barnholt realized that much of this cultural transformation depended on the development of HR practices that supported the new business identity. To do this, a program called "Vantage" was developed to transform HR practices within Agilent. Stage 1 of the Vantage process involved selecting seventy-five critical thought leaders within the new organization to help identify those aspects of HR that needed changing to support the new culture—and to suggest what those changes should be and how to implement them.

From these seventy-five thought leaders came suggestions for a variety of new and highly integrated HR systems. A reward philosophy was developed that focused on (1) an employee's track record over time, (2) the extent to which the employee exhibited key Agilent values, (3) the potential the employee had for development and growth within the firm, and (4) how critical the skills were that the employee possessed in the attainment of Agilent's business goals. A new performance measurement system was developed around these four performance criteria. In addition, the base pay of Agilent employees was benchmarked against external competitors. The position of an employee within the base pay system depended not only on the nature of their job but was also linked directly to the performance measurement system. A variety of pay-for-performance systems were implemented including a bonus system linked to overall firm and divisional performance. Employee stock option programs were implemented along with other means of recognizing high performance.

To complement the development of these new HR systems, an intense program to increase communication channels from management to employees and from employees to management was constructed. Of particular importance to the transformation of the Agilent culture was the development of leadership training programs to help line managers understand and implement the HR programs and related aspects of the new Agilent culture. Perhaps the most important aspect of Agilent's HR transformation was the fact that all of the programs developed—performance measurement, pay systems, communication programs, and leadership development systems—were designed around the six core concepts of the new Agilent culture. From the actions taken by Agilent Technologies, it is obvious that horizontal, vertical, and external fit of HR practices requires a step-by-step analysis of the overall mission, goals, and objectives of the organization. This must be done with the involvement of key line managers who help identify ways to link HR practices directly to critical organizational goals and values. Building a partnership between HR and line management to develop strategically relevant HR practices is very important and will be discussed later in the chapter. However, before we turn to the discussion of "HR partnership," one final issue associated with strategic fit must be discussed—the apparent conflict between strategic fit and strategic flexibility in HR practices.

HR Practices: Strategic Fit versus Strategic Flexibility

So far in this chapter, strategic fit has been portrayed as a highly desirable end state for HR managers to achieve in their organizations. However, as with many things in life, too much of a good thing might have bad consequences. It is widely recognized that organizational environments are dynamic, and when vertical, horizontal, and external fit become extremely "tight," problems may occur. HR systems that are highly intermeshed with one another and embedded within organizational strategies and structures become increasingly difficult to change.[55] There is a danger of HR systems becoming too well "fitted" to a particular business environment and strategy. An organization could become like the wooly mammoth: a fantastic, successful creature until the weather changed and—boom!—it died.

Several researchers point out that both fit and flexibility are needed for long-term competitive advantage.[56] Patrick Wright and Scott Snell argue that fit and flexibility are independent concepts, with HR managers needing to pay close attention to both.[57] They describe fit as a *temporary state* in an organization. Fit may exist at time 1, but not at time 2. On the other hand, flexibility is a *characteristic* of an organization related to its ability to meet the demands of a dynamic environment. Wright and Snell distinguish between two types of flexibility. **Resource flexibility** is the extent to which an organization can apply its resources to a variety of uses and purposes. Resource flexibility also involves the cost, difficulty, and time needed to switch resources from one use to another. For example, an organization hires employees who possess a particular skill needed for their current business strategy. There is a good fit between the skills of employees hired and current strategy. At the same time, the organization includes in its selection process measures of "trainability" or "ability to learn" to select employees who can more easily develop new skills if they are needed. In this case the organization has both resource fit and resource flexibility.

Coordination flexibility concerns the extent to which an organization has decision-making and other systems that enable it to quickly move resources from one use to another. For example, AT&T's Resource Link is a database of employee skills to which line managers have ready access. This database provides information about the skills of current employees in other areas of the firm. If "new skills" are needed in one area of AT&T, Resource Link increases the likelihood that these skills can be quickly obtained from areas where they already exist. Resource Link provides enhanced coordination flexibility within AT&T.[58] As with the development of strategic fit, the establishment of HR practices that provide both fit and flexibility is something that HR managers cannot do alone. They can accomplish this difficult task only by developing a strong **partnership** with line managers.

PARTNERSHIP

To become a business partner, the HR manager must (1) learn as much about the firm's business as possible, (2) be more responsive to and more aware of the organization's needs and direction, (3) shift away from traditional HR functions, (4) become more involved in supportive, collaborative relationships with managers throughout the organization, and (5) demonstrate how critical HR is to the success of the business.[59]

A good example of this partnership role can be found at First Tennessee National Corporation (FTNC), a financial services company that has a history of progressive HR practices. First Tennessee has been named nine times as one of the 100 best companies for working mothers by *Working Mother* magazine. The American Association of Retired Persons named First Tennessee as one of only twenty-five "best employers" for workers over fifty years of age.[60]

Back in 1998, the new director of HR, Sarah Meyerrose, was given the task of linking HR issues with bottom-line business profits. She not only had to help improve company profits through HR activities but also had to do so in a way that could be made obvious to company investors. Meyerrose began her task by collaborating closely with the firm's Chief Financial Director (CFD). Together they began a study of how the firm's HR systems linked with its business strategy. They examined data on the firm's market share, profits, perceived customer value, and customer loyalty. One of their findings was that employee turnover rates were inversely related to business unit financial performance. Units with a more stable group of employees showed better financial performance levels. The tenure of employees was linked to the availability of career paths within the firm. One of the specific actions that resulted from the study was to increase the use of lateral career moves for good employees when vertical moves were unavailable. Later studies found that these lateral moves were effective in reducing employee turnover because employees understood that these moves were intended to develop their skills—and thus increase their ability to move up vertically in the organization when opportunities arose to do so. Working together, the CFD and director of HR were able to identify financial problems that were directly linked to HR issues and then develop HR programs to increase financial performance.[61]

Lucent Technologies provides another example of a major firm's focus on the partnership between HR and line management.[62] Lucent developed a model of HR services that focused on three client service levels—individual employees, supervisors, and senior leaders. The critical role for value creation in Lucent's new HR approach was that of "HR Business Partner"; that is, HR leaders who work directly with top line managers to implement the organization's strategy. All levels of client services were measured against strict client-service standards. However, the overriding goal of HR Business Partners was to have senior executives view HR as helping them solve *their* problems in *their* businesses for *their* clients and, at the end of the year, for the executives to say that "We were very successful and couldn't have done it without HR."[63] Examples of how HR at Lucent Technologies went about transforming itself into a true business partner include the following:

- HR staff attended staff meetings to better understand the nature of the business.
- A cadre of fifty-eight HR staff was developed whose job it was to find and remove HR practices that did not add value.
- Top executives from other areas of the firm were brought in to discuss their areas with HR staff and help identify ways for HR to help grow those areas.
- A new competency model for HR staff was developed to identify the skills they needed to be more effective business partners.

The First Tennessee and Lucent Technologies examples relate clearly to the five points made at the beginning of this section about what it means for HR to become a business partner. As evidenced in the First Tennessee example, the ability of HR to measure its contribution to the organization's bottom line or other relevant measures of firm effectiveness is an essential ingredient in the development of a lasting, meaningful partnership between HR and other functional managers. Measurement of HR's contribution to the organization underlies all aspects of SHRM. Strategic HRM is really about HR practices adding value to the organization. The next section looks closely at the issue of measuring HR's contribution to organizational competitiveness and success.

MEASURING HRM

In *The HR Scorecard: Linking People, Strategy, and Performance,* the authors report the results of a survey of 968 firms. Among these firms, less than 10 percent had formal measures of the efficiency and effectiveness of HR systems.[64] HR departments have long been criticized for not providing bottom-line results for the organization. Although some have argued that such criticism is unwarranted and that measuring HR's impact is often unnecessary and sometimes detrimental (see A Different Point of View box), there has been increasing focus on how HR departments should evaluate their contribution to the organization.[65]

Inward Versus Outward HR Function Focus

A number of authors have suggested typologies of HR measurement systems, and literally dozens of individual indices have been developed to measure HR effectiveness.[66] For example, one scholar distinguished between measures that had an "inward HR function focus" and those that had an "outward focus."[67]

Inward HR Function Measures **Inward HR function measures** assess the efficiency and quality of activities within the HR function itself. **Operational measures** usually assess the quantity, quality/accuracy, cost, and speed or cycle times associated with various HR practices. Examples include average cost of filling a vacant management position, cost per training hour, amount of time required to time to fill vacant positions, or cost to process an administrative transaction. These types of measures are typically assessed relative to some standard (e.g., compared to similar measures from competitors or "best practice" firms) or examined in terms of improvement over time (e.g., lower costs to hire a manager this year than last). **Service quality measures** assess the performance of HR systems as perceived by the primary users of those systems. Service quality measures are evaluated in terms of improvement over time, to external standards, or against the preprogram expectation of the users involved. A variety of service quality dimensions can be assessed.

In *How to Measure Human Resources Management,* Jac Fitz-enz identified six measures of HR service delivery satisfaction.[68] These factors, which are presented in Table 2.6, are applicable to any form of customer service, be it HR services or services one might receive in a hotel. The factors deal with basic issues relating to the quality and speed of service as well as the ability of service providers to anticipate (not simply react to) the needs of those they serve.

Outward Focused HR Measures **Outward focused HR measures** assess the impact of HR practices on aspects outside the HR function itself. **Results measures** focus on assessment of aspects such as the extent to which the firm:

- Recruits employees with critical skills
- Retains key employees

A DIFFERENT POINT OF VIEW

Pitfalls on the Road to Measurement

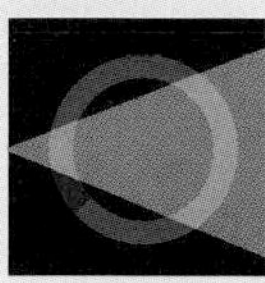

In a 1997 article in *Human Resource Management,* Jeffrey Pfeffer challenges the idea that HR managers must justify HR practices using "bottom-line," cost-versus benefit measures. Pfeffer asks:

> When was the last time you, the reader, saw the corporate General Counsel's office justify its use of resources—not whether or not it was less expensive than using outside counsel, but whether the total expenditure on legal bills was reasonable? Legal fees are seen as something necessary and inexorable . . . Ask your friends in management consulting who do strategy work the last time a corporation's strategy formulation process and associated expenses were measured in a way comparable to the measurement of human resources. (p. 359)

Pfeffer uses practices in two highly successful organizations to support his point. He notes that Singapore International Airlines (SIA) spends about $80,000,000 a year on training. Among the thirty-two participants in one of SIA's most expensive senior-level management training programs are six or seven pilots. These pilots have limited managerial responsibility. When asked why the pilots were included in this high-level *managerial* training class, the SIA people said that it was important to make pilots feel a part of the organization and to understand how it worked—therefore they were included. There was no "bottom-line" answer to the question of how SIA could justify spending managerial training resources on the pilots. SIA really did not care. Including the pilots in the program "made sense," and so they were included.

At AES Corporation, a firm that develops and operates power plants around the world, there is no formal HR staff at all. Money is spent on HR-related issues when employees, working in teams, deem it necessary. While AES measures aggregate results (e.g., profit), it does not have highly complex processes for approving HR expenditures, nor does it invest time and energy micro-measuring the cost-benefit ratio of HR activities. Pfeffer points out that one of the major problems with the current focus on measuring HR is that "unfortunately, in almost all aspects of organizational operations, what is most easily measured and what is important are often loosely related" (p. 360).

HR managers, due to cost pressures, cannot afford to spend money developing good measures of what is important. Instead they often use measures produced by the firm's accounting systems (e.g., cost of operating an HR system) or measures of the level of HR activity (e.g., number of people hired, transactions processed). Why? Because they are easy to get and to track over time.

Pfeffer identifies a number of problems with the measures that are typically used to assess HR effectiveness. Among these problems are the following:

- They don't tell us if the money is spent wisely, (e.g., whether a training budget is spent on the most critical training needs).
- They are easy to manipulate and play games with.
- They tend to encourage a drive for efficiency, which ends up as a drive for shrinkage.
- There is an assumption that somehow "less" equals "better" (e.g., Volvo is more efficient than Toyota because it employs fewer people).
- Such measures don't take into account exactly what is being done with the resources.
- The time horizon of many of these measures is extremely short term.
- They measure specific "parts" of the organization but do not help us understand the organization as a complete system.
- They tend to measure too many things to be effective in influencing individual behavior.
- They often measure things that HR cannot really influence (e.g., in the auto industry how much training is done in a particular plant is heavily determined by the nature of the technology of the production process in that plant).

Pfeffer (1997) argues that firms like SIA and AES are more likely to show high levels of economic performance than those that chase the precision of cost-benefit analysis at the expense of understanding what is really important. To Pfeffer, efforts directed toward micro-measuring the impact of HR programs in an organization are futile because "To measure everything is, at the end, equivalent to measuring nothing" (p. 362).

Source: Jeffrey Pfeffer, "Pitfalls on the Road to Measurement: The Dangerous Liaison of Human Resources with the Ideas of Accounting and Finance," *Human Resource Management,* Vol. 36 (3), 1997, pp. 357–365.

TABLE 2.6

Six Measures of HR Service Delivery

Measure	Definition
Reliability	The dependable and accurate performance of activities related to the HR activity; for example, making sure medical claims related to worker injuries on the job are filed using proper procedures with all information in the file being accurate.
Responsiveness	Indicate a willingness to help and provide prompt service; for example, providing training on interviewing techniques to a new manager when that individual is suddenly faced with recruiting new staff.
Assurance	Display skills and knowledge that generate trust and confidence within the customer; for example, an HR staff person who is expert in equal employment opportunity law shares this information with managers who are recruiting new staff.
Empathy	Provide caring, individual attention; that is, add the personal touch to service and through specific actions indicate to customers that you care about them and their problems or issues.
Tangibles	Appearance of facilities and staff and the appearance and usefulness of the published materials; for example, having clean, comfortable, well-equipped training rooms.
Anticipation	Anticipating customer needs; for example, communicate regularly with potential customers to find out what is happening in their work environment and then try to help them identify potential problems and prevent the problem from actually occurring.

Source: Adapted from lecture materials presented by Jac Fitz-enz at the 1996 HR Benchmarking Conference in Sydney, Australia, organized by HRM Consulting of Brisbane. Reprinted by permission of HRM Consulting.

- Develops employee skills, abilities, and knowledge
- Aligns individual and organizational objectives
- Shares knowledge across business units
- Enhances team performance
- Creates a positive social climate between management and workers
- Enhances employee satisfaction, motivation, loyalty, trust, and commitment and promotes working relationships across both internal and external boundaries[69]

Logically, improvement in these results measures should have an overall positive effect on business performance. **Business impact measures** can include level of improvement in the quality of the firm's products or services, cost avoidance or reduction, production efficiency indices, amount of time to produce and get a product to market, number of new products introduced, revenue and sales growth, market share, customer satisfaction and retention rates, indices of profitability, and share price.

The HR Balanced Scorecard

Increasingly, firms are incorporating into their HR assessment the **balanced scorecard approach** originally described by Robert Kaplan and David Norton in 1992. The Balanced Scorecard provides a strategic framework for assessing the effectiveness of an organization.[70] A recent survey of 1,300 firms found that 27 percent indicated they had incorporated a balanced scorecard approach to their assessment of HR activities.[71] The scorecard assesses organizational performance from four perspectives:

Financial: What is the firm's strategy for satisfying shareholders?
Customer: What does the customer want, and how must the firm be perceived by the customer to achieve its strategic objectives?
Internal, operational: What are the critical aspects of the firm's business processes, and how must they operate to be consistent with its customer objectives?
Strategic and organization learning: To achieve the firm's long-term goals, how must the organization learn and improve?

Verizon Communications, formed by the merger of GTE and Bell Atlantic, is one of the world's leading providers of wireline and wireless communications products. Verizon uses the balanced scorecard approach to assess the strategic effectiveness of its HR function.[72] Verizon HR faced five major strategic challenges. First was the imperative to enhance the talent pool within the firm. Second, leadership within Verizon had to be developed to cope with the increasingly dynamic business environment. Third, there was a need to enhance customer service and support. Fourth, Verizon needed to improve its "organizational integration" in terms of enhancing the flow of knowledge throughout the firm and to improve the organization's relationship with its unions. Finally, Verizon's HR unit needed to increase its internal capabilities to meet its own functional challenges.

Verizon's HR scorecard focused on the four basic scorecard perspectives. From a strategic perspective, Verizon HR developed measures of success for achieving the major strategic thrusts described previously. From the operations perspective, measures were developed of HR success in staffing, technology utilization, and HR administrative processes and transactions. As part of the HR scorecard, Verizon HR also developed measures of how it was viewed by its key customers. Finally, from the financial perspective, measures of how HR adds measurable financial value to the organization, including return-on-investment measures for training, staffing, technology, risk management, cost of service delivery were devised.

To ensure that HR strategy was aligned with business strategy, Verizon HR had to first define what the strategic goals of the business were. Then it had to clearly understand what HR needed to deliver to enable the business to achieve those goals. Thirdly, it had to identify strategies and actions that would enable HR to deliver the critical business requirements. Finally, it had to develop specific measures of the success of HR's strategies and actions in delivering those requirements that would be acceptable to HR's stakeholders within the firm. To achieve this, HR put together a document outlining what the firm's business strategy was and held discussions within the HR unit to come up with a list of what outcomes HR needed to produce. Following that, they conducted a line management survey to get another view of HR outcomes required. From the HR-generated and line management-generated lists, Verizon HR came up with a final list of enterprise and business unit measures to assess HR in each of the four scorecard areas (see Table 2.7). This list provided HR with a strategically linked, broad-based approach to assessing its effectiveness as a unit within the overall business.

Dollar Value of HR Programs

Another issue in assessing HR practices relates to the monetary costs and benefits of HR activities—the **dollar value of HR programs.** Dollar-value indices used to assess HR are include measures such as these:

- Cost of benefits as a percentage of total compensation
- Labor contract costs

TABLE 2.7

Verizon HR Balanced Scorecard Measures*

Scorecard	Enterprise Measures
Financial: • Maximize shareholder value • Maximize human capital performance • Minimize HR costs	• Total shareholder return • Revenue per employee • HR Return on Investment (ROI) • Total HR cost per employee • Budget variance
Customer: • Business partner • World class standards • Responsive quality service • Low cost provider	• Rating on corporate service agreement • Ranking of HR practice • Employee satisfaction survey • Benefit center satisfaction percent • HR cost factor indices
Internal Operations: • Align HR planning with business priorities • Provide quality consultative advice • Ensure a strategy focused work force • Develop and enhance world class programs • Optimize HR services through alternative delivery channels	• % strategic HR plans implemented • % HR customized recommendations implemented • % productivity improvement goals established • % compensation schemes aligned with strategy • benchmarking ranking • % programs executed • cost per delivery channel • Cycle time to fill • Cost per transaction
Strategic: • Capability: build strategic competencies • Performance based culture/climate • Organizational integration: information for decision-making leadership	• Leadership Development participation • Voluntary separation rate/cost • Rating on viewpoints survey • Organizational health index • Reporting % accurate first request • Turnaround time for ad hoc request • Leadership bench strength • Diversity • Executive coaching

*Similar ideas were developed for business unit-level measures.

Source: Adapted from Garret Walker & Randall MacDonald, "Designing and Implementing an HR Scorecard," *Human Resource Management,* Vol. 40 (4), 2001, pp. 365–377.

- Return on HR investment (HR operating expense/total operating expenses)
- Cost per hire
- Sales revenue per employee
- HR cost per sales dollar
- Cost per employee training hour[73]

Wayne Cascio describes more direct ways to assess HR cost-benefit ratios.[74] The first step, obviously, is to figure out how much some undesirable HR-related situation in the organization is costing. For example, Cascio suggests that the cost of employee absenteeism can be assigned a dollar value using the following formula:

> Cost of absenteeism = [hours lost to absenteeism × (average of wage per hour per absent employee + average of benefits per hour per absent employee)] + (total supervisory hours lost due to absenteeism × average hourly wage of supervisors) + all other incidental costs resulting from absenteeism (such as extra wages paid to hire temporary workers to replace the absent employee or wages paid in overtime to employees who have to work extra time because of the absent employee)

Using formulas similar to Cascio's, some analyses suggest that for employees earning \$30,000 per year, the average cost of absenteeism per employee-day would be around \$415.[75] Suppose that a firm has a 3 percent absenteeism rate, which means that each employee is absent about 7.8 days per year. If there are fifty employees earning \$30,000, then the firm can expect these employees to have a total of about 390 days of absenteeism per year. At \$415 per day, this level of absenteeism would cost the firm \$161,850!

Once the firm knows what absenteeism is costing, the next step is estimating the costs of the HR program developed to fix the problem. Suppose, for example, that the firm decides to implement an incentive program to reduce absenteeism. Workers who have a perfect attendance record each week have their names placed into a "lotto draw" in which one person wins \$50 each week. At the end of the year, each employee is given one lotto ticket for each week of perfect attendance. Three tickets are drawn, with the first person receiving \$1,000, the second \$500, and the third \$250. The costs of this program would include the following:

- 52 weeks × \$50 weekly prizes = \$2,600
- Materials used in the drawings such as tickets, drum, and so forth = \$250
- Administrative time associated with running the program; for example, one person earning \$100 per day (wage + benefits) working the equivalent of two days each month × 12 months = \$2,400
- Other overhead costs estimated at 30 percent of the program administrator's salary = \$720

The total cost of the program would be \$5,970. If this program resulted in a 20 percent decrease in absenteeism, the benefit gained from the program would be 20 percent × \$161,850 = \$32,370. Subtracting the cost of running the incentive program would result in total savings to the firm of \$26,400!

The preceding absenteeism example seems relatively simple and straightforward. Unfortunately, assessing the dollar costs and benefits of HR practices is not always so easy. Despite the difficulty, the pressures of a more competitive business environment will increasingly place HR practitioners in the position of having to justify the **bottom-line impact** of their practices on the organization. We will not go into great detail on costing HR programs here; rather, most chapters will include a section that describes some of the methods and formulas that may be used to assess the costs and benefits of HR programs discussed in that particular chapter.

Combining Customer Reaction, HR Impact, and Dollar Value: An Eastman Kodak Example

Eastman Kodak provides an excellent example of a firm that assesses HR using a variety of measures. Kodak developed three clusters of measures for use in assessing the impact and value of HR programs:[76]

Cluster 1: Internal operational measures (how well HR does what it does)

- Cycle time of HR practices (how long it takes to develop and run programs)
- Quality and cost of practices
- Result measures, such as acceptances versus offers in hiring
- HR client satisfaction measures
- Measures such as the ratio of HR expenses to total operating expenses of the company

Cluster 2: Internal strategic measures (how well HR practices serve strategically important initiatives in the organization)

- Leadership diversity in terms of race, gender, and so forth
- 360-degree measures of leadership competency
- Percentage of employees with documented development plans
- Number of hours devoted to development by employees
- Results of development activities assessed using four levels of training evaluation
- Clarity of performance expectations related to strategically important behaviors and adequacy of performance feedback

Cluster 3: External strategic measures (to assess how well HR practices satisfy customers and shareholders)

- Incremental sales and earnings
- Changes in customer satisfaction and commitment

The two critical elements of the Kodak system are that (1) it uses a variety of measures of customer reactions, HR impact, and dollar value and (2) it approaches the measurement of HR effectiveness from different strategic perspectives.

Benchmarking HR Practices

Another aspect of measuring the effectiveness of HR programs is through HR benchmarking. Benchmarking is important because to determine the true *competitive* advantage of HR, an organization must assess HR practices not only against some internal standard but also against the HR practices of key competitors and firms that exemplify HR excellence. **Benchmarking** is a generic term that can be defined as "a comparison with selected performance indicators from different organizations, typically in the same industry, or with comparable organizations that are considered to be 'best in class.'"[77] Benchmarking has been conducted on a wide variety of organizational practices, often relating to production methods or technology, but for the remainder of this section we use the term only as it applies to the comparison and evaluation of HR practices.

There are several different types of benchmarking.[78] **Internal benchmarking** occurs when a firm compares practices in one part of the organization against those in other internal units. For example, work and safety practices in a firm's operations in the southwestern United States might be compared with those in its New England operations. **Competitive benchmarking** is conducted against external competitors in the same markets. Firm A might compare itself with four of its competitors in terms of its employee turnover rate, ratio of HR staff to production employees, and percentage of total operating budget spent on employee training. **Generic HR benchmarking** involves the comparison of HR processes that are the same, regardless of industry. Sheraton Hotels could compare aspects of its HR practices with the HR practices at Ford Motor Company, IBM, Lucent Technologies, and Harvard University.

Regardless of which type of benchmarking is conducted, the process is essentially the same. The firm must first *understand its own performance* by developing measures of customer reactions, HR impact, or dollar value. The firm must then *decide exactly what to benchmark,* because more aspects of HR performance may be measurable than need to be benchmarked. Measures that are obtainable in the comparison firms or business units should be identified and then prioritized relative to their overall strategic importance to the role of HR in the company. An overall *plan for the program* should be developed, including the allocation of sufficient resources for the project and the establishment of a clear project calendar. The next step is to *identify firms* (or in the case of internal benchmarking, parts of the firm) that will be in the study, persuade them to participate, and then collect data. *Analyzing the data* collected involves looking for "gaps" between your firm's (unit's) practices and those of other firms (units) in the study. Recommendations on how to close these gaps should be made and then implemented.

The number of different indices of HR performance that can be benchmarked is almost limitless. Which benchmark indices should be used will depend on the specific strategy and circumstances of the firm involved. A wide variety of resources on the Internet provide firms with systems for benchmarking their HR activities. For example, the Saratoga Institute has played a large part in the development of modern HR benchmarking techniques. Its Workforce Diagnostic System is a comprehensive approach to benchmarking HR processes. Using this system, companies can benchmark and monitor a variety of HR indices including the cost of recruiting, hiring, and turnover of employees, as well as measures of the return on investment of several HR practices. Table 2.8 provides a brief outline of the types of benchmark measures included in the Workforce Diagnostic System.[79]

TABLE 2.8

Brief Summary of the Saratoga Workforce Diagnostic System

Aspect of HR Being Benchmarked	HR Indices
HR Staff and Structure	HR Headcount Ratios
	HR Investment Factors by HR Functional Area
	HR Employee Cost Factor
	HR Outsourcing and Consulting Costs
	HR Staff Breakdowns
	HRIT Investment Factor
	Training Investment Factor
	Training Staff Ratio
Compensation and Benefits	Employee Cost Factor
	Compensation as a Percentage of Revenue
	Sales Revenue and Operating Expense
	Workers Compensation Claim Factor
	Benefit Factor
	Healthcare Factor
	Benefit Plan Breakdown Costs
Staffing and Hiring	Accession Rates
	Cost per Hire by Job Level and Source
	Requisition Rates
	Time to Fill and Time to Start
	Relocation Program Cost Factor
Separation Rates	Separation Rates
	Voluntary and Involuntary Separation Rates
	Voluntary Separation Rates by Length of Service
	Planned Separation Rate
	Unplanned Separation Rate
	Separation Rate by Reason
Organization and Operations	Revenue, Expense, and Income Factors
	Earnings Factor
	Sales Revenue Factor
	Human Capital ROI (Return on Investment)
	Human Economic Value Added
	Average Tenure

Source: This outline of the Workforce Diagnostic System is found on the Saratoga Institute's Web site. The information for each of the HR aspects indicated in Table 2.8 is found at http://www.pwcservices.com/saratoga-institute/hr_staff_structure.htm; http://www.pwcservices.com/saratoga-institute/compensation_benefits.htm; http://www.pwcservices.com/saratoga-institute/staffing_hiring.htm; http://www.pwcservices.com/saratoga-institute/retention_separation.htm; http://www.pwcservices.com/saratoga-institute/operations.htm. (accessed 17 November 2003)

IS STRATEGIC HRM REALLY WORTH ALL THE TROUBLE?

Because of the magnitude of the differences between the traditional personnel perspective and strategic HRM, it is not surprising that many organizations have yet to make the leap into SHRM. The transformation from traditional HRM to SHRM is not made for a variety of reasons. The adoption of SHRM requires a highly competent and persistent SHRM leader as well as committed and supportive top management. Many firms simply do not have this type of HR leader or top management support. Political forces within the organization, accompanied by competing coalitions with different self-interests, may preclude the adoption of many SHRM practices. For example, HR systems that could help achieve particular organizational objectives may not be supported by unions. Also, firms that are not labor-intensive may be less likely to make the effort to move to a strategic HR orientation because human resources are perceived to make up a relatively small portion of the organization's potential competitive advantage.

Firms experiencing very stressful business conditions (either rapid expansion or sudden decline) often feel that they are "up to their ears in alligators" and do not have the time or resources to invest in an HRM transformation. Unfortunately, for many of these firms the lack of attention to HR issues may be one of the primary factors contributing to their business stress. For example, firms undergoing downsizing often cut HR staff because they are viewed as nonessential to the core business. However, after downsizing, employees often need extensive training to manage expanded jobs, and the selection of any new staff becomes particularly critical. Thus, at a time when HR services are most needed, they are often reduced. Additionally, highly decentralized organizations made up of autonomous business units may view the move to a corporate-wide, relatively unitary model of SRHM as both unfeasible and potentially undesirable.

The traditional role that HR has played in many organizations often makes the transition to SHRM extremely difficult. Unless HR managers are involved directly in the process of strategy formulation, any attempt by senior management to link HR activities with business strategy simply creates a cycle in which HR cannot implement the HR components of the strategy effectively, which causes HR to lose credibility with non-HR managers. This further isolates HR from the strategic planning process, making it increasingly difficult to implement strategy and so forth.

Transforming traditional HR into strategic HRM is a complex and time-consuming process. Top managers and HR practitioners are right in questioning the overall value of the SHRM transformation process. Just as we can evaluate the effectiveness of a single HR practice, we also must examine the issue of whether strategic HRM is really "worth all the trouble." There is evidence that HR practices do have a variety of positive outcomes and a direct bottom-line effect on organizational profitability.

A significant amount of recent research examines whether strategic HR practices affect a firm's overall performance as well as the processes by which this occurs. One model of how HR practices affect firm performance is presented in Figure 2.4. According to this model, how an organization goes about its HR activities will directly affect a variety of "HR outcomes," including employee satisfaction, motivation, perceived work climate, and commitment. These HR outcomes, in

FIGURE 2.4

A Model of the Link Between HR Practices and Firm Performance

Source: Paul Boselie, Jaap Paauwe, and Paul Jansen, "Human Resource Management and Performance: Lessons from the Netherlands," *International Journal of Human Resource Management*, Vol. 12 (7), 2001, p. 1110.

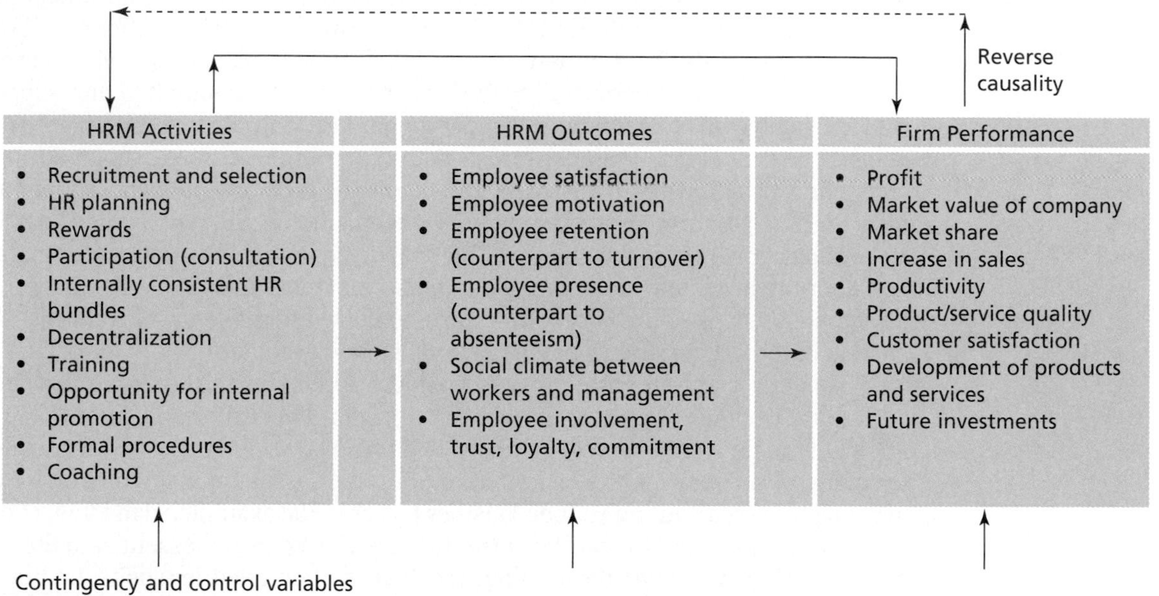

turn, affect bottom-line aspects of firm performance such as profitability, market share, and sales levels.[80]

A number of studies have found support for the impact of HR practices on a variety of outcomes. For example, one study found that "progressive" HR practices fostered a more positive work climate in a network of bank branches. Another examined the link between "innovative" HR practices and organizational commitment in 422 managers. The study found a significant link between the perception of managers that innovative HR practices had been implemented in their firms and their level of organizational commitment.[81]

In a landmark 1997 study, Mark Huselid and his colleagues assessed the level of HR "technical" and "strategic" effectiveness in 293 U.S. firms. Firm performance also was measured based on share price, net sales per employee, and gross rate of return on assets. The results of the study indicated that an increase of one standard deviation in overall HR effectiveness was associated with a 5.2 percent increase in per-employee sales volume valued at $44,380, a 16.3 percent increase in cash flow valued at $9,673 per employee, and a 6 percent increase in market value valued at $8,882 per employee.[82] Other findings in a variety of geographic locations support Huselid's contention that improved HR practices resulting from a transformation to a strategic HR perspective can have a bottom-line impact. For example, Sears found that for every 5 percent improvement in employee attitudes (resulting from various HR initiatives), customer retention rates increased by 1.3

percent and profits by 0.4 percent. A 2003 study of manufacturing plants in Germany, Italy, Japan, and the United States found a significant link between the use of "high performance work practices" and various measures of organizational performance such as unit costs and quality. Productivity measured in terms of sales per employee was related to the use of high involvement HR systems in a sample of 165 firms in New Zealand. Research on the use of high performance HR systems in Western firms operating in China found a significant correlation between the use of such HR systems and firm profitability and overall performance as rated by managers in the sample. Another study found a link between HR practices and rated overall firm performance in a Russian sample, and a study of Danish firms reported that "innovation performance" was predicted by the extent to which the firms had HR practices such as decentralized decision making, use of teams, enhanced training programs, and programs that increased information sharing throughout the firm.[83]

Although these studies vary considerably in terms of what HR practices were measured and how firm performance was operationalized, taken collectively there seems to be a strong case for promoting the improvement of HR activities as a means of affecting the financial results and other positive outcomes in many organizations. The business environment that has caused organizations to focus on human resources as a potentially enduring source of competitive advantage is likely to continue for many years. To the extent that HR practitioners become more adept at measuring aspects of customer reactions, HR program impact, the dollar value of HR practices, and comparing their own HR practices with those of their best competitors, the importance of strategic human resource management is likely to continue to grow. Is strategic human resource management really worth all the trouble? The answer is almost certainly yes.

SUMMARY OF KEY POINTS

This chapter discussed the process of how an organization can move from a traditional personnel management perspective to a strategic HRM approach. This move is necessitated by a modern business environment that is constantly changing, where technology, finance, and products can be imitated easily by competitors. Human resources are one of the few enduring sources of competitive advantage that remain for many firms. The traditional view of HR is that of an isolated, record-keeping function within the organization. Although strategic human resource management can be considered simply as the process of helping an organization achieve competitive advantage through its people, there are many different perspectives on this seemingly simple definition.

Some believe that a universal set of HR practices will always contribute to a firm's success, regardless of the business environment or the company's strategy. The role of strategic human resource managers is one of incorporating these universally effective HR practices into their firm. Others believe that SHRM involves a process of matching specific HR practices to particular aspects of the firm's strategy. Here the HR practitioner's role is to ensure a fit between HR practices and business strategy. Also, HR practices must fit with the external environment and one another. Other SHRM specialists believe that SHRM involves a process of putting together configurations of HR practices that are logically consistent with one another and are appropriate for the particular type of industry or business environment in which a firm operates. A final view of SHRM is as a means of gaining competitive advantage by putting together a unique group of human skills and abilities that other firms are unable to imitate and that give the firm special capabilities relative to its competitors.

Each of these perspectives adds to an overall view of SHRM. Taken collectively, these theoretical perspectives suggest that SHRM is a process that involves (1) internally transforming HR staff and structure, (2) enhancing HR administrative efficiency, (3) integrating HR into the strategic planning process, (4) linking HR practices to business strategy and to one another, (5) developing a partnership with line management so that HR programs meet real business needs, and (6) measuring the bottom-line impact of HR activities. Although each of these parts of the SHRM process is complex, time consuming, and difficult, research indicates that real financial benefits result from more progressive, strategic, and efficient use of human resources within modern organizations.

THE MANAGER'S VOCABULARY

administrative efficiency
balanced scorecard approach
benchmarking
best-fit perspective
bottom-line impact
business impact measures
business partner teams
central administrative service units
centralized centers of expertise
centralized HR services
compelling business case
competitive advantage
competitive benchmarking
configurational approach
coordination flexibility
delayering
dollar value of HR programs
empowered employees
environmental opportunities
environmental threats
external fit
generic HR benchmarking
horizontal fit
HR bundles
HR practice choices
human capital advantage
human capital pool
integration
internal benchmarking
inward HR function measures
mission statement
"one-stop shop"
operational measures
outsourcing
outward focused HR measures
partnership
resource-based model
resource flexibility
results measures
service quality measures
strategic human resource management (SHRM)
strategy formulation
universalistic approach
values statement
vertical fit
work systems

QUESTIONS FOR DISCUSSION

1. Defend this statement: "The business environment increasingly forces firms to make human resources a critical source of competitive advantage."
2. Discuss the environmental changes faced by Xilinx as described in the HR Challenge. What approach would you take to deal with the immediate and long-term HR implications of the change in Xilinx's financial performance?
3. Compare and contrast the universalistic, configurational, and resource-based approaches to strategic human resource management.
4. Pick a specific large organization with which most people are familiar. As best you can, determine what business strategy the organization is following. What implications does this strategy have for human resource management? What HR practice choices might make the most sense for this firm?
5. Discuss an organization you have worked for. In what ways did its HR practices facilitate or inhibit meeting the organization's goals?
6. What typical aspects of the structure of the HR function are changed when firms move to SHRM?
7. How are the skills needed by staff in a strategic HRM environment different from those needed by staff in a more traditional personnel/HR environment?

8. What is meant by the statement "Integration is a key part of the process of developing a SHRM perspective"? How would you go about integrating HR into the strategic planning process of a firm?
9. What do the terms "vertical fit," "horizontal fit," and "external fit" mean?
10. Describe how some organizations have gone about building a partnership between HR and line managers.
11. What are the differences between inward HR function measures and outward-focused HR measures? Give some examples of each.
12. Defend this statement: "Developing a tight fit between HR practices and a firm's business strategy and external environment can be detrimental to a firm's long-term success."
13. Does a move to SHRM really have a positive impact on firm performance? Defend your response, and be sure to explain how HR practices affect the financial and other aspects of firm performance.

Case 2.1
Jumbuck Enterprises

You are the vice president of HR at Jumbuck Enterprises. The new CEO of Jumbuck, Harry (also known as "Chainsaw") Price has called you into his office one fine Monday morning. Harry says to you: "[Your name], times are tough here at Jumbuck Enterprises. Things have got to change, and change in a big way. All this warm-and-fuzzy human resource management stuff is great—as long as you have the profits to spend on it. When you don't, well, then I reckon I can save the firm quite a bit of money by sacking the whole HR Department. After all, a couple of decent clerks can handle the payroll."

You gape at Chainsaw with a look of total disbelief in your eyes. You catch your breath and say, "But Chain . . . , I mean Harry, the HR Department is one of the most critical groups in the firm. How can Jumbuck Enterprises be productive and successful without a motivated, highly trained, and talented work force? Every year the efforts of the HR Department result in hundreds of thousands of dollars in added profit for the firm."

Harry raises his eyes up toward the ceiling, gives a little laugh, and says, "Oh yeah, well prove it. You've got until Friday at noon to show me how the HR Department affects the bottom-line profits of this organization. I want a ten-minute presentation from you about HR's great value to this firm. It better be good. Otherwise, by Friday at five o'clock you'll all have received your last paychecks from Jumbuck Enterprises."

You hurry back to your office and rummage through a stack of reports one of your assistants has just prepared for you from a benchmarking study. In these data your firm is compared with 200 firms in all industries in the local area. Of these 200 firms, twenty were in your industry. Given the data that follow, justify your existence as an HR unit within Jumbuck Enterprises. How have you increased profits either directly or indirectly? How have you added value?

Some Hints: Average cost of an operative leaving the firm is estimated at one-half to one times the operative's annual salary. Average cost of a manager leaving the firm is estimated as one to two times the manager's annual salary. Average cost of a day's absence by an employee earning $30,000 per year is $415 per day.

HR Expense Factor (HR operating expenses/total organization operating expenses)

Jumbuck 2002	2003	2004	All Industry Median	Your Industry Median
1.1%	.98%	.94%	1.3%	1.1%

HR Staffing Factor (Total number of full-time employees/number of full-time HR employees)

Jumbuck 2002	2003	2004	All Industry Median	Your Industry Median
54	56	55.26	55	58

Operative Absence (Total days absence/total work days)

Jumbuck 2002	2003	2004	All Industry Median	Your Industry Median
3.2%	3%	2.9%	3.77%	3.19%

Average Position Tenure in Years The average number of years an employee has been in current position.

Jumbuck	2002	2003	2004	All Industry Median	Your Industry Median
Managerial	8	4	3	3.5	3.8
Operative	12	10	9	11	10

Labor Turnover Rate

Jumbuck	2002	2003	2004	All Industry Median	Your Industry Median
Managerial	18%	14%	12%	14%	13%
Operative	22%	18%	14%	15%	16%

Managerial and Professional Start Time Time from job becoming vacant to job being filled. (Time to start in days/number of recruits)

Jumbuck 2002	2003	2004	All Industry Median	Your Industry Median
65	52	45	65.24	57

Managerial and Professional Hiring Costs Average cost of hiring managerial and professional staff. (Cost in dollars of hires/number of hires)

Jumbuck 2002	2003	2004	All Industry Median	Your Industry Median
$1,530	$1,335	$1,275	$1,800	$1,500

Recruitment Source Ratio Ratio of positions filled from within the firm to positions filled by external recruits.

Jumbuck 2002	2003	2004	All Industry Median	Your Industry Median
1:5	1:4	1:2	1:3	1:4

Managerial and Professional Career Path Ratio For example, in 2002, for every one promotion, there were twelve horizontal transfers within the firm for managerial and professional staff. (Promotions/horizontal transfers)

Jumbuck 2002	2003	2004	All Industry Median	Your Industry Median
1:12	1:8	1:5	1:6	1:8

Average Cost of Sick Leave Days Due to Accidents on the Job Includes employee absences from work plus medical costs associated with the accident.

Jumbuck 2002	2003	2004	All Industry Median	Your Industry Median
$2,775	$2,595	$2,280	$2,215	$2,325

Company Operating Expenses = $121,500,000 This has been the same for the last three years, along with the following:

Total employees	1,000
Total operative employees	800
Total management employees	200
Average operative salary	$30,000
Average management salary	$60,000
Average HR salary	$38,000
Revenue per employee	$129,000
Gross profit per employee	$7,500
Number of management hires	16

Source: Adapted from a case prepared by Pat Foley and Peter Howes and presented at the 1996 Benchmarking Conference, HRM Consulting, Ltd., Sydney, Australia, 1996. Reprinted by permission of HRM Consulting.

Exercise 2.1

HR Strategy: E-Commerce Comes to Bojangles' Book and Music Company

You are the HR director for Bojangles' Book and Music Company (BBMC) in Springhill, Louisiana. Bojangles has been a family-owned business since 1925. It has been very successful over the years, providing a wide range of books and music to its customers. Bojangles prides itself on its very high level of customer service and an ability to fully live up to its motto of "You Want It , We Got—Or We Can Get It Fast." Bojangles' operations have spread from its single store in Springhill to a total of thirty stores in Louisiana, Mississippi, Alabama, and Georgia. Bojangles locates its stores in medium-sized towns because it found competition in the larger cities was too great. It has a highly efficient distribution system to ensure that all stores can live up to the BBMC motto.

BBMC's work force is hired from the local store areas. Stores provide part-time work for local high school students, and full-time employees tend to range in age from the mid-twenties to the late thirties. BBMC provides a profit-sharing scheme to all of its full-time employees. Turnover among these staff members is relatively low, with most staying with BBMC for several years.

Over the past couple of years, BBMC's profits have been dropping. Market research conducted by a professor from Western Central Louisiana University has indicated that much of Bojangles' loss in revenue can be attributed to book and music sellers operating on the Internet. After much soul searching, Beauregard B. Goree, Bojangles' current CEO, has decided "to take Bojangles' Book and Music Company onto the World Wide Web!"

Initially, BBMC will run all of its e-commerce operations from its home site in Springhill and use its existing distribution center. As to what this move to e-commerce means for BBMC's existing storefront operations, Beauregard B. Goree will only say, "Well, we'll just have to wait and see about that!"

1. Outline BBMC's strengths and weaknesses related to this change in mode of operation.
2. Outline the opportunities and threats associated with this change in business strategy.
3. Outline the HR practice implications for staff of such a change in operations. Specifically,
   a. what changes, if any, would be needed in how people are hired and what kinds of skills and qualifications they would need to have?
   b. how would you appraise the performance of staff in the new e-commerce operations, and how would that differ from staff in the storefront sites?
   c. what changes would be required in how you paid staff?
   d. what new training and development programs would be required?

Exercise 2.2

Changes in the Business Environment, Changes in HR: A Group Project

Students work in groups of four to five. Each group is to identify an organization that has faced a major change in the business environment in which it operates—for example, AT&T during its breakup and deregulation of the telecommunications industry or airline companies after the post-9/11 downturn in the world travel economy. Students may also focus on any local firm that has undergone some major shift in its business environment.

The task of each group (this may be done in or outside class) is to do the following:

- Outline the basic nature of the old business environment in which the firm operated, and describe the likely changes the new environment may have on the business strategy of the firm.
- Identify the human resource implications of these environmental and strategy shifts in terms of the selection, training, performance appraisal, and compensation of employees.
- Identify the major problems the firm has or will likely experience in implementing these new HR activities.

- Prepare a report for presentation to the class.

For example, an airline facing the reduction in worldwide air travel following the terrorist attack of September 11, 2001, could choose to either heavily reduce its costs, service routes, and flight frequencies, *or* it might decide to become a "luxury airline" focusing on a high level of quality for business travelers (with business travel less affected by recent world events than typical tourist travel). Employees would need to be more quality and customer-service focused and have better interpersonal and communication skills when dealing with business travelers. This would have an impact on both selection and training activities as well as on performance appraisal, for which quality and customer relations behaviors would become more important. Pay and incentive systems would need to reflect these new priorities. One major problem that is likely to face HR managers is the need to terminate employees who are unable to develop new and necessary skills. Pay and incentive systems to motivate performance may be difficult to implement if the firm is highly unionized or has low profit levels that make increased incentives not feasible.

In their reports, students should stress the fit between HR activities and the firm's new strategy, business environment and type of customers, as well as the horizontal fit among the various HR activities to show that they are consistent with one another.

Exercise 2.3
Benchmarking Resources on the Web

Your company is thinking about beginning a benchmarking program in human resource management. Use the Internet to locate data and articles about benchmarking human resource management. Prepare a report to your manager on what you have learned about the advantages and disadvantages of benchmarking, how to select comparison organizations, and whether you should obtain the services of any of the benchmarking organizations or consultants you encounter on the Web.

NOTES AND REFERENCES

1. Information for this HR Challenge was obtained from the "Corporate Backgrounder" section of the Xilinx Web site http://www.xilinx.com/company/press/grounder.htm (accessed on October 14, 2003; Earnings Report: Xilinx Inc. *Computergram Weekly,* July 20, 2001, p. N; Earnings Report: Xilinx Inc., *Network Briefing Daily,* October 10, 2001, p. 4; and Willem P. Roelandts, "Whatever You Do, Hang on to Your Engineers: They're Your Best Asset," *Design News,* Vol. 58 (10), 2003, p. 20.

2. To find out what Xilinx actually did to deal with the situation, see Thomas De Long and Christina Darwall, *Xilinx, Inc. (A),* Harvard Business School Cases, No. N-403-136, January 12, 2003; Roelandts, "Whatever You Do, Hang on to Your Engineers"; and see the interview of Peg Wynn, Vice President of Human Resources at Xilinx, in "HR Heroes: HR in High Tech—Small Companies," *HR Heroes: What It Means to Be a Strategic HR Leader in the 21st Century,* DVD produced by the SHRM Foundation, Society for Human Resource Management (Available at: http://www.shrm.org) 2003.

3. Wayne Brockbank, "If HR Were Really Strategically Proactive: Present and Future Directions in HR's Contribution to Competitive Advantage," *Human Resource Management,* Vol. 38 (4), 1999, pp. 337–352.

4. Randall S. Schuler, "Repositioning the Human Resource Function: Transformation or Demise," in *HRM Reality: Putting Competence in Context,* eds. P. J. Frost, V. F. Mitchell, and W. R. Nord (Cincinnati: Southwestern, 1992), pp. 8–21.

5. Steven W. Hays and Richard C. Kearney, "Anticipated Changes in Human Resource Management: Views from the Field," *Public Administration Review,* Vol. 61 (5), 2001, pp. 585–597; Jacek Lipiec, "Human Resources Management Perspective at the Turn of the Century," *Public Personnel Manage-*

ment, Vol. 30 (2), 2001, pp. 137–146; and Alfred Walker (Ed.), *Web-Based Human Resources: The Technologies and Trends That Are Transforming HR* (New York: McGraw-Hill, 2001).
6. Dave Ulrich, *Human Resource Champions* (Cambridge, Mass.: Harvard Business School Press, 1997).
7. Bartlett & Ghoshal (2002), "Building Competitive Advantage Through People" *MIT Sloan Management Review,* Vol. 43 (2), 2002, pp. 34-41.
8. Edward E. Lawler III and Susan A. Mohrman, "Beyond the Vision: What Makes HR Effective?" *Human Resource Planning,* Vol. 23 (4), 2000, pp. 11–20; SHRM/Towers Perrin survey results reported in Wayne Cascio, "*HR Heroes: What It Means to Be a Strategic HR Leader in the 21st Century: Discussion Guide*" (Alexandria, Va.: SHRM Foundation, 2003), p. 4).
9. James Walker, *Human Resource Strategy* (Sydney: McGraw-Hill International Editions, 1992); and Ian Clark, "HRM: Prescription, Description and Concept," *Personnel Review,* Vol. 22 (4), 1993, pp. 20, 23.
10. Jeffrey Pfeffer, *The Human Equation: Building Profits by Putting People First* (Boston, Mass: Harvard Business School Press, 1998).
11. Paul Boselie, Jaap Paauwe, and Paul Jansen, "Human Resource Management and Performance: Lessons from the Netherlands, *International Journal of Human Resource Management,* Vol. 12 (7), 2001, pp. 1107–1125.
12. John Delery, "Issues of Fit in Strategic Human Resource Management: Implications for Research," *Human Resource Management Review,* Vol. 8 (3), 1998, pp. 289–309; and Patrick M. Wright, "Strategy—HR Fit: Does It Really Matter?" *Human Resource Planning,* Vol. 21 (4), 1998, pp. 56–57.
13. Casey Ichinowski and Kathryn Shaw, "The Effects of Human Resource Management Systems on Economic Performance: An International Comparison of U.S. and Japanese Plants," *Management Science,* Vol. 45 (5), 1999, pp. 704–721, at 705.
14. Sohel Ahmad and Roger G. Schroeder, "The Impact of Human Resource Management Practices on Operational Performance: Recognizing Country and Industry Differences," *Journal of Operations Management,* Vol. 21 (1), 2003, pp. 19–43.
15. Jay Barney, "Looking Inside for Competitive Advantage," *Academy of Management Executive,* Vol. 9 (4), 1995, pp. 49–61.
16. Jay Barney and Patrick Wright, "On Becoming a Strategic Partner: The Role of Human Resources in Gaining Competitive Advantage," *Human Resource Management,* Vol. 37 (1), 1998, pp. 31–46.
17. Patrick M. Wright; Benjamin B. Dunford, and Scott A. Snell, "Human Resources and the Resource Based View of the Firm," *Journal of Management,* Vol. 27 (6), 2001, pp. 701–721.
18. Ibid., p. 704.
19. Barney and Wright, "On Becoming a Strategic Partner."
20. Michael Beer, "The Transformation of the Human Resource Function: Resolving the Tension Between a Traditional Administrative and a New Strategic Role," *Human Resource Management,* Vol. 36 (1), 1997, pp. 49–56; and Steve Bates, "Business Partners," *HR Magazine,* Vol. 48 (9), 2003, pp. 45–49.
21. Beer. "The Transformation of the Human Resource Function"; Wayne Brockbank, "If HR Were Really Strategically Proactive: Present and Future Directions in HR's Contribution to Competitive Advantage," *Human Resource Management,* Vol. 38 (4), 1999, pp. 337–352; and Timothy Galpin and Patrick Murray, "Connect Human Resource Strategy to the Business Plan," *HR Magazine,* Vol. 42 (3), 1997, pp. 99–104.
22. James Walker, "Perspectives: Is Your Business Case Compelling?" *Human Resource Planning,* Vol. 25 (1), 2002, p. 12.
23. Ibid., pp. 12–14.
24. James W. Walker and William E. Reif, "Human Resource Leaders: Capability Strengths and Gaps," *Human Resource Planning,* Vol. 22 (4), 1999, pp. 21–32.
25. Connie Freeman, "Training HR Pros to Fit Your Culture," *HR Focus,* Vol. 74 (5), 1997, pp. 9–10.
26. David Jones, "Repositioning Human Resources: A Case Study," *Human Resource Planning,* Vol. 19 (1), 1996, pp. 51–53.
27. Jill Conner and Jeana Wirtenberg, "Managing the Transformation of Human Resources Work," *Human Resource Planning,* Vol. 16 (2), 1993, pp. 17–34.
28. Information concerning Tampella Power from Arja Ropo, "Towards Strategic Human Resource Management: A Pilot Study in a Finnish Power Industry Company," *Personnel Review,* Vol. 22 (4), 1993, pp. 35–53; information about Northern Telecom from James Kochanski and Phillip Randall, "Rearchitecting the Human Resources Function at

Northern Telecom," *Human Resource Management,* Vol. 33 (2), 1994, pp. 299–315; information on Benetton from Arnaldo Camuffo and Giovanni Costra, "Strategic Human Resource Management—Italian Style," *Sloan Management Review,* Vol. 34 (2), 1993, pp. 59–67; information about Siemens Rolm from Gillian Flynn, "On Track to a Comeback: Siemens Rolm Models Reengineering Done Right," *Personnel Journal,* Vol. 75 (2), 1996, pp. 58–69.

29. Gregory Kesler, "Four Steps to Building an HR Agenda for Growth: HR Strategy Revisited," *Human Resource Planning,* Vol. 23 (3), 2000, p. 24–37.

30. Ibid.; and Neil McEwen, "Transforming HR: The Practitioner's Perspective," *HR Review,* Vol. 2 (1) 2002, pp. 18–23.

31. Ulrich, *Human Resource Champions.*

32. Cited in "Going First Class," *HR Focus,* Vol. 73 (7), 1996, p. 11.

33. Described in Beer, "The Transformation of the Human Resource Function."

34. Institute of Management and Administration, *Human Resource Department Management Report,* Issue 03-04, April 2003, pp. 1, 7, 11–14.

35. Jones, "Repositioning Human Resources."

36. Institute of Management and Administration, "HRIS Managers' Forum," *Managing Human Resources Information Systems,* Vol. 2002 (5), 2002, p. 15.

37. Towers Perrin, "Web-Based Self-Service: The Current State of the Art" "at http://www.towers.com/towers/webcache/towers/United_States/publications/Reports/TP_Track_WebBasedSelfSer/TP_Track_WebBasedSelfSe.pdf, 2001 (accessed October 27, 2003); Towers Perrin, "Use of the Web for HR Service Delivery Growing Steadily," at www.towers.com/towers/, September 1, 2002 (accessed 27 October 2003); Watson Wyatt Worldwide, "eHR: Getting Results Along the Journey," at http://www.watsonwyatt.com/research/printable.asp?id=W-524, 2002 (accessed October 27, 2003); Towers Perrin, "Companies Report Big Payoffs From Web-Based HR Services," at www.towers.com/towers/, October 1, 2003 (accessed October 27, 2003).

38. Charles Greer, Stuart Youngblood, and David Gray, "Human Resource Management Outsourcing: The Decision to Make or Buy," *Academy of Management Executive,* Vol. 13 (3), 1999, pp. 85–96.

39. Craig Gunsauley, "Employers Embrace Multiservice HR Outsourcing," *Employee Benefit News,* Vol. 16 (8), 2002, pp. 17–18; Reed Executive PLC, "More Organizations Decide to Outsource," *Personnel Today,* September 3, 2002, p. 63; and Craig Gunsauley, "Mellon Goes Global," *Employee Benefit News,* Vol. 16 (8), 2002, pp. 17–18.

40. From a report by Reed Business Information Services described in "End-to-End Outsourcing," *Personnel Today,* March 25, 2003, pp. 24–25.

41. Steve Bates, "HR Outsourcing Is Not All About Money," *HR Magazine,* Vol. 48 (4), 2003, p. 14; and Dominique Hammond, "Firms Resist HR Outsourcing," *People Management,* Vol. 8 (12), 2002, p. 8.

42. Stephen Kerr, "Organizational Rewards: Practical, Cost Neutral Alternatives That You May Know, But Don't Practice," *Organizational Dynamics,* Vol. 28 (1), 1999, pp. 61–70.

43. General Electric Web site, Investor FAQs, "What is GE's mission statement?" at http://www.ge.com/en/company/investor/faqs.htm#faq12 (accessed October 28, 2003).

44. Richard L. Osborne, "Core Value Statements: The Corporate Compass," *Business Horizons,* September–October 1991, pp. 28–34.

45. IBM and Marriott examples described on pp. 8–9 of the United States General Accounting Office, *Human Capital: Key Principles from Nine Private Sector Organizations,* General Government Division, Report Number GAO/GGD-00-28, January 2000.

46. Brian Becker and Mark Huselid, "Overview: Strategic Human Resources Management in Five Leading Firms," *Human Resource Management,* Vol. 38 (4), 1999, pp. 287–301; Walker and Reif, "Human Resource Leaders"; "James Walker, "Perspectives: Is Your Business Case Compelling?" *Human Resource Planning,* Vol. 25 (1), 2002, pp. 12–14.

47. Melody Jones, "Four Trends to Reckon With," *HR Focus,* Vol. 73 (7), 1996, pp. 22–23.

48. James Baron and David Kreps, "Consistent Human Resource Practices," *California Management Review,* Vol. 41 (3), 1999, pp. 29–53.

49. P. Boxall, "Strategic HRM: Beginning a New Theoretical Direction," *Human Resource Management,* Vol. 2 (3), 1992, pp. 61–79.

50. Richard Beatty and Craig Schneier, "New HR Roles to Impact Organizational Performance: From 'Partners' to 'Players,'" *Human Resource Management,* Vol. 36 (1), 1997, pp. 29–37.

51. Ibid.
52. Wendy Boswell and John Boudreau, "How Leading Companies Create, Measure and Achieve Strategic Results Through 'Line of Sight,'" *Management Decision,* Vol. 39 (10), 2001, pp. 851–859.
53. R. Guzzo,"Introduction: At the Intersection of Team Effectiveness and Decision Making," in *Team Eeffectiveness and Decision Making in Organizations,* eds. R. Guzzo, E. Salas, and Associates (San Francisco: Jossey-Bass, 1995), pp. 1–8.
54. Information about the Agilent HR transformation was summarized from information in Grace Yokoi and Charles O'Reilly III, "Building the Culture at Agilent Technologies: Back to the Future," Graduate School of Business, Stanford University, Case Number HR-20, September 2001.
55. C. Chadwick and P. Cappelli, "Alternatives to Generic Strategy Typologies in Strategic Human Resource Management," in *Research in Personnel and Human Resource Management, Supplement 4, Strategic Human Resources Management in the 21st Century,* eds. P. Wright, L. Dyer, J. Boudreau, and G. Milkovich (Greenwich, Conn.: JAI Press, 1999), pp. 11–29; and Gerald Ferris, Wayne Hochwarter, Ronald Buckley, Gloria Harnell-Cook, and Dwight Fink, "Human Resources Management: Some New Directions," *Journal of Management,* Vol. 25 (3), 1999, pp. 385–415.
56. Chadwick and Cappelli, "Alternatives to Generic Strategy Typologies in Strategic Human Resource Management"; Ferris et al., "Human Resources Management"; and J. Milliman, M. Von Glinow, and M. Nathan, "Organizational Life Cycles and Strategic International Human Resource Management in Multinational Companies: Implications for Congruence Theory," *Academy of Management Review,* Vol. 16, 1991, pp. 318–339.
57. Patrick Wright and Scott Snell, "Toward a Unifying Framework for Exploring Fit and Flexibility in Strategic Human Resource Management," *Academy of Management Review,* Vol. 23 (4), 1998, pp. 756–772.
58. Ibid.
59. Janice Tomlinson, "Human Resources—Partners in Change," *Human Resource Management,* Vol. 32 (4), 1993, pp. 545–554.
60. ClariNews: Hot News, "First Tennessee National Corp. Makes Lists of Best Employers for Working Mothers and People Over 50," available at http://quickstart.clari.net/qs_se/webnews/wed/bp/Btn-first-tennessee.RFMG_DSN.html, September 23, 2003. (accessed October 30, 2003)
61. Steve Bates, "Business Partners," *HR Magazine,* Vol. 48 (9), 2003, pp. 45–49.
62. Brian Becker and Mark Huselid, "Overview: Strategic Human Resource Management in Five Leading Firms," *Human Resource Management,* Vol. 38 (4), 1999, pp. 287–301.
63. Ibid.
64. Brian Becker, Mark Huselid, and Dave Ulrich, *The HR Scorecard: Linking People, Strategy, and Performance* (Boston: Harvard Business School Press, 2001).
65. Jeffrey Pfeffer, "Pitfalls on the Road to Measurement: The Dangerous Liaison of Human Resources with the Ideas of Accounting and Finance," *Human Resource Management,* Vol. 36, (3), 1997, pp. 357–365.
66. Elizabeth Cabrera and Angel Cabrera, "Evaluation of Human Resource Practices in Spanish Banks," *International Journal of Management,* Vol. 18 (3), 2001, pp. 337–344: Wayne F. Cascio, *Costing Human Resources: The Financial Impact of Behavior on Organizations* (Mason, Ohio: South-Western, 1999); Wayne F. Cascio, *Costing Human Resources,* (Mason, Ohio: South-Western, 2000); Jac Fitz-enz, *How to Measure Human Resources Management* (New York: McGraw-Hill, 2002); Nancy Kaylor, Susan McLane, and Susan Schechter, "Ideas and Trends in Personnel," *Human Resources Management,* Vol. 408, June 1997, pp. 87–97; Tom Lawson and Regina Hepp, "Measuring the Performance Impact of Human Resource Initiatives," *Human Resource Planning,* Vol. 24 (2), 2001, pp. 36–44; Sunil Ramlall, "Measuring Human Resource Management's Effectiveness in Improving Performance," *Human Resource Planning,* Vol. 26 (1), 2003, p. 51; Edward Rogers and Patrick Wright, "Measuring Organizational Performance in Strategic Human Resource Management: Problems, Prospects, and Performance Information Markets," *Human Resource Management Review,* Vol. 8 (3), 1998, pp. 311–331; and Ulrich, *Human Resource Champions.*
67. James Walker, "Are We Using the Right Human Resource Measures?" *Human Resource Planning,* Vol. 21 (2), 1998, pp. 7–8.
68. Fitz-enz, *How to Measure Human Resources Management.*
69. Boselie, Paauwe, and Jansen, "Human Resource Management and Performance"; and Walker, "Are We Using the Right Human Resource Measures?"

70. Richard Beatty, Mark Huselid, and Craig Schneider, "New HR Metrics: Scoring on the Business Scorecard," *Organizational Dynamics,* Vol. 32 (2), 2003, pp. 107–121; and Robert S. Kaplan and David P. Norton, "The Balanced Scorecard—Measures That Drive Performance," *Harvard Business Review,* Vol. 70 (1), 1992, pp. 71–79.
71. SHRM and BSC survey cited in Institute of Management and Administration, "The Balanced Scorecard: One Approach to HR Metrics, *HR Focus,* Vol. 80 (10), 2003, p. S2.
72. Garret Walker and Randall MacDonald, "Designing and Implementing an HR Scorecard," *Human Resource Management,* Vol. 40 (4), 2001, pp. 365–377.
73. Nancy Kaylor, Susan McLane, and Susan Schechter, "Ideas and Trends in Personnel," *Human Resources Management,* Vol. 408, June 1997, pp. 87–97.
74. Wayne Cascio, *Costing Human Resources: The Financial Impact of Behavior in Organizations,* 4th ed. (Cincinnati, Ohio: South-Western College, 2000).
75. Lyle Spencer, *Calculating Human Resource Costs and Benefits: Cutting Costs and Improving Productivity* (Brisbane, Australia: Wiley, 1986).
76. Arthur Yeung and Bob Berman, "Adding Value Through Human Resources: Reorienting Human Resource Measurement to Drive Business Performance," *Human Resource Management,* Vol. 36 (3), 1997, pp. 321–335.
77. Jean Hiltrop and Charles Despres, "Benchmarking the Performance of Human Resource Management," *Long Range Planning,* Vol. 27 (6), 1994, p. 47.
78. Taken from lecture materials provided by Peter Howes of HRM Consulting, Inc., of Brisbane at the HR Benchmarking Conference in Sydney, Australia, 1996.
79. Information on the Saratoga Institute can be found at http://www.pwcservices.com/saratoga-institute. (accessed November 17, 2003)
80. Boselie, Paauwe, and Jansen, "Human Resource Management and Performance."
81. Tanuja Agarwala, "Innovative Human Resource Practices and Organizational Commitment: An Empirical Investigation," *International Journal of Human Resource Management,* Vol. 14 (2), 2003, pp. 174–197; and Garry A. Gelade and Mark Ivery, "The Impact of Human Resource Management and Work Climate on Organizational Performance," *Personnel Psychology,* Vol. 56 (2), 2003, pp. 383–404.
82. Mark Huselid, Susan Jackson, and Randall Schuler, "Technical and Strategic Human Resource Management Effectiveness as Determinants of Firm Performance," *Academy of Management Journal,* Vol. 40 (1), 1997, pp. 171–188.
83. Sohel Ahmad and Roger G. Schroeder, "The Impact of Human Resource Management Practices on Operational Performance: Recognizing Country and Industry Differences," *Journal of Operations Management,* Vol. 21 (1), 2003, pp. 19–43; Ingmar Bjorkman and Fan Xiucheng, "Human Resource Management and the Performance of Western Firms in China," *International Journal of Human Resource Management,* Vol. 13 (6), 2002, pp. 853–864; Carl Fey, Ingmar Bjorkman, and Antonina Pavlovskaya, "The Effect of Human Resource Management Practices on Firm Performance in Russia," *International Journal of Human Resource Management,* Vol. 11 (1), 2000, pp. 1–18; James Guthrie, Chester Spell, and Robert Nyamori, "Correlates and Consequences of High Involvement Work Practices: The Role of Competitive Strategy," *International Journal of Human Resource Management,* Vol. 13 (1), 2002, pp. 183–197; and Keld Laurssen and Nicolai Foss, "New Human Resource Management Practices, Complementarities and the Impact on Innovation Performance," *Cambridge Journal of Economics,* Vol. 27, 2003, pp. 243–263; and Yeung and Berman, "Adding Value Through Human Resources."

CHAPTER 3

Human Resource Planning

- What Is Human Resource Planning?
- Forecasting the Demand for Labor
- The Internal Supply of Labor
- The External Supply of Labor
- Planning Human Resource Programs

HR Challenge

Twenty percent of America's registered nurses are expected to retire within the next ten years. The demand for health care is rising with the aging of the population. The number of new entrants into the nursing profession, although rising slightly in recent years, is insufficient to replace those leaving, much less cater to increasing demand. The shortage of nurses is forecast to worsen through 2020.[1] *Nor is the problem limited to the United States; hospitals in England are also reporting severe shortages. Further, fully one-third of Canadian nurses are now age fifty or over, and the typical retirement age for nurses in that country is fifty-six to fifty-eight.*

These statistics sounded a warning bell for the New Hanover Health Network, a five-hospital system in southeastern North Carolina. New Hanover was experiencing difficulty recruiting nurses to service its 800 beds and anticipated even more shortages in the future. The firm's existing HR systems were simply unable to supply their needs. A proactive strategy was needed to equip the firm to acquire critical human resources in an increasingly difficult labor market. New Hanover decided to take a hard look at its staffing sources and practices and adopt a multi-pronged, strategic approach to meeting its future needs for nursing staff. Suppose you were Director of Human Resources at New Hanover Health Network. What kind of programs and practices might you implement to achieve these goals?[2]

Chapter 3 is about human resource planning (also called *work force planning*), the process by which organizations anticipate future staffing needs and plan programs to ensure that the correct number and type of employees are available when they are needed. The first section of the chapter defines and describes the nature of human resource planning. Then the discussion moves to judgmental and mathematical methods for forecasting the demand for labor within a firm and to the methods planners can use to make forecasts about the future internal supply of labor. External labor trends are highlighted next, with emphasis given to how these affect organizations. The next section of the chapter describes how to plan responses to potential shortages and surpluses so that the organization will have the number and type of human resources required to allow for effective implementation of strategy.

WHAT IS HUMAN RESOURCE PLANNING?

An organization would not build a new plant, conduct the ribbon-cutting ceremony, and then begin to worry about how to staff the facility. A firm cannot hire several hundred engineers and get them on board overnight, nor can it develop management talent in just a few weeks. Foresight is necessary to ensure that appropriately qualified staff will be available to implement an organization's future plans. The tighter the labor market, the more forward planning is required to avoid future problems due to understaffing. On the other hand, planning ahead in a declining economy is also critical in minimizing expensive overstaffing and possible layoffs. **Human resource planning** is concerned with the flow of people into, through, and out of an organization. HR planning involves anticipating the need for labor and the supply of labor and then planning the programs necessary to ensure that the organization will have the right mix of employees and skills when and where they are needed. Forecasting the future can be a very inexact science, so human resource planning also may include multiple scenarios and contingency plans.

Human resource experts can also take on a strategic role in collaboration with the top management team to plan a strategy for the firm that capitalizes on or builds the organization's unique human resource competencies.[3] For instance, Marriott Corporation's goal of being the provider of choice for food and lodging services was supplemented by the goal of becoming the "employer of choice" as well. Executives decided that unless Marriott was a very attractive employer, it would not be able to obtain the number and quality of people it needed for a growth and high-quality service strategy. The company adopted initiatives to broaden its recruiting base, but it also worked hard at retaining and motivating current employees. To that end, changes were made in career paths, job responsibilities, work teams, and reward systems.[4]

A Model for Human Resource Planning

The first step in HR planning is to collect information. A forecast or plan cannot be any better than the data on which it is based. HR planning requires two types of information: data from the external environment and data from inside the organization (see Figure 3.1).[5] Data from the external environment include information on

FIGURE 3.1

Human Resource Planning Model

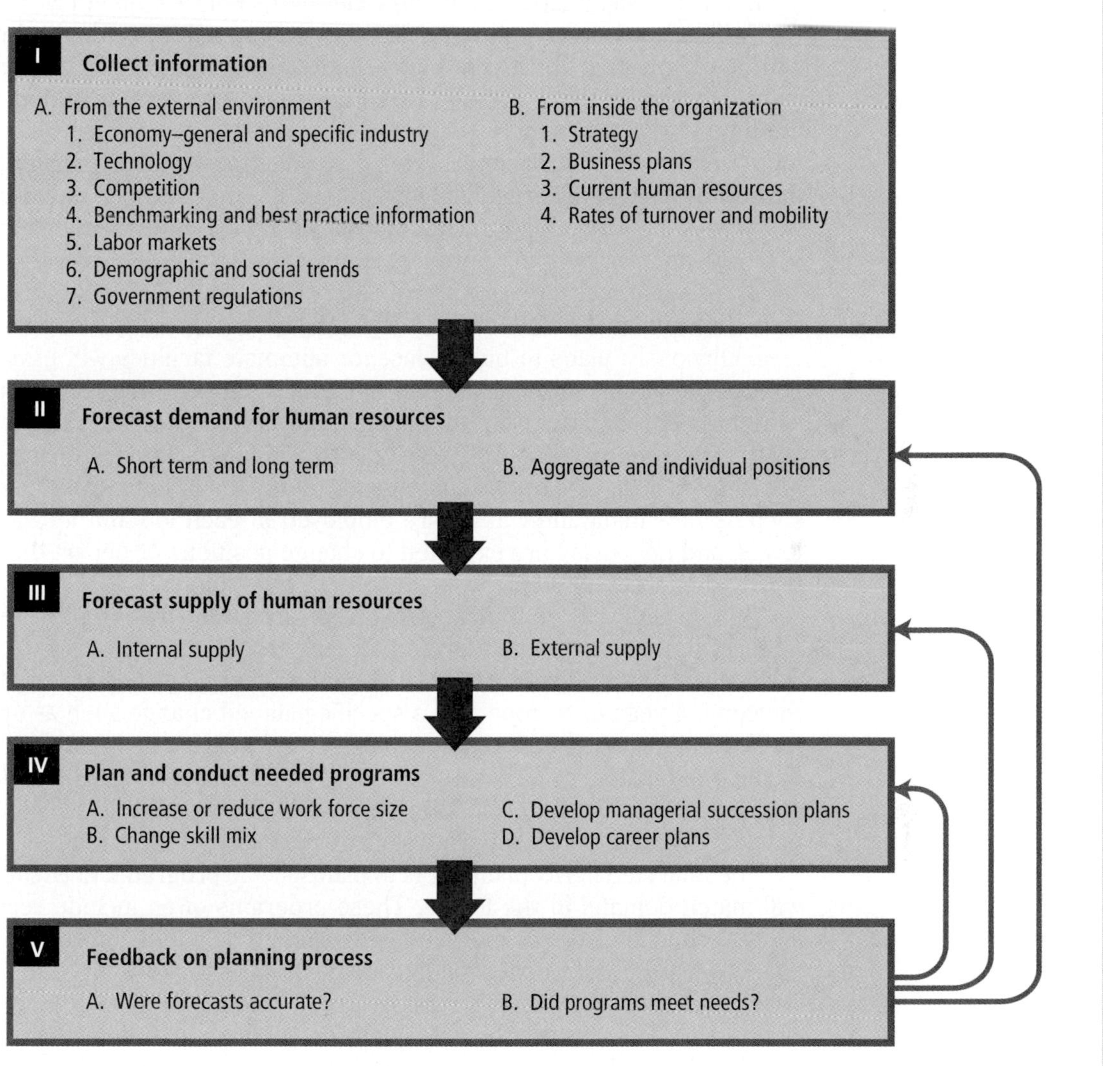

current conditions and predicted changes in the general economy, the economy of the specific industry, relevant technology, and competitor firms. Any of these may affect the organization's business direction and volume and thus the need for human resources.

Human resource planners must also be aware of labor-market conditions such as unemployment rates, skill availabilities, and the age distribution of the labor force. Finally, planners need to be aware of federal and state regulations: those that directly affect staffing practices, such as affirmative action or retirement-age legislation, and those that indirectly affect demand for services or ability to pay staff. For example, employment in the home health industry recently rose substantially due to changes in government policy and budget with regard to Medicare payments for home health services.[6] A systematic program of environmental scanning will help an organization anticipate what is likely to happen and prepare for shifts in the external environment.[7]

External benchmarking data also can be useful in human resource planning. One might, for instance, discover that other companies are doing the same work with fewer people, which could lead to a consideration of more efficient ways to work. Benchmarking efforts by Duke Power Company's consulting arm showed them new ways to organize. Historically, they had staffed projects exclusively with highly experienced (and expensive) professionals. Benchmarking showed them that other successful consulting firms used a small number of top-class experts working with a large support staff of less skilled and experienced people, and they were able to replicate this approach successfully.[8]

The second major type of information comes from inside the organization. Internal information includes short- and long-term organizational plans and strategies. Obviously, plans to build, close, or automate facilities will have HR implications, as will plans to modify the organization's structure, buy or sell businesses, and enter or withdraw from markets. A decision to compete on the basis of low cost rather than personalized service also will have staffing implications. Finally, information is needed on the current state of human resources in the organization, such as how many individuals are employed in each job and location, their skill levels, and how many are expected to change positions or depart the organization during the forecast period.

Once planners have the external and internal information they need, they can forecast the future demand for employees. At a minimum, this forecast includes relatively short-term estimates of the number of employees who will be needed in the coming year, or to cope with a specific planned change such as opening a new facility. Longer term demand forecasts several years into the future also may be made. Next, planners forecast the supply of labor: the internal supply of employees and their skills and promotability, as well as the probable availability of potential new employees with requisite skills in the external labor market.

The final step in HR planning is to plan specific programs to ensure that supply will match demand in the future. These programs often include recruiting plans and also may include training and development activities, incentives or disincentives to early retirement, modifications of career paths in the organization, changes in the way work is structured, or a variety of other HR management programs. Note that the feedback loop shown in Figure 3.1 allows for learning from past planning efforts. If demand or supply forecasts have not been as accurate as desired, forecasting processes can be improved in subsequent years. Similarly, if programs prove to be inadequate or inappropriate, they can be modified.

Who Plans?

Traditional HR planning is usually initiated and managed by the HR department. However, information is needed from all parts of the organization, and line managers must be involved in the HR planning process, with some planning methods requiring more manager involvement than others. Strategic HR planning involves top management as well as HR experts and may rely on information from many levels of management.

Not all organizations engage in HR forecasting and planning, although more and more are doing so each year. As with many other HR activities, larger firms are more likely than smaller ones to have HR planning systems.[9] Because of the large number of individuals involved, the military has been a leader in the development of sophisticated HR planning systems.

Who Is Planned For?

In designing a human resource planning system, there are several choices regarding whom to plan for. One choice is to plan at the aggregate level, for jobs or job families. **Aggregate-level planning** is typically used for jobs with multiple incumbents and for jobs at or below the middle-management level. An organization may forecast that thirty-five electrical engineers will be needed at the California development laboratory or that a total of 2,100 registered nurses will be required. The focus is on the number of persons needed for a job or job category, not on identifying the specific individuals who will fill the positions.

Many large organizations plan for each job or job family, but this may not always be necessary. The alternative is to plan only for those jobs that logic or experience indicates are important or problematic. Clearly this would include jobs that are essential in allowing the organization to implement its strategy. Other job categories that may require considerable HR planning are those in which skills needed are likely to change considerably from present requirements, employment levels are expected to increase or decrease substantially, positions are hard to fill for any reason, or jobs require a long training time to produce qualified staff.[10] For instance, a large manufacturer may need to plan carefully for scientists and engineers if there is a chronic shortage of these essential professionals. But the manufacturer may find that it does not need to engage in long-range planning for janitors or assembly personnel if they can be hired and trained quickly when demand increases.

Duke Power Company has developed a work force planning system based on pivotal roles—jobs that have the greatest strategic importance in each of its businesses. All other jobs are considered support roles and are less central to future business success. The pivotal roles identified surprised some employees—traditionally important top management and engineering jobs were not always pivotal in the new competitive environment Duke faces. Instead, the jobs of national account manager, customer service representative, and meter reader were among those identified as critical for planning purposes.[11]

In addition to aggregate planning—or instead of it—many organizations plan at the individual level. For important jobs, particularly upper-management positions, these organizations identify specific employees who are likely successors when a position becomes vacant due to promotion or retirement. A **succession plan** for a top managerial position might identify from one to three possible replacements and specify the additional training and experience each needs to become fully qualified for that position in the future.

When Is Planning Done?

Traditionally organizations mount a major HR planning effort once a year, which provides useful guidance and background data for long-term thinking, but HR planning should also be built into everyday management decision making, with plans assessed each time any kind of strategic change is considered or new information becomes available. For instance, an unexpected business downturn would indicate that near-term recruiting plans should be reconsidered. The appearance of a problem in staffing or a new strategic initiative also should trigger further planning. A large organization in the midst of downsizing may run its computerized planning models every week to monitor changes made through voluntary attrition, internal transfers, enhanced retirement packages, and layoffs.

The formal planning process can focus on one of several time horizons. For example, organizations at the elementary stage of development of the HR planning function typically plan for the short term—just one year in advance and with particular emphasis on recruiting or downsizing needs. Likewise, those operating in a very turbulent and unpredictable environment might limit their planning to the relatively near-term future. Organizations that have more experience in HR planning, have more complex needs, and operate in a more stable environment might also plan for the intermediate term—two to three years out. Some organizations engage in long-range HR planning—more than three years into the future. Plans for executive succession and the development of "high-potential" managers often incorporate these longer time horizons.[12]

FORECASTING THE DEMAND FOR LABOR

Once HR planners have collected information from both internal and external sources, they forecast the **demand for labor.** How many and what type of people will be needed to carry out the organization's plans in the future? These forecasts are grounded in information about the past and present and in assumptions about the future. Different methods of forecasting the demand for labor require different assumptions. Some of the more common assumptions are that past trends and relationships among variables will hold up in the future; that the productivity ratio is constant (or follows a known pattern) as the number of units produced increases; and that the business plans of the organization, sales forecasts, and so on are reasonably descriptive of what will actually happen. In a highly volatile business, these assumptions may not be valid. It is always wise to explicitly list one's assumptions in forecasting and to put no more faith in the forecast than in the assumptions on which it was based.

Demand forecasting methods can be divided into two categories: judgmental and mathematical. In practice, most organizations use some combination of the two methods. For example, expert judges might estimate the values of some variables and then use these values in prediction equations, or experts might integrate the results of mathematical methods with less quantifiable information into a final subjective forecast.

Judgmental Methods

Judgmental methods make use of knowledgeable people to forecast the future. Judgmental methods do consider quantitative data but also factor in intuition and expertise. Judgmental methods may be used by small organizations or by those new to HR forecasting that do not yet have the database or expertise to use some of the more complex mathematical models. Judgmental methods also may be preferred when an organization or environment is in a state of transition or turmoil; at such times, past trends and correlations cannot be used to make accurate predictions about the future.

Perhaps the simplest judgmental method is **bottom-up** (or **unit**) **forecasting:** Each unit, branch, or department estimates its own future need for employees. Ideally, managers receive some guidance and information, which they combine with their own perspectives to reach the estimates. The sum of the estimated unit needs is the demand forecast for the whole organization. HR planners may wish to review the unit forecasts carefully before summing so as to control managers' natural tendencies to exaggerate the needed size and importance of their units.[13]

Houston Lighting and Power developed a spreadsheet-based bottom-up planning system that provides line managers with information on current staffing levels in the job classes they supervise, asks for estimated changes in workload and productivity, and requests estimates of HR needs in each of the next five years. The estimates are approved by the next level of management and then forwarded to the HR planning group, which integrates them into an organization-wide forecast.[14]

Another judgmental method involves **top-down forecasting** by experienced top managers and executives. These experts meet to discuss how trends, business plans, the economy, and other factors will affect the need for human resources at various levels of the organization. Besides predicting the most likely future demand, these experts also may make separate forecasts based on best- and worst-case scenarios. For instance, they might forecast what the need for labor will be if almost everything that could go wrong does go wrong (e.g., there is a recession, the organization loses the product liability suit now being tried, and the company does not land the large government contract it has bid for). After completing such exercises, the experts can be fairly certain that the actual demand for labor will fall somewhere between their best- and worst-case predictions. Many of the mathematical forecasting methods also lend themselves to this type of what-if assessment.

One highly structured judgmental method of expert forecasting utilizes the **Delphi technique** to achieve group consensus on a forecast.[15] In using this technique, the experts do not meet face to face. This is more economical if they are assigned to different locations; it also can improve the quality of decision making by minimizing disruptive personality conflicts and preventing the loudest group member from dominating the decision process. The first step in the Delphi process is to develop an anonymous questionnaire that asks the experts for an opinion and the reasons they hold that opinion. The results of this questionnaire are compiled and returned to the experts, along with a second anonymous questionnaire. In this way, the experts can learn from one another and modify or elaborate their positions in the second questionnaire. The process continues through several more rounds until the experts agree on a judgment.

In one published test of the Delphi technique, a national retail company predicted the number of buyers needed in one year. The experts were seven managers, who responded to five rounds of questionnaires. In the first round, estimates ranged from thirty-two to fifty-five buyers. By the fifth round, estimates narrowed to between thirty-four and forty-five buyers, with a mean of thirty-eight. The Delphi predictions were not made public or used in recruitment planning that year so that the company could evaluate their accuracy compared with actual end-of-year staffing levels. At the end of the year, thirty-seven buyers were actually employed. The Delphi method proved to be much more accurate than three simple mathematical models also applied to the same forecasting problem.[16]

A complete Delphi process using several rounds of anonymous questionnaires takes time to complete, so this method may not be appropriate if results are needed very quickly. As with any expert forecasting method, participants should be knowledgeable about the topic. Their existing knowledge can be supplemented by providing information on past and current staffing, business performance, business plans, and the like.

Simple Mathematical Methods

The simplest mathematical methods of forecasting use only one factor to predict demand. For example, to predict the need for labor, one could examine staffing levels during the last few years, note the trend, and extend this trend to the upcoming year. A better method would be to use forecasts of the coming year's sales, production, or another business factor known to be related to the need for labor. This information would then be combined with productivity ratios to predict the number of direct labor employees needed.[17]

The **productivity ratio** is the average number of units produced per direct labor employee per year. Suppose a company produces sofas and knows from past history that the productivity ratio is about fifty sofas per furniture assembler per year. If the marketing department expects to sell 10,000 sofas in the coming year, then the company needs 10,000/50 = 200 furniture assemblers.

Direct-to-indirect-labor **staffing ratios** are used to calculate the number of individuals required in other jobs. For instance, if the sofa firm generally has one supervisor for every fifteen assemblers, then about thirteen supervisors will be needed for two hundred assemblers. Past experience also may show that two shipping-and-receiving clerks are required for every fifty assemblers. This means that the company needs a total of eight clerks.

Productivity and staffing ratios based on historical data may be modified judgmentally if the ratios are expected to change. For instance, if the union has negotiated a new contract requiring workdays that are thirty minutes shorter and more paid holidays, the expected productivity ratio should be adjusted downward. If an improved order-processing program will be installed in the clerks' computers, the staffing ratio may change, with fewer clerks needed to service the same number of direct workers.

Forecasting with productivity ratios is based on the assumption that the number of employees needed increases linearly with the amount of work to be done. This assumption is not always correct. Envision, for example, a company that has handled increasing demand for its product by having employees work overtime. At some point, the company will not be able to cope with increasing sales in this way and may decide to add a second shift or open a new plant. At this juncture, a large increase in staffing will occur, resulting in a discontinuous relationship between output and labor demand.

A different demand forecast method may be suitable for companies that do a great deal of contract or project work. For these firms, the amount of labor needed depends directly on how many contracts they land or how many projects go ahead. If the firms can calculate the number of people or labor hours needed for each contract, these figures can be multiplied by the estimated probability of receiving each contract and then summed to estimate the most likely aggregate labor-demand figure. Forecasts of this type tend to be accurate only if there are many pending contracts to sum over and if one can correctly estimate the probabilities of receiving various contracts.[18] One high-tech firm plots future research projects through the anticipated phases of development. The number and types of engineers and scientists needed for each phase of each project are estimated, together with the likely duration of each phase and the probability that the project will progress to the next phase. Adding across projects provides an estimate of the demand for various types of research and development staff for each future time period. Recently, a number of sophisticated work force optimization computer programs have become available to estimate needs and allocate human resources in project-based work, such as that found in IT departments and professional service firms.[19]

Complex Mathematical Methods

Some forecasting methods use more complicated statistical techniques. Large organizations with a long history of HR planning are likely to employ these methods. One such method, **multiple regression,** uses several factors that correlate with labor demand to forecast future demand. Examples of such factors include sales, profits, capital investments, and gross national product (GNP). Historical data are used to derive an equation describing the relationships of these factors to employment levels; then current or predicted values of the factors are inserted into the equation to predict future demand. This method can be applied only when sufficient historical data exist to allow for the derivation of stable regression weights, when fairly strong relationships exist between the factors and labor demand, and when no dramatic changes in productivity or product mix are anticipated.[20]

A second forecasting method employs **linear** (or **goal**) **programming** to determine optimal staffing levels given a set of constraints. Constraints might include compensation budgets, minimum and maximum ratios between various kinds of jobs, or minimum and maximum output figures. Further information on these techniques is available in most operations management textbooks.[21]

THE INTERNAL SUPPLY OF LABOR

Once the demand for labor is predicted, it is necessary to forecast the supply of labor that the organization will already have available to meet the demand. The **internal supply of labor** consists of all the individuals currently employed by an organization. These employees can help to fill future demands by remaining employed in their current positions or by being promoted or transferred to fill vacancies elsewhere in the organization. The internal supply of labor is constantly changing as new people enter and others resign, retire, or are discharged. The skill mix also changes as people move in and out and as employees develop new capabilities through training or on-the-job experience.

To keep track of the current internal supply and to predict the future supply, planners need some sort of supply information system. At a minimum, this system may consist of simple staffing tables that show the number of incumbents in each job within the organization. For small companies, a manual system may suffice, but increasingly employee information is stored and manipulated in computer programs, some of which have very sophisticated retrieval and analysis capabilities. The next sections describe two such systems: skills inventories and human resource information systems.

Skills Inventories

A **skills inventory** is a manual or computerized system designed to keep track of employees' experience, education, and special abilities.[22] Computerized skills inventories may be freestanding programs or modules of a larger human resource information system (described further in the next section). A skills inventory database will include information on employee formal qualifications and certifications, work and training history, competencies, and preferences. The inventory can be used to assess the current supply of employees of various sorts. For instance, an employer might wish to know how many people are presently working as salespersons, how many people have current or past experience in firefighting, or how many certified professional engineers are employed. The inventory also can be used to identify candidates for promotion or transfer. Suppose a large company has an opening for an experienced petroleum geologist who is willing to relocate and who speaks fluent Arabic. A personnel requisition form that describes the opening will be generated using the same standard key words that are used in the skills inventory. The inventory system will then be able to generate a list of all qualified employees in the organization. The inventory can also help to identify individuals who are ready for particular training or development courses. In addition, through items on location and position preference, the inventory can ensure that employees' own career plans and wishes are considered when the organization makes transfer or promotion decisions.

Human Resource Information Systems

A **human resource information system (HRIS)** combines in one system all the information that organizations typically keep on employees and on positions. An HRIS can streamline administration and record-keeping tasks as well as provide decision support for managers and HR specialists.[23] The last fifteen years have seen a massive movement toward full-blown, highly integrated human resource information systems that can do much more than simple skills inventory systems.[24] Even quite small firms are finding advantages in automating HR information.[25] Many of the functional components are available in modular form and can be added as demand grows. For instance, a firm might start out with pay and benefits modules, then later add modules for tracking appraisal and training. Most human resource information systems are comprised of the components and capabilities listed here and shown in Figure 3.2:

- A computerized database management system
- Screens for inputting data
- Programs for cross-checking data and transaction accuracy
- Modules for performing specific functions such as tracking applicant flows and for generating regular reports such as monthly compensation costs or positions filled versus those vacant
- Query programs for requesting special information combinations or what-if analyses
- Self-serve interfaces. Many Web-based systems now allow employees and managers to selectively access and modify records without requiring assistance from an HR clerk

FIGURE 3.2
Elements of an HRIS

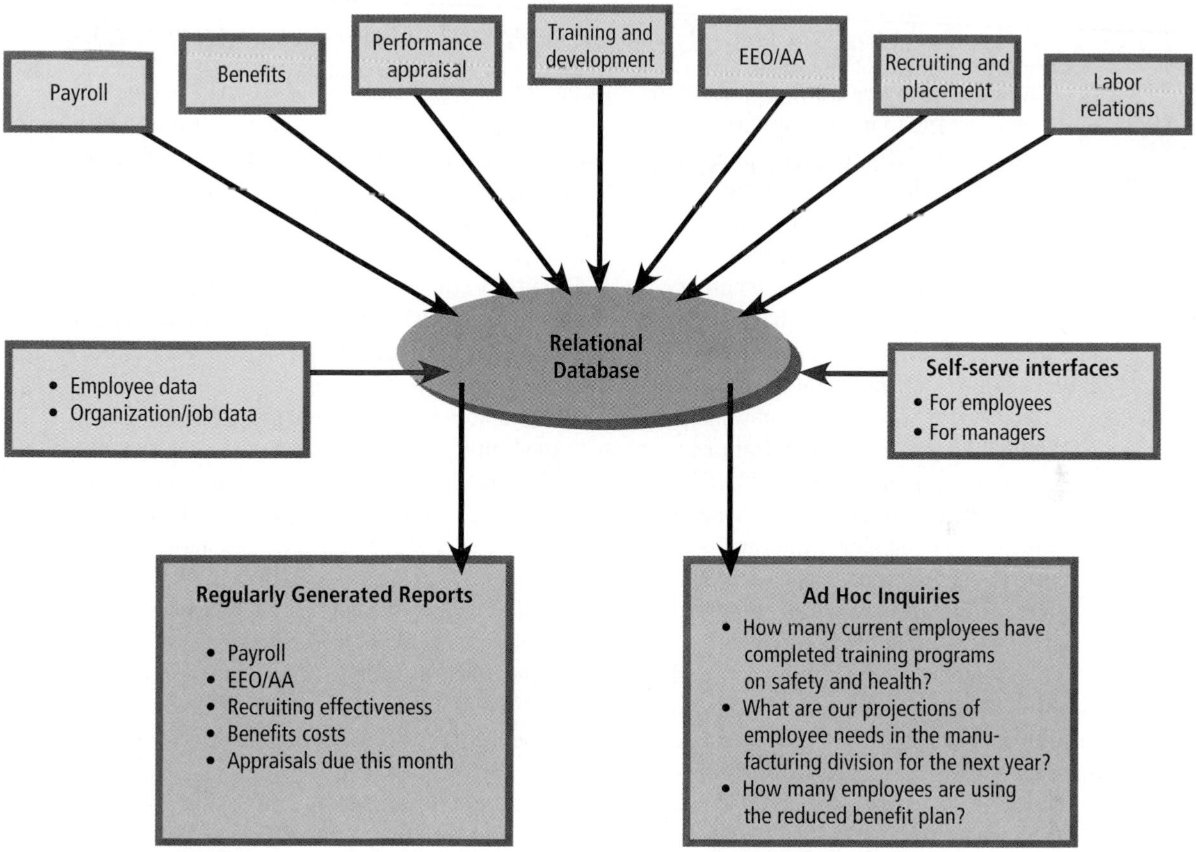

Payroll
Benefits
Performance appraisal
Training and development
EEO/AA
Recruiting and placement
Labor relations

Relational Database

- Employee data
- Organization/job data

Self-serve interfaces
- For employees
- For managers

Regularly Generated Reports
- Payroll
- EEO/AA
- Recruiting effectiveness
- Benefits costs
- Appraisals due this month

Ad Hoc Inquiries
- How many current employees have completed training programs on safety and health?
- What are our projections of employee needs in the manufacturing division for the next year?
- How many employees are using the reduced benefit plan?

One issue of concern with HRISs is the fact that organizations can so readily store and access large amounts of information about employees and applicants. Questions may arise about employee privacy, who has access to sensitive information, and whether information used to make decisions about individuals is accurate. The Ethical Perspective box explores these questions in further detail.

Leading-edge HRISs can support integrated HR record keeping and decision making across multiple locations and even across countries.[26] For instance, SAP boasts that its HRIS user interfaces are available in multiple languages, that local labor law requirements are incorporated into record fields as appropriate for each country, and that salary information can be maintained in both local currency and headquarters currency units simultaneously. Further, internal recruitment searches can be conducted worldwide at the touch of a button. Microsoft recently adopted SAP for its worldwide operations. A single human resource management system residing on one server has replaced the series of customized programs and stand-alone systems on many computers previously used in eighteen different subsidiaries in fifty-five countries. Now users need to learn only one system to access up-to-the-minute information on employment around the world.

ETHICAL PERSPECTIVE

Privacy and Accuracy of Computerized Employee Records

Privacy is an area of growing concern to employees and to human resource managers. Although there is no explicit constitutional right to privacy, certain amendments and federal laws have some relevance to this issue, and some states have enacted privacy laws. Privacy considerations, whether derived from legal requirements or from basic respect for individuals, may constrain the type and amount of information that employers gather about applicants and employees and also the way that the information is stored, used, and disseminated by organizations.

With more and more employee records stored in computers, there is some concern that unauthorized persons could gain access to employee information of a confidential nature, such as performance appraisals, salary data, home addresses, or drug test results. Employers should have privacy policies in place that clearly specify who may access what type of data and for what purposes. Technical approaches should also be used to restrict computer users' access to information that is off-limits to them. HRIS security systems include limiting physical access to terminals by unauthorized persons, such as locking offices after hours, or key card access to the human resource information center. Probably more important is multilevel password protection to limit access to data files. Some individuals will have passwords that allow them to view only selected types of information. Others may be authorized to view a wider range of information, and still others will be allowed to both view and edit information. As access to HRISs becomes more available to individuals outside the HR specialty via various self-serve interfaces, security becomes a more pressing concern.

Firms doing business in Europe have encountered the strict European Union Data Privacy Directive that went into effect in 1998. The Directive applies to both customer and employee databases. Employers who gather information must disclose to the member nation's data protection authority how information on employees is stored, processed, and sent in or out of the European Union. Firms also have to obtain the consent of employee works councils before installing new employee information systems. These approvals add months to the process of adopting new systems. Failure to comply with the privacy rules may result in heavy fines, or even an order to shut down data transmission from Europe altogether. DaimlerChrysler, with 365,600 employees worldwide and headquarters in both the United States and Germany, is working toward the installation of a global e-HR system. Managing the different privacy laws regarding the handling and transmission of personal data is a substantial challenge that they are working to overcome.

Another employee records issue is accuracy. Ideally, employees should be permitted to view their personnel records from time to time to make sure that they are timely and accurate. Some HRISs automatically produce "turnaround documents" when employees' files are modified. These are sent to employees showing the changes made and requesting correction if needed. For instance, if an employee fills out a change in his or her flexible benefits scheme, the HRIS will return a copy of the change to the employee for verification.

Sources: Ellen Messmer, "EU Data-Privacy Laws Bog Down U.S. Firms," *Network World,* December 17, 2001, p. 8; Jill Evans, "Out in the Open," *People Management,* May 29, 2003, pp. 32–33; Sandra E. O'Connell, "Security for HR Records," *HR Magazine,* September 1994, p. 37; E. R. Eddy, D. L. Stone, and E. F. Stone-Romero, "The Effects of Information Management Policies on Reactions to Human Resource Information Systems: An Integration of Privacy and Procedural Justice Perspectives, *Personnel Psychology,* Summer 1999, pp. 335–358; J. C. Hubbard, K. A. Forcht, and D. S. Thomas, "Human Resource Information Systems: An Overview of Current Ethical and Legal Issues," *Journal of Business Ethics,* September 1998, pp. 1319–1323.

HRISs are available in a wide range of prices, starting as low as $500 for a simple one-function program. An annual index and reviews of HRIS packages can be found at www.hrcensus.com. Larger organizations have been adopting **enterprise resource planning** systems from providers such as PeopleSoft, SAP, and Oracle. These systems offer complete HRISs as well as compatible systems for managing other business functions such as accounts receivable, materials management, and finance.[27]

A further recent advance in such systems is the use of **application service providers,** which host and maintain both hardware and software. Individuals at the company simply log on through a Web browser to access their HRIS or other applications. This approach is said to offer companies faster implementation, predictable costs, high reliability, and expert support compared to the less certain process of installing and maintaining an in-house system.[28]

Web-based HR systems are rapidly increasing in popularity. Self-serve HR portals allow employees and managers to access and modify information related to HR data and programs. Employees may be able to complete transactions such as schedule their vacation time, select flexible benefits, input a change of address, request information on their retirement benefits, or enroll in training programs. Managers may input position vacancies, transfers, terminations, and job title and salary changes, as well as other similar activities.[29]

Whatever its level of complexity, an HRIS should be able to provide information needed in HR planning. Up-to-date reporting of head count, positions budgeted, turnover rates, and the like can assist in forecasting internal supply. Queries might be made to assess, for instance, the number of employees who are eligible for an enhanced retirement package or who might be available to transfer to a location anticipating a skill shortage.

Predicting the Internal Supply of Labor

Given the necessary data in staffing tables, a skills inventory, or an HRIS, human resource professionals can predict the internal supply and distribution of labor in the future.

Markov analysis is a fairly simple method of predicting the internal supply of labor at some future time. The heart of Markov analysis is the **transition probability matrix,** which describes the probabilities of an incumbent staying in his or her present job for the forecast time period (usually one year), moving to another job in the organization, or leaving the organization. When this matrix is multiplied by the number of people beginning the year in each job, the results show how many people are expected to be in each job by the end of the year.

To develop the transition probability matrix, planners take the following steps:

1. Specify a mutually exclusive and exhaustive set of states that include all jobs between which people can move and an exit state for those who quit, retire, or are fired.
2. Gather data from each of the last several years on what transition rates actually occurred between each state. Such data could show, for instance, that during the past year 15 percent of the people who began the year in job A left the organization, 10 percent were transferred to job B, and 5 percent were promoted to job C.

3. Attempt to develop stable, reliable estimates of expected future transition rates. Some judgment is required at this step. Many organizations use the preceding year's transition rates. However, if the preceding year was atypical (with an unusually high or low rate of movement), planners may find it better to average the rates over the last several years. This third step is very important because the accuracy of prediction depends on using correct transition rates. If movement rates vary widely from year to year, planners may not be able to use Markov analysis to forecast internal supply.[30]

Once the transition probability matrix is developed, applying it is a simple matter (see Table 3.1). To produce predictions, the matrix is multiplied by the vector of the number of incumbents in each state. For instance, job A began the year with sixty-two incumbents. Fifteen percent of those incumbents ($0.15 \times 62 = 9$) left the organization, 10 percent ($0.10 \times 62 = 6$) moved to job B, and 5 percent ($0.05 \times 62 = 3$) moved to job C. That leaves forty-four of the original incumbents in job A. However, 15 percent of the seventy-five people ($0.15 \times 75 = 11$) in job B transferred to job A, so the total number of employees in job A at the end of the year is fifty-five (44 + 11). (These numbers have been rounded to whole digits because fractions of employees are not meaningful.)

Markov analysis describes what is expected to happen if existing transition rates remain the same. This type of analysis can also be used speculatively to as-

TABLE 3.1

Markov Analysis

Transition Probability Matrix						
		(Time 2)				
(Time 1)	Job A	Job B	Job C	Job D	Exit	
Job A	0.70	0.10	0.05	0	0.15	
Job B	0.15	0.60	0.05	0.10	0.10	
Job C	0	0	0.80	0.05	0.15	
Job D	0	0	0.05	0.85	0.10	
Matrix Applied to Incumbents[a]						
	Initial Staffing Level	Job A	Job B	Job C	Job D	Exit
Job A	62	44	6	3	0	9
Job B	75	11	45	4	8	7
Job C	50	0	0	40	2	8
Job D	45	0	0	2	38	5
Predicted end-of-year staffing level		55	51	49	48	29

[a]Numbers have been rounded to whole digits because fractions of employees are not meaningful.

sess the impact of possible modifications in transition rates. For instance, suppose that job D is going to be understaffed because of an unusually large number of retirements. In the past, this job has been filled largely by promotions from job B. Planners might use the Markov model to determine what would happen if the rate of lateral transfers from job C to job D was increased or if the rate of promotion from job B was increased. Planners could experiment with different probabilities until they found a workable solution.

Auburn University's College of Veterinary Medicine used Markov analysis to predict the impact of three HR options on the age and rank composition of the faculty. Data from 1984 to 1994 were used to model the transition rates between the states of assistant professor, associate professor, full professor, and exit. Forecasts were subsequently made for 1995 and 2004. Some of the results are shown in Table 3.2. In scenario 1, entry-level hiring continued at the usual rate over the ten-year period. In scenario 2, a hiring freeze on new employees was imposed in the first two planning years, as the newly elected governor was hinting at this course of action. In scenario 3, enhanced retirement packages were offered in the first and fifth years of the plan. The hiring freeze alternative, although saving funds in the short term, had undesirable long-term impacts—the faculty became older, the proportion of people in higher ranks increased disproportionately, and in consequence the average salary increased. Scenario 3, offering an enhanced retirement package twice, reduced the proportion of senior faculty to below what would be desirable. Further experimentation with various scenarios suggested the best combination of actions.[31]

TABLE 3.2

Academic Staff by Rank for School Years 1984 and 1994 Actual and 2004 Projected

	1984	%	1994	%	2004	%
Forecast Based on Transitional Probabilities Alone						
Assistant professor	34	40.0	26	26.5	21	19.6
Associate professor	23	27.1	35	35.7	52	48.6
Professor	28	32.9	37	37.8	34	31.8
Total	85	100	98	100	107	100
Forecast Including Simulation of a Hiring Freeze in the First Two Years						
Assistant professor	34	40.0	26	26.5	12	12.6
Associate professor	23	27.1	35	35.7	43	45.3
Professor	28	32.9	37	37.8	40	42.1
Total	85	100	98	100	95	100
Forecast Including Simulation of an Early Retirement Option in Years 1 and 4						
Assistant professor	34	40.0	26	26.5	30	28.3
Associate professor	23	27.1	35	35.7	53	50.0
Professor	28	32.9	37	37.8	23	21.7
Total	85	100	98	100	106	100

Source: E. R. Hackett, A. A. Magg, and S. D. Carrigan, "Modeling Faculty Replacement Strategies Using a Time-Dependent Finite Markov-Chain Process," *Journal of Higher Education Policy and Management,* May 1999, p. 87.

Markov analysis is widely used and easy to apply. However, it has been criticized for certain weaknesses and limitations.[32] Transition probabilities must be relatively stable or able to be estimated for Markov analysis to be accurate. Also, the probabilities will not be reliable if there are only a few incumbents in each job. Generally, Markov analysis works best if there are at least fifty people in each job or state.[33]

A second weakness is conceptual rather than statistical. Markov analysis assumes that the probability of movement is determined solely by the employee's initial job state. The probability of moving to job B depends entirely on where the employee began the year—in job A, C, or D. In actual practice, however, people move within organizations because of the pull of vacancies rather than the push of their current assignments. Thus the true probability of moving to job B also depends on the number of vacancies in job B.

An approach to predicting internal movement and supply that takes this dynamic into account is called **renewal** (or **replacement**) **analysis.** This method is driven by destination demand—the number of vacancies anticipated in higher-level jobs. Transition matrices help identify how the demand can be filled by internal movements from lower-level positions. These movements create additional vacancies and in turn drive further movement at even lower job levels.[34]

More complex methods of forecasting internal supply are available in goal programming, network analysis, and computer simulation. Simulations may use both replacement and Markov analyses, utilize the age and promotability information stored on each of thousands of employees, and allow a variety of different HR policies and assumptions to be tried out and evaluated.[35]

The U.S. Navy developed a very sophisticated HR forecasting model to help reduce civilian employment levels in eight shipyards that were being downsized. Markov analysis showed that allowing natural attrition and typical transition rates to take their course would reduce overall employment levels, but in a way that was unbalanced across critical shipyard occupations. To keep each of eighteen different occupations staffed at the desired level, attrition needed to be combined with modified transfer rates and carefully planned hiring in some areas. Adding goals to the model and predicting two years into the future on a quarterly basis allowed the reductions to be thoroughly planned and accomplished with minimal disruption of work efficiency.[36]

Choosing Forecasting Methods

A number of methods of forecasting HR demands and internal supply have been presented.[37] Not all are appropriate for all organizations and situations, so the HR practitioner must make choices about which methods best suit the organization in question. The following factors should be considered in choosing techniques for HR forecasting:

- *Stability and certainty* It is not feasible to use methods that rely heavily on past data if the organization and environment are changing rapidly and in relatively unpredictable ways. Informed human judgment may be superior in this situation. It will also be useful to forecast several scenarios, each with different sets of assumptions.
- *Availability of data* How accurate and complete are past data on employee numbers, skills, and flows? If the data are not available, some statistical approaches cannot be used.

- *Number of employees* Some statistical techniques, such as Markov analysis, are reliable only for large numbers of employees. Smaller numbers might call for judgmental methods.
- *Resources available* How much time, computing power, and statistical expertise are available to compile the forecast?
- *Time horizon* Judgmental methods may be superior at anticipating the direction of complex long-term trends, whereas statistical methods may be quite accurate in the short term.
- *Credibility to management* Will key managers accept the process and believe its predictions? Sometimes simpler methods that involve substantial management input will have more credibility, although in high-tech organizations sophisticated modeling may be readily accepted.[38] Duke Power Company faced the challenge of developing a work force planning system that would satisfy two distinct sets of clients. Managers on the utilities side of the company were used to sophisticated head-count planning models, whereas those in Duke's investment, real estate, and consulting businesses wanted something "so simple it could be outlined on a napkin."[39]

Implications of Internal Supply and Distribution

Whatever methods are chosen to make HR forecasts, the real benefit comes from the way the forecasts are used. Careful study of internal supply and distribution reports allows HR planners to anticipate and head off a variety of problems. For instance, planners might notice that a particular unit or job family contains a high proportion of employees nearing retirement age. This may signal the need to establish a high-volume training program to prepare replacements for these positions.

The Union Oil Company of California developed an internal flow model that produces statistics on the replacement ratio, or the number of employees in a given five-year age bracket who are waiting to fill each job currently held by someone in the next-older age bracket. Ratios that are too high are a concern because they mean that upward progress is blocked and younger employees are likely to become frustrated in their careers.[40] Ratios that are too low indicate a possible future shortage of experienced employees for higher-level jobs.

A British expert on HR planning, Gordon McBeath, points out that recent recruiting trends may create problems with HR flows in the future if organizations fail to anticipate the effects for their organizations. Firms that historically hired new employees straight from a university have shifted to hiring an increasing number of returning homemakers and older graduates as the supply of young graduates dwindled. Some firms have found that these mature workers have different movement patterns, being less eager to move up the hierarchy into management and expecting employment for five to ten years rather than thirty to forty. If most managers of the future will come from today's smaller crop of new college graduates, then a higher than usual percentage of new graduates will advance into management. In anticipation, one organization raised hiring standards for new graduates to ensure that more of them will have promotion potential, even though a typical response to a shortage of entry-level employees would be to lower hiring standards.[41]

Benchmarking the Internal Supply and Distribution of Labor

There are a number of ways in which an organization's internal supply and distribution of employees might be compared with that of its competitors to produce useful insights. A simple measure is revenue per employee or, alternatively, profit per employee. This varies widely across industries, so within-industry comparisons are most appropriate. If, for instance, a bank finds that its profit per employee is $20,000, whereas the industry average is $45,000, there is clearly room for improvement. Perhaps there are too many employees or they are not trained and equipped to perform their work efficiently.

Another type of benchmarking measure is the staffing ratio of front-line operating employees to managerial and professional support staff. Organizations that are top heavy and have too many managers for the number of people actually doing productive work compared with industry norms might wish to consider a flatter, less bureaucratic structure. In an Australian benchmarking survey, the finance sector averaged three operatives per manager/professional, whereas the transport industry averaged twenty-five operatives per manager/professional. The U.S. Army utilizes a similar measure—the tooth-to-tail ratio. This is the number of fighting personnel compared with the number of support staff (logistics, training, medical, maintenance, etc.) required to back them up in the field.[42]

THE EXTERNAL SUPPLY OF LABOR

As they hire new workers, lay off or discharge others, and lose current employees to other firms, organizations continuously interact with external labor markets. Therefore, to plan effectively, HR planners must understand how to assess and adjust to the **external supply of labor.**

Some Definitions

In the United States a great deal of data are collected and published monthly about the labor supply, but making sense of these data requires an understanding of a few basic concepts and definitions.[43]

The **civilian labor force** comprises all people sixteen years of age or older who are not in the military and who are employed or seeking work. The civilian labor force does not include **"discouraged" workers** who have given up looking for work or people who are institutionalized in prisons or mental hospitals. In August 2004 the civilian labor force comprised more than 147 million people, and it is forecasted to grow slowly to 158 million by 2010.[44]

The **labor force participation rate** is the percentage of the total working-age population that is currently in the labor force. In 2004 the overall participation rate was about 66 percent. For males over age 20 it was 76 percent, whereas for females in the same age range it was 60.3 percent.[45]

The **unemployment rate** is the percentage of the labor force that is seeking work rather than working. When the unemployment rate is high and many people are out of work, the labor market is described as "loose," meaning that employers can find new employees easily. Conversely, a "tight" labor market occurs when unemployment is very low and employers have great difficulty finding new workers.

The overall unemployment rate reached a thirty-year low of 4 percent in 2000, with some metropolitan areas—including Minneapolis/St. Paul, Minnesota, and Raleigh, North Carolina—having unemployment rates below 2 percent. The nationwide unemployment rate for university graduates was also under 2 percent during 1999 and 2000, sparking a short-lived bidding war for technical talent in some fields. The dot.com crash in 2001, followed by the September 11 terrorist attacks and subsequent business downturn, increased unemployment to about 6 percent in 2003.

In the United States, the Bureau of Labor Statistics conducts a monthly Current Population Survey using a representative sample of households nationwide. Each month the Bureau reports these labor force statistics in its journal, *Monthly Labor Review.* This journal also contains analyses of new developments and trends in the labor supply. Additional labor force statistics are available at the Bureau's Web site, www.bls.gov.

Labor Markets

The concept of labor markets is an important one. A **labor market** is the area from which an employer typically recruits to fill a position; this area varies according to the type of job being filled.[46] For instance, the labor market for secretaries, plumbers, cashiers, and so on is usually the immediate, surrounding geographic area. This is so because workers are seldom willing to relocate for these jobs, and employers find it unnecessary to mount a nationwide search to fill them. For these jobs, the labor market is defined by how far potential employees are willing to commute to work. For other jobs—such as college professor, chief executive officer, computer engineer, or research chemist—the labor market is nationwide or even international. There also are regional labor markets for skilled jobs for which incumbents are willing to move but for which employers need not search too widely. For example, schools in Texas may recruit teachers at Texas and Oklahoma universities, but they probably feel no need to recruit in New York. In times of employee shortages, labor markets may widen. For instance, the nursing shortage referred to in the HR Challenge has expanded the nurse labor market geographically. U.S. hospitals are now recruiting in Canada, Canadian hospitals are dealing with the ensuing shortage in their own country by recruiting in the United Kingdom, U.K. hospitals have turned to recruiting in South Africa, and South African hospitals find they need to recruit in Asia![47]

Before making decisions, employers must be sure that information is collected on the right labor markets. Knowing that the unemployment rate is very high for the country does not guarantee that a firm will be able to find sufficient new employees at any specific location. Labor markets are based on skills as well as geography. For instance, the nationwide labor market for entry-level electrical engineers may be quite a bit tighter or looser than the local labor market for secretaries or refrigeration mechanics. Data on local and regional labor-market conditions are available from state employment service offices and the BLS Web site. In summary, a great deal of data is available on current labor markets. This information might be quite helpful to the recruiter who is attempting to fill positions right now, but for most HR planning purposes, data projecting the future status of various labor markets will be more useful.

FIGURE 3.3

Composition of the U.S. Labor Force by Race and Ethnic Origin

Source: Data compiled from H. N. Fullerton Jr., "Labor Force Participation: 75 Years of Change, 1950–98 and 1998–2025," *Monthly Labor Review,* December 1999, pp. 3–12; and Mitra Toossi, "A Century of Change: The U.S. Labor Force 1950–2050," *Monthly Labor Review,* Vol. 125 (5), May 2002, pp.15–28. Values for 2025 and 2050 are estimated.

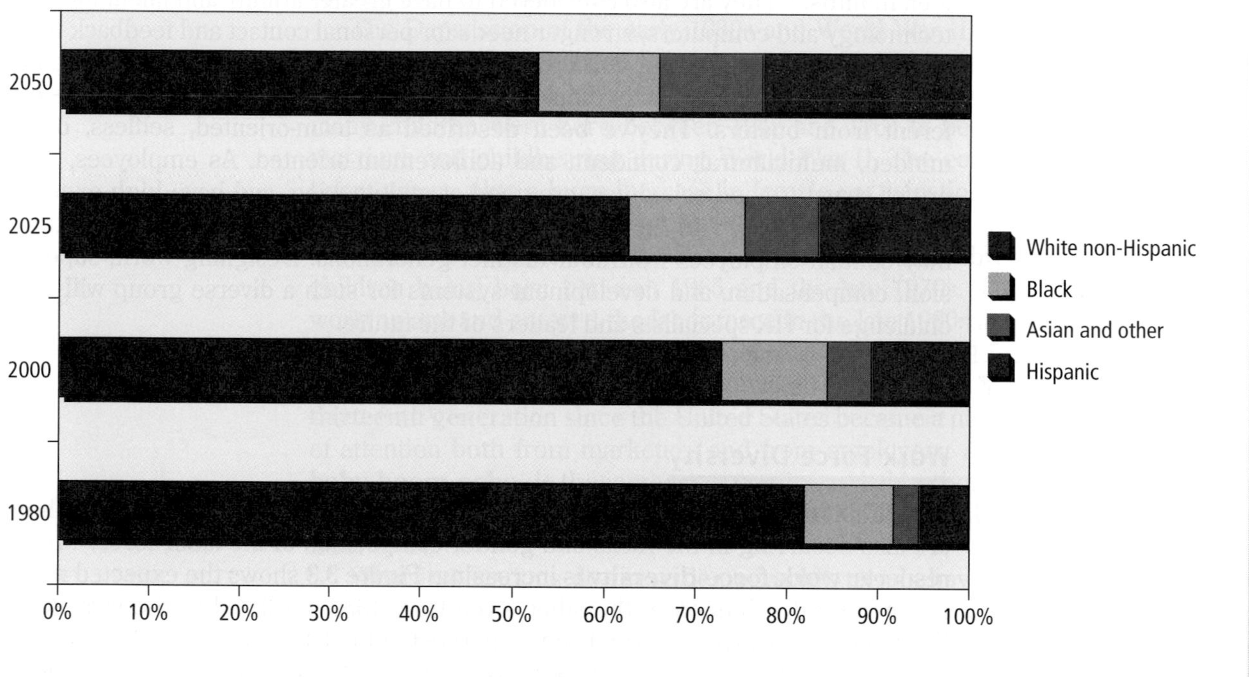

The Contingent Work Force

Much has been written in the past decade and a half about the increasing number of **contingent workers.** This term refers to employees who do not have permanent full-time jobs but are called on by companies to work when and as needed, for periods ranging from hours to years. Definitions of "contingent workers" vary, but the term is usually considered to include employees working on short-term or project contracts; those working on an on-call basis, such as substitute teachers; those working as independent contractors; and those whose services are acquired from a temporary help or employee-leasing agency.[61] Some definitions also include all part-time workers, although some part-time employees have permanent jobs. Alarmists noted the decline of "good," secure, full-time jobs during the 1990s. However, research suggests that most contingent and part-time employees have chosen this type of job because of the flexibility it offers, and they are reasonably satisfied with their situation. For organizations, contingent workers allow variations in workload to be managed without the need to lay off permanent employees.[62] As unemployment declined in the late 1990s, the upward trend in contingent workers slowed and began to reverse. Employers have become more willing to lock in scarce workers on a permanent basis.[63] However, some experts believe that contingent workers are here to stay and will probably continue to increase in number. Some of the factors contributing to this trend are as follows:[64]

- Global interdependence of economies and increased competitive pressure means firms need to be able to change headcount quickly and keep fixed labor costs down.
- There are more small businesses, who find it easier to "rent" than "own" employees due to lack of in-house HR expertise and possibly precarious finances.
- In Europe restrictive work rules make it very difficult to retrench permanent employees, whereas there are fewer limitations in shedding contingent workers.
- Changing technologies mean that firms need new skills on short notice. Being in demand and having variety in job assignments makes contingent work appealing to professionals in fields such as IT.
- Employee expectations have changed, with fewer wanting a long career with a single firm. Loyalty is more to the profession than to the employer. Contingent work offers greater flexibility in working hours and days, which suits those with family responsibilities or those in partial retirement.

Industry and Occupational Trends

The Bureau of Labor Statistics predicts which occupations and industries will be growing or declining in the near future. The fastest-growing occupations between now and 2010 are expected to be in the professional specialty field, especially in jobs such as computer and network engineer, database administrator, systems analyst, and desktop publishing specialist. Other fast-growing occupations are in the health field: medical and physician assistants, home health aides, physical and occupational therapy aides, audiologists, and fitness trainers. The largest growth in absolute numbers of new jobs is predicted for food service workers, customer service representatives, nurses, retail salespersons, computer support specialists, cashiers, and clerks.[65]

PLANNING HUMAN RESOURCE PROGRAMS

Having made demand and internal supply forecasts and considered the state of the external labor market, the HR planner can anticipate future problems with employee supply and plan programs for offsetting them. The following sections deal with planning for a new start-up and planning for labor shortages and surpluses. The final section considers managerial succession planning.

Planning for a New Establishment: Opening the Mirage

An exemplary exercise in HR planning occurred in connection with the opening of the Mirage hotel and casino in Las Vegas.[66] This property cost $635 million and has 3,049 rooms, a 105,000-square-foot casino, and twelve food and beverage outlets. All these facilities were opened virtually simultaneously. Obviously, a great deal of HR planning was necessary to carry out this feat.

Planning began two years in advance of the opening with the hiring of a vice president for human resources. His first task was to gather data on labor-market demographics, wage trends, competitors' expansion plans, and the opening experiences of other luxury hotels. Then he calculated the number of employees needed to run the facility (initially estimated at 5,000) and adjusted this figure for the expected number of no-shows (those hired before opening who did not turn up), early turnovers, and the lower-than-usual productivity of individuals just learning their jobs. These projections produced a target number of hires and allowed estimation of the number of applications (47,000) needed to produce that number of qualified staff. Later, estimates of the likely volume of business were increased, so employment projections increased as well. For the opening, 6,200 people were hired from 57,000 applications.

After making the demand forecast, the next task of the HR vice president was to consider sources of applicants. He decided that some experienced employees would come from the company's other Las Vegas casino and that the local labor market would be sufficient to supply the rest. He directed special attention to jobs known to be problematic in the area, such as housekeeper. In this case, the organization offered a cash bonus to employees who referred a friend for the job of housekeeper.

In addition to planning for numbers of employees in each job category, the HR vice president had to plan their training and schedule their starting dates. He hired forty-two middle managers early and put them through a half-year training program; he hired and trained supervisors; finally, he had each supervisor conduct training for his or her work group. The hotel and casino opened successfully six weeks ahead of the original schedule.

The careful HR planning that preceded the opening has continued. Three years after the opening, the Mirage employed more than 7,000 people in 405 job classifications. Extensive training, excellent employment conditions, and HR services that treat employees like valued customers make the Mirage a continuing success story as an employer. Turnover averages 60 percent per year in the hospitality industry, but the Mirage experienced an employee turnover rate of only 19 percent per year, which had declined to 12 percent seven years after the opening.[67]

Planning for Shortages

Clearly the Mirage had to deal with an unusually large initial labor shortage that had to be met primarily from the external labor market. Most existing businesses would also tend to go to the external labor market for new employees when demand exceeds internal supply, though this is not their only option. Figure 3.4 lists a number of potential actions to deal with shortages.

Employers are finding that recruiting qualified employees from the external environment is not always easy. Innovations in recruiting may be necessary (they are discussed further in Chapter 6), and in some cases employers may have to create qualified workers where none existed before. For instance, Barden, a ball-bearing manufacturer in Connecticut, experienced great difficulty fill-

FIGURE 3.4
Program Planning Options

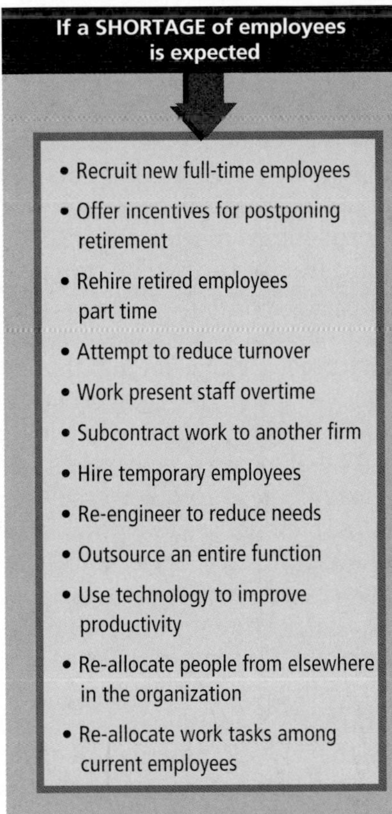
If a SHORTAGE of employees is expected
• Recruit new full-time employees
• Offer incentives for postponing retirement
• Rehire retired employees part time
• Attempt to reduce turnover
• Work present staff overtime
• Subcontract work to another firm
• Hire temporary employees
• Re-engineer to reduce needs
• Outsource an entire function
• Use technology to improve productivity
• Re-allocate people from elsewhere in the organization
• Re-allocate work tasks among current employees

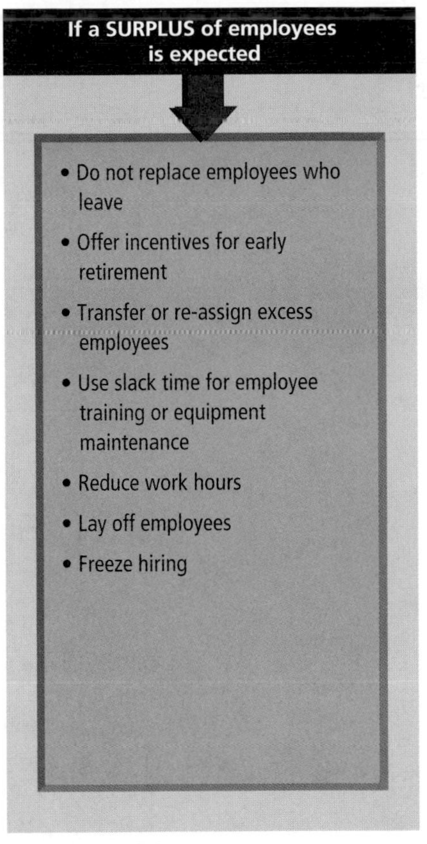
If a SURPLUS of employees is expected
• Do not replace employees who leave
• Offer incentives for early retirement
• Transfer or re-assign excess employees
• Use slack time for employee training or equipment maintenance
• Reduce work hours
• Lay off employees
• Freeze hiring

ing its labor needs in an area with an unemployment rate of only 2.5 percent. Then it discovered the answer to its labor shortage in immigrants whose English was too poor to make them attractive to other employers. The organization retained the Berlitz language training company to provide four hours of English instruction each day for three weeks. The result was competent, committed, and self-confident employees.[68]

When faced with a shortage, employers should consider other alternatives to hiring additional full-time employees. Some companies reduce labor demand by outsourcing peripheral functions—such as security, cleaning, printing, and account collection—to other firms that specialize in providing these services. Some employers encourage employees who are nearing retirement age to continue working by increasing the pension formula to reward extra years of service more heavily, or they rehire retired employees on a part-time basis. If a shortfall is caused or worsened by high employee turnover, employers should attempt to identify the causes of turnover and act to remedy them (retention strategies are discussed in Chapter 16). If successful, this course of action would save recruiting and training costs and might substantially improve employees' attitudes.

If the long-range plan suggests that demand will peak quickly and then return to a lower level, hiring new permanent employees would be unwise. For relatively short periods of increased demand, employers could pay for overtime rather than hire additional employees. Overtime work must be compensated at one and one-half times the regular hourly rate, but it may still be more economical than hiring, training, and providing benefits to new employees who are not needed over the long term. Alternatively, employers may choose to subcontract some work to another company during the demand peak or to acquire temporary workers from firms specializing in the provision of skilled short-term labor.[69]

Another response to a tight labor market is to analyze and modify the way work is done to achieve greater efficiency and thus require fewer staff. Companies have engaged in "business process reengineering" to eliminate unnecessary steps and activities that do not directly add value for the customer.[70] In some cases the work tasks performed by one employee can be reallocated across several others rather than hiring someone new. In other cases technology can reduce the demand for employees. Caroline Power & Light is providing electricity services for more customers than ever with 2,000 fewer employees through technology-driven improvements in productivity. The company installed laptops and positioning devices in service trucks; trucks can now be routed to multiple locations on one trip rather than losing time by returning to base to pick up their next assignment. Soon electricity meters will be read remotely by computer, greatly reducing the need for meter readers.[71]

New Hanover Health Network, described in the HR Challenge, has adopted a number of strategies to meet its anticipated future shortage of nursing staff. Working with the Health Care Division of an HR consulting firm (Bernard Hodes Group, www.hodes.com), New Hanover made the following changes designed to increase retention of current nursing staff as well as to attract an increasing supply of applicants:

1. It made applying easier by installing an online application process.
2. It used the consultant's expertise in résumé-mining to locate potential nursing applicants across hundreds of Web job-board sites.
3. It merged recruitment advertising with the firm's other marketing activities with the goal of creating a recognizable brand image in the minds of both customers and potential employees. Recruitment ads now look similar to other advertising done by the firm and benefit more from the image created by other marketing efforts.
4. It made a strategic decision to move away from using contract nursing employees, who tend to stay only a short while, and toward permanent staff employed directly by the hospitals. Contract employment was reduced by 47 percent in less than a year. This has helped to create a climate of long-term commitment among employees.
5. It undertook a "boomerang initiative" in which employees who have recently left the firm are invited to return. As an incentive, there is no loss of benefits or seniority if the return is within one year of departure. Six to 8 percent of nurses who quit have been recaptured by this program.

TABLE 3.3

Responses of 316 Hospital CEOs to the Nursing Shortage

Top Five Strategies for Addressing the Nursing Shortage (percent indicating very effective)	Strategies Hospitals Plan in the Next Two Years to Address the Nursing Shortage
Promote zero tolerance for verbal/physical abuse/harassment 64%	Offer refresher courses for nurses who have been out of the work force 23%
Support nurses in efforts to improve patient care resources/services 56%	Partner with educational facilities to recruit adults into the clinical professions as a second career 19%
Encourage nurses to participate in management decisions relative to workplace issues such as staffing or scheduling 52%	Accommodate the physical needs of older nurses 15%
Implement technology that reduces the amount of time nurses spend on paperwork 50%	Increase use of e-recruitment technology (i.e., using job sites to identify candidates) 14%
Promote mentoring programs that model work/life balance 49%	Increase use of nurse extenders (e.g., LPNs, nurse's aides) 10%
Strategies Hospitals Have Implemented to Address the Nursing Shortage	**Strategies Hospitals Do Not Plan to Implement to Address the Nursing Shortage**
Offer tuition reimbursement 97%	Reduce services/close units 81%
Offer recognition programs 96%	Offer profit sharing 81%
Provide a 401k/TSA plan 94%	Recruit nurses from other countries 73%
Give service awards for tenure 93%	Recruit retired nurses 67%
Increase nurse salaries 83%	Increase reliance on agency/temporary labor 62%

Source: Research Notes, *Healthcare Executive,* Vol. 18 (5), Sept/Oct 2003, p. 42.

6. It created a full-time staffing position to coordinate recruitment and retention efforts. The staffing expert works closely with nursing schools in an attempt to recruit their graduates.
7. The staffing expert implemented a mentoring program to ease the school-to-work transition for new nursing graduates. The turnover rate of new graduates has fallen dramatically, from 30 percent to 6 percent, at least partly as a result of the mentoring program.

New Hanover Health Network will still need to engage in shorter-term human resource supply and demand forecasting to guide month-to-month hiring, but this series of planned activities has paid off in the form of reduced hiring needs and a larger applicant pool over the long term.[72] Table 3.3 shows other strategies a large sample of hospital CEOs reported using or planning to use in dealing with the nursing shortage.

While not feasible in the case of hospitals, one possible response to a shortage of labor is to move work to countries in which qualified employees are more read-

INTERNATIONAL PERSPECTIVE

Manufacturing Overseas

One solution to scarce or expensive workers is to take production abroad, either by building a factory in a low-wage country or, more commonly, by contracting with existing manufacturers there. This approach has been taken by a large number of U.S. organizations as well as by many manufacturers headquartered in Japan, Taiwan, and Hong Kong. Popular sites for overseas manufacturing are the People's Republic of China, Thailand, Indonesia, the Philippines, Mexico, and India.

At first, most U.S. companies ignored any ethical issues involved in using overseas manufacturers to produce their goods. However, the potential ethical pitfalls are numerous: Overseas manufacturers may provide dangerous working conditions, require excessively long hours, hire children, and pay below-subsistence wages. In China even the inadequate safety rules are often sidestepped because officials are eager to attract new investors or are easily bribed. In Shenzhen, China, eighty-one workers were killed when fire ripped through a handicrafts factory. The factory had illegally housed workshops, workers' dormitories, and a warehouse under one roof. The situation was worsened by the fact that windows were barred and doors were locked to keep workers inside and prevent theft. A few months earlier a similar Bangkok factory fire killed nearly 200 workers.

Of course, wages are lower than in the home country, but some foreign manufacturers fail to pay even what is promised. There are reports of Chinese workers hired by foreign firms at the minimum wage of about $100 a month and then routinely "fined" more than half their wages for mistakes in production. There are allegations that a company in Bangladesh supplying shirts to a large U.S. clothing retailer pays garment workers 20 cents per hour, well below the local minimum wage of 33 cents; fails to pay overtime rates; and requires workdays of twelve and a half hours, seven days per week, in violation of local labor laws. In many cases children accompany their mothers to work and are themselves put to work at a very young age.

U.S. companies that are seen to exploit workers have come under pressure from Western trade unions, human rights groups, consumers, shareholders, and investigative journalists. Recently, students at more than 175 campuses mobilized to protest against garments bearing their university's logo being made in overseas sweatshops.

In the interest of maintaining their reputations as good corporate citizens, some large U.S. companies

ily available (and in many cases, wages are lower).[73] The maquiladora factories across the Mexican border are an example, as are the numerous factories doing production work for U.S. firms in Asia. Nike is an example of a firm that has contracted out virtually all production of its athletic shoes to manufacturers in Asia. In addition to the challenges involved in managing a labor force in another country (see Chapter 17 for more on this), there may be sticky ethical issues involved when poorer nations are used as sources of labor for wealthier nations (see the International Perspective box).

It's not just low-skilled work that is going off-shore to find readily available, lower-cost labor. India has become a popular site for software companies because of the plentiful supply of skilled programmers, and a number of white-collar and clerical jobs were exported to Ireland in the 1990s. A recent survey suggests that 3 million white-collar jobs may migrate overseas to China, India, Eastern Europe,

have adopted global sourcing guidelines in an attempt to assure that their suppliers' employees are treated humanely. Retailing giant Wal-Mart has felt the sting of ignoring the conduct of its suppliers. The company was the subject of a scathing documentary when one of its subcontractors in Bangladesh was found to be employing underage workers. In response, Wal-Mart adopted a groundbreaking supplier code of conduct. In part the code prohibits workweeks of more than sixty hours and forbids the hiring of children under age fifteen. Levi Strauss also has a stringent sourcing policy and is an acknowledged leader in efforts to raise safety and employment standards in overseas suppliers. Nike's athletic apparel products are produced in more than fifty countries in about 704 plants, none of which Nike owns. The company has adopted a detailed code of conduct for the treatment of employees in overseas plants. All plants are audited regularly by both Nike managers and independent experts. Violations of the code result in financial penalties on the supplier and ultimately the termination of the contract to provide goods for Nike.

However, the ethical issues are not as simple as they may first appear. Imposing Western-level safety or pay standards will deter foreign investment in underdeveloped economies, yet foreign investment is desperately needed to improve employment and living standards throughout these countries. Employment in foreign-owned factories is the only source of income for many families and the only source of financial independence for some Third World women—if the firms leave, these individuals suffer. Even child labor has two sides: If education simply isn't available, aren't children better off accompanying their mothers to work in foreign-owned factories than begging in the streets or being employed as virtual slaves in local cottage industries? And some child laborers are the sole supporters of their families: Is it responsible to fire them for being underage when a sourcing policy comes into effect? Firms from wealthier nations are generally being urged to remain in less developed nations and work with their suppliers to improve the pay and conditions of local workers.

Sources: Martha Nichols, "Third-World Families at Work: Child Labor or Child Care?" *Harvard Business Review,* January–February 1993, pp. 12–23; M. A. Emmelhainz and R. J. Adams, "The Apparel Industry Response to 'Sweatshop' Concerns: A Review and Analysis of Codes of Conduct," *Journal of Supply Chain Management,* Summer 1999, pp. 51–57; Stephen J. Frenkel, "Compliance, Collaboration, and Codes of Labor Practice," *California Management Review,* Fall 2002, pp. 29–49; and E. J. Schrage, *Promoting International Workers Rights through Private Voluntary Initiatives: Public Relations or Public Policy?* January 2004, http://www.uichr.org/content/act/sponsored/gwri_report.pdf. See http://www.business-humanrights.org for more information.

and the Philippines between 2003 and 2015. It's been reported that IBM Global Services is the fifth largest employer in India, and that India graduated three times as many IT majors as the United States did in 2003.[74]

Planning for Surpluses

When forecasts show that internal supply will exceed demand, employers must make plans to reduce supply. If the problem is recognized far enough in advance, a full or partial hiring freeze plus natural attrition may take care of the surplus. This alternative is the least costly in terms of both money and company reputation. If attrition is insufficient, employers can offer incentives for early retirement. (Under the Age Discrimination in Employment Act of 1967, employees cannot be forced to retire, except in individual cases where there is a documented medical or job-performance problem.)

Depending on the nature of the surplus, a firm may be able to transfer or reassign employees to jobs in parts of the organization that are still experiencing demand. Some firms have set up an internal temporary agency through which surplus employees can be borrowed by other units, allocated to work on special projects, or even sent out as temporaries to work for other organizations.[75] If the firm expects the surplus to be short lived and can afford to keep excess workers on the payroll, it can use the slack time to provide cross-training in related jobs to increase work force skills and flexibility. Alternatively, excess workers can perform equipment maintenance and overhaul or other activities that were postponed when demand was high.[76]

An option that allows retention of all or most employees but still realizes payroll savings is to reduce work hours, perhaps to a four-day, thirty-two-hour workweek. In this way, a company can spread a 20 percent decrease in demand (and in pay) equitably across the whole work force rather than keep 80 percent of employees full time and lay off 20 percent. This alternative has been especially popular in states that permit workers on partial layoff to collect unemployment compensation for the days they do not work.

As indicated in Figure 3.4, the last resort is to lay off excess employees. This action obviously is bad for the employees, but it is also bad for the employer. Laying off workers damages a company's reputation as a good place to work and can be costly. Laid-off workers are entitled to collect unemployment compensation from a state-managed fund. The fund is supported by employer contributions, and the rate at which a firm is required to contribute depends on its past history of employee claims against the fund. Thus layoffs now will convert into higher premiums in the future.

Unfortunately, studies show that layoff is often the option chosen because HR managers usually have less than two months between the time a surplus of employees is first noticed and the time that staff reductions must be completed.[77] Better planning might lengthen this interval and allow the use of other methods to reduce staff. Note that federal law (the Worker Adjustment and Retraining Notification Act) requires employers to give employees sixty days' notice before closing an entire plant or laying off fifty or more people.[78]

Many responsible companies provide outplacement services to employees who must be let go. At a minimum such services may include sessions on how to prepare a résumé and conduct a job search.[79] Chapter 16 discusses outplacement in more detail. Several studies have shown that fair and generous treatment of laid-off employees can sustain morale and performance of the employees who are not laid off. Unfair treatment may cause layoff survivors to suffer from stress, fear, and guilt.[80]

When a company must lay off some but not all employees, it should have a fair procedure for deciding who must go. For unionized employees, layoff procedures are usually specified in the contract, with seniority often being an important factor. All employers should have a **reduction in force (RIF)** policy prepared well in advance of the need to reduce employment levels. Such a policy might reward employees with longer service for their loyalty, but it also should reflect what is best for the company. This means that marginal performers or unskilled, easily replaceable employees should be released first. A firm should make every effort to retain good performers and skilled employees; although some of the latter may have to move down to less skilled jobs for a while, at least they will receive paychecks and will be available to move back up when business improves.

A special case of planning for employee redeployment and potential surpluses occurs when there is a merger or acquisition. In the late 1990s there were a record number of mergers and acquisitions, though the rate of such activities slowed down somewhat in the early 2000s.[81] A large percentage of mergers and acquisitions fail altogether or fail to perform as well as expected, and this is most often attributed to problems in dealing with the human side of the deal. Human resource executives and planners need to be involved in potential mergers from the earliest stages right through to the successful integration of the two firms.

During the due diligence pre-merger phase, HR experts need to explore the size and skills of the target work force, estimate costs and liabilities of compensation and benefit systems, investigate contractual obligations to employees and retirees, investigate potential legal or compliance problems, and assess the culture of the target organization compared to that of the acquirer.

When the decision is made to go ahead with the merger, critical decisions must be made quickly about the new organization's structure and who will staff the executive ranks. But decisions don't stop here. Employees at all levels want to know "how will this affect me?" Retrenchments are common as redundant functions and facilities are centralized. Aside from possible job loss, employees also face changed job responsibilities, derailed career plans, reduced power, and new bosses. HR planners have to work quickly to provide answers to employees who are understandably worried about their future in the new organization. A transparent and objective process based on performance, future capability, and the projected needs of the new organization should be put in place to help determine who stays and who goes. Throughout the merger or acquisition process, frequent and honest communication with the work force is essential.

A common employee response to uncertainty, perceived threat, or poor communication from the company is to quit, yet a significant share of the cash paid in the deal was to obtain the other organization's experienced work force. Thus another important HR function early in the merger process is to identify individuals with critical skills and to implement a program to retain them through the turbulent period of the merger. Retention bonuses or special grants of stock are possible choices. For those who will no longer be needed, severance arrangements and outplacement assistance should be put in place. Gaps that cannot be filled by any current employees also need to be identified so that targeted recruiting and selection can proceed. Finally, there is a great deal of work to be done in harmonizing HR systems and policies in the areas of compensation, benefits, record keeping, and so forth.[82]

Managerial Succession Planning

Regardless of expansion or contraction of the total work force in an organization, the need for good managers is critical and continuous. Many organizations plan for managerial succession and development because they have found that it takes years of systematic grooming to produce effective top managers. Some organizations have extremely formal, detailed, and long-range succession plans for specific

FIGURE 3.5
Replacement Chart

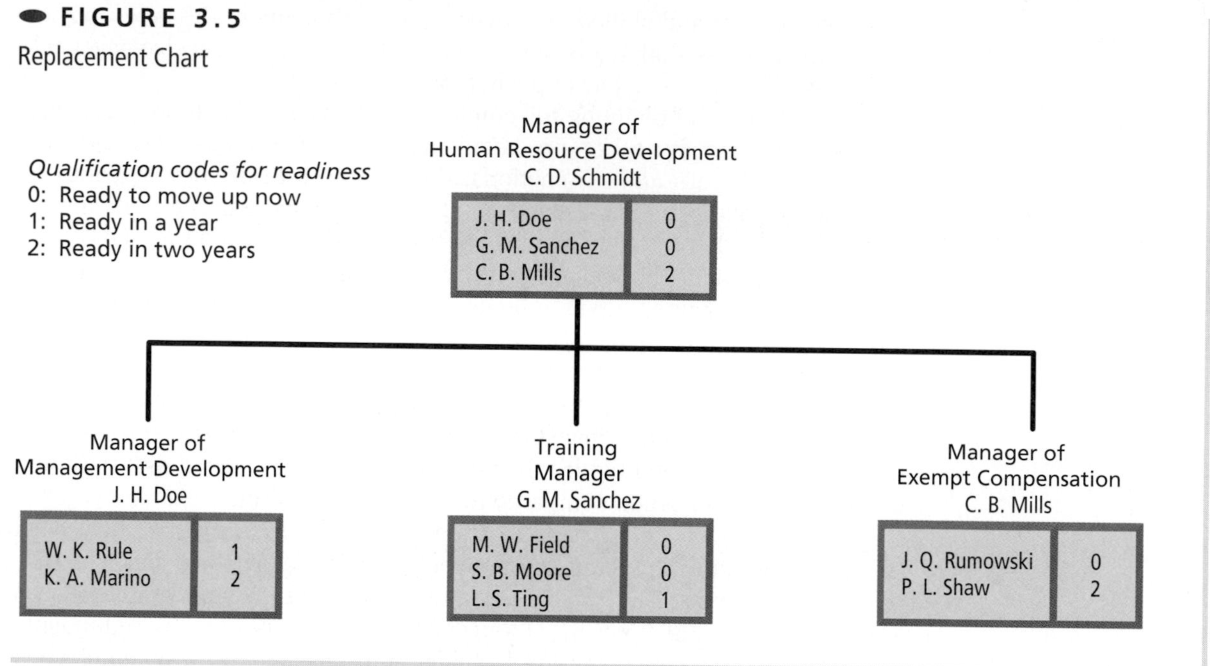

critical positions. For instance, one article reported that Exxon Corporation had already hired and was grooming the individual it expected to be chief executive officer twenty-two years later![83]

How companies practice succession planning varies.[84] Some engage in a painstaking annual process that involves gathering a great deal of data, often from 360-feedback systems, and thoroughly reviewing potential leaders. Other companies have less formal systems that are integrated with ongoing business activities. For instance, Dell Computer Corp. asks general managers and their teams to review high-potential employees every quarter as part of the business planning process. This way, individuals' needs for developmental assignments can be matched with business needs in real time.

Most managerial succession planning systems rely on committees of higher-level managers to identify high-potential candidates and plan developmental activities for them.[85] Development plans include formal training programs, helpful feedback and mentoring, and a series of job assignments leading to the target job. In addition to planning for the development of individuals, these systems can also result in the identification of viable near-term replacements for important positions. The traditional format for displaying such information is the **replacement chart.** The chart in Figure 3.5 shows how long an incumbent is expected to remain in his or her present position and lists one to three individuals who are now or soon will be ready to assume the position. In a thorough system, the chart is backed up by formal evaluations of performance and potential as well as comprehensive development plans for each possible replacement.

Traditional succession planning has come under attack in the last few years. Although many of the features discussed here are still important in identifying and developing managerial talent, the structure and emphasis of state-of-the-art succession planning systems has changed to be more broad and flexible, as shown in Figure 3.6.

FIGURE 3.6

How Succession Planning Systems Are Changing

Source: E. J. Metz, "Designing Succession Systems for New Competitive Realities," *Human Resource Planning,* Vol. 21 (3), 1998, p. 33.

BUSINESS SYSTEMS

FROM		TO
Organizational pyramids with multiple layers	➡	Flatter organization structures
Desire for "seasoned" leaders	➡	Want the "seasoning" developed sooner in careers
Stability	➡	Flexibility with faster market responsiveness

SUCCESSION SYSTEMS

FROM		TO
Groom a backup for each position	➡	Develop pools of broadly qualified candidates; have position pools
Specialty disciplines in candidates	➡	More broadly disciplined candidates
Business unit autonomy	➡	More centralization and integration of systems and information
Siloed career growth	➡	Cross-boundary fertilization to develop broader skills and perspectives
Largely human resources driven	➡	Largely line driven
Subjective and informal criteria: personality/image oriented	➡	Strategic competencies and models define success; 360 degree feedback
Technical competence a key factor	➡	Cross-functional management capability: quick learner; manage change
Tolerate marginal performers	➡	Fewer positions for development requires removing marginal blockers
Company directs and controls career	➡	Individual sets career direction
Controlled and confidential process	➡	Input from multiple sources; more open planning and development process
"Promises"	➡	No "promises"
Focus on training and seminars as primary development vehicle	➡	Sequential job assignments provide primary development experience supplemented by specific training
Take advantage of vacancies to promote candidates	➡	Create assignments for development (e.g., exchanges, trades, special projects)
Promote from within when fully qualified	➡	Promote when about 70 percent qualified; hire less experienced talent at entry level

SUMMARY OF KEY POINTS

Organizations must plan for human resources. Otherwise, they run the risk of having (1) employees of insufficient skill or number to meet the organization's needs or (2) an excess of costly employees whose pay and benefits eat into profits. HR planning is based on information about the organization's internal and external environments and on assumptions about what will happen in these environments in the future. Planning may be at the aggregate level of jobs or job families or at the individual level, as in the planning of managerial succession and development. Strategic human resource planning involves HR experts in formulating and implementing the organization's strategy in the light of HR opportunities and constraints.

HR planners may use judgmental methods, such as unit forecasting or the Delphi technique, to predict a firm's need for labor at a particular point in the future. Mathematical techniques may be used for this same purpose. HR planners predict the future internal supply of labor, drawing on skills inventories, human resource information systems, and Markov analyses to make their forecasts. Planners also gather information on relevant external labor markets to determine the availability of potential new employees.

After both demand and supply forecasts are made, planners reconcile the two to determine areas in which more or fewer employees will be needed. Then they design programs to increase or reduce the size of the work force or to change employees' skills to match the forecasted needs. A number of alternatives for dealing with employee shortages and surpluses are available. Through careful planning, an organization can anticipate needs and implement programs to meet them before the needs actually materialize and cause problems for the organization. Succession planning ensures the supply of qualified and experienced top managers for the future.

THE MANAGER'S VOCABULARY

aggregate-level planning
application service providers
baby boom
baby-boom echo
baby bust
birth dearth
bottom-up (or unit) forecasting
civilian labor force
contingent workers
Delphi technique
demand for labor
demand forecasting
"discouraged" workers
enterprise resource planning
external supply of labor
generation X
human resource information system (HRIS)
human resource planning
internal supply of labor
labor force participation rate
labor market
linear (or goal) programming
Markov analysis
millennials
multiple regression
productivity ratio
reduction in force (RIF)
renewal(or replacement) analysis
replacement chart
skills inventory
staffing ratios
succession plan
thirteeners
top-down forecasting
transition probability matrix
unemployment rate
veterans
work force diversity

QUESTIONS FOR DISCUSSION

1. Why should organizations engage in HR planning? Why do some organizations need relatively more complex and comprehensive HR planning systems than do others?
2. Describe judgmental and mathematical methods of forecasting the future demand for employees.

3. When are judgmental methods of demand forecasting preferred over mathematical methods? When is the reverse true?
4. Describe the roles that human resource information systems can play in an organization. What are the components of such systems?
5. Describe the advantages and disadvantages of Markov analysis for predicting the future internal supply of labor.
6. A low-tech organization is about to use systematic HR planning for the first time. As yet, the HR function has little power or credibility in the organization, though the head of HR is a well-trained, newly hired MBA. The organization's environment is fairly stable, and good records of past staffing levels are available. What method or methods of human resource planning would you recommend in this situation? Why?
7. What kinds of information might an HR planner want to gather about the external labor market?
8. How are changing age and ethnic demographics likely to affect organizations in the next decade?
9. From your own experience, how do boomers, busters, and millennials differ from each other in skills, attitudes and work values, and job prospects? How might these differences affect relationships between the three groups in the work setting?
10. Would you like to be part of the "contingent" work force? Why or why not? What are the advantages and disadvantages of contingent positions for employees and for employers?
11. What can an organization do when a shortage of employees is anticipated?
12. What can an organization do when it expects the internal supply of labor to exceed the demand for labor?
13. What purposes are served by managerial succession planning? What are some characteristics of an effective managerial succession planning system? How have succession planning systems changed in the past few years?

Case 3.1
Brooks Beverage Management, Inc.

Brooks Beverage Management, Inc. (BBMI) is a soft-drink bottler in Holland, Michigan. The market for some of BBMI's cold drinks always dips sharply in winter when consumers turn to hot beverages. This results in an excess of about fifty-five production-line employees between September and March. If laid off, these employees will be difficult and costly to replace. Each receives three months of training on the high-tech bottling equipment before being fully qualified. BBMI operates in a labor market with a very low unemployment rate of 3 percent, so anyone laid off will be snapped up quickly by another employer and not be available in the spring when demand picks up at the bottler. BBMI has put together a task force of representatives from all areas of the company to suggest solutions to this anticipated staffing dilemma. What ideas can you think of to ensure that the services of skilled employees are available when they are needed, year after year? Be creative!

Source: V. Frazee, "Share Thy Neighbor's Workers," *Personnel Journal,* June 1996, pp. 81–84. Reprinted by permission.

Case 3.2
Elite Small Goods

Your firm, Elite Small Goods, supplies specialty food items to delicatessens in major cities. Elite operates two small food-processing plants in New York City to supply its East Coast markets. These plants use old technology in simple and labor-intensive processes. Most of the production employees have limited English-language capability and less than a high school education. However, they are loyal to the firm; turnover is less than 10 percent per year. These operators are managed by traditional supervisors who make all the decisions and issue orders. Equipment maintenance is provided by specialized tradespeople at each plant: an electrician, a boilermaker, and an engine mechanic.

Business is good enough that management is considering modernizing one of the plants. Processing would become much more efficient, with one plant doing more work than both can do together at the present time. The older plant would be closed. The new processing equipment requires sophisticated skills from production operators, including reading technical manuals, operating computers, and performing a wide variety of other tasks. The vendor suggests that the new equipment is most effective when employees are organized into self-managed teams. The modernized plant also will require two multiskilled mechanics who can be trained to maintain all aspects of the complex equipment.

Presently, combined employment at the two plants is sixty-five. The modernized plant will require only fifty-five employees. A manager who strongly favors modernization has been heard to say that "since only ten jobs are affected, the human resource implications are minimal." The CEO has asked you to study and report on the staffing implications of the proposed plant modernization and closure. What do you do now? What information do you seek, and what use do you make of it? What type of staffing actions do you think may be necessary? What cautions might you give management?

Exercise 3.1

Human Resource Planning and the Internet

Using the Internet, locate the latest figures about the size and composition of the U.S. population, the U.S. labor force, and the unemployment rate. Attempt to locate similar information for your city or state. How might you use this type of information in human resource planning?

Search the Internet for additional information that may be relevant to human resource planning for one of the following types of organizations:

- A large nationwide moving company specializing in employee relocation
- A junior college in Houston
- A group of five hospitals in North Carolina
- A high-tech company in California's Silicon Valley

Exercise 3.2

Predicting Supply and Demand

It is now January 2007. Your task is to predict supply and demand for each job category as of January 2008 and to plan what to do to meet the demand.

1. Your 700 operatives this year will produce 100,000 products. Improvements to the plant scheduled for completion in December 2007 will enable production of 120,000 products. You plan to hire more operatives to utilize this new capacity to the fullest in 2008. The improvements to the plant also will result in an increase in productivity such that each worker will be able to produce 5 percent more next year than this year.
2. The use of a new computerized billing system will increase the productivity ratio of clerks to 135 percent of the current ratio. The workload for the clerks will not change from what it is this year.
3. Because of a large standing order, fewer salespersons will be needed. It is estimated that a sales force of forty people will be sufficient to handle business at the beginning of 2008.
4. The ratio of management and staff to operatives should be the same as it is at present.

Supply

Transition Probability Matrix

Present Number of Employees (beginning of 2007)	Operatives	Clerical	Sales	Management/Staff	Exit
700 Operatives	.80	0	0	0	.20
150 Clerical	.10	.80	0	0	.10
50 Sales	0	0	.80	.10	.10
100 Management/staff	0	0	0	.90	.10

Forecast

	Operatives	Clerical	Sales	Management/Staff
January 2008 predicted supply	________	______	____	_____________
January 2008 predicted demand	________	______	____	_____________
Gap	________	______	____	_____________

What discrepancies will exist, and how will you deal with them for each group (operatives, clerical, sales, management/staff)? Be innovative and suggest several solutions.

NOTES AND REFERENCES

1. Todd Raphael, "Behind the Nursing Shortage," *Workforce,* September 29, 2000. (Available at: www.workforce.com/ archive/article/001/07/ 16.xci); Peter I Buerhaus, Douglas O. Staiger, and David I. Auerbach, "Trends: Is the Current Shortage of Hospital Nurses Ending?" *Health Affairs,* Vol. 22 (6), Nov/Dec 2003, pp.191–198.

2. "Mounting a Strategic Recruitment Initiative"[paid advertorial], *Workforce.* (Available at: www.workforce.com/feature/00/ 07/26/)

3. Randall S. Schuler and James W. Walker, "Human Resources Strategy: Focusing on Issues and Actions," *Organizational Dynamics,* Summer 1990, pp. 4–19.

4. Dave Ulrich, "Strategic and Human Resource Planning: Linking Customers and Employees," *Human Resource Planning,* Vol. 15 (2), 1992, pp. 47–62.

5. Emily S. Bassman, "Strategic Use of Environmental Scanning Data," in *Human Resource Forecasting and Strategy Development,* ed. Manuel London, Emily S. Bassman, and John P. Fernandez (New York: Quorum, 1990), pp. 29–37.

6. J. L. Martel and D. S. Langdon, "The Job Market in 2000: Slowing Down as the Year Ended," *Monthly Labor Review,* February 2001, pp. 3–20.

7. Lorenz P. Schrenk, "Environmental Scanning," in *Human Resource Management: Evolving Roles and Responsibilities,* ed. Lee Dyer (Washington, D.C.: BNA Books, 1988), pp. 88–124.

8. J. J. Laabs, "Duke's Newest Power Tool," *Personnel Journal,* June 1996, pp. 44–52.

9. Harvey Kahalas, Harold L. Pazer, John S. Hoagland, and Amy Levitt, "Human Resource Planning Activities in U.S. Firms," *Human Resource Planning,* Vol. 3, 1980, pp. 53–66.

10. Thomas P. Bechet, *Strategic Staffing: A Practical Toolkit for Workforce Planning* (New York: AMACOM, 2002).

11. Laabs, "Duke's Newest Power Tool."

12. Susan E. Jackson and Randall S. Schuler, "Human Resource Planning: Challenges for Industrial/Organizational Psychologists," *American Psychologist,* February 1990, pp. 223–239; E. H. Burack and N. J. Mathys, *Human Resource Planning: A Pragmatic Approach to Manpower Staffing and Development* (Northbrook, Ill.: Brace-Park, 2001).

13. A. M. Bowey, "Corporate Manpower Planning," *Management Decision,* Vol. 15, 1977, pp. 421–469.
14. Daniel N. Bulla and Peter M. Scott, "Manpower Requirements Forecasting: A Case Example," in *Strategic Human Resource Planning Applications,* ed. Richard J. Niehaus (New York: Plenum Press, 1987), pp. 145–155.
15. Andre L. Delbecq, Andrew H. Van de Ven, and David H. Gustafson, *Group Techniques for Program Planning* (Glenview, Ill.: Scott, Foresman, 1975), pp. 83–107.
16. George T. Milkovich, Anthony J. Annoni, and Thomas A. Mahoney, "The Use of the Delphi Procedures in Manpower Forecasting," *Management Science,* December 1972, pp. 381–388.
17. Burack and Mathys, *Human Resource Planning.*
18. Don R. Bryant, Michael J. Maggard, and Robert P. Taylor, "Manpower Planning Models and Techniques," *Business Horizons,* April 1973, pp. 69–78.
19. Diane Rezendes Khirallah and Elisabeth Goodridge, "Working Smarter," *informationweek.com,* August 13, 2001, pp. 20–22.
20. Lee Dyer, "Human Resource Planning," in *Personnel Management,* ed. Kendrith Rowland and Gerald Ferris (Boston: Allyn and Bacon, 1982), p. 53. See Robert H. Meehan and S. Basheer Ahmed, "Forecasting Human Resources Requirements: A Demand Model," *Human Resource Planning,* Vol. 13 (3), 1990, pp. 297–308, for an example of using regression to predict demand in a public utility company.
21. Bowey, "Corporate Manpower Planning"; and Bryant, Maggard, and Taylor, "Manpower Planning Models and Techniques" For further information on linear or goal programming, see C. J. Verhoeven, *Techniques in Corporate Manpower Planning* (Boston: Kluwer, 1982); Richard C. Grinold and Kneale T. Marshall, *Manpower Planning Models* (New York: North-Holland, 1977); and Richard J. Niehaus, *Computer-Assisted Human Resources Planning* (New York: Wiley, 1979). An excellent source on planning is D. Ward, T. P. Bechet, and R. Trip, *Human Resource Forecasting and Modeling* (New York: Human Resource Planning Society, 1994).
22. D. E. Guessford, A. B. Boynton Jr., R. Laudeman, and J. P. Guisti, "Tracking Job Skills Improves Performance," *Personnel Journal,* June 1993, pp. 109–114.
23. Michael J. Kavanagh, Hal G. Gueutal, and Scott I. Tannenbaum, *Human Resource Information Systems: Development and Application* (Boston: PWS-Kent, 1990).
24. K. A. Kovach and C. E. Cathcart Jr., "Human Resource Information Systems (HRIS): Providing Business with Rapid Data Access, Information Exchange and Strategic Advantage," *Public Personnel Management,* Summer 1999, pp. 275–282.
25. R. E. Thaler-Carter, "The HRIS in Small Companies: Tips for Weighing the Options," *HR Magazine,* July 1998, pp. 30–37.
26. Scott A. Snell, Donna Stueber, and David P. Lepak, "Virtual HR Departments," In Robert L. Heneman and David B. Greenberger (Eds.) *Human Resource Management in Virtual Organizations* (Greenwich, Conn.: IAP) 2002, pp. 81–101.
27. Sam Ashbaugh and Rowan Miranda, "Technology for Human Resources Management: Seven Questions and Answers," *Public Personnel Management,* Vol. 31 (1), Spring 2002, pp. 7–20.
28. Lore Bussler and Elaine Davis, "Information Systems: The Quiet Revolution in Human Resource Management," *The Journal of Computer Information Systems,* Vol. 42 (2), Winter 2001-2002, pp. 17–20.
29. Alfred J. Walker (Ed.). *Web-Based Human Resources* (New York: McGraw-Hill) 2001; *Cedar 2003 Workforce Technologies Survey 6th Annual Edition,* 2003.
30. John A. Hooper and R. F. Catalanello, "Markov Analysis Applied to Forecasting Technical Personnel," *Human Resource Planning,* Vol. 4, 1981, pp. 41–47.
31. E. R. Hackett, A. A. Magg, and S. D. Carrigan, "Modeling Faculty Replacement Strategies Using a Time-Dependent Finite Markov-Chain Process," *Journal of Higher Education Policy and Management,* May 1999, pp. 81–93.
32. Herbert G. Heneman III and Marcus B. Sandver, "Markov Analysis in Human Resource Administration: Applications and Limitations," *Academy of Management Review,* October 1977, pp. 535–542.
33. Richard J. Niehaus, "Human Resource Planning Flow Models," *Human Resource Planning,* Vol. 3, 1980, pp. 177–187.
34. For more information, see Guy E. Miller, "A Method for Forecasting Human Resource Needs Against Internal and External Labor Markets," *Human Resource Planning,* Vol. 3, 1980, pp. 189–200.
35. Niehaus, "Human Resource Planning Flow Models"; and Bryant, Maggard, and Taylor, "Manpower Planning Models and Techniques."

36. E. S. Bres III, R. J. Niehaus, F. J. Sharkey, and C. L. Weber, "Use of Personnel Flow Models for Analysis of Large Scale Work Force Changes," in Niehaus (ed.), *Strategic Human Resource Planning Applications,* pp. 157–167; for an update on this system, see R. J. Niehaus, "Evolution of the Strategy and Structure of a Human Resource Planning DSS Application," *Decision Support Systems,* Vol. 14, 1995, pp. 187–204.
37. See Linda O'Brien-Pallas, Andria Baumann, Gail Donner, Gail Murphy, Jacquelyn Lochhaas-Gerlach, and Marcia Luba, "Forecasting Models for Human Resources in Health Care," *Journal of Advanced Nursing,* Vol. 33 (1), January 2001, pp. 120–129 for a recent review of methods used in forecasting nurse supply and demand.
38. James A. Craft, "Human Resource Planning and Strategy," in Dyer (ed.), *Human Resource Management,* pp. 47–87.
39. Laabs, "Duke's Newest Power Tool."
40. William E. Bright, "How One Company Manages Its Human Resources," *Harvard Business Review,* January–February 1976, pp. 81–93.
41. Gordon McBeath, *The Handbook of Human Resource Planning* (Oxford: Blackwell, 1992); example: p. 52.
42. *The Australian Human Resource Benchmarking Report: 1995 Edition* (Brisbane: Australian Human Resources Institute and HRM Consulting Party, Ltd., Brisbane, 995); L. M. Spencer Jr., *Calculating Human Resource Costs and Benefits* (New York: Wiley-Interscience, 1986).
43. *Handbook of Methods,* Bulletin 2285 (Washington: Bureau of Labor Statistics, 1988).
44. Howard N Fullerton Jr. and Mitra Toossi, "Labor Force Projections to 2010: Steady Growth and Changing Composition," *Monthly Labor Review,* Vol. 124, November 2001, pp. 21–38; Mitra Toossi, "A Century of Change: The U.S. Labor Force 1950–2050," *Monthly Labor Review,* Vol. 125 (5), May 2002, pp.15–28.
45. These data were retrieved from the U.S. Department of Labor, Bureau of Labor Statistics site in January 2004, covering the first eleven months of 2003. (Available at: http://www.bls.gov/cps/cpsatabs.htm)
46. M. Duane, *Customized Human Resource Planning* (Westport, Conn.: Quorom, 1996).
47. Raphael, "Behind the Nursing Shortage."
48. George T. Silvestri, "Occupational Employment: Wide Variations in Growth," *Monthly Labor Review,* November 1993, pp. 58–86.
49. Fullerton and Toossi, "Labor Force Projections to 2010: Steady Growth and Changing Composition," and *Monthly Labor Review,* August 2004, p. 71.
50. R. W. Judy and C. D'Amico, *Workforce 2020: Work and Workers in the 21st Century* (Indianapolis, Ind.: Hudson Institute, 1997); Justin A. Heet, "Beyond Workforce 2020: The Coming (and Present) International Market for Labor," (Hudson Institute White Paper, June 23, 2003). (Available at: http://irlcjr.hudson.org/files/publications/workforce_international_mkt_labor.pdf)
51. Arlene Dohm, "Gauging the Labor Force Effects of Retiring Baby-Boomers," *Monthly Labor Review,* July 2000, pp. 17–25.
52. Bob Filipczak, "It's Just a Job: Generation X at Work," *Training,* April 1994, pp. 21–27.
53. C. L. Jurkiewicz, "Generation X and the Public Employee," *Public Personnel Management,* Spring 2000, pp. 55–74.
54. Kim Macalister, "The X Generation," *HR Magazine,* May 1994, pp. 66–69.
55. Claire Raines, *Connecting Generations: The Sourcebook for a New Workplace* (Menlo Park, Calif.: Crisp Publications, 2003).
56. Joseph F. Coates, Jennifer Jarratt, and John B. Mahaffie, *Future Work: Seven Critical Forces Reshaping Work and the Work Force in North America* (San Francisco: Jossey-Bass, 1990).
57. Toossi, "A Century of Change: The U.S. Labor Force 1950–2050."
58. Maria Shao, "Diversity Training: What Is It? Who Does It? Working Together," *Boston Globe,* March 7, 1994, pp. 8–9.
59. R. Rooseveldt Thomas Jr., "From Affirmative Action to Affirming Diversity," *Harvard Business Review,* March–April 1990, pp. 107–117; Marilyn Loden and Judy B. Rosener, *Workforce America! Managing Employee Diversity as a Vital Resource* (Homewood, Ill.: Business One Irwin, 1991); David Jamieson and Julie O'Mara, *Managing Workforce 2000: Gaining the Diversity Advantage* (San Francisco: Jossey-Bass, 1991); Lee Gardenswartz and Anita Rowe, *Managing Diversity: A Complete Desk Reference and Planning Guide* (Burr Ridge, Ill.: Irwin Professional Publishing, 1993); R. M. Wentling and N. Palma-Rivas, "Current Status of Diversity Initiatives in Selected Multinational Corporations," *Human Resource Development Quarterly,* Spring 2000, pp. 35–60; and R. M. Wentling and N. Palma-Rivas, "Current Status and Future

Trends of Diversity Initiative in the Workplace: Diversity Experts' Perspective," *Human Resource Development Quarterly,* Fall 1998, pp. 235–253.
60. Justin A. Heet, "Beyond Workforce 2020: The Coming (and Present) International Market for Labor." But for a contrasting view, see Peter Cappelli, "Will There Really Be a Labor Shortage?" *Organizational Dynamics,* Vol. 32 (3), 2003, pp. 221–233.
61. A. E. Polivka, "Contingent and Alternative Work Arrangements, Defined," *Monthly Labor Review,* October 1996, pp. 3–9. Note that this entire issue of *Monthly Labor Review* is devoted to a discussion of the characteristics of the contingent labor market.
62. A. E. Polivka, "Into Contingent and Alternative Employment: By Choice?" *Monthly Labor Review,* October 1996, pp. 55–74; C. von Hippel, S. L. Mangum, D. B. Greenberger, R. L. Heneman, and J. D. Skoglind, "Temporary Employment: Can Organizations and Employees Both Win?" *Academy of Management Executive,* January 1997, pp. 93–104; R. Nardone, "Part-Time Employment: Reasons, Demographics, and Trends," *Journal of Labor Research,* Summer 1995, pp. 275–292.
63. S. Hipple, "Contingent Work: Results from the Second Survey," *Monthly Labor Review,* November 1998, pp. 22–35.
64. Peter Allan, "The Contingent Workforce: Challenges and New Directions," *American Business Review,* Vol. 20 (2), June 2002, pp. 103–110.
65. U.S. Department of Labor, Bureau of Labor Statistics "Tomorrow's Jobs," *Occupational Outlook Handbook 2002-2003 Edition.* (Available at: http://www.bls.gov/oco/oco2003.htm Bulletin 2540).
66. Information in this section comes from Robert W. Eder, "Opening the Mirage: The Human-Resources Challenge," *Cornell Hotel and Restaurant Administration Quarterly,* August 1990, pp. 25–31, at 26–27.
67. Bill Leonard, "HR Policies Ensure the Mirage Won't Vanish," *HR Magazine,* June 1992, pp. 85–91; Amy Zuber, "Mirage Rehabilitation Program Offers Former Prison Inmates a Second Chance," *Nation's Restaurant News,* Vol. 31 (31), August 4, 1997, pp. 11–12.
68. Schuler and Walker, "Human Resources Strategy."
69. Marc J. Wallace Jr., and M. Lynn Spruill, "How to Minimize Labor Costs During Peak Demand Periods," *Personnel,* July–August 1975, pp. 61–67; Leonard Greenhalgh, Anne T. Lawrence, and Robert I. Sutton, "Determinants of Work Force Reduction Strategies in Declining Organizations," *Academy of Management Review,* April 1988, pp. 241–254; and A. Halcrow, "Temporary Services Warm to the Business Climate," *Personnel Journal,* October 1988, pp. 84–89.
70. Daniel Morris and Joel Brandon, *Re-engineering Your Business* (New York: McGraw-Hill, 1993).
71. Y. J. Dreazen and J. M. Schlensinger, "A Tight Labor Market Can Spur Productivity," *Wall Street Journal Interactive Edition,* March 18, 2000. (Available at: www.careerjournal.com/ hrcenter/articles/20000216-dreazen.html)
72. "Mounting a Strategic Recruitment Initiative."
73. Robert O. Metzger and Mary Ann Von Glinow, "Off-Site Workers: At Home and Abroad," *California Management Review,* Spring 1988, pp. 101–111.
74. Steve Bates, "Overseas Outsourcing: How Big a Threat?" *HR Magazine,* Vol. 48 (9), September 2003, pp. 12–13; Bill Laberis, "Here Today, Gone Tomorrow?" *Adweek Magazines' Technology Marketing,* Vol. 23 (6), September 2003, p. 10.
75. The theme of *Personnel Journal* in June 1996 was strategies to prevent layoffs. The issue contains seven articles about various ways to avoid layoffs.
76. Rene J. Schoysman, "Planning Manpower in a Downturn Economy," *Journal of Systems Management,* May 1980, pp. 31–33.
77. J. T. McCune, R. W. Beatty, and R. V. Montagno, "Downsizing: Practices in Manufacturing Firms," *Human Resource Management,* Vol. 27, 1988, pp. 145–161.
78. "President Lets Plant Closing Become Law Without His Signature," *Ideas and Trends in Personnel,* August 9, 1988.
79. Gary B. Hansen, "Innovative Approach to Plant Closings: The UAW–Ford Experience at San Jose," *Monthly Labor Review,* June 1985, pp. 34–37.
80. Joel Brockner, "The Effects of Work Layoffs on Survivors: Research, Theory, and Practice," in *Research in Organizational Behavior,* Vol. 10, ed. Barry M. Staw and L. L. Cummings (Greenwich, Conn.: JAI Press, 1988), pp. 213–255.
81. "2002 M&A Profile," *Mergers & Acquisitions: The Dealermaker's Journal,* Vol. 38 (2), February 2003, p. 15.
82. J. W. Walker and K. F. Price, "Perspectives: Why Do Mergers Go Right?" *Human Resource*

Planning, 2000, Vol. 23 (2), pp. 6–8; R. N. Bramson, "HR's Role in Mergers and Acquisitions," *Training & Development,* October 2000, pp. 59–66; T. A. Daniel, "Between Trapezes: The Human Side of Making Mergers and Acquisitions Work," *Compensation and Benefits Review,* Winter 2000, pp. 19–37.

83. G. L. McManis and M. S. Leibman, "Succession Planners," *Personnel Administrator,* August 1988, pp. 24–30.

84. David W. Rhodes and James W. Walker, "Management Succession and Development Planning," *Human Resource Planning,* Vol. 7, 1984, pp. 157–173; S. D. Friedman, "Succession Systems in Large Corporations: Characteristics and Correlates of Performance," *Human Resource Management,* Vol. 25, 1986, pp. 191–213; and Ayse Karaevli and Douglas T. Hall, "Is Succession Planning Up to the Challenge?" *Organizational Dynamics,* Vol. 32 (1), 2002, pp. 62–79.

85. See Diana Kramer, "Executive Succession and Development Systems: A Practical Approach," in London, Bassman, and Fernandez (eds.), *Human Resource Forecasting and Strategy Development,* pp. 99–112, for detailed advice on setting up a succession planning system.

CHAPTER **4**

Job Analysis: Concepts, Procedures, and Choices

HR Challenge

Alpha Electric (formerly Alpha Defense Systems, Inc.) is converting its plant in Banksia, Tennessee, from military to commercial manufacturing. Alpha will be moving into an extremely competitive business environment where product life cycles are short and innovation, customer orientation, high quality, and cost-effectiveness are necessary to succeed.

Alpha is a former defense contractor that made computer components for use in highly sophisticated weapons systems. The Banksia plant will have to make significant changes in many of its production processes to adapt its weapons-systems technology to manufacture high-tech communications systems for nonmilitary consumers. Although some assembly-line jobs will be similar to those in the old manufacturing process, others will change significantly.

One problem that Alpha faces is how to describe these new jobs before the plant actually starts operations in order to have the information necessary to hire and train personnel for the new jobs. A second problem is that many of the jobs in the new plant will be cognitively more demanding than the old assembly-line procedures. In addition to the manufacturing processes, warehousing, shipping and receiving, and most other jobs within the plant will be converted to a team-based approach. The organizational structure will be flattened, and employees will be given more responsibility and broader powers to do their jobs. With the flatter structure, greater individual and team responsibilities, and higher levels of employee empowerment, deciding who does what job has become a much more complex task. For many areas of work, there is the question of whether traditional jobs still exist.

Given the transformation of manufacturing and other basic activities within the plant, the jobs of supervisors, mid-level managers, and even top executives will likely change. Understanding the changed nature of management and leadership within Alpha is another critical issue for the new plant. As the HR director of Alpha Electric, you are faced with the task of analyzing and helping to design the new work and management structure. What are the overall HR implications of these changes? What methods are available to help you understand and describe the nature of jobs within the new plant? What do you do? Where do you start?

A traditional solution to this HR Challenge would have involved the HR director developing a job analysis program for Alpha Electric to identify what work needed to be done and who should do it. However, in recent years, the nature and methods of job analysis have been undergoing a transition brought about by dynamic business environments, a more empowered work force, shorter product life cycles, more cognitively challenging individual and team-based work processes, and many other factors. What would have been a fairly straightforward HR problem a few years ago has now become much more difficult.

This chapter examines the role of job analysis in twenty-first century organizations. A recent survey of the use of job analysis in 250 organizations found that approximately 96 percent of public organizations, 41 percent of manufacturing firms, and 67 percent of private service-oriented firms had formal job descriptions for all positions in their organizations.[1] Such data indicate that job analysis remains a significant human resource activity. Traditionally, job analysis has been defined as the process of "obtaining information about jobs."[2] Although it has always been a complex area of human resource management to describe, an adequate discussion of job analysis has become even more difficult because the term "job" has become very contentious in modern organizations. For example, William Bridges, in his 1995 book *Job Shift,* suggested that jobs "are artificial units superimposed on this field. They are patches of responsibility that, all together, were supposed to cover the work that needs to be done."[3] To fully understand the subject of this chapter, we must first recognize that modern job analysis has a "multiple personality."

TRADITIONAL JOB ANALYSIS

Over the past fifty years, an enormous number of methodologies have been developed for measuring and understanding the nature of jobs. Part of the discipline of job analysis focuses on these traditional methods. Within this traditional approach, the goal of research and practice has been to identify better methods and measurement procedures to describe the content of jobs. In the traditional view, there is a straightforward assumption that jobs exist and can be measured. In contrast to the traditional view, **job extinction** proponents argue that *jobs* no longer exist in modern organizations due to the dynamic nature of work in rapidly changing business environments. The job extinction view argues that much of what we now know as job analysis is no longer meaningful and must be replaced with drastically different means for understanding what employees do in organizations.

One way of appreciating these two different views of job analysis is to compare how the two perspectives define "a job." Traditionally, a job has been defined using four hierarchical concepts: job, position, duty, and task. Thus a job is comprised of several similar positions; each position is made up of a set duties; each set of duties is comprised of several distinct tasks. These four concepts have the following definitions:

- A **task** is "a meaningful unit of work activity generally performed on the job by one worker within some limited time period. . . . It is a discrete unit of activity and represents a composite of methods, procedures, and techniques."[4] Example tasks for a grocery check-out employee might include ring up purchased items, take cash and make change, complete credit card transactions, and place grocery items in a bag.
- A **duty** is a loosely defined area of work that contains several distinct but related tasks performed by an individual. A duty for a grocery employee might be to check and restock shelves or to check out customer purchases.

A DIFFERENT POINT OF VIEW

Do We Really Need Job Descriptions, or Even Jobs?

In sharp contrast with traditional human resource management practice, some authors feel that to facilitate the flexibility required in today's rapidly changing environment, companies should do away with job descriptions. Tom Peters, author of the highly influential *Thriving on Chaos* and more recently *Liberation Management: Necessary Disorganisation for the Nanosecond Nineties,* explains:

> Perhaps a case could be made for job descriptions in a stable, predictable, very vertically oriented (functional) organisation. Today, in all cases the job description is a loser. . . . It is imperative today that managers and non-managers be induced to cross "uncrossable" boundaries as a matter of course, day after day. Standing on the formality of a written job description (as an excuse for inaction, or the reason you have to "check up—and up and up—the line") is a guaranteed strategy for disaster.*

An article in *Fortune* magazine makes the point even more strongly—it argues that the entire concept of "job" is becoming obsolete. "In a fast moving economy, jobs are rigid solutions to an elastic problem."† Instead of viewing organizations as a structure of jobs, they should be viewed as "fields of work," made up of constantly changing activities and projects, with a shifting complement of core and peripheral workers doing whatever needs to be done.

W. L. Gore and Associates, maker of Gore-Tex waterproof fabrics, has proved that such unconventional human resource management can be successful. Bill Gore wanted to avoid stifling his employees' initiative and constraining their interpersonal communications, so he abandoned job titles, hierarchy, and a traditional corporate structure. There are only three job titles in the organization, which employs more than 6,000 people: President, Secretary-Treasurer, and Associate. The first two titles are used only because they are required by incorporation law.

Gore's associates are expected to be flexible and adaptable. Rather than being assigned a specific job and having work flow down from above, associates are expected to commit themselves to a team to which they feel they can make the most valuable contribution—or alternatively, initiate a team themselves and lead it toward a new objective. Those who require more regimented and structured working conditions do not stay with the organization for long.

Associates at Gore can recall countless stories of newcomers who have either thrived or failed in their unusual working environment. One example is the

- A **position** is the set of tasks and duties performed by a single individual in an organization. Each person in an organization has a position; for example, Sally holds a specific position within the grocery store.
- A **job** is "a group of positions that are identical with respect to their major or significant tasks and sufficiently alike to justify their being covered by a single analysis."[5] For example, the grocery store employs twenty people in the job of check-out clerk.

In contrast to this highly structured and static view of a job is the description provided by Greg Stewart and Kenneth Carson.[6] They state that, "In general, determinations of what needs to be done and who does it are made as people evaluate themselves and others, and then enter into agreements that bind them to act in a predictable manner . . . the formation of these agreements is known as behavioral contracting. . . These contracts psychologically bind individuals to perform specific behaviors . . . behavioral contracts also differ . . . in that they are dynamic, comprehensive, and subjective, rather than static, narrow, and objective."[7] For an example of

story of Jack Dougherty. On July 26, 1976, Jack Dougherty, a newly minted MBA from the College of William and Mary, became an associate. Bursting with resolve and dressed in a dark blue suit, he presented himself to Bill Gore, shook hands firmly, looked him in the eye, and said he was ready for anything.

What happened next was the one thing for which Jack was not ready. "That's fine, Jack, fine," Gore replied. "Why don't you look around and find something you'd like to do." Three frustrating weeks later, Jack found that something. Now dressed in jeans, he loaded fabric into the maw of a machine that laminates Gore-Tex membrane to other fabrics. It was Jack's way of learning the business. And by 1982 he had become responsible for all advertising and marketing in the fabrics group.[‡]

Fundamental to the success of Gore's dynamic structure is the firm's system of sponsorship, whereby each new associate is assigned to a more senior associate, or "sponsor," who is expected to take an active interest in the new associate's progress, developing his or her strengths and providing coaching about his or her weaknesses. In the absence of a well-defined job description, such a system ensures that associates can contribute to the fullest extent of their ability and that they are recognized appropriately for their contributions. Also fundamental to the system is a strong commitment by all employees to follow four guiding principles:

1. Be fair.
2. Make commitments, and keep them.
3. Use your freedom to grow and develop.
4. Consult others when your decisions will have an impact on them or cause a potentially major problem for the company.

By following these principles, associates can regulate their behavior without any need for detailed rules and fixed responsibilities.

* Tom Peters, *Thriving on Chaos* (London: Pan, 1989), pp. 500–501.

† William Bridges, "The End of the Job." reprinted in *Time—Australia,* September 19, 1994, pp. 2–7, from *Fortune,* September 19, 1994; quote, p. 4.

‡ Frank Shipper and Charles C. Manz, "Employee Self-Management Without Formally Designated Teams: An Alternative Road to Empowerment," *Organizational Dynamics,* Winter 1992, p. 57.

Sources: John Huey, "The New Post-Heroic Leadership," *Fortune,* February 21, 1994, pp. 42–50; Tom Lester, "The Gore's Happy Family," *Management Today,* February 1993, pp. 66–68. For more information about W. L. Gore, see http://www.gore.com/siteindex.html; Tom Peters, *Liberation Management: Necessary Disorganisation for the Nanosecond Nineties* (London: Macmillan, 1992); and Frank Shipper and Charles C. Manz, "Employee Self-Management Without Formally Designated Teams: An Alternative Road to Empowerment," *Organizational Dynamics,* Winter 1992, pp. 48–61.

this sort of **behavioral contracting** in action, see the box A Different Point of View. Some authors have even argued that traditional job analysis is detrimental to organizational health. As early as 1992, two scholars suggested that the "traditional approach to job analysis assumes a static job environment. Specifically, it must be assumed that the job analyzed today will consist of the same set of duties and tasks tomorrow . . . the reliance on job analysis and the proliferation of resulting job descriptions can cripple an organization's ability to be flexible and adapt rapidly to change."[8]

One area of job analysis that falls somewhat between the traditional and job extinction points of view is that of **cognitive task analysis (CTA).** This approach has been defined as "the extension of traditional task analysis techniques to yield information about the knowledge, thought processes, and goal structures that underlie observable task performance. Some would confine the term exclusively to the methods that focus on the cognitive aspects of tasks, but this seems counterproductive. Overt observable behaviour and the covert cognitive functions behind it form an integrated whole."[9] Proponents of cognitive task analysis, like job extinction proponents, argue that traditional job analysis methods have not been adapted sufficiently to accommodate the changing nature of work. In particular, jobs today are often very cognitively focused and involve extensive and complex teamwork processes. Traditional methods do not deal with these aspects of modern jobs very well. As a result, new CTA procedures have been developed and will be discussed later in this chapter.[10] In reality, however, cognitive task analysis is not a complete repudiation of traditional job analysis. Most approaches to CTA are a combination of traditional methods of collecting information about jobs along with new techniques to better analyze the cognitive processes involved in individual and team activity.

As exemplified by cognitive task analysis methods, the reality for job analysis research and practice lies somewhere between "jobs are dead" and "let's just keep on using the same old job analysis methods." Although jobs are more dynamic now than in the past, in "most instances, people still have jobs—a definable set of activities that are performed as well as a definable set of competencies that enable their effective performance. The list of activities and competency assessments associated with a particular position may be broader than it was in the past, but it certainly still exists . . . even if 'jobs' as we have traditionally known them are dying, clearly work is not."[11]

For job analysts, the arguments of the job extinction proponents show that there is a need for more dynamic approaches to job analysis. However, traditional methods of analyzing jobs, *if properly adapted* (as evidenced in many CTA approaches), remain extremely useful. Given this, the remainder of the chapter discusses traditional methods of job analysis because this provides a solid foundation on which to develop improved techniques for analyzing twenty-first century work. Toward the end of the chapter we elaborate on the *strategic view of job analysis* and describe some of the more dynamic approaches to job analysis that already exist or are currently being developed.

THE JOB ANALYSIS PROCESS

Job analysis is defined simply as "obtaining information about jobs."[12] A job analysis typically produces a **job description,** which is a written narrative of the activities performed on a job as well as information about the job context, equipment used,

FIGURE 4.1
Job Analysis Process

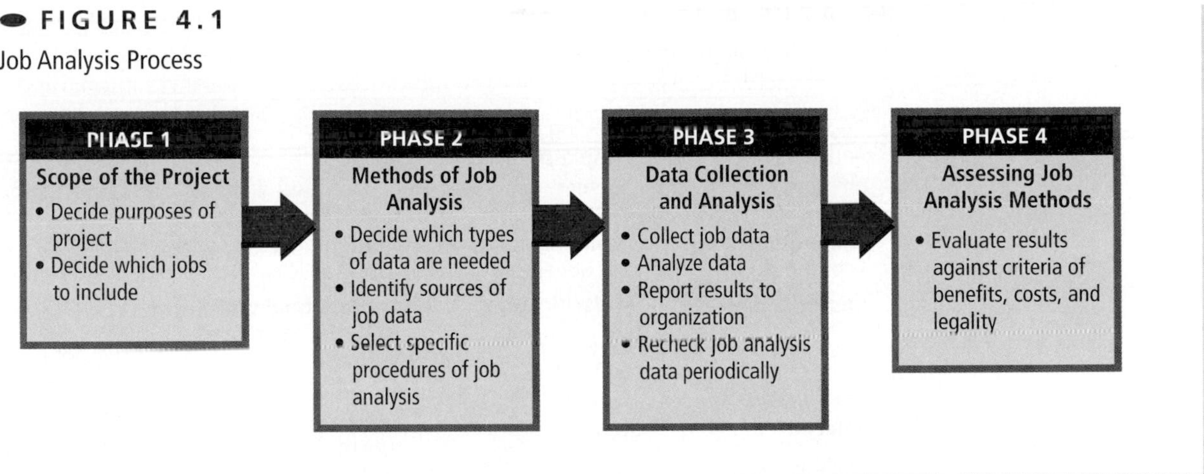
PHASE 1
Scope of the Project
• Decide purposes of project
• Decide which jobs to include
PHASE 2
Methods of Job Analysis
• Decide which types of data are needed
• Identify sources of job data
• Select specific procedures of job analysis
PHASE 3
Data Collection and Analysis
• Collect job data
• Analyze data
• Report results to organization
• Recheck job analysis data periodically
PHASE 4
Assessing Job Analysis Methods
• Evaluate results against criteria of benefits, costs, and legality

and working conditions. There is also usually a **job specification** that outlines the specific skills, knowledge, abilities, and other physical and personal characteristics necessary to perform a job. The basic job analysis process consists of ten steps, which can be grouped into the four major phases as shown in Figure 4.1.

PHASE 1: THE SCOPE OF THE JOB ANALYSIS

To determine the scope of any job analysis effort, an organization must first decide what it hopes to accomplish with the job analysis data. It must then identify the jobs or work processes that it wants to include in the analysis program. Management, both within and outside the HR function, must be involved in these decisions.

Uses of Job Analysis

Knowing what duties a job requires and what skills are needed to perform these duties is critical in setting up an appropriate selection system (test development and validation). Job analysis became even more important in selection thanks to a variety of equal employment opportunity laws, including the Americans with Disabilities Act (ADA) that went into effect in 1992 (discussed more fully in Chapter 5). For some time U.S. courts have indicated that organizations must clearly show that there are direct links between the duties that employees perform on their jobs and the knowledge, skills, and abilities that are assessed in selection procedures. The ADA outlaws discrimination against individuals with mental and physical handicaps who are able to perform the essential functions of a job, either in the usual way or with reasonable accommodation to their needs. Examples of the types of accommodations that employers may be expected to make can be found on the U.S. Department of Labor's Office of Disability Employment Policy "Job Accommodation Network" Web site.[13] To ensure that truly qualified people with disabilities are not misjudged but that those not able to do the job are properly rejected, organizations can no longer rely on job descriptions that simply list the tasks that must be performed. Instead, organizations must identify the essential

TABLE 4.1
Uses of Job Analysis

Recruiting and Selecting Employees	Developing and Appraising Employees	Compensation	Job and Organizational Design
Human resource planning Identification of internal labor markets Recruitment Selection Placement Equal employment opportunity Realistic job previews	Job training and skill development Role clarification Employee career planning Performance appraisal	Determining pay rates for jobs Ensuring equal pay for equal work Ensuring equal pay for jobs of comparable worth	Designing/ redesigning jobs to improve efficiency or motivation Determining lines of authority and responsibility Determining necessary relationships among work groups

functions or fundamental duties of jobs and link these clearly to specific physical and mental requirements.[14] Table 4.1 shows a range of other uses for job analysis.

For prospective employees, job analysis data can provide realistic information about what jobs will be like. **Realistic job previews** can reduce applicants' unrealistically high expectations about jobs and thus reduce early employee dissatisfaction and turnover. For new hires, job analysis data can help orient them to their positions.

Job analysis data also provide the information needed to develop job-relevant training programs and performance appraisal systems.[15] Such data can help supervisors and employees clarify conflicts and ambiguities in employees' roles.

Job analysis data can be used to determine the similarity of jobs and thus the feasibility of transfers between jobs. In the U.S. Air Force, job analysis data have been used to identify jobs that individuals can transfer to with minimal retraining[16] Similarly, job analysis data may be used to identify nontraditional career paths for employees. In one study, job analysis data were used to show that the skills, knowledge, and abilities essential for performance in secretarial and clerical positions are very similar to those needed in entry-level management jobs.[17] Because female employees often predominate in secretarial and clerical jobs, such information may provide employers with ways to increase the movement of women into managerial positions. From the employees' perspective, they can use job analysis information to plot career paths and to make maximum use of their past experience in moving to different, more challenging jobs.

A traditional use of job analysis has been in the area of job evaluation, to determine the relative worth of jobs and thereby develop equitable compensation structures.[18] Job analysis provides a way for organizations to determine the relative similarity of two jobs. Job analysis procedures have also been used to design jobs for maximum efficiency. Some of the oldest job analysis techniques, such as time and motion studies, were developed for this purpose.

One use of job analysis data not included in Table 4.1 is **job classification,** which is an intermediate step between the collection and use of the data. In job classification, the job analyst uses information to categorize similar jobs into a job family. The analyst can then develop selection, appraisal, pay, or other procedures for an entire job family rather than for a single job. For example, in the area of personnel selection, research has shown that cognitive ability tests may be extremely useful in selecting among job applicants across a wide variety of jobs. Using a concept referred to as synthetic validation, job analysis data can help to identify groups of jobs for which a single cognitive ability test might serve as a predictor of future job performance among job applicants.[19]

Determining Which Jobs to Analyze

A variety of factors determine which jobs in an organization should be analyzed. Likely targets of job analysis are jobs that are critical to the success of an organization. For example, quality control specialists would be critical for an organization whose business strategy focuses on providing high-quality products. Jobs that are difficult to learn and perform (and thus require extensive training) are also essential to analyze, as are jobs for which the organization is constantly having to hire new employees (because job analysis provides information on how best to select those employees). Legal considerations may also determine which jobs should be analyzed. Jobs that have few minority or female employees should be analyzed to make sure that illegal discrimination is not occurring in hiring practices. In addition, jobs should be analyzed when new technology or other circumstances suggest that the way in which the job is performed needs to be changed. When completely new jobs are added, these should be analyzed. When some jobs are eliminated and their duties distributed to other jobs within the organization, job analysis may be appropriate to clarify the nature of these expanded jobs.

Which types of jobs, the number of jobs, and the geographic dispersion of jobs are important for determining the specific method of job analysis used. For example, one way to collect job information is to observe employees actually performing the jobs. If IBM were to use this procedure for collecting information about all the jobs in IBM worldwide, this job analysis project would cost millions of dollars and take years to complete. If, on the other hand, IBM were interested only in the job of keyboard assemblers at a single plant, this observation method of collecting job information might prove quite useful.

PHASE 2: CHOOSING AMONG METHODS OF JOB ANALYSIS

To determine which methods of job analysis to use, the job analyst must decide on (1) the types of data to collect, (2) the sources of information from which to get the data, and (3) the specific type of job analysis to implement.

Types of Job Data

Several types of data can be collected in a job analysis project. Some job analysis methods focus on descriptors of specific tasks and are thus applicable to a narrow range of jobs. Other methods produce descriptors that are more generic in nature and can be used across a wide variety of jobs.

Job data can relate to various work activities and human abilities as well as to other job characteristics and information about the equipment used on the job. J. W. Cunningham and his colleagues identified three levels of work activities.[20] **Foundation work activities** are free of technological content and are applicable to a wide range of occupations. For example, a question such as "How much responsibility for people do you have on your job?" could be asked of employees in almost any type of job. **Intermediate work activities** have some technological content but are applicable across a reasonably wide range of occupations: for example, "How much of your time is spent teaching people?" Although teaching people would not be applicable to every job, a wide range of jobs might involve some level of teaching, for example, professors, personnel trainers, and supervisors in technical fields who might have to instruct subordinates. **Area work activities** are technologically oriented and quite specific to particular occupational groups such as nursing. Collecting this type of data would involve questions such as "How much time do you spend cleaning surgical equipment?" In addition to identifying this hierarchy of work activities, Cunningham and his colleagues also described a hierarchy of knowledges and skills that ranged from "fundamental" (e.g., ability to read, think, plan) to "occupation specific" (e.g., the skill needed by a surgeon to use a laser scalpel).

In addition to Cunningham's work, a number of taxonomies of human abilities have been developed over the years and are widely used in job analysis.[21] Taken collectively, these taxonomies identify four major types of abilities:

- **Psychomotor abilities,** such as manual dexterity and arm/hand steadiness
- **Physical abilities,** such as strength and stamina
- **Cognitive abilities,** such as intelligence and verbal comprehension
- **Situational abilities,** such as the ability to work under time pressure and the ability to work alone

Much recent work has been focused on identifying "core competencies" of managers and other professionals. Such studies represent efforts to develop lists of human abilities, skills, and knowledge relevant to occupational clusters or specific occupations.[22]

Many other types of information can be collected as part of a job analysis process. A good example of this can be found in the **Occupational Information Network (O*NET)** developed for the U.S. Department of Labor.[23] Data on experience requirements, occupation requirements, occupation-specific requirements, occupation characteristics, worker requirements, and worker characteristics are all part of the O*NET system. Examples of the types of data in each of these six major categories are presented in Table 4.2.

Regardless of the content of the data collected, the job analyst must also decide whether to collect data in a qualitative or quantitative format. **Qualitative data** are narrative descriptions of the work activities, abilities, characteristics, and equipment associated with the job. **Quantitative data** are numerical values that indicate the extent to which the work activities, abilities, characteristics, and equipment are involved in the performance of the job. For example, a job analyst who collects qualitative data about a job might learn that typing letters is really important on the job. By collecting data in a quantitative format, the analyst might instead find that 70 percent of an employee's time is spent typing letters.

An advantage of quantitative data is that they allow the job analyst to compare different jobs. Using qualitative data, the job analyst might find that for one job

TABLE 4.2

Types of Data in the Occupational Information Network (O*NET) Database

Experience Requirements

1. Experience and training—Specific preparation required for entry into a job and past work experience contributing to qualifications for an occupation
2. Licensing—Licenses, certificates, or registrations that are used to identify levels of skill or performance relevant to occupations

Occupation Requirements

1. Generalized work activities—General types of job behaviors occurring on multiple jobs, such as:
   a. Looking for and receiving job-related information
   b. Information/data processing
   c. Performing complex/technical activities
   d. Coordinating/developing/managing/advising others
2. Organizational context—Characteristics of the organization that influence how people do their work such as:
   a. Decision-making system
   b. Job characteristics
   c. Job stability and rotation
   d. Human resources systems and practices
   e. Social processes and roles
   f. Culture and organizational values
   g. Supervisor role
3. Work context—Physical and social factors that influence the nature of work, such as:
   a. Formality of communication
   b. Job interactions
   c. Responsibility for others
   d. Conflictual contact
4. Physical work conditions, such as:
   a. Work setting
   b. Environmental conditions
   c. Job hazards
   d. Body positioning
   e. Work attire
5. Structural job characteristics, such as:
   a. Criticality of position
   b. Pace and scheduling

Occupation-Specific Requirements

Detailed information describing the characteristics of a particular occupation, such as occupational skills and knowledge; tasks and duties; machines, tools, and equipment

Occupation Characteristics

Basic information on the nature of the industry, job opportunities, and pay within the occupation

Worker Characteristics

1. Abilities—Enduring attributes of the individual that influence performance
   a. Cognitive abilities, such as:
      i. Verbal abilities

(continued)

TABLE 4.2
Continued

ii. Idea generation and reasoning
iii. Attentiveness
b. Psychomotor abilities, such as:
i. Fine manipulative abilities
ii. Reaction time and speed abilities
c. Physical abilities, such as:
i. Endurance
ii. Flexibility, balance, and coordination
d. Sensory abilities, such as:
i. Visual abilities
ii. Auditory and speech abilities
2. Interests—Preferences for work environments and outcomes, such as:
a. Holland occupational classification
b. Occupational values
3. Work styles—Personal characteristics that describe important interpersonal and work-style requirements in jobs and occupations, such as:
a. Achievement orientation
b. Social influence
c. Interpersonal orientation
d. Conscientiousness
e. Practical intelligence

Worker Requirements

1. Basic skills—Developed capacities that facilitate learning or the more rapid acquisition of knowledge, such as:
a. Reading comprehension
b. Writing
c. Critical thinking
2. Cross-functional skills—Developed capacities that facilitate performance of activities that occur across jobs, such as:
a. Social skills
b. Complex problem-solving skills
c. Systems skills
3. Knowledge—Organized sets of principles and facts applying in general domains, such as:
a. Business and management
b. Manufacturing and production
c. Arts and humanities
d. Law and public safety
4. Education—Prior educational experience required to perform in a job

Source: Adapted from information in Norman Peterson, Michael Mumford, Walter Borman, Richard Jeanneret, Edwin Fleishman, Kerry Levin, Michael Campion, Melinda Mayfield, Frederick Morgeson, Kenneth Pearlman, Marilyn Gowing, Anita Lancaster, Marilyn Silver, and D. Donna, "Understanding Work Using the Occupational Information Network (O*NET): Implications for Practice and Research," *Personnel Psychology,* Vol. 54 (2), 2001, pp. 451–492.

"typing letters is very important" and for another job "typing letters is critical." How, then, can the job analyst compare these two jobs? Is "very important" the same as "critical"? If, instead, the job analyst were to collect quantitative data, he or she might find that typing letters is 50 percent of one employee's job but 80 percent of another's.

Sources of Job Data

Although the most direct source of information about a job is the job incumbent, a number of other sources are available. For example, other sources could include existing job descriptions, equipment maintenance records, films of employees working, or architectural blueprints of a work area. In addition to job incumbents, job data could be obtained from supervisors or other job experts. These sources might provide information that the average job incumbent cannot, thereby enabling the job analyst to question the incumbent more effectively.

The first place a job analyst should look for information is job analysis data that already exist. However, the job analyst should view these data with caution. They may have been developed using inadequate procedures, or they may no longer be valid descriptions of present-day jobs.

Although job analysts, trainers, supervisors, and other experts may never have performed a certain job, they may be knowledgeable about the content and context of the work. For instance, an engineer who designed a nuclear reactor probably could offer considerable insight into the job of a nuclear reactor operator. Regardless of which sources are used, the job analyst should ensure that (1) sources of information are the most recent available, (2) that any source used is as accurate and reliable as possible, and (3) whenever possible that data are collected from several different sources.

Having good job analysis data is important because inaccurate job analyses can cost money.[24] For example, exaggeration of job duties could result in a higher salary than the job is really worth. Inaccurate job descriptions could result in poor hiring decisions that result in lower productivity of employees in the job. The financial costs of poor job analysis data can become very apparent when organizations defend their personnel practices in court (as in the case of a sex, race, or age discrimination suit). The adequacy of the sources of job analysis information is particularly important when **subject matter experts (SMEs)**—individuals who provide job analysis information—are involved.[25]

Perhaps the most common SMEs used to provide job information are job incumbents. However, a number of researchers have identified several problems with this source of job information.[26] Getting good information from job incumbents depends heavily on the motivation of the incumbent to provide that information. Even if motivated to do so, job incumbents have been found to be good at assessing the experiential nature of their work (concrete tasks and work context) but less able to assess more abstract characteristics (e.g., complex cognitive or decision-making aspects of the job). Job complexity and the level of job satisfaction in job incumbents have also been found to affect job incumbent ratings.[27] Later in this chapter, we discuss the notion of "future-oriented" job analyses; that is, describing what the job will be at some time in the future rather than what it is now. Sanchez points out that job incumbents are probably *not* the best source of information about the future nature of jobs. Supervisors, managers, or other nonincumbent experts are likely to be better sources of future-oriented job information.

When using subject matter experts, a job analyst should select SMEs who have had an adequate opportunity to perform the job or to observe the job being performed. According to several studies, the amount of job knowledge, experience, and competence that SMEs have influences the accuracy and reliability of the information they provide.[28] Job incumbents who are interviewed should be representative of the types of people who do the job and include both males and females if both sexes perform the job. Significant differences have been found in the job analysis ratings made by males and females. It is also probably best to collect information from both high and low performers and from individuals with varying levels of experience on the job.[29]

Job Analysis Procedures

A wide variety of specific procedures can be used in analyzing a job, ranging from very simple qualitative approaches to highly complex and structured quantitative methods. In the next sections we discuss three major types of job analysis procedures.

Narrative Job Descriptions **Narrative job descriptions** and specifications are the simplest form of job analysis. The job analyst collects qualitative data from various sources of job data. Most frequently, the analyst interviews employees and supervisors or observes workers performing the job. Narrative job descriptions typically include information on job title; job identification number; name of the department or division where the job is performed; name of the job analyst; brief written summary of the job; list of the job's major duties; description of the skills, knowledge (including education), and abilities needed to perform the job; list of the machines, tools, and equipment used on the job; and an explanation of how the job relates to other jobs in the organization. In writing these descriptions, job analysts try to describe the job in a terse, direct style with concrete, simple language. They avoid technical terms (unless they are widely used on the job) and make minimal use of adjectives, gerunds, and participles. Quite a number of Web sites provide ready-made job descriptions or have software available on a fee basis to aid in writing job descriptions.[30] An example of one such narrative job description is presented in Figure 4.2.

FIGURE 4.2

Example Job Description from Internet Web Site

Source: This description was adapted from a job decription found at http://www.jobdescription.com/content/complet5.asp. (accessed December 22, 2003)

OLEC Corp: Job Description

Job title:	Personal Computer Network Technician
Department:	Information Services
Reports to:	Director of Information Systems
FLSA status:	Nonexempt
Prepared by:	Connie Sheehan
Prepared date:	January 4, 2004
Approved by:	Stephanie Marsh
Approved date:	January 12, 2004

SUMMARY

Installs, configures, and troubleshoots computer networks and associated assemblies by performing the following duties.

ESSENTIAL DUTIES AND RESPONSIBILITIES include the following. Other duties may be assigned.

1. Performs network troubleshooting to isolate and diagnose common network problems.
2. Upgrades network hardware and software components as required.

3. Installs, upgrades, and configures network printing, directory structures, rights, security, and software on file servers.
4. Provides users with network technical support.
5. Responds to the needs and questions of users concerning their access of resources on the network.
6. Establishes network users, user environment, directories, and security for networks being installed.

SUPERVISORY RESPONSIBILITIES

This job has no supervisory responsibilities.

QUALIFICATIONS

To perform this job successfully, an individual must be able to perform each essential duty satisfactorily. The requirements listed below are representative of the knowledge, skill, and/or ability required. Reasonable accommodations may be made to enable individuals with disabilities to perform the essential functions.

EDUCATION and/or EXPERIENCE

Fifth-year college or university program certificate; or two to four years related experience and/or training; or equivalent combination of education and experience.

LANGUAGE SKILLS

Ability to read, analyze, and interpret general business periodicals, professional journals, technical procedures, or governmental regulations. Ability to write reports, business correspondence, and procedure manuals. Ability to effectively present information and respond to questions from groups of managers, clients, customers, and the general public.

MATHEMATICAL SKILLS

Ability to apply advanced mathematical concepts such as exponents, logarithms, quadratic equations, and permutations. Ability to apply mathematical operations to such tasks as frequency distribution, determinations of test reliability and validity, analysis of variance, correlation techniques, sampling theory, and factor analysis.

REASONING ABILITY

Ability to solve practical problems and deal with a variety of concrete variables in situations where only limited standardization exists. Ability to interpret a variety of instructions furnished in written, oral, diagram, or schedule form.

CERTIFICATES, LICENSES, REGISTRATIONS

- Certified Netware Engineer (CNE) Certificate
- Licensed Microsoft Technician
- HP Authorized Service Person

PHYSICAL DEMANDS

- While performing the duties of this job, the employee is regularly required to stand; use hands to finger, handle, or feel; reach with hands and arms; and talk or hear. The employee frequently is required to walk and stoop, kneel, crouch, or crawl. The employee is occasionally required to sit, climb or balance, and taste or smell. The employee must frequently lift and/or move up to 10 pounds and occasionally lift and/or move up to 100 pounds. Specific vision abilities required by this job include close vision, depth perception, and ability to adjust focus.
- While performing the duties of this job, the employee is regularly required to talk or hear. The employee frequently is required to walk and sit. The employee is occasionally required to stand; use hands to finger, handle, or feel; and reach with hands and arms.

WORK ENVIRONMENT

- The work environment characteristics described here are representative of those an employee encounters while performing the essential functions of this job. Reasonable accommodations may be made to enable individuals with disabilities to perform the essential functions.
- While performing the duties of this job, the employee is occasionally exposed to risk of electrical shock. The noise level in the work environment is usually moderate.

The uses of narrative job descriptions are relatively limited. The information provided is so general that its use in developing specific performance appraisal or training content is difficult. The same problems exist for use of narrative descriptions in pay determination or job design. However, narrative descriptions are useful for recruiting and orientation, for creating realistic job previews, and for career planning.

Engineering Approaches **Engineering approaches** involve an examination of the specific body movements and procedural steps required to perform a particular task. The job analyst collects data by observing actual employees on the job, films of employees working, or both films and live employees. The analyst develops an operation chart to show the actions of an employee performing a task. The chart typically uses symbols to represent the worker's specific actions and the sequence in which they occur; through the use of symbols and brief phrases, a detailed description of the task emerges.

Micromotion studies are a particular type of engineering approach. They are used to analyze jobs that contain very short-cycle, repetitive tasks (e.g., soldering the electrical circuits on the chassis of a television set). The job analyst develops a list of basic body motions and uses it to analyze all the tasks included in the study. Several standard lists of basic body motions have been developed.[31] These lists include such motions as search, select, grasp, hold, position, inspect, assemble, and disassemble. The analyst films workers performing a task and then analyzes the film to identify the separate motions and the time required to complete each motion. The term **time and motion study,** which derives from this analysis of time and motions, is often used to describe this category of job analysis procedures.

The engineering approaches to job analysis provide detailed information about jobs. These methods concentrate on tasks and basic body movements, are relatively objective in their manner of collecting information, and usually result in some form of quantitative data. The data are particularly useful for the design of equipment to be used on the job.

Structured Job Analysis Procedures Although there are many different structured job analysis procedures, we will discuss nine that are representative. Each procedure provides a different view of jobs and is suitable for different uses.

Critical Incidents Technique J. C. Flanagan developed the **critical incidents technique (CIT)** for assembling lists of behaviors critical to job performance. The procedure consists of four steps:[32]

1. A panel of experts provides written examples of behaviors that represent effective or ineffective performance on the job. These examples describe a given incident: what led up to it, exactly what the employee did, the consequences of the behavior, and to what extent the consequences of the behavior were under the control of the employee. For example, here is a critical incident of good performance by a night security guard: The security guard heard a strange hissing sound coming from the basement. He investigated the noise and found a gas leak in the building's furnace. He immediately cut off the gas to the furnace, preventing an explosion, and called the utility company to arrange for the repair of the leak.

2. All the examples generated in step 1 are then sorted into groups of similar behaviors (e.g., handling emergency situations). This sorting may be done by either the job analyst or by a group of experts on the job.
3. The categories identified in step 2 are defined and named by either the job analyst or job experts.
4. The job behavior categories are rated according to how critical or important they are for job performance. This rating is done by a group of job experts.

Using the CIT, job analysts can identify major types of behaviors that correlate with effective or ineffective performance. The CIT is well suited for developing performance appraisal systems and also for determining the training needs of employees. However, it does not identify the common, routine behaviors performed on jobs. This limitation in Flanagan's approach can be eliminated easily by extending the CIT procedure to include statements concerning average performance and thus provide a better overall view of job behaviors.

O*NET The U.S. Department of Labor has developed the Occupational Information Network database, called O*NET. Job data for O*NET are collected using a survey method involving nine questionnaires.[33] Examples of the type of data collected were presented earlier in Table 4.2. The O*NET database system replaces the ***Dictionary of Occupational Titles (DOT)*** and includes a wide variety of occupational and career information.[34] A summary of the information available from O*Net is contained in Table 4.3. An overview of the basic O*Net products is given in Section A of the table. A particularly useful product for O*Net customers is the **Career Exploration Tools** described in Section B. Information obtained with the Career Exploration Tools can be used with the online search functions at O*NET OnLine to help individuals find jobs within the O*NET database that match up well with their own personal abilities, interests, and values. The other O*NET products represent a technologically enhanced approach to job analysis, providing a wealth of information that HR specialists can use in developing personnel selection, training, and other HR systems.[35]

Functional Job Analysis (FJA) In **functional job analysis (FJA),** trained job analysts review written materials, observe workers performing the job, and interview job incumbents and supervisors for information.[36] Others familiar with the job then review all of this information to ensure its validity and reliability. In the FJA procedure, job analysts rate each task using seven scales: three worker-function scales (see Table 4.4), a worker-instruction scale, and three scales concerning general educational development in reasoning, mathematics, and language. The worker-function scales indicate the type of behavior engaged in toward data, people, and things; these scales also indicate the percentage of time spent on each task. For example, in performing one task, an employee might spend 70 percent of the time working with people, 10 percent working with data, and the remaining 20 percent working with things.

The FJA method has been used to analyze many different jobs. It has a wide range of applications but is not particularly useful for job classification or evaluation unless combined with other techniques. One of its main advantages is that it analyzes each task separately. This characteristic provides a detailed picture of the job and makes the FJA method applicable for a variety of organizational purposes.

TABLE 4.3

O*Net Information and Web Sites

Section A: Major O*Net Products Available Online		
Product Categories	**Web Site**	**Product Description**
O*NET Career Exploration Tools	http://www.onetcenter.org/tools.html	Instruments to help individuals explore careers and make career decisions.
O*NET OnLine	http://www.onetcenter.org/online.html	Users can search the O*NET database to find occupations, search for occupations with certain skill requirements, and cross-match occupations within O*NET to other occupational classification schemes. Data for each occupation include: Tasks, Knowledge, Skills, Abilities, Work Activities, Work Context, Job Zone, Interests, Work Values, Related Occupations, and Wages and Employment.
Research and Technical Reports	http://www.onetcenter.org/research.html	Research and technical reports about the development of O*NET and the O*NET database.
Testing and Assessment Consumer Guides	http://www.onetcenter.org/guides.html	Guides developed for employers and HR specialists to aid them in developing improved personnel testing systems.
O*NET Occupational Listings	http://www.onetcenter.org/occupations.html	Listings of O*NET occupation codes, titles, and definitions, which can be sorted by occupation code, job title, etc.
O*NET Questionnaires	http://www.onetcenter.org/questionnaires.html	Questionnaires used in the O*NET Data Collection Program that have been prepared and made available for public use.
O*NET Database	http://www.onetcenter.org/database.html	This site links to the O*Net database, which contains information on several hundred variables that represent descriptors of work and worker characteristics.

Position Analysis Questionnaire (PAQ) Designed by E. J. McCormick, the **Position Analysis Questionnaire (PAQ)** consists of 194 items: 187 items focus on generic worker-oriented activities involved in performing a job, and 7 items deal with pay issues.[37] Because of its worker-oriented nature, the PAQ can be used to analyze a wide variety of jobs. The items of the PAQ are grouped in six divisions. The first division includes items on the information workers use in performing a job (e.g., use of written materials, near visual differentiation), the second division concerns the mental processes used on the job (e.g., level of decision making, coding/ decoding), and the third division identifies the actual output of the job (e.g., use of keyboard devices, assembling/disassembling). The final three divisions of the

Section B: Career Exploration Tools (found at http://www.onetcenter.org/tools.htm)		
Tool	**Web Site**	**Description**
Ability Profiler	http://www.onetcenter.org/AP.html	A paper-and-pencil test using computerized scoring to assess an individual's level on nine job-relevant abilities.
Interest Profiler	http://www.onetcenter.org/IP.html	A paper-and-pencil test to help an individual discover the type of work activities and occupations they would like and find exciting. The test measures six major occupational interest categories.
Computerized Interest Profiler	http://www.onetcenter.org/CIP.html	A computerized version of the Interest Profiler.
Work Importance Locator	http://www.onetcenter.org/WIL.html	A paper-and-pencil instrument that measures six types of work values. Individuals can identify occupations that they may find satisfying based on the similarity between their work values and the characteristics of the occupations.
Work Importance Profiler	http://www.onetcenter.org/WIP.html	A computerized version of the Work Importance Locator

PAQ deal with relationships with other persons (e.g., contacts with the public, customers), the job context (e.g., high temperatures), and other job characteristics (e.g., specified work pace, amount of job structure).

To complete the PAQ, a job analyst, supervisor, or job incumbent uses one of six rating scales. (The job analyst usually rates the PAQ items during an interview with a job incumbent or supervisor.) The six scales used to rate PAQ items are (1) extent of use, (2) importance to the job, (3) amount of time, (4) possibility of occurrence, (5) applicability, and (6) special code. The special code scales are constructed for specific items and vary in their exact format. Depending on the nature of the item, each is rated using only one of the scales. Typically, a PAQ analysis is completed for several individual positions with the same job title. The results of these analyses are then averaged to get a better, more reliable picture of the job.

The PAQ has been used extensively for personnel selection, job classification, and job evaluation.[38] However, its use in performance appraisal and training systems is limited. The worker-oriented PAQ items make analyzing a wide variety of jobs easier, but they also make it difficult to translate PAQ scores directly into specific performance standards or training content.

Task Inventory Procedure A **task inventory** is "a form of structured job analysis questionnaire that consists of a listing of tasks within some occupational field . . . and [a] provision for some type of response scale for each task."[39] A task inventory focuses on what gets done on a set of jobs in a particular occupation. Because of this, a task inventory must be developed for each group of jobs to be analyzed. In contrast to the PAQ, there is no single version of the task inventory. Developing a task inventory involves several major steps:[40]

TABLE 4.4

Worker-Function Scales in Functional Job Analysis

Data	People	Things
1. Comparing	1a. Taking instructions	1a. Handling
	1b. Serving	1b. Feeding/off-bearing
2. Copying	2. Exchanging information	2a. Machine tending I
		2b. Machine tending II
3a. Computing	3a. Sourcing information	3a. Manipulating
3b. Compiling	3b. Coaching	3b. Operating/controlling I
	3c. Persuading	3c. Driving/controlling
	3d. Diverting	3d. Starting up
4. Analyzing	4a. Consulting	4a. Precision working
	4b. Instructing	4b. Setting up
	4c. Treating	4c. Operating/controlling II
5a. Innovating	5. Supervising	
5b. Coordinating		
6. Synthesizing	6. Negotiating	
	7. Mentoring	

Note: The higher the scale number, the more complex the function. Precise definitions of worker functions can be found in the source of this table.

Source: S. A. Fine and M. Getkake, *Benchmark Tasks for Job Analysis: A Guide for Functional Job Analysis* (Mahwah, N.J.: Erlbaum, 1995).

1. *Determine the jobs to include in the inventory.* Most task inventories are developed for use in analyzing an occupation rather than a single job. For example, a task inventory might be developed to examine the occupation of "nurse" within a hospital. In reality, there are many specific nursing jobs such as surgical nurse, obstetrics nurse, neonatal nurse, and nursing supervisor. The task inventory would be designed to encompass all of these specific jobs.
2. *Construct a list of tasks.* Using written materials, as well as interviews with job incumbents and supervisors, the job analyst produces an initial list of tasks performed. A group of individuals familiar with the occupation reviews the list of task statements. A pilot study using job incumbents may be conducted with this list to ensure that all relevant tasks are included and that the wording of the task statements is appropriate.
3. *Plan the survey and analyses.* The job analyst must decide what information about tasks is needed. The analyst may collect several different types of data, such as whether the task is performed on a specific job, the importance of the task to the job, the criticalness of the task, the relative time spent performing the task, the complexity of the task, and the difficulty of learning the task. A portion of a typical task inventory is shown in Figure 4.3. Usually the analyst runs a pilot study to ensure that the instructions are clear and that the format of the inventory is appropriate and easy to use. Once the inventory is ready, the job analyst plans how it will be administered, which job incumbents will be selected to complete the inventory, and what analyses will be conducted on the data that are collected.

FIGURE 4.3

Sample Task Inventory

Source: Harry L. Ammerman, *Performance Content for Job Training,* Vol. 3 (Columbus, Ohio: Center on Education and Training for Employment, [formerly CVE], The Ohio State University). Copyright 1977. Used with permission.

DATA PROCESSING TASK INVENTORY		Page 14 of 26 pages
Listed below are duties and the tasks that they include. Check all tasks that you perform. Add any tasks you do that are not listed, then rate the tasks you have checked.	CHECK IF DONE ✔	TIME SPENT 1. Very much below average 2. Below average 3. Slightly below average 4 About average 5. Slightly above average 6. Above average 7. Very much above average
H. Operating automatic data processing equipment		
1. Analyze job steps to determine data recovery points.		
2. Analyze machine operation through use of messages received from the equipment.		
3. Analyze machine operation through use of conditions displayed.		
4. Determine cause of machine stops and malfunctions.		
5. Interrogate memory locations on the console.		
6. Load programs and data cards.		
7. Locate tapes in storage media or tape library.		
8. Maintain card files (source object, etc.).		
9. Maintain current run tapes.		
10. Maintain levels of data processing supplies.		

4. *Administer the task inventory.* The job analyst administers the inventory by handing it out to select employees during work hours or mailing it to employees. In a very large organization, hundreds of incumbents could be asked to complete the task inventory.
5. *Process the survey data.* As the inventories are returned, they are checked to make sure that they have been filled out properly. The data are then coded and analyzed to identify important tasks. Once important tasks have been identified, additional data on these tasks may be collected to determine the skills, knowledge, or abilities required to perform the tasks. Analyses may also be done to cluster similar jobs into job families.

Task inventories provide a wealth of information about the jobs within a specific occupational field. They are useful when the job analyst needs to collect data from many job incumbents who are spread over a large geographic region. Once designed, the inventories are relatively easy to complete and may be mailed to employees. When only a few employees are involved, however, task inventories are not cost-effective because they are expensive to develop. The information obtained from task inventories is very useful in the design of training programs.

No two task inventories are exactly the same, so inventory data cannot be used to compare jobs in very different occupational fields. For the same reason, task inventories are not suited for organization-wide job evaluation purposes.

Ability Requirements Scales The **ability requirements scales,** developed by E. A. Fleishman and his associates, measure abilities needed to perform jobs.[41] Job experts are asked to rate the extent to which fifty-two abilities are required to perform the job. These include abilities such as oral comprehension, number facility, night vision, dynamic flexibility, and selective attention. Job experts rate each ability using scales in which the ability is carefully defined and distinguished from other abilities. The rater uses a 7-point scale, in which each point on the scale is "anchored" with a behavioral example. For example, for rating the ability of static strength, the 1 level on the rating scale is anchored with the statement "Lift one package of bond paper," and the 7 level on the scale is anchored with the statement "Reach over and lift a seventy-pound box onto a table." Once important abilities have been identified, individual tasks on the job that require those abilities can be identified. The ability requirement scales are particularly appropriate for use in job classification and for the development of personnel selection systems.

Personality-Related Job Analysis Procedures There has been a resurgence of interest in personality characteristics as predictors of job performance using the "Big Five" personality dimensions.[42] As a result, attempts are being made to develop job analysis instruments to describe the personality requirements of jobs; that is, **personality-related job analysis procedures.** For example, Patrick Raymark and his colleagues have conducted research on the development of the **Personality-Related Position Requirements Form (PPRF).**[43] The PPRF is designed to identify aspects of jobs that are potentially related to individual differences in personality. The PPRF consists of 107 items divided into five major categories (surgency, agreeableness, conscientiousness, emotional stability, and intellectance). Factor analysis results indicated that these five categories could be divided further into twelve subfactors. The structure of the PPRF is shown in Table 4.5. Items within each of the twelve subfactors of the PPRF have a common format—that is, "Effective performance in this position requires the person to . . ."—with job experts indicating whether the personality characteristic represented by the item is "not required," "helpful," or "essential" to performance on the job. Examples of items for the "Leadership" subfactor of the surgency category include (1) lead group activities through exercise of power or authority and (2) take control in group situations. Examples of items in the "General Trustworthiness" subfactor of the conscientiousness category include (1) refuse to share or release confidential information and (2) make commitments and follow through on them.

Managerial Job Analysis Procedures A number of job analysis procedures have been designed specifically for use with managerial and professional jobs. An example of these is the **Professional and Managerial Position Questionnaire (PMPQ).** The PMPQ consists of ninety-three items, divided into three major sections: job activities, personal requirements, and other information.[44] The first section, job activities, includes items on six major types of activities: (1) planning and scheduling activities, (2) processing information and ideas, (3) exercising judg-

TABLE 4.5

Structure of the Personality-Related Position Requirements Form (PPRF)

Category 1: Surgency	**Category 3: Conscientiousness**
1. General leadership	7. General trustworthiness
2. Interest in negotiations	8. Adherence to a work ethic
3. Achievement striving	9. Thoroughness and attentiveness to details
Category 2: Agreeableness	**Category 4: Emotional stability**
4. Friendly disposition	10. Emotional stability
5. Sensitivity to interest of others	**Category 5: Intellectance**
6. Cooperative or collaborative work tendency	11. Desire to generate ideas 12. Tendency to think things through

Source: Adapted from Patrick Raymark, Mark Schmit, and Robert Guion, "Identifying Useful Personality Constructs for Employee Selection," *Personnel Psychology*, Vol. 50 (3), 1997, pp. 723–736.

ment, (4) communicating, (5) interpersonal activities and relationships, and (6) technical activities. The second section of the PMPQ concerns the personal requirements needed for job performance. This section contains personal development items dealing with the educational, training, and experience requirements of the job. The section also includes personal characteristics items used to indicate whether traits such as adaptability are needed on the job. The final section of the PMPQ, other information, includes items on the number of personnel supervised by the employee, whether the employee is a member of professional organizations or has a professional license or certification, and the salary of the employee.

Cognitive Task Analysis As noted earlier in this chapter, an area of job analysis typically known as cognitive task analysis (CTA) has been developing over the past several years. CTA methods attempt to identify the critical cognitive skills/abilities and knowledge areas associated with task performance. There are a variety of methods for conducting CTA although most of them share the following basic phases:[45]

1. *Identifying cognitively oriented tasks in the job.* Jobs are analyzed using traditional job analysis methodologies to determine which tasks need to be the subject of a cognitive task analysis. This preliminary phase may collect job information using methods such as (a) reviews and analyses of written job information; (b) unstructured or structured interviews; or (c) structured questionnaires. As with many traditional job analysis procedures, information is usually collected on the importance, typicality, and frequency of job activities.
2. *Identifying **knowledge representations.*** Subject matter experts (SMEs) are asked to identify the broad areas of knowledge involved in each task; that is, the general types of knowledge needed to perform the task successfully.
3. ***Knowledge elicitation.*** Structured interviews with SMEs and computer-aided knowledge elicitation methods are used to obtain detailed information about the type of cognitive skills and knowledge used to perform each job task. In-

cumbents can be limited in their ability to access the relevant knowledge and skills they need to perform a task. Much goes on below the conscious level, particularly when tasks are performed under extreme time pressure or when the task has significant cognitive or motor components. Because of this, **process-tracing** methods are usually used. One process-tracing method involves the observation of individuals engaged in "expert performance," which is videotaped, then carefully and elaborately analyzed and coded. Another process-tracing method is the "verbal think aloud" approach in which SMEs perform a representative set of task problems and "think aloud" as they do so. A job analyst records their thoughts, and when SMEs become silent during the performance of a task, the job analyst encourages them to verbalize the things that are going on in their minds as they complete the task.[46]

There are many specific methodologies for conducting cognitive task analysis. One of the major problems with this group of methods is that there is no consensus as to the appropriate taxonomy of cognitive skills/abilities and knowledge areas that should be used when analyzing tasks. Scholars are working on this problem and attempting to develop taxonomies of cognitive skills that are large enough to make the analysis of a wide variety of jobs possible, but not so large as to be practically unwieldy.[47] One particularly interesting area within the CTA domain has been the development of CTA procedures for use in analyzing the complex cognitive functions that occur when job performance is dependent on a team of employees. To date, these methods remain at the developmental stage, but further work in this area should prove highly useful in understanding the nature of work in the twenty-first century and beyond.[48] In general, cognitive task analysis methods represent a welcome addition to more traditional methods of job analysis.

PHASE 3: DATA COLLECTION AND ANALYSIS

The job analyst must deal with several issues related to collecting and analyzing job data. The job analyst may have made all the right decisions up to this point about the scope and method of the job analysis project. However, if the procedures used in collecting the job data and analyzing those data are incomplete or incorrect, the job analysis project will be a failure.

Collecting Job Data

The first important aspect of collecting job data is to get the organization ready. Second, the job analyst must be aware of the sources of bias that may influence the accuracy of the data collected. Finally, the job analyst must be sure that interviews, if used, are conducted in a skillful manner.

Getting the Organization Ready Before data collection can begin, the job analyst must make sure that members of the organization understand and are committed to the project. Management should be involved closely in the development of the project. The job analyst must liaise closely with the organization's internal HR unit and also with any supervisors whose employees may be involved in the data collection process. Perhaps most important, a clearly stated rationale and set of goals for the project must be provided to all organizational members who participate in the project.

Sources of Bias The primary concern in collecting data about a job is that these data provide an accurate, up-to-date, and representative picture of work activities. One major source of bias that can occur during data collection results from the sampling procedures used to select data sources. As noted earlier in this chapter in our discussion of the sources of job information, it is important to collect job data from the type of people who actually do the job. Factors such as the gender and experience of the job incumbent can influence how the job is described. Jobs also change over time. For example, the work activities of a farmer in midsummer are quite different from those in midwinter. Thus the job analysis should be sure to identify any changes in the job due to these time factors. Finally, jobs may change due to technology or other situational factors. The job of a person doing architectural drawings by hand is very different from that of a person doing the same drawing using the latest computer-assisted design software. The job of an insurance salesperson in Tampa, Florida, may change dramatically if a hurricane roars through the city. Thus the job data obtained must reflect these situationally determined changes so that they are recognized and incorporated into the overall picture of the job.

Job Analysis Interviews E. J. McCormick provides a useful set of guidelines for conducting job analysis interviews (see Figure 4.4). Although such guidelines are helpful, there are no simple methods for conducting good interviews. Interviewing is a skill that must be developed through practice.

Analyzing Job Data

Once quantitative job data are collected, numerous methods are available for analyzing them. What statistical analyses will be done should be decided before data are collected; otherwise, the job analyst may find that the data collected are not amenable to the analysis procedures chosen.

If job data are collected from several sources (e.g., several job incumbents), the job analyst should always check **inter-rater reliability;** that is, how well these sources agree on the characteristics of the job. A low level of agreement among data sources would indicate that either some sort of bias is present or major differences in the jobs of the respondents exist.[49]

Reporting and Rechecking Job Data

Once all the analyses have been completed, the job analyst prepares a report that typically includes the purpose and scope of the project, a summary of the specific methods used and why they were used, an explanation of the analyses conducted and what information they provided, and a strategy as to how the information gained from the project can be used in the future. The report should be written in a form that is easy for the average manager (with no technical expertise in job analysis methods) to understand. The very best job analysis project is worthless unless managers can understand what was done and what the results of the project were.

The final part of the job analysis process is to recheck the results of the project periodically. Jobs are dynamic, and the information collected about a job today may not accurately represent the job five years from now. Data must be updated periodically to incorporate job changes; otherwise, the organization may find itself

FIGURE 4.4

Guidelines for Job Analysis Interviewing

Source: Reprinted from *Job Analysis: Methods and Applications.* Copyright © 1979 AMACOM, a division of American Management Association. Published by AMACOM, a division of American Management Association International New York, NY. Reprinted by permission of the publisher. All rights reserved. http://www.amacombooks.org

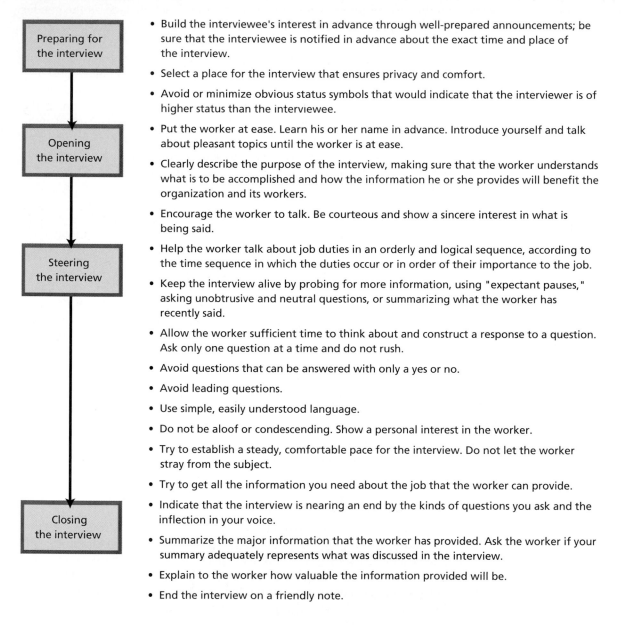

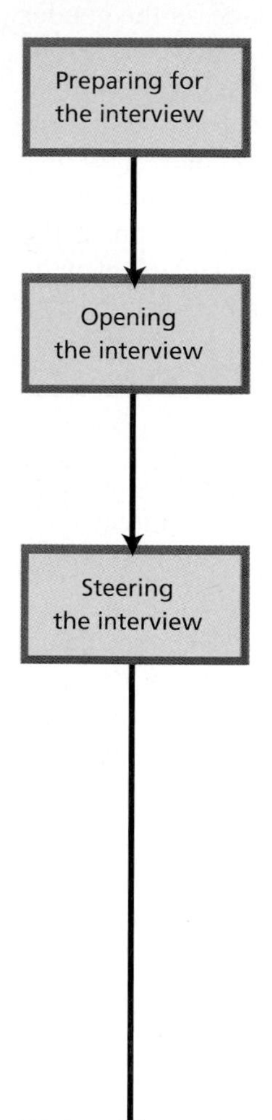

- Build the interviewee's interest in advance through well-prepared announcements; be sure that the interviewee is notified in advance about the exact time and place of the interview.
- Select a place for the interview that ensures privacy and comfort.
- Avoid or minimize obvious status symbols that would indicate that the interviewer is of higher status than the interviewee.
- Put the worker at ease. Learn his or her name in advance. Introduce yourself and talk about pleasant topics until the worker is at ease.
- Clearly describe the purpose of the interview, making sure that the worker understands what is to be accomplished and how the information he or she provides will benefit the organization and its workers.
- Encourage the worker to talk. Be courteous and show a sincere interest in what is being said.
- Help the worker talk about job duties in an orderly and logical sequence, according to the time sequence in which the duties occur or in order of their importance to the job.
- Keep the interview alive by probing for more information, using "expectant pauses," asking unobtrusive and neutral questions, or summarizing what the worker has recently said.
- Allow the worker sufficient time to think about and construct a response to a question. Ask only one question at a time and do not rush.
- Avoid questions that can be answered with only a yes or no.
- Avoid leading questions.
- Use simple, easily understood language.
- Do not be aloof or condescending. Show a personal interest in the worker.
- Try to establish a steady, comfortable pace for the interview. Do not let the worker stray from the subject.
- Try to get all the information you need about the job that the worker can provide.
- Indicate that the interview is nearing an end by the kinds of questions you ask and the inflection in your voice.
- Summarize the major information that the worker has provided. Ask the worker if your summary adequately represents what was discussed in the interview.
- Explain to the worker how valuable the information provided will be.
- End the interview on a friendly note.

selecting, training, or appraising the performance of employees for jobs that no longer exist.

PHASE 4: ASSESSING TRADITIONAL JOB ANALYSIS METHODS

Several factors have traditionally been used to assess job analysis methods. Some criteria that serve as the basis for assessments are presented in Table 4.6. Although these criteria can be helpful in comparing different methods, which method is best depends on the particular objectives of the organization as well as on cost limitations and other factors governing the project.

Legality is also a criterion that should be used to assess whether a job analysis method would be acceptable to the courts if it were used as evidence to support the personnel selection, training, performance appraisal, or pay practices of the organization. In the resolution of its employment discrimination lawsuit against Griffin Pipe Products Company, the U.S. Equal Employment Opportunity Commission required "a job analysis of each salaried position at the facility involving the supervision of union workers. The job analysis will identify those job qualifications necessary to successful performance of the job. Assessment of job candidates will be based upon these qualifications by means of interview questions or written submissions keyed to actual job behaviors."[50] In general, the history of court and EEOC actions related to job analysis suggest a number of guidelines for job analysis procedures. First, the purposes of the job analysis should be clear and the results used only for those purposes. Job data should be collected from several sources, including representative and knowledgeable human sources. A job analysis should list all tasks performed on the job and also make clear which tasks are

TABLE 4.6

Ten Criteria for Assessing Job Analysis Methods

Number	Criterion	Definition
1	Purposes served	Can the data collected be used for a variety of purposes?
2	Versatility	Can a method be used to analyze many different jobs?
3	Standardization	Does a method provide data that can be easily compared to data collected by other methods?
4	User acceptability	Do users of the method accept it as a reasonable way to collect job data?
5	Training required	How much training is needed before individuals can use it to collect data in the organization?
6	Sample size	How large a sampling of information sources is needed before an adequate picture of the job can be obtained?
7	Off the shelf	Can the method be used directly off the shelf, or must considerable development work be done to tailor it for use in a particular organization?
8	Reliability	Does the method produce reliable data?
9	Time to complete	How long does it take to analyze a job using the method?
10	Cost	How much does the method cost to implement and use?

Source: From E. L. Levine, R. A. Ash, M. Hall, and F. Sistrunk, "Evaluation of Job Analysis Methods by Experienced Job Analysts," *Academy of Management Journal*, Vol. 26 (1983), pp. 339–348. Reprinted by permission.

most important. Job analyses used to justify the use of ability, skill, or knowledge tests in selection should indicate a clear, justifiable link between tasks performed on the job and each skill, ability, and knowledge tested for in the selection process. Job analysis data should be checked regularly for reliability and validity, and the results of a job analysis should be reported in a written form that is clear and easily understood.

Of late there have been calls to concentrate more on the accuracy of the inferences made in the job analysis process than on the accuracy of the data collected. The "**job-descriptive inference**" involves the extent to which a job description and lists of tasks and duties adequately represent the work activities that underlie job performance. The "job-specification inference" involves listing knowledge, skills, abilities, and other characteristics (KSAOs) that can be tied to specific behaviors identified in a job description.[51] For example, the job of a salesperson may involve making audiovisual presentations. An inference has to be made in this instance about the extent to which an effective presentation taps into the product knowledge, communication skills, and persuasive skills of a salesperson. An organization that fails to appreciate the fact that making good presentations involves more than merely possessing good communication skills may end up hiring wrong candidates or misdirecting its training effort. No matter how accurate the data collected are (e.g., presentations *are* important), if inferences made are erroneous (e.g., oral communication skills are the *only* requirements for making presentations), then job analysis will not prove useful.

THE "NEW STRATEGIC VIEW" OF JOB ANALYSIS

As discussed in Chapter 2, there has been a substantial shift from traditional human resource management to strategic human resource management (SHRM). Perhaps the key aspect of SHRM is the linkage of HR practices to business strategy, but the SHRM approach also requires HR practitioners to be more focused on proactive, future-oriented management of human resources. This proactive, future-oriented philosophy applies to job analysis as much as it does to all other HR practices and procedures. Historically, research and practice in traditional job analysis have focused on developing better methods of measuring the content of jobs. In traditional research, the concept of "better" was typically operationalized as some set of psychometric criteria such as increased inter-rater agreement or more consistent factor structures in items across time and situations. These psychometric criteria remain essential elements of a good job analysis instrument. However, over the past ten or fifteen years, researchers have been developing job analysis methods that can adequately measure changes in the nature of jobs and predict those changes into the future. In this section we describe some of the methods of job analysis that meet the strategic HRM challenge of measuring what employees do in a rapidly changing organizational environment.

Future-Oriented, Strategic Job Analysis

The main objective of **future-oriented, strategic job analysis** is to identify the tasks, skills, abilities, and knowledge that will be needed to perform the job in the future. In one study job experts used a standard job analysis methodology to look at the future requirements of a job. Next the experts were asked to predict changes in technology, population, social values, and other social and business factors that might impinge on the nature of work in their organization. Finally, they were asked to predict how these external changes would affect the nature of jobs performed within the firm. These data were then used to describe the tasks, skills, knowledge, and abilities needed for doing the job in the future.[52]

William George reported a case in which an organization was changing its strategic focus to an increased "customer-conscious" orientation.[53] To help employees understand the nature of this strategic shift, job descriptions were altered to focus more on "what we want to be doing in the future" rather than on what was actually being done in current jobs. Most future-oriented job analyses adapt traditional job analysis methods to allow organizations to anticipate the nature of job changes. This gives organizations time to better prepare their current employees for the changes as well as time to redeploy employees to the new jobs when their old jobs disappear rather than having to terminate their current work force and hire a new one.

Job Analysis: A More Generic Approach to What We Measure

In discussing the nature of air traffic control jobs, the European Organization for the Safety of Air Navigation pointed out in 2001 that in the future more "flexibility and adaptability towards evolutionary changes in working environment and conditions will probably be required" of individuals working in that profession.[54] This statement is not only true for air traffic controllers but is also applicable to many jobs in the twenty-first century. A range of skills that enable individuals to adapt to changing work demands are increasingly important in modern jobs. As early as 1992, Cardy and Dobbins argued that job analysis should focus more on "generic personal characteristics or work behaviors that are important for competitive success."[55] They refer to this approach as **generic job analysis** and argue that the more dynamic jobs are, the more job analysis procedures must focus on broad and generic rather than narrow and task-specific measures of job content.

Although many traditional methods of job analysis focus on concrete tasks and duties, several of them include job descriptors that can be used to describe activities that are involved in a wide variety of jobs. For example, data from the Position Analysis Questionnaire (described earlier in this chapter) and the Occupational Analysis Inventory have been used to provide information about the extent to which generic human "attributes" are needed on a job. These attributes include such things as convergent and divergent thinking, intelligence, dealing with people, empathy, working alone, or dealing with concepts and information.[56] In a study of generic work behaviors in the retailing industry, the researcher was able to identify nine generic behavior dimensions (e.g., thoroughness, unruliness, attendance, theft, drug misuse) that were applicable to a wide variety of retail jobs.[57] Many of the attributes contained in the O*NET database can be considered fairly generic in nature. For example, O*NET includes data on *basic skills* that relate to an individual's capacity to learn and acquire new knowledge; *cross-functional skills* that facilitate performance across different job contexts; *abilities* that are relatively enduring basic capacities for performing a wide range of different tasks; and *work styles,* which represent a range of personality and dispositional factors (see Table

4.2). Finally, personality traits such as those measured by the Personality-Related Position Requirements Form (PPRF) are also generic in nature and can be applied to a wide variety of jobs.

Competency modeling is a process that has been increasingly popular and, as typically conducted, represents a broader, more generic approach to measuring job characteristics. Competencies are "a set of observable performance dimensions, including individual knowledge, skills, attitudes, and behaviors, as well as collective team, process, and organizational capabilities, that are linked to high performance, and provide the organization with sustainable competitive advantage."[58] Two aspects of this definition are important. First, competencies represent a broad range of characteristics. Second, competencies are those characteristics that differentiate effective from ineffective performers or are in some way critical to particular competitive strategies in which an organization may engage.

A number of major kinds of competencies have been identified.[59] These include the following:

- **Task competencies:** Abilities needed to do the tasks and activities on a job, such as sweeping a floor.
- **Results competencies:** Abilities needed to achieve some specific result on a job, such as achieving a 15 percent profit.
- **Output competencies:** Abilities needed to produce some specified output, such as designing a product.
- **Knowledge, skill, and attitude competencies:** Subject matter knowledge, process abilities, attitudes, values, orientations, or commitments needed to be effective.
- **Superior performer differentiators:** Abilities rooted in a person's intelligence and personality that are possessed by superior performers but not by other employees.
- **Attribute bundles:** A *collection* of knowledge, skills, attitudes, tasks, outputs, and results needed for effective performance, such as a "problem-solving attribute bundle" made up of some knowledge, such as technical know-how and problem-solving techniques; some skills, such as analytical skills and lateral thinking; and some attitudes, values, orientations, and commitments, such as achievement orientation and integrity.

As there are many different kinds of competencies, there are also many different methods by which the competency requirements of jobs are determined. These competency-modeling methods are very much like those used in more traditional job analysis procedures, but they are focused on a broader range of job competency requirements and typically have an orientation toward future changes in the nature of the job. Many of these methods examine those factors that distinguish between top performers and other employees. Subject matter experts are also often asked to anticipate changes in the competencies required in employees as a result of strategy changes or changes in the business environment in which a firm operates.[60]

A significant amount of competency research has focused on identifying **managerial competencies** relevant to specific managerial jobs or to the more generic

TABLE 4.7

A Summary of Managerial Competencies

Dimension	Competencies
Traditional Functions	1. Problem Awareness
	2. Decision Making
	3. Directing
	4. Decision Delegation
	5. Short-Term Planning
	6. Strategic Planning
	7. Coordinating
	8. Goal Setting
	9. Monitoring
	10. Motivating by Authority
	11. Motivating by Persuasion
	12. Team Building
	13. Productivity
Task Orientation	14. Initiative
	15. Task Focus
	16. Urgency
	17. Decisiveness
Person Orientation	18. Compassion
	19. Cooperation
	20. Sociability
	21. Politeness
	22. Political Astuteness
	23. Assertiveness
	24. Seeking Input
	25. Customer Focus
Dependability	26. Orderliness
	27. Rule Orientation
	28. Personal Responsibility
	29. Trustworthiness
	30. Timeliness
	31. Professionalism
	32. Loyalty
Open Mindedness	33. Tolerance
	34. Adaptability
	35. Creative Thinking
	36. Cultural Appreciation
	37. Emotional Control
	38. Resilience
	39. Stress Management

(continued)

TABLE 4.7
Continued

Dimension	Competencies
Communication	40. Listening
	41. Oral Communication
	42. Public Presentation
	43. Written Communication
Developing Self and Others	44. Developmental Goal Setting
	45. Performance Assessment
	46. Developmental Feedback
	47. Job Enrichment
	48. Self-Development
Occupational Acumen and Concerns	49. Technical Proficiency
	50. Organizational Awareness
	51. Quality Concern
	52. Quantity Concern
	53. Financial Concern
	54. Safety Concern

Source: Robert P. Tett; Hal A. Guterman; Angela Bleier, and Patrick J. Murphy, "Development and Content Validation of a 'Hyperdimensional' Taxonomy of Managerial Competence," *Human Performance,* Vol. 13 (3), 2000, pp. 205–251.

occupation of "manager."[61] A list of common managerial competencies is presented in Table 4.7. In addition to research studies on managerial competencies in general, many firms are using competency-modeling procedures to identify the critical competencies for managers in their firm. Often these competency models are hierarchical in nature, identifying a set of core competencies that all managers must possess as well as competencies applicable to different managerial levels within the firm. An example of such a model is presented in Figure 4.5.

The Traditional and Strategic Views of Job Analysis: Working Together

The area of competency modeling is a good example of how critical aspects of both the traditional and "new strategic view" of job analysis fit well together. As noted, competency modeling focuses on more generic characteristics required by jobs and typically takes a dynamic, future-oriented view of these characteristics. However, within this new approach, researchers have acknowledged that much work needs to be done to ensure that competency-modeling methods also meet the psychometric qualities relating to reliability and accuracy of more traditional methods. Better, easier-to-use, and more reliable methods are needed to assess job competencies and other strategic or generic aspects of jobs. The "new view" of job analysis that is really needed is one that combines the emphasis of the "strategic view" of job analysis with the methodological rigor that has long characterized more traditional methods.

FIGURE 4.5

Multilevel Corporate Competency Model

Source: Adapted from Elmer Burack, Wayne Hockwarter, and Nicholas Mathys, "The New Management Development Paradigm," *Human Resource Planning,* Vol. 80 (1), 1997, pp. 14–21.

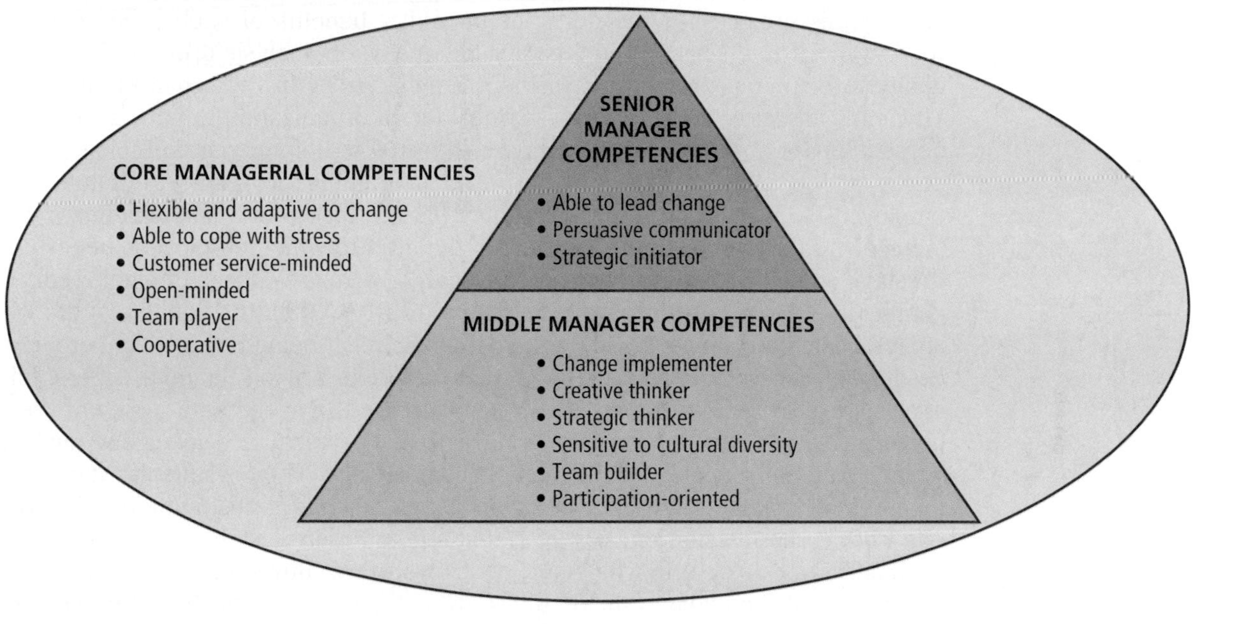

JOB ANALYSIS: ADDING VALUE TO THE ORGANIZATION

Regardless of which approach is taken to job analysis, any job analysis effort must, in the end, add value to the organization. The extent to which job analysis programs add value can be measured in many ways. The essence of any measure of value added by an HR activity is an assessment of the relative costs versus benefits of the activity. The criteria described in Table 4.6 provide insight into the likely value-adding ability of any job analysis project, at least in terms of the costs of the project. Job analysis methods that can serve several purposes, that can be used to analyze many different jobs, and that are standardized such that comparisons across jobs are made easy have more value-adding potential than job analysis systems of a more restricted nature. User acceptability relates directly to the reaction of stakeholders in the job analysis program. If users (and those whose jobs are analyzed) react negatively to the process, then the value added to the firm is reduced. Job analysis methods that are off the shelf or require relatively small sample sizes will reduce the dollar cost of job analysis programs considerably. Job analysis methods that require little training of those who use them reduce the direct costs to the organization of any training programs needed. Job analysis methods that can be completed quickly (e.g., paper-and-pencil checklist methods versus extensive interviews) also will have greater potential for adding value due to their lower cost in time and effort. The reliability of the data collected by job analysis methods also affects its value-adding potential because unreliable data have little chance of providing useful information to the organization. The cost of job analysis materials also will determine value added. Job analysis methods that have questionable legality may cost the firm many tens of thousands of dollars if the company is taken to court.

The preceding criteria can help HR managers determine the likely costs of any job analysis project, but the dollar or nondollar benefits of such programs are more difficult to assess. The ultimate value of any job analysis program lies in its ability to help employees perform their strategic roles in the organization more efficiently and effectively. Thus it is critical for an organization to have a clear understanding of how job analysis data are expected to help increase employee productivity. Job analysis data could be used in training programs to "multiskill" employees so that they can perform more varied work roles. The benefits of the job analysis data are then determined by the level to which employees better understand and perform varied tasks. If job analysis data are collected to help reduce conflict in the firm resulting from "territorial overlap," then the benefits of the job analysis data must be assessed on the basis of conflict being reduced and employees having a clearer understanding of what their roles are in relation to others. Job analysis data collected to help employees increase the speed and quality of their performance must be assessed using measures of performance speed and quality, which can then be translated into actual dollar savings. The possible list of criteria for use in determining the benefits of job analysis data is almost infinite. It is obvious from earlier discussion, however, that one criterion that must be included in such a list is the extent to which any job analysis procedure helps an organization anticipate and then adapt quickly to the dynamic environment that characterizes business life in the twenty-first century.

SUMMARY OF KEY POINTS

The nature of jobs is changing. The stable, relatively finite groups of tasks that have made up employees' jobs have become far less stable and considerably less finite. Jobs are broader and subject to frequent alteration. Because jobs are changing, the traditional approaches to job analysis may need to change as well. Greater emphasis must be placed on identifying how jobs are likely to change in the future. In situations of change, job analysis methods may have to focus more on identifying the generic personal characteristics of employees that enable them to function well in a dynamic environment. However, traditional methods of job analysis can serve as the basis for these future-oriented, strategic job analysis procedures.

Given this increasingly complex work environment, conducting a good job analysis is far more complex and difficult than it might seem. It requires that the job analyst make many important decisions. The analyst, in conjunction with management, must decide on the purpose and desired uses of the job analysis data. Job analysis may be used for human resource planning and recruitment. It also may be used to develop sound employee selection and placement procedures. Job analysis serves as the basis for developing training and performance appraisal programs and can be used to set wage rates across different jobs.

Once the organization decides how it intends to use the job analysis data, the job analyst must determine what jobs will be analyzed, what type of information is needed, and the sources of that information. Information about behavioral descriptors, ability requirements, and other job characteristics, such as the motivational nature of the job, can be collected. The job analyst also may want information concerning the machines, tools, and equipment used on the job and the working conditions in which the job takes place. The analyst can choose among a variety of human and nonhuman sources to provide these data.

Based on these decisions, the job analyst chooses from a myriad of job analysis procedures, ranging from simple narrative descriptions to highly complex micromotion or structured procedures. The functional job analysis method provides data that are useful in identifying worker traits needed to perform the job as well as information useful in developing standards for employee performance. The task inventory is excellent for collecting data from large numbers of job incumbents and is particularly helpful in developing personnel selection tests and training programs. The Position Analysis Questionnaire is an excellent method for comparing a wide variety of very different jobs. Cognitive task analysis methods are helping us to understand the increasing cognitive demands that modern jobs require.

Once job data are collected, they must be analyzed for reliability and accuracy and then summarized and used within the organization. The job analyst must recheck these data periodically and assess their overall value—their costs and benefits—to the organization, as well as their versatility.

Job analysis methods should be designed so that they can be performed reliably and in a standardized way throughout the organization. Methods should be assessed in terms of the time needed to teach individuals how to do the analysis, the time needed to complete the analysis, and the costs of collecting data. Any method used by an organization also should conform to standards set down in recent legal decisions that have specified what the courts consider a "good" job analysis procedure. It is also important to have clear measures of the expected benefits of job analysis programs, as well as the dollar costs of conducting them, so that the level of value adding achieved through job analysis projects can be assessed.

THE MANAGER'S VOCABULARY

ability requirements scales
area work activities
attribute bundles
behavioral contracting
Career Exploration Tools
cognitive abilities
cognitive task analysis (CTA)
competency modeling
critical incidents technique (CIT)
Dictionary of Occupational Titles (DOT)
duty
engineering approaches
foundation work activities
functional job analysis (FJA)
future-oriented, strategic job analysis
generic job analysis
intermediate work activities
inter-rater reliability
job
job analysis
job classification
job description
job-descriptive inference
job extinction
job specification
knowledge elicitation
knowledge representations
knowledge, skill, and attitude competencies
managerial competencies
micromotion studies
narrative job descriptions
Occupational Information Network (O*NET)
output competencies
personality-related job analysis procedures
Personality-Related Position Requirements Form (PPRF)
physical abilities
position
Position Analysis Questionnaire (PAQ)
process tracing
Professional and Managerial Position Questionnaire (PMPQ)
psychomotor abilities
qualitative data
quantitative data
realistic job preview
results competencies
situational abilities
subject matter experts (SMEs)
superior performer differentiators
task
task competencies
task inventory
time and motion study

QUESTIONS FOR DISCUSSION

1. What is behavioral contracting, and how is it different from the traditional view of the nature of jobs?
2. What is job analysis, and why is it important to an organization?
3. What is the difference between a job description and a job specification?
4. Suppose your company was hiring information systems technicians and wants to develop a method for selecting job applicants with the highest potential for doing well on the job. What types of information from the Occupational Information Network (O*NET) could be useful in setting up this selection system?
5. How do the advantages of quantitative job data compare with those of qualitative job data?
6. What general guidelines should the HR specialist use when deciding how many and what sources of job information to use in a job analysis project?
7. How does cognitive task analysis differ from more traditional methods of job analysis such as the Position Analysis Questionnaire or functional job analysis?
8. Table 4.6 lists ten criteria for assessing job analysis methods. Suppose you are the HR manager of a small company employing 150 people. Which of the ten criteria would you find most important in assessing a job analysis project? Suppose your company had 5,000 employees rather than 150. Would the list of most important criteria change for you? Why or why not?
9. According to the strategic view of job analysis, job analysis procedures need to be more future-oriented and strategic. Job analysis procedures also need to be more generic in nature. What is meant by future-oriented, strategic job analysis? What kinds of information would be collected in a generic job analysis procedure?
10. What is a "competency"? What is competency modeling, and how does it exemplify the strategic view of job analysis?

Exercise 4.1
Conducting a Job Analysis

This exercise will give you some hands-on experience in conducting a job analysis. Interview a job incumbent and use the information you collect in that interview to describe the job performed by the incumbent. It is important that the job incumbent has held the position long enough to really know what it involves. In conducting the job interview, you should first review the job analysis form and instructions provided here. In your interview, you must collect enough information about the job to complete this form. Before starting the interview, spend some time planning how you will proceed and write down some of the questions you will ask.

Option 1: Redo the job analysis you have conducted on the current job, this time describing the job as it will be ten years in the future. How will the job change? What new skills and abilities will be needed? What tasks and duties will no longer be performed or will be performed in a very different manner?

Option 2: Try your hand at process tracing for this job. Select one of the tasks that must be performed on the job that requires a high level of cognitive activity. Ask the job incumbent to do this task for you while "thinking aloud" about the knowledge and cognitive processes used to perform the task. If it is impossible for the person to actually do the task, have the individual talk you through the task step by step. At each step, the job incumbent should explain what he or she would do and what knowledge and cognitive activities he or she would be engaged in.

Instructions for Filling Out the Job Analysis Form

1. Job identification
   - Organization: name of organization
   - Incumbent: name of job incumbent interviewed
   - Analyst: name of person analyzing job
   - Date: date of interview

2. *Job summary.* Provide an overview (one to three sentences) of the job being analyzed. Do not write this job summary until you have completed the remaining parts of the job analysis form.
3. *Duties performed.* Identify the major duties performed on the job. Arrange these duties in either chronological order (i.e., in the time sequence in which the tasks are usually performed) or order of importance to the job. Indicate the percentage of time spent on each duty during a typical workday. Also indicate the importance of each duty to the job. It may be that a large amount of time is spent on tasks that are not really that important for successful job performance. You will probably need more space than provided on this sample form.
4. *Supervision given.* How many subordinates does the job incumbent supervise? What are the titles of those subordinates?
5. *Supervision received.* What is the job title of the job incumbent's supervisor? How closely is the incumbent supervised?
6. *Relationship to other jobs.* Promoted from: What position would the incumbent usually hold prior to this job? Promoted to: What is the most likely position to which the incumbent would be promoted?
7. *Machines, tools, and equipment used.* List these devices, and define any that are not commonly known.
8. *Working conditions.* Indicate the physical environment of the job (e.g., indoors or outdoors, physically hazardous surroundings).
9. *Job specifications*
   - Physical requirements: List any special physical skills or abilities needed to perform the job (e.g., being able to lift fifty pounds).
   - Educational requirements: Indicate the minimum level of education necessary *to perform the job.* Do not list what the organization specifies as the necessary educational level because organizations often require a higher level of education than is actually needed to perform the job. Also list any certificates or licenses required.
   - Special skills: List any special skills needed (e.g., the artistic skills of a musician).
   - Experience required: What previous experience is necessary to perform the job? Do not include "experience" that is easily acquired on the job.
   - Training required after hire: Indicate any specific job training that is necessary after the employee enters the job.
10. *Unusual terms.* Define any terms used in the preceding analysis that would not be commonly understood.

Job Analysis Form

1. *Job identification* ____________________
   Organization ____________________
   Job title ____________________
   Incumbent ____________________
   Analyst ____________________
   Date ____________________
2. *Job summary*
3. *Duties performed*
4. *Supervision given*
5. *Supervision received*
6. *Relationship to other jobs*
   Promoted from:
   Promoted to:
7. *Machines, tools, and equipment used*
8. *Working conditions*
9. *Job specifications*
   Physical requirements:
   Educational requirements:
   Special skills:
   Experience required:
   Training required after hire:
10. *Unusual terms*

Exercise 4.2
Planning a Job Analysis Project

For each of the following jobs and organizational situations, indicate the type of job analysis method(s) that would be most appropriate, identify from whom information about the job should be collected and what kind of data would be best to collect, and discuss any particular problems that might confront the job analyst. Be sure to indicate how your choices will help to ensure that your job analysis efforts are seen as reliable and valid by members of the organization. You may have to make assumptions about the firm. Feel free to do so, but indicate what your assumptions are.

Scenario A Pangigantic is a large firm that manufactures electronics components. Most of the work is done by assemblers at an assembly line. The jobs tend to be fairly simple and repetitive in nature. The firm has begun an effort to increase productivity by improving the design of the machinery used in manufacture as well as selecting better, more skilled people to work on the line.

Scenario B Archi-Builders, Inc. is a small firm providing architectural and interior design services to customers in a fairly limited geographic area. Projects are typically done using a "team-based" approach involving architects, engineers, interior designers, and building construction specialists. The CEO of the firm has asked you to help analyze the "job" of these project teams with the hope that work design and scheduling as well as employee selection and training can be improved.

Scenario C Bore All, Pty., Ltd. is a medium-sized Australian firm that specializes in drilling water wells (known as "bores" in Australia). Profits from the firm have been decreasing over the past four years, and the board of directors has approached you to help them design the job of and help hire the new CEO of Bore All. The chair of the board of directors indicates that in the past the CEO of Bore All has been "one of those engineer-types, great at drilling wells, but not much of an entrepreneur." It is obvious that the job of the new CEO will be very different from the typical CEO job in the past.

Exercise 4.3
*An Internet Encounter with O*NET*

The U.S. Department of Labor has developed the Occupational Information Network database, called O*NET, which is an advanced technology database system. Select a job that you would like to investigate, then use the Internet to visit the O*NET site. What sort of information is available within each of the O*NET product categories? How might organizations and individuals make use of this information? What sort of wage and salary information is available through the O*NET system? Within O*NET, find the link to the Job Accommodation Network. Visit this site. What useful information does it provide organizations? Visit the Career Exploration Tools site. Download and look at examples of the ability, interest, and work importance assessment instruments.

Option: Coordinate with your course instructor so that the ability, interest, and work importance assessment instruments along with their respective scoring software are available to the class. Take these tests, get your scores on the various ability, interest, and work importance dimensions, then go to the O*NET OnLine Web site (http://online.onetcenter.org/) and use the "skills search" application to identify occupations that require the abilities you possess and seem to match your interest and importance ratings.

NOTES AND REFERENCES

1. Anonymous, "Setting the Tone: Job Specifications and Person Specifications," *IRS Employment Review,* May 23, 2003, pp. 42–48.

2. E. J. McCormick, *Job Analysis: Methods and Applications* (New York: AMACOM, 1979), p. 20.

3. William Bridges, *Job Shift: How to Prosper in a Workplace Without Jobs* (St. Leonards, Australia: Allen & Unwin, 1995), p. 1.

4. H. L. Ammerman, *Performance Content for Job Training, Vol. 2* (Columbus, Ohio: Center for Vocational Education, Ohio State University, 1977), p. 21.

5. McCormick, *Job Analysis,* p. 19.

6. Greg Stewart and Kenneth Carson, "Moving Beyond the Mechanistic Model: An Alternative Approach for Contemporary Organizations," *Human*

Resource Management Review, Vol. 7 (2), 1997, pp. 157–184.
7. Ibid., p. 164.
8. Bob Cardy and Greg Dobbins, "Job Analysis in a Dynamic Environment," *Human Resources Division News,* Vol. 16 (1), 1992, p. 4.
9. Susan Chipman, Jan Maarten Schraagen, and Valerie Shalin, "Introduction to Cognitive Task Analysis," in *Cognitive Task Analysis,* eds. Jan Maarten Schraagen, Susan Chipman, and Valerie Shalin (Mahwah, N.J.: Lawrence Erlbaum, 2000), pp. 3–4.
10. Rosemarie Reynolds and Michael Brannick, "Is Job Analysis Doing the Job? Extending Job Analysis with Cognitive Task Analysis," *The Industrial-Organizational Psychologist,* Vol. 39 (1), 2001, pp. 63–67.
11. Cited in Allen Church, "From Both Sides Now: The Changing of the Job," *The Industrial Organizational Psychologist,* Vol. 33 (3), 1996, pp. 52–62.
12. McCormick, *Job Analysis,* p. 19.
13. U.S. Department of Labor, Office of Disability Employment Policy, Job Accommodation Network's Searchable Online Accommodation Resource (SOAR) system, http://www.jan.wvu.edu/soar/index.htm. (accessed December 22, 2003)
14. Equal Employment Opportunity Commission, *A Technical Assistance Manual on the Employment Provisions (Title I) of the Americans with Disabilities Act)* (Washington, D.C.: EEOC, 1992); and Krystin Mitchell, George Alliger, and Richard Morfopoulos, "Toward an ADA-Appropriate Job Analysis," *Human Resource Management Review,* Vol. 7 (1), 1997, pp. 5–26.
15. Jack McKillip, "Case Studies in Job Analysis and Training Evaluation," *International Journal of Training and Development,* Vol. 5 (4), 2001, pp. 283–289.
16. Roger Ballentine, J. W. Cunningham, and William E. Wimpee, "Air Force Enlisted Job Clusters: An Exploration in Numerical Classification," *Military Psychology,* Vol. 4 (2), 1992, pp. 87–102.
17. William Wooten, "Using Knowledge, Skill and Ability (KSA) Data to Identify Career Pathing Opportunities: An Application of Job Analysis to Internal Manpower Planning," *Public Personnel Administrator,* Vol. 22 (4), 1993, pp. 551–563.
18. Robert Heneman, "Job and Work Evaluation: A Literature Review," *Public Personnel Management,* Vol. 32 (1), 2003, pp. 47–71.
19. Jen A. Algera and Martin A. Greuter, "Job Analysis for Personnel Selection," in *Advances in Selection and Assessment,* eds. Mike Smith and Ivan Robertson (New York: Wiley, 1989), pp. 7–30.
20. J. W. Cunningham, D. W. Drewes, and T. E. Powell, "Framework for a Revised Standard Occupational Classification (SOC)," in *Seminar on Research Findings,* ed. Standard Occupational Classification Revision Policy Committee (No. 1995-398-319-40067) (Washington, D.C.: U.S. Government Printing Office, 1995), pp. 57–165.
21. E. A. Fleishman and M. K. Quaintance, *Taxonomies of Human Performance: The Description of Human Tasks* (Orlando, Fla.: Academic Press, 1984), pp. 162–167; E. A. Fleishman and M. D. Mumford, "Individual Attributes and Training Performance: Applications of Ability Taxonomies in Instructional Systems Designs," in *Training and Development: New Frontiers in Industrial and Organizational Psychology,* ed. I. Goldstein (San Francisco: Jossey-Bass, 1990); and L. D. Marquardt and E. J. McCormick, *Attribute Ratings and Profiles of the Job Elements of the Position Analysis Questionnaire (PAQ)* (West Lafayette, Ind.: Department of Psychological Sciences, Purdue University, 1972).
22. Timothy Athey and Michael Orth, "Emerging Competency Methods for the Future," *Human Resource Management,* Vol. 38 (3), 1999, pp. 215–226; and Robert P. Tett, Hal A. Guterman, Angela Bleier, and Patrick J. Murphy, "Development and Content Validation of a 'Hyperdimensional' Taxonomy of Managerial Competence," *Human Performance,* Vol. 13 (3), 2000, pp. 205–251.
23. Norman Peterson, Michael Mumford, Walter Borman, Richard Jeanneret, Edwin Fleishman, Kerry Levin, Michael Campion, Melinda Mayfield, Frederick Morgeson, Kenneth Pearlman, Marilyn Gowing, Anita Lancaster, Marilyn Silver, and Donna Dye, "Understanding Work Using The Occupational Information Network (O*NET): Implications for Practice and Research," *Personnel Psychology,* Vol. 54 (2), 2001, pp. 451–492.

24. Frederick Morgeson and Michael Campion, "Social and Cognitive Sources of Potential Inaccuracy in Job Analysis," *Journal of Applied Psychology,* Vol. 82 (5), 1997, pp. 627–655.
25. Douglas Pine, "Assessing the Validity of Job Ratings: An Empirical Study of False Reporting in Task Inventories," *Public Personnel Management,* Vol. 24 (4), 1995, pp. 451–460.
26. Kristin Prien, Erich Prien, and William Wooten, "Interrater Reliability in Job Analysis: Differences in Strategy and Perspective," *Public Personnel Management,* Vol. 32 (1), 2003, pp. 125–141; and Juan Sanchez, "Adapting Work Analysis to a Fast-Paced and Electronic Business World," *International Journal of Assessment and Selection,* Vol. 8 (4), 2000, pp. 207–215.
27. J. I. Sanchez, A. Zamora, and C. Viswesvaran, "Moderators of Agreement Between Incumbent and Non-Incumbent Ratings of Job Characteristics," *Journal of Occupational and Organizational Psychology,* Vol. 70, 1997, pp. 209–218.
28. J. Kevin Ford, Eleanor M. Smith, Douglas J. Sego, and Miguel A. Quinones, "Impact of Task Experience and Individual Factors on Training-Emphasis Ratings," *Journal of Applied Psychology,* Vol. 78 (4), 1993, pp. 583–590; Michael Lindell, Catherine Clause, Christina Brandt, and Ronald Landis, "Relationship Between Organizational Context and Job Analysis Task Ratings," *Journal of Applied Psychology,* Vol. 83 (5), 1998, pp. 769–796; Wendy Richman and Miguel Quinones, "Task Frequency Rating Accuracy: The Effect of Task Engagement and Experience," *Journal of Applied Psychology,* Vol. 81 (5), 1997, pp. 512–524; and Paul Spector and Suzy Fox, "Reducing Subjectivity in the Assessment of the Job Environment: Development of the Factual Autonomy Scale (FAS)," *Journal of Organizational Behavior,* Vol. 24, 2003, pp. 417–432.
29. Frank J. Landy and Joseph Vasey. "Job Analysis: The Composition of SME Samples," *Personnel Psychology,* Vol. 44 (1), 1991, pp. 27–50; Anda Papadopoulou, Elizabeth Ineson, and Derek Wilkie, "Convergence Between Sources of Service Job Analysis Data," *International Journal of Contemporary Hospitality Management,* Vol. 7 (2/3), 1995, pp. 42–47; and Wendy Richman and Miguel Quinones, "Task Frequency Rating Accuracy: The Effect of Task Engagement and Experience," *Journal of Applied Psychology,* Vol. 81(5), 1997, pp. 512–524.
30. For example: http://www.jobdescription.com/content/about; http://www.culpepper.com/subscription/jobs/default.asp; http://www.mycareer.com.au/jobseeker/home.aspx?RefTrk=Decide; http://www.workplacetoolbox.com/index.jsp.
31. McCormick, *Job Analysis,* pp. 76–77.
32. J. C. Flanagan, "The Critical Incidents Technique," *Psychological Bulletin,* Vol. 51, 1954, pp. 327–358.
33. Norman Peterson, Michael Mumford, Walter Borman, Richard Jeanneret, Edwin Fleishman, Kerry Levin, Michael Campion, Melinda Mayfield, Frederick Morgeson, Kenneth Pearlman, Marilyn Gowing, Anita Lancaster, Marilyn Silver, and Donna Dye, "Understanding Work Using the Occupational Information Network (O*NET): Implications for Practice and Research," *Personnel Psychology,* Vol. 54 (2), 2001, pp. 451–492.
34. U.S. Department of Labor, *Dictionary of Occupational Titles,* 4th ed., revised (Washington, D.C.: U.S. Government Printing Office, 1991).
35. Timothy Crespin and James Austin, "Computer Technology Applications in Industrial and Organizational Psychology," *Cyberpsychology & Behavior,* Vol. 5 (4), 2002, pp. 279–303; Leaetta M. Hough and Frederick L. Oswald, "Personnel Selection: Looking Toward the Future—Remembering the Past," *Annual Review of Psychology,* Vol. 51, 2000, pp. 631–664; and Richard Jeanneret and Mark Strong, "Linking O*NET Job Analysis Information to Job Requirement Predictors: An O*NET Application," *Personnel Psychology,* Vol. 56 (2), 2003, pp. 465–492.
36. Sidney Fine and Steven Cronshaw, *Functional Job Analysis: A Foundation for Human Resources Management* (Mahwah, NJ: Lawrence Erlbaum, 1999).
37. E. J. McCormick, P. R. Jeanneret, and R. C. Mecham, "A Study of Job Characteristics and Job Dimensions as Based on the Position Analysis Questionnaire (PAQ)," *Journal of Applied Psychology,* Vol. 56, 1972, pp. 347–368.
38. For example, see Calvin Hoffman, "Generalizing Physical Ability Test Validity: A Case Study Using Test Transport Ability, Validity Generalization, and Construct-Related Validation Evidence," *Personnel Psychology,* Vol. 52 (4), 1999, pp. 1019–1041.
39. McCormick, *Job Analysis,* pp. 117, 119.

40. Ammerman, *Performance Content for Job Training.*
41. E. A. Fleishman, *Manual for the Ability Requirements Scale (MARS, revised)* (Palo Alto, Calif.: Consulting Psychologists Press, 1991); and E. A. Fleishman and M. E. Reilly, *Human Abilities: Their Definition, Measurement, and Job Task Requirements* (Palo Alto, Calif.: Consulting Psychologists Press, 1991).
42. Michael Mount and Murray Barrick, "The Big Five Personality Dimensions: Implications for Research and Practice in Human Resource Management," *Research in Personnel and Human Resource Management,* Vol. 13, 1995, pp. 153–200; Samuel Gosling, Peter Rentfrow, and William B. Swann Jr., "A Very Brief Measure of the Big-Five Personality Domains," *Journal of Research in Personality,* Vol. 37 (6), 2003, pp. 504–528; and John Lounsbury, Eric Sundstrom, James Loveland, and Lucy Gibson, "Intelligence, 'Big Five' Personality Traits, and Work Drive as Predictors of Course Grade," *Personality & Individual Differences,* Vol. 35 (6), 2003, pp. 1231–1239.
43. Patrick Raymark, Mark Schmit, and Robert Guion, "Identifying Potentially Useful Personality Constructs for Employee Selection," *Personnel Psychology,* Vol. 50 (3), 1997, pp. 723–736.
44. J. L. Mitchell and E. J. McCormick, *Development of the PMPQ: A Structured Job Analysis Questionnaire for the Study of Professional and Managerial Positions* (West Lafayette, Ind.: Research Foundation, Purdue University, 1979).
45. Susan Chipman, Jan Maarten Schraagen, and Valerie Shalin, "Introduction to Cognitive Task Analysis," in *Cognitive Task Analysis* (see note 9), pp. 3–23.
46. David DuBois and Valerie Shalin, "Describing Job Expertise Using Cognitively Oriented Task Analyses (COTA)," in *Cognitive Task Analysis* (see note 9), pp. 41–55.
47. For example see Thomas Seamster, Richard Redding, and George Kaempf, "A Skilled-Based Cognitive Task Analysis Framework," in *Cognitive Task Analysis* (see note 9), pp. 135–146.
48. Wayne Zachary, Joan Ryder, and James Hicinbothom, "Building Cognitive Task Analyses and Models of a Decision-Making Team in a Complex Real-Time Environment," in *Cognitive Task Analysis* (see note 9), pp. 365–383.
49. Juan Sanchez and Edward Levine, "Accuracy or Consequential Validity: Which Is the Better Standard for Job Analysis Data?" *Journal of Organizational Behavior,* Vol. 21, 2000, pp. 809–818.
50. U.S. Equal Employment Opportunity Commission, "Griffin Pipe Products to Pay $100,000, and Implement Revamped Promotion Procedures: Settlement Benefits African-Americans Denied Promotion to Salaried Positions," Press Release, February 13, 2003, http://www.eeoc.gov/press/2-13-03b.html. (accessed December 24, 2003)
51. Fredrick P. Morgeson and Michael A. Campion, "Accuracy in Job Analysis: Toward an Inference-based Model," *Journal of Organizational Behavior,* Vol. 21, 2000, pp. 819–827; and Juan Sanchez and Edward Levine, "Accuracy or Consequential Validity: Which Is the Better Standard for Job Analysis Data?" *Journal of Organizational Behavior,* Vol. 21, 2000, pp. 809–818.
52. Benjamin Schneider and Andrea M. Konz, "Strategic Job Analysis," *Human Resource Management,* Vol. 28 (1), 1989, pp. 51–63.
53. William George, "Internal Marketing and Organizational Behavior: A Partnership in Developing Customer-Conscious Employees at Every Level," *Journal of Business Research,* Vol. 20, 1990, pp. 63–70.
54. European Organisation for the Safety of Air Navigation, European Air Traffic Management Programme, *Guidelines for Selection Procedures and Tests for Ab InitioTrainee Controllers (Revised),* EATMP Infocentre Reference: 010716.1, Edition 2.0, August 2001, Document Identifier HRS/MSP-002-GUI-01, EATMP Infocentre, Eurocontrol Headquarters, Brussels.
55. Cardy and Dobbins, "Job Analysis in a Dynamic Environment," p. 5.
56. J. W. Cunningham, R. R. Boese, R. W. Neeb, and J. J. Pass, "Systematically Derived Work Dimensions: Factor Analyses of the Occupational Analysis Inventory," *Journal of Applied Psychology,* Vol. 68 (2), 1983, pp. 232–252; J. W. Cunningham, Thomas Powell, William Wimpee, Mark Wilson, and Roger Ballentine, "Ability-Requirement Factors for General Job Elements," *Military Psychologist,* Vol. 8 (3), 1996, pp. 219–234; and McCormick, Jeanneret, and Mecham, "A Study of Job Characteristics and Job Dimensions as Based on the Position Analysis Questionnaire (PAQ)."

57. Steven Hunt, "Generic Work Behavior: An Investigation into the Dimensions of Entry-Level, Hourly Job Performance," *Personnel Psychology,* Vol. 49 (1), 1996, pp. 51–83.
58. Athey and Orth, "Emerging Competency Methods for the Future," p. 216.
59. Patricia McLagan, "Competencies: The Next Generation," *Training & Development,* Vol. 51 (5), 1997, pp. 40–47.
60. Ibid.
61. Robert P. Tett, Hal A. Guterman, Angela Bleier, and Patrick J. Murphy, "Development and Content Validation of a 'Hyperdimensional' Taxonomy of Managerial Competence," *Human Performance,* Vol. 13 (3), 2000, pp. 205–251.

PART 3

Acquiring Human Resources

CHAPTER 5

Equal Employment Opportunity: The Legal Environment

- The EEO Environment
- Discrimination Defined
- Legal and Regulatory Documents
- Enforcement of EEO Laws and Regulations
- Proving Illegal Discrimination
- Management's Response

HR Challenge

What does it take to be the poster company for sex discrimination? How about a suit with 1.6 million plaintiffs?—the largest civil rights action ever brought against a private employer in the United States. The potential number of plaintiffs is larger than one-quarter of the U.S. population. This is the distinction achieved by Wal-Mart in a suit alleging gender discrimination, now certified by federal Judge Martin Jenkins in San Francisco as a class action suit, allowing the lawsuit to apply to as many as 1.6 million current female employees and former female employees who worked for the company from December 1998.[1]

The original suit, filed in June 2001 by six former and current female employees, charged that the Bentonville, Arkansas, retailer systematically denies women workers equal pay and opportunities for promotion. Judge Jenkins found that the plaintiffs had enough evidence that the company had common pay and hiring practices across the country, raising the "inference that Wal-Mart engages in discriminatory practices in compensation and promotion that affect all plaintiffs in a common manner." Judge Jenkins also ruled that the class can pursue back pay for wage differences, lost earnings to those who were actually denied promotions, and punitive damages.[2] *Wal-Mart denies that it treats women differently and plans to appeal the decision of Judge Jenkins to certify the suit as a class action.*

The plaintiffs in the case claim the following:

- *Approximately two-thirds of Wal-Mart's hourly employees are women although they constitute only a little more than one-third of all its salaried managers.*

- *Full-time female hourly employees working at Wal-Mart earn 5 to 15 percent less than men in similar jobs—differences that cannot be explained by seniority or performance reviews.*
- *Female store managers earn 18 percent less than male counterparts.*
- *Women at Wal-Mart make up 89 percent of cashiers and 79 percent of department heads, both hourly nonmanagerial positions, but only 38 percent of assistant store managers and 15 percent of store managers are women at its more than 3,500 stores. In comparison, at 20 other large retailers a total of 57 percent of managers are women.*
- *Women comprise 4 percent of district managers, and few, if any, regional managers. There is only one woman among the 20 executive officers of Wal-Mart.*[3]

Of course, plaintiff allegations are a long way from findings of fact in court. However, most cases of this size and complexity are settled out of court, albeit for huge sums. For example, Home Depot, Inc. agreed to pay $104 million in 1997 to settle a class action suit on behalf of 25,000 women who claimed they were denied promotions because of their gender. Coca-Cola, in 2000, and Texaco, (now part of Chevron Texaco), in 1996, each paid well over $100 million to settle race discrimination cases.[4]

What would it take to settle this case? It is likely that Wal-Mart would have to agree to goals for boosting women in pay and rank. Such agreements were part of both the Coca-Cola and Texaco settlements. Wal-Mart has already taken steps to change its employment practices by creating a director of diversity and a compliance team. It also has restructured pay scales by providing clearly defined classes along with rules for starting wages and progress from class to class.

Clearly Wal-Mart has a long way to go to clean up its act as far as fair treatment of all employees. This leads to the question, what are the EEO standards needed to prevent being the poster company for gender discrimination? How should organizations respond to EEO complaints? More to the point, how can organizations prevent the types of issues that lead to large class action suits such as those experienced by Wal-Mart and other organizations? These important questions will be addressed as we consider the human resource legal environment.

In this chapter the term **equal employment opportunity (EEO)** is used to represent a collection of legal and social policies stating that members of U.S. society should have equal access to and treatment in employment. Since the mid-1960s, EEO laws and regulations have influenced almost every aspect of human resource management. All managers and supervisors must be familiar with EEO policies. Familiar or not, a recent survey showed a great deal of looking the other way. A survey by consulting firm KPMG of 2,300 blue- and white-collar workers in seventeen industries found that one-third of those surveyed said they had witnessed sexual harassment in the past year.[5] In addition, 36 percent of the respondents said they had observed employment discrimination. Clearly, even after forty years of EEO laws, further work needs to be done.

An organization should develop HR practices that are consistent with EEO laws and regulations for two reasons. First, equal employment opportunity is the law of the land. Companies that intentionally or unintentionally violate EEO laws are subject to a variety of penalties. These penalties include making back pay settlements of thousands of dollars, paying for the legal defense of the organization in court, paying the legal costs of the person or persons filing the charges of discrimination if the company is found guilty, and losing federal contracts that the company might have. The cases described in the HR Challenge (Home Depot, Coca-Cola, Texaco) are examples of the monetary cost of discrimination suits.[6] By any standard, settlements approaching $100 million should sound alarm bells in many corporate boardrooms.

The second reason for conforming to EEO laws and regulations is that it makes good sense from an HR perspective. The goal of human resource management is to make maximum use of all human resources available to an organization. By discriminating against individuals because of their race, sex, national origin, disability, or other characteristics, an organization is turning away potential employees who could make valuable contributions to the company. Obviously, the costs to an organization of such human resource losses are more difficult to measure than the direct monetary losses associated with court settlements. However, from the perspective of good human resource management, these human resource losses should be considered as significant as direct monetary losses.

This chapter describes the important components of the U.S. EEO environment with which all HRM specialists should be familiar to avoid both the financial and human costs inherent in violating EEO laws and regulations. In recent years, especially with the passage of the Americans with Disabilities Act, EEO laws have become increasingly complex. The descriptions provided herein should be very helpful, but organizations facing specific problems are advised to seek expert assistance.

THE EEO ENVIRONMENT

Several major components make up the EEO environment; they are shown in Table 5.1. Illegal discrimination in our society can take many forms, but this text focuses only on such discrimination in employment situations. Legal and regulatory documents include amendments to the U.S. Constitution; laws passed by the federal, state, and local governments; presidential executive orders; and guidelines prepared by government agencies. These documents define employment discrimination. Agents of enforcement include the Equal Employment Opportunity Commission, the Office of Federal Contract Compliance Programs, the Department of Justice, and the court systems. These agents can take a variety of administrative and judicial enforcement actions against organizations that discriminate illegally. The final component in the EEO environment is management and its preventive and corrective responses to EEO legislation and regulations.

DISCRIMINATION DEFINED

Many people assume that discrimination implies some form of illegal act. In fact, to "discriminate" means simply to distinguish clearly or differentiate. One example of "desirable" discrimination is the effort to achieve a distinction between good and poor workers in a company's performance management system.

TABLE 5.1

Components of the EEO Environment

	Specific Elements
Employment discrimination	Overt discrimination
	Disparate treatment
	Disparate impact
Legal and regulatory documents	U.S. Constitution and amendments
	State and local laws
	Laws passed by Congress
	Presidential executive orders
	Guidelines of U.S. government agencies
Agents of EEO enforcement	Equal Employment Opportunity Commission
	Office of Federal Contract Compliance Programs
	U.S. Department of Justice
	Federal and state court systems
Management responses	Preventive actions
	Corrective actions

Source: From *Federal Regulation of Personnel and Human Resource Management,* 2nd ed., by Ledvinka/Scarpello. Copyright © 1991 PWS-Kent. Reprinted by permission of South-Western College Publishing, a division of International Thomson Publishing, Inc., Cincinnati, Ohio 45227.

Illegal discrimination occurs when unfair actions are taken toward members of a protected class. A **protected class** or group consists of individuals who share some characteristic in common, such as their race, color, religion, sex, national origin, age, disability status, or status as military veterans. These individuals are protected by laws that prevent discriminatory employment actions against them because of the characteristic they have in common. Suppose, for instance, that most white employees in a company were rated as outstanding performers but the majority of Hispanic employees were rated as unsatisfactory performers. Such discrimination would be questionable and, if based solely on ethnicity, would be illegal.

Laws preventing discrimination have been passed when Congress or a state legislature has had evidence that individuals with some particular characteristic in common have been treated unfairly in our society. For example, during the civil rights movement of the 1960s, several laws were passed to protect citizens from racial discrimination in housing, employment, and voting rights because strong evidence existed that racial discrimination (left over from pre–Civil War days) still existed.

LEGAL AND REGULATORY DOCUMENTS

The important EEO laws and regulatory documents are summarized in Table 5.2 and described in the following sections.

TABLE 5.2

Major EEO Laws and Regulatory Documents

Law or Document	Type of Discrimination Prohibited	Employers Covered
Fifth Amendment—U.S. Constitution	Deprivation of employment rights without due process	Federal government
Fourteenth Amendment—U.S. Constitution	Deprivation of employment rights without due process	State governments
Civil Rights Act of 1866	Racial discrimination in employment	Private employers, unions, employment agencies
Civil Rights Act of 1871	Deprivation of employment rights	State/local governments
Equal Pay Act of 1963	Sex discrimination in pay	All employers, unions
Title VII—Civil Rights Act of 1964 (amended 1972)	Employment discrimination based on race, color, religion, sex, national origin	Private employers, government unions, employment agencies
Age Discrimination in Employment Act of 1967 (amended 1986)	Employment discrimination based on age (ages forty and above)	Private employers, unions, employment agencies
Vocational Rehabilitation Act of 1973	Employment discrimination based on mental or physical handicaps	Federal contractors, government
Immigration Reform and Control Act of 1986	Discrimination based on citizenship or national origin	Employers generally
Older Workers Benefit Protection Act of 1990	Expands protection of Age Discrimination in Employment Act	Private employers, unions, employment agencies
Americans with Disabilities Act of 1990 (amended 1994)	Discrimination based on physical or mental disability	Employers generally
Civil Rights Act of 1991	Discrimination based on race, color, religion, sex, or national origin	Employers generally
Family and Medical Leave Act of 1993	Provides unpaid leave for employees under certain circumstances	Larger employers generally
Executive Order 11246 (amended by Executive Order 11375)	Same as Title VII with affirmative action required	Federal contractors
Uniform Guidelines (interpretive document for EEO laws)		

The Constitution

The **Fifth Amendment** to the U.S. Constitution states that "no person shall . . . be deprived of life, liberty, or property, without due process of law." This amendment relates to the actions of the federal government toward federal employees. The **Fourteenth Amendment** applies due process to actions taken by state governments and provides state employees with "equal protection of the laws." If a government worker is fired without a due process hearing, that worker can possibly file suit in court (1) using either the Fifth or the Fourteenth Amendment as the basis for the case and (2) arguing that he or she is being deprived of property without due process of law.

Federal Legislation

Although many EEO laws have been passed by state and local governments, we will limit our discussion to those passed by the U.S. Congress. Managers, however, should be aware of state EEO laws, because these laws are sometimes more stringent than federal laws. For example, a Texas state law prohibiting age discrimination covers individuals between the ages of twenty-one and seventy. The federal age discrimination law applies only to persons who are age forty and over.

Civil Rights Acts of 1866 and 1871 The **Civil Rights Act of 1866** provides all citizens with the same right to make and enforce contracts as "white citizens" have.[7] This law has been interpreted by the courts as prohibiting racial discrimination by employers, unions, and employment agencies in making employment contracts.[8] It is often combined with the **Civil Rights Act of 1871,** which gives all people in the United States the right to sue if deprived of constitutional rights as a result of state action, custom, or conspiracy.[9]

Equal Pay Act of 1963 The **Equal Pay Act (EPA)** prohibits wage discrimination among employees on the basis of sex when the work requires equal skill, effort, and responsibility and is performed under similar working conditions.[10]

- *Skill* is defined as the experience, training, education, or other abilities needed to perform the job.
- *Effort* can be mental or physical in nature (e.g., lifting 100-pound sacks of grain or working in a job that requires constant attention to detail). It is the degree or amount, not the nature, of the effort that is considered.
- *Responsibility* is the degree of accountability for people, equipment, money, or other things that the job entails.
- *Working conditions* include the physical surroundings and hazards under which the job is performed.

Court cases indicate that jobs need not be identical to be considered substantially equal to one another.[11] These rulings prevent organizations from giving men and women different job titles and paying them different wages even though they do essentially the same work. In other words, if a female executive secretary has essentially the same job duties as a male office manager, she must be paid the same wage. However, in jobs that are substantially equal, pay differentials between some male and female employees may be allowed as long as the differences are based on one of the following factors:

- Bona fide seniority systems
- Differences in the quality of performance
- Piece-rate pay systems, where pay is tied directly to the number and quality of units produced
- Factors other than sex (such as night shifts paying more than day shifts)

When the Equal Pay Act was signed into law by President Kennedy more than forty years ago, women earned 58 cents to every dollar earned by men.[12] Although enforcement of the EPA as well as other civil rights laws have helped to narrow the wage gap, unequal pay remains a problem. In 2002 women employed full time earned, on average, 77 cents for every dollar earned by men.[13] The issue, though, is quite complex and involves, among other things, the types of work women do and their occupations. (See Chapter 11 for further discussion of the Equal Pay Act and the earnings gap.) The 106th Congress (1999–2000) considered the Paycheck Fairness Act, which would have strengthened pay equity laws and procedures. Hearings were held by the appropriate Senate committee (June 2000), but the Senate voted against this amendment.[14] This legislation continues to be discussed although the outlook for reform is uncertain.

Civil Rights Act of 1964 The most important legislation concerning equal employment opportunity is the **Civil Rights Act of 1964,** amended by the Equal Employment Opportunity Act of 1972, the Pregnancy Discrimination Act of 1978, and the Civil Rights Act of 1991.[15]

Title VII of the Civil Rights Act **Title VII** is a portion of the Civil Rights Act of 1964, as it was constituted then and exists today, that is the most important piece of legislation ever enacted by Congress to guarantee American workers equal employment opportunity.[16] The goal of Title VII was economic justice and national well-being. Regarding economic justice, Congress noted that it had been well documented that discrimination forced a marginal existence on minority employees while, at the same time, depriving the nation of the talents and skills minorities possessed. With respect to national well-being, Congress stated that:

> Aside from the political and economic considerations, . . . we believe in the creation of job equality because *it is the right thing to do.* We believe in the inherent dignity of man. He is born with certain inalienable rights. . . . All vestiges of inequality based solely on race must be removed in order to preserve our democratic society.[17] (emphasis added)

Title VII prohibits employment discrimination based on race, color, religion, sex, or national origin. It protects employees from discrimination in such terms and conditions of employment as selection, placement, promotion, discharge, training, and pay and benefits. The Equal Employment Opportunity Commission (EEOC) was created by the 1964 law to enforce the provisions of Title VII.

As amended, Title VII applies to private employers that have fifteen or more employees on each working day of twenty or more calendar weeks in the current or preceding year. Title VII also applies to labor unions, employment agencies, state and local governments and their agencies, colleges, and universities. It protects all employees and applicants for employment in these organizations. There are some exceptions to this coverage, however. Religious organizations are not covered by certain religious discrimination aspects of Title VII. Elected public officials and their staffs and members of the Communist party are not protected. Employees who apply for jobs that require national security clearance are subject to special policies.

Pregnancy Discrimination Act of 1978 The **Pregnancy Discrimination Act (PDA)** of 1978, which amended Title VII, was passed to protect pregnant women from employment discrimination.[18] This act requires employers to be nondiscriminatory in providing employee benefits such as health insurance, sick leave, pensions, and vacation time. If an employer provides sick leave and health or disability insurance to employees generally, it cannot specifically exclude childbirth and related medical conditions.[19] Other important aspects of the PDA include the following:

- Elective abortions may be excluded from health insurance plans but not from other benefits, such as sick leave. Medical problems resulting from abortions may not be excluded from medical insurance.
- Employers must provide medical benefits to the husbands of female employees if they provide benefits to the wives of male employees.
- Employers must provide leave of absence or sick leave for childbirth on the same basis as for any other medical disability.
- Employers must allow women to work until their pregnancy results in physical disability that (1) interferes with their job performance and (2) is the same level of disability that would cause workers with other medical problems to have to stop working.
- Employers must allow women to return to work after childbirth on the same basis as for other disabilities.

In 1987 the U.S. Supreme Court faced the issue of whether a state statute that required employers to provide leave and reinstatement to employees disabled by pregnancy was preempted, or overridden, by the nondiscrimination mandates of the PDA. At issue in *California Federal Savings & Loan v. Guerra*[20] was a California statute providing such pregnancy leave. The employer in the case argued that, under the law, pregnant employees are treated differently from other employees and that the California law was thus not consistent with the PDA. Justice Thurgood Marshall, writing the opinion for the Court, disagreed with this assertion and held that the PDA did not preempt this California statute. Justice Marshall wrote that the favorable treatment given to pregnant workers under the California statute was not of the kind meant to be outlawed by the PDA. The PDA was meant essentially to prevent harmful discriminatory actions being taken against pregnant employees.

Title VII and Fetal Protection Policies In the 1991 case of *United Auto Workers v. Johnson Controls,* the U.S. Supreme Court examined the validity under Title VII of a company's fetal protection policy that said that all women of childbearing age were excluded from certain jobs involving lead exposure.[21] Opponents of the policy argued that the policy constituted sex discrimination, in that fertile men were given a choice of whether or not they wanted to risk lead exposure but fertile women were not. The Supreme Court upheld this point of view, ruling that the company's fetal protection policy did constitute unlawful sex discrimination and that no valid bona fide occupational qualification (discussed later in the chapter) was advanced. The court rejected arguments that the policy was necessary for safety reasons.

Sexual Harassment Supreme Court Justice Clarence Thomas, former U.S. Senator Bob Packwood, former President Clinton, and various business leaders have all helped propel **sexual harassment** into the headlines. Because Congress did not discuss on-the-job sexual behavior in passage of Title VII, the courts originally interpreted this omission to mean that sexual behavior was not a form of sex discrimination. However, in *Barnes v. Costle* (1977), sexual harassment was recognized for the first time as a form of sex discrimination under Title VII.[22] The EEOC has defined illegal sexual harassment in the following way:

> Unwelcome sexual advances, requests for sexual favors, or other verbal or physical conduct of a sexual nature constitute sexual harassment when any of the following conditions apply:

- Submitting to or rejecting such conduct is an explicit or implicit term or condition of employment.
- Submitting to or rejecting the conduct is a basis for employment decisions affecting the individual.
- The conduct unreasonably interferes with an individual's work performance or creates an intimidating, hostile, or offensive working environment.[23]

These EEOC guidelines were upheld by the U.S. Supreme Court in the significant 1986 case of ***Meritor Savings Bank v. Vinson.***[24] In that case, the employer bank argued that Title VII's prohibition of discrimination with respect to "compensation, terms, conditions, or privileges" of employment involved only "tangible losses" of "an economic character." Essentially, the employer was arguing that only "quid pro quo" sexual harassment—that is, a situation in which continued employment or an employment benefit is conditioned on sexual conduct—should be unlawful under Title VII. Thus the case of an employee's being fired for not having sex with a boss would constitute clearly unlawful quid pro quo harassment. On the other hand, if no clear quid pro quo situation is involved, there is no legal violation.

In the *Meritor* case, the Supreme Court rejected this narrow interpretation of Title VII and held that "environmental" sexual harassment, as defined in the EEOC's guidelines, also was unlawful. In the Supreme Court's opinion, any workplace conduct that is sufficiently severe or pervasive so as to alter the conditions of an individual's employment and create an "abusive" working environment can be unlawful. Thus, under the *Meritor* case, sexual jokes, pornographic pictures, and so forth can, under certain circumstances, constitute unlawful sexual harassment under Title VII.

The Supreme Court also ruled in *Meritor* that the fact that a sexual relationship between parties at the workplace is "voluntary" may be irrelevant. The critical issue in such cases is whether the sexual advances at issue were "unwelcome" and whether they were sufficiently severe to be "abusive." If so, they may be held unlawful under Title VII.

In the *Meritor* case, the Supreme Court did somewhat duck the critical issue of when an employer is responsible for the harassing actions of its employees. A lower court hearing the case had held that employers are strictly liable for the hostile work environment created by a supervisor's sexual advances to an employee, even if the employer neither knew nor could have reasonably known of the alleged misconduct. The Supreme Court rejected this notion and held that the lower court had erred in concluding that employers are always automatically liable for acts of sexual harassment committed by their supervisors. On the other hand, the Court also rejected the notion that absence of notice to an employer necessarily insulates the employer from liability. Instead, the Court avoided issuing a definitive ruling on employer liability, holding only that the general rules regarding employer responsibility for the actions of employees should apply.

Finally, the Supreme Court in *Meritor* rejected the bank's argument that the failure of the woman to report the harassment by way of the bank's existing grievance procedure insulated the bank from liability. The Court held that the complainant may have failed to report the violation for a variety of reasons and that such a failure to report does not necessarily alter the bank's liability.

Another defining U.S. Supreme Court case was that of *Harris v. Forklift Systems,*[25] which further defined the concept of "environmental" sexual harassment. In that case, the president of the company, although not engaging in any explicit quid pro quo behavior, had clearly created a sexually harassing environment of the kind potentially unlawful under the *Meritor* case. Among other things, he had referred to the plaintiff, Teresa Harris, as a "dumb ass woman," made sexual innuendoes about women's clothing, and asked female employees to get coins from his front pants pocket. The company argued, however, that because Teresa Harris had not shown any concrete psychological harm as a result of these actions, they did not violate Title VII. The Supreme Court disagreed.

The Supreme Court held that workplace conduct need not result in concrete psychological harm in order to be actionable in court as "abusive work environment" harassment. The Court held that such conduct need only be so pervasive and severe that a "reasonable person" would perceive it to be hostile or abusive. Such a determination would turn on all relevant circumstances, including the following

- The frequency of the discriminatory conduct
- Its severity
- Whether it is physically threatening or humiliating or a mere offensive utterance
- Whether it unreasonably interferes with an employee's work performance

In sum, the Supreme Court stated that Title VII clearly comes into play before harassing conduct leads to a "nervous breakdown." (See the International Perspective box for information on what constitutes cross-cultural sexual harassment or an abusive work environment.)

Because of the vagueness of what constitutes sexual harassment, the fact that the Civil Rights Act of 1991 mandates jury trials in cases of sexual harassment, and the high level of damages permitted under that act, attorneys have become extremely aggressive in their pursuit of evidence in such cases. Questioning plaintiffs regarding abortion, sexually transmitted diseases, and past sexual activity is not generally permitted in rape cases, but such questioning is permissible, and is being conducted, in sexual harassment cases.[26]

Two relatively recent cases have gained notoriety. The first concerns the issue of same-sex sexual harassment. In the case of Joseph Onscale, a male worker on an off-shore drilling rig charged that three male coworkers sexually harassed him with physical attacks, taunts, and threats of rape. The Supreme Court, in the case of *Onscale v. Sundowner,* ruled that the Civil Rights Act of 1964 could include cases of same-sex harassment.[27] The *Onscale* case thus opened up a new area of sexual harassment litigation—that associated with same-sex harassment.[28] Interestingly, a study with mock jurors found that the harassers are likely to be judged more severely in same-sex harassment cases.[29]

The second item of note is a record-setting $10 million settlement of sexual harassment charges brought by eighty female employees. The suit against the drug maker Astra was the result of alleged sexual harassment, intimidation of employees, and destruction of records on the part of the former president, Lars Bildman, and other executives.[30] In an unusual move, Astra has filed a $15 million suit against Lars Bildman, thus attempting to collect the damages from the employee most responsible for the illegal activity.[31]

Finally, two more recent cases, *Faragher v. City of Boca Raton* and *Burlington Industries Inc. v. Ellerth,* reaffirmed long-established court guidelines.[32] The guidance for employers is as follows:

INTERNATIONAL PERSPECTIVE

Sexual Harassment—Or Is It?

A Korean salesman hired by a U.S.-based multinational company in Seoul is rotated to a U.S. office for six months of training and work experience. After a few months, an American female coworker complains of sexual harassment. It seems the Korean has refused to listen to her or respond to her questions even though they need to work closely together, has screamed at her in front of customers, and has publicly addressed her with an obscene term. At one point, she thought he was so angry that he might strike her. He also frequently tells her that women are less important than men in his culture and that he intends to treat her accordingly. The Korean insists that he has not done anything wrong or anything different from what he did while working in Asia in the past.*

A U.S. expatriate working in Mexico is subject to what she sees as unwanted advances by her superior. In addition to his making suggestive comments to her, she complains that he stands too close to her and sometimes touches her while talking. This has continued despite her consistently moving away and displaying a total lack of interest in his advances. A female colleague from Mexico tells her to lighten up—the manager's behavior is normal.

A Middle Eastern–born man is shocked when an American coworker files a formal sexual harassment complaint. He is stunned that any woman would even think of behaving so disrespectfully toward a man.

Because cultures differ in the type of behavior that is acceptable between the sexes, there seems to be considerable possibility of misunderstanding when employees of diverse cultures and genders meet in the workplace. Behavior that Americans would consider unacceptable is especially likely to occur in countries where the sexes are not equal under the law or in society.

It is possible that perfectly innocent local customs might be offensive to hypersensitive Americans. For instance, standing close and touching while speaking to others are common in Hispanic and southern European nations but could be seen as overtly sexual by those accustomed to greater personal distance.

It is clear that U.S. regulations prevail when the employees involved are working in the United States. To reduce the likelihood of incidents, firms should fully brief expatriates posted to the United States on our local practices and regulations regarding male–female behavior at work.

When the harassment takes place in an overseas establishment, it is less clear whose standards should apply—those of the host country or those of the home country. Multinational firms are often admonished to adapt their policies to local customs rather than practice "cultural imperialism." On the other hand, if freedom from unwanted sexual advances or overtly discriminatory behavior is considered a universal human right, then firms should protect this right in their operations worldwide. While relatively few countries have well-developed and enforceable prohibitions against sexual harassment in the workplace, more and more nations are moving in this direction. The European Commission recently adopted a directive to ban sexual harassment that requires member states to formulate their own regulations preventing harassment—though how harassment is defined may be culture-specific.

Note: *This first incident is a true one. The company subsequently established that the offender was a hot-tempered individual with a history of impulsive and possibly abusive behavior. Cultural values undoubtedly contributed to the situation, but they were not the whole story. One would not expect most Korean men to behave in this way.

Sources: Robyn Talbot, Eastern Hemisphere Human Resource Director, personal communication, 1997; and W. Hardman and J. Heidelberg, "When Sexual Harassment Is a Foreign Affair," *Personnel Journal,* April 1996, pp. 91–97.

- If an employer does not have a written policy against sexual harassment, it should get one that includes a clearly stated procedure for filing a complaint.
- Once an employer has a written policy and procedure, it should be made known to everyone in the organization.
- Every complaint should be investigated in accordance with the procedures.
- Every employment decision should be documented.[33]

All of this adds up to what has become known as the *Faragher/Ellerth* affirmative defense against claims of sexual harassment, namely (a) that the employer exercised reasonable care to prevent and promptly correct any sexually harassing behavior and (b) that the employee unreasonable failed to take advantage of any preventive or corrective opportunities provided by the employer or to otherwise avoid harm.[34] Even with recent decisions there are unresolved issues. For example, many people are confused about exactly what constitutes sexual harassment and the extent of the employer's obligation to prevent what most often takes place "behind closed doors."[35]

Religious Harassment With post-September 11 (2001) tensions, employers should make sure that their Arab and Muslim employees are not experiencing workplace harassment. As a result of these tensions, the Equal Employment Opportunity Commission (EEOC) has brought several post–September 11 suits alleging harassment of Muslims or Arabs in the workplace.[36] Most of these suits have been due to disparaging comments, unfair treatment, and even discharge, as a result of an employee's middle eastern ethnicity.[37] HR professionals have an obligation to pay attention to possible harassment and to take affirmative action through communication and training to make sure the workplace is harassment free.

Age Discrimination in Employment Act of 1967 The **Age Discrimination in Employment Act (ADEA)** of 1967, amended in 1986, prohibits employment discrimination against job applicants and employees aged forty years or over.[38] The legislation was designed to remedy the stereotypical perceptions and resulting restrictive practices that deemed older workers unsuitable for employment. Leading to the ADEA was a study reporting that applicants over fifty-five years of age were excluded from 50 percent of all private-sector jobs, whereas 25 percent of jobs were closed to applicants forty-five years of age or older.[39] As an effort to protect older workers, the ADEA has taken on additional significance in the twenty-first century as a result of the aging of the work force (see the discussions of work force diversity in Chapters 1 and 3).

The legislation applies to private firms that employ twenty or more people on each working day of twenty or more calendar weeks in the current or preceding year. Employment agencies, labor unions, and federal, state, and local government employees are covered by the law.[40] This law has effectively banished any mandatory retirement age. It also prohibits discrimination based on age in recruiting, hiring, promoting, firing, and laying off employees and in most other terms and conditions of employment. The federal law applies only to persons aged forty and above. A twenty-five-year-old worker is not protected by the act.

A recent court case, *O'Connor v. Consolidated Coin Caterers Corp.*, clarifies one important aspect of age discrimination.[41] The plaintiff, James O'Connor, was terminated by Consolidated at age fifty-six and replaced by a forty-year-old. Lower courts ruled that this was not age discrimination because O'Connor's replacement was in the protected class, that is, age forty or above. The Supreme Court ruled that the fact that one person in the protected class has lost out to another person in the protected class is irrelevant.[42] In other words, Mr. O'Connor's claim of age discrimination was valid.

In an important win for business as well as older workers, the Supreme Court ruled in *General Dynamics Land Systems, Inc. v. Cline et al.*[43] that the ADEA cannot be used by younger workers against employers who offer enhanced benefits to older workers. A General Dynamics unit, in agreement with the United Auto Workers union, agreed to stop providing health care coverage to future retirees, except those current employees who were at least fifty years old, who would continue to be insured upon retirement.[44] In a 6 to 3 ruling, the high court did not agree that the younger workers were being discriminated against, thus affirming the legality of what many companies have been doing in offering special incentives to older workers.

Older Workers Protection Act of 1990 The **Older Workers Protection Act** amended the ADEA to make clear that certain previously permitted age-based distinctions in employee benefits plans are unlawful. More specifically, the new law overturned the Supreme Court's 1989 decision in *Public Employees Retirement System of Ohio v. Betts,* which held that employer decisions concerning employee benefits generally were not subject to challenge under the ADEA.[45] The 1990 law also sets very strict standards regarding employee waivers and releases of age discrimination claims—that is, situations in which employees, as a condition for receiving a severance or other payment from their employer, sign a waiver, or release, giving up any future age discrimination claim. Under the new law, employees must be given at least three weeks to consider any waiver or release agreement and even then have a week after signing the agreement to revoke it.

Vocational Rehabilitation Act of 1973 The **Vocational Rehabilitation Act** requires employers who have federal contracts of $2,500 or more to take affirmative action toward qualified individuals with disabilities.[46] The laws discussed thus far require only that employers not discriminate against certain types of persons. The affirmative action components of the Vocational Rehabilitation Act and the executive orders (discussed later in the chapter) require employers to develop more active procedures for seeking out and accommodating the needs of workers protected by the laws.

Americans with Disabilities Act of 1990 The **Americans with Disabilities Act (ADA)** went into effect on July 26, 1992. The scope of this law is vast, extending far beyond the employment context. For example, all new apartment and business buildings must be made accessible to the disabled. With respect to employment, the law initially affected all employers with more than twenty-five employees. On July 26, 1994, this requirement was lowered to fifteen employees, making an estimated 400,000 more employers subject to this act. Thus the ADA is significantly broader in application than the Vocational Rehabilitation Act of 1973, which applies only to federal contractors, although the new law does not mandate any affirmative action. Simply put, the ADA prohibits discrimination on the basis of disability—in hiring and in all terms, conditions, and privileges of employment. Unlike the Vocational Rehabilitation Act, which is administered by the Department of Labor, the ADA is administered by the EEOC.

Administration by the EEOC The EEOC was deluged with charges when the ADA went into effect, receiving more than 35,000 charges from mid-1992 through 1994. As shown in Table 5.3, disabilities (ADA) charges constituted approximately 16 percent of all charges received by the EEOC in the late 1990s, with the figure dropping to approximately 14 percent in fiscal year 2000 and beyond.

As Figure 5.1 shows, the most common impairment involved in charges brought under the ADA since its inception has been emotional/psychiatric impairments, followed by back impairments.

Defining Disability At the heart of the ADA is the definition of disability. The act defines **disability** as (1) a physical or mental impairment that substantially limits one or more of the major life activities of an individual, (2) a record of such an impairment, or (3) being regarded as having such an impairment. The term "physical or mental impairment" is defined broadly. It includes any physiological disorder or condition, cosmetic disfigurement, or anatomical loss affecting one or

TABLE 5.3

Summary of Charges Received and Resolved by the EEOC

	Fiscal Year						
	1997	1998	1999	2000	2001	2002	2003
Charges Received*	**80,680**	**79,591**	**77,444**	**79,896**	**80,840**	**84,442**	**81,293**
Racial Discrimination	26.4%	26.4%	27.2%	26.5%	26.0%	26.2%	26.1%
Religious Discrimination	1.5%	1.6%	1.7%	1.8%	1.9%	2.3%	2.3%
Sex Discrimination	22.4%	22.4%	22.5%	23.1%	22.6%	22.3%	22.3%
Sexual Harassment	14.4%	14.3%	14.3%	14.5%	13.9%	12.6%	12.4%
Pregnancy Discrimination	3.6%	3.9%	3.9%	3.8%	3.9%	4.1%	4.3%
Age Discrimination	14.3%	13.9%	13.3%	14.7%	15.7%	17.4%	17.5%
Equal Pay Discrimination	1.0%	1.0%	1.0%	1.2%	1.1%	1.1%	1.1%
Disabilities Discrimination	16.4%	16.3%	16.0%	14.5%	14.8%	14.0%	14.1%
Resolutions†	**106,312**	**101,470**	**97,846**	**93,672**	**90,106**	**95,222**	**87,755**
Settlements	3.8%	4.6%	6.2%	8.5%	8.1%	8.8%	9.6%
Withdraw with Benefits‡	3.4%	3.2%	3.7%	4.0%	4.1%	4.0%	4.2%
Administrative Closure**	28.3%	26.7%	24.1%	20.5%	20.7%	20.6%	17.4%
No Reasonable Cause	60.7%	60.9%	59.5%	58.3%	57.2%	59.3%	63.1%
Reasonable Cause	3.8%	4.6%	6.6%	8.8%	9.9%	7.2%	5.7%

Notes: * The number for total charges reflects the sum of the individual charge filings; that is, the number of separate individuals filing charges. Because individuals often file charges claiming multiple types of discrimination, the actual number of charges for any given fiscal year will be less than the total of the eight types of discrimination listed.
† Resolutions include charges received from previous periods; hence resolutions can exceed charges received in a given year.
‡ Charge is withdrawn upon receipt of desired benefits or remedies.
** Closed for administrative reasons, such as failure to locate the charging party; the charging party failed to respond, and so forth.
Source: U.S. Equal Employment Opportunity Commission. (Available at: http://www.eeoc.gov/stats/enforcement.html)

FIGURE 5.1

Most Common Impairments Alleged Under ADA*

Note: This is not a complete list; therefore percentages do not add up to 100.

Blood disorders include HIV (1.6%)

*Based on charges received July 26, 1992, to September 30, 2003.

Source: U.S. Equal Employment Opportunity Commission. (Available at: http://www.eeoc.gov/stats/ada-receipts.html)

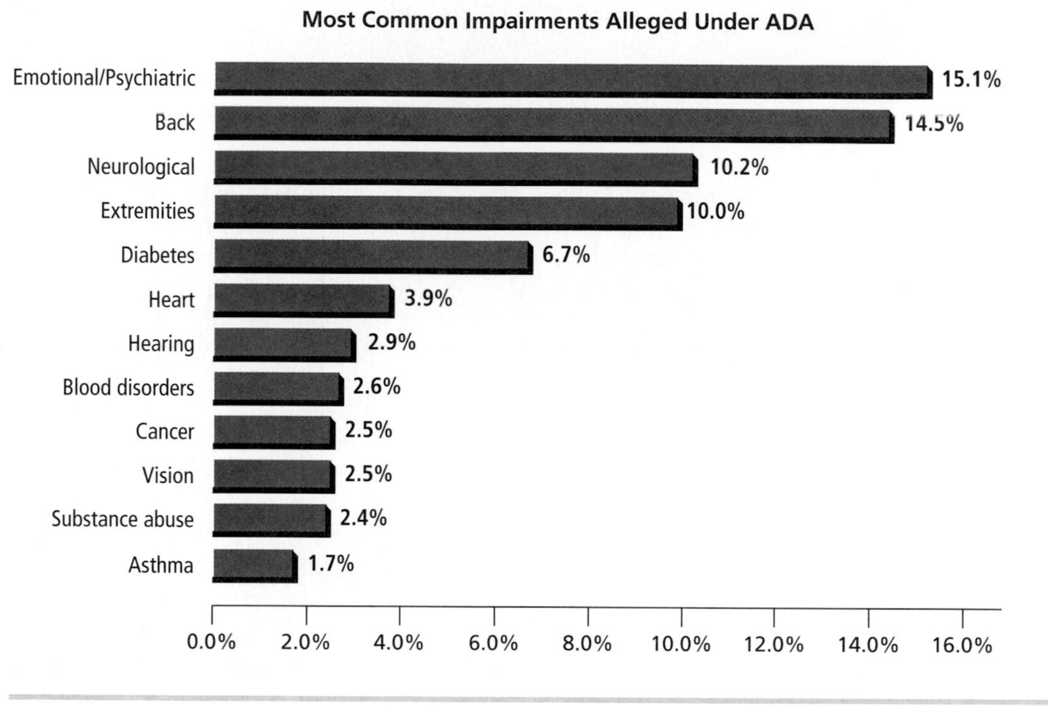

more of several body systems, as well as any mental, physical, or psychological disorder.

The definition of "mental or psychological disorder" includes emotional and mental illness, mental retardation, and learning disabilities. This definition is so broad that it includes virtually the entire spectrum of psychological disorders; as such, it prompted considerable debate in Congress during legislative consideration of the bill. At the urging of Senator Jesse Helms of North Carolina, various conditions—including kleptomania, compulsive gambling, sexual behavior disorders, and pyromania—were specifically excluded from the definition of "disability" under the ADA. Homosexuality and bisexuality were also excluded on the grounds that they are not impairments. Nevertheless, the ADA covers hundreds of psychological disorders. The act also specifically states that persons with acquired immune deficiency syndrome (AIDS) and those who are HIV-positive (infected with the human immunodeficiency virus) are protected under the ADA.

Interestingly, the ADA protects only disabilities that "substantially limit one or more major life activities." A common cold, for example, although a disability, does not "substantially limit" any "major life activities." The EEOC in its regulations has stated that it will examine the nature, severity, duration, and impact of the given impairment on a case-by-case basis to determine whether the impairment does substantially limit a major life activity and thus constitute a disability under the law. It should be noted, however, that the ADA covers people who are viewed by employers as having a substantially limiting impairment, even if the impairment does not necessarily have this effect. For example, an executive whose high blood pressure has clearly been controlled by medication probably cannot be denied a promotion for that reason.

A recent U.S. Supreme Court decision in the case of *Toyota v. Williams* seemed to narrow the definition of disability.[47] Ella Williams sued Toyota Motor Manufacturing's Georgetown, Kentucky, plant for failing to accommodate her carpal tunnel syndrome. The court ruled unanimously that Williams, even though she could not perform some tasks required by her job, was not "substantially limited" in a "major life activity" as required by the ADA, and therefore was not disabled under the law.[48] This ruling has major implications for the view of work itself as a major life activity under Title I of the ADA.[49]

Reasonable Accommodation Unlike the Vocational Rehabilitation Act, the ADA does not require affirmative action. It does impose an affirmative obligation on employers to make "reasonable accommodations" to the known disabilities of an applicant or an employee unless the employer demonstrates that this would constitute an "undue hardship." The concept of **reasonable accommodation** is not unique to the ADA. Title VII of the Civil Rights Act, for example, requires employers to reasonably accommodate the religious practices of their employees as long as such accommodations do not constitute an "undue hardship." Such accommodations may include job transfers, work-schedule changes, or other actions that allow workers to meet both their religious and their job responsibilities.

With respect to the disabled, employers are required to make reasonable accommodations of a kind that will allow individuals to perform the essential functions of the job. Reasonable accommodations often involve changes in the workplace, the job itself, and the equipment used to perform the job. For example, employers may modify elevators to include Braille or voice floor indicators, alter restrooms to meet the special needs of disabled workers, and build ramps to allow wheelchair access to buildings.

Employers are not required to accommodate the needs of workers with disabilities in every case. Employers may argue that changes necessary to accommodate a worker would cause undue hardship—that is, the accommodation would be extremely costly to the company or would disrupt the efficient, safe operation of the company. Whether or not an accommodation is reasonable or results in undue hardship for the employer depends on several factors:

- The nature of the job itself (whether it can be changed to accommodate a certain type of handicap)
- The size of the company
- Union agreements that might preclude certain types of work-schedule or work-rule changes
- The cost of the accommodation for the employer

Recent ADA U.S. Supreme Court Cases As with other EEOC issues, the courts have had a great deal to do with defining the scope of the statutes. Even though the ADA is relatively recent in the history of employment law, the courts have already done a great deal to signal both employees and employers as to the nature of the issues involved.

In a recent decision that severely limits the ADA, the Supreme Court ruled that states do not have to make "reasonable accommodations" in the workplace. In the landmark case *Board of Trustees of University of Alabama v. Garrett,* the Court ruled that the disabled could not sue state government agencies.[50] The court ruled that states' rights trump the legal rights of people with disabilities.

The case had to do with Patricia Garrett, a nurse who worked at the University of Alabama's medical center. Garrett discovered that she had breast cancer and received a leave of absence while recovering from surgery. When she returned to work, she was demoted in deference to her employer's belief that she had a disability and could no longer perform her duties satisfactorily.[51] Although the merits of Garrett's case could be debated, the decision could seriously undermine the ADA in the future—not only in the public sector but also in the private sector. All told, the Court's decision is a huge step backward for persons with disabilities seeking a fair chance to work and contribute.

The second case, *PGA Tour, Inc. v. Martin,* also had implications beyond the case itself.[52] In this case the Supreme Court ruled decisively in favor of Casey Martin, a professional golfer suffering from a progressive circulatory disorder that has caused his right leg to atrophy such that walking is not only very painful but also poses the risk of severe damage to his health. The Court ruled that Martin should be allowed to use a golf cart. Justice Stevens said the PGA Tour's walking rule was "at best peripheral" and "not an indispensable feature" of golf and "thus it might be waived in individual cases without working a fundamental alteration."[53] The broader implications of this case have to do with the Court's emphasis on the need to evaluate each case on an individual basis. According to Justice Stevens, those for whom the given rules and procedures are "beyond their capacity," not simply uncomfortable or difficult, should be accommodated.

A third case, *Barnett v. US Airways* further defined what is meant by reasonable accommodation.[54] In a 5 to 4 decision, the U.S. Supreme Court ruled that an employer is not required to grant an employee with a disability a job in place of an employee with more seniority if a seniority system normally is used as a fundamental factor in such decisions. In the case, Robert Barnett, a US Airways employee who was disabled by a back injury, claimed to be entitled to a mailroom position as a reasonable accommodation even though two other employees were ahead of him in the airline's seniority system.[55]

AIDS in the Workplace As noted earlier, AIDS is clearly defined as a disability under the ADA. Employers cannot require a test for AIDS or any other medical examination as a condition of making an offer of employment. Once an offer of employment has been made, however, employers can make the offer conditional on taking such an examination. An employer cannot generally discriminate against a job applicant who is HIV-positive, although such a person may be lawfully excluded from coverage under the employer's health insurance plan if the plan excludes other preexisting conditions. The following are some general guidelines for dealing with the AIDS issue:

- Treat AIDS like any other disease covered by state or federal laws against discrimination.
- Educate coworkers about AIDS.

- Maintain confidentiality of all medical records.
- Do not in any way discriminate against a person with AIDS.
- Do not exclude AIDS victims from training or consideration for promotion.
- Accommodate or make a good effort to accommodate the AIDS victim.

Obesity Evidence of weight-based discrimination has been observed in many studies. In fact, studies assessing the effect of both employee weight and other possible bases for discrimination (sex, specific disabilities, race, etc.) provide evidence that weight-related bias may be greater than that associated with other characteristics.[56] Whether being overweight is a legally protected impairment under the ADA remains a question.

The Rehabilitation Act decision of the U.S. Court of Appeals for the First Circuit in *Cook v. State of Rhode Island, Department of Mental Health, Retardation and Hospitals* (1993) has led some commentators to speculate that obesity is probably covered by the ADA.[57] That case involved the refusal of a state mental retardation facility to hire an individual who was 5 feet, 2 inches tall and weighed more than 320 pounds. The state facility argued that the individual's obesity compromised her ability to evacuate patients in the event of an emergency and also increased the possibility of her developing serious illnesses leading to increased absenteeism and worker compensation claims. The state government also argued that there was, in the plaintiff's obese condition, an element of voluntariness that mitigated against its being accorded legally protected status.

The federal appeals court, however, rejected these arguments. The court held that "morbid obesity," defined as being more than twice the proper body weight or more than 100 pounds overweight, constituted a legally protected impairment even if not caused by an underlying physical disorder. The court stated that a "voluntariness" test was improper, noting that impairments such as alcoholism or perhaps even diabetes could in some sense be seen as "voluntary" conditions.

With the report of the Centers for Disease Control and Prevention (CDC), the lead U.S. federal agency for protecting health and safety of citizens, that poor diet and physical inactivity are the second cause of preventable death (behind smoking), there can be little doubt that obesity is set to be the Next Big Thing.[58] More and more overweight people are taking their claims to court.[59] Even the U.S. Congress is getting involved in an effort to shield food chains and restaurants from lawsuits.[60] Finally, the National Association to Advance Fat Acceptance and other advocates seek laws that would bar employment discrimination based on physical appearance.[61]

Genetic Discrimination Discrimination based on the presence of a disability is illegal under the ADA. But what about discrimination based on genetic characteristics that predispose an individual to developing a disease, condition, or late-onset disorder? (Late-onset disorders are those that may not show visible signs until later in the individual's life.) The ADA may protect against genetic discrimination as well, because the law applies not only to people with a disability but also to people regarded as having a disability. People who experience genetic discrimination are often regarded as having a disability because they have an abnormal gene. The EEOC ruled in 1995 that genetic discrimination in employment is prohibited. More recently, the EEOC issued guidance implementing an executive order that prohibits genetic discrimination by the federal government. Although the executive order is limited to federal government employment, it represents a major step in setting the legal standard for addressing genetic discrimination in the workplace.[62]

In a "first-ever" case, the EEOC brought a workplace discrimination suit against Burlington Northern Santa Fe Railway for testing its employees for genetic defects. Burlington Northern then reached a $2.2 million settlement on behalf of thirty-six employees. The railroad tested or attempted to test workers who claimed to have job-related carpal tunnel syndrome for genetic predisposition to this syndrome.[63] As more and more tests become available, discrimination on the basis of genetic predispositions promises to become an even larger workplace issue.

Workplace Violence As noted earlier, the ADA clearly covers most psychological disorders. Anger and aggression of the type that are part of some psychological disorders, however, constitute a clear threat of possible workplace violence. Headlines about disgruntled employees gunning down coworkers alarm both employers and other employees.[64] There is, therefore, a question as to how employers are supposed to handle employees with psychological disorders, given potential correlations between workplace violence and some forms of mental illness.

It should be noted, though, that a recent congressional Office of Technology Assessment study found higher correlations between workplace violence and factors other than mental illness. Indeed, the two factors most highly correlated with workplace violence were (1) substance abuse and (2) a prior history of violence.

Nevertheless, this is not an issue employers can easily ignore. An employer may treat an employee with a disability who is prone to violence the same as any other employee, even if the misconduct resulted from the disability. For example, an employee with a mental disability may be disciplined or fired for violence or threats of violence as long as the same discipline would be imposed on an employee without a disability.[65]

Immigration Reform and Control Act of 1986 The **Immigration Reform and Control Act (IRCA)** provides penalties for companies and individuals within the companies who knowingly hire illegal aliens.[66] The IRCA covers companies with three or more employees. For first offenses, fines of $250 to $2,000 per illegal alien may be imposed. A pattern of violation by a company may result in fines of up to $10,000 and six-month jail sentences. Employers must collect sufficient information from job applicants to confirm their legal status within the United States, and both the applicant and the company must fill out an I-9 form. Companies must retain their employment records for three years after hire or for one year following termination, whichever comes first.

English-Only Rules With increasing numbers of immigrants coming into the United States, an issue of heightened importance is whether an employer can lawfully require employees to speak only English at work. Traditionally, the EEOC has considered such "English-only" work rules unlawful, representing discrimination on the basis of national origin. In June 1994, however, the Supreme Court upheld without comment a decision by the federal appeals court in San Francisco rejecting the EEOC's position that English-only rules are automatically invalid. The appeals court held that employers who require their workers to speak English on the job do not necessarily violate Title VII.

The case of *Garcia v. Spun Steak Co.* (1994)[67] involved two employees of San Francisco meatpacker Spun Steak Company who were making derogatory and racist remarks in Spanish, belittling coworkers. In response, the company adopted an English-only rule for the workplace. When the EEOC challenged this rule as automatically invalid and mandated that the employer show some "business necessity" for adopting it, the employer countered that Title VII protects against discrimination based on national origin but does not protect the right of workers to express their cultural heritage in the workplace. The appeals court agreed with the employer, noting that the EEOC's traditional policy in this regard created a new right never contemplated by Congress.

Since the *Garcia* case, there have been a number of cases and EEOC settlements suggesting that English-only policies are, more often than not, employment discrimination. For example, *EEOC v. Premier Operator Services, Inc.* involved employees who worked as telephone operators. Their ability to speak Spanish was perceived as an asset because the company services many Spanish-speaking customers, and many employees were tested for their bilingual abilities. However, Premier had an English-only policy prohibiting speaking Spanish at work except when speaking to a customer on the phone. The court ruled that the English-only policy constituted disparate treatment based on national origin. There was no evidence of business necessity for the English-only policy that was related to performance on the job. Nor was there any evidence that speaking Spanish at work caused discord among the employees.[68]

Civil Rights Act of 1991 One of the fundamental purposes of this legislation was to reverse the U.S. Supreme Court's 1989 decision in *Wards Cove Packing Co. v. Antonio.*[69] In *Wards Cove,* the Court made it more difficult for employees to prove discrimination (particularly in "disparate impact" cases, discussed later in this chapter). The new legislation overturned *Wards Cove* and essentially put into law the Supreme Court's 1971 decision in ***Griggs v. Duke Power Co.,*** which obliges employers to prove that a practice causing discrimination was required by a "business necessity."[70] The 1991 act also overturned another 1989 Supreme Court decision, which held that the Civil Rights Act of 1866 did not apply to cases in which an employee was discharged but only to those cases relating to the formation of a contract, such as hiring. The 1991 legislation made it clear that the Civil Rights Act of 1866 does indeed apply to discharge cases.

The **Civil Rights Act of 1991** also amends Title VII to provide that an employment practice may be established as unlawful by demonstrating that race, color, religion, sex, or national origin was a motivating factor for an adverse employment decision, even though other legitimate factors also motivated the decision. The act further expands the scope of Title VII and the ADA to apply to U.S. citizens employed in foreign countries by American-owned or American-controlled employers. This provision in the law overturned a 1991 Supreme Court decision, which held that Title VII did not apply outside the United States to U.S. citizens working for American-owned or American-controlled companies.

The Civil Rights Act of 1991 also amended section 703 of Title VII to explicitly prohibit "race norming" of employee or job candidate test scores—that is, altering test scores on the basis of race, sex, national origin, or other criteria. In addition, the law established a formal commission to study the artificial barriers to advancement that women and other minorities face in the workplace—the so-called **glass ceiling.**

Traditionally, damage awards under Title VII have been limited to back pay, lost benefits, and attorney's fees and costs. The 1991 act, however, provided monetary awards of compensatory and punitive damages in cases of intentional discrimination. Under the 1991 law, compensatory damages can cover emotional pain and suffering and enjoyment of life, but the amount of punitive damages that can be awarded is limited by the size of the given employer. When compensatory or punitive damages are sought, either party may demand a jury trial.

Jury Trials and the Civil Rights Act of 1991 The provision for jury trials for discrimination claims in the Civil Rights Act of 1991 constituted a radical change in the enforcement of Title VII. As noted earlier in the discussion of aggressive legal tactics in sexual harassment cases, employers and their attorneys generally feel at much greater risk in trials before juries as opposed to trials solely before federal judges. It is surmised that juries are more likely to be swayed by visceral or emotional arguments than are federal judges well familiar with Title VII law. Moreover, as Justice Scalia pointed out in his concurrence in the *Harris v. Forklift Systems* case discussed earlier, the legal standards being given to juries in such cases are often themselves quite vague and ambiguous. Although the 1991 act limits the amount of monetary award on a sliding scale according to employer size, companies are taking steps to try to keep Title VII cases away from juries.

One way employers are achieving this is by getting employees to agree, in a written agreement before they are hired, that any discrimination claim arising during the course of employment will be submitted for **arbitration** rather than to the courts. The U.S. Supreme Court in the 1991 case of *Gilmer v. Interstate/Johnson Lane* upheld such a mandatory arbitration clause in the securities industry.[71]

Recently the U.S. Supreme Court handed employers a further victory by ruling that companies can insist that workplace disputes go to arbitration rather than to court. Thus arbitration is another important enforcement vehicle for disputes that would otherwise go to court.[72] The 5 to 4 ruling by the U.S. Supreme Court in *Circuit City Stores, Inc. v. Adams* means, in essence, that an employer can enforce a signed agreement that obligates an employee to take all employment-related disputes to arbitration under the Federal Arbitration Act (FAA) rather than to court.[73] The case arose when former Circuit City employee Saint Clair Adams sued, claiming that Circuit City had discriminated against him because of his sexual orientation. As a condition of his employment, Adams had signed an agreement to submit all employment-related claims to a neutral arbitrator.[74] Employers who do not now require employment-related disputes to be resolved through arbitration are likely to look at the benefits of such a procedure now that there is no question on the basic issue of enforceability.

Family and Medical Leave Act of 1993 The **Family and Medical Leave Act (FMLA)** was signed into law by President Clinton on February 5, 1993, and became effective on August 5, 1993. The law's enactment followed eight years of congressional debate on this controversial legislation and a veto of the bill by President George H. W. Bush. The law applies to all employers with fifty or more employees. To be eligible for coverage under the act, employees must have worked for the given employer for at least 1,250 hours during a minimum of twelve months. Certain highly paid employees are exempt from coverage under the act.

Eligible employees qualify for a total of up to twelve weeks of unpaid leave during any twelve-month period in one or more of the following circumstances:

- The birth of a child to an employee and the need to care for the child
- Placement of a child with the employee for adoption or foster care

- Caring for a spouse, child, or parent with a serious health condition
- The employee's own serious health condition

Moreover, when an employee returns to work after the leave, he or she generally is entitled to return to the position formerly occupied, if that position remains available. If that position is no longer available, the employee has the right to an "equivalent" position with equivalent pay, benefits, and working conditions. Employees on leave pursuant to the act are entitled to have their health benefits maintained while on leave. However, employees are expected to give their employers thirty days' notice that leave is needed, if such notice is at all practicable. Husbands and wives both working for the same employer can take only a combined total of twelve weeks of leave during a twelve-month period for certain situations, such as the birth of a child. Some individual states have enacted leave legislation that is broader in scope than federal legislation, and employers in those states are required to follow the state laws.

Numerous policy arguments were raised during the long debate leading to the Family and Medical Leave Act. Proponents of the legislation pointed to the facts that today approximately 65 percent of mothers work outside the home and that many parents head single-parent homes. Without leave legislation, the care of a sick child is problematic. In addition, proponents of the legislation pointed to the comprehensive leave legislation existing in other countries, such as France's sixteen weeks of leave at 90 percent of normal pay.

Opponents of the legislation primarily objected to the fact that it represented a new government mandate for employers. They argued that this new cost to employers could hurt employees not in need of family leave—and also job seekers in "high-risk" leave categories because employers would be reluctant to hire such individuals.

The Family and Medical Leave Act is administered by the U.S. Department of Labor, which commissioned a study of the act's effectiveness in 2000. Two surveys were involved: (1) interviews with more than 2,500 employed U.S. residents and (2) interviews with human resource directors of more than 1,800 U.S. private business establishments. Notable findings were as follows:[75]

- More than 35 million covered and eligible workers benefited from taking leave for family and medical reasons in the first seven years of the FMLA.
- More than half (52.4 percent) of all employees who took leave did so because of their own health, 18.5 percent did so to care for a new baby (newborn, adopted, or foster child), 13 percent to care for an ill parent, and 11.5 percent to care for an ill child.
- Only 2.4 percent of employees needing leave could not take it, the most common reason being the inability to afford the leave (77.6 percent of those needing but not taking leave).
- One-sixth (16 percent) of establishments covered by the FMLA and 41 percent of employees (at both covered and noncovered establishments) were not aware of the act.
- A large majority of those taking leave said that it had positive effects on their ability to care for family members (78.7 percent), their own or family members' emotional well-being (70.1 percent), and their own or family members' physical health (63.0 percent).

- Two-thirds of those taking leave (65.8 percent) received at least some pay during their leave.
- For more than 80 percent of covered employers, the act had a positive effect, or no noticeable effect, on business productivity, profitability, and growth.

To date, the U.S. Supreme Court has ruled in two FMLA cases. In the first, *Ragsdale v. Wolverine World Wide, Inc.,* the employer, Wolverine World Wide, granted Tracy Ragsdale, who suffers from Hodgkin's disease, thirty weeks' medical leave under its more generous policy than the twelve-week leave under the FMLA.[76] However, the employer refused her request for additional leave or permission to work part time and terminated her when she did not return to work. Ms. Ragsdale argued that the thirty-week leave was not under the FLMA provisions; she had not used her FMLA leave and thus was entitled to the additional twelve weeks permitted by the FMLA. The U.S. Supreme Court ruled in favor of the employer in this case, that Ms. Ragsdale was not entitled to an additional twelve weeks leave under the FMLA.

In May 2003 the U.S. Supreme Court upheld the applicability of the FMLA to state employees.[77] William Hibbs, an employee of the Nevada Department of Human Resources, took leave under the provisions of the FMLA to care for his wife. When Mr. Hibbs did not return to work after twelve weeks, he was fired. Mr. Hibbs sued in Federal District Court seeking damages. The State of Nevada claimed it was protected by its Eleventh Amendment immunity from suit. The key question before the Court in *Hibbs* was whether applying the FMLA to the states was within Congress's power. The Court ruled that it was. Clearly the FMLA is providing the opportunity for employed individuals to respond to family needs while at the same time protecting their jobs.

Executive Orders

Presidential **executive orders** are another type of document that addresses employment discrimination. **Executive Order 11246,** issued by President Lyndon Johnson in 1965, prohibits discrimination based on race, color, religion, or national origin. **Executive Order 11375,** issued in 1967, prohibits discrimination based on sex. Both of these executive orders apply to federal agencies and companies with federal contracts of $10,000 or more. The Office of Federal Contract Compliance Programs (OFCCP) within the Department of Labor ensures that federal contractors comply with the provisions of these executive orders.

Whereas Title VII prohibits discrimination, Executive Orders 11246 and 11375 establish the concept of **affirmative action** for organizations. These executive orders require employers to take the following affirmative actions:

- Treat job applicants and employees without regard to race, color, religion, or national origin.
- State in advertisements that all applicants will be treated equally.
- Tell all labor unions and subcontractors associated with the company about the company's commitments under the orders.
- Include the equal opportunity obligation in all subcontracts and purchase orders.

- Comply with all provisions of the orders and provide information to federal agencies when requested.
- File regular compliance reports describing hiring and other employment practices.

"Glass Ceiling" Initiative and Beyond On August 9, 1991, the Labor Department issued its "Report on the Glass Ceiling Initiative." This report, the result of an intensive study by the OFCCP of nine corporate work forces, focused on the general paucity of women and minorities in top managerial positions in the nation's largest corporations. This lack of minorities and women in top positions has been termed a "glass ceiling," which women and minorities can see through but not get through. The report made recommendations regarding development, training, and other approaches designed to facilitate the movement of women and minorities into the executive suite. As noted earlier, the Civil Rights Act of 1991 established a special glass ceiling commission to study these issues further, with the latest report from 2002 showing progress but still plenty of room for improvement.[78]

Another initiative has been establishment of the Women's Bureau within the Department of Labor. The mission of the Women's Bureau is "to promote profitable employment opportunities for women, to empower them by enhancing their skills and improving their working conditions, and to provide employers with more alternatives to meet their labor needs."[79]

As concerns regarding workplace diversity have grown, attention has focused not only on invisible barriers (glass ceilings) preventing women and minorities from attaining executive positions but also on invisible barriers that may exist regarding effective communication and working relations within organizations. Clearly, such "glass walls" frequently inhibit positive interaction among individuals with differing backgrounds within organizations. An important objective for the multicultural organization of today is to work toward breaking through such barriers.[80]

Affirmative Action Plans Companies with federal contracts (of $10,000 or more) must formulate detailed **affirmative action plans (AAPs)** to ensure their compliance. Additionally, nonconstruction contractors with fifty or more employees and contracts of $50,000 or more must develop written affirmative action plans for each of their establishments. These AAPs consist of four parts:

1. A utilization analysis that shows the percentage of men, women, and minorities employed in the company
2. An availability analysis that indicates the availability of men, women, and minorities in the relevant labor market
3. An identification of problem areas (using utilization and availability data) that lists any inequities between the availability and actual representation of men, women, and minorities in the company
4. Corrective actions, with goals and timetables, that outline the employer's plans to achieve employment parity

Utilization Analysis The employer identifies the number of men, women, and minorities who are employed in each job group (utilized) within the company. The employer also may collect data on the nature of recent hiring decisions (e.g., out of twenty recent applicants hired for the job of carpenter, ten were women) and on the number of offers made to minority applicants (e.g., ten blacks were offered the job of first-line production supervisor, but only one accepted). Other data might include a work force comparison of the employer and similar companies in the same geographic region or a statistical report on the increase in the company's minority or female employees over a designated time period.

Availability Analysis In its AAP the employer must indicate the availability of men, women, and minorities in the relevant labor market. Any minority group making up 2 percent or more of the labor market should be considered. There is considerable disagreement over what geographic area constitutes the appropriate labor market from which to collect data. Factors that affect the appropriateness of the geographic region are (1) the area in which the employer presently recruits employees, (2) the area in which current employees and job applicants typically live, (3) the availability of public transportation, and (4) the type of job involved. Even when the appropriate geographic region can be determined, there remains the problem of identifying exactly how many qualified, potentially employable individuals live in that region. As a result, the availability analysis can become a fairly subjective process.

Identification of Problem Areas The employer examines utilization and availability data for instances of underutilization—that is, where utilization is less than availability—or for instances of concentration—that is, where certain jobs are filled almost exclusively by members of a particular sex or minority.

Table 5.4 presents hypothetical utilization and availability analyses for Acme Electronics Corporation. A comparison of row 2 (percent of utilization) and rows 8 and 10 shows that black women are both seeking work and qualified at a considerably higher rate than their current utilization for the job group of technicians. White men and women are somewhat overutilized. Black male utilization and availability are relatively equal—that is, parity exists for black men. This table also reflects an instance of concentration: 70 percent of the technicians are men, which shows that men are concentrated in this job group.

Corrective Actions, with Goals and Timetables If utilization problems exist, the company must develop a set of specific actions that will achieve parity. At Acme Electronics, these actions might include increasing recruitment efforts at predominantly black universities, advertising in women's magazines, or developing special training programs to help current (particularly black) female employees acquire skills that would enable them to become technicians. The employer must specify the goals it hopes to achieve by these actions and the targeted deadlines for their achievement. Acme Electronics, for example, might set the goal of increasing the number of black female technicians by 100 percent (from ten to twenty) within two years.

The Current Debate over Affirmative Action Almost forty years after the establishment of affirmative action, a debate rages over whether it has done any good or, even if it has, whether its continuation is a necessity. There is little doubt that things have changed in these four decades. In 1964, when affirmative action went into effect, the work force was comprised of 10.7 percent minority workers and 34 percent women. Today minority workers account for 30 percent and women account for almost 50 percent of the work force.[81] Despite the progress, many

TABLE 5.4

Hypothetical Utilization and Availability Analyses: Acme Electronics Corporation

Job group: Technicians
Relevant Labor Area: Standard Metropolitan Statistical Area
Prepared by: J. B. Shaw, EEO Coordinator, Date: 2/6/98

		Total	Male	Female	White Male	White Female	Black Male	Black Female
Utilization	1. Size of utilized population	500	350	150	200	140	150	10
	2. Percent of utilization	100%	70%	30%	40%	28%	30%	2%
Availability	3. Size of available population	100,000	49,000	51,000	20,000	21,000	29,000	30,000
	4. Percent of availability	100%	49%	51%	20%	21%	29%	30%
	5. Size of work force	60,000	36,000	24,000	16,200	14,400	19,800	9,600
	6. Percent of work force	100%	60%	40%	27%	24%	33%	16%
	7. Individuals seeking work	3,500	1,925	1,575	578	709	1,347	866
	8. Percent seeking work	100%	55%	45%	17%	20%	29%	24%
	9. Individuals with requisite skills in reasonable recruiting area	42,000	25,200	16,800	13,104	9,240	12,096	7,560
	10. Percent of individuals with requisite skills	100%	60%	40%	31%	22%	29%	18%

Note: In actual utilization and availability data, information would be presented for total, male, female, white male and female, black male and female, Hispanic male and female, Asian male and female, and American Indian male and female.

Source: Adapted from *EEO Compliance Manual*, 1979. Reprinted by permission of Prentice-Hall, Inc., Englewood Cliffs, New Jersey.

would argue that there continues to be a role for affirmative action. The issue today is not so much organizational entry as advancement. Even with the dawn of the twenty-first century, the overwhelming majority of senior managers are white and male.[82]

Given the past progress and current needs, why is there so much animosity surrounding affirmative action? The idea of affirmative action is an emotional issue to many on both sides of the debate. Some believe that, within reason, a preference should be given to those members of protected groups (e.g., minorities and women) who have been the objects of past discrimination. Those supporting affirmative action are not concerned that the current members of the protected groups may not, themselves, have been victims of discrimination, because the goal is a preference to correct past discrimination.

Those against affirmative action believe that employment policy should not favor one group over another. They believe that affirmative action should not be used to remedy the effects of either actual or historical discrimination in such a way as to benefit nonvictims to the detriment of those who are not members of a protected class.

To date, the most visible anti–affirmative action effort was the successful 1996 California ballot initiative, which stated:

> The state [of California] shall not discriminate against, or grant preferential treatment to, any individual or group on the basis of race, sex, color, ethnicity, or national origin in the operation of public employment, public education, or public contracting.

The fragility of affirmative action at the present time is illustrated by the case of *Board of Education of the Township of Piscataway v. Taxman.*[83] In 1989 the Piscataway (New Jersey) school board was faced with the need to lay off one of the ten teachers in the high school business department. Seniority guided the decision, but the two junior teachers, Sharon Taxman and Debra Williams, had been hired on the same day. The board, relying on its affirmative action plan, laid off Taxman, a white, in preference to Williams, the only black teacher in the department. Taxman filed suit, which the U.S. Supreme Court agreed to hear on appeal in mid-1997. Five months later a broad coalition of civil rights groups agreed to pay about 70 percent of the $433,500 needed to pay Taxman's back salary and legal bills to settle the case. The civil rights groups feared that the Court's mere acceptance of the *Taxman* case signaled its intent to end all voluntary programs designed to achieve a more diverse work force. The civil rights groups viewed the case as "atypical" and were reluctant to see it as the basis for the potential rethinking of all affirmative action in employment.

Affirmative action in school admission has been an area of controversy for almost thirty years. Colleges and universities have relied on Justice Powell's 1978 ruling in *Regents v. Bakke* to structure their diversity programs.[84] In a closely divided decision, the Court held that race could be one of the factors considered in choosing a diverse student body in university admissions decisions. Allen Bakke was an applicant to the University of California, Davis medical school, but was rejected in favor of a less qualified minority because of a 16 percent minority quota. Even though the Court held that race could be a factor, it also ruled that maintaining a quota is not proper and in this case constituted discrimination against Mr. Bakke, and thus he was admitted to the medical school.

More recently several federal courts have prohibited universities from offering scholarships to minorities solely on the basis of race.[85] Thus it was of great interest when the U.S. Supreme Court agreed to hear two cases from the University of Michigan, *Grutter v. Bollinger* and *Gratz v. Bollinger.*[86] *Grutter* dealt with the University of Michigan's Law School diversity plan and *Gratz* had to do with diversity among undergraduates. The question in both cases was whether diversity is a compelling government interest and, if it is, whether the respective admissions plans were tailored to that interest.[87] In the *Grutter* (law school) case the Court answered "Yes" to both questions. In the *Gratz* (undergraduate) case the Court ruled that the plan was not narrowly tailored and thus was illegal.

The law school plan (*Grutter*) combined objective variables (e.g., GPA, LSAT) with "soft" variables (e.g., recommendation letters, leadership, work experience, and overcoming social or economic disadvantage). The law school sought a critical mass of underrepresented minority students (a) to make each class "stronger than the sum of its parts" and (b) to prevent minority students from feeling "uncomfortable discussing issues freely based on their personal experience."[88] The law school also claimed that there was no hard and fast objective rule for admissions and no fixed percentage goal for the "critical mass."

The undergraduate admissions in *Gratz* used a "selection index" of 150 points, with 100 points required for admission. Up to 12 points were awarded for standardized scores, up to 98 points for GPA, category of school attended, and strength or weakness of the curriculum, and up to 40 points for other factors. These other factors included up to 20 points for geographical location, alumni relations, outstanding essay, personal achievement, or leadership and service activity, and up to 20 points for "miscellaneous" categories, including socioeconomic disadvantage, racial and ethnic minorities, athletic scholarship, and discretionary selection by the provost.[89]

The result of the pair of decisions, the Court's first in a generation to address race in university admissions, is a road map for taking race into account without getting crosswise with the Constitution's guarantee of equal protection.[90] As stated by Justice O'Connor, the law school engages in a "highly individualized, holistic review of each applicant's file" in which race counts as a factor but is not used in a "mechanical way."[91]

The question of how this maps onto affirmative action in the workplace is of interest. It would be ironic if the law allowed affirmative action in education, at least in part to create a diverse work force, and then prohibited comparable affirmative action in terms of entering the work force.[92] However, the Court historically has treated education and employment differently. Different legal rubrics apply.

Opponents of affirmative action think it makes the goal of a colorblind society more difficult to achieve. Affirmative action started out as a means to attain nondiscrimination and equal opportunity but wound up trying to allocate opportunities on the basis of proportionalism by using only two variables, race and gender.[93] As one observer stated, "America has been a country that corrects laws in one direction and corrects them in another, then over-corrects and over-corrects."[94] Clearly the correction is underway with respect to affirmative action, and the end result continues to be in the balance.

The Problem of Reverse Discrimination One problem organizations often face when specifying goals and timetables for affirmative action programs is **reverse discrimination.** Title VII prohibits discrimination in employment based on race, color, sex, national origin, or religion. Because previous hiring practices have often been discriminatory, many companies have implemented selection procedures designed not only to prevent discrimination but also to make up for and correct for the effects of past discrimination. For example, an organization might have established a hiring quota to increase the number of women in managerial positions; this quota might require that one female manager be hired for every male hired. Inevitably, the question before the courts has become: Do such voluntary quota systems constitute a form of illegal reverse discrimination against nonminority males?

Steelworkers v. Weber In ***Steelworkers v. Weber*** (1979), the Supreme Court ruled that a quota system used by Kaiser Aluminum and Chemical Corporation to admit persons into a training program did not constitute illegal reverse discrimination because the quota system was designed to correct the effects of the company's past discriminatory practices against blacks.[95] The *Weber* decision has been supported in several later court rulings, which have strongly backed the use of voluntary procedures to correct for past discrimination.[96]

Firefighters Local Union 1784 v. Stotts One important case indicates that actions taken as part of bona fide seniority systems may take precedence over voluntary quota systems. The city of Memphis, Tennessee, had instituted procedures to increase the number of minority firefighters in its employ. During a period of layoffs, however, a "last hired, first fired" policy was implemented, which had an adverse impact on recently hired black firefighters. In *Firefighters Local Union 1784 v. Stotts* (1984), the Supreme Court supported the seniority-based layoff policy and ruled that black firefighters could claim protection from the policy only if they had personally and directly been the object of hiring discrimination by the city of Memphis.[97] (Later in this chapter we outline some steps that management can take to minimize the possibility that a quota system set up as part of an AAP will result instead in reverse discrimination.)

City of Richmond v. J. A. Croson The city of Richmond, Virginia, had enacted an ordinance requiring prime contractors on city projects to subcontract at least 30 percent of the dollar amount to minority-owned businesses. The ordinance was passed in response to the fact that virtually none of the city's contracts had been awarded to minority businesses, even though 50 percent of the city's population was black. No direct evidence, however, was ever uncovered to prove that the city or its prime contractors actually discriminated against minorities. In *City of Richmond v. J. A. Croson* (1989), the U.S. Supreme Court ruled that the city of Richmond's program violated the equal protection clause of the U.S. Constitution because no evidence had been presented to demonstrate specific instances of minority discrimination. Set-aside programs of this kind would thus be permissible only if designed to correct demonstrable acts of past discrimination.[98] The Supreme Court's *Croson* decision put into question minority business set-aside programs in nearly forty states and 200 cities and counties throughout the United States.

Adarand Constructors, Inc. v. Pena The U.S. Supreme Court, in the case of *Adarand Constructors, Inc. v. Pena* (1995), ruled that preferential treatment based on race is almost always unconstitutional.[99] The 5 to 4 ruling was based on a case in Colorado in which Adarand, a white-owned Colorado-based highway construction company specializing in guardrail work, submitted the low bid. Gonzales Construction Company also submitted a bid and was awarded the contract based on its minority status. After losing the guardrail subcontract to Gonzales, Adarand filed suit claiming that the race-based decision violated its right to equal protection. In its decision, the Supreme Court supported Adarand's claim. A summary of affirmative action cases is provided in Table 5.5.

Uniform Guidelines

In 1978 the EEOC, along with several other government agencies, issued a set of guidelines for hiring employees. These guidelines, officially called the *Uniform Guidelines on Employee Selection Procedures* (also called the ***Uniform Guidelines***), outline what organizations should do to avoid illegal discrimination in selecting employees.[100] The EEOC has also issued special guidelines on sex, national origin, age, and religious discrimination. Although organizations are not required to follow the practices detailed in the *Uniform Guidelines,* the EEOC uses them to determine which charges of discrimination brought to it are legitimate and should be taken to court.

TABLE 5.5

Supreme Court AA Rulings by Category of Affirmative Actions

Voluntary AA	*Regents of University of California v. Bakke* (1978)
	Steelworkers v. Weber (1979)
	Wygant v. Jackson (1986)
	Johnson v. Transportation (1987)
	Gratz et al. v. Bollinger et al. (2003)
	Grutter v. Bollinger et al. (2003)
Court Ordered Affirmative Action	*Local 28 (Sheet Metal Workers) v. EEOC* (1986)
	United States v. Paradise (1987)
Court Approved Consent Decrees	*Firefighters Local Union 1784 v. Stotts* (1984)
	Local 93 (Firefighters) v. Cleveland (1986)
	Martin v. Wilks (1989)
Government Set-Asides	*Fullilove v. Klutznick* (1980)
	Metro v. FCC (1990)
	City of Richmond v. J. A. Croson (1989)
	Adarand Constructors, Inc. v. Pena (1995)

Source: Adapted from Art Gutman, "Affirmative Action: What's Going On?" *Industrial-Organizational Psychologist,* October 2002, Vol. 40 (2), pp. 59–68.

ENFORCEMENT OF EEO LAWS AND REGULATIONS

In the majority of EEO cases, individuals who believe they have been discriminated against bring complaints to the EEOC or to the OFCCP (although the OFCCP usually turns individual discrimination complaints over to the EEOC). These agencies examine the facts of each case, decide whether or not illegal discrimination has occurred, and attempt to arrange a settlement between the individual and the organization. If no settlement is reached, the agencies cannot force a settlement on an employer but may take the issue to federal court. The courts can force an organization to make changes in its selection or other HR practices.

The individual who files a complaint with the EEOC or OFCCP is called the complainant or the charging party. In court, this individual may be called the plaintiff. The organization against which the complaint is filed may be referred to as the respondent or, in court, as the defendant.

As described previously, more and more employers are likely to require employees to sign an agreement to submit all employment-related disputes to a neutral arbitrator under the Federal Arbitration Act. Thus arbitration becomes a further method of enforcing EEO regulations.

Equal Employment Opportunity Commission

In addition to Title VII problems, the EEOC handles issues related to the Equal Pay Act, the Pregnancy Discrimination Act, the Age Discrimination in Employment Act, and the Americans with Disabilities Act. The major activity of the agency is to process charges of discrimination related to these laws. Table 5.3 shows the number of private-sector charges received over a seven-year period. Charges received varied from a low of 77,444 in 1999 to 84,442 in 2002.[101] In each of the years approximately one-quarter of the charges were for racial discrimination, with sex discrimination close behind in the number of cases filed. Age, disabilities, and sexual harassment each accounted for approximately 15 percent of the charges.

Of interest, the vast majority of charges filed with the EEOC were determined to have no reasonable cause (57 to 63 percent) or were dropped administratively (17 to 28 percent). Administrative closure generally stems from the failure of the charging party to respond to EEOC communications. (Remember, given the EEOC backlog, communication may be many months after the charge was filed, and the problem may have been resolved.) The conclusion of "no cause" means that there is no reason to believe discrimination occurred based on the evidence examined. The charging party may request a review in such "no cause" findings and may exercise the right to bring private court action. Also of interest, the EEOC brings suit in less than 1 percent of cases. An example of such a suit is the case of the drug maker Astra USA, discussed earlier.

A schematic of the EEOC's charge-processing procedure is presented in Figure 5.2. Procedural steps must occur within certain time limits after the discriminatory act has occurred; these time limits are included in the figure.

The Charge A charge is filed against an organization, usually by a private individual. This charge must be made to the federal EEOC or to a state or local EEO agency within 180 days of the occurrence of the alleged discriminatory act. If the charge is first processed by a state or local agency, and if that agency's actions are not satisfactory to the individual, the individual has up to 300 days from the occurrence, or 30 days after the state or local agency has concluded its investigation and rulings, to file with the federal EEOC.[102]

The Investigation The EEOC must investigate the charge to see whether discrimination has occurred. The EEOC may interview the complainant and personnel in the organization (e.g., supervisors or coworkers) to determine the facts; the EEOC also may ask the organization to provide data (from personnel files) relevant to the charge. Once the investigation is complete, the EEOC makes a ruling. The EEOC may rule that there is reasonable cause to believe that discrimination has occurred. If reasonable cause is found, the EEOC attempts to conciliate the dispute. If no reasonable cause is found, the EEOC dismisses the case. Complainants may then, on their own, file suit against the company in federal court.

The Conciliation Meeting An EEOC mediator (conciliator) meets first with the complainant to work out an acceptable settlement and then tries to get the employer to agree to it. This process of trying to reach an out-of-court settlement is called **conciliation.** The conciliator then draws up a conciliation agreement, which is signed by the complainant, the employer, and the EEOC. The conciliation agreement is a written document that lists the violations that occurred and the agreed-upon corrective actions that will be taken by the employer. The agreement might include actions such as granting the employee a promotion that had been denied because of discrimination, giving back pay, or instituting new company policies to prevent discrimination in the future. If a conciliation agreement is not achieved, the EEOC may

FIGURE 5.2
EEOC Charge-Processing Procedure

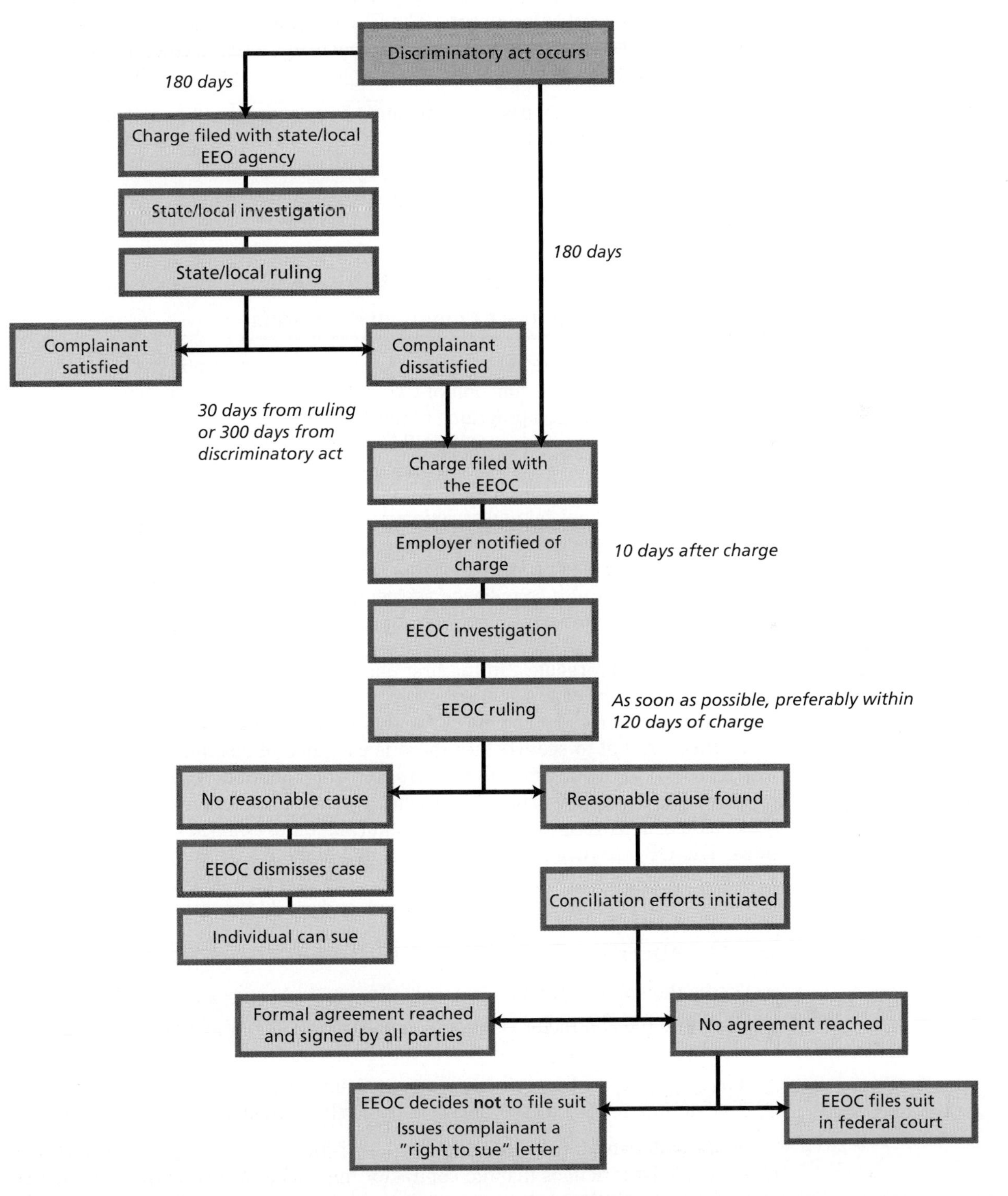

then file suit against the company in federal court or provide a **right-to-sue letter** to the complainant, who can then file suit on his or her own behalf.

EEOC and Judicial Enforcement The EEOC enforces the laws through conciliation agreements or the federal courts. The courts may order a company to take the following actions:

- Remedy the effects of past discrimination by granting back pay, promotions, or retroactive seniority to specific individuals who have been discriminated against.[103]
- Cease discrimination by modifying discriminatory policies and practices or by using temporary quotas to achieve racial balance.[104]
- Pay the attorney's fees of the complainant.

Office of Federal Contract Compliance Programs

The OFCCP enforces the provisions of executive orders relating to employment discrimination. A primary function of the OFCCP is to conduct reviews to ensure that the affirmative action programs required by executive orders are carried out. The review process used by the OFCCP is outlined in Figure 5.3.

Types of Reviews The OFCCP may conduct a complaint investigation when an individual files a complaint of discrimination against a company. The OFCCP often turns the complaint over to the EEOC but can choose to investigate the complaint itself. A pre-award review of an organization may be conducted before it receives a federal contract. A regular compliance review may be conducted of an organization covered by executive orders, even if no complaint of discrimination has been filed.

The Review Procedure In the first phase of a review—the **desk audit**—the OFCCP requests the contractor to provide relevant information about its recruitment activities, hiring practices, and the makeup of its present work force. The OFCCP reviews this material to see whether there is evidence of discrimination or whether practices dictated by the executive orders are being followed. If there is no evidence of violations, the review may end. If possible violations are found, the OFCCP conducts an on-site review and seeks other information to confirm or refute the violations. The OFCCP may request additional personnel data and conduct interviews with company employees. When the on-site review is completed, the OFCCP may take additional information from the company and conduct an off-site analysis.

OFCCP Decisions The OFCCP may take one of three actions:

- Notify the contractor that it is in compliance.
- Find that the contractor is not in compliance and turn the case over to the Justice Department for prosecution in the federal courts.
- Find that the contractor is not in compliance, issue a show-cause statement, and attempt to remedy the violations through additional OFCCP involvement.

A **show-cause statement** includes a list of the violations that the OFCCP has identified, a list of actions that the contractor must take to correct these violations, and a request that the contractor reply in writing as to how it will correct the violations or present further evidence to prove that no violations have actually occurred.

FIGURE 5.3

OFCCP Review Procedure

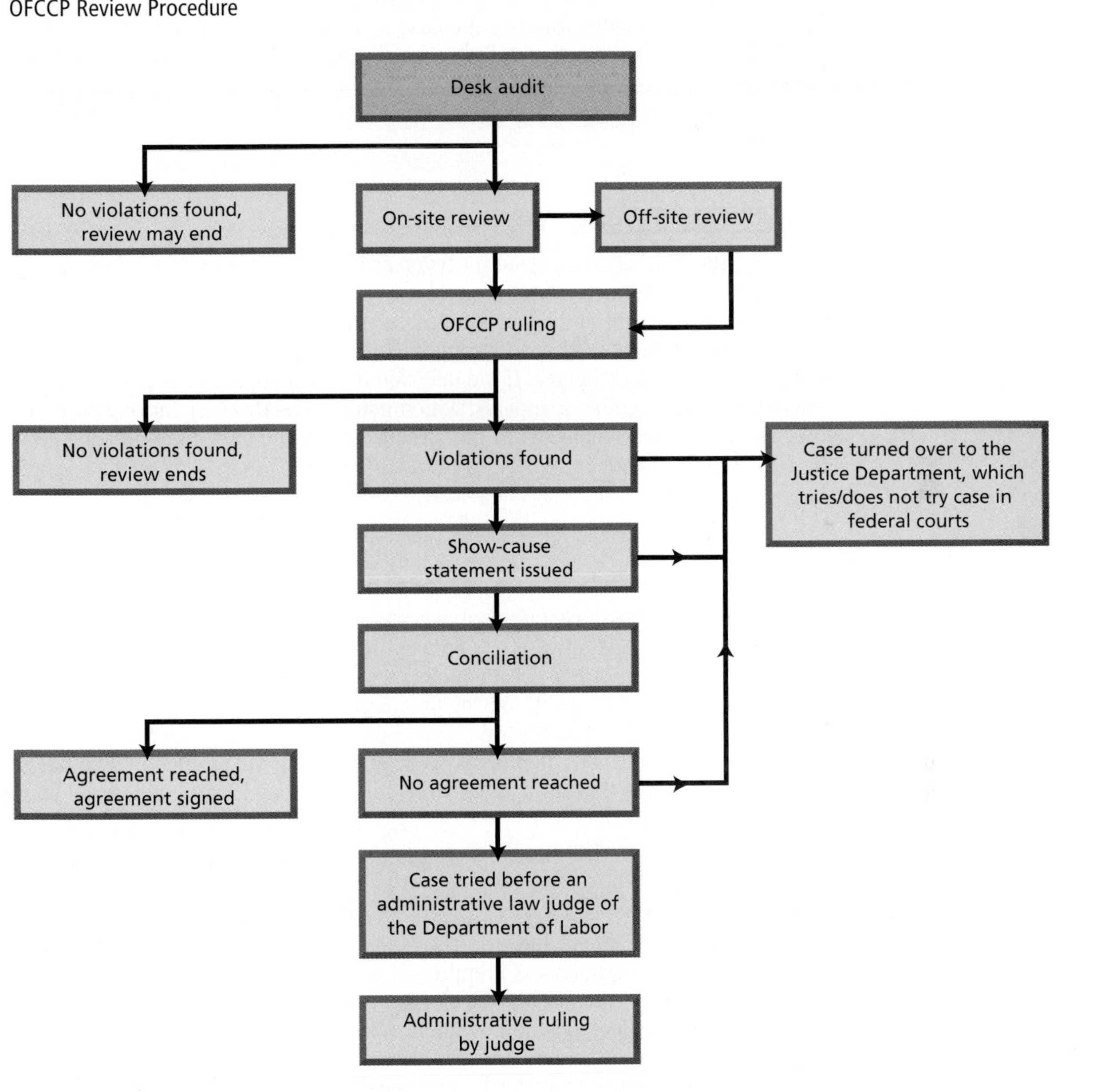

If a satisfactory agreement is not reached, the OFCCP may enforce its decision using administrative procedures or turn the case over to the Justice Department.

Administrative and Judicial Enforcement The OFCCP may enforce its rulings by taking the case to an administrative law judge within the Department of Labor. This judge can rule against the company and (1) cancel the company's federal contract, (2) suspend the company from receiving contracts for a specified time period, (3) permanently prevent the company from receiving federal contracts, or (4) take other appropriate actions.

Alternatively, the OFCCP can turn the case over to the Justice Department at several junctures before or after a show-cause statement has been issued. The Justice Department decides whether the case is strong enough to take to court. The court can provide "injunctive relief"—that is, make the company stop acting in ways that violate the executive orders—suspend or cancel the company's federal contracts, or institute other actions similar to the methods of EEOC enforcement discussed earlier.

The Federal Courts

Typically, the federal court system serves as the final step in the enforcement of EEO laws. A discrimination suit may pass through three levels in the federal court system. First, the suit is filed in a federal district court. The Civil Rights Act of 1991 allows discrimination cases to be brought to a jury. Previously all Title VII cases were decided by judges. If the decision is appealed, the case goes to the federal district circuit court of appeals, which usually has three or more judges hear the case as a panel. Finally, from the circuit courts, the case may be appealed to the U.S. Supreme Court.

PROVING ILLEGAL DISCRIMINATION

The court system has a very formal process for establishing guilt in EEO cases. This process is associated with the concept of burden of proof. The plaintiff provides evidence to indicate a **prima facie case** of discrimination. *Prima facie* simply means "on the face of it" or "at first sight." The evidence presented must suggest, at first sight, that the employer has discriminated. Once a prima facie case has been established, the burden of proof shifts to the employer, who has the opportunity to show that its actions were not illegal and are justified for sound business reasons.

The Prima Facie Case

The most direct way to establish a prima facie case is to show that the employer overtly discriminated against a member of a protected class. Statements by the employer such as "We do not hire blacks as managers" or job advertisements such as "Management trainee position: women need not apply" would make a convincing prima facie case. But rarely do such blatant examples of discrimination exist. A prima facie case is usually established by proving disparate treatment or disparate impact.

Disparate Treatment (*McDonnell Douglas Corp. v. Green*) **Disparate treatment** occurs when one employee is treated differently from other workers because of his or her race, sex, national origin, or the like. In such a situation, different standards are applied to different types of people. The court case that most clearly describes how illegal discrimination can be proven in a case of disparate treatment is ***McDonnell Douglas Corp. v. Green*** (1973).[105] In this case, Green, a black mechanic/technician at McDonnell Douglas Corporation, was laid off as part of a company-wide work force reduction. Green protested that his layoff was racially motivated and joined protests against McDonnell Douglas that included blocking highway accesses to the McDonnell Douglas plant. Green was arrested for these protest activities. In 1965 McDonnell Douglas placed job advertisements for qualified mechanics/technicians. Green applied for the job but was rejected. He filed a case of racial discrimination against McDonnell Douglas. In deciding this case, the Supreme Court said that, first, Green had to prove a prima facie case of discrimination by showing the following:

- He was a member of a protected class.
- He applied for a job for which he was qualified.
- He was rejected.
- The employer continued to seek applicants for the job.

These criteria for showing a prima facie case of discrimination have become known as the *McDonnell Douglas v. Green* rule. Green's situation met the requirements of this rule and indicated a prima facie case of racial discrimination. The Supreme Court stated, however, that simply showing a prima facie case of discrimination did not end the process: The employer had to be given the chance to defend its actions. In this case, McDonnell Douglas defended itself by stating that Green had been rejected because he had participated in illegal actions against the company (the blocking of highways to the plant). The Supreme Court accepted this defense as reasonable. The Court then stated that Green should have the opportunity to prove that the organization's rationale for his rejection was, in fact, a cover-up for a racially discriminatory decision. The Court suggested that data showing that McDonnell Douglas had rehired white workers, but not black workers, who had committed acts of similar seriousness against the company would be useful in invalidating the company's defense. Data showing that McDonnell Douglas had a general pattern of discriminatory practices against blacks (e.g., that McDonnell Douglas hired very few minority workers for any jobs) also would be useful. The Court indicated that Green had not provided sufficient evidence to refute the company's rationale for rejecting his application.

Disparate Impact (*Griggs v. Duke Power Co.*) In *Griggs v. Duke Power Co.* (1971),[106] the Supreme Court established the concept of disparate impact as a type of discrimination. The *Griggs* approach was specifically upheld by Congress in the Civil Rights Act of 1991. **Disparate impact,** also called **adverse impact,** occurs when the same standards are applied to all employees but have very different consequences for particular groups. In the *Griggs* case, Willie Griggs, a black man, applied for the job of coal handler at the Duke Power Company. The company, which required that all coal handlers have high school diplomas, rejected Griggs because he did not. Griggs filed a suit against the company, claiming that the diploma requirement had nothing to do with a person's ability to do the job and that it discriminated against blacks because a lower percentage of blacks had high school diplomas than did whites. In this case of adverse impact, the Supreme Court ruled that in proving a prima facie case of discrimination, Griggs did not have to show that Duke Power Company intended to discriminate against blacks but simply that the policies of the company had an adverse impact on them. The *Griggs* ruling and other court decisions have held that at least three types of data can be used to show a prima facie case of disparate impact.[107] These types of data are presented in Table 5.6.

TABLE 5.6

Types of Data Used to Show Disparate Impact

Comparison/ Type of Data	Ratio 1				Ratio 2				Ratio1/Ratio 2
1. *Comparison of Actual Impact*	*Minorities[a] Hired*	*Minority Applicants*	*Ratio Hired*	*Percent Hired*	*Majorities Hired*	*Majority Applicants*	*Ratio Hired*	*Percent Hired*	*60% Minorities Hired* / 68.2% Majorities Hired
Hiring data	60	100	60/100	60%	75	110	75/110	68.2%	
2. *Comparison of Potential Impact*	*All Minorities in Labor Market*	*Qualified[b] Minorities in Labor Market*	*Ratio of Potentially Hireable Minorities*	*Percent of Potentially Hireable Minorities*	*All Majorities in Labor Market*	*Qualified Majorities in Labor Market*	*Ratio of Potentially Hireable Majorities*	*Percent of Potentially Hireable Majorities*	*50% Potentially Hireable Minorities* / 80% Potentially Hireable Majorities
Labor-market data	10,000	5,000	5,000/ 10,000	50%	25,000	20,000	20,000/ 25,000	80%	
3. *Comparison of Work Force to Population*	*Minorities in Company Work Force*	*Total Company Work Force*	*Minority Ratio to Total Work Force*	*Minority Percent of Total Work Force*	*Minorities in Local Population*	*Total Local Population*	*Minority Ratio to Population*	*Minority Percent of Population*	*6% Minorities in Work Force* / 41.7% Minorities in Population
Population and company data	30	500	30/500	6%	25,000	60,000	25,000/ 60,000	41.7%	

[a] "Minorities" means protected classes such as blacks, Hispanics, or women.

[b] In this context, the term "qualified" means that the person has some specific qualification that the employer seeks in hiring workers (e.g., a high school diploma).

A comparison of the actual impact of selection procedures may be used to determine whether disparate impact exists. In comparison 1 of Table 5.6, the minority members hired–minority applicants ratio is compared with the majority members hired–majority applicants ratio. If these ratios are radically different from each other, the difference would indicate that discrimination might have occurred somewhere in the selection process. Alternatively, if an organization had some specific qualification that it required of employees—a high school diploma in the case of Duke Power Company—disparate impact could be shown by looking at the potential effect the requirement would have on minority and majority applicants.

In comparison 2 of Table 5.6, only 50 percent of the minorities in the labor market have a high school education, as opposed to 80 percent of the majorities. A significant adverse impact could occur if an organization used a high school education as a selection requirement.

The third type of disparate impact data involves comparing the proportion of minorities in the company's work force with the proportion of minorities in the local population. If minorities comprise 41.7 percent of the local population but only 6 percent of the company's work force, for example, this inequity might constitute a prima facie case of discrimination.

In *Griggs v. Duke Power Co.*, the prima facie case of discrimination was established using data that showed the potential impact of the hiring requirement on black applicants (see comparison 2 of Table 5.6). In rebutting the prima facie case, the company argued (1) that the hiring requirement was fair because it was applied to all applicants and (2) that there was no intention to discriminate. The good intent of the company was demonstrated by its practice of helping to fund the education of workers who attempted to complete their high school education. The Court rejected this defense, saying that impact, not intent, was the key issue in determining discrimination. Furthermore, the company had no proof that having a high school diploma had any fundamental relationship to on-the-job performance of employees.

Four-Fifths Rule A major question related to proving disparate impact is: How do we decide when the impact is adverse enough to be considered discriminatory? The EEOC has developed a rule of thumb for determining adverse impact. It is called the **four-fifths rule.** The EEOC applies this rule to actual impact data to determine whether a prima facie case of discrimination exists.[108] The rule states that if the minorities hired–minority applicants ratio is less than four-fifths (80 percent) of the majority members hired–majority applicants ratio, then a prima facie case of discrimination exists. For example, in comparison 1 of Table 5.6, the minority ratio is 60/100 (60 percent, or .60), and the majority ratio is 75/110 (68.2 percent, or .682). To compare the two selection rates, 0.60 is divided by 0.682, yielding 0.879 (or 87.9 percent). Thus the minority ratio is greater than four-fifths (or 80 percent) of the majority ratio, and no prima facie case exists.

Retaliation A special form of disparate treatment is **retaliation.** Employers cannot retaliate—by firing, demoting, harassing, or otherwise treating employees unfairly—because employees have filed discrimination charges. In *EEOC v. Union Bank of Arizona* (1976), the Court ruled that protection against retaliation should be extended even to employees who suffered retaliation because their employer mistakenly believed that they had filed a charge.[109] In *United States v. City of Socorro* (1976), a federal district court ruled that it was illegal discrimination to retaliate against an employee whose spouse had filed a charge of discrimination.[110] Employees who are retaliated against can get injunctive relief from the retaliation.[111] Section 706 of Title VII of the Civil Rights Act of 1964 allows the EEOC to seek immediate relief from retaliation for an individual filing a charge of discrimination, even though the EEOC has not completed its processing of the charge.

Rebutting a Prima Facie Case

A company can defend itself against a prima facie case of adverse impact or treatment by using the defenses of job relatedness, bona fide occupational qualification, bona fide seniority system, or business necessity.

Job Relatedness Showing **job relatedness** is a defense that is appropriate in situations in which an apparently neutral practice of the organization has a disparate impact on some protected class. The company must show that its procedures are related to employee performance. For example, an employer may be able to justify the adverse impact on women caused by a 6 foot, 2 inch height requirement by showing that individuals who are less than 6 feet, 2 inches tall have difficulty performing the job. The height requirement would not constitute illegal discrimination because it relates directly to the ability of workers to perform their job.

If an employer can show that individuals who score below seventy on an ability test have difficulty performing the job, then hiring only applicants with scores of seventy or above may be justified, even if this selection requirement adversely affects black applicants. However, proving that a particular hiring requirement is job related is not easy. In ***Albermarle Paper Company v. Moody*** (1975), Albermarle had used test scores of verbal and nonverbal intelligence in selecting job applicants.[112] The company had hired an industrial psychologist to determine the job relatedness of these tests, and the psychologist had found a significant correlation between test scores and supervisor ratings of employee performance. Moody, a black employee of Albermarle, filed a charge of racial discrimination against the company and successfully proved that the tests had an adverse impact on black job applicants. In ruling on the case, the Supreme Court stated that to show job relatedness, a company must first analyze and document the tasks and responsibilities of the job. The Court also stated that performance standards must be clear and unambiguous so as to allow the employer to accurately determine which employees are high (or low) performers. Albermarle had met neither of these requirements. No systematic job analysis had been conducted, and the performance ratings used were highly subjective and ambiguous in nature. The Court ruled in favor of Moody. A detailed description of how an organization can show the job relatedness of hiring requirements is provided in the *Uniform Guidelines* and is discussed further in Chapter 7.

Bona Fide Occupational Qualification Another defense against a prima facie case of adverse treatment is the **bona fide occupational qualification (BFOQ).** The BFOQ defense has been interpreted narrowly by both the EEOC and the courts and can be based on age, sex, religion, or national origin but not on race or color. An employer claiming its conduct was based on a BFOQ admits sex-based treatment, for example, but maintains that the differential treatment is necessary to promote legitimate business objectives. Thus, requiring that only male actors be considered for the role of Julius Caesar would be justifiable because "maleness" is an inherent part of the character of Julius Caesar. In *Dothard v. Rawlinson* (1977), the Supreme Court held that refusing to hire females as prison guards in an all-male prison was justifiable as a BFOQ.[113] Because the BFOQ defense involves the direct use of age, sex, religion, or national origin in making selection decisions, organizations hoping to use this defense must have very convincing evidence to support their cases. In *Diaz v. Pan American World Airways* (1971), the company had used sex (only women were hired) as a BFOQ for hiring flight attendants.[114] Pan Am did not have any strong evidence to prove that only women were capable of performing flight attendants' essential duties of serving food and drinks and providing for the safety of the passengers. A federal court ruled that sex was not a BFOQ for the job of flight attendant.

Bona Fide Seniority System A third possible defense is the **bona fide seniority system.** Organizational actions that result in disparate treatment or disparate impact may be justified if the actions are part of a bona fide seniority system. In *Teamsters v. United States* (1977), the Supreme Court decided that seniority systems that had the effect of locking minorities into lower level jobs were valid as long as the intent of the seniority systems was not to discriminate.[115] The definition of a bona fide seniority system as one that does not intend to discriminate has been supported in other court decisions.[116] In *Firefighters Local Union 1784 v. Stotts,* discussed earlier, the "last hired, first fired" policy used by the city of Memphis in laying off firefighters had an adverse impact on black employees. Nevertheless, the Supreme Court ruled that the policy was justified because it was part of a bona fide seniority system.

Business Necessity A final defense is **business necessity.** Employers may justify practices that result in disparate treatment or disparate impact if the actions are essential to efficient and safe operation of the company. In *Furnco Construction Corporation v. Waters* (1978), the Supreme Court accepted the company's practice of requiring job applicants to possess certain experience, skills, and training because improper performance of the job could result in serious physical harm to employees.[117] These requirements had an adverse impact on black job applicants but were justified by business necessity. Employers using the business necessity defense generally have been required to prove that there existed an overriding necessity, not simply a convenience for their actions.[118]

MANAGEMENT'S RESPONSE

The final factor in the EEO environment is management and the responses it makes to EEO laws and regulations. In this section we examine the actions that management should take to deal effectively with equal employment opportunity.

Take Control

The most important step in dealing effectively with EEO activities is for management to take control of them in the organization.[119] The key elements of control are information, policy, and communication. An organization should regularly conduct a self-analysis to examine the status of minority, female, and disabled workers. The company may wish to develop and regularly update special logs

FIGURE 5.4

Discipline/Discharge Log

Source: Adapted from V. Grossman, *Employing Handicapped Persons: Meeting EEO Obligations.* Reprinted by permission of BNA Books, Washington, D.C.

Location: ______________________ From: ______________________ To: ______________________

Name	Race / Sex	Handicap / Age	A. Type of discipline	B. Job-related reason for discipline	C. Job-related reason for discharge	D. Type of separation	Reason for other type of separation	Date recalled or returned if laid off or on leave of absence

Place proper symbols, numbers, or answers in each column.

Race: M—Minority
NM—Non-minority
Sex: F—Female
M—Male
Handicapped—H
Age—Put age if employee is 40 years of age or older

A. Type of Discipline
1—Verbal warning
2—First written warning
3—Second written warning
4—Demotion
5—Suspension (specify number of days)
6—Discharge

B. Job-Related Reason for Discipline
1—Unsafe work performance
2—Ineffective work performance
3—Failure to obey a supervisor
4—Failure to obey the employer's policy
5—Interfering with the work performance of other employees
6—Unexcused lateness or tardiness
7—Unexcused absences
8—Other (specify)

C. Job-Related Reason for Discharge
1—Did not receive written recommendation to work from drug or alcoholism counselor or physician
2—Did not receive written recommendation to work from physician or counselor because of mental, physical, or emotional condition
3—Unsafe work performance
4—Ineffective work performance
5—Failure to obey a supervisor
6—Failure to obey the employer's policy
7—Interfering with the work performance of other employees
8—Unexcused tardiness
9—Unexcused absences

D. Type of Separation
1—Resignation
2—Layoff
3—Sick leave
4—Other leave of absence
5—Death
6—Retirement
7—Disability
8—Discharge

on a variety of personnel decisions. A sample data log of employee discipline/discharge decisions is presented in Figure 5.4. This information allows the company to identify areas in which disparate impact or disparate treatment may be occurring and provides the basis for a defense of company policies in discrimination suits.

An organization should collect information concerning the potential impact new HR policies may have on its work force. For example, organizations forced to make layoffs should evaluate the likely impact of these layoffs on minorities, women, and older workers. If need be, the companies could take steps to lessen the adverse effect of the layoffs on these protected groups and thus prevent discrimination complaints.

All organizations should develop formal, written policies concerning equal employment opportunity. An example of such a policy against sexual harassment is presented in Figure 5.5. However, policies are effective only to the extent that they are understood by employees. The Ethical Perspective box addresses another problematic policy area—anti-nepotism rules.

The last element of control is communication. The organization should make sure that EEO policies are displayed widely and prominently throughout the company. The organization should develop special training programs to transmit knowledge of EEO issues and the company's EEO policies to managers, first-line supervisors, and other key employees.

Make Procedures Objective and Job Related

Employers' decisions about hiring, firing, promoting, and providing benefits to employees must be objective and job related. Testing procedures used to hire employees should be validated using techniques consistent with the EEOC's *Uniform Guidelines.* (These techniques are discussed in more detail in Chapter 7.) When decisions are based on performance evaluations of employees, the procedures

FIGURE 5.5

A Corporate Policy against Sexual Harassment of Employees

Policy of Acme Electronics Corporation

Corporate policy is that all employees have the right to work in an environment free of discrimination. One form of discrimination is sexual harassment. Corporate policy concerning sexual harassment is as follows:

Any employee found engaging in sexual harassment will be subject to:

—Official reprimands that will be placed in the employee's permanent personnel file
—Suspension from work without pay
—Demotion to a lower-paying job assignment
—Discharge from the company
—Other appropriate action

No supervisor shall explicity or implicity threaten that a subordinate's refusal to submit to sexual advances will result in adverse effects on the worker's employment, pay, promotions, assigned duties, or any other condition of employment. Acme employees are prohibited from engaging in behavior of a sexual nature that would create an offensive, unpleasant, or otherwise hostile work environment; e.g., telling jokes of a sexual nature, offensive flirtations, sexual advances or propositions, comments concerning the bodies of members of the opposite sex, or using sexually explicit words that might be considered offensive.

Acme Corporation encourages any employee who feels he/she has been the victim of sexual harassment to report the incident to his/her supervisor or to Bob Farrow, chair of the EEO Compliance Committee (456-2534, Room 423 in the Personnel Office). The incident will be investigated, and corrective action will be taken if appropriate. Acme management is committed to eliminating this type of behavior from our company and will take every step necessary to protect individuals from it.

ETHICAL PERSPECTIVE

Anti-Nepotism Rules—Fair or Unfair?

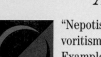

"Nepotism is the practice of showing favoritism to relatives and close friends."* Examples would include hiring or promoting a relative largely because of the relationship and at the expense of more qualified candidates who are not related to the decision maker. The authors of a text on business ethics, William Shaw and Vincent Barry, point out that this action "would raise a number of moral concerns; chief among them would be disregard both of managerial responsibilities to the organization and of fairness to all other applicants."†

To prevent this potential conflict of interest and the unfairness that may arise when relatives are hired, a number of organizations have adopted anti-nepotism rules. The most extreme form of the rule prohibits the employment of a relative of an employee anywhere in the organization, even at another site. Less extreme rules prohibit the employment of related people at the same site or in the same department. The most limited type of anti-nepotism rule is a no-supervision rule, which states that one may not have decision-making authority (regarding job assignment, appraisal, hiring, or compensation) over a relative.

Anti-nepotism rules were invented to prevent abuses and served this role reasonably well until the explosion in the number of dual-career couples in the 1970s. Suddenly, rules that were intended to prevent hiring unqualified relatives were prohibiting the employment of highly qualified individuals who just happened to be married to current employees. If the spouse is qualified on his or her own merits, a rule intended to ensure fairness in employment now causes unfairness.

A more difficult situation arises when coworkers marry. Presumably both were hired on their own merits, but a no-spouse rule may now decree that one must transfer to another department or leave the organization altogether. Somehow, the presence of one's spouse is presumed to have an immediate and deleterious effect on one's ability to perform the job properly.

Most no-spouse rules are written in sexually neutral language (no spouses, as versus no wives of male employees), but some have been challenged in court. Title VII–based challenges focus on the fact that anti-nepotism rules often have an adverse impact on women. In the case of coworkers who marry, the Fifth and the Fourteenth Amendments, which protect the right to marry, have been invoked. With some exceptions, no-spouse rules have been upheld by the courts. Legality, however, does not guarantee fairness.

Even more complex problems can be created when intimate relationships short of marriage take place between coworkers or between a superior and a subordinate. Should no-spouse rules be applied to coworkers who are cohabiting? Dating? When a boss is romantically involved with a subordinate, perceptions of favoritism may occur, and if the relationship goes sour, sexual harassment charges are a possibility. On the other hand, most people feel that legal off-the-job

used to assess performance should be as objective and directly related to the job as possible. Job analysis should be used to determine the important aspects of job performance. Performance should be assessed by persons who have been trained in performance-rating techniques and have had adequate time to observe the performance of the individual(s) being rated. (The details of how to set up a good performance appraisal system are discussed in Chapter 10.)

Develop Grievance Procedures

In cases of discharges, promotions, or sexual, racial, ethnic, or religious harassment, the availability of formal grievance procedures often aids in resolving complaints of discrimination so that the EEOC's involvement is not necessary. Every

behavior such as dating is a private matter and none of the employer's business.

Some organizations are accommodating dual career couples by relaxing stringent anti-nepotism rules that were adopted before large numbers of married women entered the labor force. They find that these antiquated rules deny them the services of potentially excellent employees and also complicate recruiting professionals, who are often married to other professionals. A sensible policy for many organizations seems to be to emphasize ability and merit, rather than relationship or nonrelationship, in all personnel decisions and, if necessary, to adopt a no-supervision-of-spouses rule. This prevents any suspicion of favoritism and reassures employees who are not related to the boss that evenhanded treatment will prevail. Effective anti-nepotism policies also specify exactly which relationships are covered (stepchildren? third cousins?) and which procedures will be followed should one member of a related pair need to be transferred or terminated.

An alternate approach is taken by firms such as Steelcase, Inc., which intentionally hires married couples and relatives. Usually 10 to 18 percent of new hires are sons or daughters of employees. Quad/Graphics, a large printing company in Wisconsin, reports that over half its employees are related in some fashion. Allowing the employment of relatives helps to create a family-like work atmosphere and may be the only option when a firm is one of few major employers in a small community. However, an exclusive emphasis on hiring relatives might limit diversity and equal opportunity for members of minority groups not traditionally employed by the firm.

Note that in the international arena, nepotism takes on a whole different flavor. In a great many countries, especially those with a collectivist culture, individuals have a positive duty to look after their relatives and friends by employing them. Failing to do so would be a breach of their moral responsibilities. In countries such as Thailand, India, Mexico, Korea, and Indonesia, who you know is said to be more important than what you know, especially in hiring for small and medium-sized organizations. Expatriate managers must be sure they understand the local context before passing harsh judgment on nepotistic practices that would be problematic back home.

Notes: *William Shaw and Vincent Barry, *Moral Issues in Business* (Belmont, Calif.: Wadsworth, 1989), p. 240.
†Ibid.

Sources: Len Bierman and Cynthia D. Fisher, "Anti-Nepotism Rules Applied to Spouses: Business and Legal Viewpoints," *Labor Law Journal,* 1984, pp. 634–642; J. M. Steiner and S. P. Steinberg, "Caught Between Scylla and Charybdis: Are Anti-Nepotism Policies Benign Paternalism or Covert Discrimination?" *Employee Relations,* Autumn 1994, pp. 253–267; Richard K. Zuckerman and Sharon N. Berlin, "Romance in the Workplace: Employers Can Make Rules If They Serve Legitimate Needs," *New York State Bar Journal,* September–October 1999; and Bless Stritar Young, "In the Family Way: Drafting Your Anti-Nepotism Policy," *ABA Law Practice Management,* February 2001. (Available at: www.abanet.org/lpm/newsarticle11695_front.shtml)

employer should have a formal grievance procedure that employees can use to deal with possible cases of discrimination. Such a procedure is usually available in unionized companies. Nonunionized organizations also should develop a formal grievance procedure. Figure 5.6 shows how such a procedure might work. Moreover, as noted earlier, some companies have adopted internal procedures culminating in binding outside arbitration.

Act Affirmatively

If evidence of discrimination exists in the organization, management should develop policies to correct the situation. These plans should be consistent with guidelines set forth by the OFCCP and the EEOC. In developing these plans, organizations

FIGURE 5.6

EEO Grievance Procedure for Sexual Harassment Complaint

Source: Reprinted with permission from *EEO Today,* Vol. 5, Spring 1978. Copyright 1978 by Executive Enterprises, Inc., 22 West 21st Street, New York, N.Y. 10010-6904. All rights reserved.

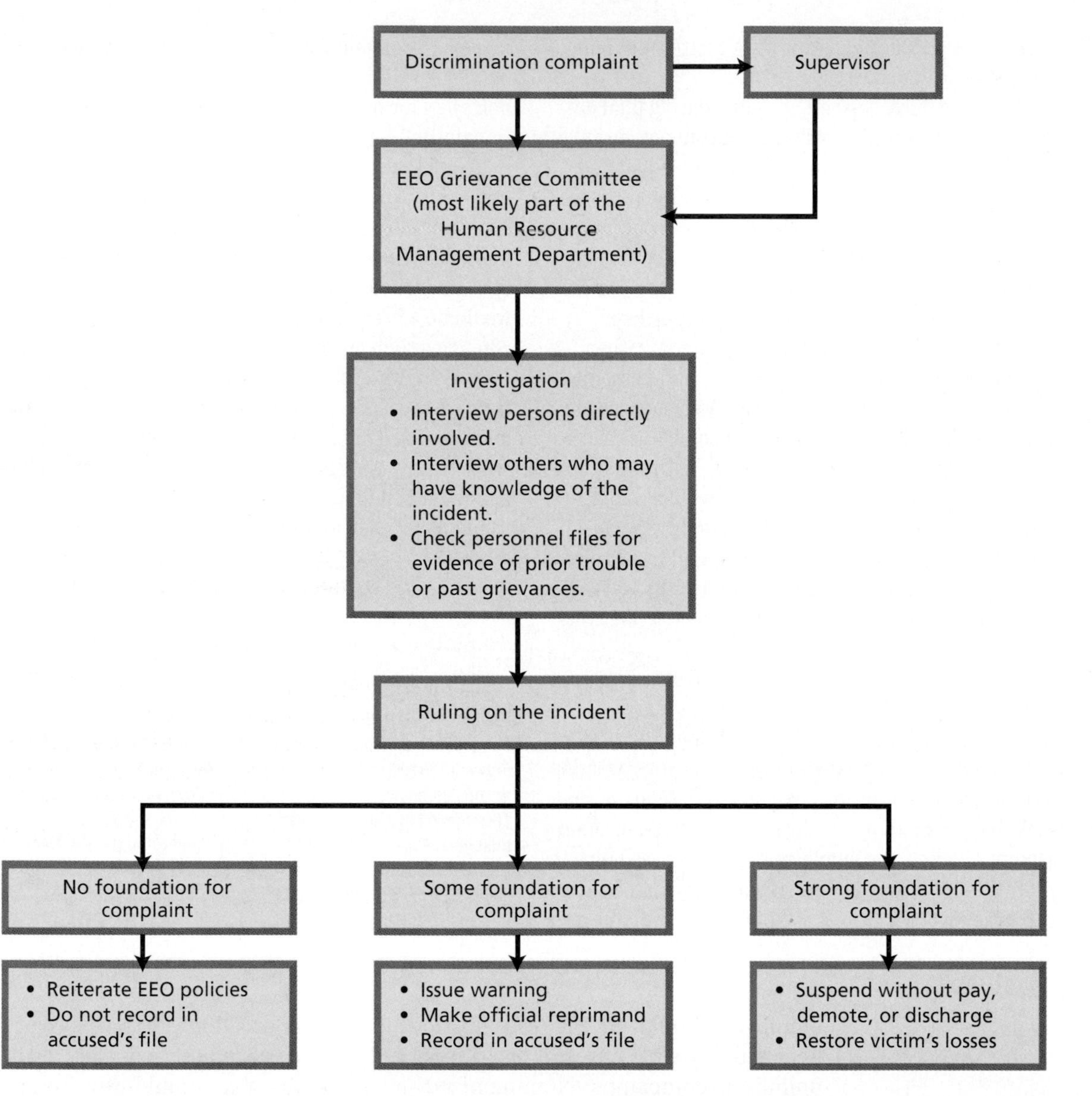

should make use of the minority, female, and disabled workers already in the company. These employees, formally brought into the process, can provide useful insights and information about how best to recruit and retain minority, female, and disabled workers. Employers should take into account the Supreme Court decision in *Steelworkers v. Weber,* discussed earlier in this chapter. In that case, the Court ruled that voluntary quota systems are acceptable to the extent that employers do the following:

- Avoid quota systems when no evidence of past discrimination exists.
- Develop plans that do not require the discharge of or have other significant ill effects on majority workers.
- Avoid setting minority quotas of greater than 50 percent.
- Develop plans that are temporary in nature and will end once the negative effects of past discrimination are corrected.[120]

If a Complaint Is Filed

If, despite the best efforts of the organization, an employee files a discrimination complaint with the Equal Employment Opportunity Commission, the actions of management remain critical. Management should make some of the following responses:

1. When notified by the EEOC that a charge has been filed, ask for a copy of the charge to find out precisely what the company has allegedly done.
2. Conduct an internal investigation to see if the charge is valid. During the investigation, take great care not to pressure or harass the individual who made the charge. Such harassment might result in the company being charged with retaliation.
3. Respond to the charge in writing. The response should be absolutely accurate and clearly state the organization's position. If the internal investigation shows that discrimination actually occurred, management should attempt to reach an equitable settlement with the employee.
4. Cooperate within reasonable limits with the EEOC or the OFCCP. During the EEOC's fact-finding investigation or the OFCCP's compliance review, the agency may ask for a large number and great variety of personnel documents. Management should take the position that it will gladly cooperate but will provide only documents that are relevant to the case at hand. Management need not turn over every available personnel document. Which data are turned over should result from a negotiation between management and the investigators. By providing unrestricted access to personnel data, the saying "Give me enough time and documents, and I'll find something illegal" will surely apply.

Summary of Key Points

There are many different aspects of discrimination under EEO law. These range from broad concepts, such as disparate treatment and disparate impact, to more specific instances, such as sexual harassment, pregnancy discrimination, discrimination against the disabled, and reverse discrimination. The U.S. Constitution, the laws passed by Congress and state legislatures, presidential executive orders, and guidelines of U.S. government agencies all provide protection against these various types of discrimination. The process by which an individual can prove discrimination by an employer has been clearly set out in the courts. This process requires the plaintiff to initially prove a prima facie case of discrimination, using data that show (1) that he or she has been treated differently from other employees because of his or her race, sex, religion, color, national origin, or disabled status or (2) that company policies have an adverse impact on some protected class. The organization then has an opportunity to defend its actions, on the basis of a BFOQ, seniority system, job relatedness, or business necessity.

Along with state and federal court systems, the Equal Employment Opportunity Commission, the Office of Federal Contract Compliance Programs, and the Justice Department help enforce the laws and executive orders that prohibit discrimination. These agents of enforcement can use a wide array of potential sanctions against organizations that discriminate. Increasingly, cases in this area are being subject to jury trials, and partly because of this, there has been a considerable growth in interest in the use of arbitration and other alternative methods to resolve disputes.

The final element in the EEO environment is management. By taking control, making HRM procedures objective and job related, setting up procedures to handle discrimination complaints when they arise, and acting affirmatively, management can prevent itself from becoming the object of discrimination lawsuits. Companies also may be able to purchase insurance policies to protect themselves against EEO lawsuits. By taking these steps, management can make maximum use of all the human resources available to it.

The Manager's Vocabulary

adverse impact
affirmative action
affirmative action plans (AAPs)
Age Discrimination in Employment Act
Albermarle Paper Company v. Moody
Americans with Disabilities Act
arbitration
bona fide occupational qualification (BFOQ)
bona fide seniority system
business necessity
Civil Rights Act of 1866
Civil Rights Act of 1871
Civil Rights Act of 1964
Civil Rights Act of 1991
conciliation
desk audit
disability
disparate impact
disparate treatment
equal employment opportunity (EEO)
Equal Pay Act
Executive Order 11246
Executive Order 11375
executive orders
Family and Medical Leave Act
Fifth Amendment
four-fifths rule
Fourteenth Amendment
glass ceiling
Griggs v. Duke Power Co.
Immigration Reform and Control Act
job relatedness
McDonnell Douglas Corp. v. Green
Meritor Savings Bank v. Vinson
Older Workers Protection Act
Pregnancy Discrimination Act
prima facie case
protected class
reasonable accommodation
retaliation
reverse discrimination
right-to-sue letter
sexual harassment
show-cause statement
Steelworkers v. Weber
Title VII
Uniform Guidelines
Vocational Rehabilitation Act

Questions for Discussion

1. What could Wal-Mart have done to prevent the charges of sex discrimination?
2. What are some of the reasons an organization should be interested in complying with EEO regulations? How is Wal-Mart an example of the necessity to comply?
3. In the context of discrimination laws, what is a protected class? Can someone who is not a member of a protected class claim discrimination in employment?
4. What sorts of practices are prohibited by the Equal Pay Act of 1963?
5. Do you agree with the U.S. Supreme Court's decision in the *Meritor* case? What is "environmental" sexual harassment? How do you prove its existence? To what extent should courts be permitted to hear evidence regarding the private sex lives of plaintiffs bringing harassment charges?
6. Suppose a friend of yours has been exposed to the AIDS virus and is HIV-positive. Your friend's

employer learns about this and fires your friend. Is this illegal employment discrimination?

7. Title VII of the Civil Rights Act of 1964 prohibits discrimination in employment based on race, color, sex, religion, or national origin. Executive Orders 11246 and 11375 require employers with federal contracts to act affirmatively in hiring employees. What is the difference between not discriminating and acting affirmatively?
8. In what ways is the Americans with Disabilities Act of 1990 (ADA) different from other civil rights legislation? In what ways is it the same?
9. A faculty member at your college requests a leave under the Family and Medical Leave Act of 1993 (FMLA) to help her daughter, who is expecting twins. Would such a request be covered by FMLA? How should the college respond?
10. What is affirmative action? Why is it controversial at the present time?
11. Is affirmative action permissible at your college to promote a more diverse student body?
12. What is a bona fide occupational qualification (BFOQ)? Can race be a BFOQ? Why or why not?
13. What are the roles of the Equal Employment Opportunity Commission (EEOC) and the Office of Federal Contract Compliance Programs (OFCCP)?
14. To prove that an organization has illegally discriminated against a person, the individual(s) must first show evidence of a prima facie case of discrimination. How is this done in a situation where disparate treatment has occurred? Where adverse impact has occurred?
15. Why are the Supreme Court cases *Griggs v. Duke Power Co.* (1971) and *Albermarle Paper Co. v. Moody* (1975) important to understanding discrimination in employment?
16. How would you rule if an employee fired for bringing a gun to work sued the employer under the ADA, claiming he had a "mental disability"?

Case 5.1
"What Is Reasonable Accommodation?"

You are the HR manager of the South Hampton plant of ABC Foods. One of your employees, Sarah Wentworth, operates a cereal packaging machine. Sarah transferred from another ABC Foods plant when it closed and has been a good worker on the day shift at South Hampton.

You are aware that Sarah is under a doctor's care for a mild form of epilepsy. Once or twice in a three-month period Sarah has daytime seizures that cause no problem in her work. She can feel the onset of a seizure and sits down near her machine until it passes. The seizures normally last a couple of minutes and cause shaking and a blank expression. After the seizure ends, Sarah is able to return to her machine and continue her work.

As Sarah completed her second year at the South Hampton plant, it was announced that the Valley Forge Plant of ABC Foods was closing and workers would be given the option of transferring into South Hampton on a seniority basis. This policy of allowing more senior employees to displace less senior employees under such circumstances is a common policy in many companies and was a long-standing policy at ABC Foods. Soon it became clear that a worker with twenty years Sarah's seniority from the Valley Forge plant would displace Sarah at South Hampton. Sarah was given the opportunity to transfer to the night shift.

When Sarah learned that she would be moved to the third (night) shift, she presented a letter to you (as HR manager). The letter from her physician stated that transferring shifts would cause a disturbance of her sleep pattern and thus worsen her seizures. Sarah requests that she be "accommodated" under the Americans with Disabilities Act (ADA) and be allowed to continue on the day shift.

You consult the ABC Foods' physician who disagrees, stating that Sarah's sleep pattern will not be disrupted so long as she is not assigned rotating shifts. On that basis, you decide to respect the seniority system and assign Sarah to the night shift.

1. Is Sarah disabled under the Americans with Disabilities Act (ADA)? Why or why not?
2. If you believe that Sarah is disabled, is ABC Foods required to accommodate her in accordance with the ADA? Why or why not?
3. If Sarah is not technically disabled under the ADA, should ABC Foods accommodate the request just the same?

Source: Adapted from *EEOC v. Sara Lee Corp.*, No. 00-1534 (4th Cir. January 9, 2001).

Exercise 5.1
Interviewing Under the ADA

As discussed throughout the chapter, the Americans with Disabilities Act, which became effective in July 1992, has had a monumental impact on the administration of equal employment opportunity laws. In general, employers may not, under the ADA, make pre-employment inquiries as to whether, or to what extent, an individual is disabled. Employers may, however, ask job applicants whether they can perform the "essential functions" of the job. The EEOC recently issued guidelines with regard to pre-employment inquiries under the ADA in an attempt to clarify what types of questions may be asked legally of job applicants. Some observers have countered, though, that these guidelines and the sample questions included with them have made matters even less clear. After each of the following sample questions, mark whether you think the question is *legal* or *illegal.*

1. How many days were you sick last year? __________
2. What physician-prescribed medications are you currently taking? __________
3. Are you able to lift things? __________
4. How well can you handle stress? __________
5. Can you perform this job function with or without reasonable accommodation? __________
6. When do you expect to recover completely from your broken arm? __________

Exercise 5.2
Affirmative Action Update

Your employer is interested in keeping up with the latest on affirmative action. As part of your job, you provide quarterly summaries of legislation, lawsuits, and court rulings. Using the following Web site, provide this quarter's summary (remember, the focus is on affirmative action only): http://www.shrm.org/hrlinks/legal.htm (HR Links, Society for Human Resource Management).

Exercise 5.3
Affirmative Action Debate

As a class, divide into an even number of groups to debate the proposition: *Affirmative action laws are largely a thing of the past in the modern workplace and mandating affirmative action can now be retired.*

1. Odd-numbered groups should prepare to make a case that affirmative action laws continue to be needed.
2. Even-numbered groups should prepare to make a case that affirmative action laws can now be retired.

Notes and References

1. Ann Zimmerman, "Wal-Mart Faces Class Action in Sex-Discrimination Case," *Wall Street Journal,* June 22, 2004. (Available at: http://online.wsj.com/article_print/0,,SB108790740256243925,00.html); Steven Greenhouse, "Judge Certifies Suit Accuses Wal-Mart of Sex Discrimination," *New York Times,* June 22, 2004. (Available at: http://www.nytimes.com/2004/06/22/business/22CND-BIAS.html)

2. *Dukes et al. v. Wal-Mart,* U.S. District Court for the Northern District of California, C 01-02252 MJJ, June 21, 2004.

3. Zimmerman, "Wal-Mart Faces Class Action"; Greenhouse, "Judge Certifies Suit"; *Dukes et al. v. Wal-Mart.*

4. Wendy Zellner, "A New Pay Scheme at Wal-Mart," *Business Week,* June 3, 2004. (Available at: http://www.businessweek.com/@@maC8CmUQzm*AsQYA/premium/content/04_24/b3887045_mz011.htm?se=1); Wendy Zeller, "A Wal-Mart Settlement: What It Might Look Like," *Business Week,* July 5, 2005. (Available at: http://www.businessweek.com/@@maC8CmUQzm*AsQYA/premium/content/04_27/b3890047_mz011.htm?se=1); Jonathan D. Glater, "Attention Wal-Mart Plaintiffs: Hurdles Ahead," *New York Times,* June 27, 2004. (Available at: http://www.nytimes.com/2004/06/27/business/yourmoney/27walm.html).

5. Jennifer Gill, "Ain't Misbehaving? Not at Work," *Business Week,* June 7, 2000. (Available at: http://www.businessweek.com/careers/content/jun2000/ca2000067_401.htm)

6. Joshua M. Javits, "It's the Real Thing: $192.5 Million," *Legal Report,* March–April 2001, pp. 1–2.

7. Civil Rights Act of 1866, Section 1981 (401 FEP Manual 81).

8. *Johnson v. Railway Express Agency,* U.S. Supreme Court, 10 FEP 831 839 847 (1975).

9. Civil Rights Act of 1871, Section 1983 (401 FEP Manual 81).

10. Equal Pay Act of 1963 (401 FEP Manual 451).

11. *Schultz v. Wheaton Glass Co.,* 421 F. 2d 259 (3rd Cir. 1970).

12. Council of Economic Advisers, *Explaining Trends in the Gender Wage Gap* (Washington DC: The Council of Economic Advisors, 1998) (Available at: http://clinton4.nara.gov/WH/EOP/CEA/html/gendergap.html)

13. Carmen DeNavas-Walt, Robert W. Cleveland, Bruce H. Webster Jr., "Income in the United States: 2002," September 2003. (Available at: http://www.census.gov/hhes/www/income02.html)

14. National Women's Law Center, "The Paycheck Fairness Act: Helping to Close the Women's Wage Gap," May 2003. (Available at: http://www.nwlc.org/pdf/PaycheckFairnessMay2003.pdf)

15. Civil Rights Act of 1964 (401 FEP Manual 1); 401 FEP Manual 11.

16. Benjamin W. Wolkinson and Richard N. Block, *Employment Law: The Workplace Rights of Employees and Employers* (Cambridge, Mass.: Blackwell, 1996), p. 10.

17. House Judiciary Committee Report, 88th Congress, Report 914, Part 2, December 2, 1963. Interesting that Congress talks about the dignity of "man" and "his" rights.

18. *General Electric Co. v. Gilbert,* 423 U.S. 822 (1976).

19. Gillian Flynn, "Watch Out for Pregnancy Discrimination," *Workforce,* November 2002, Vol. 81 (12), pp. 84–85.

20. *California Federal Savings & Loan v. Guerra,* 479 U.S. 272 (1987).

21. *United Auto Workers v. Johnson Controls,* 111 S. Ct. 1196 (1991).

22. *Barnes v. Costle,* 561 F. 2d 983 (D.C. Cir. 1977); *Fisher v. Flynn,* 598 F. 2d 663 (1st Cir. 1979); and *Williams v. Civiletti,* 487 F. Supp. 1389, 22 FEP 1311 (1980).

23. Discrimination Because of Sex, Title VII of the Civil Rights Act of 1964, as amended; Adoption of Final Interpretive Guidelines, 29 CFR Part 1604, Section 1604, 11(a), 1980.

24. *Meritor Savings Bank v. Vinson,* 477 U.S. 57 (1986).

25. *Harris v. Forklift Systems,* 114 S. Ct. 367 (1993).

26. See Ellen E. Schultz and Junada Woo, "Plaintiffs' Sex Lives Are Being Laid Bare in Harassment Cases," *Wall Street Journal,* September 15, 1994, p. A1.

27. *Onscale v. Sundowner Offshore Services, Inc.,* U.S. Supreme Court, (96-568) 83 F.3d 118, reversed and remanded. (March 4, 1998).

28. Kenneth M. Jarin and Ellen K. Pomfret, "New Rules for Same Sex Harassment," *HR Magazine,* June 1998, pp. 114–123.

29. Julie Holliday Wayne, Christine M. Riordan, and Kecia M. Thomas, "Is All Sexual Harassment Viewed the Same? Mock Juror Decisions in Same- and Cross-Gender Cases," *Journal of Applied Psychology,* 2001, Vol. 86 (2), pp. 179–187.

30. Mark Maremont, "Abuse of Power: The Astonishing Tale of Sexual Harassment at Astra USA," *Business Week,* May 13, 1996, pp. 86–98; U.S. Equal Employment Opportunity Commission, "Astra USA Agrees to Provide $10 Million to Victims of Discrimination," February 5, 1998. (Available at: http://www.eeoc.gov/press/2-5-98.html)

31. Mark Maremont and Rochelle Sharpe, "Astra Expected to Pay over $10 Million to Settle Charges of Sexual Harassment," *Wall Street Journal,* February 5, 1998, p. A4.

32. *Farager v. City of Boca Raton,* 524 US 775 (1998); and *Burlington Industries, Inc. v. Ellerth,* 524 US 742 (1998).

33. Debbie Rodman Sandler, "Sexual Harassment Rulings: Less Than Meets the Eye," *HR Magazine,* October 1998, pp. 136–143.

34. Robert K. Robinson, Neal P. Mero, and Dave L. Nichols, "More than Just Semantics: Court Rulings Clarify Effective Anti-Harassment Policies," *Human Resource Planning,* 2001, Vol. 24 (4), pp. 36–47.

35. Paul Gibson, "The Future of Sexual Harassment Suits," *HR Magazine,* October 1998, pp. 142–143.

36. "EEOC Sues Chicago Area Hospital for Post-9/11 Backlash Discrimination," April 7, 2003. (Available at: http://www.eeoc.gov/press/4-7-03.html)

37. Karyn-Siobhan Robinson, "Employers Should Be Aware of Possible Anti-Muslim, Anti-Arab Sentiments in the Workplace," *Society for Human Resource Management,* April 25, 2003. (Available at: http://www.shrm.org/hrnews_published/archives/CMS_004341.asp)

38. Age Discrimination in Employment Act of 1967 (401 FEP Manual 351).

39. Daniel P. O'Meara, *Protecting the Growing Number of Older Workers: The Age Discrimination in Employment Act* (Philadelphia: Wharton School, 1989), p. 13.

40. "Supreme Court Clarifies Proof Required for Age Discrimination Claims," *Employment Law Briefs,* Vol. 4 (2), October 1996, p. 3.

41. *O'Connor v. Consolidated Coin Caterers Corp.,* 116 S. Ct. 1307 (1996).

42. Ibid.

43. *General Dynamics Land Systems, Inc. v. Cline* (02-1080) 296 F.3d 466 (2004).

44. Robert S. Greenberger, "Justices Limit Use of Age-Bias Laws," *Wall Street Journal,* February 25, 2004, p. D2.

45. *Public Employees Retirement System of Ohio v. Betts,* 109 S. Ct. 2854 (1989).

46. Vocational Rehabilitation Act of 1973 (401 FEP Manual 501).

47. *Toyota Motor Mfg., Ky., Inc. v. Williams,* 534 U.S. 184 (2002) 224 F.3d 840.

48. Michael Barrier, "A Line in the Sand," *HR Magazine,* July 2002, pp. 35–43; Michael T. Zugelder and Paul J. Champagne, "Responding to the Supreme Court: Employment Practices and the ADA," *Business Horizons,* January-February 2003, Vol. 46 (1), pp. 30–36; Art Gutman, "Two January 2002 Supreme Court Rulings: *Toyota v. Williams & EEOC v. Waffle House," Industrial-Organizational Psychologist,* April 2002, Vol. 39 (4), pp. 58–65.

49. Note this does not mean that working cannot serve as a major life activity under other Titles of the ADA. See Gutman, "Two January 2002 Supreme Court Rulings."

50. *Board of Trustees of University of Alabama v. Garrett* (99–1240) 531 U.S. 356 (2001) 193 F.3d 1214, reversed. (February 21, 2001)

51. John M. Williams, "The High Court's Low Blow to the Disabled," *Business Week,* March 7, 2001. (Available at: http://www.businessweek.com/bwdaily/dnflash/mar2001/nf2001037_455.htm)

52. *PGA Tour, Inc., v. Martin,* 532 U.S. 121 S. Ct 1879 (2001).

53. Cited in Linda Greenhouse, "Golf: Disabled Golfer May Use a Cart on the PGA Tour, Justices Affirm," *New York Times,* May 30, 2001, p. A1.

54. *US Airways, Inc. v. Barnett,* (00-1250) 228 F.3d 1105 (2002)

55. Art Gutman, "The Supreme Court Ruling in *US Airways v. Barnett," Industrial-Organizational Psychologist,* June 2002, Vol. 40 (1), pp. 90–95.

56. Mark V. Roehling, "Weight-Based Discrimination in Employment: Psychological and Legal

Aspects," *Personnel Psychology,* Vol. 52, 1999, pp. 969–1016.

57. *Cook v. State of Rhode Island, Dept. of Mental Health, Retardation and Hospitals,* 10 F. 2d 17, 2 AD 1476 (1st Cir. 1993).

58. Centers for Disease Control and Prevention, National Center for Chronic Disease Prevention, "Actual Causes of Death in the United States, 2000." (Available at: http://www.cdc.gov/nccdphp/factsheets/death_causes2000.htm)

59. Steven Greenhouse, "Overweight, But Ready to Fight; Obese People Are Taking Their Bias Claims to Court," *New York Times,* August 4, 2003, p. B1.

60. "House Likely to Back Fat Lawsuit Limits," *CNN.* (Available at: http://www.cnn.com/2004/LAW/03/10/fat.lawsuits.reut/index.html)

61. See National Association to Advance Fat Acceptance at http://www.naafa.org/.

62. "DNA: Handle with Care," *Harvard Business Review,* April 2001, Vol. 79 (4), pp. 30–32.

63. Sarah Schafer, "Railroad Agrees to Stop Gene-Testing Workers," *Washington Post,* April 19, 2001, p. E1.

64. Mike France and Michael Arndt, "Office Violence: After the Shooting Stops," *Business Week,* March 12, 2001, pp. 98–100.

65. Janet Wiscombe, "Vigilance Stops Violence—and Lawsuits," *Workforce,* October 2002, Vol. 81 (10), pp. 38–44.

66. Immigration Reform and Control Act of 1986, 8 USC 1324 (a).

67. *Garcia v. Spun Steak Co.,* 62 FEP 525, FEP 1856 (1994).

68. *EEOC v. Premier Operator Services, Inc.,* 113 F.Supp.2d 1066 (N.D. Tex, 2000).

69. *Wards Cove Packing Co. v. Antonio,* 109 S. Ct. 2115 (1989).

70. *Griggs v. Duke Power Co.,* 401 U.S. 424, 3 FEP 175 (1971).

71. *Gilmer v. Interstate/Johnson Lane Corp.,* 500 U.S. 20, 111 S. Ct. 1647 (1991).

72. Linda Greenhouse, "Court Says Employers Can Require Arbitration of Disputes," *New York Times,* March 22, 2001, p. C1.

73. *Circuit City Stores, Inc. v. Adams,* (99–1379) 194 F. 3d 1070.

74. Margaret M. Clark, "Supreme Court Supports Arbitration Agreements," *HR News,* Vol. 20 (5), May 2001, pp. 1, 20.

75. U.S. Department of Labor, "FMLA Survey," January 2001. (Available at: http://www.dol.gov/asp/fmla/toc.htm; http://www.dol.gov/asp/fmla/chapter8.htm)

76. *Ragsdale v. Wolverine World Wide, Inc.* (00-6029) 218 F.3d 933 (2002).

77. *Nevada Department of Human Resources v. Hibbs* (01-1368) 273 F.3d 844, affirmed (2003).

78. U.S. Equal Employment Opportunity Commission, "Glass Ceilings: The Status of Women as Officials and Managers in the Private Sector." (Available at: http://www.eeoc.gov/stats/reports/glassceiling/index.html)

79. U.S. Department of Labor, Women's Bureau. (Available at: http://www.dol.gov/wb/info_about_wb/mission.htm)

80. Taylor Cox Jr., "The Multicultural Organization," *Academy of Management Executive,* May 1991, Vol. 5 (2), pp. 34–47.

81. U.S. Census Bureau, "National Population Projections." (Available at: http://www.census.gov/population/www/projections/natsum-T3.html); U.S. Department of Labor, Bureau of Labor Statistics, "The Employment Situation: February 2004."(Available at: http://stats.bls.gov/news.release/pdf/empsit.pdf)

82. The U.S. Equal Employment Opportunity Commission, "Glass Ceilings."

83. *Taxman v. Piscataway Township Bd. of Educ.,* 91 F.3d 1547 1551 (3d. Cir. 1996).

84. *Regents of University of California v. Bakke,* 438 US 265 (1978).

85. *Hopwood v. The University of Texas,* 95 F. 3d 53 (1996); *Johnson v. Board of Regents of University of Georgia* (CA11 201) 263 F.3d 1234.

86. *Gratz et al. v. Bollinger et al.* (02-516) 188 F.3d 394 (2003); *Grutter v. Bollinger et al.* (02-241) 288 F.3d 732 (2003).

87. Art Gutman, "The Grutter, Gatz & Costa Rulings," *Industrial-Organizational Psychologist,* Vol. 41 (2), October 2003, pp. 117–127.

88. Ibid.

89. Ibid.

90. Linda Greenhouse, "Supreme Court Splits on Diversity Efforts at University of Michigan," *New York Times,* June 23, 2003, pp. A1.

91. *Gratz et al. v. Bollinger et al.*

92. Jonathan A. Segal, "Diversity: Direct or Disguised?" *HR Magazine,* October 2003, pp. 123–132;

Matt Murray, "Corporate Goal: Ethnic Variety, No Quotas," *Wall Street Journal,* June 24, 2003, p. B1.
93. Charlene Marmer Solomon, "Affirmative Action: What You Need to Know," *Personnel Journal,* August 1995, pp. 56–67
94. Ibid., p. 58.
95. *Steelworkers v. Weber,* 443 U.S. 193, 20 FEP 1 (1979).
96. *Edmonson v. U.S. Steel Corp.,* District Ct. Alabama, 20 FEP 1745 (1979); *Moseley v. The Goodyear Tire & Rubber Co.,* 612 F. 2d 187, 22 FEP 121 (1980); and *Wright v. National Archives and Records Service,* 4th District California, 21 FEP 8 (1979).
97. *Firefighters Local Union 1784 v. Stotts,* U.S. Supreme Court, 34 FEP 1702 (1984).
98. *City of Richmond v. J. A. Croson,* 109 S. Ct. 707 (1989).
99. *Adarand Constructors, Inc. v. Pena,* 515 U.S. 200 (1995).
100. *Uniform Guidelines on Employee Selection Procedures,Title 29 Code of Federal Regulations,* Part 1607 (1978).
101. U.S. Equal Employment Opportunity Commission. (Available at: http://www.eeoc.gov/stats/enforcement.html)
102. On November 20, 1990, the EEOC announced that it would consider charges by "testers" in the investigation and prosecution of job discrimination claims. Testers are individuals who seek employment in an attempt to prove discrimination but without the intention of actually accepting employment if it is offered. Although the use of testers to prove discrimination has become a well-accepted practice in the housing discrimination context, using such testers in the employment context is quite controversial. The U.S. Chamber of Commerce, for example, has expressed concern over the EEOC policy, noting that it will cause employers to expend needless time, effort, and money interviewing individuals who are not really interested in employment.
103. *Albermarle Paper Co. v. Moody,* 422 U.S. 405, 10 FEP 1181 (1975).
104. *Clark v. American Marine Corp.,* 437 F. 2d 959, 3 FEP 155 (1971).
105. *McDonnell Douglas Corp. v. Green,* 411 U.S. 792, 5 FEP 965 (1973).
106. *Griggs v. Duke Power Co.,* 401 U.S. 424, 3 FEP 175 (1971).
107. The other court decisions include *Hazelwood School District v. United States,* 433 U.S. 299, 15 FEP 1 (1977), and *Teamsters v. United States,* 431 U.S. 324, 14 FEP 1514 (1977).
108. Although the concept of a prima facie case was developed in the court system, the type of evidence that indicates a prima facie case is also the type that the EEOC and OFCCP look for in their own investigations of organizations. The agencies look for evidence of disparate treatment and disparate impact. Of course, the OFCCP also examines the extent to which organizations are following the actions set forth in their affirmative action programs.
109. *EEOC v. Union Bank of Arizona,* 12 FEP 527 (D. Arizona, 1976).
110. *United States v. City of Socorro,* 25 FEP 815 (D. New Mexico, 1976).
111. *Drew v. Liberty Mutual Insurance Co.,* 480 F. 2d 69, 5 FEP 1077 (1973).
112. *Albermarle Paper Co. v. Moody,* 422 U.S. 405, 10 FEP 1181 (1975).
113. *Dothard v. Rawlinson,* 433 U.S. 321, 15 FEP 10 (1977).
114. *Diaz v. Pan American World Airways,* 442 F. 2d 385, 3 FEP 337 (1971).
115. *Teamsters v. United States,* 431 U.S. 324, 14 FEP 1514 (1977).
116. *Pullman-Standard v. Swint,* 456 U.S. 273, 28 FEP 1073 (1982); and *American Tobacco Co. v. Patterson,* 456 U.S. 63, 28 FEP 713 (1982).
117. *Furnco Construction Corp. v. Waters,* 438 U.S. 537, 17 FEP 1062 (1978).
118. *Robinson v. P. Lorillard Co.,* 444 F. 2d 829, 3 FEP 653 (1971); and *Bethlehem Steel Co. v. United States,* 446 F. 2d 652, 3 FEP 589 (1971).
119. R. Peres, *Dealing with Employment Discrimination* (New York: McGraw-Hill, 1978), p. 133.
120. L. S. Kleiman and R. H. Faley, "Voluntary Affirmative Action and Preferential Treatment: Legal and Research Implications," *Personnel Psychology,* Vol. 41, 1988, pp. 481–496.

CHAPTER 6

Recruiting and Job Search

- Overview of the Recruitment Process
- Strategic Issues in Recruiting
- Internal Recruiting
- External Recruiting
- The Applicant's Point of View
- Evaluation and Benchmarking of Recruitment

HR Challenge

The Police Department in Odessa, Texas, employs 178 officers and 84 civilian staff, serves more than 90,000 residents, and responds to more than 130,000 calls each year. The department needs to hire an average of sixteen qualified police officers each year, in a labor market that has become increasingly competitive. At present, the officer recruitment process consists of eight phases, from first application through interview and background check, to medical, psychological, and drug testing, and takes about 117 days from first contact with an applicant to appointment as an officer. The department is attracting a reasonable number of applicants to begin the process. Only 10 percent of those who apply are eventually hired, though about 20 percent are probably qualified. A number of potentially good candidates drop out of the lengthy recruitment process to accept jobs elsewhere. Because the recruitment process is slow, the department is chronically understaffed, and officers, candidates, and recruiters are frustrated.[1] You are a consultant called in to help remedy the situation. What information would you need to collect to better understand the police recruitment problem? How can the department improve the recruitment process?

Recruiting is the process by which organizations locate and attract individuals to fill job vacancies. Most organizations have a continuing need to recruit new employees to replace those who leave or are promoted, to acquire new skills, and to permit organizational growth. Recruiting is an even more important activity when unemployment rates are low and economic growth is strong, as firms compete to attract the qualified employees they need to succeed. Recruiting can be quite expensive. A large survey in 2002 found that U.S. companies spend, on average, $3,546 recruiting each nonexempt employee and nearly $7,000 recruiting each exempt employee.[2]

Recruitment follows HR planning and goes hand in hand with the selection process by which organizations evaluate the suitability of candidates for various jobs. Without accurate planning, organizations may recruit the wrong number or type of employees. Without successful recruiting to create a sizable pool of candidates, even the most accurate selection system is of little use. This chapter concentrates on how to plan and conduct a successful and cost-effective recruiting effort. It highlights methods that can be used to locate candidates from within the organization and from the outside labor market. It also focuses on the job applicant and the ways in which a candidate looks for and chooses a job. The chapter closes with a discussion of the measures that can be used to evaluate the effectiveness of the recruitment process.

OVERVIEW OF THE RECRUITMENT PROCESS

Figure 6.1 presents an overview of the recruitment process from the perspectives of the organization and the candidate. This flow chart displays the process as it unfolds over time. When a vacancy occurs and the recruiter receives authorization to fill it, the next step is a careful examination of the job and an enumeration of the skills, abilities, and experience needed to perform the job successfully. Existing job analysis documents can be very helpful in this regard. In addition, the recruitment planner must consider other aspects of the job environment—for example, the supervisor's management style, the opportunities for advancement, pay, and geographic location—in deciding what type of candidate to search for and what search methods to use. After carefully planning the recruiting effort, the recruiter uses one or more methods to produce a pool of potentially qualified candidates.

A firm can generate candidates *internally,* from among its present employees who desire promotion or transfer, or *externally,* from the labor market. The organization then screens the candidates, evaluates some of them more thoroughly, and offers the best the position. Throughout the recruitment process, the organization attempts to "sell" itself to the more promising candidates—that is, to convince them that the organization is a good place to work and that it offers what they want in the way of both tangible and intangible rewards.

Candidates searching for an employer go through a parallel set of activities—first acquiring occupational skills and experience, next searching for job openings through a variety of methods, and then applying for jobs that appear to be a suitable match for their qualifications. As the process continues, applicants attempt to "sell" organizations on their abilities while at the same time collecting information that helps them evaluate companies and jobs. Eventually, they decide to accept or reject job offers.

In the recruitment and selection process, the organization's and the individual's objectives may conflict. The organization is trying to evaluate the candidate's

FIGURE 6.1
The Recruitment Process

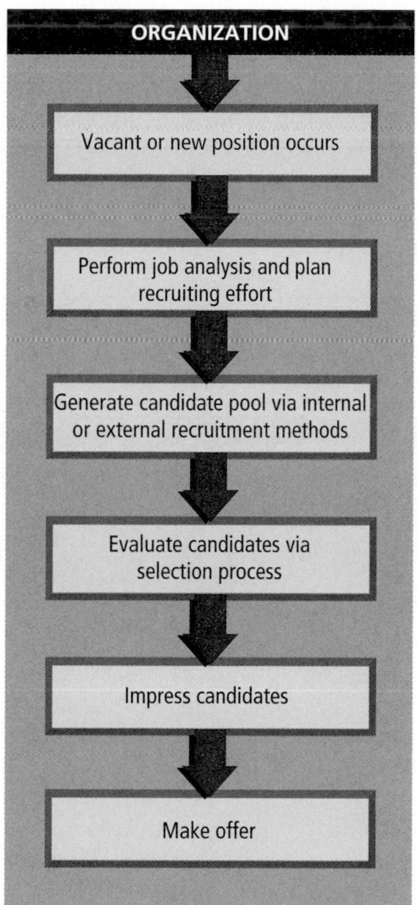
ORGANIZATION
Vacant or new position occurs
Perform job analysis and plan recruiting effort
Generate candidate pool via internal or external recruitment methods
Evaluate candidates via selection process
Impress candidates
Make offer

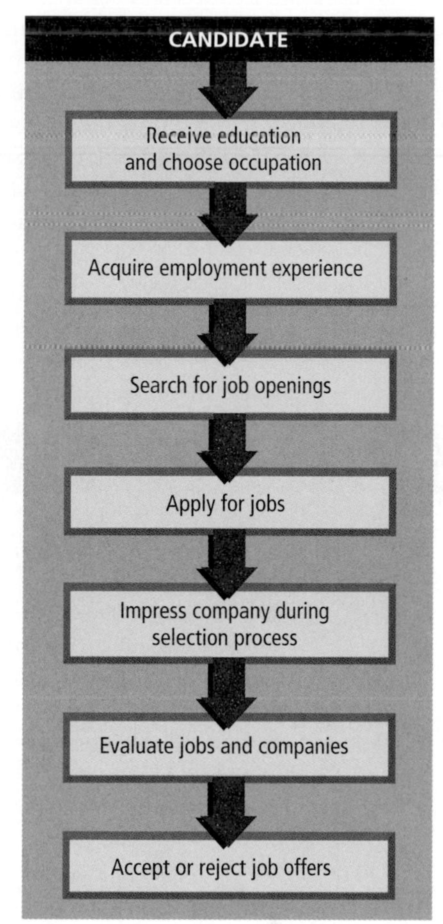
CANDIDATE
Receive education and choose occupation
Acquire employment experience
Search for job openings
Apply for jobs
Impress company during selection process
Evaluate jobs and companies
Accept or reject job offers

strengths and weaknesses, but the candidate is trying to present only strengths. Conversely, although the candidate is trying to ferret out both the good and the bad aspects of the prospective job and employer, the organization may prefer to reveal only positive aspects. In addition, each party's own objectives may conflict. The organization wants to treat the candidate well to increase the probability of job-offer acceptance, yet the need to evaluate the candidate may dictate the use of methods that may alienate the prospect, such as background investigations or stress interviews. Analogously, the applicant wants to appear polite and enthusiastic about the organization to improve the probability of receiving an offer, but he or she may also want to ask penetrating questions about compensation, advancement, and the company's financial health and future.[3]

STRATEGIC ISSUES IN RECRUITING

The nature of a firm's recruiting activities should be matched to its strategy and values as well as to other important features such as the state of the external labor market and the firm's ability to pay or otherwise induce new employees to join.

In this section we discuss the varied goals that can be served by recruiting, how a recruitment philosophy based on corporate values can guide recruiting choices—including the critical choice of whether to recruit internally or externally—and how innovative recruiting can achieve a competitive advantage in attracting scarce employee resources. Many of the issues to be discussed here are summarized in Figure 6.2. The Partnerships for Strategic Success feature provides an example of how recruitment and training are aimed at somewhat different targets in two companies in the same industry that pursue different strategies for competitive success.

PARTNERSHIPS FOR STRATEGIC SUCCESS

Strategic Recruitment in the Bookstore Industry

The two major bookstore super chains, Borders and Barnes & Noble, have taken quite different strategic routes to success. Borders has focused on carrying a wide range of sometimes esoteric books and using a sophisticated inventory tracking system to deeply understand and forecast the interests of their customers. Up to half the inventory of each store is unique to the area and customer base it serves. The inventory system plus the input of knowledgeable floor staff attuned to local requirements keeps the product mix fine-tuned. In contrast, Barnes & Noble has focused on selling mainstream best-sellers at reduced prices. Each store has many copies of fewer but more popular books, with deep discounts offered on slightly older stock. Efficient (but perhaps not inspired) advising of customers and fast cashiering are highly valued. These strategies have translated into different human resource practices, as the two chains value somewhat different qualities in their floor staff.

Borders hires well-educated booklovers with a passion for a specialized field of literature, cinema, or music. Zany individualism is valued, with employees often sporting tattoos, long hair, piercings, and nontraditional clothing at work. Diversity in styles and interests are valued. At frequent staff meetings, employees are encouraged to share information about interesting books they are reading. They are able to borrow books from the store and also receive a monthly allowance to buy books. Individuals within a store often specialize, with customer inquiries directed by other staff to the most knowledgeable person in that field. Ask a Borders seller to recommend a book, and his or her depth of knowledge and enthusiasm quickly shine through. Customers are likely to get very specific and well-informed advice from a staff member who shares their excitement about a particular area.

Barnes & Noble hires rather buttoned-down and conservative staff members. Deep knowledge of a particular area of literature is less important than prior experience in retailing. In contrast to Borders' more specialized approach, at Barnes & Noble all store staff are trained to provide basic services throughout the store, including giving advice to customers, making coffee, stocking shelves, and cashiering. The emphasis is on speed and efficiency of service for a generally less scholarly clientele.

There is little competition for talent between the two companies because they are seeking quite different types of employees. It is rare for Borders to hire away a Barnes & Noble employee or vice-versa. Clearly, each company has managed to institute human resource practices in the areas of recruitment, selection, and training that provide the types of employees needed to execute their differing strategies.

Sources: D. M. G. Raff, "Superstores and the Evolution of Firm Capabilities in American Bookselling," *Strategic Management Journal,* Vol. 21, 2000, 1043–1059; S. F. Gale, "The Bookstore Battle," *Workforce,* http://www.workforce.com/archive/feature/23/49/48/index.php; S. F. Gale, "Are the Bookstores Actually Different? *Workforce,* http://www.workforce.com/archive/feature/23/49/48/234950.php.

FIGURE 6.2
Strategic Decisions in Recruiting

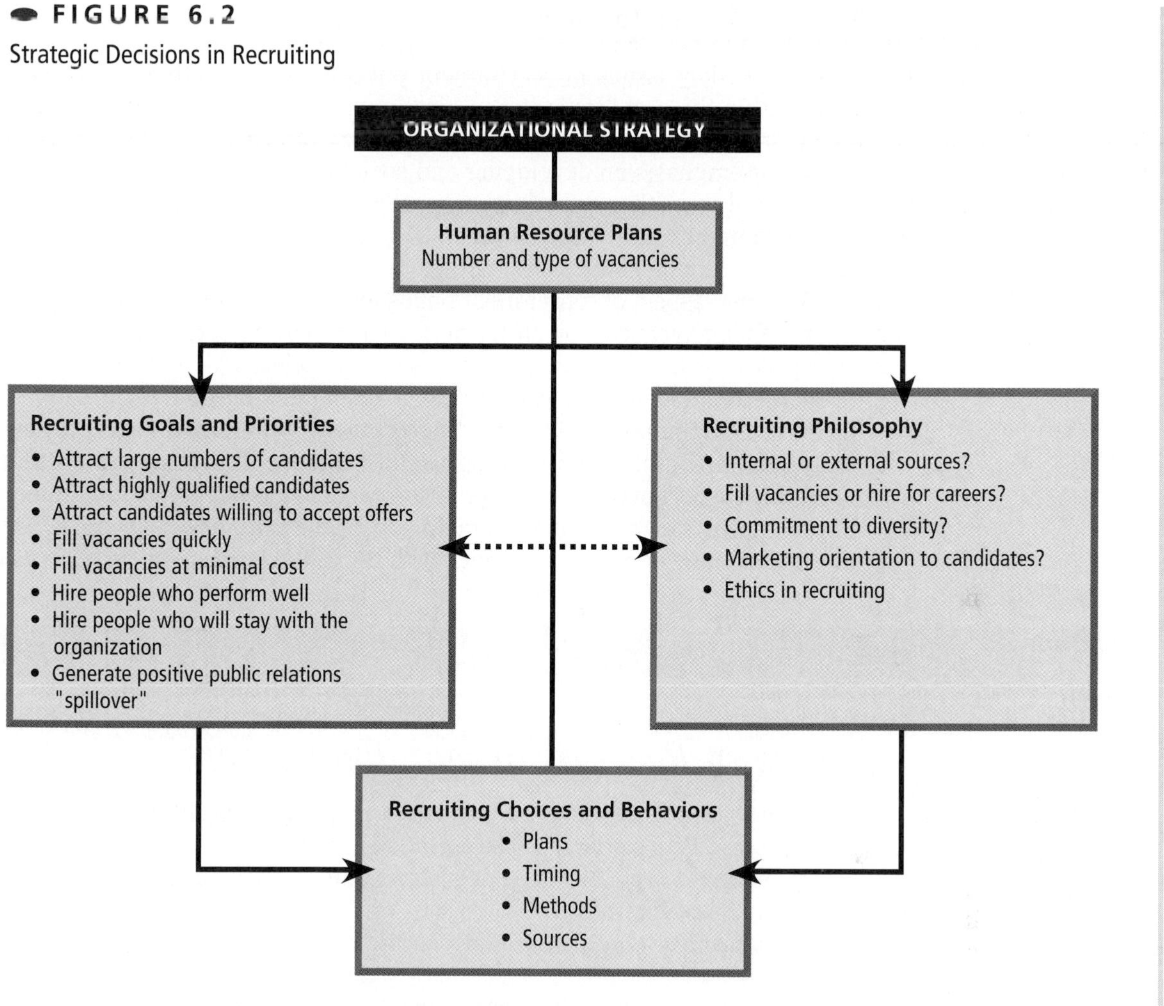
ORGANIZATIONAL STRATEGY
Human Resource Plans
Number and type of vacancies
Recruiting Goals and Priorities
• Attract large numbers of candidates
• Attract highly qualified candidates
• Attract candidates willing to accept offers
• Fill vacancies quickly
• Fill vacancies at minimal cost
• Hire people who perform well
• Hire people who will stay with the organization
• Generate positive public relations "spillover"
Recruiting Philosophy
• Internal or external sources?
• Fill vacancies or hire for careers?
• Commitment to diversity?
• Marketing orientation to candidates?
• Ethics in recruiting
Recruiting Choices and Behaviors
• Plans
• Timing
• Methods
• Sources

Recruitment Goals

A good recruiting program needs to serve many and sometimes conflicting goals. A commonly mentioned goal is to attract a large pool of applicants, but applicant pools can be too large and thus costly to process. Recruiting must also attract a high proportion of well-qualified candidates who are seriously interested in accepting a job offer. Post-hiring goals also must be considered—the recruiting process must yield workers who are good performers and who will stay with the organization for a reasonable length of time. An additional goal is that recruiting efforts should have beneficial "spillover" effects; that is, the organization's general image should be enhanced, and even unsuccessful applicants should develop positive attitudes toward the company and its products. Further, all the preceding goals should be reached with the greatest speed and at the least possible cost to the organization.[4] Balancing these varied goals against one another should be done with reference to the organization's overall strategy and values. As a part of this process of prioritizing goals, the organization may develop a recruitment philosophy.

Recruitment Philosophy

One of the key issues in recruitment philosophy is whether to promote largely from within the organization or to hire from the outside for vacancies at all levels. Some organizations, such as General Electric Company and United Parcel Service, put great emphasis on developing and socializing managers within the firm, from the ground up. Other organizations prefer to hire proven talent from the outside. The advantages and disadvantages of internal and external recruiting are discussed later in the chapter.

A second aspect of recruitment philosophy concerns where the emphasis is: on merely filling vacancies or on hiring for long-term careers. Does the organization seek people with skills sufficient for present vacancies, or does it try to attract the type of talented candidates who can feed the management pipeline of the future? A short-term view may emphasize filling vacancies quickly, whereas a long-term view may tolerate delay in the interests of finding just the right people to bring in for the long haul.[5]

A third aspect of recruitment philosophy concerns depth of commitment to seeking and hiring a diverse range of employees. Some firms are still at the EEO/affirmative action stage of mere compliance with the law, whereas others, such as Corning

ETHICAL PERSPECTIVE

Ethics in Recruiting and Job Search

A number of ethical challenges can arise in the recruiting process. Both parties to recruiting may be motivated to present their best sides while concealing their weaknesses, and this may lead to a temptation to lie or mislead by omission or commission. Applicants may engage in résumé fraud, though most organizations have a policy of firing employees if significant résumé fraud is later detected. Firms sometimes emphasize the most positive aspects of jobs while failing to mention less pleasant aspects, and in extreme cases, firms have been sued for fraudulent recruiting. In one case, a firm enticed an individual to relocate with promises of a bright future. However, the firm knew that its financial condition was very shaky and that there was a good probability that the new employee would soon be laid off. A jury later awarded the employee damages of $250,000.

Honesty is a central value in most ethical systems, so blatant lying would probably be regarded by both employers and applicants as unacceptable. However, the morality of other recruiting behaviors is not so clear-cut and may be defined situationally by common practice in the industry. Theft of property would be rejected by most people, but what about theft of employees and their organization-specific knowledge? When one organization raids a competitor by hiring away its best talent, has an unethical act been committed by the raider? What if the new hire passes on critical insider knowledge of the strategies, customers, or technology of the former employer? "Noncompete" agreements signed on hiring are efforts to prevent employees, if they later quit, from using their organization-specific knowledge to the disadvantage of their former employer, but such agreements are not always legally enforceable. Recently, firms including Wal-Mart and PaineWebber have filed corporate-raiding lawsuits against other firms they claim have made attempts to damage them by wholesale poaching of important staff. In another case, an employer sued their former director of recruiting, who they allege tried to use his insider knowledge of the firm's compensation system to lure staff to his new employer.

In some industries, raiding is commonplace and accepted. But do some firms go too far? Recruiters in the information technology industry have been known to loiter in the parking lots of competitors to pitch job opportunities to employees as they leave work. Others pay thousand-dollar bribes to obtain in-house phone directories. Some recruiters have been known to tele-

Incorporated, Digital Equipment Corporation, and Avon Products, Inc., have graduated to valuing diversity as a central principle of organizational life. Their recruiting practices, both internal and external, actively encourage participation by all types of people. Perhaps more important, extensive training and consultative processes strive to create a climate that is welcoming to and supportive of all candidates.[6]

A fourth aspect of recruitment philosophy is whether applicants are viewed as commodities to be purchased or as customers to be wooed. Organizations that adopt a **marketing orientation to recruiting** will spend substantial time and money to determine what their customers (potential applicants) want and to tailor their recruiting practices and messages to various segments of the market. For instance, NEC Information Systems hired a research firm to explore what systems analysts and marketing graduates wanted in a job and then incorporated these features successfully into the company's advertising campaign.[7] Swiss Bank and Ingersoll-Rand have used focus groups of university students to obtain a better understanding of the needs of the campus recruiting market.[8]

A fifth aspect of recruitment philosophy involves ethics in terms of fairness and honesty in the recruitment process. This theme is further developed in the Ethical Perspective box.

phone companies and lie about their identity as they try to obtain names and contact details for valuable employees. One recruiter represented himself as a producer from a nationally syndicated talk show and asked for the company's chief financial officer's name and phone number, ostensibly so he could be interviewed on the program.

A firm called Advanced Internet Recruitment Strategy (AIRS) runs popular seminars designed to teach recruiters how to search company Web sites and associated links to locate potential candidates. Techniques such as "X-ray," "peelback," "flipping," and "domain search" enhance access to employee information not intended for the public. Companies are advised to keep employee information and company directories behind firewalls and to supply only generic contact information (such as sales@companyname.com) rather than specific employee names on public Web sites. DePaul University ethicist Laura Hartman argues that the onus shouldn't be solely on the employer to protect employee data behind firewalls. Rather, she contends that it is unethical for recruiters to use advanced search techniques to poach employees, just as it would be unethical to steal from a person's home just because the person forgot to lock the door.

A recent survey of human resource specialists asked which of a number of questionable recruiting methods they thought were ethical. The survey was provoked by an incident in which twenty employees of one retailer were caught cruising the aisles of a competitor's store trying to lure away employees. Only 8 percent of respondents thought this was ethical. Ten percent thought that recruiting in a competitor's parking lot was ethical, 13 percent felt that contacting employees via e-mail addresses found on the employer's intranet was acceptable, and 17 percent had no problems with calling employees at home using phone numbers obtained from an ex-employee of the competitor. Fifty-one percent of respondents felt that all four actions were unethical.

Sources: M. Geyelin and W. Green, "Companies Must Disclose Shaky Finances to Some Applicants," *Wall Street Journal,* April 20, 1990, p. B8; M. Ronald Buckley, Donald B. Fedor, Shawn M. Carraher, Dwight D. Frink, and David Marvin, "The Ethical Imperative to Provide Recruits Realistic Job Previews," *Journal of Managerial Issues,* Winter 1997, Vol. 9 Issue 4, pp. 468–485; S. Kuczynski, "You've Got Job Offers," *HR Magazine,* March 1999, pp. 50–58; G. Flynn, "Raid the Competition for Workers, Not Their Secrets," *Workforce,* December 1998, pp. 121–123; Eilene Zimmerman, "Fight Dirty Hiring Tactics," *Workforce,* May 16, 2001, www.workforce.com/feature/00/17/14; and "What Types of Recruiting Are Ethical," *Workforce,* May 30, 2001, www.workforce.com/cgi-bin/iu.pl.

Internal or External Sources?

Deciding whether the position is to be filled internally or externally is often an early task in recruitment planning for a specific vacancy. In some cases, there is no decision to be made. For instance, entry-level jobs must be filled externally, but for other positions, the company's policy or union contract may require that internal sources be used first. Most organizations use a mixture of internal and external sources—promoting from within when qualified employees are available and recruiting from external sources when new skills are needed or growth is rapid. Each type of source has its advantages and disadvantages.

Advantages of Internal Recruiting When **internal recruiting** is used, the vacancy is filled by a person of known ability. Because the employer has observed the employee in one position, there is less guesswork involved in assessing his or her suitability for a second position. In contrast, assessments of external recruits are based on less reliable sources, such as references, and on relatively brief encounters, such as interviews. Another advantage of promoting from within is that doing so motivates current employees. Skilled and ambitious employees are less likely to quit and more likely to become involved in developmental activities if they believe promotion is likely.[9] Also, training and socialization time is reduced when openings are filled internally because a current employee has less to learn about the organization and its idiosyncratic procedures than a newcomer. Recruiting may also be faster and less expensive if an internal candidate can be found. Finally, in times of impending retrenchment, filling as many jobs as possible internally maximizes job security for present employees.

Tesco, the leading retailer in the United Kingdom, has implemented an innovative "store swap" program to reduce their external recruiting costs, enhance employee retention, and benefit cash-strapped part-time employees who are also university students. A single phone call to a national hotline allows students to transfer from the store where they normally work during the school year to a store in their home town during the holidays, then transfer back when university classes resume. The program helps to retain trained staff by making temporary internal recruiting as easy as possible.[10]

Disadvantages of Internal Recruiting If the organization is expanding rapidly, there may be an insufficient internal supply of qualified individuals above the entry level. This situation may result in people being promoted before they are ready or not being allowed to stay in a position long enough to learn how to do a job well. Also, when one vacancy is filled internally, a second vacancy is created—the position of the individual who was promoted or transferred to fill the first vacancy. If this slot is also filled internally, then another vacancy occurs. This movement of personnel is called the **ripple effect.** In one organization, 195 initial vacancies eventually resulted in 545 job movements.[11] Another disadvantage of internal recruiting is that some organizations' internal recruiting procedures are extremely cumbersome. They may involve a bureaucratic nightmare of forms, waiting times, eligibility lists, and requirements of permission to interview from the candidate's current superior.[12] Still another disadvantage of internal recruiting is that an organization can become inbred and lose flexibility if all its managers are homegrown. Finally, meeting affirmative action goals usually can be accomplished only by aggressive external recruiting.

Advantages of External Recruiting **External recruiting** can bring in new ideas and viewpoints, avoid the confusion that accompanies the ripple effect, meet affirmative action goals, and cope with the demands of rapid growth without overusing inexperienced personnel. Another advantage may be savings in training costs. Hiring experienced workers away from other companies may cut down on the need for a comprehensive training and development program in-house. Finally, there may be instances that require a severe shakeup or turnaround. Particularly at the upper-management level, an outsider with no prior commitment to present employees or ongoing projects may be the only individual with enough objectivity (and even ruthlessness) to bring about needed changes and enunciate a new vision for the organization.[13]

Disadvantages of External Recruiting One disadvantage of external recruiting is the cost. Because the external labor market is much larger and harder to reach than the internal one, recruiting externally usually takes longer and costs more. With external recruiting, there is also the risk of hiring a candidate who does not live up to the apparent high potential displayed during the selection process. Finally, too much external recruitment is discouraging to current employees because it reduces their chances to move up in the organization.

Countercyclical Hiring

One strategic issue relevant to external recruiting is when to do it. Most firms recruit each year to meet that year's needs. They attempt to hire many people in a boom year and hire very few during years when the industry, economy, or company is on a down cycle. Human resource planners at Union Oil Company of California realized that such short-range recruitment planning was not efficient. In boom years the company was attempting to hire many people at the same time that its competitors were also recruiting heavily. This high demand drove up starting salaries and resulted in lower quality hires. During the leaner years of the cycle, top graduates were willing to work for lower starting salaries and were readily available because competitors were not hiring. Consequently, Union Oil began to plan campus recruiting on a five-year schedule, spreading its hiring evenly over the period and thus maximizing applicant quality while controlling salary costs.[14] Research suggests that the firms most likely to engage in **countercyclical hiring** emphasize human resource planning to avoid shortages, strive to maintain a regular age distribution of managers, and value training and development. They also are firms that can afford to hire in downturns because they are stronger financial performers.[15]

Alternatives to Traditional Recruiting

Traditional recruiting is not always the answer to a firm's human resource needs. This section explores a number of options that may either replace or supplement what we normally think of as "recruiting." Suppose, for example, that a recruiting campaign brings in too few qualified applicants. A traditional approach is to intensify essentially similar recruiting efforts—to run yet another advertisement, extend a contract with an employment agency, or recruit in a larger geographic region. Sara Rynes, a leading recruitment researcher, suggests that in this situation organizations should broaden their focus from recruiting activities to the concept of applicant attraction.

In addition to doing "more of the same" in the way of recruiting, firms can attempt to attract applicants by improving or changing the nature of inducements, perhaps increasing wages, or providing flexible work arrangements or stock options. New benefits in the race to attract technical professionals have included signing bonuses of up to $20,000, paid sabbaticals, casual dress codes, concierge services, being allowed to bring one's pet to work, reduced summer hours, and massages in the office. Public-sector organizations have had to work very hard to attract information technology professionals, as they cannot offer stock options and sky-high salaries. Fairfax County, Virginia, has had success attracting new employees by offering flextime and job sharing, as well as playing up the facts that very little travel is required and that working hours are reasonable (as opposed to the travel, very long hours, and weekend work common in the private sector).[16] See the Flexibility in the Workplace feature for more detail on new ways to attract candidates.

A third strategy is to change the focus of recruiting to labor pools that are relatively more plentiful and underutilized; for example, to recruit from retirees, people with disabilities, disadvantaged urban residents, mothers with young children, and so on. Inducements as well as recruiting methods and messages will have to be tailored to the needs and desires of these groups. In some cases, employees from these pools may need assistance with adaptive devices or arrangements, transportation to work, or extra training.[17]

Another alternative for finding scarce professionals in technical fields is to sponsor their permanent or temporary immigration from other countries. Many nations offer employer-sponsored visa programs to allow domestic employers to recruit needed talent from abroad.[18]

Cisco Systems used yet another approach to acquire talent on a large scale when IT professionals were in short supply. It purchased entire companies (twenty-five in 2000 alone), largely to obtain the intellectual capital and product development expertise embedded in these organizations' work forces.[19]

There are even more distinct alternatives to traditional recruiting, which include not hiring at all. Many firms have no desire to repeat the painful retrenchments of the 1980s and early 1990s and are reluctant to recruit enough full-time staff to meet all their needs. Instead, they have adopted the staffing strategy of keeping a small cadre of permanent employees (who are relatively insulated from layoff), along with a buffer of temporary or contract workers. This strategy is also employed in large Japanese companies and has allowed them to offer lifetime employment to selected groups of employees.

Several alternatives to recruiting and hiring employees directly have increased in popularity. The first is to use temporary workers obtained from a temporary help agency. The temporary help industry has been expanding rapidly since the 1970s.[20] **Temporaries** are particularly helpful for covering peak demand periods, especially in an uncertain economic climate when demand could drop precipitously. Temporaries may cost more per hour worked, but they are paid only for the time they actually work. Another advantage of using temporaries is that they are quickly and easily available; therefore, recruiting costs are minimal. In addition, the temporary help agency has already selected and trained the temporaries; thus training costs are low because the temporaries require only a brief orientation to the company. It is not uncommon for firms to offer successful temporaries a

FLEXIBILITY IN THE WORKPLACE

Family Friendly Policies Attract Applicants

Employees' work and nonwork lives are increasingly interdependent. There are more two-career families, some professional jobs require far more than 40 hours of work per week, and technology sometimes makes it possible to work extra hours from home. Work requirements seem increasingly likely to intrude into family time, yet employees are more concerned with work–life balance than ever before. In response, creative mechanisms to allow more freedom for employees to honor both work and family responsibilities are becoming more widespread. These "family friendly" policies have the potential to attract candidates who are not available for a standard nine to five, five day per week job. Employers who are able to offer these options may be more successful in recruiting than those who do not. Let's look at three such policies: job sharing, flextime, and telecommuting.

In **job sharing** two people do one full-time job. They share the salary, but often both are entitled to full benefits. Sears, Roebuck and Co. has adopted a job-sharing plan for its in-house corporate attorneys. One job sharer in the pair works Monday to Wednesday, the other Wednesday to Friday. The company has benefited by being able to attract experienced, top quality lawyers who just happen to have significant child-care responsibilities at the moment. Job sharing also benefits employees by keeping their skills up to date while allowing them more time with a young family.

Flextime is not a new idea, but it is becoming more widespread, with 58 percent of companies now offering it to some employees. In flextime, employees work the same number of hours each week (often forty) but have some freedom to determine when those hours are. Often there are "core" hours when everyone is expected to be in the office, such as 10:00 a.m. to 2:00 p.m. Other than this, employees are free to begin their workday very early and leave early, or start later and stay later. This allows employees to avoid peak commuting times as well as juggle family responsibilities or to accommodate study or recreational activities before or after work. One study found that a job advertised as allowing flextime was more attractive to job candidates who experienced high work–family conflict, apparently because they believed flextime would help ease the conflict.

Telecommuting or **teleworking** is another increasingly popular way of offering flexibility to employees. This allows the employee to work from home or another remote location rather than requiring their physical presence in an office five days per week. Some telecommuters work exclusively from home; other are in the office one or more days per week but have some leeway about where they work the rest of the time. With widespread availability of broadband Internet access, working at home has become more feasible and popular for a wide range of jobs, with 37 percent of organizations offering some teleworking opportunities in 2001, up from 20 percent in 1997. Full-time telecommuting can expand the geographic labor market from which an employer can draw while eliminating relocation costs and reducing expenses for office facilities. It also allows employees to live in their preferred location while "virtually" working elsewhere. Surprisingly, one study found that the option to telecommute was more attractive to single and child-free candidates than to those with greater family commitments. This may be because working at home can create even more frequent conflicts between work and other roles when children are present.

These flexible arrangements can provide benefits to employer and employee alike, but all require considerable care and forethought in implementation. Coordination and management of staff can become problematic when individuals are not always physically present at the same time. Expectations must be clearly spelled out in terms of hours worked and performance standards accomplished. Telecommuters require suitable equipment and broadband access, together with policies covering the private use of such facilities. Safety for individuals working at home is also a concern.

Sources: B. L. Rau and M. M. Hyland, "Role Conflict and Flexible Arrangements: The Effects on Applicant Attraction," *Personnel Psychology,* 2002, pp. 111–136; T. L Honeycutt and B. Rosen, "Family Friendly Human Resource Policies, Salary Levels, and Salient Identity as Predictors of Organizational Attraction," *Journal of Vocational Behavior,* 1997, Vol. 50, pp. 271–290; Kelley R. Bowers, "Sears Lures Attorneys In-house with Job Sharing Program," *Corporate Legal Times,* January 1997, Vol. 7 (62), p. 22–23; "Telecommuting Can Help Attract, Retain Staff," *Staff Leader,* November 2003, Vol. 17 (3), pp. 1–4; Michelle M. Robertson, Wayne S. Maynard, and Jamie R. McDevitt, "Telecommuting: Managing the Safety of Workers in Home Office Environments," *Professional Safety,* April 2003, Vol. 48 (4), pp. 30–36.

permanent position. Essentially, firms can "try before they buy" to be sure a candidate is qualified and fits in. Some temporary agencies charge a "conversion fee" when their employees are hired within thirty to ninety days of initial placement.[21]

Historically, temporaries have been used primarily in jobs such as assembler, laborer, secretary, clerk, or truck driver. In today's work environment, however, they are available for a variety of other professions, including nursing, computer programming, engineering, and accounting.[22] There is even a trend toward "interim executives"—high-caliber, experienced managers who can be brought in for a few months to oversee a turnaround, liquidation, or special project.[23]

Employee leasing is a way to obtain the services of individuals over a longer time period than would normally be the case with temporaries. An employee leasing firm recruits, hires, trains, and compensates employees, and the organization that leases them provides their work facilities, direct daily supervision, and duties. For example, a nursing services firm employs many nurses and provides them to hospitals on a contract basis. This arrangement relieves the hospitals of a great deal of HRM responsibility. In the future, a number of HR professionals may find themselves working in employee-leasing firms rather than in large production-oriented companies. Employee leasing provides the organization with flexibility to change the number of employees easily and without actual layoffs.[24]

Yet another alternative to recruiting and hiring to staff a function within the organization is to hire an outside firm to perform the entire function, either on or off the organization's premises. Strategic management experts suggest that unless an organization can perform a support function extremely well, it should consider subcontracting that function so that the organization can concentrate all available resources on building unique core competencies. By hiring out such functions as maintenance, security, and office services, the organization can achieve greater efficiency by having these activities performed by specialists. Also, the organization can place competitive pressure to perform on the supplier as the current supplier can always be replaced by another supplier. This type of incentive is not present when the function is performed in-house.

A similar solution is for the organization to contract with a single individual or consultant on a project basis. For instance, a firm may award a contract to a freelance computer consultant to do a piece of programming rather than hire an additional full-time programmer. Not infrequently, the individuals providing these services are former employees who have become self-employed.[25]

All these options—temporaries, employee leasing, subcontracting—reduce an organization's employment levels and thus its recruiting needs. Another approach to reducing the need to recruit is to attempt to increase the retention of current employees. Loss of talented, experienced staff to voluntary turnover can be very costly and disruptive to an organization. Chapter 16 discusses strategies to enhance employee retention.

INTERNAL RECRUITING

Most companies fill vacancies internally whenever possible. A number of internal recruiting methods are used for different levels of jobs. Lower level jobs such as manual and clerical jobs are called **nonexempt jobs** because their incumbents are not exempt from the minimum wage and overtime provisions of the Fair Labor

Standards Act (discussed more in Chapter 11). These people typically are paid an hourly wage. In contrast, higher level administrative, managerial, and professional employees are paid on a salary basis and are **exempt** from the overtime provisions of the Fair Labor Standards Act. The following discussion considers the internal recruiting methods used for each category of job in turn.

Internal Recruiting for Nonexempt Positions

Some small or nonunionized companies have an informal system for locating promotable employees. When openings occur, the hiring manager may rely on memory to suggest candidates or may ask supervisors to recommend employees who appear qualified. The obvious drawbacks of such a system are that (1) good candidates may be overlooked, (2) favoritism may be displayed, and (3) qualified candidates may be hoarded by a supervisor who prefers to keep them in the department rather than recommend them for deserved promotions elsewhere. A more systematic method involves the use of a skills inventory system to locate all viable candidates. Figure 6.3 is an example of the many steps in an internal recruitment process in one organization. In this situation, the human resource department searches the organization's records to locate possible candidates; then a long series of steps is followed to determine whether the candidate fits the opening.

The most commonly used system for internal recruitment is **job posting and bidding.** The HR manager posts openings on bulletin boards, publishes them in an in-house newspaper, or posts them on the company's intranet. Employees nominate themselves if they are interested in being considered for an opening. Many large or unionized companies use this method, and all but the very top civil service jobs are filled internally by this method.[26]

Job postings describe the positions, locations, pay rates, and qualifications and encourage all interested employees to apply. The hiring manager and an HR representative evaluate the candidates and make the selection decision. Employees who apply but are not selected often receive feedback. This feedback loop demonstrates that the system operates in an open and fair manner and helps rejected candidates understand how to improve their qualifications for future openings.[27]

In unionized companies, the basis of selection and other details of the posting-and-bidding process are spelled out in the union contract. Two types of clauses are common. The first type says that the hiring manager will select the applicant with the most seniority if he or she is at least minimally qualified. The second type says that the hiring manager will select the most qualified person but that if there are two equally qualified candidates, the hiring manager will choose the one with more seniority. In nonunionized organizations, policies may state that the selection decision will be based primarily on the applicant's ability to do the vacant job and secondarily on the applicant's performance, attendance, and seniority in his or her present job.[28]

Internal Recruiting for Exempt Positions

The posting-and-bidding process is relatively rare as a method of internal recruiting for professional and managerial positions in the private sector, although a few organizations have used it successfully.[29] Organizations trying to fill vacant managerial slots might identify candidates by consulting replacement charts or by

FIGURE 6.3

Internal Recruitment Process

Source: Reprinted with permission from Bernhard Welle, Vice President, Human Resources, Dial Corp., Phoenix, Ariz.

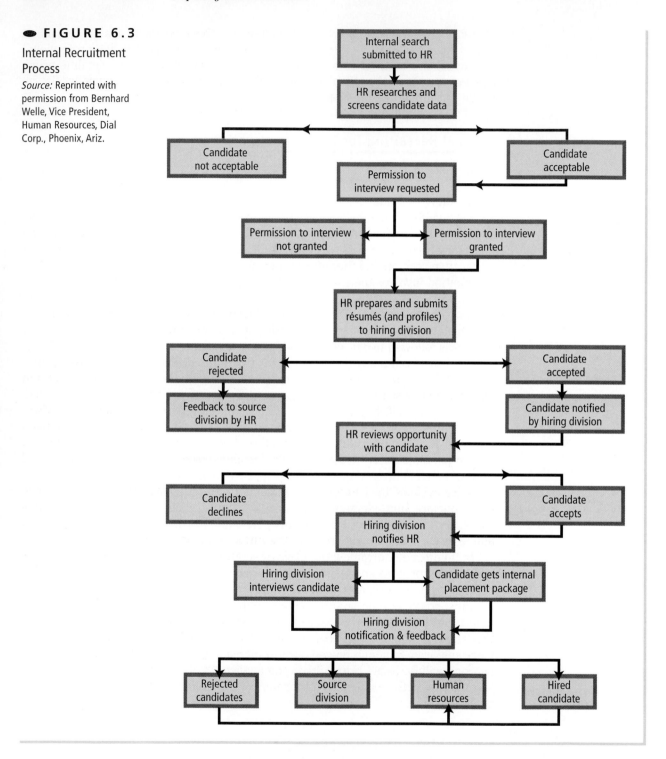

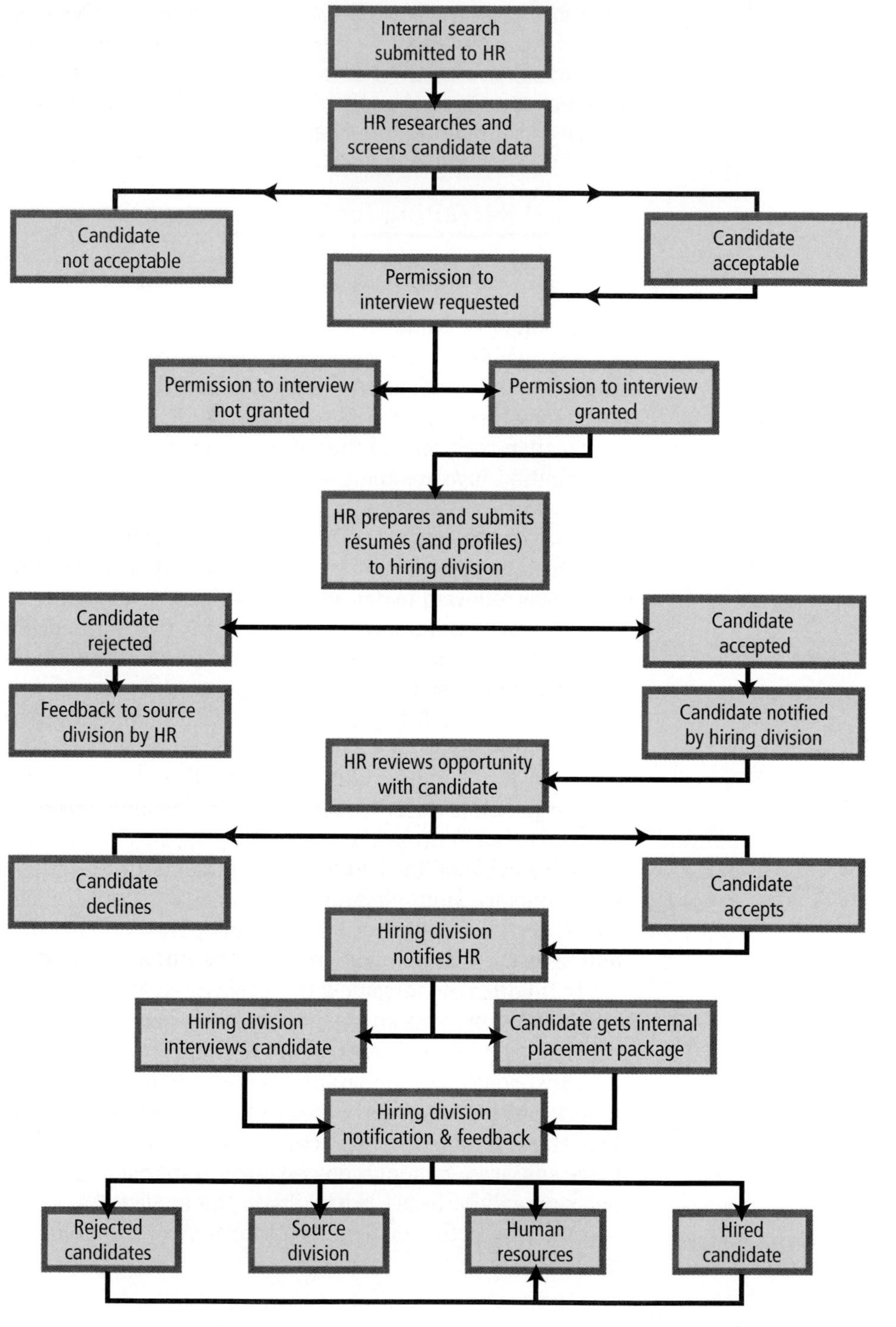

forming a nominating committee of higher managers who pool their information to generate a slate of candidates. Larger organizations, however, have found that they need a more systematic method of identifying candidates, particularly if they wish to encourage transfers across divisional lines. These firms use managerial succession planning processes and human resource information systems to locate suitable candidates. (Succession planning was discussed in Chapter 3.)

EXTERNAL RECRUITING

External recruiting may be seen as having three crucial steps. First, reasonable numbers of well-qualified candidates must be attracted to apply for the job. Second, these candidates must be motivated to maintain their status as applicants by remaining interested in the job while the organization screens and evaluates them. Finally, chosen candidates must be motivated to accept job offers when made.[30] Deficiencies at any stage of this process may result in lower quality or insufficient hires.

A successful external recruiting effort requires careful planning and coordination. In most medium-sized and large organizations, HRM professionals do most of the recruiting. These people may be human resource generalists who spend some of their time performing recruitment activities or full-time recruiters who specialize in seeking and screening potential new employees. Recruiters may make hiring decisions for some lower level jobs, but ordinarily they locate, evaluate, and then refer the most qualified candidates to the manager (or sometimes the team) of the unit in which the vacancy exists. This manager, called the hiring manager, makes the final hiring decision, often in consultation with other managers. To find the right kind of candidates, recruiters must work closely with hiring managers throughout the recruitment process.

The recruiter's first step after receiving an assignment is to meet with the hiring manager to find out more about the position to be filled. The two of them must work out specifications in terms of the education, skills, and experience needed and desired.[31] In addition to obtaining information about the job's requirements, the recruiter must also identify what might attract candidates to the job. With this information, the recruiter can begin to plan where to look for applicants, how many to look for, and how to screen them.

Throughout the recruiting process, the hiring manager should stay in close touch with the recruiter. The hiring manager should examine résumés or applications that have passed initial screening by the recruiter and should also review some of the applications that the recruiter rejected during the first step. Such involvement on the part of the hiring manager provides feedback to the recruiter on whether his or her decisions are consistent with the hiring manager's preferences.

Planning for External Recruiting

Before beginning the recruiting effort, the recruiter must plan which methods to use, how intensively to use them, and when to begin recruiting to produce the required number of candidates at the time they are needed. As a rule, higher level positions take longer to fill. A recent survey by the Society for Human Resource Management found that exempt positions took an average of thirty-five days from opening to first day on the job, whereas nonexempt positions took twenty-one days.[32] Several other factors, including the following, may make recruiting more difficult or time consuming:

- The need for a confidential search or the requirement that no advertising be done
- A technically complex position for which qualified individuals are hard to find
- Competition in the marketplace for the type of candidates needed
- A poor industry, company, or division reputation
- Low pay relative to what other firms are offering to similarly qualified individuals
- An unclear job description or confusing reporting relationships
- No housing assistance or relocation costs paid by the company
- An undesirable location

These factors either make it difficult to locate candidates or make candidates less willing to entertain offers.[33] Under any of these conditions, recruiters should begin the search early, consider using a wider than usual range of recruiting methods, and perhaps target nontraditional segments of the labor market.

If data from past recruiting efforts are available, recruiters should calculate, for different types of positions, the average time between the first contact with an applicant and the first day on the job. Such data can help in determining how far in advance to begin the recruiting process.[34]

Recruiting goals are usually expressed in terms of the number of positions to be filled. However, knowing that the Odessa Police Department needs to hire sixteen officers over the course of a year does not immediately tell a recruiter how extensively to search or when to begin looking. What the recruiter really needs to know is how many applications or initial interviews will be needed to locate sixteen police officers who are not only able to pass all the selection hurdles but also willing to accept a job offer. Based on previous years' experience, the recruiter may be able to calculate yield ratios. A **yield ratio** is the number of candidates who pass each stage of the selection process and then choose to proceed to the next stage compared with the number who entered each stage to begin with. Yield ratios for the eight steps in the Odessa Police Department's recruiting process are shown in Figure 6.4. Assume sixty candidates begin the process by turning in a complete application. Of these, 72 percent, or forty-three individuals, usually pass the written test and are allowed to continue to the next stage. Sixty-one percent of these, or twenty-six, pass the background investigation; 58 percent, or fifteen people, pass the oral interview; 70 percent of the survivors, eleven candidates, pass the polygraph; 77 percent, or eight people, pass the medical exam; 72 percent, or six people from the original sixty applicants, pass the psychological exam; and all who have passed the first seven hurdles typically pass the final drug test and accept job offers. This means that under its current system, to produce sixteen hires, the department will have to process 160 applications each year.

The department decided to study its recruitment system further in an attempt to improve the timeliness of hires and to reduce the loss of potentially qualified candidates who could not afford to wait nearly four months for a decision. They assessed the time it took to administer each stage of the process in an effort to locate the constraint, or bottleneck, that was slowing down the recruitment system. These times are shown in the third column from the left in Table 6.1. The problem

FIGURE 6.4
Recruiting Yield Pyramid

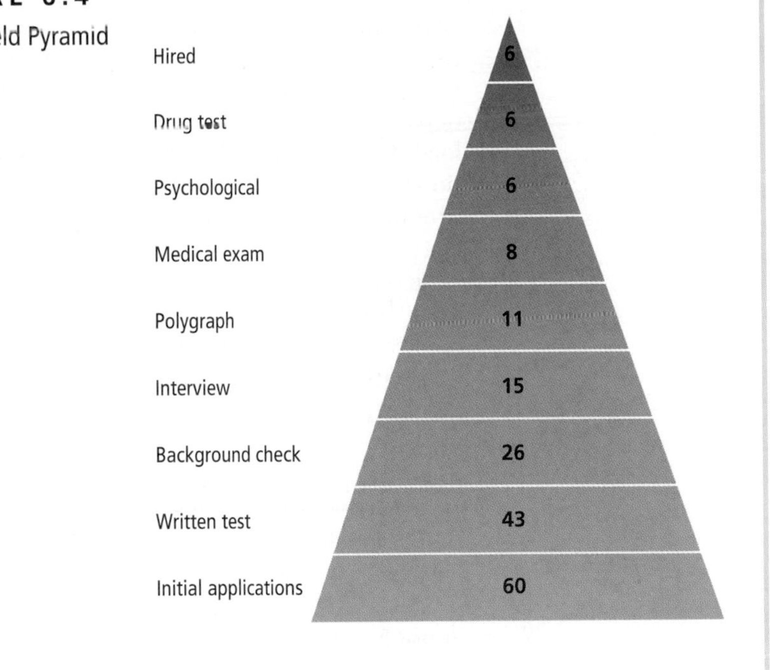

TABLE 6.1
Recruitment Process at the Odessa Police Department

Original Recruitment Process	Candidates Processed per Day (Capacity)	Total Days Required to Process Survivors of Entering Cohort of Sixty	Revised Recruitment Process	Candidates Processed per Day (Capacity)	Total Days Required to Process Survivors of Entering Cohort of Sixty
Application	60	1	Application	60	1
Written exam	30	2	Written exam	30	2
Background investigation	.25	104	Brief background investigation	20	2
Interview	4	4	Interview	4	4
Polygraph	8	2	Polygraph	8	2
Medical exam	8	1	Medical exam	8	1
Psychological exam	4	2	Psychological exam	4	2
Drug test	60	1	Drug test	60	1
			Detailed background investigation	7	1
Total days per cohort		117			16

Source: Data from Lloyd J. Taylor III, Brian J. Moersch, and Geralyn McClure Franklin, "Applying the Theory of Constraints to a Public Safety Hiring Process," *Public Personnel Management,* Fall 2003, Vol. 32, pp. 369 and 380.

was found to be at the third step, the intensive background check (military, credit, criminal, work, and educational records, interviews with neighbors, etc.), which took the lone full-time investigator four days per candidate to complete. The recommended solution was to take advantage of the thirty-three other people in the department who were capable of doing background checks as part of their workload, but also to shift to a less comprehensive one-day background check as the third step in the hiring process, and save the remaining three-day detailed background investigation until the very last (now ninth) step in the process when there were fewer candidates and nearly all who had unsuitable backgrounds had failed at an earlier step in any case. These two fairly simple changes reduced the recruitment time to just sixteen days, meaning that very few good candidates were lost, quality of hires remained high, and the department was at full strength most of the time rather than being perpetually short-staffed while waiting for a lengthy recruitment process to bear fruit.[35]

Recruitment Information and Résumé-Tracking Systems

Before beginning to recruit candidates, the HR professional must have a system for tracking applicants as they move through the recruitment and selection process. The system may be manual or computerized, depending on the number of applicants handled. An efficient recruitment information system must ensure that candidates do not get lost but instead move through the process and stay informed of their status. An applicant who is deemed unsuitable should receive a polite letter to that effect as soon as possible after the decision.[36] Good candidates who are pending should receive encouraging letters or e-mails to keep them interested in the organization. Such conscientious communication enhances an organization's image, even among candidates who are eventually rejected.[37]

The recruitment information system must be able to generate reports on applicant characteristics to determine whether an adverse impact is occurring or whether affirmative action efforts have broadened the applicant pool as intended. The statistics generated must cover the percentages of black, other minority, and female applicants to various job categories. The recruitment information system also should be able to provide data necessary to calculate yield ratios, average time from first contact to first day on the job, and other indices helpful in planning and evaluating recruiting.[38]

The pace of recruiting and the volume of applications received have skyrocketed with the spread of Internet recruiting. Recruiters need help to quickly screen out résumés of the many individuals who are not qualified and to enable a very fast response to the most promising candidates. The best candidates may be hired by someone else unless a telephone interview is arranged within twenty-four to seventy-two hours of the electronic submission of a resume.[39] In the past few years, **résumé-tracking software** programs have been developed to store and search résumés electronically. Résumés are either submitted electronically or scanned in from paper copies.[40] An artificial intelligence program picks out and catalogs key words from the documents. Recruiters can search their résumé database for needed qualifications, and the programs create ranked lists of potentially qualified candidates. The U.S. Navy has adopted Resumix to help manage the more than 1,000 Internet resumes it receives every day.[41] Recently, more advanced **hiring management systems** have been developed to facilitate internal and external posting of jobs, sort and manage incoming résumés, and integrate corporate recruiting Web sites with commercial job boards. Some of these programs maintain lists of past applicants and "push" relevant information about new job openings to them.[42]

Informal Methods

External recruiting methods are often grouped into two classes: informal and formal. **Informal recruiting methods** tap a narrower labor market than formal methods. Informal methods include rehiring former employees or former cooperative education students, hiring people referred by present employees, and hiring from among those who have applied without being solicited (such applicants are called walk-ins or **gate hires**). **Formal recruiting methods** search the labor market more widely for candidates with no previous connection to the company.

Employee referral, also known as **word-of-mouth advertising,** is quick, effective, and usually inexpensive. Because employees who refer their friends and acquaintances as candidates have their own credibility on the line, they tend to refer people who are well qualified and well motivated and then to mentor these individuals once they are hired. APX International, an engineering firm in Michigan, finds 80 percent of its new hires by employee referral. Each time employees receive their paycheck, they are given information about current job openings. In essence, the firm has as many recruiters as it has employees.

Some companies give bonuses to employees who refer a good candidate. For example, the pharmaceutical company McGaw pays $2,000 for a successful referral for a sales job. Half is paid after the first month of employment and the remainder after six months if both the new hire and the referrer are still working for the company.[43] PeopleSoft has paid as much as $5,000 for referrals in hard-to-find specialties, and Canadian technology giant Nortel has run a $1 million cash and prizes scheme to encourage employee referrals. At Texas Instruments, employees who successfully refer others receive cash bonuses as well as entry into a raffle for a new car.[44]

One significant drawback of word-of-mouth advertising is that this method may reduce the likelihood of a firm meeting its affirmative action goals. If a firm's work force is primarily nonminority, then the friends referred by present employees are likely to be nonminority as well. Thus companies should supplement informal methods with formal methods that reach a more diverse audience. Word-of-mouth advertising is also unlikely to generate the large numbers of candidates that might be needed for a major expansion.

Formal Methods

Formal methods of external recruiting entail searching the labor market for candidates who have no previous connection to the firm. These methods traditionally have included newspaper advertising, use of employment agencies and executive search firms, and campus recruiting. Posting job ads on the Internet, on the company's own site or on a commercial job board, has also become extremely popular in the last decade. Table 6.2 shows the recruiting methods used by a sample of HR professionals and a sample of job seekers in a 2001 survey. Historically, newspaper advertising has been the most commonly used method of recruiting. It remains popular, though expenditures on newspaper ads have fallen substantially as Internet recruitment has spread. Table 6.2 also shows the effectiveness of various recruiting methods as perceived by both parties on a scale from 1 (not at all effective) to 5 (extremely effective). Although HR professionals and job seekers do not agree perfectly on all methods, both find informal methods including referrals and personal contacts highly useful, and both find some usefulness in Internet postings. Advertising in newspapers, professional and trade journals, and headhunters and agencies are seen as moderately useful. Because this survey featured experienced employees, campus recruiting was not rated. However, this method is usually seen as quite useful by recruiters of new graduates.[45]

Recruitment Advertising A traditionally common formal recruiting method is newspaper advertising. Ads placed in newspapers are accessible to everyone and thus do not discriminate against any groups in disseminating information about job openings. Recruitment advertising has an obvious target—people who are seeking work—and an obvious goal—attracting these job seekers to apply for a job at a particular company. Newspaper ads, however, reach a much wider audience. Estimates are that only 10 to 20 percent of the readers of help-wanted ads are currently seeking work. Other readers are not actively looking for jobs but skim the ads regularly to see what is available. These readers are unlikely to apply immediately but are developing images of the employers whose ads they see. A well-designed, informative advertisement may help convince these people to con-

TABLE 6.2

Extent of Use and Rated Effectiveness of Recruitment Methods as seen by HR Professionals and Job Seekers

	HR Professionals		Job Seekers	
Recruitment/Search Method	**% Use**	**Effectiveness***	**% Use**	**Effectiveness***
Internet job postings	88%	3.6	96%	3.2
Personal contact/networking	95	3.7	95	4.1
Ads in newspapers	96	3.3	95	2.8
Employee referrals/employee referral program	91	3.5	92	3.8
Online or Web site job applications	49	3.2	90	2.9
Headhunters	74	3.5	89	3.2
Employment agencies	76	3.0	81	2.8
Ads in professional and trade journals	67	3.2	78	3.1
Job fairs	70	2.8	76	2.7
Open houses	36	2.3	69	2.2
Internet advertisements (e.g., banners and links)	29	3.0	68	2.2
Job hotlines	30	2.6	67	2.5
Temp-to-hire	75	3.0	65	3.1
Walk-ins	76	2.1	62	2.2
Radio/TV advertising	26	2.6	54	2.3
Minority job fairs	51	2.6	42	2.5

*Mean effectiveness ratings are based on a scale where 1 is "not at all effective" and 5 is "extremely effective."
N = 566 HR professionals and 439 job seekers.
Source: Data from: Search Tactics Poll, at SHRM/CareerJournal.com, 2001.

sider the company at some later date when they are interested in a new job. Another audience for ads includes clients, stockholders, brokers, activists, and regulators, all of whom may have some interest in an organization's activities. The final audience for ads is a company's own employees. When one company discontinued its regular recruitment advertising, it found that its employees were suddenly nervous and that rumors of layoffs were circulating.[46] A well-designed advertising campaign can reinforce confidence and pride among current employees. However, the U.S. Army found that the reverse can also occur. Soldiers reported uniformly negative reactions to the Army's "Be All You Can Be" ad campaign, feeling that it was misleading and unrealistic and failed to emphasize such important values as patriotism and self-sacrifice.[47]

The main purpose of a recruitment ad is to generate a **qualified response**—that is, to produce applications from candidates who are at least minimally qualified for the job. A good ad should also make screening applications easy by clearly telling applicants what sort of information to provide in their application package. To elicit a qualified response, the ad must contain enough information about the job, necessary qualifications, location, and pay rate to allow uninterested or unqualified people to make the decision not to apply. At the same time, the ad must attract qualified candidates by conveying a good impression of the company or division and by emphasizing the advantages of the particular job. To achieve its objectives, an ad must not misrepresent the job and raise unrealistic expectations in candidates. Rather, it should clearly describe the legitimate attractions of the job.[48] See the International Perspective box for how ad content for the same job varies across countries, reflecting cultural differences in the types of persons organizations in those countries wish to attract.

One form of advertisement is a **blind ad,** in which the company does not identify itself but rather asks candidates to reply to an anonymous post office box. A company may use blind ads when it does not want competitors to know that it is planning an expansion, when it does not want its own employees to know that one of them may be replaced, or when it has a poor reputation as an employer. Blind ads typically yield a significantly lower response rate than nonblind ads and should not be used unless there is a very good reason. A survey conducted in Europe discovered that 75 percent of job ad readers said that the organization's name was a crucial piece of information that should always be included in a job advertisement.[49]

The greatest concentration of ads usually appears in Sunday newspapers in larger cities. For a firm seeking a person whose skills are relatively common in the general population (such as a bookkeeper, secretary, laborer, or salesperson), the newspaper is a good place to advertise. Local papers may be most appropriate if the firm does not expect to assist in employee relocation. If, however, a company is seeking a person with a specialized skill or unusual knowledge in a geographically dispersed labor market, it should choose advertising sources that specifically target the population of qualified persons, such as publications and conventions of professional organizations.[50] For example, universities looking for new faculty for the management department could advertise in the Academy of Management Placement Roster, the Academy's placement Web site, and conduct screening interviews at the Academy's annual professional meeting.

Internet Recruiting **Internet recruiting** has grown at a phenomenal rate over the past few years.[51] Ninety-four percent of *Fortune* Global 500 companies

INTERNATIONAL PERSPECTIVE

Job Ads—A Window on the National Soul

National culture can influence the traits desired in job candidates, and hence the content of recruitment ads. Even in the European Union, striving to become a single labor market, there are substantial national differences in the content of recruitment ads across countries. One study examined these differences in newspaper ads for the job of manager. The differences in ad content seem to reflect national and cultural differences in the behavior expected from successful managers, traditional sources of management candidates, and typical human resource practices.

In the United Kingdom, a general management background is desired, individuals need not necessarily have advanced or specialized educational qualifications in management, and the focus is on making a profit, showing initiative, and having leadership and interpersonal skills. Desired age is never mentioned in ads. These criteria are consistent with the U.K.'s individualistic and relatively low-power distance culture.

In France, coming from one of the elite universities (grandes ecoles) is essential and continues a long tradition in management recruitment. Abstract academic skills are valued above "mundane" practical skills. Managers are expected to be authoritarian and closely supervise their subordinates, with people skills being unimportant in rigid formal hierarchies. A desired age range for candidates is often specified. French ads commonly invite candidates to submit a résumé and a hand-written letter of application, because the French are fond of using graphology (handwriting analysis) as a method of selection.

In Germany, ads tend to emphasize specific technical qualifications, usually in the form of an engineering degree. Practical skills are highly valued, and an apprenticeship plus engineering degree is the optimal combination. Skills for working in a team to get the job done are important, and letters of reference attesting to strong ability to get along with colleagues are expected as part of the application package. These desired managerial attributes are consistent with Germany's higher level of collectivism and lower level of power distance compared to France.

The three countries also differ in the amount of information newspaper ads contain about compensation. Most ads for managerial posts in the U.K. contain detailed information on salary and a variety of other benefits such as a car. Clearly, these items are important, a basis on which employers compete against each other, and perfectly legitimate to discuss publicly. In Germany salary is less commonly mentioned, perhaps because the culture is egalitarian and almost everyone receives the same set of attractive benefits. In France salary is virtually never mentioned in advertisements. Apparently it is inappropriate to publicly discuss pay and perquisites because there are often large differences in remuneration across organizational levels (reflecting a high-power distance culture), and across individuals even in the same job (reflecting an emphasis on personalized power and influence). Too much mention of salary and benefits risks raising issues of inequity with other employees.

These differences suggest that a single pan-European staffing policy is unlikely to fit expectations equally well in all countries and that recruitment ads should be tailored to local practice and expectations.

Sources: Christine Communal and Barbara Senior, "National Culture and Management: Messages Conveyed by British, French, and German Advertisement for Managerial Appointments," *Leadership and Organizational Development Journal,* Vol. 20, 1999, pp. 26–35; Michael Segalla, Alfonso Sauquet, and Carlo Turati, "Symbolic vs. Functional Recruitment: Cultural Influences on Employee Recruitment Policy," *European Management Journal,* Vol. 19, 2001, pp. 32–42.

had a dedicated careers Web site in 2003, and an increasing number are only accepting applications over the Internet. Entire new job titles—such as Internet Sourcer, Internet Recruiting Specialist, and Internet Recruiting Manager—have come into being in the past few years. Companies find that Internet recruiting is much less expensive and much faster than traditional methods. It is by far the most economical way to reach a nationwide or worldwide audience of job candi-

FIGURE 6.5

How Has the Internet Changed the Way You Recruit? Responses of 228 HR Managers

Note: Percentages do not add up to 100 as multiple responses were allowed.

Source: D. Gere, E. K. Scarborough, and J. Collison, *2002 Recruiter Budget/Cost Survey.* (Alexandria, Va.: Society for Human Resource Management, 2002) p. 16, Chart 19.

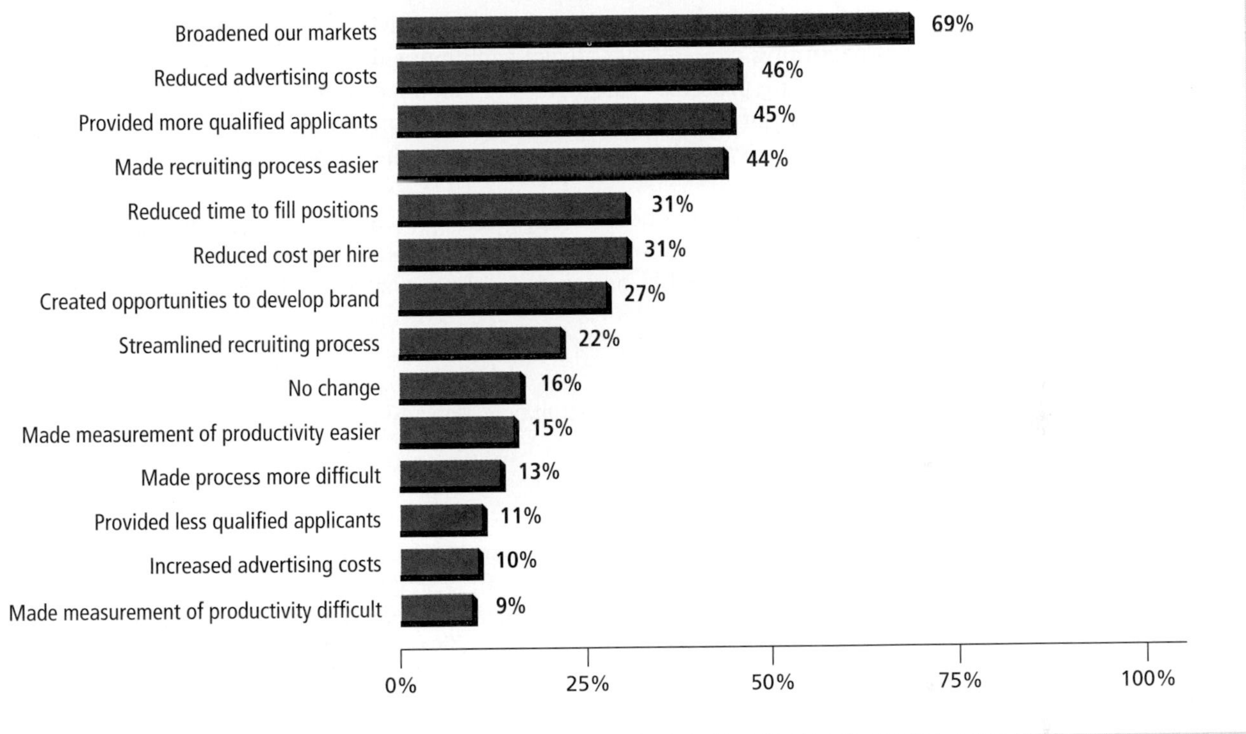

dates. A survey of HR managers in 2002 documented the ways the availability of the Internet has changed the recruiting process (see Figure 6.5 for details).[52] A drawback can sometimes be the very large number of résumés that are submitted, many of which are not at all suited to the positions listed.

At first, Internet recruiting was used largely to reach candidates in the information technology and engineering fields. Each year, as more and more people have gained access to the Internet, a wider and wider range of jobs have been advertised and successfully filled via this recruitment medium. New graduates are especially active in using the Web to locate job opportunities, apply online, and research companies as potential employers. There are a number of ways in which the Internet is used by both job seekers and employers, including the following:

- Large job boards that post jobs and résumés
- Niche boards specializing in particular industries, locations, or occupations
- Company Web sites that contain job listings and facilities for online submission of résumés to that company

When Internet recruiting first began, recruiters used the Web much as they would use a newspaper—they posted job ads on Internet **job boards,** the e-equivalent of the classified section of the Sunday paper. Job boards attract a great deal of traffic, but some recruiters feel that many of the résumés posted are out of date and that the best candidates have already been taken or have not posted their résumés in the first place. Companies are increasingly customizing their Internet recruiting, combining some use of big job boards with focused use of niche boards and a strong careers site attached to their company's homepage.

Table 6.3 provides suggestions for an effective company careers Web site. Internet recruiting may initially attract candidates to apply, but this is only one step in the recruiting process. Candidates still need face-to-face time with company representatives before they make a decision to switch employers, and employers also need to meet the candidate in person to assess the individual's suitability to the job and the company.

Internet recruiting is not the best choice for all recruiting needs. Jobs requiring lower levels of education, paying less, and likely to be filled from a single local labor market are probably better suited to newspaper ads, local employee refer-

TABLE 6.3

Criteria for Designing an Effective Recruitment Web Site

Navigation

1. Easy for job seekers to find. Many links from other relevant noncompany Web pages to the company homepage, many links from other company Web pages to the careers page.
2. A clear navigation structure that guides users back and forth through the site, site map, and obvious links to more specific relevant pages.

Content

1. Current and credible content that supports the company's recruitment brand.
2. Detailed company information on products and services, unit descriptions, management, and office locations.
3. Discussion of company culture and the value proposition to candidates.
4. Little or no use of fancy graphics and flash video that take a long time to load and that some users can't read.
5. Plenty of white space to separate and contrast blocks of content.

Functionality

1. Online résumé submission.
2. List of open jobs with detail on job content and hiring requirements, searchable on multiple levels (specialty, location, experience, etc.).
3. Personalization features such as résumé builders, culture tests, and so forth.

Other Features

1. Five mouse clicks or less from the company homepage to a specific job opening.
2. Prompt e-mail acknowledgment of résumé submissions.
3. For some companies, a subsite for students/new graduates is very helpful. The site might provide extra advice on the job search and selection process for those who are relatively new to this activity.

Source: Ideas from Texas Instruments Incorporated and Michael Foster, *Recruiting on the Web: Smart Strategies for Finding the Perfect Candidate* (New York: McGraw-Hill Trade, 2002).

rals, or a public job service agency. For example, gift catalog company Lillian Vernon Corp. uses Internet recruiting for management information systems and engineering jobs but uses local newspaper and television ads, billboards, and an airplane towing a banner to recruit locally each year when its employment swells from 1,000 to 5,000 for the Christmas rush.[53]

Employment Agencies Another formal method of recruiting is to use an employment agency. An agency finds and prescreens applicants, referring those who seem qualified to the organization for further assessment and final selection. An agency can screen effectively only if it has a clear understanding of the position it is trying to fill. Thus it is very important that an employer be as specific and accurate as possible when describing a position and its requirements to an employment agency.

Employment agencies are covered by Title VII of the Civil Rights Act and thus are forbidden to discriminate in screening and referring candidates on the basis of race, color, sex, religion, or national origin. Sometimes, however, agencies have been known to discriminate at the request of firms. For instance, in a survey of recruiters for executive search firms, 14 percent reported having been asked not to refer Jewish candidates for certain positions.[54]

Alternatively, an employment agency may discriminate without the client organization's knowledge if the agency's recruiters mistakenly believe that a certain race or sex of candidate is more likely to be welcomed or if the agency uses an invalid selection device with an adverse impact in screening. In this case, both the agency and the client organization could face discrimination charges.[55]

Agencies that provide employment services can be publicly funded or for-profit agencies. On occasion, unions provide employment services as well.

Public Job Service Agencies Every state has a publicly funded agency that is affiliated with the U.S. Employment Service (USES). These **public job service agencies** have a number of offices throughout each state. In addition to administering unemployment compensation, public job service agencies attempt to find jobs for those seeking work. In most cases, able-bodied persons who are collecting unemployment compensation must register with the job service agency; however, anyone who is seeking work may register as well.

State job service agencies interview job seekers to find out about their skills, experience, and preferences. Employers call in their vacant jobs and describe the job specifications. The agency then matches applicants and refers qualified persons to the employer for interviews. State job service agencies may also test applicants when requested to do so by employers.

Public job service agencies fill primarily blue-collar and clerical positions. Sometimes, however, the agencies are able to fill higher level openings. They are also able to recruit nationally through their Web site, America's Job Bank (www.ajb.dni.us). This site lists both openings and résumés of job seekers. One day in February 2005, America's Job Bank listed 665,421 individuals seeking work and 1,245,969 jobs to be filled. State and USES employment agencies offer their services with no direct charge to either the job seeker or the employer.

Private, For-Profit Agencies Organizations use for-profit, **private employment agencies** to produce a set of prescreened candidates; job seekers use them to locate a suitable position. For each successful placement, agencies charge a fee that can range from 10 to 30 percent of the employee's first-year pay. The fee may be paid by either the applicant or the employer, depending on the labor market. Employment agencies specializing in administrative support personnel typically handle jobs paying under $40,000 per year, whereas those filling professional/technical jobs in accounting, finance, data processing, retail, software engineering, and technical sales cover jobs paying $40,000 to $80,000 annually.[56] Private employment agencies are presently under threat from Internet job boards and the ability of companies to recruit directly through their own Web sites. Table 6.4 shows the fees charged for some specific positions by selected agencies in 1999. A contingency fee means that the fee is payable only if the position is successfully filled. The "retained" fee listed against the Director of Business Development position is paid for a search by an executive recruitment (headhunter) firm, regardless of the outcome of the effort.

Unions Unions sometimes provide employment services for their members. For construction workers and stevedores, labor contracts may specify that employers first seek candidates at the union hiring hall before recruiting elsewhere. The union hall refers union members seeking jobs to companies for evaluation and selection.

Additional Recruiting Methods As employers have had to contend with labor shortages in some regions and occupations, they have used more innovative recruitment methods. Some of these include job fairs, TV or radio ads, direct mail, point-of-sale recruitment advertising (on the assumption that those who buy your product may be interested in making or selling it), and employment hotlines to provide job information twenty-four hours a day. Another increasingly common method is "telecruiting," whereby potential candidates who are already employed are phoned in an effort to build their interest in changing employers. Table 6.5 shows additional methods of attracting employees that complement traditional recruiting activities.

Another way to innovate when job candidates are scarce is to consider bringing them in from an area where employees are more readily available. An example of a company that did this effectively is the Opryland Hotel in Nashville. When the hotel doubled in size, 1,500 more workers were needed. With 3 percent unemployment in the local labor market, traditional recruiting sources and methods would not yield the required number of qualified employees. Therefore, Opryland Hotel went to a place where unemployment stood at 12 percent—Puerto Rico. Two hun-

TABLE 6.4

Examples of Employment Agency and Executive Search Fees

Position	Salary	Fee	Fee Type
Administrative assistant	$ 30,000	$ 6,000	Contingency
Small company controller	$ 65,000	$16,250	Contingency
Director of business development	$200,000	$66,000	Retained
Underwriter	$ 58,000	$18,000	Contingency
Receptionist	$ 19,000	$ 3,600	Contingency

Source: Available at www.bankrate.com/brm/news/biz/tcb/19990916a.asp.

TABLE 6.5

Innovative External Recruiting Methods

Telecruiting Phone calls to potential candidates, with names obtained from mailing lists of professional associations, schools, and mailing list companies.

Direct mail Using lists from above sources.

Point-of-sale recruiting messages (posters, literature, messages on the back of cash register tapes) Useful if customers are potentially qualified applicants.

Talent scout cards One organization in need of customer-oriented service staff gave its managers "talent scout" cards inviting prospective candidates to apply for jobs. Managers were asked to distribute the cards to exceptionally friendly, helpful customer service personnel they encountered while doing their shopping.

Posters Displayed on community bulletin boards, parks, laundromats, banks, and so forth.

Door hangers Useful for recruiting in a specified geographic area.

Radio Alone or to refer candidates to open houses or large newspaper ads.

Billboards Fixed highway displays or electronic billboards with varying messages.

Hotlines and 800 numbers Telephone lines with either recorded job vacancy messages or live interviewers. Live lines are increasingly being made available on Sundays, when most newspaper ads appear and candidates have the time to follow up on openings.

Information seminars On job-hunting skills or on topics specific to one's industry, such as new developments in artificial intelligence. The latter may attract qualified professionals who would be reluctant to attend an open house or job fair, where the recruiting purpose is more explicit.

Welcome Wagon, relocation consultants, realtors These organizations are aware of newcomers to the community. Increasingly, spouses of individuals transferred into the community are seeking work and can be located through these sources.

Referral program Employee referral systems are common, but now some firms are encouraging their customers and suppliers to refer candidates as well.

Outplacement firms and local layoffs Skilled employees who have lost their jobs through no fault of their own may be found by contacting outplacement firms and by monitoring the local paper for layoffs at other establishments in the community.

Event recruiting Attend, sponsor, or supply free refreshments or gifts at trendy events such as bike races, marathons, and grand openings of microbreweries. Cisco Systems has successfully used event participation to establish a reputation as a "cool" place to work by participating in the types of events popular with the people they wish to employ.

Re-recruiting former employees Especially in high tech, good individuals may be recruited away by a new challenge or more money. A few years later, they may again be willing to move and can bring their newly honed skills back to a former employer. This requires companies to get over any hang-ups about "disloyal" employees and face the new realities of career paths in the twenty-first century.

Source: Compiled from Catherine D. Fyock, "Expanding the Talent Search: 19 Ways to Recruit Top Talent," *HR Magazine*, July 1991, pp. 32–35. Reprinted with permission from *HR Magazine*, published by the Society for Human Resource Management, Alexandria, Va. Additional ideas from K. Wheeler "Non-Traditional Recruiting Methods, Revised: Some Ideas and Examples," November 29, 2000, available at www.erexchange.com/articles.

dred and fifty employees were hired and relocated in the first year. Because Puerto Rico has a strong hospitality industry and relatively high unemployment, the company was easily able to find qualified staff.[57]

Recruiting Targeted Groups

In this section we discuss directing recruiting methods to specific segments of the labor market, such as executives, new college graduates, the disadvantaged, minorities, and older workers. In each case, these groups are better served with focused methods than with generic newspaper advertising. The more carefully one can specify the group being targeted, the better aimed one's recruitment methods can be. One example of excellent targeting is provided by United Airlines at Boston's Logan Airport. The company was having a hard time filling food service jobs. Because the airline could offer free travel as a benefit, it decided to target people who would have a particular desire to fly: immigrants who had family members overseas. To reach this audience, the airline used recruiting posters placed along mass-transit routes serving immigrant sections of the city. The method was a great success, and the airline's applicant shortage was relieved.[58]

Executive Search Firms **Executive search firms** recruit managerial talent for positions paying more than $80,000 per year. They view the organization rather than the candidate as their client. In fact, most executive search firms are not interested in receiving unsolicited applications or résumés. Instead, they conduct a separate nationwide or even international search for each position that they contract to fill.

Most of the *Fortune 1,000* companies and many public-sector organizations make some use of executive search firms, or **headhunters.**[59] These firms charge employers substantial fees, usually equal to one-third the estimated first-year cash compensation (salary and bonus) for the position, plus search expenses. Many headhunters charge this fee whether or not the search results in a candidate being hired. They see themselves as professionals who are paid to use their skills to make the search rather than to guarantee its outcome.

One survey showed that about 40 percent of all executive searches were completed successfully within the time specified by the contract. An additional 15 to 20 percent were eventually completed, and 40 percent failed.[60] Among the many reasons a search might fail to produce an acceptable candidate are the following:

- Unclear or unrealistically high job specifications
- Poor company or industry reputation
- Internal politics in the hiring organization
- Insufficient research staff at the search firm
- Use of an overly specialized search firm[61]

Most of these reasons need no further explanation, but it might be helpful to understand a little more about overly specialized search firms. Typically, a firm hired to conduct a search agrees not to raid the client organization for a period of two years. The agency is barred from calling on that organization's employees as prospects in subsequent searches for other organizations. Executive search firms that have been very successful in writing a lot of contracts or that are highly specialized in a discipline (e.g., data-processing management) or in an industry (e.g., the petroleum industry) eventually may find themselves forbidden to recruit from the most likely sources of candidates, compromising their ability to conduct effective searches.

Companies use executive search firms for several reasons. First, search firms are better at locating candidates who are already employed and who may not be actively considering a job change. Second, they are very good at the "high-touch" relationship building necessary to woo executives from one company to another. Third, using search firms tends to be faster for a company than if it were to do its own recruiting. The search firm may already have extensive files of possible candidates and is experienced in locating additional names. Search firms claim they can fill a position in about half the time that a company would need to do its own recruiting. Fourth, the search firm can keep the hiring company's name a secret until the final referral stage if the company does not want others to know that staffing changes are contemplated in important positions. A final reason is that directly seducing a competitor's employees is considered bad form, but hiring a third party to do it is more acceptable.

The search process consists of several steps. Most search firms begin by drawing on the files accumulated in previous searches. Some firms claim to have extensive databases. Executive recruiters also search published sources, such as business periodicals and alumni directories of prestigious schools.[62] In addition, they contact organizations, trying to acquire information about managers who may fit the profile they are looking for.[63] Finally, recruiters phone prospects and try to interest them in the job. Recruiters proceed to interview the better prospects and check references before referring the top candidates to the hiring company for final selection. Occasionally, the search firm may continue its involvement in the process by serving as a mediator while the chosen candidate and the employer negotiate the details of the employment contract.[64]

The executive search industry grew rapidly in the 1990s but is now facing significant challenges.[65] Perhaps the largest of these is the rise of the Internet, which allows savvy computer users to replicate search firms' extensive proprietary databases with relative ease. Although high-end recruiting will continue to require a personal touch, big search firms such as Korn/Ferry, Heidrick & Struggles International, and LAI Worldwide have hedged their bets by entering the Internet market themselves.[66]

Campus Recruiting **Campus recruiting** is widely used by large and medium-sized firms that need highly educated entry-level employees. Campus recruiting can be very productive for an organization, because many good candidates can be interviewed in a short period of time and at a single location. Furthermore, it is convenient because the university recruitment center provides both space and administrative support.[67] Campus recruiting is moderate in cost. It is more expensive than word-of-mouth recruiting, gate hiring, or limited advertising, but it can be less expensive than using employment agencies (when the company pays the fee).[68]

One disadvantage of campus recruiting is that candidates are available to start work only at certain times of the year. Other disadvantages include the lack of experience and the inflated expectations often held by new graduates, the high cost of hiring graduates for positions that may not really require a college degree, and the difficulty of evaluating candidates who do not possess much relevant work history. Over the past few years when the market has been right, another cost of campus recruiting in high-demand fields has been the hefty signing bonuses required to attract candidates.[69]

In planning a firm's university recruiting program, the recruiter must first decide how many schools to visit. Experts advise that more intensive recruiting at a smaller number of appropriately selected schools tends to be more effective than brief visits to a larger number of schools. Recruiters usually choose universities on the basis of the company's past experience with their graduates, the degrees offered, the reputation of the school, the demography of the student body (e.g., sex, age, and minority composition), the geographic location, and the quality of the college placement office.[70]

After targeting a subset of schools, the recruiter makes an effort to build up the company's reputation with students and disseminates detailed information on the types of careers available before making the interview visit. A key role in attracting students may be played by the recruiting brochure distributed prior to the interview visit. A British survey has found that a good brochure addresses students' most pressing information needs: what the job duties will be, starting salary ranges, where the company is located, training and career development policies, opportunity for promotion, and the disciplines and degrees required.[71] One study found that students' perceptions of the company's brand image influenced their choice to apply when recruiters came to campus. Image was enhanced by pre-recruitment visit publicity (favorable new articles about the company), company sponsorship of on-campus activities, word-of-mouth endorsements by former students and faculty, and advertising and distribution of recruiting brochures at the university.[72] By visiting the same schools year after year, the firm can develop visibility and maintain an ongoing relationship with placement center officials as well as increase the likelihood of positive word-of-mouth from prior recruits. A top-class company Web site is also very important in attracting university students to events both on and off campus.[73]

Although campus interviewers may be full-time HR professionals, they often are people who work in some other capacity during most of the year. For instance, engineering managers may be pressed into service to conduct campus interviews with engineering students for a few weeks each year. J.C. Penny sends younger staff members to recruit on campus on the assumption that they will relate better to students.[74] Candidates usually value the opportunity to be interviewed by someone in their own specialty, but this practice can backfire if the interviewer is not well trained for the role.[75] Before embarking on recruiting tours, managers should receive in-depth training on how to conduct interviews and should be made aware of EEO issues. They also need to be able to sensibly answer candidates' questions about career opportunities, the company's compensation and benefits packages, and procedures during the remainder of the selection process.

Campus interviews are usually followed by site-visit or plant-trip invitations to the best candidates. The firm should plan these visits carefully to make a good impression. For instance, the firm should pay all travel expenses in advance. The trip itself should be well organized, with interviews, meals, and tours carefully scheduled so that candidates are not left at loose ends. Candidates particularly enjoy having a sponsor to shepherd them through the entire trip. They also like talking to employees in positions similar to the one for which they are being considered.

Some organizations are dropping the term "campus recruiting," which implies a one-dimensional activity conducted a few weeks a year, in favor of the concept of a "university relations program." The latter brings home the importance of maintaining year-round visibility on selected campuses using a variety of methods.[76]

University cooperative education programs or internships are excellent methods of recruiting that provide companies with the opportunity to assess the ability of new professionals and get an inside track on hiring the best ones. Young professionals can be very impressed by a properly structured internship experience and may strongly desire to return to the same company full time after graduation. Kraft General Foods hires 300 interns each year and finds that the internship program provides a competitive edge in attracting top graduates.[77] A side benefit of cooperative and internship programs is that they keep the company well publicized on campuses at no additional cost.[78]

Recruiting Older Workers Older workers are often mentioned as a possible solution to labor shortages. Individuals are retiring at younger ages but are remaining in the work force in some fashion for years after their formal retirement.[79] Some older workers want full-time employment; others seek part-time work to keep them busy, renew social contacts, or supplement income; and still others are looking for opportunities to develop new skills and experience personal growth. Some individuals stay with their preretirement employer under different terms, while others seek different employers or different types of work. Employers say they value older workers because of their skills, scheduling flexibility, low absenteeism, high motivation and loyalty, and ability to mentor younger workers.

Older workers may not be reached by traditional recruitment advertising because they tend to assume that employers are not interested in them. Thus recruitment messages should specifically mention the value placed on experience and maturity, the chance to build a second or third career, the opportunity for flexible scheduling, and the opportunity to work while keeping one's Social Security benefits. These messages can be delivered through the senior employment networks in operation in many areas; through clubs, organizations, and publications for seniors; and also through more general advertising outlets.[80] One expert suggests holding "unretirement" parties or "second-career fairs" as well as including pictures of older workers on recruiting literature.[81]

Recruiting Disabled Workers The 43 million Americans with some form of disability comprise another large but often neglected source of workers. Some of these have become disabled in adulthood and have valuable prior work experience. If a disability does not interfere with a person's ability to perform the essential function of the job (either with or without accommodation), the employer may not discriminate against the person. In fact, people with disabilities often make excellent employees, displaying a high level of motivation and commitment and possessing skills commensurate with those of the nondisabled population. McDonald's hired more than 9,000 people with physical or mental disabilities as part of a special recruiting and development program.

As with older workers, recruiting the disabled is a matter of getting information about jobs to them and making them feel welcome as applicants. This may mean supplementing standard methods with contacts, advertising, and visits to organizations, networks, rehabilitation facilities, and training schools for various disabilities, as well as making sure that recruiting literature portrays acceptance of workers with disabilities. When assessing candidates with disabilities, it is critical to test them only on "essential functions" of the job and to provide necessary accommodation during assessment so that applicants can display their capabilities fully.[82]

Crestar Bank of Richmond, Virginia (now SunTrust Bank Mid-Atlantic), received an award for its efforts to hire employees with disabilities for its call centers in Richmond and Norfolk. The bank worked extensively with the Virginia Department of Rehabilitative Services and other public agencies to identify candidates and assess the accommodations needed to allow them to perform the job. The vast majority of accommodations (such as changing the height of a desk to suit a wheelchair) cost less than $1,000. In cases where the cost was higher (for example, to provide special software for a blind employee), the public agency partner was able to assist.[83]

Recruiting Disadvantaged Workers One largely underutilized source of workers is people in inner cities who may lack some job skills and also lack convenient employment opportunities because many jobs have migrated to suburban areas. With training and attention to other needs such as transportation, these individuals can make fine employees. For instance, when Pizza Hut in New Jersey couldn't find enough local people to staff its suburban stores, it recruited in nearby cities where youth unemployment was high and then organized transportation from the city to the suburban stores.[84]

Urban youth, the homeless, and individuals recently released from prison have a very high unemployment rate. These employees may also need considerable training and support, with respect to both on-the-job behavior (why it is necessary to report to work on time, why and how to be polite to customers, how to dress for work) and off-the-job living arrangements (rent money during the transition to employment, transportation to work, etc.). Firms that have successfully hired from these labor pools recommend partnering with a nonprofit social service agency that can provide the extra training, support, and counseling that may be needed.[85] For instance, United Parcel Service installations in northern New Jersey successfully hired 1,500 employees through the Main Street Counseling Center, a community-based organization in Essex, New Jersey.[86] In some cases, employers are eligible for tax credits or subsidies for a portion of initial wages and training costs when hiring from specified groups.

Affirmative Action Recruiting Organizations with government contracts of more than $100,000 must have a written affirmative action plan (AAP). This document includes goals for increasing the number of women and minorities in job classes in which they are currently underutilized by the organization. Thus many organizations are attempting to increase their hiring of women for upper level or nontraditional jobs and their hiring of minorities for a wide range of jobs.

To hire minorities, firms must first find and attract applicants. Advertising is one way to do this. Firms should design ads carefully so that they do not convey stereotypes or preferences for male or nonminority applicants; the ads should also carry a line about the employer's commitment to equal employment opportunity. When seeking candidates for jobs not usually performed by one sex, companies should run ads that are sexually neutral or, from time to time, ads that are specially worded for affirmative action.[87] The Maryland State Police found that using a picture of a black officer on a recruiting billboard produced more minority applicants in two months than all other methods combined had produced during the preceding two years.[88] A recent study found that it was not sufficient just to show black employees in an ad, but rather to depict them in supervisory or managerial roles.[89]

In addition to advertising content, location is very important. Firms should place ads in minority and foreign-language newspapers, as well as in major dailies in cities with large minority populations. Firms also should consider advertising in military publications because the armed forces are disproportionately nonwhite and individuals finishing a tour of duty often make excellent employees. Other effective locations for ads are on minority or foreign-language radio stations, as well as in newsletters of professional organizations (e.g., the Association of Black Psychologists or the Society of Women Engineers) that reach a desired audience.

Other affirmative action recruiting methods include recruiting on predominantly minority or female junior college and college campuses, using the public job service office, placing banner ads on Web sites that cater to minority interests, and using private employment agencies that specialize in minority placement.[90]

Once candidates are attracted to apply, it is important to convey the feeling that the company is seriously committed to valuing diversity. Recruiting teams should include minority-group members, and interviewers should be trained to communicate effectively with all kinds of people and focus on job-relevant abilities rather than on race- or gender-related attributes.

Recruiting Passive Job Seekers Potential job candidates can be categorized by their level of activity in seeking a new job, according to a recent survey of 3,000 professionals and executives. Some are actively seeking employment, either because they are currently unemployed (2 percent) or employed but looking for a change (9 percent). These candidates will proactively read job ads in newspapers and on the Web, use informal contacts to obtain job leads, post their résumés on job boards, and readily apply for jobs. Most traditional recruiting activities are aimed at this group of active candidates. Other people (53 percent) are not looking to make a job move—they are happy where they are or for some other reason not at all interested in pursuing employment alternatives. There is little point in targeting recruiting efforts at this group. However, there is increasing interest in recruiting from among what have been called **passive job seekers.**[91] These individuals are not actively looking but would change jobs within the next six months if the right opportunity came along. They will not post their résumés on job boards, list with an employment agency, or regularly read employment ads, yet they are often highly desirable as employees. Methods that attract this group most effectively are probably employee referral, networking, general PR releases about the company, banner ads for the company's recruitment Web site at other Web sites likely to be visited by individuals in the desired profession, and headhunters. Some companies have developed skills in locating potential passive candidates on the Web by using meta–search engines to locate résumés on individuals' homepages, lurking in newsgroups and e-forums to see who sounds clever, finding posted professional association membership rosters, and accessing electronic in-house directories of competitors.[92]

THE APPLICANT'S POINT OF VIEW

This section discusses the methods candidates use to search for jobs, the ways applicants evaluate job offers and make decisions about accepting jobs, and a technique that helps applicants make better decisions and produces more suitable employees for organizations.

Job Search

Research on the methods job seekers use to find work indicates that the majority of jobs are obtained through informal sources. One survey determined that 60 to 90 percent of blue-collar employees found their jobs informally, as did 60 to 84 percent of managers, professionals, and technicians. Contacting employers directly (in person, by phone, or by letter) and seeking help from friends and relatives seem to be the most effective methods of job search for many types of candidates.[93]

Private employment agencies are also effective in finding jobs.[94] Generally, using multiple search methods, using them frequently, beginning to search for work as early as possible, making many contacts, and not interrupting one's search for a vacation or other reason all help to reduce the duration of unemployment.[95] Being financially insecure or having a family to support are also correlated with speed of job finding, probably because individuals in such situations are more likely to take the first offer they receive.[96] In addition to just finding a job, candidates should be mindful of finding a job and an organization that fit their skills, abilities, preferences, and values, as this increases the likelihood of later satisfaction with both the job and organization.[97]

Job Choice

How do people decide which of several job offers to accept? There has been a fair amount of theorizing on this topic over the years. Early work in this field assumed that job offers were simultaneous and candidates simply picked the best job. In real life, however, candidates seldom have more than one or two offers at the same time. Thus their decision process is more complicated; it is sequential rather than simultaneous. As a result, it seems likely that job seekers "satisfice," or take the first offer that is at least minimally acceptable on all important dimensions, rather than optimize, or engage in a very long and costly search to find the best possible job.[98]

Which factors do job seekers look at when evaluating a job offer? The research literature offers three views:

1. Individuals make rational choices based on objective factors such as pay, location, and opportunity for advancement.
2. People form gut-level preferences for one organization over another based on subjective factors that they may not even be aware of.
3. When job seekers do not have enough information to differentiate on the basis of either objective or subjective factors about the company or job, they tend to be influenced by certain recruiting factors, such as the interviewer's skill or politeness.[99]

Objective Factors Approach

According to the **objective factors approach,** candidates evaluate job offers largely on their merits. If a firm wishes to take a marketing orientation toward recruiting, it is necessary to find out which aspects of jobs are desirable to candidates and then provide and publicize those aspects. Table 6.6 shows how 1,000 U.S. employees ranked the importance of ten job factors. Note that pay was ranked only fifth. Other studies also have found that pay comes in at about fifth when individuals rank their own preferences but is almost always ranked first in importance to "other people" or to "subordinates." Researchers agree that pay is probably quite important to most people but that it may be socially undesirable to admit this publicly.[100]

In the study cited in Table 6.6, male and female employees had very similar preferences. However, there were pronounced differences in the ranks given to various job characteristics by employees of different age groups and income levels. Employees under age thirty ranked pay at the top of their list. Those aged thirty-one to forty ranked job security first, those aged forty-one to fifty felt that

TABLE 6.6

Average Rank of Importance of Ten Job Characteristics to American Employees

Job Characteristic	All Employees	Under Age 30	Ages 31–40	Ages 41–50	Age Over 50	Earnings <$25,000	Earnings $40,000–$50,000
Interesting work	1	4	2	3	1	5	1
Full appreciation of work done—others show appreciation of my work	2	5	3	2	2	4	3
A feeling of being "in on things," being well informed and involved	3	6	4	1	3	6	2
High job security	4	2	1	4	7	2	4
Good wages	5	1	5	5	8	1	6
Promotion and growth in my skills within the organization	6	3	6	8	9	3	5
Good working conditions	7	7	7	7	4	8	7
Personal loyalty to employees from superiors and the organization	8	9	9	6	5	7	8
Tactful discipline from superiors	9	8	10	9	10	10	9
Sympathetic help with personal problems from superiors	10	10	8	10	6	9	10

Source: Data compiled from K. Kovach, "Employee Motivation: Addressing a Crucial Factor in Your Organization's Performance," 1994. Reprinted by permission of Dr. Kenneth A. Kovach, George Mason University, Fairfax, Virginia.

"being in on things" was most important, and those over age fifty most preferred interesting work. Employees earning less than $25,000 per year placed good wages and job security at the top of their list, whereas those earning $40,000 to $50,000 put interesting work and being in on things in the top two positions. A 1999 survey of graduating college students asked which of four items respondents valued most in making a career decision. The winner by a large margin, selected by 42 percent of respondents, was balancing work and personal life. This was followed by money (26 percent), advancement potential (23 percent), and location (9 percent).[101] A 2001 survey of employees between ages twenty and thirty-nine found that more than 80 percent of both male and female respondents put time with the family at the top of their work–life priority list.[102]

Research generally supports objective job factors as the primary determinants of applicants' final job choice decisions.[103] The recruiting implications of the objective job factors approach are straightforward. Organizations and recruiters need to find out which job factors are important to most candidates and then attempt to make these factors available. The most important and influential factors should receive the most emphasis in recruiting literature and in other communications with candidates. In other words, recruiters need to apply market research techniques to the task of selling the organization's merits to job candidates and also to improving the "product" they are trying to sell.[104]

Subjective Factors Approach The **subjective factors approach** says that applicants also evaluate the "perceived ability of a firm to provide satisfaction for [their] deep-seated and often unrecognized emotional needs."[105] There is some support for the idea that individuals are attracted to organizations whose images or climates match their personality and values.[106] For instance, security-minded individuals might gravitate toward paternalistic organizations. From a recruiting standpoint, this approach suggests that applicants must have enough contact with the organization to assess whether or not the subjective aspects of the organization fit their own needs. Recruiting literature also might discuss the organization's culture and prevailing values to help applicants assess the fit with their own preferences.

Recent research verifies that graduates are more likely to apply for an interview with firms that have a good image or reputation.[107] Among the determinants of image are previous contact with the firm, use of the firm's product, studying the organization in class, and amount of useful information in the recruiting literature.[108] This research confirms our earlier recommendation that firms should try to be highly visible on campus in a variety of ways to support their campus recruiting efforts.

Recruiting Factors Approach The **recruiting factors approach** holds that candidates may not have enough knowledge of either organizations or jobs to make a decision between relatively similar job offers. This lack of discriminating information causes job seekers, particularly inexperienced ones, to be influenced by recruiting factors such as the interest and concern the recruiter shows or the smoothness with which the recruiter handles paperwork. These recruiter behaviors are taken as indicators of the likely characteristics of the rest of the organization.[109]

A great deal of research verifies that recruiting factors do have some impact on job choice decisions. For instance, students are more impressed when the recruiter has the title Director of Recruiting than when the same person uses no title. Students are unfavorably impressed by interviewers who are lacking in verbal fluency (who pause, repeat themselves, or stumble when asking questions).[110] Other studies have found that interviewers who are pleasant, conduct interviews in an organized fashion, are knowledgeable about the job, have read the applicant's résumé before the interview, and show interest in the candidate make a better impression and increase the probability of job offer acceptance.[111] Interviewers who present a balanced (positive and negative) picture of the job are perceived as being more credible and trustworthy than those who present only positive information.[112] Long time lags between selection steps (e.g., a wait of two months after a screening interview before the applicant is invited on a plant trip), poorly organized site visits, and stress interviews tend to sour applicants on a company.[113] Finally, a recruiter who stays in touch with a candidate after an offer is extended helps increase job offer acceptances and increase the rate at which candidates who have accepted actually show up to begin work.[114]

The recruiting factors approach to job choice clearly points to the importance of a highly professional recruiting function. Interviewers need to be trained or selected for both style and substance. More specifically, it has been suggested that effective recruiters "must possess an image and appearance that reflects favorably on the organization: an outgoing nature; flexibility, willingness to take necessary risks, ability to think on one's feet, skill in setting priorities; self-motivation, and salesmanship," as well as communication, interpersonal abilities, and familiarity with the organization.[115] In addition to these personal traits and skills, which aid in making a good impression, recruiters must be sure that contacts with candidates are timely and informative and that site visits are well choreographed. Computerized hiring management systems can also assist by providing candidates with regular e-mailed updates on their progress and the company's continuing interest in them.

The three views of the applicant decision process are beginning to be integrated, as shown in Figure 6.6. It appears that recruiting factors have their greatest impact on applicant reactions early in the recruiting process, at the initial inquiry and first interview stage. Good treatment here means that candidates are more likely to decide to pursue their application with the organization. Also, a competent recruiter can influence candidate perceptions of the objective factors in the job by providing greater amounts of relevant information. Subjective factors are not always accurately perceived by applicants, but these factors and the candidate's perceptions of them become much more important as candidates learn more and move closer to their final decision about which job to accept.[116] Although recruiting factors may not always directly affect final job choice decisions, a professional approach to recruiting is necessary to attract and sustain the interest of desirable job candidates.

Realistic Job Preview

Once a new employee has been recruited and selected, he or she must adjust to the new job and organization. There may be problems at this step, as evidenced by the high rate of turnover among new hires in their first few months. One reason for the turnover may be that the job did not match the newcomer's expectations or desires.[117] The recruitment process may be partly responsible for this mismatch,

FIGURE 6.6
Factors Affecting Job Choice

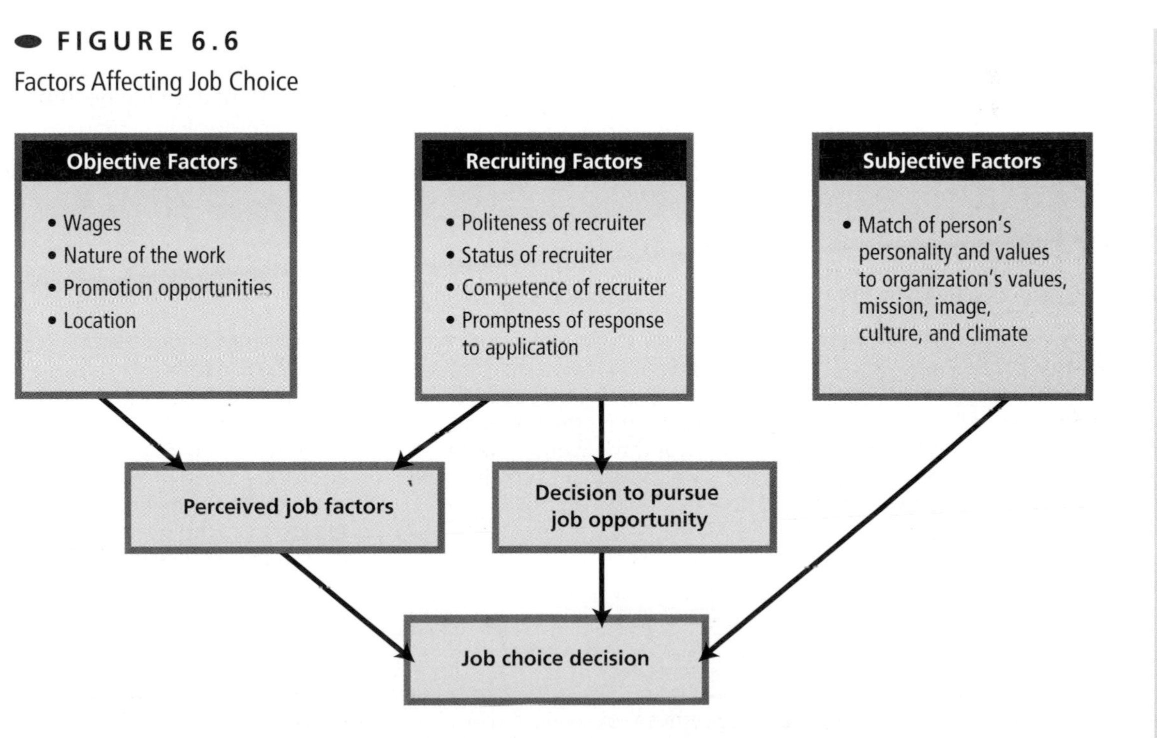

because recruiters tend to present jobs in very favorable terms to increase candidates' offer acceptance rate.

One way to reduce these problems is to use a **realistic job preview (RJP),** a down-to-earth presentation of both the favorable and unfavorable aspects of the job. Ideally, each stage of recruiting is honest and realistic. An RJP may take the form of a booklet or film about the job, realistic information delivered by an interviewer, or a work-sample test that exposes the candidate to actual job conditions and activities. Table 6.7 contrasts the contents of an RJP recruiting film with the contents of an unrealistically positive film that was shown to telephone operator applicants.

Many studies have compared the attitudes and behaviors of realistically recruited employees with those of unrealistically recruited persons. Overall, these studies show that RJPs sometimes reduce turnover, lower recruits' expectations about the job, slightly reduce the job offer acceptance rate, and slightly increase job satisfaction and commitment to the organization among new hires.[118] Although the beneficial effects of RJPs are not always pronounced, the cost of forestalling just a few early turnovers may justify the use of the technique. Several reasons for the effects of RJPs have been suggested and have received varying degrees of support in the literature:[119]

1. *Self-selection:* If the RJP helps the candidate realize that the job will not be personally satisfying, the candidate may choose to drop out of the selection process or decline an offer if one has been received. Without this realistic information, the candidate might have accepted the offer and could have become an early turnover statistic.
2. *Commitment to the decision:* When the RJP is presented before the candidate accepts or rejects the job offer, the candidate feels that he or she has made an informed decision about the job. Having accepted a job known to include difficult moments or distasteful duties, a newcomer feels less justified in reversing the decision and quitting when an unpleasant event actually occurs.
3. *Lowered expectations:* The aim of an RJP is to lower, or make more realistic, the expectations the newcomer holds about the job. One theory of job satisfac-

TABLE 6.7

A Comparison of a Realistic Job Preview Film and a Traditional Recruiting Film

Material in Both Films	Material in Traditional Film	Material in RJP Film
Customers can be quite unfriendly at times; work is fast-paced; helping customers can be satisfying; dealing with others is a large part of the job. Action shots of operators handling an emergency call, a "wise-guy" call, a credit card call, an overseas call, a "nasty" customer, and a directory-assistance request.	Everyone seems happy at work; the work is exciting, important, and challenging.	The job is routine, lacks variety, and may become boring. Supervision is close and there is little freedom and limited opportunity to make friends with coworkers. Employees are criticized for poor performance but seldom praised for good performance. The job is challenging at first, but once it is learned, it is easy.

Source: Reprinted from *Personnel,* July–August 1975.

tion states that dissatisfaction is a function of the discrepancy between what one expects on a job and what one actually gets. Lowering expectations reduces the gap between expectations and reality; consequently, dissatisfaction decreases. Since dissatisfaction is one cause of turnover, this mechanism can explain both attitudinal and behavioral differences between RJP and no-RJP groups.

4. *Coping:* Research has shown that unpleasant events are less stressful and dealt with more effectively if they are expected than if they are surprises. It is possible that the RJP operates by improving the ability of new hires to cope with negative aspects of the job. The RJP may stimulate newcomers to mentally rehearse their reactions to anticipated job problems and so increase their ability to deal with problems when they occur.

RJPs are most useful when recruiters present them early in the recruiting process (so that the self-selection and commitment processes can occur). RJPs are particularly effective for jobs in which there tends to be early high turnover and for complex jobs in which applicants are unlikely to have an accurate picture of the job or occupational field prior to applying.[120] RJPs make the most sense when there are plenty of applicants for the available openings; if some decide to decline offers, the jobs can still be filled. In addition, RJPs are most effective in reducing turnover when unemployment is low. In this situation, candidates will be most likely to turn down a job offer that does not suit them because other jobs are readily available.[121] Finally, RJPs should include both positive and negative information. Overly negative presentations may have a disproportionate effect in driving away well-qualified candidates.[122]

EVALUATION AND BENCHMARKING RECRUITMENT

A firm should evaluate its recruitment process along with all its other human resource management activities. Collecting appropriate evaluation measures on past recruiting efforts can help an organization predict the time and budget needed to fill future openings, identify the recruiting methods that yield the greatest number or the best quality of candidates, and evaluate the job performance of individual recruiters. Benchmarking against similar firms can also be informative. The granddaddy of all recruiting evaluation measures is cost per hire, though speed of filling vacancies is also an important measure. One recent study suggests that the size of the applicant pool initially attracted is also a key metric. Larger pools tend to contain more qualified individuals. Without a sufficiently large and qualified initial pool, even firms that effectively retain applicants through the selection process and motivate candidates to accept offers will be left with poorer quality outcomes.[123]

Nationwide Insurance, a large insurance and financial services firm, recently benchmarked its recruiting methods and subsequently made a number of improvements to the process. Its time to hire averaged forty-five days, and a survey showed that hiring managers were not particularly satisfied with the service they were receiving. Fifteen to twenty thousand applications were received per month. With this volume, there were delays in processing, some candidates fell through the cracks, and most did not receive a timely acknowledgment of their application. Hiring managers were receiving lists of fifteen candidates per position, placing too much of a burden of assessment and rejection on them. Improvements to the recruitment system included online résumé submission with instant acknowledgment and another e-mail thanking the candidate for his or her interest within twenty-four hours. Those who haven't been invited for an interview for their job of choice receive a later e-mail asking whether they are still interested in Nationwide and would like to remain in the candidate pool for future jobs. Recruiters are doing more prescreening, and now hiring managers are sent only the top three candidates. At some job fairs, Nationwide is almost hiring on the spot. Candidates can talk to a prescreener, then have a complete interview, then talk to the head of the hiring unit in a single day. If they pass these hurdles, they are told that Nationwide is very interested in hiring them. The required drug tests and background checks are undertaken within the next forty-eight hours, and a final offer is made within just a few days. The time to hire has come down substantially, and hiring managers report much greater satisfaction with recruiting services since these changes were instituted.[124]

Measures Used to Evaluate Recruiting Sources

When a number of sources or methods of recruiting have been used, it makes sense for the HR manager to evaluate each to see whether some are consistently superior to others. Inefficient sources can be dropped from future recruiting efforts. Some of the criteria that are used to evaluate sources and methods are total cost, cost per hire, number of applicants generated, yield ratios, and eventual job tenure and performance of hires. As a rule, gate hires and employee referrals tend to be quick and low in cost. Advertising and campus recruiting take the longest and cost more. Recruiting through agencies is intermediate in terms of the time it takes to fill positions, but it is often the most costly method.[125] Internet recruitment can be relatively fast, and through increased use of the company's own site rather than job boards, costs can be quite reasonable.

Differences in the Quality of Recruiting Sources

Research on the quality of different recruiting sources offers some interesting viewpoints. Stephen Mangum asserts that the best jobs are filled internally or through informal recruiting methods, such as word of mouth, and that the best candidates also find new jobs informally, through a network of contacts who are aware of their abilities. He suggests that only the least desirable jobs and least employable people are left to be matched through formal methods, such as newspaper ads, employment agencies, and Internet job boards.[126] Although this argument may be overstated, a body of research supports the idea that informal sources do produce the best candidates. A series of studies of employee tenure indicate that candidates who are referred by a current employee, who are rehired, or who turn in an unsolicited application stay in their new jobs significantly longer than those hired through agencies or newspaper ads.[127] The research on the job performance of hires from different sources is less extensive and less conclusive than that on turnover, but some evidence for similar differences does exist.[128]

Two rationales for differences in the applicant quality of recruiting sources have been advanced. One, based on RJP research, suggests that informal sources, such as rehires and employee referrals, yield candidates who have been told about both the good and bad aspects of the job and thus have a lower turnover rate. The second explanation is that sources may simply tap into different kinds of people in terms of ability level, motivation, or experience. Anyone can read a newspaper or surf the Net, but perhaps it takes a candidate with a bit more initiative to research a company enough to make an unsolicited application or to find out about an opening from contacts. In addition, more experienced employees may be more likely to have and use a network of informal sources, whereas new labor force entrants may tend to use newspapers and agencies to find positions; we know that younger people also have higher turnover rates.[129] There is some support in the research literature for all these propositions.[130]

Ideally, each firm should conduct its own analysis of source quality for each type of job. Recruiting sources that are of low quality can be used less intensively or eliminated altogether in future recruiting. In one study of recruiting sources for bank tellers, the researcher estimated that by discontinuing use of the three worst sources, the bank could save $180,000 over four years in reduced turnover, recruiting, and training costs.[131]

Summary of Key Points

Individuals seeking jobs and organizations seeking good employees may have conflicting objectives during the recruiting process. These may lead each side to emphasize the positive and conceal the negative about itself.

Organizational recruiting plans should be guided by good human resource planning and keyed to the strategy and values of the organization. A company's recruiting philosophy and goals will influence the approach it takes to recruiting. In some cases, recruiting may not be necessary if a company explores creative ways of dealing with labor shortages, such as outsourcing, temporaries, or employee leasing.

One of the first decisions a company must make in filling a vacancy is whether to seek a current employee through internal recruiting or seek a new hire from the external labor market. Internal and external recruiting have their own advantages and disadvantages. A firm that chooses internal recruiting has several methods available, including the job posting-and-bidding (self-nomination) process, nomination by superiors, and searches of the human resource information system.

Recruiting should be planned carefully so that the correct scope and timing of activities can be undertaken. Companies also need a means of tracking applicants, searching résumés, and producing applicant flow statistics. These activities can be accomplished manually or by computerized systems of varying levels of sophistication.

If a firm chooses external recruiting, it must plan carefully and may consider a wide variety of methods. Informal methods, such as gate hires and employee referrals, are inexpensive and often produce very good candidates. Formal methods include recruitment advertising (either in print or on the Internet), using employment agencies, and campus recruiting. Advertising makes vacancies known to a large number of potential applicants. Properly written ads can produce qualified applicants, help a firm meet its affirmative action goals, and enhance a company's public image. Employment agencies and executive search firms may be used to locate and prescreen applicants. Using private agencies and search firms is costly but may bring a company results significantly faster than if the company did its own recruiting. Recruiting through the firm's own career Web site is rapidly increasing in popularity and effectiveness. Campus recruiting is used by many organizations to hire entry-level professional and technical employees. A carefully planned university relations program can make campus recruiting very effective. Special recruitment campaigns targeting, for example, older people or the disadvantaged also have proven effective in attracting employees in tight labor markets.

From the job seeker's point of view, organizations and jobs may be evaluated on the basis of objective factors about a job, subjective factors such as an organization's image or culture, or recruiting factors such as recruiter behavior and informativeness. Ideally, job seekers should be given realistic job previews that help them to select jobs they will like and to reduce turnover and dissatisfaction due to unmet expectations.

After a company completes a recruiting effort, it should evaluate the outcomes, its recruiters, and the sources and methods used. In this way, the firm can improve the quality, success, and cost-effectiveness of future recruiting efforts.

The Manager's Vocabulary

blind ad
campus recruiting
countercyclical hiring
employee leasing
employee referral
executive search firms
exempt job
external recruiting
flextime
formal recruiting methods
gate hires
headhunters
hiring management systems
informal recruiting methods
internal recruiting
Internet recruiting
job boards
job posting and bidding
job sharing
marketing orientation to recruiting
nonexempt job
objective factors approach
passive job seekers
private employment agencies
public job service agencies
qualified response
realistic job preview (RJP)
recruiting factors approach
résumé-tracking software
ripple effect
subjective factors approach
telecommuting
teleworking
temporaries
word-of-mouth advertising
yield ratio

Questions for Discussion

1. Explain how the organization's and candidate's objectives in the recruiting process might conflict. How might these conflicts affect the eventual success of the recruiting and job search process?
2. What factors might go into a company's recruiting philosophy? How might the recruiting philosophies of a major international accounting firm and a small family-owned convenience store differ?
3. What are the pros and cons of using temporary or leased employees rather than hiring permanent employees?
4. Suppose a regional sales manager who needs to hire four salespeople delegates recruiting and initial screening to the regional HR office. What types of information must be exchanged between the sales manager and the recruiter to maximize the likelihood of a successful recruiting effort?
5. How are yield ratios used in recruitment planning?
6. How does internal recruiting for a nonexempt position typically differ from internal recruiting for an exempt position?
7. Think of a job that seems hard to fill in your local labor market. Using a wide variety of methods, design a recruitment campaign to attract candidates to this job.
8. Describe the ways in which companies and applicants can use the Internet for recruitment and job search. What are the qualities of an effective company career Web site?
9. Describe the services provided by various types of employment agencies and search firms. Why might a company use these organizations rather than doing its own recruiting?
10. If an organization planned to recruit at your university on a regular basis, what sorts of activities might it pursue to maximize recruiting success? Are some companies particularly visi-

ble and effective in recruiting on your campus? How did they get that way?

11. Pick one nontraditional labor market and plan a campaign to reach members of this market in your area.
12. Describe three views of how candidates evaluate organizations when choosing among job offers. What are the recruiting implications of each view?
13. Based on the data in Table 6.6, write a recruiting ad for a job paying $75,000 per year and requiring twelve to fifteen years of postuniversity experience (probably meaning that many candidates would be in their mid-thirties). Now rewrite the ad supposing that the same job paid $30,000 and was likely to be filled by someone just graduating from a junior college. How will you modify the contents of the ads to appeal to the likely job characteristic preferences of these different groups of candidates?
14. What is a realistic job preview? Describe the effects it has and the four possible explanations for these effects. Have you ever had a realistic job preview? What effect did it have on your decision to accept the job? What effect did it have on your decision to stick with the job if you accepted it?
15. How and why should recruiting methods and sources be evaluated?
16. What are some of the ethical issues that can arise in recruiting? Have you observed what you consider to be either bad manners or bad ethics on the part of companies seeking employees? What effect did this have on you?

Case 6.1
Inova Health System

Inova Health System is a Falls Church, Virginia, provider of health care. Its 10,000 employees provide services in three hospitals, seven outpatient centers, two long-term care facilities, and also provide home nursing visits. Historically, each of these units has managed its own recruiting. As health care budgets tightened, HR administrators at Inova wondered whether decentralized recruiting was still appropriate. Some of the problems encountered with each unit doing its own recruitment advertising and screening were the following:

- Duplication of advertising expenses—$500,000 in the past year
- Units competing with one another to recruit from the same labor market
- Candidates interested in jobs common to several facilities (such as nursing) needing to apply and interview separately at each facility
- Lack of internal mobility for current employees across units due to lack of knowledge of openings
- A less-than-consistent corporate identity projected to candidates and the community by unit-specific recruitment advertising
- Inability to measure recruiting effectiveness or keep accurate EEO/AA statistics because of varying record-keeping systems across units
- Inefficiencies because each unit is too small to support sophisticated recruitment technologies such as a twenty-four-hour jobs hotline or a computerized résumé scanning-and-tracking system

You are part of a task force of experienced recruiters drawn from Inova's larger units. The task force is charged with recommending what, if anything, should be done to improve the recruitment function at Inova.

1. How would you begin to study this problem?
2. Might you use benchmarking in any way? How?
3. Would you choose to centralize the recruitment function? Why or why not?
4. If you do recommend a centralized recruiting office, what services would it provide?
5. If you centralize recruiting, what benefits would you anticipate for (a) the company and (b) the applicants?
6. What barriers might you encounter in implementing a centralized system?

Source: "HR at Inova Reengineers Recruitment Process" by Phyllis A. Savill, copyright June 1995. Used with permission of ACC Communications Inc. *Personnel Journal* (now known as *Workforce*), Costa Mesa, California.

Case 6.2
Recruiting at Health Source

Your organization, Health Source, Inc., owns four large drugstores in Houston, Texas, and will open two more stores in the next year. One of the new stores will be located in suburban Houston, and the other will represent your first venture into the Dallas market. Each store will require about twenty-five employees at the start, including five pharmacists, four cosmeticians, a manager, an assistant manager, and a number of clerks.

1. How would you go about locating and recruiting the fifty employees needed for the new stores? What are your options? How do the recruiting methods you considered compare with one another in terms of cost, and how effective do you think each will be? How long will the recruiting process take? Are there any possible legal or ethical ramifications to think about?
2. Would your recommendations for recruiting be the same or different if (1) Health Source plans no further expansion after these two new stores, or (2) if Health Source plans to pursue an aggressive expansion policy for several years?

Exercise 6.1
Developing Recruiting Plans

Design a recruiting campaign for several of the following situations. Include an explicit definition of the labor market you intend to reach; then select the method(s) you would use to reach this target audience. How would you attract qualified candidates to apply? Justify why your recruiting plan is appropriate and cost effective for the particular job you are trying to fill. Explain why your recruiting plans differ from one another.

1. Chili's restaurant chain would like to grow faster and has a target of growing by 10 to 12 percent per year. The main impediment to meeting this target is the difficulty of recruiting enough qualified restaurant managers.[132]
2. The Transportation Security Administration was charged by Congress to hire 55,000 highly reliable airport security staff within just ten months.[133] How would you suggest that such a mass hiring operation be successfully managed?
3. A U.S.-based manufacturer of agricultural chemicals needs to appoint a regional manager to spearhead its entry into the Southeast Asian market.
4. A seventy-outlet women's clothing store chain needs to fill two middle-management positions at its headquarters. The HR director realizes that all the current middle managers are white males.
5. The local 7-Eleven store needs two part-time clerks.

Exercise 6.2
Recruiting on the Internet

1. For the occupation and job of your choice, search the Net for employment opportunities. Which sites seem most useful for a job seeker in this occupational area? What advice would you give to a novice user who is seeking job opportunities via the Internet?
2. Suppose you would like to work for a specific major company. Search the Net for that company's careers site and any other sources of information about the company that would be useful to you as a job seeker. How many different locations did you find and use?

3. Suppose you are the director of recruiting for the company you chose in item 2. How would you strengthen your company's presence and recruiting effectiveness on the Internet?

Notes and References

1. Lloyd J. Taylor III, Brian J. Moersch, and Geralyn McClure Franklin, "Applying the Theory of Constraints to a Public Safety Hiring Process," *Public Personnel Management,* Vol. 32, Fall 2003, pp. 367–382.

2. Society for Human Resource Management, "2002 SHRM/EMA Staffing Metrics Study," 2002, http://www.shrm.org/hrresources/surveys_published/SHRM_EMA%202002%20Staffing%20Metrics%20Survey%20Cost-per-Hire.pdf.

3. Lyman W. Porter, Edward E. Lawler III, and J. Richard Hackman, *Behavior in Organizations* (New York: McGraw-Hill, 1975); Kevin D. Carlson and Mary L. Connerley, "The Staffing Cycles Framework: Viewing Staffing as a System of Decision Events," *Journal of Management,* Vol. 29, 2003, pp. 51–79.

4. Sara L. Rynes and Alison E. Barber, "Applicant Attraction Strategies: An Organizational Perspective," *Academy of Management Review,* April 1990, pp. 286–310.

5. The first two aspects are based on James A. Breaugh, *Recruitment: Science and Practice* (Boston: PWS-Kent, 1992).

6. R. Rooseveldt Thomas, "From Affirmative Action to Affirming Diversity," *Harvard Business Review,* March–April 1990, pp. 107–117.

7. Steven D. Maurer, Vince Howe, and Thomas W. Lee, "Organizational Recruiting as Marketing Management: An Interdisciplinary Study of Engineering Graduates," *Personnel Psychology,* Winter 1992, pp. 807–833; and Albert H. McCarthy, "Research Provides Advertising Focus," *Personnel Journal,* August 1989, pp. 82–87.

8. S. P. Talbott, "Boost Your Campus Image to Attract Top Grads," *Recruitment Staffing Sourcebook* (supplement to the March 1996 issue of *Personnel Journal*), pp. 6–8.

9. Dave R. Dahl and Patrick R. Pinto, "Job Posting: An Industry Survey," *Personnel Journal,* January 1977, pp. 40–42; and W. Chan, "External Recruitment versus Internal Promotion," *Journal of Labor Economics,* Vol. 14 (4), 1996, pp. 555–570.

10. "Tesco Extends 'Store Swap' Scheme Across UK," *Personnel Today,* June 24, 2003, p. 6.

11. Elmer H. Burack and Nicholas J. Mathys, *Human Resource Planning: A Pragmatic Approach to Manpower Staffing and Development* (Lake Forest, Ill.: Brace-Park Press, 1980); and D. Geoffrey John, "Staffing with Temporary Help," *Personnel Administrator,* January 1987, pp. 96–99.

12. J. Scott Lord, "Internal and External Recruitment," in *Human Resource Planning, Employment, and Practice,* ed. Wayne F. Cascio (Washington, D.C.: Bureau of National Affairs, 1989), pp. 73–102.

13. K. H. Chung, M. Labatkin, R. C. Rogers, and J. E. Owers, "Do Insiders Make Better CEOs Than Outsiders?" *Academy of Management Executive,* November 1987, pp. 325–331; and A. Gupta, "Contingency Perspectives on Strategic Leadership: Current Knowledge and Future Research Directions," in *The Executive Effect: Concepts and Methods for Studying Top Managers,* ed. D. C. Hambrick (Greenwich, Conn.: JAI Press, 1988).

14. William E. Bright, "How One Company Manages Its Human Resources," *Harvard Business Review,* January–February 1976, pp. 81–93.

15. Charles R. Greer and Timothy C. Ireland, "Organizational and Financial Correlates of a 'Contrarian' Human Resource Investment Strategy," *Academy of Management Journal,* December 1992, pp. 956–984.

16. C. Cunningham, "Reeling in IT Talent in the Public Sector," *InfoWorld,* May 15, 2000, pp. 78–79.

17. Rynes and Barber, "Applicant Attraction Strategies." See Margaret L. Williams and George F. Dreher, "Compensation System Attributes and Applicant Pool Characteristics," *Academy of Management Journal,* August 1992, pp. 571–595, for evidence that firms improve their pay and benefit systems when they have had trouble filling vacancies.

18. L. A. West Jr. and W. A. Bogumil Jr., "Foreign Knowledge Workers as a Strategic Staffing Option," *Academy of Management Executive,* November 2000, pp. 71–83.

19. R. Barner, "Talent Wars in the Executive Suite: Six Trends Shaping Recruitment," *The Futurist,* May–June 2000, pp. 35–41.

20. Gladys Fazio Garlitz, "Temporary Workers: A Changing Industry," *Personnel Administrator,* March 1983, pp. 47–48; and J. L. Simonetti, N. Nykudym, and L. M. Sell, "Temporary Employees: A Permanent Boom?" *Personnel,* August 1988, pp. 50–56.

21. V. Frazee, "The Try-Before-You-Buy Method of Hiring," *Recruitment Staffing Sourcebook* (supplement to the August 1996 issue of *Personnel Journal*), pp. 6–8.

22. Garth Mangum, Donald Mayall, and Kristin Nelson, "The Temporary Help Industry: A Response to the Dual Internal Labor Market," *Industrial and Labor Relations Review,* July 1985, pp. 599–611; and Max Messmer, "Right-Sizing Reshapes Staffing Strategies," *HR Magazine,* October 1991, pp. 60–62.

23. Stephenie Overman, "Hired to Take Charge Temporarily," *HR Magazine,* June 1993, pp. 52–53.

24. John Ross, "Effective Ways to Hire Contingent Personnel," *HR Magazine,* February 1991, pp. 52–54.

25. Martin M. Greller and David M. Nee, *From Baby Boom to Baby Bust: How Business Can Meet the Demographic Challenge* (Reading, Mass.: Addison-Wesley, 1989), chap. 4.

26. Sharon M. Tarrant, "Setting Up an Electronic Job-Posting System," *Training & Development,* January 1994, pp. 39–42.

27. Dahl and Pinto, "Job Posting."

28. Garry G. Wallrapp, "Job Posting for Non-Exempt Employees: A Sample Program," *Personnel Journal,* October 1981, pp. 796–798.

29. James T. Gunn, "An Open Job-Bidding System for Professionals and Managers: Fact or Fiction," *Human Resource Planning,* Vol. 2, 1979, pp. 187–195.

30. A. E. Barber, *Recruiting Employees: Individual and Organizational Perspectives* (Thousand Oaks, Calif.: Sage, 1998).

31. Robert Half, *Robert Half on Hiring* (New York: Crow, 1985).

32. Letty Kluttz, "2002 Staffing Metrics Survey, Time to Fill/Time to Start," Society for Human Resource Management, March 2003, http://www.shrm.org/hrresources/surveys_published/SHRM_EMA%202003%20Staffing%20Metrics%20-%20Time%20to%20Fill_Start.pdf.

33. Donn L. Dennis, "Evaluating Corporate Recruiting Efforts," *Personnel Administrator,* January 1985, pp. 21–26.

34. Roger H. Hawk, *The Recruitment Function* (New York: American Management Association, 1967).

35. Taylor, Moersch, and Franklin, "Applying the Theory of Constraints to a Public Safety Hiring Process"; see Robert L. Armacost and Rohne L. Jauernig, "Planning and Managing a Major Recruiting Project," *Public Personnel Management,* Summer 1991, pp. 115–126, for another example of recruitment planning.

36. See S. W. Gilliland, M. Groth, R. C. Baker IV, A. F. Dew, L. M. Polly, and J. C. Langdon, "Improving Applicants' Reactions to Rejection Letters: An Application of Fairness Theory," *Personnel Psychology,* 2001, pp. 669–703, for advice on how to obtain more positive responses to rejection letters.

37. M. Gibelman, "Managerial Manners—Notably Lacking in Personnel Recruiting," *Administration in Social Work,* Vol. 20, 1996, pp. 59–72.

38. This section draws on Christine White and Abbie W. Thorner, *Managing the Recruitment Process* (New York: Law and Business, 1982).

39. Scott Hays "Hiring on the Web," *Workforce,* Vol. 78 (8), August 1999, pp. 76–84.

40. W. H. Baker, K. DeTeinne, and K. L. Smart, "How *Fortune* 500 Companies Are Using Electronic Resume Management Systems," *Business Communication Quarterly,* September 1998, pp. 8–19.

41. S. P. Talbott, "Get the Most from Automated Résumé-Tracking Software," *Recruitment Staffing Sourcebook* (supplement to the March 1996 issue of *Personnel Journal*), pp. 18–20.

42. J. Meade, "Where Did They Go?" *HR Magazine,* September 2000, pp. 81–84.

43. K. Tyler, "Employees Can Help Recruit New Talent," *HR Magazine,* September 1996, pp. 57–60.

44. J. D. McCool, "Harnessing the Power of Employee Referrals," August 2, 2000. (Available at: www.wetfeet.com/employer/articles)

45. D. Terpstra, "The Search for Effective Methods," *HR Focus,* May 1996, pp. 16–17.

46. Van M. Evans, "Recruitment Advertising in the 80's," *Personnel Administrator,* December 1978, pp. 21–25, 30.

47. L. Shyles and J. E. Hocking, "The Army's 'Be All You Can Be' Campaign," *Armed Forces & Society,* Spring 1990, pp. 369–383.

48. Margaret Magnus, "Recruitment Ads That Work," *Personnel Journal,* August 1985, pp. 42–63; Martin Asdorian Jr., "Drowning in Résumés," *HR Magazine,* September 1992, pp. 59–62; and Karel De Witte, "Recruitment Advertising," in *Assessment and Selection in Organizations,* ed. Peter Herriot (Chichester, England: Wiley, 1989), pp. 205–217.

49. De Witte, "Recruitment Advertising."

50. Robert A. Martin, "Employment Advertising—Hard Sell, Soft Sell, or What?" *Personnel,* May–June 1971, pp. 33–40.

51. Michael Foster, *Recruiting on the Web: Smart Strategies for Finding the Perfect Candidate* (New York: McGraw-Hill Trade, 2002); "Research Demonstrates Success of Internet Recruiting," *HR Focus,* April 2003, p. 7.

52. D. Gere, E. K. Scarborough, and J. Collison, "2002 Recruiter Budget/Cost Survey." (Alexandria, Va.: Society for Human Resource Management, 2002).

53. Marlene Piturro, "The Power of e-cruiting" *Management Review,* Vol. 89 (1), January 2000, pp. 33–37.

54. S. L. Slavin and M. A. Pradt, *The Einstein Syndrome: Corporate Anti-Semitism in America Today* (Lanham, Md.: University Press of America, 1982).

55. Stephen Rubenfeld and Michael Crino, "Are Employment Agencies Jeopardizing Your Selection Process?" *Personnel,* September–October 1981, pp. 70–77.

56. P. Falcone, "Maximize Your Recruitment Resources," *HR Magazine,* February 1999, pp. 92–93.

57. S. P. Talbott, "Creative Staffing Drives Success," *Recruitment Staffing Sourcebook* (supplement to the March 1996 issue of *Personnel Journal*), pp. 12–13.

58. T. Chauran, "Get High Mileage from Your Advertising Dollar," *Recruitment Today,* February–March 1989, pp. 48–51.

59. C. Rush, "Executive Search: Recruiting a Recruiter," *Public Management,* July 1995, pp. 20–22.

60. William Dee, "Evaluating a Search Firm," *Personnel Administrator,* March 1983, pp. 41–43, 99–100.

61. Loretta D. Foxman and Walter L. Polsky, "Career Counselor," *Personnel Journal,* February 1985, pp. 21–22, and March 1985, pp. 14–16. See also John Wareham, "The Search," *Across the Board,* September 1979, pp. 28–31.

62. Florence Berger, "Executive Search: The Headhunter as Matchmaker," *Cornell Hotel and Restaurant Administration Quarterly,* May 1983, pp. 55–61.

63. John C. Perham, "How Recruiters Get the Lowdown," *Dun's Business Month,* May 1985, pp. 60–61.

64. Larry Reibstein, "Offers and Counteroffers: Attitudes Change in Executive Search Game," *Wall Street Journal,* May 5, 1986, p. 21. For more information about executive search firms, see Stephanie Jones, *The Headhunting Business* (London: Macmillan, 1989).

65. S. J. Wells, "Slow Times for Executive Recruiting," *HR Magazine,* April 2003, pp. 61–68.

66. J. Reingold, E. C. Baig, L. Armstrong, and W. Zellner, "Headhunting 2000," *Business Week,* May 17, 1999, p. 74.

67. This section draws on Stephen D. Bruce, *College Recruiting* (Stamford, Conn.: Bureau of Law and Business, 1983). See also B. Leonard, "The Sell Gets Tough on College Campuses," *HR Magazine,* June 1995, pp. 61–63; J. Phillips, *Recruiting, Training, and Retaining New Employees* (San Francisco: Jossey-Bass, 1987); M. E. Scott, "A Case for College Relations and Recruitment," National Association of Colleges and Employers, Bethlehem, Penn.

68. "National Association of Colleges and Employers (NACE) Year 2000 Employer Benchmark Survey," National Association of Colleges and Employers, Bethlehem, Penn.

69. A. C. Poe, "Signing Bonuses: A Sign of the Times," *HR Magazine,* September 1999, pp. 104–112.

70. Maury Hanigan, "Key Campus Strategies," *HR Magazine,* July 1991, pp. 42–44.

71. Philip Schofield, "The Difference a Graduate Recruitment Brochure Can Make," *Personnel Management,* January 1991, pp. 36–39.

72. C. J. Collins and C. K. Stevens, "The Relationship between Early Recruitment-Related Activities and the Application Decisions of New Labor-Market Entrants: A Brand Equity Approach to Recruitment," *Journal of Applied Psychology,* 2002, Vol. 87 (6), pp. 1121–1133.

73. Jobtrak.com survey, June 12, 2000. Available at: http://static.jobtrak.com/mediacenter/press_poll_061200,html.

74. A. C. Poe, "Face Value," *HR Magazine,* May 2000, pp. 60–68.

75. John W. Boudreau and Sara L. Rynes, "Giving It the Old College Try," *Personnel Administrator,* March 1987, pp. 78–83; and Sara L. Rynes and John W. Boudreau, "College Recruiting in Large Organizations: Practice, Evaluation, and Research Implications," *Personnel Psychology,* Vol. 39, 1986, pp. 729–757.

76. Lord, "Internal and External Recruitment."

77. Harriet Edleson, "Innovative Internships," *HR Magazine,* July 1991, pp. 39–41; and Talbott, "Boost Your Campus Image to Attract Top Grads."

78. Robert E. Hite, "How to Hire Using College Internship Programs," *Personnel Journal,* February 1986, pp. 110–112.

79. D. C. Feldman and S. Kim, "Bridge Employment During Retirement: A Field Study of Individual and Organizational Experiences with Post-Retirement Employment," *Human Resource Planning,* Vol. 23 (1), 2000, pp. 14–25.

80. This section draws on two publications by the American Association of Retired Persons: *How to Recruit Older Workers* (1993) and *The Older Workforce: Recruitment and Retention* (1993).

81. Catherine D. Fyock, "Finding the Gold in the Graying of America," *HR Magazine,* February 1994, pp. 74–76.

82. Mary Cook, *The AMA Handbook for Employee Recruitment and Retention* (New York: AMACOM, 1992), pp. 57–61; Susan J. Herman, *Hiring Right: A Practical Guide* (Thousand Oaks, Calif.: Sage, 1994); and V. Frazee, "Focusing Your Recruiting Efforts on Disabled Workers," *Recruitment Staffing Sourcebook* (supplement to the August 1996 issue of *Personnel Journal*), pp. 10–12.

83. S. Overman, "Winning Ways," *HR Magazine,* July 2000, pp. 87–96.

84. J. A. Tannenbaum, "Firms Try Busing to Ease Labor Shortage," *Wall Street Journal,* December 30, 1988, p. B2.

85. S. Overman, "Put Overlooked Labor Pools on Your Recruiting List," *HR Magazine,* February 1999, pp. 87–90.

86. Andrew S. Bargerstock and Gerald Swanson, "Four Ways to Build Cooperative Recruitment Alliances," *HR Magazine,* March 1991, pp. 49–51, 79.

87. Sandra L. Bem and Daryl J. Bem, "Does Sex-Biased Job Advertising Aid and Abet Sex Discrimination?" in *Contemporary Problems in Personnel,* ed. W. Clay Hamner and Frank L. Schmidt (Chicago: St. Clair Press, 1977), pp. 445–455.

88. The remainder of this section is based on Robert Calvert Jr., *Affirmative Action: A Comprehensive Recruitment Manual* (Garrett Park, Md.: Garrett Park Press, 1979).

89. D. R. Avery, "Reactions to Diversity in Recruitment Advertising—Are Differences Black and White?" *Journal of Applied Psychology,* 2003, Vol. 88, pp. 672–279.

90. M. N. Martinez, "Looking for Young Talent? Inroads Helps Diversify Efforts," *HR Magazine,* March 1996, pp. 73–76.

91. L. Sewell, "Passive Candidates: Who They Are and How to Find Them." (Available at: http:// www.wetfeet. com/employer/ articles/article. asp?aid=377)

92. S. Boehle, "Online Recruiting Gets Sneaky," *Training,* May 2000, pp. 66–74; Foster, *Recruiting on the Web: Smart Strategies for Finding the Perfect Candidate.*

93. Michael C. Keeley and Philip K. Robins, "Government Programs, Job Search Requirements, and the Duration of Unemployment," *Journal of Labor Economics,* July 1985, pp. 337–362; Bradley R. Schiller, "Job Search Media: Utilization and Effectiveness," *Quarterly Review of Economics and Business,* Winter 1975, pp. 55–63; and Samuel J. Yeager and Thomas Vocino, "Sources of Information Used by Professionals in Government to Find Jobs: Effectiveness and Impact," *Review of Public Personnel Administration,* Fall 1983, pp. 100–113; D. C. Feldman and B. S. Klass, "Internet Job Hunting: A Field Study of Applicant Experiences with On-line Recruiting," *Human Resource Management,* Summer 2002, pp. 175–192.

94. Steven M. Bortnick and Michelle Harrison Ports, "Job Search Methods and Results: Tracking the Unemployed, 1991," *Monthly Labor Review,* December 1992, pp. 29–35.

95. Lee D. Dyer, "Job Search Success of Middle-Aged Managers and Engineers," *Industrial and Labor Relations Review,* April 1973, pp. 969–979; and Graham L. Reid, "Job Search and the Effectiveness of Job Finding Methods," *Industrial and Labor Relations Review,* July 1972, pp. 479–495.

96. Dyer, "Job Search Success of Middle-Aged Managers and Engineers," pp. 479–495; see also R. Kanfer, C. R. Wanberg, and T. M. Kantrowitz, "Job Search and Employment: A Personality-Motivational Analysis and Meta-Analytic Review," *Journal of Applied Psychology,* 2002, Vol. 86 (5 0, pp. 837–855.

97. A. M. Saks and B. E. Ashforth, "Is Job Search Related to Employment Quality? It All Depends on the Fit," *Journal of Applied Psychology,* 2002, Vol. 86 (4), pp. 646–654.
98. Donald P. Schwab, "Recruiting and Organizational Participation," in *Personnel Management,* eds. Kendrith M. Rowland and Gerald R. Ferris (Boston: Allyn and Bacon, 1982), pp. 103–127; Donald P. Schwab, Sara L. Rynes, and Ramon J. Aldag, "Theories and Research on Job Search and Choice," in *Research in Personnel and Human Resources Management,* eds. Kendrith M. Rowland and Gerald R. Ferris (Greenwich, Conn.: JAI Press, 1987), pp. 129–166; and A. E. Barber, C. L. Daly, C. M. Giannantonio, and J. M. Phillips, "Job Search Activities: An Examination of Changes Over Time," *Personnel Psychology,* Vol. 47, 1994, pp. 739–766.
99. Orlando Behling, George Labovitz, and Marion Gainer, "College Recruiting: A Theoretical Base," *Personnel Journal,* January 1968, pp. 13–19.
100. Clifford E. Jurgenson, "Job Preferences (What Makes a Job Good or Bad?)," *Journal of Applied Psychology,* June 1978, pp. 267–276.
101. JobTrak.com Career Value Poll. (Available at: http://static.jobtrak.com/mediacenter/press_polls/poll_121499.html>)
102. Cite in N. R. Lockwood, "Work/Life Balance: Challenges and Solutions," *Society for Human Resource Management Research Quarterly,* June 2003, http://www.shrm.org/research/quarterly/0302worklifepdf.asp.
103. Sara L. Rynes, "Recruitment, Job Choice, and Post-Hire Consequences: A Call for New Research Directions," in *Handbook of Industrial and Organizational Psychology,* Vol. 2, 2nd ed., eds. M. D. Dunnette and L. M. Hough (Palo Alto, Calif.: Consulting Psychologists Press, 1991), pp. 399–444; S. Highouse and J. R. Hoffman, "Organizational Attraction and Job Choice," in *International Review of Industrial and Organizational Psychology,* Vol. 16, eds. C. L. Cooper and I. T. Robertson (New York: John Wiley & Sons, 2001), pp. 37–64.
104. Hanigan, "Key Campus Strategies."
105. Behling, Labovitz, and Gainer, "College Recruiting."
106. Victor R. Tom, "The Role of Personality and Organizational Images in the Recruiting Process," *Organizational Behavior and Human Performance,* September 1971, pp. 573–592; D. M. Cable and T. A. Judge, "Person–Organization Fit, Job Choice Decisions, and Organizational Entry," *Organizational Behavior and Human Decision Processes,* September 1996, pp. 294–311; A. M. Saks and B. E. Ashforth, "A Longitudinal Investigation of the Relationships between Job Information Sources, Applicant Perceptions of Fit, and Work Outcomes," *Personnel Psychology,* Summer 1997, pp. 395–426; T. A. Judge and D. M. Cable, "Applicant Personality, Organizational Culture, and Organizational Attraction," *Personnel Psychology,* Summer 1997, pp. 359–394; and J. D. Werbel and S. W. Gilliland, "Person–Environment Fit in the Selection Process," *Research in Personnel and Human Resources Management,* Vol. 17, 1999, pp. 209–243.
107. D. B. Turban and D. M. Cable, "Firm Reputation and Applicant Pool Characteristics," *Journal of Organizational Behavior,* Vol. 24, 2003, pp. 733–751.
108. Robert D. Gatewood, Mary A. Gowan, and Gary J. Lautenschlager, "Corporate Image, Recruitment Image, and Initial Job Choice Decisions," *Academy of Management Journal,* April 1993, pp. 414–427.
109. Sara L. Rynes, Robert D. Bretz Jr., and Barry Gerhart, "The Importance of Recruitment in Job Choice: A Different Way of Looking," *Personnel Psychology,* Autumn 1991, pp. 487–521; J. A. Breaugh and M. Starke, "Research on Employee Recruitment: So Many Studies, So Many Remaining Questions," *Journal of Management,* 2000, Vol. 26 (3), pp. 405–434.
110. Donald P. Rogers and Michael Z. Sincoff, "Favorable Impression Characteristics of the Recruitment Interviewer," *Personnel Psychology,* Autumn 1978, pp. 495–504.
111. Neal Schmitt and Brian W. Coyle, "Applicant Decisions in the Employment Interview," *Journal of Applied Psychology,* April 1976, pp. 184–192; Daniel B. Turban and Thomas W. Dougherty, "Influences of Campus Recruiting on Applicant Attraction to Firms," *Academy of Management Journal,* December 1992, pp. 739–765; and Steven D. Maurer, Vince Howe, and Thomas W. Lee, "Organizational Recruiting as Marketing Management: An Interdisciplinary Study of Engineering Graduates," *Personnel Psychology,* Winter 1992, pp. 807–833.
112. Cynthia D. Fisher, Daniel R. Ilgen, and Wayne D. Hoyer, "Source Credibility, Information Favorability, and Job Offer Acceptance," *Academy of Management Journal,* March 1979, pp. 94–103.
113. W. R. Boswell, M. V. Roehling, M. A. LePine, and L. M. Moynihan, "Individual Job-Choice Deci-

sions and the Impact of Job Attributes and Recruitment Practices: A Longitudinal Field Study," *Human Resource Management,* Spring 2003, pp. 23–37.
114. Thomas Bergmann and M. Susan Taylor, "College Recruitment: What Attracts Students to Organizations," *Personnel,* May–June 1984, pp. 34–46; and Sara L. Rynes, Herbert G. Heneman III, and Donald P. Schwab, "Individual Reactions to Organizational Recruiting: A Review," *Personnel Psychology,* Autumn 1980, pp. 529–542.
115. Lord, "Internal and External Recruitment," p. 82.
116. Michael M. Harris and Laurence S. Fink, "A Field Study of Applicant Reactions to Employment Opportunities: Does the Recruiter Make a Difference?" *Personnel Psychology,* Vol. 40, 1987, pp. 765–784; M. Susan Taylor and Thomas J. Bergmann, "Organizational Recruitment Activities and Applicants' Reactions at Different Stages of the Recruitment Process," *Personnel Psychology,* Vol. 40, 1987, pp. 261–286; and Gary N. Powell, "Applicant Reactions to the Initial Employment Interview: Exploring Theoretical and Methodological Issues," *Personnel Psychology,* Spring 1991, pp. 67–83.
117. Robert J. Vandenberg and Vida Scarpello, "The Matching Model: An Examination of the Processes Underlying Realistic Job Previews," *Journal of Applied Psychology,* February 1990, pp. 60–67; L. M. Shore and L. E. Tetrick, "The Psychological Contract: An Explanatory Framework in the Employment Relationship," in *Trends in Organizational Behavior,* Vol. 1, eds. C. L. Cooper and D. M. Rousseau (Chichester, England: Wiley, 1994), pp. 91–109.
118. Steven L. Premack and John P. Wanous, "A Meta-Analysis of Realistic Job Preview Experiments," *Journal of Applied Psychology,* November 1985, pp. 706–719; and J. M. Phillips, "Effects of Realistic Job Previews on Multiple Organizational Outcomes: A Meta-Analysis," *Academy of Management Journal,* Vol. 41, 1998. pp. 673–690.
119. James A. Breaugh, "RJPs: A Critical Appraisal and Future Research Directions," *Academy of Management Review,* October 1983, pp. 612–619.
120. Richard R. Reilly, Barbara Brown, Milton R. Blood, and Carol Z. Malatesta, "The Effects of Realistic Previews: A Study and Discussion of the Literature," *Personnel Psychology,* Winter 1981, pp. 823–834.
121. John P. Wanous, *Organizational Entry* (Reading, Mass.: Addison-Wesley, 1992), p. 60.
122. S. Highouse and J. R. Hoffman, "Organizational Attraction and Job Choice."
123. K. D. Carlson, M. L. Connerley, and R. L. Mecham III, "Recruitment Evaluation: The Case for Assessing the Quality of Applicants Attracted," *Personnel Psychology,* 2002, pp. 461–490.
124. Todd Raphael, "Nationwide Speeds Up Hiring, Increases Satisfaction," *Workforce,* May 23, 2001.
125. Ibid.
126. Stephen L. Mangum, "Recruitment and Job Search: The Recruitment Tactics of Employers," *Personnel Administrator,* June 1982, pp. 96–104.
127. James A. Breaugh, "Relationships Between Recruiting Sources and Employee Performance, Absenteeism, and Work Attitudes," *Academy of Management Journal,* March 1981, pp. 142–147; Martin J. Gannon, "Source of Referral and Employee Turnover," *Journal of Applied Psychology,* June 1971, pp. 226–228; Phillip J. Decker and Edwin Cornelius III, "A Note on Recruiting Sources and Job Survival Rates," *Journal of Applied Psychology,* August 1979, pp. 463–464; C. J. Simon and J. T. Warner, "Matchmaker, Matchmaker: The Effect of Old Boy Networks on Job Match Quality, Earnings, and Tenure," *Journal of Labor Economics,* Vol. 10, 1992, pp. 306–329; and G. S. Taylor, "The Relationship between Sources of New Employees and Attitudes Toward the Job," *Journal of Social Psychology,* Vol. 134, 1994, pp. 99–110.
128. Breaugh, "Relationships between Recruiting Sources and Employee Performance, Absenteeism, and Work Attitudes"; David F. Caldwell and Austin Spivey, "The Relationship between Recruiting Source and Employee Success: An Analysis by Race," *Personnel Psychology,* Spring 1983, pp. 67–72; and J. D. Werbel and J. Landau, "The Effectiveness of Different Recruitment Sources: A Mediating Variable Analysis," *Journal of Applied Social Pscyhology,* Vol. 26, 1996, pp. 1337–1350.
129. De Witte, "Recruitment Advertising."
130. James A. Breaugh and R. B. Mann, "Recruiting Source Effects: A Test of Two Alternative Explanations," *Journal of Occupational Psychology,* Vol. 57, 1984, pp. 261–267; Maureen A. Conard and Steven D. Ashworth, "Recruiting Source Effectiveness: A Meta-Analysis and Re-Examination of Two Rival Hypotheses," paper presented at the First Annual Conference of the Society for Industrial and

Organizational Psychology, Chicago, April 1986; and Philip G. Swaroff, Lizabeth A. Barclay, and Alan R. Bass, "Recruiting Sources: Another Look," *Journal of Applied Psychology,* November 1985, pp. 720–728; Breaugh and Starke, "Research on Employee Recruitment: So Many Studies, So Many Remaining Questions." Some studies report differences in applicant characteristics from different sources but do not find differences in subsequent performance or tenure; see R. P. Vecchio, "The Impact of Referral Sources on Employee Attitudes: Evidence from a National Sample," *Journal of Management,* 1995, pp. 953–965; C. R. Williams, C. E. Labig Jr., and T. H. Stone, "Recruitment Sources and Posthire Outcomes for Job Applicants and New Hires: A Test of Two Hypotheses," *Journal of Applied Psychology,* Vol. 78, 1993, pp. 163–172.

131. Gannon, "Source of Referral and Employee Turnover."

132. Rachel King, "Chili's Hot Interview Makeover," *Workforce,* September 1, 2003. (Available at: htts://www.workforce.com/archive/article/23/47/90)

133. Ken Gordon, "Big, Fast, and Easily Bungled," *Workforce,* August 11, 2003. (Available at: http://www.workforce.com/section/06/feature/23/49/38)

CHAPTER 7

Measurement and Decision-Making Issues in Selection

- Statistical Methods in Selection
- Reliability
- Validity
- Decision Making in Selection
- Utility of a Selection System

HR Challenge

Dingo Doggie Bites (DDB) is an Australian dog food manufacturer that has been operating primarily along the eastern seaboard of Australia; that is, in Sydney, Brisbane, Rockhampton, and Cairns. DDB is planning to expand operations significantly and open new production facilities in other areas of Australia—specifically, Melbourne, Adelaide, Darwin, and Alice Springs. The company is family owned and has, in the past, hired production workers on the basis of an interview, a thirty-item test of basic math skills, a standardized verbal ability test, and a "work task simulation" that the developers, Aussie Psychometrics, Ltd., have assured DDB's management will test the essential psychomotor skills needed to perform production line jobs. Job applicants tend to be relatives or friends of current employees.

There are approximately 200 production workers in the four existing production plants. The new CEO of Dingo Doggie Bites, Peter Bettie, is concerned about the effectiveness of current selection procedures. Considerable competitive pressure is being placed on DDB by American and British firms entering the Australian dog food market. To put it bluntly, workers at DDB generally perform at an "adequate" level, but productivity almost certainly will have to improve to meet the new threat from foreign competitors.

Antidiscrimination laws and legislation on "unfair dismissals" provide additional incentives for firms such as DDB to improve their selection procedures. In the Melbourne and Adelaide plants, job applicants are expected to come from a wide variety of ethnic groups, including Chinese, Vietnamese, Greek, Croatian, Serbian, and individuals from a variety of Middle Eastern nations. A significant proportion of applicants in Darwin and Alice Springs will likely be Australian Aborigines.

You are a widely respected expert on EEO and human resource selection issues in the United States. Although EEO legislation in Australia is somewhat less extensive than that in the United States, there are many similarities between the two countries in their basic approach to equal employment opportunity. An Australian friend of yours, Larry Springboard, has invited you to join him for a round of golf at Le Grande Tres Cher Country Club. Playing with you that day is Peter Bettie. After finding out what you do for a living, Peter starts telling you about his situation and seeks your help. What should he do? Where should he start? What are the critical issues he should seek advice about from local HR consultants?

Human resource selection is a process of measurement, decision making, and evaluation (see Figure 7.1). The goal of a personnel selection system is to bring into an organization individuals who will perform well on the job. A good selection system also should be fair to minorities and other protected groups.

To have an accurate and fair selection system, an organization must use reliable and valid measures of job applicant characteristics. Although such a statement would seem obvious—any HR practitioner would want a reliable, valid selection process—some research indicates that what happens in the real world is not as ideal as one might like. For example, a research study done in New Zealand found that the *more* valid a selection test was, the *less* likely personnel consultants in New Zealand were to use it! Thirty-three percent of those surveyed did not even understand what the term "validity" meant in reference to personnel selection.[1] In addition to validity and reliability, a good selection system must combine information about applicant characteristics in a rational way and produce correct hire and no-hire decisions. Finally, a good selection system should add to the overall effectiveness of the organization (see the Partnerships for Strategic Success box for an example of one organization that has spent an enormous amount of effort to ensure its selection procedures are excellent and continually improving).

In this chapter we address each of these areas in turn. First, we introduce the statistical methods needed to understand reliability and validity. Second, we consider why reliability of selection instruments is important and offer examples of common methods of assessing reliability. Next the discussion moves to the ways in which selection tests can be validated so that the results can be used to make hiring decisions. Then, we describe several methods of using test scores to make these decisions. The final sections examine the factors that affect the costs of selection systems and describe the many benefits that can be realized from a properly designed selection process.

FIGURE 7.1
The Selection Process

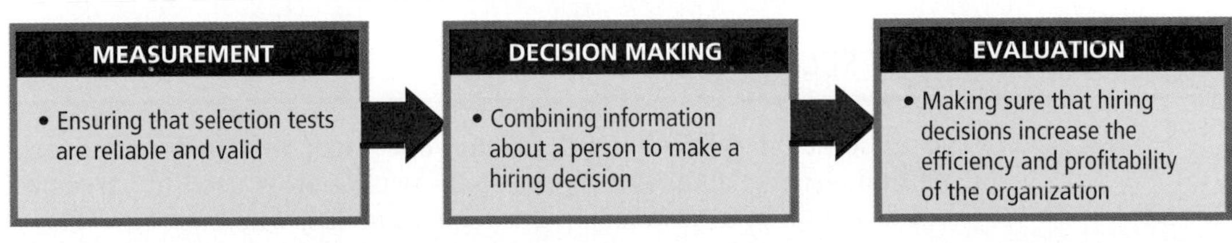

PARTNERSHIPS FOR STRATEGIC SUCCESS

Improving the Selection of Prison Correction Officer Trainees in Pennsylvania

Over the years, government and military organizations have often been leaders in the development of sophisticated selection techniques due to the large numbers of people these organizations hire/induct each year. A 2001 article by Charles Sproule and Stephen Berkley provides a good example of selection procedures development in one civil service organization. These two authors describe a process begun in 1968 by the Research and Special Projects Unit of the Pennsylvania Civil Service Commission to monitor and constantly improve the selection processes used for hiring Prison Correction Officer Trainees (COT). During a typical year, between 4,000 and 6,000 individuals apply for COT jobs. Half to two-thirds of the applicants are tested and between 500 and 700 are hired. In 1997 the hiring process cost nearly $1,300 per successful job applicant—a significant amount of money in any organization. The history of the COT job testing process exemplifies an organization that has consciously and actively reacted to new situations in its operational environment and attempted to improve its testing program. This process also exemplifies many of the concepts discussed in this chapter.

In 1981 hiring was accomplished using equally weighted written and oral tests. The written test assessed visual memory (using photographs), associative memory (using mug shots and names), and reading comprehension. The oral test measured motivation and job interest; poise and self-confidence; communication skills; and judgment. The selection process also included physical tests, medical checks, police background checks, and pre-employment tours of prison facilities. Psychological screening (background investigations and pre-employment testing with the Minnesota Multiphasic Personality Inventory—MMPI) was added to the hiring process in 1982 after a corrections officer murdered thirteen innocent victims and there was significant external political pressure to take action to prevent such occurrences in the future.

In 1984 a predictive validation study was conducted on the selection process using a sample of 442 newly hired correction officer trainees. This study found that both the written and oral tests in the selection system were significantly related to job performance, whereas a personality test (the Jackson Personality Research Form), which had been tested in the study, showed no such relationship. Despite the lack of support for the use of personality tests, the study showed that the use of the current selection system saved the State of Pennsylvania several million dollars per year compared to random selection.

Further improvements to the selection process were made in the early 1990s. In 1991 interviews were conducted with incumbent corrections officers and other Department of Corrections staff to determine how the screening process could be improved. Subsequently, the COT job analysis was updated, and a report was issued recommending ten improvements in the assessment, selection, and training of COTs. A new COT examination was developed in 1992 that included three parts: a written test (weighted 45 percent); a writing exercise (weighted 10 percent); and a structured oral test (weighted 45 percent). The written test initially contained seventy multiple-choice questions.

STATISTICAL METHODS IN SELECTION

To understand reliability and validity, one must first understand two statistical methods—correlation and regression. Correlation is used to assess the strength and direction of a relationship between variables, whereas regression makes use of the relationship to predict scores on one variable from scores on one or more

Two parts of the test, observation ability and ability to follow oral instructions, were video based and showed incidents and events in correctional settings to which the job applicant had to respond.

Additional analyses of the 1992 test were conducted in 1993, 1995, and 1996. The 1995 study found small test performance differences by race, with whites outperforming blacks on the written test and the writing exercise test, and blacks outperforming whites on the oral test. Gender-related differences in test performance were trivial in nature. The written test had the largest score difference by race. Differential item analyses of the 1992 COT test showed that in the last two test sections there were nine test items with differences of 15 or more percentage points by race. Seven items favored whites, and a disproportional percentage of blacks did not complete the test. The researchers found evidence that test "burnout" may have been contributing to this black–white difference, and as a result, the number of test items in the final two sections of the test was reduced from fifteen to ten (which reduced the total number of test items from seventy to sixty-five).

A validation study of the COT conducted in 1996 found that the written test was an excellent predictor of job success, correlating .39 with a combined performance rating criterion measure. The oral test and writing exercise scores to written test scores only marginally increased the correlation between test performance and measures of performance. Thus the value of the oral test and writing exercise was put into question, and these two components of the selection procedure were dropped. The COT examination had been costing the Commonwealth of Pennsylvania around $641,000 annually. The test costs could be broken down as follows: written test = $91,000, writing exercise = $40,000, and oral test = $510,000. Each hire was costing the Commonwealth of Pennsylvania $1,300. This did not include the cost of recruitment, interviews, drug screening, medical screening, physical fitness testing, and background investigations. Although video production costs, including staff time, associated with the COT were around $233,000, the exclusion of the writing exercise and oral test from the exam saved $550,000 each year. Thus, a one-time investment of $233,000 for the production of the video test content was offset by savings of more than half a million dollars annually.

The basic nature of the testing procedures continues today, with new medical and physical ability testing procedures introduced in 1999. The important point in this history of the Correctional Officer Trainee selection process is the ability of the Pennsylvania Civil Service Commission and its Research and Special Projects Unit to conduct high-quality analyses of the test program's performance, including subgroup and differential item analyses. As a result of this process of continuous test improvement, the Civil Service Commission has been able to enhance its ability to hire good people into a very demanding job while at the same time decreasing unnecessary costs to the taxpayers of Pennsylvania. Many private organizations could learn much from this example.

Source: Charles Sproule and Stephen Berkley, "The Selection of Entry-Level Corrections Officers: Pennsylvania Research," *Public Personnel Management,* Vol. 30 (3), 2001, pp. 377–418.

other variables. Only a brief discussion of these methods is offered here; those desiring more detail should refer to a basic statistics textbook.

Correlation Analysis

Correlation analysis is used to determine the degree of relationship between two variables. For example, an HR specialist may wish to know whether scores on a mechanical ability test are related to job performance. If a relationship exists, then a mechanical ability test given to job applicants might be useful in deciding who should be hired.

The **Pearson product moment correlation coefficient** (represented by the symbol *r*) is a numerical index that indicates the direction and degree of linear relationship between two variables. The Pearson correlation coefficient has several important characteristics:

- The numerical value of *r* ranges from –1.0 to +1.0.
- The sign of the correlation (– or +) indicates the direction of the relationship.
- The magnitude of *r* indicates the strength of the relationship.
- This numerical index is appropriate only for describing linear (straight-line) relationships.

Several different strengths and directions of correlations are presented in Figure 7.2. When $r = +1.0$, a perfect positive linear relationship exists between two variables

FIGURE 7.2

Examples of Strengths and Directions of Correlations

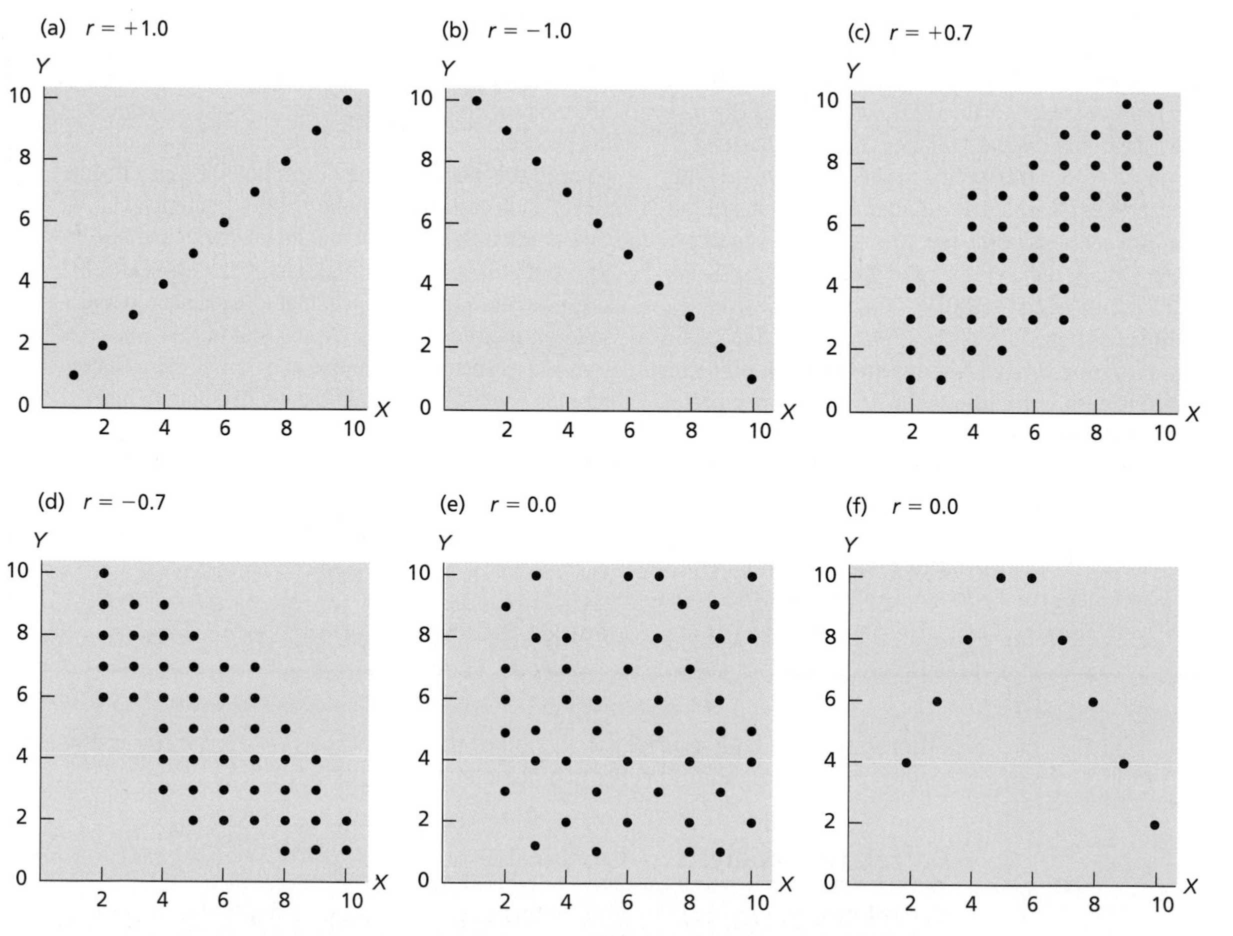

(see Figure 7.2a). As variable X increases, variable Y increases in some exactly proportional manner. When $r = -1.0$, a perfect negative relationship exists, but in this case, as variable X increases, variable Y decreases in the same manner (see Figure 7.2b). When $r = +.70$ or $-.70$ (see Figures 7.2c and d), a relationship between X and Y exists, but it is not as strong (not as exactly proportional) as when $r = +1.0$ or -1.0. Figure 7.2e depicts a zero relationship between X and Y. In the right corner (see Figure 7.2f), r also equals 0.0, but for another reason. In this case, X and Y are related but the relationship cannot be represented by a straight line. (The Pearson correlation coefficient is appropriate only for describing linear relationships.)

Regression Analysis

Regression analysis allows HR specialists to use a known relationship between variables to predict an individual's future behavior. The Pearson correlation coefficient indicates how close to a straight line the relationship between two variables is. Regression analysis answers the question, "To which straight line is the relationship closest?" Regression analysis does this by identifying the equation for the line that best fits a set of data (data for several individuals on two variables, X and Y). If a correlation exists between mechanical ability and job performance, HR specialists can use regression analysis to predict the future performance of an individual whose mechanical ability is known.

The job performance and mechanical ability levels of ten individuals are represented in Figure 7.3. In Figure 7.3a, the line that best fits these data has been drawn. In Figure 7.3b, a non-best-fitting line has been drawn. A complex mathematical formula is used to compute the equation for the best-fitting line. By means of this formula, the HR specialist would find that the equation for the best-fitting line (shown in Figure 7.3a) is

$$Y_p = .128X + 1.9$$

where Y_p = predicted performance

X = mechanical ability

.128 = the slope of the line (i.e., for every unit that X increases, Y increases .128 units)

1.9 = the Y-intercept (i.e., the point where the line crosses the Y-axis).

The HR specialist can use the regression equation to predict performance of a job applicant by inserting the measured mechanical ability of the applicant into the formula. If Joe scored 35 on the mechanical ability test, then Joe's predicted performance would be $Y_p = .128(35) + 1.9 = 6.38$. How accurately the regression equation actually predicts Joe's performance depends on the strength of the relationship between mechanical ability and performance. As the strength of the relationship increases (r approaches +1.0 or −1.0), the accuracy of prediction increases. If $r = 0.0$, then predictions based on a regression equation would be no better than random guesses.[2]

Rarely in personnel selection do HR specialists predict the performance of job applicants by using information about only one ability or characteristic. Information used in selecting employees usually includes data from multiple sources, such as interviews, application blanks, references, and ability tests. Multiple correlation and regression analyses are simply extensions of the correlation and regression

FIGURE 7.3

Best-Fitting and Non-Best-Fitting Regression Lines

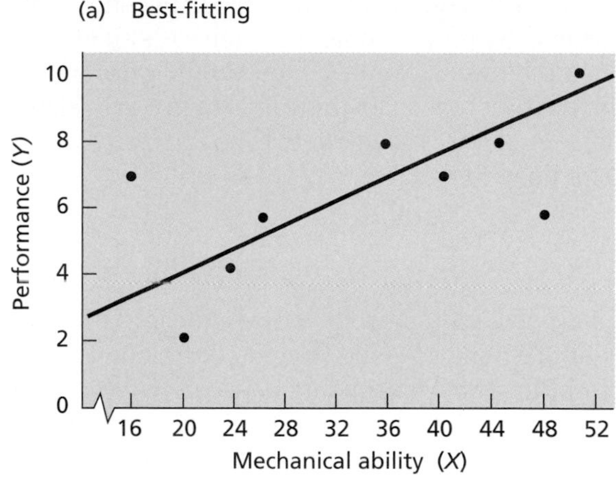

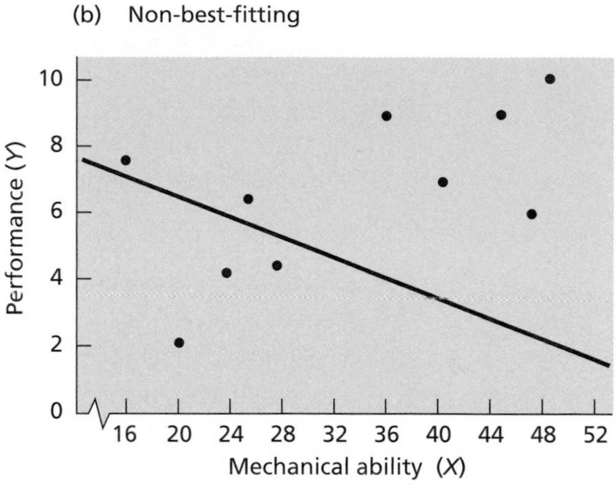

analyses described here. A multiple correlation indicates the degree of relationship between one variable (e.g., job performance) and a set of other variables, whereas multiple regression analysis allows the HR specialist to develop a "best-fitting" equation using these multiple variables to predict later job behavior.

RELIABILITY

An organization's personnel selection system should use reliable and valid measures of a job applicant's characteristics to make correct hiring decisions. **Reliability,** discussed in this section, refers to consistency of measurement.[3] For instance, an individual should get about the same score if his or her intelligence is measured with the same test twice, a few weeks apart. If the person scored 75 on Monday and then scored 145 three weeks later, would this test be a good measure of the person's general intelligence? The answer—not at all! Validity, discussed in the next section, has to do with whether or not the test measures what it is supposed to measure (intelligence) and whether test scores are significantly correlated with job performance (e.g., does intelligence correlate with success in the job of college professor? shoemaker? truck driver?).

In our discussion, the terms "test," "measure," or "instrument" may apply to any form of measurement that takes place in the selection process. Thus an interview is considered as much a test as a paper-and-pencil measure of intelligence. The concept of reliability applies equally to both.

Systematic Error versus Random Error

Any time a measure is taken of an individual there will be some error in that measurement. For example, if a thermometer were used to take the temperature of a patient, the observed temperature could consist of the true body temperature of the patient, some systematic error or bias in the temperature reading, and/or random error affecting the reading.[4] For example, **systematic error** could occur if the thermometer were faulty and thus always measured the temperatures of patients one degree higher than their true temperatures. **Random error** would occur if a patient did not hold the thermometer in the right place in the mouth for the appropriate length of time or if a patient had taken a hot or cold drink just before measurement. At different times, a patient could get a temperature reading lower or higher than his or her true internal body temperature.

The key difference between systematic error and random error is that systematic error affects measurement in a consistent, predictable fashion, whereas random error, by definition, is inconsistent or variable in its effect. Ideally, the HR specialist wants tests that have neither systematic nor random error. However, from the viewpoint of reliability, random error, due to its inconsistent nature, is the greatest problem.

Methods of Measuring Reliability

The most important methods of assessing reliability for HR specialists are test–retest, inter-rater, and internal consistency.[5] In each of these methods, the correlation coefficient (or similar method) is used as the index of reliability. Typically, a correlation of about .80 or higher is considered good reliability. Not all these methods must be used in every situation, and in some instances a particular method may be totally inappropriate.

Test–Retest The **test–retest method** examines the consistency of a test over time. A single group of people take a test (time 1). Later, the same people take the same test again (time 2). The correlation (called the **coefficient of stability**) is computed between the time 1 and the time 2 scores. Test–retest reliability is important when we are measuring something that we normally would assume is a relatively stable trait of an individual. For example, intelligence is a fairly stable characteristic of a person, and we would not normally expect that a person's intelligence would vary wildly from one time to another. As we noted earlier, an intelligence test that indicated a dramatically different level of intelligence for a person from one time to another would be a pretty suspect measure of intelligence and would be unlikely to predict subsequent behavior or performance.

Inter-Rater Reliability Suppose a job applicant is interviewed by several different interviewers. The interviewers rate the applicant separately on several dimensions. In this case, each interviewer can be viewed as a form of "interview test." It is therefore important to know how one interviewer's rating of the candidate correlates with the other interviewers' ratings of the same candidate. This correlation among evaluators who are sizing up the same set of applicants is referred to as **inter-rater reliability.** One caution should be noted about inter-rater reliability: Sometimes inter-rater reliability is low, and that is okay. Suppose an applicant is being interviewed by three different people—a midlevel manager, a technical specialist, and a person who would be a subordinate of the applicant if the applicant were hired. The inter-rater agreement among these three interviewers could be quite low because they bring to the interview situation different perspectives of the job for which the applicant is being considered. A low level of agreement among the interviewers would not necessarily mean that our interview procedure is faulty. On the other hand, if all three interviewers were technical specialists, a lack of agreement would probably indicate reliability problems.

Internal Consistency The third method of assessing reliability is **internal consistency.** This type of reliability assesses whether all the items on a test measure the same trait or ability; that is, whether the test's content is internally consistent. In the most common way of assessing internal consistency, a group of people are given a test. A coefficient is computed that represents the average correlation of each item on the test with each other item. This is called **coefficient alpha** and is the preferred measure of internal consistency in most situations.[6] Coefficient alpha will be high (.80 or above) if most of the items on the test measure the same thing.

Having reliable measures is critical. Reliability information can be obtained from several sources: (1) reliability studies conducted by the organization that will use the tests, (2) reliability information provided by commercial test publishers that sell the tests, (3) data from other companies that have used the same tests in their selection systems, or (4) published data from scholars who have used the tests in research studies.

Reliability serves as the foundation for the validity of a test. If a test cannot measure people consistently, it cannot possibly be valid. The next section discusses the concept of test validity.

VALIDITY

The *Standards for Educational and Psychological Testing* defines **validity** as the "degree to which accumulated evidence and theory support specific interpretations of test scores entailed by proposed uses of a test." The important notion here is that when we "validate" a predictor test for selection purposes, we are not validating the test itself but rather the inferences and actions we take as a result of test scores.[7] In personnel selection, tests are used to measure some characteristic—for instance, mechanical ability—that is believed to relate to how well a person will be able to perform a job. In this situation, we are inferring that the test actually measures mechanical ability and that on the basis of how an applicant scores on the test, we can also infer whether the individual will be able to perform the job. We then take action based on an applicant's test scores (we hire or do not hire the person). Validity deals with the issues of (1) whether the test is an adequate measure of the characteristic it supposedly measures and (2) whether inferences and actions based on test scores are appropriate. **Validation** is the process of providing evidence to support the adequacy of our measure and the inferences and actions we take based on test scores.

Note that nothing in the law requires organizations to validate all selection tests. The organization would need validity evidence only if an applicant were to file a complaint and was able to establish a prima facie case of adverse impact. Then the employer might use validity data to show that the test was a good selection device that was necessary to improve the quality of hiring. However, techniques for validation were developed long before the passage of EEO laws. It makes sense to validate, even if a test has no adverse impact and the validity data will never be needed in court. No organization would want to spend time and money using a selection device that is not useful. Validation shows the usefulness of a test in identifying applicants who will make good employees.

In the past it was common for HR researchers to identify three separate and distinct types of validity: construct validity, content validity, and criterion-related validity.[8] As noted previously, the current view is that validity is a single concept related to the adequacy of interpretations drawn about test scores, and that construct, content, and criterion-related "validity" simply represent different sources of information for providing evidence of a measure's overall validity. We shall look at only two of these validation approaches—content and criterion-related—because they are of the most significant practical concern to the HR specialist.

Content Validation

Content validation provides evidence of whether or not a test is representative of some construct's "domain." Content validation is most appropriately done when the construct being measured consists of readily observable behaviors. Suppose, for instance, that an organization develops a technical math test for use in selecting engineering technicians. The test includes math problems in addition, subtraction, division, and multiplication. However, the job of an engineering technician in the organization requires an individual to work on advanced trigonometry, geometry, and calculus problems. Is the math test a representative sample of the types of math problems that are performed on the job? Content validity deals with this issue. In the preceding example, the math test is not content valid. Although it does measure some aspects of technical math, it does not adequately sample all aspects of the domain of technical math problems confronted on the job.

Determining the content validity of a test is primarily a judgmental process that should begin with a thorough job analysis.[9] Test items are evaluated on the degree to which they correspond to the skills and knowledge needed to perform critical job tasks. For instance, a typing test may be purchased or constructed for the job of secretary, and a test for knowledge of construction and electrical standards may be written for the job of building inspector. One approach to judging the content validity of such tests was developed by Charles Lawshe in 1975. Lawshe's approach uses a panel of experts to rate the items on a test as to whether each represents essential aspects of the same domain. The experts must be highly knowledgeable about the job.[10] These ratings yield a content validity score for each item. This allows the HR specialist to compare the content validity of one test item with that of another and to delete poor items. By averaging the content validity scores across all test items, an index of the content validity for the whole test can be obtained. This index can be used to compare several proposed tests to identify the test that most closely corresponds to the performance domain of a given job. Content validity indicates whether test items reflect critical aspects of job performance; it thus helps HR professionals determine whether inferences and actions (hire/not hire) based on test scores are warranted.

Criterion-Related Validation

In the **criterion-related validation** of a test, the HR specialist determines whether test scores are statistically related to some important criterion variable. The criterion variable is simply whatever aspect of an individual's behavior the HR specialist is trying to predict, such as job performance, absenteeism, or turnover.

Most frequently, the criterion variable is some measure of job performance (for the remainder of the discussion on validity, we will assume this is the case). In using a test in personnel selection, we are making an inference that applicants who score in a particular manner on the test will be better performers than those who score in some other way. Criterion-related validation procedures directly test the appropriateness of that inference.

In conducting a criterion-related study, the first step is to analyze the job. Information about the nature of the job helps the HR specialist choose one or more tests that seem likely to predict job performance. For instance, after analyzing the job of entry-level computer programmer, the HR specialist may choose tests of scheduling and planning, information processing, and problem solving.[11] Information from the job analysis is also used to develop a criterion measure of job performance. The criterion measure might be job-performance rating scales filled out by the supervisor or objective measures of the quality and quantity of output produced by individuals. A validity study is then conducted to determine whether the tests correlate with the job-performance criterion as expected.

Two major procedures of criterion-related validation are concurrent validation and predictive validation. A comparison of the concurrent and predictive validation procedures is presented in Figure 7.4.

Concurrent Validation **Concurrent validation** involves the use of current employees. The procedure involves three steps:

1. Select a sample of current employees.
2. Give each employee the proposed selection test and simultaneously collect information on the criterion variable.
3. Compute the correlation between test scores and criterion scores.

In the case of 200 currently employed computer programmers, for instance, this procedure might indicate a statistically significant correlation of .35 between scheduling-and-planning test scores and supervisory ratings of performance over the past month. This suggests that the scheduling-and-planning test may be useful to select computer programmers who will be high performers.

Although concurrent validation seems relatively simple, it has two major problems. The first problem concerns the representativeness of the sample of employees. Current employees may vary considerably from actual job applicants in their demographic characteristics, motivation, abilities, and job experience.[12] The question that arises is this: Does the relationship between test and performance scores for present employees apply equally well to job applicants? Ultimately, it is job applicants about whom we want to make inferences.

The second major problem with concurrent validation is called **restriction of range.** Since present employees are used, it is unlikely that the sample will include individuals who are extremely poor performers (they would already have quit or been fired). The absence of very low performers results in a restriction of range on the performance scores found in the validation sample. If, in addition, the test is related to job performance, a restriction of range in the test scores also can occur because low performers, who would probably do poorly on the test, are absent from the sample. The effect of this double-edged restriction of range is to cause the correlation between the test scores and performance scores in the validation sample to appear lower than it should be.[13]

FIGURE 7.4
Concurrent and Predictive Validation Procedures

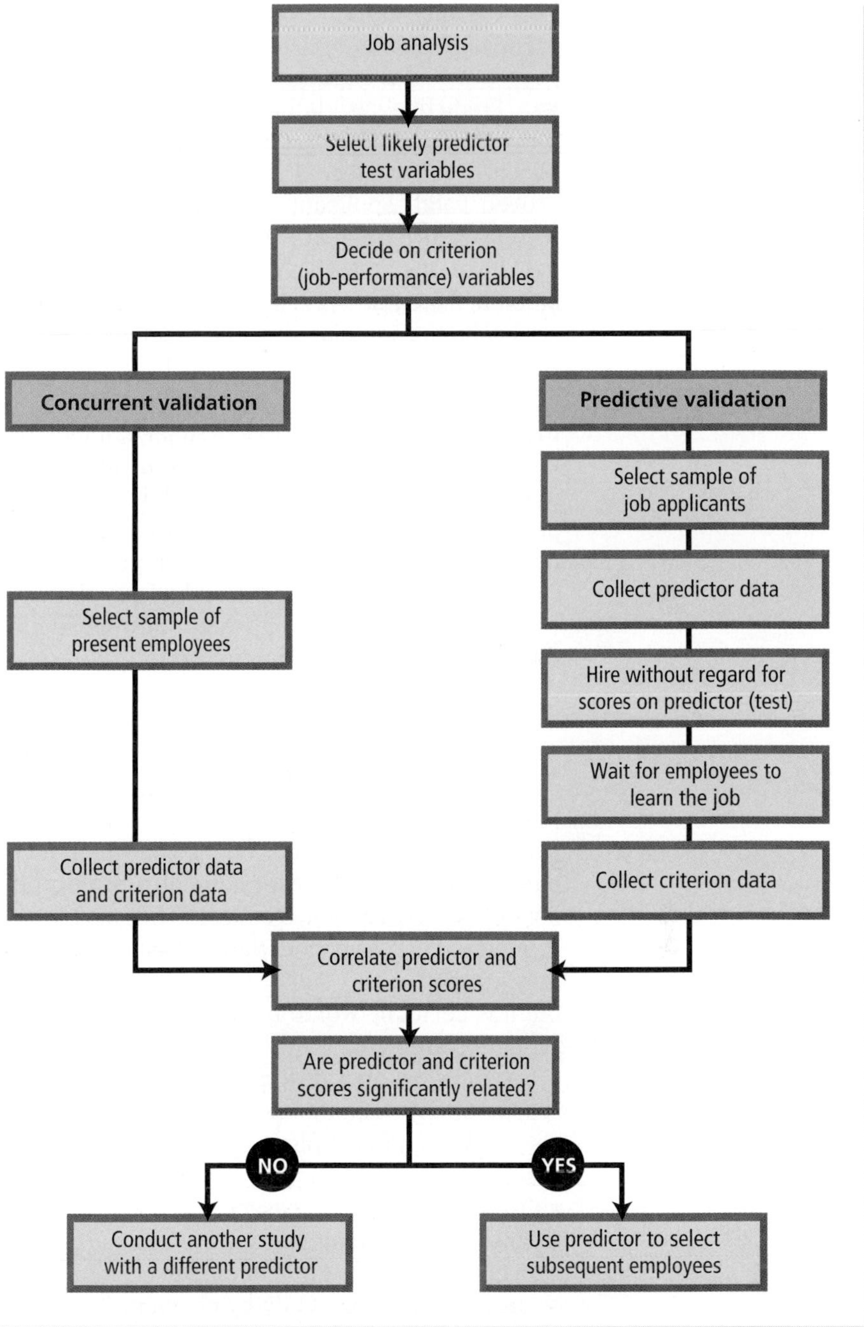

Restriction of range is a problem because it may cause the HR specialist to conclude that a test is not related to job performance when it really is. By selecting a representative sample to participate in the validation study, the HR specialist can reduce restriction of range, although not eliminate it entirely. Also, the HR specialist can use statistical methods developed specifically to estimate what the correlation between variables would be if no restriction of range were present.

Considerable care must be taken, however, in exactly how and when these statistical adjustments are used.[14]

Predictive Validation Another method of criterion-related validation is through **predictive validation,** a procedure that uses the scores of actual job applicants who are tested (time 1) and then hired. Because the test has not yet been proved valid, applicant test scores are not used by HR specialists in deciding whom to hire. Instead, the HR specialist measures the job performances of the new hires after they have been on the job for a while and then computes the correlation between time 1 test scores and time 2 performance scores.[15]

Problems associated with predictive validation are the sample size and the time required to perform a typical predictive study. At one time, researchers thought a predictive study could be conducted if thirty applicants were tested and hired for the same job. However, such small samples often result in these studies having very low "statistical power," which means the relationship between test and performance is difficult to detect. This low power then reduces the confidence we can place in the results of our study. Considerably larger sample sizes (e.g., 200) are needed to obtain adequate levels of power.[16] Obtaining large samples of job applicants may be impossible for all but the biggest companies. If, for instance, an advertising firm hires about twenty new advertising designers a year, it would take the firm years to acquire data from a large number of individuals. However, depending on the overall size of the firm, a concurrent validation study *might* be feasible because all presently employed designers could be used.

Another problem with predictive validation relates to the time interval between collecting predictor scores and measuring the criterion. Some studies have found that predictive validity correlations tend to decline in magnitude as the time between predictor and criterion measurement increases. Thus a problem-solving test may correlate $r = .30$ with computer programmer performance ratings if the ratings of performance are collected no more than one month after the test is taken. If, instead, performance were measured six months after testing, the correlation may be only $r = .20$. There is some controversy about whether this problem exists, but it is certainly worth taking into account in designing and evaluating predictive validation studies.[17]

In the case of criterion-related validity, the HR specialist should be wary of the results of any validation study that has been done on just one sample of individuals—unless that sample is extremely large. The HR specialist should recheck the results of a validity study on another sample, a process referred to as **cross-validation.** This is necessary because the relationship between test scores and criterion measures may result from unique or chance factors in a particular sample. The hope is that a true relationship between test scores and criterion measures will occur in all samples. Only by checking this assumption, however, can the HR specialist confidently apply testing procedures to future samples of job applicants.[18]

The HR specialist also should recheck the validity of tests after the selection system has been implemented. The need to recheck validity is due to two phenomena. The first is referred to as the **dynamic criterion.**[19] Over time, there may be systematic changes in the critical behaviors needed on a job. Likewise, the performance appraisal system used in the organization may change.[20] The second phenomenon is called **item parameter drift.**[21] This occurs when job applicants respond differently to individual items on a test due to educational, technological, cultural, or other changes that have occurred during the life of the test. Suppose, for example, that a test of "computer knowledge" was designed in 1995. On the test were several items dealing with use of the Internet. In 1995 it was found that these items tended to help differentiate between individuals with high versus low levels of computer knowledge. However, in 2005, given the increased familiarity with the Internet by most people in developed countries, these same items would probably not be as effective in distinguishing between job applicants with high versus low computer knowledge as everyone would get the items right. As a result of both dynamic criteria and item parameter drift, tests that adequately predicted job performance in 1995 may not predict performance as well in 2005. Therefore, the HR specialist should revalidate selection tests periodically to ensure that the test remains useful over time.

Special Concerns in Validation

Showing that tests have good content and criterion-related validity is not the only task of the HR specialist. The legal context in which selection systems operate requires that any "valid" selection system must also be examined for potential unfairness or bias toward minority-group members. One issue that has received a lot of research attention is the presence of majority and minority subgroup differences in average scores on many selection tests. This research has focused on whether subgroup differences actually exist and, if they do exist, then why. The *Principles for the Validation and Use of Personnel Selection Procedures* of the Society of Industrial and Organizational Psychologists (SIOP) identifies a number of other fairness/bias issues of relevance to HR practitioners. Among these are equity of treatment in test situations, differential validity and prediction, and measurement bias. Each of these issues is discussed separately in the following sections.[22]

Test Fairness and Subgroup Differences in Mean Test Scores A large body of research has found significant differences in the mean scores of black and white job applicants on a number of common ability tests. In most cases, the tests measure some form of cognitive ability. For example, one study found that whites scored higher than blacks on general cognitive ability, verbal ability, quantitative ability, spatial ability, memory ability, and mental processing speed.[23] It is less likely that such differences exist on noncognitive tests, such as tests of interpersonal abilities or personality.[24] Even in the case of cognitive tests, the magnitude of differences seems to be affected by the nature and size of the black–white samples, the exact trait being measured, the motivation of test takers, differences in test anxiety, level of self-efficacy, perceptions of the credibility of the specific test involved, and other non-ability-related factors.[25]

The presence of mean test score differences presents a substantial problem to test users. Obviously, one reason for such differences may be that one subgroup has a higher true ability than the other. However, mean score difference may instead reflect bias or unfairness in the selection test toward one subgroup. It is often difficult to determine whether true ability differences or bias is the cause of any subgroup differences. Therefore, when subgroup differences are likely to occur, use one of these strategies to decrease any potential bias in the testing situation:

1. Use non–cognitively oriented tests—such as personality tests or work samples—in the selection process that have been shown through content or criterion-related validation studies to be closely linked to job performance.

2. For any cognitive tests used, analyze individual test items and remove any that are "culturally laden."
3. Use alternative means to present test materials; subgroup members may find computer or video technology more familiar and easier to use than traditional paper-and-pencil tests.
4. Change the way in which the test and test items are presented to subgroup members so that their test-taking motivation is enhanced.
5. Use coaching or orientation materials that inform examinees about the test and thus help facilitate their test performance.[26]

Although these actions may not be effective in every case, they do provide some added assurance that the firm testing job applicants is providing as fair a testing situation as is possible. This may benefit the firm if its testing procedures are challenged in court, and it may also help identify applicants who truly have (or do not have) the ability to perform the job.

Test Fairness as Equitable Treatment One aspect of test fairness can be defined in terms of the extent of **equitable treatment in testing** conditions. To be fair, majority and minority group members must be treated comparably in terms of access to practice materials, the amount of performance feedback they receive, their opportunities to retake the test, as well as other features of test administration such as accommodating test takers with disabilities.

Test Fairness as Differential Validity and Prediction The SIOP *Principles* also define test fairness as a lack of differential predictive bias. Two aspects of predictive bias are important. **Differential validity** exists when the correlation between test scores and performance for one group is significantly lower than the correlation for another group.[27] Differential validity is presented graphically in Figure 7.5. In Figure 7.5a it is clear that for majority employees, a strong relationship exists between performance and scores on a problem-solving test. This is not the case for minority employees. In Figure 7.5b no differential validity exists. The relationship between problem-solving test scores and performance for both groups is essentially equal, although minority-group members tend to score lower on the test. Also, if a regression equation were developed using all the employees, the predictions based on that equation would not systematically over- or underpredict for either group.

In Figure 7.5c no differential validity exists. However, if a regression-line equation were developed using the total sample (line T), this equation would tend to systematically underpredict minority-group performance but overpredict majority-group performance. This is referred to as **differential prediction.**[28] Although differential validity and differential prediction are issues that should be investigated in every criterion-related validation study, in reality these problems occur infrequently.[29]

Validity Generalization Differential validity and differential prediction focus on whether the validity of selection tests changes depending on the types of people tested. There has also been a long-standing assumption that validity varies from one job to another and from one organization to another. This assumption is based on many studies that have found a test that validly predicts performance in a job does not correlate significantly with performance in a different job in the same

FIGURE 7.5

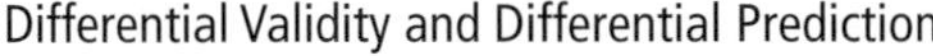

Differential Validity and Differential Prediction

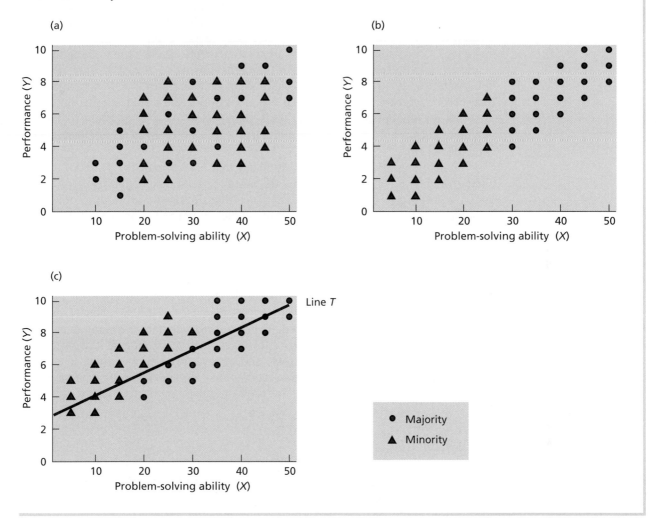

organization or in a similar job in a different organization. Over the past two decades, strong arguments have been made against this assumption of **situational specificity.** The argument against situational specificity is called **validity generalization**—that is, that test validity is readily applicable across a variety of organizations and similar jobs. This approach suggests that most differences in the observed validity of tests across situations result from methodological and statistical problems rather than from true differences in the strength of relationships between predictor and criterion. Proponents of validity generalization submit that if these problems are controlled, tests found to be valid predictors of performance for a job will be useful for selecting for that job in all organizations.[30]

Proponents of validity generalization argue that tests of general cognitive ability are particularly good predictors of job performance across a wide variety of jobs. General cognitive ability predicts whether an individual will be able to adequately learn a job; the level of competency then influences job performance.

Although many of the validity generalization studies have been conducted in the United States, a recent study found similar strong support for the generalized validity of cognitive ability tests in firms in the European Union.[31] In a review of the validity generalization research, Kevin Murphy noted that "it is now widely accepted that (a) professionally developed ability tests, structured interviews, work samples, assessment centers, and other structured assessment techniques are likely to provide valid predictions of future performance across a wide range of jobs, settings, etc.; (b) the level of validity for a particular test can vary as a function of characteristics of the job (e.g., complexity) or the organizations, but validities are reasonably consistent across settings; and (c) it is possible to identify abilities and broad dimensions of personality that are related to performance in virtually all jobs."[32]

Validity generalization research suggests that HR specialists may draw on published validity generalization studies to identify potential selection tests for "local" use. However, care must be taken to ensure that the predictor method of interest to a particular firm is the same kind of predictor method represented in validity generalization studies. Thus a firm seeking support for use of a highly structured, behavioral description interview should not rely on validity generalization studies that have examined another type of selection interview or "interviews in general." Even if such care is taken, there are still problems in using a validity generalization approach. Perhaps the most obvious is that it seems to contradict EEOC guidelines for development of selection tests because no job analysis is required and situational specificity is ignored. There are also certain advantages in doing one's own validation study. It allows the organization to look at the predictive power of unique combinations of tests and of tests predicting unique local measures of job performance. Validation studies also enable the organization to develop local norms and cutoff scores for the tests to use in hiring decisions.[33]

DECISION MAKING IN SELECTION

Generally, the HR specialist collects several types of information about job applicants before making a selection decision. The HR specialist still has the problem of how to use these sources of information to make the best final hire/no-hire decision. At least four different methods exist for combining information and making a selection decision: additive models, multiple cutoff, multiple hurdle, and profile matching.

Additive Models

Additive models are a purely statistical approach to selection decision making.[34] When using additive models, the HR specialist simply converts test scores received by a job applicant to some common metric and then adds them up. The job applicants with the highest totals are hired. In some additive procedures, the test scores are weighted in some manner so that performing well on one test may contribute more to an applicant's total than scoring well on another test. Multiple regression (mentioned earlier in this chapter) is a special form of additive procedure in which an equation is derived, using statistical procedures, that best represents the linear relationship between some criterion variable and a set of predictor variables that have been weighted so as to maximize their relationship with the criterion. Many other approaches to weighting tests in an additive model have been suggested.[35]

Suppose that an HR specialist developed an additive model in which performance = 2 (problem-solving ability) + 3 (scheduling-and-planning ability) + 1 (interview rating). Three individuals apply for the job. They are given the problem-solving test and scheduling-and-planning test and then are interviewed by the HR manager, who rates each applicant on a 10-point scale. Their scores are as follows:

	Problem-Solving Ability	Scheduling-and-Planning Ability	Interview Rating
Joe	20	5	9
Al	5	15	7
Sally	25	4	5

Joe's predicted performance score is 2(20) + 3(5) + 1(9) = 64. Al's and Sally's predicted scores are 62 and 67, respectively. If one job opening exists, Sally would be hired.

Additive models are compensatory in that a high score on one characteristic can make up for a low score on another characteristic. Sally's high level of problem-solving ability compensated for her low levels of scheduling-and-planning and interview performance. The HR specialist must be certain that this assumption of compensatory characteristics is reasonable for the position being filled.[36]

Multiple Cutoff

If the assumption of a compensatory relationship among predictor variables is inappropriate, other decision-making methods are needed. In the **multiple cutoff method,** job applicants are required to have some minimum level of each predictor variable. Multiple cutoff is a noncompensatory model of selection. In the preceding example with Joe, Al, and Sally, suppose that a multiple cutoff procedure is used. Cutoffs for each of the three predictor variables are set so that the minimum level of problem-solving ability needed is 10, a score of 5 on the scheduling-and-planning test is required, and an interview rating of 5 is necessary. Using this approach, Joe, not Sally, would be hired, because Sally does not meet the minimum standard for scheduling and planning. An advantage of the multiple cutoff method is that it is conceptually simple and easy to explain to managers. In operation, however, it is more difficult than it seems.

If only a single predictor test is used, the cutoff score can be set using data on (1) how many job openings are likely to occur over a set time period, (2) how many job applicants are likely to apply during that period, and (3) the likely distribution of scores for applicants on that predictor test. The number of job openings and applicants can be obtained from company files on past openings and applicant flow. The likely distribution of test scores can be obtained from situations in which the test was given to other groups of job applicants. If twenty job openings will occur in the next year and 200 people are likely to apply for them, then the appropriate cutoff would be the 90th percentile score on the predictor—that is, the score that passes the top 10 percent of job applicants. Although this procedure, called the **predicted yield method,** is relatively easy when dealing with a single-predictor test, it becomes dramatically more difficult as the number of tests increases. When several tests are used, the setting of cutoffs tends to become a trial-and-error procedure.

In general, cutoff scores should enable the organization to select qualified candidates who are capable of learning the job and performing it in a safe, efficient manner; at the same time the firm should be sensitive to the possible adverse impact of a particular cutoff score on minority groups. Luckily for HR specialists, the courts have accepted the fact that cutoff scores are somewhat imprecise. Thus the courts do not require evidence that a person who scores 1 point below the cutoff would be a poor performer whereas an individual who scores 1 point above the cutoff would perform well. As will be discussed in more detail later in this chapter, the use of predictor score "bands" is acceptable. This is where all persons within a score band are considered as having the same score.[37]

Multiple Hurdle

In both additive and multiple cutoff approaches, decision making is nonsequential. Each applicant takes all predictor tests, and the organization then makes the decision about whom to hire. More often, however, selection is a sequential process, in which applicants pass through several selection stages (with individuals being rejected at each stage) before some are hired. The **multiple hurdle method** can be described as a sequential multiple cutoff approach. Using the preceding example with Joe, Al, and Sally, suppose that all three applicants take the scheduling-and-planning test. This would be the first hurdle in the selection process. Sally would not pass this hurdle and would be rejected. Joe and Al both clear this first hurdle and move on to the second stage of selection, the problem-solving test. Joe successfully meets the minimum level of problem-solving ability required; Al does not. Al would be rejected. The HR specialist then interviews Joe and eventually hires him.

One advantage of the multiple hurdle approach is that it can be more cost effective than either additive models or the multiple cutoff method. To illustrate, suppose that (for each applicant) the scheduling-and-planning test costs \$10, the problem-solving test costs \$25, and the interview costs \$50. Using an additive model or multiple cutoff method, the total cost of processing 100 applicants would be $\$85 \times 100 = \$8{,}500$. Suppose, instead, that a multiple hurdle approach is used. Of the hundred applicants, only fifty pass the first hurdle (scheduling and planning) to go on to the second, problem solving. Of these fifty, only ten go on to the interview. The cost to the organization of this selection system would be $\$10(100) + \$25(50) + \$50(10) = \$2{,}750$. This method represents considerable savings over additive models and the multiple cutoff method.

One problem with the multiple hurdle approach is restriction of range. In the first step of the process, the sample of job applicants is relatively unrestricted. As the applicants move through the process, more and more are rejected. By the time the final group of applicants reaches the last hurdle, they represent a very select sample of people, making validation studies of the final hurdles very difficult. Selection procedures that are sufficiently sensitive to differentiate among the individuals in this final group are difficult to design.

Profile Matching

The three preceding methods of decision making assume that more is better. Given two people who meet the minimum cutoff on some predictor, the individual with the higher level of that predictor will be selected. In additive models, the person with the highest predicted score will be hired. **Profile matching** assumes that there is some ideal level of predictor variables that an applicant should have rather than some minimum level that must be met or exceeded. In profile matching, groups of good and poor employees are identified. Individuals in these groups are measured on several likely predictor variables. If good performers score differently from poor performers on a characteristic, then the variable is useful in selecting good performers. Once several variables that differentiate between good and poor performers have been identified, an ideal profile of the successful employee is developed. For example, the ideal employee might have average intelligence, good social skills, a low need for dominance over others, and a high level of planning ability. In profile matching, the job applicants hired are those who most closely match the profile of a successful employee.

A comparison of the decisions made by profile matching, the additive model, and the multiple cutoff method is presented in Table 7.1. One common procedure for determining the degree of profile match is to sum the squared differences between an applicant's score on each predictor variable and the profile score for that variable. Thus Bill's profile-matching score would be $(16 - 20)^2 + (43 - 50)^2 + (6 - 5)^2 = 66$. If you calculate the match scores for George and Maria, you find that their scores are larger than Bill's. The smaller the score, the closer the match; therefore, Bill would be hired if the profile-matching procedure is used.

The results reached by these decision-making procedures are quite different. In deciding which procedure to use, the HR specialist must take into account whether a compensatory or noncompensatory model is more appropriate. The number of applicants and the cost of testing are also important considerations. It

TABLE 7.1

Hiring Decisions Based on Three Decision-Making Methods

	Test 1	Test 2	Test 3
Weights	.6	.3	.1
Average score of successful job incumbents	20	50	5
Minimum cutoff score set by job experts	15	45	5
George's scores	70	44	65
Maria's scores	50	47	45
Bill's scores	16	43	6

If only one job opening is available:

- An additive model would select George because his predicted performance of 61.7 is greater than Maria's 48.6 or Bill's 23.1.
- Multiple cutoff would select Maria because George and Bill do not meet the minimum cutoff for test 2.
- Profile matching would select Bill because his pattern of scores most closely matches that of successful job incumbents.

may be possible to combine several of the methods within a single selection system. Applicants could be given several tests early in the hiring process. These test scores could be combined using an additive model to decide which applicants go on to the second phase of selection. In the second phase, several more tests could be given and a multiple cutoff procedure used. In the third phase, a profile matching procedure could be employed to make the hire/no-hire decisions. All three steps of this process, taken together, form a multiple hurdle approach to selection.

Adjusting Test Scores of Minority-Group Members

As noted earlier, no tests are completely reliable or valid. They are, to varying degrees, imprecise predictors of an applicant's potential job performance. Additionally, there is some evidence that the validity and predictive power of selection tests may vary for majority- and minority-group members. In the past, some HR practitioners adopted the practice of adjusting the scores of minority-group members before selection decisions are made. These adjustments were made to enhance the diversity of the work force, affirmatively correct past hiring discrimination, or alleviate specific test bias or other imperfections in the testing process that tend to primarily affect minority-group members.

However, the adjustment of minority-group scores in most cases is illegal. Section 106 of the Civil Rights Act of 1991 prohibits the adjustment of test scores on the basis of race, color, religion, sex, or national origin. Thus adding bonus points to the scores of minority-group members, using separate cutoffs for different groups, or using top-down selection from separate lists to choose majority- and minority-group members are legally questionable procedures because they are directly based on the sex, race, color, or national origin of applicants. Rather than simply abandoning tests that have some level of bias, practitioners may do a number of things to keep the tests in their selection battery.[38] Test users can attempt to justify the use of a test based on "business necessity" (e.g., a test that measures an ability essential to safe performance of the job) or very obvious job relatedness. Practitioners may also modify a test to reduce its level of bias. For example, as noted earlier in the discussion of reducing subgroup differences in mean test scores, there is some evidence that performance on selection tests may be enhanced for minority subgroup members by using a computer or video-based method of testing rather than a paper-and-pencil format.[39] Another study found that highly structured interviews reduce differences in ratings between black and white applicants compared to less structured interview procedures.[40]

Another approach to rescuing tests with some level of bias is through the use of **banding.**[41] In a banding approach, people within a certain range of test scores are treated as if they had all scored exactly the same. In traditional approaches to banding, the range of scores (band width) depends on the reliability of the predictor test. If a test is highly reliable, then the band width is quite narrow; if the reliability is low, then the band is quite wide.

There are two general banding methods. In **fixed banding** a band is set relative to the initial highest score observed and the bands are fixed from that point on. Individuals are selected until a band is depleted; then persons from the next lower band are selected. Alternatively, **sliding bands** can be used—a new band is established each time the highest scoring person is hired or eliminated from the applicant pool. Sliding bands generally provide more opportunity for lower scoring individuals to be hired. However, the proportion of minority-group members in the applicant pool, the mean difference between minority- and majority-group members, and the standard deviations of the two group distributions will determine the level of impact banding has on minority-group selection.[42] For example, if the number of minority group members in the applicant pool is low and the mean difference between majority- and minority-group member test scores is large, banding may have little practical effect on the rate of minority selection. Minority members will still be unlikely to be selected. From a legal perspective, the critical issue when using banding is to base the hiring of individuals *within a band* on factors other than sex, race, color, or national origin.[43]

UTILITY OF A SELECTION SYSTEM

In evaluating a selection system, the HR specialist needs to know if the system has utility for the organization. **Utility** concerns the overall value of the selection system to the organization; it is analogous to cost-benefit analysis. The economic benefit of a properly developed selection system can be impressive. For example, in a situation where there are twenty-five new hires a year for five years, one analysis calculated the increased value of a structured interview procedure (compared to a traditional unstructured interview) as $1,121,250![44] The HR specialist should evaluate the potential utility of a selection system not only after it is ready to be implemented but also throughout its development. Asking the right questions at the right time can save time, effort, and money.

The traditional view of the utility of a selection system is that it is composed of three major factors: the efficiency of selection, the standard deviation of performance in dollars, and the costs associated with selection. These factors are discussed next. However, for an alternative view of factors that contribute to utility see A Different Point of View.

Efficiency of Selection

Whenever an organization makes hiring decisions, some of those decisions are correct and some are not. The results of a selection process are presented graphically in Figure 7.6a. This scattergram represents the relationship between *X*, some predictor variable, and *Y*, the known future performance of a group of job applicants. All applicants above the horizontal line are successful performers, whereas those below the line are unsuccessful. The vertical line represents a cutoff score on the predictor variable set by the organization. Individuals who score to the right of the cutoff would be hired; those to the left would not. Four types of selection decisions are represented in Figure 7.6a:

Quadrant A: **True-positive decisions,** in which the individuals who are hired turn out to be good performers

Quadrant B: **False-negative decisions,** in which individuals are not hired but would have turned out to be good performers (e.g., a National Football League team does not draft a particular college player, and later this player becomes a star running back for another team)

Quadrant C: **True-negative decisions,** in which individuals who would have been unable to perform the job are not selected

A DIFFERENT POINT OF VIEW

There's More to Utility Than Meets the Eye

Many authors have criticized the traditional view of utility for being too narrow in its focus on what factors affect utility. They also suggest that the definition of "utility" primarily in terms of dollar costs versus dollar benefits may be too restricting. This alternative view can be called the *multi-attribute approach* to utility analysis. In addition to the traditional factors affecting utility, there are other, more strategic influences on selection-program value. Craig Russell and his associates argue that fully understanding utility requires HR practitioners to take into account the "strategic impact" of personnel selection systems. They cite an example of this problem in a retail chain store. A new selection system resulted in the hiring of managers who were approximately $3,000 per quarter "better" than those previously hired. Unfortunately, the average retail store was losing $3,660 per quarter. Even with the new, improved selection system, the stores would remain unprofitable. Did the new selection system meet the strategic needs of the firm (i.e., make the stores profitable)? Obviously not!

The labor market also influences utility. A hiring procedure that selects high-performing employees has considerable utility. However, these employees may demand higher salaries, especially if such workers are scarce in the current labor market. The increased costs in salaries would reduce the overall utility of the hiring procedure. Another complicating factor is that employees hired using a selection procedure typically work for the firm for more than one year. Thus one selection procedure might result in hiring employees who are very productive early in their tenure with the firm but less so as time progresses. Another selection procedure might result in hiring employees who have less initial value to the firm but whose productivity increases the longer they stay. Which selection procedure has the highest utility over the life of the employee?

A fourth strategic issue that complicates our view of utility relates to the distribution of performance across employees. Traditional views of utility assume that the ideal situation for a firm is to have an employee work force comprised exclusively of high performers. This may be an inappropriate assumption. A situation creating optimal value to the firm may require a "mix" of performance levels among employees. If we draw an analogy to American football teams, good teams have a mix of skill levels among players. Someone must be willing to sit on the bench while others serve as first-string players. A team filled only with star athletes most likely would (1) cost the owners a horrendous amount in salaries and (2) be filled with such dissension and low morale that, in the end, the team probably would not be very good. Such a team needs a set of complementary abilities among its members.

The final issue included in the multi-attribute view of utility is that of adverse impact on minority-group members. In the traditional view of utility, the higher the validity of a selection test, the better its utility. Some scholars argue, however, that tests with high validity may also have high adverse impact on minority-group members. For example, a test with a correlation of .40 with job performance may be found to exclude 90 percent of minority-group members from selection. Another test may correlate .25 with job performance but exclude only 20 percent of minority-group members from the selection process. Which test has higher overall utility? These scholars suggest that, for many organizations, the test with lower validity but also lower adverse impact might be viewed as having higher overall value to an organization.

Sources: J. W. Boudreau, "Utility Analysis for Decisions in Human Resource Management," in *Handbook of Industrial and Organizational Psychology,* Vol. 2, 2nd ed., eds. M. D. Dunnette and L. M. Hough (Palo Alto, Calif.: Consulting Psychologists Press, 1991), pp. 621–745; John P. Campbell, "Modeling the Performance Prediction Problem in Industrial/Organizational Psychology," in *Handbook of Industrial and Organizational Psychology,* Vol. 2, 2nd ed., eds. M. D. Dunnette and L. M. Hough, (Palo Alto, Calif.: Consulting Psychologists Press, 1990), pp. 687–732; Calvin Hoffman and George Thornton III, "Examining Selection Utility Where Competing Predictors Differ in Adverse Impact," *Personnel Psychology,* Vol. 50 (2), 1997, pp. 455–470; Philip Roth and Philip Bobko, "A Research Agenda for Multi-Attribute Utility Analysis in Human Resource Management," *Human Resource Management Review,* Vol. 7 (3), 1997, pp. 341–368; Craig Russell, Adrienne Colella, and Philip Bobko, "Expanding the Context of Utility: The Strategic Impact of Personnel Selection," *Personnel Psychology,* Vol. 46 (4), 1993, pp. 781–801; and C. J. Russell and D. R. Domm, "On the Validity of Role Congruency–Based Assessment Center Procedures for Predicting Performance Appraisal Ratings, Sales Revenue, and Profit," paper presented at the fifty-fourth annual meeting of the Academy of Management, San Francisco, August 1990.

FIGURE 7.6
Efficiency in Selection Decision Making

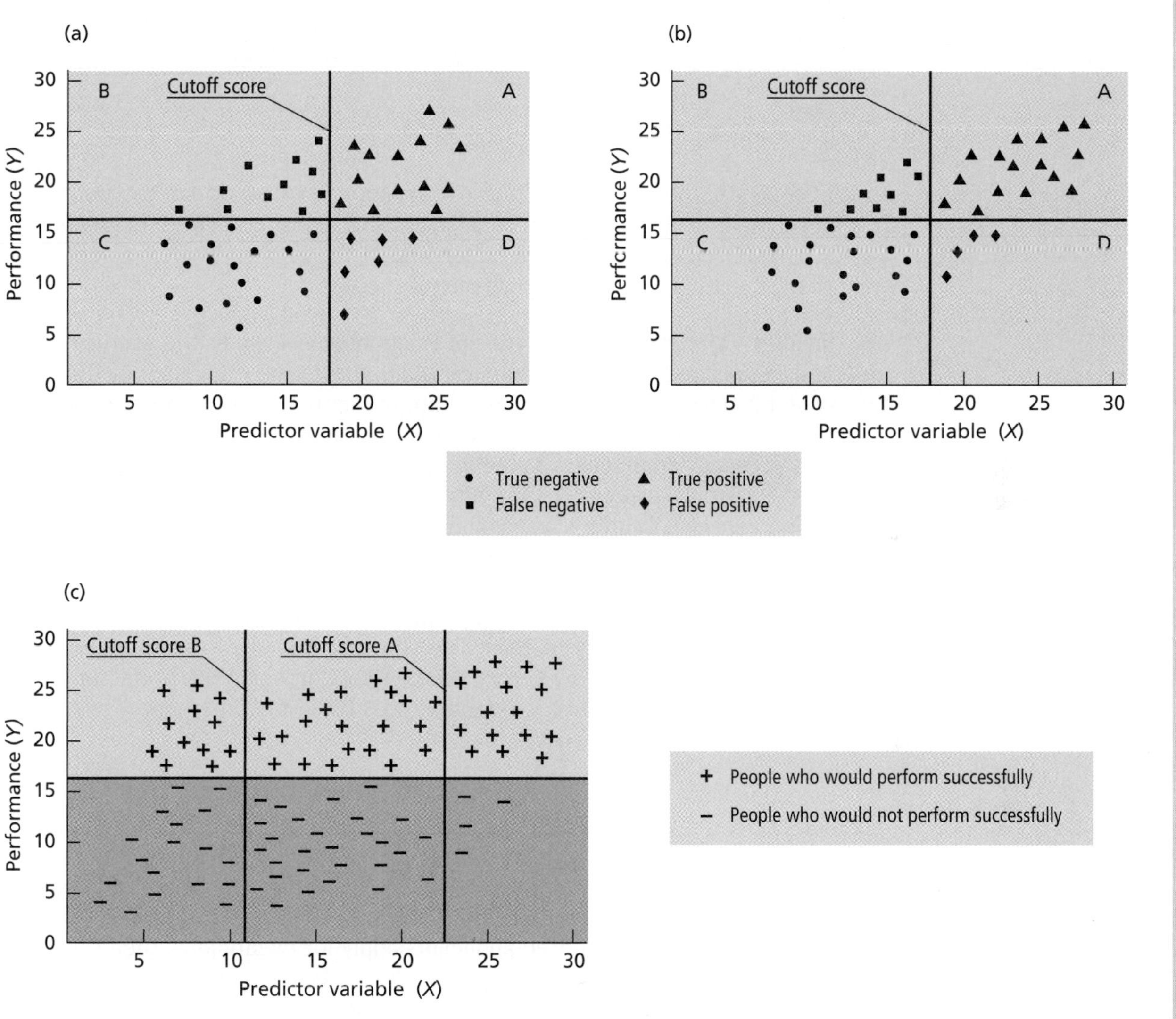

Quadrant D: **False-positive decisions,** in which individuals who are hired turn out to be poor performers

If no selection system is used (ignore the cutoff line) and the organization simply hires people on a random basis, the proportion of successful performers hired to unsuccessful performers hired would equal $(A + B)/(A + B + C + D)$. If scores on the predictor variable are used to select employees, the proportion of successful to unsuccessful persons selected would equal $A/(A + D)$. The efficiency of the selection system can thus be defined as

$$\text{Efficiency} = [A/(A+D)] - [(A+B)/(A+B+C+D)]$$

Efficiency of selection is the extent to which the system increases the proportion of successful selections. This definition assumes that no selection procedures are presently being used by the organization. If the organization is using some existing system, then the efficiency of the new system can be defined as:

$$E = [A/(A+D)]_n - [A/(A+D)]_o$$

where n = new selection system

o = old selection system

In this equation, the only goal of the organization is to maximize the number of true-positive decisions and minimize false-positive decisions. There is no concern for false-negative decisions. Three factors affect the efficiency of a selection system: validity, selection ratio, and base rate of success.

Validity The validity, or degree of relationship between the predictor variable and job performance (criterion) variable, affects the efficiency of the selection system.[45] The stronger the relationship, the more "valid" is the predictor and the greater is the accuracy of the selection decisions based on that predictor. Figure 7.6b presents graphically the relationship of validity to efficiency. (Figures 7.6a, b, and c use the same predictor cutoff and success points.) In Figure 7.6a, the correlation between X and Y is approximately .50; the efficiency of the predictor is .20. That is, with random selection, 50 percent of the persons hired are successful, but with a predictor test as the basis for selection, 70 percent of the persons selected are successful ($E = .70 - .50 = .20$). In Figure 7.6b, the validity of the predictor is .75, and the efficiency increases to .30. In other words, random selection yields successful employees 50 percent of the time, but using the predictor test increases the percentage of successful employees hired to 80 percent. Thus, as validity increases, so does efficiency.

Selection Ratio A second factor that affects efficiency is the selection ratio.[46] The **selection ratio (SR)** is defined as the number of job openings divided by the number of job applicants. If the organization has to fill twenty job openings and a hundred people apply for them, SR = 20/100 = .20. Figure 7.6c illustrates the relationship between the selection ratio and efficiency. Assume that the correlation between X and Y is .50. If a hundred applicants apply for twenty jobs, then the cutoff score (A) on the predictor test is set so that the top twenty applicants are selected. Of those selected, 80 percent will turn out to be successful employees, whereas if no selection test is used, only 50 percent of those hired will be good performers. If seventy job openings have to be filled from a hundred applicants, the cutoff score (B) is set to hire the top seventy applicants. In this case, about 54 percent of those selected will be successful performers. When SR = .20, $E = .80 - .50 = .30$. When SR = .70, $E = .54 - .50 = .04$. Thus, generally, as the selection ratio decreases, efficiency increases—if the validity of the test is constant. However, if SR is very small (e.g., 1 job and 1,000 applicants), the sheer cost of testing the applicants may outweigh any gain due to selecting the one right person for the available job.

Base Rate of Success The **base rate of success (BRS),** the third factor that affects efficiency, is the proportion of applicants who perform a job successfully when they are hired randomly, without the use of a selection system.[47] Suppose that Acme Paper Company decides to set up a selection system for the job of packer/stacker. The job requires an employee to place five-pound stacks of paper into boxes, seal the boxes with tape, and stack the boxes on top of other boxes. If Acme Paper hires people randomly, what proportion will be able to perform the job of packer/stacker? Nearly everyone. Acme Paper Company will gain very little from the use of a selection test. Suppose, instead, that Acme Paper Company is interested in developing a selection system for a job in which only 1 of 10,000 people performs successfully—that is, a job with a very low BRS. Although the efficiency of the system that could select this single person would be very great, Acme Paper faces a problem. It will probably be impossible to devise such a sensitive system. Generally, midlevel BRSs (.40 to .60) have the highest potential for increased selection efficiency.

The **Taylor-Russell tables** have been developed to show how efficiency varies as a function of validity, selection ratio, and base rate of success.[48] Table 7.2 contains a portion of these tables. The entries in the table represent the proportion of applicants selected who will be successful. Three different base rates of success are represented, along with four different levels of validity and selection ratios ranging from .05 to .95. Taylor-Russell tables can be used to determine the efficiency of a selection system compared with no selection system, or they can be used to compare one selection system with another. For each base rate of success, the row corresponding to $r = 0.00$ represents the use of no selection system, and each entry in this row equals the base rate. Suppose Acme Paper Company has no present selection procedures and that BRS = .50. If the company develops a selection test (test A) where SR = .40 and where validity = .25, the proportion of successful employees selected will rise to .60, and the efficiency will be .10 ($E = .60 - .50$).

TABLE 7.2

Examples from the Taylor-Russell Tables

Base Rate of Success (BRS)	Level of Validity	Selection Ratio (SR)										
.30	*r*	.05	.10	.20	.30	.40	.50	.60	.70	.80	.90	.95
	.00	.30	.30	.30	.30	.30	.30	.30	.30	.30	.30	.30
	.25	.50	.47	.43	.41	.39	.37	.36	.34	.33	.32	.31
	.50	.72	.65	.58	.52	.48	.44	.41	.38	.35	.33	.31
	.75	.93	.86	.76	.67	.59	.52	.47	.42	.37	.33	.32
.50	*r*	.05	.10	.20	.30	.40	.50	.60	.70	.80	.90	.95
	.00	.50	.50	.50	.50	.50	.50	.50	.50	.50	.50	.50
	.25	.70	.67	.64	.62	.60	.58	.56	.55	.54	.52	.51
	.50	.88	.84	.78	.74	.70	.67	.63	.60	.57	.54	.52
	.75	.99	.97	.92	.87	.82	.77	.72	.66	.61	.55	.53
.70	*r*	.05	.10	.20	.30	.40	.50	.60	.70	.80	.90	.95
	.00	.70	.70	.70	.70	.70	.70	.70	.70	.70	.70	.70
	.25	.86	.84	.81	.80	.78	.77	.76	.75	.73	.72	.71
	.50	.96	.94	.91	.89	.87	.84	.82	.80	.77	.74	.72
	.75	1.00	1.00	.98	.97	.95	.92	.89	.86	.81	.76	.73

Source: Adapted from H. C. Taylor and J. T. Russell, "The Relationship of Validity Coefficients to the Practical Effectiveness of Tests in Selection," *Journal of Applied Psychology*, Vol. 23, 1939, pp. 565–578.

If an alternative predictor test (test B) is available—where validity = .75, BRS = .50, and SR = .40—the proportion of successful employees selected will be .82. The increased efficiency of using test B instead of test A would be $E = .82 - .60 = .22$. Whether Acme Paper Company decides to use test A or test B might then depend on the cost of testing. If test A costs $0.50 per applicant to administer and test B costs $50 per applicant, the gain in efficiency might not be worth the additional cost of test B. Obviously, efficiency is not the only factor that determines the utility of a selection system.

Standard Deviation of Performance in Dollars

Utility models require another concept before utility can be calculated: the **standard deviation of performance in dollars (SDP$).** This variable is much more difficult to measure than the selection ratio or base rate. It assumes that an employer can put a dollar value on the performance of an employee. Many researchers have attempted to measure performance in terms of this dollar criterion.[49]

Proponents of the dollar criterion suggest that an organization should be able to measure the output of an employee and place a dollar value on that output (e.g., an employee produces 600 widgets that are each sold for a profit of $0.50). The organization also should be able to compute the cost of the employee to the company (e.g., salary and fringe benefits). The dollar value of the employee would be equal to the profits attributable to that employee minus the costs to the company of employing that person.

Unfortunately, few jobs allow for such an easy computation of costs versus profits. For example, how can an organization calculate the dollar value of a mid-level manager or of an assembly-line worker whose performance is directly affected by the actions of employees farther up the line? Sometimes cost-accounting procedures have been used to estimate the dollar value of employee performance. Other researchers have suggested that cost-accounting procedures are simply not appropriate. These researchers have developed more subjective procedures that assess SDP$ using ratings made by job experts.[50] One procedure has shown that the difference in dollar value of an employee performing at the 85th percentile level and an employee performing at the 50th percentile level is equal to about 40 percent of the salary of the job.[51]

The greater the standard deviation of performance in dollars, the greater is the utility of a given selection test. A **standard deviation** is a statistic that measures the variability of a distribution of scores. A large standard deviation of performance in dollars means that the dollar value of a high performer is much greater than that of a low performer. A low standard deviation of performance in dollars indicates little difference in the value of high and low performers. Selection systems developed for jobs in which there is a low standard deviation of performance in dollars will be of less overall utility than for jobs where performance differences reflect very different levels of employee dollar value.

However, the total payoff to the organization also depends on the number of persons hired. For instance, a valid test for selecting mail clerks may produce less payoff per hire than another test of equal validity used to select vice presidents. This is so because the value to the organization of hiring a good versus a poor mail clerk is probably substantially less than the value of hiring a good versus a poor vice president. However, if fifty good mail clerks are hired using a valid test, their combined contribution to the organization may exceed the utility gained by hiring one good vice president.

To summarize the preceding discussion, a test is more likely to have utility if the following conditions are present:

- Validity is high.
- The selection ratio is reasonably low.
- The base rate of success is moderate.
- The job has a large standard deviation of performance in dollars.
- Many positions are to be filled.

Costs Associated with Selection

Several costs are associated with any selection system. One of the most obvious is the **cost of testing,** which includes the value of testing materials and the dollar value associated with the time of individuals involved in setting up and running the selection process. Among the setup costs are those associated with developing, monitoring, and analyzing validation studies conducted prior to implementing a new selection system. These validation costs would include the costs of consultants or internal staff to develop the validation procedures, monitor the study as it progresses, and then analyze the data collected in the study, as well as the paid time of employees involved in the study. Given two selection procedures of equal validity, the test that costs less will provide the organization with the greater value for its investment in selection. Furthermore, if either the selection ratio or base rate of success is extremely low, the organization is faced with the cost of testing many applicants when only a few of them will actually be hired.

Another cost issue relevant to selection utility is the differential costs associated with making specific types of selection errors. Consider the costs of making a false-positive hiring decision—that is, hiring someone who is not a successful performer. These costs are (1) recruiting and testing costs, (2) induction and orientation costs, (3) training costs, (4) employee relations costs when the employee is fired, (5) costs associated with firing the employee (e.g., severance pay), and (6) any damage done by the employee while he or she was working (e.g., loss of clients, disruption of team functioning).

Analogously, false-negative hiring decisions also entail certain costs. These include (1) competitive advantage costs (e.g., the football team that fails to draft a particular player later loses in the Super Bowl because that player scores the winning touchdown against them) and (2) legal costs. False-negative applicants are often minority-group members or women. If these individuals file suit against the company and are able to prove that they really were qualified for the job, both actual and reputation costs to the company can be high. These types of costs associated with false-negative decisions are often referred to as the "social consequences" of selection decisions.[52] A selection procedure that has high dollar utility to the firm but that results in a lot of false-negative errors may be less desirable to management than one that has lower dollar utility but that minimizes false-negative errors.

Traditionally, HR specialists have tried to avoid false-positive errors but have paid little attention to false-negative ones. Thus HR specialists have set selection-test cutoffs to minimize the number of false-positive errors. If the costs associated with both types of selection errors are taken into account, however, employers can achieve the greatest utility by setting cutoff scores that reduce the overall number of both false-positive and false-negative hiring decisions.[53]

Utility: A Critical Issue in Strategic HRM

In Chapter 2 one of the defining features of strategic HRM was that HR practices must "add value" to the organization. Utility lies at the heart of this concept. In our discussion here, utility may seem a relatively easy aspect with which to deal. After all, in relation to selection systems, the concept of utility simply indicates that a selection system should:

- Make correct decisions about whom to hire and not hire
- Be developed only when there are enough applicants to warrant it
- Not be used for jobs that are really easy to do well
- Be used only for jobs where the level of performance is important from a financial perspective
- Not be too expensive to use

These "simple" concepts are, however, more difficult to assess than they seem to be. If we add to this picture other factors affecting the utility of a selection system such as those discussed in A Different Point of View on page 304, utility becomes a devilishly complex aspect of SHRM. Nevertheless, HR practitioners must attempt to assess the utility of their HR activities as best they can to provide some measure of the "value added" by HR procedures.

Summary of Key Points

A personnel selection system requires effective measurement, decision-making, and evaluation methods. The first requirement of a selection instrument is that it be a reliable measure. Reliability can be assessed over time, between raters, or within the context of a single test. If an instrument does not measure something consistently (reliably), it cannot possibly predict a criterion—so it cannot be valid. Validity is usually established by using one of the criterion-related methods (predictive or concurrent) or by proving that the content of the selection device matches critical job content. Additional concerns about validation include whether the results of the validation study are stable and useful in subsequent samples of applicants and whether the test predicts the job performance of minority- and majority-group members with equal accuracy and fairness.

Given valid measures, HR specialists must choose a decision-making strategy that takes into account the nature of the job, the number of applicants and job openings, and the costs of testing. Strategies include additive models, multiple cutoff, multiple hurdle, and profile matching. Approaches such as banding may be used in selection decision making in an effort to adjust individual scores so that the imprecise nature of testing can be taken into account.

For any selection system, the organization must make an attempt to evaluate the utility of the system. The organization should not wait until after the selection system has been developed and implemented to judge its likely utility. The company should evaluate data on probable validities, selection ratios, previous base rates of success, the standard deviation of performance in dollars, and the cost of tests before the development procedure begins. In addition, a number of broader strategic issues determine the value of a selection system to an organization. By analyzing these factors before spending the time, effort, and money to develop a selection system, HR specialists can more wisely develop and use selection procedures in their organizations.

The Manager's Vocabulary

additive models
banding
base rate of success (BRS)
coefficient alpha
coefficient of stability
concurrent validation
content validation
correlation analysis
cost of testing
criterion-related validity
cross-validation
differential prediction
differential validity
dynamic criterion
efficiency of selection
equitable treatment in testing
false-negative decisions
false-positive decisions
fixed banding
internal consistency
inter-rater reliability
item parameter drift
multiple cutoff method
multiple hurdle method
Pearson product moment correlation coefficient
predicted yield method
predictive validation
profile matching
random error
regression analysis
reliability
restriction of range
selection ratio (SR)
situational specificity
sliding bands
standard deviation
standard deviation of performance in dollars (SDP$)
systematic error
Taylor-Russell tables
test–retest method
true-negative decisions
true-positive decisions
utility
validation
validity
validity generalization

Questions for Discussion

1. Why are the Pearson correlation coefficient and regression analyses important statistical methods in human resource selection?
2. The reliability of a test indicates the extent to which random error influences test scores. Why is this factor of concern to the HR specialist who is setting up a selection system?
3. What are the different ways of assessing reliability?
4. What is validity?
5. How are the predictive and concurrent methods for criterion-related validation similar to or different from one another?
6. What is content validation? What sort of information might be sought in a content validation process?
7. Why should the results of a validation study always be "rechecked"?
8. If the proponents of validity generalization are correct, what implications does this assumption have in developing selection systems in organizations?
9. HR specialists can take either a compensatory or a noncompensatory approach to combining information about a job applicant when making a final hire/no-hire decision. How do these two approaches to decision making differ from one another?
10. What is banding? Why might an organization use it?
11. If there is a significant difference in the mean test score of majority and minority subgroups on a selection test, what actions could an HR practitioner take to eliminate or reduce this difference to ensure that the test is as fair to both subgroups as possible?
12. What is the utility of a personnel selection system? What factors influence the utility of a selection system?

Case 7.1
The Delta Intelligence Test

For the past ten years, Eastern Amalgamated Paper Company (EAPCO) has used the Delta Intelligence Test (DIT) to select employees for its unskilled production jobs. There are approximately 1,000 employees in these jobs, and the average turnover rate in EAPCO plants is high—about 35 percent each year. Pay for employees in these jobs is around $30,000 per year. Job applicants have been considered for employment only if they score above the national average score of all employees taking the DIT. This national average score is published yearly by Selection Systems, Inc. (SSI), the developer of the DIT, and is based on the test scores of more than 100,000 job applicants. This year's national average score was 22. Test–retest reliability data are also available from SSI. Some regular users of the DIT are asked to give the DIT to a sample of their employees twice, with the second administration following the first by one week. Typical test–retest data reported by SSI indicate coefficients of stability of around .85.

In analyzing the hiring patterns of the company, Paul Hawke, the new manager of human resources for EAPCO, noticed that a large number of black applicants failed the test. Out of every hundred white applicants, eighty-five passed the DIT, and approximately fifty were hired for positions in the company. In contrast, out of every hundred black applicants, thirty passed the DIT, and only ten were hired. Hawke was concerned about the potential legal implications of this hiring system. He found no evidence that systematic job analyses had been conducted on the unskilled production jobs or that EAPCO had validated the DIT against any measure of job performance. Validity data on the DIT were available from SSI. These data typically consisted of the results of concurrent validation studies conducted by other organizations using the DIT. Hawke decided it was time for an internal EAPCO validation study to be done.

Hawke contacted Validation Consulting, Inc. (VCI), a local firm, and hired it to conduct the study. One week later, Steven Peabody-Reynolds, a partner at VCI, arrived at Hawke's office. Peabody-Reynolds spent the morning discussing the current selection system with various managers and first-line supervisors. He returned one week later and presented Hawke with a plan for validating the DIT. The study was designed as a concurrent validation procedure. Peabody-Reynolds recommended using just the Kentucky plant in the study to save money. There were a hundred unskilled production workers at the Kentucky plant—ninety whites and ten blacks. Most of the employees had been with the company for quite some time and had not taken the DIT since their initial hiring. Fifteen of the employees in the proposed study (all white) had been at the Kentucky plant for eighteen years or more. Hawke agreed to the plan, and one week later the study was conducted at the Kentucky plant.

All employees in the study were given the DIT (time 1). One week later (to allow VCI to check the test–retest reliability of the DIT), the same employees were given the DIT again (time 2), and their supervisors were asked to rate their overall work performance using a 7-point scale where 1 = very unsatisfactory performer, 2 = unsatisfactory performer, 3 = satisfactory performer, 4 = good performer, 5 = very good performer, 6 = excellent performer, and 7 = truly exceptional performer. Performance ratings and DIT scores were returned to Peabody-Reynolds. He conducted statistical analyses on the data and reported to Hawke that he had found a significant correlation (.52) between DIT (time 2) scores and performance ratings. Hawke concluded that the DIT was related to job performance and was a valid test for use in screening employees to fill unskilled production jobs.

Six months after the study was completed, James Wilson, a black job applicant, took and failed the DIT. He then filed a charge of racial discrimination against EAPCO. The EEOC attempted to conciliate between Wilson and EAPCO, but the company refused to offer any sort of settlement that was acceptable to Wilson. The EEOC decided to file suit against EAPCO in federal court. Hiring data from EAPCO's personnel files clearly indicate a prima facia case of discrimination. However, the company is basing its case on the arguments that the use of the DIT is justifiable because DIT scores are related to job performance and that use of the DIT has substantial utility. With around 1,000 applications for unskilled production jobs each year, EAPCO feels that the DIT is an important, inexpensive ($20 per applicant) screening device in the hiring process. The data from the validation study conducted by Steven Peabody-Reynolds are presented in the table that follows. In the table, ID = the employee ID number; Race = race of the employee where 1= White and 2 = Black; Tenure = tenure at the Kentucky plant where 1 = less than eighteen years and 2 = eighteen years or more; DIT1 = Delta Intelligence Test score for the employee taken at time 1, DIT2 = Delta Intelligence Test score for the employee taken at time 2, and Perf. = the performance rating of the employee.

Through various legal maneuvers, the case against EAPCO has been delayed several times. During this period, Paul Hawke has resigned as human resource manager, and Bronwyn Downer, a local HR consultant with significant HR experience in a variety of industries, has been hired as Hawke's replacement. The CEO of EAPCO has indicated some concern as to whether Paul Hawke was handling the Wilson case in the best interests of the company. The CEO has asked Ms. Downer to review the situation and make a recommendation as to whether EAPCO should seek to settle the discrimination case with Wilson. EAPCO's lawyers have indicated that they believe Wilson will accept a settlement of around $200,000. The CEO has asked Ms. Downer, in making her analysis of the situation, to consider all the important issues. These include the following:

- The reliability of the DIT
- The validity of the DIT (including differential validity)
- The adequacy of the validation study conducted by Peabody-Reynolds
- The efficiency and utility of the current selection system based on the DIT

The CEO wants Ms. Downer to make a recommendation, based on her analysis of these critical issues, as to how EAPCO should proceed in the case brought against them by Mr. Wilson. Put yourself in the position of Ms. Downer. Conduct your analysis and make a recommendation, supported by sound arguments, to the CEO.

Option 1 Your instructor will provide you with the following information taken from the data collected by Steven Peabody-Reynolds:

1. The correlation (coefficient of stability) between DIT scores collected at time 1 and those collected at time 2
2. The correlation between DIT (time 2) and performance ratings for
   a. The total sample
   b. White employees (Race = 1)
   c. Black employees (Race = 2)
   d. Employees with eighteen years' experience or more (Tenure = 2)
3. The average DIT (time 2) score for each level of performance rating
4. The average performance of employees scoring above 22 on the DIT (time 2)
5. The average performance of employees scoring 22 or less on the DIT (time 2)
6. EAPCO's typical selection ratio
7. An estimate of the base rate of success for job applicants
8. An estimate of the standard deviation of performance in dollars (SDP$)

Option 2 Using the data provided in the following table, conduct your own statistical analyses. You will need to calculate all of the information listed in Option 1. Information necessary for estimating the selection ratio and SDP$ is given in the text of the case. Discuss with your instructor how you might use the performance rating data in the table to estimate the base rate of success. You can conduct your statistical analyses using any spreadsheet package such as Microsoft Excel or Lotus 1-2-3 or with a more advanced statistical analysis package such as SPSS for Windows. You also can do the necessary calculations on a hand calculator (it will take a while, though). Just look up the "computational formula" for a correlation in any standard statistics text. The rest is just averaging numbers for different groups.

ID	Race	Tenure	DIT1	DIT2	Perf.
143	2	1	21	20	2
144	1	1	18	18	6
145	1	1	19	20	7
146	1	1	19	18	5
147	1	2	22	19	4
148	1	1	16	17	4
149	1	2	21	19	5
150	1	1	17	18	6
151	1	2	21	20	6

ID	Race	Tenure	DIT1	DIT2	Perf.
152	1	1	21	20	5
153	1	1	20	19	5
154	1	1	20	20	4
155	1	2	22	19	3
156	2	1	23	22	2
157	1	1	13	15	3
158	1	1	19	20	5
159	1	1	24	25	5
160	1	2	18	18	2
161	1	1	23	23	6
162	1	1	23	24	6
163	1	1	19	18	3
164	1	1	19	19	5
165	1	1	19	18	2
166	1	1	14	25	6
167	1	1	28	29	5
210	1	1	22	24	6
211	1	1	23	23	6
212	1	1	27	28	5
213	1	1	26	25	6
214	1	1	24	25	5
215	1	2	33	32	7
216	1	1	25	26	6
217	2	1	20	21	3
218	1	1	31	30	4
219	1	1	28	30	6
220	2	1	20	22	3
221	1	1	23	25	4
222	1	1	20	22	5
223	1	2	31	25	7
224	1	2	26	22	6
225	1	1	23	24	6
226	1	1	20	20	3
227	1	2	22	24	5
228	1	1	16	15	3
229	1	1	25	24	6
248	1	1	20	20	3
249	1	1	16	15	3
250	1	2	17	18	3
251	1	1	21	22	6
252	1	1	18	16	3
253	1	1	22	22	4
254	1	1	27	28	6
255	1	2	22	31	6
256	1	1	21	20	4

ID	Race	Tenure	DIT1	DIT2	Perf.
257	1	1	23	22	4
258	1	2	20	20	4
259	1	1	13	14	3
260	1	1	23	25	6
261	1	1	18	20	3
262	1	1	19	22	5
263	1	1	18	18	3
264	1	1	25	27	6
265	1	1	21	20	3
266	1	1	24	24	6
267	1	1	17	15	3
268	2	1	21	21	2
269	1	1	20	22	5
270	1	1	22	21	5
271	1	1	25	24	6
272	2	1	20	25	1
273	2	1	17	18	1
274	1	1	20	23	6
275	1	1	24	19	5
276	1	1	20	20	5
277	1	1	19	23	6
280	2	1	22	22	3
282	1	1	21	20	4
283	1	1	21	22	5
285	1	1	22	23	5
286	2	1	20	19	3
289	1	1	24	24	5
290	1	1	22	22	5
297	2	1	18	20	3
300	1	1	20	19	4
430	1	1	15	13	3
432	1	1	20	18	6
433	1	1	25	28	6
434	1	1	27	29	5
435	1	2	27	23	6
436	1	1	22	24	4
437	1	1	30	30	5
439	1	2	28	18	5
440	1	1	26	25	5
441	1	2	26	25	5
442	1	1	30	28	6
443	1	1	31	30	6
444	1	1	18	17	4
445	1	1	18	18	4
446	1	1	21	22	6

Exercise 7.1
Finding Test Information on the Internet

It is clear from Chapter 7 that an HR professional needs to collect a substantial amount of information about potential selection tests before actually using the tests in hiring decisions. Many specialist consulting firms have developed selection tests for use by organizations, and many of these firms advertise their test products on the Internet. The following exercise will give you an opportunity to use the Internet to locate some of these test publishers and examine the types of information they provide about their selection-test products.

Instructions

1. Decide on some general occupational group that will be your focus in this exercise. For example, you might focus on hospitality, general clerical, computer programming, or midlevel managerial jobs.
2. Using the key words of "employment test publishers," use one of the Web search engines to identify several firms that publish employment tests. You can use other key words to help expand your search (e.g., personnel tests or personnel testing).
3. Identify firms that publish tests that seem of potential relevance to hiring people into your focal occupational group.
4. Identify which kinds of information these firms provide on the Internet about their test products (e.g., reliability information, cost of the tests, or type of people for whom the tests are appropriate).
5. From what you have learned in Chapter 7, what other types of information would you need to obtain from these employment test publishers before making a rational decision about whether their test would be useful in hiring people into the occupational group?

Exercise 7.2
Valid Selection on a Small Scale

Brian Warne is an entrepreneur who owns a small chain of seven restaurants. The restaurants serve family-style meals at moderate prices. Unfortunately, Brian is having a very difficult time with the managers of the outlets; they are not performing well. Brian has hired three new managers in the last eighteen months, and none of them is working out. Brian feels that they just cannot "put two and two together" the way he'd expect of any normal manager. They are unable to make decisions and seem to lack the ability to find quick and creative solutions to problems that arise in the restaurants. Brian is deeply concerned about the quality of the current managers and wants to improve the selection system so that in the future he can hire better managers for his existing restaurants and support his goal of opening three new restaurants each year.

On the weekend, Brian happened to run into a consulting industrial psychologist, Shane Lara, at a cocktail party. Brian explained his problem briefly and made an appointment to see Shane the next week. At the meeting, Brian stated that the managers' decision making was so poor it almost seemed they were mentally disabled, and he asked Shane whether it was possible to test future applicants for mental disability to avoid hiring any more losers.

You are Shane Lara. You decide that Brian needs a quick tutorial on some fundamental concepts about creating a legally defensible and valid selection system.

- Draw on all relevant material you have studied in this book to date to decide what to tell Brian.
- Recommend what steps should be taken next. How might it be possible to develop a valid selection system for such a small organization?
- You explain to Brian that your rates for doing the work are $250 per hour, and that approximately forty hours will be needed to complete the steps you recommend. What kinds of things should Brian consider when deciding whether hiring you to do the work makes sense from a utility perspective?

Notes and References

1. Richard Sisley, "The Recruitment Gamble: Improving the Odds," *Management,* Vol. 44 (4), 1997, pp. 22–24.
2. For a more detailed description of correlation and regression analysis, see J. Cohen and P. Cohen, *Applied Multiple Regression/Correlation Analysis for the Behavioral Sciences* (Hillsdale, N.J.: Erlbaum, 1975), pp. 73–122.
3. R. M. Guion, *Personnel Testing* (New York: McGraw-Hill, 1965), chap. 2.
4. J. C. Nunnally, *Psychometric Theory* (New York: McGraw-Hill, 1967), p. 172.
5. American Educational Research Association, American Psychological Association, National Council on Measurement in Education, *Standards for Educational and Psychological Testing* (Washington, D.C.: American Educational Research Association, 1999); and Robert Guion, *Assessment, Measurement, and Prediction for Personnel Decisions* (Mahwah, N.J.: Erlbaum, 1998).
6. L. J. Cronbach, "Coefficient Alpha and the Internal Structure of Tests," *Psychometrika,* Vol. 16, 1951, pp. 297–334.
7. American Educational Research Association et al., *Standards for Educational and Psychological Testing,* p. 184; and Guion, *Assessment, Measurement, and Prediction for Personnel Decisions.*
8. See these earlier versions of the *Uniform Guidelines on Employee Selection Procedures* (Washington, D.C.: Bureau of National Affairs, 1979); and Society for Industrial and Organizational Psychology, *Principles for the Validation and Use of Personnel Selection Procedures,* 3rd ed. (Bowling Green, Ohio: SIOP Publications, 1987).
9. Guion, *Assessment, Measurement, and Prediction for Personnel Decisions.*
10. Charles Lawshe, "A Quantitative Approach to Content Validity," *Personnel Psychology,* Vol. 28, 1975, pp. 563–575.
11. This example is based on reports from a validation study of computer adaptive testing by Randall Overton, Harvey Harms, Rogers Taylor, and Michael Zickar, "Adapting to Adaptive Testing," *Personnel Psychology,* Vol. 50 (1), 1997, pp. 171–185.
12. American Educational Research Association et al., *Standards for Educational and Psychological Testing,* p. 18.
13. Ibid., p. 19.
14. Paul Sackett, Roxanne Laczo, and Richard Arvey, "The Effects of Range Restriction on Estimates of Criterion Interrater Reliability: Implications for Validation Research," *Personnel Psychology,* Vol. 55 (4), 2002, pp. 807–825.
15. For a description of several other versions of the basic predictive validity procedure, see R. M. Guion and C. J. Cranny, "A Note on Concurrent and Predictive Validity Designs: A Critical Reanalysis," *Journal of Applied Psychology,* Vol. 67, 1982, pp. 239–244.
16. F. L. Schmidt, J. E. Hunter, and V. W. Urry, "Statistical Power in Criterion-Related Validity Studies," *Journal of Applied Psychology,* Vol. 61, 1976, pp. 473–485; Frank Schmidt, "Statistical Significance Testing and Cumulative Knowledge in Psychology: Implications for Training of Researchers," *Psychological Methods,* Vol. 1, 1996, pp. 115–129.
17. Gerald Barrett, Ralph Alexander, and Dennis Doverspike, "The Implications for Personnel Selection of Apparent Declines in Predictive Validities over Time: A Critique of Hulin, Henry, and Noon," *Personnel Psychology,* Vol. 45 (3), 1992, pp. 601–617; and C. Hulin, R. Henry, and S. Noon, "Adding a Dimension: Time as a Factor in the Generalizability of Predictive Relationships," *Psychological Bulletin,* Vol. 107, 1990, pp. 328–340.
18. American Educational Research Association et al., *Standards for Educational and Psychological Testing,* p. 20
19. G. V. Barrett, M. S. Caldwell, and R. A. Alexander, "The Concept of Dynamic Criteria: A Critical Reanalysis," *Personnel Psychology,* Vol. 38, 1985, pp. 41–56.
20. D. L. Deadrick and R. M. Madigan, "Dynamic Criteria Revisited: A Longitudinal Study of Performance Stability and Predictive Validity," *Personnel Psychology,* Vol. 43, 1990, pp. 717–744.
21. Kim-Yin Chan, Fritz Drasgow, and Linda Swain, "What Is the Shelf Life of a Test? The Effect of Time on the Psychometrics of a Cognitive Ability Test Battery," *Journal of Applied Psychology,* Vol. 84 (4), 1999, pp. 610–619.
22. Leaetta Hough, Fredrick Oswald, and Robert Ployhart, "Determinants, Detection and Amelioration of Adverse Impact in Personnel Selection Procedures: Issues, Evidence and Lessons Learned,"

International Journal of Selection and Assessment, Vol. 9 (1/2), 2001, pp. 152–194; and Society for Industrial and Organizational Psychology, *Principles for the Validation and Use of Personnel Selection Procedures* (Bowling Green, Ohio: Society for Industrial and Organizational Psychology, Inc., 2003)

23. Hough, Oswald, and Ployhart, "Determinants, Detection and Amelioration of Adverse Impact in Personnel Selection Procedures."

24. Ibid.; and Harold Goldstein, Kenneth Yusko, and Vasiliki Nicolopoulos, "Exploring Black-White Subgroup Differences of Managerial Competencies," *Personnel Psychology,* Vol. 54 (4), 2001, pp. 783–808.

25. R. E. Ployhart and M. G. Ehrhart, "Modeling the Practical Effects of Applicant Reactions: Subgroup Differences in Test-Taking Motivation, Test Performance, and Selection Rates," *International Journal of Selection & Assessment,* Vol. 10 (4), 2002, pp. 258–270; Philip Roth, L. Craig Bevier, A. Philip Bobko, Fred Switzer III, and S. Peggy Tyler, "Ethnic Group Difference in Cognitive Ability in Employment and Educational Settings: A Meta-Analysis," *Personnel Psychology,* Vol. 54 (2), 2001, pp. 297–330; and Ann Marie Ryan, "Explaining the Black-White Test Score Gap: The Role of Test Perceptions," *Human Performance,* Vol. 14 (1), 2001, pp. 45–75.

26. P. R. Sackett, N. Schmitt, J. E. Ellingson, and M. B. Kabin, "High Stakes Testing in Employment, Credentialing, and Higher Education: Prospects in a Post-Affirmative Action World," *American Psychologist,* Vol. 56 (4), 2001, pp. 302–317.

27. L. G. Humphreys, "Statistical Definitions of Test Validity for Minority Groups," *Journal of Applied Psychology,* Vol. 58, 1973, pp. 1–4.

28. Society for Industrial and Organizational Psychology, *Principles for the Validation and Use of Personnel Selection Procedures,* p. 32.

29. For example, see D. Broach, W. L. Farmer, and W. C Young, *Differential Prediction of FAA Academy Performance on the Basis of Race and Written Air Traffic Control Specialist Aptitude Test Scores* (Washington, D.C.: Federal Aviation Administration Office of Aviation Medicine, 1999), Report No. DOT/FAA/AM-99/16; and Maria Rotundo and Paul Sackett, "Effect of Rater Race on Conclusions Regarding Differential Prediction in Cognitive Ability Tests, *Journal of Applied Psychology,* Vol. 84 (5), 1999, pp. 815–822.

30. Paul Sackett, "The Status of Validity Generalization Research: Key Issues in Drawing Inferences from Cumulative Research Findings," in *Validity Generalization: A Critical Review,* ed. K. R. Murphy (Mahwah, N.J.: Erlbaum, 2003), pp. 91–114.

31. Jesus Salgado, Neil Anderson, Silvia Moscoso, Cristina Bertha, and Filip de Fruyt, "International Validity Generalization of GMA and Cognitive Abilities: A European Community Meta-Analysis," *Personnel Psychology,* Vol. 56 (3), 2003, pp. 573–605.

32. Kevin Murphy, "Impact and Assessments of Validity Generalization and Situational Specificity on the Science and Practice of Personnel Selection," *International Journal of Selection and Assessment,* Vol. 8 (4), 2000, pp. 194–206, at 194–195.

33. S. Messick, "Validity," in *Educational Measurement,* ed. R. L. Lim (New York: American Council on Education/Macmillan, 1989), pp. 13–103.

34. Cohen and Cohen, *Applied Multiple Regression/Correlation Analysis for the Behavioral Sciences,* pp. 73–122.

35. Winfred Arthur, Dennis Doverspike, and Gerald Barrett, "Development of a Job Analysis–Based Procedure for Weighting and Combining Content-Related Tests into a Single Test Battery Score," *Personnel Psychology,* Vol. 49 (4), 1996, pp. 971–985; and Kevin Murphy and Ann Shiarella, "Implications of the Multidimensional Nature of Job Performance for the Validity of Selection Tests: Multivariate Frameworks for Studying Test Validity," *Personnel Psychology,* Vol. 50 (4), 1997, pp. 823–854.

36. W. F. Cascio, E. R. Valenzi, and V. Silbey, "Validation and Statistical Power: Implications for Applied Research," *Journal of Applied Psychology,* Vol. 63, 1978, pp. 589–595; W. F. Cascio, E. R. Valenzi, and V. Silbey, "More on Validation and Statistical Power," *Journal of Applied Psychology,* Vol. 65, 1980, pp. 135–138.

37. David Arnold, "Seventh Circuit Rules Favorably Regarding Use of Banding," *Industrial/Organizational Psychologist,* Vol. 39 (1), 2001, p. 153.

38. Guion, *Assessment, Measurement, and Prediction for Personnel Decisions.*

39. David Chan and Neal Schmitt, "Video-Based versus Paper-and-Pencil Method of Assessment in Situational Judgment Tests: Subgroup Differences in Test Performance and Face Validity Perceptions," *Journal of Applied Psychology,* Vol. 82 (1), 1997, pp. 143–159.

40. Allen Huffcutt and Philip Roth, "Racial Group Differences in Employment Interview Evaluations," *Journal of Applied Psychology,* Vol. 83 (2), 1998, pp. 179–189.
41. Michael Campion, James Outtz, Sheldon Zedeck, Frank Schmidt, Jerard Kehoe, Kevin Murphy, and Robert Guion, "The Controversy over Score Banding in Personnel Selection: Answers to 10 Key Questions," *Personnel Psychology,* Vol. 54 (1), 2001, pp. 149–185.
42. Kevin Murphy, Kevin Osten, and Brett Myors, "Modeling the Effects of Banding in Personnel Selection," *Personnel Psychology,* Vol. 48 (1), 1995, pp. 61–84.
43. Arnold, "Seventh Circuit Rules Favorably Regarding Use of Banding."
44. Philip Roth and Philip Bobko, "A Research Agenda for Multi-Attribute Utility Analysis in Human Resource Management," *Human Resource Management Review,* Vol. 7 (3), 1997, pp. 341–368.
45. H. E. Brogden, "On the Interpretation of the Correlation Coefficient as a Measure of Predictive Efficiency," *Journal of Educational Psychology,* Vol. 37, 1946, pp. 64–76.
46. L. J. Cronbach and G.C. Gleser, *Psychological Tests and Personnel Decisions.* (Urbana: University of Illinois Press, 1965).
47. P. E. Meehl and A. Rosen, "Antecedent Probability and the Efficiency of Psychometric Signs, Patterns, or Cutting Scores," *Psychological Bulletin,* Vol. 52, 1955, pp. 194–216.
48. H. C. Taylor and J. T. Russell, "The Relationship of Validity Coefficients to the Practical Effectiveness of Tests in Selection," *Journal of Applied Psychology,* Vol. 23, 1939, pp. 565–578.
49. H. E. Brogden and E. K. Taylor, "The Dollar Criterion—Applying the Cost Accounting Concept to Criterion Construction," *Personnel Psychology,* Vol. 3, 1950, pp. 133–154; and Victor Catano and V. W. Johnston, "Estimating the Dollar Value of Performance for a Complex Military Occupation: The Influence of Supervisory Rank and Experience," *Military Psychology,* Vol. 5 (4), 1993, pp. 201–218.
50. W. F. Cascio and J. R. Morris, "A Critical Reanalysis of Hunter, Schmidt, and Coggin's 'Problems and Pitfalls in Using Capital Budgeting and Financial Accounting Techniques in Assessing the Utility of Personnel Programs'," *Journal of Applied Psychology,* Vol. 75, 1990, pp. 410–417; W. F. Cascio and V. Silbey, "Utility of the Assessment Center as a Selection Device," *Journal of Applied Psychology,* Vol. 64, 1979, pp. 107–118; S. F. Cronshaw and R. A. Alexander, "Why Capital Budgeting Techniques Are Suited for Assessing the Utility of Personnel Programs: A Reply to Hunter, Schmidt, and Coggin," *Journal of Applied Psychology,* Vol. 76, 1991, pp. 454–457; and J. E. Hunter, F. L. Schmidt, and T. D. Coggin, "Problems and Pitfalls in Using Capital Budgeting and Financial Accounting Techniques in Assessing the Utility of Personnel Programs," *Journal of Applied Psychology,* Vol. 73, 1988, pp. 522–528.
51. F. L. Schmidt, J. E. Hunter, R. C. McKenzie, and T. W. Muldrow, "Impact of Valid Selection Procedures on Work Force Productivity," *Journal of Applied Psychology,* Vol. 64, 1979, pp. 609–626.
52. S. Messick, "Validity," in *Educational Measurement,* ed. R. L. Lim (New York: American Council on Education/Macmillan, 1989), pp. 13–103.

CHAPTER 8

Assessing Job Candidates: Tools for Selection

- Overview of the Selection Process
- Application Blanks and Biodata
- Tests
- The Interview
- Physical Testing
- Reference and Background Checks
- Selecting Managers
- Criteria for Choosing Selection Devices

HR Challenge

The U.S. Border Patrol, part of the U.S. Department of Homeland Security, hires about 1,000 new agents each year. New hires attend eighteen weeks of intensive training at the Border Patrol Academy located at Federal Law Enforcement Training Center, Glynco, Georgia. To graduate, they must pass assessments in Spanish, immigration law, physical fitness, driver training, firearms training, and operations. Without careful selection, many candidates would fail to complete the training. This is very expensive and can result in serious understaffing problems in the field. In the past, there has been a particular problem with predicting whether prospective agents would be able to learn Spanish, which is required of all Patrol agents.

What kind of selection methods and practices would you recommend be used to select recruits for the Border Patrol Academy? In what order would you use them? How can you be sure that these practices are both legal and effective?

Selection follows the recruitment of a pool of job applicants. The selection process involves assessing the applicants to decide who will be hired. Ideally, the people who are hired will be better employees, on average, than those who are rejected. If the selection devices used to assess applicants have been chosen and validated properly, this goal should be realized. Chapter 8 discusses the benefits of proper selection, the selection process itself, and the range of selection devices available to human resource professionals.[1]

OVERVIEW OF THE SELECTION PROCESS

Organizations vary in the complexity of their selection systems. Some merely skim application blanks and conduct brief, informal interviews, whereas others engage in testing, repeated interviewing, lengthy assessment centers, background checks, and so on. Although the latter course is more costly per applicant, many benefits are realized from careful, thorough selection.

A prominent sociologist has pointed out that organizations need to have members who are both skilled and motivated to perform their organizational roles. Such members can be identified by careful selection or developed after hire by extensive training and socialization. Thus cursory selection may increase training and monitoring costs greatly, whereas spending more on the selection process will reduce these post-hire expenses by bringing well-qualified people into the organization to begin with.[2]

Benefits of Careful and Strategic Selection

The cost of hiring the wrong person can be very large. Removing a bad hire from the organization can be fraught with legal difficulties, and during that person's tenure the organization may suffer from lost sales and missed opportunities, dissatisfied customers, and low morale among disenchanted coworkers, to say nothing of wasted managerial time, training expenditures, and the inept employee's salary and benefit costs. To replace the poor hire, costs are incurred in advertising, selection, relocation, and training of a successor. One estimate of the cost of replacing a poor hire in a job requiring a high school education is $14,000, whereas for a job requiring a university graduate the cost is closer to $66,000. Yet another study suggests that the cost of hiring a bad sales representative is three times the rep's annual compensation, including salary, commission, expenses, and benefits.[3]

On the other hand, the dollar savings (utility) of appropriate selection procedures can be very large.[4] Researchers estimated that using cognitive ability tests for selection could yield the 5,000-member Philadelphia Police Department $18 million in savings from increased performance for each year's hires. Similarly, the U.S. government, by improving selection strategies for its work force of 3 million people, could save $15.6 billion annually.[5]

Selecting the right people is also critical to successful strategy implementation. The organization's strategy may affect job duties and design, and the job should drive selection. For instance, if a company plans to compete on the basis of prompt, polite, personalized service, service and communication skills should be featured in the job specification, and selection devices that can identify these skills in front-line applicants should be chosen. This argument is based on the assumption that the organization's strategy is clear, well known, and stable enough that people who fit the strategy can be selected. However, some scholars have pointed out that in a rapidly changing, uncertain world, not all organizations are able to stick to a single strategy long enough for staffing practices to catch up and bear fruit.

Another approach to strategic staffing suggests that human resources come first and drive strategy rather than the reverse: "Companies are beginning to realize that the foundation of their competitive strategy is the quality of their human capital."[6] Having a top-notch, flexible, innovative staff may be a competitive advantage that is more sustainable than technological or marketing advantages. Such people will be able to generate and implement a wide range of new strategies to respond quickly to a changing environment. This suggests hiring the best individuals one can find rather than hiring those who fit a specific job or strategy that exists today but may be gone tomorrow. "Best" in this new context means best in intelligence, best in interpersonal skills, and best in motivation. Many jobs in today's rapidly changing organizations involve self-management, continuous learning, teamwork, negotiation, and relationship management.

FIGURE 8.1
Typical Order in Which Selection Devices Are Used

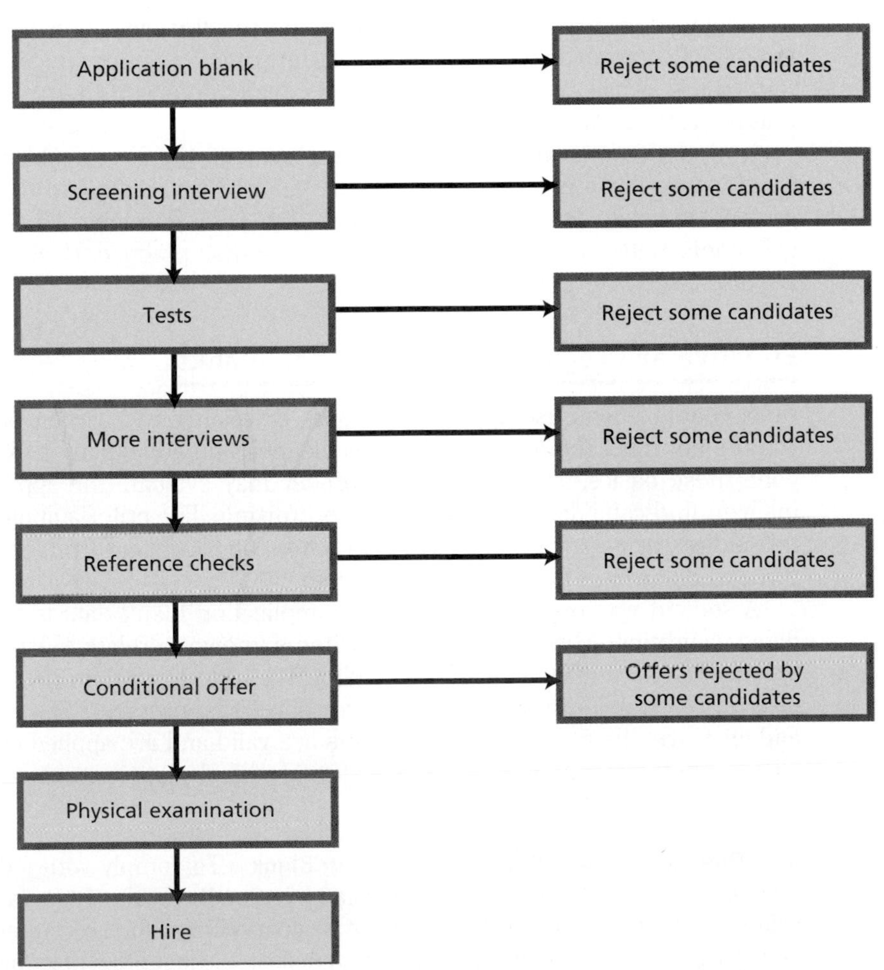

The Process of Selection

Most organizations use more than one selection device to gather information about applicants. Often these devices are used sequentially, in a multiple hurdle decision-making scheme: Candidates must do well on an earlier selection device to remain in the running and be assessed by later devices. Figure 8.1 shows a fairly typical order in which selection devices might be used. Less expensive devices such as application blanks and some written tests tend to be used for the initial screening of large numbers of applicants. More costly procedures such as interviews and assessment centers are used later in the process for candidates who have passed the earlier assessments. The HR department often takes responsibility for the first few hurdles, and one or more managers or supervisors interview the survivors of these hurdles and choose from among the short-listed candidates. Pending satisfactory reference checks, offers are made, medical examinations are completed, and hiring is finalized. The following sections explore the use and benefits of a variety of selection devices.

APPLICATION BLANKS AND BIODATA

The application blank or résumé represents the first selection hurdle for most jobs. Application blanks typically request information about education, work history, and skills, as well as the names and contact details of the applicant and several references. Most of the information requested is factual and can be verified, such as degrees earned or dates of employment. Application blank or résumé fraud is not uncommon. Some studies have found that a significant proportion of candidates falsify or slightly inflate some of their credentials.[7] Thus, seeking outside confirmation of important credentials is a wise practice. Background checks are discussed later in the chapter.

Effective and Legal Use of Application Blanks

Most organizations use application blanks or résumés to screen out candidates who do not meet the minimum job specifications on education or experience. Beyond these basics, a manager or HR officer may evaluate the applications informally to find candidates who look most promising. The criteria applied in making this judgment may not be explicit, job related, or consistent from one screener to the next and thus may pose a legal problem.

A second way organizations can use application blank data is to apply a validated weighting scheme, in which only items known to relate to later job success are scored and utilized in decision making. **Weighted application blank (WAB)** procedures have been shown to produce scores that predict performance, tenure, and employee theft. Because the weights are valid and are applied consistently to all applicants, this method of using application blank data is more defensible than an informal evaluation.

Questions to Avoid on an Application Blank To comply with federal employment laws, a firm must not discriminate in hiring on the basis of age, race, color, sex, religion, or national origin. This does not mean it is illegal for a recruiter to ask about age, religion, and so on in the selection process; it is just illegal for the recruiter or interviewer to act on this information in a discriminatory fashion. In the interests of playing it safe, however, interviewers should avoid questions about any of these subjects unless they are clearly job related. Further, such questions may be illegal under state or city human rights laws. One study of application blanks from eighty-eight organizations found that each blank included at least two "inadvisable" items; on average, there were 7.2 inadvisable items per application blank.[8]

The Americans with Disabilities Act of 1990 specifically prohibits asking questions about disabilities or the present or prior health status of candidates before making a job offer. Inquiries can be made about the candidate's ability to perform essential functions of the job but not broadly in regard to disabilities.[9] For example, if lifting is an essential feature of the job, candidates may be asked whether they are able to perform this function, but they may not be asked in general about "back problems" or past workers' compensation claims.

In addition, application blanks and interviews should avoid questions that appear neutral but cause disparate impact if used as selection standards—for example, questions about height and weight. Examples of inquiries that tend to exclude a disproportionate share of minorities are those concerning arrest record, type of military discharge, credit rating, and home ownership.[10] Table 8.1 lists some

TABLE 8.1

Problematic and Acceptable Questions of Job Candidates

Topic	Problematic Questions	Acceptable Questions
Name	Do you prefer the title Mr., Ms., Miss, or Mrs.? What is your maiden name?	Are your recent work records in another name?
Age	What are your age, birthdate, and year of high school graduation?	Are you age 18 (21) or over? (if legally required minimum age, such as to serve alcohol)
Marital/family status	What are your marital status, number and age of children, plans for having future children, child-care arrangements?	Only after hiring for insurance and tax purposes
Birthplace/national origin	Where were you born, when were you naturalized, what is your mother's tongue?	Do you have permission to live and work in the United States?
Organization membership	List all the clubs and organizations you belong to.	List memberships and offices held in relevant professional organizations.
Gender	What is your gender?	Only if bona fide occupational qualification.
Religion	What is your religion, what religious holidays do you observe? Please give pastor or rabbi's name as a reference.	Are you available to work the following required schedule?
Criminal record	List all arrests and convictions.	List job-related and recent convictions.
Physical characteristics	What are your height and weight? Please supply a photo.	Photo is permissible only after hire, height and weight only if bona fide occupational qualification.
Handicap	Do you have any handicaps? Provide full medical history. Have you received workers' compensation?	Explain job requirements and ask if candidate is able to perform them with or without reasonable accommodation.

permissible and inadvisable questions. Employers should bear in mind that they can and should ask any truly job-related questions. Accordingly, when interviewing candidates for the job of bank guard, the recruiter for the bank should ask about armed robbery convictions; when hiring for a job that involves control of money, the recruiter should ask about embezzlement convictions; and when selecting truck drivers, the recruiter should ask about traffic violations.

Constructing a Weighted Application Blank (WAB) There are several procedures for deriving valid application blank weighting schemes. In most of them, the first step is deciding which criterion to predict and defining high and low levels of this criterion. For instance, if tenure is the criterion of interest, "high" could be defined as staying at least two years after hire and "low" as leaving before the end of one year. The steps involved in deriving weights are described in Figure 8.2 and Table 8.2. The aim is to identify the questions and answers that reliably distinguish

FIGURE 8.2

Steps in Constructing a Weighted Application Blank

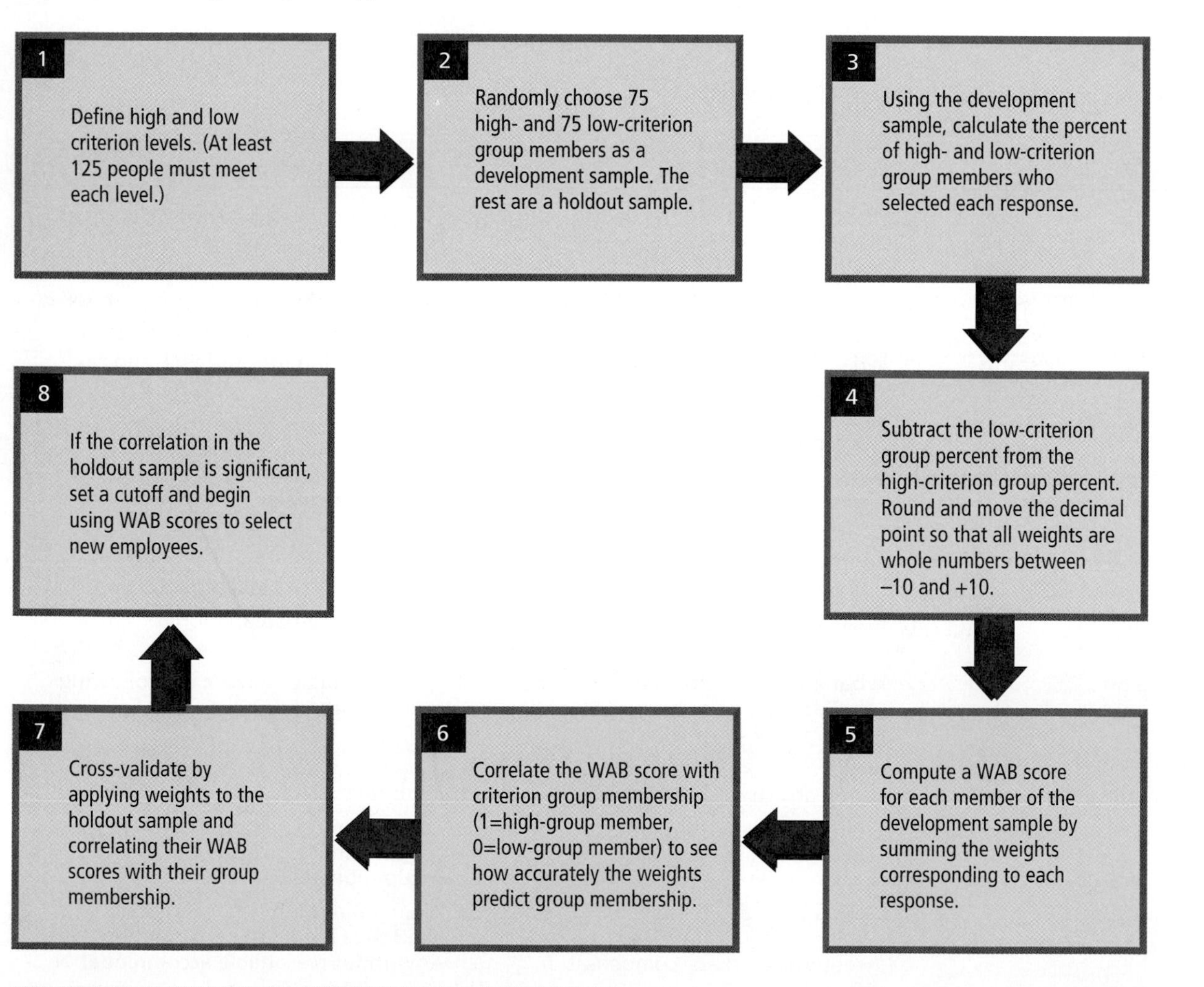

TABLE 8.2

Application Blank Responses and Corresponding Weights

	Percent of Responses			
	Criterion			
Items	Low	High	Difference in Percents	Weight
1. Number of jobs held in last five years:				
1	10%	50%	40	4
2	30%	30%	0	0
3 or more	60%	20%	-40	-4
2. Reason for leaving last job:				
Better opportunity	10%	40%	30	3
Dissatisfied	20%	10%	-10	-1
Laid off	40%	40%	0	0
Fired	30%	10%	-20	-2
3. Number of languages spoken:				
1	70%	60%	-10	-1
2	30%	30%	0	0
3	0%	10%	10	1

between the low- and the high-criterion groups. Before these questions are used to screen new applicants, the weights must be cross-validated to ensure that they are stable and generalizable to a different sample rather than merely the result of chance relationships in the development sample.

Relatively few organizations use WABs, even though WABs tend to be quite helpful in predicting performance. WAB development procedures can be quick and easy to apply, given a suitable sample size, though more complex biodata instruments require professional assistance for design and analysis.[11]

Using Biodata, Experience, and Accomplishment Records for Selection

Biodata is a term used to refer to any type of personal history, experience, or education information. Some organizations use a biographical information questionnaire instead of, or in addition to, the usual application blank. Biodata questionnaires may be much more detailed than application blanks and may be scored with keys based on very sophisticated statistical analyses.[12] Sample questions might include, "Do you repair mechanical things in your home, such as appliances?" "As a child, did you collect stamps?" "How many times did your family move while you were growing up?" One such biodata question—"Did you ever build a model airplane that flew?"—was almost as powerful a predictor of success in flight training during World War II as the entire U.S. Air Force battery of selection tests.[13] The life insurance industry trade association (LIMRA) has been developing and validating biodata instruments since the 1930s. Biodata characteristics that have been found helpful in selecting life insurance agents include educational attainment, financial success and stability, and "natural market"—that is, whether the candidate's friends and acquaintances are the type of people who tend to buy life insurance.[14] Some firms have moved to using Web-based biodata forms very early in the screening process. This can result in substantial cost savings as only suitably qualified candidates are admitted to the next step in the selection process.

Validity of Biodata In most studies that compare the validity of different types of predictors, empirically scored biodata are among the most effective predictors of subsequent job behavior.[15] Biodata have predicted success in occupations as diverse as U.S. Navy underwater demolitions expert, pilot, office worker, engineer, research scientist, salesperson, accountant, supervisor, and manager.[16] There are many potential explanations for the high predictive power of biodata:

1. *Nonfiction explanation:* Reporting on the verifiable aspects of one's past history reveals the truth about one's entire relevant past. A person's past history probably provides a sounder basis for predicting future behavior than does a short experience such as the interview, in which candidates are on their best behavior and can present an artificially positive picture of themselves.
2. *Relevant-item explanation:* Weighted application blanks and biodata questionnaires are valid because the only items that receive weights are those that are individually valid. Thus every item is related to the criterion. In contrast, in most tests only the total score is validated against the criterion. If some individual items do not predict job success, they are still part of the total score and may depress the overall validity of the test.
3. *Point-to-point explanation:* Biodata use past behavior to directly predict future behavior of the same type. There is no need to hypothesize or measure intervening constructs that may be imperfectly related to behavior, either past or future. For instance, high school grade point average (GPA) is the best predictor of college GPA. There is no need to measure an abstract trait such as verbal ability or intelligence to predict college GPA.[17] However, biodata instruments may measure important constructs or traits, and some construct-based methods of developing and validating the instruments do exist.[18] The next two explanations are examples of constructs that may be assessed in biodata instruments.
4. *Personality explanation:* Many biodata items serve as indicators of important personality traits such as "will to achieve" or conscientiousness.[19] These stable traits may both underlie past performance and contribute to future performance.
5. *Cognitive and noncognitive explanation:* Biodata measures may tap both cognitive and noncognitive traits and abilities. That is, past activities and achievements reflect skill and intelligence as well as personal qualities such as motivation or leadership.[20] Such broad measurement of a variety of important qualities may contribute to the predictive power of biodata instruments.

Experience and Accomplishment Records When candidates have job-related experience, appropriate measures of that experience can be valid predictors of subsequent job performance.[21] Rather than relying on informal methods of evaluating job experience and accomplishments, some organizations use content-valid

job experience questionnaires to screen candidates for technical and professional jobs. The usual procedure is to conduct a job analysis by the task inventory method to identify the most important or time-consuming tasks. The results of this job analysis are turned into questions about past work experience with each task or with each type of equipment used. Usually a content-evaluation panel of job experts verifies the job relatedness of each question.[22]

Applicants answer each question by rating the frequency, complexity, or recency of their experience with each task. To discourage inflated self-ratings, the questionnaire may ask applicants to list the names and addresses of people who can verify their experience with each task.[23] The California State Personnel Board is using an

FIGURE 8.3

Sample Dimension of an Accomplishment Record

Source: From Leaetta M. Hough, "Development and Evaluation of the 'Accomplishment Record' Method of Selecting and Promoting Professionals," *Journal of Applied Psychology,* February 1984, pp. 135–146. Copyright 1984 by the American Psychological Association. Reprinted by permission of the author.

Using Knowledge

General definition Interpreting and synthesizing information to form legal strategies, approaches, lines of argument, etc.; developing new configurations of knowledge, innovative approaches, solutions, strategies, etc.; selecting the proper legal theory; using appropriate lines of argument, weighing alternatives, and drawing sound conclusions.

Guidelines for rating In using knowledge, accomplishments at the lower levels are characterized by the resolution of legal issues that lack impact and importance or issues easily resolved by existing case law or precedent. At progressively higher levels, the accomplishments describe the formulation of increasingly complex legal strategies or the resolution of difficult legal issues that may be included in a case or procedures of substantial import. At the highest levels, accomplishments may refer to the assumption of significant personal responsibility in drafting major rules, regulations, proposed statutes, or like materials. Awards or commendations are likely.

Time period:

General statement of what you accomplished:

I was given the task of transferring our antitrust investigation of ___________ into a coherent set of pleadings presentable to ____________ and the Commission for review and approval within the context of the Commission's involvement in shopping centers nationwide.

Description of exactly what you did:

I drafted the complaint and proposed order and wrote the underlying legal memo justifying all charges and proposed remedies. I wrote the memo to the Commission recommending approval of the consent agreement. For the first time, we applied antitrust principles to this novel factual situation.

Awards or formal recognition:

none

The information verified by: ______________________________

Internet-delivered experience questionnaire as the first step in screening candidates for correctional officer and property appraiser (see http://exams.spb.ca.gov).[24]

When selecting experienced professionals to hire or promote, a firm may find it helpful to use a structured, content-valid **accomplishment record** for soliciting information about candidates' past specific achievements. A federal regulatory agency demonstrated the feasibility of this approach by developing such a form for promoting attorneys. The procedure followed in developing the form had several steps. First, a job analysis was performed using the critical incident method. Incidents were sorted into eight job dimensions, including research, oral communication and assertive advocacy, independent work, and use of legal knowledge. Three hundred current attorneys then provided examples of their accomplishments on each dimension. Next, a group of job experts used these examples to generate keys and guidelines for scoring applicant accomplishments. The agency trained evaluators to use the keys reliably. Finally, the agency applied the system to assess the accomplishments of attorneys seeking promotion. Figure 8.3 shows one of the dimensions from the accomplishment record, guidelines for scoring that dimension, and a specific accomplishment submitted by a candidate for promotion.[25]

TESTS

A test is a means of obtaining a standardized sample of behavior. Tests are standardized in content, scoring, and administration. That is, every time the test is given, its questions are identical or, in the case of tests with more than one form, equivalent. The scoring rules are constant. The administration is also the same: All test takers get the same instructions, have the same length of time to work, and take the test under similar conditions. Because tests are standardized, they provide information about job candidates that is comparable for all applicants. Other aspects of competing candidates cannot be compared so readily. For instance, grade point averages could be compared, but if candidates went to different schools or took somewhat different courses, this measure would not mean exactly the same thing for all applicants. In 2000 about 60 percent of companies surveyed by the American Management Association used some form of testing for selection.[26]

Testing and EEO

Before Title VII of the Civil Rights Act became law, quite a number of firms tested applicants for blue-collar jobs. General intelligence and mechanical comprehension tests were especially popular, although they were seldom empirically validated for the jobs in question. As Title VII was interpreted by the courts over the years, the doctrine of disparate impact developed, along with the requirement to demonstrate the job relatedness (validity) of tests that excluded a disproportionate share of minority applicants. When the courts rejected some reasonably well-conducted validity studies as inadequate, many firms simply gave up testing to avoid the possibility of litigation and the cost of further validation. Instead, they used unscored and subjective procedures for hiring and promotion decisions. However, in 1988 the U.S. Supreme Court ruled that informal and subjective methods of making employment and advancement decisions were not immune from legal challenge if they created adverse impact.[27] This ruling opened the door for a return to testing on the basis that a properly validated test would be more effective and stand up to legal challenge better than an informal decision-making procedure.

There have been allegations that tests are culturally biased and thus unfair to minority applicants. Ability tests often do display mean differences in scores across racial groups and are more likely to have an adverse impact than selection devices such as biodata forms, structured interviews, and personality tests.[28] Extensive research, however, indicates that properly constructed ability tests do predict the job performance of different races with equal accuracy.[29]

Cognitive Ability Tests

Properly chosen **cognitive ability tests** have been found to have high validity and utility in the selection process.[30] Such ability tests are usually developed by psychologists and are purchased by organizations from test publishers. Tests that are readily available cover such abilities as general intelligence, numerical ability, verbal ability, clerical ability, abstract reasoning, and mechanical aptitude.[31] There is substantial evidence that general cognitive ability, or intelligence, underlies scores on a number of different specific ability tests and that general cognitive ability is a good predictor of success in nearly all jobs.[32] It is a particularly effective predictor in more complex jobs.[33] Figure 8.4 shows sample items from two commercially available clerical skills tests. Some large organizations or industry associations employ psychologists to develop and validate tests suited to their particular needs, such as computer programming aptitude or stockbroker aptitude. The Partnerships for Strategic Success box provides an example of a language learning ability test developed by the Office of Personnel Management (the peak personnel body for U.S. government employment) for the U.S. Border Patrol.

Choosing Tests As discussed in Chapter 7, the procedure for empirical validation begins with job analysis, followed by selection of potential predictors, development of criteria, and collection and analysis of validity data. If validity is to be established nonempirically, via content validation or validity generalization, job analysis becomes even more important.

The selection of potential predictors is a critical step. Because so many published tests are available, a firm must collect information and consider it carefully before selecting several tests for a validation effort. The choice process should involve reading test reviews written by knowledgeable people and carefully reading the **test manual,** which details test content, purpose, administration, scoring, and developmental procedures.[34] Among the several characteristics to look for in a published test are the following:[35]

- *Specific ability assessed:* The test should measure aptitudes or abilities that make sense for the job in question. For instance, for the job of proofreader, a firm might try a test of spelling ability. Table 8.3 gives one test publisher's recommendations of which of their basic skills tests to use for different types of clerical jobs.
- *Reliability:* The test should have high internal consistency reliability and reliability over time. Tests that are used to make important decisions about individuals, as in the selection process, must have high reliability (at least .80 but preferably much higher).

FIGURE 8.4

Sample Items from Paper-and-Pencil Skills Tests

Source: Basic Skills Tests, available from Psychological Services, Inc., Glendale, Calif. Reprinted by permission.

(a) Sample item from the Coding Test of the Basic Skills Tests battery. The entire Coding Test contains 72 items with a time limit of 5 minutes.

The examinee reads a table containing a list of items that are classified into three or four categories; each item has a unique code. The examinee then reads a new set of information and selects the correct code from five alternatives for each item in the set.

Look at the sample table of codes. The sample table lists codes for Department, Department Size, and Travel Budget. Below the tables are two sample problems. In the problems, mark the circles below the codes that correspond to the information found in the table.

Department	Department Size	Travel Budget
31 Marketing	**1** 1–9 employees	**A** $500–999
25 Operations	**2** 10–19 employees	**B** $1,000–2,499
42 Accounting	**3** 20–39 employees	**C** $2,500–5,999
11 Research & Dev.	**4** 40–59 employees	**D** $6,000–7,999
28 Personnel	**5** 60 or more employees	**E** $8,000–10,000

Accounting Dept., staff of 10, $3,000 Travel Budget

Department	Department Size	Travel Budget
11 25 28 31 42	**1 2 3 4 5**	**A B C D E**
○ ○ ○ ○ ○	○ ○ ○ ○ ○	○ ○ ○ ○ ○

Marketing Dept., staff of 45, $9,500 Travel Budget

Department	Department Size	Travel Budget
11 25 28 31 42	**1 2 3 4 5**	**A B C D E**
○ ○ ○ ○ ○	○ ○ ○ ○ ○	○ ○ ○ ○ ○

(b) Sample item from the Following Written Direction Test of the Basic Skills Tests battery. The entire Following Written Directions Test includes 36 items with a time limit of 5 minutes.

The examinee reads a set of rules, determines what action to take in various situations by applying the rules, and selects the correct answer.

Read the sample set of rules below. Answer the problems by following the rules.

Rules for Determining Type of Mail Delivery

The three types of delivery used for mailing packages are regular, freight, and express. Listed below are the rules for deciding which type of delivery to use.

- ☐ Regular or freight delivery should be used for packages that do not need to be received urgently.
- ☐ Express delivery should be used for packages that need to be received urgently.
- ☐ Freight delivery should be used for large packages only.
- ☐ Regular delivery should be used for small packages only.
- ☐ Express delivery may be used for large or small packages.

	Regular	**Freight**	**Express**
Large crate, not urgent	○	○	○
Small package, urgent	○	○	○

PARTNERSHIPS FOR STRATEGIC SUCCESS

The Office of Personnel Management and the U.S. Border Patrol

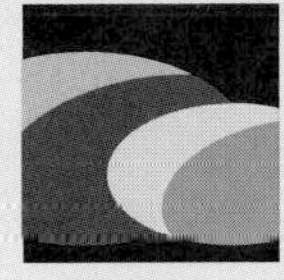

The HR Challenge asked how you would select potential agents for the U.S. Border Patrol. Clearly, this is an important task that must be accomplished well. A carefully developed and validated multistep process is used for this purpose.

First, candidates apply by Internet (http://staffing.opm.gov/BPA/) or telephone. There are some basic requirements used for screening at this step. Successful applicants must be U.S. citizens, under thirty-seven years of age, have a valid driver's license, not have been convicted of a crime that prohibits them from carrying a firearm in the future, and have an appropriate combination of work experience and formal education. Note that the age requirement is legal for law enforcement positions.

Those who pass go on to the second step, a written test. The test takes about four hours and includes several sections. One section requests further biographical information on experience and accomplishments. Another is a logical reasoning test. Border Patrol agents must read and understand complex legal papers and be able to make sound judgments on what may or may not be concluded from any given set of evidence or circumstances. This test assesses these abilities in a way that is independent of specific job knowledge, which will be learned later at the Academy. The final section of the test is related to Spanish. If the candidate already speaks Spanish, he or she takes a Spanish language proficiency exam. However, many candidates do not know the language and will need to learn it during their training.

The Office of Personnel Management worked closely with the Border Patrol to develop and validate a test of language learning ability, called the Artificial Language Test, for candidates who did not already speak Spanish. This test introduces a fictional language that has grammatical rules similar to Spanish. For instance, nouns are either feminine or masculine, rules describe how to make words plural, and verbs are conjugated in predictable ways. The test materials include a vocabulary list ("boy" is "ekaplek") and set of grammatical rules (the plural of a word is formed by adding "oz" to the singular form). Candidates study the rules and then may refer to rules and vocabulary lists as they answer the fifty-question test (Which of the following is the word for boys? A. ekaplekir, B. ekaplekoz, etc.).

The percent of recruits who failed training due to problems with learning Spanish was more than 11 percent before the introduction of the Artificial Language Test. The failure rate fell to under 3 percent when the test was used to select applicants. Given that about 1,000 candidates are trained each year at a cost of more than $18,000 each, it is estimated that approximately $1.5 million in training costs have been saved each year due to improved selection for language learning ability.

The third step for individuals who have passed the written test is a structured interview with a panel of interviewers. Interviewers assess candidates on judgment and decision making, emotional maturity, interpersonal skills, and cooperativeness and sensitivity to the needs of others. Candidates must receive a rating of Pass on each of these criteria to proceed to the final step.

The last step before the job offer is confirmed involves a medical examination that includes hearing and vision tests, a drug test, and a background investigation.

Sources: C. D. Diane, F. S. Brogan, and D. E. McCauley, *A Validation of Artificial Language Tests for Border Patrol Agents* (Washington, D.C.: U.S. Office of Personnel Management, 1991). Preparation Manual for the U.S. Border Patrol Test is available at: http://www.customs.gov/ImageCache/cgov/content/careers/border_5fpatrol/prep1896_2epdf/v3/prep1896.pdf

TABLE 8.3

Test Publisher's Recommendations for Combinations of Basic Skills Tests to Use for Various Types of Clerical Jobs

	General Clerk	Receptionist/ Information Clerk	Secretary Administrative Clerk	Figure Clerk	Typist Clerk	Bookkeeping Clerk	Machine Operator Clerk	Comprehensive Clerical Battery
BST 1 Language skills	✓	✓			✓			✓
BST 4 Computation			✓	✓	✓			✓
BST 5 Problem solving						✓		
BST 7 Following oral directions			✓					
BST 8 Following written directions							✓	✓
BST 9 Forms checking			✓		✓			
BST 11 Classifying	✓	✓						
BST 12 Coding						✓		✓
BST 15 Visual speed and accuracy				✓			✓	

Source: Brochure on the Basic Skills Tests, available from Psychological Services, Inc., Glendale, Calif. Reprinted by permission.

- *Proper test development procedures:* Developing a test entails much more than writing questions on a piece of paper. HR managers should check to be sure that thorough test-development procedures have been followed. These procedures include applying item and factor analysis, trying out successive versions of the test on large samples of people, developing evidence for the construct validity of the test, and compiling normative data on large samples of people.
- *Administrative ease:* HR professionals must consider whether the test can be given to a group of people at the same time or whether it must be administered individually; perhaps whether the test is suitable for administration by computer or over the Internet: how much time and expertise are required to administer, score, and interpret the test; and how much the test materials will cost.
- *Past success:* HR specialists should find out whether past empirical validation studies of the test on similar jobs have been successful, the extent to which the test is being used in the industry, and the record (if any) of the test in EEO proceedings.

Work-Sample and Trainability Tests

Work-sample and trainability tests ask applicants to do a portion of the job to demonstrate that they have the skill and knowledge to perform or the ability to learn the job. Because these tests are developed directly from a thorough job analysis and are double-checked by one or more panels of job experts, they are said to have a "point-to-point correspondence" with the job and are considered content valid. Properly developed tests of this sort need not be validated empirically. Note that the work-sample test does not need to represent the entire job. Some skills may be better assessed by an interview or an ability test. Simple job skills or information that can be readily taught to new hires also should not be included on the test.

Work-Sample Tests **Work-sample tests** are used when the applicant is expected to possess one or more crucial job skills—skills that the organization does not intend to teach to new hires. After conducting a thorough job analysis to verify the level and need for these kinds of skills, the HR specialist can construct a carefully standardized work-sample test. For example, if 80 percent of the job of secretary requires typing manuscripts from handwritten copy, then the work-sample test should include typing from handwritten copy. The tester should give all candidates the same copy, equipment, instructions, and length of time to complete the test. Scoring standards that have been developed in advance should be applied consistently for all applicants.

In one application of work-sample testing, a company developed a set of four role plays for selecting telemarketing representatives. Candidates for telephone sales jobs made two simulated "cold calls" and returned two calls to hypothetical clients who had already indicated interest in the product. The supervisor playing the role of the client was trained to follow each of the four scripts fairly closely. This supervisor and another trained supervisor who also listened to the calls rated the candidate on communication, social sensitivity, sales ability, and overall performance.[36] In a concurrent validation design, a composite of these ratings significantly predicted telephone sales performance. See Table 8.4 for further examples of work-sample tests.

Work-sample tests also may be paper-and-pencil tests of job knowledge. For instance, the HR specialist might develop a written test assessing knowledge of electrical standards to help select building inspectors. Some firms have used technical reading comprehension tests to assess candidates applying for jobs in which employees need to obtain critical information from manuals or other written sources.[37] Others have had very good results from what are called **situational judgment tests.** Using critical incidents from the job and a panel of subject matter experts, a set of questions is developed to assess whether candidates make good choices when faced with typical dilemmas on the job.[38] Two items from situational judgment tests are shown in Figure 8.5. Situational judgment tests have been found to add to the accuracy of selection over and above tests of job knowledge, cognitive ability, job experience, and the personality trait of conscientiousness.[39]

Trainability Tests **Trainability tests** are used for semiskilled jobs in which the candidate is not expected to know the skill when applying for the job. They are intended to assess the ease with which a candidate can learn the type of skill required by the job. The first part of a trainability test consists of a carefully standardized period of instruction during which the trainer introduces a task, explains and demonstrates each step, and has the candidate perform the task once or twice while being coached. The second portion is the actual test, during which the candidate performs the task several times without coaching. The trainer observes and

TABLE 8.4

Work-Sample Tests

	Test of Skill	Definition
Construction superintendent	Blueprint reading	Locate errors in blueprints
	Scrambled subcontractors' test	Correctly order the desired sequence of thirty building subcontractors needed to construct a building from start to finish.
	Construction-error recognition test	Locate errors (twenty-five in all) built into a small test building.
	Planning and scheduling exercise	Matching employee skills to job and schedule demands in a written exercise.
	Structured interview	Questions focusing on security of tools and materials, site safety, relationships to building inspector and other regulators, and ethical issues in dealing with subcontractors.
Police emergency operator/dispatcher	Listening, recording, and spelling test	Listen to tape-recorded emergency calls and correctly record important information on forms provided.
	Memory test	Recall information on locations and activities of several patrol units after information has been presented orally.
	Phone call simulation	Role play handling calls from distraught callers in simulated emergency situations. Callers are role played with experienced operators trained to behave consistently with all applicants. Scores are based on skill and judgment in calming the caller and eliciting the most important information.

Sources: For construction superintendent example, David D. Robinson, "Content-Oriented Personnel Selection in a Small Business," *Personnel Psychology,* Spring 1981, pp. 77–87. For police emergency operator/dispatcher example, Neal Schmitt and Cheri Ostroff, "Operationalizing the 'Behavioral Consistency' Approach: Selection Test Development Based on a Content-Oriented Strategy," *Personnel Psychology,* Spring 1986, pp. 91–108.

uses a checklist to record errors. At the conclusion of the performance period, the instructor rates the overall trainability of the candidate.

Figure 8.6 is an instructor's evaluation form used in trainability tests for overlock sewing machine operators who have been taught to sew a simple bag. Trainability tests have also been used successfully for electronic assemblers, bricklayers, carpenters, lathe operators, milling machine operators, and a variety of simple U.S. Navy jobs. In addition, they have been used to select current employees for advanced training on new digital equipment in the telephone industry.[40]

Advantages of Work-Sample and Trainability Tests Work-sample and trainability tests have many advantages. First, when empirical validation studies have been conducted, the predictive power of work-sample tests has been found to be quite high.[41] Trainability tests have shown moderate validities with job success, though the strength of the correlations sometimes diminishes over time, indicating that eventually even less trainable employees are able to learn the job. Second, work-sample and trainability tests can be developed and used even for very small samples, unlike tests requiring empirical validation. Third, these tests tend to have

FIGURE 8.5

Items from Situational Judgment Tests

Source: J. A. Weekley and C. Jones, "Further Studies of Situational Tests," *Personnel Psychology,* Vol. 52, 1999, pp. 679–700.

For each question, applicants are to indicate which response they believe is best under the circumstances, and which response is worst. Points are gained for correctly identifying best and worst choices.

From a test for the job of retail clerk:

A customer asks for a specific brand of merchandise the store doesn't carry. How would you respond to the customer?

a) Tell the customer which stores carry that brand, but point out that your brand is similar.
b) Ask the customer more questions so you can suggest something else.
c) Tell the customer that the store carries the highest quality merchandise available.
d) Ask another sales person to help.
e) Tell the customer which stores carry that brand.

ANSWER: Best is (b), worst is (d)

For a job in a hotel:

You are the only bellcap at the front of the hotel because your coworker just left for a short break. A guest asks you to get him some fresh towels. What would you do?

a) Ask the guest to inform someone inside of the hotel of the request.
b) Leave your door to get the towels for the guest.
c) Wait until your coworker returns and then take care of the request.
d) Explain to the guest that you are unable to leave your post.
e) Get someone else to help the guest and follow-up.

ANSWER: Best is (e), worst is (a)

less adverse impact than cognitive ability tests.[42] Fourth, they possess excellent face validity; thus applicants who do poorly can readily understand why they are being rejected and probably will not file complaints of unfair treatment. Finally, because work-sample and trainability tests embody important aspects of the job, they can serve as realistic job previews. Candidates who do not enjoy the work sample may choose to turn down a job offer, thus sparing the organization the expense of hiring, training, and then losing an employee to early turnover.[43]

Personality Tests

About 15 percent of companies in a recent American Management Association survey reported using personality tests for selection.[44] Unlike the tests already described, personality tests do not have *correct* answers. The intent of these tests is to elicit *self-descriptive* answers. Measures of personality must be developed as carefully as measures of cognitive ability. In evaluating such measures, one would

FIGURE 8.6

Instructor's Scoring Sheet for a Trainability Test

Source: From I. T. Robertson and R. M. Mindel, "A Study of Trainability Testing," *Journal of Occupational Psychology,* June 1980, pp. 131–138. Reprinted by permission.

Overlock Trainability Assessment Form

Factory ______________________ *Assessor* ______________________

Name ______________________ *Date* ______________________

	Bag 1	Bag 2	Bag 3
Aligns wrong seam first			
Presents incorrect corner			
Forgets to position cloth correctly			
Forgets to align seam			
Puts thumb on top			
Does not use fingers of left hand correctly			
Does not use fingers of right hand correctly			
Seam not completed in one sew			
Does not remember cutting method on last seam			

Other errors (please describe)

Total errors

Overall ratings

Positioning of hands good	always	generally	sometimes	rarely
Positioning of feet good	always	generally	sometimes	rarely
Notices errors and subsequently corrects	always	generally	sometimes	rarely

Please circle appropriate letter.

A Extremely good. The assessor would expect him/her to become a very good machinist in a short time.

B Fairly good without being outstanding. The assessor would expect him/her to reach 100 performances in a reasonable time.

C Good enough for simple work. The assessor would expect him/her to become a steady worker on a simple machine or task.

D Would have difficulty in training. The assessor would expect him/her to take longer training and to perform a simple task.

E Would not be trainable. Even with a great deal of attention, he/she would not make the grade, even on an easy operation.

expect to see a complete test manual detailing extensive development work utilizing large samples, followed by evidence of validity against job-performance criteria. A number of personality tests on the market amount to little more than quackery, so potential buyers must take care.

Personality inventories are sets of objectively scored questions or statements to which the test taker responds *yes* if the item is self-descriptive and *no* if it is not. Some personality inventories are long—up to 400 questions or more—and some ask extremely personal questions about religious beliefs, sexual fantasies, and other non-work-related issues that an interviewer would never even consider asking. Applicants may justifiably feel that their privacy has been invaded when asked to take some personality tests. In the case of *Soroka v. Dayton Hudson Corporation,* Target stores in California agreed to cease using a personality test for security guards because some of the questions seemed non–job related, invasive, and potentially discriminatory.[45] Despite this decision and the apparent irrelevance of isolated questions on some tests, remember that well-developed personality tests sum up a large number of questions to produce reliable scores on well-defined dimensions of personality. Items that lack face validity for job performance may still be helpful in assessing important basic personality traits, and these traits may predict behavior on the job.

A number of well-developed personality inventories are available. Most give scores on several traits, such as extraversion, self-esteem, authoritarianism, neuroticism, and conscientiousness. Even though these inventories are scored objectively, their proper interpretation may require special training. Users should also be aware that tests that specifically diagnose mental illnesses rather than relative standing on normal personality traits may be illegal in preemployment screening under the Americans with Disabilities Act.[46]

Historically, predictive validities have been low and inconsistent for personality tests. Low validities were attributed to (1) the transparency of some personality inventories, which may invite efforts to "fake good" by applicants eager to be hired; (2) the "shotgun" approach of attempting to find relationships between many personality dimensions and job performance without giving much thought to the actual demands of the job; and (3) the fact that very few jobs require one and only one type of personality for success. There may be several ways to do the same job well, perhaps by being diligent or creative or persuasive. Thus for many years industrial psychologists recommended that personality tests not be used for employee selection. Since 1990, however, a number of studies have shown that appropriately chosen personality measures often do help predict interpersonal, motivational, and noncognitive aspects of job success, although cognitive ability measures remain the best predictors of task performance.[47] Because personality measures are usually uncorrelated with ability measures, adding an appropriate personality test to a selection battery of ability tests may well increase the overall validity of the selection system.

Advances in understanding the dimensions of personality are bearing fruit in the selection arena. Until about 1990, there was no agreement on the structure of personality, hence little consensus on which of many possible personality traits might be useful in selection. Since 1990, psychologists have learned that much of the variance in personality is accounted for by the **"Big Five" personality dimensions** defined in Table 8.5. When past selection research is summarized into these five factors, some personality dimensions are consistently related to success in most jobs. For instance, conscientiousness is related to success in job training,

TABLE 8.5

The Big Five Personality Dimensions

1. Extraversion ↔ Introversion
2. Friendliness, agreeableness ↔ Hostility, noncompliance
3. Neuroticism ↔ Emotional stability
4. High conscientiousness, high dependability, and high self-control ↔ Low conscientiousness, low dependability, and low self-control
5. High intellect, high openness to experience and new ideas ↔ Low intellect, low openness to experience and new ideas

Source: Table designed from material appearing in J. M. Digman, "Personality Structure: Emergence of the Five-Factor Model," *Annual Review of Psychology,* Vol. 41, 1990, fig. 1, p. 421.

to job performance, and to personnel data such as absenteeism and disciplinary actions in virtually all jobs.[48] The Big Five (except agreeableness) are modest but significant predictors of managerial and leadership success.[49] There is also evidence that personality-type measures of "customer service orientation" can be useful in predicting the performance of service employees.[50] The correlations between personality and desirable behavior on the job tend to be small to moderate in size but are of use when combined with appropriate ability measures.

Emotional Intelligence

The concept of **emotional intelligence** has received a great deal of attention from scholars, consultants, and the popular press over the past decade. Some conceptualizations of emotional intelligence treat it as a personality trait that can be measured by self-report (see sample items in Table 8.6); others view it as a set of skills that should be assessed more objectively. There are many definitions of emotional intelligence, ranging from virtually anything that is not a cognitive or physical skill, including many already well-studied aspects of personality, to a more nar-

TABLE 8.6

Sample Items Assessing Emotional Intelligence as a Personality Trait

When I experience a positive emotion, I know how to make it last.
I find it easy to understand the nonverbal messages of other people.
When I am in a positive mood, I am able to come up with new ideas.
I use good moods to help myself keep trying in the face of obstacles.
I am able to control my temper and handle difficulties rationally.
I am sensitive to the feelings and emotions of others.
I have a good sense of why I have certain feelings most of the time.

Source: Items adapted from N. S. Schutte, J. M. Malouff, L. E. Hall, D. J. Haggerty, J. T. Cooper, C. J. Golden, and L. Dornheim, "Development and Validation of a Measure of Emotional Intelligence," *Personality and Individual Differences,* Vol. 25, 1998, pp. 167–177; and C. Wong and K. S. Law, "The Effects of Leader and Follower Emotional Intelligence on Performance and Attitudes: An Exploratory Study," *Leadership Quarterly,* Vol. 13, 2002, pp. 243–274.

rowly defined set of specific social and self-management competencies. Emotional intelligence involves the ability to recognize emotions in oneself and others, manage emotions in oneself and others, and use emotions appropriately in solving problems.[51] The construct is new and still being developed, but it may have some potential to predict aspects of work performance above and beyond cognitive ability. Some scholars contend that emotional intelligence is especially important for success at higher levels of management.[52]

Integrity Tests

Many employers today are interested in screening out job candidates who may be likely to steal from them. Estimates of the cost to American business of employee theft, pilferage, or unexplained inventory shrinkage range up to $200 billion per year.[53] Employers who subscribe to the "bad apple" theory believe that rejecting potential thieves and hiring only honest employees will greatly reduce losses. This view is only partly correct: Research has shown that post-hire factors such as pay equity, job satisfaction, and opportunity to steal also play a role in determining actual theft.[54]

Traditionally, two types of **integrity tests** have been used to identify potentially dishonest employees: polygraph examinations and paper-and-pencil tests. The **polygraph,** or lie detector, measures and graphs respiration, blood pressure, and perspiration while the person being tested answers questions. Doubts about the validity of the polygraph and horror stories of honest individuals who were discharged or denied employment because of erroneous polygraph results have led to legal restrictions on the use of polygraphs.

The Employee Polygraph Protection Act of 1988 prohibits private-sector employers from using polygraph tests on applicants or employees, with a few exceptions. Companies that provide security services or manufacture and distribute controlled drugs may continue to use polygraphs; polygraph tests may also be used for investigating specific crimes against the employer, such as theft or embezzlement. In no case, however, may a company discharge or discipline an employee solely on the basis of polygraph results.[55]

Since polygraph testing has been restricted, paper-and-pencil integrity tests have increased in popularity. There are two types of written integrity tests on the market: overt integrity tests that assess attitudes toward theft and ask about past dishonest behavior, and personality-oriented integrity tests that focus on broader traits such as dependability, rule-following, impulse control, and conscientiousness. Most available tests have satisfactory reliability and reasonable validity in identifying individuals who have been caught stealing in the past or who will be caught stealing in the future.[56] Nordstrom, Inc. and Home Depot use the Reid Report, an overt integrity test, to select store employees. These companies find that the test helps identify candidates who will cause problems or be likely to quit if hired.[57] Personality-oriented tests predict not only theft but also composite measures of other types of counterproductive behavior, such as abuse of sick leave, excessive grievance filing, drug use at work, and rule breaking.[58] These behaviors are more common than outright theft and can cost organizations a great deal of money and aggravation. Another behavior that these measures predict—workplace violence—is discussed in Chapter 14.

Technological Advances in the Administration of Selection Devices

Technology and the Internet are having a major and growing impact on the way organizations select employees using the selection devices mentioned previously. An increasing number of assessment devices can be administered over the Internet rather than requiring job candidates to come to a central testing site. Biodata forms and experience records are well suited to being administered and instantaneously scored over the Internet as the first step in selection. Some firms also conduct ability testing over the Internet but often require a follow-up test for qualifying individuals in a monitored testing center. For example, a Web-based Call Center Aptitude Test for preselection of call center agents has recently been developed and validated. The test consists of a biodata form, a cognitive speed test, a personality inventory, and a multimedia situational judgment test.[59] Those who pass the test continue on to additional selection steps before final hiring decisions are made. This type of innovation is generating substantial savings in time and money for both companies and applicants.[60]

Another way technology can facilitate testing a particular skill is to have the computer create a customized test for each test taker by selecting items from the item pool on the basis of the correctness of past answers. For instance, if a moderately difficult item is answered correctly, the computer will next present a more difficult item. If the test taker fails this item, the computer will next choose an item between the first and second in difficulty. Called **adaptive testing,** this method quickly zeros in on the person's true ability level by selecting the most diagnostic items for the person being tested. This method can provide an accurate test score in about half the number of items needed to produce an equally accurate score via nonadaptive methods in which everyone answers all questions.[61]

THE INTERVIEW

Virtually all organizations use interviews as a selection device for most jobs. Most commonly, candidates are interviewed by at least two people before being offered a job. Typically, an HR specialist and the individual who will be the candidate's immediate supervisor conduct these interviews. For managerial and professional jobs, it is common for the candidate to have a third interview with one or more higher level managers.

A recent trend in interviewing is to conduct preliminary interviews with distant candidates via videoconferencing or telephone. International executive search firm Korn/Ferry has been using videoconferencing for several years and finds that it speeds up searches by two to four weeks, as well as saving travel costs.[62] The Gallup Organization has developed and validated procedures for structured telephone interviewing for a number of jobs. Their procedures allow all screening interviews for large multisite organizations to be conducted centrally from a single office using highly trained interviewers and scorers.[63] However, job candidates tend to prefer face-to-face interviews to those mediated by technology.[64]

Because the interview is so popular, one might expect that it is a highly useful selection device. Interviews can be valid if done properly, but this is not always the case. The next two sections consider the reliability and validity of the interview.

Reliability of the Interview

In the interview context, reliability is consensus, or agreement, between two interviewers on their assessments of the same candidates. This is called **inter-rater reliability**. Research shows that it is usually rather weak. Interviewers might agree fairly well on the overall assessment of a candidate (e.g., one is outstanding, another is a dismal prospect) and on factual issues (e.g., the candidate has or has not worked on a similar job in the past), but interviewers seem unable to agree on more subjective or future-oriented characteristics (e.g., whether the candidate is creative or will be able to work without close supervision).[65]

Validity of the Interview

Historically, the predictive validity of the interview has been thought to be quite low. Research in the 1970s and 1980s suggested that the average validity of the interview for predicting job performance was as low as .14.[66] However, recent research has suggested that some interview procedures can yield reasonable validity.[67] Interviews also tend to capture somewhat different aspects of a person than do cognitive ability tests, so that a properly conducted interview can add to the prediction of job performance over and above tests.[68]

Still, many interviews are relatively ineffective. What can go wrong in the typical interview to cause interviewers to make inaccurate predictions? It seems that interviewers often commit judgmental and perceptual errors that can compromise the validity of their assessments.[69]

- **Similarity Error** Interviewers tend to be positively predisposed toward candidates who are similar to them (in hobbies, interests, or personal background). They tend to be negatively disposed toward candidates who are unlike them. When the dissimilarity or similarity is not job related, it may still color the interviewer's judgment and introduce invalid variance into the interviewer's ratings.

- **Contrast Error** When several candidates are interviewed in succession, raters tend to compare each candidate with the preceding candidates rather than with an absolute standard. Thus an average candidate might be rated as higher than average if he or she comes after one or two poor candidates and as lower than average if he or she follows an excellent interviewee.

- **Overweighting of Negative Information** Interviewers tend to see their job as a search for negative or disqualifying information about candidates. Thus they may overreact to a single minor piece of negative information. In addition, they are more likely to change their initial opinion of a candidate from positive to negative than from negative to positive.[70]

- **Race, Sex, and Appearance Bias** Interviewers may be more or less positive about a candidate on the basis of the candidate's race, sex, or age. In general, interviewers rate blacks more favorably than similarly qualified whites and females lower than comparable males. There is some evidence that sex interacts with the nature of the job. For example, interviewers assess men and women who are applying for jobs traditionally held by their sex positively but less positively when these same individuals are applying for jobs held predominantly by the opposite sex.[71] Finally, there is evidence of a "beautyism" bias—that is, physically attractive male and female candidates receive more positive ratings.[72] Overweight candidates are viewed less favorably, particularly if they are female.[73]

First Impression Error Some interviewers tend to form a first impression of candidates rather quickly, based on a review of the application blank or on the first few moments of the interview. Even though this impression is based on relatively little information about the candidate, their initial judgment may be resistant to change as more information or contradictory information is acquired. In addition, interviewers may choose subsequent questions based on the first impression in an attempt to confirm the positive or negative impression.[74] The result is **first impression error.**

Traits Rated and Halo Error **Halo error** occurs when the interviewer's overall impression or strong impression of a single dimension spreads to influence his or her rating of other characteristics. For instance, if a candidate impresses the interviewer as being very enthusiastic, the interviewer might tend to rate the candidate high on other characteristics, such as job knowledge, loyalty, and dependability. This is especially likely to happen when the interviewer is asked to rate many traits or to rate traits that are difficult to observe in a short interview. Research has shown that only a few traits, such as intelligence and sociability, are accurately assessed in the typical interview.[75]

Nonverbal Factors Many studies have demonstrated that interviewers are influenced by nonverbal factors in the interview. Candidates who wear appropriate clothing, make eye contact, smile, show animation, speak fluently, and modulate their voices make more positive impressions on interviewers.[76] For jobs involving technical skill and low contact with others, this interviewer tendency probably weakens validity. On the other hand, it may contribute valid variance to the prediction of success in jobs involving a great deal of public contact.

Faulty Listening and Memory An interviewer may miss a substantial portion of what the interviewee says because of poor listening habits or preoccupation with what to ask next. Immediately after the interview, an interviewer who has not taken notes may have forgotten up to 75 percent of the information given by the candidate.[77] It is therefore recommended that interviewers take notes during the interview and review them when making a decision.[78]

Differences between Interviewers Evidence suggests that interviewers selecting for the same job differ from one another in many ways, including the following:

- Different selection criteria and weights. They look for different qualities in applicants and disagree on which qualities are most important.
- Different definitions of what the ideal candidate looks like.
- Different recommended hire rates. Some recommend most of the candidates they see; others are very choosy.
- Different decision strategies. Some are analytical and consider many separate criteria in reaching a final decision; others are more intuitive and rely mainly on overall impressions.
- Different abilities to build rapport with the candidate. Those who build more rapport are able to elicit more information during the interview.[79]

These differences contribute to low inter-rater reliability and undoubtedly reduce the validity of the interview as a selection tool. Despite all of these problems, interviewers tend to believe they are "good judges of character" and "can spot a winner at fifty paces." Managers like using interviews because they feel interviews allow them more flexibility and control over selection decisions compared with more rigid and quantitative methods such as ability tests and biodata questionnaires.[80]

Types of Interviews

Interviews can be classified by their degree of structure or the extent to which interviewers plan the questions in advance and ask the same questions of all the candidates for the job. Three types of interviews, based on three degrees of structure, can be defined: unstructured, semistructured, and structured interviews.

Unstructured Interviews In the **unstructured interview,** questions are not planned in advance, and interviews with different candidates may cover quite different areas of past history, attitudes, or future plans. Unstructured interviews have low inter-rater reliability and overall have the lowest validity. Because questions are not planned, important job-related areas may remain unexplored, and illegal questions may be asked on the spur of the moment. Interviewers may also rely too much on single favorite questions of dubious validity, such as "If you were in a salad, what type of vegetable would you be?" Unstructured interviews are unfortunately still widely used but are generally not recommended for evaluating job candidates.[81]

Semistructured Interviews The **semistructured interview** involves some planning on the part of the interviewer but also allows flexibility in precisely what the interviewer asks candidates. This permits interviews to be customized to explore the differing backgrounds and aspirations of candidates. Semistructured interviews may be used for higher level positions or for final interviews for short-listed candidates following more structured interviews. Semistructured interviews are likely to be more valid than unstructured ones but not as valid as highly structured interviews.

In an excellent book on semistructured interviewing techniques, Thomas Moffatt suggests that interviewers plan their objectives in terms of what they hope to learn about the candidate and then use a "cone" approach to elicit this information.[82] A cone is a mini-interview on a particular topic, such as the candidate's last job, feelings about working in groups, or military experience. Each cone is introduced by a very broad question, which is followed by more specific questions on aspects of the topic. These questions may vary from interviewee to interviewee but all pertain to the topic of the cone. The interviewer might plan to include four to eight cones in an hour-long interview.

In the cone approach, most questions are designed to elicit a reasonably lengthy response. As in all types of interviews, leading questions are avoided. Leading questions are those that imply a correct answer, such as "You don't plan to remain a secretary for your whole life, do you?" Finally, yes–no and short answer questions are used sparingly because they tend to turn the interview into an interrogation and do not provide as much useful information as longer answers. Figure 8.7 is a partial example of a cone on the candidate's last job.

FIGURE 8.7
Cone Method of Semistructured Interviewing

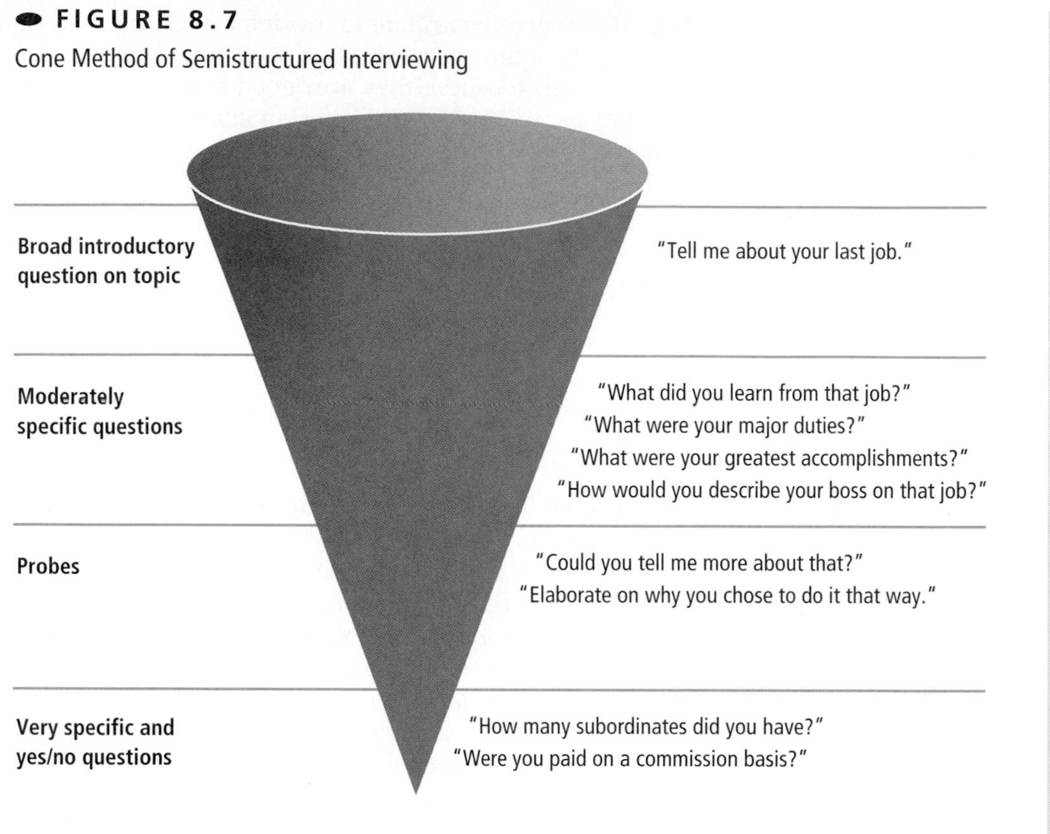
Broad introductory question on topic
"Tell me about your last job."
Moderately specific questions
"What did you learn from that job?"
"What were your major duties?"
"What were your greatest accomplishments?"
"How would you describe your boss on that job?"
Probes
"Could you tell me more about that?"
"Elaborate on why you chose to do it that way."
Very specific and yes/no questions
"How many subordinates did you have?"
"Were you paid on a commission basis?"

Structured Interviews Research shows conclusively that the highest reliability and validity are realized in the structured interview.[83] In a **structured interview,** questions are planned in advance and are asked of each candidate in the same way. The only difference between interviews with different candidates might be in the probes, or follow-up questions, if a given candidate has not answered a question fully. Interviews that feature structured questions usually also provide structured rating scales on which to evaluate applicants after the interview. At least three types of structured interviews have been discussed in the research literature: the patterned interview, the situational interview, and the behavior description interview.

In the traditional **patterned interview,** questions tend to focus on past work activities, education, career goals, and so on. The questions may be job related, or they simply may be questions that interviewers typically ask, such as "What are your strengths and weaknesses?" or "What do you plan to be doing five years from now?" This type of structure does increase inter-rater reliability and may prevent the interviewer from talking too much, but it does not necessarily result in high validity.

High predictive validity depends on eliciting from the candidate relevant information on the skills, abilities, and attitudes needed for job success. The **situational interview** and the **behavior description interview** attempt to collect and properly evaluate job-relevant information. Both of these structured approaches begin with a thorough job analysis. Interview questions are based directly on the job analysis and are double-checked by job experts so that the interview is demonstrably content valid. In some cases, empirical validation work is also conducted to identify interview questions and answers that best differentiate between successful and unsuccessful employees.[84] The situational interview focuses mainly on future-oriented questions about what the candidate *would do* if faced with a hypothetical job situation, whereas the behavior description interview asks about past behaviors—what the candidate actually *did do* in past situations similar to those likely to occur on the job. The evidence to date suggests that both approaches work, though behavior description questions may be superior for predicting success on higher level jobs.[85]

Situational interview questions ask the candidate what he or she would do in a particular job situation. For instance, the interviewer might ask a candidate for camp counselor how he or she would respond to a child who was very homesick or who was disruptive.[86] As the job experts develop the questions, they also write good, average, and poor sample responses. This answer key helps interviewers give more reliable ratings of candidates' answers. Usually a panel of three or more interviewers conducts all the interviews. The interviewers do not attempt to reach a consensus on each candidate. Instead, their independent ratings are averaged to produce an overall score for each candidate.

The behavior description approach to structured interviewing is based on the assumption that "the best predictor of future performance is past performance in similar circumstances."[87] Traditionally, interviewers often applied this principle by asking candidates about experience with tasks similar to those of the job for which they are applying. However, interviewers often fall into the "experience equals excellence fallacy" by assuming that if a candidate has performed a task at all, he or she has performed it well. Behavior description interviewing overcomes this problem by requiring candidates to give specific examples of how they performed job duties or handled job problems in the past.

Job experts derive behavior description interview questions from the critical incidents technique of job analysis. Suppose, for example, that the job expert, using this technique, identifies one dimension of a sales job as "establishing new client contacts." Then, based on this dimension, a behavior description item for experienced candidates might be, "Tell me about the most difficult new client contact you have made in the last six months." After the candidate has described a specific incident, the interviewer's next questions might be, "What was the obstacle you faced? What did you say when you were stumped? What did you do to overcome the difficulty?"[88] Research has shown that behavior description interviews are much more valid than unstructured interviews.[89] Behavior description interviewing has been widely adopted in organizations throughout the English-speaking world. In fact, Chili's restaurant chain is administering a written form of behavior description interview online to candidates for restaurant manager jobs. Recruiters read candidates' responses to questions such as "Describe the most effective idea you've implemented to boost employee morale," and decide whom to invite for an in-person interview. The company saves both time and travel expenses by using this method.[90]

Improving the Interview

Clearly, the interview can be a useful selection device, though often its potential is not used properly. Ideally, the interview should (1) be based on a thorough job analysis, (2) be structured, (3) contain either situational or behavior description items, and (4) be conducted by a panel of interviewers who have been trained to avoid common errors.[91] Validity seems to be enhanced if interviewers act more as information gatherers than as decision makers. Also, the statistical combination of interviewer item or dimension ratings often yields more valid predictions than overall subjective judgments of individual interviewers or panels.[92] To be effective, the interview should have the well-planned and reasonable objective of assessing important applicant characteristics that cannot be better evaluated by other selection methods.[93]

PHYSICAL TESTING

The Physical Examination

One of the final steps in the selection process may be a physical examination or test. A survey in 2000 found that 52 percent of firms required medical examinations of all new hires, while an additional 15 percent required exams for some jobs.[94] The examination is required by law for jobs such as pilot, interstate truck driver, and any position that involves handling food. Note that under the Americans with Disabilities Act, an employer may not require physical examinations (or other health-related information) until *after* the candidate receives a conditional offer of employment.

Information gained from physical examinations can serve several purposes:

1. To revoke conditional employment offers to persons who are found to be physically unable to perform the essential functions of the job, even with reasonable accommodation
2. To place individuals in jobs that they are fit enough to handle—for instance, to place individuals with chronic bronchitis in jobs in which they will not be exposed to high concentrations of dust or irritating fumes
3. To prevent the spread of contagious diseases to current employees or customers
4. To document preexisting injuries and illnesses to prevent fraudulent group insurance or workers' compensation claims

As with all selection devices, reliability, validity, and utility are relevant in the evaluation of physical examinations. Reliability may not be extremely high. Physicians who are not knowledgeable about job demands may not be able to agree on whether a candidate is fit enough or can perform essential job functions. Moreover, some physiological measures, such as blood pressure, are not highly reliable over time. The validity of the physical examination for assessing strength or endurance is also questionable. When jobs require unusual strength or stamina, actual physical tests are likely to be more valid than a physician's opinion. In terms of utility, physical examinations are expensive because they must be administered individually by a costly tester.

Additional limitations are placed on the physical examination as a selection device by the Americans with Disabilities Act. This act states that individuals may not be rejected due to physical inability to perform a "marginal" job function. "Marginal" means infrequent and nonessential. Thus determinations of physical ability to do the job must be based on a clear understanding of which job duties are essential and which are marginal. An employer that uses a physical examination must give the examination to all candidates who have been offered the job, not just to those who appear to have disabilities.[95] Further, information generated from the examination must be treated confidentially and must be stored in a file separate from other employee records.

Strength and Fitness Testing

For physically demanding jobs, employers may be wise to directly measure applicant strength or fitness as part of the selection process. Most police and fire departments test recruits for fitness. Research has shown that strength and fitness are positively related to the successful completion of training and negatively related to the incidence of lower back injuries for steelworkers, underwater demolition divers, and telephone and outdoor craftworkers. It has also been found that a person's maximum oxygen uptake (aerobic power) should be at least 2.5 times the level required on a continuing basis during an eight-hour shift.[96] Thus, ability to perform a demanding job during a brief work sample does not necessarily mean that a person is fit enough to do the same job all day.

It is possible to put together a battery of physical tests that will be content valid.[97] The procedure is based on a very thorough job analysis, then developing realistic simulations of the type of activities required in the job. For instance, a firefighter may need to drag a 175-pound person down a flight of stairs, and a police officer may need to run a mile faster than the suspect he or she is likely to be pursuing, while wearing 10 pounds of equipment and body armor. A construct approach to test validation is also possible. The process may involve objective measures of the heart rates or oxygen uptakes or other fitness measures among current employees.[98] Based on this information, appropriate tests of strength, endurance, flexibility, or aerobic capacity can be selected and cutoff points can be established.

Employers should be aware that physical testing frequently has an adverse impact on female candidates and older candidates. Consequently, the validity of the tests and the appropriateness of the cutoff scores must be carefully established.[99]

Drug Testing

The 2002 National Survey on Drug Use and Health released by the U.S. Department of Health and Human Services showed that 75 percent of America's 16.6 million adult users of illicit drugs were employed. The same survey found that 80 percent of the nation's 66 million binge and heavy alcohol users were employed.[100] There may be good reasons for avoiding hiring substance abusers. Some studies suggest that drug and alcohol abusers have higher rates of absenteeism and accidents. Furthermore, employers may be liable for negligent hiring if a drug-using employee causes an accident that harms others. The cost of substance abuse at work has been estimated at $7,000 per employee per year in lost productivity and quality, or as much as $75 billion annually, though these estimates have been criticized by others.[101]

To cope with this situation, some employers have adopted drug and alcohol screening programs for applicants and current employees. Initial and random testing of all individuals involved in safety-sensitive jobs such as truck driver and airline pilot is required by law, but employers often test other categories of employees as well. Approximately 60 percent of employers drug-test applicants during the final stages of hiring, and 40 percent periodically test current employees. Companies spent $757 million drug testing employees and applicants in 2002, with the average test costing $25 to $35.[102] Because use of illegal drugs is not considered a disability, drug testing is perfectly legal under the Americans with Disabilities Act. Unlike medical examinations, drug testing may be conducted before a conditional offer of employment is made.

Drug tests appear to be reasonably reliable, but usually a second, more sophisticated confirmatory test is performed when a sample gives an initial positive reading. To be fair to candidates, it is important to choose a properly certified laboratory to conduct drug tests. It is also necessary to have a step-by-step procedure to ensure that samples are labeled properly and actually have been provided by the person being tested.[103]

Overall, drug testing is a relatively expensive and invasive procedure. Whether it has utility (cost-effectiveness) in a given setting depends on the extent to which drug users are represented in the applicant pool and the extent to which drug use actually compromises job performance, attendance, or safety on the job in question.[104]

A number of researchers have evaluated job candidates' attitudes toward drug testing. They have found that drug users are more negative than nonusers to the idea of drug testing but that most job candidates say they are less likely to apply to an organization that requires drug testing than to one that does not. As might be expected, candidates give less approval to alcohol testing than to testing for illegal drugs. Attitudes toward testing also vary with the job involved. Testing is much more strongly approved for jobs involving danger to the incumbent or risk to others, such as airline pilot, surgeon, police officer or firefighter, air traffic controller, nuclear engineer, and truck driver, than for jobs less likely to put other people's lives in jeopardy, such as janitor, salesperson, or secretary. Finally, testing for candidates and incumbents is more acceptable when the system is seen as providing "procedural justice." This means that the system is perceived as fair and open, retesting is available, the reasons for testing are clearly explained, testing is announced and scheduled in advance rather than being random and unannounced, and current employees who test positive once are referred for treatment rather than immediately discharged.[105]

REFERENCE AND BACKGROUND CHECKS

Most organizations check candidates' references in varying degrees of detail as part of the selection process. In one survey, more than 80 percent of firms said they regularly checked the references of executive, professional, administrative, and technical job candidates. Sixty-eight percent checked references for skilled laborers, 57 percent for part-time employees, and about 40 percent for temporary and seasonal workers.[106] The goal in reference checking is often to verify information that the candidate has already given the organization, such as academic degrees, dates of employment, job responsibilities, and salary. It has been estimated that between 10 percent and 30 percent of applicants falsify their résumés in some way, so such verification is a reasonable precaution. Reference and **background**

checks are also used to discover new information on the history or past performance of the candidate, such as relevant criminal convictions or reasons for leaving a previous job.

Obtaining Reference Information

Reference information is usually collected by HR specialists from a candidate's former employers or teachers or from other knowledgeable persons the candidate lists. In addition to verifying dates of employment, type of work, and salary, firms often ask why the candidate left their employment, whether he or she would be rehired, how well the employee performed and got along with colleagues, and how often the employee missed work.[107] Ideally, an organization should seek additional reference information from people other than those the candidate names. To get additional references, an employer should ask the listed references for the names of other people who might know the candidate well enough to comment on his or her qualifications. Information from references may be solicited in writing, in a phone interview, or in a face-to-face interview. Generally, letters are the least useful. Because writers have time to carefully censor what they say, their letters are nearly always positive and relatively unrevealing. Interviewing the references can be more helpful because an interview allows the interviewer to establish rapport with the reference, note voice tones that may convey doubts about the candidate, and probe more deeply into important issues.[108] Phone interviews are more common and more economical than face-to-face interviews with references. As with any interview, the reference interview should be planned carefully in advance and focus on job-related issues.[109]

Obtaining Background Information

Background investigations may be performed by the organization or by an investigative services firm hired by the employer. When an outside agency is hired to do the investigation, the Fair Credit Reporting Reform Act requires employers to disclose to applicants that credit or background checks may be performed, to obtain written authorization, and to inform applicants if the investigation influenced a decision not to hire them.[110] Background information may be solicited from neighbors, credit agencies, and court or police records. A traditional basic background check by an investigative services firm typically costs between $50 and $200.[111] Some firms now specialize in providing quick and inexpensive Internet background checks of credit histories and criminal records, and there are an increasing number of "do it yourself" Web resources for checking the backgrounds of job candidates.

Validity and Legality of Reference Information

Studies of the validity of reference information agree that predictive validity tends to be low but is sometimes significant.[112] The most informative references are former or current superiors who know the candidate's work well and who have observed the candidate perform in a similar job. In addition, reference information may be more accurate if (1) the reference knows that the candidate is being thoroughly assessed and (2) if the reference has no hidden motivations, such as to keep the candidate from leaving the present job or to unload a problem employee on an unsuspecting new employer. References may be more useful to screen out candidates who have falsified their credentials or who have had behavioral problems on several past jobs than to predict the job performance of reasonably qualified candidates.

There are several potential legal problems associated with references and background checks. The first involves the new employer. If an employer hires someone who subsequently causes injury to another—and the employer should have known, through appropriate reference and background checks, about the employee's propensity for committing injurious acts—then the employer is liable for **negligent hiring.** For instance, a carpet cleaning company had to pay more than $11 million in damages when a woman was murdered by a carpet cleaner the firm had sent to her home. The firm had failed to discover that the employee had a history of violent crime. In Texas, a reserve deputy sheriff was hired without a background check. He injured a citizen on a routine traffic stop his first week on the job. It was subsequently discovered that he had prior convictions for assault and battery, had an outstanding arrest warrant, and was on probation at the time he was hired.[113]

There may also be legal problems for employers who give references. One involves possible lawsuits for defamation when an employer or former employer gives a negative reference. Thus many companies are discouraging candidates' superiors from giving any reference information at all. Instead, these firms are handling all requests for reference information centrally, from the personnel office, and they are limiting the information to facts such as dates of employment and job title.[114] Although this policy may appear wise for an employer or former employer, it complicates the task of the potential future employer who would like a frank assessment of a candidate, and it creates a second possible legal problem. By remaining silent about a problem employee, the former employer may be liable for negligent referral, or for violating a duty to warn, if the candidate is hired and subsequently causes harm to others.[115]

Because reference information can be helpful in identifying potential problem employees, moves have been made to reduce the risks of both giving and seeking references. By mid-2000, thirty-five states had passed "job reference immunity statutes" protecting employers who provide reference information in good faith.[116] Further, a large majority of organizations now require candidates to sign a release authorizing the company to contact referees and waiving the right to legal action against current or former employers who provide reference information.

Employee Reactions to Reference and Background Checks

A large survey of employees after 9/11 showed that most respondents generally approved of employers carefully scrutinizing the backgrounds of job applicants. In fact, it was the single most frequent recommendation by managers in response to a question about what their organization could do to enhance security in the workplace. However, not all types of investigations were equally acceptable to survey respondents (see Figure 8.8 for details).[117] Most employees find it very reasonable for a potential employer to check educational credentials and prior work history, but reactions to background checks on other types of information are sometimes less positive. Some questions can be seen as intruding unnecessarily into one's

FIGURE 8.8

Percent of Employees Approving of Background Check Data

Source: Data from "The Mind and Mood of American Employees on Workplace Privacy and Security," *ChoicePoint,* May 2002. (Available at: http://www.choicepoint.net/choicepoint/business/pre_employ/WPSWhitePaper.pdf)

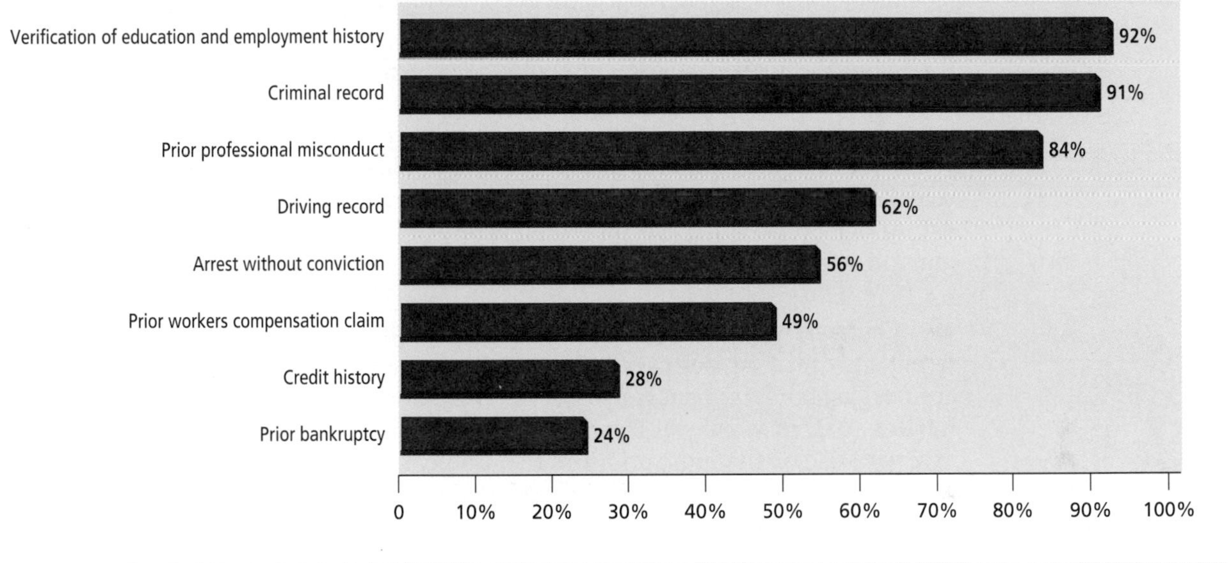

private life or perhaps assessing personal history that has little bearing on ability to perform the job in question. Further, reference and background investigations seem to provoke a disproportionate number of court challenges compared to medical examinations or drug tests.[118] Employers are probably wise to check relevant aspects of applicants' backgrounds but to avoid collecting data not likely to be job related.

SELECTING MANAGERS

The selection of managers for hire or promotion is a particularly important and difficult task. Estimates of American managers who are incompetent range from 50 to 75 percent, and 30 to 50 percent of all appointments at the executive level end in firing or resignation.[119] Clearly, there is room for improvement in managerial selection practices. There are many different ways to be a successful manager, but one thing is certain: Managing requires a wide range of skills. Thus single-factor ability tests are seldom very useful in selecting managers. Nevertheless, some studies have found significant correlations between mental ability tests and managerial performance, and some personality characteristics such as extraversion, need for power, need for achievement, conscientiousness, emotional stability, or general activity have some predictive success.[120] Emotional intelligence is also thought to be important for managerial success. As a rule, the best predictors of managerial success tend to be relatively broad measures, such as supervisor ratings of promotion potential or assessment center ratings.

Assessment Centers

An **assessment center** is a content-valid work sample of the managerial job, most often used to select nonmanagerial employees for promotion to low-level management positions. Because these individuals are not currently performing managerial duties, an appraisal of their work performance is not likely to predict success in the job of manager or supervisor. Hence there is a need for a work-sample test for the managerial job. Assessment centers also have been used to select salespersons, higher level managers, and supervisors who will succeed in a team environment.[121] One survey found that more than 500 U.S. organizations used assessment centers.[122] The technique is also popular in public-sector organizations that must select and promote on some form of merit. Assessment centers can last from one day to one week and have three characteristics: multiple means of assessment, multiple assessees, and multiple assessors.

Characteristics of Assessment Centers Multiple means of assessment or different situational exercises and tests cover a wide range of activities and skills that are performed by a manager. Assessment centers virtually always include an **in-basket test,** in which the candidate is given a stack of letters and messages to deal with. He or she must prioritize the problems and act on each by making a decision or an appointment, referring, delegating, or asking for more information.

Assessment centers also include some sort of **leaderless group discussion** exercise, because so much of a manager's time is spent in meetings or groups of some sort. Assessment centers may also include two-person role playing (e.g., salesperson with customer, supervisor with problem subordinate), management games, interviews with assessors, written tests of intelligence or personality, and possibly preparing and delivering a speech. Throughout all these exercises, assessees are observed and evaluated on dimensions such as decision making, planning, leadership, persuasiveness, energy, interpersonal sensitivity, and communication. The choice of assessment dimensions and exercises is based on a careful job analysis of the type and level of managerial job for which candidates are being evaluated.

If group exercises are used, more than one candidate must be assessed at the same time. Typically, six to twelve candidates will form an assessment center class, and three to six assessors will observe and evaluate the performance of the candidates. Assessors are usually managers two to three levels higher than the job for which they are assessing candidates.

Assessors undergo training on the exercises and assessment dimensions, observe candidates during the exercises, and then meet for one or two days after the candidates leave to determine ratings and to hammer out an assessment report on each candidate's managerial potential and development needs. There is some evidence that serving as an assessor has the side benefit of improving a manager's interviewing and communication skills.[123] Table 8.7 provides further detail on how to construct an effective assessment center by highlighting ten errors that can undermine the usefulness of assessment centers for selection and promotion decisions.

Validity and Utility of Assessment Centers Studies have shown that assessment center data do predict both short- and long-term success and advancement in management positions. Validities are often relatively high. Furthermore, assessment centers are equally valid for both sexes and all races and do not seem to produce adverse impact.[124] There are some questions about the construct validity of

TABLE 8.7

Ten Common Errors in Designing and Using Assessment Centers

	Error	Explanation/Example
1	Poor planning	Insufficient support from top management or potential assessors, underestimating the time and effort required to develop and use the center, unresourcing, no agreement on how to use the results.
2	Inadequate job analysis	Assessment center activities and procedures must be closely linked to job demands to be content valid and legally defensible.
3	Weakly defined dimensions	Dimensions to be rated by assessors (e.g., oral communication skill, prioritization) must be clearly defined and closely related to the job analysis.
4	Poor exercises	Exercises should be job related and allow the demonstration of skills on the dimensions to be rated. Clear and consistent instructions and standards for administering exercises must be developed and used every time the center is run.
5	No pretest evaluations	Prior to use, exercises and all procedures should be tried out and fine-tuned.
6	Unqualified assessors	Assessors should be one to two levels above assessees and should themselves possess the skills being assessed.
7	Inadequate assessor training	Assessors must be trained to understand the dimensions to be rated, to observe and record behavior properly, and to prepare assessment reports.
8	Inadequate candidate preparation	Candidates should be thoroughly briefed on assessment center procedures in advance of participation.
9	Sloppy behavior documentation and scoring	Assessors must document candidate behavior carefully and objectively rather than just forming an overall opinion of the candidate.
10	Misuse of results	Center results should be used only for the previously stated purpose (e.g., selection or development). Assessment center results should be combined with information from other selection devices to make the most accurate decisions about candidates.

Source: These points are made and explained more fully in C. Caldwell, G. D. Thornton III, and M. L. Gruys, "Ten Classic Assessment Center Errors: Challenges to Selection Validity," *Public Personnel Management*, Vol. 32, 2003, pp. 73–88.

assessor ratings,[125] but despite these issues, well-designed centers do seem to be effective in identifying management potential. Assessment centers are probably the most expensive selection device in common use. However, the relatively high validity and the potential losses from hiring an incompetent manager seem more than enough to offset the cost, leading to the conclusion that assessment centers are likely to offer high utility.[126]

Other Selection Methods for Managers

When the use of an assessment center is not feasible, careful reference checking and behavior description interviewing by a panel probably hold the most promise as selection methods for managers. Following a careful job analysis, behavior description interview formats should be developed for both candidates and their references. A thorough investigation of candidates' past behavior in situations similar to those of the new job should provide the most useful information.

Some organizations hire a consulting clinical or organizational psychologist to provide **individual assessments** of candidates for middle- and upper-level management positions. The assessment process normally includes gathering information about the job and organization and then gathering information from the candidates by means of a personal history questionnaire, cognitive and personality tests, and a clinical interview. Finally, all this information is combined judgmentally, and the assessor writes a report detailing the candidate's strengths, weaknesses, and suitability for the job. There are no empirical data available on the validity of these judgments because sample sizes are very small. Unfortunately, however, there is evidence that inter-rater reliability is low when more than one expert assesses the same candidate.[127]

Finally, in selecting higher level managers, an organization or subunit may find that its business strategy and environment are important in determining the type of managerial skills needed.[128] Table 8.8 lists some recommendations for candidate skills and attitudes that best match various business situations and strategies.

TABLE 8.8

Suggestions for Selecting Executives Who Match Business Strategy

Situation	Major Job Thrusts	Specific Characteristics of Ideal Candidates
Start-up	Creating vision of business	Vision of finished business
	Establishing core technical and marketing expertise	Hands-on orientation: a "doer"
	Building management team	In-depth knowledge in critical technical areas Organizing ability Staffing skills Team-building capabilities High energy level and stamina Personal magnetism and charisma Broad knowledge of all key functions
Turnaround	Rapid, accurate problem diagnosis	"Take charge" orientation: strong leader
	Fixing short-term and, ultimately, long- term problems	Strong analytical and diagnostic skills, especially financial Excellent business strategist High energy level Risk taker Handles pressure well Good crisis management skills Good negotiator
Liquidation/divestiture of poorly performing business	Cutting losses	Callousness: tough-minded, determined—willing to be the "bad guy"
	Making tough decisions	Highly analytical regarding costs-benefits—does not easily accept current ways of doing things
	Making the best deal	Risk taker Low glory seeking; willing to do dirty jobs—does not want glamour Wants to be respected, not necessarily liked

Source: Reprinted from "Strategic Selection: Matching Executives to Business Conditions," by Marc Gertstein and Heather Reisman, *Sloan Management Review,* Winter 1983, pp. 33–49, by permission of the publisher. This material is an adaptation of a full table.

Behavior description and situational interview questions might be used to assess these characteristics.

CRITERIA FOR CHOOSING SELECTION DEVICES

A large number of selection devices have been described in this chapter. Conscientious human resource managers are faced with the daunting task of choosing which measures to use.[129] Some of the criteria that may be applied to this decision are discussed next.

Validity Traditionally, validity or job relatedness has been recommended as the most important single characteristic of a selection device. The middle column of Table 8.9 shows the results of meta-analyses of the validities of different kinds of selection devices for predicting job performance. Validity is usually assessed against *individual performance on a specific job.* However, as organizations change, we may see some redefinition of what types of validity matter—predicting the single best individual performer on a specified job, predicting who will fit best with an existing work team, predicting who will fit with the organization's strategy, culture, and values, or predicting who has the social and intellectual flexibility to adapt to new demands as jobs change over time. Another consideration is **incremental validity.** This is the extent to which an additional selection device contributes over and above those selection devices already in use by a firm. Incremental validity depends on both the validity of the new device and the extent to which it measures something relevant to job performance but different than what is already

TABLE 8.9

Average Validity and Incremental Validity for Common Selection Devices

Selection Device	Validity for Predicting Overall Job Performance (estimated true population correlation)	% Increase in Validity When a Device Is Added to a General Mental Ability Test
Work-sample tests	.54	24%
General mental ability tests	.51	—
Structured interviews	.51	24%
Job knowledge tests	.48	14%
Integrity tests	.41	27%
Unstructured interviews	.38	8%
Assessment centers	.37	4%
Biodata measures	.35	2%
Conscientiousness tests	.31	18%
Reference checks	.26	12%

Source: Data from F. L. Schmidt and J. E. Hunter, "The Validity and Utility of Selection Methods in Personnel Psychology: Practical and Theoretical Implications of 85 Years of Research Findings," *Psychological Bulletin,* Vol. 124, 1998, pp. 262–274. Note that the correlations in the second column are correct upwards to account for restriction in range and unreliability in the measurement of performance.

measured by existing devices. The final column of Table 8.9 shows the estimated improvement in validity when a given selection device is added to a general mental ability test.

Utility Utility models remind us that factors other than validity are also important in assessing the total contribution of a new selection device to the organization. Factors such as the costs of developing and using the device, the tenure of those selected, the base rate of success, the standard deviation of performance in dollars, and the selection ratio all affect the benefits obtained from an additional selection device. The devices discussed in this chapter vary widely in cost, from simple application blanks to days-long assessment centers. Some devices are costly to develop initially, such as empirically scored biodata questionnaires or custom-designed ability tests, but relatively inexpensive to use once developed.

Legality and Likelihood of Legal Challenge It goes without saying that selection devices must be legal, complying in their design, administration, and use with the relevant local, state, and federal laws. A review of federal court cases showed that structured interviews, work samples, assessment centers, and biographical information blanks were less likely to be challenged in court than were unstructured interviews and cognitive and physical ability tests.[130]

Acceptability to Managers Credibility among managers is another criterion that appears to be used in choosing selection devices. Unfortunately, managers' views of the usefulness of selection devices often do not parallel the research findings about validity (witness the popularity of the unstructured interview).[131] One study found a strong relationship between managers' and consultants' *beliefs* about the validity of various selection methods and their frequency of use. However, there was almost no correlation between the frequency of use of selection devices and their actual empirical validity. Another study found that organizations seemed to prefer selection methods that were traditional rather than new and that were nontechnical and hence easy to use.[132] Note that the same selection devices have different levels of popularity and acceptability to both managers and employees across nations. See the International Perspective box for more information on this.

Applicant Reactions Applicants do not respond equally positively to all selection devices. There is concern that unpopular or intrusive devices, or those that do not seem fair, may tend to alienate good applicants and perhaps make them less likely to accept a job offer.[133] The way applicants are treated before, during, and after selection devices are applied can also influence their reactions. A scale to measure applicant reactions to the fairness of a selection device has recently been developed. Sample items from each dimension of the scale are shown in Table 8.10. This can serve as a checklist for managers to assure that their practices are perceived as fair, in addition to having validity and utility.

Devices that can be problematic include stress interviews, drug tests, background investigations, personality inventories, and honesty tests. These may be seen as violating privacy or not being job related, even though in fact they may be valid. The following selection methods are ones applicants tend to like:

- Those with unmistakable face validity—such as work-sample tests, assessment centers, and ability tests containing job-related questions

INTERNATIONAL PERSPECTIVE

Selection Techniques Around the World

Is it reasonable for a large multinational company to use identical selection methods in every country in which it operates? One might argue that if the jobs are the same or similar, then the same KSAs will be required, so the same properly chosen selection devices should be valid and effective anywhere. There is often pressure to standardize practices across the various nations in which a large company does business. However, research has shown that the popularity of different selection methods varies substantially across countries. Candidates may not like or perform to their full potential on unfamiliar selection devices. Multinationals should be aware of local practices and consider whether they should either tailor their selection practices to local expectations or make an extra effort to explain to local candidates why they use the methods they do.

Some countries have a strong tradition of empirical research on selection and work psychology (the U.S., the U.K., and Germany) and tend to have more research-based, valid, and systematic procedures for selection. In particular, these countries make greater use of cognitive ability tests, assessment centers, and structured interviews than do other countries in Europe and Asia.

Italian companies rely almost exclusively on interviews. French employers also make extensive use of interviews, usually multiple unstructured interviews, and of projective personality tests (which are notoriously unreliable). A significant share of French enterprises also use graphology (handwriting analysis) in the selection process despite the fact that is has been shown to possess zero validity. Graphology is very rarely used for selection elsewhere in the world.

The United States is the only country to place much emphasis on integrity and drug testing. These methods would likely be seen as highly inappropriate and intrusive elsewhere.

The reasons for these differences may be economic (advanced selection devices and associated research can be expensive), historical (strong versus weak tradition of work psychology), or cultural. As an example of the latter, countries vary on emotionality and the extent to which emotions are seen as legitimate information versus biases to be eliminated in selection decision making. In Britain and the United States, whether you "like" a candidate is often dismissed as a bias, whereas in Southern European countries, liking may be seen as a highly relevant criterion for selection decisions.

Cultures also differ in their emphasis on achievement versus ascription. The former put great weight on what an individual has accomplished and focus on grades, work achievements, and measures of individual ability and skill in selection. Ascription cultures focus on who a person is rather than what the individual has accomplished. Ascription cultures such as Poland, Japan, and Korea may place more weight on family background, social status/class/caste, status of school attended, and the importance of those who refer or recommend candidates than on individuals' objective accomplishments.

Even when the same methods are used, interpretations or keys may be culture specific. Consider a behavior description question about one's role and contribution to a team's success. Individualistic cultures may value a response that highlights the importance of the candidate's contribution as a "star," whereas collectivist cultures may find a self-effacing response that shares credit with the team more appropriate.

Sources: S. Newell and C. Tansley, "International Uses of Selection Methods," *International Review of Industrial and Organizational Psychology,* Vol. 16, eds. C. L. Cooper and I. T. Robertson (Chichester, England: John Wiley & Sons Ltd., 2001), pp. 195–213; A. M. Ryan, L. McFarland, H. Baron, and R. Page, "An International Look at Selection Practices: Nation and Culture as Explanations for Variability in Practice," *Personnel Psychology,* Vol. 52, 1999, pp. 359–391; Y. P. Huo, H. J. Huang, and N. K. Napier, "Divergence or Convergence: A Cross-National Comparison of Personnel Selection Practices," *Human Resource Management,* Vol. 41 (1), 2002, pp. 31–44.

TABLE 8.10

Dimensions and Sample Items from the Selection Procedural Justice Scale

Dimension	Item
Job relatedness, predictive	Doing well on this test means a person can do the job well.
Job relatedness, content	The content of the test was clearly related to the job.
Information known	I understood in advance what the testing processes would be like.
Chance to perform	This test allowed me to show what my job skills are.
Reconsideration opportunity	I was given ample opportunity to have my test results rechecked, if necessary.
Feedback	I had a clear understanding of when I would get my test results.
Consistency	The test was administered to all applicants in the same way.
Openness	I was treated honestly and openly during the testing process.
Treatment	The test administrators treated applicants with respect during today's testing process.
Two-way communication	I was able to ask questions about the test.
Propriety of questions	The test itself did not seem too personal or private.

Note: "Test" may be replaced with the specific name of any selection device, such as "interview" or "reference check," to assess reactions to various selection devices.
Source: Items and dimensions are extracted from T. N. Bauer, D. M. Truxillo, R. J. Sanchez, J. Craig, P. Ferrara, and M. A. Campion, "Applicant Reactions to Selection: Development of the Selection Procedural Justice Scale (SPJS)," *Personnel Psychology*, Vol. 54, 2001, pp. 387–419.

- Those that are so traditional that applicants expect to encounter them, such as the interview or an application blank
- Those on which applicants expect to perform well[134]

Societal Impact There may be an inherent conflict in what is good selection for the organization and what may be good for our multicultural society. Research clearly shows that using selection tests of general cognitive ability will improve the quality and performance of hires. However, cognitive ability tests are quite likely to produce adverse impact on minority groups, so their use is not without controversy.[135] One approach to reducing adverse impact is to use tests in combination with other valid selection devices that display smaller race differences, such as structured interviews and work-sample tests.[136]

Benefits of Proper Selection Systems

Although the preceding criteria can be applied to choosing individual selection devices, there is much to be gained from having a coherent selection system made up of several state-of-the-art devices. Using a larger number of "good selection practices" is related to a firm's financial success. In one study, whether or not firms used five good selection practices was measured. The practices were assessment of recruiting source quality, validation of predictors, structured interviews, use of cognitive aptitude and ability tests, and use of biodata or weighted application blanks. The average number of good practices used by firms was only 1.36, so there is considerable room for improvement. There was a significant positive correlation between the number of practices used and the annual profit and profit growth of the companies. This relationship was especially strong for service and financial organizations. Clearly, where people deliver services directly, there is a substantial payoff from good selection processes.[137]

The most accurate selection should occur where several valid selection devices are used together to assess different aspects of candidates' abilities and motivation to do the job. An increasing amount of research has verified that different types of individually valid selection devices can complement each other to add unique information about applicants' likelihood of success. For instance, personality and biodata both explain variability in performance beyond that explained by general mental ability, and structured interviews add to the validity of a selection system beyond mental ability and conscientiousness.[138] One comprehensive review of selection devices suggests that the best prediction will normally be obtained from a combination of a test of general mental ability, a work sample, and an integrity test. For inexperienced employees for whom the work sample is not appropriate, a structured interview can be used instead.[139]

Summary of Key Points

A wide variety of selection devices may be used to assess job applicants. One of the most common is the application blank. This device may be used informally for screening or systematically through the weighted application blank procedure. Biodata—whether obtained through application blanks, biodata questionnaires, or experience and accomplishment records—are often impressively valid predictors of job success. Properly chosen tests of cognitive ability are also excellent predictors, as are work-sample and trainability tests.

Personality tests are making a comeback and can have modest but consistent validity for some aspects of job success. The delineation of the Big Five dimensions of personality has helped clarify the underlying relationships between personality and some aspects of job performance. Integrity tests are being used increasingly to screen out employees who may steal from their employers or otherwise present behavioral problems.

Interviews are a widely used selection device. The traditional interview is not especially valid because interviewers make errors and may not ask job-related questions. More current interview techniques, such as situational and behavior description interviewing, are effective when interviewers are trained properly and are prepared to conduct a structured, content-valid interview.

The physical examination is often the final step in the hiring process. The Americans with Disabilities Act requires that a conditional job offer be made before a physical examination is given. A few companies use strength or fitness tests as predictors of success in physically demanding jobs. Many more use drug tests as screening devices.

Because résumé fraud is not uncommon, organizations find it a wise practice to verify important credentials before making job offers. In addition to verifying credentials, reference checks and background investigations may be used to discover additional information about job candidates.

Selecting managers is an especially difficult task because managerial jobs are highly complex and require many different skills. The assessment center, though expensive, can be a content-valid way to identify management talent. Other methods include interviews, tests, reference checks, and individual assessment by a psychologist.

A number of criteria might be considered in choosing a selection device. Among these are validity, utility, legality, acceptability to management, applicant reactions, effect on society, and incremental validity beyond devices already in use.

The Manager's Vocabulary

accomplishment record
adaptive testing
assessment center
background check
behavior description interview
Big Five personality dimensions
biodata
cognitive ability test
contrast error
emotional intelligence
first impression error
halo error
in-basket test
incremental validity
individual assessment
integrity test
inter-rater reliability
job experience questionnaire
leaderless group discussion
negligent hiring
patterned interview
personality inventory
polygraph
semistructured interview
similarity error
situational interview
situational judgment test
structured interview
test manual
trainability test
unstructured interview
weighted application blank (WAB)
work-sample test

Questions for Discussion

1. What are the steps in a typical selection process? Compare the selection process on your last job with that shown in Figure 8.1.
2. Describe how to construct a weighted application blank (WAB). Why do WABs tend to have high validity?
3. What are some questions that should not be included in an application blank? Why?
4. Explain how experience and accomplishment records can be used in selection. How would you construct these so as to ensure content validity?
5. What qualities would you look for in a test if you were picking one for a validation effort in your organization?
6. How would you go about designing a work-sample test for the job of pizza delivery driver?
7. How does a trainability test differ from a work-sample test? What are the advantages of each type of test? Can you think of any disadvantages?
8. What role should personality testing play in selection for most jobs?
9. What types of integrity tests are available, and when might they be most useful?
10. What types of errors are committed by interviewers?
11. What is meant by the degree of structure in an interview? How does structure affect reliability and validity?
12. How do patterned, situational, and behavior description interviews differ from one another?
13. How is technology changing or facilitating the selection process?
14. Why would an organization choose to use a physical examination as the last step in the selection process? In what ways must the organization be cautious in using the examination?
15. Debate both sides of this thesis: All job candidates should be screened for the use of illegal drugs.
16. How and why should reference information be collected about job candidates? What legal problems can arise with giving and collecting references?
17. What issues arise in the use of background checks in the selection process?
18. What are the special problems and procedures involved in hiring managers?
19. Consider the type of job you wish to obtain after graduation from your current course of study. How should incumbents for this type of job be selected to maximize their chances of being successful performers? How does your

proposed selection system stack up against the criteria listed in the last section of this chapter?

20. You are HR Director for a large global company with manufacturing plants in five different countries around the world. Jobs are quite similar from plant to plant. Does it make sense to use an identical selection process in all the plants? Why or why not?

Exercise 8.1
How Should You Have Been Hired?

Working alone or in a group, do the following:

1. Pick a job that you or another member of your group has held.
2. Consider the knowledge, skills, abilities, and experience needed to perform that job. List the attributes you believe an employer should look for in hiring a new employee for that job.
3. Determine how you would go about measuring these attributes in an applicant.
4. Now, assume that you have decided to use an interview to assess some of the attributes.
5. Plan a cone-type semistructured interview for the job.
6. Suppose you have decided to use a structured interview. Write some situational and behavior description questions that would be useful in selecting employees for that job.
7. Write questions for a reference interview with a candidate's former supervisor.
8. If you are working in a group, conduct one or more interviews with one another for the target job and one or more reference interviews.
9. Go to the Web and locate one or more do-it-yourself free background checking sites. See what you can find out about yourself if you were the applicant. Would this site provide useful information for selection given the job in question?

Exercise 8.2
Hiring at Health Source

You are human resources director at Health Source, a drugstore chain that is preparing to open new stores in Dallas and Houston. Each store will require about fifteen clerks. Your recruiting efforts have been successful, and each store has attracted about 100 applicants for those fifteen jobs. You have performed a job analysis and concluded that the clerks must be able to learn to operate a cash register and make change accurately, take the initiative in providing friendly assistance to customers, and show up for work on time. In addition, because of the presence of controlled drugs on the premises, you want clerks who have no history of drug problems or theft. Recommend a complete selection system for Health Source.

1. How will you go about selecting clerks?
2. What legal considerations will affect your decisions?
3. How many selection devices will you use, and in what order?
4. How much is each selection device likely to cost, and—on the basis of the literature—how valid might you expect it to be?
5. Suppose that you have a strong preference for work-sample or trainability tests as a part of the selection system. How might you use work samples for this job? Lay out your system and its scoring key in as much detail as possible.
6. How would you handle the integrity/drug use portion of the selection system?
7. How do you expect applicants to react to the selection process at Health Source?

Exercise 8.3
Preparing to Conduct an Interview

Your job responsibilities have just expanded to include interviewing job applicants. The first interviews will take place in about ten days. Fortunately, there are up-to-date job descriptions available for the jobs for which you will be conducting interviews. Still, you feel a bit uncertain of exactly how to proceed. You decide to check the Internet for advice on how to conduct interviews.

1. Locate resources that would be useful to you in learning how to conduct interviews.
2. Find and work through an interviewer training simulation online.
3. Write a brief report of what you have learned about how to conduct an effective job interview.

Notes and References

1. See H. G. Heneman III, T. A. Judge, and R. L. Heneman. *Staffing Organizations,* 3rd ed. (Middleton, Wis.: Mendota House/Irwin-McGraw-Hill, 2000), for more detail on employee selection.

2. A. Etzioni, *A Comparative Analysis of Complex Organizations* (New York: Free Press, 1975); C. L. Mulford, G. E. Klonglon, G. M. Beal, and J. M. Bohlen, "Selectivity, Socialization, and Role Performance," *Sociology and Social Research,* Vol. 53, 1968, pp. 68–77; Lawrence M. Rudner, "Pre-Employment Testing and Employee Productivity," *Public Personnel Management,* Summer 1992, pp. 133–150.

3. G. Cornick, "The Cost of a Poor Hire." (Available at: www.shrm.org/peoplewise/1099cornick.htm)

4. For more detail on calculating the utility of a selection device in a given situation, see W. F. Cascio, *Costing Human Resources: The Financial Impact of Behavior in Organizations,* 4th ed. (Cincinnati, Ohio: Southwestern, 2000).

5. John E. Hunter and Frank L. Schmidt, "Ability Tests: Economic Benefits versus the Issue of Fairness," *Industrial Relations,* Fall 1982, pp. 293–308.

6. Charles C. Snow and Scott A. Snell, "Staffing as Strategy," in *Personnel Selection in Organizations,* eds. N. Schmitt and W. C. Borman and Associates (San Francisco: Jossey-Bass, 1993), pp. 461.

7. "Recruiters Beware: Lying Is Common among Applicants," *HR Focus,* October 1992, p. 5; Irwin L. Goldstein, "The Application Blank: How Honest Are the Responses?" *Journal of Applied Psychology,* October 1971, pp. 491–492; and Thomas E. Becker and Alan L. Colquitt, "Potential versus Actual Faking of a Biodata Form: An Analysis Along Several Dimensions of Item Type," *Personnel Psychology,* Vol. 45, 1992, pp. 389–408.

8. Stephen J. Vodanovich and Rosemary H. Lowe, "They Ought to Know Better: The Incidence and Correlates of Inappropriate Application Blank Inquiries," *Public Personnel Management,* Fall 1992, pp. 363–370.

9. Adin C. Goldberg, "What You Can and Cannot Ask," *HR Focus,* July 1992, p. 6; and *CCH's Explanation of the Americans with Disabilities Act of 1990* (Chicago: Commerce Clearing House, 1990).

10. For more information, see Clifford M. Koen Jr., "Guide to Pre-Employment Inquiries Interview Questions: What You Can and Cannot Ask," *HR Focus,* June 1995, pp. 4–5; and W. E. Barlow, "Pre-Employment Interviews: What You Can and Can't Ask," *Personnel Journal,* January 1996, p. 99.

11. See J. E. Harvey-Cook and R. J. Raffler, "Biodata in Professional Entry-Level Selection: Statistical Scoring of Common Format Applications," *Journal of Occupational and Organizational Psychology,* 2000, Vol. 73, pp. 103–118, for an example of using a WAB to predict the success of newly hired staff in accounting firms.

12. M. D. Mumford and Garnett S. Stokes, "Developmental Determinants of Individual Action: Theory and Practice in Applying Background Measures," in *Handbook of Industrial and Organizational Psychology,* Vol. 3, 2nd ed., eds. M. D. Dunnette and L. M. Hough (Palo Alto, Calif.: Consulting Psychologists Press, 1992), pp. 61–138; Garnett S. Stokes, Michael D. Mumford, and William

A. Owens (eds.), *Biodata Handbook* (Palo Alto, Calif.: CPP Books, 1994).

13. James J. Asher, "The Biographical Item: Can It Be Improved?" *Personnel Psychology,* Summer 1972, pp. 251–269.

14. "Spotting a Winner in Insurance," *Business Week,* February 12, 1979, pp. 122, 127; M. A. McManus and M. L. Kelly, "Personality Measures and Biodata: Evidence Regarding Their Incremental Predictive Value in the Life Insurance Industry," *Personnel Psychology,* Vol. 52, 1999, pp. 137–148.

15. R. R. Reilly and G. T. Chao, "Validity and Fairness of Some Alternative Employee Selection Procedures," *Personnel Psychology,* Spring 1982, pp. 1–62; J. E. Hunter and R. F. Hunter, "Validity and Utility of Alternative Predictors of Job Performance," *Psychological Bulletin,* Spring 1984, pp. 72–98; and M. K. Mount, L. A. Witt, and M. R. Barrick, "Incremental Validity of Empirically Keyed Biodata Scales over GMA and the Five Factor Personality Constructs," *Personnel Psychology,* Vol. 53, 2000, pp. 299–323.

16. Russell J. Drakely and Peter Herriot, "Biographical Data, Training Success, and Turnover," *Journal of Occupational Psychology,* Vol. 61, 1988, pp. 145–152; Hannah R. Rothstein, Frank L. Schmidt, Frank W. Erwin, William A. Owens, and C. Paul Sparks, "Biographical Data in Employment Selection: Can Validities Be Made Generalizable?" *Journal of Applied Psychology,* April 1990, pp. 175–184; and Craig J. Russell, Joyce Mattson, Steven E. Devlin, and David Atwater, "Predictive Validity of Biodata Items Generated from Retrospective Life Experience Essays," *Journal of Applied Psychology,* October 1990, pp. 569–580; K. D. Carlson, S. E. Scullen, F. L. Schmidt, H. Rothstein, and F. Erwin, "Generalizable Biographical Data Validity Can Be Achieved without Multi-Organizational Development and Keying," *Personnel Psychology,* 1999, Vol. 52, pp. 731–755.

17. Asher, "The Biographical Item."

18. G. S. Stokes and L. A. Cooper, "Content/Construct Approaches in Life History Form Development for Selection," *International Journal of Selection & Assessment,* 2001, Vol. 9, pp. 138–151.

19. F. A. Mael and A. C. Hirsch, "Rainforest Empiricism and Quasi-Rationality: Two Approaches to Objective Biodata," *Personnel Psychology,* Winter 1993, pp. 719–738; Garnett S. Stokes and Sarita Reddy, "Use of Background Data in Organizational Decisions," in *International Review of Industrial and Organizational Psychology,* Vol. 7, eds. C. L. Cooper and I. T. Robertson (Chichester, England: Wiley, 1992); and M. D. Mumford, D. P. Costanza, M. S. Connelly, and J. F. Johnson, "Item Generation Procedures and Background Data Scales: Implications for Construct and Criterion-Related Validity," *Personnel Psychology,* Summer 1996, pp. 361–398.

20. B. K. Brown and M. A. Campion, "Biodata Phenomenology: Recruiters' Perceptions and Use of Biographical Information in Résumé Screening," *Journal of Applied Psychology,* Vol. 79 (6), 1994, pp. 897–908.

21. M. A. Quinones, J. K. Ford, and M. S. Teachout, "The Relationship between Work Experience and Job Performance: A Conceptual and Meta-Analytic Review," *Personnel Psychology,* Vol. 48, 1995, pp. 887–910; and P. E. Tesluk and R. R. Jacobs, "Toward an Integrated Model of Work Experience," *Personnel Psychology,* Vol. 51, 1998, pp. 321–355.

22. For a detailed treatment of scoring systems for training and experience measures, see R. A. Ash, J. C. Johnson, E. L. Levine, and M. A. McDaniel, "Job Applicant Training and Work Experience Evaluation in Personnel Selection," *Research in Personnel and Human Resource Management,* Vol. 7, 1989, pp. 183–226.

23. Cathy D. Anderson, Jack Warner, and Cassie C. Spenser, "Inflation Bias in Self-Assessment Examinations: Implications for Valid Employee Selection," *Journal of Applied Psychology,* November 1984, pp. 574–580; David C. Myers and Sidney A. Fine, "Development of a Methodology to Obtain and Assess Applicant Experiences for Employment," *Public Personnel Management Journal,* Spring 1985, pp. 51–64; and Ronald D. Pannone, "Predicting Test Performance: A Content-Valid Approach to Screening Applicants," *Personnel Psychology,* Autumn 1984, pp. 507–514. See also Michael A. McDaniel, Frank L. Schmidt, and John E. Hunter, "A Meta-Analysis of the Validity of Methods for Rating Training and Experience in Personnel Selection," *Personnel Psychology,* Vol. 41, 1988, pp. 283–309.

24. K. Coffee, J. Pearce, R. Nishimura, "State of California: Civil Service Testing Moves into Cyberspace," *Public Personnel Management,* Summer 1999, pp. 283–300.

25. Leaetta M. Hough, "Development and Evaluation of the 'Accomplishment Record' Method of

Selecting and Promoting Professionals," *Journal of Applied Psychology,* February 1984, pp. 135–146. See C. W. Von Bergen and B. Soper, "The Accomplishment Record for Selecting Human Resource Professionals," *SAM Advanced Management Journal,* Autumn 1995, pp. 41–46, for an example of how to use accomplishment records to select HR generalists.

26. American Management Association, "2000 AMA Survey on Workplace Testing: Basic Skills, Job Skills, and Psychological Measurement." (Available at: www.amanet.org)

27. *Watson* v. *Fort Worth Bank and Trust,* 47 FEP Cases 102, U.S. Sup. Ct., No. 86–6139 (June 29, 1988).

28. J. L. Outtz, "The Role of Cognitive Ability Tests in Employment Selection," *Human Performance,* 2002, Vol. 15, pp. 161–171; P. L. Roth, C. A. Bevier, P. Bobko, F. S. Switzer III, and P. Taylor, "Ethnic Group Differences in Cognitive Ability in Employment and Educational Settings: A Meta-Analysis," *Personnel Psychology,* 2001, pp. 297–330.

29. J. E. Hunter, F. L. Schmidt, and R. Hunter, "Differential Validity of Employment Tests by Race: A Comprehensive Review and Analysis," *Psychological Bulletin,* July 1979, pp. 721–735; Alexandra K. Wigdor and Wendell Garner (eds.), *Ability Testing: Uses, Consequences, and Controversies,* Part I (Washington, D.C.: Committee on Ability Testing, National Research Council, National Academy Press, 1982), pp. 145–147. Subsequent reviews have reached similar conclusions, see J. A. Hartigan and A. K. Wigdor, *Fairness in Employment Testing* (Washington, D.C.: National Academy Press, 1989); U. Neisser, G. Boodoo, T. J. Bouchard, A. W. Boykin, N. Brody, S. Ceci, D. Halpern, J. Loehlin, R. Perloff, R. Sternberg, and S. Urbina, "Intelligence: Knowns and Unknowns" *American Psychologist,* Vol. 51, pp. 77–101; and D. Lubinski, "Scientific and Social Significance of Assessing Individual Differences," *Annual Review of Psychology,* Vol. 51, 2000, pp. 405–444.

30. F. L. Schmidt and J. E. Hunter, "The Validity and Utility of Selection Methods in Personnel Psychology: Practical and Theoretical Implications of 85 Years of Research Findings," *Psychological Bulletin,* Vol. 124, 1998, pp. 262–274.

31. Joyce Hogan and Robert Hogan (eds.), *Business and Industry Testing: Current Practices and Test Reviews* (Austin, Tex.: Pro.ed, 1990).

32. John Hawk, "Real World Implications of g," *Journal of Vocational Behavior,* Vol. 29, 1986, pp. 411–414; John E. Hunter, "Cognitive Ability, Cognitive Aptitudes, Job Knowledge, and Job Performance," *Journal of Vocational Behavior,* Vol. 29, 1986, pp. 340–362; Schmidt and Hunter, "The Validity and Utility of Selection Methods in Personnel Psychology"; Arthur R. Jensen, "g: Artifact or Reality?" *Journal of Vocational Behavior,* Vol. 29, 1986, pp. 301–331; M. J. Ree, J. A. Earles, and M. S. Teachout, "Predicting Job Performance: Not Much More than g," *Journal of Applied Psychology,* Vol. 79, 1994, pp. 518–524.

33. Schmidt and Hunter, "The Validity and Utility of Selection Methods in Personnel Psychology"; and J. F. Salgado, N. Anderson, S. Moscoso, C. Bertua, F. de Fruyt, and J. S. Rolland, "A Meta-Analytic Study of General Mental Ability Validity for Different Occupations in the European Community," *Journal of Applied Psychology,* 2003, Vol. 88, pp. 1068–1081.

34. One source for finding out about tests is B. S. Plake and J. C. Impara (eds.), *The Fourteenth Mental Measurements Yearbook* (Lincoln, Neb.: University of Nebraska Press, 2001).

35. C. Paul Sparks, "How to Read a Test Manual," in *Business and Industry Testing,* eds. Hogan and Hogan, pp. 36–47.

36. Paul Squires, Steven J. Torkel, James W. Smither, and Margaret R. Ingate, "Validity and Generalizability of a Role-Play Test to Select Telemarketing Representatives," *Journal of Occupational Psychology,* Vol. 64, 1991, pp. 37–47.

37. Rosemarie J. Park, Rene V. Davis, Elizabeth K. Rengel, and Rebecca L. Storlie, "The Selection and Validation of a Reading Test to Be Used with Civil Service Employees," *Public Personnel Management,* Fall 1985, pp. 275–284; and Lyle F. Schoenfeldt, Barbara B. Schoenfeldt, Stanley R. Acker, and Michael R. Perlson, "Content Validation Revisited: The Development of a Content-Oriented Test of Industrial Reading," *Journal of Applied Psychology,* October 1976, pp. 581–588.

38. J. A. Weekley and C. Jones, "Further Studies of Situational Tests," *Personnel Psychology,* Vol. 52, 1999, pp. 679–700; M. A. McDaniel, F. P. Morgeson, E. B. Finnegan, M. A. Campion, and E. P. Braverman, "Use of Situational Judgment Tests to Predict Job Performance: A Clarification of the Literature," *Journal of Applied Psychology,* 2001, Vol. 86, pp. 730–740.

39. J. Clevenger, G. M. Pereira, D. Wiechmann, N. Schmitt, and V. S. Harvey, "Incremental Validity of Situational Judgment Tests," *Journal of Applied Psychology,* 2001, Vol. 86, pp. 410–417.

40. I. T. Robertson and R. M. Mindel, "A Study of Trainability Testing," *Journal of Occupational Psychology,* June 1980, pp. 131–138; Arthur I. Siegel, "The Miniature Job Training and Evaluation Approach: Additional Findings," *Personnel Psychology,* Spring 1983, pp. 41–56; and Richard R. Reilly and Edmund W. Israelski, "Development and Validation of Minicourses in the Telecommunication Industry," *Journal of Applied Psychology,* Vol. 73, 1988, pp. 721–726.

41. James J. Asher and James A. Sciarrino, "Realistic Work Sample Tests: A Review," *Personnel Psychology,* Winter 1974, pp. 519–533; Ivan Robertson and R. S. Kandola, "Work Sample Tests: Validity, Adverse Impact, and Applicant Reaction," *Journal of Occupational Psychology,* September 1982, pp. 171–183; and Schmidt and Hunter, "The Validity and Utility of Selection Methods in Personnel Psychology."

42. N. Schmitt and A. E. Mills, "Traditional Tests and Job Simulations: Minority and Majority Performance and Test Validities," *Journal of Applied Psychology,* 2001, Vol. 86, pp. 451–458.

43. J. L. Farr, B. S. O'Leary, and C. J. Bartlett, "Effect of a Work Sample Test upon Self-Selection and Turnover of Job Applicants," *Journal of Applied Psychology,* October 1973, pp. 283–285; K. A. Hanisch and C. L. Hulin, "Two-Stage Sequential Selection Procedures Using Ability and Training Performance: Incremental Validity of Behavioral Consistency Measures," *Personnel Psychology,* Vol. 47, 1994, pp. 767–786; M. Callinan and I. T. Robertson, "Work Sample Testing," *International Journal of Selection & Assessment,* 2000, Vol. 8, pp. 248–260.

44. American Management Association, "2000 AMA Survey on Workplace Testing."

45. *Soroka v. Dayton Hudson Corp.,* 6 Ind. Empl. Rights Cas. (BNA) 1491 (Cal. Ct. App. 1991); see also Daniel P. O'Meara, "Personality Tests Raise Questions of Legality and Effectiveness," *HR Magazine,* January 1994, pp. 97–100.

46. D. C. Brown, "EEOC Issues Revised Policy on Medical Examinations Under the ADA," *Industrial and Organizational Psychologist,* January 1996, pp. 107–108.

47. Murray R. Barrick and Michael K. Mount, "The Big Five Personality Dimensions and Job Performance: A Meta-Analysis," *Personnel Psychology,* Spring 1991, pp. 1–26; M. K. Mount and M. R. Barrick, "The Big Five Personality Dimensions: Implications for Research and Practice in Human Resource Management," *Research in Personnel and Human Resource Management,* Vol. 13, 1995, pp. 153–200; T. A. Judge and R. Ilies, "Relationship of Personality to Performance Motivation: A Meta-Analytic Review," *Journal of Applied Psychology,* 2002, Vol. 87, pp. 797–807; T. A. Judge and J. E. Bono, "Relationship of Core Self-Evaluations Traits—Self-Esteem, Generalized Self-Efficacy, Locus of Control, and Emotional Stability—With Job Satisfaction and Job Performance: A Meta-Analysis," *Journal of Applied Psychology,* 2001, Vol. 86, pp. 80–92.

48. Barrick and Mount, "The Big Five Personality Dimensions and Job Performance"; Mount and Barrick, "The Big Five Personality Dimensions"; and D. S. Ones and C. Viswesvaran, "Bandwidth-Fidelity Dilemma in Personality Measurement for Selection," *Journal of Organizational Behavior,* Vol. 17, 1996, pp. 609–626. For dissenting opinions on the Big Five, see Leaetta M. Hough, "The 'Big Five' Personality Variables—Construct Confusion: Description versus Prediction," *Human Performance,* Vol. 5, 1992, pp. 139–155; R. J. Schneider, L. M. Hough, and M. D. Dunnette, "Broadsided by Broad Traits: How to Sink Science in Five Dimensions or Less," *Journal of Organizational Behavior,* Vol. 17, 1996, pp. 639–655; and T. A. Judge, C. A. Higgins, C. J. Thoresen, and M. R. Barrick, "The Big Five Personality Traits, General Mental Ability, and Career Success across the Life Span," *Personnel Psychology,* Vol. 52, 1999, pp. 621–652.

49. T. A. Judge, J. E. Bono, R. Ilies, and M. W. Gerhardt, "Personality and Leadership: A Qualitative and Quantitative Review," *Journal of Applied Psychology,* 2002, Vol. 87, pp. 765–780.

50. M. A. McDaniel and R. L. Frei, "Validity of Customer Service Measures in Personnel Selection: A Meta-Analysis," paper presented at the Ninth Annual Conference of the Society for Industrial and Organizational Psychology, Nashville, April 1994.

51. J. D. Mayer, P. Salovey, D. R. Caruso, and G. Sitarenios, "Emotional Intelligence as a Standard Intelligence," *Emotion, 2001,* Vol. 1, pp. 232–242; J. V. Ciarrochi, A.Y. C. Chan, and P. Caputi, "A Critical Evaluation of the Emotional Intelligence Construct," *Personality & Individual Differences, 2000,*

Vol. 28, pp. 539–561; V. Dulewicz, M. Higgs, and M. Slaski, "Measuring Emotional Intelligence: Content, Construct and Criterion-Related Validity," *Journal of Managerial Psychology,* 2003, Vol. 18, pp. 405–420.

52. D. Goleman, "What Makes a Leader?" *Harvard Business Review,* Vol. 76 (6), November-December 1998, pp. 93–102; see www.eiconsortium.org for more on emotional intelligence.

53. S. Greengard, "Are You Well Armed to Screen Applicants?" *Personnel Journal,* December 1995, pp. 84–95; and B. P. Niehoff and R. J. Paul, "Causes of Employee Theft and Strategies the HR Managers Can Use for Prevention," *Human Resource Management,* Spring 2000, pp. 51–64.

54. Richard C. Hollinger and John P. Clark, *Theft by Employees* (Lexington, Mass.: Lexington Books, 1983).

55. "Congress Clears Lie-Detector Ban," *Congressional Quarterly Weekly Reports,* June 11, 1988, p. 1630.

56. D. S. Ones, C. Viswesvaran, and F. L. Schmidt, "Comprehensive Meta-Analysis of Integrity Test Validities: Findings and Implications for Personnel Selection and Theories of Job Performance," *Journal of Applied Psychology,* Vol. 78, 1993, pp. 679–703; H. J. Bernardin and D. K. Cooke, "Validity of an Honesty Test in Predicting Theft among Convenience Store Employees," *Academy of Management Journal,* Vol. 36, 1993, pp. 1097–1108; J. E. Wanek, P. R. Sackett, and D. S. Ones, "Towards an Understanding of Integrity Test Similarities and Differences: An Item-Level Analysis of Seven Tests," *Personnel Psychology* Vol. 56, 2003, pp. 873–894.

57. Greengard, "Are You Well Armed to Screen Applicants?"; http://www.hrstndassociates.com/integritytesting.html.

58. Joyce Hogan and Robert Hogan, "How to Measure Employee Reliability," *Journal of Applied Psychology,* April 1989, pp. 273–279.

59. U. Konradt, G. Hertel, and K. Joder, "Web-Based Assessment of Call Center Agents: Development and Validation of a Computerized Instrument," *International Journal of Selection and Assessment* Vol. 11, 2003, pp. 184–193.

60. J. M. Stanton, "Validity and Related Issues in Web-Based Hiring," *Industrial Psychologist,* January 1999, pp. 69–77; J. Mooney, "Pre-Employment Testing on the Internet: Put Candidates a Click Away and Hire at Modem Speed," *Public Personnel Management,* Vol. 31 (1), Spring 2002, pp. 41–52; J. W. Jones and K. D. Dages, "Technology Trends in Staffing and Assessment: A Practice Note," *International Journal of Selection and Assessment,* Vol. 11, 2003. pp. 247–252; D. S. Chapman and J. Webster, "The Use of Technologies in the Recruiting, Screening, and Selection Processes for Job Candidates," *International Journal of Selection and Assessment,* Vol. 11, 2003, pp. 113–120.

61. N. Schmitt, S. W. Gilliland, R. S. Landis, and D. Devine, "Computer-Based Testing Applied to Selection of Secretarial Applicants," *Personnel Psychology,* Vol. 46, 1993, pp. 149–165; F. Drasgow, J. B. Olson, P. A. Keenan, P. Moberg, and A. D. Mead, "Computerized Assessment," *Research in Personnel and Human Resource Management,* Vol. 11, 1993, pp. 163–206; and R. C. Overton, H. J. Harms, L. R. Taylor, and M. J. Zickar, "Adapting to Adaptive Testing," *Personnel Psychology,* Vol. 50, 1997, pp. 171–185.

62. "Solve the Long-Distance Hiring Dilemma," supplement to the August 1996 issue of *Personnel Journal,* pp. 18–20; and K. O. Magnusen and K. G. Kroeck, "Videoconferencing Maximizes Recruiting," *HR Magazine,* August 1995, pp. 70–72.

63. F. L. Schmidt and M. Rader, "Exploring the Boundary Conditions for Interview Validity: Meta-Analytic Validity Findings for a New Interview Type," *Personnel Psychology,* Vol. 52, 1999. pp. 445–464.

64. D.S. Chapman, K.L. Uggerslev, and J. Webster, "Applicant Reactions to Face-to-Face and Technology-Mediated Interviews: A Field Investigation," *Journal of Applied Psychology,* 2003, Vol. 88, pp. 944–953; S. G. Straus, J. A. Miles, and L. L. Levesque, "The Effects of Videoconference, Telephone, and Face-to-Face Media on Interviewer and Applicant Judgments in Employment Interviews," *Journal of Management,* Vol. 27, 2001, pp. 363–381.

65. J. M. Conway, R. A. Jako, and D. F. Goodman, "A Meta-Analysis of Interrater and Internal Consistency Reliability of Selection Interviews," *Journal of Applied Psychology,* Vol. 80 (5), 1995, pp. 565–579; and Eugene C. Mayfield, Steven H. Brown, and Bruce W. Hamstra, "Selection Interviewing in the Life Insurance Industry: An Update of Research and Practice," *Personnel Psychology,* Winter 1980, pp. 725–740.

66. Tom Janz, Lowell Hellervik, and David C. Gilmore, *Behavior Description Interviewing* (Boston: Allyn and Bacon, 1986); Hunter and Hunter, "Validity and Utility of Alternative Predictors of Job Performance."

67. M. McDaniel, D. Whetzel, F. Schmidt, and T. Maurer, "The Validity of Employment Interviews: A Comprehensive Review and Meta-Analysis," *Journal of Applied Psychology,* August 1994, pp. 599–616; S. Moscoso, "Selection Interview: A Review of Validity Evidence, Adverse Impact and Applicant Reactions," *International Journal of Selection and Assessment,* Vol. 8, 2000, pp. 237–247.

68. M. A. Campion, J. E. Campion, and J. P. Hudson Jr., "Structured Interviewing: A Note on Incremental Validity and Alternative Question Types," *Journal of Applied Psychology,* Vol. 79 (6), 1994, pp. 998–1002; and E. D. Pulakos and N. Schmitt, "Experience-Based and Situational Interview Questions: Studies of Validity," *Personnel Psychology,* Vol. 48, 1995, pp. 289–308.

69. Richard Arvey and James Campion, "The Employment Interview: A Summary and Review of Recent Research," *Personnel Psychology,* Summer 1982, pp. 281–322; Neal Schmitt, "Social and Situational Determinants of Interview Decisions: Implications for the Employment Interview," *Personnel Psychology,* Spring 1976, pp. 79–101; R. A. Posthuma, F. P. Morgeson, and M. A. Campion, "Beyond Employment Interview Validity: A Comprehensive Narrative Review of Recent Research and Trends over Time," *Personnel Psychology,* 2002, pp. 1–81.

70. M. M. Okanes and H. Tschirgi, "Impact of the Face-to-Face Interview on Prior Judgments of a Candidate," *Perceptual and Motor Skills,* February 1978, pp. 46, 322.

71. Richard D. Arvey, "Unfair Discrimination in the Employment Interview: Legal and Psychological Aspects," *Psychological Bulletin,* July 1979, pp. 736–765.

72. M. Hosoda, E. F. Stone-Romero, and G. Coats, "The Effects of Physical Attractiveness on Job-Related Outcomes: A Meta-Analysis of Experimental Studies," *Personnel Psychology,* Vol. 56, 2003, pp. 431–462.

73. R. Pingitore, B. L. Dugoni, R. S. Tindale, and B. Spring, "Bias against Overweight Job Applicants in a Simulated Employment Interview," *Journal of Applied Psychology,* Vol. 79 (6), 1994, pp. 909–917.

74. John F. Binning, Mel A. Goldstein, Mario F. Garcia, and Julie H. Scattaregia, "Effects of Pre-Interview Impressions on Questioning Strategies in Same- and Opposite-Sex Employment," *Journal of Applied Psychology,* Vol. 73, 1988, pp. 30–37; Therese Hoff Macan and Robert L. Dipboye, "The Relationship of Interviewers' Preinterview Impressions to Selection and Recruiting Outcomes," *Personnel Psychology,* Winter 1990, pp. 745–768; and T. W. Dougherty, D. B. Turban, and J. C. Callender, "Confirming First Impressions in the Employment Interview: A Field Study of Interviewer Behavior," *Journal of Applied Psychology,* Vol. 79 (5), 1994, pp. 659–665.

75. M. R. Barrick, G. K. Patton, and S. N. Haugland, "Accuracy of Interviewer Judgments of Job Applicant Personality Traits," *Personnel Psychology,* Winter 2000, pp. 925–951.

76. See Sandra Forsythe, Mary Frances Drake, and Charles E. Cox, "Influence of Applicant's Dress on Interviewers' Selection Decisions," *Journal of Applied Psychology,* May 1985, pp. 374–378; Robert Gifford, Cheuk Fan Ng, and Margaret Wilkinson, "Nonverbal Cues in the Employment Interview: Links between Applicant Qualities and Interviewer Judgments," *Journal of Applied Psychology,* November 1985, pp. 729–736; Thomas V. McGovern and Howard E. A. Tinsley, "Interviewer Evaluation of Interviewee Nonverbal Behavior," *Journal of Vocational Behavior,* October 1978, pp. 163–171; and T. DeGroot and S. J. Motowidlo, "Why Visual and Vocal Interview Cues Can Affect Interviewers' Judgments and Predict Job Performance," *Journal of Applied Psychology,* Vol. 84, 1999, pp. 986–993.

77. Though forcing interviewers to take notes may not be helpful, see J. R. Burnett, C. Fan, S. J. Motowidlo, and T. DeGroot, "Interview Notes and Validity," *Personnel Psychology,* Vol. 51, 1998, pp. 375–396.

78. C. H. Middendorf and T. H. Macan, "Note-Taking in the Employment Interview: Effects on Recall and Judgments," *Journal of Applied Psychology,* Vol. 87 (2), 2002, pp. 293–303.

79. L. M. Graves and R. J. Karren, "The Employee Selection Interview: A Fresh Look at an Old Problem," *Human Resource Management,* Vol. 35, Summer 1996, pp. 163–180.

80. A. H. Church, "From Both Sides Now: The Employee Interview—The Great Pretender," *Industrial and Organizational Psychologist,* July 1996, pp. 108–117.

81. K. I. Van der Zee, A. B. Bakker, and P. Bakker, "Why Are Structured Interviews so Rarely Used in Personnel Selection?" *Journal of Applied Psychology,* Vol. 87 (1), 2002, pp. 176–184.

82. Thomas L. Moffatt, *Selection Interviewing for Managers* (New York: Harper and Row, 1979).

83. A. L. Huffcutt and W. Arthur, Jr. "Hunter and Hunter (1984) Revisited: Interview Validity for Entry-Level Jobs" *Journal of Applied Psychology,* Vol 79, 1994, pp. 184–190. and McDaniel, Whetzel, Schmidt, and Maurer, "The Validity of Employment Interviews."

84. Schmidt and Rader, "Exploring the Boundary Conditions for Interview Validity."

85. McDaniel, Whetzel, Schmidt, and Maurer, "The Validity of Employment Interviews"; and Campion, Campion, and Hudson, "Structured Interviewing: A Note on Incremental Validity and Alternative Question Types"; A. I. Huffcutt, J. A. Weekley, W. H. Wiesner, T. G. Degroot, and C. Jones, "Comparison of Situational and Behavior Description Interview Questions for Higher-Level Positions," *Personnel Psychology,* 2001, pp. 619–644; E. D. Pulakos and N. Schmitt, "Experience-Based and Situational Interview Questions: Studies of Validity," *Personnel Psychology,* Vol. 48, 1995, pp. 289–308.

86. Gary P. Latham, Lise M. Saari, Elliot D. Pursell, and Michael A. Campion, "The Situational Interview," *Journal of Applied Psychology,* August 1980, pp. 442–427; Elliott D. Pursell, Michael A. Campion, and Sarah R. Gaylord, "Structured Interviewing: Avoiding Selection Problems," *Personnel Journal,* November 1980, pp. 907–912; Michael A. Campion, Elliott D. Pursell, and Barbara K. Brown, "Structured Interviewing: Raising the Psychometric Properties of the Employment Interview," *Personnel Psychology,* Vol. 41, 1988, pp. 25–42; and Jeff A. Weekley and Joseph A. Gier, "Reliability and Validity of the Situational Interview for a Sales Position," *Journal of Applied Psychology,* Vol. 72, 1989, pp. 484–487.

87. Janz, Hellervik, and Gilmore, *Behavior Description Interviewing.*

88. Ibid., pp. 64–65.

89. Tom Janz, "Initial Comparisons of Patterned Behavior Description Interviews versus Unstructured Interviews," *Journal of Applied Psychology,* October 1982, pp. 577–580; Janz, Hellervik, and Gilmore, *Behavior Description Interviewing;* Christopher Orpen, "Patterned Behavior Description Interviews versus Unstructured Interviews: A Comparative Validity Study," *Journal of Applied Psychology,* November 1985, pp. 774–776; S. J. Motowidlo, G. W. Carter, M. D. Dunnette, N. Tippins, S. Werner, J. R. Burnett, and M. J. Vaughn, "Studies of the Structured Behavioral Interview," *Journal of Applied Psychology,* Vol. 77, 1992, pp. 571–587.

90. Rachel King, "Chili's Hot Interview Makeover," *Workforce,* September 1, 2003. (Available at: http://www.workforce.com/archive/article/23/47/90.php)

91. M. Dixon, S. Wang, J. Calvin, B. Dineen, and E. Tomlinson, "The Panel Interview: A Review of Empirical Research and Guidelines for Practice," *Public Personnel Management,* Vol. 31, 2002, pp. 397–428.

92. Frank Landy, "The Validity of the Interview in Police Officer Selection," *Journal of Applied Psychology,* April 1976, pp. 193–198; T. W. Dougherty, R. J. Ebert, and J. C. Callender, "Policy Capturing in the Employment Interview," *Journal of Applied Psychology,* Vol. 71, 1986, pp. 9–15; Y. Ganzach, A. N. Kluger, and N. Klayman, "Making Decisions from an Interview: Expert Measurement and Mechanical Combination," *Personnel Psychology,* Vol. 53, 2000. pp. 1–20.

93. A. I. Huffcutt, J. M. Conway, P. L. Roth, and N. J. Stone, "Identification and Meta-Analytic Assessment of Psychological Constructs Measured in Employment Interviews," *Journal of Applied Psychology,* Vol. 86 (5), 2002, pp. 897–913.

94. American Management Association. *AMA Survey on Workplace Testing—Medical Testing.* (Available at: www.amanet.org)

95. Jonathan A. Segal, "Pre-Employment Physicals Under the ADA," *HR Magazine,* October 1992, pp. 103–107.

96. Michael A. Campion, "Personnel Selection for Physically Demanding Jobs: Review and Recommendations," *Personnel Psychology,* Autumn 1983, pp. 527–550; and B. R. Blakley, M. A. Quinones, M. S. Crawford, and I. A. Jago, "The Validity of Iso-

metric Strength Tests," *Personnel Psychology,* Summer 1994, pp. 247–274.

97. R. D. Arvey, T. E. Landon, S. M. Nutting, and S. E. Maxwell, "Development of Physical Ability Tests for Police Officers: A Construct Validation Approach," *Journal of Applied Psychology,* Vol. 77, 1992, pp. 996–1009; Larry T. Hoover, "Trends in Police Physical Ability Selection Testing," *Public Personnel Management,* Spring 1992, pp. 29–40; Blakley, Quinones, Crawford, and Jago, "The Validity of Isometric Strength Tests."

98. Edwin A. Fleishman, "Evaluating Physical Abilities Required by Jobs," *Personnel Administration,* June 1979, pp. 82–90; J. C. Hogan, "Physical Abilities," in *Handbook of Industrial and Organizational Psychology,* eds. Dunnette and Hough.

99. C. C. Hoffman, "Generalizing Physical Ability Test Validity: A Case Study Using Test Transportability, Validity Generalization, and Construct-Related Validation Evidence," *Personnel Psychology,* Vol. 52, 1999, pp. 1019–1041; and D. Biddle and N. S. Sill, "Protective Service Physical Ability Tests: Establishing Pass/Fail, Ranking, and Banding Procedures," *Public Personnel Management,* Summer 1999, pp. 217–225; R. J. Shephard and J. Bonneau, "Assuring Gender Equity in Recruitment Standards for Police Officers," *Canadian Journal of Applied Physiology,* Vol. 27 (3), 2002, pp. 263–295.

100. Department of Health and Human Services, Substance Abuse and Mental Health Services Administration, Office of Applied Studies, "Results from the 2002 National Survey on Drug Use and Health: National Findings." (Available at: http://www.oas.samhsa.gov/nhsda/2k2nsduh/Results/2k2Results.htm#chap3)

101. A. Meisler, "Drug Testing's Negative Results," *Workforce Management,* October 2003, pp. 35–40 (Available at: http://www.workforce.com/archive/feature/23/53/63/235365.php)

102. *Ibid.;* Jacques Normand, Stephen D. Salyards, and John J. Mahoney, "An Evaluation of Preemployment Drug Testing," *Journal of Applied Psychology,* December 1990, pp. 629–639.

103. Mark D. Uhrich, "Are You Positive the Test Is Positive?" *HR Magazine,* April 1992, pp. 44–48; J. F. Atwood, "Applicant Drug Testing: An Intriguing Odyssey," *Public Personnel Management,* Summer 1992, pp. 119–132; and W. Arthur Jr., and D. Doverspike, "Employment-Related Drug Testing: Idiosyncratic Characteristics and Issues," *Public Personnel Management,* Spring 1997, pp. 77–87.

104. Russell Cropanzano and Mary Konovsky, "Drug Use and Its Implications for Employee Drug Testing," *Research in Personnel and Human Resource Management,* Vol. 11, 1993, pp. 207–257.

105. Michael Crant and Thomas S. Bateman, "An Experimental Test of the Impact of Drug-Testing Programs on Potential Job Applicants' Attitudes and Intentions," *Journal of Applied Psychology,* April 1990, pp. 127–131; Mary A. Konovsky and Russell Cropanzano, "Perceived Fairness of Employee Drug Testing as a Predictor of Employee Attitudes and Job Performance," *Journal of Applied Psychology,* October 1991, pp. 698–707; Kevin R. Murphy, George C. Thornton III, and Kristin Prue, "Influence of Job Characteristics on the Acceptability of Employee Drug Testing," *Journal of Applied Psychology,* June 1991, pp. 447–453; Kevin R. Murphy, George C. Thornton III, and Douglas H. Reynolds, "College Students' Attitudes Toward Employee Drug Testing Programs," *Personnel Psychology,* Autumn 1990, pp. 615–631; and B. J. Tepper, "Investigation of General and Program-Specific Attitudes Toward Corporate Drug-Testing Policies," *Journal of Applied Psychology,* Vol. 79, 1994, pp. 392–401; M. E. Paronto, D. M. Truxillo, T. N. Bauer, and M. C. Leo, "Drug Testing, Drug Treatment, and Marijuana Use: A Fairness Perspective," *Journal of Applied Psychology,* Vol. 87 (6), 2002, pp. 1159–1166.

106. Report available from the "1998 SHRM Reference Checking Survey." Society for Human Resource Management, 1800 Duke St. Alexandria, VA, 22314.

107. See E. C. Andler, *The Complete Reference Checking Handbook,* 2nd ed. (New York: AMACOM, 2003) for more detail, including recommended reference check questions.

108. Paul Dobson, "Reference Reports," in Peter Herriot (ed.), *Assessment and Selection in Organizations* (Chichester, England: John Wiley and Sons, 1989), pp. 455–468.

109. For detailed advice on conducting the references interview, see Susan J. Herman, *Hiring Right: A Practical Guide* (Thousand Oaks, Calif.: Sage, 1994).

110. For more information, see www.ftc.gov.

111. For more on reference checking, see Greengard, "Are You Well Armed to Screen Applicants?"

112. James C. Baxter, Barbara Brock, Peter C. Hill, and Richard M. Rozelle, "Letters of Recommendation: A Question of Value," *Journal of Applied Psychology,* June 1981, pp. 296–301; Alan Jones and Elizabeth Harrison, "Prediction of Performance in Initial Officer Training Using Reference Reports," *Journal of Occupational Psychology,* March 1982, pp. 35–42; M. G. Aamodt, D. A. Bryan, and A. J. Whitcomb, "Predicting Performance with Letters of Recommendation," *Public Personnel Management,* Spring 1993, pp. 81–90; Schmidt and Hunter, "The Validity and Utility of Selection Methods in Personnel Psychology."

113. Ann Marie Ryan and Marja Kasek, "Negligent Hiring and Defamation: Areas of Liability Related to Pre-Employment Inquiries," *Personnel Psychology,* Summer 1991, pp. 293–319; and B. T. McMillan and M. Muraco, "Background Checks: Prudent Practice or Legal Requirement?" (Available at: www.shrm.org/ peoplewise/0700mcmillan.htm); C. Lachnit, "The Costs of Not Checking," *Workforce,* February 2002, p. 52.

114. Charles S. White and Lawrence S. Kleiman, "The Cost of Candid Comments," *HR Magazine,* August 1991, pp. 54–56; and Betty Southard Murphy, Wayne E. Barlow, and D. Diane Hatch, "Job Reference Liability of Employers," *Personnel Journal,* September 1991, pp. 22, 26.

115. P. P. Stokes, "Is There a Duty to Disclose in Employment References?" *Business Forum,* Vol. 25 (3/4), Summer/Fall 2000, pp.11–16; J. Swerdlow, "Negligent Referral: A Potential Theory for Employer Liability," *California Law Review,* Vol. 64, 1991, p. 1645.

116. C. Hirschman, "The Whole Truth," *HR Magazine,* June 2000, pp. 87–92.

117. ChoicePoint, " The Mind and Mood of American Employees on Workplace Privacy and Security," May 2002. (Available at: http://www.choicepoint.net/choicepoint/business/pre_employ/WPSWhitePaper.pdf)

118. D. E. Terpstra, R. B. Kethley, R. T. Foley, and W. Limpaphayom, "The Nature of Litigation Surrounding Five Screening Devices," *Public Personnel Management,* Vol. 29, 2000, pp. 43–54.

119. R. Hogan, G. J. Curphy, and J. Hogan, "What We Know about Leadership: Effectiveness and Personality," *American Psychologist,* June 1994, pp. 493–504; and C. Fernandez-Araoz, "Hiring without Firing," *Harvard Business Review,* July–August 1999, pp. 109–120.

120. I. T. Robertson and P. A. Iles, "Approaches to Managerial Selection," in *International Review of Industrial and Organizational Psychology,* Vol. 3, ed. C. L. Cooper and I. Robertson (Chichester, England: Wiley, 1988), pp. 159–211; Glen Grimsley and Hilton F. Jarrett, "The Relationship of Past Managerial Achievement to Test Measures Obtained in the Employment Situation: Methodology and Results," *Personnel Psychology,* Spring 1973, pp. 31–48; and Michael J. Stahl, "Achievement, Power, and Managerial Motivation: Selecting Managerial Talent with the Job Choice Exercise," *Personnel Psychology,* Winter 1983, pp. 775–789.

121. A. Armstrong, "Using Assessment Centres to Select Team Leaders," *Asia Pacific Journal of Human Resources,* Vol. 35 (2), 1977, pp. 67–79.

122. A. C. Spyychalski, M. A. Quinones, B. B. Gaugler, and K. Pohley, "A Survey of Assessment Center Practices in Organizations in the United States," *Personnel Psychology,* Spring 1997, pp. 71–90.

123. Robert V. Lorenzo, "Effects of Assessorship on Managers' Proficiency in Acquiring, Evaluating, and Communicating Information about People," *Personnel Psychology,* Winter 1984, pp. 617–634.

124. Barbara B. Gaugler, Douglas B. Rosenthal, George C. Thornton III, and Cynthia Bentson, "Meta-Analyses of Assessment Center Validity," *Journal of Applied Psychology,* August 1987, pp. 493–511; Joel L. Moses and Virginia R. Boehm, "Relationship of Assessment Center Performance to Management Progress of Women," *Journal of Applied Psychology,* August 1975, pp. 527–529; J. R. Huck and D. W. Bray, "Management Assessment Center Evaluations and Subsequent Job Performance of White and Black Females," *Personnel Psychology,* Spring 1976, pp. 13–30; and P. G. W. Jansen and B. A. M. Stoop, "The Dynamics of Assessment Center Validity: Results of a 7-Year Study," *Journal of Applied Psychology,* Vol. 86, 2001, pp. 741–753.

125. Richard Klimoski and Mary Brickner, "Why Do Assessment Centers Work? The Puzzle of Assessment Center Validity," *Personnel Psychology,* Vol. 40, 1987, pp. 243–260; F. Lievens, "Trying to Understand the Different Pieces of the

Construct Validity Puzzle of Assessment Centers: An Examination of Assessor and Assessee Effects," *Journal of Applied Psychology,* Vol. 87, 2002, pp. 675–686.
126. Wayne F. Cascio and V. Sibley, "Utility of the Assessment Center as a Selection Device," *Journal of Applied Psychology,* April 1979, pp. 107–118; K. Dayan, R. Kasten, and S. Fox, "Entry-Level Police Candidate Assessment Center: An Efficient Tool or a Hammer to Kill a Fly?" *Personnel Psychology,* 2002, pp. 827–849.
127. Ann Marie Ryan and Paul R. Sackett, "A Survey of Individual Assessment Practices by I/O Psychologists," *Personnel Psychology,* Autumn 1987, pp. 455–488; Ann Marie Ryan and Paul R. Sackett, "Exploratory Study of Individual Assessment Practices: Interrater Reliability and Judgments of Assessor Effectiveness," *Journal of Applied Psychology,* August 1989, pp. 568–579; and S. Highhouse, "Assessing the Candidate as a Whole: A Historical and Critical Analysis of Individual Psychological Assessment for Personnel Decision Making," *Personnel Psychology,* 2002, pp. 363–396.
128. James P. Guthrie and Judy D. Olian, "Does Context Affect Staffing Decisions? The Case of General Managers," *Personnel Psychology,* Summer 1991, pp. 263–292; A. K. Gupta, "Executive Selection: A Strategic Perspective," *Human Resource Planning,* Vol. 15, 1992, pp. 47–61; and M. S. Van Clieaf, "Strategy and Structure Follow People: Improving Organizational Performance Through Effective Executive Search," *Human Resource Planning,* Vol. 15, 1992, pp. 33–46.
129. Relatively little is known about how or why organizations chose various selection devices. See S. L. Wilk and P. Cappelli, "Understanding the Determinants of Employer Use of Selection Methods," *Personnel Psychology,* Vol. 56, 2003, pp. 103–124, for a recent article on this subject.
130. D. A. Terpstra, A. A. Mohamed, and R. B. Kethley, "An Analysis of Federal Court Cases Involving Nine Selection Devices," *International Journal of Selection and Assessment,* Vol. 7 (1), 1999, pp. 26–34.
131. S. L. Rynes, A. E. Colbert, and K. G. Brown, "HR Professionals' Beliefs about Effective Human Resource Practices: Correspondence between Research and Practice," *Human Resource Management,* Vol. 41, No. 2, 2002, pp. 149–174.
132. S. Dakin and J. A. Armstrong, "Predicting Job Performance: A Comparison of Expert Opinion and Research Findings," *International Journal of Forecasting,* Vol. 5, 1989, pp. 187–194; and Mike Smith and Morton Abrahamsen, "Patterns of Selection in Six Countries," *The Psychologist,* May 1992, pp. 205–207.
133. A. M. Ryan and R. E. Ployhart, "Applicants' Perceptions of Selection Procedures and Decisions: A Critical Review and Agenda for the Future," *Journal of Management,* Vol. 26 (3), 2000, pp. 565–606; see also a special issue of the *International Journal of Selection and Assessment* Vol. 12, May 2004, on this topic.
134. Sara L. Rynes, "Who's Selecting Whom? Effects of Selection Practices on Applicant Attitudes and Behavior," in *Personnel Selection in Organizations,* eds. Schmitt and Borman and Associates, pp. 240–274; J. W. Smither, R. R. Reilly, R. E. Millsap, K. Pearlman, and R. W. Stoffey, "Applicant Reactions to Selection Procedures," *Personnel Psychology,* Vol. 46, 1993, pp. 49–76; A. N. Kluger and H. R. Rothstein, "The Influence of Selection Test Type on Applicant Reactions to Employment Testing," *Journal of Business and Psychology,* Fall 1993, pp. 3–25; T. H. Macan, M. J. Avedon, M. Paese, and D. E. Smith, "The Effects of Applicants' Reactions to Cognitive Ability Tests and an Assessment Center," *Personnel Psychology,* Vol. 47, 1994, pp. 715–738; S. L. Rynes and M. L. Connerley, "Applicant Reactions to Alternative Selection Procedures," *Journal of Business and Psychology,* Spring 1993, pp. 261–277; and D. D. Steiner and S. W. Gilliland, "Fairness Reactions to Personnel Selection Techniques in France and the United States," *Journal of Applied Psychology,* April 1996, pp. 134–141.
135. K. R. Murphy, B. E. Cronin, and A. P. Tam, "Controversy and Consensus Regarding the Use of Cognitive Ability Testing in Organizations," *Journal of Applied Psychology,* Vol. 88, 2003, pp. 660–671.
136. Outtz, "The Role of Cognitive Ability Tests in Employment Selection."
137. D. E. Terpstra and E. J. Rozell, "The Relationship of Staffing Practices to Organizational Level Measures of Performance," *Personnel Psychology,* Vol. 46, 1993, pp. 27–48.
138. Judge, Higgins, Thoresen, and Barrick, "The Big Five Personality Traits, General Mental Ability,

and Career Success Across the Life Span"; Mount, Witt, and Barrick, "Incremental Validity of Empirically Keyed Biodata Scales over GMA and the Five Factor Personality Constructs"; J. M. Cortina, N. B. Goldstein, S. C. Payne, H. K. Davison, and S. W. Gilliland, "The Incremental Validity of Interview Scores Over and Above Cognitive Ability and Conscientiousness Scores," *Personnel Psychology,* Vol. 53, 2000, pp. 325–351; and McManus and Kelly, "Personality Measures and Biodata."

139. Schmidt and Hunter, "The Validity and Utility of Selection Methods in Personnel Psychology."

PART 4

Building and Motivating Performance

CHAPTER 9

Human Resource Development

- Human Resource Development: An Introduction
- The Needs Assessment Phase
- The Design and Development Phase
- The Evaluation Phase

HR Challenge

Suppose you are an HR executive for the state of Idaho. The state has historically promoted into management jobs good technical performers who appeared to have management potential. These individuals may have had little past training or experience at supervision, management, or leadership. For the most part, they learned to manage on the job by trial and error. It is likely that more systematic development would enhance their effectiveness as managers. Furthermore, your department has forecast that more than half of Idaho's executive level managers and 28 percent of managers below the executive level will be retiring within the next five years. There is a need to develop the skills of current managers and to build management skills in a substantial number of nonmanagers who will be promoted to fill the vacancies expected to occur over the next few years. The state has committed resources to this project, and a team of human resource development professionals has been assembled to plan an approach. You need to move quickly, and within your modest budget. What must the team do first, before a sound development program can be designed?[1]

The training function, now often called **human resource development (HRD)** or **workplace learning and performance,** coordinates the provision of training and development experiences in organizations.[2] This chapter examines the role of training in modern organizations and describes a model for the training process. The model begins with the diagnosis of training needs and the establishment of clear objectives for the training effort. The next step is to design and deliver learning activities that use appropriate methods and procedures to maximize the learning and subsequent job performance of trainees. Finally, training efforts are evaluated to see whether they met their objectives and were cost effective. Further information about the HRD profession can be found on the homepage of the American Society for Training and Development (http://www.astd.org).

HUMAN RESOURCE DEVELOPMENT: AN INTRODUCTION

Scope and Cost of Human Resource Development

In recent years the scope of HRD has broadened from simply providing training programs to facilitating learning throughout the organization in a wide variety of ways. There is increasing recognition that employees can and should learn continuously, and that they can learn from on-the-job experience, from each other, and from short, readily available online tutorial modules as well as from more formally structured learning opportunities. However, formal training is still essential for most organizations. Employers provide training for many reasons: to orient new hires to the organization or teach them how to perform in their initial assignment, to improve the current performance of employees who may not be working as effectively as desired, to prepare employees for future promotions and increased responsibilities, or to enable employees to deal with changes in the design, processes, or technology of their present jobs.

Table 9.1 summarizes the specific types of training U.S. organizations with more than 100 employees report having provided to their employees in 2003. Computer applications training and new employee orientation were the most popular training topics. Various management and supervisory skills such as leadership, performance appraisal, interviewing, and problem solving were also commonly taught. Note that many organizations train employees about sexual harassment and diversity to reinforce the organization's policies with respect to fair treatment. Seventy-four percent of organizations provide "train-the-trainer" courses for superiors or peers who will in turn provide on-the-job training to others. In addition to being one of the most important HRM functions, HRD is also one of the most expensive. The same survey revealed that in 2003 these organizations spent $51.3 billion on formal training for their employees.[3]

Strategy and HRD

Training can help an organization succeed in a number of ways. Ultimately, it is employee knowledge and skill that produce the organization's product or service. An organization that can produce more qualified, up-to-date employees in less time will have a competitive advantage. Training facilitates the implementation of strategy by providing employees with the capability to perform their jobs in the manner dictated by the strategy. Training must be tailored to fit the organization's

TABLE 9.1

Percentages of U.S. Firms Providing Each Type of Training to Employees in 2003

Training Topic	% Providing
Computer systems/applications	96%
New hire orientation	96
Management development	91
Technical training	90
Communication skills	89
Sexual harassment	88
Supervisory skills	88
Leadership	85
New equipment operation	85
Performance management/appraisal	85
Team building	82
Customer service	81
Product knowledge	79
Safety	77
Managing change	75
Problem solving/decision making	75
Train-the-trainer	74
Diversity/cultural awareness	72
Hiring/interviewing	71
Quality/process improvement	65
Public-speaking/presentation skills	62
Ethics	61
Wellness	54
Outplacement/retirement	41

Source: Data from T. Galvin, "2003 Industry Report," *Training,* Vol. 40, October 2003, pp. 31–32.

strategy and structure. For instance, an organization whose strategy involves providing exceptional service through a committed, long-service cadre of extremely well-qualified employees will need more complex training and career development systems than an organization that competes on the basis of simple, low-cost services provided by transient, unskilled employees. The latter will need a highly efficient new employee orientation and basic training scheme. Team-based high-involvement organizations find that extensive training in team skills as well as in technical job skills is necessary to make innovative organizational structures function as intended. When strategy changes, training is often needed to equip employees with the skills to meet new demands. For instance, Case Corp., a manufacturer of farm equipment in Wisconsin, decided to change the role of its sales representatives in Europe from just selling equipment to dealers to acting as business consultants who help advise dealers on how to succeed over the long run. Careful thinking about the competencies required in this new strategic role resulted in new selection standards as well as extensive development activities for current employees.[4]

Training is seen as pivotal in implementing organization-wide culture-change efforts, such as developing a commitment to customer service or making a transition to self-directed work teams. Pace-setting HRD departments have moved from simply providing training on demand to proactively solving organizational problems. Trainers see themselves as internal consultants or performance-improvement specialists rather than just instructional designers or classroom presenters. Training is only one of the remedies that may be applied by the new breed of HRD practitioners.

In an age of network organizations, alliances, and long-term relationships with just-in-time suppliers, leading companies are finding that they need to train people other than their own employees. Some organizations offer quality training to their suppliers to ensure the quality of critical inputs. Organizations with a strong focus on customer service may provide training for purchasers of their product. For example, 68 percent of respondents in the training industry survey in 2003 said they provided some customer education. Increasingly, the need to train and update employees, distributors, and clients around the world has pushed organizations toward e-learning solutions as part of the training mix.

A Systems Model of the Training Cycle

Because the objective of HRD is to contribute to the organization's overall goals, training programs should be developed systematically and with true business needs in mind. However, often they are not. Instead, training objectives may be undetermined or hazy, and the programs themselves may not be evaluated rigorously or at all. In fact, it sometimes seems that what is important is that the training program is "attention getting, dramatic, contemporary, or fun. Whether or not [the program] changes behavior becomes secondary."[5]

One solution to this haphazardness is to develop training programs following an **instructional systems design (ISD)** model such as the one presented in Figure 9.1. The model shows four phases: (1) needs assessment, (2) design and de-

FIGURE 9.1

An Instructional Systems Design Model

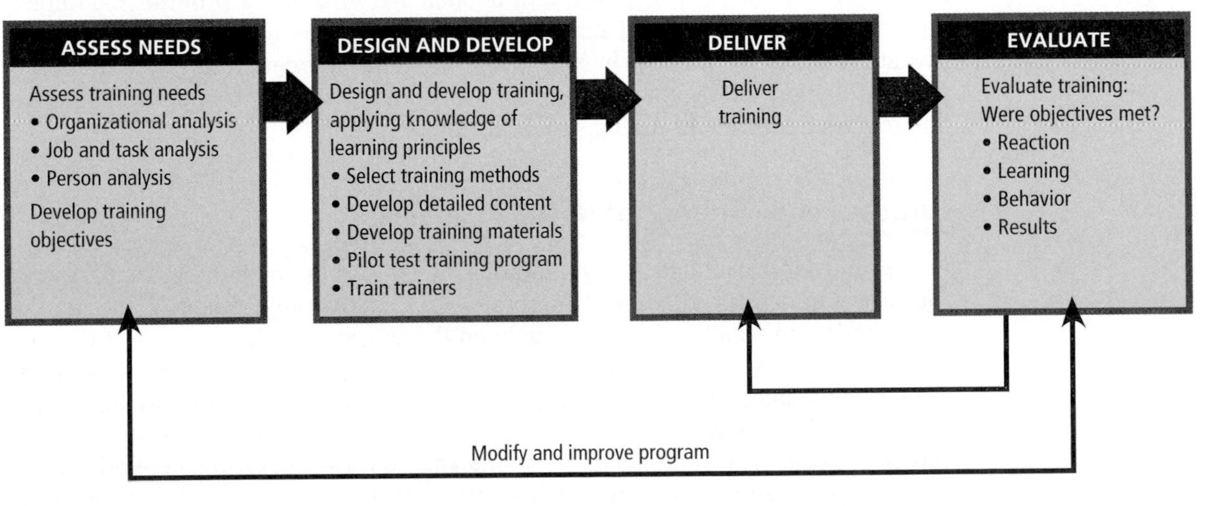
ASSESS NEEDS
Assess training needs
• Organizational analysis
• Job and task analysis
• Person analysis
Develop training objectives
DESIGN AND DEVELOP
Design and develop training, applying knowledge of learning principles
• Select training methods
• Develop detailed content
• Develop training materials
• Pilot test training program
• Train trainers
DELIVER
Deliver training
EVALUATE
Evaluate training: Were objectives met?
• Reaction
• Learning
• Behavior
• Results
Modify and improve program

velopment of training, (3) delivery of training, and (4) evaluation of training. If each step is carefully implemented, effective and relevant training is likely to be the result. The rest of this chapter focuses on these phases of the training cycle.

Note that systematically planning and implementing a training program involves more than just HRD specialists. Employees are often involved in needs assessment activities, and management must approve major new training initiatives and expenses. There is often yet another party involved, as many organizations use consultants in the development or delivery of training. The in-house HRD specialist may participate with a consultant in conducting a needs analysis and designing a customized program, which may be delivered either by the consultants or by trainers from the organization. In other cases the HRD specialist may select off-the-shelf programs from outside vendors to meet the training needs he or she has identified. An increasing amount of training seems to be outsourced in recent years.[6] Reasons given for outsourcing are to access the latest technological expertise and most experienced trainers, and to obtain increased efficiency of delivery, better service, and sometimes lower cost.

THE NEEDS ASSESSMENT PHASE

Successful training begins with a thorough **needs assessment** to determine *which employees* need to be trained and *what* they need to be trained to do. Allison Rossett and Joseph W. Arwady state: "The question is not *whether* you will solicit this kind of information through needs assessment. It's *how much* of it you will do and using which tools."[7] The culmination of the assessment phase is a set of objectives specifying the purpose of the training and the competencies required in trainees after they complete the program.

Needs assessment takes time and money. Unfortunately, a great many organizations undertake training without this necessary preliminary investment.[8] Often there is little effort to predict future training needs or to determine if perceived needs and problems really exist and can be addressed properly by training. Not infrequently, an organization undertakes training as a knee-jerk reaction to a perceived problem or as a response to a popular fad in training programs. Training undertaken without a careful analysis of whether it is needed is likely to be ineffective and a waste of money. Inappropriate training also can sour the attitudes of trainees toward all organizationally sponsored training and reduce their motivation to attend future and perhaps more useful programs.

Purposes and Methods of Needs Assessment

An organization can use many methods of gathering information and several sources of information for needs assessment, as shown in Table 9.2.[9] The choice of methods and sources depends partly on the purpose of the training. If the purpose is to improve employees' performance in their present job, then clearly the trainer must begin by looking at present performance and identifying performance deficiencies or areas where there seems to be room for improvement compared to desired levels. Sources of information on performance deficiencies include supervisors' and clients' complaints, performance appraisal data, objective measures of output or quality, and even performance tests given to determine the

TABLE 9.2

Methods and Sources of Information for Needs Assessment

Methods of Gathering Data for Needs Assessment	Sources of Information
Search of existing records	Existing records (e.g., output, quality, waste, downtime, complaints, accident reports, requests for training, exit interviews, performance appraisals, equipment operation manuals, procedures manuals, job descriptions, hiring criteria, personnel files, competency models and profiles)
Individual interviews	Incumbents
Group interviews	Superiors
Questionnaires	Subordinates
Performance tests	Subject matter experts
Written tests	Clients
Assessment centers	
Observation	
Collection of critical incidents	
Job analysis	
Task analysis	

current knowledge and skill level of employees. In addition, HRD specialists might collect critical incidents of poor job performance and look at accident reports to locate possible skill or knowledge problems.

Individual or group interviews with superiors, incumbents, or even clients are another means of gathering information on performance discrepancies and perceived training needs. Group techniques are especially helpful for anticipating future training needs, for prioritizing training demands, or for ambiguous situations. A group of executives, for instance, might work together to predict and prioritize the new skills that will be needed by top managers in the organization over the next decade.

When a large number of potential trainees are involved, or when they are geographically dispersed, a subsample may be selected for needs assessment interviews, or a questionnaire on needs assessment may be developed for wider distribution. Typically, existing data will be scrutinized and some interviews will be held prior to designing the questionnaire. An important advantage of methods that involve large numbers of superiors and potential trainees in the assessment phase is that such early participation may enhance acceptance and commitment to the eventual training product.

Once the organization has identified a performance deficiency, the next step is to determine whether the deficiency should be addressed by training. In some cases, motivation, constraints, or poor task design cause the deficiency. In such situations, training in job skills would not solve the performance problem.[10] For instance, if the employee used to be able to perform as desired, he or she may simply need practice, performance feedback to facilitate self-correction, or a job aid (such as a checklist of steps) rather than full-blown training. If employees need more information (for instance, to correctly respond to clients in a call center), it may be possible to provide them with a computerized **performance support system** that enables them to quickly located needed information. This may be a more efficient and effective approach than using extensive training in an attempt to store volumes of rapidly changing information inside of employees' heads.[11] If the employee could do the job correctly if his or her life depended on it, then motivation rather than skills or knowledge may be the problem. Perhaps good performance is being ignored or even punished, while poor performance is accepted without criticism. In these cases, the solution is to act on the environment and the reward system rather than to train the employee.

If training is being planned for current employees destined for promotion or transfer, needs assessment is more complex. The training specialist must measure the demands of the future job and then attempt to assess the ability of the employees to meet those demands. Because the employees being assessed do not yet hold the future job, their current level of performance may or may not indicate their ability to do the future job. Therefore, the training specialist may have to use special techniques to assess the employees' level of skill and knowledge relative to the demands of the future job. Such techniques include assessment centers (for candidates under consideration for management jobs) and tests or supervisory ratings of relevant abilities. Organizations that have developed and applied competency models to their managerial jobs (see Figure 4.5) are finding that measuring the developmental needs of managers against the requirements of future jobs has become easier and more systematic.[12]

When training is being designed for new hires, the methods used must be slightly different. Training is designed on the basis of a careful analysis of job content and the assumed characteristics of the trainees. If the trainees are not yet hired, it is difficult to assess their current level of knowledge. Thus the training specialist must coordinate closely with the staffing manager as the latter sets hiring criteria and evaluates candidates.

Three Levels of Needs Assessment

Regardless of the specific methods used to evaluate needs, any thorough assessment effort must address three key areas: the organization, the job and tasks, and the individual.

Organizational Analysis

Organizational analysis looks at the proposed training within the context of the rest of the organization. Table 9.3 provides a list of issues that may be explored in the organizational analysis portion of the needs assessment. The key consideration is whether the training addresses a genuine business need. Is the proposed training compatible with the organization's strategy, goals, and culture, and will employees be likely to transfer the skills they learn in training to their actual jobs? Corporate-culture compatibility is especially important for management training and executive development. Efforts to train managers to lead, make decisions, or communicate in ways that are not valued or expected by powerful others in the work environment are doomed to failure.

The impact that the training of one unit has on other related units must also be considered in an organizational analysis. For instance, if the accounting group is

TABLE 9.3

Issues in Organizational Analysis

- What are the training implications of the organization's strategy?
- Where in the organization is training needed?
- How are various units performing compared with expectations or goals?
- In which units is training most likely to succeed?
- Is this training program closely linked to the organization's goals and business needs?
- Which units should be trained first?
- Can the organization afford this training?
- Which training programs should have priority?
- Will this training adversely affect untrained people or units?
- Is this training consistent with the organization's culture?
- Will this training be accepted and reinforced by others in the organization, such as the trainees' superiors and subordinates?

trained to produce different measures of financial performance, then groups that either provide input to the accounting group or use the reports produced by this group also may need some orientation.

If training is to be provided to a large number of employees throughout the organization, the organizational analysis may ask which units should receive the training first. The answer may be the units that need it most. Alternatively, one may decide to begin with units known to be especially receptive to training to develop a record of success and a positive image for the training program before extending it to other units in the organization. When a cultural or value change is the aim of the training, it is often a good idea to train from the top down, so that each group of trainees is managed by individuals who have already learned about and accepted the change. Quite often, the higher level managers who were trained first become the trainers as the change is cascaded down the organization.

The organization's future plans must also be considered. For instance, a training specialist would not want to plan a massive training effort for a product or process that top management plans to discontinue in a year or two. Finally, the availability of trainers, facilities, and financial resources and the priorities of competing training programs must be considered as part of the organizational analysis.

Job and Task Analysis The duties and responsibilities of the job, together with the knowledge, skills, and abilities needed to perform them, are the focus of the second stage of needs analysis. Several approaches for analyzing jobs are available (see Chapter 4). Although any of these methods could be used as inputs into training needs assessment, the task inventory and critical incident methods are especially helpful. Task inventories can pinpoint specific tasks performed on the job, and the critical incidents method helps identify tasks that are not being performed correctly.

Once the preceding methods have identified the duties or tasks for which training may be needed, the next step is to develop a detailed analysis of each task. The purpose of this step is to verify that the task is important and should be the object of training and to develop in-depth information about the task knowledge and procedures that should be taught. The trainer will need to call on **subject matter experts** such as superiors and high-performing employees to generate **task analysis** information. Some of the questions to ask the experts are shown in Table 9.4. Written documents such as equipment instruction manuals and procedures manuals are another source of detailed task information.

Individual Analysis The final level of analysis looks at the individuals to be trained. (See A Different Point of View for more on the role of individual strengths and weaknesses in identifying training needs.) The **individual analysis** attempts to determine which employees should receive training and what their current levels of skill and knowledge are. The trainer may single out individuals on the basis of their past performance or select an entire work group or all incumbents with a specific job title. Then the trainer assesses, or at least estimates, the skill and knowledge levels of the chosen trainees so that the training is neither too simple nor too complex.

Attention must focus on prerequisite basic skills as well as on existing job-related skills and knowledge. For instance, one company conducted a training program on statistical quality control for a number of its employees. Later the company found that the employees were unable to use the techniques they had been taught. Careful investigation revealed that many of the employees were unable to do basic mathematics but had been too embarrassed to make this known during the training.[13] If a better individual analysis had been conducted before the quality control program was initiated, the trainer could have included basic math at the start of the course, and the employees would have been better prepared to benefit from the training. If individual analysis indicates a wide range of trainee skills and knowledge, trainers may wish to group employees into remedial and advanced groups. Alternatively, trainers could choose a training method that allows for self-paced learning or individualized instruction. Whenever possible, this kind of variance should be recognized and planned for before the training begins so that all trainees can have an appropriate and satisfying learning experience.

TABLE 9.4

Some Task Analysis Questions

- How hard is this task?
- Can it be learned on the job, or should it be taught off the job?
- How important is it that incumbents be able to do this task from the very first day on the job?
- What are the consequences of performing this task incorrectly?
- What knowledge, skills, information, equipment, materials, and work aids are needed to do this task?
- What signals the need to perform this task?
- Exactly what are the steps in performing this task?
- How can the incumbent tell if the task has been performed correctly?

A DIFFERENT POINT OF VIEW

Fixing Weaknesses or Building Strengths?

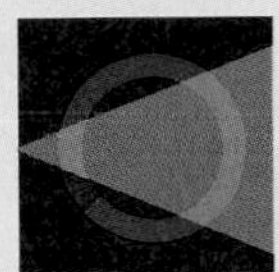

A traditional approach to training and development, and to self-development, is to discover what an individual is bad at and work to improve these weaknesses. The implicit assumption is that everything is fixable, anyone can be trained to do anything relatively well, and the best payoff of training dollars is to fix weaknesses.

Recently, a very different approach has emerged. The **human strengths** view suggests that we are all different and possess our own pattern of talents. The Gallup organization has conducted extensive research to identify thirty-four distinct kinds of human strengths. Examples include empathy, adaptability, command, competition, intellection, and strategic. One can build a natural talent into a strength with training and practice, and because of the underlying natural ability in a particular area, one can learn to produce consistent near-perfect performance. Training and development activities aimed at turning talents into strengths will pay off rapidly in major gains because individuals are so good at learning and growing in their areas of natural talent. However, learning is slow and painful in areas in which one does not possess much talent, and an individual is unlikely to become more than passable no matter how much effort is expended. There may be times when remedial attention to weaknesses is necessary and helpful, but the payoff will generally be better for directing attention toward enhancing strengths.

Organizations can maximize performance by assigning and developing individuals in areas related to their strengths and allowing them to manage around or outsource to others those activities that are not their natural forte. This approach suggests that great attention be paid to the individual analysis phase of needs assessment to appreciate the genuine differences that exist between people; to job transfer, job redesign, and correct initial placement to match job requirements with natural talent; and to training directed mainly at enhancing strengths rather than merely at fixing weaknesses. (Note, however, that every instance of poor performance does not indicate lack of talent. It may just be that the talent has not yet had the opportunity to be honed into a strength.)

Source: M. Buckingham and D. O. Clifton, *Now, Discover Your Strengths* (New York: Free Press, 2001); www.strengthsfinder.com.

Identifying Training Objectives

The final step in the assessment phase is to translate the needs identified by the organizational, task, and individual analyses into measurable objectives that can guide the training effort. Training can be evaluated at four levels: reaction to the training, learning measured at the end of training, changes in on-the-job behavior, and bottom-line performance or financial results. Analogously, objectives can be written for each of these levels.[14] For instance, "reaction" refers to how the trainees felt about the training—whether it was interesting and satisfying. A reaction objective might be to have an average rating of 4 on a 5-point scale of trainee satisfaction. At the opposite end of the evaluation continuum, a results level objective might be to reduce by 20 percent the total number of products that fail inspection.

Reaction and results objectives are not very useful for specifying exactly what must go on in the training program or what individual trainees must master. **Behavioral objectives** specify these critical requirements—that is, what the trainee will learn and how that learning will be demonstrated after training. A behavioral objective states *what* the person will be able to do, *under what conditions,* and *how* *well* the person will be able to do it.[15] The following examples are *inadequate* behavioral objectives:

- Be able to perform as a project supervisor after training.
- Develop an appreciation of statistical quality control techniques.

These objectives fail to specify what behaviors the trainee will display at the end of the training or when the individual is back on the job. They also do not specify how well or under what conditions the trainee will be able to perform and so are not helpful in designing the training program.

On the other hand, the following examples meet all the requirements for *good* behavioral objectives:

- Within one minute, point to the seven emergency exits on a Boeing 747 airliner.
- Within five minutes, strip a bed and remake it with clean sheets to hotel standards (hospital corners, tucked in tautly all around, top sheet folded over blanket, spread centered and one inch above floor all around).

With these behavioral objectives in hand, the training specialist can begin to design the training and simultaneously to plan the evaluation phase of the training cycle.

Needs Assessment in Action

The HR Challenge at the beginning of this chapter describes a situation in which needs assessment is an extremely important first step. A development program for Idaho state managers could not be designed without a thorough understanding of the nature of the managerial job and the most commonly occurring performance gaps among current incumbents. The team of HR professionals utilized two main sources of information in their needs assessment. First, they looked closely at an existing training program used in some other states, the Certified Public Manager program. This provided an initial typology of public manager competencies and a framework for organizing the data they collected themselves. Their own data came from twenty focus groups held around the state with groups of managers and HR professionals at a variety of levels. Focus groups were considered to be a fast and efficient way to obtain the opinions of managers and to raise the importance and visibility of the upcoming development program. Participants in focus groups were asked to discuss questions such as these:

- What training topics are most important for state managers?
- If you were on a selection panel for a new manager in your department, what skills and abilities would you look for?
- Describe the worst (best) manager you have ever experienced. What accounted for his or her failure (success)?
- What training do you wish you had had that you have not received?
- What was the most helpful training you have ever had for your management job?
- What was the most important experience you have had that taught you about management?

- What format, duration, and structure would be most suitable for a Certified Public Manager program in this state?

Analysis of responses resulted in a prioritized list of training topics organized into seven levels from first-line supervisor to top executive.[16]

THE DESIGN AND DEVELOPMENT PHASE

Once the training specialist has identified training needs and prepared objectives, the next step is to develop a training program that will achieve those objectives. This is accomplished by selecting training methods and developing training materials that convey the knowledge and skills identified in the behavioral objectives. The later stages may involve pilot testing the program and training the trainers.[17] The evaluation of the training program must also be planned before the training is delivered. To design an effective training program, it is necessary to understand how people learn.

Learning Principles

Nearly 100 years of research on human and animal learning have led to the discovery of a number of principles that underlie and facilitate learning. This section briefly examines these principles.

Preconditions for Learning For training to be most successful, two **preconditions for learning**—readiness and motivation—should be cultivated. **Trainee readiness** means that trainees possess the background skills and knowledge necessary to learn the material that will be presented to them. For instance, knowing basic math is a prerequisite for learning statistical quality control techniques. Some top U.S. business schools feel that several years of work experience constitute a prerequisite that enhances readiness to learn in M.B.A. programs. The other precondition for learning is **trainee motivation.**[18] Trainees learn best if they see a need for the new skills and understand how successful training will benefit them. There are several ways to increase trainee motivation.

Research has shown that the attitudes and expectations of trainees as they begin a training program can affect their reactions to the program and the amount they learn.[19] Individuals who freely choose to attend a training program learn more than those who are required to attend.[20] Moreover, individuals who are committed to their careers and have engaged in career planning seem to respond better to training.[21] Organizations can influence the attitudes of potential trainees by involving them in the needs assessment phase and by giving them a realistic training preview—a synopsis of what they can expect from the training program and how it fits into their career plans.

Two additional ways to increase motivation are goal setting and self-efficacy enhancement. A number of studies have shown that when individuals set specific goals for themselves, they perform better than when they have no goals or vague goals.[22] For a long training program, trainees should have a clear picture of their final desired goal but should also set intermediate goals, allowing them to get a feeling of success and progress as they increase their mastery of different components of the training program. **Self-efficacy expectations** are simply a belief that one will be able to perform the tasks successfully. These beliefs are a strong determinant of persistence and eventual success in learning difficult tasks.[23] Thus it has been suggested that trainers attempt to increase the efficacy expectations of trainees by (1) *persuasion*—telling the trainees that they can do it, that there is a high rate of success in the program; (2) *modeling*—showing the trainees (in person or on videotape) others like themselves who have succeeded in training; or (3) *enactive mastery*—causing the trainees to experience success in the early stages of training.[24] Mastery is the most potent method for increasing efficacy expectations, and trainers should structure early success opportunities into the training program and provide positive feedback on initial performance improvements.

In addition to the two preconditions for learning—trainee readiness and motivation—several other important learning principles must be considered in the design of a training program. These learning principles involve the following:

- Conditions of practice
- Knowledge of results
- Overcoming interference
- Transfer of training
- Adult learning principles

Conditions of Practice Actively practicing the skill or task is essential for efficient learning and mastery. Lack of opportunity for active, hands-on practice is a critical downfall of many training programs, especially those conducted in a classroom setting. The training designer must always ask "How much practice is enough?" and be sure to include at least enough to move trainees to the performance level specified in the behavioral objectives. Sometimes, however, practicing even more is desirable. **Overlearning** is practicing far beyond the point at which the trainee has mastered and performed the task correctly several times. Overlearning is particularly useful for critical tasks that are performed infrequently or under stress, such as cardiopulmonary resuscitation (CPR) or an airline crew's activities during a flight emergency. Overlearning should be used when the trainee is learning a task in which the first reactions must be absolutely correct. Overlearning is important for several reasons:[25]

- It increases retention over time.
- It makes the behavior more automatic.
- It increases the quality of performance under stress.
- It helps trainees transfer what they have learned to the job setting.

Another aspect of practice is deciding whether to have the **whole** task taught and practiced as one unit or to break down the task into separately learned and practiced **parts.** If the task is simple, it can be learned and practiced as a whole. If the task is complex, it probably should be broken down into component parts that can be taught and practiced as separate elements. Another condition of practice that the trainer must consider is whether the practice should be **distributed** (divided into spaced segments with time or some other activity in between) or **massed** (scheduled in one long session). Cramming the night before an examination is an example of massed practice. Research has shown that when information must be remembered over a long period of time, distributed practice is generally better than massed practice.[26] Classroom training is often massed, as trainees are trained for hours or days on end after being brought into the training center.

Knowledge of Results For effective learning to take place, trainees need to receive **feedback,** or **knowledge of results,** on how they are performing. Feedback is critical for both learning and motivation.[27] If feedback is not provided, trainees may learn the technique incorrectly or lose the motivation to learn. Because feedback makes the learning process more interesting for trainees, it maximizes trainees' willingness to learn. Feedback is also necessary if goals for maintaining or improving performance have been set.

The trainer should plan to give plenty of feedback and encouragement early in the training program. At first, the trainer should praise any improvement at all. Gradually, as trainees' skills increase, the trainer should raise the performance level required to receive positive feedback. Later in the program, the trainer should teach trainees how to evaluate their own performance, and trainees should move toward reliance on self-generated feedback rather than feedback from others. This increases the likelihood that trainees will be able to continue to perform correctly when back on the job.

Overcoming Interference **Interference** occurs when habits or learning acquired prior to training make it difficult for the trainee to absorb new material. Interference is most severe when the trainee has learned a strong stimulus–response connection in the past and now has to learn a totally different response to the same or similar stimulus. One of the authors of this book experienced a great deal of interference when attempting to learn to sail a boat. Many years of daily horseback riding had established a strong connection between the stimulus "sensation of excessive speed" and the response "pull back on the reins." When the sailboat picked up too much speed, she automatically pulled back on the rope attached to the boom. Unfortunately, this action can be counted on to make sailboats increase speed and tip over. Despite understanding the principles of sailing and knowing that the correct response was to slacken the rope, the old habit of pulling back was almost irresistible.

Interference can be a special problem when the new correct response must be performed reliably under stress. Under stress, individuals have a tendency to revert to their old habitual responses. Suppose, for example, that an individual who learned to drive in the United States visited England and began to drive on the left-hand side of the road. In an emergency situation, the driver's strong habit of keeping to the right would probably take over.

The trainer should try to anticipate any inappropriate habits that trainees might bring with them to the learning situation and explicitly address them in the training program. To overcome interference, the trainer should clearly teach the principles underlying the new correct response and provide a great deal of practice to increase the strength of the new stimulus–response connection.

Transfer of Training If learning that has occurred in the training session is not transferred to the job, the training program has been a waste of company resources. Many training programs have been criticized for their lack of impact on trainees' actual behavior on the job.[28]

Traditional learning theory recommends a number of ways to maximize **transfer of training.** Dealing mainly with training content and methods, these recommendations include maximizing the similarity between training and work settings, teaching the principles that underlie the practice being taught, building in time for overlearning, using a variety of job-related examples so that trainees can see how to apply the skill in a wide range of situations, and making sure that the material really is relevant to trainees' on-the-job needs. In addition to these guidelines for training content and methods, organizations can follow a variety of other procedures to enhance transfer. Some of these occur during training, whereas others have to do with the pre- and post-training environment.

During training, the trainer should work on building trainee self-efficacy because it has been shown that self-efficacy at the end of training predicts the extent to which trainees attempt to use their new skills when back on the job.[29] In addition, as trainees learn skills, the trainer should ask them to develop an action plan, including measurable goals, for performing the new behaviors back on the job. After the training, trainees should be encouraged to assess themselves against these personal goals on a regular basis.[30]

A model borrowed from addiction research has been adapted to facilitate transfer of training back to the job. Called the **relapse-prevention model,** its goal is to help trainees avoid relapsing into their old behavior patterns. This model suggests that training time should be devoted both to anticipating situations that could cause relapse and to planning strategies for dealing with these situations in advance.[31] For instance, if managers who have just been taught to use a participative leadership style expect a relapse to the old autocratic style when working under a tight deadline, they can plan how to avoid the relapse.

Back on the job, a number of factors can affect transfer. One important factor is the opportunity to perform trained tasks. If one is taught how to use a new computer program but does not have on-the-job access to the program for several months after the training, clearly some benefits of the training will be lost. One study of Air Force jet mechanics found that, on average, trainees had performed only about half the trained tasks in the four months following training. Some had performed only four of thirty-four trained tasks during this period![32]

Another key factor is the extent of support for the new behavior in the workplace. If superiors and peers do not accept or reward new behaviors by trainees, the new behaviors will be given up quickly or may not be tried at all. If superiors do not themselves receive the training, they should be briefed on what their subordinates are learning and how they can support use of the new skills. To facilitate transfer, trainees should be counseled both before and after the training by their immediate superior and receive encouragement to follow through with what they have learned.[33]

Whenever possible, groups or teams that will be working together should be trained together so that they can learn both the training content and how to apply it in the unique mix of personalities and abilities found in their own team. Training intact groups should also facilitate the development of group norms that support the new behaviors.

If a training program is held in several sessions over the course of weeks or months, trainees can be given homework assignments that require them to apply what they are learning to an actual work problem and report back at the next session. Some training programs are structured to include an initial classroom component, followed by an on-the-job application project, and then a presentation of project results to the rest of the class and to higher-ups. (When applied to training managers, this is called *action learning,* which is discussed in more detail later.)

This sequence ensures serious efforts to learn and apply the new skills to solving real-world problems.

Another method of enhancing transfer is to provide reminders or job aids to cue and to support performance. If employees have been taught time-management techniques, a cue might be a screen message to each computer user first thing in the morning asking, "Have you made your to-do list today?" Trainers should plan as carefully for transfer of training as they do for the formal portion of the training. The key concept is **embedding.** Recent research clearly shows that training programs are more effective when they are thoroughly embedded in the work setting. Programs must address genuine business needs; be consistent with the organization's culture and values; be understood, sold to, and supported by trainees' superiors beforehand; be integrated with career planning systems; and be reinforced by peers, superiors, opportunities, and reward systems afterward.[34]

Adult Learning Principles Most instructional techniques are based on the well-researched science of teaching children, which is called **pedagogy.** Some educators believe that different techniques are more effective with adult learners. The science of teaching adults has been labeled **andragogy.** Andragogy is based on assumptions about key differences between adult and child learners. First, adults already have a great deal of knowledge and experience that they can learn from and share with others. Second, adults want to take responsibility for themselves and their learning. Third, adults are problem centered; they want to learn things that have immediate usefulness in solving current problems.[35] These characteristics mean that adults may resent being treated like children, as when a trainer assumes they know very little, their experience is irrelevant, and they should learn exactly and only what the trainer tells them to learn.

Andragogy suggests that learning should be active and student centered rather than passive and instructor centered. Instructor-centered teaching occurs when teachers decide what students should learn, present that content as they think best, and then test the learners' mastery of it. A student-centered approach allows learners to be involved in diagnosing their own training needs, picking their own learning goals and objectives, and even structuring their own evaluation, thus ensuring that trainees consider the program relevant.[36] Andragogy also recommends that training focus on real-world problems, perhaps through techniques such as case studies, role playing, and action learning. Finally, andragogy acknowledges and uses the experience and knowledge that adults bring with them. Group discussions can be very effective in getting learners to share relevant experiences and to explicitly discover principles that they already know on an intuitive level. According to one adult trainer, "Never teach an adult something he or she already knows, and never tell a group anything you can get from the group itself."[37]

However, the principles of andragogy have been challenged.[38] There is no concrete evidence that the learning process is truly different for adults as compared with children; some children respond well to student-centered learning, and sometimes adults prefer direction and instructor-imposed structure to self-diagnosis and personal responsibility for learning. Thus a pure andragogical approach is not always appropriate for adults. Particularly in the case of organizational training, the organization often must dictate training content relevant to organizational needs or required certifications. However, andragogical principles can contribute much to the design of training programs and can be used in varying degrees to increase the motivation and personal responsibility of trainees. Switching between instructor-centered methods such as lectures, student-centered methods such as group discussion of past relevant experience or current challenges, and practical activities and case studies can help ensure relevance and maintain learner interest.

There may be other characteristics of learners aside from chronological age that influence which teaching approach is most successful. For instance, learners with short attention spans should receive a wide range of different teaching methods, whereas those with low self-confidence should be exposed to new material more slowly and with a chance for early success in an easy application. Highly instrumental trainees should receive minimal theory and plenty of opportunity to practice clearly job-related skills, and low-interest trainees should be started off with graphic examples of how the training content can help them.[39]

In conclusion, all the learning principles discussed here must be considered in the design of training programs. If these principles are ignored, an effective training program is much less likely to result.

Training Methods

With training objectives defined and learning principles in mind, the trainer must choose appropriate training methods and design the sequence of events in the training program. Perhaps the first decision to be made is whether to conduct the training on the job or away from the job. In many cases the decision is to do some of both. Figure 9.2 diagrams two training options. In each case the right circle represents what an employee already knows when hired. The left circle is what he or she needs to know to be a fully effective employee. If the person was hired because he or she already possessed some relevant skill and knowledge, there will be overlap between the circles, and this content need not be trained. The remaining area of job skill is what the employee must learn. Some aspects of this can be learned informally by on-the-job practice and informal coaching, whereas some

FIGURE 9.2
Deciding Where and How to Train

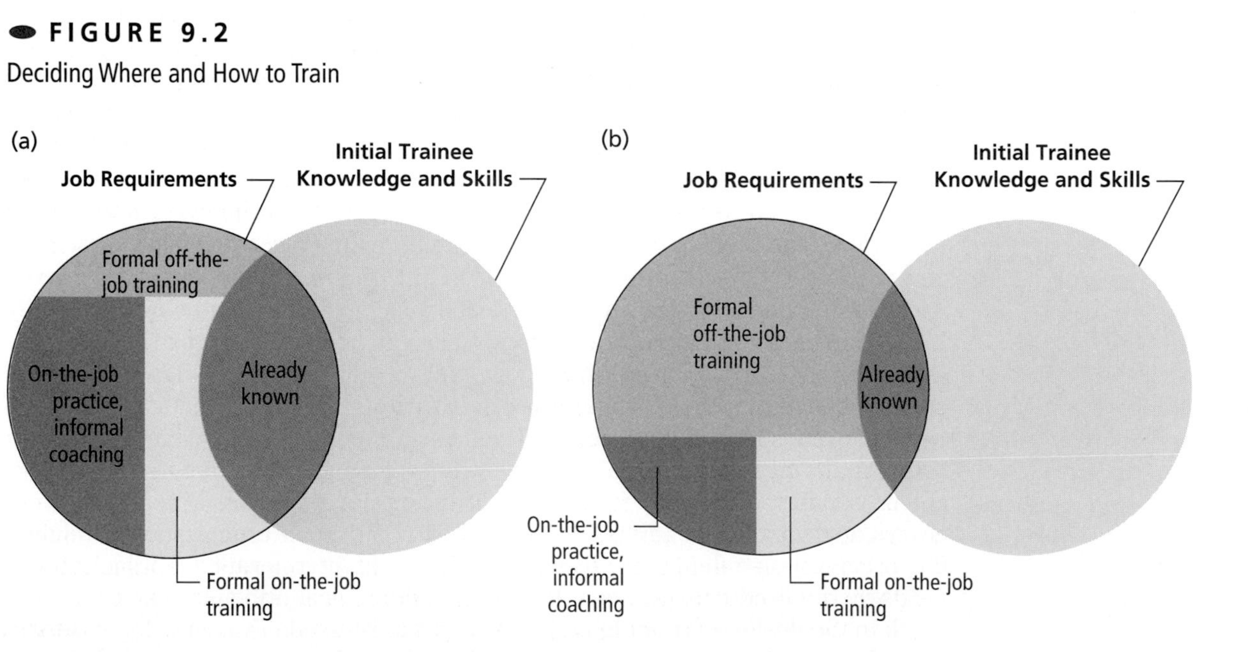

should be taught formally. The formal instruction could be structured on-the-job training, off-the-job classroom training, Web-based coursework or other prescribed self-study courses, or some combination. Figure 9.2(a) diagrams a job that is largely learned on the job, perhaps waiting tables in a pizza restaurant. Figure 9.2(b) shows a job in which more off-the-job training is required—perhaps tax return preparation. The final increment in speed, confidence, and dealing with unusual nuances always happens with on-the-job practice and coaching, but many principles and laws must first be taught in a more formal context.

On-the-Job Training Formal **on-the-job training (OJT)** is conducted at the work site and in the context of the actual job. The vast majority of all industrial training is conducted on the job, often by the trainee's immediate superior or a nominated peer trainer. On-the-job training has several advantages:

1. Because the training setting is also the performance setting, the transfer of training to the job is maximized.
2. The costs of a separate training facility and a full-time trainer are avoided or reduced.
3. Trainee motivation remains high because it is obvious to trainees that what they are learning is relevant to the job.
4. Trainees generally find on-the-job training more valuable than classroom training.[40]

A formal OJT program should be constructed as carefully as a classroom training program. Ideally, the supervisor or peer who acts as the trainer will be taught how to introduce and explain new tasks. The trainer should consider carefully the order in which to introduce new tasks and should use a written checklist and objectives for each stage of the training process. Periodically, the trainer should give the trainee performance tests to ensure that the material is being mastered and to maintain trainee motivation through feedback.[41] **Job instruction training,** a procedure developed to train new defense plant workers during World War II, is outlined in Table 9.5. This is a proven and systematic way to teach a new task.

On the negative side, OJT may suffer from frequent interruptions as the trainer or trainee is called away to perform other duties. Moreover, what many organizations call OJT is really very little training at all. Employees are abandoned on the job and expected to pick up necessary skills as best they can. Often these employees are not informed about important but infrequent events (such as emergency procedures or annual maintenance) and may learn bad habits and unsafe procedures from coworkers.

On-the-job training is taking on increased importance as more and more organizations move toward **multiskilling** or **cross-training,** often in a team context. In these systems, workers first learn their own jobs and then learn one or more of the other jobs performed by members of their team. This provides more interesting work variety, allows for more flexibility in getting work done when team members are absent, and enables workers to better understand the entire work process—all of which are beneficial for continuous improvement and quality efforts. The majority of such cross-training is accomplished on the job using peer coaching and prepared self-paced learning materials (manuals, audiotapes, self-tests, etc.).[42]

Researchers have recently begun to explore informal learning on the job and are finding that unstructured learning from peers sometimes is more effective

TABLE 9.5

Job Instruction Training Procedure

How to Get Ready to Instruct	
1. Have a timetable. —How much skill you expect and when. 2. Break down the job. —List the important steps. —Pick out the key points. 3. Have everything ready. —The right equipment, material, and supplies. 4. Have the workplace properly arranged. —As you would expect the worker to maintain it.	
How to Instruct	
Step 1: *Prepare the Worker* a. Put the worker at ease. b. Find out what he or she knows. c. Arouse interest. d. Place the worker correctly.	Step 3: *Try Out Performance* a. Have the worker perform the operation. b. Have the worker explain the key points. c. Correct errors. d. Reinstruct as needed.
Step 2: *Present the Operation* a. Tell. b. Show. c. Explain. d. Demonstrate	Step 4: *Follow-up* a. Put the worker on his or her own. b. Encourage questioning. c. Check frequently. d. Taper off assistance.

Source: K. Wexley and G. Latham, *Developing and Training Human Resources in Organizations,* 2nd ed. (Figure 6.2 from page 150). © 1991 Addison Wesley Longman Inc. Reprinted by permission of Addison Wesley Longman.

than formally structured classroom training programs. In some cases the knowledge is so subtle and tacit that it cannot be abstracted into general principles and taught in the classroom, or the knowledge is needed immediately rather than months later after a course is designed. Leading organizations are intentionally facilitating **communities of practice,** sets of individuals who share information and develop skills and solutions through informal interaction and communication.[43] For instance, Caterpillar's Knowledge Network supports more than 2,300 communities of practice involving employees, dealers, and suppliers. One of the communities concentrates on bolted joints and fasteners. Individuals with questions or problems related to this topic can post questions and very quickly receive helpful input from other community members.[44]

Apprenticeship Training **Apprenticeship training** is a combination of on- and off-the-job training. The Department of Labor regulates apprenticeship programs, and management and unions often jointly sponsor apprenticeship training. Apprenticeship programs require a minimum of 144 hours of classroom instruction each year, together with on-the-job experience working with a skilled worker. These programs can last from two to five years, depending on the complexity of the skill being taught. Skilled trades usually learned through apprenticeship training include bricklaying, sheet metal, carpentry, plumbing, and electrical.[45]

Off-the-Job Training **Off-the-job training** is conducted in a location specifically designated for training. It may be near the workplace or away from work at a special training center, resort, or laboratory. Conducting the training away from the workplace minimizes distractions and allows trainees to devote their full attention to the material being taught. However, off-the-job training programs may not provide as much transfer of training to the actual job as do on-the-job programs. Many people equate off-the-job training with the lecture method, but in fact a wide variety of methods can be used either in or outside the classroom. Table 9.6 lists a number of potential training methods and activities.

Selecting a Training Method Table 9.7 shows the most commonly used instructional methods, based on a 2003 survey of U.S. companies. The vast majority of organizations always or often use live classroom instruction and workbooks and manuals, though the use of Internet and other technology-mediated training methods (e-learning) has increased rapidly in recent years.

Given the wide range of possible training methods, how does a trainer select the best methods for a particular course? Clearly, one must consider the cost of the method; the number of individuals to be trained; the location and availability of trainees, training rooms, and training technology; and the skill and preference of the trainer and the instructional designer. It is also important to consider trainee preferences, expectations, and likely reactions. Reactions to training content and methods vary across cultures, so training that will be presented in overseas locations requires special consideration (see the International Perspective box). Among the most important criteria in selecting a training method is its match with the training content. The methods chosen must convey needed information and allow trainees to engage in the appropriate type and amount of practice for the skills they are trying to learn. For example, lectures, Web-based training, and assigned readings can be used to convey factual content but may be inadequate for teaching physical or interpersonal skills. A group interaction method would be better suited for teaching interpersonal skills, whereas on-the-job training might be best to teach a physical skill.[46]

Adult learners need variety and involvement, so methods should be as active as possible and change frequently over the course of a training day to maintain attention. Table 9.8 demonstrates how a variety of methods might be used for different topics in a one-day classroom training program on win–win negotiation. Often it is desirable to use different training methods at different points during the training process. For instance, the first step may require a method that is good for conveying information or an overview (lectures, videotapes), whereas later steps may require hands-on practice alternating with discussion of how one might apply the principles being taught on the job. It is increasingly common (and efficient) to use e-learning methods to convey principles and information to trainees, followed by face-to-face training, practice, or mentoring to develop skills based on the knowledge learned in the first stage. This mixture of e-learning and live instruction is called **blended learning.**

TABLE 9.6

Some Off-the-Job Training Methods and Activities

Action planning Often a closing activity asking participants to specify or set goals about exactly what they will do differently back on the job.

Behavior-modeling training Use of a videotape to demonstrate the steps in a supervisory activity (such as conducting a disciplinary interview), followed by role-played skill practice and feedback.

Behavioral simulation Large-scale multiperson role play, noncomputerized business game.

Brainstorming Creative idea-generation exercise in which no criticism is allowed.

Business game Computerized business simulation that requires participants to make decisions about strategy and investments and then provides financial results based on the decisions.

Buzz group Small-group discussion of several minutes' duration on an assigned topic.

Case study From a one-paragraph vignette to a fifty-page Harvard-style case.

Demonstration

E-learning Web-based courses or tutorials, CD-ROM courses, virtual classrooms, interactive TV, satellite broadcasts, and so forth.

Experiential exercise

Field trip

Group discussion

Guest speaker

Guided teaching Drawing from the group the points the lecturer otherwise would make him- or herself.

Ice breaker Get-acquainted exercise.

Information search Asking trainees to locate the answers to questions in the training materials or manuals provided.

Intergroup exchange Small groups share their ideas or findings with another group.

Learning game Competition between teams in a quiz show format.

Lecture

Mental imagery Asking participants to close their eyes and visualize or recall something or engage in mental rehearsal of a physical or interpersonal skill.

Outdoor leadership training Team activities that may include hiking, rope courses, or other physical challenges along with problem-solving activities.

Pair and trio discussion tasks

Panel discussion

Problem-solving activities

Role play

Self-assessment instrument or quiz An example is a conflict resolution–style inventory.

Team building A series of group activities and sometimes surveys used to develop team skills and role clarity in a team of people who must work together closely on the job.

Videotapes Can be used alone or for self-study, but are most effective if embedded in discussion and practice.

Workbooks Workbooks and other written self-study materials.

TABLE 9.7

Frequency with Which Instructional Methods Are Used

	Always	Often	Seldom	Never
Case studies	3%	37%	46%	14%
CD-ROM, DVD	1%	44%	47%	8%
Computer-based games, simulations	1%	9%	47%	44%
Instructor-led classroom	19%	72%	8%	1%
Internet/intranet	7%	56%	30%	7%
Non-computer-based games, simulations	2%	23%	40%	35%
Public seminars	2%	40%	48%	10%
Role play	5%	30%	44%	21%
Satellite/broadcast TV	1%	11%	33%	55%
Self-study, non-computer-based	2%	21%	52%	25%
Videoconferencing	2%	20%	40%	38%
Videotapes	4%	48%	36%	11%
Virtual classroom with instructor	2%	19%	40%	39%
Web-based self study	5%	39%	43%	13%
Workbooks and manuals	19%	60%	19%	2%

Source: Adapted from T. Galvin, "2003 Industry Report," *Training*, Vol. 40, October 2003, pp. 30–31.

E-learning As can be seen in Table 9.7, a large share of firms are using technology in the training delivery process. **E-learning** methods include training delivered by CD-ROM, intranet, or Internet; satellite broadcasts; virtual classrooms; and digital collaboration between trainees. Information provided may vary from a single needed fact or procedure, to a module on a narrow topic, to a broader training course, to a full university degree. Most firms using e-learning to a significant extent have invested in a **learning management system.** These systems provide a single log-on point for all e-learning opportunities offered through the company, as well as functioning as a human resource development information system. In the latter capacity, they manage course registration and scheduling, generate reports of training activities, and track employee completions of both e-learning and traditional training activities throughout the organization.[47]

Many e-learning resources are entirely self-paced, allowing employees to initiate and pursue training when they need it and when they have time. However, some e-learning courses have set start and end dates and interactivity with an instructor and sometimes classmates. In **synchronous e-learning programs,** all participants must log on to discussion groups or attend broadcasts in a virtual classroom at the same time. In **asynchronous e-learning programs,** students work in their own time but may interact with the instructor or other students by e-mail, discussion groups, or blackboard programs throughout the duration of the course.

There are many advantages to e-learning in terms of logistics, cost, and efficiency of learning (see Table 9.9). It has been suggested that e-learning is ideal for work forces with high diversity in age, learning speed, and skill, which could cause difficulty in a traditional classroom setting. There is some evidence that

TABLE 9.8

Outline for a Training Program on Win–Win Negotiating

Activity	Time (minutes)	Method
I. Opening activities		
A. Agenda review	5	Presentation
B. Things we have in common	30	Icebreaker
C. Interactive overview of conflict resolution	45	Intergroup exchange
II. What you bring to conflict situations		
A. Feelings about conflict	20	Physical continuum
B. Looking at your conflict style	20	Game
C. Assessing your conflict style	30	Questionnaire
D. Experiencing different approaches to conflict	30	Role play
E. Conflict behavior is situational	10	Checklist
F. Misunderstandings in conflict situations	15	Lecturette
G. Viewing others objectively	15	Writing task
III. Conflict-resolution effectiveness		
A. Stating complaints and requesting change	30	Skills practice
B. Anatomy of an argument	30	Information search
C. Dealing with difficult people	25	Mental imagery
D. Reframing conflict scenarios	20	Dyadic discussion
E. The steps of negotiation	45	Skills practice
F. Putting it all together	30	Role play
G. What to do when negotiation fails or never gets started	20	Intergroup exchange
IV. Closing activities		
A. Action planning	30	Writing task
B. Obstacle assessment	20	Mental imagery

Source: From M. Silberman's *Twenty Active Training Programs*. Copyright © 1992 Pfeiffer/Jossey-Bass. Reprinted by permission.

training time is reduced with e-learning, as more knowledgeable trainees can skip sections they know and progress more quickly than they could in a classroom. E-learning allows many employees to be trained in a short period of time, and learning management systems can easily track whether required training has been completed. KPMG has gone from 90 percent classroom to 70 percent electronic training in the past few years. The company says that classroom training is too expensive and too slow to keep their people worldwide up to date on the latest things they need to know.[48] The Internal Revenue Service and the Department of Defense's Acquisitions, Technology, and Logistics group are also making serious investments in e-learning.[49] See the Partnerships for Strategic Success box for another example of the benefits of a correctly targeted and implemented e-leaning approach.

However, there are disadvantages to e-learning. The start-up costs for equipment can be high. Standards are evolving, but it is still common to experience compatibility problems between learning management systems, off-the-shelf

TABLE 9.9

Advantages of E-Learning

- Training can be conducted at remote or international sites, 24/7.
- Training is available on demand, when needed or when the work schedule permits.
- Costs for trainers and travel are very limited.
- New programs and updates can be delivered worldwide simultaneously.
- Very large numbers of people can receive the training at the same time.
- Learning management systems can keep and update records on who has commenced or completed which programs.
- When self-paced, the average time to complete a learning unit is usually considerably less than when the same material is presented using traditional classroom methods.
- Programs can provide online assessment/certification and immediate feedback to learners.
- Involvement and active practice may be higher than in the classroom, where some students can "tune out" or become lost in the crowd.
- If on CD-ROM or a company intranet, review of previously studied material is readily available when a refresher is needed.

courses from various vendors, and programs on individual users' computers.[50] Custom-designed courses are expensive and time consuming to develop. Some commercially available e-learning programs are very good, but others are little more than text on a screen.[51] When employees are offered the opportunity to take commercial or university-based courses online, there are often problems with quality of instruction, choosing among the many programs available, and flagging learner motivation.[52] There are also concerns that employers may "require" employees to complete e-learning programs on their own time, without the compensation that may be legally due to them.[53]

Will e-learning eventually replace classroom training? The demise of the traditional training room has been predicted (wrongly) since the first primitive teaching machine was developed half a century ago. However, it finally seems likely that a significant share of routine training will come to be delivered electronically, and that face-to-face training will be used more selectively as the situation warrants. As mentioned previously, e-learning is often used as a complement to face-to-face training rather than as a complete replacement for it. For instance, cardiopulmonary resuscitation might best be taught in an e-learning theory session concluding with a test on the content, followed by classroom practice on resuscitation dummies.[54] Such "blended" learning experiences can be very effective when both knowledge and skill need to be learned.[55]

Management Development

Because managerial work is important, complex, and challenging, many organizations provide regular management training. Training for executives, managers, and supervisors accounts for the lion's share of training dollars spent, despite the

INTERNATIONAL PERSPECTIVE

Intercultural Issues in Training

Interesting problems can arise when a trainer or consultant goes on the road to deliver training programs to trainees overseas, or addresses trainees from other countries in a virtual classroom. Training programs that have been very successful in one country can be a disaster elsewhere for a number of reasons:

- Training content does not transfer across cultures.
- Content is acceptable, but the methods of delivery are not culturally appropriate.
- Norms about training session behavior may be different.
- The trainer's personal behavior may be inappropriate.
- Equipment problems may occur.

Especially in the case of management training, cultural assumptions and practices may mean that the content of a training program is simply wrong for that culture. For instance, it may be inappropriate to attempt to teach supervisors in a very high power distance country to use participative decision making. In these countries, the leader is supposed to have all the answers, and inviting subordinates to become involved is regarded as a sign of weakness and incompetence. Likewise, a program on how to give clear negative feedback in a disciplinary interview may be unsuitable in a culture in which saving face is critically important.

More often, the content may be relevant but the highly interactive and egalitarian training methods often recommended in the English-speaking West do not suit local learners. In high power distance cultures, subordinates generally will not speak out in a group with people of mixed levels or status—only the most senior person will speak. Trainers often like to stimulate vigorous debate, but this approach will fall flat when trainee status is unequal or in a culture that values harmony. Competitive games that pit one individual or team against another are also not suited to collective or high-harmony cultures. Active learning methods involving role plays or other public practice methods can be very threatening in a culture sensitive to saving face. For example, behavior-modeling training is not well received in Hong Kong because of the substantial amount of role playing involved. Learners from cultures that are sensitive to saving face and to power distinctions are often more comfortable with teacher-centered methods such as lectures than with participative methods.

We have found that cultures seem to vary as to whether inductive or deductive methods are best for

fact that there are many more nonmanagerial employees than managers. The results of all this training, however, are not always clear because management development programs are seldom evaluated rigorously. A comprehensive review of the evaluations that have been done concluded that many types of management development programs do have a beneficial impact on job behavior.[56] Among these programs, those that provide carefully designed training linked to a thorough needs assessment should be more effective than faddish programs purchased from vendors of canned, one-size-fits-all management development packages.[57]

Figure 9.3 reflects research showing that managers learn their craft in a number of ways. Most say that they have learned the greatest amount not through studying for university degrees or from company-sponsored management training, but from actually doing the job and interacting with others in the work environment. Managers say that the most intense learning occurs from job assignments that are very difficult and challenging, such as building a new start-up operation or turning around a failing operation; from assignments that represent a major change or increase in responsibility, such as moving from a staff to a line position,

presenting new material. In the English-speaking West, we tend to present a theory first and then give some examples of how it might be applied (deduction). During a management development course in Brunei, it seemed that supervisors were confused when the theory was introduced first but caught on when several concrete examples preceded the presentation of a general principle (induction). A sensitive cross-cultural trainer should be prepared to switch strategies upon noticing differences like these.

Norms about training session behavior may vary across cultures. For instance, in Germany, training is *not* supposed to be fun; it is serious business. The trainer who opens a session with a joke and uses games as teaching aids quickly loses credibility. There are also norms about formality and punctuality. In much of Europe it would be impolite to call people one had just met by their first names. Titles are important, so name badges should show their wearer's company position as well as full name. In Germany, training sessions should begin and end on time and be clearly structured. In Spain, France, and Italy, time must be allowed for socializing and networking because relationships are very important in these cultures.

Trainers must behave in ways that are culturally appropriate. This may mean dressing more formally than they might for training sessions at home. Female trainers should dress very modestly in conservative countries (the Middle East, Asia). In Japan, teachers are very highly respected and must act in a way deserving of such respect rather than being casual and overly friendly. In cultures sensitive to saving face, the trainer should be careful not to put people on the spot by singling them out or asking for an answer before they have had time to prepare.

Finally, there can be equipment problems in cross-cultural training. Electrical systems differ, and high-tech training equipment may not be available or electrically compatible. A clever international trainer will be prepared with back-up methods and activities in case the VCR does not work or the intended methods just do not seem to be getting through to the audience. The trainer will also do a lot of homework before traveling to learn as much as possible about the culture and organization in which he or she will be teaching.

Sources: P. S. Kirkbride and S. F. Y. Tang, "The Transferability of Management Training and Development: The Case of Hong Kong," *Asia Pacific Human Resource Management,* February 1989, pp. 7–19; G. Adler, "The Case of the Floundering Expatriate," *Harvard Business Review,* July–August 1995, pp. 24–40; and B. Filipczak, "Think Locally, Train Globally," *Training,* January 1997, pp. 41–48.

moving to a different functional area, or moving to a job with greatly increased responsibilities for people, dollars, or units; and from hardships, such as a personal or business failure or dealing with very difficult individuals. Thus a complete program of management development should include a job assignment and succession system that continuously presents new challenges.[58]

Formal training of supervisors and junior managers is often done by in-house trainers or by training consultants. These employees may need basic skills in planning, leading, organizing, and controlling. Methods such as lectures, behavior modeling training, case studies, behavioral simulations, experiential exercises, and role plays are commonly used. Mentoring is also important to new managers. Some mentorship relations develop informally; other companies assign more senior managers to coach one or more junior managers on their job performance and advise them on career plans.[59]

Higher level managers and executives usually have basic managerial skills already and need a qualitatively different type of development. Table 9.10 summarizes some recent trends in state-of-the-art executive development.[60] Mini-M.B.A.

PARTNERSHIPS FOR STRATEGIC SUCCESS

The Learning Revolution at Rockwell Collins

Rockwell Collins is a manufacturer of instruments and communication systems for aircraft. The Cedar Rapids–based company has 17,000 employees in sixty-three domestic and overseas locations. In 1998 the company had serious training problems. Nearly all training was delivered in classrooms at its Cedar Rapids headquarters, from 8:00 a.m. to 5:00 p.m. The 60 percent of employees working elsewhere, and those working evening and night shifts, found it difficult and expensive to attend training, and often could not or did not do so. Courses were not seen as relevant to actual job needs, and supervisors did not regard training as "real work" or a legitimate use of time. Needs analysis was seldom done, with HRD staff merely responding to requests for training by hiring an outside vendor. Further, many highly skilled senior technicians were nearing retirement age, and there was concern about losing their knowledge when they left. Mechanisms were needed for capturing this knowledge and passing it on to others, and for delivering timely and relevant training on an equal basis to employees at all locations. Further, a shift in the corporate attitude toward training was required.

Cliff Purington was hired in 1998 with the mission of addressing these concerns. In partnership with a consultant and a number of vendors, he produced an amazing turnaround, increasing the amount of training provided by 400 percent, reducing costs by 40 percent, and saving more than $31 million in four years. E-learning was a large part of the solution, but it only succeeded because of careful groundwork to correctly identify business needs, address cultural issues, involve managers, and continuously refine and sell the changes to employees.

In the first year of a three-year plan, 30 percent of classroom training was shifted to e-learning delivery. This comprised readily available off-the-shelf programs that addressed widespread and genuine needs. In each of the next two years, a further 20 percent of classroom topics were migrated to e-learning mode. Many of these programs were custom-designed to meet Rockwell Collin's specific technical needs. E-learning programs were delivered by self-paced Web-based programs, CD-ROM programs, and live training in online virtual classrooms.

As soon as a program was available in e-learning mode, Purington stopped offering it in the classroom, thus encouraging staff to use the new system. Given supervisors' attitudes toward training, it was judged unlikely that employees would be able to undertake meaningful training while at their desks, where they were expected to be working instead. So Purington installed nineteen learning centers around the company where employees could go to concentrate on completing a learning module.

One spectacular success story was a training program on electromagnetic interference—critical knowledge to design engineers, the lack of which was creating major problems for the company. It would have taken thirteen years to deliver the twenty-hour course to the 2,500 engineers who needed it using traditional classroom methods. Instead, three months were devoted to developing an eight-hour-long CD-ROM course covering the same material. Just six months after the course was released, 1,300 engineers had completed it, and EMI issues were no longer causing problems for the company. Another success story was the 500 "QuickLearns" created for less than $4,000 each. These are CD video modules of no more than twenty minutes duration that show an experienced employee performing and explaining a single important task. Text explaining the process is also provided, along with self-test quizzes. QuickLearns helped capture the knowledge of the most experienced technicians before they retired and were also useful for training and refreshing knowledge of common procedures that many employees needed to be taught.

Source: C. Purington and C. Butler, with S. F. Gale, *Built to Last: The Inside Story of How Rockwell Collins Became a True Learning Organization* (New York: AMACOM, 2003).

FIGURE 9.3
How Managers Learn

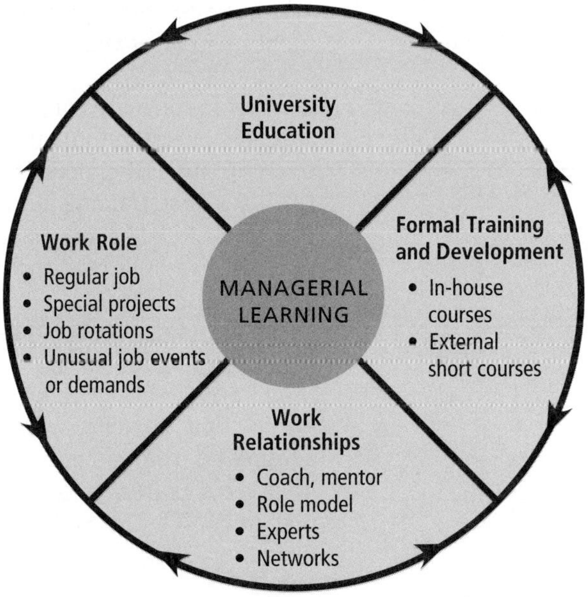

and similar programs that focus on teaching functional skills such as accounting and marketing have been on the decline for the past fifteen years. In their place are customized in-house programs that are closely tied to important business needs, including managing change and strategic leadership. Many of the largest and most successful organizations have what amounts to their own "university,"

TABLE 9.10
Trends in State-of-the-Art Executive Development

There is less:
- Use of university-based programs and mini-MBAs.
- Focus on functional knowledge (marketing, accounting, finance).

There is more:
- Use of personal coaches.
- Emphasis on customized, in-house programs and corporate universities.
- Emphasis on strategic leadership and change management.
- Use of 360-degree feedback programs to motivate learning and build learning experiences customized to individuals.
- Use of action learning.
- Training driven by strategic and business needs.
- Training of entire top management teams.
- Use of executives as trainers rather than professors or training specialists.
- Cascading of training from the top down.
- Use of multicompany consortia for developing top talent.
- Use of competency models to drive an integrated program of selection, appraisal, and training.

such as General Electric's highly regarded Crotonville Management Development Institute in New York State.

Another trend over the past ten years is the use of **competency models.** Competency models are carefully derived organization-specific lists of the skills or competencies needed to manage effectively in that organization. The models are used to integrate HR practices so that selection, performance appraisal, 360-degree feedback instruments, and training programs are all aimed at building the same essential skills. Managers understand the competencies valued by their organization, receive appraisal and 360-degree feedback on their possession of these competencies, attend formal training programs aimed at improving key competencies, and can engage in self-directed learning or receive individual coaching to build their standing on specific competencies.[61]

Action Learning An increasingly common method of middle and upper management development combines on- and off-the-job learning. **Action learning** has been used in Europe for more than thirty years and has become increasingly popular in the United States over the past fifteen years. The underlying idea is that formal training is good at conveying factual knowledge but poor at teaching individuals to seek out and use knowledge to solve complex problems in innovative ways . . . yet it is the latter that is most crucial for managerial success. Action learning programs usually feature some classroom instruction together with an applied project tackled by a team of trainees. They investigate and solve a real organizational problem that is outside their area of expertise and very complex. They struggle to analyze the problem—learning from fellow trainees and tutors, collecting data, and reading from the literature as necessary to discover a solution. In the process, they develop specific managerial competencies along with learning how to learn.[62] Action learning programs usually culminate in trainee presentations of their conclusions to an audience of senior executives.[63]

New Employee Orientation

A very common type of training is new employee orientation. All employees, whether managerial or nonmanagerial, should be provided with a systematic orientation when they first join an organization. Newcomers have much to learn about their supervisors and coworkers, the demands of their job, company rules and procedures, and the organization's culture and assumptions. Until employees learn enough to feel comfortable in these areas, they can experience uncertainty and stress.[64] A good orientation program may help newcomers feel part of the company and the team, build loyalty, help them get up to speed more quickly, and even reduce early employee turnover.[65]

A thorough introduction to the organization's culture and mission is especially important when employees must convey the culture to clients through their actions. For example, new hires ("cast members") at Walt Disney World in Orlando, Florida, spend their first day and a half at Disney University taking a course called Traditions 1. They learn about the history of the company, the special language used, and the importance of cheerful and informative interactions with guests.[66]

Employees usually say that their best source of information about the organization is coworkers. Thus, if at all possible, newcomers should be assigned a "buddy" or be given a position in which they have plenty of access to friendly coworkers.[67] In addition, the organization should provide formal orientation training.

TABLE 9.11

Content of a Two-Phase New Employee Orientation System

Administered by the Supervisor	Administered by a Trainer, with Guest Appearances by Company Leaders
About the department:	*About the organization:*
• Relationships to other units	• History
• Mission and goals	• Products
• Procedures	• Goals
• Work flow	• Organization structure
• Facilities	• Who's who in the organization
• Schedule	• Culture, ethical principles
• Introduction to coworkers	*Rules and procedures:*
About the job:	• Employee handbook
• Workstation	• Work hours
• Duties	• Vacation and leave
• Goals/performance standards	• Provision of pay and benefits
• Tools and equipment	• Discipline system
• Where to go, whom to ask for help	• Complaint/suggestion systems
• On-the-job training	
Human resource issues:	
• Performance appraisal process	
• Promotion criteria	
• Salary increase schedule and criteria	
• Training plans	

Source: Based on G. Dessler, *Personnel Management* (Reston, Va.: Reston Publishing Company, 1984), pp. 223–277.

An employee orientation program might feature two parts: (1) an introduction to the specific job and department, provided by the supervisor, and (2) one or more sessions of general orientation to the company, coordinated by the HRM department. Supervisors should be trained to orient new employees and should use a checklist to be sure that they cover all important points. Table 9.11 lists sample contents for both parts of the orientation process.[68] Increasingly, orientation programs are being delivered using more than one method. Live presentations, tours, videotapes, Web-based training, buddy systems, one-on-one sessions with the manager, and more may form part of the orientation process. Note that a "one size fits all" approach to new employee orientation is probably not appropriate. Although core material is relevant to all employees, orientations should be somewhat customized to the job and organizational level of participants.[69]

THE EVALUATION PHASE

The third step in the instructional systems design model (see Figure 9.1) is to deliver the training that has been designed in the second step to meet the needs identified in the first step. We will not discuss delivery specifically in this chapter but will proceed to the final step in the training cycle, which is **evaluation.**[70] Evaluation is the determination of the extent to which the training activities have met their goals. Unfortunately, the evaluation is often done poorly or ignored altogether. One reason for this is that managers simply tend to assume that training will work. Another is that a manager who champions a training program may feel threatened by the prospect of an objective evaluation of the program's effectiveness.[71]

The basic approach to evaluation should be to determine the extent to which the training program has met the objectives identified prior to the training. Planning for the evaluation should start at the same time that planning for the training program begins. If the goals of the program are clearly stated as specific objectives, the appropriate evaluation method can be implemented at the same time as the program.

Evaluation Levels and Purposes

Donald Kirkpatrick developed the best-known and most widely used framework for the evaluation of training programs.[72] **Kirkpatrick's four levels of evaluation** are shown in Figure 9.4. Each level answers a very important but different question about the effectiveness of the program.

Reaction The first level involves **reaction measures,** or the participants' feelings about the program. Reaction information is usually gathered by questionnaire during or immediately after the program. At least two aspects of reaction should be assessed: whether trainees *enjoyed* the program, and whether they think the program will be *useful* to them. Figure 9.5 shows the training evaluation questionnaire used by Black & Decker in their Eastern Hemisphere locations.

Learning The second level of evaluation has to do with learning. **Learning measures** assess the degree to which trainees have mastered the concepts, information, and skills the training tried to impart. Learning is assessed during or at the end of the training program with paper-and-pencil or computerized tests, performance tests, and graded simulation exercises. In addition to assessing the success of the training program, learning measures are essential when the training is aimed at certifying individual employees as proficient in a particular skill.

Behavior On-the-job behavior is the third level of evaluation in Kirkpatrick's approach. **Behavior measures** ask whether employees are doing things differently on the job after training, whether they are visibly using what they have been taught. In essence, this is transfer of training. On-the-job behavior can be assessed by any of the performance evaluation techniques discussed in Chapter 10. Behavior ratings can be collected from the superior, peers, subordinates, or clients of the trained employees.

Results The final level of evaluation involves **results measures.** At this level the impact of the training program on the work group or organization as a whole is assessed objectively. The appropriate objective measures to use depend on the content and objectives of the training. Sample measures of results might include sales, productivity, quality, accidents, turnover, customer complaints, and employee attitudes.

Kirkpatrick suggests that the last three levels of evaluation may form a hierarchy. Change farther up the hierarchy of outcomes is unlikely unless change has occurred lower in the hierarchy. That is, if no learning has occurred, it is unlikely

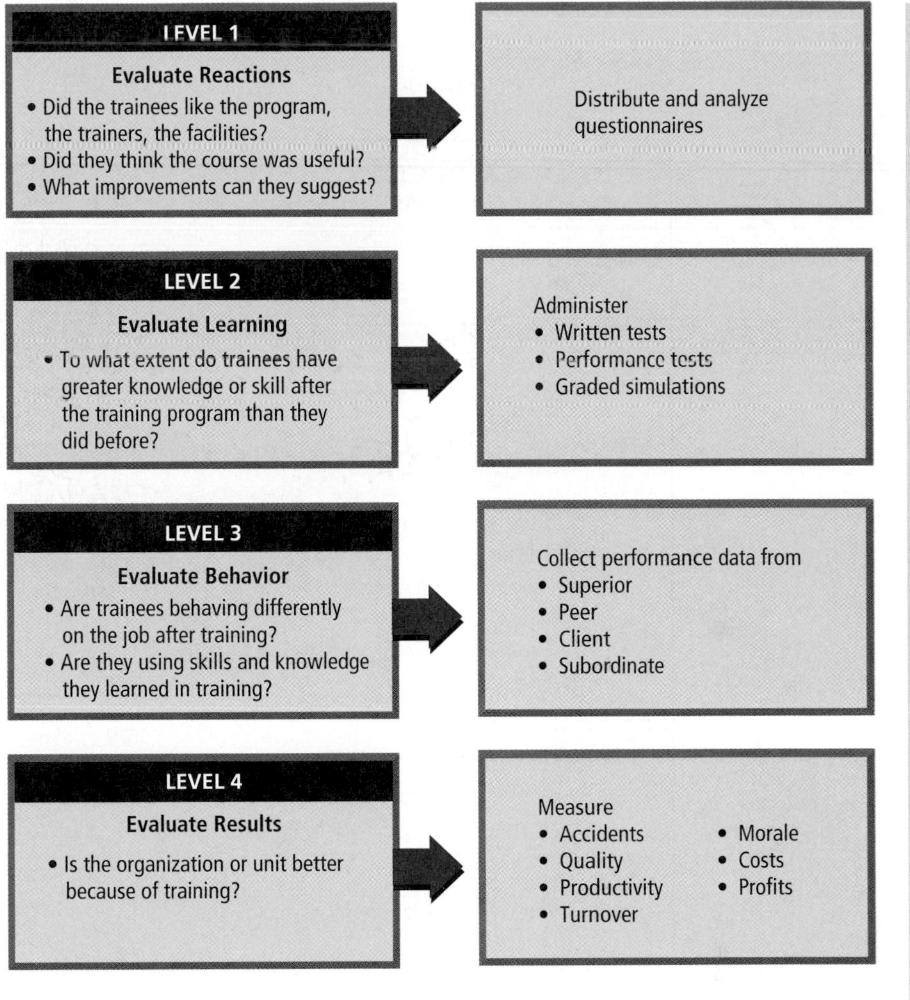

FIGURE 9.4

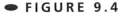

Kirkpatrick's Four Levels of Training Evaluation

Source: Reprinted with permission from the November 1983 issue of *Personnel Administrator,* copyright, 1983, the Society for Human Resource Management, Alexandria, Va.

that on-the-job behavior will change. If behavior does not change, it is unlikely that measurable improvements in results will be observed. However, a favorable reaction is not necessarily a prerequisite to learning—a fun program may or may not be a useful one.[73]

A thorough evaluation would include measurements at all four of these levels. Such a thorough evaluation should be undertaken for expensive or strategically important training programs where there is an opportunity to use the data to improve the program in the future. However, for an inexpensive program offered only once to a small group of employees, a simple reaction questionnaire may provide all the evaluation needed.[74]

Evaluation Designs

Designing a good evaluation effort involves knowing when to collect evaluation measures and which groups to collect them from.[75] Together these factors define the experimental design used to assess the impact of the training.

FIGURE 9.5

Training Evaluation Form

Source: Reprinted with the permission of The Black & Decker Corporation.

BLACK & DECKER
EASTERN HEMISPHERE

TRAINING EVALUATION FORM

NAME OF PARTICIPANT : ______________________ (OPTIONAL)

COURSE TITLE : ______________________

COURSE PROVIDER : ______________________

INSTRUCTOR (S) : ______________________

COURSE DURATION : ____________ TO ____________

Scale
1 Poor
2 Fair
3 Meet Expectations
4 Exceed Expectations
5 Outstanding

1. CONTENT — *Please circle your response*

To what extent did this course meet your learning objectives? 1 2 3 4 5

Remarks: ______________________

2. TRAINING METHODOLOGY

a) lectures/exercises were comprehensive & appropriate 1 2 3 4 5

b) visual aids reinforced the learning 1 2 3 4 5

c) handouts/manual were well written & will be a useful reference 1 2 3 4 5

Remarks: ______________________

3. INSTRUCTOR EFFECTIVENESS

a) was well prepared and organized 1 2 3 4 5

b) able to communicate the concepts & impart skills effectively 1 2 3 4 5

c) encourages participation and learning in class 1 2 3 4 5

Remarks: ______________________

4. OVERALL RATING OF THE COURSE 1 2 3 4 5

5. Would you recommend this course to others in the organization? ( )Yes ( ) No ( )Maybe

Remarks : ______________________
(Please suggest names/designation where appropriate)

6. COMMENTS

Which three(3) aspects of the course were most helpful? In what way was it most helpful?

____

____

____

Which three(3) aspects of the course could be improved? Please elaborate.

____

____

____

Additional Comments

____

To be filled in by the Immediate Supervisor(for external programs)

7. SHARING OF LEARNINGS

☐ not applicable

☐ will share his/her learnings with at least one colleague

☐ will share his/her learnings in the department meeting

SIGNATURE OF IMMEDIATE SUPERVISOR DATE

Because reaction measures assess whether participants like the training and think it will be useful, these measures are collected during or immediately after the training. Ideally, an additional reaction questionnaire should be sent to participants several months after the training to see if they still believe the training has been of use in their jobs.

The purpose of learning, behavior, and results measures is quite different from that of reaction measures, in that the trainer is trying to discover whether or not a *change* has occurred in the variable being measured—that is, do trainees know more, behave differently, or produce better results after than before the training? If there has been a change, the trainer will want to know whether it can be attributed to the training program—that is, did the training program bring about the change?

There are two basic strategies for determining whether a change has occurred. The first is to compare the trainees after the training to the way they were before the training. At the very least, this comparison involves the collection of evaluation measures at two points in time. The second strategy is to compare the learning, behavior, or results of the trained group to the learning, behavior, or results of a group that has not been trained but is otherwise as similar as possible to the trained group. The strongest evaluation designs draw on both these strategies. There are many complex and highly effective designs for evaluating training. This section covers only a few of the more straightforward ones (see Figure 9.6).

One-Shot Posttest-Only Design In the **one-shot posttest-only design,** training evaluation measures are collected only from the trained group, after the training has been conducted. Because there is no pretraining measure and no untrained group for purposes of comparison, there is no way to determine whether a change has occurred or whether any change has been caused by the training. However, if the aim is to determine whether a desired standard of performance has been reached, this simple design might produce some useful data. For instance, one might be able to verify that 90 percent of the trainees passed the learning test at the end of training, that after the training program customer complaints averaged one per thousand transactions, or that Bob, Harry, and Sue earned their certificate in CPR.

One-Group Pretest–Posttest Design Another very simple design is the **one-group pretest–posttest design,** in which the training group is assessed both before and after the training. For instance, the productivity of the trained group might be found to be 5 percent higher after training than it was before training. Although this design does allow a trainer to determine if there has been a change, it does not enable the trainer to conclude with absolute certainty that the training brought about the change. A change from one time period to another can be caused by anything that occurs between measurements, not just by the training. For instance, there might be a new supervisor, revised work methods, a change in the quality of raw materials, an increase in workload, employee turnover, a change in the pay system, or union activity. Any of these or similar factors could affect behavior or results measures and cause the training evaluation to be misleading. If nontraining concurrent events seem unlikely to account for a change from before to after training, then the trainer can gain some useful information about the effectiveness of the training from this simple design.

FIGURE 9.6
Designs for Evaluating Training

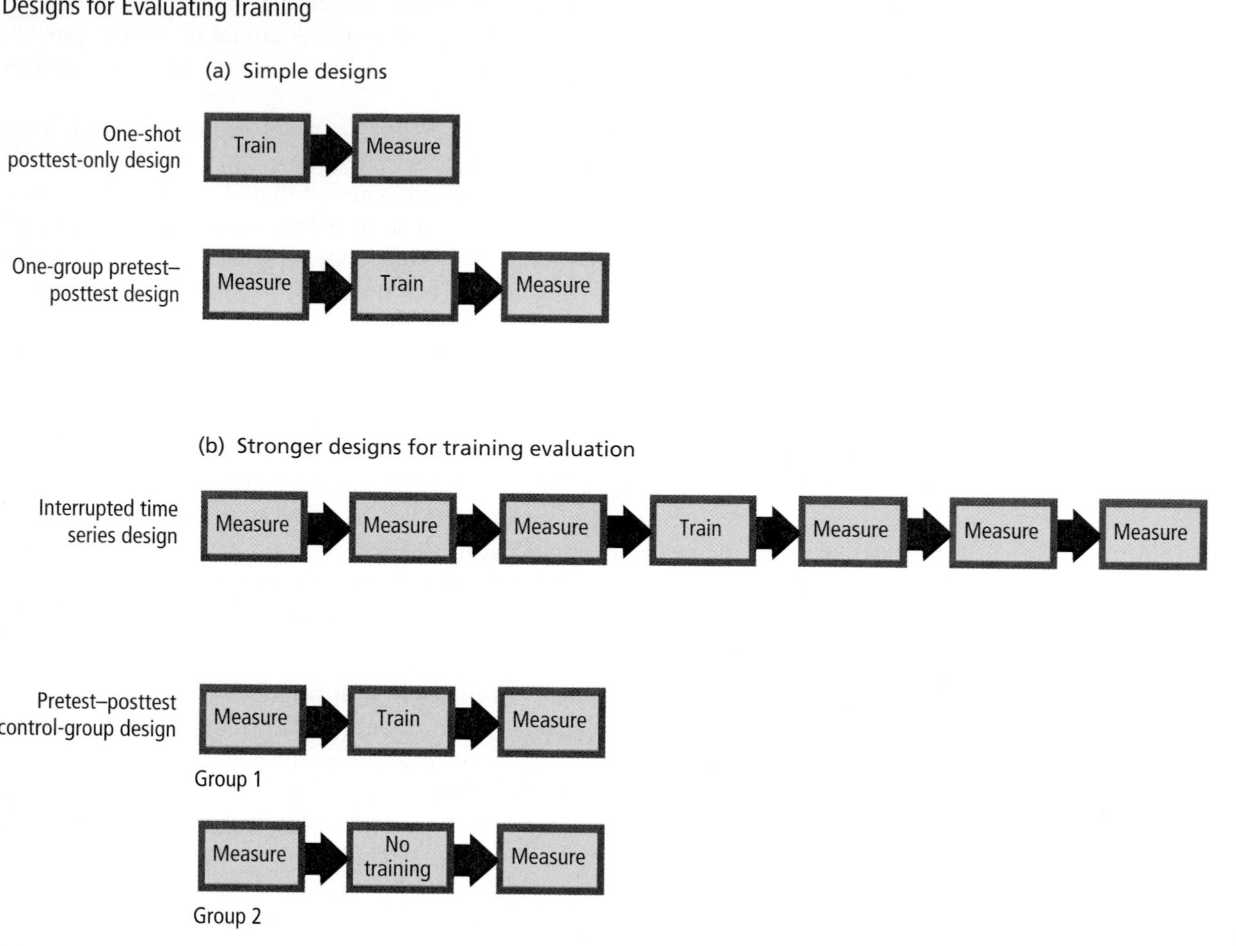

Interrupted Time Series Design An improved evaluation design that avoids some of the above-mentioned problems is the **interrupted time series design.** In this design, the trainer measures the group several times both before and after the training. The trainer probably should not use an obtrusive measure, such as a questionnaire or learning test, or trainees could improve over time just because they are gaining practice with the measure. Objective measures of behavior or results (such as sales volume, quality, or customer complaints) are less obtrusive, and they are easy to collect repeatedly.

The interrupted time series design allows the trainer to observe trends in performance and to see if there is a change in the trend immediately after the training. For instance, a trainer may find that employees are slowly improving with experience over time but that a jump in performance occurs shortly after the training. This design is the best one to use if all employees are to be trained simultaneously, leaving none to serve as a control group.

Pretest–Posttest Control-Group Design An even better design uses a control group of employees who are very similar to the training group except that they do not receive the training (at least not yet). In the **pretest–posttest control-group design,** both the group to receive the training and the control group are measured at least once before and once after the training. This design allows the trainer to draw quite firm conclusions about (1) whether any change has occurred and, (2) if it has, whether the change was due to the training.

The trainer might normally expect to find that the trained group improves from pretest to posttest, whereas the control group stays the same. However, other patterns of results also can be interpreted under this design. For instance, if the training group is the same after the training as before, but the control group is worse on the posttest than on the pretest, then the training probably was effective in preventing a decline in performance that would otherwise have occurred.

Using the Evaluation to Improve Training

Information from the training evaluation can be used in making decisions about whether to continue the training program or how to improve it. Modifying the training based on reaction measures is fairly straightforward. A boring speaker can be replaced, a video rated as irrelevant dropped, or a caterer changed, depending on the feedback received. If a sound evaluation design was used, additional modifications of the training program might be suggested by trainees' scores on the learning, behavior, or results measures.

If insufficient learning occurred, the training presentation itself may have been at fault. Information may have been presented unclearly, or inadequate time and practice may have been allowed for trainees to absorb the material. Alternatively, trainee readiness or motivation may have been deficient so that an otherwise well-designed training experience had no real impact on the trainees.

If behavior on the job did not improve despite gains in learning, the fault could lie in the needs assessment, the training program itself, or the work environment. If the initial needs assessment was not performed correctly, trainees might have mastered material that was not relevant to the demands of their jobs. Thus, although they might have learned something from the training, what they learned is not something they can use. Another possibility is that the training content might have been appropriate, but there was insufficient emphasis either on transfer of training to the job or on relapse prevention. Finally, the fault could lie in the work environment if supervisors or the environment do not facilitate the use of new skills.

When learning and behavior change, but results do not improve, the appropriateness of the training or validity of the results measures should be scrutinized. If people are behaving differently, but the behavior has no impact on the bottom line, then the training may be teaching the wrong things. This problem could stem from a poor needs assessment. If, on the other hand, the trained behaviors are better and more effective than the behaviors used previously, then the problem may be simply that the results measures are too coarse or contaminated to register their beneficial effect. Results measures such as profit and turnover are affected by many factors outside the organization, including general economic and labor-market conditions. Perhaps a training program does have a beneficial impact, but the impact is simply not visible against larger trends in global results measures.

Utility of Training Programs

In Chapter 7 the concept of utility, or cost-benefit analysis, was applied to selection systems. **Utility** is the net dollar gain realized by an organization as a result of adopting a given HRM practice, and it can be calculated for training programs as well as for selection systems.[76] Jack Phillips has championed adding a fifth level to Kirkpatrick's training evaluation hierarchy, **return on training investment.**[77] Phillips believes the benefits of training should be carefully quantified and compared to the cost of delivering the training to justify training expenditures and evaluate the relative worth of different training programs. A program could produce learning, behavior change, and results, but still not be a good investment. For instance, a sales training program might increase sales but have been so expensive that there is no return on investment.[78]

Calculating utility or return on investment requires both assessing the costs of the training and putting a dollar value on the benefits of the training. Some cost categories associated with the development and delivery of classroom training are shown in Table 9.12. They include one-time costs incurred in developing the program initially, costs that are incurred each time the program is repeated, and costs incurred for each person trained. It is harder to put a dollar value on the benefits of training than it is to assess the costs. First, one must estimate how much better a trained employee will perform than an untrained employee. The dollar payback of a certain percentage of improvement in performance depends on the importance of the job. It is probably worth more to an organization to increase an executive's performance by 10 percent than to increase a secretary's performance by 10 percent. The amount gained per trainee per year is multiplied by the number of persons trained.

Next, the duration of the training's impact must be estimated. Because the benefit of training an employee is lost when that employee quits, turnover rates are often built into utility calculations. However, even if an employee stays with the organization, the effects of some kinds of training gradually wear off as trainees forget what they have learned or the knowledge becomes obsolete. Thus an estimate of the "half-life" of the training intervention also must be factored in.[79]

TABLE 9.12

Costs of Designing and Delivering Classroom Training

One-Time Costs
- Needs assessment costs
- Salaries of training designers or consultants
- Purchase of reusable training equipment and materials
- Full-scale evaluation of the program when first offered

Per-Session Costs
- Trainer salaries, travel, and lodging
- Facilities rental

Per-Trainee Costs
- Trainee wages or salary during training
- Transportation, food, and lodging for trainees during training
- Nonreusable training materials, handouts, etc.

The final step in calculating utility is to subtract the total costs from the total benefits of a particular training program given to a specified number of people. Estimating the necessary parameters and calculating utility can be extremely complex, but by doing so an employer can build a solid justification for a training program on purely economic grounds.

Properly conceived and implemented training programs can have definite effects on organizational performance and profits.[80] An extensive study of the utility of several training programs in a large pharmaceutical company found that training programs varied widely in their impact. Managerial training programs had an average return on investment of 45 percent, whereas sales and technical training had an average return on investment of 156 percent. Information of this sort can be used to decide where to direct training resources to produce the largest impact.[81]

Summary of Key Points

Human resource development professionals are concerned with facilitating learning and performance in an organization to foster achievement of organizational goals. Learning and performance can be improved in many ways, including performance support systems, communities of practice, on-the-job experience and mentoring, and formal training activities. The instructional systems design approach to training involves four phases: needs assessment, design and development of training programs, delivery of programs, and evaluation. The assessment phase determines who needs to be trained and what they need to be trained to do. Assessment involves organizational analysis to be sure that the training addresses a genuine business need, task analysis to understand exactly what employees need to know, individual analysis to understand what trainees already know and what methods might suit them best, and identification of clear and measurable training objectives to guide program development and evaluation.

The design and development phase includes choosing appropriate training methods and developing training materials. The design of a training program must consider issues such as conditions of practice, knowledge of results, interference, transfer of training, and adult learning principles. A large number of training methods are available, and training can be delivered on or off the job. Methods should be chosen to assure that content is delivered clearly, appropriate opportunities for practice occur, and sufficient variety is provided to the trainee. E-learning encompasses a range of methods and is rapidly increasing in popularity. Learning management systems can facilitate employee access to e-learning opportunities as well as manage information about other training activities in the organization.

Management development is intended to improve the present and future performance of managers. Many millions of dollars are spent on formal management training each year, although managers probably do most of their learning from on-the-job experiences. This suggests that a complete management development system should include both training courses and challenging job assignments. Action learning programs combine on- and off-the-job learning for managers.

In the evaluation phase, the training is evaluated (1) to determine whether it has achieved its objectives and (2) to make improvements in the training program. Four levels of evaluation measures should be collected for a thorough evaluation: reaction, learning, behavior, and results. A sound experimental design should be used to assess the impact of the training. Finally, the utility of a training program can be calculated by assessing its costs and putting a dollar value on its benefits to the organization.

The Manager's Vocabulary

action learning
adult learning principles
andragogy
apprenticeship training

asynchronous e-learning program
behavior measure
behavioral objectives
blended learning
community of practice
competency model
cross-training
distributed practice
e-learning
embedding
evaluation
feedback
human resource development (HRD)
human strengths
individual analysis
instructional systems design (ISD)
interference
interrupted time series design
job instruction training
Kirkpatrick's four levels of evaluation
knowledge of results
learning management system
learning measure
massed practice
multiskilling
needs assessment
off-the-job training
on-the-job training (OJT)
one-group pretest–posttest design
one-shot posttest-only design
organizational analysis
overlearning
part learning
pedagogy
performance support system
preconditions for learning
pretest–posttest control-group design
reaction measure
relapse-prevention model
results measure
return on training investment
self-efficacy expectations
subject matter experts
synchronous e-learning program
task analysis
trainee motivation
trainee readiness
transfer of training
utility
whole learning

Questions for Discussion

1. In what ways does the HRD function relate to the organization's strategy?
2. What methods might you use in analyzing the needs of present employees in their present jobs?
3. What are some possible causes of performance deficiencies other than a need for training?
4. What concerns are addressed at the organizational analysis phase of training needs assessment?
5. How would you conduct the task analysis phase of training needs assessment for the job of movie theater ticket seller?
6. What are the training implications of the human strengths view, and how do these differ from the traditional view?
7. What are the characteristics of a good behavioral objective? What purpose do training objectives serve?
8. What can a trainer do to build trainee motivation before and during a training course?
9. What is self-efficacy, why is it important in training, and how can trainers influence it?
10. What is massed practice? What effect does massed practice have on retention?
11. What is overlearning? When and why should it be used?
12. Suppose you are planning a training course on customer service for front-line staff. How would you go about embedding this course in the organization to maximize its effectiveness and transfer?
13. Redesign this class using the principles of adult learning. Would you prefer the course to be run along adult learning lines or in a more traditional teacher-centered fashion? Why?
14. What are the advantages and disadvantages of on-the-job training? Discuss your personal experiences being trained on the job. Was it done well or poorly? What improvements would you suggest?
15. Suppose you were being sent overseas to deliver a training program for your company. What factors would you want to consider as you prepared for this training assignment?
16. What are the advantages and disadvantages of e-learning?

17. How would you go about selecting and sequencing training methods for a day-long training program on the topic of "conducting the employment interview"?
18. Suppose you were asked to teach a group of somewhat experienced but not formally trained supervisors how to conduct a disciplinary interview with a subordinate who has performed badly or broken a rule. Come up with ten different methods or activities you could use to do this. Which method do you think would be most effective? How might you combine several methods for the best effect?
19. What is action learning?
20. Develop the outline for an orientation program for a new secretarial employee at your college or business school.
21. Explain four levels at which training can be evaluated.
22. The career center at you university is preparing to offer a one-day course for graduating students on how to find a job. They have asked you to plan an evaluation of the effectiveness of this training program. Which of Kirkpatrick's levels of evaluation would you use? Which specific measures would you collect? Which research design would you use?
23. Explain how utility concepts can be used to estimate the net dollar value of a training program.

Case 9.1
Management Development Systems at Resort Wear of California

You are part of a consulting group that has been hired by Resort Wear of California, a chain of twelve upscale women's clothing shops located between San Diego and San Francisco. The owner of the business is worried about the quality of store managers. Some are good, some are promising but inexperienced, and some do not seem to be very effective. The owner plans to double the number of stores starting next year and would like to build up the skills of store managers and assistant managers to support this expansion.

The owner is willing to commit a reasonable amount of money to develop managers, but you do not have a blank check (you can't afford to send them all to a university or even bring them together physically more than once or twice). It is also necessary to keep all stores running while management training is occurring.

Your team has been retained to design a management development strategy to be implemented over the next two years. Using what you know about both on- and off-the-job management development, decide how you should proceed and what you might recommend to the owner. Consider training content as well as methods.

Case 9.2
Training New Employees at Health Source

The drugstore chain Health Source needs to train staff for the two new stores that will soon be opening in Dallas and Houston. Approximately fifty new employees will need to be oriented, and the thirty of them who are clerks need to learn how to operate a cash register, stock shelves, and provide quality customer service "The Health Source Way." Being a small firm, Health Source does not have a full-time training officer. However, it does have an HR director (you) and a number of experienced Houston-based supervisors and employees. Plan how you will accomplish the necessary training for the clerks at the two locations. How will you determine exactly what content must be taught? Which skills will be taught on the job? Which should be taught in the classroom or by other off-the-job methods? What must be taught prior to opening, and what can be taught later? Which training methods are likely to be most successful with the clerks? Who will the trainers be?

Health Source has never had a formal employee orientation program before, but it also has never needed to orient so many people at the same time. If expansion continues beyond these two stores, a formal orientation program will be useful again and again. What material should go into the orientation program for all new employees? Who should deliver the program, and how?

Exercise 9.1
Applying Learning Principles

You are designing a two-day workshop to teach intact teams of managers to use systematic group problem-solving methods. The managers include several state managers and their three to five immediate subordinates, each of whom manages an area within a state. These individuals are required to attend the training program. The content of the program includes several steps in the problem-solving process (defining the problem and generating decision criteria, generating alternatives, choosing an alternative, action planning for implementation, and evaluating success) and several types of skills (listening, consensus seeking, brainstorming, cause-and-effect analysis, force-field analysis, action planning).

How will your training program incorporate or deal with each of the following learning principles or conditions? Are there any that will not concern you? Which may be most crucial in this situation?

1. Readiness
2. Motivation
3. Interference
4. Feedback
5. Overlearning
6. Distributed versus massed practice
7. Whole versus part learning
8. Transfer of training

Notes and References

1. W. D. Patton and C. Pratt, "Assessing the Training Needs of High-Potential Managers," *Pubic Personnel Management,* Vol. 31, 2002, pp. 465–484.
2. P. Galagan, "The Future of the Profession Formerly Known as Training," *Training and Development,* December 2003, pp. 26–38.
3. T. Galvin, "2003 Industry Report," *Training,* October 2003, pp. 19–45.
4. R. Zemke and S. Zemke, "Putting Competencies to Work," *Training,* January 1999, pp. 70–76.
5. J. R. Hinrichs, "Personnel Training," in *Handbook of Industrial and Organizational Psychology,* ed. M. D. Dunnette (Chicago: Rand McNally, 1976), p. 830.
6. T. W. Gainey, B. S. Klaas, and D. Moore, "Outsourcing the Training Function: Results from the Field," *Human Resource Planning,* Vol. 25 (1), 2002, pp. 16–22.
7. Allison Rossett and Joseph W. Arwady, *Training Needs Assessment* (Englewood Cliffs, N.J.: Educational Technology Publications, 1987), p. 68.
8. L. A. Digman, "Determining Management Development Needs," *Human Resource Management,* Winter 1980, pp. 12–17; and Lise M. Saari, Terry R. Johnson, Steven D. McLaughlin, and Denise M. Zimmerle, "A Survey of Management Training and Education Practices in U.S. Companies," *Personnel Psychology,* Winter 1988, pp. 731–743.
9. For a detailed treatment of needs analysis methods, see Irwin L. Goldstein and K. Ford, *Training in Organizations* (Belmont, Calif.: Wadsworth, 2002). See also C. E. Schneier, J. P. Guthrie, and J. D. Olian, "A Practical Approach to Conducting and Using the Training Needs Assessment," *Public Personnel Management,* Summer 1988, pp. 191–205; and P. J. Taylor, M. P. O'Driscoll, and J. F. Binning, "A New Integrated Framework for Training Needs Analysis," *Human Resource Management Journal,* Vol. 8 (2), 1998, pp. 29–50.
10. Robert F. Mager and Peter Pipe, *Analyzing Performance Problems,* 3rd ed. (Atlanta, Ga.: Center for Effective Performance, 1997).
11. A. Rossett and E. Mohr, "Performance Support Tools: Where Learning, Work, and Results Converge," *Training and Development,* February 2002, pp. 35–39.

12. Zemke and Zemke, "Putting Competencies to Work." For more on competency models, see J. S. Shippmann, R. A. Ash, M. Battista, L. Carr, L. D. Eyde, B. Hesketh, J. Kehoe, K. Pearlman, E. P. Prien, and J. I. Sanchez, "The Practice of Competency Modeling," *Personnel Psychology,* Autumn 2000, pp. 703–740.
13. V. S. Kaman and J. P. Mohr, "Training Needs Assessment in the 80's: Five Guideposts," *Personnel Administrator,* October 1984, pp. 47–53.
14. F. O. Hoffman, "The Hierarchy of Training Objectives," *Personnel,* August 1985, pp. 12–16.
15. Robert F. Mager, *Preparing Instructional Objectives* (Belmont, Calif.: Lake Publishing, 1975).
16. Patton and Pratt, "Assessing the Training Needs of High-Potential Managers."
17. See K. G. Brown and M. W. Gerhardt, "Formative Evaluation: An Integrative Practice Model and Case Study," *Personnel Psychology,* 2002, pp. 951–983, for advice on evaluating and pilot testing training as it is being designed.
18. J. A. Colquitt, J. A. LePine, and R. A. Noe, "Toward an Integrative Theory of Training Motivation: A Meta-Analytic Path Analysis of 20 Years of Research," *Journal of Applied Psychology,* Vol. 85, 2000, pp. 678–707.
19. R. A. Noe, "Trainees' Attributes and Attitudes: Neglected Influences on Training Effectiveness," *Academy of Management Review,* October 1986, pp. 736–749, For more on trainee motivation and pretraining influences of training effectiveness, see T. T. Baldwin and R. J. Magjuka, "Training as an Organizational Episode: Pretraining Influences on Trainee Motivation," pp. 99–127, and J. E. Mathieu and M. W. Martineau, "Individual and Situational Influences on Training Motivation," pp. 193–221, both in *Improving Training Effectiveness in Work Organizations,* ed. J. K. Ford (Mahwah, N.J.: Erlbaum, 1997).
20. W. D. Hicks and R. J. Klimoski, "Entry into Training Programs and Its Effects on Training Outcomes: A Field Experiment," *Academy of Management Journal,* September 1987, pp. 542–552; and Timothy T. Baldwin, Richard J. Magjuka, and Brian T. Loher, "The Perils of Participation: Effects of Choice of Training on Trainee Motivation and Learning," *Personnel Psychology,* Vol. 44 (1), Spring 1991, pp. 51–65.
21. R. A. Noe and N. Schmitt, "The Influence of Trainee Attitudes on Training Effectiveness: Test of a Model," *Personnel Psychology,* Autumn 1986, pp. 497–523.
22. Edwin A. Locke and Gary P. Latham, *A Theory of Goal Setting and Task Performance* (Englewood Cliffs, N.J.: Prentice-Hall, 1990).
23. A. Bandura, "Self-Efficacy: Toward a Unifying Theory of Behavioral Change," *Psychological Review,* Vol. 84, 1977, pp. 191–215.
24. Marilyn E. Gist, Catherine Schwoerer, and Benson Rosen, "Effects of Alternative Training Methods on Self-Efficacy and Performance in Computer Software Training," *Journal of Applied Psychology,* December 1989, pp. 884–891; John E. Mathieu, Jennifer W. Martineau, and Scott I. Tannenbaum, "Individual and Situational Influences on the Development of Self-Efficacy: Implications for Training Effectiveness," *Personnel Psychology,* Vol. 46, 1993, pp. 125–147; and Marilyn E. Gist and Terence R. Mitchell, "Self-Efficacy: A Theoretical Analysis of Its Determinants and Malleability," *Academy of Management Review,* Vol. 17, 1992, pp. 183–211.
25. James E. Driskell, Ruth P. Willis, and Carolyn Copper, "Effect of Overlearning on Retention," *Journal of Applied Psychology,* Vol. 77, 1992, pp. 615–622.
26. Frank N. Dempster, "The Spacing Effect: A Case Study in the Failure to Apply the Results of Psychological Research," *American Psychologist,* August 1988, pp. 627–634; and J. J. Donovan and D. J. Radosevich, "A Meta-Analytic Review of the Distribution of Practice Effect: Now You See It, Now You Don't," *Journal of Applied Psychology,* Vol. 84, 1999, pp. 795–805.
27. D. R. Ilgen, C. D. Fisher, and M. S. Taylor, "Motivational Consequences of Individual Feedback on Behavior in Organizations," *Journal of Applied Psychology,* August 1979, pp. 349–371; and Joseph J. Martocchio and Jane Webster, "Effects of Feedback and Cognitive Playfulness on Performance in Microcomputer Software Training," *Personnel Psychology,* Vol. 45, 1992, pp. 553–578.
28. For more detail on transfer of training, see S. W. Kozlowski and E. Salas, "A Multilevel Organizational Systems Approach for the Implementation and Transfer of Training," in *Improving Training Effectiveness in Work Organizations,* ed. Ford; and E. F. Holton III and T. Baldwin, (Eds.), *Improving Learning Transfer in Organizations.* (San Francisco, Calif.: Jossey-Bass, 2003).

29. Thomas Hill, Nancy D. Smith, and Millard F. Mann, "Role of Efficacy Expectations in Predicting the Decision to Use Advanced Technologies: The Case of Computers," *Journal of Applied Psychology,* Vol. 72, 1987, pp. 307–313.

30. K. N. Wexley and T. T. Baldwin, "Posttraining Strategies for Facilitating Positive Transfer: An Empirical Exploration," *Academy of Management Journal,* September 1986, pp. 503–520; Timothy T. Baldwin and J. Kevin Ford, "Transfer of Training: A Review and Directions for Future Research," *Personnel Psychology,* Spring 1988, pp. 63–105.

31. R. D. Marx and L. A. Burke, "Transfer Is Personal," in *Improving Learning Transfer in Organizations,* eds. Holton and Baldwin, pp. 227–242; and L. A. Burke and T. T. Baldwin, "Workforce Training Transfer: A Study of the Effect of Relapse Prevention Training and Transfer Climate," *Human Resource Management,* Fall 1999, pp. 227–242.

32. J. Kevin Ford, Miguel A. Quinones, Douglas J. Sego, and Joann Speer Sorra, "Factors Affecting the Opportunity to Perform Trained Tasks on the Job," *Personnel Psychology,* Vol. 45, 1992, pp. 511–527.

33. J. B. Tracey, C. I. Tannenbaum, and M. J. Kavanagh, "Applying Trained Skills on the Job: The Importance of the Work Environment," *Journal of Applied Psychology,* April 1995, pp. 239–252; Holton and Baldwin, *Improving Learning Transfer in Organizations.*

34. "Support Systems for Training," in *Designing Training Programs,* eds. L. Nadler and Z. Nadler (Houston: Gulf Publishing, 1994), pp. 212–233; E. Salas, "The Science of Training: A Decade of Progress," *Annual Review of Psychology,* Vol. 52, 2001, pp. 471–499; S. Rynes and B. Rosen, "A Field Survey of Factors Affecting the Adoption and Perceived Success of Diversity Training," *Personnel Psychology,* Vol. 48, 1995, pp. 247–270; J. D. Facteau, G. H. Dobbins, J. E. A. Russell, R. T. Ladd, and J. D. Kudisch, "The Influence of General Perceptions of the Training Environment on Pretraining Motivation and Perceived Transfer," *Journal of Management,* Vol. 21, 1995, pp. 1–25; Tracey, Tannenbaum, and Kavanagh, "Applying Trained Skills on the Job."

35. Malcolm Knowles, *The Adult Learner: A Neglected Species* (Houston: Gulf Publishing, 1978); for more on adult learning, see Robert Burns, *The Adult Learner at Work* (Sydney, Australia: Business and Professional Publishing, 1995).

36. For more on managing student-centered learning experiences, see Jill Baldwin and Hank Williams, *Active Learning: A Trainer's Guide* (Oxford, England: Blackwell, 1988).

37. R. F. Crapo, "It's Time to Stop Training . . . And Start Facilitating," *Public Personnel Management,* Winter 1986, pp. 443–449. Quote from p. 446.

38. D. Feuer and B. Geber, "Uh-oh . . . Second Thoughts About Adult Learning Theory," *Training,* December 1988, pp. 31–39; Sharon B. Merriam, "Adult Learning and Theory Building: A Review," *Adult Education Quarterly,* Summer 1987, pp. 187–198; and R. Zemke and S. Zemke, "Adult Learning: What Do We Know For Sure?" *Training,* June 1995, pp. 31–40.

39. John W. Newstrom and Mark L. Lengnick-Hall, "One Size Does Not Fit All," *Training and Development Journal,* June 1991, pp. 43–48.

40. D. Schaff, "What Workers Really Think About Training," *Training,* September 1998, pp. 59–66.

41. R. L. Jacobs, *Structured On-the-Job Training,* 2nd ed. (San Francisco: Berrett-Koehler, 2003): W. J. Rothwell and H. C. Kazanas, *Improving On-the-Job Training: How to Establish and Operate a Comprehensive OJT Program* (San Francisco: Jossey-Bass, 1994).

42. Margaret Kaeter, "Cross-Training: The Tactical View," *Training,* March 1993, pp. 35–39; and Bob Filipczak, "Frick Teaches Frack," *Training,* June 1993, pp. 30–34.

43. E. Wenger, R. McDermott, and W. M. Snyder, *Cultivating Communities of Practice.* (Boston: Harvard Business School Press, 2002).

44. T. Galvin and H. Johnson, "Best Return on Training," *Training,* December 2003, pp. 24–28.

45. For more on apprenticeship training, see the Department of Labor Employment and Training Administration Web site at http://www.doleta.gov/atels_bat/.

46. Carol Rocklin Kay, Sue Kruse Peyton, and Robert Pike, "Diagnosing the Training Situation: Matching Instructional Techniques with Learning Outcomes," *The 1987 Annual: Developing Human Resources* (San Diego: University Associates, 1987), pp. 203–212.

47. H. Johnson, "Prescription for Success," *Training,* October 2003, pp. 52–55.

48. K. Dobbs, "Who's in Charge of E-Learning?" *Training,* June 2000, pp. 55–58.

49. J. Schettler, "Weapons of Mass Instruction," *Training,* February 2003, pp. 20–30; and M. Gold,

"IRS Goes E," *Training and Development,* May 2003, pp. 76–82.
50. M. Hequet, "Things You Need to Know about E-Learning Standards," *Training,* October 2003, pp. 46–50.
51. For good advice on designing Web-based programs, see M. Driscoll, *Web-Based Training: Creating E-Learning Experiences.* (San Francisco: Jossey-Bass/Pfeiffer, 2002); and K. G. Brown and J. K. Ford, "Using Computer Technology in Training," in *Creating, Implementing, and Managing Effective Training and Development,* ed. K. Kraiger (San Francisco: Jossey-Bass, 2002), pp. 192–233.
52. D. Zielinski, "Can You Keep Learners on Line?" *Training,* March 2000, pp. 64–75; S. Boehle, "My Exasperating Life as an Online Learner," *Training,* June 2000, pp. 64–68; and K. G. Brown, "Using Computers to Deliver Training: Which Employees Learn and Why?" *Personnel Psychology,* 2001, pp. 271–296.
53. D. Zielinski, "The Lie of Online Learning," *Training,* February 2000, pp. 38–40.
54. H. Johnson, "Prescription for Success."
55. G. Johnson, "Brewing the Perfect Blend," *Training,* December 2003, pp. 30–34.
56. M. J. Burke and R. R. Day, "A Cumulative Study of the Effectiveness of Managerial Training," *Journal of Applied Psychology,* May 1986, pp. 232–245; for a recent nonempirical review, see Timothy T. Baldwin and Margaret Y. Padgett, "Management Development: A Review and Commentary," in *International Review of Industrial and Organizational Psychology,* Vol. 8, eds. C. L. Cooper and I. T. Robertson (Chichester, England: Wiley, 1993), pp. 35–85.
57. See D. A. Ready and J. A. Conger, "Why Leadership-Development Efforts Fail," *MIT Sloan Management Review,* Spring 2003, pp. 83–88, for more on how to design appropriately targeted management development systems.
58. Morgan W. McCall Jr., M. M. Lombardo, and A. M. Morrison, *The Lessons of Experience: How Successful Executives Develop on the Job* (Lexington, Mass.: Lexington Books, 1988); G. Cattegno and R. Millwood, "Work-Based Learning for Managers," in *Enterprising Nation,* Research Report Vol. 1 (Commonwealth of Australia, 1995), pp. 75–114; Jean M. Bartunek and Meryl Reis Louis, "The Design of Work Environments to Stretch Managers' Capacities for Complex Thinking," *Human Resource Planning,* Vol. 11 (1), 1988, pp. 13–22; and Gail S. Robinson and Calhoun W. Wick, "Executive Development That Makes a Business Difference," *Human Resource Planning,* Vol. 15, 1992, pp. 63–75.
59. B. R. Ragins and J. L. Cotton, "Mentor Functions and Outcomes: A Comparison of Men and Women in Formal and Informal Mentoring Relationships." *Journal of Applied Psychology,* August 1999, pp. 529–550; D. B. Peterson, "Management Development: Coaching and Mentoring Programs," in *Creating, Implementing, and Managing Effective Training and Development,* ed. Kraiger, pp. 160–191.
60. For more on trends in executive development, see J. A. Conger and K. Xin, "Executive Education in the 21st Century." *Journal of Management Education,* Vol. 24, 2000, pp. 73-101; J. Zenger, D. Ulrich, and N. Smallwood, "The New Leadership Development," *Training and Development,* March 2000, pp. 22–27; W. Lawler, "The Consortium Approach to Grooming Future Leaders," *Training and Development,* March 2000, pp. 53–57; and J. D. Olian, C. C. Durham, A. L. Kristof, K. G. Brown, R. M. Pierce, and L. Kunder, "Designing Management Training and Development for Competitive Advantage: Lessons from the Best," *Human Resource Planning,* Vol. 21 (1), 1998, pp. 20–31; and H. Mintzberg, "Third Generation Management Development," *Training and Development,* March 2004, pp. 28–38.
61. R. J. Mirabile, "Competency-Based Strategies," *Handbook of Business Strategy* (New York: Faulkner & Gray, 1997), pp. 297–305; D. Giber, L. Carter, and M. Goldsmith (Eds.), *Linkage, Inc.'s Best Practices in Leadership Development Handbook* (Lexington, Mass.: Linkage Inc. 2000); and Olian, Durham, Kristof, Brown, Pierce, and Kunder, "Designing Management Training and Development for Competitive Advantage."
62. D. L. Dotlich and J. L. Noel, *Action Learning* (San Francisco: Jossey-Bass, 1998).
63. Joseph A. Raelin and Michele LeBien, "Learning by Doing," *HR Magazine,* February 1993, pp. 61–70; V. Marsick, "Experience- Based Learning: Executive Learning Outside the Classroom," *Journal of Management Development,* Vol. 9, 1990, pp. 50–60; J. L. Noel and R. Charan, "Leadership Development at GE's Crotonville." *Human Resource Management,* Vol. 27, 1988, pp. 433–447; P. Froiland, "Action Learning: Taming Real Problems in

Real Time," *Training,* January 1994, pp. 27–34; and J. A. Raelin, "The Design of the Action Project in Work-Based Learning," *Human Resource Planning,* Vol. 22 (3), 1999, pp. 12–28.

64. C. D. Fisher, "Organizational Socialization: An Integrative Review," *Research in Personnel and Human Resources Management,* Vol. 4, 1986, pp. 101–145.

65. Daniel C. Feldman and Jeanne M. Brett, "Coping with New Jobs: A Comparative Study of New Hires and Job Changers," *Academy of Management Journal,* June 1983, pp. 258–272; and H. J. Klein and N. A. Weaver, "The Effectiveness of an Organizational-Level Orientation Training Program in the Socialization of New Hires," *Personnel Psychology,* Spring 2000, pp. 47–66.

66. Michelle Neely Martinez, "Disney Training Works Magic," *HR Magazine,* May 1992, pp. 53–57.

67. M. R. Louis, B. Z. Posner, and G. N. Powell, "The Availability and Helpfulness of Socialization Practices," *Personnel Psychology,* Winter 1983, pp. 857–866.

68. For more advice on planning an orientation program, see Mary F. Cook (Ed.), *The AMA Handbook for Employee Recruitment and Retention* (New York: AMACOM, 1992), chap. 7.

69. For more on orientation, see D. M. Sims, *Creative New Employee Orientation.* (New York: McGraw-Hill, 2002).

70. Good sources on training delivery skills are J. E. Eitington, *The Winning Trainer* (Houston: Gulf Publishing, 1996); and B. L. Delahaye and B. J. Smith, *How to Be an Effective Trainer* (New York: Wiley, 1998).

71. For recent thinking on training evaluation, see S. M. Brown and C. J. Seidner (Eds.), *Evaluating Corporate Training: Models and Issues* (Boston: Kluwer Academic Publishers, 1998); and K. Kraiger, "Decision-Based Evaluation," in *Creating, Implementing, and Managing Effective Training and Development,* ed. Kraiger, pp. 331–375.

72. D. L. Kirkpatrick, "Four Steps to Measuring Training Effectiveness," *Personnel Administrator,* Vol. 28, 1983, pp. 19–25; D. L. Kirkpatrick, *Evaluating Training Programs: The Four Levels* (San Francisco: Berrett-Koehler, 1994).

73. G. M. Alliger, S. I. Tannenbaum, W. Bennett Jr., H. Traver, and A. Shotland, "A Meta-Analysis of the Relations among Training Criteria," *Personnel Psychology,* Vol. 50, 1997, pp. 341–358.

74. S. I. Tannenbaum and S. B. Woods, "Determining a Strategy for Evaluating Training: Operating within Organizational Constraints," *Human Resource Planning,* 1992, Vol. 15 (2), pp. 63–81.

75. This section is based on C. D. Fisher, "Laboratory Research," in *Method and Analysis in Organizational Research,* eds. T. S. Bateman and J. R. Ferris (Reston, Va.: Reston Publishing Co., 1984), pp. 169–185; T. D. Cook and D. T. Campbell, "The Design and Conduct of Quasi-Experiments and True Experiments in Field Setting," in M. D. Dunnette (ed.), *Handbook of Industrial and Organizational Psychology* (Chicago: Rand-McNally, 1976), pp. 223–326.

76. W. Cascio, *Costing Human Resources.* (Cincinnati: South-Western, 2000).

77. Jack J. Phillips, *Handbook of Training Evaluation and Measurement Methods* (Houston: Gulf Publishing, 1991).

78. *Diederick Stoel* [interviewer], "The Evaluation Heavyweight Match," *Training & Development,* January 2004, pp. 46–48.

79. F. L. Schmidt, J. E. Hunter, and K. Pearlman, "Assessing the Economic Impact of Personnel Programs on Work Force Productivity," *Personnel Psychology,* Summer 1982, pp. 333–347.

80. J. S. Russell, J. R. Terborg, and M. L. Powers, "Organizational Performance and Organizational Level Training and Support," *Personnel Psychology,* Winter 1985, pp. 849–863.

81. C. C. Morrow, M. Q. Jarrett, and M. T. Rupinski, "An Investigation of the Effect and Economic Utility of Corporate-Wide Training," *Personnel Psychology,* Spring 1997, pp. 91–119.

CHAPTER 10

Performance Assessment and Management

- The Performance Assessment and Management Process
- Strategic Importance of Performance Assessment
- Functions of Performance Assessment
- Criteria for a Good Assessment System
- Deciding What Types of Performance to Measure
- Methods of Appraising Performance
- Raters of Employee Performance
- Enhancing the Measurement of Employee Performance
- Feedback of Results: The Performance Assessment Interview

HR Challenge

The current trend is for organizations and workers to support pay for performance; that is, employees put part (or all) of their pay at risk depending on results. Obviously such an approach requires an acceptable method of appraising performance. Although popular in private industry, pay for performance is largely unknown in the public sector, which is characterized by the 1949 general schedule (GS) system, with its guaranteed, annual across-the-board raises. The GS approach tends to reward longevity, not performance.

Yet beginning mid-2004, the Central Intelligence Agency (CIA) is transitioning to a pay-for-performance system. Yes, the CIA will roll out a uniform performance appraisal system—a first for the CIA.[1] Bob Rebelo, CIA chief of human resources, is quoted as saying that a standard performance appraisal system is "the foundation that has to be laid and cemented in place."[2] The new performance appraisal system will replace a hodgepodge of employee evaluation methods used in the agency. According to a study by a six-member independent panel of business executives from various private sector backgrounds, the GS system has no element of accountability. Employees are rewarded automatically and do not have to perform.[3] As a result, managers do not have to manage.

The CIA goal is to replace the multiple performance appraisal systems now in use with a single, standard system that can be tailored to the individual, the occupation, and the specific assignment. The new form features a clear statement of expectations and standards discussed with the employee at the start of the performance cycle, a mandatory midcycle performance review, employee input in the final evaluation, and an overall rating. The standards and expectations for each employee are tailored to the employee's skill level and expertise. Managers are responsible for providing feedback to employees at every stage of the year-long performance review.[4]

Interestingly, this is a well-planned initiative. The panel of business executives proposed performance and pay plans that reflect the best practices in the private sector.[5] *The proposed pay-for-performance system was then piloted in the office of the CIA's chief financial officer (CFO). In the pilot, 700 CFO employees were converted from the GS system to the pay-for-performance system. The CFO employees were guaranteed a 1.72 percent raise, similar to the cost-of-living adjustment provided GS employees. The balance of the raise was determined by a new pay decision process driven by employee ratings and management reviews.*

CFO employees wrote up their accomplishments, and supervisors described why the accomplishments made a difference at the CIA. In turn, CFO employees received raises that were generally competitive with what was provided to GS employees with one important difference. High-performing employees got higher raises than the GS would have allowed.[6] *Preliminary findings from the pilot show that linking pay to performance increased work force efficiency. Employees cleared up a backlog of work and kept pace with new work.*[7]

What do you think? Does the new CIA system provide advantages over the more common GS system? Can the positive results in the CFO be sustained over a longer period? Does the new system promote worker productivity and managerial excellence? Can the new pay-for-performance system be successful in other offices within the CIA? What will it take to ensure this success?

A critical factor related to an organization's long-term success is its ability to measure how well employees perform and to use that information to ensure that performance meets present standards and improves over time. This process is referred to as performance management, the handy umbrella term for all of the organizational activities involved in managing people on the job—performance measurement along with programs to influence performance.[8] The measurement portion of the system is called *performance assessment, performance appraisal,* or *performance evaluation.* It is a complex task that is difficult to do, and it is not done well by most organizations.[9]

This chapter explains some of the ways that sound assessment information can be collected and used to improve performance; it also explores the difficulties of developing a **performance assessment and management** system. Several different methods of assessing performance are examined. Another part of the chapter focuses on one particularly important part of an assessment system: the process by which performance feedback is provided to employees.

THE PERFORMANCE ASSESSMENT AND MANAGEMENT PROCESS

Performance Management

Performance management is the integration of performance appraisal systems with broader human resource systems as a means of aligning employees' work behaviors with the organization's goals. Performance management should be an ongoing, interactive process designed to enhance employee capability and facilitate productivity. The performance management cycle is illustrated in Figure 10.1.

There is no one way to manage performance. Whatever system is adopted needs to be congruent with the culture and principles that pervade the organization.[10] However, most systems of performance management have several parts:

1. *Defining performance:* It is desirable to carefully define performance so that it supports the organization's strategic goals. Setting clear goals for individual employees is a critical component of performance management.
2. *Appraisal process:* It is important to conceptualize an appraisal process that will be steady across the organization and consistent with the culture of the organization. There are many ways of appraising employee performance, and the system adopted has to be one that will work in the context of the particular organization involved.
3. *Measuring performance:* Measuring performance does not need to be narrowly conceived but can bring together multiple types of performance measured in various ways. The key is to measure often and use the information for midcourse corrections.
4. *Feedback and coaching:* To improve performance, employees need information (feedback) about their performance, along with guidance in reaching the next

FIGURE 10.1
Performance Management Cycle

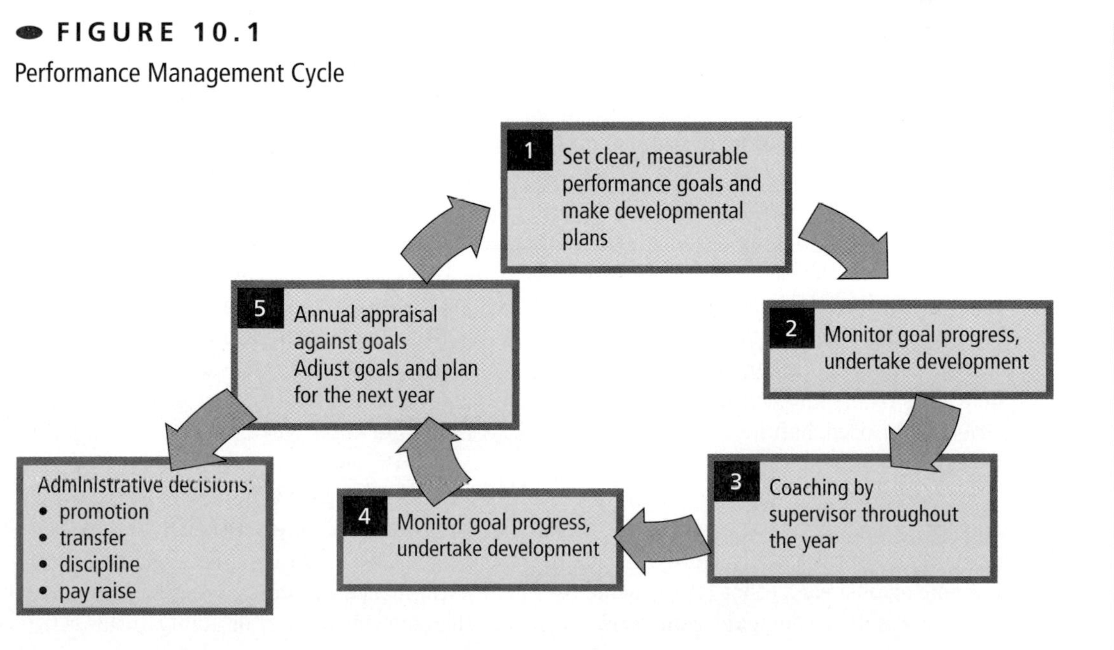

level of results. Without frequent feedback, employees are unlikely to know that their behavior is out of synchronization with relevant goals or what to do about it.[11]

The purpose of performance management is to make sure that employee goals, employee behaviors used to achieve those goals, and feedback of information about performance are all linked to the corporate strategy. An effective process can benefit an organization, but creating, implementing, and maintaining a system is no easy task. For instance, less than 20 percent of businesses accomplish their performance management goals, and less than 10 percent judge their systems to be effective.[12]

A DIFFERENT POINT OF VIEW

Does the Downside of Performance Appraisal Outweigh the Benefits?

In the last fifty years, performance appraisal has been accepted as a vital and widely used tool of effective management. However, appraisal systems remain controversial, with a few scholars believing they do more harm than good.

As long ago as 1957, Douglas McGregor (creator of the famous concepts of Theory X and Theory Y) expressed his uneasiness with the use of appraisal systems. Conventional performance appraisal, "unless handled with consummate skill and delicacy, constitutes something dangerously close to a violation of the integrity of the personality. Managers are uncomfortable when they are put in the position of playing God."*

Perhaps the most vocal critic of appraisals was quality guru W. Edwards Deming, who claimed that appraisals are devastating to individuals and destructive to organizations. An annual appraisal rating system "nourishes short-term performance, annihilates long-term planning, builds fear, demolishes teamwork, nourishes rivalry and politics. It leaves people bitter, crushed, bruised, battered, desolate, despondent, dejected, feeling inferior, some even depressed, all unfit for work for weeks after receipt of rating, unable to comprehend why they are inferior."† Other effects may be that appraisals "discourage risk taking and pit people against each other for the same rewards. . . . The result is a company composed of prima donnas, of sparring fiefdoms. People work for themselves, not the company."‡ There is evidence that appraisals that are perceived as unfair can contribute to stress and job burnout.

Researchers at American Cyanamid Company asked employees for reactions to their forced-distribution appraisal system. Employees expressed largely negative reactions: "Until it is my turn, I can't get a better rating no matter what I do," said one of the employees. Another didn't take performance appraisal seriously: "It's a Mickey Mouse numbers game. My superior and I just laugh at it, we get through it as soon as we can."** Other criticisms are that those who get low ratings become discouraged rather than motivated. Further, they may lose so much confidence in their abilities that they stay in the organization for years as substandard performers rather than braving the labor market in search of a job that might fit them better.

Opponents of performance appraisal attack it on a variety of grounds. Some seem to feel that the idea of appraisal is sound but the execution weak (the wrong things are rated, the forced distribution is inappropriate for the group in question, supervisors aren't trained to prepare accurate appraisals or give feedback effectively, etc.). Others feel that the very concept is flawed. For instance, Deming believes much of performance variability is due to system factors rather than individual effort or ability. If this is true, then ap-

Performance Appraisal

Performance appraisal is that part of the performance assessment and management process in which an employee's contribution to the organization during a specified period of time is assessed. Performance feedback lets employees know how well they have performed in comparison with the standards of the organization. Delivering and receiving **performance feedback** can be an emotionally laden process that dramatically affects employees' attitudes toward the organization and themselves. If used effectively, performance assessment and management can improve employee motivation and performance. If used inappropriately, it can have disastrous effects. (See A Different Point of View for more on possible

praisal systems that hold individuals accountable for results that actually are beyond their control would certainly be seen as unfair and demotivational.

A number of organizations have revamped their appraisal systems in a bid to reduce possible negative outcomes. In some cases this has involved dropping numerical rating systems that required raters to make very fine (and potentially divisive) distinctions among people in favor of more qualitative, narrative approaches. American Cyanamid has abandoned its forced-distribution, ten-grade system and now uses only three grades: unacceptable (rarely used), good (for the vast majority of employees), and exceptional (for astonishingly good performance). For employees rated as good, pay raises are based on seniority and position in the pay range rather than on merit. Bonuses are available to those rated as exceptional.

On the other hand, forced-ranking systems have also become more popular, with 20 percent of companies estimated to be using them. Employees call them "rank and yank" systems, because people at the bottom are targeted for retrenchment. Employees may feel that their placement depends partly on how persuasive their manager is in ranking meetings or that horse trading in these meetings determines their future. ("OK, I'll accept Fred moving down to the satisfactory category if you'll agree to Janet moving into the excellent category.") At Enron, employees were classified as superior (5 percent), excellent (30 percent), strong (30 percent), satisfactory (20 percent), and needs improvement (15 percent), with ranking done every six months. Those in the lowest category received coaching and drafted an improvement plan—if their performance wasn't up to standard in six months, they were terminated. Although the system produces some tension and grumbling, many of the companies using it (e.g., GE and Microsoft) are top performers.

Appraisal is a complex issue, and it is clear that to be effective a system must be designed and implemented with great care. It is also clear that in some situations a poorly conceived appraisal system will create more problems than it solves.

Notes: *Douglas McGregor, "An Uneasy Look at Performance Appraisal," *Harvard Business Review,* September–October 1972, pp. 133–138; quote: p. 134.

†W. E. Deming, *Out of the Crisis* (Cambridge, Mass.: MIT Press, 1986), p. 37.

‡Mary Walton, *The Deming Management Method* (London: Mercury Books, 1989), pp. 88–89.

**Tom Peters, *Thriving on Chaos* (London: Pan Books, 1989), p. 495; and Saul W. Gellerman and William G. Hodgson, "Cyanamid's New Take on Performance Appraisal," *Harvard Business Review,* May–June 1988, pp. 36–37, quote: p. 37.

Sources: Clinton O. Longenecker and Steven J. Goff, "Performance Appraisal Effectiveness: A Matter of Perspective," *SAM Advanced Management Journal,* Spring 1992, pp. 17–23; Gerald T. Gabris and Douglas M. Ihrke, "Does Performance Appraisal Contribute to Heightened Levels of Employee Burnout?: The Results of One Study," *Public Personnel Management,* Summer 2001, pp. 157–172; and John Greenwald, "Rank and Fire," *Time,* June 18, 2001, pp. 46–48.

negative consequences of assessment.) An anonymous quote published by James Bowman provides a humorous definition of the process: "Personnel Appraisal (pers_-n-el a-pra_-zel) *n*: given by someone who does not want to give it to someone who does not want to get it."[13]

Assessment and feedback can occur informally, as when a supervisor notices and comments on a good or poor performance incident. A more formal method is the structured annual performance review, in which a supervisor assesses each employee's performance using some official assessment procedure. Larger organizations tend to use both formal and informal methods, whereas many smaller organizations use only informal supervisory feedback.

Over the years, a great deal of research has been devoted to performance assessment systems. This research has looked at who should do the assessment, what methods of appraising are best, when and how often assessments should be done, and for what purposes assessment information should be used.

STRATEGIC IMPORTANCE OF PERFORMANCE ASSESSMENT

Strategically, it is hard to imagine a more important HR system than performance assessment and management. As shown in Chapter 1 (Figure 1.2) and clarified in subsequent chapters, organizations strive to do the following at all levels:

- Design jobs and work systems to accomplish organizational goals.
- Hire individuals with the abilities and desire to perform effectively.
- Train, motivate, and reward employees for performance and productivity.

It is this sequence that allows organizations to disperse their strategic goals throughout the organization.

Within this context, the evaluation of performance is the control mechanism that provides not only feedback to individuals but also an organizational assessment of how things are progressing. Without performance information, managers and employees can only guess as to whether they are working toward the right goals, in the correct way, and to the desired standard.[14] For example, one study surveyed thousands of managers and found that those from high-performing companies applied more attention, discipline, and resources to identifying performance differences than their lower performing counterparts.[15]

Consistency between Organizational Strategy and Job Behavior

Performance assessment plays another important role in organizational strategy, that of ensuring strategy-consistent behavior.[16] A truism of organizational life is that people engage in the behaviors that they perceive will be rewarded.[17] Employees want to be rewarded and will try to do those things that the organization is emphasizing. For example, if the focus is on service, employees will behave in ways that gain the rewards associated with service delivery. If the focus is on cost control, employees will seek ways to control cost and thus be recognized and rewarded. If the focus is on rewarding productivity, employees will strive for productivity. Performance assessment becomes a means of knowing whether employee behavior is consistent with the overall strategic focus; it also brings to the fore any negative consequences of the strategy–behavior link. For example, a single minded productivity focus may include potential negative consequences, such as decreased quality and cooperation. Performance assessment is an important organizational mechanism to elicit feedback about the consistency of the strategy–behavior link.

Consistency between Organizational Values and Job Behavior

Performance assessment is also a mechanism to reinforce the values and culture of the organization. For example, how is an organization that articulates the value of developing its people to know whether managers throughout the organization share this value? A history of developing people or communication from the highest executives is not enough. Managers typically have more to do than time to get it done and will let slide what is not reinforced. If managers are held accountable for developing their people by being judged on this task in their own performance assessment, they will be likely to spend more time developing subordinates.

A further element in the strategic importance of performance assessment is in the alignment of the assessment with the organizational culture. For example, many organizations have adopted a more team-oriented focus; in such a culture, the stress is on team management, teamwork, and more open and trusting relationships among all employees. In a team-oriented system, the traditional assessment that rates one employee in comparison with others may be counterproductive.[18] Such a system will engender competition rather than teamwork among employees. In such a setting, an assessment system that emphasizes coaching and development, and involves feedback from coworkers, may be more appropriate than the traditional supervisor-based rating.

FUNCTIONS OF PERFORMANCE ASSESSMENT

One survey delineated a large number of purposes, divided into four major categories, for which formal performance assessment or appraisal can be used. These multiple uses are illustrated in Table 10.1. Goal setting and **developmental uses** of assessment focus on setting goals and improving employees' capability to reach these goals, whereas **administrative uses** of assessment include decision making about merit raises and promotions. Assessment information is also used to contribute to organizational well-being (e.g., to anticipate HR needs) and for documentation (e.g., to provide criteria for validation research).[19] Each of these applications of performance assessment and assessment information is explored in this section.

Performance Assessment as a Goal-Setting and Employee Development Tool

Performance assessment can be used in several ways to help employees set goals, to assess the congruence of their efforts toward these goals, and then to assess tools needed to achieve these targets. It plays a role in reinforcing and improving performance and in determining career paths and training needs.

TABLE 10.1

Multiple Organizational Uses for Performance Information

General Applications	Specific Purposes
Goal-setting and developmental uses	Set clear, measurable performance goals
	Monitor goal progress
	Identify individual training needs
	Provide performance feedback and coaching
	Determine transfers and job assignments for developmental purposes
	Identify individual strengths and developmental needs
Administrative uses/decisions	Salary
	Promotion
	Retention or termination
	Recognition of individual performance
	Layoffs
	Identification of poor performers
	Discipline
Organizational maintenance/objectives	Human resource planning
	Determine organization training needs
	Evaluate organizational goal achievement
	Provide information for goal identification
	Evaluate human resource systems
	Reinforce organizational development needs
Documentation	Document human resource decisions
	Help meet legal requirements

Source: J. N. Cleveland, K. R. Murphy, and R. E. Williams, "Multiple Uses of Performance Appraisal: Prevalence and Correlates," *Journal of Applied Psychology*, Vol. 74, 1989, pp. 130–135. Copyright © 1989 by the American Psychological Association. Adapted with permission.

Goal Setting The managers work with employees and agree on a set of goals to achieve during a specified period of time. Goals should be quantifiable and should include an agreed-upon target. It is important that employees then be empowered to achieve these goals. For example, a retail manager's goal might be to reduce customer returns to no more than 3 percent of the dollar amount of sales; that is, no more than $300 in returns for every $10,000 in sales. Consistent with company policy, the manager then should be empowered in specific methods of achieving this goal. Extensive research suggests that when employees have a voice in the appraisal process, as in setting performance goals, they are more satisfied with the appraisal results.[20]

Reinforcing and Sustaining Performance Using performance assessment as an employee development tool can place supervisors in the role of reinforcing and sustaining performance. By providing feedback on past performance, supervisors can encourage employees to continue on a positive trajectory. Praise can augment any financial rewards that the employee may receive. In our Western culture, virtually all employees like to be told when they are doing a good job.

Improving Performance The supervisor can use performance assessment data to suggest ways in which employees might perform better in the future. The supervisor can point out strengths and weaknesses and help employees identify more effective ways to accomplish important tasks. Additionally, the supervisor can discuss work goals with the employee and agree on a timetable for achieving these goals. A more detailed discussion of how to use performance feedback to improve employee performance is provided later in this chapter.

Determining Career Progression Goals The performance assessment session gives supervisors and employees an opportunity to discuss employees' long-term career goals and plans. The supervisors can advise employees on the steps to take to reach these goals. On the basis of past skills, supervisors can give employees short-term, specific suggestions on how to improve performance in ways that will help employees achieve longer term career goals. As a result, employees may become more highly motivated to perform well in their present position because it is seen as a necessary step toward an ultimate goal.

Determining Training Needs Performance assessment can determine the training needs of individual employees. If particular employees are not performing up to expectations, a training program may enable them to correct any skills or knowledge deficiencies. Employees who are performing above the requirements of the position can be placed in a development program that will prepare them for promotion to a higher level job. Performance assessment also supplies information useful in developing training programs that will fit the needs of most employees. For example, if employees' communication skills are rated uniformly low, the company can develop a program to address this need.

Performance Assessment as an Administrative Tool

In addition to employee development uses, performance assessments also play a role in administrative decision making. Performance assessments are used to link rewards to performance and to evaluate the effectiveness of HR policies and practices.

It is worth noting that performance assessments used for administrative purposes are, on average, scored considerably higher than those used for development. In a review and summary (meta-analysis) of twenty-two studies and a total sample of more than 57,000 ratings, it was found that evaluations were much more lenient when those ratings were "for keeps."[21] These results are an indication of the discomfort raters experience when rewards hang in the balance. Of course, it is to the advantage of both the organization and the individual that ratings be honest and accurate, topics addressed in the following sections.

Linking Rewards to Performance Performance assessments are part of the reward and punishment system of an organization. Employees who receive favorable evaluations tend to receive organizational rewards, such as merit pay increases and bonuses, whereas those with unfavorable evaluations receive organizational sanctions, including demotions or discharge. Other personnel decisions commonly linked to performance assessments include promotions, layoffs, transfers, and discipline decisions.

INTERNATIONAL PERSPECTIVE

Performance Appraisal and Performance-Based Rewards in China

Performance appraisal and performance-based pay have been a feature of U.S. HR systems for many decades and are consistent with American individualistic values that people should be rewarded on the basis of their contribution. However, neither performance appraisal nor performance-based pay are universal practices. China provides a case in point.

Until fairly recently, employment practices in the People's Republic of China were described as "the iron rice-bowl." Labor was not regarded as a commodity, so there could be no labor market. There was no unemployment, as all workers were assigned by the state to an employer. Employers could not fire employees, and employees could not choose their workplace. An employer provided a job for life and cradle-to-grave welfare (housing, education, medical care, pension) for employees and their families. All employees "ate out of one big pot," meaning they received pay and benefits on an egalitarian basis, regardless of their contribution. Wage differentials were based on position and age rather than performance. Further, wage structures were flat, with top managers in state-owned enterprises making only two or three times as much as junior technical workers. Managerial advancement was based more on proper political beliefs than on performance on the job. In a system like this, Western-style performance appraisal was simply unnecessary, as there was no possibility of differential treatment on the basis of merit.

Since reforms began in the late 1970s, Chinese HR practices have been changing gradually. Foreign-invested joint ventures are leading the changes, but state-owned enterprises are updating their HR practices as well. Central Committee recommendations for managerial performance appraisal were issued in late 1979; throughout the 1990s the government endorsed movement toward fixed-term labor contracts, rather than lifetime employment, and also encouraged more widespread adoption of performance-based rewards at all levels.

The recommended appraisal system for white-collar employees ("cadres") includes ratings on a 4-point scale of the following dimensions:

- "Good moral practice" (appropriate political beliefs, extent of complying with government directives)
- "Adequate competence" (educational qualifications, leadership and management skills, and physical status including age)
- "Positive working attitude" (diligence, attendance, initiative, sense of responsibility)
- "Strong performance record" (actual results including quantity and quality of output)

In addition, some employees are assessed against annual goals and objectives set for their position.

Blue-collar workers are also assessed following a scheme set down by the government. Correct ideological and political beliefs are part of the appraisal system (and their weighting was increased after the Tiananmen Square incident in 1989), but work achievements are also emphasized.

Compensation rates used to be set by the central government and did not take account of either individual or organizational performance. Since the mid-1980s, state-owned enterprises have been made more accountable, and wages can now vary with the performance of the enterprise. The payment of bonuses based on individual performance is also encouraged, though a legacy of egalitarianism means that nearly identical bonuses are sometimes given to everyone at the same level to prevent jealousy. Foreign-invested enterprises, which have more leeway in compensation rates and methods, have been more successful in implementing pay-for-performance systems.

Sources: K. Goodall and M. Warner, "Human Resources in Sino–Foreign Joint Ventures: Selected Case Studies in Shanghai, Compared with Beijing." *International Journal of Human Resource Management,* Vol. 8, 1997, pp. 569–594; J. Child and Y. Lu (eds.) *Management Issues in China,* Vol. 2 (New York: Routledge, 1996); C. J. Zhu and P. J. Dowling, "Managing People During Economic Transition: The Development of HR Practices in China," *Asia Pacific Journal of Human Resources,* Vol. 28 (2), 2000, pp. 84–106; and D. Z Ding, K. Goodall, and M. Warner, "The End of the 'Iron Rice-Bowl': Whither Chinese Human Resource Management?" *International Journal of Human Resource Management,* April 2000, pp. 217–236.

The goal in linking pay to performance and to other personnel decisions is to motivate employees to perform better. Unfortunately, matching performance and reward is much easier said than done. The performance of individuals must be assessed accurately, the rewards provided must truly be of value to employees, and the organization must develop a performance-based reward system that employees perceive as being administered fairly. The system will fail if employees believe managers and supervisors distribute rewards on the basis of favoritism or political considerations.

Evaluating HRM Policies and Programs Performance assessment data can also be used to evaluate the effectiveness of HRM programs. Assessments can be performed before and after an intervention to measure the amount of change that has occurred. Interventions that might be evaluated with performance assessment data include training programs, job enrichment or redesign, quality circles, and the like. Recall from Chapter 7 that the empirical validation of selection devices requires scores on a job performance criterion. This information is usually collected by some method of performance assessment.

Of course, in some cultures, performance assessment and the applications illustrated are either shunned or take on a different role. Performance appraisal in China is a case in point. (See the International Perspective box for more on performance appraisal and performance-based rewards in China.)

CRITERIA FOR A GOOD ASSESSMENT SYSTEM

As mentioned previously, surveys find that the overwhelming majority of both private- and public-sector organizations use some type of performance assessment.[22] At the same time, "in almost every major survey most employees who get . . . evaluations and most supervisors who give them rate the process a resounding failure."[23] Another survey, conducted in 2000 on behalf of the Society for Human Resource Management, found that only one in three respondents were satisfied with their system of performance assessment.[24] Sadly, many assessment systems are poorly designed and poorly implemented. The Ethical Perspective box gives some advice for designing assessment systems that employees perceive as fair and just.

The fundamental decisions about what type of performance to assess and how to measure that performance should be shaped by four desirable criteria: validity, reliability, freedom from bias, and practicality, including user acceptance.

Validity

A good measure of performance should measure important job characteristics (relevancy) and be free from extraneous or contaminating influences; it also should encompass the whole job (not be deficient).[25] As discussed in Chapter 7, a measure is content-valid if it measures important parts of a job and does so in a representative way. A measure is construct-valid if it measures what it claims to measure—in this case, job performance. The relationship between these two types of validity and the concepts of relevance, contamination, and deficiency is quite clear. A relevant measure assesses aspects of performance that are truly

ETHICAL PERSPECTIVE

Developing a Procedurally Just Performance Appraisal Process

When organizations make decisions about people—such as whom to hire or promote, what appraisal ratings or merit raise to give, or how to discipline a particular infraction—it is very important that the decisions be seen as fair and just. Research has shown that at least two aspects of justice influence employees' job satisfaction and organizational commitment, and both must be considered in organizational decisions.

The first type is "distributive justice," or the perceived fairness of particular outcomes. It has to do with the distribution of rewards and punishments across people. Distributive justice would exist if employees agreed that the best person had been chosen for a promotion, that the punishment fit the crime in a discipline case, or that the size of merit raises accurately reflected true differences in performance across the people involved. Distributive justice is specific to a particular decision—we might agree that one promotion decision was fair, but that is no guarantee that we will think the next one is fair. This is because distributive justice doesn't include evaluation of the fairness of the method or process by which the decision was made. The latter is called "procedural justice." Presumably, a just policy or procedure should help assure equitable outcomes every time, whereas a single instance of distributive justice could occur by chance, favoritism, or some other unfair process.

What makes an allocation procedure just? Following are six rules for procedural justice:*

- *Consistency rule:* Allocation procedures should be consistent across persons and over time.
- *Bias suppression rule:* Personal self-interest in the allocation process should be prevented.
- *Accuracy rule:* Decisions must be based on accurate information.
- *Correctability rule:* Opportunities must exist to enable decisions to be modified.
- *Representativeness rule:* The allocation process must represent the concerns of all recipients.
- *Ethicality rule:* Allocations must be based on prevailing moral and ethical standards.

Performance appraisal is a situation in which decisions are made about individuals (allocation of ratings or rankings and associated rewards), and the potential for misunderstandings and feelings of injustice are great. This means that a very fair and clear process should be adopted.

Research has shown that appraisals are seen as more fair when consistent standards are applied to all ratees; there is a system by which the ratee can appeal or rebut the evaluation; and raters are familiar with the ratee's work, solicit employee input before assigning ratings, provide prompt feedback, and allow two-way communication in the appraisal interview. In addition, procedures are more likely to be perceived as fair if employees understand the rating dimensions and the superior's expectations well before the rating takes place. Ideally, ratees should also have input into determining the rating criteria.

These appraisal procedures meet most of the six rules given above and should help assure that the emotionally laden process of performance appraisal is seen as fair, insofar as is humanly possible.

Note: *Folger and Greenberg, p. 146.

Sources: Robert Folger and Jerald Greenberg, "Procedural Justice: An Interpretive Analysis of Personnel Systems," *Research in Personnel and Human Resource Management*, Vol. 3, 1985, pp. 141–183; and Robert Folger and Russell Cropanzano, *Organizational Justice and Human Resource Management* (Thousand Oaks, Calif.: Sage, 1998).

important in determining job effectiveness. For example, a relevant measure for assessing the performance of a college professor would include teaching performance. A measure is not deficient if it measures all-important aspects of performance. In the case of the college professor, the measure of performance would be deficient unless it assessed such factors as service and intellectual contributions (research and publications) as well as teaching performance. A measure is free of contamination if it avoids assessing constructs other than performance. If the professor's performance rating included an assessment of how well the professor's shoes were shined, the measure would be contaminated by this irrelevant content. The relationships between relevance, deficiency, and contamination are presented graphically in Figure 10.2.

A performance assessment system must be valid. It is essential that a good job analysis be conducted before developing the performance measure so that all relevant aspects of performance are covered and irrelevant factors do not contaminate the assessment measure.

Reliability

Inter-rater reliability is the most relevant type of reliability for performance assessment. Reliability is high when two or more raters agree on the performance of an employee and low when they do not. Inter-rater reliability is usually quite good when performance raters come from the same level of the organization, such as two superiors or two peers of the person being rated. However, there is often legitimate disagreement between raters at different levels, such as a peer and a

FIGURE 10.2

Relationships among Relevance, Deficiency, and Contamination

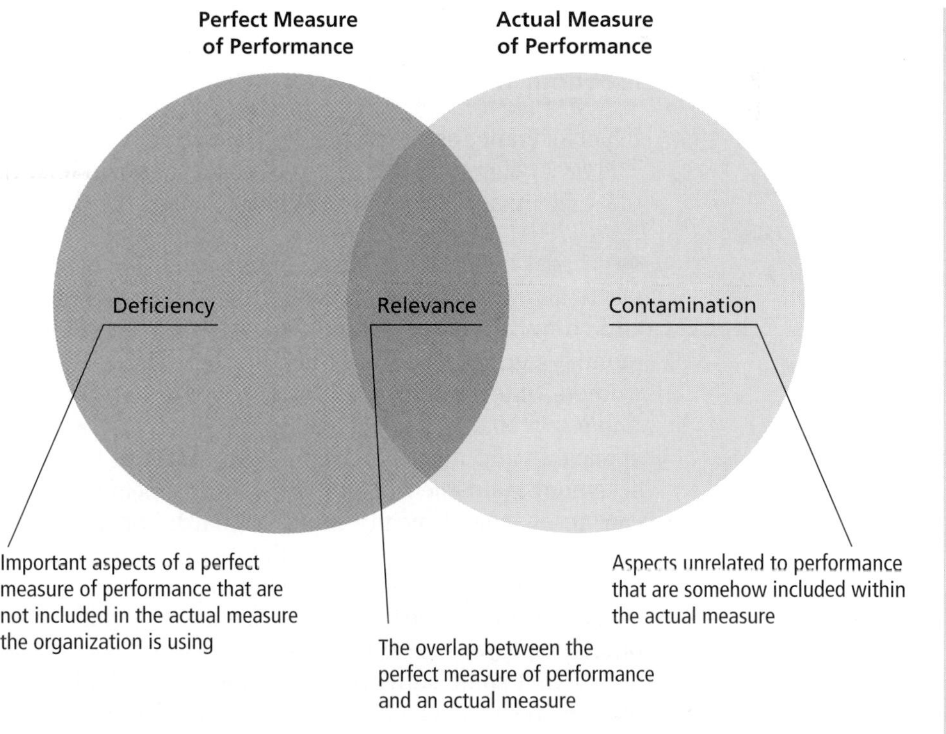
Perfect Measure of Performance
Actual Measure of Performance
Deficiency
Relevance
Contamination
Important aspects of a perfect measure of performance that are not included in the actual measure the organization is using
The overlap between the perfect measure of performance and an actual measure
Aspects unrelated to performance that are somehow included within the actual measure

superior or a superior and a subordinate. Thus high inter-rater reliability is expected only among raters at the same organizational level.

In a study of almost 10,000 employees from seventy-nine organizations, Hannah Rothstein found that inter-rater reliabilities—that is, the correlation (see Chapter 7) between two raters observing the same employee—typically ranged from 0.65 to 0.73, a high enough level to lend confidence to the stability of the rating process.[26] Another study observed lower values (from 0.45 to 0.63), with the lowest ratings being of communication and interpersonal skills (0.45 and 0.47, respectively).[27] Ratings for the dimensions of productivity, quality, and administrative skill were all in the high 0.50s or low 0.60s, again at a high enough level to know that there is consistency in observation. In the latter study, agreement among peers was notably lower, generally ranging between 0.33 and 0.42, suggesting that any system involving peers needs to incorporate extensive training.[28]

Internally consistent reliability and reliability over time are not especially important in performance assessment because performance itself may not be internally consistent or stable over time. A person may be very good at certain aspects of a job but quite weak at others, so a measure that accurately gauged these different aspects of performance would not show high internal consistency. Similarly, because performance may improve with experience or training and fluctuate with effort or luck, strong stability over time is not necessarily expected.[29]

For more objective measures of performance, another aspect of reliability is important. Suppose absenteeism from work is used as one measure of an employee's performance. If the supervisor sometimes records when the employee is absent and sometimes does not, then this measure of performance is unreliable. Thus, when evaluating the reliability of performance assessments, it is very important to know exactly what type of measure was used and, in the case of subjective ratings of performance, who was making the ratings.

Freedom from Bias

In performance assessment, the criterion of freedom from bias has two components. The first concerns legal issues of fairness to employees; the second has to do with the subjectivity of one person's judgments about the performance of others.

Legal Issues of Fairness In one sense, an assessment is free from bias if it is fair to all employees regardless of their race, sex, national origin, disability status, and so on. Employment legislation permits employers to use a bona fide assessment system but not one that has an unjustifiably adverse impact on minorities, women, older employees, or other protected groups of people.[30] In *Brito v. Zia Company* (1973), the court ruled that the *Uniform Guidelines* (see Chapter 5) were applicable and must be followed in evaluating the adequacy of a performance assessment instrument.[31] In other words, a performance assessment is a "test" and can be evaluated by the same standards. Spanish-surnamed workers were reinstated with back pay because the company had used a performance assessment instrument of questionable validity to make layoff decisions. In addition, Spanish-surnamed employees had been promoted significantly less frequently than were other employees. The court was critical of Zia's subjective assessment process, noting that some supervisors making ratings had never directly observed the employees' performance. Zia Company failed to present evidence of the validity of its assessment procedure.

In June 1989 the Supreme Court reaffirmed the importance of objective standards in performance assessment in the case of *Price Waterhouse v. Hopkins.*[32] Ann B. Hopkins filed charges of sex discrimination against the accounting firm of Price Waterhouse after being turned down for promotion to partner despite high performance. Hopkins charged that gender stereotyping was involved in the decision: she had been told she would have "to walk more femininely, talk more femininely, dress more femininely, wear makeup, have her hair styled, and wear jewelry" to be considered for promotion.[33] The Court ruled in Hopkins's favor, stating that her obligation to show that gender was a factor in the employment decision had been satisfied, whereas Price Waterhouse had failed to show that the same decision would have been made in the absence of gender as a factor. The Court's decision dealt with the effect of gender stereotyping in the workplace and the need for objectivity in performance evaluation.[34]

Although there is no legal mandate for an organization to have and use an assessment system that meets some state-of-the-art requirement for soundness, the methods of assessment that an organization employs should not have an adverse impact on groups protected by the law. If challenged, the organization will seek to defend itself on the basis of the soundness, objectivity, and validity of its assessment system.[35] Most performance assessment systems currently in use probably would not fare too well if they were subjected to legal challenge. A system can be discriminatory for any of the following reasons:

1. The rating content is not job related or valid.
2. The content of the ratings is not developed from a thorough job analysis.
3. The raters do not observe ratees performing their work.
4. Ratings are based on raters' evaluations of subjective or vague factors.
5. Ratings are not collected and scored under standardized conditions.[36]

An employer can reduce the probability of a legal challenge in several ways. A primary rule is to use only assessment systems that are based on a thorough job analysis. The assessment process should incorporate only those duties or characteristics that are important for job performance. Supervisors must be trained to use the rating instrument properly, and the results and rationale for all evaluations must be carefully documented.[37] If possible, formal appeal mechanisms should be established, and upper level or human resource managers should review ratings.[38] Finally, some form of counseling should be offered to help poor performers improve.

Race Differences There has been a long-standing interest in the effects of rater and ratee race on performance ratings. Recently, several large-scale studies[39] have examined this issue, with one of the larger studies finding that black raters (whether peers, subordinates, or supervisors) assigned more favorable ratings to ratees of their own race.[40] Results for white raters differed according to the particular rating source. White supervisors assigned more favorable ratings to ratees of their own race, but white subordinates and peers did not. White and black managers received higher ratings from black raters than from white raters.[41] Through training and other procedures, employers should take special care to ensure that race bias is understood and then eliminated from performance ratings.

Age Differences It is worth noting that cases brought under the federal Age Discrimination in Employment Act (ADEA; see Chapter 5) have not scrutinized defendant organizations' assessment systems. The intent of the ADEA is to protect those aged forty or over from discriminatory employment decisions. A study of more than fifty-three age discrimination cases found that in contrast to Title VII cases, the outcome of ADEA cases was not influenced by the soundness of the performance assessment system.[42] Formal performance evaluation procedures were not required by the courts for an employer to mount a successful defense; instead, less reliable sources of employee performance information have been accepted as conclusive evidence substantiating an employer's claim of nondiscrimination in employment decisions. However, employers would be wise to have a sound, objective, and valid assessment system to defend ADEA charges should they arise. It should be added, too, that research generally has shown that there is no relationship between age and performance, despite the prevalence of a stereotype of older workers being less effective.[43]

Freedom from Rating Errors When an assessment system requires individuals to make subjective judgments about the performance of others, the second component of freedom from bias becomes important. Ratings may be biased, either intentionally or unintentionally. Common rating errors are described next and shown graphically in Figure 10.3. Some of these errors also occur in interviewing—another situation in which one person judges and evaluates another.

Leniency Errors Sometimes raters give employees more positive performance ratings than they deserve. For example, an analysis of U.S. Marine Corps officer fitness reports showed that on a 9-point scale, with 9 representing "outstanding performance," the average performance ratings for a sample of more than 2,000 officers was 8.2.[44] Although officers are well trained and devoted to their service, it is difficult to believe that almost all of them are truly outstanding. For the military in general and the Marines in particular, leniency is part of the assessment organizational culture.

With a large number of employees, one would expect the true distribution of performance ratings to approximate a bell-shaped curve (see the curve indicating true distribution of performance in Figure 10.3a). Of course, assuming modestly successful recruiting (see Chapter 6), selection (see Chapters 7 and 8), and development (see Chapter 9), the true distribution of performance may be negatively skewed. When **leniency errors** occur, most employees receive very high performance ratings (see the curve indicating leniency error in Figure 10.3a). Leniency is a very common type of rating bias, although recent research suggests that it is a stable characteristic of raters that could be predicted using measures of individual differences.[45]

Severity Errors Sometimes raters evaluate employees more unfavorably than their performance warrants. When such **severity errors** occur, as shown in Figure 10.3a, the distribution of performance ratings shifts dramatically to the left of the true distribution of performance. Severity error is the reverse of leniency error.

Central Tendency Errors Sometimes a supervisor rates all employees near the midpoint of a performance scale. Few if any employees receive very high or very low ratings. As Figure 10.3b shows, such **central tendency errors** result in a rating distribution that is highly compressed around the middle. Central tendency errors are often caused by the rater's failure to observe or ambiguity caused by poor descriptions of the performance dimensions.

FIGURE 10.3

Leniency, Severity, Central Tendency, and Halo Errors

(a) Leniency and severity errors

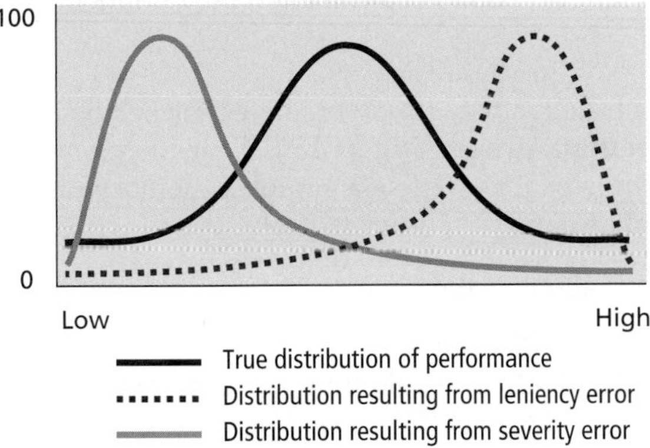

True distribution of performance
Distribution resulting from leniency error
Distribution resulting from severity error

(b) Central tendency error

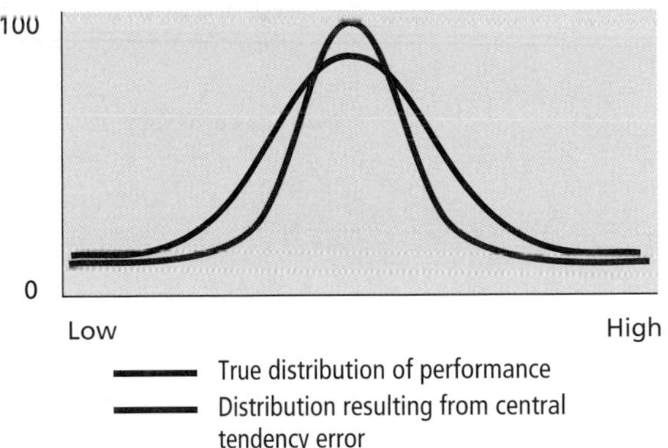

True distribution of performance
Distribution resulting from central tendency error

(c) Halo error

Employee's *true* performance on five dimensions:

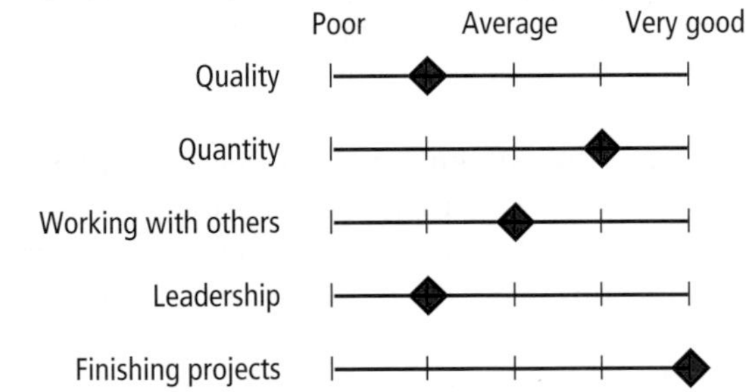

Employee's *rated* performance on five dimensions:

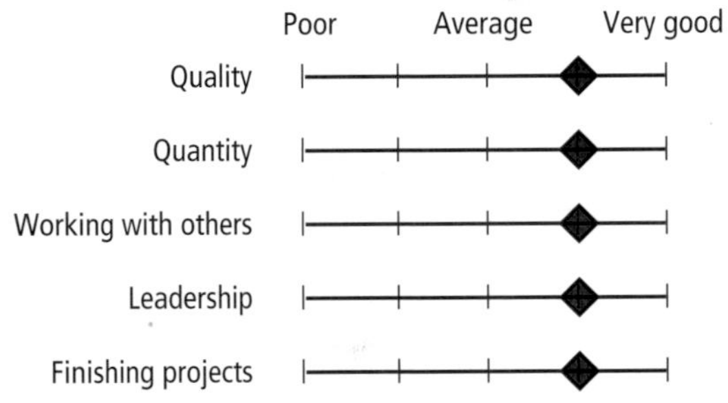

When central tendency, leniency, or severity errors are frequent, an assessment system cannot accomplish its purpose of differentiating between good and poor workers. When one of these errors occurs, nearly everyone receives the same rating—a high, low, or average score, depending on the type of error.

Halo Errors Whereas leniency, severity, and central tendency errors occur when several employees are appraised, **halo errors** involve the rating of a single individual on several aspects of performance. This pervasive form of rating error has been long recognized yet is not well understood.[46] Jack M. Feldman defines halo error as a very high correlation among ratings across several performance areas or, more simply put, the tendency of raters to color performance judgments by general feelings toward the individual.[47] For example, a supervisor may be asked to rate an employee on quality and quantity of performance, working with coworkers, leadership, and finishing projects on time. In general, one would expect an employee to be good at some tasks, average at others, and perhaps weak in some performance areas. The individual would receive some high ratings, some low, and some average, depending on the performance area. The correlation among those ratings would be moderate to low. When halo error occurs, an employee receives nearly identical performance ratings on all performance areas, and the resulting correlation among the ratings is very high.[48] An example of halo error is given in Figure 10.3c.

Why Do Rating Errors Occur? Rating errors occur through both unintentional and intentional processes.

Unintentional Errors One way to examine why rating errors occur is to use the approach called **cognitive information processing (CIP).** Proponents of CIP argue that performance assessment is best viewed as a complex memory task in which the assessors must do the following:

- Acquire performance information about an employee.
- Encode and store that information in their memory.
- Retrieve that information at a later date when asked to assess the employee's performance.
- Weigh and combine the information into an overall performance judgment.[49]

The amount of performance information available about an employee is enormous. Raters can notice and recall only a limited amount of information on each employee, and research has shown that they use a variety of methods to condense the information they do receive.[50] This can result in a variety of memory and judgment errors in assessment. One cognitive shortcut that people use in processing information about others is the schema. **Schemas** are simply mental categories that an individual uses to organize information and classify people.[51] For example, a supervisor might use two schemas in classifying employees: the good worker schema and the bad worker schema. Associated with each schema is a set of attributes, called a **prototype** that represents the essential characteristics associated with that schema.[52] Thus the prototype for the supervisor's good worker schema might include the following: never absent, writes well, always gets projects done on time, and gets along well with coworkers. A ratee need not exhibit all the prototype characteristics to be classified into the schema. For instance, noticing that an employee is never absent from work, the supervisor might categorize that person as a good worker, even without direct evidence that the employee writes well, hands in projects on time, or gets along well with coworkers. It should be added that this is an example of failure to observe all categories of employee behavior as well as of pre-existing category construction.

When asked to assess the performance of an employee, a supervisor searches his or her memory to determine into which schema the employee has been placed. The supervisor recalls information about the employee, *including the schema prototype.* The supervisor's judgment of the employee is based not only on the precise behaviors observed but also on the prototype associated with the schema. This recollection of behavior that never actually occurred (but that fits a particular schema) is the source of halo error. Often an employee rated high on work attendance will also receive positive ratings on all other aspects of performance *even though he or she may not have actually performed well in these areas.* Similarly, an employee originally categorized as a poor worker may be rated low on all criteria even though the supervisor may not really have observed poor performance in some areas. This process is shown in Figure 10.4.

FIGURE 10.4

How Cognitive Information Processing Causes Rating Errors

Prototype of a "Good Worker"

Employee's Actual Behavior Observed by Supervisor

Supervisor's Later Appraisal of Employee (applies prototype)

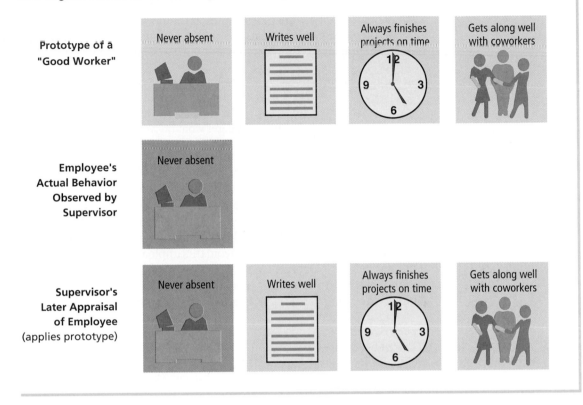

Leniency and severity errors may also be influenced by the nature of schema prototypes. If a supervisor's prototype characteristics for the good worker are so extreme that few employees will ever exhibit behavior that allows them to be classified as good workers, severity error may occur. If some of the prototype characteristics of a good worker are very easy for most employees to exhibit, leniency error may occur.

Intentional Errors Sometimes supervisors intentionally rate employees inaccurately for political or other reasons. A company vice president summarized one common view of the politics of assessment:

> As a manager, I will use the review process to do what is best for my people and the division. . . . I've got a lot of leeway—call it discretion—to use this process in that manner. . . . I've used it to get my people better raises in lean years, to kick a guy in the pants if he really needed it, to pick up a guy when he was down or even to tell him that he was no longer welcome here. It is a tool that the manager should use to help him do what it takes to get the job done. I believe most of us here operate this way regarding appraisals. . . . Accurately describing an employee's performance is really not as important as generating ratings that keep things cooking.[53]

A term for the approach exhibited by this VP is *backfilling*—that is, deciding on the end evaluation result and then rigging the numbers to achieve the predetermined end. As stated by one researcher, "It would be naïve to think of performance appraisal as anything other than a political process. Rating accurately is not always the goal of appraisers and there are many situations where providing inaccurate appraisal data is sound management."[54] While many would find this reprehensible, such actions are probably more common than is admitted.

The preceding approach to performance assessment can lead to cynicism on the part of employees. One employee's view is expressed as follows:

> In the end it still comes down to this: My boss can give me any rating he wants and there isn't a lot I can do about it. I can hit my numbers, but he might think I should have exceeded them. . . . Perhaps he didn't like my style or the way I handled a certain deal. In the end I'll get what he wants me to have.[55]

Recent work has begun to shed some light on how political factors affect performance assessments.[56] For example, intentional leniency error can occur for several reasons. Supervisors may feel that having subordinates with high performance ratings will make them look good to their own superiors, or they may fear that their working relationship with employees will be ruined by an unfavorable assessment.[57] Also, supervisors simply may find it difficult to give negative feedback to their employees and may inflate ratings to avoid this unpleasant task.[58] For these reasons, intentional leniency error is far more prevalent than severity error, although some intentional severity error can occur. The common reasons supervisors give for inflating or deflating performance ratings are summarized in Table 10.2.

TABLE 10.2

Why Supervisors Inflate and Deflate Ratings

Reasons for Inflating
To maximize the merit raise an employee is eligible to receive, particularly when the merit raise ceiling is low.
To protect or encourage an employee whose performance has suffered because of personal problems. The supervisor feels sorry for the employee.
To avoid "hanging out dirty laundry" that would reflect badly on the supervisor or unit.
To avoid creating a written record of an employee's poor performance that becomes part of the employee's permanent record.
To avoid a confrontation with an employee.
To reward an employee who has shown improvement in performance, even though performance is still not high.
To increase the likelihood that an employee whom the supervisor does not like will be promoted out of the supervisor's work unit.
Reasons for Deflating
To shock an employee back onto a higher performance track.
To teach a rebellious employee a lesson about who is in charge.
To send a message to an employee that he or she should consider leaving the organization.
To build a strongly documented, written record of poor performance so that an employee can be fired.

Source: Based on C. O. Longenecker, H. P. Sims, and D. A. Gioia, "Behind the Mask: The Politics of Employee Appraisal," *Academy of Management Executive,* Vol. 1, 1987, pp. 183–193.

Practicality

It takes time, effort, and money to develop, implement, and use a performance assessment system. The benefits to the organization of using the system must outweigh its costs. The assessment system should also be relatively easy to use and should have a high degree of employee and managerial acceptance. Even the best-developed assessment system is futile if it is not used.[59]

The development and use of an assessment system can be an expensive undertaking. Table 10.3 shows the estimated costs of developing a performance assessment system that were reported in a study by M. A. Jones. The costs required to develop the system were distinguished from those needed to implement and run it within the organization. In all, the assessment system that Jones analyzed would cost just under $700,000 (adjusted to 2002 dollars) to develop and implement. (This is likely a modest estimate for a limited appraisal system.)

Because dollar costs are high, an important practical criterion on which to judge an assessment system is the savings it might bring to the organization.[60] The process of measuring dollar return to an organization, called *utility analysis*, was discussed earlier in connection with both selection and training. Feedback, like training and careful selection, can improve employee performance. Estimates of performance improvement following feedback range from 8 percent to as much as 26 percent. The dollar value of improvements can be calculated using an estimate of the standard deviation of performance in dollars.[61] In one study, the cost of developing and implementing an assessment system was estimated at $700 per employee. Subtracting the costs of conducting assessments and giving feedback

TABLE 10.3

Costs of Developing and Implementing an Appraisal System

Item	Development	Implementation
Operating Costs		
Production and development	$116,500	$39,100
Data-entry hardware	N/A	$900
Paper	$3,600	$1,800
Mailing/distribution	$1,100	$14,400
Training	N/A	$55,100
Human Resource Costs		
Job analysis/experts	$79,900	N/A
Clerical	$24,200	$24,000
Professional coordinator	N/A	$15,600
Consultant	$55,100	$3,200
Rater time	N/A	$174,300
Ratee time	N/A	$64,400
Total	$280,400	$392,800
Grand total		$673,200

Source: Adapted from M. A. Jones, "Estimating Costs in the Development and Implementation of a Performance Appraisal System," paper presented at the First Annual Scientist-Practitioner Conference in Industrial-Organizational Psychology, Old Dominion University, Norfolk, Virginia, 1980. Reprinted by permission. Dollar figures (adjusted to 2002 dollars) have been rounded to the nearest $100.

from the estimated dollar value of performance improvements, analysts estimated that an organization in which 500 managers were appraised and provided with feedback could realize benefits of $5.3 million in the first year.[62] Thus, even though assessment systems are expensive to develop and implement, they offer great potential benefits.

DECIDING WHAT TYPES OF PERFORMANCE TO MEASURE

The criteria for evaluating performance assessment systems described earlier provide the basis for making important decisions when developing an assessment system. One crucial choice is simply what type of performance to assess. There are three basic categories of performance information.

1. *Trait-based systems* assess the abilities or other personal characteristics of an employee. For example, in a performance management system, it might be important that a service employee have a pleasant personality.
2. *Behavior-based systems* measure the extent to which an employee engages in specific, relatively well-defined behaviors while on the job. For example, in a performance management system, it might be important that an employee be a positive contributor to a team.
3. *Results-based systems* measure the "bottom line" associated with an employee's work: Did the job get done? Were the financial results positive?[63] For example, in a performance management system, a store manager's goal might be to reduce returns to 3 percent of sales.

Each type of assessment system has some advantages and disadvantages. Figure 10.5 illustrates the three types of systems.

Trait-Based Appraisals

Trait-based appraisals are used to assess the personality or personal characteristics of employees, such as their ability to make decisions, loyalty to the company, communication skills, or level of initiative. This type of assessment asks a lot about what a person is but relatively little about what he or she actually *does* and, as such, concerns "who" performs the job. Although trait-based assessments are easy to construct, the disadvantages of focusing on traits are significant.

Trait-based approaches have questionable validity. Traits assessed in this type of approach often do not relate well to how employees really behave on the job because job behavior is strongly influenced by situational and environmental factors. An employee who is usually boisterous and aggressive with coworkers may act in a restrained, considerate manner when dealing with clients. Because the link between personal traits and actual job behavior is weak, trait-based systems are potentially more susceptible to charges of unfairness by minorities, women, and other protected groups. Trait-based systems are not as likely to be accepted by the courts. As noted earlier, court decisions such as *Price Waterhouse v. Hopkins* have made it very clear that what is assessed in a performance assessment system should have a clear link to effectiveness on the job.[64]

A further problem is that the inter-rater reliability of trait-based ratings is often low. The traits are difficult to define accurately, and the different frames of refer-

FIGURE 10.5
Examples of Trait-, Behavior-, and Results-Based Performance Appraisal Systems

A. Trait-based appraisal

Rate the employee on each of the following traits:

1. Loyalty to company	very low	low	average	high	very high
2. Communication ability	very low	low	average	high	very high
3. Cooperativeness	very low	low	average	high	very high

B. Behavior-based appraisal

Using the scale below, rate the frequency with which the employee exhibits the following behaviors:

1 = never 3 = sometimes 5 = almost always
2 = rarely 4 = frequently

_____ 1. Greets customers in a pleasant and friendly manner.
_____ 2. Is able to explain technical aspects of a product to a customer.
_____ 3. Fills out charge card slips correctly, getting approval from supervisor for all charges above $300.

C. Results-based appraisal

From your production and employee files, please provide the following information for this employee:

1. Number of units produced this month: _____
2. Number of units produced that were rejected and scrapped by quality control: _____
3. Number of units produced that were rejected and returned for repair by quality control: _____
4. Days this month the employee was absent without certified medical cause: _____

ence used by different raters make agreement among raters unlikely. A final disadvantage is that trait-based assessments are not helpful for providing feedback to employees. For example, telling an employee that he or she is too shy is not very useful. The information does not indicate how the employee can be less shy. Also, the basic personality traits of individuals are relatively well fixed by the time they are hired by an organization and are very difficult to alter.

Behavior-Based Appraisals

Assessment can consider the behavior of employees rather than their personal traits or "how" the job is done. Behavior measures are appropriate when the process used to accomplish the job is very important, and thus behavior measures are used to emphasize how a job is done. For example, a salesperson should greet customers as they enter the store, help them find what they are looking for, take their payment promptly, and thank them for their business. It is possible that a salesperson who did not greet or assist customers might complete sales, but this individual would not be representing the store in the way managers preferred. A sound behavior-based assessment would note the salesperson's failure to follow the preferred process.

In **behavior-based appraisals,** employees are assessed on how they do their job. Such assessments are more acceptable to the courts than trait-based assessments. Behavior measures can be very useful for feedback purposes because they indicate exactly what an employee should do differently. For instance, although a shy employee may always be shy, a behavior-based assessment might point out particular things that the person could do differently, such as contributing ideas at regularly scheduled staff meetings.

Deficiency may be a problem with some behavior-based assessments because they often will not include all behaviors that could lead to job effectiveness. For some jobs, effective performance can be achieved using a variety of different behaviors. For example, one salesperson may sell twenty cars a month using an aggressive, "pushy" style. Another salesperson may sell just as many cars using a reserved, considerate, fact-oriented approach. An assessment system that assumes that an aggressive sales style is best would unfairly assess the performance of the second salesperson. Of course, if the aggressive style is most consistent with the dealer's organizational approach, the salesperson with the reserved manner may want to find an employer with a culture more consistent with this style, for example, a Saturn dealership.

Results-Based Appraisals

Another approach to performance assessment measures the results of work behavior. This approach deals with bottom-line issues such as how many cars an employee sold or how much profit the employee brought into the organization during the month. When it is not important how results are achieved, or when there are many different ways to succeed, a **results-based appraisal** is appropriate. Under this approach, both car salespersons described earlier would receive the same evaluation, even though they achieved their results using very different means.

Despite their intuitive appeal, results-based assessments pose questions of practicality, contamination, and deficiency. Results-based measures may be difficult to obtain for some jobs. What are the performance results of a high school teacher's behavior? Furthermore, results are not always under the control of an individual employee. Equipment breakdowns, a change in the economy, bad luck, inadequate budgetary or staff support, or other factors not directly controlled by an employee may greatly affect the job results.[65] Results measures are therefore contaminated by these external factors. Another problem is that results-based assessments may foster a "results at all cost" mentality among employees.[66] For example, in an organization that evaluated its telephone order takers on the basis of sales, employees on the telephone bank learned to hang up on customers calling to cancel orders or arrange returns because these counted against sales. Obviously, such a practice was not what the organization intended and would hurt customer satisfaction and repeat sales.

Teamwork among employees may suffer if individuals are preoccupied with their own *personal* results and will not take the time to help coworkers. Results-based measures are deficient in that they may not tap such aspects of performance as cooperation, which may have important benefits for the organization. A final disadvantage is that results-based assessments are less helpful for employee development. Although they may indicate that results are below acceptable levels, they do not always provide clear information on how to improve work performance.

Care must be taken in deciding what type of performance is appropriate to assess for a specific job. Unless a clear link between traits and job effectiveness can be shown, trait-based assessments should be avoided; in general, fewer legal problems are associated with behavior- and results-based systems. A carefully constructed combination of behavior- and results-based approaches may be most appropriate for many jobs.

The next section of this chapter describes some specific methods of assessing performance. Some of these techniques are, by their nature, suited to assessing only one type of performance information. Others, particularly those involving subjective ratings, may be used to assess more than one performance type.

METHODS OF APPRAISING PERFORMANCE

Performance can be measured in many different ways. Most of the performance measures currently in use can be characterized as either objective or subjective. Objective measures are typically results-based measures of physical output, whereas subjective measures can be used to assess traits, behaviors, or results.

Objective Measures

Objective measures assess performance in terms of numbers, such as the amount of a product an employee produces or sells, the number of defective products produced, the number of times an employee is absent or late to work, or some other direct numerical index of how well or quickly an employee can perform certain tasks. Some job measures are more objective than others, but none are truly objective. For example, the number of defective products produced may be the result of a machine defect or the quality of raw materials received from the supplier. Most workers are quick to report that many of the "objective" measures of job performance really relate to job elements beyond their control.

There are five major types of objective measures: production measures, dollar sales, personnel data, performance tests, and business unit measures.

Production Measures The manufacturing industry has used production measures for at least the last 100 years. These measures simply involve counting the number of items produced by an employee or the number of defective units made or obtaining some other quantitative index of production. Production measures can be used appropriately when an employee produces a measurable, physical product. As with any results-based assessment, production measures may not be available for many of the jobs in an organization, or they may be influenced by factors beyond an employee's control. For example, if a coworker is habitually late in getting raw materials to an employee, that employee's production rate could be slowed down. Or a worker may be assigned to an older piece of equipment or a machine that is prone to break down. For a production measure to be a valid measure of performance, three conditions must be met: (1) production should be on a repetitive basis, (2) the amount of product should be measurable, and (3) the employee should be primarily responsible for the amount produced; that is, production needs to be sensitive to the employee's ability and effort, not system-driven.

Dollar Sales Sales performance is usually measured by the dollar amount of sales made in a given period of time. Typically, some minimum acceptable level of sales is defined, and performance beyond that quota is rewarded more highly. Sales measures are also results-based and suffer from many of the same shortcomings as production measures. For example, a salesperson assigned to a rural territory may have to spend many hours traveling from town to town, whereas a salesperson assigned to a large city can devote more time to actual client contact. The salesperson in the city will probably sell more than the salesperson in the rural area, even if both work equally hard and are equally skilled. The sales measure is contaminated by this difference in sales territory, which creates a so-called **opportunity bias.**[67] Thus it is appropriate to use dollar sales as an index of performance only when individuals have substantial control over their sales performance or when it is possible to adjust for contaminants such as differences in sales territory.

Personnel Data Information from an employee's personnel file is sometimes used in performance assessment. **Personnel measures** include such particulars as the number of times an employee has been absent or late to work and the number of reprimands or disciplinary actions taken against the individual.

Serious problems arise in the use of personnel data. One is **contamination.** If an employee is absent from work because of illness or is late to work because of a flat tire, does this mean the employee is a poor performer? Personnel data are of questionable relevance. If an employee is habitually late to work but consistently produces more and better-quality products than coworkers, is the employee a poor performer? Personnel measures may also be unreliable because some supervisors record absenteeism or tardiness more carefully than others. Personnel data should be used as a measure of performance only when a clear link can be made between the measure (e.g., tardiness) and actual job effectiveness, such as the delay of the start of business as a result of an employee's tardiness.

Performance Tests Performance tests are work samples or simulations under standardized conditions. For example, telephone operators may all receive the same set of scripted calls and be evaluated on speed, accuracy, and courtesy of service. Pilots fly periodic "check rides" in flight simulators to assess their ability to handle both routine and emergency procedures.

Performance tests are useful when it is difficult to collect comparable or uncontaminated performance data in any other way, but they suffer from three major problems. First, they tend to be deficient because only some aspects of a job can be realistically simulated. Second, if employees know they are being tested on their job effectiveness, they are likely to work very hard to perform the test well. Performance tests then become a measure not of typical performance but of maximum employee capability. For example, whereas pilot inattentiveness is a cause of many air emergencies, how many pilots will be inattentive while being observed in a simulator? The final problem is that of practicality. Many jobs simply do not lend themselves to this kind of assessment, and for those that do, performance tests are generally expensive and time consuming to develop and implement.

Business Unit Performance Measures The preceding objective measures are seldom useful for managers. However, the performance of upper level managers and executives is sometimes assessed by objective measures of the performance of the business unit that they head. Measures might include stock price, return on equity, profit, or market share. Clearly, these measures can be contaminated by economic factors beyond the manager's control, but they can often be valuable when benchmarked against the industry.

Overall Value of Objective Measures Each type of objective measure has its own strengths and weaknesses. For instance, objective measures have the advantages of being free from the types of errors and biases that plague subjective measures. However, objective measures seldom capture the individual's total contribution to the organization. Measures of quantity, quality, attendance, and even profit may represent important dimensions of performance but are **deficient** in that they ignore dimensions such as cooperation or willingness to contribute in ways that go beyond the job description. Most organizations believe subjective assessments are more complete in their representation of performance and thus use subjective measures of performance either to supplement or to replace objective measures in the assessment system.

Subjective Measures

Because they rely on human judgment, **subjective measures** are prone to the rating errors discussed earlier. Most performance assessment systems place heavy emphasis on subjective ratings of performance. One study reported that among ninety-six police departments in major cities, nearly 90 percent used supervisory ratings as their primary performance assessment tool.[68] Anyone who has the opportunity to observe an employee's performance—including superiors, peers, subordinates, clients, and the employees themselves—can make subjective ratings. For the vast majority of organizations, however, it is the immediate supervisor who judges performance. Advantages and disadvantages of using other sources of performance judgments are considered later in this section.

Unlike objective measures, subjective judgments can be used even when the employee does not produce a measurable physical product. Subjective ratings can be used to measure the behavior or personal traits of employees as well as results. The major problem with subjective measures of performance is that the raters have to observe and evaluate job-related behavior. Raters may not have the chance to observe relevant behavior, and even if they do, their ratings may be biased. Several different types of subjective measures can be used. Generally, they can be classified as either comparative procedures (ranking) or assessments against absolute standards (rating).

Comparative Procedures Subjective comparison of the overall work performance of individual employees can yield a rank ordering of employees from best to worst. Three kinds of **comparative procedures** are used in performance assessments: ranking, paired comparisons, and forced distributions.

Ranking When **ranking** is used, employees are compared directly against one another. Ranking is easy to explain, understand, and use. It is generally not time consuming and is less expensive than other evaluation techniques. The simplest ranking procedure is **straight ranking,** in which the evaluator arranges employees in order from best to worst on the basis of their overall performance. First, the best employee is identified, then the second best, and so on until the worst employee is assigned the lowest rank. A variation is called **alternate ranking.** In this procedure, the evaluator first ranks the best employee, next the worst employee, then the second best, then the second worst, and so on until all employees are ranked.

In **paired-comparison ranking,** all possible pairs of employees are formed. The evaluator indicates which individual in each pair is the better performer. An employee's rank is determined by the number of times he or she is chosen as the better performer in a pair. The person chosen most often is ranked first. Use of this method requires the comparison of many pairs even when the total number of employees is not large. The formula for the number of possible pairs of employees is $n(n-1)/2$, where n = the number of employees. For example, if there are 10 employees in a work group, $10(9)/2 = 45$ judgments must be made. In the case of 20 employees, 190 pairs must be compared. Paired-comparison ranking is more complicated than straight ranking, but the process is believed to result in more consistent, reliable ranks than the straight-ranking approach.

A variation of this approach is to present pairs of statements, allowing the rater to choose the statement that best describes the employee's performance. In a recent study a group of researchers modified this form of paired-comparison rating of performance to a computerized adaptive rating scale (CARS).[69] The computer presents pairs of statements, but then moves on to the next employee when a stable estimate of performance is obtained. The advantage of the procedure is that it is interactive and adaptive. In this way, superior rating accuracy can be achieved with fewer comparisons.

Forced Distribution When using a **forced-distribution method,** also called **forced-ranking method,** the evaluator has to place a certain percentage of employees into each of several performance categories. An example of such a system was the forced distribution system used by Ford Motor. Ford's performance management process required that 10 percent of its employees receive A's, 80 percent B's, and 10 percent C's (the lowest grade).[70] The approach taken by Ford generated a great deal of controversy and several lawsuits.[71] Ford is not the only company relying on forced rankings to differentiate employees. For example, Hewlett-Packard, General Electric, and Microsoft have also adopted such systems, either as part of work-force reduction programs or as indicative of the competitive cultures they sought to engender. General Electric's former CEO, Jack Welch, is among the most vocal and articulate advocates of performance management systems that force turnover of the lowest performing employees each year.[72] At GE the bottom 10 percent of employees are supposed to be eliminated.

Forced-distribution judgments are usually based on an overall assessment of employees' performance. Examples of performance levels and distribution targets in a forced-distribution procedure are presented in Table 10.4.

Advantages and Disadvantages of Comparative Procedures Comparative procedures are easy to explain and use; help in making layoff, promotion, and merit raise decisions; and serve as controls for leniency, severity, and central tendency errors. They have a number of disadvantages, however:

TABLE 10.4

Forced-Distribution Appraisal Method

Performance Level	Distribution Target
Level 1: Employee is below acceptable performance standards.	5% of unit
Level 2: Employee meets acceptable performance standard but has room for improvement.	15% of unit
Level 3: Employee shows a uniformly good level of performance.	50% of unit
Level 4: Employee shows a very high level of performance.	20% of unit
Level 5: Employee consistently shows outstanding performance.	10% of unit

Note: Each of the employees in a work unit is allocated to one of the performance levels shown in the table. Associated with each performance level is a "distribution target" that is used in allocating employees to the various levels.

- Employees are evaluated according to their overall performance rather than on a number of distinct aspects of performance. Comparative procedures provide no clue as to the absolute difference in performance among employees. It is impossible to tell whether the top-ranked employee in a group is a lot or just a little better than the second-ranked person.
- It is not possible to compare across work groups. The person ranked third in a good group may be better than the person ranked first in a weaker group.
- Comparative methods also require that one evaluator know the performance of every employee in a unit. In large groups, this may not be possible.

Because comparative procedures generally do not focus on specific job-related behaviors, they risk legal challenge. The courts have ruled against companies when comparative methods have had an adverse impact on minorities or women. Another problem is that comparative methods are not useful for employee development. An employee learns how he or she compares with other employees, but this feedback does not indicate how to improve performance. Comparative procedures may foster competition and resentment among employees. After all, only one person can receive the top ranking.

A major problem with forced distributions is that a group of employees may not conform to the predefined distribution used in the procedure; in highly selected groups, a majority of employees truly may be outstanding. Furthermore, performance may not be distributed normally if the organization has made successful efforts to reward and retain high-rated employees while encouraging poor performers to leave. Employees are often unhappy with forced-distribution systems because most employees believe they are above average.[73] A forced-distribution system allows only a few to receive the ratings that most think they deserve. Supervisors generally dislike forced-distribution systems because they limit the rater's discretion. Of course, in most cases, it was the inappropriate use of this rater "discretion" in the form of excessive leniency that caused the organization to institute the forced-distribution system in the first place.

Finally, many companies, including those that recently adopted forced-distribution systems, are trying to emphasize team-oriented work. Forced-distribution systems are generally not consistent with the team concept, leading a spokesperson for a company that previously used the system to state, "My recollection is it created 10 problems for every one it solved." Others view the system as a Band-Aid approach to dealing with work-force performance issues.[74]

Despite their drawbacks, comparative methods can be a useful component of an overall performance assessment system. They are useful in forcing evaluators to make distinctions between employees when differential rewards are to be distributed. In most situations, it may be best to combine comparative methods with other forms of performance assessment, such as the absolute standard approaches discussed next. A recent research article described how the global assessments resulting from comparative methods can be improved through a process of priming; that is, using the global assessment as a lead-in to more specific job ratings.[75] In this way, one may have the advantages of both an accurate global assessment and meaningful assessments of specific job behaviors.

Absolute Standards Instead of comparing an employee's performance with that of fellow employees, an assessment system can be based on absolute performance standards for the job. Each employee is evaluated against the standards. **Absolute standards** facilitate comparison of employees from different departments. Performance is measured on a number of specific dimensions so that employees can be given more helpful feedback than is generated by comparative procedures. Variations of the absolute standards technique include graphic rating scales, weighted checklists, the critical incidents technique, behaviorally anchored rating scales, and behavioral observation scales.

Graphic Rating Scales **Graphic rating scales** are the most widely used evaluation technique. The rater evaluates an employee on each of several performance dimensions using a continuum made up of clearly defined scale points. Figure 10.6 gives some examples of graphic rating scales for measuring performance along the dimension of quality. The rating dimensions should be based on a careful job analysis.

In the graphic rating scale method, the rater describes an employee as falling at some point on a performance continuum—such as unsatisfactory, average, or outstanding—on each dimension. The scale points can be assigned scores (e.g., ranging from 5 points for outstanding to 0 points for unsatisfactory), and a total score for an employee can be computed by summing the ratings across all dimensions rated. If some characteristics are more important than others, the rating on these dimensions can be multiplied by an appropriate weight before the total is calculated.

Graphic rating scales have several advantages. They are relatively easy to develop and use, more than one performance dimension can be included, employees' scores can be compared, and the method is well accepted by raters. If properly developed for relevance and clarity, graphic rating scales can be just as reliable and valid as more complicated techniques. On the other hand, this method offers little protection from rating errors, such as leniency, severity, central tendency, and halo errors. Graphic rating scales are often criticized because the performance dimensions on which the employee is rated and the scale anchors used in making the rating may be ill defined and vague. In Figure 10.6, scale A does not define the dimension being rated, and the scale anchors are ambiguous and uninformative. Scales D and E provide more definition of the dimension and levels of performance assessed.

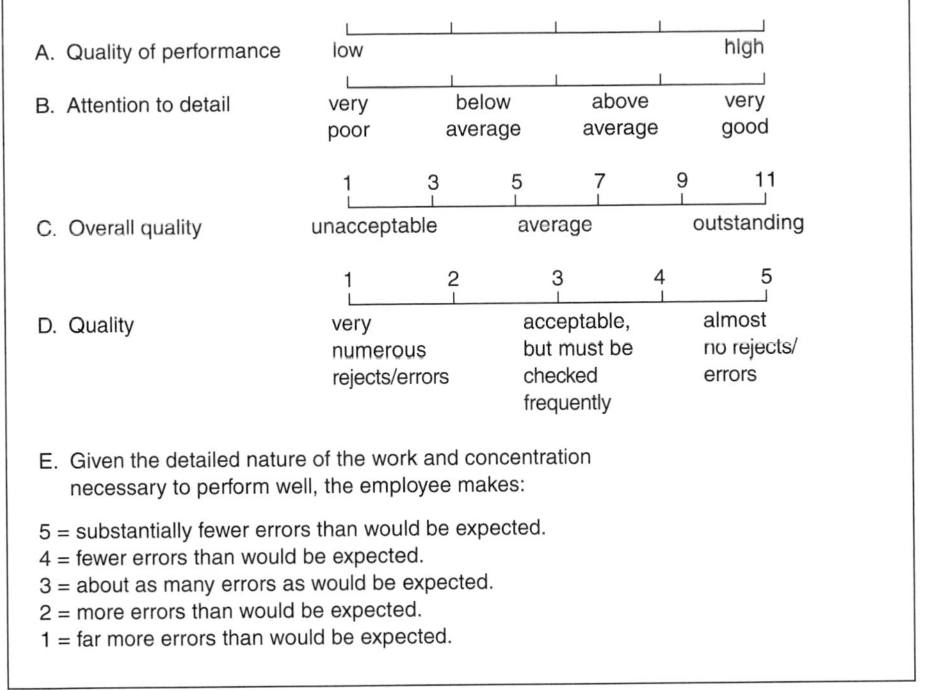

A. Quality of performance
low
high
B. Attention to detail
very poor
below average
above average
very good
1 3 5 7 9 11
C. Overall quality
unacceptable
average
outstanding
1 2 3 4 5
D. Quality
very numerous rejects/errors
acceptable, but must be checked frequently
almost no rejects/errors
E. Given the detailed nature of the work and concentration necessary to perform well, the employee makes:
5 = substantially fewer errors than would be expected.
4 = fewer errors than would be expected.
3 = about as many errors as would be expected.
2 = more errors than would be expected.
1 = far more errors than would be expected.

FIGURE 10.6
Examples of Typical Graphic Rating Scales

Mixed standard scales represent an effort to make graphic rating scales more effective. In this method, three statements are written to define low, medium, and high levels of performance along each dimension.[76] In Figure 10.7, for example, item 7 represents good performance on a dimension that might be called "efficiency of work"; item 5 represents average performance on this dimension; and item 2 represents poor performance. The rating form presents these three items in mixed order, along with items from other dimensions. Raters complete the scales by deciding whether the employee is worse than, equal to, or better than each of the performance statements. A special scoring procedure, shown at the bottom of Figure 10.7, is used to assign a performance score for each dimension. For example, if the employee is rated better than all three of the statements representing a particular dimension, he or she receives a score of 7. If the employee is rated worse than all three statements, a score of 1 is assigned. In the example shown the employee is better than the "poor" statement for dimension 2, equal to the "average" statement for dimension 2, and worse than the "good" statement, for a score of 4.

Mixed standard scales are supposed to reduce halo, leniency, and severity errors because the scale items are mixed randomly throughout the rating form and do not present a clear hierarchy from good to bad performance. Unfortunately, however, it is still easy to bias one's ratings. There have been several comparisons of ratings from mixed standard scales with ratings from other formats, and no strong evidence was found suggesting that this format is superior to others.[77]

Mixed standard scales also allow the detection of careless or inconsistent ratings. For example, suppose a rater indicated that an employee was worse than the statement representing a low level of work efficiency but also rated the employee

FIGURE 10.8

Weighted Checklist for Supervisory Job, with Example Evaluation of One Supervisor

Source: James B. Shaw, Abdul Jalil bin Ismail, and Cynthia D. Fisher, "A Cognitive Categorization Approach to Managerial Performance Appraisal: Analysis of the Singapore Manager," paper presented at the First International Conference on Personnel/Human Resource Management, National University of Singapore, December 1987. Reprinted by permission.

Instructions:

Check those statements that represent the typical actions of the employee.

	Statement	Value[a]
✓	Acts decisively when encountering problems	4.9
___	Is fair to all subordinates in his/her promotion decisions	5.0
___	Provides temporary solutions to problems that keep appearing	3.0
✓	Assesses the mood of subordinates before pursuing a subject that would damage relationships	3.9
✓	Evaluates performance once or twice a year	4.1
✓	Is unwilling to point out subordinates' poor work performance	2.2
___	Conducts detailed discussions with worker to solve problems	4.6
___	Checks subordinates' work thoroughly and is sharp at finding errors	4.2
✓	Gives merit increment to a poor performer	2.0
___	Carries out the policies of the company without regard to individual welfare or circumstances	2.3
✓	Signs subordinates' work without carefully checking it	2.0
___	Is unable to provide guidelines for making decisions when faced with a problem	2.3
✓	Maintains very good relations with other supervisors in the division	5.0
___	Shows concern for employee welfare but does not act on it	2.7

Performance
Score for employee = (4.9 + 3.9 + 4.1 + 2.2 + 2.0 + 2.0 + 5.0) = 24.1

[a]High values indicate that the statement represents good performance. These values would not be included on the actual rating form.

this chapter. Recent research has shown that structured diaries of specific incidents produced ratings with less leniency and more fine-grained distinctions.[79] The log also helps the supervisor provide specific examples when explaining ratings to subordinates.

Behaviorally Anchored Rating Scales Some assessment systems use graphic rating scales on which anchor points are defined in considerable detail, using examples of behavior that represent particular levels of performance. Such a **behaviorally anchored rating scale (BARS)** is developed for each of several important performance dimensions. Raters are asked to mark the scale point that best represents the performance of an employee. Figure 10.9 illustrates a BARS developed for the performance dimension "problem solving/decision making" for the job of mid-level manager.

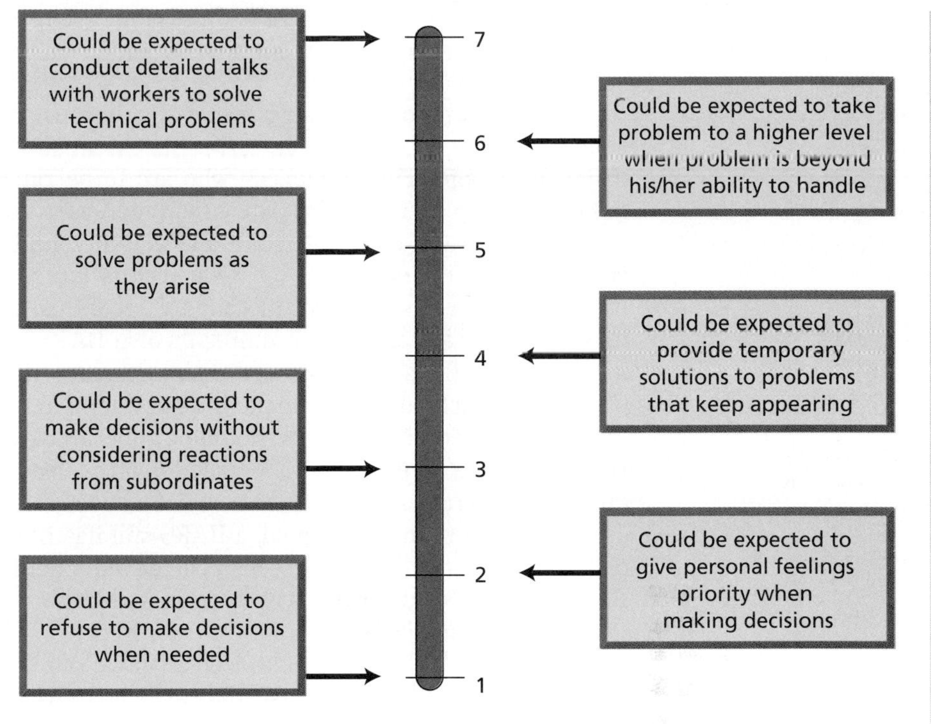

FIGURE 10.9

Example of Behaviorally Anchored Rating Scale for the Performance Dimension of Problem Solving/Decision Making

Source: James B. Shaw, Abdul Jalil bin Ismail, and Cynthia D. Fisher, "A Cognitive Categorization Approach to Managerial Performance Appraisal: Analysis of the Singapore Manager," paper presented at the First International Conference on Personnel/Human Resource Management, National University of Singapore, December 1987. Reprinted by permission.

The development of a BARS is a time-consuming and costly process that involves the efforts of many people. The steps are as follows:

1. A group of knowledgeable employees (perhaps including both workers and supervisors) identifies the important dimensions that make up effective performance. This group writes a clear definition for each dimension.
2. A second group comes up with as many critical incidents as it can to illustrate effective, average, and ineffective performance for each dimension.
3. A third group is given the list of dimensions and a stack of cards, each containing one of the critical incidents. The task of each member of this group is to assign each critical incident to the dimension it seems to characterize. This is called "retranslation." Critical incidents that are not placed in the same dimension by a majority of the retranslation group are discarded as unclear.
4. A fourth group rates the level of performance each remaining incident represents. For example, suppose that the incident "smiles and greets customers" has been reliably sorted into the "customer service" dimension of performance. Members of the fourth group then rate this incident as to whether it represents outstanding, above-average, average, or below-average performance. The mean and standard deviation of these ratings are computed for each critical incident. Items are discarded if group members are unable to agree on the performance level represented. From the remaining items, incidents are chosen to anchor each point along the BARS. Each anchor is worded "Could be expected to . . ." so that it can be selected by a rater who has observed similar, but not precisely identical, behavior in an employee.
5. As a final step, the rating scale is pilot tested in the organization.

Note that a BARS can be developed with only two groups rather than four. In this case, the first group carries out steps 1 and 2, and the second group completes steps 3 and 4.

A BARS is time consuming to develop because the development process involves so many people. Interestingly, this potential weakness is also the method's major advantage. The employees who are to be rated with the scales may have helped develop them. Their involvement increases the chance that the BARS will be a valid measure of performance and that the employees will accept its use. Because a BARS is necessarily job related, it is less vulnerable to legal challenges than many other assessment methods. Use of this method may not be practical, however. Each job category requires its own BARS, which may not be possible in many organizations either for economic reasons or because there are too few employees in a particular job to make the development technique feasible.

It would seem that a BARS should be superior to other assessment techniques. However, some research has concluded that the use of a BARS does not always reduce rating errors and in some cases introduces a new form of bias not found in other forms of rating.[80] Even so, a BARS still has the advantage of increasing employee involvement in the assessment development process. In constructing a BARS, employees and supervisors may clarify their understanding about the nature of the job and how it should be performed.

A variant of BARS is computerized adaptive rating scales (CARS). The CARS is a paired-comparison rating task that uses adaptive testing principles to present pairs of the type of scaled behavioral statements produced using BARS.[81] (See the discussion of paired-comparison ratings earlier in the chapter.) The procedure is that the initial presentation would be two behavioral statements associated with a dimension, one reflecting somewhat below average performance and the other reflecting somewhat above average performance. Depending on which statement the rater indicated was more descriptive of the rate, two additional behavioral statements would be presented, one with a scaled effectiveness level somewhat above the effectiveness value of the statement picked first as the more descriptive and the other with a scaled effectiveness level somewhat below the effectiveness value of the initially chosen statement. The advantage is economy of the rater's time in that statements presented reflect the effectiveness values previously indicated. A study using CARS found both higher degrees of reliability and validity, thus demonstrating the potential for such an approach.[82]

Behavioral Observation Scales Raters who use a BARS may find it difficult to select a single scale point to represent the performance of an employee who sometimes engages in some very positive behaviors but at other times performs poorly. **Behavioral observation scales (BOS)** were developed partly in response to this problem (see Figure 10.10).

To develop BOS, job experts first identify groups of similar behavioral incidents and form them into performance dimensions. In Figure 10.10, several behavioral incidents have been grouped to form a performance dimension called "communicating with subordinates." Job experts evaluate the behavioral incidents to make sure they are relevant to the dimension and important for distinguishing between successful and unsuccessful employees. If experts cannot agree about an incident's relevance, it is discarded. A 5-point frequency-of-occurrence scale is attached to each incident, which raters use to indicate how frequently each employee engages in the behavior.[83]

FIGURE 10.10

Example of Behavior Observation Scale for the Performance Dimension Communicating with Subordinates

Source: James B. Shaw, Abdul Jalil bin Ismail, and Cynthia D. Fisher, "A Cognitive Categorization Approach to Managerial Performance Appraisal: Analysis of the Singapore Manager," paper presented at the First International Conference on Personnel/Human Resource Management, National University of Singapore, December 1987. Reprinted by permission.

	Almost never				Almost always
Puts up notices on bulletin board when new policies or procedures are implemented	1	2	3	4	5
Maintains eye contact when talking to employees	1	2	3	4	5
Uses both written memos and verbal discussions when giving instructions	1	2	3	4	5
Discusses changes in policies or procedures with employees before implementing them	1	2	3	4	5
Writes memos that are clear, concise, and easy to understand	1	2	3	4	5

Total Performance Level	
Below adequate	5–9
Adequate	10–14
Good	15–19
Excellent	20 +

Behavioral observation scales have many advantages. They are based on a careful analysis of the job. The content validity of BOS incidents is evaluated directly and BOS are likely to be found acceptable to the courts. BOS can also be helpful in providing performance feedback to employees. Because they use frequency scales rather than simply indicating the one behavior that best represents an employee's performance, BOS may provide a greater depth of performance information than a BARS. Research, however, has not shown BOS to be clearly superior.[84]

Management by Objectives

A previously popular individualized method of evaluating the performance of managers and professionals was **management by objectives (MBO).** The MBO process involves three steps:

1. The employee meets with his or her superior and agrees on a set of goals to achieve during a specified period of time. Goals should be quantifiable and should include an agreed-upon target.
2. Throughout this period, progress toward the goals is monitored, though the employee is generally left free to determine how to go about meeting them.
3. At the end of the period, the employee and superior again meet to evaluate whether the goals were achieved and to decide together on a new set of goals.

Of course, if this sounds like performance management, it is because much of MBO has been subsumed under performance management as described previously.

MBO has several advantages similar to those of the broader approach, performance management. Observable, results-oriented goals replace the difficult-to-observe, subjective traits sometimes used in other measures of performance. MBO can encourage innovation and creativity because employees are free to determine how they will meet their goals. Such a process can be valuable in gaining the commitment of employees because they are actively involved in setting goals. It can also empower employees because they have a degree of latitude in deciding how to meet their goals.

Management by objectives can lead to performance improvement, particularly if goals are specific, moderately difficult, and accepted by the employees—and if the procedure has top management commitment. A summary of seventy studies of MBO programs found that when the commitment of top management was high, the average gain in productivity was 56 percent. When commitment was low, the average gain in productivity was only 6 percent.[85] When properly established and supported by top managers, MBO can lead to positive results.

RATERS OF EMPLOYEE PERFORMANCE

In most organizations, supervisors provide subjective ratings of employee performance. However, there are several other potential sources for performance ratings, including employees themselves, peers, subordinates, and customers both internal (e.g., the customers of HRM) and external to the organization. Each of these sources has its own advantages and disadvantages.

A consistent finding in the performance assessment literature is that ratings obtained from different rating sources have only partial agreement.[86] Self-ratings tend to be most dissimilar from those of other sources, probably the result of individuals rating themselves higher (leniency error) than other comparison groups (supervisor, subordinate, or peer).[87] In one study peer ratings correlated 0.62 with those of supervisors[88] and in another the correlation was 0.79,[89] both very substantial degrees of relationship. Finally, a further study involved a single instrument containing forty-eight behaviorally oriented items representing ten dimensions of managerial performance. The items were presented separately rather than as scales. The study found no difference in the way self, peer, supervisor, and subordinate groups organized the items to the scales. In other words, the ten scales were seen as analogous irrespective of the group doing the rating.[90]

Self-Evaluation

Employees are sometimes asked to evaluate themselves. It seems logical that individuals would be the best judges of their own performance, particularly if supervisors cannot observe them on a regular basis. If employees are asked to evaluate themselves, they may respond by becoming more motivated and involved in the evaluation process.

Self-ratings tend to show more leniency error than supervisor ratings, although halo errors are lower.[91] **Self-evaluations** have become popular as part of the management by objectives process when the supervisor and the subordinate jointly evaluate goal attainment. Self-evaluation seems most appropriate when it is used as an employee development tool rather than to make administrative decisions.[92] It also may serve as an important input into a supervisory assessment. An employee's self-assessment may provide important information of which the supervisor was not aware. The supervisor can then factor this information into his or her performance ratings of the employee.

Peer Evaluation

Compared with supervisory ratings, peer or coworker evaluations are more stable over time, can tap more dimensions of performance, are better able to distinguish effort from performance, and can focus more on task-relevant abilities. One study has concluded that peer ratings may be the most accurate evaluations of employee performance.[93] **Peer evaluations** can be particularly useful when supervisors do not have the opportunity to observe an individual's performance but fellow employees do.

Peers sometimes resist evaluating one another. An individual may not want to give a fellow employee a favorable evaluation for fear of looking inferior in comparison. On the other hand, an individual may not want to jeopardize a good working relationship by giving an unfavorable rating to a colleague.[94] Friendship bias may lead an employee to rate his or her friends higher than other employees. Finally, if resources are finite, as for salary increases, workers in a unit may see peer evaluation as a win–lose scenario.

A survey of 218 industrial employees who had used a peer evaluation system for more than a year found a high degree of user acceptance.[95] It seems, however, that peer evaluations, like self-evaluations, are best used for employee development rather than for administrative decisions. The same survey found that users were more favorable in their attitudes toward peer assessments that were used for developmental rather than for evaluative purposes.

When teamwork, participation, and cohesiveness are part of the organization's culture, peer evaluations can work well. In organizations that are competitive and have a low level of trust among employees, peer evaluations may be little more than a way for employees to enhance themselves by belittling their fellow employees.

Subordinate Evaluation

Evaluation by subordinates may provide valuable information. Subordinates know how well a supervisor performs with respect to leading, organizing, planning, delegating, and communicating. In fact, evaluating the boss is becoming a popular mechanism in many organizations.[96]

Subordinates, however, may inflate their rating of a supervisor, especially if they think the supervisor will be able to discern who has given a particular rating. Complete anonymity is essential if this technique is to provide valid ratings.[97] However, some systems of subordinate evaluation tend to compromise anonymity. For example, in one organization, supervisor evaluations by employees on a series of open-ended performance questions go to the supervisor's manager. The manager's secretary organizes the comments of each person in order. In other words, the comments of employees 1 through 15 are given for the first item, for the second item in the same order, and so forth. The supervisors and manager can then read all the comments of employee 1 for each item, all the comments of employee

2, and in this way have a good idea as to the identity of each of the fifteen employees. Of course, this could be remedied easily by having the secretary scramble the employee responses so that they are in a different order for each item. As it turned out, both the supervisor and the manager appreciated the semblance of anonymity (rather than real anonymity) in reviewing the comments.

Open channels of communication and an abundance of trust between supervisors and subordinates are also needed if this type of evaluation is to be worthwhile. Like self- and peer evaluations, **subordinate evaluation** is useful for development[98] but historically has not been used widely for making administrative decisions. In fact, one study looked at subordinate ratings and found that managers whose initial level of performance was moderate or low improved over time, thus showing that upward feedback had the desired effect.[99]

Customer Evaluation

Another source of assessment information comes from customers or clients. Such assessments are popular in the context of service delivery where there is a high degree of client involvement and the service employee is relatively removed from other employees or supervisors.[100] Customers can be internal or external to the organization. For example, the "customer set" for human resource professionals includes the employees of the organization.

As an example of external customers, it would be difficult for the owner or manager of a carpet cleaning company to know whether the service was performed to the company's standards and to the customer's satisfaction in the absence of feedback from the customer. This feedback could be obtained through a phone interview with the customer or a formal survey. Alternately, customer feedback can be through "shoppers," individuals who appear to be regular customers but who are actually hired to carefully observe and rate the service using a predefined protocol.

360-Degree Assessment

An estimated 90 percent of *Fortune 1000* firms use some form of **360-degree assessment,** where performance ratings are collected simultaneously from subordinates, peers, supervisors, and employees themselves.[101] Although we generally view enough snapshots of ourselves so that there are few surprises, a profile or the view from the back may show us some features we had not expected. In one study, those appraised using the 360-degree approach reported that 25 percent of the feedback was expected positive feedback, 30 percent was unexpected positive feedback, 20 to 30 percent was expected negative feedback, and 15 to 20 percent was unexpected negative feedback.[102] For most of those appraised, the varying perspectives will ensure surprises as well as useful learning.

Such assessments can be used for any of the purposes described in Table 10.1, although many researchers[103] and practitioners[104] maintain that it is best for development and feedback purposes rather than for salary or other administrative uses. The focus on development assures those participating—groups such as subordinates, peers, and customers—that the 360-degree assessment is being done to improve all involved and is not part of the competitive win–lose scenario that so often accompanies salary and promotion decisions. The focus is on evaluation of skills and competencies relevant for job performance in useful behavioral terms. Information can be collected through rating forms, open-ended comments, or some combination of both. The 360-degree approach works best when results are filtered through a coach and combined with self-evaluation. Although many firms are using 360-degree assessments, they are most successful in organizations that offer open and participative climates as well as active career development systems.[105]

Studies have reported improvement in performance following 360-degree feedback, with the most notable results for those who initially rated themselves higher than the ratings they received from others.[106] The assumption of the 360-degree feedback process is that negative or discrepant feedback—that is, ratings lower than one's self-ratings—can create an awareness of the need to improve in specific ways. Although this is certainly the desired result, other studies have shown that it is not always the case. Some researchers have found that in approximately one-third of the cases negative feedback caused those who received it to be discouraged or to see the results as less accurate, particularly when the feedback concerned personal characteristics rather than task behaviors.[107] The results of some of these studies call into question the widely held assumption about 360-degree feedback that negative feedback and results discrepant from one's self-ratings motivates positive change.[108]

The 360-degree system is believed to have a number of advantages over traditional assessment systems. Supervisors, peers, subordinates, and employees themselves typically differ in their ability to appraise various dimensions of performance. These raters observe different behaviors and may interpret them with divergent standards. Thus each source has access to unique information about performance.[109] Perhaps the best approach is to use as many different sources as possible to maximize the breadth of information and cancel out biases unique to a particular source. Multiple sources can be used regardless of which specific subjective method of measuring performance is adopted.

360-Degree Assessment at Lloyd Investment[110] As 360-degree gained in prominence, Lloyd Investment implemented such an assessment system for 2,000 professional employees on a worldwide basis. The development and implementation of the system cost more than $1.5 million. The system involved feedback from superiors, peers, subordinates, internal clients, and the professionals themselves through a self-evaluation.

The 360-degree procedure began with the professional being evaluated selecting an evaluation director (ED), typically the person's manager or supervisor, to coordinate all aspects of the process. The evaluee then worked with the ED to identify those people within the firm with whom he or she regularly interacted and who would be in a position to provide substantive feedback on the evaluee's performance.

Four broad categories were evaluated, although each was tailored to the particular job, tasks, and divisions involved: (1) market/professional skills, (2) management and leadership, (3) commercial orientation, and (4) teamwork, including cooperation with all Lloyd Investment units and employees. The list of evaluators, called the evaluation request form, was submitted to the Office of Development, which undertook the following series of steps:

1. First, the appropriate evaluation form was structured for each evaluator.
2. The evaluators were then directed to the intranet address where they were to provide their evaluative feedback to the professional undertaking the 360-degree assessment.[111] (The Office of Development used the computer to make sure

evaluators were not overloaded with assessments. If a professional sought the rating of someone who had already done ten ratings, he or she received a notice that the individual was not available.)

3. The system then audited responses as they were submitted and checked to see that they fell within predefined limits, preventing invalid input from being submitted.
4. A computer program was then used to create a ten- to twenty-page book of results for each professional from the evaluative feedback received.
5. Finally, this anonymous raw data was sent to the evaluation director to be interpreted and synthesized before being reviewed with the professional being evaluated.

Lloyd Investment clearly believed in the value of multiple perspectives in developing its professionals. Lloyd Investment's commitment to the process and results included the following:

1. The initial cost of developing and implementing the system
2. Creation of an Office of Development to coordinate all administrative aspects of each 360-degree evaluation
3. The time and effort of employees throughout the firm in participating in the 360-degree evaluation of others
4. The commitment of the 2,000 professionals and their managers or supervisors (in serving as EDs)

There is little doubt that 360-degree assessment has received much attention in the past decade. A growing number of U.S. firms have implemented 360-degree programs. Lloyd Investment is exemplary of an organization that is committed to 360-degree feedback and is willing to do what is necessary to assure the integrity of the process.

A variety of individual and organization improvement goals have been attributed to these assessment processes. However, despite the attention given to 360-degree assessment, there has been much more discussion about how to implement such programs than about why organizations have rushed to jump on the bandwagon or even what they expect to accomplish.[112] There has been little critical evaluation of the outcomes of 360-degree appraisal or the changes desired.[113] For example, Lloyd Investment provided a window into the type of commitment necessary to implement and sustain a 360-degree appraisal system. One might ask how many of the business firms rushing to adopt 360-degree assessment have the same commitment to the system to assure its success.

Self-Managed Teams

More and more companies are looking to self-managed teams as the productivity and quality-of-work-life breakthrough of the twenty-first century.[114] A survey showed that teams of various types are in use in nearly all of the *Fortune 1000* companies.[115] Teams come in many forms. They may vary on the following characteristics:

- Temporary versus permanent
- Parallel to the existing organizational structure (most often used for temporary teams) versus incorporated into it

- Autonomous, semiautonomous, or working under the direction of a supervisor versus working independently
- Cross-functional—that is, made up of workers from several functional areas (e.g., product design, manufacturing, and marketing)—versus functionally homogeneous workers
- Full time versus part time (e.g., committees, quality circles)

Self-managed teams create special challenges for performance assessment. When teams perform highly interdependent activities, evaluating them using an assessment system that focuses only on individual results may be inappropriate as well as discouraging to the teamwork necessary to get results.[116] In addition, when teams are working effectively, they manage themselves. There is no supervisor, yet historically it is the supervisor who has made performance assessment judgments about employees. For example, one company reorganized from a traditional structure of a supervisor for each group of fifteen to twenty hourly employees to semiautonomous teams with one division manager responsible for 150 workers.[117] There is no way a division manager can have sufficiently detailed knowledge of 150 employees to accomplish the specific goals of performance assessment illustrated in Table 10.1. Consequently, teams must assume responsibility either for

TABLE 10.5

A Partnership Approach to Team Appraisals

The performance appraisal team consists of the

- Team member being evaluated, the **evaluee.**
- Performance appraisal **chairperson,** the evaluee's advocate. The chairperson is selected by the evaluee.
- **Committee members,** two individuals selected by the chairperson from a list of all team members.
- **Management consultant** to both provide input into the evaluee's performance and facilitate the process.

Steps in the performance appraisal process include:

1. Evaluee selects the performance appraisal chairperson.
2. PA chairperson selects two committee members.
3. Evaluee provides chair, committee members, and consultant with a list of accomplishments and training for the previous year.
4. The PA team members provide feedback on the evaluee's accomplishments and training to the chair and the evaluee.
5. The evaluee writes his or her own performance appraisal document from the input received and sends a copy of the PA document to the committee for their review.
6. Following the committee's review of the PA document, the committee and evaluee meet. A final rating is determined, and the committee jointly sets goals for the evaluee for the next year.
7. The PA chairperson writes a summary of the meeting, including the ratings and recommendations. The completed document is signed by the committee members (including the management consultant) and forwarded to human resources.

Source: Adapted from Carol A. Norman and Robert A. Zawacki, "Team Appraisals—Team Approach," *Personnel Journal*, September 1991, pp. 101–104.

developing a performance assessment system for their members or for applying an existing system to suit the purposes of the team.

As an example, one team-oriented organization uses a partnership approach to performance assessments, including self-assessments and ratings from peers.[118] The process, described in Table 10.5, is initiated when the team member, the evaluee, chooses an advocate of his or her work to lead the performance assessment. The advocate then assembles a committee to participate with the evaluee in completing the performance review and setting goals for the coming year.

It is important that both team and individual performance be measured. Understanding the team's objectives and each member's responsibility toward those objectives is one of the keys to successful team evaluation.[119] The team must begin by understanding its customers and the work process that will be followed to satisfy customer needs. Otherwise, processes for team performance evaluation are not that different than those for individual assessment. Methods used to appraise performance should be free from (system and personal) bias and should be designed to enhance performance. Finally, team members must be trained to collect and act on the information: feeding it back to other team members, addressing performance issues, setting goals, and so forth.[120]

ENHANCING THE MEASUREMENT OF EMPLOYEE PERFORMANCE

In developing a performance assessment system, particularly one that involves subjective evaluations of performance, a number of serious problems must be overcome. Training evaluators and giving them feedback are ways to improve raters' ability to make accurate assessments.

Training Evaluators

Several rater training programs have been developed that aim to help evaluators produce reliable and accurate performance ratings. Programs can generally be classified into three types: rater-error training, frame-of-reference training, and information-processing training.

Rater-Error Training People can be taught how to reduce rating errors, such as leniency, severity, central tendency, and halo errors.[121] In **rater-error training (RET),** evaluators view examples of the common errors and receive suggestions on how to avoid them. RET has been found effective in reducing common rating errors. One study found that the effectiveness of error training was a function of the ability and disposition of trainees. Individuals with more ability or those more open to ideas derived greater benefit from the training.[122]

Several critics, however, have argued that error reduction often comes at the expense of rating accuracy.[123] For example, if a supervisor has many high-performing employees, all of them should be rated high. If the supervisor decides to avoid the appearance of leniency error by lowering the ratings of some employees, the evaluations become less accurate. In this manner, a risk of training is replacing one response set (leniency) with another (reduced accuracy).

Frame-of-Reference Training Attempts have been made to reduce errors by developing a common frame of reference among raters for evaluating performance.[124] Examples of actual employee behavior in the organization are used to develop norms for good and poor performance. Raters are then trained to observe these behaviors and use them as the standard against which to judge the performance of employees. The goal is the development of a common appraisal language, including agreed-upon labels and a shared nomenclature.

In a review of the effectiveness of rater training programs, four of seven studies using **frame-of-reference (FOR) training** were reported to have reduced leniency error. Only three of ten studies using FOR training to reduce halo error reported positive results.[125] Another study focused on implementation problems associated with FOR training, including procedures to identify incidents and then to understand differences between supervisors and subordinates with respect to appropriate frames of reference.[126] It appears that many of the implementation issues associated with FOR training can be overcome but that FOR training is most useful in improving rating accuracy when combined with other methods.[127]

Information-Processing Approaches Some training efforts focus on how performance raters observe, store, recall, and use information. In a 1980 study, raters were trained to avoid eight different "errors of observation."[128] Their accuracy in observing and remembering behavior improved, but no measures of rating error or rating accuracy were taken. Another study introduced two information-processing methods of rater training that did increase rater accuracy.[129] **Observation training** (similar to the approach used in the 1980 study) focused on helping raters to improve the way they observed the behavior of employees and to identify important performance activities. **Decision-making training** introduced raters to good strategies for use in decision making and helped them identify mistakes in inference that supervisors often make when appraising performance. (Given several accurate pieces of information, a supervisor may make inappropriate inferences about them and their relation to one another and end up making a bad decision.)

Which Training Method Is Best? Because rater-error training and frame-of reference training have had limited success, information-processing approaches may be the most promising methods for improving rating accuracy. However, regardless of the training method used, raters who are actively involved in their training programs are more likely to learn to reduce rating errors. Involvement may be in the form of group discussions or of practice rating an employee whose performance has been videotaped. Practice rating is followed by feedback on what the most accurate rating would have been. Both practice and feedback seem to be essential for effective training. Neither discussion nor lecture without practice and feedback has been shown to reduce rating errors.[130] Ultimately, it comes down to rater motivation to rate accurately, and, as discussed previously (see the section on intentional errors), accurate ratings frequently lead to more challenges for already overworked managers.[131]

Feedback to Evaluators

Feedback is an important component of successful training programs, and rating the raters may be a good way to reduce systematic bias.[132] One approach is to structure an evaluator's own performance assessment so that it pays attention to how well and accurately he or she rates the performance of others; that is, supervisors should be assessed on how well they appraise their subordinates. This approach should enhance motivation for the rating process and let raters know what others think of their evaluations. Another possibility is to require that their own superiors endorse supervisors' assessment ratings. Called a one-over-one review, to connote the two levels of evaluation, this is a common method of achieving additional accountability and the accuracy associated with it.[133] In this manner the person doing the rating of subordinates has to defend them to at least one other person. The superiors provide quality control by helping prevent extreme leniency, severity, or central tendency errors in the ratings. The second level of review also assures a degree of consistency in evaluations across departments within an organization.

FEEDBACK OF RESULTS: THE PERFORMANCE ASSESSMENT INTERVIEW

One of the potentially most important aspects of performance management is providing performance feedback to employees. To improve performance, employees need information (feedback) about their performance along with guidance in reaching the next level of results. Most theories of work motivation point out that before employees can improve their performance, they must know how well they are currently doing.

In the usual situation, neither the supervisor nor the employee looks forward to the assessment interview.[134] It can be an uncomfortable and anxiety-provoking experience for both parties. One would expect a supervisor to be apprehensive about discussing a negative evaluation with an employee, but most managers see little or no practical value in conducting performance assessment interviews, no matter what the evaluation.[135] Conducting a good interview requires a great deal of effort and skill on the part of the supervisor. In addition, perceptions of the results by the employee can be influenced by his or her positive or negative attitudes toward the organization, the job, or the supervisor.[136] This section considers several types of feedback interviews, problems that can occur in giving feedback, and ways to improve the process.

Types of Feedback Interviews

The feedback interview is a discussion between the supervisor and the employee concerning the employee's past performance and how that performance can be improved in the future. The three main approaches to feedback discussion are often referred to as "tell and sell," "tell and listen," and "problem solving."

Tell and Sell In a **tell-and-sell feedback interview,** the supervisor tells the employee how good or bad the employee's performance has been and then attempts to persuade the employee to accept this judgment. The employee has no input into the evaluation. Because it is very directive and one-sided, the tell-and-sell interview can lead to defensiveness, resentment, and frustration on the part of the subordinate. It fails to recognize the possibility that the employee may have information pertinent to the evaluation—information of which the supervisor is unaware. The employee may not accept the results of the interview and may not be committed to achieving the goals that are set. This may lead to poor performance in the future.

For new employees or those who have little desire for participation, the tell-and-sell interview can be effective in providing feedback and improving performance. New employees often feel unqualified to judge their own performance and prefer to be told how they are doing and what is expected of them.[137]

Tell and Listen In the **tell-and-listen approach** to the feedback interview, the supervisor tells the employee what has been right and wrong with the employee's past performance but then gives the employee a chance to react. The extent of the subordinate's participation in the interview can vary widely. The subordinate may simply be given an opportunity to react to the supervisor's statements or may be permitted to offer a full self-assessment, challenging the supervisor's assessment. There is evidence that subordinates prefer even very limited participation to none at all.[138]

Problem Solving The employee has much more control over the **problem-solving interview.** Employees evaluate their own performance and set their own goals for future performance. The supervisor is primarily a helper and colleague rather than a judge and offers observations and advice in a noncritical manner. An active and open dialogue ensues, in which goals for improvement are established mutually. The problem-solving interview is more difficult for the supervisor than the other types of interviews, but it is more likely to result in employee acceptance and commitment to the established goals. Training can help supervisors learn to conduct such interviews effectively. A drawback of problem-solving interviews is that some employees may prefer a more direct approach. Some may be hesitant to discuss poor performance with their supervisor, particularly if personnel decisions such as salary increases will be based on the interview.

The problem-solving approach is most consistent with the goals of performance management; that is, an ongoing, interactive process designed to enable an employee to develop to his or her full potential. For those employees uncomfortable in taking the lead, a tell-and-listen approach will get the discussion going before transitioning into a problem-solving approach for discussing employee development issues and planning for future performance.

Problems with the Feedback Interview

Two major problems complicate the process of giving feedback to subordinates: disagreement about the rated level of performance and the use of the feedback interview for multiple purposes.

Disagreement and Defensiveness Supervisors and subordinates often disagree about how well the subordinate has performed. One review of studies found that the average correlation between subordinate and supervisor ratings was only 0.22.[139] Subordinates in the United States usually rate their performance higher than do supervisors. In only one of the eighteen studies reviewed were supervisors' ratings of subordinate performance higher than the subordinates' ratings of their own performance.

Even when supervisor and subordinate agree on the level of performance, they often disagree about its causes. Supervisors tend to feel that subordinates are personally responsible for their performance, especially poor performance. On the other hand, subordinates often (sometimes legitimately) blame poor performance on situational factors such as bad luck, lack of resources, or insufficient cooperation from others.[140]

Disagreement on either level of performance or cause sets the stage for subordinate defensiveness. The subordinate makes excuses for past performance and argues with the supervisor's rating. The subordinate becomes unable to listen and learn from any legitimate points the supervisor may have. Note that defensiveness is not restricted to employees who receive a low performance rating. One study found that subordinates who were judged "satisfactory" had lower satisfaction and commitment because they had expected higher ratings.[141]

Another author maintains that the traditional manager-to-subordinate performance assessment feedback is an authoritarian procedure—a parent–child type of exchange. It is suggested that as organizations move toward involvement-oriented working, a performance discussion based on the subordinate's self-review may be more appropriate.[142] Further, such a review has the advantage of forcing the manager into a counseling and coaching mode rather than a largely judicial one.[143]

Multiple Purposes Assessment interviews are often used to review past performance, convey administrative decisions, plan for future work goals, and discuss the employee's career goals and development needs.[144] This is a great deal to accomplish in a single meeting. In addition, supervisors must play two incompatible roles, judge and coach, in a multipurpose interview. For merit raise decisions to have credibility, they must be clearly linked to past performance. Thus it is wise to couple these two purposes in the assessment interview. However, conventional wisdom holds that it is counterproductive to discuss future goals and development in that same interview. Criticism of past work or announcement of a smaller-than-expected raise may make the subordinate defensive and unwilling to address performance-improvement issues seriously. Thus a separate interview a few weeks later has been recommended for developmental issues. This recommendation, however, which is accepted as gospel by many HR practitioners, is based on only a single study conducted in 1965.[145]

More recent research has challenged this view.[146] Two studies in field settings found that discussing salary issues did not hurt the developmental aspects of a feedback interview and, in fact, had some positive effects. Including salary discussion in the assessment interview may force the supervisor to give more specific feedback to back up the decision. Salary discussion can also energize the interview and elicit more subordinate participation. Perhaps, with sufficient skill and tact on the part of the supervisor, both administrative and developmental purposes can be served in the same assessment interview. A compromise position may be best. The supervisor can plan to talk about past performance, merit pay decisions, future performance goals, and development in a single interview. However, if the subordinate becomes defensive or upset after discussing past performance and salary, the supervisor can postpone the discussion of the future.

Impression Management in the Feedback Process Recent research has emphasized the role of impression management in the feedback process.[147] **Impression management** refers to behaviors by an employee designed to control how he or she appears to the supervisor. For example, impression management tactics could include (1) taking sole credit for positive events even when credit should be shared, (2) making the supervisor aware of one's accomplishments, (3) arriving early or staying late to give the impression of being a hard worker, or (4) taking an interest in the supervisor's personal life and perhaps doing personal favors.[148]

Poorly performing employees use impression management strategies to minimize the amount of negative feedback they receive. For the employee, the goal is to maintain positive self-esteem. At the same time, such strategies on the part of the employee meet the needs of the supervisor, who generally has an underlying reluctance to give negative performance feedback. In any case, impression management tends to skew the assessment and feedback interaction.[149] Several researchers have examined procedures for minimizing impression management in the appraisal process.[150] Suggestions to control the effects of politics and impression management are given in Table 10.6.

TABLE 10.6

Recommended Steps to Control Impression Management in Performance Appraisal

Steps to Minimize Dysfunctional Politics and Impression Management

- Make sure appraisal has a single clear purpose—multiple purposes create potential conflicts.
- Make sure the appraisal criteria are well defined, specific, and relevant to the job—generic measures create more opportunities for distortion.
- Train raters on use of the appraisal and sensitize raters to impression management and its effects.
- Use developmental appraisals—they are less prone to politics.
- Use more than one rater and make raters accountable to upper level review.
- Conduct appraisals in a climate of mutual trust and respect.
- Build top management support for appraisal system integrity.

Steps to Maximize Impression Management That Supports Organizational Goals

- Clearly communicate the goals of the appraisal process.
- Create consensus on the goals of the appraisal process.
- Make sure that appraisal processes are perceived to be uniform across the organization—perceptions that other units are more lenient or less lenient lead to dysfunctional politics.
- Build an organizational culture and climate that promotes integrity and consistency with organizational goals; e.g., the motivation of employees.
- Foster a climate of openness to encourage employees to be honest about weaknesses so as to promote self-improvement.
- Recognize employee accomplishments that are not self-promoted.
- Consider a separate rating process for appraisals that are linked to important outcomes.
- Give raters some flexibility to recognize ratees for value-added contributions that are not well-defined performance criteria.

Source: Adapted from Steve W. J. Kozlowski, Georgia T. Chao, and Robert F. Morrison, "Games Raters Play: Politics, Strategies, and Impression Management in Performance Appraisal," in *Performance Appraisal: State of the Art in Practice*, ed. James W. Smither (San Francisco: Jossey-Bass, 1998).

Improving the Performance Assessment Interview

Feedback is most effective in improving performance when it is specific, when the employee accepts it, and when it helps define clear goals for future performance.[151]

Feedback Specificity Feedback is particularly helpful if it comes from a behaviorally based assessment instrument and if the performance rating is backed up with specific examples of good or poor performance. A critical incidents log can be useful in providing this type of specific feedback. **Specific feedback** helps employees determine exactly what they should do differently to improve performance. Research has shown that subordinates prefer specific feedback in the assessment interview, even if it concerns poor performance, to assessments that contain only vague performance information.[152]

Subordinate Acceptance For feedback to be accepted by a subordinate, it must come from a credible, trustworthy source. Credibility is enhanced when the evaluator is seen as being knowledgeable about the subordinate's job, has had adequate opportunity to observe the behavior of the subordinate, and has clearly taken the time to prepare carefully for the assessment interview. Research has shown that feedback is more likely to affect subsequent performance when it comes from a believable source.[153] In addition, feedback should be given often and as soon as possible after both good and bad performance events so that employees always know where they stand and can quickly take any necessary corrective action. The formal interview should be the culmination of the ongoing, continual process of informal performance feedback. Nothing in the annual assessment interview should come as a surprise to the subordinate.

It may be particularly difficult for the subordinate to accept negative feedback. Destructive criticism and threats to the subordinate are ineffective and may cause subsequent performance to deteriorate.[154] Thus the supervisor should discuss specific incidents of poor performance in a considerate, constructive way. Two studies have shown that when the supervisor attributes poor performance to situational causes, the subordinate is better able to accept negative feedback.[155] For example, a supervisor may note that a salesperson fell far below sales goals but also acknowledge that the economy was in a downturn (a possible external cause of poor performance). The supervisor can then proceed to discuss what the subordinate might do differently to improve performance even when economic conditions are poor. This approach will help to minimize defensiveness on the part of the salesperson.

A number of studies support the notion that satisfaction with and acceptance of assessment feedback are a function of the subordinate's degree of contribution and participation in the assessment discussion.[156] Anything that moves the interview from an authoritarian boss–subordinate interaction to a discussion between two knowledgeable and committed individuals will enhance acceptance of the results.

Setting Clear Goals The process of goal setting has already been discussed in the context of performance management and MBO and as a productivity enhancing technique. Whatever assessment system has been used, assessment discussions should culminate in specific goals that focus the subordinate's attention on performance improvement. Later the supervisor should follow up on goal progress and give additional feedback when necessary to help the subordinate achieve the desired level of performance.

Summary of Key Points

Performance management can serve a strategic function by focusing employee efforts on the types of behaviors required to successfully attain organizational goals. Performance management should be an ongoing, interactive process that is designed to enhance employee capability and facilitate productivity. The measurement portion of the system is called performance appraisal. Appraisals are also used (1) to make administrative decisions about employees, (2) to provide feedback for employee development, and (3) to evaluate HR policies and programs.

A good appraisal system should measure important job characteristics (relevancy), be free from extraneous or contaminating influences, and encompass all important aspects of the job (not be deficient). It should be reliable and avoid rating errors. Appraisal systems must be fair to minorities, women, and other protected groups. Appraisals must also be practical. Meeting all these criteria in an appraisal system is a challenge.

Performance measures can be characterized as objective or subjective. Objective and subjective measures can be used in combination. Subjective measures can compare employees with each other (ranking), or they can judge performance against absolute standards for the job (rating). A number of types of rating procedures can be used, including graphic rating scales, mixed standard rating scales, behaviorally anchored rating scales (BARS), and behavioral observation scales (BOS). Ratings may be obtained from subordinates, peers, or the employee being assessed, although most commonly the only rater is the employee's supervisor. An additional assessment system, management by objectives (MBO), features joint superior and subordinate goal setting and performance assessment against these individualized standards.

Traditionally, when one thinks of performance appraisal, it is in terms of supervisors evaluating subordinates. In addition to supervisors, raters of employee performance include the employees themselves, peers, subordinates, and customers, including "customers" internal to the organization. A new approach to performance assessment is 360-degree assessment, using many or all of the sources of feedback described.

Performance assessment is an important tool for motivating and improving employee performance. Unfortunately, its potential is seldom fully realized. Assessments can be improved by careful development of an appropriate assessment instrument, by training raters to use the system properly, and by providing feedback to raters as to how well they are performing their assessment and development functions with their own subordinates. The annual performance assessment interview is a valuable opportunity for supervisor and subordinate to communicate about past performance, current concerns, and goals for the future. This meeting does not have to be an unpleasant confrontation and can enhance the relationship between the supervisor and the subordinate. When giving performance feedback to subordinates, supervisors must ensure that the feedback is credible, specific, constructive, and accompanied by concrete examples of poor or good performance. They should also allow an appropriate degree of participation and ensure that goals for future performance are set.

The Manager's Vocabulary

360-degree assessment
absolute standards
administrative uses of performance assessment
alternate ranking
behavior-based appraisals
behavioral observation scales (BOS)
behaviorally anchored rating scale (BARS)
central tendency errors
cognitive information processing (CIP)
comparative procedures
contamination
critical incidents technique
decision-making training
deficient
developmental uses of performance assessment
forced-distribution method
forced-choice system
forced-ranking method
frame-of-reference (FOR) training
graphic rating scales
halo errors

impression management
leniency errors
management by objectives (MBO)
mixed standard scales
objective measures
observation training
opportunity bias
paired-comparison ranking
peer evaluations
performance appraisal
performance assessment and management
performance feedback
performance management
personnel measures
problem-solving interview
prototype
ranking
rater-error training (RET)
results-based appraisals
schemas
self-evaluations
severity errors
specific feedback
straight ranking
subjective measures
subordinate evaluation
tell-and-listen approach
tell-and-sell feedback interview
trait-based appraisals
weighted checklist

Questions for Discussion

1. In what ways can performance assessment and management assist an organization in ensuring congruence between strategic goals and the behavior of employees?
2. What strategic goals of the Central Intelligence Agency (CIA) were served by adopting an effective performance management system? What was the CIA trying to achieve?
3. What purposes can be served by performance assessment and management?
4. How can an organization design a performance assessment or change one already in use to make it more consistent with legal mandates?
5. What types of errors characterize the performance assessment process?
6. If you were an employee, would you want to be evaluated by traits, behavior, or results? Why?
7. Why would a supervisor intentionally distort performance ratings of a subordinate? What can be done to prevent intentional distortion of performance ratings?
8. What are some of the advantages and disadvantages of using trait-, behavior-, and results-based types of assessment?
9. Compare and contrast ranking versus rating systems of assessment and management in terms of their advantages and disadvantages.
10. What are mixed standard scales, how do they work, and what special purposes do they serve?
11. What is the difference between a BARS and a BOS? Which do you think is better and why?
12. What does the cognitive information processing approach to performance assessment say about how to improve assessment?
13. What is 360-degree assessment? In what types of organizations will it work best?
14. What are some of the impressive aspects of 360-degree assessment used by Lloyd Investment?
15. Who should rate the performance of employees? Explain your answer.
16. Why is the performance assessment interview important?
17. What is the range of styles in which a performance assessment interview might be conducted? For which situations might each style be best?
18. Is it possible for a supervisor to include discussions of past performance, merit raise, and future performance goals in the same assessment interview?
19. How can superiors increase the effectiveness of the feedback they give to subordinates?
20. How does the evaluation of teams differ from the evaluation of individuals? What evaluation challenges do teams create?

Case 10.1
Performance Management at Jet Food Services

It is now the end of Teresa Ross's first year as regional manager for Jet Food Services. As regional manager, Teresa supervises a total of ten districts, each of which has a manager responsible for sales and service to customers in that area.

Jet Food provides contract food services for hospitals, schools, colleges, business firms, and other institutions that need meals prepared on site but that do not wish to be responsible for operating such services. Jet Food Services hires all necessary kitchen employees, purchases all supplies, and prepares meals in accordance with specifications agreed on with customers. The district manager is responsible for coordinating all customer activities. This includes planning, budgeting, hiring and supervising Jet's on-site representative (customer service manager), customer satisfaction, and contract renegotiations.

Teresa was recruited after years of experience as director of food services for a multi-campus university. In that job, she had oversight responsibility for the food services at several campuses. The Jet Food position offered an opportunity for continued growth and advancement.

In her first year, Teresa has concentrated on getting to know the district managers and the customers with whom they work. She spent more than a week with each district manager and visited each customer with him or her. At this point, she feels comfortable with her job and the knowledge she has gained of both operations and personnel, and it is time to appraise the performance of the district managers and to schedule review meetings with these employees.

Teresa's Assessment of Blake Mack Blake Mack is the longest term district manager in Teresa's region. He completed less than one year of college, held several short-term jobs, and then joined Jet as a shift supervisor of the company's services at a large college. At present, he is completing twelve years of employment with Jet. He has been a district manager for three years.

In working with Blake, Teresa has observed his strengths, along with some problems. Blake has a talent for working with people, Jet employees and customers alike. In fact, in his years with Jet, no customer he worked with has ever switched to a competitor. Many on-site supervisors recruited, trained, and supervised by Blake have gone on to become managers of other districts.

On the other hand, Blake's unhealthful eating habits—despite doctors' warnings—have contributed to some serious medical difficulties. During the past year, Blake was out of work for three months with gall bladder and heart problems, attributable in part to obesity. And Blake's behavior toward others can be overbearing. Teresa kept track of her phone calls from district managers during the year, and there were more calls (or messages) from Blake than from the other nine district managers taken together—calls to promote or advertise his own efforts.

Although Blake can be charming, he has started to be loud and rude with regional personnel whom he perceives as excessively rule-oriented. All in all, Blake's style and appearance have become entirely different from what Teresa is accustomed to in colleagues and employees.

Further, it has been announced that Teresa's region is going to be expanded and that a new position, that of assistant regional manager, will be created. Blake has made it clear that as Jet's longest tenured district manager in the region, he feels entitled to this promotion. However, Teresa does not feel she could work with Blake as the assistant regional manager. She feels that their management styles are too different and that Blake's behavior might irritate regional and corporate personnel.

As Teresa looks over Jet's performance assessment and management instrument, she realizes that her honest assessment of Blake's performance in his current job is generally excellent. She glances at the last page of the assessment and management form and the overall ratings from which she will have to choose. Jet's overall rating system is on a 1–10 scale, with 10 as outstanding; 7–9, different degrees of excellent performance; 5–6, satisfactory; 3–4, below average; and 1–2, unacceptable. Teresa is uncertain as to what overall rating to assign. If she gives Blake too high a rating, he will expect to be promoted. If the rating is too low, Blake will doubtless be angry, feeling that an injustice has been done.

Blake Mack's Self-Assessment Blake sees himself as different from the other district managers. An outgoing, gregarious type, he loves to visit his customer locations and work with his company's personnel. His idea of a successful day is one spent teaching a customer service manager a new operating procedure or management technique. In fact, Blake is known to roll up his sleeves and teach Jet employees a new recipe or how to improve an existing dish.

Blake has worked for several district managers and has always liked to keep them informed about his activities, sometimes phoning two or three times each day. From discussions with Teresa, he is aware that she thinks many of these calls are not necessary, but he wants her to know how things are going with his employees and customers. He is also aware of Teresa's views regarding his ignoring medical advice.

Blake is proud of his career and of what he has been able to do without much higher education. He feels he is qualified to become a regional manager, and he looks forward to the possibility of promotion to the new assistant regional manager position as a step toward this ultimate goal.

Blake's Assessment Rating In reviewing the situation, Teresa decides to give Blake an overall rating of 6. She feels justified, given that Blake did miss months of work as a result of neglecting his health. She knows that Blake will expect a higher overall rating, but she is prepared to stand behind her evaluation. Teresa then goes back to considering the separate ratings she will assign and to making plans for their feedback review.

1. How would you describe Teresa Ross's approach to the assessment and management of Blake's performance?
2. Are Teresa's concerns with Blake's performance legitimate? Will Blake have justifiable reasons for feeling dissatisfied with the assessment and management results?
3. How could Jet Food's system of performance assessment and management be improved? If you were Jet's vice president of human resources, what changes would you suggest?

Exercise 10.1
Assessing a Performance Assessment and Management Measure

This exercise is designed to give you hands-on experience in evaluating measures of performance that are actually being used by organizations.

Step 1. Two or three weeks before doing the exercise, obtain from an organization in your local area a copy of the assessment and management instrument that is used in assessing employee performance. If possible, find out something about how the instrument was developed. Also find out for which jobs the assessment and management instrument is used. Be sure to remove the name of the company from all materials to ensure confidentiality. At least one week before the exercise, bring to class the assessment and management instrument, a description of how it was developed (if possible), and a list of jobs for which it is used.

Step 2. In class, break into groups of three or four. The instructor will have reviewed the assessment and management instruments and made an overhead transparency of each instrument. Each group will be given one instrument, the description of the development process, and the list of jobs for which it is used.

Step 3. Each group will assess its assessment and management instrument and prepare a brief analysis of it for the class. Among the issues that should be addressed in the analysis are the following:

- What type of performance information is being obtained—traits, behaviors, results, a combination?
- To what extent did supervisors, subordinates, and other job experts participate in the development process?

- Are the performance dimensions measured reasonable for the jobs involved?
- Are there any apparent deficiencies, irrelevant dimensions, or possible contaminants?
- Are the performance dimensions and rating anchors defined clearly enough so that raters will understand exactly what they are rating?
- Who should make the ratings—supervisor, peers, subordinates?
- Do any of the performance dimensions lend themselves to a more accurate rating by a particular type of rater or to more objective assessment?
- How would your group members feel if their performance were assessed using the instrument?
- How can the instrument be improved?

Exercise 10.2
Developing a Measure of Performance

Brief descriptions of three jobs are provided. In doing the exercise you may wish to fill in information about a job from your own knowledge or experience. Keep a record of any information you add to the description provided.

Step 1. Divide into groups of three to five. Your instructor will assign one of the jobs to your group. Read the description of the job assigned to you.

Step 2. Your group's task is to develop a system for appraising the performance of employees on this job. Prepare a brief presentation to give to your fellow students. In this presentation, you must specify the following:

- The types of performance information you will collect—traits, behaviors, results.
- The exact method by which you will collect the information and, in the case of subjective ratings, who will make those ratings.
- The steps you will take to ensure that the information collected is reliable and valid.
- How often the measure(s) of performance will be obtained.

Job Descriptions

Post Office Clerk. Receives letters and parcels and sells postage stamps and money orders. Weighs packages to determine charges. Computes cost of insuring and registering mail. Answers questions concerning postal regulations and procedures. Places mail into slots after sorting by mail code or destination. Takes complaints regarding lost mail or mail theft, fills out forms, and submits for investigation.

Emergency Dispatcher/Operator. Answers telephone calls from the public regarding emergency situations that require police, fire, or medical assistance. Gathers pertinent information from callers using an oral questionnaire and records data on a computer. Communicates with police, fire, or medical units in the field, dispatching them to appropriate locations. Monitors location and activities of all field units continuously. On request from field units, checks warrants for arrest, stolen vehicle reports, runaway reports, and so forth using computer.

Animal Keeper (Zoological Garden). Cleans animal enclosures by hosing, sweeping, raking, scrubbing, and removing manure, soiled bedding, and unused food. Maintains enclosure materials such as nest boxes, plants, decorative materials, and bedding. Feeds and waters animals, preparing diet as instructed by the animal manager. Inspects and monitors animals and reports injuries, illnesses, or unusual behavior. Assists veterinarian in capturing and immobilizing animals when necessary.

Exercise 10.3
Performance Assessment and Management Update

The president of your company would like an update on business articles being written on performance assessment and management. Proceed with the following steps:

1. Find the Pathfinder homepage at http://www.pathfinder.com/
2. Search using the following: performance <and> assessment and management.
3. Read and summarize an article on employee performance assessment and management.

Exercise 10.4
Computers in Performance Evaluation

Your organization is considering ways to use computers to streamline performance evaluation. Proceed with the following steps:

1. Find the SuccessFactors product page at http://www.successfactors.com/sf/products/index.shtml
2. Of the several computer-based products for employee performance evaluation, which do you think would work best?
3. Summarize the features of the product you have chosen, and explain why you think it is best.

Notes and References

1. Stephen Barr, "Pay-Personnel System Another Frontier for CIA," *Washington Post,* April 4, 2004, p. C02.
2. Ibid.
3. Business Executives for National Security, "Pay for Performance at the CIA: Restoring Equity, Transparency, and Accountability," Central Intelligence Agency, January 2004. (Available at: http://www.bens.org/images/CIA_Reform%20Report.pdf)
4. Ibid.
5. Ibid.
6. Barr, "Pay-Personnel System Another Frontier for CIA."
7. Ibid.
8. Leslie A. Weatherly, "Performance Management: Getting It Right from the Start," *SHRM Research Quarterly,* 2004, pp. 2–10.
9. "Taming the Performance-Management Monster," *Training and Development,* June 1994, pp. 9–10; and Donald J. McNerney, "Improved Performance Appraisals: Process of Elimination," *HR Focus,* July 1995, pp. 1, 4–5.
10. Jai Ghorpade and Milton M. Chen, "Creating Quality Driven Performance Appraisal Systems," *Academy of Management Executive,* Vol. 9, 1995, pp. 32–39.
11. Robert L. Cardy and Gregory H. Dobbins, "Performance Management," in *Blackwell Encyclopedic Dictionary of Human Resource Management,* eds. Lawrence H. Peters, Charles R. Greer, and Stuart A. Youngblood (Malden, Mass.: Blackwell, 1997).
12. James S. Bowman, "Performance Appraisal: Verisimilitude Trumps Veracity," *Public Personnel Management,* Vol. 28, 1999, pp. 557–576.
13. Ibid, p. 557.
14. Martha Gephart, "The Road to High Performance," *Training and Development,* June 1995, pp. 30–38.
15. Beth Axelrod, Helen Handfield-Jones, and Ed Michaels, "A New Game Plan for C Players," *Harvard Business Review,* January 2002, pp. 80–88.
16. Allan M. Mohrman Jr., Susan M. Resnick-West, and Edward E. Lawler III, *Designing Performance Appraisal Systems—Aligning Appraisals and Organizational Realities* (San Francisco: Jossey-Bass, 1989); and Dick Grote, *The Performance Appraisal Question and Answer Book: A*

Survival Guide for Managers (New York: AMACOM, 2002).

17. Steve Kerr, "On the Folly of Rewarding A, While Hoping for B," *Academy of Management Journal,* Vol. 18, 1975, pp. 766–783.

18. Douglas G. Shaw and Craig Eric Schneier, "Team Measurement and Rewards: How Some Companies Are Getting It Right," *Human Resource Planning,* Vol. 18, 1995, pp. 34–49; and Susanne G. Scott and Walter O. Einstein, "Strategic Performance Appraisal in Team-Based Organizations: One Size Does Not Fit All," *Academy of Management Executive,* Vol. 15 (2), 2001, pp. 107–116.

19. Nancy M. Somerick, "Strategies for Improving Employee Relations by Using Performance Appraisals More Effectively," *Public Relations Quarterly,* Vol. 38 (3), Fall 1993, pp. 537–539.

20. Brian D. Cawley, Lisa M. Keeping, and Paul E. Levy, "Participation in the Performance Appraisal Process and Employee Reactions: A Meta-Analytic Review of Field Investigations," *Journal of Applied Psychology,* Vol. 83, 1998, pp. 615–633.

21. I. M. Jawahar and Charles R. Williams, "Where All the Children Are Above Average: The Performance Appraisal Purpose Effect," *Personnel Psychology,* Vol. 50, 1997, pp. 905–925.

22. Alan H. Locher and Kenneth S. Teel, "Appraisal Trends," *Personnel Journal,* Vol. 67 (9), 1988, p. 139.

23. Timothy D. Schellhardt, "It's Time to Evaluate Your Work and All Involved Are Groaning," *Wall Street Journal,* November 19, 1996, p. A1.

24. Society for Human Resource Management (SHRM), "Development Components Lacking in Performance Management Systems," December 15, 2000. (Available at: http://my.shrm.org/press/releases/default.asp?page=001215.htm)

25. See H. E. Brogden and E. K. Taylor, "A Theory and Classification of Criterion Bias," *Educational and Psychological Measurement,* Vol. 10, 1950, pp. 159–186; see also Jeffrey S. Kane and Edward E. Lawler III, "Performance Appraisal Effectiveness: Its Assessment and Determinants," in *Research in Organizational Behavior,* ed. Barry M. Staw (Greenwich, Conn.: JAI Press, 1979), pp. 425–478.

26. Hannah R. Rothstein, "Interrater Reliability of Job Performance Ratings: Growth to Asymptote Level with Increasing Opportunity to Observe," *Journal of Applied Psychology,* Vol. 75, 1990, pp. 322–327.

27. Chockaliangam Viswesvarar, Deniz S. Ones, and Frank L. Schmidt, "Comparative Analysis of the Reliability of Job Performance Ratings," *Journal of Applied Psychology,* Vol. 81, 1996, pp. 557–574.

28. Ibid.

29. David A. Hofmann, Rick Jacobs, and Steve J. Gerras, "Mapping Individual Performance Over Time," *Journal of Applied Psychology,* Vol. 77, 1992, pp. 185–195.

30. Hubert S. Feild and William H. Holley, "The Relationship of Performance Appraisal Characteristics to Verdicts in Selected Employment Discrimination Cases," *Academy of Management Journal,* Vol. 25, 1982, pp. 392–406.

31. *Brito v. Zia Company,* 478 F. 2d 1200 (10th Cir. 1973); and Gerald V. Barrett and Mary C. Kernan, "Performance Appraisal and Terminations: A Review of Court Decisions since *Brito v. Zia* with Implications for Personnel Practices," *Personnel Psychology,* Vol. 40, 1987, pp. 489–503.

32. *Price Waterhouse v. Hopkins,* 109 S.Ct 1775 (1989); and Bill Shaw, "Employee Appraisal Discrimination Cases, and Objective Evidence," *Business Horizons,* September–October 1990, pp. 61–65.

33. *Price Waterhouse v. Hopkins.*

34. Paul R. Sackett, Cathy L. Z. DuBois, and Ann Wiggins Noe, "Tokenism in Performance Evaluation: The Effects of Work Group Representation on Male–Female and White–Black Differences in Performance Ratings," *Journal of Applied Psychology,* Vol. 76, 1991, pp. 263–267.

35. Jon M. Werner and Mark C. Bolino, "Explaining U.S. Courts of Appeals Decisions Involving Performance Appraisal: Accuracy, Fairness, and Validation," *Personnel Psychology,* Vol. 50, 1997, pp. 1–24.

36. W. H. Holley and H. S. Feild, "Performance Appraisal and the Law," *Labor Law Journal,* Vol. 26, 1975, pp. 423–430.

37. J. T. Austin, P. Villanova, and H. Hindman, "Legal Requirements and Technical Guidelines Involved in Implementing Performance Appraisal Systems," in *Human Resource Management: Perspectives and Issues,* 3rd ed., eds. G. R. Ferris, K. R. Rowland, and M. R. Buckley (Boston: Allyn and Bacon, 1995).

38. Werner and Bolino, "Explaining U.S. Courts of Appeals Decisions."

39. K. Kraiger and J. K. Ford, "A Meta-Analysis of Ratee Race Effects in Performance Ratings," *Journal of Applied Psychology,* Vol. 70, 1985, pp. 56–65; and P. R. Sackett and C. L. Dubois, "Rater–Ratee

Race Effects on Performance Evaluation: Challenging Meta-Analytic Conclusions," *Journal of Applied Psychology,* Vol. 76, 1991, pp. 873–877; Philip L. Roth, Allen I. Huffcutt, and Philip Bobko, "Ethnic Group Differences in Measures of Job Performance: A New Meta-Analysis," *Journal of Applied Psychology,* Vol. 88 (4), 2003, 694–706.

40. Michael K. Mount, Marcia R. Sytsma, Joy Fisher Hazucha, and Katherine E. Holt, "Rater–Ratee Race Effects in Developmental Performance Ratings of Managers," *Personnel Psychology,* Vol. 50, 1997, pp. 51–69.

41. Ibid.

42. Christopher S. Miller, Joan A. Kaspin, and Michael H. Schuster, "The Impact of Performance Appraisal Methods on Age Discrimination in Employment Act Cases," *Personnel Psychology,* Vol. 43, 1990, pp. 555–578.

43. Glenn M. McEvoy and Wayne F. Cascio, "Cumulative Evidence of the Relationship between Employee Age and Job Performance," *Journal of Applied Psychology,* Vol. 74, 1989, pp. 11–17; and Bruce J. Avolio, David A. Waldman, and Michael A. McDaniel, "Age and Work Performance in Nonmanagerial Jobs: The Effects of Experience and Occupational Type," *Academy of Management Journal,* Vol. 33, 1990, pp. 407–422.

44. Cynthia D. Fisher and James B. Shaw, "Analysis of Officer Fitness Reports," prepared for U.S. Marine Corps, Office of Naval Research [research grant], unpublished.

45. Jeffrey S. Kane, H. John Bernardin, Peter Villanova, and Joseph Peyrefitte, "Stability of Rater Leniency: Three Studies," *Academy of Management Journal,* Vol. 38, 1995, pp. 1036–1051; and Peter Villanova, John Bernardin, S. A. Dahmus, and R. Sims, "Rater Leniency and Performance Appraisal Discomfort," *Educational and Psychological Measurement,* Vol. 53, 1993, pp. 789–799.

46. Brian E. Becker and Robert L. Cardy, "Influence of Halo Error on Appraisal Effectiveness: A Conceptual and Empirical Reconsideration," *Journal of Applied Psychology,* Vol. 71, 1986, pp. 662–671; R. Jacobs and S. Kozlowski, "A Closer Look at Halo Error in Performance Ratings," *Academy of Management Journal,* Vol. 28, 1985, pp. 201–212; and Barry R. Nathan and Nancy Tippins, "The Consequences of Halo 'Error' in Performance Ratings: A Field Study of the Moderating Effect of Halo on Test Validation Results," *Journal of Applied Psychology,* Vol. 75, 1990, pp. 290–296.

47. Jack M. Feldman, "A Note on the Statistical Correction of Halo Error," *Journal of Applied Psychology,* Vol. 71, 1986, pp. 173–176.

48. Nathan and Tippins, "The Consequences of Halo 'Error' in Performance Ratings"; William K. Balzer and Lorne M. Sulsky, "Halo and Performance Appraisal Research: A Critical Examination," *Journal of Applied Psychology,* Vol. 77, 1992, pp. 975–985; and Andrew L. Solomonson and Charles E. Lance, "Examination of the Relationship between True Halo and Halo Error in Performance Ratings," *Journal of Applied Psychology,* Vol. 82, 1997, pp. 665–674.

49. For examples, see Kevin J. Williams, Angelo S. DeNisi, Bruce M. Meglino, and Thomas P. Cafferty, "Initial Decisions and Subsequent Performance Ratings," *Journal of Applied Psychology,* Vol. 71, 1986, pp. 189–195; and Cynthia Lee, "Increasing Performance Appraisal Effectiveness: Matching Task Types, Appraisal Process, and Rater Training," *Academy of Management Review,* Vol. 10, 1985, pp. 322–331.

50. Daniel R. Ilgen, Janet L. Barnes-Farrell, and David B. McKellin, "Performance Appraisal Process Research in the 1980s: What Has It Contributed to Appraisals in Use?" *Organizational Behavior and Human Decision Processes,* Vol. 54, 1993, pp. 321–368.

51. S. T. Fiske and S. E. Taylor, *Social Cognition* (New York: Random House, 1984).

52. J. Crocker, S. T. Fiske, and S. E. Taylor, "Schematic Bases of Belief Change," in *Attitudinal Judgment,* ed. R. Eiser (New York: Springer-Verlag, 1984), pp. 197–226.

53. Cited in C. O. Longenecker, H. P. Sims, and D. A. Gioia, "Behind the Mask: The Politics of Employee Appraisal," *Academy of Management Executive,* Vol. 1, 1987, pp. 183–193.

54. Neil M. A. Hauenstein, "Training Raters to Increase the Accuracy and Usefulness of Appraisals," in *Performance Appraisal: State of the Art in Practice,* ed. James W. Smither (San Francisco: Jossey-Bass, 1998).

55. Cited in Dennis S. Gioia and Clinton O. Longenecker, "Delving into the Dark Side: The Politics of Executive Appraisal," *Organizational Dynamics,* Vol. 22 (3), 1994, pp. 47–57.

56. Beverly Geber, "The Hidden Agenda of Performance Appraisals," *Training,* June 1988, pp. 142–146.

57. Peter Villanova and John Bernardin, "Impression Management in the Context of Performance

Appraisal," in *Impression Management in the Organization,* eds. R. Giacalone and P. Rosenfeldt (Hillsdale, N.J.: Erlbaum, 1989).

58. Cynthia D. Fisher, "Transmission of Positive and Negative Feedback to Subordinates: A Laboratory Investigation," *Journal of Applied Psychology,* Vol. 64, 1979, pp. 533–540.

59. Gary P. Latham, Daniel Skarlicki, Diane Irvine, and Jacob P. Siegel, "The Increasing Importance of Performance Appraisals to Employee Effectiveness in Organizational Settings in North America," *International Review of Industrial and Organizational Psychology,* Vol. 8, 1993, pp. 87–132.

60. Frank J. Landy, James L. Farr, and Rick R. Jacobs, "Utility Concepts in Performance Measurement," *Organizational Behavior and Human Performance,* Vol. 30, 1982, pp. 15–40.

61. Ibid.

62. Ibid.

63. Gary P. Latham and Kenneth N. Wexley, *Increasing Productivity through Performance Appraisal* (Reading, Mass.: Addison-Wesley, 1982).

64. *Brito v. Zia Company.*

65. Larry H. Peters and Edward J. O'Connor, "Situational Constraints and Work Outcomes: The Influence of a Frequently Overlooked Construct," *Academy of Management Review,* Vol. 5, 1980, pp. 391–397; Peter Villanova and Marie A. Roman, "A Meta-Analytic Review of Situational Constraints and Work-Related Outcomes: Alternative Approaches to Conceptualization," *Human Resource Management Review,* Vol. 3 (2), 1993, pp. 147–175; and Peter Villanova, "Predictive Validity of Situational Constraints in General versus Specific Performance Domains," *Journal of Applied Psychology,* Vol. 81 (5), 1996, pp. 532–547.

66. Latham and Wexley, *Increasing Productivity through Performance Appraisal.*

67. H. John Bernardin and Richard W. Beatty, *Performance Appraisal: Assessing Human Behavior at Work* (Boston: Kent Publishing, 1984).

68. Frank J. Landy and James L. Farr, "Police Performance Appraisal," *JSAS Catalog of Selected Documents in Psychology,* Vol. 6, 1976, p. 83.

69. Walter C. Borman, Daren E. Buck, Mary Ann Hanson, Stephan J. Motowidlo, Stephen Stark, and Fritz Drasgow, "An Examination of the Comparative Reliability, Validity, and Accuracy of Performance Ratings Made Using Computerized Adaptive Rating Scales," *Journal of Applied Psychology,* Vol. 86, 2001, pp. 965–973.

70. Joann Muller, "Ford: Why It's Worse Than You Think," *Business Week,* June 25, 2001, pp. 80–89.

71. Mark Truby, "Forced Rankings Stirs Fierce Debate," *Detroit News,* April 29, 2001. (Available at: http://detnews.com/2001/autos/0104/29/a10-218163.htm)

72. Jack Welch and John A. Byrne, *Jack: Straight from the Gut* (New York: Warner Business Books, 2001).

73. Herbert H. Meyer, "Self-Appraisal of Job Performance," *Personnel Psychology,* Vol. 33, 1980, pp. 291–296.

74. Truby, "Forced Rankings Stirs Fierce Debate."

75. R. Blake Jelley and Richard D. Goffin, "Can Performance-Feedback Accuracy Be Improved? Effects of Rater Priming and Rating-Scale Format on Rating Accuracy," *Journal of Applied Psychology,* Vol. 86 (1), 2001, pp. 134–144.

76. Garry L. Hughes and Erich P. Prien, "An Evaluation of Alternate Scoring Methods for the Mixed Standard Scale," *Personnel Psychology,* Vol. 39, 1986, pp. 839–847.

77. F. E. Saal and F. J. Landy, "The Mixed Standard Scale: An Evaluation," *Organizational Behavior and Human Performance,* Vol. 18, 1977, pp. 19–35.

78. Bernardin and Beatty, *Performance Appraisal,* p. 98.

79. Angelo S. DeNisi and Lawrence H. Peters, "Organization of Information in Memory and the Performance Appraisal Process: Evidence from the Field," *Journal of Applied Psychology,* Vol. 81, 1996, pp. 717–737.

80. T. A. DeCotiis, "An Analysis of the External Validity and Applied Relevance of Three Rating Formats," *Organizational Behavior and Human Performance,* Vol. 19, 1977, pp. 247–266; Kevin R. Murphy and J. I. Constans, "Behavioral Anchors as a Source of Bias in Rating," *Journal of Applied Psychology,* Vol. 72, 1987, pp. 573–577; and Michael J. Piotrowski, Janet L. Barnes-Farrell, and Francine H. Esrig, "Behaviorally Anchored Bias: A Replication and Extension of Murphy and Constans," *Journal of Applied Psychology,* Vol. 74, 1989, pp. 823–826.

81. Walter C. Borman, Daren E. Buck, Mary Ann Hanson, Stephan J. Motowidlo, Stephen Stark, and Fritz Drasgow, "An Examination of the Comparative Reliability, Validity, and Accuracy of Performance Ratings Made Using Computerized Adaptive Rating Scales," *Journal of Applied Psychology,* Vol. 86 (5), 2001, pp. 965–973.

82. Ibid.
83. Latham and Wexley, *Increasing Productivity through Performance Appraisal.*
84. Ibid.
85. Robert Rodgers and John E. Hunter, "Impact of Management by Objectives on Organizational Productivity," *Journal of Applied Psychology,* Vol. 76, 1991, pp. 322–336.
86. Michael K. Mount, Timothy A. Judge, Steven E. Scullen, Marcia R. Sytsma, and Sarah A. Hezlett, "Trait, Rater and Level Effects in 360-Degree Performance Ratings," *Personnel Psychology,* Vol. 51, 1998, pp. 557–576; and Chockalingam Viswesvaran, Frank L. Schmidt, and Deniz S. Ones, "The Moderating Influence of Job Performance Dimensions on Convergence of Supervisory and Peer Ratings of Job Performance: Unconfounding Construct-Level Convergence and Rating Difficulty," *Journal of Applied Psychology,* Vol. 87 (2), 2002, pp. 345–354.
87. G. C. Thornton III, "Psychometric Properties of Self-Appraisals of Job Performance," *Personnel Psychology,* Vol. 33, 1980, pp. 263–271; and M. K. Mount, "Psychometric Properties of Subordinate Ratings of Managerial Performance," *Personnel Psychology,* Vol. 37, 1984, pp. 687–702.
88. M. M. Harris and J. Schaubroeck, "A Meta-Analysis of Self–Supervisor, Self–Peer, and Peer–Supervisor Ratings," *Personnel Psychology,* Vol. 41, 1988, p. 43–62.
89. J. M. Conway and A. I. Huffcutt, "Psychometric Properties of Multisource Performance Ratings: A Meta-Analysis of Subordinate, Supervisor, Peer, and Self-Ratings. *Human Performance,* Vol. 10, 1997, pp. 331–360.
90. Jeffrey D. Facteau and S. Bartholomew Craig, "Are Performance Appraisal Ratings from Different Rating Sources Comparable?" *Journal of Applied Psychology,* Vol. 86, 2001, pp. 215–227.
91. George C. Thornton III, "Psychometric Properties of Self-Appraisals of Performance," *Personnel Psychology,* Vol. 33, 1980, pp. 263–271; Harris and Schaubroeck, "A Meta-Analysis of Self–Supervisor, Self–Peer, and Peer–Supervisor Ratings"; and Brian W. Schrader and Dirk D. Steiner, "Common Comparison Standards: An Approach to Improving Agreement between Self and Supervisory Performance Ratings," *Journal of Applied Psychology,* Vol. 81, 1996, pp. 813–820.
92. Donald J. Campbell and Cynthia Lee, "Self-Appraisal in Performance Evaluation: Development versus Education," *Academy of Management Review,* Vol. 13, 1988, pp. 302–314.
93. Kenneth N. Wexley and Richard Klimoski, "Performance Appraisal: An Update," in *Research in Personnel and Human Resources Management,* Vol. 2, eds. Kendrith M. Rowland and Gerald R. Ferris (Greenwich, Conn.: JAI Press, 1984), pp. 35–80.
94. John A. Drexler Jr., Terry A. Beehr, and Thomas A. Stetz, "Peer Appraisals: Differentiation of Individual Performance on Group Tasks," *Human Resource Management,* Vol. 40 (4), Winter 2001, pp. 333–345.
95. Glenn M. McEvoy and Paul F. Buller, "User Acceptance of Peer Appraisals in an Industrial Setting," *Personnel Psychology,* Vol. 40, 1987, pp. 785–797.
96. Joann S. Lubin, "Turning the Tables: Underlings Evaluate Bosses," *Wall Street Journal,* October 4, 1994, pp. B1, B14; Sue Shellenbarger, "Reviews from Peers Instruct and Sting," *Wall Street Journal,* October 4, 1994, pp. B1, B4; "Companies Where Employees Rate Executives," *Fortune,* December 17, 1993, p. 128; Joyce E. Santora, "Rating the Boss at Chrysler," *Personnel Journal,* May 1992, pp. 41–45; and Oren Harari, "How Am I Doing?" *Management Review,* November 1992, pp. 55–57.
97. David Antonioni, "The Effects of Feedback Accountability on Upward Appraisal Ratings," *Personnel Psychology,* Vol. 47, 1994, pp. 349–356.
98. Gary J. Greguras, Chet Robie, Deidra J. Schleicher, and Maynard Goff III, "A Field Study of the Effects of Rating Purpose on the Quality of Multisource Ratings," *Personnel Psychology,* Vol. 56, 2003, pp. 1–21.
99. James W. Smither, Manuel London, Nicholas L. Vasilopoulos, Richard R. Reilly, Roger E. Millsap, and Nat Salvemini, "An Examination of the Effects of an Upward Feedback Program Over Time," *Personnel Psychology,* Vol. 48, 1995, pp. 1–34.
100. Leonard L. Berry and A. Parasuraman, *Marketing Services: Competing through Quality* (New York: Free Press, 1991).
101. Leanne Atwater and David Waldman, "Accountability in 360-Degree Feedback," *HR Magazine,* May 1998, pp. 96–104.
102. David Antonioni, "Designing an Effective 360-Degree Appraisal Feedback Process," *Organizational Dynamics,* Vol. 25, Autumn 1996, pp. 24–38.
103. David W. Bracken, Maxine A. Dalton, Robert A. Jako, Cynthia D. McCauley, and Victoria Pollman, *Should 360-Degree Feedback Be Used Only for*

Developmental Purposes? (Greensboro, N.C.: Center for Creative Leadership, 1997); Ellen Van Velsor, Jean Brittain Leslie, and John W. Fleenor, *Choosing 360: A Guide to Evaluating Multi-Rater Feedback Instruments for Management Development* (Greensboro, N.C.: Center for Creative Leadership, 1997); and Walter W. Tornow and Manuel London (eds.), *Maximizing the Value of 360-Degree Feedback* (San Francisco: Jossey-Bass, 1998).
104. Brian O' Reilly, "360-Degree Feedback Can Change Your Life," *Fortune,* October 17, 1994, pp. 93–100; Peter Ward, *360-Degree Feedback* (London, Institute of Personnel and Development, 1997); Atwater and Waldman, "Accountability in 360-Degree Feedback"; and Susan J. Wells, "A New Road: Traveling Beyond 360-Degree Evaluation," *HR Magazine,* September 1999, pp. 83–91.
105. Bob Cardy and Greg Dobbins, "The Changing Face of Performance Appraisal: Customer Evaluations and 360° Appraisals," *Human Resources Division News,* Vol. 16, Spring 1993, pp. 17–18; and David A. Waldman, Leanne E. Atwater, and David Antonioni, "Has 360-Degree Feedback Gone Amok?" *Academy of Management Executive,* Vol. 12 (2), 1998, pp. 86–94; David W. Bracken, Carol W. Timmreck, and Allen H. Church, *Handbook of Multisource Feedback: The Comprehensive Resource for Designing and Implementing MSF Processes* (San Francisco: Jossey-Bass, 2000).
106. L. E. Atwater, P. Roush, and A. Fischthal, "The Influence of Upward Feedback on Self- and Follower Ratings of Leadership," *Personnel Psychology,* Vol. 48, 1995, pp. 35–60; J. W. Johnson and K. L. Ferstl, "The Effects of Interrater and Self–Other Agreement on Performance Improvement Following Upward Feedback," *Personnel Psychology,* Vol. 52, 1999, pp. 271–303; and R. R. Reilly, J. W. Smither, and N. L. Vasilopoulos, "A Longitudinal Study of Upward Feedback," *Personnel Psychology,* Vol. 49, 1996, pp. 599–612.
107. A. N. Kluger and A. DeNisi, "The Effects of Feedback Interventions on Performance: A Historical Review, a Meta-Analysis, and a Preliminary Feedback Intervention Theory," *Psychological Bulletin,* Vol. 119, 1996, pp. 254–284; Joan F. Brett and Leanne E. Atwater, "360° Feedback: Accuracy, Reactions, and Perceptions of Usefulness," *Journal of Applied Psychology,* Vol. 86, 2001, pp. 930–942; and Bruce Pfau and Ira Kay, "Does 360-Degree Feedback Negatively Affect Company Performance?" *HR Magazine,* June 2002, pp. 55–59.
108. Brett and Atwater, "360° Feedback."
109. Kane and Lawler, "Performance Appraisal Effectiveness"; David W. Bracken, "Straight Talk about Multirater Feedback," *Training and Development,* September 1994, pp. 44–51; and David W. Bracken, Carol W. Timmreck, John W. Fleenor, and Lynn Summers, "360-Degree Feedback from Another Angle," *Human Resource Management,* Vol. 40 (1), Spring 2001, pp. 3–20.
110. Fictitious company as an example of 360-degree appraisal.
111. Jim Meade, "Visual 360: A Performance Appraisal System That's 'Fun'," *HR Magazine,* July 1999, pp. 118–122; G. Douglas Huet-Cox, Tjai M. Nielsen, and Eric Sundstrom, "Get the Most from 360-Degree Feedback: Put It on the Internet," *HR Magazine,* May 1999, pp. 92–103; and David W. Bracken, Lynn Summers, and John Fleenor, "High-Tech 360," *Training and Development,* August 1998, pp. 42–45.
112. Waldman, Atwater, and Antonioni, "Has 360-Degree Feedback Gone Amok?"
113. A. S. DeNisi and A. N. Kluger, "Feedback Effectiveness: Can 360-Degree Appraisals Be Improved?" *Academy of Management Executive,* Vol. 14, 2000, pp. 129–139; and J. Ghorpade, "Managing Five Paradoxes of 360-Degree Feedback," *Academy of Management Executive,* Vol. 14, 2000, pp. 140–150.
114. S. Jay Liebowitz and Kevin T. Holden, "Are Self-Managing Teams Worthwhile? A Tale of Two Companies," *SAM Advanced Management Journal,* Spring 1995, pp. 11–17.
115. Edward Lawler and Susan Cohen, *American Compensation Journal,* Vol. 1, 1992, pp. 16–19.
116. Susanne G. Scott and Walter O. Einstein, "Strategic Performance Appraisal in Team-Based Organizations: One Size Does Not Fit All," *Academy of Management Executive,* Vol. 15 (2), 2001, pp. 107–116.
117. Shaw and Schneier, "Team Measurement and Rewards."
118. Carol A. Norman and Robert A. Zawacki, "Team Appraisals—Team Approach," *Personnel Journal,* September 1991, pp. 101–104.
119. Scott and Einstein, "Strategic Performance Appraisal in Team-Based Organizations"; Janice S. Miller, "Self-Monitoring and Performance Appraisal Satisfaction: An Exploratory Field Study," *Human Resource Management,* Vol. 40 (4), Winter 2001, pp. 321–332.

120. Robert C. Liden, Sandy J. Wayne, and Maria L. Kraimer, "Managing Individual Performance in Work Groups," *Human Resource Management,* Vol. 40 (1), Spring 2001, pp. 63–72.
121. H. John Bernardin, "Effects of Rater Training on Halo Errors in Student Ratings of Instructors," *Journal of Applied Psychology,* Vol. 63, 1978, pp. 301–308.
122. Stanley M. Gully, Stephaine C. Payne, K. Lee Kiechel Koles, and Jon-Andrew K. Whiteman, "The Impact of Error Training and Individual Differences on Training Outcomes: An Attribute-Treatment Interaction Perspective," *Journal of Applied Psychology,* Vol. 87 (1), 2002, pp. 143–155.
123. H. John Bernardin and M. R. Buckley, "Strategies in Rater Training," *Academy of Management Review,* Vol. 6, 1984, pp. 205–212; Jerry W. Hedge and Michael J. Kavanagh, "Improving the Accuracy of Performance Evaluations: Comparison of Three Methods of Performance Appraiser Training," *Journal of Applied Psychology,* Vol. 73, 1988, pp. 68–73; and Kevin R. Murphy and William K. Balzer, "Rater Errors and Rating Accuracy," *Journal of Applied Psychology,* Vol. 74, 1989, pp. 619–624.
124. H. John Bernardin, "Rater Training: A Critique and Reconceptualization," *Proceedings of the Academy of Management,* August 1979, pp. 131–135; Bernardin and Buckley, "Strategies in Rater Training."
125. David E. Smith, "Training Programs for Performance Appraisal: A Review," *Academy of Management Review,* Vol. 11, 1986, pp. 22–40.
126. Neil M. A. Hauenstein and Roseanne J. Foti, "From Laboratory to Practice: Neglected Issues in Implementing Frame-of-Reference Rater Training," *Personnel Psychology,* Vol. 42, 1989, pp. 359–378.
127. Lorne M. Sulsky and David V. Day, "Frame-of-Reference Training and Cognitive Categorization: An Empirical Investigation of Rater Memory Issues," *Journal of Applied Psychology,* Vol. 77, 1992, pp. 501–510; David V. Day and Lorne M. Sulsky, "Effects of Frame-of-Reference Training and Information Configuration on Memory Organization and Rating Accuracy," *Journal of Applied Psychology,* Vol. 80, 1995, pp. 158–167; and David J. Woehr and Allen I. Huffcutt, "Rater Training for Performance Appraisal: A Quantitative Review," *Journal of Occupational and Organizational Psychology,* Vol. 67, 1994, pp. 189–205.
128. George C. Thornton and S. Zorich, "Training to Improve Observer Accuracy," *Personnel Psychology,* Vol. 29, 1980, pp. 351–354.
129. Hedge and Kavanagh, "Improving the Accuracy of Performance Evaluations."
130. Bernardin, "Effects of Rater Training"; Robert D. Bretz Jr., George T. Milkovich, and Walter Read, "The Current State of Performance Appraisal Research and Practice: Concerns, Directions, and Implications," *Journal of Management,* Vol. 18, 1992, pp. 321–352.
131. Michael M. Harris, "Rater Motivation in the Performance Appraisal Context: A Theoretical Framework," *Journal of Management,* Vol. 20, 1994, pp. 737–756.
132. R. R. Sims, J. G. Veres, and S. M. Heninger, "Training Appraisers: An Orientation Program for Improving Supervisory Performance Ratings," *Public Personnel Management,* Vol. 16, 1987, pp. 37–46.
133. Neal P. Mero and Stephan J. Motowidlo, "Effects of Rater Accountability on the Accuracy and the Favorability of Performance Ratings," *Journal of Applied Psychology,* Vol. 80, 1995, pp. 517–524.
134. Jay M. Jackman and Myra H. Stober, "Fear of Feedback," *Harvard Business Review,* Vol. 81 (4), April 2003, pp. 101–107.
135. N. K. Napier and G. P. Latham, "Outcome Expectancies of People Who Conduct Performance Appraisals," *Personnel Psychology,* Vol. 39, 1986, pp. 827–837; Yitzhak Fried, Robert B. Tiegs, and Alphonso R. Bellamy, "Personal and Interpersonal Predictors of Supervisors' Avoidance of Evaluating Subordinates," *Journal of Applied Psychology,* Vol. 77, 1992, pp. 462–468; and Manuel London, "Giving Feedback: Source-Centered Antecedents and Consequences of Constructive and Destructive Feedback," *Human Resource Management Review,* Vol. 5, 1995, pp. 159–188.
136. Simon S. K. Lam, Michelle S. M. Yik, and John Schaubroeck, "Responses to Formal Performance Appraisal Feedback: The Role of Negative Affectivity," *Journal of Applied Psychology,* Vol. 87 (1), 2002, pp. 192–201; and Lin Grensing-Pophal, "Motivate Managers to Review Performance," *HR Magazine,* March 2001, pp. 45–48.
137. J. M. Hillery and K. N. Wexley, "Participation in Appraisal Interviews Conducted in a Training Situation," *Journal of Applied Psychology,* Vol. 59, 1974, pp. 168–171.
138. Mary Beth DeGregorio and Cynthia D. Fisher, "Providing Performance Feedback: Reactions to Alternate Methods," *Journal of Management,* Vol. 14, 1988, pp. 605–616.

139. Harris and Schaubroeck, "A Meta-Analysis of Self–Supervisor, Self–Peer, and Peer–Supervisor Ratings."
140. T. R. Mitchell and L. S. Kalb, "Effects of Job Experience on Supervisor Attributions for Subordinate's Poor Performance," *Journal of Applied Psychology,* Vol. 67, 1982, pp. 81–188.
141. Jone L. Pearce and Lyman W. Porter, "Employee Responses to Formal Performance Appraisal Feedback," *Journal of Applied Psychology,* Vol. 71, 1986, pp. 211–218.
142. Herbert H. Meyer, "A Solution to the Performance Appraisal Feedback Enigma," *Academy of Management Executive,* Vol. 5, 1991, pp. 68–76.
143. Donald L. Kirkpatrick, *How to Improve Performance through Appraisal and Coaching.* (New York: American Management Association, 1982).
144. M. W. McCall Jr., and D. L. DeVries, "Appraisal in Context: Clashing with Organizational Realities," prepared for the Center for Creative Leadership [technical report], 1977.
145. Herbert H. Meyer, E. Kay, and J. French, "Split Roles in Performance Appraisal," *Harvard Business Review,* Vol. 43, 1965, pp. 123–129.
146. J. B. Prince and Edward E. Lawler III, "Does Salary Discussion Hurt the Developmental Performance Appraisal?" *Organizational Behavior and Human Decision Processes,* Vol. 37, 1986, pp. 357–375.
147. James R. Larson Jr., "The Dynamic Interplay between Employees' Feedback-Seeking Strategies and Supervisors' Delivery of Performance Feedback," *Academy of Management Review,* Vol. 14, 1989, pp. 408–422; Gerald R. Ferris, Timothy A. Judge, Kendrith M. Rowland, and Dale E. Fitzgibbons, "Subordinate Influence and the Performance Evaluation Process: Test of a Model," *Organizational Behavior and Human Decision Process,* Vol. 58, 1994, pp. 101–135; Sandy J. Wayne and Robert C. Liden, "Effects of Impression Management on Performance Ratings: A Longitudinal Study," *Academy of Management Journal,* Vol. 38, 1995, pp. 232–260; Sandy J. Wayne, Robert C. Liden, Isabel K. Graf, and Gerald R. Ferris, "The Role of Upward Influence Tactics in Human Resource Decisions," *Personnel Psychology,* Vol. 50, 1997, pp. 979–1006; and Thomas E. Becker and Scott L. Martin, "Trying to Look Bad at Work: Methods and Motives for Managing Poor Impressions in Organizations," *Academy of Management Journal,* Vol. 38, 1995, pp. 174–199.
148. S. J. Wayne and K. M. Kacmar, "The Effects of Impression Management on the Performance Appraisal Process," *Organizational Behavior and Human Decision Processes,* Vol. 48, 1991, pp. 70–88.
149. Elizabeth Wolfe Morrison and Robert J. Bies, "Impression Management in the Feedback-Seeking Process: A Literature Review and Research Agenda," *Academy of Management Review,* Vol. 16, 1991, pp. 522–541.
150. Steve W. J. Kozlowski, Georgia T. Chao, and Robert F. Morrison, "Games Raters Play: Politics, Strategies, and Impression Management in Performance Appraisal," in *Performance Appraisal: State of the Art in Practice,* ed. James W. Smither (San Francisco: Jossey-Bass, 1998).
151. Barry R. Nathan, Allan M. Mohrman Jr., and John Milliman, "Interpersonal Relations as a Context for the Effects of Appraisal Interviews on Performance and Satisfaction: A Longitudinal Study," *Academy of Management Journal,* Vol. 34, 1991, pp. 352–369; and Daniel R. Ilgen, Cynthia D. Fisher, and M. Susan Taylor, "Consequences of Individual Feedback on Behavior in Organizations," *Journal of Applied Psychology,* Vol. 64, 1979, pp. 349–371.
152. Meyer, "A Solution to the Performance Appraisal Feedback Enigma"; Daniel R. Ilgen, Terence R. Mitchell, and J. W. Frederickson, "Poor Performers: Supervisors and Subordinates' Response," *Organizational Behavior and Human Performance,* Vol. 27, 1981, pp. 386–410.
153. P. Christopher Earley, "Trust, Perceived Importance of Praise and Criticism, and Work Performance: An Examination of Feedback in the United States and England," *Journal of Management,* Vol. 12, 1986, pp. 457–473.
154. Robert A. Baron, "Negative Effects of Destructive Criticism: Impact on Conflict, Self-Efficacy, and Task Performance," *Journal of Applied Psychology,* Vol. 73, 1988, pp. 199–207.
155. Brendan D. Bannister, "Performance Outcome Feedback and Attributional Feedback: Interactive Effects on Recipient Responses," *Journal of Applied Psychology,* Vol. 71, 1986, pp. 203–210.
156. Campbell and Lee, "Self-Appraisal in Performance Evaluation."

CHAPTER 11

Compensation System Development

- Employee Satisfaction and Motivation Issues in Compensation Design
- Establishing Internal Equity: Job Evaluation Methods
- Establishing External Equity
- Establishing Individual Equity
- Legal Regulation of Compensation Systems
- Administering Compensation Systems
- The Issue of Comparable Worth

HR Challenge

As VP of HR for Nanotech, Inc., you are proud of your contributions to this pioneering endeavor. Nanotech, Inc., founded five year ago by Dr. Karl Wang, CEO, now has more than 150 employees working on molecular-level machines designed to maneuver individual atoms into the position needed to build future generations of miniaturized semiconductors. Nanotech, Inc. is at the forefront of an entirely new technology.

From the beginning you knew that the compensation system would be important to attract the type of specialized talent Nanotech, Inc. was seeking. Toward that end you developed a flexible, market-based system to keep salaries competitive.

Traditionally, pay plans evaluate jobs in terms of knowledge, skills, and abilities and then group similar positions together in ranges. Employees are then assigned a range and move up within that classification. As employees gain experience, they progress to a higher range requiring greater skills.

In thinking through compensation, you felt the traditional systems were too bureaucratic and were not consistent with the flexibility needed for employee assignments in such an innovative organization. As a result, key jobs at Nanotech were identified, and salaries for these jobs were pegged to those of other high-tech firms. Market rates replaced pay ranges, with base pay being equivalent to the median of competitive pay at comparison firms.

The market-based system seemed to be working well for Nanotech. In fact, a professional journal featured an article about the innovative system you developed. Thus you were surprised when Jerry Foxton, a twenty-eight-year-old computer specialist, stopped by to see you. Jerry was concerned about his salary. He had found salary.com and used this source to compare his salary with median salaries of computer specialists in the same geographic area, the Research Triangle of North Carolina. Jerry handed you the reports from salary.com indicating that his salary was $5,000 lower than the lowest number listed as a median range.

You are confused. You use many salary surveys in establishing market rates and do not understand how they could be so wide of the mark. Further, although the reports from salary.com look impressive, you do not know much about what goes into the calculations. You are wondering how to proceed to gather the information needed to respond to Jerry. In addition, how will the information Jerry found influence the perceptions of others at Nanotech, Inc? Will some of the most talented professionals, those like Jerry, think of looking elsewhere?

An organization exists to accomplish specific goals and objectives. The individuals hired by the organization have their own needs. One is for money, which enables employees to purchase a wide variety of goods and services available in the marketplace. Hence there is a basis for an exchange: The employee provides knowledge, skills and abilities desired by the organization to meet its goals in return for money, goods, and services. Taken together, the money, goods, and services the employer provides for employees constitute the compensation.[1]

The system an organization uses to reward employees can play an important role in the organization's efforts to gain a competitive advantage and to achieve its major objectives. Compensation systems should do the following:

- Signal to employees (and others) the major objectives of the organization—such things as quality, customer focus, teamwork, and other goals—by emphasizing these through compensation.
- Attract and retain the talent an organization needs.
- Encourage employees to develop the skills and abilities the organization needs.
- Motivate employees to perform effectively.
- Support the type of culture (e.g., entrepreneurial) the company seeks to engender.[2]

Ideally, a reward system should align individual objectives with important strategic goals of the organization, but for most organizations the reality falls far short of this ideal. The design and implementation of a compensation system constitute one of the most complex activities for which human resource managers are responsible. The intricacy of compensation inspired the observation by one researcher that "reward systems are one of the most prominent and frequently discussed features of organizations."[3] Here are some of the factors that contribute to this complexity:

- Although other aspects of human resource systems (e.g., training, career management, appraisal systems, and quality-of-work-life programs) are important to some employees, compensation is considered crucial by virtually everyone.

- One goal of a compensation system is to motivate employees, yet there is tremendous variation in the value different individuals attach to a specific reward or package of rewards. Further, an individual's values also may change over time.
- The jobs in most organizations involve an almost endless variety of knowledge, skills, and abilities and are performed in situations with a wide range of demands.
- Compensation systems consist of many elements in addition to pay for time worked; these components must be coordinated to work together.

A DIFFERENT POINT OF VIEW

Some Myths About Pay

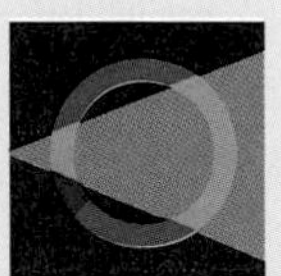

Jeffrey Pfeffer has written an article claiming that managers often believe things about pay that are incorrect and, consequently, make ineffective decisions about how much to pay people and on what basis to pay them.

The first myth is: "Labor rates and labor costs are the same." That is, managers assume that they will save money by paying a lower hourly labor rate—that paying $17 per hour is bound to cost less than paying $21 per hour. This is not necessarily true. Total labor costs depend on productivity and the number of employees being paid as well as the hourly pay rate. If the employees a firm can attract for $21 are much more skilled and efficient than those it can get for $17, it may take fewer of them and fewer labor hours to produce the same amount of output. The labor cost per unit of output may actually be less at the higher wage rate!

Hence myth number two: "You can lower your labor costs by cutting labor rates." As we have seen, hiring the cheapest labor available is not always a good strategy. These individuals may lack skills and motivation; the organization may incur costs due to high employee turnover (see Chapter 16); and customer service, quality, and productivity may be compromised.

Myth number three is: "Labor costs constitute a significant proportion of total costs." Although this is true in some industries (such as consulting, accounting, and legal services), in many others raw materials, plant, equipment, and distribution are much more expensive than labor. Trying to realize large overall savings by cutting labor costs is bound to fail if labor is a relatively small portion of total cost.

Another reason to avoid just targeting labor costs in an effort to become more competitive is myth number four: "Low labor costs are a potent and sustainable competitive weapon." Anyone can offer low rates of pay. It is better in the long run to compete on a basis that cannot be so readily copied, such as innovation in design, high quality, or outstanding service. None of these three, by the way, are likely to be achieved by firms paying bottom dollar for talent.

Myth five is: "Individual incentive pay improves performance." While individual incentives certainly can motivate performance, there can also be some negative side effects from poorly designed incentive systems. This issue is addressed in more detail in A Different Point of View in Chapter 12.

The final myth is: "People work for money." While it is certainly true that very few people will work without being paid at all, Pfeffer points out that individuals desire a lot more from work than just a paycheck. Firms that assume money is the only motivator may fail to provide other outcomes that are actually very important in attracting, keeping, and motivating high-quality employees. For example, the SAS Institute has a very low turnover rate of sales and information technology staff. SAS pays competitive rates, but it does not offer stock options and the chance to become an overnight millionaire common in other IT companies. Instead, SAS focuses on providing meaningful work in a family-friendly atmosphere with stimulating colleagues and the latest high-tech equipment. The organizational culture and the satisfying day-to-day work activities and challenges keep people loyal, not the paycheck.

Source: Jeffrey Pfeffer, "Six Dangerous Myths about Pay," *Harvard Business Review,* May–June 1998, pp. 108–119.

- Employee compensation is a major cost of doing business—up to 80 percent for service firms—and can determine the competitiveness of a firm's products or services.
- A number of federal and state regulations affect compensation systems. Failure to abide by the laws can be very costly for the organization.
- Employees, either directly or through collective bargaining arrangements, may desire to participate in the determination of compensation.
- The cost of living varies tremendously in different geographic areas, an important consideration for firms with multiple locations.

These factors lead to many myths about pay. Leading researcher Jeffrey Pfeffer's ideas concerning the myths about pay are discussed in A Different Point of View.

In most organizations, the compensation system involves a multifaceted package, not just pay for work and performance. The components of the compensation system can be roughly divided into direct (wages) and indirect (benefits) forms of compensation (see Figure 11.1). This chapter discusses procedures for designing and administering a compensation system. Chapter 12 examines the special

FIGURE 11.1

Components of the Compensation System

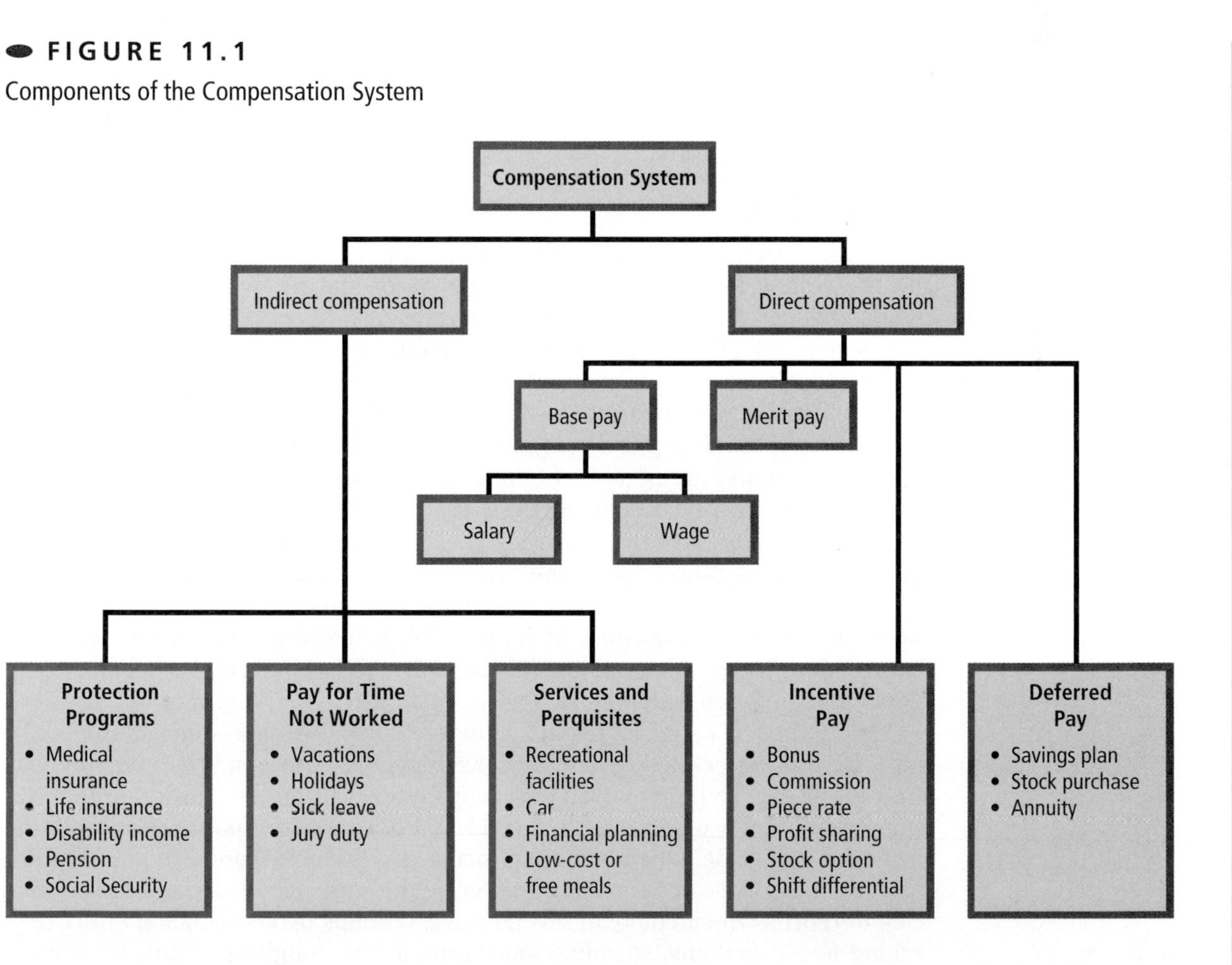

aspects of pay-for-performance (also called incentive) systems. Chapter 13 considers indirect compensation or benefits. Taken together, direct compensation, incentive pay, and benefits define **total compensation.**

EMPLOYEE SATISFACTION AND MOTIVATION ISSUES IN COMPENSATION DESIGN

People have no basic or instinctive need for money; it is important only to enable people to satisfy other needs. Organizations frequently overestimate the value workers place on monetary reward.[4] For example, if money were the primary motivation for working, why would hourly employees object to overtime, given the premium rate of pay associated with it?[5] Yet this is just what we see happening, as workers at several companies have strenuously objected to the amount of overtime they have been asked to put in.[6] In fact, when surveyed, just over half of Americans said they would rather have more free time even if it meant less money.[7]

Many supervisors become frustrated and disillusioned when pay increases do not produce a corresponding rise in productivity. Still more troublesome is the fact that the rewards that effectively motivate some workers do not succeed with others. Equity and expectancy theories (see Chapter 12) can help explain employees' reactions to compensation systems.

Equity Theory

Employees want to be treated fairly. *Equity* is the balance between the inputs an individual brings to a job and the outcomes he or she receives from it. Employee inputs include experience, education, special skills, effort, and time worked. Outcomes include pay, benefits, achievement, recognition, and any other rewards.

Individuals use a complex process to determine what is fair. Inputs are continually compared with outcomes—the individual's special skills and efforts are weighed against the pay and recognition given by the organization. However, inputs and outcomes are in different units and are hard to compare with each other directly. Thus **equity theory** suggests that individuals determine whether they are being treated fairly by comparing their own outcomes/inputs ratio with the outcomes/inputs ratio of someone else. This other person (or group of people) may be in the same job or in other jobs, in the company or outside the company, in the same industry or outside the industry. A sense of inequity arises when the comparison process uncovers an imbalance between inputs and outcomes of the employee compared with others.

Equity theory suggests that individuals will usually make some attempt to relieve the tension created by any perceived inequity.[8] An employee may perceive the ratio of his or her rewards and contributions to be less favorable than the ratio prevailing for others (see Figure 11.2). For example, a police officer may believe that he or she expends more effort at greater risk than is required of firefighters in the same community who receive the same pay. The police officer may seek to redress the inequity in several ways, perhaps by (1) reducing effort (e.g., writing fewer citations, spending more time in the doughnut shop), (2) working

FIGURE 11.2
Equity Theory

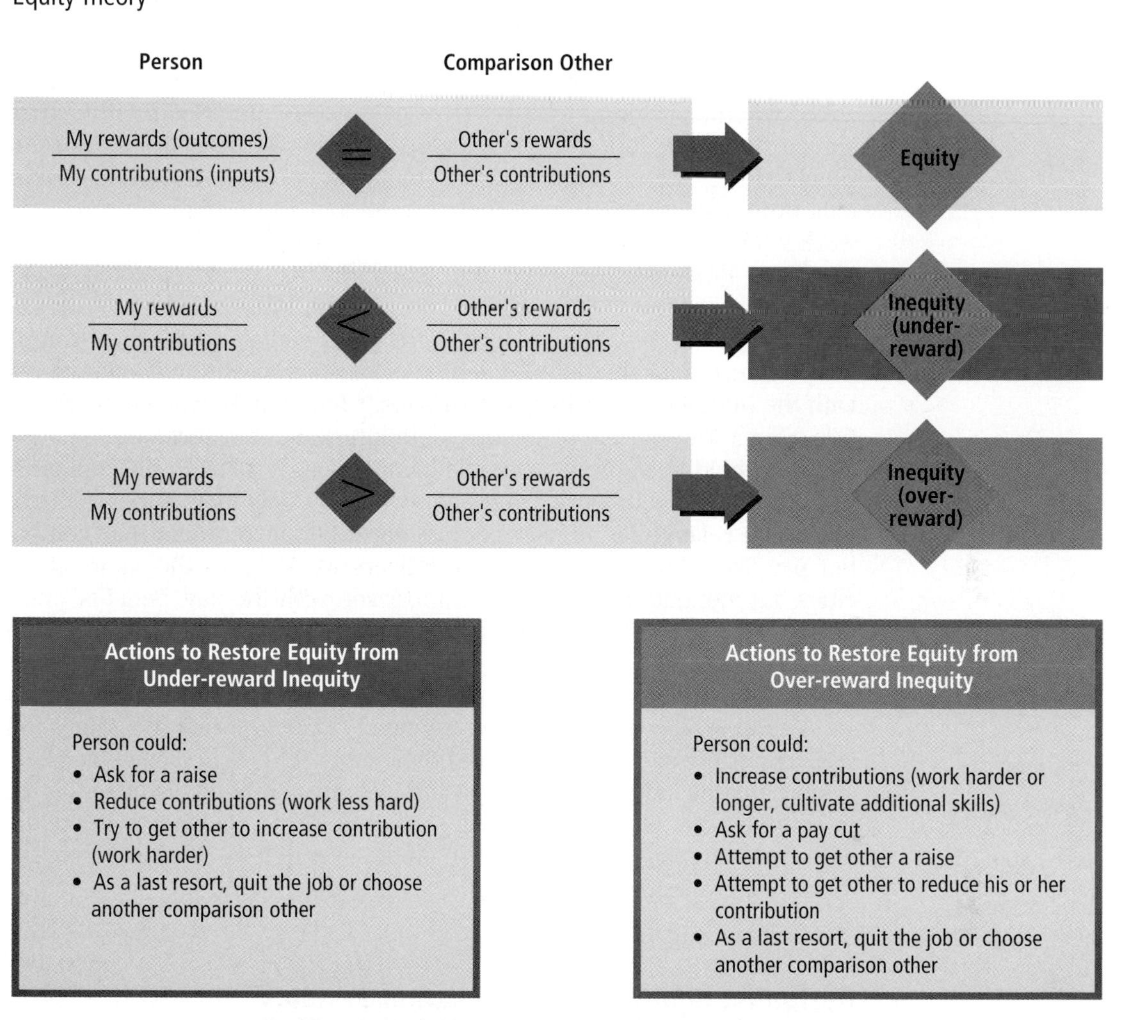
Person
Comparison Other
My rewards (outcomes)
My contributions (inputs)
=
Other's rewards
Other's contributions
Equity
My rewards
My contributions
<
Other's rewards
Other's contributions
Inequity (under-reward)
My rewards
My contributions
>
Other's rewards
Other's contributions
Inequity (over-reward)
Actions to Restore Equity from Under-reward Inequity
Person could:
• Ask for a raise
• Reduce contributions (work less hard)
• Try to get other to increase contribution (work harder)
• As a last resort, quit the job or choose another comparison other
Actions to Restore Equity from Over-reward Inequity
Person could:
• Increase contributions (work harder or longer, cultivate additional skills)
• Ask for a pay cut
• Attempt to get other a raise
• Attempt to get other to reduce his or her contribution
• As a last resort, quit the job or choose another comparison other

with colleagues to lobby the city council for higher pay for police officers, or (3) seeking employment in a community where police officers are paid more than firefighters. The desire to achieve equity even extends to the point of employee theft as a reaction to underpayment. A study measured employee theft rates before, during, and after a period in which pay was temporarily reduced by 15 percent. Theft increased markedly in plants where pay was reduced; it returned to prior levels when normal pay was resumed.[9]

People also notice when they are rewarded excessively in relation to others. In such a case, the individual might work harder than he or she did previously or volunteer for an extra assignment to eliminate the perceived inequity. Research has also shown that motivation from being overcompensated is relatively short-lived. Most individuals quickly decide that they deserve whatever pay rate they receive and do not try to sustain a higher level of performance.[10]

Satisfaction with Pay

Survey data regularly show compensation to be one of the areas of employment with which employees are least satisfied.[11] For example, a recent study involving more than 50,000 employees from U.S. manufacturing and service organizations asked whether workers felt they were paid fairly compared to others performing similar work for different employers. Nearly 60 percent of those surveyed reported they were dissatisfied with their pay.[12] It is not unusual to find individuals otherwise satisfied with their career and the organization for which they work who believe their compensation leaves something to be desired. For example, Jerry Foxton of Nanotech, Inc. (see HR Challenge) was likely very satisfied with his career and the rewards he received until his experience with salary.com. Sometimes it seems that employees are never satisfied with their compensation.

One reason for the reduced degree of satisfaction with compensation has to do with the number of possible comparisons.[13] Individuals seek comparison information from a wide variety of sources, both internal and external to the organization, and then hold to the least favorable comparison. If unfavorable comparisons with those in their line of work are not found, individuals may compare themselves to those in a related line of work. For example, a police officer may compare his or her pay favorably with other police officers working for the same city and other cities but feel under-rewarded in comparison with the pay, benefits, and work expectations of federal marshals. Highly paid executives frequently attempt to justify their compensation by comparing it with that of top-level entertainers or sports figures, who earn even more.

A successful compensation system needs to incorporate the equity concerns of all participants in the employment relationship. This is achieved by establishing a system that includes both external and internal comparisons in setting pay levels. In addition, it is important to focus on the specific employees who are dissatisfied with their compensation rather than on the overall level of satisfaction. If poor performers are dissatisfied, this may be the intended result.

Designing Equitable Compensation Systems

Three elements of equity can be distinguished: internal, external, and individual. **Internal equity** refers to the relationship among jobs within a single organization. Employees expect the president of a company to earn more than the executive vice president, who in turn earns more than the plant manager, and so on. Among other things, compensation is presumed to be correlated with the level of knowledge, skill, and experience required to do the job successfully. Thus no one is surprised that people high in the organizational structure earn more than lower level employees do. Internal equity exists when the pay differentials between different jobs within the organization are perceived as fair—differences that are neither too large nor too small.

External equity refers to comparisons of similar jobs in different organizations (e.g., the pay received by presidents of various electrical manufacturing firms). It would be no surprise to learn that the president of a firm with annual sales of $1 billion earns more than the president of a $500 million firm. Presumably a doubling of company size requires more knowledge, skill, and experience on the part of its leader. Location matters, as well as industry and company size.

When the administrative assistant working for an electrical manufacturing plant manager worries about external equity, the comparison is likely to be with administrative assistants at the automobile plant across town rather than with electrical manufacturers nationwide.

The final element, **individual equity,** refers to comparisons among individuals in the same job within the same organization. In many ways this is the most critical question. If it is not answered satisfactorily, attention to internal and external equity will have been wasted. For example, suppose the human resource manager establishes, through internal and external comparisons, that all administrative assistants in the organization should receive between $2,000 and $2,500 per month. The problem now is to determine the pay rate of each administrative assistant. Should long-service administrative assistants be paid more than those who have just been hired? If yes, what is the value of each additional year of service? Should pay differences be based on job performance? If so, how will performance be measured? How will the differences in performance be translated into pay differences? Employees must perceive that these questions are answered fairly for individual equity to exist.

There are accepted procedures for establishing internal, external, and individual equity within an organization. These procedures are reviewed in the following sections.

ESTABLISHING INTERNAL EQUITY: JOB EVALUATION METHODS

The major purpose of job evaluation is to determine the relative worth of the jobs within an organization. A systematic comparison can define an internal job hierarchy that ranks jobs in terms of their relative contribution to the organizational objectives.

Fulfillment of a company's objectives depends more on the job done by its president than that done by its plant manager. But how much is the differential worth? There is no direct way to measure the value of jobs in relation to organizational objectives, so rewards are usually based on important components generally agreed to make one job worth more than another. These aspects, called *compensable factors,* may include such things as skills, effort, and education required; amount of responsibility involved; and working conditions.

Approximately 75 percent of all companies employ some form of job evaluation.[14] To be most effective, the process should involve the employees whose jobs are affected. The following questions need to be considered:

- Which of several possible evaluation procedures is to be used?
- Will one evaluation procedure be used throughout the organization, or will different procedures be used for broad classes of jobs (e.g., exempt versus nonexempt)?
- If the procedure selected takes into account several compensable factors, which of these factors are to be included, and how are they to be weighted?

The five most frequently used job evaluation methods are (1) job ranking, (2) job grading or classification, (3) the point method, (4) the Hay plan, and (5) factor comparison. As shown in Figure 11.3, these methods can be classified on the basis of the approach taken. Along one dimension are job ranking and factor

FIGURE 11.3

Job Evaluation Procedures

Source: John M. Ivancevich, "Job Evaluation Procedures," from *Foundations of Personnel*. Copyright © 1992 by Richard D. Irwin. Reprinted by permission.

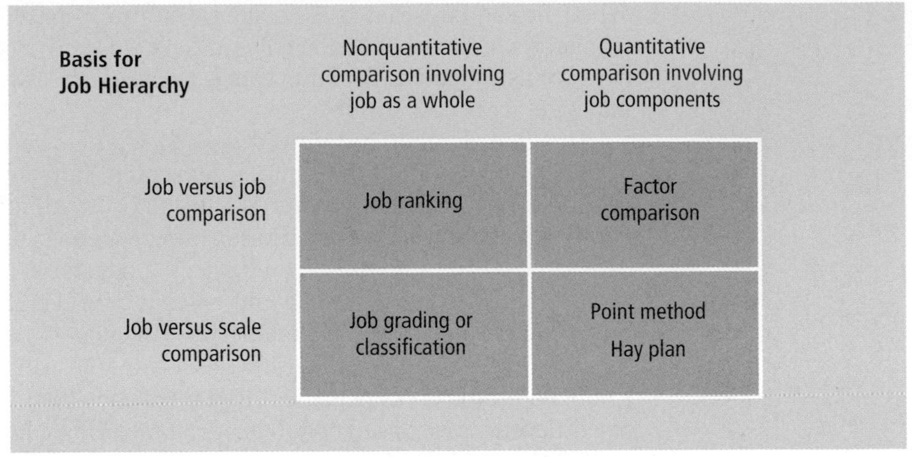

comparison, which compare one job with another, versus the other methods that compare the job with one or more rating scales. The other dimension considers the quantitative sophistication of the procedures.

Job Ranking

Job ranking, the simplest way to evaluate jobs, is used primarily in small organizations. Normally, a committee of managers reviews all the job descriptions and ranks them in order of their relative worth or importance to the organization. The ranking method is simple, inexpensive, fast, and easy to understand. However, it is nonquantitative and rather subjective. Although jobs are compared with one another, no explicit set of compensable factors is used in this comparison. Additionally, simple ranking gives no information about the distances between jobs, making it difficult to assign salary levels. Even though there may be agreement that job A is more valuable than job B, the magnitude of the difference is not known. A final difficulty is purely practical. Except in a very small organization, no one may be knowledgeable about every single job in the organization, which is necessary for meaningful ranking.

A special method of ranking is the paired-comparison technique. This method was discussed in Chapter 10 as a means of comparing employees with one another on the basis of overall performance. In the job evaluation context, the content and importance of different jobs, not the performance of incumbents, is the object of comparison. In this approach, each job is compared directly against every other job, using a matrix of the type shown in Table 11.1. Reading across each row, an X is marked each time the job is ranked more highly than the job in that column. (For example, the executive secretary job is ranked higher than computer operator but not higher than systems analyst.) The totals column records the number of comparisons in which the job is ranked higher. This total determines the job's overall rank. Although this technique is somewhat more systematic than simple ranking, the number of comparisons increases quite rapidly as the number of jobs increases. Some evidence suggests that the paired-comparison approach is more reliable than simple ranking.[15]

TABLE 11.1

Paired-Comparison Ranking Table

	Messenger	Data-Processing Manager	Data-Entry Operator	Executive Secretary	Computer Operator	Systems Analyst	Control Clerk	Pro-grammer	File Clerk	Assistant Director	Tota
Messenger											0
Data-Processing Manager	X		X	X	X	X	X	X	X	X	9
Data-Entry Operator	X								X		2
Executive Secretary	X		X		X		X	X	X		6
Computer Operator	X		X				X		X		4
Systems Analyst	X		X	X	X		X	X	X		7
Control Clerk	X		X						X		3
Programmer	X		X		X		X		X		5
File Clerk	X										1
Assistant Director	X		X	X	X	X	X	X	X		8

Instructions: Place X in space where job in row is more important than job in column.

Source: Richard Henderson, *Compensation Management: Rewarding Performance*, 5th ed., © 1989, p. 199. Adapted by permission of Prentice-Hall, Inc., Englewood Cliffs, New Jersey.

Job Grading or Classification

The **job grading** or **job classification** method is a nonquantitative job evaluation technique that compares the whole job with a predetermined standard. In this approach, jobs are assigned to predefined grades or classes. Job grading is common in the public sector. The federal government's General Schedule (GS) has eighteen grades: fifteen grades into which most jobs are classified and three top "supergrades" that cover senior executives. Employees in the supergrade are eligible for special bonuses and allowances. GS 11 through GS 15 include general management and highly specialized jobs, GS 5 through GS 10 are for management trainees and lower level managers, and GS 1 through GS 4 are for clerical and nonsupervisory personnel. Table 11.2 contains representative examples of the type of grade descriptions used by the federal government. In the private sector, job classification is commonly used in managerial and scientific or engineering jobs.[16]

It is usually fairly easy for organizations to group jobs and for employees to accept the classifications. Flexibility is another advantage of the job classification method. It can be applied to a large number and wide variety of jobs. As the num-

TABLE 11.2

Grade Descriptions and Representative Job Titles from the Classification System Used by the Federal Government

Grade Level	Grade Description	Jobs Included in Grade
GS 1	Includes those classes of positions the duties of which are to perform, under immediate supervision, with little or no latitude for the exercise of independent judgment: —the simplest routine work in office, business, or fiscal operations; or —elementary work of a subordinate technical character in a professional, scientific, or technical field.	Typist, messenger
GS 2	Includes those classes of positions the duties of which are —to perform, under immediate supervision, with limited latitude for the exercise of independent judgment, routine work in office, business, or fiscal operations, or comparable subordinate technical work of limited scope in professional, scientific, or technical field, requiring some training or experience; or —to perform other work of equal importance, difficulty, and responsibility, and requiring comparable qualifications.	Engineering aide
GS 5	Includes those classes of positions the duties of which are —to perform, under general supervision, difficult and responsible work in office, business, or fiscal administration, or comparable subordinate technical work in a professional, scientific, or technical field, requiring in either case —considerable training and supervisory or other experience; —broad working knowledge of a special subject matter or of office, laboratory, engineering, scientific, or other procedure and practice; and —the exercise of independent judgment in a limited field; —to perform other work of equal importance, difficulty, and responsibility, and requiring comparable qualifications.	Chemist, accountant, engineer (civil), statistical clerk

Source: From *The Management of Compensation* by Alan N. Nash and Stephen J. Carroll (Copyright © 1976 by Wadsworth, Inc.) Reprinted by permission of the author.

ber of jobs in the organization grows, these new jobs can easily be assigned to the grades that already exist.

The job classification method has been criticized because subjective judgments are used to place jobs into the grades (e.g., when a job seems to fall between two grades). A related disadvantage is that the job classification method relies heavily on the use of job titles rather than on a more detailed examination of job content.

Point Method

As seen in Figure 11.3, unlike job ranking or classification, the **point method** breaks the job into components and evaluates each of these job elements against specially constructed scales. A quantitative approach, the point method is rather complex to design but relatively simple to understand and administer once it is in place. It is the most widely used method of job evaluation; well over half the organizations that use job evaluation use the point method.

Four steps are followed in applying the point method: selection of compensable factors, establishment of factor scales, assignment of points to degrees, and application to organizational jobs.

Compensable Factors **Compensable factors** are those job dimensions or job requirements that will be the basis for paying employees. Organizations select three to twenty-five compensable factors, with the typical point method using about ten factors. The plan developed by the National Electrical Manufacturers Association (NEMA) involves eleven factors grouped into the following four dimensions: (1) skill (education, experience, knowledge), (2) effort (physical demand, mental or visual demand), (3) responsibility (equipment or process, material or product, safety of others, work of others), and (4) job conditions (working conditions, hazards).

Factor Scales Once the compensable factors have been chosen, scales reflecting different degrees within each factor are constructed. Examples of the scales for the knowledge factor are defined in some detail in Table 11.3. As much as possible, each degree is defined to be equidistant from the adjacent degrees.

Assigning Points to Degrees The next step is to assign points to degrees. First, however, the job evaluation committee decides on the relative importance of the different factors. For instance, in the system in Table 11.4, the committee has decided that experience is the most important factor and has awarded it the largest number of points (110 for the highest degree). Education and knowledge are next in importance, followed by physical demand and working conditions, and then the remaining factors. Once the highest degree of each factor is given a point allocation reflecting its importance, the lower degrees are assigned proportionately lesser point values in accord with factor importance.

Note that the determination of factors and the assignment of points to these factors become an important mechanism for communicating to employees what is valued in the organization. The typical plan illustrated in Table 11.4 tells employees that experience, education, and knowledge are equal to all the other factors taken together. For example, an employee wanting to know what it takes to

TABLE 11.3

Defining a Compensable Factor and Associated Degrees: An Illustration

Knowledge

This factor measures the knowledge or equivalent training required to perform the job duties.

1st Degree: Use of reading and writing, adding and subtracting of whole numbers; following of instructions; use of fixed gauges, direct reading of instruments, and similar devices; where interpretation is not required.

2nd Degree: Use of addition, subtraction, multiplication, and division of numbers including decimals and fractions; simple use of formulas, charts, tables, drawings, specifications, schedules, wiring diagrams; use of adjustable measuring instruments; checking of reports, forms, records, and comparable data; where interpretation is required.

3rd Degree: Use of mathematics with the use of complicated drawings, specifications, charts, tables; various types of precision measuring instruments. Equivalent to one to three years' applied trades training in a particular or specialized occupation.

4th Degree: Use of advanced trades mathematics, together with the use of complicated drawings, specifications, charts, tables, handbook formulas; all varieties of precision measuring instruments. Equivalent to complete accredited apprenticeship in a recognized trade, craft, or occupation; or equivalent to a two-year technical college education.

5th Degree: Use of higher mathematics involved in the application of engineering principles and the performance of related practical operations, together with a comprehensive knowledge of the theories and practices of mechanical, electrical, chemical, civil, or like engineering field. Equivalent to complete four years of technical college or university education.

Source: Adapted from *Compensation,* 3rd ed. by George T. Milkovich and Jerry M. Newman. Copyright © 1990 by Richard D. Irwin. Reproduced with permission of The McGraw-Hill Companies.

progress from the loading dock to more responsible and rewarding positions might think about evening courses at the community college.

Application to Jobs Once the compensable factors have been identified, defined, and assigned points, jobs can be evaluated and "scored." In this process, the job evaluation committee thoroughly reviews job analysis data and perhaps observes the job or speaks with incumbents. Then it will determine which degree of each factor best describes that job. The points associated with these degrees are summed for each job. An example of this procedure is given in Table 11.5.

Note that the points assigned to a job do not need to exactly match those of the plan (see knowledge factor in Table 11.5). In this example, the level of knowledge required by loading dock workers is between the first and second degrees (see Table 11.3), resulting in 21 points. Often jobs with similar point totals are later grouped together for administrative convenience. For instance, all jobs with 150 to 180 points may form a single pay grade.

In principle, the point method could be used to develop a single set of factors and weights for all the jobs in the organization. In practice, however, organizations tend to use several different point plans. There may be one plan for office and clerical employees, another for production workers, and a third for managerial staff.

TABLE 11.4

A Typical Point Plan

Factors	Degrees	1st	2nd	3rd	4th	5th
Skill						
1. Education		14	28	42	56	70
2. Experience		22	44	66	88	110
3. Knowledge		14	28	42	56	70
Effort						
4. Physical demand		10	20	30	40	50
5. Mental demand		5	10	15	20	25
Responsibility						
6. Equipment/process		5	10	15	20	25
7. Material/product		5	10	15	20	25
8. Safety of others		5	10	15	20	25
9. Work of others		5	10	15	20	25
Job conditions						
10. Working conditions		10	20	30	40	50
11. Hazards		5	10	15	20	25

Source: Richard Henderson, *Compensation Management: Rewarding Performance,* 5th ed., © 1989, p. 204. Adapted by permission of Prentice-Hall, Inc., Englewood Cliffs, New Jersey.

TABLE 11.5

Application of a Point System to Two Jobs

	Loading Dock Workers		Forklift Repair Mechanics	
Compensable Factors	**Degree**	**Points**	**Degree**	**Points**
Education	1	14	2	28
Experience	1	22	3	66
Knowledge	1-2	21	3	42
Physical demand	4	40	2	20
Mental demand	1	5	3	15
Responsibility for equipment/process	2	10	3	15
Responsibility for material/product	2	10	1	5
Responsibility for safety of others	1	5	1	5
Responsibility for work of others	1	5	1	5
Working conditions	3	30	2	20
Hazards	4	20	3	15
Total points		182		236

Rarely do the same compensable factors apply to jobs at widely different levels. For example, the job condition factors shown in Table 11.4 are not equally applicable to office/clerical, production, and managerial workers. In such a case, it may make sense to replace factors that do not apply with those more meaningful to the jobs involved. Physical demands and hazards, for instance, seldom appear in point systems for managerial jobs.

The Hay Plan

Hay Associates, one of the largest compensation consulting firms in the world, developed a well-known version of the point method. The **Hay plan** is used for evaluating managerial and executive positions by a large number of organizations worldwide.[17]

The universal factors used by the Hay plan are know-how, problem solving, and accountability. These factors, along with the associated subfactors, are described in Table 11.6. *Know-how* is the total of all the knowledge and skills required to do the job; it includes the subfactors of technical knowledge, management responsibility, and responsibility for motivating others. *Problem solving* is the amount of original thinking required by the job for arriving at decisions; it includes the subfactors of degree of freedom and type of mental activity. *Accountability* is defined as being answerable for actions taken on the job; its three subfactors are freedom to act, dollar magnitude, and impact. The Hay guide chart allows the evaluator to assign a point value for each factor. The total of the points across all factors is the value of the job.[18]

Factor Comparison

The **factor-comparison method** is a method of quantifying the job versus job comparison (see Figure 11.3). It is the least commonly used method of job evaluation.[19] The first step is to select key jobs to help anchor the system. Key jobs are those that are found in many organizations and that have relatively stable job content; they also have to be jobs for which the prevailing wage rates are known.[20] The second step is to rank the key jobs on a few compensable factors, such as skill, effort, responsibility, and job conditions. In Table 11.7, job 1 has lower skill requirements than all other jobs but is ranked highest on working conditions. The third step is to determine for each key job the amount of the present pay rate that is attributable to each of the factors. Of job 1's total rate of \$7.75, \$1.75 is allocated for its level of skill, \$1.75 for effort, \$1.25 for responsibility, and \$3.00 for working conditions.

The factor-comparison method can be applied to other jobs by comparing their standings on each factor with that of the key jobs and summing the associated dollar values to arrive at an hourly rate. For example, suppose that a new job, job X, is being evaluated. Job X is determined to have the same level of skill requirements as job 3 (\$4.25), the same level of responsibility as job 4 (\$3.75), somewhat more hazardous working conditions than job 2 (\$2.00), and somewhat greater effort requirements than job 4 (\$3.00). Thus the appropriate hourly pay for job X would be \$13.00.

The procedure is rather cumbersome and requires constant updating; hence the relative infrequency of its use. Organizations interested in a quantitative

TABLE 11.6

The Factors of the Hay Plan

Know-How	Problem Solving (Mental Activity)	Accountability
The sum total of all knowledge and skills, however acquired, needed for satisfactory job performance (evaluates the job, not the person).	The amount of original, self-starting thought required by the job for analysis, evaluation, creation, reasoning, and arriving at conclusions:	The measured effect of the job on company goals.
Know-how has three dimensions:	Problem solving has two dimensions:	Accountability has three dimensions:
• The amount of practical, specialized, or technical knowledge required.	• The degree of freedom with which the thinking process is used to achieve job objectives without the guidance of standards, precedents, or direction from others.	• Freedom to act, or relative presence of personal or procedural control and guidance; determined by answering the question, "How much freedom has the job holder to act independently?"; for example, a plant manager has more freedom than a supervisor under his or her control.
• Breadth of management, or the ability to make many activities and functions work well together; the job of company president, for example, has greater breadth than that of a department supervisor.	• The type of mental activity involved; the complexity, abstractness, or originality of thought required.	• Dollar magnitude, a measure of the sales, budget, dollar value of purchases, value added, or any other significant annual dollar figure related to the job.
• Requirement for skill in motivating people.	Problem solving is expressed as a percentage of know-how for the obvious reason that people think with what they know. The percentage judged to be correct for a job is applied to the know-how point value; the result is the point value given to problem solving.	• Impact of the job on dollar magnitude, a determination of whether the job has a primary effect on end results or has instead a sharing, contributory, or remote effect.
Accountability is given a point value independent of the other two factors.		
Using a chart, a number can be assigned to the level of know-how needed in a job. This number—or point value—indicates the relative importance of know-how in the job being evaluated.		

Note: The total evaluation of any job is arrived at by adding the points for know-how, problem solving, and accountability. The points are not shown here.

Source: From *Effective Personnel Management,* 3rd ed., by Schuler, Buetell, and Youngblood © 1989. Reprinted by permission of South-Western College Publishing, a division of Thomson Learning. Fax 800-730-2215.

TABLE 11.7

A Factor Comparison Scale

Rate	Skill	Effort	Responsibility	Working Conditions
$1.00				Job 3
1.25			Job 1	Job 4
1.50				Job 2
1.75	Job 1	Job 1		
2.00	Job 2	Job 3	Job 3	(Job X)
2.25		Job 2		
2.50		Job 4		
2.75			Job 2	
3.00		(Job X)		Job 1
3.25				
3.50	Job 4			
3.75			Job 4 (Job X)	
4.00				
4.25	Job 3 (Job X)			
4.50				
4.75				
5.00				
5.25				
5.50				

Hourly rates: job 1, $7.75; job 2, $8.50; job 3, $9.25; job 4, $11.00

approach to job evaluation are more likely to rely on a point system, which tends to be more straightforward, resulting in greater flexibility.

Computerized Job Evaluation

The most popular job evaluation procedures were developed at a time when greater value was placed on having accurate narrative job descriptions. The most frequent means of collecting job data was by having analysts interview incumbents or observe work performed and then write job descriptions. This process is labor intensive, generates a tremendous amount of qualitative data, and must be updated frequently.

A recent trend is the computerization of job evaluation.[21] Typically, after some training, incumbents complete structured questionnaires, such as the Position Analysis Questionnaire (see Chapter 4) or a task-oriented questionnaire (see Figure 11.4), which are then checked by supervisors. Supervisors also may complete the questionnaires for the jobs they supervise. Responses about time spent on and importance of various tasks are then incorporated into a statistical (regression) technique to calculate job points and the appropriate location of a job in the salary structure. Services that score the Position Analysis Questionnaire also provide job evaluation information.

FIGURE 11.4

Sample Segment of Structured Job Evaluation Questionnaire

Source: Reprinted with permission of Panel Publishers, Inc., 36 West 44th St., New York, N.Y. 10036, from *Topics in Total Compensation, Vol. 3: Computerizing Job Evaluation for Greater Efficiency and Effectiveness*, p. 248. Copyright 1989.

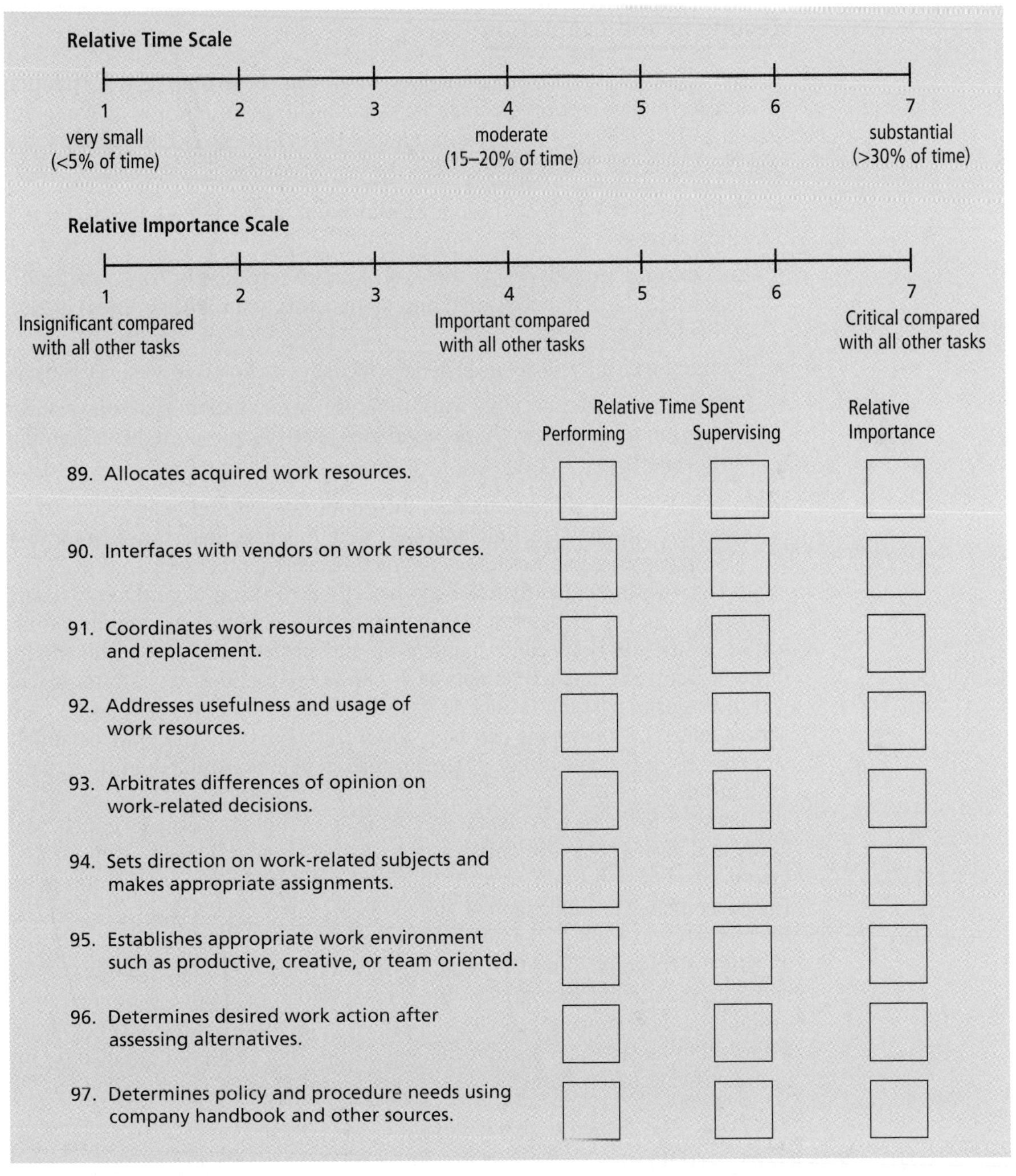

Relative Time Scale

1 very small (<5% of time) — 2 — 3 — 4 moderate (15–20% of time) — 5 — 6 — 7 substantial (>30% of time)

Relative Importance Scale

1 Insignificant compared with all other tasks — 2 — 3 — 4 Important compared with all other tasks — 5 — 6 — 7 Critical compared with all other tasks

	Relative Time Spent: Performing	Relative Time Spent: Supervising	Relative Importance
89. Allocates acquired work resources.	☐	☐	☐
90. Interfaces with vendors on work resources.	☐	☐	☐
91. Coordinates work resources maintenance and replacement.	☐	☐	☐
92. Addresses usefulness and usage of work resources.	☐	☐	☐
93. Arbitrates differences of opinion on work-related decisions.	☐	☐	☐
94. Sets direction on work-related subjects and makes appropriate assignments.	☐	☐	☐
95. Establishes appropriate work environment such as productive, creative, or team oriented.	☐	☐	☐
96. Determines desired work action after assessing alternatives.	☐	☐	☐
97. Determines policy and procedure needs using company handbook and other sources.	☐	☐	☐

Other computer-based procedures operate in similar fashions. That is, they facilitate a survey of jobs, evaluation of jobs, and the aggregation of market data for comparisons (see the next section, on external equity).[22] More and more, computers are playing an important role in removing the drudgery from salary determination.

Results of Job Evaluation

To some, job evaluation is exemplary of all that is wrong with a traditional approach to human resources. This is, in part, the point of view of Nanotech, Inc. (see the HR Challenge at the beginning of this chapter). To its critics, job evaluation is seen as the following:

- Being an overly bureaucratic procedure that allows jobs to be placed in hierarchical boxes[23]
- Encouraging employees to focus on how to advance in the organization at a time when there may be only limited opportunity for advancement as the result of downsizing[24]
- Promoting an internal focus instead of focusing on how best to serve the customer
- Being unsuitable for a forward-thinking organization that has reorganized twenty job titles as, say, three broad jobs (see discussion of broadbanding later in this chapter)

Many ask: Why not simply establish the going rate through wage surveys (see the next section) and use this information to guide salary decisions? In other words, why not bypass the process of evaluating jobs as Nanotech, Inc. has done?

In fact, this is frequently done and is termed **ranking to market.**[25] Salaries are based on a survey of salaries paid by competitors. Although expedient—and useful for many jobs, especially managerial and professional jobs—the method has disadvantages. First, such an approach allows competitors, not strategic decisions within the organization, to dictate salaries. Second, not all jobs can be compared across firms. Comparisons can be made for key jobs and then pay established for similar jobs, but this slotting of similar jobs is best accomplished by means of job evaluation.

Ranking to market is useful for some jobs, but for large organizations with many and varied jobs, the only way to construct a sound basis for the wage structure is through job evaluation. At the same time, methods such as broadbanding (discussed later in this chapter) and skill-based pay (covered in Chapter 12) have been seen as making job evaluation less relevant to restructured organizations.

Once decisions about the relative value of jobs are made, the next step is assigning actual dollar amounts to the points, ranks, or grades produced by the job evaluation. The concept of external equity is very important in this process; pay levels must be set that consider the "going rate" for that type of job and employee in the relevant labor market.

ESTABLISHING EXTERNAL EQUITY

Just as there is no given price for a pound of apples, there is no absolute rate of pay for a job. You expect to pay less for apples at a farmers' market than at a supermarket and less at a supermarket than at a convenience store. Because orchards produce more small apples than large ones, you expect small apples to cost less per pound than large ones. You expect to pay more for apples in some seasons than in others and more in New York City than in Albany, New York. And if the price for apples seems too high, there is always the possibility of buying other, less expensive fruit.

Pay to employees reflects the same dynamics that underlie the price of apples and consumers' reactions to these price differences. Just as you probably would not consistently shop at a store that charges higher prices, unless there is some special reason, you probably would not work for a company that offers less pay than you could receive at a nearby organization (again, unless there is some special reason). Employers need to compete for the skills and knowledge they require to operate their businesses to attract workers with needed skills and to motivate and retain those already employed. They use wage and salary surveys to find out what other organizations are paying for particular skills. Then, in setting pay rates, they seek to integrate the external information with what they have learned through the internal evaluation of jobs. This process is called **pricing the wage structure.**

Wage and Salary Surveys

To establish a competitively priced wage structure, organizations typically rely on wage and salary survey data collected from other organizations. The survey process involves identifying the jobs to be included, selecting the organizations to be surveyed, and then actually collecting the data. The data must then be interpreted so that wage rates can be set within the context of the organization's pay policy. Well over 90 percent of all companies regularly use wage and salary survey data in setting their own pay standards.

Identifying Key Jobs In practice, employers do not seek market data on all jobs. Instead, they gather survey information only for key jobs, which generally have the following characteristics:

- The job content is relatively stable over time.
- The jobs occur frequently both in the organization and in the surveyed organizations.
- The jobs can be defined quite precisely.
- The jobs are performed in a similar manner in most organizations.

Key jobs should span the range of positions to be included in the wage structure. For example, it would not be desirable to identify only entry-level positions as key jobs. Jobs at the middle and upper levels also need to be included. Moreover, jobs need to be carefully defined. For example, the job of secretary would seem to meet all the characteristics of a key job. However, in today's computer age, the secretarial job has been transformed. It is necessary to be specific as to the skills and responsibilities involved. Data may be collected on several clearly defined types or levels of secretaries.

One question one might ask with respect to Nanotech, Inc. is how the jobs were selected for the market comparison. If computer jobs were underrepresented, this might explain why Mr. Foxton's pay came into question.

Selecting Organizations to Survey Identifying organizations to survey can be important. In considering how to price its apples, a supermarket in New York City is not particularly concerned about supermarket prices in Albany because it will not lose any business to an Albany competitor. In the same way, organizations tend to be most interested in rewards offered by their competitors in the same labor market.

Organizations to be covered in a wage survey typically include those that (1) employ workers with the same skills, (2) are within geographic distances that would make employees willing to commute or relocate, and (3) are in the same or similar industry. However, the considerations that go into selecting a set of organizations to be surveyed vary for different jobs. For example, it is far less important that these organizations be in the same industry when the survey focuses on wages of common jobs such as secretary or truck driver. However, industry is crucial in establishing competitive pay for industry-specific jobs, for instance, petroleum engineers. The geographic area to be surveyed also depends on the job. For secretaries, all the relevant organizations competing for the skills are likely to be in the local area. For more complex jobs requiring sophisticated qualifications, however, the geographic area increases. Competition for managerial, professional, and technical jobs tends to be carried out at the regional, national, or—in some instances—international level.[26]

Other special considerations also may arise in selecting a sample of organizations to survey. For instance, suppose an organization makes wheel covers for General Motors Corporation at a plant in rural West Virginia. A local wage survey may show that wages for blue-collar workers in the area are generally quite low. However, because of intermittent activism by employees interested in being organized by the United Auto Workers, the management of this plant also needs to collect information on the pay and benefits of UAW members in plants elsewhere in the country. The wage level actually chosen may reflect both area and industry considerations.

This raises another question related to Nanotech, Inc. Specifically, what organizations were used for the market-comparison system? Were comparison companies as cutting-edge and high-tech as Nanotech? If not, Nanotech salaries could be off the mark.

Collecting Data Rather than running their own wage survey, many organizations obtain the results of surveys undertaken by industry associations (e.g., the American Assembly of Collegiate Schools of Business), professional associations (e.g., the American Chemical Society or the American Management Association), government agencies (e.g., the Bureau of Labor Statistics), or consulting firms (e.g., Hay Associates, Hewitt Associates, or Towers, Perrin, Foster, and Crosby). Numerous annual surveys cover a wide choice of job families and industries. At local levels, chapters of the Society for Human Resource Management or Chambers of Commerce often undertake surveys for their membership.

Self-Surveys For a company that wants to collect and analyze its own data, it is important to obtain information on the characteristics of the responding organization, as well as on both direct and indirect compensation (see Figure 11.1). The organizational information (e.g., total number of employees, sales, return on investment, product lines) is needed to judge the comparability of the competitor in terms of size, products, and financial condition. It is also crucial to know the types and amounts of benefits offered (e.g., fully covered medical plan versus plan supported in part by employee contributions), as well as incentives and hourly pay. Hourly pay rates or salaries may be misleading if bonuses for which employees are likely to qualify are not taken into account.

Online Surveys The Internet is increasingly popular as a source of information for salary benchmarks as exemplified by Nanotech's employee, Jerry Foxton. Salary.com is one of several Web sites providing survey data. Some sites, such as the Bureau of Labor Statistics (www.bls.gov), provide extensive information on how data are collected and analyzed. Other sites provide less information, bringing into question their reliability and validity. As one professional stated, "Internet data are easy to get—but impossibly difficult to evaluate."[27] For example, it is impossible to know when data obtained from salary.com and similar sites were collected.[28] Although popular, information from Internet sites is difficult to use without knowing the quality of the data.

Government Surveys A salary survey report can take several forms. Table 11.8 illustrates a report published by the U.S. Bureau of Labor Statistics as part of its ongoing program of wage surveys in major geographic areas. The table gives information on a sample of jobs in metropolitan Charlotte, North Carolina, and is based on establishments employing fifty workers or more in the white- and blue-collar occupations shown. The Bureau of Labor Statistics also provides information on compensation rates in other countries (see the International Perspective box).

Interpreting the Data The report shows a detailed frequency distribution of hourly wage rates for each job, along with the median wage. If the workers in a given occupation were ordered from highest earnings to lowest earnings, the earnings of the person in the middle would represent the median. The mean is not given in Table 11.8 but can be computed by adding the earnings of all workers and dividing the total by the number of workers surveyed.

Of the two summary measures, the median is the most useful in setting wage ranges. The mean can easily become distorted if a few workers are paid at extreme rates. The median is not subject to such distortion. For an employer hiring a secretary (see Administrative support), such information can be of value in suggesting that wages of close to $18.50 per hour would be required to be competitive. A wage between $21 and $23 per hour would assure the employer that top applicants would seek the job with a good chance that they would accept it if offered.

Avoiding Antitrust The U.S. Department of Justice and the Federal Trade Commission have questioned the legality of salary surveys under antitrust laws. The fear is that employers that compete for the same labor pool may use the results to collectively fix the wages of employees. For example, the hospitals in a metropolitan area could share wage information through a salary survey in an effort to avoid competing with one another for available talent.

As a result of investigations, federal antitrust agencies have indicated that they will not scrutinize compensation surveys that are consistent with these four guidelines:[29]

1. Survey data need to be collected by an independent third party, such as a consultant, not by the competing employers themselves. (Employers would be

TABLE 11.8

Hourly Wages for Selected Occupations, Full-Time Workers, Charlotte-Gastonia-Rock Hill, North Carolina–South Carolina, June 2003

Occupation[3]	10	25	50	75	90
All	$8.50	$10.92	$15.86	$22.54	$31.49
All excluding sales	8.73	11.05	16.00	22.37	31.11
White collar	9.97	13.00	18.96	27.77	38.46
White collar excluding sales	10.70	13.69	19.35	27.48	37.60
Professional specialty and technical	15.09	18.35	23.94	31.25	39.39
Professional specialty	16.76	19.87	25.00	31.85	38.46
Engineers, architects, and surveyors	23.43	26.52	30.40	38.92	42.57
Mathematical and computer scientists	21.00	24.83	31.01	35.22	37.75
Health related	17.50	19.07	21.62	25.60	42.94
Registered nurses	17.50	18.86	21.78	25.34	28.30
Teachers, college and university	22.12	26.76	32.08	36.85	48.43
Other postsecondary teachers	17.92	21.96	28.21	33.88	40.58
Teachers, except college and university	17.29	19.69	23.81	28.83	33.63
Prekindergarten and kindergarten	11.48	17.58	21.97	26.14	31.63
Elementary school teachers	17.29	19.34	23.11	27.87	32.01
Secondary school teachers	17.58	19.67	23.29	28.22	32.53
Teachers, special education	20.25	23.94	28.83	33.34	35.25
Librarians, archivists, and curators	—	—	—	—	—
Technical	13.49	15.75	18.98	25.09	50.06
Licensed practical nurses	14.46	16.18	17.50	18.14	19.36
Engineering technicians, n.e.c.	15.99	17.31	23.44	30.36	33.39
Executive, administrative, and managerial	17.70	21.85	27.89	36.96	46.15
Executives, administrators, and managers	20.19	24.98	31.91	41.83	58.17
Management related	16.16	20.10	24.97	29.09	35.00
Accountants and auditors	15.54	16.16	21.15	27.15	27.40
Personnel, training, and labor relations specialists	15.52	20.80	24.18	25.53	27.78
Management related, n.e.c.	12.25	16.35	22.28	33.02	37.38
Sales	7.00	8.00	10.61	31.25	45.00
Supervisors, sales	13.50	15.00	31.25	45.00	45.00
Sales workers, other commodities	7.50	8.25	8.50	10.00	10.61
Cashiers	6.75	7.00	7.76	8.88	10.04
Administrative support, including clerical	9.33	10.85	13.21	16.25	19.71
Secretaries	10.80	13.65	18.41	20.91	22.84
Receptionists	6.83	10.00	11.00	13.00	14.73
Bookkeepers, accounting and auditing clerks	10.30	11.75	13.25	13.73	14.71
Teachers' aides	8.58	8.92	9.42	10.71	12.53
Blue collar	8.54	10.37	14.08	19.00	23.20
Precision production, craft, and repair	11.08	14.54	18.50	21.77	25.26
Supervisors, mechanics and repairers	18.93	19.00	21.15	27.89	30.14
Bus, truck, and stationary engine mechanics	13.83	15.33	16.49	19.25	21.77

(continued)

Occupation[3]	10	25	50	75	90
Industrial machinery repairers	13.02	15.89	20.07	22.78	25.12
Electrical power installers and repairers	17.13	20.42	21.18	23.79	24.50
Construction trades, n.e.c.	9.67	10.45	12.00	13.51	15.34
Machine operators, assemblers, and inspectors	8.30	9.50	12.16	17.38	21.66
Transportation and material moving	10.50	11.85	14.08	17.75	20.50
Truck drivers	11.40	13.00	14.21	17.11	18.75
Industrial truck and tractor equipment operators	9.75	10.60	12.24	15.79	20.90
Handlers, equipment cleaners, helpers, and laborers	7.25	8.73	10.00	12.45	17.13
Groundskeepers and gardeners, except farm	8.70	9.75	10.00	11.00	12.05
Stock handlers and baggers	6.75	7.20	8.75	10.40	22.82
Machine feeders and offbearers	6.50	6.50	9.22	13.08	14.37
Laborers, except construction, n.e.c.	7.50	8.00	9.40	10.66	12.60
Service	5.40	7.50	9.27	13.34	22.99
Protective service	11.05	12.50	15.22	20.74	24.01
Supervisors, police and detectives	18.24	20.49	23.58	31.38	31.38
Police and detectives, public service	13.35	14.66	17.07	21.78	25.21
Correctional institution officers	11.54	11.75	12.85	14.01	15.23
Food service	2.18	4.50	7.25	8.60	10.00
Waiters, waitresses, and bartenders	2.13	2.13	2.28	2.75	7.00
Waiters and waitresses	2.13	2.13	2.28	2.38	7.21
Other food service	6.25	6.90	8.25	9.05	10.35
Cooks	7.00	8.00	8.50	9.40	10.35
Food preparation, n.e.c.	6.72	7.05	8.35	9.00	9.54
Health service	8.12	8.61	9.85	10.95	11.96
Health aides, except nursing	8.12	8.33	9.84	11.93	12.79
Nursing aides, orderlies and attendants	8.17	8.99	9.85	10.78	11.33
Cleaning and building service	7.00	7.75	8.51	9.46	11.12
Janitors and cleaners	6.60	7.90	8.57	9.32	10.50

Source: Selected Occupations from "Charlotte-Gastonia-Rock Hill, NC-SC National Compensation Survey June 2003," U.S. Department of Labor, Bureau of Labor Statistics, Bulletin 3120-53, March 2004, Table 6-1. (Available at: http://www.bls.gov/nes/ocs/compub.htm)

wise to avoid undertaking their own salary surveys or relying on surveys of local trade groups, such as the local hospital board. They could, of course, use the information reported by the Bureau of Labor Statistics in Table 11.8.)

2. Salary information provided by survey participants needs to be more than three months old.
3. For each job on which statistics are provided (e.g., x-ray technician, nurse), data need to be contributed by at least five employers.
4. Any information disseminated must be sufficiently aggregated so that recipients cannot attribute specific data to a particular employer.

Fortunately, these guidelines are consistent with sound practice in developing salary survey data for market comparisons.

International Compensation Comparisons

Substantial variation in compensation rates can be seen around the world; costs tend to be lower in the developing economies compared with those that are more developed. A number of European countries pay more than the United States. The U.S. Bureau of Labor Statistics has developed comparative measures of manufacturing compensation costs, allowing for international comparisons. These statistics provide a general indication of the relative total compensation cost in each country. Total compensation cost is made up of payment for time worked, holiday pay, and the cost of providing required benefits such as health insurance, pensions, workers' compensation, and unemployment insurance. To make a direct comparison, the United States is used as the benchmark country with defined costs at 100. The rest of the countries are reported relative to this standard. Note that fluctuations in the strength of each nation's currency against the U.S. dollar affect these data. The table illustrates how other countries compare with the United States in terms of manufacturing compensation costs.

In 2002 U.S. manufacturing costs averaged $21.37 per hour. Norway had the highest compensation costs, at 127 percent of the United States' level. Second was Denmark, followed by Germany. Taken together, the newly industrialized Asian economies came in at about one third of U.S. labor costs.

There are differences in compensation structures among the countries, such as variations in levels of paid leave and bonuses. For example, holiday pay and bonuses accounted for approximately 30 percent of total compensation costs in Japan, compared with some European countries, where it accounts for 15 to 20 percent of costs, and the United States, where it accounts for 6 percent. In Japan an annual bonus of three months' pay is typical, whereas in Europe an annual bonus of one to two months' pay is common.

Mexico is often seen as a low-wage country, and since passage of the North American Free Trade Agreement, many companies have tried to take advantage of this by opening facilities in Mexico. Some of them have found that actual wage costs are greater than anticipated. While the official minimum wage is low, very few people actually work for the minimum wage. In addition, there are legally required cash allowances: fifteen days' pay for a Christmas bonus (though most employers pay a full month), a vacation premium of 25 percent beyond regular pay, and required sharing of 10 percent of pretax profits. Overtime must be paid at twice the normal rate. A number of additional bonuses, such as fifteen to twenty days' pay as a reward for perfect attendance over one year, are not mandatory but are widely used and hence necessary to attract and keep good employees.

Hourly Compensation Costs for Production Workers in the Manufacturing Sector, 2002

Americas	
United States	100
Brazil	12
Canada	75
Mexico	12
Asia and Oceania	
Australia	72
Hong Kong	27
Japan	89
Korea	42
New Zealand	40
Singapore	34
Sri Lanka	2
Taiwan	27
Europe	
Austria	97
Belgium	107
Denmark	118
Finland	102
France	81
Germany	114
Ireland	73
Israel	51
Italy	71
Netherlands	102
Norway	127
Portugal	24
Spain	95
Switzerland	113
United Kingdom	84

Sources: Fay Hansen, "An Update on International Labor Costs," *Compensation and Benefits Review,* Nov/Dec 2000, pp. 14–19; Gillian Flynn, "HR in Mexico: What You Should Know," *Personnel Journal,* August 1994, pp. 34–44; "International Comparisons of Hourly Compensation Costs for Production Workers in Manufacturing, Revised Data for 2002," U.S. Department of Labor, Bureau of Labor Statistics, May 2004, http://www.bls.gov/fls/hcompreport.htm.

Pay-Level Policy

Once an organization has completed an internal job evaluation and obtained wage survey data, it needs to translate this information into pay rates for each class of job. This process involves interpreting survey results, merging job evaluation and survey data, and considering the organization's pay-level policy.

The first step in merging the internal and external data is a strategic decision on the organization's positioning in terms of the competition. The three fundamental options are to match, lead, or lag behind the market.

By setting its pay levels at the market rate, or **matching the competition,** an organization tries to keep its labor costs comparable with those of competitors. Such an approach tends to neutralize pay as a factor in attracting, retaining, and motivating employees while ensuring that labor costs are competitive.[30]

In adapting a **lead policy**—that is, paying a higher wage rate than its competitors—a firm hopes to attract and retain higher quality employees while maximizing satisfaction of its current employees. Firms with a lead policy want to be the preferred employer so that they can select the best applicants while making it costly for competitors to persuade current employees to leave.[31] Frequently, such organizations have labor costs that represent a small proportion of the cost of production or have higher levels of productivity—making such a policy affordable.

Some organizations follow a **lag approach,** setting their pay rates below those of their competitors. On the surface, it might seem that such a policy would inevitably lead to difficulties in attracting, motivating, and retaining qualified employees. Some companies, however, have other ways to attract applicants, such as employment security (as with government jobs), superior benefits (e.g., holidays, vacation time, tuition reimbursement), or an enjoyable environment (e.g., Disney World). Some organizations—because of the nature of the business (e.g., entertainment, airlines), social or business philosophy (e.g., Ben and Jerry's),[32] or excellent reputation (e.g., Harvard University)—will attract well-qualified applicants even at below-market wages. Still other organizations may adopt a lag approach because they simply cannot afford to pay competitive salaries.[33] Research has shown that pay policy decisions often involve a complex mixture of factors.[34]

Figure 11.5 diagrams how the three policies might be put into practice. The diagonal market line illustrates the gradual increase of market wage rates as different organizations implement changes at various times. At the beginning of the planning cycle (a year in this case), a firm with a lead policy sets its wage rates at the level that the market will reach only at the end of the year. A typical lag policy, by contrast, begins the year at a level equal to the market and is well below it by the end of the year. An organization with a match policy is actually paying wages equivalent to competition only at midyear. As can be seen, the match rate is above the market level at the start of the year and below it at the end.

Finally, an organization need not have one policy for all jobs. For example, an organization that can count on a steady supply of clerical and trade employees might adopt a policy of lagging behind the competition for these groups. However, to attract the top professional talent, the same firm might adopt a lead policy in compensation for these groups. What policy should Nanotech, Inc. adopt— lead, match, or lag? Should they have the same policy for all positions?

Because wages paid by competitors are constantly changing, survey results are inevitably out of date when they reach the organization. For example, a survey initiated in mid-2005 might be compiled and ready for distribution by the end of the year. An organization that intended to use these data to set pay for mid-2006 would need to

FIGURE 11.5

Pay Policies over Time: Lag, Match, and Lead Pay Structures

Source: Richard Henderson, *Compensation Management: Rewarding Performance,* 5th ed., Copyright © 1989, p. 477. Reprinted by permission of Prentice-Hall, Inc., Englewood Cliffs, N.J.

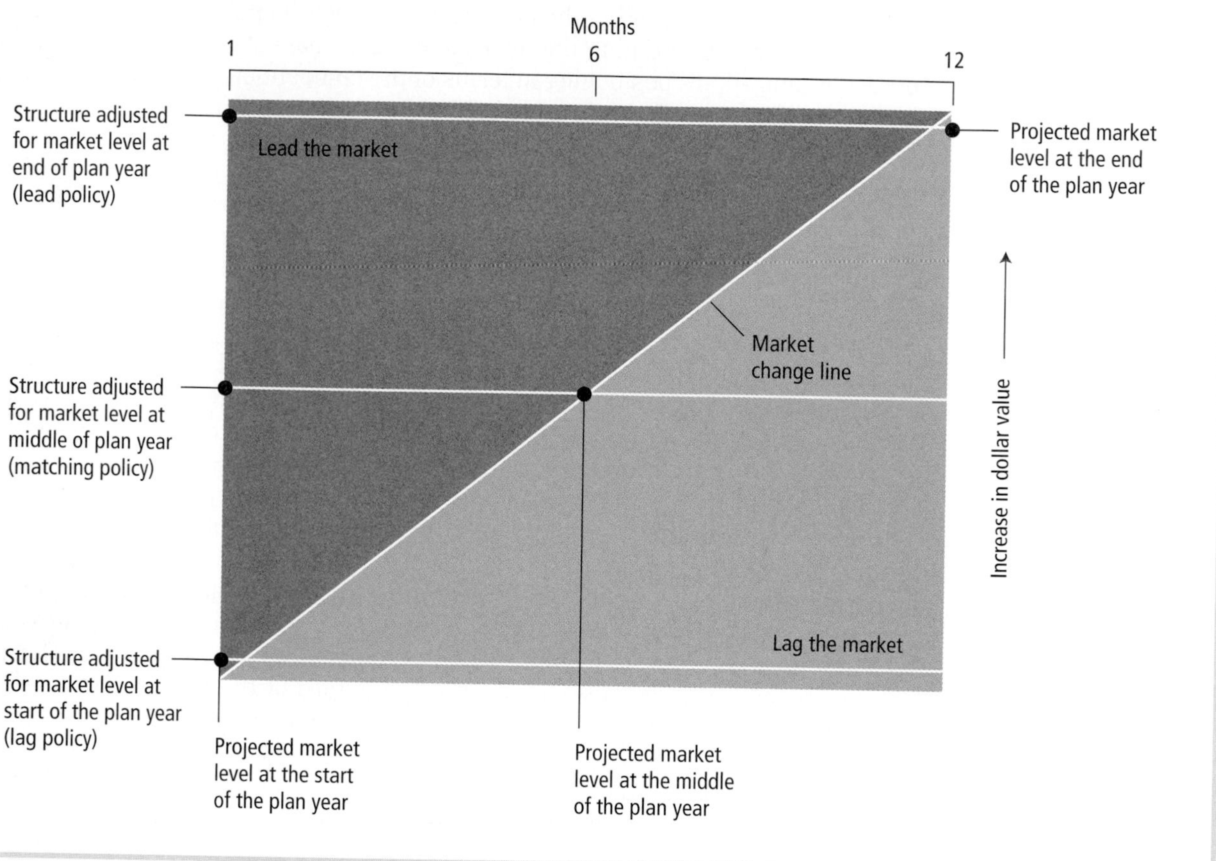

make adjustments to reflect changes between the time of data collection and the plan period (mid-2005 to mid-2006 in the example discussed). The adjustment is based on historical trends from previous years, economic forecasts (e.g., productivity trends, cost-of-living changes), and judgment as to any special circumstances. In the example, figures from mid-2005 will need to be projected twelve months ahead to obtain the market level as of mid-2006, the start of the 2006–07 plan. Assuming that inflation and other factors will increase the market wage level at an annual rate of 4.5 percent, survey data should be multiplied by 1.045 to obtain the market rates for July 1, 2006, the beginning of the 2006–07 plan year.

ESTABLISHING INDIVIDUAL EQUITY

As mentioned earlier, jobs evaluated as having nearly the same value are usually combined into a single wage grade. It would be cumbersome to have fifty different wage rates for fifty different job titles or a slightly higher rate for a job evaluated at

205 points versus one at 200 points. Thus wage grades are established (e.g., all jobs between 200 and 225 points would be a grade), and all jobs within the grade are paid identically. A single wage may be selected for each grade and paid to every person whose job falls in that grade. More commonly, however, a range of pay rates is set for each grade. When a range is set, the issue of individual equity becomes salient, and the organization must have a system for determining where in the range the compensation of each employee should be.

Designing Pay Ranges

The range associated with a pay grade sets the upper and lower bounds of possible compensation for individuals whose jobs fall in the grade. There is no optimal number of pay grades for a wage structure, although most organizations define ten to sixteen pay grades.[35]

Establishing Pay Ranges The first step is to define the pay policy line linking pay to job evaluation points. Think of a graph with wage grades along the horizontal axis and pay (dollars) along the vertical axis (see Figure 11.6). The policy line

FIGURE 11.6

Pay Ranges

Source: Reproduced from Marc J. Wallace Jr., and Charles H. Fay, *Compensation Theory and Practice,* 2nd ed. With the permission of South-Western College Publishing. Copyright © 1988 PWS-Kent Publishing Company. All rights reserved.

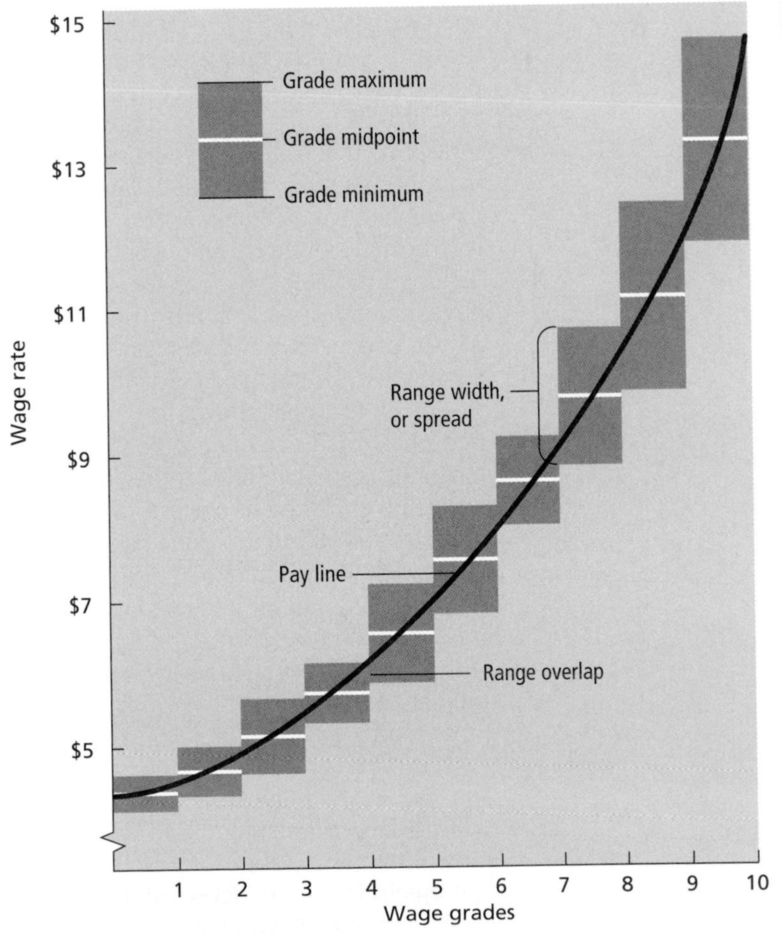

is based on salary survey data, appropriately adjusted and taking into consideration the firm's policy (lead, match, or lag). The points on the line will represent the midpoints of the **wage ranges,** which are calculated next.

Each grade has a minimum, a maximum, and a midpoint. The spread around the midpoint may vary, with 10 to 20 percent on either side being typical, as shown in Figure 11.6.[36] The percentage spread is frequently greater for higher level positions on the assumption that there is more leeway to make an outstanding or very poor contribution in these more important jobs.

It is important that adjacent grades overlap, as shown in Figure 11.6, because an experienced employee in a lower grade may make a greater contribution than a relatively new employee in the next higher grade. Well over half of a given pay range may overlap the adjacent pay grade.

Although each range has a maximum, the structure is dynamic. Ordinarily, the pay policy line and all the ranges are adjusted upward each year as inflationary and competitive pressures push wages upward. At some point, the top-performing employees will eventually reach the maximum within a range. They should then be considered for promotion to a higher grade. If the overlap between grades is too large, even a promotion may not bring a large enough salary increase to have incentive value.

Broadbanding The concept of **broadbanding** was developed in an effort to make job evaluation more compatible with the downsizing and delayering that characterize many restructured organizations. An increasing number of companies are using broadbands or are considering applying this concept as a way to remove the artificial barriers created by job grades.[37] An advantage of broadbanding is in the flexibility it provides and the signals it sends to employees. For example, an employee may be interested in a job but be reluctant to explore moving into it if it is not at a higher grade. With broadbanding, the position may be in the same band, so the employee can focus on the content of the job, its challenges, and its developmental opportunities rather than on its grade level. In this way the employee can learn new skills and better contribute to the team without the possible stigma of a demotion or reduction in pay.[38]

In the example shown in Figure 11.7, four wage grades have been combined into one broad grouping of jobs. In this way, career growth would be defined in terms of responsibilities rather than through upward advancement.[39] Individuals would be expected to perform several of the activities, previously defined as jobs, that now fall within the same band. Instead of the 25 percent (50 percent range) on either side of the midpoint defining the minimum and maximum of a range, the spread from minimum to maximum would be 110 percent.

Broadbanding is not right for all companies. Managers must be trained to deal with banding's broader salary ranges and fewer control points. Workers may resist the absence of frequent, if small, symbols of their increased value through movement to higher grades.[40]

Above- and Below-Range Employees When the wage structure is formed initially, it is not unusual to find employees who are currently being paid above the maximum for a range or below the minimum. Those below the minimum are "green-circled," and increased to be within the range. If for some reason the gap is large between the employee's current rate and the minimum rate of the range, this increase may be over a period of time rather than all at once.

FIGURE 11.7
Illustration of a Typical Broadband

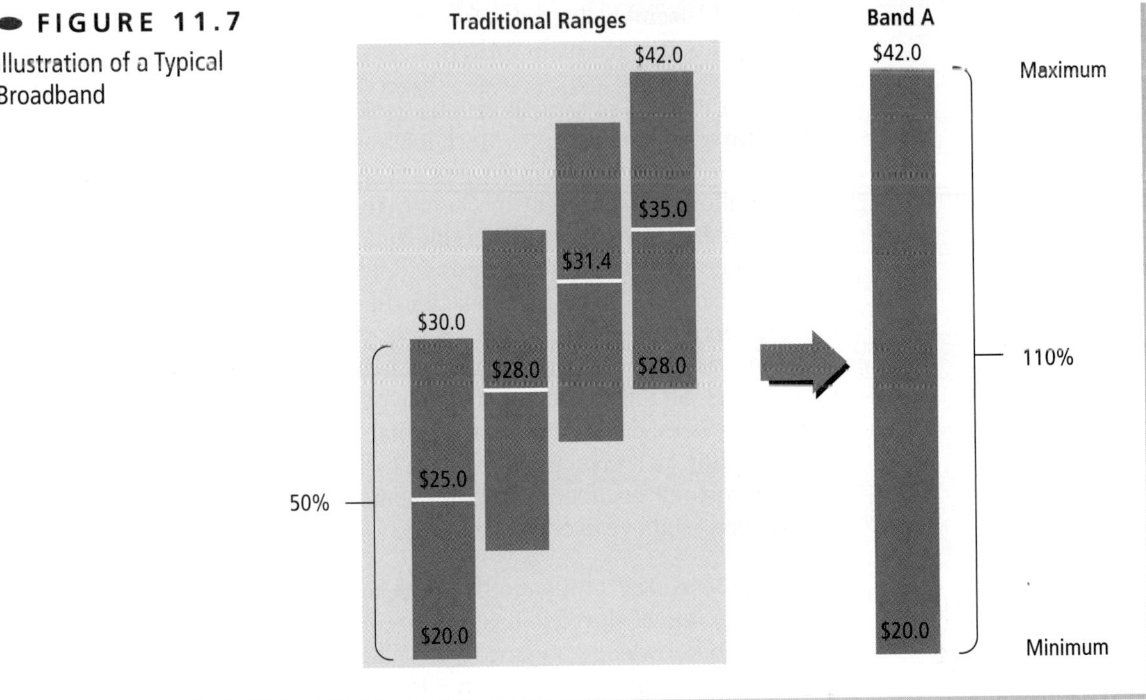

If employees earning more than the maximum qualify for promotion, they can be moved to a job in a higher range commensurate with their existing pay. If promotion is not possible, the employee is "red-circled"; that is, his or her pay is frozen at its present level until the range moves up, through annual increases, to include the individual. It is generally regarded as less than ideal to cut an employee's pay as a result of job evaluation. That said, cutting pay is not unheard of, although one needs to be aware of what such cuts are communicating to the employee. Ideally, no one's pay is cut as a result of job evaluation.

Setting Individual Pay

Individual equity requires that rewards to employees be allocated fairly across individuals performing the same job. The two commonly used approaches to determine how workers are placed and progress through the pay ranges are seniority and merit. A newer method bases increments on the number of skills mastered.

Seniority When based on seniority, pay increases depend solely on the employee's experience or length of service on the job. Individuals all start out with equal pay and then progress through steps with each year of service. In addition to the step increases, the entire range (i.e., the entry rate and each of the steps) is adjusted to reflect the results of salary surveys and economic trends.

The **seniority-based pay** system rewards a stable, experienced work force. Seniority systems are often used when employees are unionized, when employees do not accept or trust the concept of merit pay, when differences in performance are difficult to measure accurately, or when jobs call for very similar work performance or output. Assembly-line jobs, for example, typically require similar work performance and output from all workers.

Merit Pay Many organizations try to link compensation to actual job performance through **merit pay.**[41] Merit increases are given, usually on an annual basis, with better-performing employees receiving larger raises. In theory, merit increases allow management to use pay to motivate employees to higher levels of performance. However, considerable data suggest that merit pay may not be as desirable, as easy to implement, or as widely used as is commonly believed. The next chapter discusses in more detail the theory and practice of using incentives, including merit pay.

Many workers distrust merit reward systems because they do not feel that their pay is actually reflective of their performance level. After comparing notes with their peers, employees may feel that they have not been treated fairly, usually because they perceive their own performance as being relatively high. In one study across all occupational groups, more than 95 percent of employees rated themselves as above average.[42]

Skill-Based Pay Still another basis for establishing individual pay rates has to do with the knowledge one has mastered on the job.[43] **Skill-based pay** plans analyze the job knowledge an employee will need to progress. All employees begin at an entry-level rate. As they learn additional skills, and as the learning is verified through demonstration or tests, they qualify for increments in pay. Skill-based pay is especially compatible with broadbanding because employees can be rewarded for gaining additional skills within a broader array of job activities. Skill-based pay, along with the incentives it engenders for employees, is described further in the next chapter.

LEGAL REGULATION OF COMPENSATION SYSTEMS

The major factors influencing an organization's reward system include job content (assessed by job evaluation), market forces (e.g., supply of labor, competition for labor, prevailing wages, and employer's ability to pay), and the pay policy of the organization. Certain legal constraints also influence all compensation systems. In fact, the recent increase in government regulations has made legal constraints a major factor in planning and administering a compensation system.

Legal issues related to direct compensation (e.g., pay rates, hours, and so forth) are considered in this chapter. Legislation that affects indirect compensation (e.g., pensions, Social Security, and so on) is discussed in Chapter 13.

The Fair Labor Standards Act

The **Fair Labor Standards Act (FLSA)** of 1938 is the major law affecting direct compensation. Its provisions on the minimum wage, hours of work, and equal pay directly affect the design of compensation systems. Sections of the FLSA dealing with child labor and record-keeping requirements are also important but have fewer direct consequences and are not considered in this chapter.

Because the Constitution empowers Congress and the federal government to regulate interstate commerce, virtually all employers are covered by the FLSA. The act applies to all employers producing goods for interstate commerce or having employees who handle, sell, or otherwise work on such goods or materials. This means that any organization that uses a product produced in another state (e.g., a day-care facility using disposable diapers made in another state) is covered.

The terms "exempt" and "nonexempt" are crucial for understanding and complying with the FLSA. **Exempt employees,** also called "white-collar" employees, include executive, administrative, and professional employees who are exempt from the minimum wage, work hours, and overtime provisions of the FLSA. **Nonexempt employees,** also termed "blue-collar" employees, are subject to the provisions of the FLSA.

For more than sixty years the FLSA provided that to be exempt as an executive an employee must supervise two or more employees, have the authority to hire and fire, and otherwise exercise independent judgment. Administrators need not supervise other employees but do need to exercise independent judgment in carrying out top management policies. Professionals are exempt under the definition of the FLSA if they perform nonstandardized artistic or intellectual work of a varied nature that requires independent judgment.

Correctly determining the exempt or nonexempt status of a job is important, although it is not always easy.[44] For instance, we tend to think of accountants and engineers as professionals, but in some cases they are not professionals under the FLSA guidelines. A lower level accountant who applies accounting principles with little independent judgment or a newly hired engineer who does setup work for other engineers is not exempt. Under the law, their employer is liable for overtime pay for these individuals.

Things became more complicated in March 2003 when the Department of Labor proposed regulations that would overhaul the FLSA "white-collar" exemptions. These regulations, dubbed the "Fair Pay" initiative, became effective in August 2004 and were intended to streamline guidance for employers as to who is exempt.[45] The regulations include the following revisions:

1. A new minimum salary of $23,660 per year ($455 per week) to be defined as exempt regardless of duties.
2. A requirement that those in the "executive" exemption have the authority to hire, fire, and discipline their employees.
3. To qualify for the administrative exemption under the new rule, the employee must have the primary duty of performing office or nonmanual work directly related to the management or general business operations of the employer or the employer's customers, which must include the exercise of discretion and independent judgment with respect to matters of significance.[46]

Although the new regulations come with up-to-date examples and clearer guidance for employers, the regulations themselves are not that different. The goal of the new FLSA regulations is to "stem a tide of lawsuits against employers that deny workers overtime by classifying them as professionals."[47] It is too early to say whether this goal will be achieved.

Minimum Wage The **minimum wage** provisions of the FLSA establish the lowest pay an employer can offer an employee. The minimum wage was first set at $0.25 in 1938 to prevent the exploitation of workers and establish a "level playing field" for all employers. The law establishing the federal minimum wage called for a balancing act that is relived each time there is a discussion of increasing the minimum wage. The legislation stipulated that workers be paid at least enough to maintain a "minimum standard of living necessary for health, efficiency and general wellbeing." At the same time, though, it sought to do this "without substantially curtailing employment."[48]

After many years with the minimum wage set at $3.35 per hour, President George Bush (the 41st president) signed a bill raising the minimum wage to $3.80 in 1990 and then to $4.25 in 1991. In 1996 President Bill Clinton signed legislation authorizing two $0.45 increases, bringing the minimum wage to $5.15 per hour by 1997. Although the minimum wage increased $1.80 in nominal dollars during the 1990s, the increase (to 1999) was actually $0.27 when adjusted for inflation and more than 30 percent below what it was in 1978.[49] The economic growth and tight labor conditions of the 1990s thinned the ranks of minimum wage workers to only about 1 percent of hourly employees earning exactly $5.15 per hour, down from 9 percent in 1980.[50] At the same time, more than 11 million Americans still hover around the pay floor, earning from $5.15 to $6.64 an hour. Each year Congress or the president discusses proposed increases in the minimum wage, but there have been no increases since 1996.[51]

Despite the wide coverage of the minimum wage provisions, it does not apply to all nonexempt workers. Employers need not pay the minimum wage to apprentices or agricultural workers. If employees receive more than $30 per month in tips, employers may reduce the hourly wage below the minimum by a specified amount.

Hours of Work The overtime provisions of the FLSA require payment of one and one-half the regular hourly rate for work over forty hours per week. Union contracts may specify greater amounts (e.g., twice the regular hourly rate) or lower thresholds (e.g., overtime after thirty-five hours per week) that supersede the FLSA provisions.

Employers may pay overtime to exempt employees (e.g., executives and professionals) but are not obligated to do so. Salaried nonexempt employees are covered; to calculate appropriate overtime pay, their salary is converted into an hourly rate. Employers of nonexempt employees are required to keep thorough records of the hours worked to be sure that employees receive overtime payment when it is due.[52]

The Wage and Hour Division of the Department of Labor has responsibility for enforcing the FLSA. Most inspections are triggered by an employee complaint, but once the inspection begins, all records for all employees may be scrutinized and back pay for all affected workers can be ordered. In addition, the Wage and Hour Division targets certain "low-wage" industries for scrutiny, including restaurants, hotels/motels, garment manufacturing, health care, and agricultural processing. These industries have had repeated violations in the past. For example, in 2003 the Department of Labor recovered $39 million in back wages for more than 80,000 workers in "low-wage" industries.[53] Therefore, it is wise for employers to know the provisions of the FLSA and to follow them carefully.[54]

Equal Pay Act

Passed as an amendment to the FLSA, the Equal Pay Act (EPA) of 1963 requires an organization to offer equal pay for equal work, regardless of the sex of the employee. The Equal Pay Act defines equal work as (1) requiring equal skill, (2) requiring equal effort, (3) requiring equal responsibility, and (4) being performed under similar working conditions. Thus men and women performing the same job in the same location for the same employer must be offered the same pay, all other things being equal. The use of two job titles for what is essentially the same job as a pretext for paying one group less than the other is not permitted (e.g., calling men "office managers" and women "senior secretaries" when their duties are identical).

Equal pay is not required if differences in the average pay of men and women arise because of a seniority system, a merit system, or a system that measures earnings by quantity or quality of production. In other words, the customary approaches used to establish individual pay are acceptable even if they create unequal pay between men and women. Such discrepancies would arise, for example, if an organization based individual pay on seniority and most of its female employees were more recently hired.

The Equal Pay Act would seem to be a natural basis for pursuing the issue of comparable worth, a topic discussed later in this chapter. In fact, the rather strict requirements of identical skill, effort, responsibility, and working conditions have made it difficult to use this legislation as the basis for insisting on equal pay for work of comparable worth.

Other Laws Affecting Compensation

Other legal regulations that affect reward systems have to do with discrimination, wages paid by contractors who work for the U.S. government, and wage garnishment. In addition, some states have their own wage and hour laws.

Title VII of the Civil Rights Act prohibits discrimination on the basis of race, color, sex, national origin, and religion in all aspects of employment, including compensation. Thus it would be illegal to pay minority employees less than similarly qualified nonminority employees for doing the same job in the same location.

Several laws (Davis–Bacon Act of 1931, Walsh–Healy Public Contracts Act of 1936, and McNamara–O'Hara Service Contract Act of 1965) require that suppliers of goods or services to the federal government pay at least the "prevailing wage" to their employees. In practice, the prevailing wage usually has been set by the Department of Labor as the average wage of unionized workers in an area or industry. The intent of these laws is to prevent the government from buying "sweatshop" goods and thus indirectly exploiting workers. Some argue that this causes wages to be artificially raised and costs the government more than it would have to pay without this law.[55]

The Consumer Credit Protection Act of 1968 covers wage garnishment, the procedure by which a creditor can get a court order compelling the employer to pay over a portion of an indebted employee's earnings. The act limits the amount that can be ordered withheld from each paycheck and prohibits an employer from firing an employee for the first incident of garnishment.

A final law, the Sarbanes-Oxley Act of 2002, requires Chief Executive Officers (CEOs) and Chief Financial Officers (CFOs) of companies that restate their accounts because of "misconduct" to give up their bonus and stock option gains.[56] The act does not require that the Securities and Exchange Commission (SEC) connect the executives to the misdeeds.

The regulatory context has a powerful influence on organizational reward systems. The human resource manager must carefully obey the law in many aspects of establishing and administering a compensation system. Regulatory constraints are equally significant with respect to benefits, a topic covered in the next chapter.

ADMINISTERING COMPENSATION SYSTEMS

Even the best-designed compensation system will be ineffective if it does not gain employee acceptance, and this acceptance is often determined by the way the reward system is administered. This section discusses several of the major issues associated with the administration of compensation systems.

Pay Secrecy

The process by which a compensation system is formulated and administered is critical to the organization. One important administrative issue concerns the availability of compensation information to employees. Unfortunately, in most organizations, the tendency is toward secrecy. **Pay secrecy** is an administrative strategy that may increase the manageability of the system in that less information has to be communicated and fewer challenges to fairness may have to be heard.

Studies by Edward E. Lawler have shown that employees regularly misperceive the pay of others, including subordinates, peers, and superiors.[57] For example, superiors were perceived as receiving less than their actual salary, whereas subordinates and peers were thought to receive more than they actually did. Another study showed that managers make different pay allocation decisions when pay is secret than when it is open.[58] Secrecy makes it easier for allocators to use whatever criteria they wish because their decisions are less likely to be known by others.

Just how much and what types of information about pay should be provided to employees are questions that are troubling to compensation professionals. These are not simple questions to answer. Much has been written about the effects of secrecy on the behavior and attitudes of employees.

On one end of the spectrum is a policy of full, or open, disclosure; that is, information regarding individual salaries is available on request. When the government is the employer, full disclosure is the norm because pay policies and even individual salaries are a matter of public record. Similarly, most union contracts spell out wages on the basis of job title and time in grade.

Most other employees are provided with very little information about pay. In a survey conducted by the Bureau of National Affairs, only 18 percent of responding companies said that managers had knowledge of the salaries of their superiors or peers.[59] Open systems with regard to pay are the exception, not the rule. In fact, in some organizations, as a condition of employment, employees are asked to sign a contract stating that salary is to be regarded as confidential and that violation of this condition can lead to discharge.

The goals of achieving equity and, to the extent possible, participant satisfaction would seem to call for telling employees about pay policies and levels.[60] For merit systems to have a motivating effect, employees need to know how effort translates into rewards. Information about the maximum and the average raise should be made available each year. Each employee should be told what the midpoint is for his or her job, as well as the pay range. In addition, the organization should explain how it arrived at the pay structure. Allowing employees to see where their jobs are located in the wage structure should not create significant problems for an employer that has a well-designed job evaluation plan.

Employee Participation

People tend to be more committed to programs they had a hand in developing. When employees help create compensation plans, there is generally less resistance, and the plan is much more likely to be a successful motivator than a plan imposed by management.[61]

It is appropriate to involve employees in many phases of a reward system. For example, a wide variety of employees should serve on job evaluation committees. If a point plan is adopted, it is reasonable to involve employees in identifying the compensable factors to be used and the weight to be assigned to each factor. Employees are also likely to have good insight into which competitor firms should be included in a wage survey.

There are several mechanisms for employee involvement. At the broadest level, employees can be surveyed to learn their preferences. Employee task forces can help integrate these preferences into a system. Such groups are usually an excellent way to involve employees in the decisions associated with a reward system.

The decision to involve employees in designing or administering a compensation system should not be made without deliberation, however. This approach is unlikely to work well unless the organization has already established an overall philosophy of participative management, as well as a reasonable climate of organizational trust. Participation takes considerable time, so if time and trust are limited, a more traditional, top-down approach might be more appropriate.

Wage Compression

Wage compression, rated as the top compensation problem at the present time, results when wages for new hires are increasing faster than the wages of people already on the payroll.[62] As a result, the pay differentials between individuals become very small or nonexistent. For example, a business school may find that to be competitive it needs to offer inexperienced assistant professors $70,000 for nine months. At the same time, assistant professors with two or three years' experience are earning between $66,000 and $68,000, and several associate professors with as much as ten years' experience are earning only $77,000. Constrained by a limited budget, the dean chose to use the limited available funds primarily to recruit new faculty, who were getting attractive offers from other schools. This meant that the traditional wage differentials between ranks could not be maintained. The dean elected to create internal inequities in the interest of external competitiveness for new faculty.

Although wage compression often must be accepted in the short run, it can be extremely counterproductive if allowed to continue. In the business school example, senior faculty became dissatisfied and searched for new jobs at other universities. Because the best qualified could most easily secure new positions, the average quality of the school's remaining faculty was at risk.

Much of employers' resistance to increases in the minimum wage is not directly related to additional costs for entry-level jobs but to the threat of wage compression and the cost of preventing it. Similarly, managers frequently experience wage increases indirectly as a result of union negotiations. As wages of union members increase, the company raises salaries of lower- and middle-level managers to prevent wage compression.

Impact of Inflation

Even well-designed compensation systems can have major problems in inflationary or deflationary times. In the late 1970s many firms were limited to giving 10 percent merit raises to their best people even though the inflation rate was 13 to 14 percent. Employees felt that they were losing purchasing power. At a minimum, they hoped to keep even with inflation.

In the early 1980s firms began catching up, giving raises in the 12 and 13 percent range. Once inflation had been checked, salary increases soon fell back to 7 percent. In the 1990s and thus far in the twenty-first century, merit budgets have averaged 4 percent or less. Under these circumstances, it has been difficult to convince employees that current salary increase levels are sufficient when expectations had adjusted to higher levels.[63] To maximize the perception of fairness, it is essential to have good communication with employees about their compensation package and salary increases.

All-Salaried Work Force

As part of the move to increase employee participation at all organizational levels, many firms have moved to an all-salaried work force. All employees, even the blue-collar workers, receive the agreed-upon salary each pay period, and the size of their checks does not depend primarily on the number of hours worked. That is, employees are not docked for lateness or other absences. This policy is meant to eliminate the feeling of hourly employees that they are second-class citizens.

The employer remains responsible for enforcing the Fair Labor Standards Act, however, and from this perspective, nonexempt salaried employees are still paid by the hour. Employers must keep a record of hours worked (presumably by less obtrusive means than a time clock) and pay overtime to all nonexempt employees who work more than forty hours in any one week, whether or not they are otherwise treated as salaried employees by the employer.

Wage Concessions

It is not unusual to read about a strike resulting from an impasse in collective bargaining. Typically, the contract has expired, and the union and management cannot agree on wages. Perhaps the union is asking for a 14 percent increase over the three years of the contract period, but the final management offer is 10 percent. Difficult economic times bring a new twist to this scenario. Until recently it was almost inconceivable that a well-entrenched union would agree to concessions (or reductions) in wages and benefits, yet this is exactly what is happening. In the automobile, steel, and other manufacturing industries, less expensive foreign labor has forced American manufacturers to bring their costs in line. Wage concessions have been one part of the strategy. In other industries, such as transportation, deregulation opened routes and business to new competition. Low-cost, nonunionized airlines were flying many of the same routes, forcing the established unionized carriers to slash labor costs.[64]

One solution adopted by some companies and unions was the two-tier wage contract. In this type of agreement, current employees continue to receive their existing wage rates, but any new hires after a specified date are paid at a much lower rate. This has proven to be a shortsighted solution because it creates substantial internal inequity, and individuals hired at the lower rate do not feel fairly treated by either the union or the company. The problems intensify the longer the system is in effect, as the lower paid workers increase in number and in seniority.

THE ISSUE OF COMPARABLE WORTH

A policy of equal pay for equal work was mandated by the Equal Pay Act of 1963. The notion of comparable worth goes further, calling for equal pay for jobs of comparable work. **Comparable worth** is based on the idea that traditionally female-dominated jobs are underpaid relative to traditionally male-dominated jobs that require the same level of (although perhaps a different) skill and make an equally valuable contribution to the employer. At times, the ideological and political debate surrounding comparable worth has been fierce. This section examines the elements of this controversy.

The Earnings Gap

The comparable worth debate centers on what has come to be known as the **earnings gap.** Each year the Bureau of the Census reports on the difference between women's and men's median incomes. As shown in Table 11.9, women employed full time earned about $0.76 per hour for each dollar men earned in 2002.[65] Despite the gap between men and women, the 2002 figure is quite an improvement from 1979, when women earned $0.60 for each dollar men earned. Questions about the earnings gap include the following: (1) Does the earnings gap represent discrimination against women by a male-dominated economic system? (2) Does it reflect the voluntary choices women make regarding education and occupation, as filtered through the elements of supply and demand in the labor market? Although there is no complete answer to these questions, there are relevant data.[66]

There can be no doubt that women have made progress. Figure 11.8 shows that between 1964 and 1999 women's jobs doubled in nine of ten industry groups (every industry except nondurable manufacturing) whereas men's jobs doubled in only three of ten groups (services, retail trade, and finance). This indicates that opportunities for women have increased rather dramatically in the past four decades.

Even with the expanded opportunity for women, part of the reason for the wage gap is that women tend to hold different jobs from men, even within an occupational category. For instance, women are more likely to be nurses than physicians, both of which are part of the services industry, specifically professional health occupations. Table 11.10 shows that twenty occupations (of 427 census-defined occupations) account for almost 43 percent of the women employed full time. Further, the twenty occupations employing half of all working women are among the lowest paying occupations.[67] More recent reports reaffirm that men and women gravitate toward different kinds of jobs.[68] Further, jobs dominated by females

TABLE 11.9

Women's Earnings as a Percentage of Men's Earnings, 1979–2002

Year	Annual %
1979	59.7%
1980	60.2
1981	59.2
1982	61.7
1983	63.6
1984	63.7
1985	64.6
1986	64.3
1987	65.2
1988	66.0
1989	68.7
1990	71.6
1990	69.9
1991	69.9
1992	70.8
1993	71.5
1994	72.0
1995	71.4
1996	73.8
1997	74.2
1998	73.2
1999	72.2
2000	73.0
2001	76.0
2002	76.0

Source: U.S. Women's Bureau and the National Committee on Pay Equity. (Available at: http://infoplease.com/ipa/A0193820.html)

traditionally pay less because supply exceeds demand.[69] For example, more than 45 percent of today's women are in the service sector (all of the occupational categories from Table 11.10 plus many others), where wages are frequently below average.[70]

Women in their late twenties or early thirties tend to earn as much as men in the same occupation and with similar qualifications.[71] The discrepancy in earnings comes when women have children, for it is then that they cut back on work time and make different choices within career options. Overall, when occupation is included as a variable, up to 90 percent of the earnings gap between men and women can be explained.[72] This means that males and females in the same occupation with comparable seniority are closer in income, whether as word processors, assembly-line workers, or physicians. This does not mean that there are no differences within occupations. A report from the U.S. Census Bureau found a substantial gap in median earnings between men and women in the 35 to 54 age

FIGURE 11.8

Changes in Employment for Men and Women by Occupation: 1964–1999

Source: "Women's Jobs 1964–1999: More Than 30 Years of Progress," U.S. Department of Labor, Women's Bureau. (Available at: http://www.dol.gov/dol/wb/public/jobs6497.htm)

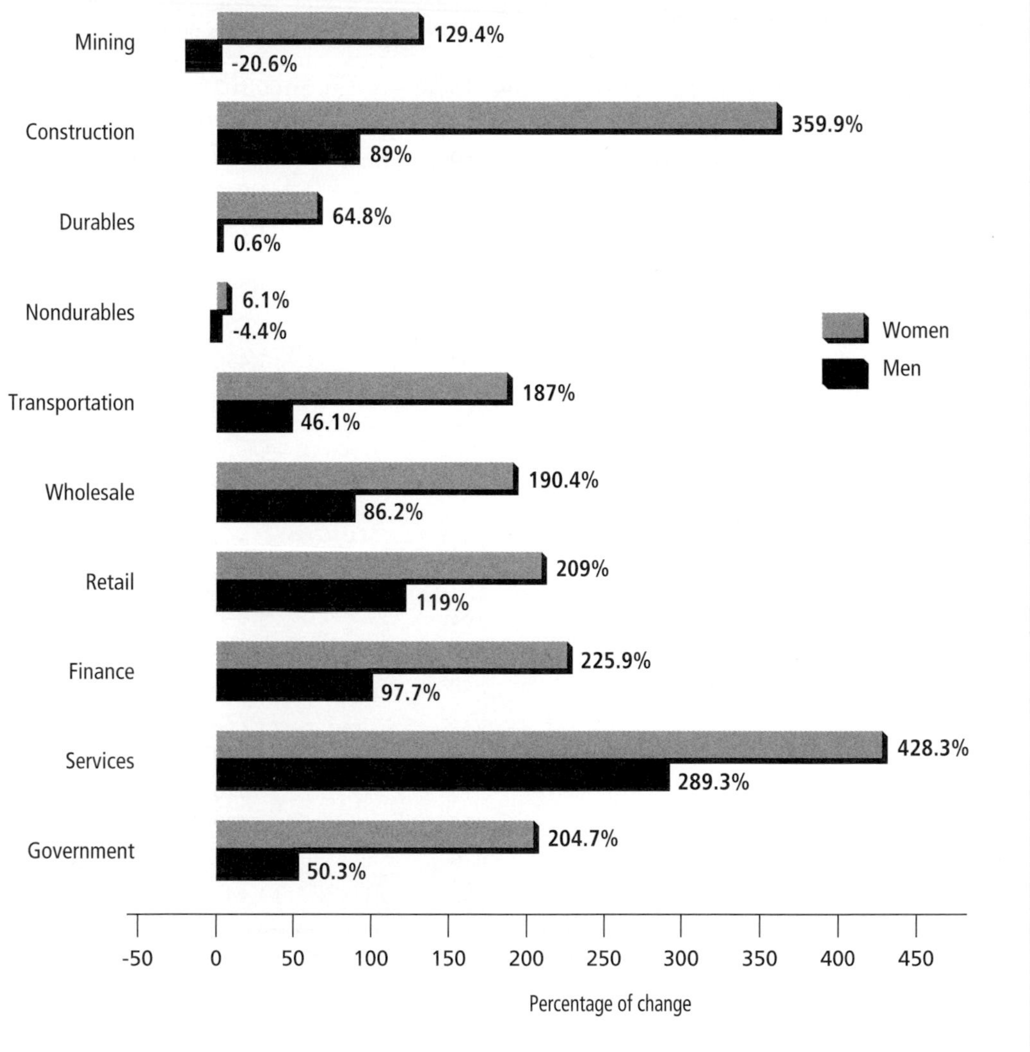

range that is unexplained after controlling for work experience, education, and occupation.[73] Just as there are differences in earnings among the twenty leading occupations of employed women (Table 11.10), there are differences within occupations, even when trying to control for experience and education. Many factors may influence occupational choices and selection of a particular job within that occupation. For example, one study found that regardless of field of occupation, women had different standards for fair pay than men and expected to earn less than men.[74]

Still another explanation could have to do with types of employers preferred by men and by women. It could be that more men than women are employed by organizations with greater ability to pay. For instance, female lawyers may tend to seek

TABLE 11.10

Twenty Leading Occupations of Employed Women in 2003

Occupations	Women Employed (in thousands)	Total Employed (men and women)	Percent Women	Women's Median Weekly Earnings
Total, sixteen years and over (full time)	44,076	100,302	43.9	$552
Secretaries and administrative assistants	2,692	2,794	96.3	531
Elementary and middle school teachers	1,780	2,208	80.6	757
Registered nurses	1,650	1,829	90.2	887
Nursing, psychiatric, and home health aides	1,144	1,285	89.0	372
Cashiers	1,040	1,378	75.5	315
Customer service representatives	1,038	1,503	69.1	503
First-line supervisors/managers of office and administrative support	984	1,450	67.9	609
First-line supervisors/managers of retail sales workers	938	2,259	41.5	496
Bookkeepers, accounting, and auditing clerks	894	978	91.4	512
Receptionists	831	892	93.2	446
Accountants and auditors	784	1,344	58.3	756
Retail salespersons	765	1,840	41.6	382
Maids and housekeeping cleaners	682	806	84.6	317
Secondary school teachers	540	1,009	53.5	824
Waitresses and waiters	528	775	68.1	318
Teacher assistants	527	580	90.9	344
Office clerks	511	610	83.8	502
Financial managers	491	952	51.6	823
Preschool and kindergarten teachers	476	484	98.3	493
Cooks	452	1,149	39.3	317

Source: "20 Leading Occupations of Employed Women Full-Time Wage and Salary Workers 2003 Annual Averages," Department of Labor, Women's Bureau. (Available at: http://www.dol.gov/dol/wb/public/wb/factsheets/20lead2003.htm)

jobs with public or legal aid organizations rather than with private law firms. Finally, differences reflect possible discriminatory promotion practices and related factors.

Two classic examples illustrate why the comparable worth debate has aroused such passion. In 1981 in the city of San Jose, California, positions of senior legal secretary (predominantly female) and senior carpenter (predominantly male) were both assigned 226 job evaluation points, yet the secretaries earned $665 per month, whereas the carpenters earned $1,040 per month. In other words, the senior secretaries' earnings were only 64 percent of the senior carpenters'—despite equivalent job evaluation points.[75] The same (1981) San Jose study found that librarians (a predominantly female job) and street sweeper operators (predominantly male) received equivalent pay of $750 per month, even though librarians were assigned many more job evaluation points than sweeper operators.

Legal and Judicial Developments

The Equal Pay Act has not been conducive to redressing issues of comparable worth. Instead, most court cases have relied on Title VII of the Civil Rights Act. Courts generally have held that Title VII incorporates the equal pay for equal work standard (skill, effort, responsibility), along with the four affirmative defenses for pay differentials (seniority, merit, quality or quantity of work, or any condition other than sex), and allows a broader inquiry into compensation practices of defendants. The argument has been that workers in predominantly female jobs are paid less than workers in predominantly male jobs and that this is discriminatory because the jobs, although different in content, are of comparable worth to the employer.

The early pay discrimination cases showed clearly that employers had to pay workers at the same rate if those jobs required substantially the same work performed, knowledge, and skill as jobs filled predominantly by men. In *Schultz v. Wheaton Glass Co.*,[76] men and women inspected and boxed empty bottles, yet men received 10 percent more for occasionally stacking boxes and performing other duties. The difference was ruled to be sex biased. In *Hodgson v. Brookhaven General Hospital*,[77] female aides claimed that their jobs were equal to those performed by more highly paid male orderlies. However, the hospital presented evidence that the duties performed by men were different, and the pay discrepancy was found to be legal.

Christensen v. State of Iowa was a major comparable worth case. Clerical workers (predominantly female) at the University of Northern Iowa argued that their jobs were equivalent to those of physical plant workers (predominantly male) in terms of job evaluation points, yet physical plant workers were paid at a higher rate. The university's defense was that conditions in the local labor market required it to pay physical plant workers more to be competitive. The court sided with the university, noting:

> The value of the job to the employer [job evaluation] represents but one factor affecting wages. Other factors may include the supply of workers willing to do the job. . . . We find nothing in the text and history of Title VII suggesting that Congress intended to abrogate the law of supply and demand or other economic principles that determine wages for various kinds of work. We do not interpret Title VII as requiring an employer to ignore the market in setting wage rates for genuinely different work classifications.[78]

The courts have consistently rejected comparable worth claims. The specific reasons for final rulings have varied but seem to reflect a sense that comparable worth is not a viable legal theory under Title VII.

Even though the courts have not been sympathetic to comparable worth, twenty states have specifically enacted legislation or adopted policies implementing comparable worth standards in the state civil service.[79] Minnesota's law is among the most stringent, requiring all public employers (state, county, school district, and so on) to establish equitable compensation relationships between female- and male-dominated jobs.[80]

Alternatives

One argument against comparable worth is that it would be a threat to the labor-market process of establishing wages based on supply and demand. Many contend that market rates accurately reflect job worth.[81] Market forces create many kinds of pay differences, not just between men and women. For example, college teachers in the liberal arts are paid less than engineering faculty, even though both jobs require similar skill, effort, and responsibility. The market forces that affect the two groups are quite different. Universities are locked in fairly high-level competition with private-sector firms to attract doctoral engineers to join their faculties, whereas competition for doctoral philosophers is far less acute, primarily because there are fewer nonacademic opportunities.

Further, it would be financially and motivationally ineffective for a university to equalize salaries of the engineering and liberal arts faculty. Running counter to market trends would create its own set of perceived inequities. For example, chemical engineering faculty members would see that liberal arts faculty members were being given an above-market premium while they were not. As a result, the engineers would become more likely to seek higher paying industry positions, whereas liberal arts faculty members may not have such opportunities. In turn, academic institutions would need to raise salaries of chemical engineers to attract faculty, and the cycle would continue.

Ultimately, no job or group of jobs has an intrinsic economic worth. In the energy boom of the mid-1980s, one oil company found that accountants, attorneys, and petroleum engineers were similar in terms of job complexity, education required, and other job evaluation factors. However, the company found that it could hire all the accountants and attorneys it wanted for $22,000 to $24,000 a year but could not hire a petroleum engineer for less than $32,000. A few years later, when the energy slump hit, thousands of petroleum engineers were out of work. The company could then hire engineers for less than accountants.

Prospects for the Future

We still have not explained why jobs held predominantly by women, almost without exception, are paid less than those held predominantly by men. Are women's jobs fairly valued using existing procedures? Even though the courts and the federal legislation process have not implemented the notion of comparable worth, a number of states have proceeded in that direction.

The most aggressive approach has been in the province of Ontario, Canada. The Pay Equity Act of 1987, passed by the Ontario Legislative Assembly, was designed to redress systemic gender discrimination in compensation for female jobs.[82] The law covers every company with more than ten employees. Most organizations, especially larger organizations, re-evaluated jobs, using the point method or a computer-based evaluation procedure, to bring salaries of those in predominantly female jobs to the level of those males in equivalent jobs. The following observations were made in a follow-up survey of twenty-seven Toronto private-sector employers with a combined total of more than 45,000 employees:

1. Pay equity did not have a pronounced effect on the compensation of females. Rather the effect was modest both with respect to the proportion of females receiving adjustments and the size of the average adjustment.
2. A large majority of the firms surveyed (81 percent) reported no important effects on productivity, morale, turnover, or job satisfaction.
3. Many firms (44 percent) had major difficulties with or complaints about the job evaluation process. It was difficult to separate the person from the job in

that the person doing the job evaluation would tend to overvalue a job if he or she thought the employee was a good performer and vice-versa if the employee was a poor performer.[83]

Comparable worth has been the subject of several legislative proposals at the federal level. The "Paycheck Fairness Act," proposed as an amendment to the FLSA and introduced in 2001 and 2003 but not passed by Congress, encourages employers to develop comparable worth pay systems as a means of raising women's wages. Specifically, the bill would allow the U.S. Secretary of Labor to establish voluntary job evaluation guidelines. Employers would be encouraged to compare the wages paid to similarly rated jobs and identify pay disparities between those occupations dominated by women and those dominated by men.[84]

The experience of the U.S. public sector in twenty states, along with the results in Ontario, suggests that comparable worth may yet become a significant issue. As a result, many major organizations are quietly working to reduce the gap between the pay of men and women.[85]

Summary of Key Points

Compensation is an important human resource function. Pay issues are of concern to managers because of the high cost of labor to the company. Managers are also concerned about developing pay policies and methods that will help them attract, retain, and motivate employees.

The main problems in designing a direct compensation system revolve around internal, external, and individual equity. Internal equity is based on paying jobs of equal value the same amount and paying jobs of different value an acceptable set of differentials. Internal equity is established through job evaluation.

Four general approaches to job evaluation have been discussed. The two nonquantitative methods that evaluate jobs as a whole are job ranking and job classification. The other two job evaluation methods break jobs down into compensable factors to evaluate their worth. These methods are the point and factor-comparison methods. The Hay plan and computerized job evaluation procedures are variations of the point method. Job evaluation results in a wage structure or hierarchy of jobs.

The next step is to price the wage structure, being aware of external equity, or how the organization's wage rates compare with those of other employers in the labor market. Wage surveys are used to find out what other employers are paying for various jobs and to set equitable midpoints and ranges for each wage grade.

The final equity concern centers on setting the pay of individuals within a wage grade. Typical bases for this decision include seniority, merit, and skill. Merit pay systems have the potential to motivate high performance, but they are difficult to administer in a way that employees perceive as fair.

There are numerous legal constraints on compensation practices. The most important of these concern minimum wage and overtime pay and are found in the Fair Labor Standards Act and its many amendments. Additional issues in compensation include the secrecy or openness of pay systems, employee involvement in compensation decisions, and the concept of comparable worth.

The Manager's Vocabulary

broadbanding
comparable worth
compensable factors
earnings gap
equity theory
exempt employees
external equity
factor-comparison method
Fair Labor Standards Act (FLSA)
Hay plan
individual equity
internal equity

job grading (or job classification)
job ranking
lag approach
lead policy
matching the competition
merit pay
minimum wage
nonexempt employees
pay secrecy
point method
pricing the wage structure
ranking to market
seniority-based pay
skill-based pay
total compensation
wage ranges

Questions for Discussion

1. Identify at least four reasons why designing and implementing reward systems constitute one of the most complex HRM activities.
2. What is total compensation, and what are its components?
3. What does equity theory say about the way individuals evaluate and respond to their pay level?
4. What are the three elements of compensation equity? Why is each important?
5. What are the purposes of job evaluation? Why do organizations use job evaluation?
6. What are the major methods of job evaluation? Which is the most popular? Explain how each works.
7. For what types of jobs would the Hay method of job evaluation most likely be used?
8. Recommend a job evaluation system for a small family-owned business with six job titles and thirty incumbents. Recommend a system for an oil refinery with 800 employees in managerial, technical, and blue-collar jobs. Why do your recommendations differ?
9. Why do some believe job evaluation is not necessary, and even counterproductive, to the operation of a modern organization?
10. How would you go about designing a survey for setting the pay of trade employees (e.g., plumbers, electricians, and welders) on your campus?
11. How would you go about designing a survey for setting the pay of faculty members on your campus? In what ways would the survey for faculty members differ from that for trade employees?
12. Define the term "pay-level policy," and discuss the three types of policies. Under what circumstances would each pay-level policy be used?
13. Which pay policy for trade employees would you recommend to your university? What circumstances faced by your university influenced your recommendation?
14. Identify three major reasons employees doing the same job in an organization might receive different compensation.
15. What is the major purpose of the Equal Pay Act? What does it require of employers?
16. What are the advantages and disadvantages of a policy of pay openness versus pay secrecy?
17. What is wage compression? How does wage compression relate to the impact of inflation?
18. Why might two people disagree about whether or not a given pay system is fair? What are three factors on which distributive justice can be based?
19. What is meant by comparable worth, and how does this issue affect the design of a compensation system?
20. To what extent are there differences in the level of pay of men and women? Identify four possible reasons for these differences.

Case 11.1
A Dilemma for Magnolia State Bank

Magnolia State Bank, serving a small community, has successfully bid to take over the insolvent City Bank and Trust in a large city fifty miles away. The president of Magnolia State is anxious to examine the comparability of the wage plan of the newly acquired branch with that of the Magnolia headquarters location.

Tellers and clerks, the majority of the work force at Magnolia State Bank, receive a starting wage of $375 a week ($19,500 per year), which can increase to $425 ($22,100 per year) with experience. The cost of living in Magnolia is low, and Magnolia State Bank stands virtually alone as a prestigious employer with good working conditions. In fact, the low-wage structure at Magnolia State Bank is part of the competitive strategy that has allowed the bank to maintain its position as the sole bank in the community.

City Bank and Trust is one of many banks in the large, nearby city. The cost of living is higher, and numerous reputable employers are competing for available talent. As a result, City Bank and Trust has found that it must start clerks and tellers at $500 ($26,000), with ranges up to $575 ($29,900), to attract and retain employees with needed skills.

1. Could Magnolia State Bank justify continuing the approximate 35 percent wage differences that exist between Magnolia and the newly acquired branch?
2. If yes, how would you, as president of Magnolia State Bank, explain the differences to employees in Magnolia? Given what you know about equity theory, how would employees be likely to respond? How would you address employee concerns?
3. If no, how would you proceed to merge the systems? What effect would wage reductions have on attracting and retaining employees at the city branch? What effect would wage increases have on the competitive position of the bank in Magnolia?

Case 11.2
The Case of Frontier Steel

Marvin Smith took pride in the company he founded, Frontier Steel, a small steel fabricator in the St. Louis area. He developed the company to its current 125 employees and considered each employee as a friend. In the early 1980s he decided that having some employees paid by the hour and others as salaried employees created an unnecessary division within his "family." As a result, he sought help from a consultant and followed the recommendation to create an all-salaried work force at Frontier Steel. The time clock used by hourly employees was removed, and all employees were paid a fixed monthly salary.

Recently, Mary Jones, a long-time employee, was dismissed as a result of differences with her supervisor. Smith was surprised to learn that Jones had filed a federal wage-and-hour claim seeking back pay for the overtime she had worked over a five-year period. More specifically, approximately five years before Jones was dismissed, she asked and was granted permission to arrive at work thirty minutes early every day so that she could ride to the plant with her husband. Jones was now claiming that these approximately 600 extra hours worked over the five years were overtime, a potential cost of $7,200. More troubling to Smith was the fact that many employees had been given permission to vary their schedules in the same way that Jones had done.

1. What are the rules governing an all-salaried work force?
2. Would Frontier Steel be liable for back overtime pay for all employees who worked extra hours? If yes, why? If no, what would determine liability?
3. What should Frontier Steel have done to avoid the type of claim Mary Jones filed?

Source: Adapted from Kent Banning, "Know the Rules on Pay and Hours." Reprinted by permission, *Nation's Business*, April 1991. Copyright 1991, U.S. Chamber of Commerce.

Exercise 11.1
Class Debate: The Earnings Gap between Men and Women

One (or more) class meetings before this debate, divide the students into groups of six or eight each. Within each group, form two teams: one to speak "for" (affirmative) and the other "against" (negative) the proposition below. Each team should prepare an opening statement, arguments for their position, rebuttals to likely points from the other side, and a closing statement. In addition, a group of three students should be selected to serve as judges. The judges should study the issues but instead of debating would evaluate the quality of the arguments "for" and "against" the proposition by the debaters.

Proposition: The difference in men's and women's annual earnings (see Table 11.9) is primarily the result of discrimination against women.

Debate Format

1. Affirmative: Opening argument and facts to support argument. (3 minutes)
   2 minutes silence
2. Negative: Opening argument, facts to support argument, and identify errors in affirmative's argument. (3 minutes)
   2 minutes silence
3. Affirmative: Respond to criticisms of negative, identify errors in logic or facts of negative team, return to original argument, and show how it is still correct. (1 minute)
   2 minutes silence
4. Negative: Respond to criticisms of affirmative speaker, identify errors in logic or facts of affirmative team, return to original argument, and show how it is still correct. (1 minute)
   1 minute silence
5. Affirmative: Closing argument mentioning strongest points along with major weaknesses in negative argument. (1 minute)
   1 minute silence
6. Negative: Closing argument mentioning strongest points along with major weaknesses in affirmative argument. (1 minute)
   3 minutes silence
7. Judges: Identify which facts are unsupported by the evidence presented (or by evidence independently researched by the judge) along with conclusions not logically supported. (3 minutes)

Resources It is suggested that class members look for sources using the following search terms: (a) pay equity; (b) comparable worth; and (c) earnings gap:

- Google.com or some other search engine
- Library databases such as Ebsco or ABInform

Other resources include:

Daniel H. Weinberg, "Evidence from Census 2000 about Earnings by Detailed Occupation for Men and Women," U.S. Census Bureau, May 2004. (Available at: http://www.census.gov/prod/2004pubs/censr-15.pdf)

June Ellenoff O'Neill, "Comparable Worth," The Concise Encyclopedia of Economics. (Available at: http://www.econlib.org/library/Enc/ComparableWorth.html)

Exercise 11.2
Standard-of-Living Adjustment

Your company is transferring an employee from Atlanta, Georgia, to open a new office in Los Angeles, California. The employee owns a home in Atlanta, is currently making $55,000 in Atlanta, and is concerned about how far that salary will go in Los Angeles. What income will the employee need in Los Angeles to own a home and have an income equivalent to the current Atlanta income? To answer this question, proceed as follows:

1. Locate the Web site http://www.homefair.com/.
2. On the tools bar, click the "salary calculator."
3. On the state screen, enter the respective states of Georgia and California. Then click "show cities."
4. On the cities screen, enter the salary, $55,000, and the respective cities, Atlanta and Los Angeles. For housing preference, select "own."
5. At the bottom of the cities screen, click "calculate" and note the Los Angeles income needed for a standard of living equivalent to the standard of living in Atlanta.

Source: Adapted from Georganna Hall and Gemmy Allen, *The Internet Guide for Human Resources* (Cincinnati, Ohio: South-Western College Publishing, 1997).

Exercise 11.3
External Equity

Your instructor will provide you with average weekly earnings for two positions at your college:

- Entry-level secretary
- Entry-level computer systems analyst

Using the "Wages, Earnings, & Benefits" section of the Web site http://stats.bls.gov, answer the following questions:

1. Using the geographic areas where your campus is located, how do the earnings for these two entry-level positions compare with the region?
2. How do the entry-level earnings for these two positions compare with the U.S. average?

Notes and References

1. Greg Cornish and Garry Adams, "Trends in Remuneration: The Concept of Total Quality Pay," *Asia Pacific Human Resources,* Vol. 31, 1993, pp. 75–86.
2. Elizabeth J. Hawk, "Culture and Rewards: A Balancing Act," *Personnel Journal,* April 1995, p. 37.
3. Edward E. Lawler, "The Design of Effective Reward Systems," in *Handbook of Organizational Behavior,* ed. J. W. Lorsch (Englewood Cliffs, N.J.: Prentice-Hall, 1987), p. 255.
4. F. A. Heller and L. Porter, "Perceptions of Managerial Needs and Skills in Two National Samples," *Occupational Psychology,* Vol. 40, 1966, pp. 1–13.
5. "The High Price of Overtime," *Los Angeles Times,* January 16, 1990, pp. A1, A20–A21.
6. Douglas Lavin and Gabriella Stern, "GM-UAW End 3-Day Strike at Parts Plant," *Wall Street Journal,* January 23, 1995, p. A2; and Sunil Babbar and David J. Aspelin, "The Overtime Rebellion: Symptom of a Bigger Problem?" *Academy of Management Executive,* Vol. 12, 1998, pp. 68–76. Note: Rebellion against overtime has been a phenomenon of better economic times. With high unemployment most workers are more concerned about a good paying job rather than some of the requirements of the job.
7. John Marks, "Time Out," *U.S. News & World Report,* December 11, 1995, pp. 85–96.
8. J. Stacy Adams, "Toward an Understanding of Inequity," *Journal of Abnormal and Social Psychology,* October 1963, pp. 422–436.
9. Jerald Greenberg, "Employee Theft as a Reaction to Underpayment Inequity: The Hidden Cost of Pay Cuts," *Journal of Applied Psychology,* Vol. 75, 1990, pp. 561–568.
10. Edward E. Lawler, *Motivation in Work Organizations* (Pacific Grove, Calif.: Brooks/Cole, 1973).
11. Edward E. Lawler, *Strategic Pay* (San Francisco: Jossey-Bass, 1990).
12. "Majority of Workers Are Dissatisfied with Pay," *HR Magazine,* June 2001, pp. 35, 37.
13. Robert W. Rice, Suzanne M. Phillips, and Dean B. McFarlin, "Multiple Discrepancies and Pay Satisfaction," *Journal of Applied Psychology,* Vol. 75, 1990, pp. 386–393.
14. Bureau of National Affairs, *Wage and Salary Administration* (Washington, D.C.: U.S. Government Printing Office, 1990), p. 6.
15. L. Dyer, D. P. Schwab, and R. D. Theriault, "Managerial Perceptions Regarding Salary Increase Criteria," *Personnel Psychology,* Vol. 29, 1976, pp. 233–242.
16. Robert B. Pursell, "R&D Job Evaluation and Compensation," *Compensation Review,* Vol. 2, 1972, pp. 21–31; and T. Atchinson and W. French, "Pay Systems for Scientists and Engineers," *Industrial Relations,* Vol. 7, 1967, pp. 44–56.
17. Pursell, "R&D Job Evaluation and Compensation."
18. Edward N. Hay and Dale Purves, "The Profile Method of High Level Job Evaluation," *Personnel,* September 1951, pp. 162–170.
19. Hewitt Associates, *Total Compensation Data Base CompBook 1989–1990* (Lincolnshire, Ill.: Author, 1990).
20. Donald P. Schwab, "Job Evaluation and Pay Setting: Concepts and Practices," in *Comparable Worth: Issues and Alternatives,* ed. E. Robert

Livemash (Washington, D.C.: Equal Employment Advisory Council, 1980).
21. N. Fredric Crandall, "Computerizing Job Evaluation for Greater Efficiency and Effectiveness," *Topics in Total Compensation,* Vol. 3, 1989, pp. 241–250.
22. Denise Barry and Kara McLaughlin, "A S.M.A.R.T. Method for Comp Analysis," *HR Magazine,* May 1996, pp. 80–83.
23. Lawler, *Strategic Pay.*
24. Jay R. Schuster and Patricia K. Zingheim, *The New Pay: Linking Employee and Organizational Performance* (Lexington, Mass.: Lexington Books, 1992).
25. Ibid.
26. Emily Pavlovic, "Choosing the Best Salary Surveys," *HR Magazine,* April 1994, pp. 44–48.
27. "How Reliable Are Online Salary Data?" *HR Focus,* Vol. 78 (10), October 2001, pp. 5–6.
28. Alison Stein Wellner, "Salaries in Site," *HR Magazine,* May 2001, pp. 89–96.
29. Anthony J. Dennis, "Avoiding the Antitrust Traps," *HR Focus,* September 1995, p. 11.
30. Lester C. Thurow, *Generating Inequity: Mechanisms of Distribution in the U.S. Economy* (New York: Basic Books, 1975); Caroline L. Weber and Sara L. Rynes, "Effects of Compensation Strategy on Job Pay Decisions," *Academy of Management Journal,* Vol. 34, 1991, pp. 86–109; and Brian S. Klass and John A. McClendon, "To Lead, Lag, or Match: Estimating the Financial Impact of Pay Level Policies," *Personnel Psychology,* Vol. 46, 1996, pp. 121–141.
31. Daniel J. B. Mitchell, "How to Find Wage Spillovers (Where None Exist)," *Industrial Relations,* Fall 1982, pp. 392–398; and H. Gregg Lewis, "Union Relative Wage Effects: A Survey of Macro Estimates," *Journal of Labor Economics,* January 1983, pp. 1–27.
32. See http://www.benjerry.com.
33. Thomas A. Mahoney, *Compensation and Reward Perspectives* (Homewood, Ill.: Irwin, 1979).
34. Chockalingam Viswesvaran and Murray R. Barrick, "Decision-Making Effects on Compensation Surveys: Implications for Market Wages," *Journal of Applied Psychology,* Vol. 77, 1992, pp. 588–597.
35. Kenneth S. Law and James R. Carlopio, "Two Statistical Aids for Determining the Optimal Number and Width of Pay Grades," *Asia Pacific Human Resources,* Vol. 30, 1992, pp. 60–71.
36. Ibid.
37. Larry Reissman, "Nine Common Myths about Broadbands," *HR Magazine,* Vol. 40 (8), 1995, pp. 79–86.
38. Peter V. LeBlanc and Michael McInerney, "Need a Change? Jump on the Banding Wagon," *Personnel Journal,* January 1994, pp. 72–78.
39. Frank H. Wagner, "Broadbanding in Practice: Hard Facts and Real Data," *Journal of Compensation and Benefits,* Vol. 10, July–August 1994, pp. 27–34.
40. Karen Jacobs, "A New Approach to Pay Scales Gives Employers Flexibility," *Wall Street Journal,* April 10, 1997, p. A10.
41. W. A. Evans, "Pay for Performance: Fact or Fable," *Personnel Journal,* September 1970, pp. 726–729.
42. Herbert H. Meyer, "The Pay-for-Performance Dilemma," *Organizational Dynamics,* Winter 1975, pp. 71–78.
43. H. Tosi and L. Tosi, "What Managers Need to Know about Knowledge-Based Pay," *Organizational Dynamics,* Vol. 14 (3), 1986, pp. 52–64.
44. Michelle Conlin, "Revenge of the 'Managers,'" *Business Week,* March 12, 2001, pp. 60–61.
45. DOL's FairPay Overtime Initiative. (Available at: http://www.dol.gov/esa/regs/compliance/whd/fairpay/main.htm)
46. Ibid.
47. Aaron Bernstein, "Too Stingy with the Overtime," *Business Week,* December 22, 2003. (Available at: http://www.businessweek.com/@@6GjJcYYQTHTAsQYA/magazine/content/03_51/b3863112.htm); Gillian Flynn, "Overtime Lawsuits: Are You at Risk?" *Workforce,* October 2001, pp. 36–42.
48. Rick Wartzman, "Devalued: How Minimum Wage Lost Its Status as a Tool of Social Progress," *Wall Street Journal,* July 19, 2001, pp. A1, A10–A11.
49. "Minimum Wage Legislation & Living Wage Campaigns." (Available at: http://www.financeprojectinfo.org/mww/minimum.asp)
50. Wartzman, "Devalued."
51. Richard S. Dunham, "The GOP Squabbles, and Business Suffers," *Business Week,* March 2, 1998, pp. 38–39; and Wartzman, "Devalued."
52. Gillian Flynn, "Overtime Compensation Isn't as Simple as It Seems," *Personnel Journal,* December 1995, p. 104.
53. "DOL WHD: 2003 Statistics Fact Sheet." (Available at: http://www.dol.gov/esa/whd/statistics/200318.htm)
54. Margaret M. Clark, "Employer, Audit Thyself," *HR Magazine,* February 2003, pp. 65–71.

55. Marc J. Wallace Jr., and Charles H. Fay, *Compensation Theory and Practice* (Boston: PWS Kent, 1988), pp. 136–138.
56. Paula Dwyer, "Making Execs Give Back the Cash," *Business Week,* August 26, 2002. (Available at: http://www.businessweek.com/@@a2*x14YQWXTAsQYA/magazine/content/02_34/b3796038.htm)
57. Edward E. Lawler, "Managers' Perception of Their Subordinates' Pay and of Their Superiors' Pay," *Personnel Psychology,* Vol. 18, 1965, pp. 413–422.
58. L. H. Kidder, G. Bellettirie, and E. S. Cohn, "Secret Ambitions and Public Performances," *Journal of Experimental Social Psychology,* Vol. 13, 1977, pp. 70–80; and Kathryn M. Bartol and David C. Martin, "Effects of Dependence, Dependency Threats, and Pay Secrecy on Managerial Pay Allocations," *Journal of Applied Psychology,* Vol. 74, 1989, pp. 105–113.
59. Bureau of National Affairs, *Wage and Salary Administration* (Washington, D.C.: U.S. Government Printing Office, 1990), p. 6.
60. Lin Grensing-Pophal, "Communication Pays Off," *HR Magazine,* May 2003, pp. 77–82.
61. E. E. Lawler III and J. R. Hackman, "The Impact of Employee Participation in the Development of Pay Incentive Plans: A Field Experiment," *Journal of Applied Psychology,* Vol. 53, 1969, pp. 467–471.
62. Thomas J. Bergmann, Frederick S. Hills, and Laurel Priefert, "Pay Compression: Causes, Results, and Possible Solutions," *Compensation Review,* Vol. 15 (2), 1983, pp. 17–26; "How to Handle Today's Pay Challenges," *HR Focus,* Vol. 79 (7), July 2002, pp. 3–5.
63. Labor Letter, "A Special Report on People and Their Jobs in Offices, Fields, and Factories: Top Officers' Pay Slowed in 1982, But Fringes Abound," *Wall Street Journal,* April 26, 1983, p. 1.
64. Micheline Maynard, "For Airlines, a Long Argumentative Summer," *New York Times,* June 30, 2004. (Available at: http://nytimes.com/2004/06/30/business/30labor.html); and "Delta Seeking $1B from Pilots?" *CNN Money,* July 6, 2004. (Available at: http://money.cnn.com/2004/07/06news/fortune500/delta/index.htm?cnn=yes)
65. U.S. Women's Bureau and the National Committee on Pay Equity. (Available at: http://infoplease.com/ipa/A0193820.html)
66. Edwin G. Dolan, *Economics of Public Policy,* 5th ed. (St. Paul, Minn.: West/Wadsworth, 1995).
67. Mary V. Moore and Yohannan T. Abraham, "Comparable Worth: Is It a Moot Issue?" *Public Personnel Management,* Vol. 21, 1992, pp. 455–472.
68. Kathleen Schalch, "Ending Male/Female Income Inequality," National Public Radio, April 2, 1998. (Available at: http://www.npr.org/rundowns/rundown.php?prgId=3&prgDate=2-Apr-1998)
69. Marlene Kim, "Women Paid Low Wages: Who They Are and Where They Work," *Monthly Labor Review,* September 2000, pp. 26–30.
70. Ibid.
71. Schalch, "Ending Male/Female Income Inequality."
72. Dolan, *Economics of Public Policy;* Erica L. Groshen, "The Structure of the Female/Male Wage Differential: Is It Who You Are, What You Do, or Where You Work?" *Journal of Human Resources,* Vol. 26, 1991, pp. 457–472; and Schalch, "Ending Male/Female Income Inequality."
73. Daniel H. Weinberg, "Evidence from Census 2000 about Earnings by Detailed Occupation for Men and Women," U.S. Census Bureau, May 2004. (Available at: http://www.census.gov/prod/2004pubs/censr-15.pdf)
74. Linda A. Jackson, Philip D. Gardner, and Linda A. Sullivan, "Explaining Gender Differences in Self-Pay Expectations: Social Comparison Standards and Perceptions of Fair Pay," *Journal of Applied Psychology,* Vol. 77, 1992, pp. 651–663.
75. Ronnie J. Steinberg, "Identifying Wage Discrimination and Implementing Pay Equity Adjustments," in *Comparable Worth: Issue for the 80's,* Vol. I (Washington, D.C.: U.S. Commission on Civil Rights, 1985).
76. *Schultz v. Wheaton Glass Co.,* 421 F. 2d 259 (1970).
77. *Hodgson v. Brookhaven General Hospital,* 436 F. 2d 719 (5th Cir. 1970).
78. *Christensen v. State of Iowa,* 16 FEP Cases 232 (1977).
79. Thomas J. Patten, *Fair Pay* (San Francisco: Jossey-Bass, 1988).
80. Richard D. Arvey and Katherine Holt, "The Cost of Alternative Comparable Worth Strategies," *Compensation and Benefits,* Vol. 20, 1988, pp. 37–46.
81. Kenneth A. Kovach and Peter E. Millspaugh, "Comparable Worth: Canada Legislates Pay Equity," *Academy of Management Executive,* Vol. 4, 1990, pp. 92–101; and Lynne Kilpatrick, "In Ontario, 'Equal Pay for Equal Work' Becomes a Reality, but

Not Very Easily," *Wall Street Journal,* March 9, 1990, p. B1.
82. Kenneth A. Kovach and Peter E. Millspaugh, "Comparable Worth: Canada Legislates Pay Equity," *Academy of Management Executive,* Vol. 4, 1990, pp. 92–101; and Lynne Kilpatrick, "In Ontario, 'Equal Pay for Equal Work' Becomes a Reality, But Not Very Easily," *Wall Street Journal,* March 9, 1990, p. B1.
83. Judith A. McDonald and Robert J. Thornton, "Private-Sector Experience with Pay Equity in Ontario," *Canadian Public Policy,* Vol. 24 (2), 1998, pp. 185–208.
84. SHRM Governmental Affairs Department, "Equal Pay/Comparable Worth," July 2002. (Available at: http://www.shrm.org/government/factsheets_published/CMS_001904.asp)
85. Aaron Bernstein, "Comparable Worth: It's Already Happening," *Business Week,* April 28, 1986, pp. 52, 56.

CHAPTER 12

Incentive Compensation

- Strategic Importance of Variable Pay
- Linking Pay to Performance
- Individual Incentives
- Group Incentives
- Barriers to Pay-for-Performance Success
- Summary: Making Variable Pay Successful
- Executive Compensation

HR Challenge

When sales slip, why would a company eliminate commissions paid to sales people—commissions designed to drive customers to the checkout register? That is exactly what the electronics retailer Circuit City did on what sales representatives refer to as "Bloody Wednesday." Not only did Circuit City eliminate commissions and switch all sales representatives to hourly pay, but they laid off 3,900 highly paid commissioned sales people.[1] That's right, Circuit City laid off the 3,900 people who sold the most.

The salespeople did what they were expected to do—sell product. Many were in the Million Dollar Club, meaning that they sold more than $1 million in computers and consumer electronics per year. Using an approach which is generally legal, Circuit City turned around and hired more than 2,000 lower paid hourly workers to replace those with higher pay who were laid off.

The problem, as Circuit City saw it, was that the company needed to economize. Circuit City felt they could no longer afford to pay big commissions to its sales staff while its rivals, such as Best Buy, Wal-Mart, and CompUSA, sold more with service representatives paid by the hour. In the early 1990s Circuit City's sales were twice that of Best Buy. More recently, Best Buy's sales have been more than twice that of Circuit City.

Further, customers seemed to prefer self-service to having a salesperson "encouraging" them one way or another. To deal with falling prices and an eroding customer base, Circuit City decided that high-paid sales representatives no longer fit the times. In so doing, Circuit City said that the change will allow it to simplify store operations, cut operating costs, and serve customers better.[2]

Circuit City's experience illustrates that incentive pay can be effective in encouraging employees to engage in behaviors that produce the desired results. However, at the same time, incentive pay can be counterproductive in the larger scheme of things. This experience is an example of the need to be careful of what you pay for.

Global competition has posed a difficult challenge for organizations in general and for human resource specialists in particular.[3] HR managers must try to develop human resource programs that improve productivity and enhance organizational effectiveness. Attaining these goals will help ensure that American businesses will be competitive in national and world arenas.

One popular approach to enhancing productivity has been linking rewards to performance through various forms of **incentive pay.**[4] In fact, the idea of incentive pay is so widely accepted that most organizations say they pay for performance. A survey by Hewitt Associates, a compensation and benefits consulting firm, found that in 2003–2004, 77 percent of the 1,200-plus companies surveyed were using incentive pay for nonexecutive employees based on some measure of performance.[5] According to the Hewitt survey, the most common types of incentive pay were the following:

- *Special recognition* to acknowledge outstanding individual or group achievements with small cash awards or merchandise (e.g., gift certificates)
- *Individual performance* rewards based on specific employee performance criteria
- *Business incentives,* which are awards to employees for a combination of financial and operational measures for company, business unit, department, plant, or individual performance
- *Stock ownership* rewards to professionals who meet specific goals

Incentive pay went from 4 percent of total compensation (for salaried workers) to almost 11 percent in the 1990s.[6] Most managers and many workers believe performance should be the most important factor in determining salary increases.[7] In addition, studies indicate that linking pay to performance can lead to better employee performance.[8]

The goal of performance-based reward systems is to reward participants in direct relation to their individual performance and contribution to organizational success. In the past, compensation practice was dominated by traditional (fixed) pay plans, in which pay increases were given across the board or based on the cost of living or seniority.

The preceding chapter defined *organizational rewards* as the money, goods, and services provided by an employer to its employees. Thus the reward system includes more than just direct compensation, and direct compensation may include more than just base pay (salary or wage). This chapter explores the elements of direct compensation that go beyond fixed salary and wages—specifically, various types of individual and group incentive systems. The implementation and administration challenges associated with both incentives are examined. (The Ethical Perspective box provides a cautionary note for managers attempting to use reward systems to motivate appropriate employee behavior.) Chapter 13 focuses on indirect compensation, particularly legislatively mandated benefits (such as Social Security and workers' compensation) and optional benefits (such as insurance, pensions, vacations, and sick leave).

ETHICAL PERSPECTIVE

Reward Systems and Inappropriate Behavior

When individuals are caught in organizational wrongdoing, there is a tendency to blame the individual for some sort of character weakness and to suggest that the appropriate remedy is to hire more ethical employees. However, in many cases the organizational reward system is at least partly at fault. Steven Kerr, in a classic article entitled, "On the Folly of Rewarding A While Hoping for B," points out that employees are very good at figuring out what really gets rewarded, and doing (or appearing to do) those things, regardless of what the organization officially says it wants employees to do. If the reward system pays off for cutthroat behavior, this is what the organization will get, despite upper management protestations that teamwork and cooperation should be the order of the day. If the organization wants high-quality work but measures only attendance and tardiness, it will get prompt attendance but probably not high-quality work.

Commission payments often constitute a large share of direct compensation for sales positions. Commission systems do enhance the motivation to sell, but if poorly designed, sales may occur at the expense of other important and longer term goals for the organization and the client. As an example, in the brokerage industry, commission systems can potentially create problems as follows:

- Some firms pay more for sales from new accounts than from existing accounts to incentivize seeking new customers. However, this may mean that less attention is devoted to providing good service to loyal longer term customers.
- Brokers who advise investors to buy a stock are paid commissions when the sale is made, but investors only find out if the advice was sound months or years later.
- Brokers are usually paid only when shares are traded, but sometimes the best advice to give a client is to hold their current portfolio.
- Brokers should get to know their clients' needs, goals, and risk propensities, then recommend a portfolio suited to each client's particular profile. However, this takes time, which is not directly compensated. The match of a portfolio to client goals is seldom subject to external assessment for reward purposes.

The HR practitioner must remember that reward systems are very potent. They can be harnessed to assess and encourage desired behavior. However, they also can (either intentionally or unintentionally) motivate behavior that is interpersonally, organizationally, or socially dysfunctional. Careful attention to the design of appraisal and reward systems is necessary to ensure that they do in fact elicit the type of behavior the organization really wants from its employees.

Sources: Steven Kerr, "On the Folly of Rewarding A While Hoping for B," *Academy of Management Journal*, December 1975, pp. 769–783; J. Settel and N. B. Kurland, "Can We Create a Conflict-Free Commission Payment System?" *Business & Society Review*, September 1998, pp. 33–44; R. Coughlan, "Toward a Conflict-Free Compensation System: Lessons from Hospitality," *Business & Society Review*, Winter 1999, pp. 355–365.

STRATEGIC IMPORTANCE OF VARIABLE PAY

E. E. Lawler gave the name **new pay** to reward programs that seek to align compensation with organizational goals, values, and culture, as well as with the challenges of the global economy.[9] New pay goes beyond individual or group incentive pay and seeks to provide a mechanism for an organization to use all elements of compensation, direct (cash compensation) and indirect (benefits), to help forge a partnership between the organization and its employees. The aim is employees who exhibit the following qualities:

- Understand the goals of the organization
- Know their role in accomplishing these goals
- Become appropriately involved in decisions of the organization
- Accept that their rewards are related to their contribution to the goal attainment of the organization[10]

Having determined their goals, objectives, and values, how do organizations signal these elements to their employees? Assuming an organization has selected the right individuals, trained these individuals, and established appropriate work systems, it is still a challenge to have these employees understand what needs to be done. A major mechanism for indicating the organizational goals and objectives is the compensation system. This can best be understood from examples of misalignment:

- What is being signaled to coworkers when well-intentioned but ineffective employees are given above-average merit increases?
- What is being signaled to employees when executives are given large bonuses after the organization has had a below-average year, and only small increases are given to other workers?
- What is being signaled if high commissions and other incentives are paid to field sales representatives, but there is no monitoring of sales practices?
- What is being signaled if an organization has an established bonus system, does not attain the profits necessary to trigger the bonuses in a given year, but decides to pay them anyway "because it was a tough year"?

Basic to the effective functioning of any organization is the way it uses its system of total compensation to communicate to employees both what needs to be done and their role in accomplishing these objectives. The preceding examples of misalignment are frequently well-intentioned actions on the part of managers, but obviously they are not consistent with the desired alignment between rewards and organizational objectives. Any system of compensation is highly visible and becomes central to the very fabric of the organization.[11]

LINKING PAY TO PERFORMANCE

Employers believe that reward systems in general and incentive systems in particular influence performance.[12] Among respondents to an Institute of Management and Administration (IOMA) survey of 156 U.S. executives, for example, the vast majority believed that various incentive pay systems have a very positive effect on performance (see Table 12.1). In addition, many workers prefer that pay be linked to performance, reinforcing the motivation to use such reward systems.

Reasons to Link Pay to Performance

Motivation Several studies, including research based on free agency and final-offer arbitration in major league baseball,[13] have indicated that when pay is contingent on performance, individual and group performances are consistently higher than when this contingency is not present.[14] Vroom's **expectancy theory**

TABLE 12.1

Ratings of the Effectiveness of Various Incentive Pay Reward Programs

Plan Type	% Who Rate as Highly or Moderately Effective
Skill- or knowledge-based pay	95%
Special one-time spot awards (after the fact)	90
Profit-sharing (apart from retirement programs)	89
Long-term incentives (executive level)	88
Individual incentives	84
Profit-sharing (as part of retirement program)	83
Group incentives (not team-based)	83
Competency-based pay	82
Long-term incentives (below executive levels)	81
Team-based pay	79
Lump-sum merit pay	70
Gainsharing	69
ESOP/stock plan	66
Pay for quality	65

Note: Based on an Institute of Management and Administration (IOMA) survey of 156 U.S. executives. Not all companies used all reward programs. Executives only rated the effectiveness of programs used in their companies.
Source: HR Focus, Vol. 78 (4), April 2001, pp. 3–4.

suggests that a pay–performance link is essential for motivating performance.[15] Among approaches to understanding work motivation, expectancy theory is widely accepted and has fairly strong empirical support in applied and theoretical settings.[16] As shown in Figure 12.1, the expectancy model has three major components, each of which is based on a series of fairly straightforward observations.

1. **Expectancy:** The individual's perceptions of the probability that effort will lead to task accomplishment or performance
2. **Instrumentality:** Perceptions of the probability that performance will result in receiving rewards (such as pay or recognition)
3. **Valence:** The subjective value or desirability that the individual places on the attainment of a certain reward

The expectancy model can be summarized as

$$M = E \Sigma (I V)$$

Where M = motivation, E = expectancy, I = instrumentality, and V = valence.

As an example of how expectancy theory works, consider the case of an organization sponsoring a contest to motivate its salespersons. A trip around the world will be awarded to the salesperson with the greatest dollar volume of sales for the calendar year. According to expectancy theory, the motivational impact of this contest would depend on individual salespersons' expectancy (perceived chance of being the top salesperson), instrumentality (belief that the company will actually award the prize), and valence (desirability of the round-the-world trip). A salesper-

FIGURE 12.1
Major Elements of Expectancy Theory

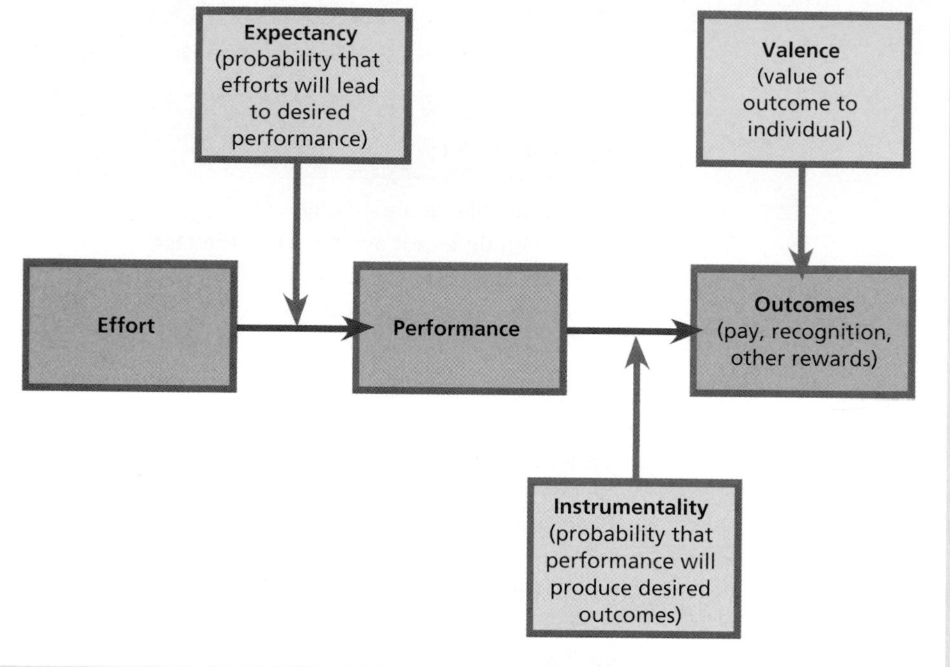

son who thinks she has a decent chance to win, believes the trip will be awarded, and has a strong desire to travel should be highly motivated by this contest. A second salesperson who believes that she has absolutely no chance of being the top seller (zero expectancy) probably will make little effort to win, even if she would greatly enjoy the trip. A third salesperson may have a very low instrumentality, believing that the company will not really award such an expensive prize. Mistrustful of the offered bargain, he will not be motivated by the contest. Also unresponsive will be a salesperson who feels that the reward is not positively valent (e.g., if he hates to travel and is terrified of airplanes).

To produce maximum motivation, all three components of the expectancy model must be high. Incentive compensation systems are designed to raise two of the three components. Instrumentality beliefs should be strengthened by making rewards contingent on good performance, and valence should be high because more money is a reward that most people find highly attractive.[17]

Expectancy theory offers useful guidelines to diagnose possible problems in incentive systems. First, one must ask whether employees believe that they can be good performers if they try. Are they properly selected, trained, and equipped to do the job? Do they get feedback so that they know where they stand and can take corrective action as necessary? Second, one must be sure that employees perceive a link between their performance and their rewards (instrumentality). Do they truly believe that better performance will make more money, or does a higher salary seem to be more a function of luck or politics? Finally, the offered reward must be of value (valence) to employees. They must be able to earn something they strongly desire, such as a promotion or a sizable raise. The prospect of a small merit raise may not be enough to motivate superior performance over an extended period of time.

Extended even further, pay may not be the most important motivating factor. People will often put recognition above pay as a reward.[18] Linux, the open-source software, relies on independent programmers around the world to contribute, generally without pay, to creating and refining the system.[19] In this way, programmers whose best work is usually well hidden have a chance to showcase their talents and receive credit.

Retention Linking pay to performance is likely to help improve work force composition. High performers will tend to gain a larger share of compensation resources and thus be motivated to stay with the organization. Below-average performers will become discouraged and will tend to leave the organization. Reward systems that are not linked to performance tend to have the opposite effect and thus result in the worst of both possibilities. Well-paid poor performers may stay with the organization: They are well rewarded and will not be sought by other organizations. By contrast, top performers feel under-rewarded and are likely to be sought by organizations that appropriately value their contributions.

Some organizations link rewards to performance by using commissions as the primary or exclusive basis for compensation. Top performers in real estate, insurance agencies, and stock brokerage houses, for example, may earn ten times more than poor performers. It is not surprising that the top performers desire to continue earning several hundred thousand dollars each year, whereas the poor performers leave the profession quickly.

Productivity When performance is linked to rewards, those capable of doing what will lead to top productivity are motivated to do so. In the real estate, insurance, and stock brokerage organizations mentioned earlier, nobody becomes productive by waiting for business to come along. The top performers make the extra effort that will result in productivity when they know they will share in the rewards of their productivity. In the financial services business, the "extras" that result in productivity frequently involve working evenings, entertaining clients, soliciting business, and volunteering in community activities, to name a few. Technical competence is important, but as one top performer was heard to say, "Not 1 in 500 makes it to the top ranks on technical skills alone." This may be an overestimate.

Cost Savings An obvious benefit of pay for performance is the capability to link compensation costs with productivity results. By basing pay on performance, employers can ensure that compensation costs, typically a major cost of doing business, will be tied to organizational results. When the results are poor and the organization is less able to pay, compensation costs are lower. With a salaried or hourly work force, compensation costs are not related to business results and, even worse, continue to grow each year as cost-of-living and merit increases are added.

Organizational Objectives It is always a challenge to make sure all employees understand organizational objectives. Because of their important influence on motivation and satisfaction, reward systems have the ability to communicate organizational objectives.[20] By linking pay to organizationally defined performance, it is also possible to ensure that individual objectives are in line with organizational

A DIFFERENT POINT OF VIEW

Do Rewards Motivate Performance?

Author Alfie Kohn has been making waves by claiming that rewards and pay-for-performance systems are fundamentally flawed and incapable of motivating improved performance. In a controversial *Harvard Business Review* article, "Why Incentive Plans Cannot Work," Kohn summarized his book, *Punished by Rewards: The Trouble with Gold Stars, Incentive Plans, A's, Praise, and Other Bribes.*

Kohn claims that rewards elicit temporary compliance at best and do not motivate sustained changes in attitude or commitment. He believes rewards are as manipulative and controlling as the threat of punishment, stating that "Do this and you'll get that" is not really very different from "Do this or here's what will happen to you." He cites laboratory research showing that people become less interested in performing inherently interesting tasks after being paid contingently than when paid at an hourly rate or not paid at all.

Agreeing with W. Edwards Deming, Kohn believes individual incentives breed unhealthy competition among coworkers; reduce teamwork, risk taking, and creativity; and lead to political behavior, short-term fixes, and cover-ups of errors. He claims that managers use incentives as a cheap and easy way to increase employee effort when they should be concentrating instead on deeper causes of performance problems, such as poor job design, lack of feedback, and ineffective leadership.

These arguments seem to be of two kinds: first, that the concept of using rewards to motivate performance is simply wrong, and second, that some individual incentive plans are badly designed and reward the wrong thing. Let us consider the first type of argument—that rewards simply cannot work, no matter how well designed. It is true that most people resent being closely controlled by others and that some reward systems, especially piece-rate incentives or systems that rely on subjective judgments by highhanded superiors, can be seen as very controlling. However, there is also research showing that performance-contingent pay actually can increase employees' feelings of control, by giving them the ability to determine how much they earn. Further, most pay-for-performance systems provide more than just the extrinsic reward of dollars. Earning more money under these systems also conveys feedback and recognition that a job was done

objectives. Employees whose efforts are not synchronized with organizational objectives will not enjoy an equal share of the rewards.

Reasons Not to Link Pay to Performance

Linking pay to performance is not always possible or successful. As noted in A Different Point of View, pay-for-performance systems can be misguided. An example of performance-based pay gone awry occurred when Sears Auto Centers in California acknowledged having made unnecessary repairs on customers' cars. The compensation system used by Sears Auto Centers based rewards on services and parts sold. As a result, California investigators charged Sears with defrauding its customers by selling unnecessary parts and services. Sears subsequently settled for approximately $15 million, an expensive lesson on the double-edged nature of performance-based pay.[21]

Pay-for-performance systems also take more time to administer successfully than do traditional reward systems. With fixed compensation (salary or wage), it

well and is appreciated. Research shows that when the information/feedback value of a reward is seen as more salient than its controlling aspects, intrinsic motivation is enhanced.

Much of the research that shows intrinsic motivation being undermined by payment has explored the effect of monetary incentives on enjoyable leisure-time activities for which people would not normally expect to be paid. In this case, the novelty of payment seems to make people stop and think about why they are engaging in the activity and conclude that since they are being paid to engage in it, it must not be much fun or very interesting. Other research shows that when pay is a normal, expected part of a setting, it does not harm and may even increase intrinsic motivation. For instance, poker and casino games are much more fun when the possibility of monetary gain is present. Certainly people expect to be paid for their performance at work, so money need not reduce intrinsic motivation in that context. Thus it seems that the concept of rewards for performance is not flawed.

However, the execution of reward systems can leave much to be desired, and negative consequences sometimes do flow from poorly designed incentive systems. A few companies have dropped commission systems for salespeople because they found that sales staff were becoming too aggressive in their approach and that these hard-sell tactics were driving away customers. When managers focus too much attention on installing the perfect incentive system, they may neglect to explore other causes of, and solutions for, performance problems. A balanced approach is needed, bearing in mind that it is possible to design incentive systems to reward teamwork and creativity and that group-oriented profit-sharing or gain-sharing systems can increase commitment and interest in business performance among employees.

Sources: Alfie Kohn, "Why Incentive Plans Cannot Work," *Harvard Business Review,* September-October 1993, pp. 54–63; "Rethinking Rewards," *Harvard Business Review,* November-December 1993, pp. 37–49; Edward L. Deci and Richard M. Ryan, *Intrinsic Motivation and Self-Determination in Human Behavior* (New York: Plenum Press, 1985); Alfie Kohn, *Punished by Rewards: The Trouble with Gold Stars, Incentive Plans, A's, Praise, and Other Bribes* (Boston: Houghton Mifflin, 1993); Cynthia D. Fisher, "The Effects of Personal Control, Competence, and Extrinsic Reward Systems on Intrinsic Motivation," *Organizational Behavior and Human Performance,* Vol. 21, 1978, pp. 273–288; and Jeffrey Pfeffer, "Six Dangerous Myths about Pay," *Harvard Business Review,* May-June 1998, pp. 108–119.

is often a case of "set it and forget it." With pay for performance, one needs to re-evaluate the motivation, retention, productivity, and organizational objectives continually, with the idea of fine-tuning the system to make sure rewards are aligned with desired performance.

A union's position on this type of reward system may also influence the feasibility of instituting a pay-for-performance system in a particular organization. Historically, unions have opposed performance-based pay systems. Although some unions are willing to back this type of compensation, most see no need to differentiate the pay of union workers who are doing the same job. Unions believe pay differences based on subjective supervisor assessments of employee performance may foster discrimination or favoritism. Unions favor objective methods of determining pay increases, such as across-the-board increases or seniority increases. Unions also believe merit pay plans may weaken solidarity because employees compete against their fellow union members to receive the highest rewards. Unions may be more receptive to group incentive plans because they tend to result in cooperation rather than competition. Thus a union would more likely favor a bonus plan for all employees based on a company's profitability.

Factors Affecting the Design of Incentive Systems

There are numerous ways of linking pay to performance, each with its own advantages and drawbacks. One consideration is the level of aggregation of the incentive pay: Will the incentive be based on the performance of the individual employee, the work group, the division, or the entire organization? Another consideration is the degree of objectivity involved in measuring performance. Qualifying to receive the incentive may be based on a subjective supervisory rating of performance or on purely objective measures such as sales, production, or profit. A further complication is the fact that it is not unusual for companies to have several incentive systems; for example, one system based on work group performance and another as a function of organizational performance.

Other considerations in the design of an incentive system relate to the strength of the performance–pay linkage, the potential for negative side effects, whether the system encourages cooperation, and employee acceptance. The results of Edward E. Lawler's analysis of incentive plans with respect to these criteria are shown in Table 12.2. Objective measures of performance (productivity and cost savings) tend to have greater employee acceptance and credibility. Individual incentive programs are often reported to yield higher productivity than group incen-

TABLE 12.2

Ratings of Pay Incentive Plans*

	Basis for Reward	Tie Pay to Performance	Produce Negative Side Effects	Encourage Cooperation	Employee Acceptance
Salary reward					
Individual plan	Productivity	4	1	1	4
	Cost-effectiveness	3	1	1	4
	Superiors' rating	3	1	1	3
Group plan	Productivity	3	1	2	4
	Cost-effectiveness	3	1	2	4
	Superiors' rating	2	1	2	3
Organizational plan	Productivity	2	1	3	4
	Cost-effectiveness	2	1	2	4
Bonus					
Individual plan	Productivity	5	3	1	2
	Cost-effectiveness	4	2	1	2
	Superiors' rating	4	2	1	2
Group plan	Productivity	4	1	3	3
	Cost-effectiveness	3	1	3	3
	Superiors' rating	3	1	3	3
Organizational plan	Productivity	3	1	3	4
	Cost-effectiveness	3	1	3	4
	Profit	2	1	3	3

*On a scale of 1 to 5, 1 = low and 5 = high.

Source: E. E. Lawler, *Pay and Organization Development,* © 1981 Addison Wesley Longman, Inc. Reprinted by permission of Addison Wesley Longman.

tives. One explanation is that linking individuals' pay to the group's performance diffuses the connection between pay and each person's effort. Some individuals may have a tendency to "free-ride" (let others in the group do the work for them).[22] Research has shown that group members are especially likely to free-ride if their contribution to group performance is not readily identifiable and their loafing is unlikely to be noticed.[23]

On the other hand, group plans have some advantages not generally attainable with an individual incentive system. Group systems often result in more cooperation and coordination. They are better suited for organizations in which performance is difficult to measure at the individual level and success depends on effective teamwork.

INDIVIDUAL INCENTIVES

When individual productivity is measurable, individual incentives are most successful in boosting performance through a fairly direct link between performance and rewards. The adoption of individual incentives has accelerated in recent years. Popular individual incentive plans discussed in this section include piece-rate incentive, commissions, and bonuses. Skill-based pay—a highly acclaimed recent innovation in individual incentives—and merit raises are also discussed.

Piece-Rate Incentive

Piece-rate incentive is the most common form of individual enticement for production workers. Employees are paid a fixed rate for each unit of output produced. The amount to pay per unit of output is determined as follows: First, the typical pay rate for the job is determined, probably by a wage survey. Then the typical output per day is measured. A time and motion study by industrial engineers may also provide information on the number of units that an employee should be able to make per day. The average daily wage is divided by average units per day to produce the price paid per piece. For example, if the average daily rate is $96 and each employee ought to be able to produce 96 units per day, the rate paid for each piece will be $1.00.

Some piece-rate systems pay only on the basis of units produced, so an employee who made only 70 units would receive $70 for that day. Many piece-rate systems, however, guarantee a base wage equal to the standard output level, so that all employees making 96 or fewer units receive $96. (Of course, employees who are consistently below the standard may not continue on the job.) The incentive is paid for all units in excess of the standard. Thus an employee who made 110 units would receive $96 plus $14 (14 extra units × $1.00), or $110.

The major shortcoming of the typical piece-rate incentive is in the signal it sends. Instead of suggesting a partnership between the goals of the individual and those of the organization, it implies that the organization actually distrusts the individual. As a result, a piece-rate system is likely to encourage behaviors opposite to those sought. Workers may restrict output because of the possible adverse consequences associated with high productivity.[24] For example, workers may fear layoffs if all employees dramatically increase their output. Other workers may fear being ostracized by colleagues if they try to produce at a higher-than-normal level.

Finally, workers may fear that if they consistently produce at a high rate—say, 150 units per day—the time and motion study will be redone, thereby increasing the production standards and reducing the rate paid per piece. They would then have to work harder to earn the same pay.

As suggested previously, these negative views of the piece-rate incentive can be traced to the adversarial nature of management–worker relations that it signals. On the other hand, Lincoln Electric in Cleveland, Ohio, represents a long-standing example of a successful piece-rate incentive system, a plan first introduced in 1934. Lincoln pays factory workers for each acceptable piece that is produced. In addition, each employee receives a year-end bonus based on a yearly merit rating of his or her dependability, ideas, productivity, and product quality. Lincoln's success is related to the partnership it signals. The pay of every employee from the CEO on down is at risk—contingent on individual and corporate performance.

An incentive system sometimes can lead to overemphasis on one dimension of a job and neglect of other important job elements. For instance, a piece-rate system may increase output but also increase the number of units that fail to pass inspection. Other aspects of the job that do not directly convert into units of output, such as machine maintenance, housekeeping activities, or training new employees, may be ignored under a piece-rate system.

The Taylor Plan A variation of the piece-rate system was developed by Frederick W. Taylor around the turn of the century. Unlike the straight piece-rate plan, the **Taylor plan** offers differential piecework rates. In the preceding example, the Taylor plan might specify \$1.00 per unit up to 96 units per day but reward workers producing 125 percent of standard or more (120 units) with the higher rate of \$1.25 for each unit over 96.

Standard Hour Plan The **standard hour plan** is similar to the straight piecework plan except that the standard is set in time units. Automobile repair shops often use such systems. If the customer wants to know the cost of replacing an engine timing belt, for example, he or she will be given an estimate based on the mechanic's hourly rate multiplied by the average time needed to replace the component on cars of that type. If the charge is \$45 per hour and the replacement of the timing belt requires six hours on average, the expected labor cost would be \$270. This is the labor cost quoted to the customer before work begins. An experienced mechanic may complete the job in five hours. The customer is still charged \$270, and the mechanic is paid for six hours' work (the standard time allotted for the job). If complications arise and the job takes longer than estimated (e.g., the mechanic strips a bolt and has to repair the error), charges to the customer and payment to the mechanic are still based on six hours' work. In this case, auto repair shops have manuals with the standard hours for each type of repair. Standard hour plans are generally used with longer cycle operations that are nonrepetitive.

Commissions

Commission reward systems, which are usually found in sales jobs, allow the salesperson to receive a percentage of his or her gross receipts (e.g., 5 percent of all sales). About two-thirds of all salespersons are paid on a **commission** basis—either straight commission or a base salary plus commission.

Commission payments offer a very clear link between pay and worker performance and therefore are an effective financial incentive. Commission plans are easy to administer and justify because there is no subjective element, and rewards are purely a function of performance. Because of this clear link, department stores are converting thousands of hourly sales employees to straight commission.[25] The retailers hope that the potential for higher rewards to those with strong sales skills will motivate current staff and attract better salespersons in the future.

As has been illustrated by the earlier discussion of the double-edged nature of incentives, commissions, more than most other incentive systems, require active control on the part of management. For example, commission payment may reduce cooperative teamwork. Employees may compete with one another for individual sales or for the most lucrative sales territory. The result is that several salespersons besiege customers as soon as they enter the area.

In the case of department stores shifting to straight commission, sales staff may give customers a hard time on refunds or exchanges. If an employee's pay is based strictly on sales, all other coworker- and company-related considerations may be secondary. For example, the salesperson who works hard to sell the customer a computer may not want to take the time to instruct him or her in its use. After the sale, service may not be what is expected or needed, resulting in a dissatisfied customer.

Of course the experience of Circuit City (see the HR Challenge) stands out as a special case. In this case, the sales commissions were effective in motivating sales except that competitors were achieving even better results with lower cost hourly sales employees.

In the case of financial services, incentive-based pay has frequently led to churning customer accounts to generate commissions or to emphasizing products not in the best interest of the customer. The need for management controls with commission rewards was illustrated in the instance of Baring Brothers and Company, a British bank. A quest by a Baring Brothers' employee to maximize his rewards led to losses of almost $1 billion—and the failure of the bank.[26]

From the employee's point of view, a disadvantage of commission-based compensation is the unpredictable amount of take-home pay from week to week. Any number of things outside the employee's control—such as weather, economic conditions, or the amount spent on advertising—may influence the number of sales and therefore the amount of reward. However, assuming that the salesperson can tolerate this kind of risk, commission plans offer considerable advantage to the organization by directly linking performance to rewards and keeping labor costs in line. Furthermore, for the employees who are effective, the rewards are far greater than they would otherwise be—perhaps even several times the amount that the employees could have expected if compensated by salary or wage. As an example, successful Nordstrom sales employees typically earn several times more than their counterparts with other department stores.

Bonuses

One of the most popular trends in compensation is the use of **bonuses:** one-time lump-sum payments given for meeting a performance goal. Bonuses can be based on objective goal attainment or a subjective rating. In some organizations all employees share in the bonus awards if organizational goals are met, whereas in others the size of the bonus is tied to each individual's performance. An example of the former approach is Ford Motor Company. In a plan agreed to by the United Auto Workers and Ford in the early 1980s, all hourly and salaried employees receive profit-sharing bonuses when Ford achieves its projected goals. As shown in Figure 12.2, the results have varied considerably as a function of Ford's success or lack thereof. The high-water mark was 1999 with $8,000 bonuses for each employee, no small amount to be sure. In addition to the several years of $4,000 or more bonuses were six years of zero (or near zero) bonuses as well. Another example of a bonus based on individual performance is the clause in some baseball players' contracts that specifies that they will receive a bonus (usually several thousand dollars) if voted onto the all-star team or if they reach some other performance standard.

Table 12.3 shows a sample award distribution chart for lump-sum bonuses based on both organizational and employee performance. Plans such as this also might assign different bonus ceilings to levels within the organization. For instance, top managers might be eligible to earn up to 50 percent more than their salary, middle managers 25 percent, and lower level employees 10 percent.

Bonuses not only help the employer control costs but appear to improve employee satisfaction. A company that gives a raise to an employee is making a permanent change that improves his or her pay now, in the future, and also in retirement, through a pension. This is a more costly commitment than a one-time bonus payment. Because bonuses arrive in one lump sum, they may feel to the

FIGURE 12.2

Annual Employee Bonuses at Ford Motor Company

Source: Adapted from *Detroit News*, January 28, 2000. (Available at: http://www.detnews.com/2000/autos/0001/29/01280128.htm)

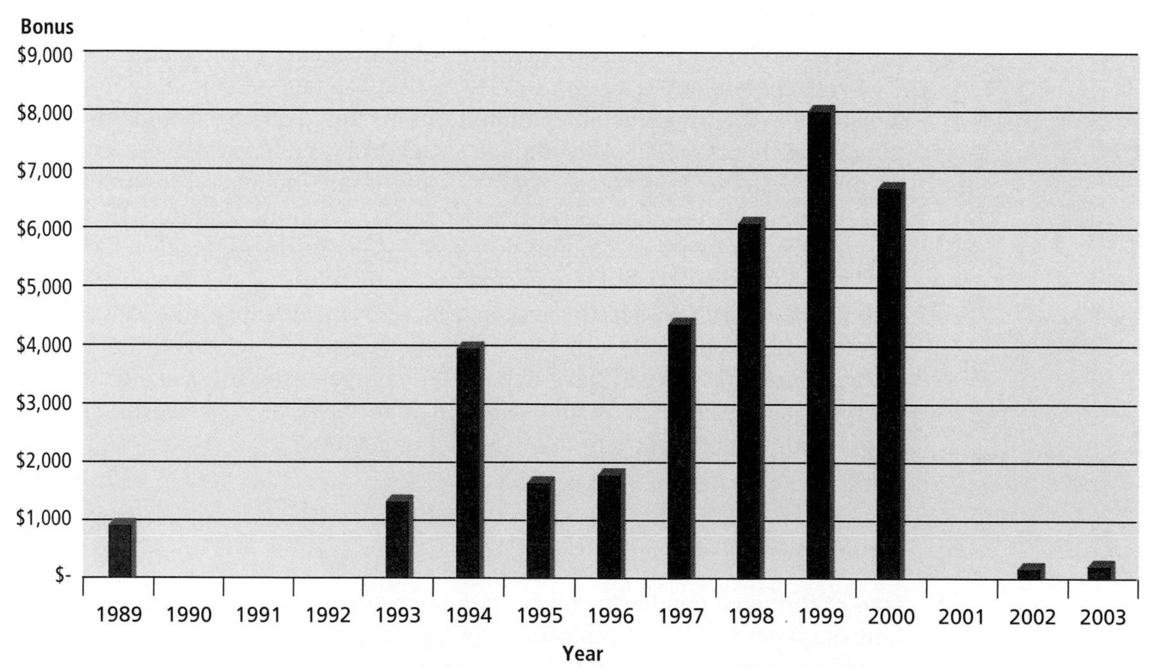

TABLE 12.3

Lump-Sum Award Determination Matrix

	The Organization's Performance (Weight = .50)				
The Employee's Performance (Weight = 50)	Outstanding (1.00)	Excellent (.80)	Commendable (.60)	Acceptable (.40)	Marginal or Unacceptable (0)
Outstanding (1.00)	1.00	.90	.80	.70	.50
Excellent (.80)	.90	.80	.70	.60	.40
Commendable (.60)	.80	.70	.60	.50	.30
Acceptable (.00)	–0–	–0–	–0–	–0–	–0–
Unacceptable (.00)	–0–	–0–	–0–	–0–	–0–

Instructions: To determine the dollar value of each employee's incentive award, (a) multiply the employee's annual, straight-time wage or salary by his or her maximum incentive award and (b) multiply the resulting product by the appropriate percentage figure from this table. For example, if an employee had an annual salary of $20,000 and a maximum incentive award of 10%, and if her performance and the organization's performance were both "excellent," the employee's award would be $1,600 ($20,000 × .10 × .80 = $1,600).
Source: Republished with permission of American Management Association, from "The Future of Merit Pay Programs" by John F. Sullivan, *Compensation and Benefits Review,* May/June 1988. Permission conveyed through Copyright Clearance Center, Inc.

employees like more money than a comparable-sized raise. Suppose an employee earning $30,000 is given a $1,500 bonus. The sizable bonus check is equal to 5 percent of the salary. If a raise of the same size were given, the $1,500 would be distributed across 52 weeks, and the employee would see less than $30 more per week in his or her paycheck. Bonus plans are easy to maintain because they do not require much documentation and are quite flexible.[27] As shown in the Ford Motor example (Figure 12.2), a major advantage of a bonus plan is that it is based partly on organizational performance; in a bad year, when corporate performance is down and resources are strained, bonuses will be much smaller or even nonexistent. Of course, on the other hand, when bonuses cannot be paid, as with Ford, it tends to hurt morale.[28]

Skill-Based Pay

Skill-based pay (or **pay for knowledge**) is a reward system that pays employees on the basis of the work-related skills they possess rather than associating rewards with performance levels or seniority.[29] Under a typical skill-based pay plan, an employee is hired and receives initial training on one job. He or she then joins a work group at the entry level rate of pay and has the opportunity to learn new job-related skills through on-the-job experience and further training. As the employee demonstrates mastery of different jobs performed by other group members, his or her pay is increased.[30] Typically, a minimum of four to five years is required for employees to top out—that is, master all the skills.[31] Skill-based pay frequently is used in conjunction with autonomous work groups or other job enrichment programs.[32]

Several models are used to design skill-based pay plans. The *stair-step model* is applicable when the learning progression is fairly logical. Successive skill levels are defined, and pay is increased as the learning of additional skills is verified. The *job-point accrual model* is used when a wide variety of jobs must be learned. The varied jobs are given a relative point rating based on value added or learning difficulty, and the points for each job mastered then determine the employee's pay grade. The *cross-department model* places a premium (in terms of rewards) on employees who learn the skills required to fill in at another department as needed.[33]

The single biggest advantage of skill-based pay is increased flexibility. Because workers know more than one job, they can move to provide expertise when and where needed.[34] Tying pay increases to skill acquisition creates an incentive for learning, self-improvement, and performance.[35]

The success of such plans depends on the needs of the organization and the employee. Skill-based pay should be implemented only if the organization has a commitment to employee training and development and has something to gain from increased flexibility. This system also rests on the assumption that employees want to grow and to improve their job skills.

Although a creative approach to compensation, skill-based pay is not for everyone.[36] For those companies that do use skill-based pay, part of the reason for its popularity lies in what it indicates to employees. For example, skill-based pay has the following qualities:

- It is associated with work teams or self-managed work groups.
- It is prevalent in organizations committed to egalitarian principles—high involvement or all-salaried work forces.
- It is embraced by reorganized organizations that have adopted a broadened conceptualization of the job.
- It is associated with organizations seeking employee involvement through total quality, continuous improvement, and similar initiatives.[37]

Merit Pay

Merit pay, because it is the standard procedure for attempting to tie pay increases to individual performance, is a major motivational device for employees at all levels—managerial, professional, and hourly.[38] **Merit pay** is an annual increment tied to the employee's performance during the preceding year. For example, during periods of low inflation and competitive pressures on corporations' costs, a top performer may receive a 5 percent increase, whereas an average performer receives 3 percent and a below-average performer receives no increase.

Even though merit pay continues to be used widely, it has come under major criticism.[39] Merit raises represent a permanent commitment to an increased salary (pay is virtually never reduced if performance falls), thereby creating an annuity that can be an expensive fixed cost to an organization during economic downturns. Suppose a top-performing employee with a salary of $40,000 receives an increase of 2 percent more than that of an average employee. If paid bi-weekly, this employee would see about $31 more in each paycheck than the average employee would. This amount is so small that the top employee is likely to feel that his or her performance has not been rewarded, yet the organization has made a fairly expensive commitment. The commitment is in the form of continuing this increase for as long as the employee remains, no matter what the future performance. For example, assuming no further increases in future years, the organization will pay $20,000 more over ten years. Compounding by future pay increases magnifies the value. Assume in this example that if for each of the next ten years the top employee meets expectations and receives a 4 percent base pay increase; the organization will be paying an additional $24,012 (in today's dollars). Finally, if benefits directly related to base pay are 30 percent of base, the compounded increase will be $31,216 for the ten-year period. The result is a potential lose–lose situation—an expensive annuity for the organization and a top-performing employee who does not feel rewarded.[40]

In practice, the size of merit raises usually depends on both performance and the employee's current position in the salary range established for that job. If all top performers were given large raises, within a few years outstanding employees might be making more than the allowable maximum for their jobs—more than the jobs are worth, no matter how well they are performed. Thus merit increase guidelines, like those shown in Table 12.4, are often used. Among employees in the same part of the pay range, better performers receive a larger percentage increase. However, an excellent performer near the maximum of the range allowed for the job will receive a smaller percentage increase than an excellent performer earning below the midpoint of the range.

Several important difficulties are involved in using merit increases to link pay to performance. First, merit increases are almost always based on the supervisor's subjective evaluation, so employees may perceive a weak link between performance and pay. Many employees like the idea of a merit system but feel that the system in their organization is not implemented in a completely fair, unbiased manner. Recall from Chapter 10 that supervisors can make a number of intentional and unintentional errors in judging performance. These errors may lead to perceived inequities in the way merit money is distributed. Second, merit increases are usually awarded annually, so they do not immediately follow the specific instances of good performance that the organization wishes to reinforce. Third, variations in the size of merit raises are generally not large enough to be highly motivating. For example, using the guidelines illustrated in Table 12.4, an excellent performer would receive a 5 to 8 percent raise, whereas a poor performer would receive nothing. Yet the excellent performer certainly makes more than an 8 percent difference, possibly even a 100 percent difference, in terms of contribution to the organization. Fourth, the size of the total merit budget may vary

TABLE 12.4

Merit Increase Guidelines

	Performance Level			
Current Position in Range	**Excellent**	**Good**	**Average**	**Poor**
Top quarter	5%	3%	1%	0
Third quarter	6%	4%	2%	0
Second quarter	7%	5%	3%	0
Lowest quarter	8%	6%	4%	0

substantially from year to year so that the same performance level does not always earn the same reward. As a result of a smaller merit pool, this year's top performer may receive a 6 percent increase, whereas last year's was awarded 9 percent.

Edward E. Lawler aptly stated the bottom line with respect to merit pay:

> The combined effect of year-to-year differences in salary-increase budgets and the annuity feature of merit raises almost always creates a situation in which the total compensation of individuals is unrelated to their performance at any point in time.[41]

According to Lawler, the best-paid individuals are likely to be those employees who are among the most senior and who have performed adequately over a period of time.

One prescription for a successful merit system defines the following requirements:

1. A high level of trust in the management of the organization
2. A correct and current job evaluation system and wage structure (alleviating the tendency to use supposed merit money to correct distortions caused by a wage structure that is incorrect or out of touch with the market)
3. Performance criteria agreed to by all levels of employees
4. Job-specific, results-based criteria to reduce subjective bias
5. Accurate performance appraisals (Since no single performance appraisal format is appropriate in all situations, alternate formats should be adopted for different situations.)
6. Appropriate administrative practices, such as minimizing the time between the performance appraisal and pay increase, to maximize the reinforcement principle
7. Skillfully administered feedback during the performance appraisal session to ensure that employees are aware of expected performance
8. Managers trained in the correct use of the compensation system[42]

Despite the problems with merit pay, it is likely to remain a staple of compensation systems. At the same time, it is likely that in the future merit programs will be supplemented with other types of individual or group incentives. Organizations will rely on merit pay for the broad range of adjustments but will reward top performers with individual bonuses or all employees with a group incentive based on company performance.[43]

GROUP INCENTIVES

Group incentives are designed to accomplish the same objectives as individual incentives—that is, to link rewards to performance. The difference is that performance is measured on the level of an organizational unit and is viewed as resulting from the combined efforts of a group rather than from individual effort. As illustrated by the Lincoln Electric example described previously, individual and group incentives are not mutually exclusive but can be combined to emphasize the desired mix of individual and group linkage of rewards to performance. Lincoln Electric successfully uses a piece-rate system (individual bonus) as well as an annual profit-sharing bonus (group incentive).

A group incentive system was developed and evaluated by the Navy Personnel Research and Development Center for the Pearl Harbor Naval Shipyard.[44] Shipyard production workers typically work together in gangs of ten to twenty employees. Thus it seemed reasonable that the work gang be the basis for assessing productivity. Work gangs were studied to develop a baseline measure of person-hours needed to complete various assignments. Performance efficiency was then calculated by dividing the hours expected by the actual hours needed. The shipyard paid out half the cost savings associated with performance efficiency to gang members as incentive awards. In addition to performance improvement and cost savings, the project produced other positive benefits, including more sophisticated labor cost accounting and improved allocation of people. Surveys of participants revealed that 80 percent of the workers had a favorable opinion of the system.

In another study, production workers on a series of tightly interconnected assembly lines in a unionized iron foundry participated in a group incentive program.[45] Productivity standards were established for each assembly line, and credit was given for output above the established standard. The researchers found a sustained trend of increasing productivity over several years following implementation of the incentive system. Sharp early increases in output were due to increased effort, whereas continued small increases over the years were attributed to employee innovations. The presence of the incentive encouraged employees to continuously develop new and more efficient ways to complete their group tasks.

Group incentives, like those for individuals, have possible negative aspects. If the group is too large, employees may feel that their efforts will have little effect on total performance. Group members may also become concerned about overproduction and thus restrict output.

Profit Sharing

Profit sharing is an incentive system in which designated employees share the business profits. Profit-sharing plans differ from gain-sharing plans (to be discussed next) in two respects:

1. They are often implemented corporation-wide, whereas gain sharing is often at the unit level.
2. They use a formula based on profit rather than on productivity improvement.

The usual profit-sharing program establishes a base-level profit target. Once this target is achieved, a percentage of additional profits is set aside in a bonus pool to be distributed to participants. Sometimes the bonus pool is distributed in equal dollar shares to all employees. At other times the distribution is made according to organizational level or salary/wages.

There are three broad types of profit-sharing plans:

1. *Current distribution plans* (or cash plans), which pay a share of the company's profits in cash or in company shares
2. *Deferred payout plans,* in which an employee's share of the company's profits is placed in a trust fund to be distributed at a later date (usually on retirement, disability, death, or termination)
3. *Combination plans,* which provide both cash payments and deferred payments[46]

Some features of profit-sharing plans are very attractive. First, when there are no profits, the company bears no costs for this type of reward system. These plans also make employees more aware of the organization's competitive position in its industry and facilitate a cooperative atmosphere. Although profit sharing may be best suited to smaller companies, where the line of sight from individual performance to corporate profits is more evident, such plans are easy to administer in larger companies as well. The profit-sharing deferment plan allows employees to postpone taxation and therefore increase rewards.

One disadvantage of profit-sharing plans is the fact that when companies have had a bad year, even good employees may go unrewarded. Low profits may be due to factors beyond the employees' control, such as economic conditions. Another drawback is that deferred payout plans may have less incentive value because of the long time lapse between the good performance and the eventual payment. Also, employees' shares of the profits are seldom tied to individual performance. Most commonly, all employees share in the profits, either equally or in proportion to their base pay. Thus there is virtually no line of sight between how hard individuals work and the size of their profit-sharing payoffs, especially if the organization is large. For all these reasons, the link between pay and performance is very weak.

Assumptions about management practices, employee participation, and productivity targets, as they relate to profit-sharing plans, are summarized in Table 12.5.

Gain-Sharing Plans

Gain sharing is a type of group incentive in which a portion of the *gains* the organization realizes from group effort is *shared* with the group. The concept also implies an organizational philosophy that engenders the kind of cooperativeness and trust needed to facilitate group efforts.[47]

Many organizations are seeking productivity and quality improvement through gain-sharing plans.[48] Other important reasons for adopting gain-sharing plans have to do with employee relations, labor costs, and a desire to link pay to performance.[49]

Scanlon Plan One very popular and widely used form of gain sharing is the **Scanlon plan,** which was first implemented in the late 1920s. Its developer, Joseph Scanlon, was a union leader who was trained in cost accounting and had a strong concern for management–labor cooperation. Scanlon believed the average worker was a great reservoir of untapped information concerning labor-saving methods. Workers needed a mechanism permitting them to "work smarter, not harder."[50]

The Scanlon plan involves employee participation in reducing labor costs. The two main features are a system of departmental and plantwide screening committees to evaluate and implement employee cost-saving suggestions and sharing labor cost savings with employees as an incentive. Savings are determined as the ratio of payroll to sales value of production and are usually calculated monthly and compared with baseline months to determine the bonus to be shared.[51] A typical distribution of savings would be 50 percent to employees, 25 percent to the employer, and 25 percent retained for an emergency fund to reimburse the company for any months when the actual wage bill is larger than the baseline. Remaining emergency funds are distributed to workers at the end of each year.

TABLE 12.5

Principal Features of Gain-Sharing and Profit-Sharing Programs

	Scanlon	Rucker	Improshare	Profit Sharing	Winsharing
Management practices	Participative system highly stressed	Participative systems recommended	Reduction in conflict between labor and management recommended	Better education and communications recommended	Successful participative management
Employee participation	Suggestion committees or work teams	Rucker committees	Good ideas used when they occur	None specified	Recommendations and improvements solicited and used in each unit
Productivity target	Reduction in cost and/or labor	Cost reduction with emphasis on labor	Reduction in labor time, direct and indirect	Improved profit	Business goals, including productivity levels, are established
Bonus basis	Ratio of costs to sales value of production	Labor: percentage of value added	Hours saved compared with standard weekly	Share of profit	Financial results in excess of business goals
Bonus frequency	Monthly to quarterly	Monthly to quarterly	Weekly	Annually— usually deferred	Quarterly, semiannually, or annually
Participants	All employees	Hourly employees— others optional	Hourly employees only	All employees	All employees

Source: Robert Doyle, *Gainsharing and Productivity: A Guide to Planning, Implementation, and Development*. Copyright © 1983 by AMACOM, a division of American Management Association. Sections adapted from Jay R. Schuster and Patricia K. Zingheim, *The New Pay: Linking Employees and Organizational Performance* (Lexington, Mass.: Lexington Books, 1992).

Rucker Plan The **Rucker plan** is similar to the Scanlon plan, but the bonus formula includes the dollar value of all materials, supplies, and services used to make the product. The resulting formula is

$$\frac{\$\text{ value of personnel costs}}{\$\text{ value of production} - \$\text{ value of materials, etc.}}$$

The resulting bonus formula is the value added to a product per labor dollar. The Rucker plan provides an incentive to save on all inputs, both human and material.

Improshare Another noteworthy approach to gain sharing is the **Improshare** (*Im*proved *Pro*ductivity through *Shar*ing) **plan** developed by Mitchell Fein and first used in 1974.[52] Whereas the Scanlon and Rucker plans are first-generation gain-sharing plans, Improshare is considered second generation as a result of its expanded scope.

Improshare is similar to the previously discussed plan at the Navy shipyard, but at an organizational level. A standard of the number of person-hours required to produce an expected level of output is developed. This standard could be determined from a base period (as with the Scanlon plan) or through time and motion studies. For example, the base may be established as 5,000 hours of labor (direct and indirect) to produce 1,000 units each week, or 5 hours per unit. If in a given week 5,000 hours are used to produce 1,300 units, 1,500 hours have been saved (300 units at 5 hours per unit). The company splits the gains fifty-fifty with its employees, giving a bonus for 750 hours. Since the 750 hours represent 15 percent of the 5,000 hours worked (750/5,000), employees receive a 15 percent bonus for the week.

Winsharing **Winsharing,** the third generation in gain sharing, is an attempt to blend gain sharing and profit sharing.[53] One of the problems with first- and second-generation gain-sharing plans is that they cannot respond to economic and market changes. A possible result is highly productive employees producing products that the organization cannot sell. Winsharing expands the set of objectives to include profit, quality, customer value, and productivity performance.

Winsharing pays out to all employees in the group on the basis of group performance compared with predetermined goals. Business goals are established, goals that may or may not include performance improvements. The plan is designed so that financial awards are shared with employees once the organization has achieved the business goal. Above the goal, 50 percent of the financial results are shared with employees, and 50 percent reverts to the organization. Quality comes into play in that the cost of poor quality (i.e., cost of rework, rejects, and warranty expense as a percentage of volume) over a budgeted amount is subtracted from the winsharing fund. Winsharing differs from profit sharing in that group measures in addition to profit determine funding. The goal is to use a broader range of business goals as the basis of plan funding and award determination.

Summary Except for winsharing, the gain-sharing plans seem much the same. The Scanlon, Rucker, and Improshare plans all base the bonus paid on the savings resulting from productivity improvement. However, as shown in Table 12.5, there are differences. For example, with the Scanlon plan, the sales value of production (i.e., the amount received for the produced products) is part of the bonus calculation. With the Improshare plan, the standard is the number of hours required to produce an expected level of output. With all three plans, it is possible that sales or price fluctuations will overshadow productivity improvements. Winsharing is designed to incorporate business and profit goals with productivity targets.

Gain-sharing plans generally work best with smaller firms or units (e.g., divisions or plants) that have fairly stable production processes, good labor–management relations, and a culture emphasizing employee participation.[54] In smaller firms or units there is a **line of sight** from individual performance to firm or unit improvement. Individual employees can see that their efforts make a difference. A stable production process is necessary because any cost-savings plan that involves comparisons with a base period will be misleading if technology is continually changing or if production varies for reasons beyond the employees' control.

Employee Stock Ownership Plans (ESOPs)

In many companies, employees at all levels own stock in the organization for which they work. Changes in the federal tax laws since the late 1970s have made **employee stock ownership plans (ESOPs)** a common vehicle for profit sharing and the funding of pension plans. ESOPs also have been used by employees to buy out firms that might otherwise have been sold or closed.

Typically, a public company borrows money to buy its own stock, either from the company treasury or on the market, and places the shares in its ESOP. As the loan is paid down, a trustee allocates stock to individual employees, usually in the form of a deferred pension benefit.[55] According to the National Center for Employee Ownership (NCEO), as of 2003, there were approximately 11,000 ESOPs in force involving 8.8 million employees and a total of more than $400 billion of assets.[56] ESOPs are popular in both publicly and privately held companies. The top ten companies that are over 50 percent employee-owned through an ESOP, stock purchase plan, or other broad-based ownership plan are shown in Table 12.6 and include several well-know names, such as Publix Supermarkets, Price Chopper, and Graybar.

The popularity of ESOPs has less to do with employee participation than with tax breaks, restructuring, and pension paring. The more stock a company's ESOP holds, the better the company can fend off a raider, proceed with a leveraged buyout, or undertake other forms of reorganization. Some companies use an ESOP to reduce or replace benefits, such as pension benefits, thus leading to considerable savings.

There is some evidence that employee ownership may increase employee commitment, loyalty, and motivation, but such benefits are by no means preordained.[57]

TABLE 12.6

Largest U.S. Companies More Than 50 Percent Employee Owned

Company	City	Plan	Industry	Number of Employees
Publix Supermarkets	Lakeland, Fl.	ESOP, stock purchase	supermarkets	121,500
Science Applications Intl.	San Diego, Calif.	ESOP, others	R&D, computer systems	41,000
Hy-Vee	West Des Moines, Iowa	profit sharing	supermarkets	40,000
Price Chopper	Schenectady, N.Y.	ESOP	supermarkets	20,000
Lifetouch	Minneapolis, Minn.	ESOP	photography studios	12,000
Nypro	Clinton, Mass.	ESOP	plastics manufacturing	11,000
CH2M Hill, Inc.	Denver, Colo.	Stock purchase	engineering, construction	10,500
Brookshire Brothers	Lufkin, Tex.	ESOP	supermarkets	10,200
Graybar	St. Louis, Mo.	Stock purchase	electric equipment wholesale	10,000
Amsted Industries	Chicago, Ill.	ESOP	industrial product manufacturing	9,000

Source: "The Employee Ownership 100," National Center for Employee Ownership, July 2004. (Available at: http://www.nceo.org/library/eo100.html)

A study of the performance of public companies with more than 10 percent broad employee ownership showed that they returned 106 percent between 1992 and 1997.[58] This is compared with 83 percent growth in the Dow and 70 percent growth in the S&P 500 during this same period.

The key to gaining the benefits is to combine ownership with the line-of-sight link between individual and organizational performance.[59] As was seen with profit sharing, especially deferred profits, the link between employee effort and company results is frequently weak.[60] With ESOPs, this relationship is further diminished because success is a function not only of profits but also of the whims of Wall Street with respect to the valuation the financial markets put on companies—a factor employees find difficult to control. Burlington Industries, the textile giant, is an example of an ESOP gone wrong as employees watched the price of the stock go from $38 at the time of the employee buyout to $15 and then to near zero as Burlington filed for bankruptcy, thus greatly devaluing retirement nest eggs for individual employees.[61]

BARRIERS TO PAY-FOR-PERFORMANCE SUCCESS

There is tremendous disparity between theory and reality when organizations try to use pay to motivate performance. The anticipated benefits of pay-for-performance systems, in terms of motivation and satisfaction, are extremely elusive. Success may be made difficult by the nature of the task, performance measurement, the amount of payout, and the failure to achieve a credible link between pay and performance.

Nature of the Task

The design of a pay-for-performance system requires consideration of the employee's task. If the purpose is to engender motivation, the employee needs to feel that he or she can influence results—that is, control the performance that is being measured.[62] This simple principle can be a major stumbling block in practice. For example, imagine twenty-five data-entry specialists, each working at a terminal and paid on the basis of the number of characters entered per hour (piece rate). Is some of the data entry more challenging than others, for example, from handwritten data sheets versus printed material? Are the twenty-five terminals equivalent—the same make and model and purchased at the same time and with the same amount of use? Do some of the entry-stations work better than others? Are some areas of the work location better than others in terms of lighting, ventilation, and freedom from glare or distractions? Are there variations in the comfort of the workstations? Although data entry is a good example of a job where effort is tied to results (performance), some level of opportunity bias still exists—unevenness in opportunity of the data-entry operators to produce at their respective maximum levels as a result of situational differences.

Very few employees have total control over their own performance. Direct pay-for-performance incentives should be adopted only when employee skill and effort have a substantial impact on output. Skill-based pay and bonus or profit-sharing approaches are more appropriate if employees are less able to control performance.

Performance Measurement

Any pay-for-performance system presumes accurate and fair measurement of performance. Subjective measures of performance are notorious for their lack of validity. As a result, individuals are likely to feel that their rewards are not related to their effort but instead are a function of the judgments of their particular supervisor. Objective measures are not always better, as suggested by the example of the data-entry specialists. Almost any individual whose pay is a function of "objective" performance, such as sales, can point to numerous inequities or contaminants in the measurement procedures.

Amount of Payout

To be effective, the incentive reward for successful performance needs to be significant. Studies show that to truly motivate employees, one needs to offer them an award for outstanding performance that is at least 15 to 20 percent above their base salary.[63] Although improving, incentive compensation—including bonuses, stock options, and profit sharing—on average accounts for only 10 percent of base compensation; thus the size of the payout is frequently a barrier to the successful linkage of pay and performance. For example, recent merit pay increases have about equaled the rate of inflation, between 3 and 4 percent during the past few years. A company fortunate enough to be able to offer 5 percent average increases during this period, almost a best-case scenario, typically would have 75 percent of its employees receive increases between 2 and 7 percent. How many employees will go all out all year long for a 7 percent increase when they could receive 2 or 3 percent for minimal effort and 5 percent for average effort?

The amount of payout and frequency of payout are linked. Although motivational theory argues for frequent reward opportunities, it is generally true that the more frequent the rewards, the smaller each reward will be. For this reason, it is often better to pay lump-sum rewards over a longer period of time, such as quarterly or annually. In this way, rewards will be larger and will have a greater impact on behavior.

Frailty of the Linkage

Pay-for-performance systems tend to focus attention on monetary rewards to the exclusion of other potential rewards. In fact, managers have the opportunity to influence employees in more ways than they may realize. Depending on the position and organization, the manager may be able to manipulate a large number of job elements to link tangible and intangible rewards with performance. There may be twenty-five to thirty "rewards" or job features at stake, each of which can make an employee's life easier and more enjoyable or, alternately, more difficult. Table 12.7 lists the job elements that a university department head might use to influence or motivate a faculty member. A similar list could be developed for other types of organizations, and most supervisors would be surprised at the length of the list.

To have the maximum motivational impact, both money and these other rewards should be closely tied to performance. Unfortunately, managers who do not understand all the rewards they control may unintentionally send mixed signals to their subordinates. Thus an employee who is evaluated as a below-average performer and is given a low merit increase may later be granted a request to attend a

TABLE 12.7
Rewards for University Faculty

1. Base salary/salary increases
2. Number of courses assigned to teach
3. Types of courses assigned to teach
4. Schedule of courses assigned to teach
5. Location of courses assigned to teach
6. Amount of secretarial support
7. Technical capability of secretarial support
8. Amount of student assistant support
9. Level of qualification of student assistant support
10. Office location/size
11. Furniture for office
12. Permission to travel
13. Resources to travel (professional conventions, etc.)
14. Consulting referrals
15. Permission to consult
16. Funds to use mainframe computer
17. Supplies
18. Telephone access (including long distance)
19. Photocopy access
20. Access to equipment
21. Funds to attend workshops
22. Parking location
23. Availability of department head and dean for meetings
24. Committee assignments within department and college
25. Contact with distinguished visitors to department
26. Invitations to social events
27. Nominations for awards/honors
28. Support for promotion
29. Involvement in activities of department
30. Praise

prestigious conference. The manager believes the low annual merit increase has successfully linked performance to rewards. Understandably, the employee is not so sure.

The situation is no different for top-performing employees. A good employee who is given an undesirable office, the worst administrative assistant, or the greatest number of extraneous assignments may well wonder about the value of his or her contribution, whatever the size of the annual merit increase. The manager is then shocked to find that the employee who received the top merit increase has decided to quit and join a competitor. These situations are all too typical. Most of the week-to-week activities of the manager convey to the employee the absence of a link between performance and rewards.

SUMMARY: MAKING VARIABLE PAY SUCCESSFUL

Pay-for-performance systems are problematic. In some organizations, the forces tending to weaken and negate the links outweigh the factors that enhance and strengthen the relationship between pay and performance. Some of the characteristics of successful incentive systems are as follows:[64]

- *Employee–organization partnerships* designed to ensure that the organization achieves measurable financial gain when the employees receive awards
- *Employee empowerment* to make decisions that influence how work is performed

- *Relevant, simple measures* that are meaningful to the organization and clear enough for employees to understand quickly
- *Effective communication* about the variable pay program and progress toward goals
- *Balance between short- and long-term performance factors* so that the organization does not sacrifice the future for the present
- *Line-of-sight considerations* through focusing as much as possible on performance measures that are within the direct control of plan participants

The typical pay-for-performance system, whether individual incentive or organization-wide bonus, is perceived positively as long as payouts are forthcoming. When individual or organizational performance decreases and payouts are reduced or eliminated, employee commitment and trust in the system begin to wane. At this point, the motivational capacity of the pay-for-performance link is greatly diminished. Variable pay plans are not "everlasting." Even in the conceptualization of an incentive pay plan, it is important to envision that circumstances are going to change and that the plan will need to be adapted to the new circumstances.

Despite the problems, the idea of pay for performance remains popular in the United States. New pay organizations find a way to have some pay of all employees at risk. Typically, this translates to competitive base pay (as described in Chapter 12) plus individual or group incentives. For these organizations, the attempt to link pay and performance represents an important competitive quest, an effort to attract, motivate, and retain talented individuals in the work force.[65]

EXECUTIVE COMPENSATION

For more than fifty years, a spring issue of *Business Week* has reported on executive pay at publicly held companies, a total of 365 in the 2004 report (for the year 2003). In addition to reporting executive pay, *Business Week* also rates the performance of these companies for the most recent three years and the often-tenuous links between company performance and chief executive officer (CEO) pay. For some forty years of this survey, most readers (and others) were not overly concerned with executive pay. Until recently, people were interested and even envious, but most understood that these executives represented a special resource to organizations because of their potential to influence results and hence deserved quite high pay.

All of this changed in the 1990s when executive pay became a highly charged topic. The reason for the intense interest can be summed up in two words, "equity" and "excess," as evidenced by these statistics:[66]

- CEO cash compensation increases averaged 9.1 percent in 2003, far ahead of the approximate 3 percent cost-of-living increase.[67]
- In 1993, the average CEO earned $3,841,273. In 1997, just four years later, CEO pay more than doubled to an average $7.8 million. In 2000, despite weakening returns, U.S. CEOs earned on average a princely $13.1 million.[68] The result of the weakening returns led to the first decreases in more than a decade in the early 2000s with the 2003 average of CEO salary, bonus, and long-term compensation at $8.1 million.[69]

- Reuben Mark, CEO, Colgate-Palmolive, was the top-paid CEO with a total pay of $141.1 million. This at a time when Colgate-Palmolive saw a –19 percent return in the three-year period ending in 2003.[70] The *Business Week* report rated Mr. Mark as one of the CEO's "who gave the least" in terms of pay for performance.[71]
- In 1980 CEO pay was 42 times the pay of the ordinary factory worker; by 1991 this ratio had increased to 104; by 1993 to 149; by 1997 to 326; and was 531 times the average worker in 2001. As a result of the collapsing stock market, this ratio fell to 282 in 2002.[72]
- In the period from 1990 to 2003, CEO pay rose 313 percent. During that time the S&P 500 stock index rose 242 percent, corporate profits increased 128 percent, the average worker's pay climbed 49 percent, and inflation rose 41 percent.[73] If the minimum wage had risen as much as CEO pay over the thirteen years, it would be more than $15.00 per hour instead of the current rate of $5.15.

Extremely high executive compensation compared with the wages being earned by lower level participants in organizations has led to perceptions of unfairness and low distributive justice. One example of the injustice was found at AMR Corporation (American Airlines), which revealed that CEO Donald Carty secretly put in place an executive bonus retention (worth twice the annual salary of each executive) and pension trust (worth $41 million) at the same time he was negotiating with American's unions about wage and benefit givebacks as well as lay-offs to avoid bankruptcy.[74] As a result of the furor, AMR's board of directors accepted Mr. Carty's resignation.

Goals of Executive Compensation

The theory of compensating the top people in an organization is straightforward: What is in the best interest of the shareholders also should be what brings the greatest reward to the executives. In most organizations, executive pay is not supposed to be based on individual performance measures but rather on unit or organizational performance because an executive's own performance is assumed to be directly reflected in measures of unit or corporate performance. Of course, situations differ, but shareholders want the executives to take the organization forward; that is, to improve things, both in the short and the long term. This wish translates into executive compensation being based on both short-term incentives (e.g., annual bonuses) and long-term ones (e.g., stock options). Consideration must be given to the structure of the incentive arrangements and the performance measures on which incentive compensation will be based.

In practice, incentives are important in determining executive compensation. Although various performance measures are used to determine payouts, most management incentive plans are "formula-driven" plans based on financial measures such as return on equity, profit before or after taxes, and return on invested capital. However, these attempts to tie executive compensation to organizational performance have not proved as effective as intended.[75] A number of studies have found no correlation between a company's stock performance and its compensation of executives.[76] The study reported in the popular book by Jim Collins, *Good to Great,* examines eleven companies who went from good to great and then outperformed their industry competition over a sustained period of time. In looking at that leap, Collins expected to find that executive compensation played a key role in creating great results. The findings were just the opposite. To quote Collins:[77]

> We found no systematic pattern linking executive compensation to the process of going from good to great. The evidence simply does not support the idea that the specific structure of executive compensation acts as a key lever in taking a company from good to great. (p. 49)
>
> Yes, compensation and incentives are important, but for very different reasons in good-to-great companies. The purpose of a compensation system should be . . . to get the right people . . . and to keep them. (p. 50)

The proliferation of stock-option grants, combined with the rise of unbelievable retirement deals, sign-on bonuses, and ironclad severance packages for CEOs have made a mockery out of attempts to truly link pay to performance. The result, irrespective of talent or lack thereof, is that virtually all CEOs have seen their net worth rise by at least several million dollars.

Several special considerations complicate the process of determining executive compensation. For example, because executives generally enjoy a high base salary, compensation arrangements seek to minimize their income tax liability. Attention to tax considerations can make a large difference in the after-tax income of an executive. Another consideration has to do with nonfinancial incentives—the perquisites associated with the executive position.

Executive Bonus Plans

Bonuses play an important role in today's competitive executive payment programs. This type of incentive is usually short term (annual) and based on performance. Consequently, the definition of performance is especially critical.

There are almost as many bonus systems as there are companies using this form of executive compensation. In some systems, the annual bonus is tied by formulas to objective measures, such as gross or net profits, earnings, share price, or return on investment. Other executive bonus plans are based on the subjective judgment of the board of directors and CEO. More complex systems establish certain targets—for example, a 10 percent increase in corporate earnings from the previous year—and generate a bonus pool after the target is attained. The bonus is then distributed, either in accordance with a preset formula or on the basis of subjective judgments.

As an example, consider the bonus plan of Michael Dell, who received only 25 percent of his possible 2001 bonus even though Dell Computer far outperformed its peers on stock price. The company did not meet other important internal targets, including operating-profit margin and customer-satisfaction measures.[78]

Long-Term Incentives

Publicly held organizations in the United States have been criticized for their focus on the short term. To encourage a longer perspective, many boards of directors are adopting programs of **long-term incentives** for executives. The most popular approach is to give stock or stock options to executives. Reports suggest that options constitute as much as 55 percent of the average CEO's pay with as many as 98 percent of large firms awarding options to executives.[79] General Electric CEO

Jeffrey Immelt's compensation is an example. Under the new GE plan, Immelt received a 2003 grant of rights to 250,000 GE stock shares with a value of $7.5 million. These shares cannot be sold for at least four years and then only if GE's cash flow from operating activities has grown an average of 10 percent or more per year over the period. This is a tough test; more than 60 percent of Mr. Immelt's compensation is fully at risk and linked to performance measures directly aligned with long-term investor interests.[80]

Table 12.8 illustrates the upsides and downsides of stock options from the view of the recipient, the company, and the shareholders. The options are valuable as long as the price of the stock keeps increasing. However, the stock purchased (or the right to buy stock) can decrease in value and even become worthless if the company goes bankrupt. Executives of many large companies have suffered this fate in recent years.

Stock options are also attractive to shareholders. First, an option is not a bonus. Executives must use their own resources to exercise their right to purchase the stock. Second, the executives are assuming the same risk as all other shareholders: namely, that the price could move in either direction. Options are a form of profit sharing that links the executive's financial success to that of the shareholders. Finally, stock options are one of the few ways to offer large rewards to executives without cost to the company.[81]

That said, stock options are also controversial as a result of their role in the corporate scandals of the early 2000s.[82] In the cases of Enron, World Com (now MCI), Qwest Communications, and Global Crossing, among others, executives are alleged to have illegally manipulated the price of stock, in part, to allow exercise of their options.[83] From these scandals it seems as though stock options have replaced money itself as the root of all evil. A number of solutions have been proposed, including momentum to require companies to expense options. Although

TABLE 12.8

Stakeholder Views on Stock Options

	Recipient	Company	Shareholders
Upsides	• Flexible • Can receive lower capital gains tax rates • Large potential gains possible	• No cost to company • Positive cash flow on employee exercise • Corporate tax deduction on employee exercise	• Encourages appropriate risk taking • Better incentive alignment through (potential) ownership • Focuses management behavior on the long term
Downsides	• Improper tax-related decisions can be catastrophic • Underdiversified wealth possibilities • Investment risk if stock prices decline	• Underwater options can reduce employee morale • Falling stock prices can reduced ability to attract and retain employees	• Dilution of equity • Repurchases may lead to less investment in long-term projects that would benefit shareholders • Performance gaming • Limited long-term ownership by executives

Source: Pamela Brandes, Ravi Dharwadkar, and G. Victor Lemesis, "Effective Employee Stock Option Design: Reconciling Stakeholder, Strategic, and Motivational Factors," *Academy of Management Executive*, Vol. 17 (1), 2003, pp. 77–93.

not yet required as part of accounting standards, dozens of companies, including Coca-Cola, General Electric, and Microsoft, have announced plans to do so voluntarily. The thought is that stock options should not be viewed as a free good (see Table 12.8) and that the value of the options should be reflected in the profit and loss statement of the company. If the cost of options reduces profitability when granted, presumably companies will be more cautious in awarding them, although there are mixed reviews on this topic.[84] Had Coca-Cola treated options as an expense in 2001, the year before they changed their policy, profits would have been reduced by $202 million.[85] Presumably one would want to believe that there would be value before spending over $200 million.

Perquisites

Perquisites, better known as **perks,** are the extras that frequently go with executive status. Used to supplement the basic benefit package, perks range from such amenities as special parking and plush offices to pay for vacation travel, automobile expenses, and company-paid memberships in clubs. More personal perks, such as low-cost loans and personal use of company facilities (e.g., airplanes), have been slowly disappearing over the last ten years as various tax and regulatory agencies have ruled that their value must be included in the executive's taxable income. However, the list of perks offered is long and will remain an expected feature of the upper levels of the executive ladder. A *Business Week* survey found that the twenty-five most highly paid CEOs received average perks valued at more than $930,000 in 2003.[86] Speaking of perks, in 2000 Apple Computer's CEO, Steve Jobs, received the ultimate nonfinancial incentive—a $90 million Gulfstream V jet of his own.[87]

Determining Executive Compensation

Who determines the pay of the top people in a publicly held organization? Obviously, it would be a conflict of interest to have the CEO determine the reward structure for the top executives, including him- or herself. Most publicly held companies in the United States have a compensation committee composed of members of the board of directors who are not officers of the firm. The compensation committee makes recommendations to the board on overall organizational pay policies, including salaries, incentives, and perquisites for top officers. Frequently, the compensation committee seeks advice from consultants who specialize in salary and rewards for executives.

Reforming Executive Compensation

To quote one author, "We are entering a new era in executive compensation, in which companies increasingly will have to sell their executive-pay programs to stockholders."[88] Having a committee of shareholders develop a plan that combines salary, annual bonus for short-term performance, and longer term stock options sounds like a good way to align executive interests with those of critical constituencies, including shareholders, the investment community, and employees. In the recent past, however, this approach has not worked as envisioned for several reasons.[89]

Frequently, the members of the board of directors, including those serving on the compensation committee, are not independent. This lack of independence can have several causes. For instance, members of the board may be appointed by the chairman and CEO. Or the members of the board may be attorneys or investment bankers who receive fees from the company. It is not unusual for a CEO to have the CEO of another company on the board and, in turn, serve on the other CEO's board. All this leads to potential conflicts of interest.[90]

Research on the role of the board of directors and CEO salary is mixed. One study showed that the longer the tenure of the CEO, the less of a link there is between compensation and company performance—a result of the CEO's ability to build influence within the board and use this influence to weaken incentive alignment mechanisms.[91] More recent research found no evidence that director independence (or lack thereof) led to greater levels of, or changes in, CEO compensation.[92] The latter researchers argue that directors, regardless of their level of independence, are ever mindful of their obligations to shareholders. Perhaps this is reinforced by a third study that showed that CEO compensation in companies whose stock is popular with institutional investors (e.g., large mutual or pension funds) tends to be more in line with shareholder preferences.[93] As extremely large investors or shareholders, institutional investors pressure the board of directors to do what is right with respect to CEO compensation.

Incentives are frequently not what they seem. Whereas shareholders have something at risk—namely, their investment in purchasing the shares—many of the forms of long-term incentives and options offered to executives have only upside potential. For example, stock appreciation rights and restricted stock require no investment or risk.[94] In other cases, boards have been known to reprice stock options to allow executives to reap benefits even though performance targets were not realized.[95] For example, options are issued to an executive when the stock is at $50, but then it falls to $30. Instead of allowing the executive to be out of the money, as should be the case, the board may cancel the $50 options and issue new ones at $30.

Several important executive compensation reforms have been implemented:

1. The Securities and Exchange Commission now requires disclosure of executive pay and trends in executive pay in proxy statements and allows shareholders a nonbinding vote on corporate pay policies.[96] Pay of top executives is now reported annually in a prescribed and relatively straightforward manner. As a result, all aspects of executive compensation are now clearly disclosed.
2. Legislation now imposes a $1 million cap on the amount of executive pay that is deductible (by the corporation). The idea behind the legislation is that any payment beyond this amount must be earned by stock options and bonus arrangements linked to performance standards. Some have argued that this has not slowed the growth in executive pay but has instead created a minimum wage for executives.[97]

All the signs point to heightened sensitivity to executive pay on the part of executives, board members, and shareholders. For example, many board of directors compensation committees now keep a closer eye on compensation and use the opinions of independent experts when designing executive compensation systems. Several organizations hold the CEO's base salary to a multiple of the average worker's salary. (For instance, CEO salary and bonus at Herman Miller is limited to twenty times the average paycheck.)[98]

Summary of Key Points

Performance-based rewards are an attempt to link compensation to performance. It is hard to underestimate the strategic importance of using variable pay to align compensation with organizational goals and to signal to employees what the major organizational values are.

Other reasons for seeking such a linkage are employee preferences and the motivational aspects of tying pay to performance. Linking pay to performance also provides an increased incentive for top performers to remain with the organization, a means of reinforcing organizational objectives, and a method of keeping labor costs in line with productivity.

As illustrated in A Different Point of View, there also are reasons to carefully consider the approach to linking rewards to performance. In some instances, programs linking rewards to performance are a "quick and dirty" substitute for good management. Furthermore, some programs attempting to link pay to performance have potential negative consequences, such as an emphasis on quantity over quality.

Pay can be linked to performance at the individual, group, or organizational levels. Individual plans can be used only where individual performance is measurable. Group systems are important where worker cooperation and coordination are necessary.

Individual plans include piecework, commission, individual bonus, and merit salary increases. In addition, an increasing number of organizations are basing pay on the number of different skills or jobs mastered as a way of motivating continued learning and flexibility.

Group incentives may be piece rates based on group output, gain-sharing plans, or profit-sharing plans. Profit sharing is an incentive system in which designated employees share the business profits. Gain-sharing plans include the Scanlon plan, Improshare, and the Rucker plan, all of which seek employee suggestions to cut costs and then share the savings with the employees. These plans work best in small to medium-sized organizations. Winsharing is a gain-sharing program that attempts to incorporate profits in addition to motivating productivity improvements.

Though linking pay to performance has its advantages, a number of factors may hinder its successful implementation. First, linking pay to performance is not going to work if employees have only limited control over performance, as is often the case. Second, performance is frequently difficult to measure. Third, many incentive rewards are not large enough to be motivational. Finally, many managers think incentive systems alone will provide the necessary linkage between pay and performance, and they may ignore many other aspects of the work or work-related environment that can reinforce the association between performance and rewards.

Executives are especially important to organizations and thus usually operate with a somewhat different system of compensation and incentives. Frequently, executive reward packages include bonus plans based on organizational performance and long-term incentives in the form of stock options. Executives may have perks such as company-paid automobiles, club memberships, and other considerations associated with their role. Executive pay has been criticized as being excessive in amount and inequitable when compared with organizational performance. Furthermore, executive pay has increased much faster than the pay of the average worker or than inflation.

The Manager's Vocabulary

bonus
commission
cost containment
employee stock ownership plans (ESOPs)
expectancy
expectancy theory
gain sharing
Improshare plan
incentive pay
instrumentality
line of sight
long-term incentives
merit pay
new pay
pay for knowledge
perks
perquisites
piece-rate incentive
profit sharing
Rucker plan
Scanlon plan

skill-based pay
standard hour plan
stock options
Taylor plan
valence
winsharing

Questions for Discussion

1. Did commission pay accomplish its intended purpose at Circuit City? If so, why did Circuit City decide to pay sales staff an hourly rate with no commission?
2. What is new pay? Why is it important?
3. In what ways can the expectancy theory of motivation be used to improve compensation systems?
4. What are the advantages of linking pay to performance? The disadvantages?
5. What are some of the reasons employees tend to resist piece-rate incentive systems?
6. What are the five major individual incentives described? How would each be best matched with the following groups of employees: (a) production workers, (b) sales employees, (c) professional employees, (d) electronics assembly workers, (e) managers, (f) scientists/engineers?
7. What is line of sight? How do individual and group incentives differ in line of sight?
8. What are some of the considerations involved in using individual versus group incentives?
9. Describe the advantages and disadvantages of the various gain-sharing plans.
10. What are the major barriers to successfully linking pay to performance? Which barriers are most associated with each type of incentive?
11. What are the advantages of skill-based pay?
12. Why does E. E. Lawler believe that merit pay, after a period of several years, will end up creating differences in employee pay unrelated to performance?
13. What is an ESOP? How would an ESOP improve employee motivation?
14. What are stock options? Why have they had minimal impact on linking CEO pay to performance?

Case 12.1
The Gyro Chemical Corporation

The Gyro Chemical Corporation produces and sells a broad line of more than 400 high-quality industrial cleaning and custodial products to companies throughout the United States. Sales are made through a network of 1,500 sales representatives. The sales representatives are compensated entirely by commission.

An effective sales force is the key factor in Gyro's profitability. It is important that each of the sales territories be fully staffed with trained, effective sales representatives. A number of sales representatives are extremely successful and earn between $150,000 and $350,000 each year in commissions. At the same time, the firm has recruited, hired, and trained many others (at a cost of $15,000 each), only to find that they are not suited to commission sales.

About 100 sales managers, each assigned to a district, are responsible for recruiting, hiring, supervising, and field-training approximately fifteen sales representatives each. Initial training of sales representatives is through a ten-day program at Gyro headquarters. The sales managers find that they spend so much time recruiting and hiring that the daily supervision and field training of current salespeople are neglected.

In an effort to remedy this situation, Gyro's top management has decided to hire twelve professional recruiters, one for each of the sales regions. The recruiters will be responsible for finding job candidates, performing initial screening, and proposing final candidates to sales managers. Hiring decisions will continue to be the responsibility of the sales managers.

The commission system that underlies the compensation of sales representatives provides the impetus for various incentive plans that pervade all levels of the organization. Even though the recruiters have a limited role, they represent an important component in assisting the sales managers. Naturally, Gyro wants the compensation of the recruiters to have an incentive component of some type.

1. What are the individual incentive alternatives for compensating the recruiters, along with the advantages and disadvantages of each? Pay particular attention to possible dysfunctional aspects of each alternative.
2. Should incentive payments to recruiters be based on (a) the number of candidates interviewed, (b) the number of candidates recommended to sales managers, (c) candidates recommended and hired, (d) candidates hired and successful? What are the advantages and disadvantages of each possibility?
3. What compensation arrangement, including combination of base and incentive pay, would you recommend for the recruiters?
4. How might sales managers be compensated to motivate them to choose and nurture highly effective salespeople?

Case 12.2
Incentive Pay for Fox Geomapping

Fifteen years ago, when John Fox started Fox Geomapping, the idea of using computers in planning school, election, and other political districts was in its infancy. Fox's idea was to store residential information about a city or county in a computer and then use mathematical models to optimize the boundaries desired in government planning (e.g., schools or election districts). The challenge was to incorporate the entire scope of census information—streets, dwellings, numbers of residents, occupations, and incomes—into a computer and then manipulate the information to satisfy the multiple goals of planning officials. The software was complex and needed to recognize logical division points, such as major highways, rivers, and political boundaries, in developing solutions.

At first, the procedures Fox used were rudimentary and ad hoc. Information was collected and stored and then processed by a series of programs adapted from other applications. One program tracked numbers and distances. Another program placed this information on computer representations of city maps. Programs adapted from operations research employed optimization routines to develop solutions. The work was tedious and cumbersome.

Over the years, hardware and software developments streamlined the process, but still the sequence was complex. At first Fox lined up the projects and then did the work. However, as the demand for the services grew, Fox Geomapping needed employees for all phases of the business. At the present time, Fox Geomapping has ten young professionals from various backgrounds involved in the many projects under way.

As Fox began to hire employees, he realized that virtually no one had the range of skills needed to run the many projects that were waiting to be done. Workers needed specialized skills in computers, understanding of mathematical modeling, knowledge of census procedures, as well as expertise in city planning. Mr. Fox was hiring college graduates, but whatever the major of those hired, two to three years of training were needed before an employee could understand the entire scope of the effort and be productive at even a minimal level. Fox was hiring talented people, was paying above-market salaries for their majors, and was then hoping they would learn enough in the first two or three years to become valued contributors to Fox Geomapping.

The problem was that many of the most talented employees left for better jobs within the first two years. Fox became convinced that he needed some type of incentive system that increased an employee's commitment to Fox Geomapping, particularly in the first several years of employment.

1. What types of incentive systems would be possible for Fox Geomapping?
2. What would be the advantages of each system Fox might consider? What would be the disadvantages?
3. Fox Geomapping has a benefit package, but Fox wonders what role increased benefits might have in gaining employee commitment. What role might benefits play in retaining professional employees?
4. Given these facts, what incentive compensation system would you recommend for Fox Geomapping, and why?

Exercise 12.1
Executive Pay Update

As a compensation specialist with a major pharmaceutical company, you are interested in executive pay. The vice president of human resources asks you for figures on the total compensation of CEOs of the following pharmaceutical companies: Abbott Laboratories, Baxter International, Bristol-Myers Squibb, Johnson & Johnson, Lilly, Merck, Pfizer, and Wyeth. Go to http://www.paywatch.org for the compensation information, then answer the following questions.

1. If you wanted a more complete picture, what else would you need to know beyond the information given at www.paywatch.org? Where could you find this additional information?
2. Find additional information for two of the CEOs. Why is the more detailed information important?

Notes and References

1. Carlos Tejada and Gary McWilliams, "Circuit City Salesmen Zapped on 'Bloody Wednesday'," *The Wall Street Journal Classroom Edition,* September 2003. (Available at: http://www.wsjclassroomedition.com/archive/03sep/bigb_circuitcity.htm)
2. "Be Careful What You Pay For," Lead Well Institute. (Available at: http://leadwell.com/db/1/4/222/)
3. Wayne Brockbank, "HR's Future on the Way to a Presence," *Human Resource Management,* Vol. 36 (1), 1997, pp. 65–69.
4. Thomas B. Wilson, *Innovative Reward Systems for the Changing Workplace* (New York: McGraw-Hill, 1995).
5. Hewitt Associates, "U.S. Salary Increase Survey: 2003 and 2004." (Available at: https://was4.hewitt.com/compensationcenter/AppController?FUNCTION=download&ACTION=5&doc_code=05823-9087&mime_type=application/pdf&atch_num=1&lang_id=1).
6. Ibid.
7. L. Dyer, D. P. Schwab, and R. D. Theriault, "Managerial Perceptions Regarding Salary Increase Criteria," *Personnel Psychology,* Vol. 29, 1976, pp. 233–242.
8. George Graen, "Instrumentality Theory of Work Motivation," *Journal of Applied Psychology,* Vol. 53, 1965, pp. 1–25; R. D. Prichard, D. W. Leonard, C. W. Von Bergen Jr., and R. J. Kirk, "The Effects of Varying Schedules of Reinforcement on Human Task Performance," *Organizational Behavior and Human Performance,* Vol. 16, 1976, pp. 205–230; and Hewitt Associates, "U.S. Salary Increase Survey: 2003 and 2004."
9. E. E. Lawler III, *The New Pay* [CEO Publication G84-7(55)] (Los Angeles: Center for Effective Organizations, University of Southern California, 1986); and Edward E. Lawler III, *Rewarding Excellence: Pay Strategies for the New Economy* (San Francisco: Jossey-Bass, 2000).
10. Edward E. Lawler III and G. Douglas Jenkins Jr., "Strategic Reward Systems," in *Handbook of Industrial and Organizational Psychology,* 2nd ed., Vol. 3, eds. Marvin D. Dunnette and Leaetta M. Hough (Palo Alto, Calif.: Consulting Psychologists Press, 1992).
11. Sara L. Rynes and Barry Gerhard (eds.). *Compensation in Organizations: Current Research and Practice.* (San Francisco: Jossey-Bass, 2000).
12. Diane Cadrain, "Put Success in Sight," *HR Magazine,* May 2003, pp. 85–92.
13. Joseph W. Harder, "Equity Theory versus Expectancy Theory: The Case of Major League Baseball Free Agents," *Journal of Applied Psychology,* Vol. 76, 1991, pp. 458–464; and Robert D. Bretz Jr. and Steven L. Thomas, "Perceived Equity, Motivation, and Final-Offer Arbitration in Major League Baseball," *Journal of Applied Psychology,* Vol. 77, 1992, pp. 280–287.
14. Deborah A. Mohr, James A. Riedel, and Kent S. Crawford, "A Group Wage Incentive System Can Boost Performance and Cut Costs," *Defense Management Journal,* second quarter 1986, pp. 13–17; B. S. Georgopolous, G. M. Mahoney, and M. W. Jones, "A Path Goal Approach to Productivity," *Journal of Applied Psychology,* Vol. 41, 1957, pp. 345–353; and D. P. Schwab and L. Dyer, "The Motivational Impact of a Compensation System on Em-

ployee Performance," *Organizational Behavior and Human Performance,* Vol. 9, 1973, pp. 215–225.
15. V. H. Vroom, *Work Motivation* (New York: Wiley, 1964); Edwin A. Locke and Gary P. Latham, "What Should We Do about Motivation Theory? Six Recommendations for the Twenty-First Century," *Academy of Management Review,* Vol. 29 (3), 2004, pp. 388–403.
16. T. R. Mitchell, Mabmoub A. Wabba, and Robert J. House, "Expectancy Theory in Work Motivation: Some Logical and Methodological Issues," *Human Relations,* Vol. 27 (2), 1974, pp. 121–147.
17. Donald P. Schwab, "Impact of Alternative Compensation Systems on Pay Valence and Instrumentality Perceptions," *Journal of Applied Psychology,* Vol. 58 (3), 1973, pp. 308–312.
18. Janet Wiscombe, "Rewards Get Results," *Workforce,* April 2002, pp. 42–48; "How Avis Tries Harder to Reward Its Employees," *HR Focus,* Vol 80 (6), June 2003, pp. 4–5.
19. Robert D. Hoff, "Tech Outfits Should Take Notes," *Business Week,* March 3, 2003. (Available at: http://www.businessweek.com/magazine/content/03_09/b3822613_tc102.htm)
20. J. L. Kerr and J. W. Slocum, "Managing Corporate Culture through Reward Systems," *Academy of Management Executive,* Vol. 1, 1987, pp. 99–108.
21. F. Filipczak, "Why No One Likes Your Incentive Program," *Training,* August 1993, p. 21.
22. N. L. Kerr and S. E. Bruun, "Dispensability of Member Effort and Group Motivation Losses: Free-Rider Effects," *Journal of Personality and Social Psychology,* Vol. 44 (1), 1983, pp. 78–94.
23. B. Latané, K. Williams, and S. Harkins, "Many Hands Make Light the Work: The Causes and Consequences of Social Loafing," *Journal of Personality and Social Psychology,* Vol. 37 (6), 1979, pp. 822–833.
24. Edward E. Lawler, *Pay and Organizational Effectiveness* (New York: McGraw-Hill, 1971).
25. Amy Dunkin and Kathleen Kerwin, "Now Salespeople Really Must Sell for Their Supper," *Business Week,* July 31, 1989, pp. 50, 52.
26. "The Bank That Disappeared," *The Economist,* March 4, 1995, pp. 11–12.
27. Daniel C. Rowland, "Incentive Pay: Productivity's Own Reward," *Personnel Journal,* March 1987, pp. 48–57.
28. Reed Abelson, "Market Fallout: Year-End Bonuses Are No Longer Routine," *New York Times,* September 4, 2001, p. C9.
29. Dale Feuer, "Paying for Knowledge," *Training,* May 1987, pp. 57–66; and Richard L. Bunning, "Skill-Based Pay: Restoring Incentives to the Workplace," *Personnel Administrator,* June 1989, pp. 65–70.
30. Edward E. Lawler and Gerald E. Ledford Jr., "Skill-Based Pay: A Concept That's Catching On," *Compensation and Benefits Review,* January–February 1986, pp. 54–61.
31. Gerald E. Ledford Jr., "Three Case Studies on Skill-Based Pay: An Overview," *Compensation and Benefits Review,* March–April 1991, pp. 11–22.
32. N. Gupta, G. D. Jenkins Jr., and W. P. Curington, "Paying for Knowledge: Myths and Realities," *National Productivity Review,* Spring 1986, pp. 107–123.
33. Richard L. Bunning, "Models for Skill-Based Pay Plans," *HR Magazine,* February 1992, pp. 62–64.
34. Lawler and Jenkins, "Strategic Reward Systems."
35. Edward E. Lawler, "The New Plant Revolution Revisited," *Organizational Dynamics,* Autumn 1990, pp. 4–14; and Edward E. Lawler, "The New Plant Approach: A Second Generation Approach," *Organizational Dynamics,* Summer 1991, pp. 4–14.
36. Robert S. Nadel, "Compensation Alternatives: Changes in Business Strategy, Plans and Expectations," July 2001. (Available at: http://www.shrm.org/whitepapers/ documents/default.asp?page=61440.asp)
37. John Dantico, "Skill Based Pay," Society for Human Resource Management White Paper, July 2001. (Available at: http://www/shrm.org)
38. Edward E. Lawler, G. E. Ledford, and S. A. Mohrman, *Employee Involvement in America* (Houston: American Productivity and Quality Center, 1989).
39. Edward E. Lawler, *Strategic Pay* (San Francisco: Jossey-Bass, 1990), pp. 71–85.
40. Steve Bates, "Top Pay for Best Performance," *HR Magazine,* January 2003, pp. 31–38.
41. Lawler, Ibid., p. 73.
42. Nathan B. Winstanley, "Are Merit Increases Really Effective?" *Personnel Administrator,* Vol. 4, 1982, pp. 23–31; regarding requirement 5, see also Michael Keeley, "A Contingency Framework for Performance Evaluation," *Academy of Management Review,* July 1978, pp. 428–438.

43. John F. Sullivan, "The Future of Merit Pay Programs," *Compensation and Benefits Review,* Vol. 20, May–June 1988, pp. 22–30.
44. Mohr, Riedel, and Crawford, "A Group Wage Incentive System," pp. 13–17.
45. John A. Wagner III, Paul A. Rubin, and Thomas J. Callahan, "Incentive Payment and Nonmanagerial Productivity: An Interrupted Time Series Analysis of Magnitude and Trend," *Organizational Behavior and Human Decision Processes,* Vol. 42, 1988, pp. 47–74.
46. Don Nightingale, "Profit Sharing: New Nectar for the Worker Bees," *Canadian Business Review,* Spring 1984, pp. 11–14.
47. Brian E. Graham-Moore and Timothy L. Ross, *Gainsharing: Plans for Improving Performance* (Washington, D.C.: Bureau of National Affairs, 1990).
48. *People, Performance, and Pay.* (Houston, TX-American Productivity & Quality Center, 1987).
49. Susan C. Hanlon, David C. Meyer, and Robert R. Taylor, "Consequences of Gainsharing: A Field Experiment Revisited," *Group and Organizational Management,* Vol. 19 (1), 1994, pp. 87–111.
50. Brian E. Graham-Moore and Timothy L. Ross, *Productivity Gainsharing* (Englewood Cliffs, N.J.: Prentice-Hall, 1983).
51. A. J. Geare, "Productivity from Scanlon Type Plans," *Academy of Management Review,* Vol. 1 (3), 1976, pp. 99–108.
52. W. C. Freund and E. Epstein, *People and Productivity* (Homewood, Ill.: Dow Jones–Irwin, 1984).
53. Jay R. Schuster and Patricia K. Zingheim, *The New Pay: Linking Employee and Organizational Performance* (Lexington, Mass.: Lexington Books, 1992).
54. Charles R. Gowen and Sandra Jennings, "The Effects of Changes in Participation and Group Size on Gainsharing Success: A Case Study," *Journal of Organizational Behavior and Management,* Vol. 11, 1990, pp. 147–169; Denis Collins, Larry Hatcher, and Timothy L. Ross, "The Decision to Implement Gainsharing: The Role of Work Climate, Expected Outcomes, and Union Status," *Personnel Psychology,* Vol. 46, 1993, pp. 77–104; Woodruff Imberman, "Gainsharing: A Lemon or Lemonade?" *Business Horizons,* January–February 1996, pp. 36–40; and Darlene O'Neill, "Blending the Best of Profit Sharing and Gainsharing," *HR Magazine,* March 1994, pp. 66–70.
55. "ESOPs: Are They Good for You?" *Business Week,* May 15, 1989, pp. 116–123.
56. "A Statistical Profile of Employee Ownership," December 2003. (Available at: http://www.nceo.org/library/eo_stat.html)
57. "ESOPs Broaden Employee Stock Ownership," *Wall Street Journal,* January 7, 1987, p. 1; and J. L. French, "Employee Perspectives on Stock Ownership: Financial Investment or Mechanism of Control?" *Academy of Management Review,* July 1987, pp. 427–435; W. Jack Duncan, "Stock Ownership and Work Motivation," *Organizational Dynamics,* Vol. 30 (1), 2001, pp. 1–11.
58. "A Statistical Profile of Employee Ownership."
59. Lawler, *Strategic Pay,* pp. 26–27.
60. "ESOPs: Are They Good for You?"
61. "This Is Some Way to Build Employee Loyalty," *Business Week,* March 2, 1992, p. 84.
62. Gene Milbourne Jr., "The Relationship of Money and Motivation," *Compensation Review,* second quarter 1980, pp. 33–44.
63. Thomas J. Hackett, "Seven Steps to Successful Performance-Based Rewards," *HR Focus,* September 1999, p. 11–13.
64. Schuster and Zingheim, *The New Pay.*
65. Drew Robb, "Automation Gives Variable Compensation a Boost," *HR Magazine,* August 2002, pp. 73–80.
66. A. Farnham, "The Trust Gap," *Fortune,* December 4, 1989, pp. 76–78; "What, Me Overpaid? CEOs Fight Back," *Business Week,* May 4, 1992, pp. 142–148; "That Eye-Popping Executive Pay," *Business Week,* April 25, 1994, pp. 52–58; and "CEO Pay: Ready for Takeoff," *Business Week,* April 24, 1995, pp. 88–94.
67. Louis Lavelle, Jessi Hempel, and Diane Brady, "Executive Pay," *Business Week,* April 19, 2004, pp. 106–110.
68. Louis Lavelle, "Executive Pay," *Business Week,* April 16, 2001, pp. 76–80.
69. Lavelle, Hempel, and Brady, "Executive Pay."
70. Ibid.
71. Ibid, p. 109.
72. "U.S. CEO Pay Gap Widens Again," *CBS MarketWatch,* April 14, 2004. (Available at: http://cbs.marketwatch.com/news/story.asp?dist=¶m=archive&siteid=mktw&guid=%7B67824A06%2DFF21%2D45E8%2DAE96%2D2A1FF8C6AF44%7D)
73. Ibid.
74. Orit Gadiesh and Marcia Blenko, "Executive Pay: The Same Old Saw?" *Wall Street Journal,* April 29, 2003. (Available at: http://online.wsj.com/PA2VJBNA4R/article/0,,SB105158242527820900-search,00.html)

75. Jennifer Reingold, "The Folly of Jumbo Stock Options," *Business Week,* December 22, 1997, pp. 36–37; Charles Elson, "What's Wrong with Executive Compensation?" *Harvard Business Review,* January Vol. 81 (1), 2003, pp. 68–77.
76. Jeffery Kerr and Richard A. Bettis, "Boards of Directors, Top Management Compensation and Shareholder Returns," *Academy of Management Review,* December 1987, pp. 645–664; C. J. Loomis, "The Madness of Executive Compensation," *Fortune,* Vol. 106 (1), 1982, pp. 42–52; M. Haire, E. E. Ghiselli, and M. E. Gordon, "A Psychological Study of Pay," *Journal of Applied Psychology Monograph,* Vol. 51, 1967; and John L. Pearce, William B. Stevenson, and James L. Perry, "Managerial Compensation Based on Organizational Performance: A Time Series Analysis of the Effects of Merit Pay," *Academy of Management Journal,* Vol. 28, 1985, pp. 261–278.
77. Jim Collins. *Good to Great: Why Some Companies Make the Leap and Others Don't.* New York: HarperCollins, 2001.
78. Gadiesh and Blenko, "Executive Pay."
79. Catherine M. Daily, S. Trevis Certo, and Dan R. Dalton, "Executive Stock Option Repricing: Retention and Performance Reconsidered," *California Management Review,* Vol. 44 (4), Summer 2002, pp. 8–23.
80. Steve Gelsi, "GE Changes CEO Pay," *CBS MarketWatch,* September 17, 2003. (Available at: http://cbs.marketwatch.com/news/story.asp?dist=¶m=archive&siteid=mktw&guid=%7B5AC6D896%2D87A6%2D45B3%2D95C8%2D1600458BD255%7D
81. Pamela Brandes, Ravi Dharwadkar, and G. Victor Lemesis, "Effective Employee Stock Option Design: Reconciling Stakeholder, Strategic, and Motivational Factors," *Academy of Management Executive,* Vol. 17 (1), 2003, pp. 77–93.
82. Louis Lavelle, "Commentary: How to Halt the Options Express," *Business Week,* September 9, 2002. (Available at: http://www.businessweek.com/@@BN5kMIcQcIjAsQYA/magazine/content/02_36/b3798085.htm)
83. Roger L. Martin, "Taking Stock," *Harvard Bsuiness Review,* January 2003, Vol. 81 (1), p. 19.
84. William A. Sahlman, "Expensing Options Solves Nothing," *Harvard Business Review,* December Vol. 80 (12), 2002, pp. 90–96, Zvi Bodie, Robert S. Kaplan, and Robert C. Merton, "For the Last Time: Stock Options are an Expense," *Harvard Business Review,* March Vol. 81 (3), 2003, pp. 63–71.
85. Floyd Norris and Sheei Day, "Coke to Report Stock Options as an Expense," *New York Times,* July 15, 2002. (Available at: http://query.nytimes.com/search/restricted/article?res=F10715F93D5D0C768DDDAE0894DA404482)
86. Lavelle, Hempel, and Brady, "Executive Pay," p. 110.
87. Geoffrey Colvin, "The Great Pay Heist." *Fortune,* June 25, 2001, pp. 64–70.
88. John D. McMillan, "Executive Pay a New Way," *HR Magazine,* June 1992, pp. 46–48.
89. Colvin, "The Great Pay Heist."
90. "Comp Committees, or Back-Scratchers-in-Waiting?" *Business Week,* May 4, 1992, pp. 146–147.
91. Charles W. L. Hill and Phillip Phan, "CEO Tenure as a Determinant of CEO Pay," *Academy of Management Journal,* Vol. 34, 1991, pp. 707–717.
92. Catherine M. Daily, Jonathan L. Johnson, Alan E. Ellstrand, and Dan R. Dalton, "Compensation Committee Composition as a Determinant of CEO Compensation," *Academy of Management Journal,* Vol. 41, 1998, pp. 209–220.
93. David Parthiban, Rahul Kochhar, and Edward Levitas, "The Effect of Institutional Investors on the Level and Mix of CEO Compensation," *Academy of Management Journal,* Vol. 41, 1998, pp. 200–208.
94. Graef S. Crystal, "Incentive Pay That Doesn't Work," *Fortune,* August 28, 1989, pp. 101, 104.
95. Shaifali Puri, "Pay for Underperformance," *Fortune,* December 8, 1997.
96. Kevin G. Salwen, "SEC Unveils New Rules on Disclosures of Corporate Executives' Pay Packages," *Wall Street Journal,* February 14, 1992, p. A4.
97. "That's Some Pay Cap, Bill," *Business Week,* April 25, 1994, p. 57.
98. "Herman Miller Links Worker–CEO Pay," *Wall Street Journal,* May 7, 1992, pp. B1, B8.

PART 5

Maintaining Human Resources

CHAPTER 13

Benefits

- The Role of Benefits in Reward Systems
- Types of Benefits
- Issues in Indirect Compensation

HR Challenge

What is the sound of pension plans as they tumble like falling dominos? We are about to find out as one company after another reneges on its pension obligations toward current and future employees. For example, in mid–2004 the U.S. government announced it would not guarantee bankrupt United Airlines' (UAL, Corp.) loans. Among UAL's debts is a total of $4.1 billion in pension payments by the end of 2008, along with another $1 billion for retiree health care benefits.[1] All of this represents obligations United Airlines cannot begin to meet; hence its filing with the Federal Bankruptcy Court in Chicago to terminate its four employee pension plans—a drastic move that it said is needed to attract the financing that would allow it to emerge from bankruptcy protection.[2]

The next domino in line is US Airways, which is facing a cash shortage and seeks permission to stretch out $67.5 million in contributions it owes to the pensions of two unions.[3] If not granted, US Airways, which emerged from bankruptcy in April 2003, could again face bankruptcy and possible liquidation. Close behind is Continental Airlines, the fifth-largest U.S. carrier. Continental announced that it would skip contributions to employee pension plans to help defer $250 million in expenses.[4]

If United Airlines, US Airways, and Continental find a way to renege on their promises, you can be sure that the other major airlines—American Airlines, Delta Air Lines, and Northwest Airlines—will try to do the same.

The sound of these pension plans tumbling is that of Captain Tim Baker, a 19-year veteran of US Airways. Mr. Baker, like many working for US Airways or other major airlines, may get less than 50 cents on the dollar of what his pension would have provided.[5] What should companies faced with escalating cost of retirement plans do to meet the challenge? Is there any way that such companies can be competitive without jeopardizing their commitment to their employees? Is this threat to airline pension plans similar to the front end of the $150 billion savings and loan crisis that hit the U.S. economy in the late 1980s?[6] These are important questions associated with pensions in the twenty-first century.

Issues related to employee benefits have become a major topic not only in most organizations but also at the national level. Greater interest in benefits stems from the overall cost, fifty cents for every dollar in payroll in many cases; the rapid increases in the expense of some programs; the effectiveness of various programs; and an increase in legislation associated with benefit programs. Employee benefits include mandatory protection programs, compensation for time not worked, optional protection programs, and private retirement (pension) plans.

Mandatory protection programs include Social Security, unemployment compensation, and workers' compensation. Unemployment compensation provides benefits to out-of-work employees who are actively looking for work. Workers' compensation is a type of no-fault insurance for occupational injuries, disabilities, and death. Both unemployment compensation and workers' compensation systems are operated by the states, whereas Social Security is a federal program.

Many employees receive pay for holidays and vacations. Pay for time not worked may also include sick leave, personal days, and leaves for maternity and infant or elder care. Other protection programs include health insurance, life insurance, and disability insurance. As a result of the skyrocketing costs of health care, employers have been forced to redesign plans by increasing deductibles, splitting some costs with employees (coinsurance), and exploring alternatives such as preferred provider and health maintenance organizations.

Pension plans are funds established by employers to provide income to employees after retirement. Some plans require contributions by employees in addition to those of employers. Plans vary, with most being defined contribution, where benefits are a function of investment growth. Others define benefits based on length of service and average earnings. In addition, many employers provide other types of capital accumulation plans, such as thrift plans or 401(k) plans that allow employees to invest pretax dollars toward retirement.

In the past twenty years a variety of federal laws and regulations regarding benefits have been implemented. ERISA specifies vesting and fiduciary standards to which private pension plans must adhere. COBRA requires the extension of group medical benefits to terminated employees, at the employees' expense.

Benefits raise several important issues, including cost containment, flexible benefit options, and work–family issues. As benefit costs have increased more rapidly than inflation, employers have had to resort to innovative ways of containing costs. Some companies have resorted to self-insurance by establishing funds to cover benefit costs and thus eliminating the segment of premiums that goes to insurance companies. Flexible benefits provide an important means of tailoring benefits to employee needs. Such programs have additional administrative costs and are difficult to communicate to employees; however, if used effectively, they can enhance the organization's reputation as a progressive, employee-oriented firm. Finally, work–family benefits are also achieving increased prominence as employers realize that work issues affect families, and vice versa.

THE ROLE OF BENEFITS IN REWARD SYSTEMS

Once a largely neglected issue, the topic of benefits has become daily news, frequently on the front page, in the past decade. Child care, health care costs and coverage, Social Security, and changes in pension benefits are among the best-known compensation topics today.

A major reason for the increased attention to benefits is cost.[7] In the middle of the last century, indirect compensation cost less than 5 percent of the direct compensation offered to most employees. As shown in Figure 13.1, increases in wages and salaries have averaged just over 3 percent over the last ten years. The cost of benefits has increased at a faster rate, averaging more than 5 percent since the turn of the century. As can be seen in Figure 13.1, this year-over-year difference in the rate of increase in wages/salaries and benefits makes for a large separation of the trend lines.

At the present time, benefits equal almost 50 percent of the cost of direct compensation for companies with 500 or more employees.[8] Most of the increase does not reflect new benefits but rather the higher costs of legally required payments (e.g., the employer's share of Social Security) and optional benefits (especially health insurance); the costs for both doubled over a twenty-year period. The breakdown of the cost of benefits is shown in Table 13.1.

The increased cost of benefits has created something of a value gap—as the cost has gone up, employee satisfaction with benefits has gone down, and the value of benefits in meeting strategic organizational goals has diminished.[9] Because benefits are contingent on membership in the organization, they help a company attract and retain employees. Benefit programs do not directly motivate increased employee performance, for the link between performance level and benefit level is virtually zero. All employees receive similar benefit coverage, regardless of their performance levels.

Employees gain several advantages by receiving part of their compensation in this indirect form. For example, even though employees may contribute to or even pay the entire cost of benefits such as insurance, the cost associated with the group coverage of all employees is likely to be considerably lower than equivalent insurance purchased individually. In addition, some benefits are given favorable

FIGURE 13.1

Employment Cost Index for Civilian Workers, Mid-1993 to 2004

Source: Bureau of Labor Statistics, Employment Cost Index. (Available at: action=EC ectbrief)

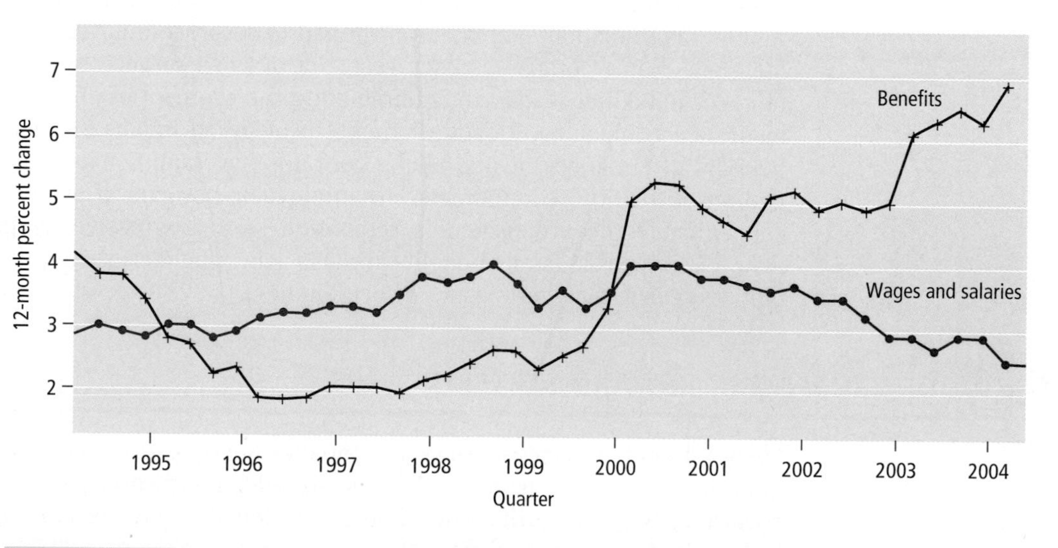

TABLE 13.1

Benefits in Relation to Total Compensation

	All Companies		Small Companies (1–99 workers)		Large Companies (500+ workers)	
	$	%	$	%	$	%
Total compensation	$24.96		$19.72		$33.31	
Wages and salaries	$17.70	70.9	$14.61	74.1	$22.52	67.6
Total benefits	$7.26	29.1	$5.11	25.9	$10.80	32.4
Mandated benefits*	$2.03	8.1	$1.87	9.5	$2.49	7.5
Pay for time not worked†	$1.66	6.6	$1.05	5.3	$2.69	8.1
Health benefits	$1.93	7.7	$1.21	6.1	$2.65	8.0
Pensions	$1.01	4.1	$0.46	2.3	$1.82	5.5
Other benefits	$0.63	2.6	$0.50	2.6	$1.15	3.5

Notes: *Mainly Social Security, Medicare, and workers' compensation.
†Includes vacation and other paid leave.
Source: "Employer Costs for Employee Compensation," Bureau of Labor Statistics, June 2004. (Available at: http://stats.bls.gov/news.release/archives/ecec_09152004.pdf)

tax treatment; the employee need not pay tax on the value of health insurance, for example. The following section reviews many of the common benefit plans currently in use and discusses related issues such as cost containment and legal considerations.

TYPES OF BENEFITS

The major categories of benefits include mandatory protection programs, pay for time not worked, optional protection programs, private retirement plans, and a wide variety of other services.

Mandatory Protection Programs

Several benefits are provided to employees because either the federal or the state government mandates them. The most notable required protection program is specified by the Federal Insurance Contribution Act (FICA) of 1935, better known as the Social Security Act. Social Security is designed to protect employees and their dependents by providing retirement income, disability income, health care (Medicare), and survivor benefits. Other mandated protection programs include workers' compensation and unemployment compensation.

Social Security For many employers and employees, **Social Security** is the most expensive benefit purchased. Two-thirds of the workers in the United States pay more toward Social Security/Medicare than they pay in income tax.

As of 2004, both employee and employer contribute 7.65 percent—15.3 percent in all—of earnings up to a maximum of $87,500, for a combined total of as much as $13,387. A total of 6.2 percent of the tax rate is for Social Security; 1.45 percent is for Medicare. The 2004 earnings maximum of $87,500 is indexed and increases every year. The maximum will increase to $90,000 in 2005. Employees who earn more than $87,500 must continue to pay the Medicare portion, with matching employer contributions. Beginning with 1994, there is no limit on the amount of wages that are subject to Medicare tax.

Social Security is not funded on an actuarial basis, as are most pension or insurance programs. In other words, the contributions are not invested in such a way as to grow and thereby cover the promised pension. Instead, money collected from currently employed individuals is used to meet the program's monthly obligations to those who are now retired or disabled. In the late 1970s, it was realized that changing demographics (a rapid increase in the elderly population) would mean too few workers to support those entitled to payments. Accordingly, Social Security has undergone major changes, the most significant being the 1983 amendments to the Social Security Act. These changes increased both the percentage of earnings contributed and the maximum earnings base. At the same time, some benefits were eliminated, and future benefits were scaled back. For example, an earnings test was added such that Social Security beneficiaries aged sixty-five to seventy could earn $10,200 a year without penalty; benefits are then cut $1 for every $3 earned above that amount. As of January 2000, the Retirement Earnings Test has been eliminated for individuals aged sixty-five to sixty-nine. It remains in effect for those aged sixty-two through sixty-four. A modified test applies for the year an individual reaches age sixty-five.

The future of Social Security is now the subject of increasing and vocal controversy. Social Security was designed for a world that no longer exists; some of the issues are as follows:

- *Longevity:* In 1940 a twenty-year-old worker could expect to enjoy 8.3 years of retirement (assuming he or she retired at sixty-five years of age). In 2000 a twenty-year-old worker can expect to enjoy 14.6 years of retirement and in 2060, 17.7 years of retirement.[10] Thus the number of years of retirement has increased 76 percent between 1940 and the present.
- *Numbers of retirees:* Current retirees not only live longer but are a larger percent of the population. In 1950 there were 13 million retirees, in 2000 there were 34.8 million, and the estimated number in 2050 is 83.7 million.[11]
- *Retirement age:* Currently, those born in 1937 or earlier could retire at age sixty-five and qualify for full Social Security benefits. Those born in 1938 can receive full benefits at age sixty-five and two months. The age of full benefits will shift upward, to sixty-seven years in 2027 for those born in 1960 or later.
- *Ratio of workers to retirees:* In 1950 there were 6.46 workers paying taxes for every retiree collecting benefits. In 2000, 4.48 workers were paying taxes to support each retiree. By 2030, there will be only 2.46 workers to support each retiree.[12]

At the present time there is much discussion on how to fix Social Security. In 2003 the 12.4 percent payroll tax (6.2 percent from employees and an equal amount from employees) raised $632 billion, $471 billion of which went right back into benefits.[13] Around 2018 annual payouts will exceed annual revenues, and by 2042 the system as it exists will no longer be able to pay all promised benefits.[14] Two types of "fixes" are being discussed, adjustments to payments or benefits or private accounts.

- *Adjustments to Payments or Benefits:* The 12.4 percent payroll tax is already regressive and is unlikely to be increased. However, additional funds could be raised by increasing or eliminating maximum income subject to payroll deductions. One proposal is to tax those above the maximum income at a lower rate, say 3.9 percent (instead of 12.4 percent).[15] This would make Social Security deductions comparable to Medicare deductions, which have no income limit. Another proposal is to continue to increase the age for full retirement benefits to seventy years of age.
- *Private Accounts:* President Bush has suggested diverting some portion of payroll taxes to private accounts. Today's promised benefits work out to about a 2 percent annual return on payroll taxes. The same funds invested in a conservative portfolio of equities might earn 5 percent.[16] The biggest catch is the cost of moving from the existing system. If workers shift 2 percent of payroll tax to private accounts, the government would have to find some other money to pay benefits to current retirees. The transition cost would be at least $1 trillion over a decade.

One thing is certain: The Social Security system will continue to be analyzed and debated.

Unemployment Compensation The Social Security Act of 1935 also established a system of **unemployment compensation insurance (UCI)** in the United States. UCI provides benefits, at the rate of 50 to 80 percent of normal pay, to out-of-work employees who have been laid off and who are actively looking for work. Those seeking benefits must be registered with the state employment office in their area and are expected to accept work commensurate with their skills. The benefit period is a function of the length of prior employment, up to a maximum of twenty-six weeks of benefits. Workers who are fired for misconduct, quit voluntarily, or do not actively seek employment generally are not eligible for UCI benefits.

Unlike Social Security, which is managed by the federal government, UCI is handled by the states in accordance with federal guidelines. As a result, the exact details of employer contributions, employee eligibility for coverage, and amount of benefits vary considerably. In most states, employers finance this benefit by paying a small tax on the first $7,000 of an employee's wages. The size of the employer's contribution varies on the basis of past claims against that employer, thus providing an incentive to employers to avoid frequent layoffs. The experience-based tax rate also provides an inducement for employers to keep careful records of the reasons employees leave and to document all discharges due to misconduct.

In periods of an extended economic downturn, it is not unusual for the twenty-six-week limit on benefits to be extended. In 2002 just such an extension was enacted by Congress and signed by the president as part of the economic stimulus for unemployed workers in the aftermath of the September 11, 2001, terrorist attack.

Workers' Compensation As the United States became increasingly industrialized in the late 1800s and early 1900s, disabling worker injuries and worker deaths became more common. Most workers had no avenue of redress and no employee benefits if they were injured on the job. Injured workers and their families simply went without compensation, and employers were not accountable for workplace hazards, which were often very great.

The first **workers' compensation,** a type of no-fault insurance for occupational disabilities and death, was initiated in the early 1900s, and most states have had such a program since 1920. Currently, all states have some form of workers' compensation, which offers reasonable and prompt benefits when workers are injured or killed on the job, regardless of fault. Workers do not need to bear the expense of time-consuming court action against their employers.

As with most insurance, the cost to employers is based on injury experience. The costs of medical treatment, rehabilitation programs, and disability income can be high, especially in cases of serious injuries. As a result, employers have an incentive to encourage employee safety. Unlike other mandated protection programs, workers' compensation is handled entirely by the state, with no federal standards or involvement. Consequently, the specific benefit provisions vary from state to state.

Many organizations and states are experiencing problems with workers' compensation. As presently conceived, there is substantial discontent with workers' compensation—discontent on the part of workers with job-related injuries, the organizations they work for, and insurers.[17] Workers' compensation incidents inevitably involve medical treatment; thus the organizational and insurer discontent is related to rapidly escalating medical costs.[18] Employee discontent is related to concerns over possible loss of income because workers' compensation benefits are generally less than actual income. Additional worker concerns have to do with job security as well as possible medical and legal hassles.

States have been forced to deal with issues relating to workers' compensation because it is an important factor in business decisions to locate or expand in a particular area. For example, in 2003, mainly as a result of workers' comp costs that had tripled for some companies, California ranked forty-sixth on the Small Business Survival Committee's yearly index, a state-by-state comparison that charts the relative difficulties small businesses face.[19] To address the problem, Governor Schwarzenegger called a special legislative session to reduce workers' compensation costs by establishing HMO-like networks of insurer-approved doctors.[20]

Compensation for Time Not Worked

Almost all employers provide full-time employees with some payments for time not worked. Figure 13.2 illustrates a wide range of such benefits.

Holidays Virtually all employers pay employees for major national holidays. Some employers have additional holidays, such as Presidents' Day (February), Columbus Day (October), or Veterans' Day (November), whereas others observe religious holidays such as Good Friday and Rosh Hashanah. Employers that must operate on holidays (e.g., hospitals or police departments) generally provide overtime pay to employees who work on holidays. The International Perspective box points out how much holiday and other benefit policies vary by region and country.

Vacation Most employers offer paid vacations to their permanent employees, the amount depending on length of service. A majority of employers stagger vacation schedules to remain well staffed throughout the year, but others schedule a plant shutdown and have all employees take vacation at that time.

Sick Leave A usual pay-for-time-not-worked benefit is sick leave. Many employees accrue sick leave in proportion to days worked. For instance, one half-day

FIGURE 13.2

Payment for Time Not Worked

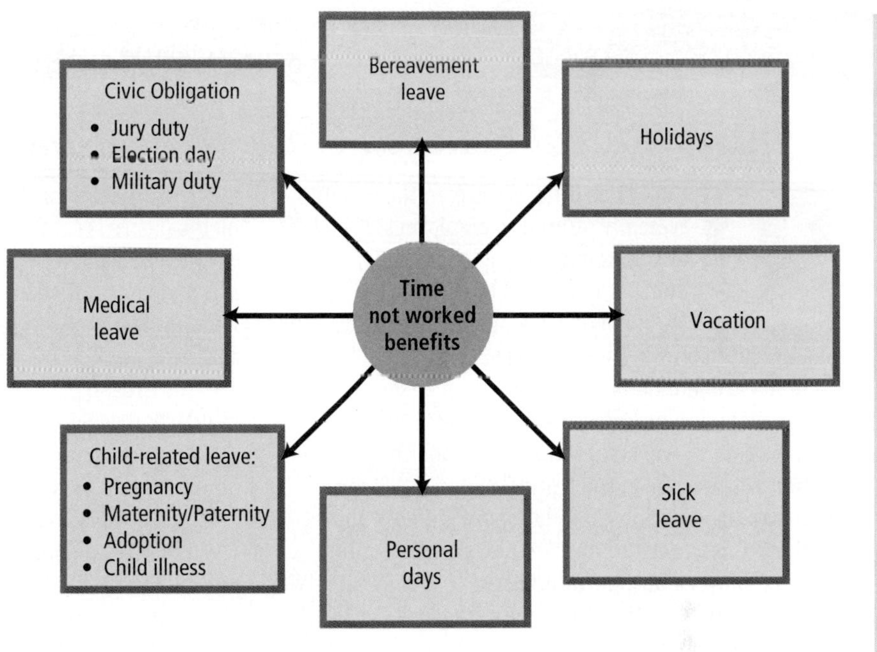

of paid sick leave may be given for each fifteen days worked. Some firms allow unused sick leave to accumulate over the years, to be used in case of extended illness. Another popular alternative is to pay employees for unused sick leave as an incentive to come to work regularly and to use sick leave only when it is really needed.

Personal Days Some employers offer one or two personal holidays each year. Employees can decide when to use these days off—for instance, to celebrate a birthday. Personal days off are sometimes called "mental health days"—for the occasional times when one has to get away from work or "go crazy."

Other Leaves In 1993 the Family and Medical Leave Act became law. This act mandates unpaid leave of up to twelve weeks, with benefits and reinstatement rights, in the event of the birth or adoption of a child or a serious illness in the immediate family, including parents. Health benefits must be maintained for employees on this type of leave. Leave is available to employees who have worked at least 1,250 hours in the previous twelve months of employment with the same employer. The importance of leave and other child-care benefits was highlighted in September 1992, when a consortium of 137 companies and nonprofit groups, including 11 major corporations, announced that they had formed the American Business Collaboration for Quality Dependent Care. The goal of the consortium is to raise $25 million to fund a variety of child- and elder-care projects across the United States.[21] In 1995 the collaboration expanded their commitment to $125 million. In the first ten years of the collaboration, more than 1,500 child- and elder-care projects were funded affecting more than 135,000 children and elders.[22]

As indicated in Figure 13.2, additional leave benefits can include medical, civic, and bereavement leave. Medical leave allows employees extended time off for major medical reasons. Frequently, such leave is unpaid and takes effect when all

INTERNATIONAL PERSPECTIVE

International Benefits: Comparisons and Complications

Countries differ greatly in the benefits typically offered to employees. These differences may be due to cultural preferences, values, and traditions; local law and tax codes; economic conditions; and many other factors. In some cases, particular levels of benefits are mandated by law; in other cases, they are simply common practice. Paid vacation is a good example. There is no legal requirement for any paid vacation whatsoever in the United States. All other industrialized nations mandate paid holidays and vacations. Customarily, however, new permanent full-time employees in the United States typically earn two weeks of paid vacation after one year of service. Employees may need to work for the same employer for five or ten years to become entitled to three weeks vacation, and fifteen to twenty years to obtain four weeks paid vacation per year. In the European Economic Community, the legally mandated minimum paid vacation for all employees is four weeks. Austria, Denmark, Finland, France, and Spain require more—a minimum of thirty days per year. Many employers give more than the required minimum. Although Germany requires twenty-four days paid holiday, most employers give thirty days (six weeks). In Europe all employees are eligible for the full amount of paid vacation, from the very first year of employment.

In addition to holidays, the popularity of other benefits also varies around the globe. In China a very desirable benefit is employer-subsidized housing. In Brazil luxury company cars are an essential benefit to attract and keep managers. When excellent publicly funded medical care is available, employer-provided health insurance becomes a much less relevant benefit, whereas it is a high priority for most U.S. employees. In particularly high tax regions, such as Scandinavia, perquisites that are tax-effective are often more attractive than increases in cash payments, and this must be kept in mind when designing compensation systems.

Another complication in administering pay and benefits multinationally is the issue of "acquired rights." In some countries in Europe and Latin America, any extra incentive, benefit, or perquisite that is offered for a period of time (two years in Brazil) becomes an acquired right and cannot be unilaterally discontinued by the employer.

For companies having employees all over the world, issues of local practice and expectation versus fairness and equality of treatment can become an issue, especially when employees around the world communicate daily by e-mail and have many opportunities to notice discrepancies in pay and benefits. Many large firms use the services of specialized consulting firms to advise them on issues surrounding international compensation and benefits.

Source: "Global Compensation and Benefits in Transition," *Compensation and Benefits Review,* January-February 2000, pp. 28–38; Steven E. Gross and Per L. Wingerup, "Global Pay? Maybe Not Yet!" *Compensation and Benefits Review,* July-August 1999, pp. 25–34; and H. Jorgensen, "Give Me a Break: The Extent of Paid Holidays and Vacation," *Center for Economic and Policy Research,* September 3, 2002. (Available at: http://www.cepr.net/give_me_a_break.htm)

sick leave days have been exhausted. Leave for civic obligations includes time off for jury duty, part (or all) of the day off to vote in national elections, and leave for military duty, such as National Guard or reserve military service. Bereavement leave allows the employee time off for a death in the immediate family.

Optional Protection Programs—Health Insurance

Optional protection programs are not mandated by law but are offered to make the employer more competitive in the labor market and to improve employee satisfaction and quality of life. Medical or health insurance is a major optional protection benefit offered by most employers. The goal of **health insurance** is to provide partial or complete coverage of medical expenses incurred by the employee and the employee's family. In practice, this means either paying directly or reimbursing the employee for hospital charges, surgery, and other personal or family medical expenses. Many plans also pay for dental care.

Health plans vary in their comprehensiveness of coverage and specifics of funding, but rapidly rising costs have made health insurance a major concern in most organizations. As shown in Figure 13.3, health insurance premiums have continued to rise at a faster rate than either workers' earnings or the consumer price index (overall inflation).[23] For example, in 2003 health insurance increased by 14 percent while workers' earnings and overall inflation remained relatively flat with a 2 to 4 percent increase. The 2003 increase means that health insurance premiums increased at seven times the rate of inflation.[24] The simple fact is that most organizations cannot afford to provide as much coverage as they have done in the past. Cost-containment strategies have included the redesign of medical plans, a search for funding alternatives, and other approaches aimed at slowing the increase in health care costs.[25]

FIGURE 13.3

Percent Change in Health Insurance Premiums Compared to Other Indicators, 1999 to 2004

Source: The Kaiser Family Foundation and Health Research and Educational Trust, *Employer Health Benefits 2004 Annual Survey* (Menlo Park, Calif.: Henry J. Kaiser Family Foundation, 2004).

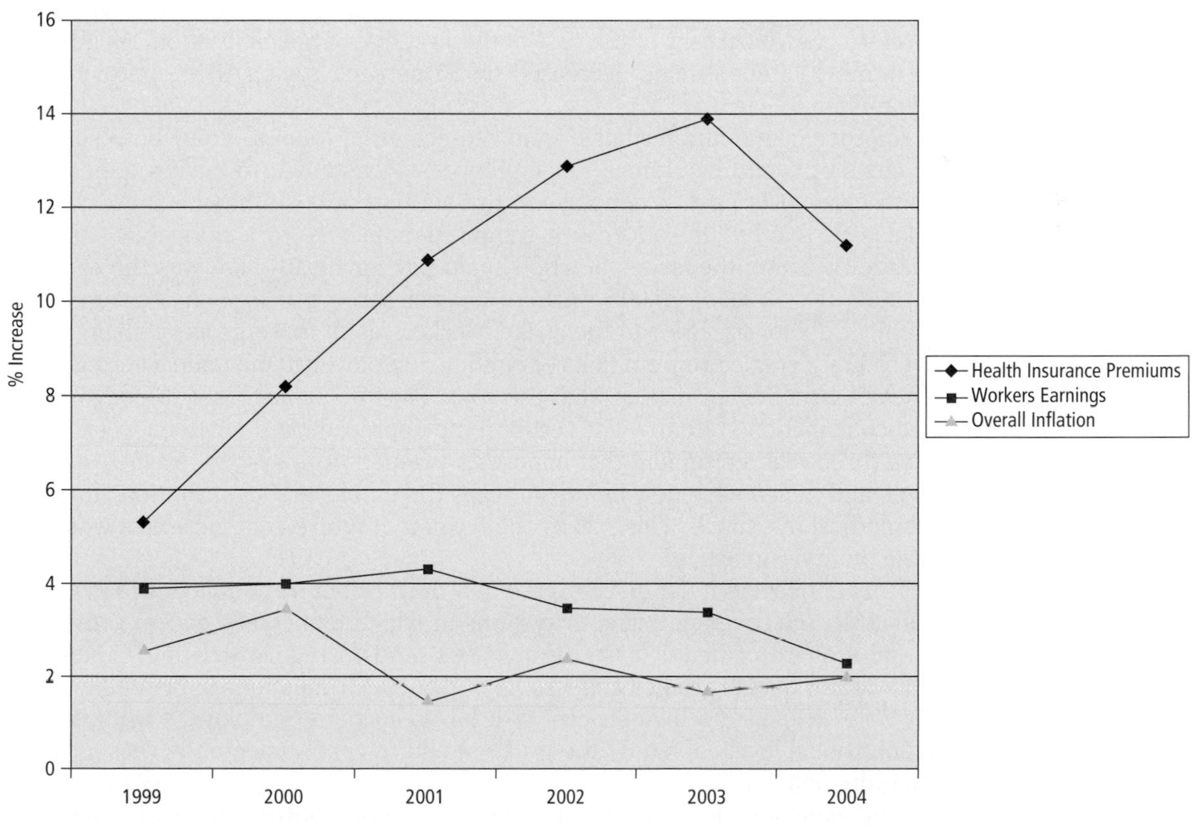

Health Plan Redesign In the past, health care insurance was typically regarded as a total package shielding employees from all health care costs. Increasingly, however, the goal is shifting to protection of employees against major and catastrophic costs. Instead of reimbursing employees for all medical bills, many employers have begun using deductibles, copayments, and coordinated coverage as ways of containing costs.

Many medical plans have a **deductible** of $100 to $400 or more for each family member each year. Only expenses over this amount will be reimbursed by the insurance fund. Thus a person in good health, who makes only one or two medical or dental visits in a year, may receive no reimbursement.

Coinsurance means that expenses beyond the deductible are shared, usually in a ratio between 50:50 and 80:20. Thus an employee submitting a bill of $500 for simple surgery in the doctor's office would receive reimbursement for $400, assuming an 80:20 split and no deductible. To take care of catastrophic expenses, costs beyond a maximum of several thousand dollars are then reimbursed 100 percent under most coinsurance plans. For example, an individual with bills of $75,000 for heart surgery might pay 20 percent of the first $5,000 (or $1,000), with insurance covering the remaining $74,000. Copayment plans have the advantage of making employees more aware of health care costs. Also, because the employee pays some of each expense, copayments tend to discourage unnecessary use of health insurance benefits.

The hospitalization segment of IBM's health plan is an example of carefully identified cost sharing. IBM's health plan provides fifty-two weeks of hospitalization for plan participants. Analysis of hospitalization showed that 31 percent of the hospitalizations were for only two days. The cost-sharing change required an employee to pay 40 percent of the cost of the first day of hospitalization. As a result, the number of admissions decreased by 36 percent, saving IBM approximately $100 million a year.[26]

Another common alternative is to require employees to contribute some of the costs of health insurance. For employees accustomed to having their entire health care costs paid by employers, the shifting of costs has become an emotional issue that has, in some cases, triggered employee work stoppages (strikes). In large measure, the issues of who should pay for health care was the cause of the 2003–04 strike of 85,000 workers against three grocery chains, mostly in Southern California. Prior to the strike, workers at all three grocery chains were covered by a single program that required the employer to maintain a certain level of health benefits, no matter what the cost. The companies want to convert to a fixed-contribution system.[27] The result of the unprecedented nineteen-week strike was a three-year agreement that imposes a two-tier wage system, slashes starting wages and benefits for new hires, and caps the employers' contributions to workers' medical insurance. This means the burden of future cost increases would be borne by the employees.

Thus employers must be very careful if they switch from noncontributory, no-deductible, full-coverage plans to systems in which employees become responsible for a share of health costs. Employees tend to regard existing benefits as rights rather than privileges and strongly resent any reductions in benefit levels. It may help to appoint a benefits-cost task force, including employees from various organizational levels, to study the problem and to communicate the reasons for a cost-reduction move.

Employers are increasingly concerned with **coordinating benefits** as a way of containing costs. The objective is to prevent duplicate payment for the same health care service. For instance, an employee may be covered both by his or her employer's plan and by a working spouse's benefits. Careful checking is necessary to ensure that reimbursement is made only once.

Health Funding Alternatives Another approach to cost containment has been to seek funding alternatives. Instead of relying on insurance companies such as Blue Cross/Blue Shield, some employers have begun to self-insure or to use preferred provider organizations or health maintenance organizations. By self-insuring, an employer sets aside funds to pay health claims in lieu of insurance coverage. If the base of employees is large enough to spread the risk, the employer can achieve significant savings.[28]

A **preferred provider organization (PPO)** is a limited group of physicians and hospitals that agree to provide services in accordance with competitive fee schedules negotiated in advance. The physicians and hospitals benefit from knowing that they have a guaranteed customer base. Employees are free to use any physician or hospital that is part of the PPO or another provider if they are willing to pay any difference. Many employers have organized PPOs in communities located near their facilities.[29]

A **health maintenance organization (HMO)** provides complete medical care for employees and their families at a fixed annual fee. Supplemental policies typically cover hospitalization for those HMOs not associated with hospitals. Because doctor visits are not charged on a per-visit basis, individuals are more likely to seek preventive care, thus reducing the incidence and costs of more serious illness.

Health savings accounts, created by the Medicare bill enacted by Congress in late 2003, are 401(k)-like accounts for health care. Employees with a qualified high-deductible health plan can also save their own money tax free each year in a health savings account.[30] To qualify, insurance policies must have an annual deductible of at least $1,000 for individuals or $2,000 for families. Annual tax-free contributions can be no more than the deductible, up to a maximum of $5,100 for individuals and $10,200 for families.[31] Both contribution and deductible levels will rise with inflation.

Health savings account funds are then invested in stocks, bonds, or mutual funds and are available to pay medical costs. Any money not spent continues to be invested and to be available for health care in future years. Some companies, while switching from traditional medical to high-deductible plans, are encouraging employees to establish health savings accounts by matching employee contributions at fifty cents on the dollar. For the company it is a means of controlling medical costs. As a bonus, employees become knowledgeable consumers in shopping for health care as the first dollars are theirs rather than reimbursed by insurance.[32]

Defined Contribution Health Coverage Another variation on the traditional health insurance is **defined contribution health coverage,** which is designed to cuts costs to employers by giving workers more control over their health care choices. Defined contribution coverage is typically a three-part product: the employer's contribution, the employee's payments, and catastrophic coverage. Employees contribute a fixed annual amount per employee into an account, which employees draw on as needed to pay for medical care.[33] Unused balances remain in the account for future health care costs. If the account is depleted, the employee picks up the remaining costs. If expenses are especially large, insurance takes over to cover catastrophic situations. As with health savings accounts, the theme is common: a means to allow companies to get out from under health cares costs, which in many cases are eating them alive, by shifting a fixed amount to employee accounts and allowing employees to shoulder more of the responsibility.[34]

Legal Requirements for Health Care Health benefits programs have been relatively free from government regulation, although health care and the public role in its delivery have been the topic of widespread public debate in the last several years. The Health Maintenance Organization Act of 1973 requires that companies with at least twenty-five employees living in an area served by an HMO offer HMO membership as an alternative to regular group health coverage. Consequently, the number of HMOs and their participants has increased dramatically. Further, a more recent trend has been a merging of HMOs to form giant managed care facilities serving millions of people in multistate territories.[35]

In 1985 the Consolidated Omnibus Budget Reconciliation Act (COBRA) was passed to prevent gaps in health care coverage. It requires employers with twenty or more employees to provide extended health care coverage for up to eighteen months to employees who are terminated and up to thirty-six months for widowed or divorced spouses and dependent children of former or current employees. The employer may pass along the full cost of the premium to the employee or employee's family, along with a 2 percent administrative fee.

Health Benefits for Retirees Companies that provide health coverage for employees typically provide continuing coverage for retirees. Such continuing coverage is coordinated with Medicare, which provides certain benefits beginning at age sixty-five. Companies try to cover the costs—and there are many—not paid by Medicare.

In an effort to clarify the potential costs of retiree medical coverage, in 1992 the Financial Accounting Standards Board (FASB) adopted Financial Accounting Standard 106, which requires organizations to subtract a portion of their obligations from their annual earnings reports. Organizations were required to (1) set up a huge "catch-up" reserve for current and retired employees and (2) accrue, or set aside, a reserve each year for postretirement medical benefits for employees currently working. The cost was staggering for many organizations. For example, General Motors had a one-time charge of $16 billion to $24 billion, an amount equal to 60 to 88 percent of GM's equity or total value. In addition, GM will have a continuing charge of $2 billion to $2.3 billion—a 22 to 33 percent reduction in pretax profits.[36] In 1999 IBM capped retiree health care at $7,500 per year of each employee's annual medical insurance costs.[37] Although IBM is not in financial distress, it says that its medical costs have been rising faster than revenue. For example, in 2003 IBM spent $335 million on retiree health care.[38]

Retiree medical benefits have gone from a long-accepted and little-noticed element of a benefit package to a front-burner issue in terms of impact on profits. The strategic, legal, accounting, and financial constraints will be weighed against general HR practices of doing nice things for retirees as organizations re-evaluate the level of medical benefits they will provide for retired workers.[39]

Health Benefits for Nonfamily Members Given the general trend to control and cut back on the expense of health care, why would organizations offer to extend coverage to people other than employees and their legal dependents? Recently many companies have moved to provide what are called domestic-partner benefits; that is, the same benefits for the long-term same-sex partners of employees as it provides for the spouses of heterosexual employees. In 1998 just 13 percent of *Fortune 500* companies offered domestic-partner benefits for same-sex partners of their employees.[40] In 2004 that number increased to 40 percent, with companies such as General Electric, Lockheed Martin, Merck, Pepsi, Sears, Wal-Mart, and UPS recently joining the list.[41]

The rationale for domestic-partner benefits is simple: Studies showed that committed same-sex couples are at no greater risk of illness, including the catastrophic illness of AIDS, than are married heterosexual pairs. A survey of companies offering domestic-partner benefits found that the cost was less than 1 percent of the total benefit costs. Most companies are relatively conservative (e.g., Wal-Mart), and those offering domestic-partner benefit plans are not doing so as part of a socially progressive agenda. Rather, on a cost-benefit basis, those companies offering such benefits feel that the value in terms of attracting and retaining employees outweighs the cost of the coverage.

Optional Protection Programs—Life and Disability Insurance

Many companies offer life insurance as a benefit, providing support for the employee's family in the case of the death of the wage earner.[42] By purchasing a group package, the employer can obtain coverage at far lower rates than would be available to individuals. Coverage is generally based on annual earnings, and for many employees coverage is offered for twice annual earnings. Some organizations allow employees to purchase additional life insurance at the group rate.

Many employers provide long-term disability insurance to guarantee income for employees who become disabled and are unable to work—an event far more likely than death of the wage earner. Disabled employees and their families are entitled to payments from Social Security, but most need additional income to approach replacement of prior earnings. Long-term disability payments typically do not begin until the employee has been unable to work for a specified period, usually three to six months.

Private Retirement/Pension Plans

A very important benefit to most employees is a private pension plan. In some cases pensions are funded entirely by employer contributions, but most involve both employer and employee contributions. A **pension** is essentially an investment to which contributions are added at regular intervals. Invested funds, along with interest, dividends, and capital gains, grow and accumulate to provide income during retirement. Under some plans, an account identified as belonging to the employee is established. With other pensions, funds are pooled, with a known share reserved for the employee on retirement. Pensions are subject to intricate financial, legal, and tax rules and considerations.

Virtually all pensions are "qualified"—that is, they conform to stringent Internal Revenue Service requirements. Both employer and individual contributions to qualified plans are exempt from income tax, and interest, dividends, and gains are allowed to accumulate tax free. Retired employees must pay income tax on the pension payments they receive, but often their tax rate is lower than when they were working and had a larger income. Thus employee contributions are a valuable means of deferring tax on income. In this context, pensions are deferred wages: rewards for long service. However, if an employer wishes to implement a pension plan for a select group of employees, such as key executives, the plan must be nonqualified.[43] This approach is frequently used to provide supplemental retirement benefits for executives.

Retirement plans are expensive, costing the employer an estimated 10 percent of payroll (see Table 13.1), including the company contribution to Social Security and pensions. The amount that the employee will receive on retirement is usually based on length of service with the company and salary level. Benefits average 20 to 30 percent of preretirement salary for most plans. (Remember that the retired employee also will qualify for Social Security.) The pension plans in use today can be categorized into three broad types: defined contribution plans, defined benefit plans, and capital accumulation plans.[44]

Defined Contribution Plans The most widely used type of pension is the **defined contribution plan,** also termed a **money purchase plan.** More than 90 percent of private pension plans are defined contribution. Contributions are made at a fixed rate to an account established for the employee. Benefits are a function of contributions plus gains (or losses) as a result of interest, dividends, or capital gains. Profit-sharing plans and ESOPs fall into this category. Defined contribution plans offer less security and predictability of retirement benefits because the employee, not the company, assumes the risk of investment performance. On the plus side, after vesting, there is no penalty to leaving the employer to work elsewhere.

Defined Benefit Plans The **defined benefit plan** is the most prevalent type of public pension and is also used by some (less than 10 percent of) private companies. Under a defined benefit plan, also called "final average pay," retirement benefits depend on a formula that includes length of service and average earnings in the final years of employment and, as such, tend to reward tenure.[45] Such plans have the advantage that employees know the amount of their retirement benefits ahead of time. Employer and employee contributions are determined by actuarial calculations.

Capital Accumulation Plans Through **capital accumulation plans,** employees have the opportunity to establish individual retirement accounts. The principal capital accumulation vehicles are thrift plans and 401(k) plans. Employees may make tax-deferred contributions, which, under thrift plans, may be matched by the organization. A common matching rate would be $1 of employer contribution for every $2 contributed by the employee.

Thrift plans were popular in some industries for many years and then became the basis for 401(k) plans as a part of the Internal Revenue Act of 1978.[46] Although they involve no employer match, 401(k) plans allow employees to set aside salary and participate in tax-deferred earnings. As a result of the Economic Growth and Tax Relief Reconciliation Act (EGTRRA) of 2001, the maximum pre-tax contribution limit is $14,000 in 2004 and $15,000 in 2005. After 2006, the maximum pretax contribution limit is indexed in $500 increments for inflation. Also beginning in 2006, 401(k) contributions will be eligible to be made on a post-tax basis and to be placed in a tax-free account similar to a Roth IRA. In addition to the increased contribution and benefit limits, the EGTRRA provides for catch-up contributions for older workers, tax credit for low-income workers, and speeded-up vesting.[47]

At present about 42 million workers have 401(k) plans. Their average age is forty-two years, and 44 percent have no other retirement plans.[48] The average account balance is about $50,000, and most investments are in mutual funds.

Other Types of Pension Plans A type of pension plan that has gained in popularity is the **cash-balance plan,** a method that combines the benefit formula of a defined contribution plan with the investment security of a defined benefit plan.[49] Benefits are expressed as "accounts" and credited with contributions and interest annually, as is done with defined contribution or capital accumulation plans.[50] As with defined benefit plans, the employer remains on the hook for all contributions. Companies rushed to adopt these new plans in the mid to late 1990s, ostensibly to allow employees to better see their benefits. However, many of the first companies to convert to such plans took the opportunity to reduce future benefits for employees nearing retirement, thus creating a political furor along with charges of age discrimination.[51]

Regulations Governing Retirement Plans

Private employer retirement plans were subject to little government regulation before 1974. Employers had great latitude in establishing and administering pension plans for their employees. As it turned out, many of the pension plans were not sound because of either poor actuarial planning or company economic reversals. Thus many employees believed they were accruing pension rights when in fact they were not. In response to these problems, during the last twenty years a wide array of legislation has been enacted, and IRS regulations have been formulated with respect to pensions.

ERISA The initial legislation setting standards in pensions was the **Employee Retirement Income Security Act of 1974 (ERISA),** which established reporting requirements and fiduciary standards, along with rules regarding plan participation, vesting, funding, and pension plan termination. Favorable tax treatment of employer contributions is available only for plans that meet ERISA guidelines. (Note that employers are not required to offer private pensions.)

In terms of participation, ERISA requires that employees who are at least twenty-one years old and have completed one year with the company be eligible to participate in the pension plan. Another important concept is **vesting,** the right to receive pension benefits contributed on the employee's behalf by the company even if the employee leaves the company before retirement. ERISA established complex alternate rules regarding vesting but basically ensured that any employee would have rights to at least 50 percent of the employer's contributions after ten years of service and would be 100 percent vested after fifteen years. Thus employees can be assured of certain pension levels if they have worked a minimum number of years, even if they leave the company before retirement. Vesting rules also prevent company abuses, such as firing long-service employees shortly before retirement to avoid paying them a pension. Vesting applies only to employer contributions. Employees retain rights to any contributions they make and can withdraw them or roll them over into another private pension plan if they leave the company.

Before ERISA, many private pension plans were not protected if the company went bankrupt. To protect employees and retired employees, ERISA created **pension plan termination insurance** and a government agency, the Pension Benefit Guaranty Corporation (PBGC), to administer the program. The insurance is funded with the assets of the plans it takes over and the premiums paid by employers with traditional pension plans. However, the rash of failing pension plans, as described in the HR Challenge, is putting pressure on the PBGC. The PBGC guarantees the pensions of 44 million Americans and has taken on more than $62 billion in pension promises, and in so doing it lost $12 billion in fiscal 2004 as its long-term deficit rose to $23.3 billion.[52]

The long-range goals of ERISA are to make private pensions equitable and to put them on a firm financial footing. The burden imposed on employers or pension trustees is substantial. As a result, in the initial years of ERISA, many employers terminated their pension plans rather than comply with the law.

Single-Sex Pension Benefits A final legal issue concerning pensions involves sex bias. Prior to 1978 it was common to use actuarial tables in planning pension contributions and payouts. Women as a group live longer than men; as a result, under most pension plans, they were required to make greater contributions to receive retirement benefits equal to those of men. Alternately, women were forced to accept lower monthly benefits after retirement than men, again because statistically they can expect to collect benefits for more years.

In 1978 the U.S. Supreme Court found this practice illegal.[53] The Court extended this concept in 1983, forcing pension plan administrators to eliminate sex distinctions in mortality tables used to determine pension benefits.[54] The Retirement Equity Act of 1984 was passed to bring legislation in line with these Court decisions. As a result, there is now no distinction in the benefits received by men and women.

GATT Treaty (1994) When Congress agreed to liberalize world trade by passing the General Agreement on Tariffs and Trade (GATT), little noticed were 129 pages of pension legislation added at the end. Many believe this bill constitutes "the most significant pension funding changes in twenty years."[55] Companies with underfunded pension plans will have to contribute more, and faster, or pay higher insurance premiums to the Pension Board Guarantee Corporation. For example, General Motors and Ford Motor, taken together, must now speed up plans for narrowing a $20 billion underfunding of their pension obligations.[56] There were other changes as well. As shown in Table 13.2, many old-line companies have large pension deficits.

Why was this pension legislation a provision of GATT? The liberalized trade legislation, GATT, meant less income for the United States through tariff cuts. Budget rules required that this diminished income be offset—hence pension revisions that promised $1 billion in new income.

Other Benefits

Many organizations offer additional benefits, some of which provide innovative opportunities for employees. Included are such benefits as vision care, prescription drugs, concierge services (e.g., dry-cleaning pickup/delivery), legal counseling, and financial counseling.[57] Many organizations have established employee assis-

TABLE 13.2

Pension Deficits of Major Companies

Company	2003 Pension Deficit (in billions)	Deficit as a % of Market Capitalization
Ford Motor	$11.7	69.1
General Motors	8.6	28.8
Delta Airlines	5.7	379.1
Delphi	4.0	69.5
AES	1.3	79.2
Navistar International	1.0	35.7
Visteon	0.9	64.8
Cummins	0.7	33.9
Hercules	0.4	38.3
Allegheny Technologies	0.3	51.1

Source: Nanette Byrnes, "The Benefits Trap," *Business Week*, July 19, 2004, pp. 64–72.

tance programs (EAPs), offering short-term counseling for employees under stress as a result of work or nonwork problems.[58] EAPs are discussed in more detail in Chapter 14. Other important benefits include those described in the sections that follow. Companies choose to offer the additional benefits most desired by their employees, most attractive to new employees, or that in some way reinforce their corporate culture and values. The Partnerships for Strategic Success feature describes the unusual benefits Patagonia provides that underscore its corporate culture.

Wellness Programs In an effort to stimulate wellness, many employers provide exercise or recreational facilities for employees or reimburse employees for health club memberships. Other companies provide incentives in the form of monthly stipends or similar payments for employees to participate in exercise programs, quit smoking, lower blood pressure or cholesterol, or take similar steps toward good health.[59]

Educational Assistance Another important benefit is **educational assistance.** Typically, employees are reimbursed for tuition and possibly for books or other associated costs. In general, educational assistance is limited to courses or degree programs that are job related.

Child-Care Assistance If they do not already do so, it is likely that more and more major companies will soon consider offering child-care assistance as an employee benefit. Such assistance can take the form of on-site child care, financial assistance, or information and referral. The number of women in the labor market has increased dramatically. Since 1975 the labor force participate rate of mothers with children under age eighteen has grown from 47 percent to 72 percent.[60] The biggest increase in working mothers occurred among women with children under age three. A total of 61 percent of this group was working in 2002 versus only 34 percent in 1975.

PARTNERSHIPS FOR STRATEGIC SUCCESS

Benefits Match the Culture at Patagonia

Patagonia, a California-based maker of sporting equipment for climbing, running, mountain biking, paddling, and skiing, has a strong and unique corporate culture. Mountaineer Yves Chouinard founded the company to make climbing hardware that would not damage rock. The company has always valued the environment and sought to inspire others to do the same. For instance, since 1985 Patagonia has donated a self-imposed "Earth tax" of 1 percent of sales to grassroots environmental groups each year. Donations have totaled more than $19 million to date. The company also founded the Conservation Alliance to encourage other companies to do the same. Patagonia virtually created the pesticide-free cotton industry in the United States to supply their T-shirt needs, pioneered recycling plastic soda bottles into synthetic fleece fabric, and installed solar and wind power electricity generation equipment in many of their corporate buildings.

Patagonia hires keen outdoor sport enthusiasts and values a laid-back "dirt bag" or "surf bum" culture. Consistent with the culture, Patagonia offers an unusual set of benefits to its employees. Employees are encouraged to pursue their chosen outdoor sport and can purchase Patagonia gear at greatly reduced prices. Their goal is to wear out the extremely durable products as well as seek input on design and quality from fellow sportsmen and women to feed back to the company.

Patagonia's headquarters is close to a surfing beach. Many employees bring their boards to work and are free to go for a surf when the waves are up during the day. The dress code at work is casual, and bare feet are not uncommon in the headquarters building. Most Patagonia facilities have employee showers to make biking, surfing, or working out during lunch easy. Patagonia is also family friendly, with on-site child care at headquarters and children welcome in the staff lunchroom and offices.

After one year of employment, employees become eligible for an Enviro Internship. They can volunteer 100 percent of their time for up to two months to the environmental group of their choice while receiving full pay and benefits from Patagonia. More than 350 employees have undertaken an internship since the program began in 1993. Patagonia also offers a $2,000 rebate to employees who buy a hybrid electric vehicle. Another unusual benefit is that Patagonia will pay an employee's bail if he or she is arrested in the course of a nonviolent environmental protest!

The culture and benefits are so appealing that Patagonia has low employee turnover and large numbers of applicants to choose from when a vacancy does occur. Patagonia's approach to being an environment- and employee-friendly company has resulted in its being listed as one of the 100 best companies to work for in America, and it has won the Workforce Optimas Award for Quality of Life.

Source: J. Laabs, "Mixing Business with Passion," *Workforce,* March 2000, pp. 80–85.

Furthermore, satisfaction with child-care arrangements has been found to be related to less work–family conflict and to lower levels of absenteeism, but it is unrelated to performance.[61] A recent survey also found that absenteeism on daytime shifts costs companies $789 per worker per year. However, responding companies that provided child care for extended-hour employees saw absenteeism costs drop an average of $300.[62]

Direct corporate involvement was stimulated by what has been called the "child-care crisis"—the finding that more than 70 percent of day care is mediocre and 12 percent is poor. The economics of day care are such that even mediocre care is expensive—almost $5,000 per year to provide services for one child. This $5,000 represents 8 percent of the median U.S. family pretax income for a dual-career family and 23 percent of earnings for families headed by a single working parent.[63]

Another avenue of corporate involvement has been through corporate–community partnerships. As part of the American Business Collaboration for Quality Dependent Care, described previously, more than 1,500 child- and elder-care projects were funded, affecting more than 135,000 children and elders.[64]

Because child-care needs and preferences are extremely diverse, multifaceted, and changing, employers are advised to undertake a systematic needs assessment of employees before developing specific programs.[65] Many employers find that the best method of assisting a diverse work force is through referral services. Such services allow employees to more readily find the type of child care best suited to their needs.

Of the companies with some type of child-care benefit, approximately half provide financial assistance, typically through a dependent-care option in a flexible benefits plan. Organizations can help employees pay for dependent care through pretax salary deductions. The Internal Revenue Code specifies that up to $5,000 of employee payments for dependent-care expenses may be excluded from an employee's annual taxable income. For example, if the proper administrative arrangements are established, an employee needing dependent care could agree to have the employer reduce his or her salary by $300 per month ($3,600 per year), with this amount then being directed to an account to pay for dependent care. Although there are administrative costs, there is no direct cost to the employer, and the employee is, in effect, paying for dependent care with pretax dollars. Without this type of plan, $3,600 worth of dependent care would cost a family earning $40,000 a total of $5,000—$3,600 for care and about $1,400 for federal income tax. Thus the savings involved can be significant. The only drawback is that any balance in a dependent-care account cannot be refunded directly or carried forward at the end of the plan year. Also, to take advantage of the tax savings, care providers need to have a Social Security number or an employer identification number. Thus the dependent care provided by the student wife from Spain cannot be paid for with before-tax contributions to a dependent-care account.

Note that such plans can be used for any qualified dependents, not just children. Many families need to arrange day care for elderly parents. Elder care was clearly one of the new benefits issues of the 1990s, and its importance is expected to increase in the twenty-first century as the population ages.[66]

Finally, some research suggests that offering child-care benefits can cause resentment among childless workers or workers with children who do not take advantage of the benefits.[67] A recent study found that current, past, and anticipated future use of child-care programs was related to more positive attitudes to child-care programs, but not to more general attitudes or behaviors. The so-called family-friendly backlash was not a serious problem.[68]

ISSUES IN INDIRECT COMPENSATION

Cost Containment

Because of the rapidly increasing costs of health care, pensions, and other benefits, employers must focus on strategic **cost containment** if they are to survive. A *Wall Street Journal* article related the story of the impact on hospital and insurance costs of a single patient who spent thirty-four days in the hospital, with a resulting bill of $5.2 million.[69] This example is dramatic, but benefit packages can add more than 50 percent to the cost of direct compensation. A tradeoff analysis can help in evaluating benefit possibilities. In one case a firm with 5,000 employees had high productivity, but rising health insurance costs were eroding profits.[70] Premiums had increased 75 percent, and a 20 percent increase—to $8.5 million—was projected. The executives were determined to reduce costs by 10 percent while identifying potential improvements in the system.

After the initial analysis, a decision was made to limit tradeoffs to health benefits. Employee satisfaction with alternative tradeoffs was solicited by inviting a 15 percent sample from all levels of the organization to participate in half-hour discussion meetings. Employees rated how much less satisfied they would be with their benefits if each alternative were implemented. The "satisfaction loss" (expressed as a percentage) for each of the potential reductions is shown in Table 13.3. Similarly, satisfaction gains were identified for suggested improvements to the plan. The satisfaction losses and gains were then divided by the percentage of premium saved (or spent) for each change. The resulting column, "Satisfaction Loss per Dollar Saved," provided guidance for changes in medical coverage that could yield the needed savings with minimal dissatisfaction from employees. As can be seen, the first choice was to add the requirement of precertification prior to hospitalization as a means of eliminating unneeded hospital days. With regard to the deductible for hospitalization, the satisfaction loss doubled in going from $100 to $200, but the loss per dollar saved was equivalent for these two alternatives. The organization decided to select the $200 deductible. The clear preference, in terms of both satisfaction loss and loss per dollar saved, was for a $150 major medical deductible. The same was true with dependent coverage options; a charge of $10 had the least satisfaction loss per dollar saved. The result was a 13.3 percent reduction in cost, with 1.4 percent then being allocated to three new plan improvements with high satisfaction gain per dollar spent. The net result was four plan reductions with a projected savings of just over $1 million, along with an added premium of $119,000 for plan improvements, for a total savings of 10.9 percent in benefit costs. The tradeoff analysis guided the effort in selecting health plan changes that would produce the savings with minimal employee dissatisfaction.

Two methods of reducing costs of benefits are through copayments and self-insurance. Both alternatives have already been discussed as funding alternatives for health insurance, but they apply more broadly. Plans with a copayment require that the employee contribute to the benefit costs. This technique is cost-effective and also an indirect way of communicating the high cost of benefit packages to employees. When copayments make employees aware of the costs of medical care, a reduction in unnecessary or abusive uses of the available benefits may result. There is some evidence that employees view benefits as part of their employment rather than as a privilege. For this reason, care must be taken when switching to a copayment plan to ensure that employees do not see this as a reduction in the compensation package.

Larger organizations can establish a fund to cover some benefit costs and thus avoid the premium expenses. In addition to the potential savings, self-insurance allows organizations to become familiar with the benefit program through in-depth knowledge of day-to-day claims and other issues related to use. In this way, still further areas of potential savings may be discovered.

TABLE 13.3

Example of Tradeoff Analysis to Evaluate Potential Health Care Savings

Plan Reductions					
Benefit	**Change (from/to)**	**Satisfaction Loss**	**Employer Savings (% of premium)**	**Satisfaction Loss per Dollar Saved**	**Cumulative Savings (% of premium)**
Precertification	Not. Req./Req.	11.4%	4.0%	2.85	4.0%
Hospital deductible	None/$100	5.7%	1.7%	3.35	7.4%
	None/$200	11.4%	3.4%	3.35	
Major medical deductible	$100/$150	11.4%	2.5%	4.56	9.9%
	$100/$200	32.9%	5.0%	6.58	
Dependent coverage	$5/$10	14.3%	2.4%	5.96	12.3%
	$6/$15	31.4%	4.7%	6.68	
Hospital coinsurance	100%/95%	18.6%	3.0%	6.20	
	100%/90%	41.4%	6.0%	6.90	
Surgical coinsurance	100%/90%	27.1%	1.0%	27.10	
	100%/80%	50.0%	2.0%	25.00	

Source: "Benefits: Profiting from Trade-Off Analysis," by Jesse A. Sherman and Michael Carter, reprinted with permission from *Personnel Journal*, Costa Mesa, California.

Partial self-insurance can be incorporated into health plans for small businesses. For example, one small business provides health insurance to three key employees. When premiums were slated for a 20 percent increase, $200 per month, the company increased the deductible for large claims (serious illnesses, not routine treatment) from $500 to $2,000, with a commitment to pay the difference ($1,500).[71] The maximum liability would be $4,500 if all three employees had major claims, as from surgery or serious illness. So far, in two years, there have been no such claims, saving the company $4,800.

Finally, as described previously, health savings accounts offer the opportunity for companies to adopt high annual deductible (up to $5,000) health care policies while at the same time encouraging employees to adopt, and in some cases contribute to, health savings accounts.[72] In this way employer coverage would be used for only the most serious medical events, and employees would be responsible for most or all of the routine coverage.

Flexible Benefit Options

One way to increase employee satisfaction with benefits and overall job satisfaction without increasing the cost of the compensation package is by offering a **flexible benefit package,** also termed a **cafeteria-style benefit plan.**[73] Under this plan, employees are automatically given a core plan with minimum coverage in medical insurance and retirement benefits. In addition, they receive benefit credits each year, which they can "spend" on additional benefits of their choice (e.g., more vacation time, more life insurance, or more dental insurance).

Flexible benefit plans are very effective and popular because they recognize that employees of different ages and life situations have differing personal needs. Flexible benefits allow individual employees to choose the benefits they want. Most companies provide a request form annually, allowing employees to modify their package.

A flexible benefit program involves several additional costs. First, communication of benefit options is more difficult. As many organizations can attest, it is extremely difficult to get the word out on a single benefit package. When there are multiple packages, as with flexible benefits, the communication problem is far more difficult. Administrative costs also increase with the number of options.

For companies willing to invest the extra effort to ensure that flexible benefit programs will work, the advantages outweigh the disadvantages. Flexible benefit programs enhance an organization's reputation for progressive treatment of its employees.

Communicating about Benefits

The main goal of both direct and indirect compensation should be to achieve company goals by providing rewards that are valued by employees. Employers must weigh both the costs of implementing benefit packages and the employee reaction to such plans, which may include behaviors such as turnover. Communication is critical for the successful administration of benefits. Organizations that do not invest effort in communicating a specific benefit might be better off not offering the benefit in the first place.

If the employer's intention is to attract entry-level employees, marketing immediate benefits such as a longer vacation or educational incentives may be more effective than advertising the pension plan, a benefit that will be more likely to reduce midcareer turnover. Also, if employees are to be satisfied with their benefit package, they must first be able to appreciate what goes into it. Although benefits may equal 40 percent or more of direct compensation, employees often grossly underestimate their cost and value.[74]

Organizations have at least two ways to correct the undervaluing of benefits. The first is to explain clearly to employees the objective costs of these benefits, pointing out why particular benefits may be of greater value than direct payment (e.g., because of tax considerations and favorable group insurance rates). Second, one study reported that employees know the value of their specific benefits almost to the penny when they make contributions to the fund.[75] Thus contributing and copayment systems not only reduce the organization's costs but have communication and educational advantages as well.

Communicating about benefits is not an easy task. Plans and options can be quite complex, and employees tend to have little interest in benefits until they need to use them. There are several ways to improve communication about benefits. First, written communication should be in plain language, not insurance jargon. Second, communication should be frequent and timed to occur when employees are likely to listen. Describing benefits when employees first begin work is unlikely to be effective because new employees have many more pressing issues to attend to in the first few weeks on the job. Finally, communication should be directed not just to the employee but also to other consumers of the benefit—most commonly, the spouse.

Work–Family Issues

More companies, especially larger firms, are trying to help their employees balance work and family demands. Studies have shown that work conflict leads to family conflict and that family conflict has a significant negative influence on an individual's attendance and quality of work.[76] These research findings, confirmed by organizational observations, have resulted in increasing employer sensitivity to the well-being of employees.[77] There can be little doubt that job and life satisfaction are related.[78]

The greatest increase in organizational response has been through child-care benefits, but other work–family benefits also are popular. Table 13.4 presents the results of a survey of just over 2,600 HR professionals regarding the most popular family–workplace initiatives.[79] Clearly, larger organizations are leading the way, but work–family benefits are on the rise among all organizations.

Work and family issues have gained a great deal of attention. For example, *Business Week* has now had two surveys of family-friendly corporate policies, the most recent being September 1997.[80] As part of the survey, companies were graded on their programs and strategies as well as on employee response. The grading criteria and results are shown in Table 13.5. Work–family issues are the problem of the twenty-first century. We can expect that more and more companies will take up the issues identified in the survey as they attempt to become more family friendly.

TABLE 13.4

Most Popular Family–Workplace Initiatives

	All Companies	Company Size (number of employees)				
		<100	101–500	501–2,500	2,501–5,000	>5,000
Dependent care flexible spending account	69%	55%	68%	79%	77%	88%
Flextime	58%	64%	51%	60%	71%	75%
Telecommuting	37%	41%	30%	43%	45%	50%
Compressed workweek	31%	21%	30%	36%	45%	53%
Paid family leave (other than FLMA)	26%	25%	23%	33%	29%	25%
Job sharing	25%	19%	20%	33%	55%	38%
Domestic-partner benefits (opposite-sex partners)	25%	28%	27%	22%	23%	19%
Ability to bring child to work in emergency	24%	39%	25%	12%	19%	9%
Child-care referral service	20%	13%	18%	26%	39%	34%
Scholarships for employees' families	20%	10%	16%	31%	32%	41%
Elder-care referral service	19%	13%	18%	17%	39%	31%
Adoption assistance	16%	10%	14%	19%	32%	34%
Domestic-partner benefits (same-sex partners)	16%	14%	17%	15%	19%	28%
Location program/designated area	16%	11%	16%	18%	29%	28%
Emergency sick child care	13%	11%	11%	14%	42%	25%

Source: Adapted from Society for Human Resource Management, "2001 Benefits Survey," April 2000. (Available at: http://www.shrm.org/surveys/results/default.asp?page=01benefits.asp)

TABLE 13.5

The Family-Friendly Grades of Top-Scoring S&P and Non-S&P Companies

S&P 500 Companies	Programs and Strategies	Employee Response	Non-S&P 500 Companies	Programs and Strategies	Employee Response
1. MBNA America	A	A	First Tennessee Bank	A-	A
2. Motorola	A-	A-	Sequent Computer Systems	A-	A-
3. Barnett Banks	A-	A-	Calvert Group	A-	A
4. Hewlett-Packard	B+	A-	SAS Institute	B-	A
5. UNUM	B	B+	Eddie Bauer	B	A
6. Lincoln National	B+	B+	Edward D. Jones	B-	A-
7. Merrill Lynch	B+	B+	Commercial Financial Services	C+	A
8. Dupont	A-	B	BE&K Brokerage	B	B+
9. TRW	B	B+	Lancaster Labs	B	B
10. Cigna	B	B	KPMG Peat Marwick	B	B

Scoring Criteria

Programs and Strategies		Employee Response	
Programs	**Percent**	**Employee Assessment**	**Percent**
Flexible work arrangements	25%	Quality of work life	30%
Family and dependent care	20	Job flexibility	30
Other programs	15	Family-friendly culture	30
Work-family organizational infrastructure	10	Overall family friendliness	10
Availability of programs to hourly and part-time workers	10		
Strategic and business rationale	20		

Source: Reprinted from September 15, 1997, issue of *Business Week* by special permission, copyright © 1997 by The McGraw-Hill Companies, Inc.

Summary of Key Points

Issues related to employee benefits have become a major topic not only in most organizations but also at the national level. Greater interest in benefits stems from the overall cost, fifty cents for every dollar in payroll in many cases; the rapid increases in the expense of some programs; the effectiveness of various programs; and an increase in legislation associated with benefit programs. Employee benefits include mandatory protection programs, compensation for time not worked, optional protection programs, and private retirement (pension) plans.

Mandatory protection programs include Social Security, unemployment compensation, and workers' compensation. Unemployment compensation provides benefits to out-of-work employees who are actively looking for work. Workers' compensation is a type of no-fault insurance for occupational injuries, disabilities, and death. Both unemployment compensation and workers' compensation systems are operated by the states, whereas Social Security is a federal program.

Many employees receive pay for holidays and vacations. Pay for time not worked may also include sick leave, personal days, and leaves for maternity and infant or elder care. Other protection programs include health insurance, life insurance, and disability insurance. As a result of the skyrocketing costs of health care, employers have been forced to redesign plans by splitting some costs with employees (coinsurance), and exploring alternatives such as preferred provider and health maintenance organizations. High deductible health care policies coupled with health saving accounts are increasing in popularity as a way of controlling costs.

Pension plans are funds established by employers to provide income to employees after retirement. Some plans require contributions by employees in addition to those of employers. Plans vary, with most being defined contribution, with benefits being a function of investment growth. Others define benefits based on length of service and average earnings. Defined benefit plans are popular in the public sector. In addition, many employers provide other types of capital accumulation plans, such as thrift plans or 401(k) plans that allow employees to invest pretax dollars toward retirement.

In the last twenty years, there have been a variety of federal laws and regulations regarding benefits. ERISA specifies vesting and fiduciary standards to which private pension plans must adhere. COBRA requires the extension of group medical benefits to terminated employees, at the employees' expense.

Benefits raise several important issues, including cost containment, flexible benefit options, and work–family issues. As benefit costs have increased more rapidly than inflation, employers have had to resort to innovative ways of containing costs. Some companies have resorted to self-insurance by establishing funds to cover benefit costs and thus eliminating the segment of premiums that goes to insurance companies. Flexible benefits provide an important means of tailoring benefits to employee needs. Such programs have additional administrative costs and are difficult to communicate to employees, but if used effectively, they can enhance the organization's reputation as a progressive, employee-oriented firm. Finally, work–family benefits are also achieving increased prominence as employers realize that work issues affect families, and vice versa.

The Manager's Vocabulary

cafeteria-style benefit plan
capital accumulation plans
cash-balance plan
coinsurance
coordinating benefits
cost containment
deductible
defined benefit plan
defined contribution health coverage
defined contribution plan
educational assistance
Employee Retirement Income Security Act of 1974 (ERISA)
flexible benefit package
health insurance
health maintenance organization (HMO)
health savings accounts
money purchase plan
pension
pension plan termination insurance
preferred provider organization (PPO)
Social Security
unemployment compensation insurance (UCI)
vesting
workers' compensation

Questions for Discussion

1. What are some of the reasons employee benefits as a proportion of total labor costs have increased substantially in the past several years?
2. Why is Social Security controversial? What are some of the ideas for solving problems with Social Security? Which solution do you favor and why?
3. What is the federal government's role in regulating benefits?
4. What are the differences between unemployment compensation and workers' compensation, both as to the purpose of the programs and how they are administered?
5. Define each of the following medical insurance terms.
   a. Deductible
   b. Coinsurance
   c. Coordinated benefits
   d. Self-insurance
   e. PPO
   f. HMO
6. What are domestic-partner benefits, and why do so many companies offer them?

7. What is the difference between defined benefit and defined contribution pension plans?
8. What is a 401(k), and what advantages does it offer?
9. What is ERISA, and what impact does it have on private pension plans?
10. What are the advantages and disadvantages of flexible benefits over standard benefit packages?
11. What are the key elements of communicating benefits to employees? Why is communication so important?
12. What are some of the reasons for increased interest in family-friendly corporate policies? Is this interest a fad or the start of a trend, and why?

Exercise 13.1
Controlling Medical Benefit Costs

A company finds that the cost of its medical benefits has increased far beyond what was expected, and further increases are projected.

1. List the alternatives available to bring medical costs under control.
2. Compare and contrast the advantages and disadvantages of each alternative for controlling costs.
3. What input, if any, should employees have in evaluating various alternatives to contain health care costs?
4. How can employee input best be solicited? How can decisions, once reached, best be communicated to employees?

Exercise 13.2
Flexible Benefit Decisions

You have just been hired by Pico Electronics. In addition to salary or wages, Pico Electronics has a flexible benefit arrangement for each employee. Employees have a benefit account and can draw from this account to fund various benefits.

Your salary and position entitle you to $1,000 per month in benefit dollars to allocate among the various choices. If your total benefit cost is less than $1,000 per month, you will keep half the difference as a monthly cash bonus. If your total is more than $1,000 per month, the difference is deducted from your salary. Under normal circumstances, benefit options, once selected, cannot be altered for five years.

Go through the benefit choices listed in this table and indicate how much of your $1,000 in monthly benefit dollars you will allocate to each benefit. Place a 0 for benefits you do not wish to purchase. Then total the allocated amounts and place the total in the last row.

Benefit	Cost	Amount Allocated
Pension plan	Up to $500/month, matched 50:50 by Pico	___
Paid vacations	$50/month for 2 weeks/yr	___
Paid holidays	$50/month for 10 days/yr	___
Paid sick leave	$50/month for 10 days/yr	___
Medical insurance	$250/employee, $350/family/month	___
Health maintenance organization	$200/employee, $250/family/month	___
Legal insurance	$50/month for 100% legal needs	___
Vision care	$50/month	___
Subsidized child care	$60/month per child for on-site care	___

Credit union	$25/month	___
Subsidized company cafeteria	$50/month for free lunches	___
Tuition reimbursement	$50/month for 100% of tuition	___
Funeral leave	$50/month for 3 days/year	___
Life insurance	$50/month for $100,000	___
Disability insurance	$75/month to cover salary if disabled	___
Dental insurance	$50/month for all checkups and required care	___
Parking	$50/month (local lots charge $75/month)	___
Total		___

1. What assumptions did you make about your situation now and for the immediate future? (For example: Married? Children? Further education?) How were these assumptions reflected in your choices?
2. Was your goal to use all of the $1,000 (and possibly more) to purchase options needed and desired or to maximize the amount left over each month?
3. What three benefit options are worth the most to you? Why?
4. What three benefit options are worth the least to you? Why?
5. Do you perceive any of the options as "too good to pass up"? Why or why not?

Source: From *Personnel/Human Resource Management,* 3rd ed., by Michael E. Carrell, Frank E. Kuzmis, and Norbert F. Elbert. Merrill, MacMillan Publishing Company. © 1989. Adapted by permission of the authors.

Exercise 13.3
Evaluating Company Benefit Plans

Visit the career/benefits Web sites of these four well-known companies: Coca-Cola, Kraft Foods, IBM, and Microsoft. IBM and Microsoft are high-tech firms. Coca-Cola and Kraft are consumer goods firms.

http://www2.coca-cola.com/careers/employee_benefits.html
http://www.kraftfoods.com/careers/benefits/index.htm
http://www-306.ibm.com/employment/us/pb_benefits.shtml
http://www.microsoft.com/careers/mslife/benefits/default.mspx

Examine the benefits of all four companies and answer the following questions:

1. How do the four companies compare in the two biggest benefits, health care and pensions? What types of plans does each of the companies have? How much is the employee expected to pay, if any?
2. What other benefits are provided by each company?
3. How do the two consumer goods firms, Coca-Cola and Kraft, compare?
4. How do the two high-tech firms, IBM and Microsoft, compare?
5. Is there a difference in benefits offered, and who pays, between the consumer goods firms and the high-tech firms?
6. Of the four companies, which benefits package would be most attractive to you and why?

Notes and References

1. Nanette Byrnes, "The Benefits Trap," *Business Week,* July 19, 2004, pp. 64–72.
2. Micheline Maynard and Mary Williams Walsh, "United Warns It May Jettison Pension Plans to Stay Afloat," *New York Times,* August 20, 2004. (Available at: http://www.nytimes.com/2004/08/20/business/20air.html

3. Micheline Maynard, "US Air to Seek 5-Year Extension for Pension Fund Payments," *New York Times,* August 17, 2004. (Available at: http://query.nytimes.com/search/restricted/article?res=F40817F7385B0C748DDDA10894DC404482)
4. Lynne Marek, "Continental to Skip Pension Payment," *Washington Post,* September 4, 2004, p. E02.
5. Byrnes, "The Benefits Trap."
6. Bert Ely, "Savings and Loan Crisis," *The Concise Encyclopedia of Economics.* (Available at:); Rob Jameson, "Case Study: US Savings and Loan Crisis," *E Risk,* August 2002. (Available at: http://www.erisk.com/Learning/CaseStudies/ref_case_ussl.asp)
7. Robert J. Greene and Russel G. Roberts, "Strategic Integration of Compensation and Benefits," *Personnel Administrator,* May 1983, pp. 79–81.
8. *Employer Costs for Employee Compensation.* Bureau of Labor Statistics, June 2004. (Available at: http://stats.bls.gov/news.release/archives/ecec_09152004.pdf)
9. Emmett Seaborn, "Strengthen Links between Benefits and Strategy," *HR Focus,* June 1999, pp. 11–14.
10. Richard Burkhauser et al., "Implications of Raising the Social Security Retirement Age," *Social Security Advisory Board,* October 13, 1998. (Available at:)
11. Robert C. Pozen, "Arm Yourself for the Coming Battle over Social Security," *Harvard Business Review,* Vol. 80 (11), November 2002, pp. 52–62.
12. Ibid.
13. Howard Gleckman, "What's Ahead for Social Security?" *Business Week,* November 22, 2004, pp. 44–45.
14. Ibid.
15. Prozen, "Arm Yourself for the Coming Battle."
16. Gleckman, "What's Ahead for Social Security?"
17. "First Aid for Workers' Comp," *Business Week,* March 18, 1996, p. 6; Karen Roberts and Sandra E. Gleason, "What Employees Want from Workers' Comp," *HR Magazine,* December 1991, pp. 49–53; and Annmarie Geddes Lipold, "The Soaring Costs of Workers' Comp," *Workforce,* February 2003, pp. 42–48.
18. James A. Swanke Jr., "Ways to Tame Workers' Comp Premiums," *HR Magazine,* February 1992, pp. 39–41.
19. Edward Popper, "California's State of Uncertainty," *Business Week,* November 21, 2003. (Available at: http://www.businessweek.com/smallbiz/content/nov2003/sb20031121_9014_sb014.htm)
20. Ronald Grover and Christopher Palmeri, "Arnold Is Hitting His Marks," *Business Week,* July 5, 2004, pp. 42–44.
21. "Family Care: Tips for Companies That Are Trying to Help," *Business Week,* September 28, 1992, p. 36.
22. "About the ABC." (Available at:)
23. The Kaiser Family Foundation and Health Research and Educational Trust, *Employer Health Benefits 2004 Annual Survey* (Menlo Park, Calif.: Henry J. Kaiser Family Foundation, 2004).
24. Ibid.
25. Jeff Goldsmith, "The New Health-Cost Crisis," *Harvard Business Review,* Vol. 79 (10), November 2001, pp. 20–21; Todd Raphael, "Using Carve-Outs to Shave Health Costs," *Workforce,* December 2001, pp. 40–42; and Mary S. Case, "A New Model for Controlling Health-Care Costs," *Workforce,* July 2001, pp. 44–48.
26. Anthony J. Rucci and John J. Sinnott, "Health Care," *Human Resource Management,* Vol. 31, Spring–Summer 1992, pp. 69–79.
27. Aaron Bernstein and Ronald Grover, "Health Care Is Making Labor Sick," *Business Week,* November 13, 2003. (Available at: http://www.businessweek.com/bwdaily/dnflash/nov2003/nf20031113_4031_db038.htm)
28. Ronald Bryan, "A Primer on Self-Funding Health Care Benefits," *Personnel Administrator,* April 1983, pp. 61–64.
29. William E. Wymer, George Faulkner, and Joseph A. Parente, "Achieving Benefit Program Objectives," *HR Magazine,* Vol. 37, March 1992, pp. 55–62.
30. Howard Gleckman, "Your New Health Plan," *Business Week,* November 8, 2004, pp. 88–96; and Jay Greene, "Assessing the Health Savings Option," *HR Magazine,* April 2004, pp. 103–108.
31. Howard Gleckman, "How Will the Plans Work?" *Business Week,* November 8, 2004, pp. 96–98.
32. Annmarie Geddes Lipold, "Structuring a New Health Plan," *HR Magazine,* March 2003, pp. 59–63; Michael T. Bond and Deborah Erdos Knapp, "The Financial Impact of Medical Savings Account Plans," *Business Horizons,* January–Feburary 2001, pp. 77–83.
33. Carolyn Hirschman, "More Choices, Less Cost?" *HR Magazine,* January 2002, pp. 36–41.

34. Kathryn Tyler, "Meet Your New Health Plan Option," *HR Magazine,* December 2002, pp. 63–66.
35. George Anders and Ron Winslow, "The HMO Trend: Big, Bigger, Biggest," *Wall Street Journal,* March 30, 1995, pp. B1, B4.
36. New Medical-Benefits Accounting Rule Seen Wounding Profits, Hurting Shares," *Wall Street Journal,* April 22, 1992, pp. C1–C2.
37. Byrnes, "The Benefits Trap."
38. Ibid.
39. Dale Buss, "Shoulder the Burden," *HR Magazine,* April 2003, pp. 48–52.
40. John Simons, "Gay Marriage: Corporate America Blazed the Trail," *Fortune,* June 2, 2004. (Available at:)
41. Ibid; and "What You Need to Know to Provide Domestic Partner Benefits," *HR Focus,* Vol. 80 (8), August 2003, pp. 3–4.
42. Jerry S. Rosenbloom and G. Victor Hallman, *Employee Benefit Planning,* 2nd ed. (Englewood Cliffs, N.J.: Prentice-Hall, 1986).
43. James W. Herlihy Jr. and Jamie D. Owens, "Methods to Implement a Nonqualified 401(k) Plan," *HR Magazine,* January 1992, pp. 52–56.
44. Allen Stiteler, "Finally, Pension Plans Defined," *Personnel Journal,* February 1987, pp. 44–53.
45. Lin Grensing-Pophal, "A Pension Formula That Pays Off," *HR Magazine,* February 2003, pp. 59–62.
46. Barbara Rudolph, "Shelter from April Showers," *Time,* February 22, 1988, p. 51.
47. Carolyn Hirschman, "The Taxman Giveth," *HR Magazine,* October 2001, pp. 71–78.
48. Carolyn Hirschman, "Growing Pains," *HR Magazine,* June 2002, pp. 31–38.
49. Elayne Demby, "Cash Balance Makes a Comeback," *Workforce,* Vol. 82 (5), May 2003, pp. 40–43.
50. Lin Grensing-Pophal, "The Challenge of Cash Balance Plans," *HR Magazine,* February 2003, p. 61.
51. Mary Maury and Victoria Shoaf, "The Effects of Adopting Cash-Balance Pension Plans," *Business Horizons,* Vol. 44 (2), March-April 2001, pp. 67–74.
52. Nanette Byrnes, "Time to Tackle the Pension Crisis," *Business Week,* November 16, 2004. (Available at: http://www.businessweek.com/bwdaily/dnflash/nov2004/nf20041116 1507_db016.htm)
53. *Los Angeles v. Manhart,* 435 U.S. 702 (1978).
54. *Arizona Governing Committee v. Norris,* 103 U.S. 3492 (1983).
55. Albert R. Karr and Ellen E. Schultz, "Pension Rules Tacked Quietly on Trade Bill Portend Vast Changes," *Wall Street Journal,* March 15, 1995, pp. A1, A8.
56. Byrnes, "The Benefits Trap."
57. Alarice Huang, "Concierge Services Free Employees from Distractions," *HR Focus,* July 1999, p. 6; "50 Benefits and Perks That Make Employees Want to Stay Forever," *HR Focus,* July 2000, pp. S2–S3; and "What Benefits Are Companies Offering Now?" *HR Focus,* June 2000, pp. 5–7.
58. Commerce Clearing House, *Employee Assistance Programs: Drug, Alcohol, and Other Problems* (Chicago: Author, 1986).
59. "Paying Workers for Good Health Habits Catches on as a Way to Cut Medical Costs," *Wall Street Journal,* November 26, 1991, p. B1; Robert J. Grossman, "Countering a Weight Crisis," *HR Magazine,* March 2004, pp. 42–51; Ellen Ernst Kossek, Cynthia Ozeki, and Deidre Wasson Kosier, "Wellness Incentives: Lessons Learned about Organizational Change," *Human Resource Planning,* Vol. 24 (4), 2001, pp. 24–35.
60. *Women in the Labor Force: A Databook,* Report 973. (Washington, D.C.: U.S. Department of Labor, February 2004). (Available at: http://www.dol.gov/wb/media/reports/main.htm)
61. Pamela Mendels, "Kiddie Care Doesn't Have to Break the Bank," *Business Week,* September 1, 1997. (Available at: http://www.businessweek.com/1997/35/b3542039.htm); Stephen J. Goff, Michael K. Mount, and Rosemary L. Jamison, "Employer Supported Child Care, Work/Family Conflict, and Absenteeism: A Field Study," *Personnel Psychology,* Vol. 43, 1990, pp. 793–809; Ellen Ernst Kossek and Victor Nichol, "The Effects of On-Site Child Care on Employee Attitudes and Performance," *Personnel Psychology,* Vol. 45, 1992, pp. 485–509; and Judith G. Gonyea and Bradley K. Googins, "Linking the Worlds of Work and Family: Beyond the Productivity Trap," *Human Resource Management,* Vol. 31, 1992, pp. 209–226.
62. "Onsite Child Care Can Reduce Absenteeism, Turnover," Society of Human Resource Management News Brief, September 9, 2003. (Available at: http://www.shrm.org/hrnews_published/archives/CMS_005486.asp#P16_1721)
63. Michele Galen "Honey, We're Cheating the Kids," *Business Week,* February 20, 1995. (Available at: http://www.businessweek.com/archives/1995/b341248.arc.htm)
64. "About the ABC."

65. Shirley Hand and Robert A. Zawacki, "Family-Friendly Benefits: More Than a Frill," *HR Magazine,* October 1994, pp. 79–84; and Ellen Ernst Kossek, "Diversity in Child Care Assistance Needs: Employee Problems, Preferences, and Work-Related Outcomes," *Personnel Psychology,* Vol. 43, 1990, pp. 769–791.
66. "The 'Baby Boomers' Triple Whammy," *Business Week,* May 4, 1992, pp. 178–179; Neville Tompkins, "Child Care and Elder Care Assistance," *HR Horizons,* Winter 1991, pp. 53–55; Bette Ann Stead, "Eldercare: Personal Triumph! Professional Downfall?" *Business Horizons,* May–June 1991, pp. 72–76; and Jeff L. Lefkovich, "Business Responds to Elder-Care Needs," *HR Magazine,* June 1992, pp. 103–108.
67. D. Harris, "The Fairness Furor," *Working Mother,* September 1997, pp. 28–32; and L. Jenner, "Family-Friendly Backlash," *Management Review,* May 1994, p. 83.
68. Teresa J. Rothausen, Jorge A. Gonzalez, Nicole E. Clarke, and Lisa L. O'Dell, "Family-Friendly Backlash—Fact or Fiction? The Case of Organizations' On-Site Child Care Centers," *Personnel Psychology,* Vol. 51, 1998, pp. 685–706.
69. Ron Winslow, "A $5.2 Million Bill for 34 Days in the Hospital," *Wall Street Journal,* August 2, 2001, p. A1.
70. Jesse A. Sherman and Michael Carter, "Benefits: Profiting from Trade-Off Analysis," *Personnel Journal,* August 1987, pp. 120–122.
71. Alison Stein Wellner with Joshua Kendall, "The Health Care Crisis: Why Small Companies Are Getting Hit So Hard and What You Can Do about It," *Business Week,* July 10, 2000. (Available at: http://www.businessweek.com/2000/00_28/b3689040.htm?$se)
72. Gleckman, "Your New Health Plan," Ibid.
73. Alison E. Barber, Randall B. Dunham, and Roger A. Formisano, "The Impact of Flexible Benefits on Employee Satisfaction: A Field Study," *Personnel Psychology,* Vol. 45, 1992, pp. 55–75.
74. Marie Wilson, George B. Northcraft, and Margaret A. Neale, "The Perceived Value of Fringe Benefits," *Personnel Psychology,* Vol. 38, 1985, pp. 209–320.
75. Ibid.
76. Christopher Alan Higgins, Linda Elizabeth Duxbury, and Richard Harold Irving, "Work–Family Conflict in the Dual Career Family," *Organizational Behavior and Human Decision Processes,* Vol. 51, 1992, pp. 51–75; and "Link Absenteeism & Benefits and Help Cut Costs," *HR Focus,* April 2000, pp. 5–6.
77. Hal Morgan and Frances J. Milliken, "Keys to Action: Understanding Differences in Organizations' Responsiveness to Work-and-Family Issues," *Human Resource Management,* Vol. 31, 1992, pp. 227–248.
78. M. Tait, M. Y. Padgett, and T. T. Baldwin, "Job and Life Satisfaction: A Reevaluation of the Strength of the Relationship and Gender Effects as a Function of the Date of the Study," *Journal of Applied Psychology,* Vol. 74, 1989, pp. 502–507; and Teresa J. Rothausen, "Job Satisfaction and the Parent Worker: The Role of Flexibility and Rewards," *Journal of Vocational Behavior,* Vol. 44, 1994, pp. 317–366.
79. Society for Human Resource Management 2001 Benefits Survey, April 2001. (Available at: http://www.shrm.org/surveys/results/default.asp?page=01benefits.asp)
80. "Work and Family," *Business Week,* September 15, 1997, pp. 96–99.

CHAPTER 14

Safety and Health: A Proactive Approach

- Occupational Safety and Health Legislation
- Management's Role in Maintaining Safety and Health
- Safety and Health Issues in the Workplace
- Violence in the Workplace
- Employee Fitness and Wellness Programs

HR Challenge

As the new HR manager of TriWorld, Inc., a chemical and fertilizer manufacturing company with 400 employees, you are conducting an audit of the firm's safety practices. The plant manager has requested the audit as he is very concerned about a spate of recent accidents at the plant. In one, an employee mistakenly opened the wrong valve and released high-pressure gas. The gas ignited, and the resulting fire killed the employee and damaged equipment nearby.

In addition, recent terrorist bombings in Warsaw, London, Paris, Sydney, Chicago, and Portland, Oregon, have the plant manager very concerned. Both of the U.S. bombings were carried out using diesel-and-fertilizer bombs. The Occupational Health and Safety Administration recently sent notices to firms around the country encouraging them to assess whether they might be targets of terrorist activities. Because TriWorld is one of the largest manufacturers of ammonium nitrate-based fertilizer in the United States, it seems possible that TriWorld might be of interest to terrorists. After all, fertilizer bombs seem to be one of their favorite instruments of destruction. The plant manager said to you, "What if someone hijacked a truckload of our product? There's enough ammonium nitrate in one of our typical shipments to blow up half of a small city."

Your audit of safety procedures at TriWorld so far has uncovered a number of troublesome facts:

- *Many long-time employees are unable to read.*
- *Because of their years of service, senior operators have often been "passed through" the extensive safety training program put in place several years previously.*

- *An informal buddy system has been established where some of the younger, more skilled operators are covering for those who lack certain fundamental abilities.*
- *Required written safety procedures are not always prominently visible at operating sites. Drivers and many others handling and loading fertilizer shipments are hired without any background checks.*
- *Little concern has been given to the safety of shipments as they travel to their destinations. There are reports that containers are often left unlocked and that shipments are sometimes left sitting in parking lots overnight while their long-haul drivers sleep.*

These facts cause you great concern. George Shrub, the owner of TriWorld, has always insisted on safety first. Until recently, TriWorld's manufacturing safety record has been good. You wonder what could have gone wrong. What could account for such divergence from the ideals TriWorld has always sought to attain? Is TriWorld likely to be of interest to terrorists? Could some of TriWorld's fertilizer one day be used to kill dozens or even hundreds of innocent citizens?

A total of 4.7 million American workers in private industries suffered from disabling injuries or illnesses on the job during 2002, and there were 5,524 workplace fatalities. This amounts to a fatal injury every ninety-five minutes and a disabling injury every seven seconds. The four leading causes of fatalities were transportation-related incidents (45 percent), contact with objects and equipment (16 percent), assaults and violent acts (15 percent), and falls (13 percent). Although workplace homicides fell to their lowest level in ten years, they remained the third-leading cause of death on the job, with a total of 608 workplace homicides reported in 1998. For women workers, homicide is the leading cause of death on the job. Of 441 fatalities among female employees, 31 percent were due to homicide.[1] (See the International Perspective box for a worldwide comparison of job-related deaths and injuries.)

Most organizations are very much concerned about providing a safe and healthy workplace. Part of this concern is simple humanitarianism. Few firms would knowingly send unprotected employees into a dangerous situation. Aside from altruism, there are two other reasons for corporate concern about safety and health in the work environment.

First, there are definite bottom-line financial consequences of workplace injuries and illness. According to the Liberty Mutual 2003 Workplace Safety Survey, the direct cost of serious work-related injuries and illnesses grew from $44.2 billion in 2000 to $45.8 billion in 2001. This is equivalent to more than $880 million per week! The top five causes of injuries accounted for almost 70 percent of this amount. These were (1) overexertion, $12.5 billion; (2) falls on the same level, $5.7 billion; (3) injuries due to bodily reaction (bending, tripping, slipping, etc.), $4.7 billion; (4) falls to a lower level, $4.1 billion; and (5) being struck by an object, $3.9 billion. Unfortunately, the direct cost of injuries represents only the "tip of the iceberg" for most organizations. In an earlier Liberty Mutual study, managers indicated that each dollar in direct costs due to injuries resulted in an additional $3 to $5 in indirect costs related to overtime, training, and lost productivity resulting from an injured employee not being able to perform his or her normal work.[2]

Many organizations have reported significant savings from actively promoting safety in the workplace. For instance, Hard Rock Café's U.S. operation saved almost $400,000 in 2001 and 2002 by reducing workplace injuries at a faster rate than the restaurant industry as a whole.

In addition to bottom-line results, the other major incentive for companies to be concerned with employee safety and health is to avoid the penalties for violating occupational safety laws. Before 1970, a company that was a dangerous place to work might have had higher insurance rates. Since then, however, the penalties have become more severe. For example, Pieper Electric in Milwaukee was fined $193,500 for failing to adequately protect workers from electrical hazards. In addition to fines, top managers can be sent to prison for criminal negligence when unsafe conditions cause the death of a worker.[3]

In this chapter we provide an overview of occupational health and safety legislation and the role of the Occupational Safety and Health Administration in enforcing that legislation. In addition, we look at the role of managers and employees in making sure that their workplace is safe. We examine the types of safety issues organizations face in the twenty-first century, including the new threat posed by international terrorists, and provide examples of how some firms are meeting safety challenges by proactively promoting employee physical and mental health.

OCCUPATIONAL SAFETY AND HEALTH LEGISLATION

Worker health and safety has been the subject of much state and federal legislation. Between 1911 and 1948, states passed workers' compensation laws requiring businesses to compensate employees injured on the job, and all states still have such laws in effect. Compensation includes some replacement of lost income while injured, medical and rehabilitation expenses, payments (lump sums) for certain permanent disabilities, and death benefits for survivors. Most employers participate in an insurance plan to cover these expenses. Because premiums go up if there are many injury claims, workers' compensation laws provide some incentive for employers to maintain a safe work environment. However, workers' compensation laws also limit employers' liability for injuries and deaths to the amounts specified by state law. Employees who accept workers' compensation benefits give up their right to sue the employer. Thus, workers' compensation laws somewhat reduce an organization's need to be concerned with workplace safety. This fact provided part of the impetus to pass a variety of federal workplace safety laws.

By far the dominant piece of federal safety and health legislation is the **Occupational Safety and Health Act of 1970.** The purpose of this act was to centralize the regulation of workplace safety and to expand coverage to include all organizations in the United States. In passing the act, Congress declared its purpose to be "to assure so far as possible every working man and woman in the nation safe and healthful working conditions and to preserve our human resources."[4]

INTERNATIONAL PERSPECTIVE

Decent Work—Safe Work: The International Picture

In a 2002 report, Jukka Takala of the International Labour Office described the status of occupational injuries and illness around the world. Mr. Takala opened the report with a statement from Mr. Kofi Annan, Secretary-General of the United Nations, who stated that the "safety and health of workers is a part and parcel of human security. . . . Safe work is not only sound economic policy, it is a basic human right." This was followed by a statement from Mr. Juan Somavia, Director-General, International Labour Office, indicating that "current estimates point to some 2 million men and women who lose their lives through occupational accidents and work-related diseases each year." Obviously there is a significant gap between the U.N.'s goal of "safe work—decent work" for all, and the reality of the international workplace. The following table shows the International Labour Organization's estimates of work-related fatalities and accidents for the year 2002. These estimates are based on the latest data readily available and are "estimates" due to the fact that the true number of fatalities and accidents worldwide is unknown—and probably unknowable. These data indicate that nearly 271 million workers were injured in work accidents in 2002.

As can be seen in the table, fatality rates in different regions can vary widely. This is the case for a num-

Global Estimates of Fatal and Other Occupational Accidents, 2002

	Estimated Total Employment	Estimated Fatalities	Estimated Accidents	Actual Fatal Accidents Reported to the ILO	Actual, All Accidents Reported to the ILO
Established market economies	380,833,643	16,170	12,340,216	14,608	7,646,585
Formerly socialist economies of Europe	162,120,341	21,425	16,350,868	8,665	590,952
India	419,560,000	48,176	36,765,877	211	211
China	699,771,000	73,615	56,179,742	17,804	93,577
Other Asia and Islands	404,487,050	83,048	63,378,830	5,631	258,130
Sub-Saharan Africa	Not available	54,705	41,748,723	1,675	48,780
Latin America and the Caribbean	114,604,962	29,594	22,584,726	6,998	1,706,105
Middle Eastern Crescent	48,635,240	28,019	21,383,071	1,876	193,040
World		354,753	270,732,052	57,468	10,537,380

Who Is Covered by the Occupational Safety and Health Act?

The Occupational Safety and Health Act of 1970 covers all private employers and their employees in the fifty states and in all territories and jurisdictions under federal authority. As defined by the Occupational Safety and Health Act, an employer is any *"person engaged in a business affecting commerce who has employees, but does*

ber of reasons, including the mix of industries present in each country. Some industries are inherently more dangerous than others. For instance, the mining and quarrying industries tend to have the highest fatality rate in most countries, and construction, transportation, utilities, and agriculture have moderately high rates. The retail trade, banking, and social service industries generally have many fewer fatalities.

Caution must be taken in comparing rates of occupational accidents and injuries across countries. Nations follow different reporting standards regarding what constitutes an injury and whether it must be reported. Even for workplace fatalities, which should be less ambiguously reported than injuries, variation in methods makes cross-national comparisons difficult. For instance, some countries include deaths that occur when a person is traveling to or from work; some do not count deaths from occupational disease.

Cross-national differences in workplace accident and fatality rates are also due to differences in legislation and the power of unions in various countries. Traditionally, in Europe unions have had far more power to control work safety issues. In the United States many laws protect worker health, with the Occupational Safety and Health Administration granted considerable powers in enforcing these laws. Unfortunately, in many developing countries, such protections are not present.

This is a situation of grave concern to international organizations such as the ILO. Recently, the ILO issued a set of guidelines intended to help governments and organizations around the world develop better workplace safety and health policies. Although the guidelines are somewhat general in nature, they provide a foundation on which organizations and governments around the world can construct more effective safety and health policies and practices. Aspects of these guidelines include the following:

1. The employer, in consultation with workers and their representatives, should set out clearly, in writing, an occupational safety and health (OSH) policy.
2. The policies should be compatible with and integrated into other management systems.
3. Worker participation should be an essential element in the OSH management system.
4. The senior management should allocate responsibility, accountability, and authority for the development, implementation, and performance of the OSH management system and the achievement of the relevant OSH objectives.
5. Formal structures and processes should be established to ensure OSH policies are implemented, monitored, and modified as needed.

Source: International Labour Office, *Guidelines on Occupational Safety and Health Management Systems,* International Labour Organization, CH-1211 Geneva 22, Switzerland, Report Number, ILO-OSH 2001; and Global Estimates of Fatal and Other Occupational Accidents, 2002 found in Annexure p. 3 of Jukka Takala, "Introductory Report: Decent Work—Safe Work," XVI World Congress on Safety and Health at Work, Vienna, May 27, 2002 (Available at: www.ilo.org/safework, accessed March 23, 2004).

J. K. M. Grevers, "Worker Participation in Health and Safety in the EEC: The Role of Representative Institutions," *International Labour Review,* July–August 1983, pp. 411–428; David C. E. Chew, "Effective Occupational Safety Activities: Findings in Three Asian Developing Countries," *International Labour Review,* Vol. 127 (1) 1998, pp. 111–124; and Michael B. Bixby, "Emerging Occupational Safety Issues in the United States, Europe, and Japan," in *Proceedings of the Third Conference on International Personnel and Human: Volume 1, Section 5, Concurrent Session II-A* (Berkhamstead, England, International Human Resource Conference, 1992).

not include the United States or any State or political subdivision of a State."[5] The act does not cover the self-employed or immediate members of farming families who do not employ outside workers. It does not cover employees whose working conditions are regulated by other federal agencies under other federal statutes, such as mine workers, certain truckers and railroad workers, and atomic energy workers. Public employees in state and local governments also are not covered.[6]

Three Agencies Created by the Occupational Safety and Health Act

The Occupational Safety and Health Act created three autonomous but related agencies to ensure occupational safety and health: the Occupational Safety and Health Review Commission, the National Institute for Occupational Safety and Health, and the Occupational Safety and Health Administration.[7] The basic activities of these three agencies are shown in Figure 14.1.

The **Occupational Safety and Health Review Commission (OSHRC)** is based in the Department of Labor. It is "an independent Federal agency created to decide contests of citations or penalties resulting from OSHA inspections of American work places. The Review Commission, therefore, functions as an administrative court, with established procedures for conducting hearings, receiving evidence and rendering decisions by its Administrative Law Judges (ALJs)."[8] Organizations can

FIGURE 14.1

Development of the Occupational Safety and Health Act

Source: Reproduced from James Ledvinka and Vida G. Scarpello, *Federal Regulation of Personnel and Human Resource Management,* 2nd ed., with the permission of South-Western College Publishing Company, a division of International Thomson Publishing, Inc. Copyright © 1991 PWS-Kent Publishing Company. All rights reserved.

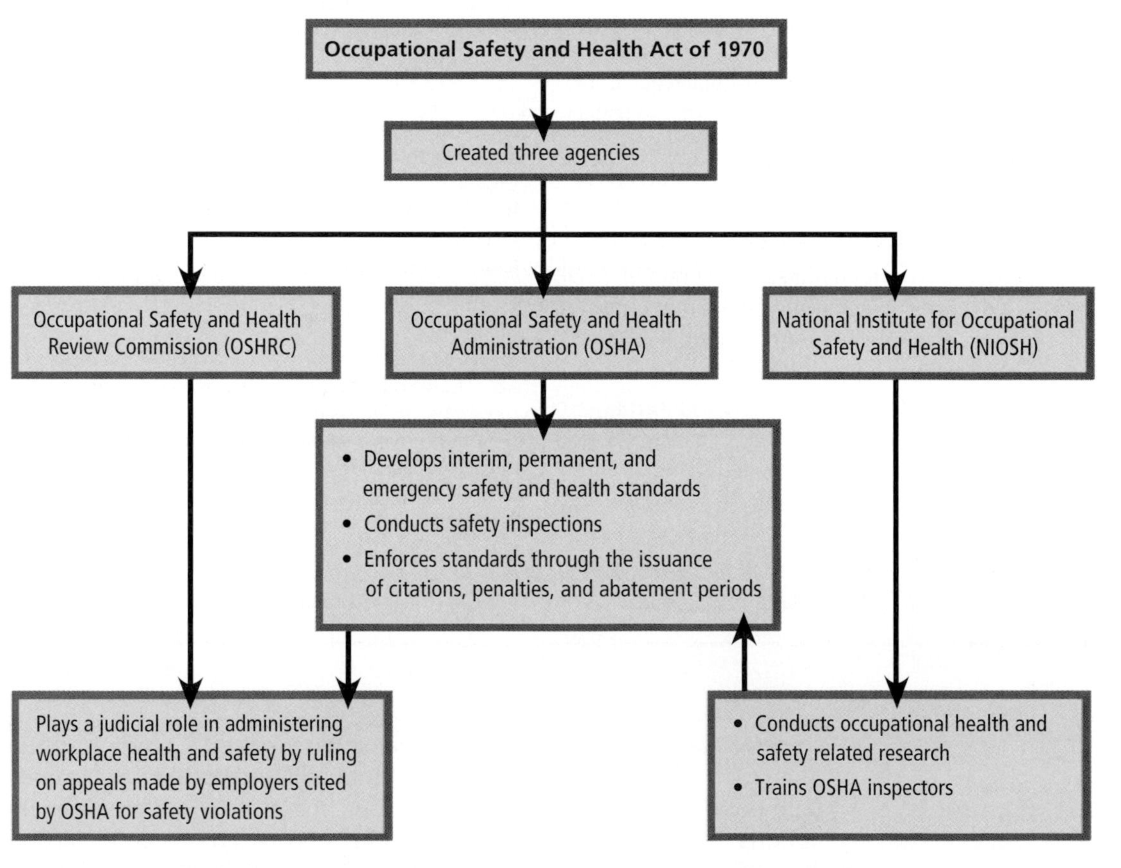

appeal a safety or health citation by requesting a review by OSHRC. If dissatisfied with an OSHRC ruling, an employer may appeal through the federal court system. The OSHRC homepage can be found at http://www.oshrc.gov/.

The **National Institute for Occupational Safety and Health (NIOSH)** has primary responsibility for conducting and coordinating research on workplace safety and health. This research could be to determine safe levels of particular chemicals in the atmosphere, for example, or what decibel level of machine noise requires ear protection to prevent injury. NIOSH's research provides the basis for making recommendations to the Occupational Safety and Health Administration concerning possible regulations. The NIOSH homepage can be found at http://www.cdc.gov/niosh/homepage.html.

The **Occupational Safety and Health Administration (OSHA)** was established as a branch of the Department of Labor. It is by far the most visible of the three agencies because it is responsible for formulating and enforcing the regulations for on-the-job safety and health. In the past several years, OSHA has enhanced its focus on being a customer service and results-oriented organization, with a view to acting more as a partner with business to improve safety rather than as a heavy-handed enforcer of sometimes trivial regulations.[9] OSHA's Web site can be visited at http://www.osha.gov.

OSHA's Primary Tasks

Immediately after OSHA was established, its first task was to develop health and safety standards and regulations. With the help of research provided by NIOSH, developing new safety and health standards and reviewing current standards remains a major OSHA activity today.

Enforcing health and safety regulations is the second responsibility of OSHA. The agency conducts workplace inspections for this purpose. Given the millions of workplaces in the United States, it is impossible for one government agency to inspect all employers. Not all inspections are performed by OSHA. OSHA allows a state to take over responsibility for inspections and enforcement of workplace safety if its laws are at least as stringent as the federal standards. However, workplace inspections remain a primary task for OSHA.[10]

Originally, OSHA was allowed to inspect any work area at any "reasonable" time. Business objected to OSHA's liberal interpretation of the legislation, and the Supreme Court ruled to curb OSHA's freedom. Employers may now deny OSHA inspectors access to all or part of a worksite. Additionally, employers are not required to turn over every document requested by an OSHA inspector. To gain access to work areas and documents denied by an employer, OSHA has to obtain a legal search warrant (assuming a negotiated agreement cannot be reached with the employer for access).[11] OSHA performs two basic types of inspections. **Programmed inspections** are based on national scheduling programs that target employers or industries with the highest injury and illness rates. OSHA gathers data on workplace and injury rates and focuses on workplaces that are among the most dangerous in the United States. The second type of inspection, **unprogrammed inspections,** occurs when there is a report to OSHA of imminent dangers or fatalities in a workplace or when OSHA receives specific complaints about safety or health hazards from employees or others.[12]

There are also two ways in which OSHA can conduct an investigation. An off-site **phone/fax investigation** may be conducted when a lower priority hazard is involved. OSHA telephones the employer, describes the alleged hazards, and then follows the telephone call with a fax or letter. The employer must respond in writing within five days, identifying any problems found and noting corrective actions taken or planned. If the response is adequate, OSHA generally will not conduct an on-site inspection. The employee or employee representative who filed the original complaint receives a copy of the employer's response and, if still not satisfied, may then request an on-site inspection. **On-site inspections** occur (1) when a safety or health hazard situation has already resulted in disabling injuries or illnesses, (2) when there is an imminent danger situation, (3) when there are written, signed complaints requesting an on-site inspection, (4) when an employer has responded inadequately to a phone/fax investigation, or (5) as part of a programmed inspection process.[13]

An OSHA on-site inspection may involve either a comprehensive inspection of the workplace—that is, a complete examination of all potentially high hazard areas of the firm—or a partial inspection limited to certain potentially hazardous areas, operations, conditions, or practices at the establishment. (See Table 14.1 for an "anatomy" of an OSHA inspection along with some tips for employers in handling the inspections.)[14] As indicated previously, an employer is not required by law to allow an OSHA inspector onto a worksite. However, the advice from most experts on OSHA procedures is for employers to be cooperative but also to exert their rights relating to OSHA inspection procedures. In an inspection, the OSHA inspector looks for unsafe conditions and violations of OSHA standards. Typically, the inspector is accompanied by representatives of both management and labor. If a violation is discovered, the OSHA inspector will issue a citation, identifying the specific violation and stating a time by which the employer must correct the situation. If a violation is not corrected in the allotted time, OSHA will levy a fine against the employer. The types of citations issued and related penalties are shown in Table 14.2. However, if the employer acts in good faith and remedies the unsafe situation quickly, the fines may be reduced.[15]

OSHA has increasingly taken on a third responsibility—to work cooperatively with business to improve safety outside the inspection/penalty system. OSHA offers no-cost consulting to organizations that ask for assistance in improving workplace safety and health systems. OSHA has run the **Voluntary Protection Program (VPP)** for more than twenty years to encourage and recognize organizations that do an outstanding job with safety. In a VPP, OSHA and an employer create a formal agreement to operate a safety and health program that includes elements such as worksite analysis, hazard prevention and control, and safety and health training. OSHA verifies the program, then removes the site from its list of routinely scheduled inspections. Through VPP, firms are encouraged to partner with OSHA and proactively improve workplace health and safety[16]

The federal agencies set up as part of the Occupational Safety and Health Act of 1970 represent only one side of the equation in determining employee health and safety in the workplace. Obviously, management plays a critical role in influencing the health and safety of workers. In the next section of this chapter we examine that role.

TABLE 14.1

Anatomy of an OSHA Inspection

Inspection Stage	What Happens	What Management Should Do
Initial contact	• Inspectors arrive, present their credentials.	• Refer inspector to your OSHA coordinator.
	• If management is not on site, the inspector is responsible for attempting to contact management.	• Check inspector's credentials.
	• If management is not available within an hour, the inspector may begin an inspection without management there.	• Ask why inspector is inspecting your workplace.
		• If there is a complaint, you are entitled to know if the complainant is a current employee, but not his or her name.
		• Notify your lawyer, who should review all OSHA requests for documents, interviews, and anything you provide to OSHA.
		• Employer may decide to deny inspector access.
Opening conference	• Inspector explains purpose of inspection and may provide copies of complaints; the conference is open to designated employee representatives.	• Designate at least one representative to accompany the inspector.
	• Inspector outlines the scope of the inspection (which physical facilities and which employees will be involved).	• Discuss the procedure for protecting trade secrets, conducting employee interviews, and producing documents.
	• Employees may also appoint a representative to accompany the inspector.	• Show the inspector that you have safety programs in place.
Walk-around inspection	• Accompany the inspector and take notes.	• Inspectors can view things that are "in plain view" but cannot walk over to things that are "not in plain view" without the consent of management.
	• If inspector takes a photo or video, you should too.	• Request another conference if you feel that the inspector is expanding the inspection beyond that already discussed.
	• Ask the inspector for copies of physical samples and all test results.	
	• Be helpful and cooperative, but don't volunteer information.	
	• If possible, immediately correct any violations identified.	
Closing conference and after inspection	• This can occur immediately after the inspection or later over the telephone.	• Notify OSHA when the corrections are complete.
	• Inspector describes violations observed.	• Ask for an extension of the time period for corrections if necessary (describe reasons for extension and actions already taken).
	• If citations are issued for safety violations, OSHA specifies a period during which corrections must be made.	• Appeal the citation if appropriate.
	• OSHA may schedule follow-up inspections.	

Sources: Adapted from William Atkinson, "When OSHA Comes Knocking," *HR Magazine,* Vol. 44 (10), 1999, pp. 35–38; Robert Grossman, "Handling Inspections: Tips from Insiders," *HR Magazine,* Vol. 44 (10), 1999, pp. 41–45; U.S. Department of Labor, Occupational Safety and Health Administration, *All About OSHA,* Report Number OSHA 2056-07R (Washington D.C.: U.S. Department of Labor, Occupational Safety and Health Administration, 2003), pp. 23–24; U.S. Department of Labor, Occupational Safety and Health Administration, *OSHA Inspections,* Report Number OSHA-2098, 2002 (Washington D.C.: U.S. Department of Labor, Occupational Safety and Health Administration, 2002).

TABLE 14.2

Types of OSHA Violations and Their Maximum Penalties

Type of Violation	Maximum Penalty per Violation
Other-than-serious	$7,000
Serious	$7,000
Violation of posting requirements	$7,000
Willful	$70,000
Willful with fatality, first conviction	Fine of up to $250,000 for an individual; up to $500,000 for a corporation; or six months in prison; or both
Willful, with fatality, second conviction	$250,000/$500,000 or one year in prison; or both
Repeated violations	$70,000
Failure to abate cited violation beyond the prescribed abatement date	$7,000 per day
Falsifying records, reports, or applications (if convicted in court)	$10,000 or six months in prison; or both
Assaulting a compliance officer or otherwise resisting, opposing, intimidating, or interfering with a compliance officer in the performance of his or her duties	$5000; three years in prison; or both

1. *Other-than-serious:* A violation that affects job safety and health but would probably not cause death or serious physical harm.
2. *Serious:* A violation where there is substantial probability that death or serious physical harm could result and that the employer knew, or should have known, of the hazard.
3. *Violation of posting requirements:* Failure to post required safety documents at the workplace.
4. *Willful:* An employer intentionally and knowingly violates the law. Employers either know they are engaging in a violation or are aware of a hazardous condition but make no reasonable effort to eliminate it.
5. *Repeated violations:* Prior violation of the same standard constitutes a "repeated violation."

Source: U.S. Department of Labor, Occupational Safety and Health Administration, *All About OSHA*, Report Number OSHA 2056-07R (Washington D.C.: U.S. Department of Labor, Occupational Safety and Health Administration, 2003), pp. 26–27.

MANAGEMENT'S ROLE IN MAINTAINING SAFETY AND HEALTH

In meeting the health and safety needs of its employees, management may take either a minimalist or a more proactive stance. In the **minimalist approach to safety and health,** management complies with the legal responsibilities placed on it by the Occupational Safety and Health Act and other state and federal regulations. In general, these responsibilities fall within three areas: (a) providing a safe workplace for employees, (b) informing and training employees about health and safety issues, and (c) complying with specific regulations or directives of OSHA. Table 14.3 shows a more detailed list of these employer responsibilities.

TABLE 14.3

Some Responsibilities of an Employer Under the Occupational Safety and Health Act of 1970

Providing a safe work environment

- Meet general duty to provide a workplace free from recognized hazards.
- Evaluate workplace conditions.
- Make sure employees have and use safe, properly maintained tools and equipment (including appropriate personal protective equipment).
- Establish or update operating procedures and communicate them to employees.
- Minimize or eliminate potential hazards.

Informing and training employees about safety and health issues

- Keep workers informed about OSHA and safety and health matters with which they are involved.
- Communicate operating procedures to employees.
- Make copies of safety and health standards available to employees for review upon request.
- Warn employees of potential hazards.
- Provide training required by OSHA standards.
- Post a copy of the *OSHA 300—Log and Summary of Occupational Injuries and Illnesses* for the prior year each year during the period February 1 to April 30.
- Post, at a prominent location within the workplace, specific OSHA information that informs employees of their rights and responsibilities.

Complying with specific safety and health regulations and directives

- Be familiar with mandatory OSHA standards.
- Comply in a responsible manner with standards, rules, and regulations issued under the Occupational Safety and Health Act.
- Report within eight hours any accident that results in a fatality or the hospitalization of three or more employees.
- Keep OSHA-required records of work-related injuries and illnesses, unless otherwise specified.
- Provide access to employee medical records and exposure records.
- Cooperate with OSHA compliance officers.
- Do not discriminate against employees who properly exercise their rights under the Occupational Safety and Health Act.
- Post OSHA citations and abatement verification notices at or near the worksite involved.
- Abate (i.e., correct) cited violations within the prescribed period.

Source: Adapted from U.S. Department of Labor, Occupational Safety and Health Administration, *All About OSHA,* Report Number OSHA 2056-07R (Washington D.C.: U.S. Department of Labor, Occupational Safety and Health Administration, 2003), pp. 4–5.

Obviously, to meet OSHA requirements, all employers must have some safety rules. However, many organizations go well beyond these minimal requirements with a more **proactive approach to safety and health.** In these firms, health and safety programs are based on a strategic human resource philosophy: Workers represent a valued asset of the organization and a significant source of the firm's competitive advantage. As a result, safety and health issues and programs designed to deal effectively with them have become a way for organizations to protect one of the firm's most valuable competitive assets—its people (see the Partnerships for Strategic Success box).

A number of characteristics distinguish successful, proactive programs from all the rest. To make sure that these characteristics exist in their safety and health programs, management must play five key roles.

PARTNERSHIPS FOR STRATEGIC SUCCESS

Safety at NexTech is SHARP

NexTech is a manufacturer producing products in an environment with extremely high temperatures, sharp-edged metal sheets, and overhead cranes in constant motion. It processes semifinished steel into a zinc-coated material used to produce metal buildings, garage doors, and ceiling grids. Despite the nature of NexTech's work environment, in 2003 NexTech managed to exceed eighteen months without a lost-time accident. NexTech has also retained 70 percent of its original employees ten years after the plant opened.

One aspect of NexTech's success is its participation in OSHA's Safety and Health Achievement Recognition Program (SHARP), which recognizes small employers who operate high-quality safety and health programs. NexTech integrates safety and health into all aspects of its operations. All employees are actively involved in safety committees, inspections, and reviews of any issues of concern. The plant-level safety committee, which includes twelve hourly employees, meets once a month to review current safety programs, identify potential hazards, and develop and implement new safety ideas. The twelve hourly employees rotate on and off the committee so that during a two-year period every employee has an opportunity to serve.

Critical to the overall program is an extensive in-house safety training program. The company also contracts with external consultants to provide mandatory safety training, including an eight-hour class that provides employees with real-life examples of incidents where people were seriously injured on the job. There is also a thirty-two-hour safety class for all employees that focuses on OSHA standards. The program makes sure all employees understand OSHA standards and how to use them. As part of the training process, employees from one of NexTech's plants are sent to its other plants to identify job hazards.

The benefits from NexTech's program are many. The incident of "days-away-and-restricted-time" due to workplace injuries is well below the national average. Sales staff use the firm's safety record as a selling point in their interactions with clients. NexTech's successful participation in the SHARP program frees it from announced OSHA inspections—although OSHA inspects the facilities every other year to ensure NexTech maintains SHARP program standards. In addition to these obvious tangible benefits, NexTech's management say that another very important part of their safety and health program is simply the satisfaction everyone gets from "doing the right thing" for their employees.

Source: Shelly Bishop, "NexTech: Safety on the Leading Edge," *Job Safety and Health Quarterly,* Vol. 14 (3), 2003. (Available at: http://www.osha.gov/Publications/JSHQ/spring2003/leadedge.htm, accessed April 12, 2004)

Leading from the Front

One of the most important roles for management is that of leading from the front. Managers must take the initiative in safety and health issues. Employees must see managers as proactive rather than reactive. If top management pays only lip service to safety, workers will follow this lead and regard safety policies as unimportant. As part of management's leadership role, managers must accept accountability for the results of safety and health programs.[17]

Involving Employees

Involving employees in the development of safety and health programs is the second key role of management.[18] Doing so will improve the overall quality of safety and health programs because employees who work "at the coal face" are most likely to understand the nature of work hazards and their possible solutions. One of the most common and effective strategies for involving employees is the use of company **safety committees** consisting of management and non-management employees. These committees identify safety hazards through self-inspections, statistical analyses, and employee input. Typically, they also attempt to find solutions to hazards that have been identified or suggest that experts be hired to resolve a problem. Taken collectively, this process is referred to as a **job hazard analysis.** Table 14.4 gives a detailed example of potential hazards in grinding castings, the causes of those hazards, and possible remedies to reduce or remove the hazards. Safety committees also arrange for training seminars and other activities to increase employee awareness of safety.

Analyzing Data

The third major role of management is to ensure that a thorough analysis of the health and safety environment in the workplace is undertaken. Not doing this may lead a firm to "solve the wrong problem." For example, a midwestern firm developed a wellness program for employees to help reduce health care costs and absenteeism. The centerpiece of the program was a new fitness center. Unfortunately,

TABLE 14.4

Sample Job Hazard Analysis: Grinding Castings

Step	Hazard	Cause	Preventive Measure
1. Reach into right box and select casting	Strike hand on wheel	Box is located beneath wheel	Relocate box to side of wheel
	Tear hand on corner of casters	Corners of casters are sharp	Require wearing of leather gloves
2. Grasp casting, lift and position	Strain shoulder/elbow by lifting with elbow extended	Box too low	Place box on pallet
	Drop casting on toe during positioning	Slips from hand	Require wearing of safety shoes
3. Push casting against wheel, and grind burr	Strike hand against wheel	Wheel guard is too small	Provide larger guard
	Wheel explodes	Incorrect wheel installed	Check rpm rating of wheel
		Cracked wheel	Inspect wheel for cracks
	Flying sparks/chips	Wheel friction with caster	Require wearing of eye goggles
	Respirable dust	Dust from caster metal and wheel material	Provide local exhaust system
	Sleeves caught in machinery	Loose sleeves	Provide bands to retain sleeves
4. Place finished casting into box	Strike hand on castings	Buildup of completed stock	Remove completed stock routinely

Source: Adapted from U.S Department of Labor, Occupational Safety and Health Administration, *Job Hazard Analysis,* Report No. OSHA-3071 (Washington, D.C.: U.S. Department of Labor, 2002), pp. 8–11.

the new program did little to reduce employee health problems or absenteeism. After surveying employees, the firm found that most employees were already physically active and that the majority of workers were women of childbearing age. Many employees smoked. What the firm needed was a smoking-cessation program and programs that focused on the health issues of women—not a gymnasium. This is a good example of the negative results that may occur from not analyzing the work environment *and* not encouraging employee participation early enough in the process.[19]

Motivating Safe Behavior

Most employees know how to use safety devices and protective equipment properly. However, a significant problem for an organization is to motivate employees to follow safety rules on a daily basis. Doing things in a less safe way may be faster and require less effort. As a result, safety precautions may be ignored, even though most employees know about them. Thus the fourth role of management in developing effective safety and health programs is to motivate safe work behavior in employees. At least five different approaches are being used by organizations to motivate employees to work safely:[20]

1. *Programs that reward results:* These programs provide employees with cash or other tangible incentives for reaching certain safety goals.
2. *Programs that recognize results:* These programs have the same basic approach as rewarding results; however, meeting safety goals leads only to forms of "social recognition" through dinner events, "safe-employee-of-the-month" certificates, and the like.
3. *Programs that reward behaviors:* These programs provide employees with cash or other tangible incentives for engaging in behaviors that have been shown to reduce or prevent accidents and injuries (e.g., wearing hardhats and safety belts) or that promote safety and health in the workplace (e.g., participating in specific safety training programs).
4. *Programs that recognize behaviors:* These programs have the same basic approach as those rewarding behaviors, but programs that merely recognize safe behaviors have the same limitations as those that merely recognize results (see item 2 above).
5. *Programs that focus on expecting behavior:* In these programs employees are shown the value of working safely. They are taught how to work safely, how to observe coworkers to see if they are working safely, and how to discuss safety observations with coworkers. No formal rewards are given.

There is no definitive evidence that one type of program is superior to the others. One of the major problems with rewarding or recognizing results is that this may lead employees to hide or underreport health and safety problems. Programs that focus on behavior rather than results should avoid this problem. Proponents of the "expecting-behaviors" approach to motivating safety in the workplace argue that external rewards or recognition should not be necessary because safety and health have intrinsic value to employees. There are obviously financial and administrative advantages to these programs relative to systems in which results or behaviors have to be closely monitored and rewarded or recognized.[21]

Although the arguments of the behavior-versus-results and expecting-versus-rewarding/recognizing proponents seem well founded, effective results on safety have been achieved through all of these types of programs. For example, Denark, a Tennessee construction company, has developed a safety incentive program that distributes about $60,000 a year in safety bonuses to employees. Denark won the Associated General Contractors of America's 2003 Annual Safety Award. In the previous year, Denark employees completed 1 million work hours without a single lost-time accident. This focus on safety is reflected in the company's bottom line. Workers' compensation insurance premiums have been reduced by 26 percent over the last six years. Denark is able to pass these savings on to its clients through lower insurance costs, which makes the company more competitive in bidding for future contracts. The company grows; employees work in a safe environment; everyone wins.[22]

Innovating

With management leadership, employee participation, careful data analysis, and motivation, any firm is well on its way to achieving successful programs in safety and health. However, one last management role needs to be mentioned—innovating. A key role for management is to be creative in its approach to safety and health programs. Fonterra, a New Zealand dairy company, recently won a Corporate Road Safety Award for its "Milk Supply Road Safety Initiative." The program included establishment of a contact center and toll-free number for members of the public to relay any concerns about milk tankers. Each of the firm's tankers now carries a large unique fleet number, which allows those driving the tankers to be individually identified. The company also appointed national training and development coordinators to help improve the skills and knowledge of drivers. The program also included regular driver assessments, a review of workplace injuries, regular vehicle safety assessments, and education of drivers about fatigue, seatbelts, and other health issues. As a result of this new integrated program, Fronterra has reduced injury accidents among the company's tanker fleet by 63 percent.[23]

The five roles of management described here will help ensure that programs designed to enhance workplace safety and health are successful. Firms in which management takes on these five roles in relation to occupational safety and health receive numerous benefits. As is evidenced in some of the examples provided so far, good safety and health programs can have significant bottom-line benefits. Firms implementing such programs are also more likely to create a cooperative working relationship with OSHA officials. Cooperation between management and OSHA will reduce the likelihood that the firm will be inspected, and if inspections occur, the probability of citations or fines will be reduced. All of this should result in a safer, healthier, and more productive workplace—and thus enhance the overall competitive advantage of a firm in the marketplace.

Thus far this chapter has described the legislative environment related to occupational safety and health in which organizations must operate. The roles that both federal agencies and an organization's management and employees play in safety and health programs have also been discussed. The remainder of this chapter identifies specific safety and health issues that are the focus of OSHA standards and regulations.

SAFETY AND HEALTH ISSUES IN THE WORKPLACE

The Occupational Safety and Health Administration focuses on several aspects of workplace safety and health. Among the most prominent of OSHA's concerns are on-the-job injuries, exposure to hazardous chemicals, a broad range of occupational diseases, and injuries or death due to workplace violence. In addition to on-the-job injuries, occupational diseases including issues related to smoking in the workplace, and workplace violence, a variety of other health and safety issues in the workplace are worthy of discussion. These include acquired immune deficiency syndrome (AIDS) and other bloodborne pathogens, drug use in the workplace, and a variety of issues that fall within the general topic of employee psychological health. This section of the chapter discusses the nature of these safety issues.

On-the-Job Injuries

The reduction of on-the-job injuries is one of the main goals of the Occupational Safety and Health Act of 1970. Although injury rates over the past decade have been decreasing, far too many accidents and injuries still occur. Table 14.5 presents data on the number of some of the common types of injuries that resulted in lost work time during the period 1994–2002. Research indicates that more than 80 percent of accidents involving employee error result from misjudging the degree of hazard.[24] Regardless of whether an employee violates a safety regulation knowingly or unknowingly, if an accident occurs, it is legally the responsibility of the employer.

Figure 14.2 shows factors that have been statistically related to worksite accidents. Aside from employee disregard for safety regulations, accidents are related to several other employee factors. New workers show a higher incidence of accidents than senior employees, perhaps because they do not have enough training or experience to fully comprehend workplace dangers. Workers under severe

TABLE 14.5

Number of Occupational Injuries and Illnesses (in thousands) Involving Time Away from Work by Selected Nature of Injury and Illness, 1994 to 2002

	1994	1998	2002
Sprains, strains, tears	963.5	760.0	617.2
Bruises, contusions	212.0	153.1	117.0
Cuts, lacerations	164.6	137.6	110.2
Fractures	138.5	115.4	99.2
Heat burns, scalds	37.3	28.4	21.5
Chemical burns	16.5	11.7	8.3
Amputations	12.2	10.2	8.8

Source: Department of Labor, Bureau of Labor Statistics. "Lost Worktime Injuries and Illnesses: Characteristics and Resulting Time Away from Work," USDL 00-115,1998. (Available at: http://stats.bls.gov/oshhome.htm)

FIGURE 14.2

Factors Related to Accidents at Work

Source: Robin C. Ballau and Roy M. Buchen, "Study Shows That Gender Is Not a Major Factor in Accident Etiology," *Occupational Health and Safety,* September 1978, pp. 54–58.

Individual Factors

- Worker inexperience
- Worker stress
- Worker carelessness
- Use of improper techniques
- Underestimation of risks
- Use of inappropriate tools
- Disregard for safety rules

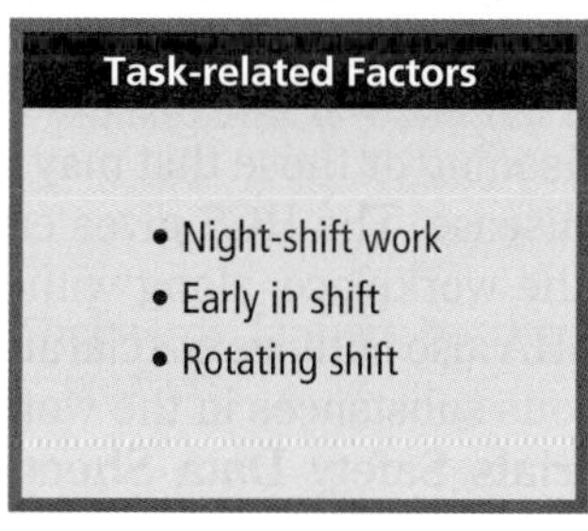

Task-related Factors
• Night-shift work
• Early in shift
• Rotating shift

Organizational Factors

- Medium-sized organization
- Specific dangerous industries

stress also appear to have more accidents on the job. More dangerous yet are practices in which employees either remove or bypass safety devices, such as taping back the guards on saw blades or disconnecting automatic cutoff switches. All these factors can be controlled to some degree by the employer through increased awareness and proper employee training.

Task-related factors also appear to contribute to workplace accidents. For example, there is a much higher incidence of accidents on night shifts than on day shifts. This discrepancy may be attributable to the typically smaller supervisory staff on night shifts, as well as to employee drowsiness and inattentiveness. Accidents also tend to occur early in shifts rather than after breaks or toward the end of shifts. Also, employees on rotating shifts have more accidents.[25]

The size of the firm is an organizational factor that is related to on-the-job accidents. Moderate-sized organizations—with 50 to 100 employees—have higher accident rates than do smaller or larger companies. This statistic may reflect the fact that smaller companies supervise their employees closely and personally and that larger organizations can afford comparatively elaborate safety programs.

Finally, because of their work processes, certain industries experience more risks than others. For example, banks and insurance companies are usually safer than construction sites or industrial plants. The tools used, the environments in which they are operated, and the tasks that need to be performed contribute to this difference.

Although a company may be in a dangerous industry, it does not have to be a dangerous place to work. DuPont, through massive safety programs, has an accident record that is many times lower than its industry's average. Thus a corporate commitment to safety—through training, increasing safety awareness, and developing safe practices for employees—may go a long way toward reducing accidents, even in an inherently dangerous industry.

Hazardous Substances

Hazardous substances represent a special category of agents that can inflict injuries on the job. The **Hazard Communication Standard (HCS)** of OSHA, implemented in the mid-1980s, requires a hazard communication program to train

In the United States, workplace costs associated with smoking are high. It is estimated that businesses pay an average of $2,189 in workers' compensation costs for smokers compared with $176 for nonsmokers. In addition, smokers miss on average 6.16 days of work per year compared with the 3.86 days missed by nonsmokers. Many U.S. firms are creating tough smoking bans that require employees to leave their workplace property to smoke. The stance on smoking in some countries is becoming even tougher than U.S. standards. In late March of 2004 Ireland implemented legislation banning all smoking from pubs and bars—quite a step in a country where having a smoke and a pint of beer in the local pub is seen by many as an integral part of Irish culture.[32]

Musculoskeletal Disorders In 2002 work-related **musculoskeletal disorders (MSD)** accounted for 34 percent of all occupational injuries and illnesses reported to the Bureau of Labor Statistics. The cost of these injuries can be enormous. For example, a study of MSDs in the State of Oregon estimated that the trucking and courier industry alone had lost almost $110 million due to MSD injuries between 1990 and 2000. The cost to hospitals was estimated at $92.9 million over the same period. Nationwide, in 2002 employers reported 487,900 incidents of MSDs, with the median time away from work as a result of the injury being nine days.[33] Among these musculoskeletal injuries, **cumulative trauma disorders (CTDs)**—also called **repetitive strain injury (RSI)**—was the fastest-growing workplace injury in the United States, having increased more than 770 percent from 1988 to 1998. Estimates of the annual cost of CTDs in the United States exceed $100 billion annually.[34]

CTDs seem to be caused by repeating the same movement many times without a break. Low-back problems are common among employees who repeatedly lift objects. Butchers in meatpacking plants frequently suffer CTDs of the hands and arms, and word-processing and data-entry operators also report the problem fairly often. Automation seems to be a culprit—it simplifies the motions needed and removes the chance to take breaks. For instance, keyboard operators type constantly for hours on end. In past years, these employees would have alternated their activities by inserting paper into a typewriter, manually erasing errors, and returning the typewriter carriage. Carpal tunnel syndrome is the CTD that occurs most commonly in people working with computer keyboards. It results in pain and loss of grip strength in the hands and arms due to swelling of tissues and subsequent pressure on nerves that run through the carpal bones of the wrist.

CTDs have reached epidemic proportions in some areas and, as a result, have attracted a great deal of research interest. It has been found that non-task factors such as previous personal injury or illness, hobbies, job satisfaction, and physical condition are just as important as work-related conditions. For example, one study found that the prevalence of CTDs was more than seven times greater among morbidly obese as compared with slender individuals. At the same time, the prevalence of CTDs was six times higher among those who exercise minimally or lightly as compared with those who exercise vigorously.[35] Further, some apparent cases of CTD are not due to the workplace at all but may be an expression of mental distress or an attempt to malinger by employees.

OSHA recognizes CTDs along with other musculoskeletal disorders as major health problems. In 1999 OSHA proposed new ergonomic workplace regulations, which were adopted in final form in November 2000.[36] More recently it has initiated a four-pronged comprehensive approach to workplace ergonomics. The science of **ergonomics** investigates the interactions between humans and mechanical systems. Ergonomically designed tools and work processes can greatly reduce the incidence of CTDs and other musculoskeletal disorders. Something as simple as a curved handle on a knife—so that the wrist does not have to be bent at an angle for long periods—can reduce the incidence of CTD in butchers. OSHA will develop industry or task-specific ergonomic guidelines for a number of industries based on current incidence rates and available information about effective and feasible solutions. It will conduct inspections for ergonomic hazards and issue citations under the General Duty Clause and issue ergonomic hazard alert letters where appropriate. OSHA will provide additional assistance to businesses, particularly small businesses, to help them reduce ergonomic problems in the workplace.[37]

Ergonomics does have a great deal to contribute to the effective design of equipment and workplaces. Figure 14.3 shows how to properly position computing equipment to minimize strain on the back, neck, shoulders, wrists, and eyes. Consideration of ergonomic work design may help prevent workplace accidents as well as occupational disease. The human errors that cause so many accidents may themselves be due to poorly designed equipment. For instance, injuries may occur when trying to repair or service equipment that is mounted too high or too close to other equipment. Poorly designed switches or gauges may violate intuitive expectations and thus cause errors in the confusion of an emergency situation. In the United States and Canada, the "up" position on switches is generally expected to mean "on" or "open" or "start," whereas "down" means "off." The opposite is true in Europe.[38]

The impact of ergonomics programs can be quite dramatic. For example, cumulative trauma disorders (CTDs) accounted for 35 percent of total recordable

FIGURE 14.3

Minimizing Musculoskeletal Strain at the Keyboard

Source: Occupational Safety and Health Administration, Department of Labor, *Working Safely with Video Display Terminals,* OSHA Publication No. 3092, 1996 (revised), p. 8. (Available at: http://www.osha.gov/oshpubs/osha3092.pdf)

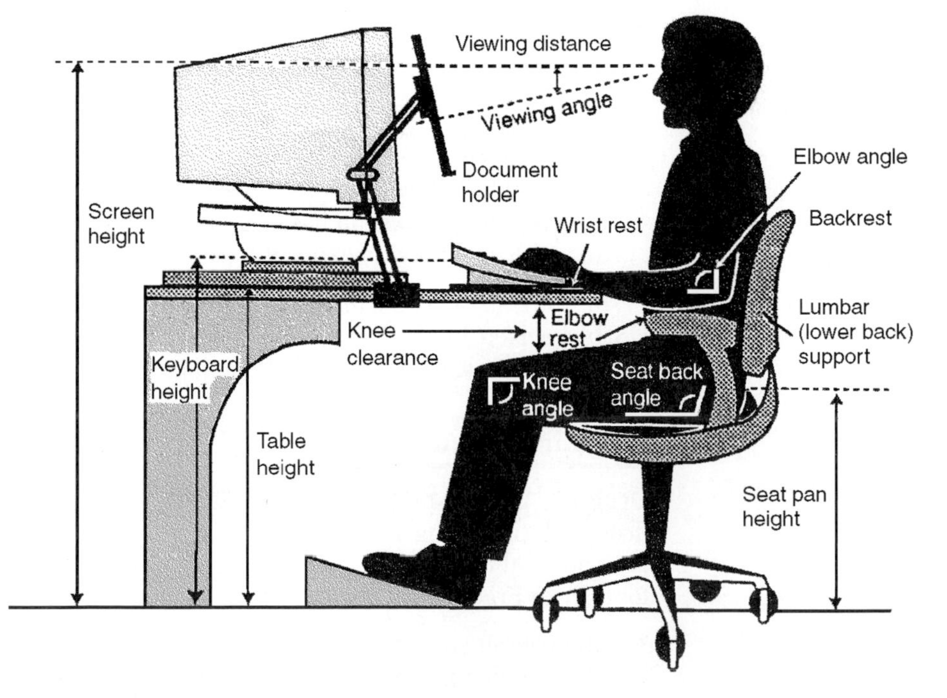

injuries and illnesses over a four-year period at Duracell's Lagrange, Georgia, facility. The company formed an ergonomics committee to identify the causes of the CTDs and to develop methods to reduce the CTD incident rate as well as the total number of accidents. The committee reviewed OSHA accident logs and compiled data related to the cost of the injuries. They implemented a number of incident reduction measures including automation of unloading and loading stations, work height adjustments, redesign of work stations, elimination of some portable equipment, the provision of antifatigue floor mats, rotation of jobs, and ergonomically designed chairs. In addition, the facility's occupational health nurse received additional training to better manage and prevent CTDs. A variety of other measures including an ergonomics survey of all production jobs in the plant were also undertaken. As a result of Duracell's actions, CTD incident rates were reduced by 90 percent, and the total accident rate was reduced by 81 percent.[39]

AIDS and Other Bloodborne Pathogens

Acquired immune deficiency syndrome (AIDS) is a handicap covered by legal statutes. Employees who have AIDS or who test positive for the HIV virus that causes AIDS must be considered handicapped and must be accommodated.[40] Despite the fact that there is little evidence that AIDS can be spread through casual contact in the workplace, OSHA has issued a set of **Bloodborne Pathogen Standards.** The standards cover "all employees who can be 'reasonably anticipated' as the result of performing their job duties to face contact with blood and other potentially infectious materials." The standards require employers to do the following:

- Identify, in writing, job duties that may expose employees to blood or other bodily fluids.
- Establish procedures for evaluating incidents when exposure to potentially harmful bodily fluids occurs.
- Establish procedures for handling and shipping infectious materials.
- Provide employees, at no cost, with personal protective equipment.
- Establish procedures for evaluating and following up on employees who have been exposed to infectious materials.
- Place warning labels on hazardous waste containers and train employees to reduce the likelihood of exposure.

In 2001, as a result of the new **Needlestick Safety and Prevention Act,** OSHA revised its Bloodborne Pathogens Standard to improve management of needle devices and record keeping on injuries from such objects.[41]

Drugs in the Workplace

Drug use in the workplace is of continuing concern to employers. The impact of drug use (including alcohol abuse) in the workplace is great. Some disturbing facts about the impact of workplace drug abuse has been provided by the Institute for a Drug-Free Workplace:

- The overall cost to employers of illicit drug abuse in 2000 was estimated to be $160.7 billion, with 69 percent of these costs due to productivity losses as a result of drug-related illnesses and deaths.

- Alcoholics and problem drinkers are absent from work as much as 8 times more often than normal, and regular users of other drugs miss work an average of five days per month due to drug use.
- Light and moderate drinkers cause 60 percent of tardiness, absenteeism, and poor quality work as a result of alcohol consumption, and heavy drinkers cause the remaining 40 percent.
- Substance abusers are 33 percent less productive and cost their employers $7,000 per year with these productivity losses, amounting annually to $640 for every American worker.
- Up to 40 percent of industrial fatalities can be linked to alcohol abuse and alcoholism.
- Drug-using employees are 3.6 times more likely to be involved in workplace accidents.
- Substance abusers are 3 times more likely to use company medical benefits than other employees.
- Eighty percent of drug abusers steal from their workplaces to support their drug use.
- Substance abuse is the third leading cause of workplace violence.[42]

More and more employers are concerned about drugs in the workplace and the potential for serious accidents caused by drug-impaired employees. Under the 1988 federal Drug-Free Workplace Act, federal contractors must certify that they maintain a drug-free workplace.[43] Among other things, this certification includes enforcing a drug-free policy, providing awareness programs, and making absence of substance abuse a condition of employment.

Many employers are testing applicants or current employees for drug abuse. It is important that organizations have appropriate policies for testing either applicants or current employees. Such policies need to involve (1) informed consent, (2) scheduling, (3) assurance of test validity, and (4) confidentiality. Even with good policies and sophisticated drug testing methods, the ability of employees to deceive drug tests is increasing. For example, the "Whizzinator" is an easy-to-conceal, simple-to-use drug test deception device that has a realistic prosthetic penis with an adjustable belt, a 4-ounce vinyl bag, dehydrated toxin-free urine, and organic heat pads—all for only $149.95. By far the most popular method of fooling drug tests is drug dilution, which requires the individual to consume large amounts of water to help reduce the relative volume of drugs present in the body. Other approaches include the use of chemicals that can be added to a urine specimen to make the drugs undetectable.[44] Employers seeking to achieve a drug-free workplace will continue to face many challenges in the future.

Psychological Health

We have seen that employers have clear responsibilities regarding employees' physical health, but what about their mental health? The employer's responsibility for the psychological well-being of employees has been addressed mainly by case law rather than by formal regulation. Employers are sometimes held responsible for mental and psychological distress that is work related, just as they are for on-the-job physical injury. In *Brickner v. N.Y. State DOT,* the court ruled that an employee who experienced stress-related physical problems in a new job and had lost work hours was entitled to workers' compensation benefits because the injury was a direct consequence of stress encountered in the new job. In the *Brickner* case, there was an obvious financial loss to the employee as a result of job stress. However, the loss experienced by the employee may not always need to be so tangible. The courts have maintained that individuals may obtain damage awards when they experience distress due to intentional or reckless acts of the employer that degrade or humiliate the employee. This principle may cover a wide range of possible actions, including sexual harassment. For example, in *City Market, Inc. v. Industrial Claim Appeals Office* the court ruled in favor of a plaintiff who argued that her employer was liable for her mental stress, which resulted from a supervisor's sexual advances. The court held it was good public policy to force the employer to pay.[45] It does seem, however, that in order to hold employers responsible for mental health-related work injuries, the employee must show that the stress was substantial in nature and that there is a very clear link between work duties and the injury incurred. For example, in *Spencer v. Time Warner Cable,* a worker who suffered a stress-related injury as a result of transfer failed to show that her stress was any greater than that of any other worker in her situation. As a result, the court denied her claim for compensation for the injury.[46]

As evidenced by these court cases, employers should be aware of their potential liabilities for stress-related illnesses, as well as the loss in employee productivity that can occur when workers are overstressed for a long period. Hewlett-Packard is an excellent example of an organization that puts considerable effort into *de-stressing* the workplace. One author described Hewlett-Packard's practices as follows:

> Hewlett-Packard takes its leisure goals seriously, requiring employees to meet personal goals as defined. If they fall short, supervisors are held accountable. Here's how it works: At monthly meetings, team members are asked to list three business goals and three personal ones. When a staff member achieves a milestone, such as leaving at 2 p.m. to take a daughter roller-blading, co-workers are encouraged to applaud with the same enthusiasm they would applaud someone landing a sales order.[47]

Hewlett-Packard also encourages its management to reduce employee stress by making sure they take the stress out of jobs. Managers are asked to examine the quantitative workload of their employees and redistribute work where needed. Managers also engage in open and regular communication with employees about job stress. As part of an overall approach, HP employees are encouraged to take mini-vacations, for example, going to an aerobics class at 3:00 P.M. as a means of reducing stress on the job.[48] Some companies have recognized that something as simple as encouraging employees to eat lunch away from their desks can help reduce job stress. One way to do this is for companies to provide a desirable place for employees to have lunch. Highland Cellular's 100 employees are offered an indoor kitchen with microwave, stove, sink, and dining area, as well as an outdoor dining area with benches and a gazebo.[49] Conscientious employers try to keep workplace stressors such as overwork, harassment, conflict, and bad supervision at bay. An increasing number of employers use more formal programs to mitigate employee stress and health problems in the form of employee assistance plans (see Chapter 13) and employee wellness programs.

VIOLENCE IN THE WORKPLACE

The National Institute for Occupational Safety and Health (NIOSH) defines **workplace violence** as "any physical assault, threatening behavior or verbal abuse that occurs in the work setting. Acts such as obscene phone calls, an intimidating presence and harassment of any kind are covered by this definition."[50] Unfortunately, violence in the workplace has become an important safety and health issue in the United States. There is some good news, however. According to the Bureau of Labor Statistics, workplace homicides were 5 percent lower in 2002 compared to 2001 with 643 in 2001 and only 609 in 2002. Workplace homicides in 2002 were the lowest recorded in the history of its workplace fatality census and represented a 44 percent decline from a high of 1,080 in 1994. Despite these encouraging figures, the level of violence in the workplace is still too high. The Department of Justice's 2002 National Crime Victimization Survey found that about 746,000 workplace crimes of violence occurred in the United States. In 2002 approximately 560,000 simple assaults, 147,000 aggravated assaults, 25,000 rapes and sexual assaults, and 14,000 robberies occurred in the workplace.[51]

Who Commits Acts of Violence?

Violence in the workplace does not simply involve one employee assaulting another. In fact, there are at least four sources of violence in work settings.[52]

- **Violence Due to Criminal Intent** Two men entered a fast-food outlet in Flushing, New York, with the intent to rob the restaurant. They left with $2,400 in cash after shooting seven employees. Five of the employees died, and two others were seriously injured. This is an extreme example of one type of workplace violence: violence committed by strangers during a robbery or similar crime. In these incidents the perpetrator does not have any legitimate connection to the business; the motive is usually theft; there is often a deadly weapon involved; and workers who exchange cash with customers as part of the job, work late night hours, or work alone are at greatest risk.

- **Violence by Customer/Client** Rhonda Bedow, a nurse who worked in a state-operated psychiatric facility in Buffalo, New York, was attacked by an angry patient who had a history of threatening behavior, particularly against female staff. He slammed Bedow's head down onto a counter after learning that he had missed the chance to go outside with a group of other patients. In this type of incident, the perpetrator is generally either a "regular" customer who becomes violent during the course of a normal transaction or is an "unwilling" client, such as a prison inmate who attacks a guard or a crime suspect who injures a police officer. In these incidents the violent act generally occurs in conjunction with the worker's normal duties, and the risk of violence to some workers (e.g., mental health workers, police) may be routine.

- **Violence by Worker-on-Worker** A postal employee opens fire on his coworkers killing fourteen and wounding seven. Coworkers had expressed concern about this individual for several years. Thanks to sensational incidents like this, the phrase "going postal," has come to refer to workplace violence in which an employee attacks his or her coworkers. In these incidents the perpetrator is an employee or former employee, and the motivating factors are often interpersonal or work-related disputes. There do not appear to be any occupations or industries more or less prone to worker-on-worker violence, although managers and others who supervise workers may be at greater risk of becoming victims.

Violence Due to a Personal Relationship Pamela Henry, an employee of an answering service firm in San Antonio, had decided to move out of the area due to the abusive behavior of her ex-boyfriend. The abuse had spilled over from her home to her workplace, where her boyfriend appeared one day in July and assaulted her. She obtained but then withdrew a protective violence order against her boyfriend thinking it was unnecessary due to her imminent departure from the area. In October her boyfriend arrived at her workplace and opened fire with a rifle, killing Henry and another female employee before killing himself. These incidents usually occur as a result of a spillover from domestic violence to the workplace: The perpetrator generally has no current or former connection to the workplace, and women significantly more often than men are the victims.

Job Factors and Organizational Factors Associated with Violence

The risk of being a victim of workplace violence depends significantly on the occupation in which one is employed. Figures from the recent National Crime Victimization Survey presented in Table 14.7 show that, not surprisingly, being in law enforcement carries a much higher risk of being a victim of violence than does being a teacher. In addition to occupation, a number of other factors have been identified as increasing the likelihood that someone will become a victim of workplace violence. Among these are the following:[53]

- Having contact with the public
- Being involved in the exchange of money
- Delivering passengers, goods, or services
- Having a mobile workplace, such as a taxicab or police cruiser

TABLE 14.7

Crime Victimization Risk Rates by Occupation in Selected Years, 1993 to 1999

	Rate per 1,000			
Occupational Field	**1993**	**1995**	**1997**	**1999**
Medical	20.3	16.0	8.4	10.0
Mental health	64.4	56.7	39.7	46.1
Teaching	25.8	15.4	14.9	12.4
Law enforcement	163.1	157.2	122.0	74.1
Retail sales	21.9	22.2	22.5	14.1
Transportation	20.6	13.8	15.4	8.4

Source: Detis D. Duhart, "Violence in the Workplace: 1993–1999," U.S. Department of Justice, Office of Justice Programs, Bureau of Justice Statistics, Special Report, December 2001. (Available at: http://www.ojp.usdoj.gov/bjs/pub/pdf/vw99.pdf, accessed April 6, 2004)

- Working with unstable or volatile persons in health care, social services, or criminal justice
- Working alone or in small numbers
- Working late at night or during the early morning hours
- Guarding valuable property or possessions
- Working in community-based settings

In addition to these job-related factors, several organizational factors may increase the probability that a violent incident will occur.[54] Poorly trained supervisors who exhibit aggressive behavior or reinforce such behavior in their subordinates may enhance the likelihood of violence. Highly authoritarian company cultures that tend to deprive employees of dignity and respect may also increase violence in the workplace. Organizations undergoing downsizing or in which employees are frequently fired are more likely to experience violent acts. Finally, violence is more likely to occur in firms that do not have clear policies about what types of behavior are acceptable and unacceptable and systems that guide the behavior of employees who find themselves harassed by others.

The Cost of Workplace Violence

The cost of violence for employers is enormous. One estimate indicated that each act of violence committed resulted in an average of 3.5 days of lost work time per incident. The cost of this lost time would be worth $55 million or more in wages across all incidents reported in the study. One study found that the annual cost of workplace violence to American businesses exceeded $36 billion per year. The calculations included the monetary cost of lost productivity, loss of life, injuries, counseling, legal fees, court awards, management time spent dealing with the crises, and other factors resulting in actual cash losses to businesses suffering from any type of workplace violence.[55]

Workplace Violence Prevention Programs

In addition to financial reasons for firms to be interested in reducing workplace violence, there are specific legal reasons for doing so. The **general duty clause,** Section 5(a) (1) of the Occupational Safety and Health Act of 1970, requires employers to provide employees with a place of employment that "is free from recognizable hazards that are causing or likely to cause death or serious harm to employees." Within the interpretation of this clause, an employer that has experienced acts of workplace violence, or has become aware of threats, intimidation, or indicators of potential violence in the workplace, would need to take action to reduce the likelihood that employees become the victims of violent acts. Given this legal requirement, along with the staggering financial cost of workplace violence, many employers are developing **workplace violence prevention programs (WVPP)** within their firms (see Table 14.8 for examples of workplace violence prevention strategies). The basic components of these programs should include a written violence prevention statement; establishment of a threat assessment team; a process for hazard assessment, control, and prevention; programs for employee training and education; a system for reporting, investigating, and following up on incidents; and some means of evaluating the overall effectiveness of the violence prevention program.[56]

Violence Prevention Statement In a **workplace violence prevention policy statement,** an organization should make it clear that adequate authority and budgetary

TABLE 14.8
Examples of Workplace Violence Prevention Strategies

Administrative/Legal Actions
A zero tolerance policy (immediate termination) in place for employee acts of violence
A zero tolerance policy (immediate termination) in place for employee threats of violence
Monitor employee e-mails or phone calls for threats or harassment
Aid employees in obtaining restraining orders against potential aggressors
The organization itself obtains restraining orders against potential aggressors
Counseling and Behavior-Oriented Strategies
Refer potential victims of domestic abuse to an EAP or counseling
Refer potentially violent employees to an EAP or counseling
Provide employees training on conflict resolution (e.g., with other employees and customers)
Provide employees training on your organization's workplace violence policy
Offer access to legal counseling or advice
Offer anger management classes
Provide employees training to identify potential victims of violence
Provide employees self-defense training
Enhancing Security in the Work Environment
Limited public access to all or portions of the building
Added a check-in or sign-in desk to screen visitors
Increased lighting on the grounds and parking lot
Installation of access card entry systems
Issued ID cards to employees and visitors
Video surveillance inside the building
Video surveillance outside the building
Security guards patrol grounds and parking lot
Placed security guards inside the building
Escort service to and from parking lot for employees after hours
Placed metal detectors at building entry points
Cabs for employees working late

Source: Adapted from Table 10 and Table 20, Evren Esen, *Workplace Violence Survey* (Alexandria, Va.: Society for Human Resource Management, 2004) pp. 11, 23.

resources will be assigned to the WVPP and those in charge of it. The statement should encourage employee participation in the design and conduct of the program. The policy should state that the organization will not tolerate violence in the workplace and that workplace violence prevention policies will be applied consistently and fairly to all employees, including supervisors and managers. The policy should also include statements about the need for prompt and accurate reporting of violent incidents. A strong, clear statement that the firm will not discriminate against victims of workplace violence is a critical part of the policy document. An example of a workplace violence prevention policy statement is given in Figure 14.4.

FIGURE 14.4

Sample Violence in the Workplace Prevention Policy

Source: Adapted from CCH, Inc. "Sample Workplace Violence Prevention Policy." (Available at: http://www.toolkit.cch.com/tools/violpo_m.asp, accessed April 8, 2004)

Zero tolerance

This company has a policy of zero tolerance for violence. If you engage in any violence in the workplace, or threaten violence in the workplace, your employment will be terminated immediately for cause. No talk of violence or joking about violence will be tolerated. "Violence" includes physically harming another, shoving, pushing, harassing, intimidating, coercing, brandishing weapons, and threatening or talking of engaging in those activities.

Workplace security measures

In an effort to fulfill this commitment to a safe work environment for employees, customers, and visitors, a few simple rules have been created. These are: Access to the company's property is limited to those with a legitimate business interest. All employees and employee vehicles entering the property must display company identification. All visitors and visitor vehicles must register and display identification while on the property.

All weapons banned

The company specifically prohibits the possession of weapons by any employee while on company property. This ban includes keeping or transporting a weapon in a vehicle in a parking area, whether public or private. Employees are also prohibited from carrying a weapon while performing services off the company's business premises. Weapons include guns, knives, explosives, and other items with the potential to inflict harm. Appropriate disciplinary action, up to and including termination, will be taken against any employee who violates this policy.

Inspections

Desks, telephones, and computers are the property of the business. We reserve the right to enter or inspect your work area including, but not limited to, desks and computer storage disks, with or without notice. The fax, copier, and mail systems, including e-mail, are intended for business use. Under conditions approved by management, telephone conversations may be monitored and voice mail messages may be retrieved in the process of monitoring customer service. Any private conversations overheard during such monitoring, or private messages retrieved, that constitute threats against other individuals can and will be used as the basis for termination for cause.

Reporting violence

It is everyone's business to prevent violence in the workplace. You are encouraged to report any incident that may involve a violation of any of the company's policies that are designed to provide a comfortable workplace environment. Concerns may be presented to your supervisor. All reports will be investigated and information will be kept confidential.

Training and programs

As part of its commitment to preventing workplace violence, the company has established training programs for all employees. Training will be included as part of your orientation. Thereafter, you will be scheduled for annual refresher training during the month that you initially joined the business. Please be advised that training is mandatory and attendance will be taken.

Employee assistance program

The company provides an employee assistance program (EAP) for all full-time and part-time employees. This EAP offers services to these employees and their eligible dependents. While we receive periodic reports on the number and types of visits or calls made to the EAP, we do not receive information about individual contacts with the EAP. If you have difficulty handling drugs or alcohol, the EAP can provide information on treatment. The EAP is a confidential service to be used when you need help.

Violence prevention team

We have created a violence prevention team to create and implement our workplace violence prevention program. The team will also handle the consequences of any incidents of violence that we experience, providing assistance to employees and information to the media. The team will take the steps necessary to continue or resume business. If you have suggestions for ways to improve the safety and security at work, please pass them along to a team member or leave a suggestion in any one of their mail boxes.

Threat Assessment Team A **threat assessment team** should be formed to assess the vulnerability of the workplace to violence. This team should be comprised of both management and employee representatives and include individuals from key functions within the organization, such as security, human resources, finance, and legal affairs. Typical activities of the assessment team are to review current records relating to violent incidents that have occurred, to conduct a workplace security analysis of the organization, and to survey employees in an attempt to identify potential security problems. This function might be performed by an organization's general safety committee, but given the special and complex nature of workplace violence, a special team to examine this issue might be warranted.

Once an assessment of security risks has been made, the threat assessment team's next function is to recommend actions to control and prevent workplace violence. The National Institute for Occupational Safety and Health has identified three major categories of actions that firms typically take to control or prevent workplace violence. As seen in Table 14.8, firms may alter the environmental design of the workplace, institute specific administrative controls, or train employees in a variety of behavioral strategies to enhance their safety in the workplace.

Employee Training Employee training is an important part of any violence prevention program. Training should be focused on at least three groups of employees. First, workers in jobs or locations with a high risk for violent incidents should be provided with specialized training to deal with this risk. Second, managers and supervisors should be trained to recognize potentially hazardous situations and to take corrective action to eliminate or reduce the hazard. Managers and supervisors should also be trained to prevent employees from being placed in dangerous situations in the first place. Managers and supervisors may also need training in special interpersonal skills to effectively deal with employees who have been victims of violence. Obviously, managers and supervisors should be totally familiar with all aspects of the policies and procedures associated with the firm's workplace violence prevention policy. Finally, security personnel need to be trained in their specific job duties, the facility layout in which they work, the proper use of security equipment on the premises, and any actions they may need to take to prevent violence from occurring in specific high-risk jobs.[57]

Incident Reports As part of a WVPP, an organization must develop procedures for reporting incidents. The procedures should focus not only on violent acts in which physical injury has occurred but also on situations involving verbal abuse, threats, or other menacing acts. Incident reports should be in writing, and employees making these reports should be assured of confidentiality. Management must do all it can to encourage employees to bring their concerns to management without fear of reprisal. If a violent incident is reported, a thorough investigation should be conducted to identify the causes of the incident and recommend corrective actions to be taken. Follow-up of the incident investigation should occur to make sure that any actions recommended have indeed been taken. Follow-up of an incident may also involve providing medical and psychological help to employees affected by the violence. Careful records of all incidents should be kept so that a historical picture of violence in the workplace can be obtained and this information used by threat assessment teams to improve workplace safety in the future. An overall evaluation of the WVPP should take place periodically to ensure that the program is having a desirable effect.[58]

Workplace Security: The Legacy of September 11, 2001

As seen in Table 14.8, a workplace violence prevention program may involve increasing the physical security of a work location. However, due to a continuing threat of terrorist activities in the United States, OSHA has taken special initiatives related to potential terrorist attacks. OSHA provides a risk assessment list to employers to help them assess their firm's risk level based on a variety of terrorism risk factors. Using the **work risk assessment list** and OSHA's new **zone pyramid system** (see Figure 14.5), employers can determine whether their firm's risk level is in the green, yellow, or red zone.[59] To determine a firm's zone level, the nature of the firm's **terrorism vulnerabilities** are identified, the chance that each event will actually occur is rated, and the potential consequences of such an event happening are determined. The overall risk level is then based on a combination of workplace vulnerabilities, the potential of a recognized threat occurring, and the anticipated consequences of such an event. Definitions of these different risk zones are also shown in Figure 14.5.[60]

FIGURE 14.5

Work Risk Assessment List and Risk Zone Levels

Sources: South Carolina Governor's Workplace Security Advisory Committee, *Prepare, Prevent, Protect South Carolina: Best Practices Workplace Security—A Report from the Governor's Workplace Security Advisory Committee,* May 23, 2002. (Available at: http://www.llr.state.sc.us/workplace/Full%20Report.pdf); U.S. Department of Labor, Occupational Safety and Health Administration, "Evacuation Planning Matrix." (Available at: http://www.osha.gov/dep/evacmatrix/index.html, accessed March 30, 2004); and U.S. Department of Labor, Occupational Safety and Health Administration, "Planning for Emergencies: OSHA's New Evacuation Planning Matrix Helps Employers Assess Their Risk and Plan for Emergency Evacuations," *Job Safety and Health Quarterly,* Vol. 14 (4), 2003, p. 12. (Available at: http://www.osha.gov/Publications/JSHQ/jshq-v14-4-summer_fall2003.pdf, accessed March 30, 2004)

Work Risk Assessment List:

Does your worksite USE, HANDLE, STORE, OR TRANSPORT **Hazardous Materials**? **Yes No** *If YES, what category of Hazard?*

☐ **Chemicals**
- Flammable liquids, solids, or gases
- Toxic or poisonous materials
- Corrosive materials
- Reactive materials
- Oxidizers or organic peroxides

☐ **Biological/Infectious Materials**
- Select agents

☐ **Radioactive Materials**
- Licensed materials

☐ **Explosives**

☐ **Other Potential Hazards**

____
____
____
____
____

Does your worksite **Provide Essential Service**? **YES NO** *If YES, which of these services fits your worksite?*

☐ **Utility Provider**
- Electricity, Sub-stations, etc.
- Fuels, pipelines, etc.

☐ **Communications**
- Telephone, Internet, Radio, TV, Computer Systems

☐ **Sewer Treatment Facility**

☐ **Emergency Services**
- Law Enforcement, Fire Services, Health Care, Public Health

☐ **Food or Water Provider**
- Water Treatment/Supply
- Food Processing
- Food Service

☐ **Other**

Does your worksite have a **High Volume of Pedestrian Traffic**? **YES NO** *If YES, what type of facility creates the traffic?*

☐ **Airport**

☐ **Sports Facility**
- Open stadium
- Inside arena

☐ **Hospital**

☐ **High-Rise Office Complex**

☐ **Auditorium**
- Entertainment event

☐ **School/University**

☐ **Large Shopping Mall**

☐ **Tourist Attraction**
- Entertainment park
- Resort/recreation area

☐ **Other**

Does your worksite have a **Limited Means of Egress**? **YES NO** *If YES, which describes the reason for limitation?*

(continued)

FIGURE 14.5
Continued

☐ **High-Rise Complex** ☐ **Underground Operations** ☐ **Other**

Does your worksite have a **High Volume of Incoming Materials**? **YES NO** *If YES, what type of materials?*

☐ **Mail and Small Packages** ☐ **Bulk Packages, Materials, Equipment** ☐ **Raw Materials**

☐ **Import and Export of Materials** ☐ **Other**

Is your worksite considered a **High Profile Site**? **YES NO** *If YES, what is near your worksite?*

☐ **Located Close Proximity (1/4 mile) to Other Characterized Sites** ☐ **Higher Media/Public Relations Impact (Landmark etc.)** ☐ **Classified Site**

☐ **Other**

☐ **Water Dams** ☐ **Military Installation**

Is your worksite considered **Transportation Related**? **YES NO** *If YES, what type of transportation?*

☐ **Airlines** ☐ **Bus Lines** ☐ **Train/Rail**

☐ **Shipyard/Port/Cruise Ships** ☐ **Trucking** ☐ **Vehicle Rental/Lease**
- Cars, trucks, etc.

☐ **Transportation Affiliated**
- Bridges/tunnels
- Major traffic activities

☐ **Other**

Terrorist Attack Risk Levels:

Green Zone: Workplaces that are unlikely to be a target for a terrorist attack because they are characterized by limited vulnerability, limited threat, *and* the consequences of any attack would be limited.

Yellow Zone: Workplaces that may be targets because they are characterized by *not more than one* of the following: high vulnerability *or* high threat *or* the consequences of any attack would be significant.

Red Zone: Workplaces that are most likely to be targets because they are characterized by two or more of the following: high vulnerability, high threat, and the consequences of any attack would be catastrophic.

OSHA's Evacuation Planning Matrix also helps employers develop plans to evacuate employees if a terrorist threat arises. OSHA recommends that employers in "red zone" workplaces develop plans for sheltering employees within the work location if a terrorist event occurs and also develop an evacuation plan. OSHA also suggests that red zone firms establish a terrorist incident response team with employees assigned specific roles.

EMPLOYEE FITNESS AND WELLNESS PROGRAMS

Fitness programs involve employees in some form of controlled exercise or recreation activities. Fitness programs range from subsidized membership in a local health club to company softball teams to very sophisticated company-owned (or company-shared) facilities. For example, Nova Chemicals Corporation shares a fitness facility with TransCanada, Husky, and Nova Gas Transmission in a building in downtown Calgary, in Alberta, Canada. It is an 18,000-square foot facility with two aerobic floors, a running track, three international squash courts, racquetball and volleyball courts, as well as treadmills, bicycles, and rowing machines. The facility is fully staffed with qualified fitness experts. Nova Chemicals Corporation has invested $3 million to $4 million in the facility. Although Nova Chemicals partially subsidizes its employees' use of the facility, employees contribute approximately $15 per month for their use. Nova believes its investment in employee health and wellness, specifically its employees' use of the fitness center, has contributed to significant reductions in stress levels, improved teamwork, and an increased work ethic. Another proponent of employee fitness programs is PepsiCo, Inc. which has invested $2 million in its fitness center. PepsiCo estimates that for every $1 invested in the program it receives $3 in return.[61] These claims about the benefits of employee fitness programs are impressive, but employers should conduct a careful analysis of employee health problems and needs before deciding that fancy gyms and swimming pools are the solution. Wellness programs may represent more effective means of enhancing employee health.

Wellness programs promote employee health by providing education on health issues, encouraging lifestyle changes (weight loss, smoking cessation) designed to reduce the risk of illness, or providing early warning of developing health problems through screening for high blood pressure, high cholesterol, and the like. According to the Wellness Council of America, more than 81 percent of businesses with fifty or more employees have some form of health promotion program—the most popular being exercise, stop-smoking classes, back-care programs, and stress management.[62]

Benefits of Fitness and Wellness Programs

Organizations can benefit in several ways from sponsoring employee fitness and wellness programs. The more elaborate the programs, the greater the potential benefits. One of the basic gains is in employee morale. Employees view the activities as fun, and they feel better about themselves. There is some evidence that employee job satisfaction can increase. Besides enhancing group spirit and corporate identification, fitness programs can help the organization attract high-quality job applicants.

Employers may receive some very direct benefits from having healthier employees. Absenteeism due to illness may decrease. Reduced employee turnover has also been shown to be a benefit of wellness programs. Johnson and Johnson reduced their absenteeism rate by 15 percent within two years of introducing their wellness program. The annual employee turnover rate for wellness program participants of the Canada Life Assurance Company of Toronto was 1.8 percent, compared to the company-wide average of 18 percent. If employees are healthier, medical and insurance rates may decrease. Waste Management, Inc. implemented a pilot stress management program for employees and their families, and the outcome was a reduced total number of medical claims. The firm estimated its dollar savings as being between $3,750 and $15,000 per participant, per year. Wellness programs may also improve overall employee productivity. A NASA study reported a 12.5 percent increase in the productivity of fitness program participants versus nonparticipants. Finally, there is considerable evidence that employee fitness and wellness programs have a significant overall return on investment. Since 1980 there have been more than fifty studies of comprehensive worksite health promotion and disease prevention programs. Of the more than thirty that were analyzed for cost outcomes, twenty-nine proved to be cost effective, with the return on each $1 invested ranging from $1.81 to $6.15.[63]

The benefits of wellness and fitness programs may, however, depend on the nature and content of the program because these factors seem to determine whether employees consistently participate. One study compared four experimental wellness program models over a three-year period. The four models were implemented at different but similar sites. The interventions and respective per-employee costs were (1) health education only ($17.68), (2) physical fitness only ($39.28), (3) health education and follow-up counseling ($30.96), and (4) health education, follow-up counseling, and plantwide organization to encourage and support employees ($38.57). Intervention 2, for physical fitness only, showed the lowest percentage of employees exercising regularly at the end of the three-year period. In contrast, interventions 3 and 4 used systematic outreach and follow-up counseling, and they were more cost effective in terms of both engaging employees at risk and reducing their risks. This is consistent with findings from another study that showed offering fitness programs alone is not enough. Intervention must reach out by working to reduce the perceived work- and health-related barriers to participation.[64]

Summary of Key Points

Organizations try to create a safe and healthy work environment for their employees for three reasons. The first is altruism; that is, the organization genuinely cares for its members. The second is the financial and nonfinancial benefits for the company: lower absenteeism and turnover, higher productivity, reduced insurance rates, improved employee morale, and enhanced appeal to job applicants. The third reason is compliance with federal, state, and local regulations. Violations of health and safety laws can mean large fines, bad publicity, and even jail sentences for top managers.

A century of social awareness preceded passage of the Occupational Safety and Health Act of 1970. This act covers all private employers in the fifty states and several federal territories and jurisdictions. The Occupational Safety and Health Act of 1970 created three separate federal agencies for administering the law. The Occupational Safety and Health Administration (OSHA) is responsible for developing and enforcing regulations. OSHA enforces its regulations by inspecting workplaces and issuing citations for violations. The Occupational Safety and Health Review Commission (OSHRC) holds hearings on employers' appeals of citations and penalties. The third agency, the National Institute of Occupational Safety and Health (NIOSH), conducts research on workplace safety and health.

OSHA is the lead agency for formulating workplace safety and health regulations and enforcing those regulations on the job. OSHA conducts two types of safety inspections. Unprogrammed inspections are in response to accident reports and complaints. Programmed inspections are part of regular enforcement activities that target high-risk employers. OSHA also provides free assistance to employers and works with them in voluntary cooperative programs to improve safety.

In meeting the health and safety needs of its employees, management may take either a minimalist or more proactive stance. Proactive approaches to safety and health require management to lead from the front, involve employees in program design and implementation, carefully analyze data related to safety and health problems, motivate workers to behave safely, and be innovative in approaches to workplace safety and health.

The Occupational Safety and Health Administration focuses on several aspects of workplace safety and health. Among the most prominent of these are on-the-job injuries, exposure to hazardous chemicals, a broad range of occupational diseases, and injuries or death due to workplace violence. OSHA has also recently focused on helping firms deal with the worldwide threat of violence from terrorist acts.

Hazardous substances represent a special category of agents that can inflict injuries on the job. OSHA has issued special standards to ensure that firms manage these substances carefully. These standards include procedures for inspecting workplaces and identifying the hazardous chemicals that are present. Standards also help protect workers from the effects of these substances through regulation of protective equipment and procedures for handling and disposing of the materials.

Occupational diseases are health problems caused by long-term exposure to something at the worksite, such as chemicals that cause cancer or loud noises that may lead to hearing loss. Smoking in the workplace can affect both those who smoke and those who must breathe the tobacco smoke exhaled by others. Musculoskeletal disorders make up about one-third of all occupational injuries. Cumulative trauma disorder is the most commonly occurring type of occupational disease. This is an umbrella term for musculoskeletal problems such as tendonitis, carpal tunnel syndrome, and low-back problems caused by repeating the same series of motions again and again in a way that eventually stresses the body.

Workplace violence is an increasingly important issue in safety and health on the job. Violence against an employee can be perpetrated by a stranger, a customer or client, another employee, or a person who has some personal relationship to the employee. Workplace violence can also affect nonemployees, such as customers visiting a workplace. Workplace violence prevention programs are an important aspect of providing a safe work environment for many organizations. OSHA has recently been forced by world events to turn its attention to helping firms deal effectively with the threat of terrorist attack.

Employers also bear responsibility for a variety of other issues related to employees' health on the job. AIDS, drug use on the job, and employee psychological health are among the issues that concern management in modern organizations. Many firms are now developing employee fitness and wellness programs aimed at improving employee health and well-being.

The Manager's Vocabulary

acquired immune deficiency syndrome (AIDS)
Bloodborne Pathogen Standards
cumulative trauma disorder (CTD)
environmental tobacco smoke (ETS)
ergonomics
fitness programs
general duty clause
Hazard Communication Standard (HCS)
job hazard analysis
Materials Safety Data Sheets (MSDS)
minimalist approach to safety and health
musculoskeletal disorders
National Institute for Occupational Safety and Health (NIOSH)
Needlestick Safety and Prevention Act
Occupational Safety and Health Act of 1970
Occupational Safety and Health Administration (OSHA)
Occupational Safety and Health Review Commission (OSHRC)
on-site inspections
phone/fax investigation
proactive approach to safety and health
programmed inspections
repetitive strain injury (RSI)
safety committee
terrorism vulnerabilities
threat assessment team
unprogrammed inspections
Voluntary Protection Program (VPP)
wellness program
workplace violence
workplace violence prevention policy statement
workplace violence prevention programs (WVPP)
work risk assessment list
zone pyramid system

Questions for Discussion

1. Why should organizations be concerned about health and safety in the workplace?
2. Broadly, what are the requirements of the Occupational Safety and Health Act of 1970?
3. What are the major activities of the Occupational Safety and Health Administration?

4. How does OSHA enforce workplace safety?
5. What roles must management play in developing effective safety and health programs in an organization?
6. What factors tend to cause on-the-job injuries?
7. Think of a job you have held, and list the specific aspects of that job and work setting that could contribute to injuries. What actions, if any, did the employer take to minimize the risk of accidents and injuries?
8. What is a cumulative trauma disorder? How can the incidence of CTDs be reduced?
9. What are the Bloodborne Pathogens Standards, and to whom do they apply?
10. What factors contribute to an employee's risk of becoming a victim of workplace violence?
11. What are the main components of a workplace violence prevention program?
12. What is OSHA's new zone pyramid system? What factors affect whether a firm is classified in the green, yellow, or red zone of this pyramid?
13. Why do some organizations offer employee fitness and wellness programs? What features do these programs usually offer?

Case 14.1

Refusing to Work in "Unsafe" Conditions

The Occupational Safety and Health Act states that employers have a specific duty to comply with safety regulations and standards promulgated under the act, as well as a "general duty" to provide a workplace free of recognized hazards that are likely to harm employees. The act further prohibits employers from discriminating against employees who exercise their rights under the law. Rights include notifying OSHA of unsafe conditions and talking with inspectors. An additional regulation issued by the Secretary of Labor states that an employee may refuse to perform a task that he or she reasonably believes would pose a serious threat to safety or life if he or she is unable to notify OSHA of the problem immediately. Of course, under the general duty clause, an employer should not ask any employee to perform a highly dangerous task. However, people may differ in their perceptions of whether a task is dangerous, and employers do have a right to assign work and to discipline employees for insubordination.

Discuss the following situation. Do you think the employee has the right to refuse the work, or is the employer justified in imposing discipline? Why?

The Situation: Bambi Clark had been a secretary for Central States Manufacturing for six months. One morning she appeared at work in a very agitated state. She told her office manager, Diane Holmes, that she and her husband were trying to start a family and that she had just read in the *National Inquirer* that prolonged exposure to video-display terminals causes mutations and birth defects. Clark was quite upset, worried that she might already have conceived a monster. She flatly refused to turn on her computer and begin work. Holmes called the chief safety engineer, who assured Clark that the terminals did not give off harmful radiation. In his professional opinion, there was absolutely no danger to her or to her potential offspring in working with a video screen. Clark still refused to operate the computer or even to perform other duties in the office where other secretaries worked on computers. Holmes gave her one last chance to change her mind and then suspended her without pay for the rest of the day.

Case 14.2

Employer Responsibility for Job Stress

The General Duty Clause of the Occupational Safety and Health Act of 1970 requires employers to provide employees with a safe working environment. In situations where employees are harmed by work-related factors, the employer may be liable to provide the employee and his or her family with compensation for that harm. Read the following case and decide whether Major Pitts' widow should be compensated by the employer.

Situation: In 1997 Major Oscar Vernon Pitts suffered a stroke at his job with the City of Rome Police Department. For several months before his stroke, Pitts had not felt well, was often tired, and had increased his smoking habit from one and one-half packs of cigarettes per day to two or more packs daily. He also had a history of medical problems, including heart attacks in 1982 and 1983.

Several witnesses at the trial testified that a number of problems on his job had caused Major Pitts some frustration. However, Pitts generally seemed to enjoy his work activities. Nonwork factors were also relevant to the case. Prior to his stroke, Major Pitts' son had been convicted for drug trafficking. Pitts believed the arresting officers had tampered with the evidence and that the ten-year sentence his son received was too harsh. He also blamed his son's arrest and the sentence on his position with the Rome Police Department.

Medical evidence indicated that Major Pitts' stroke had resulted from a cardiac embolism—a blood clot from his heart that had traveled to his brain. The neurologist who treated Pitts following the stroke testified that stroke risk factors include advancing age, high blood pressure, heart disease, diabetes, smoking, and . . . a genetic history as well as a previous history of vascular disease. The neurologist agreed that Pitts had several risk factors at the time of his stroke but also indicated that Major Pitts' massive stroke was exaggerated by his job as a police captain with extreme stress and fatigue from this position. His blood pressure and heart condition were also worsened by these work-related factors. In all, Mr. Pitts was at risk for major cardiovascular events given his high-stress occupation.

Note: After you have made your decision about Major Pitts' situation, use your library's legal cases database to find the *Pitts v. City of Rome* case (see source) and read what the court decided.

Source: Adapted from *Pitts v. City of Rome,* A02A0031, Court of Appeals of Georgia, 256 Ga. App. 278; 568 S.E.2d 167; 2002 Ga. App. LEXIS 893; 2002 Fulton County D. Rep. 2164, July 2, 2002.

Exercise 14.1
Ensuring a Safe Workplace

Divide into groups of no more than four or five students per group. Half of the groups should do Option 1 while the other half do Option 2:

Option 1: Restaurant Safety

1. Develop a list of the types of hazards and accidents that can happen to restaurant employees.
2. Visit a restaurant in the community. Seek information about the extent of employee hazards and accidents and steps the restaurant takes to reduce incidents. How does each restaurant handle safety training, accident reports, and other aspects of maintaining a safe work environment?
3. Report to the class and compare results.

Option 2: Safety from Terrorism

1. Interview the health and safety officer at a local firm that your group feels might have characteristics that would put it at risk of terrorist activity (e.g., a firm that manufacturers and distributes hazardous chemicals). In your interview, use the work risk assessment list to identify the types of general risks that exist at the firm.
2. After your interview, use the definitions for green, yellow, and red zone classifications found in Figure 14.4 to assess that organization's overall terrorism risk level. You can find more detail about the assessment process by getting the full report upon which Figure 14.4 is based (see source). To determine whether it is a green, yellow, or red zone firm, you will need to analyze the general risks you identified in your interview in a much more detailed manner. You must (a) clarify and define exactly what could happen, (b) assess the severity of the damage that would occur if the risk event actually happened, (c) estimate the likelihood that the risk could occur, and (d) identify steps that could be taken to reduce high-level risks. Use the following rating scales to help you in this assessment.

	Rating
Severity of Event	
Catastrophic (possibility of human fatality, multiple injuries, or massive destruction/disruption)	3
Medium (no fatalities expected, moderate destruction/disruption)	2
Low (nuisance, little to no injuries or destruction/disruption)	1
Likelihood of Event	
High	3
Medium	2
Low	1

For a company manufacturing hazardous chemicals, such an analysis might look something like this:

What could happen: A tanker carrying ammonia could be blown up.

Severity of the event: Catastrophic (rating 3). The release of the gas and vapor would be damaging to the general population, resulting in eye irritation, difficulty breathing, or death, depending on the amount released.

Likelihood of event occurring: Medium (rating 2). The firm is located near Washington, D.C., which is an area of prime terrorist interest. Its shipments of ammonia travel through this area frequently.

Threat reduction measures: Increase plant security; review procedures for storing, handling, and transferring ammonia; keep inventory of ammonia supplies at a low level within the plant; have alarm system monitoring the ammonia storage area; vary the routes by which ammonia supplies are shipped by truck; do careful background checks on ammonia truck drivers; have an emergency action plan with drills and assessment of drills for the plant; educate community on hazards and actions to take if ammonia is released; make local security officials aware of the nature and route of your shipments.

Source: Rating scales and threat analysis are adapted from procedures describe in South Carolina Governor's Workplace Security Advisory Committee, *Prepare, Prevent, Protect South Carolina: Best Practices Workplace Security—A Report from the Governor's Workplace Security Advisory Committee,* May 23, 2002. (Available at: http://www.llr.state.sc.us/workplace/Full%20Report.pdf)

Exercise 14.2
Safety and Health Programs

Divide into six groups. Each group should investigate and report on one of the following programs at their university. Specifically, what is your university doing in each of the following areas?

1. *Smoking in the workplace:* Does the university have a formal policy? When was it developed? What problems or issues led to the development of the policy? Are there plans to review or alter the current policy? How do employees feel about the policy?
2. *Workplace injuries:* What does the university do to prevent workplace injuries? Is there a safety specialist? What is this individual's training? What responsibilities does this individual have? Who is responsible for first aid in the event of an injury?
3. *AIDS in the workplace:* Does the university have a formal policy concerning employees or students with AIDS? When was the policy developed? What problems led to its development? How has it worked?
4. *Hazardous chemicals:* What hazardous chemicals are used in the university? Who is responsible for maintaining and distributing Materials Safety Data Sheets? Obtain several of these sheets and note their contents.
5. *Occupational disease:* Have there been instances of repetitive strain injuries among employees at the university? What has been done to reduce problems associated with repetitive strain? Have there been concerns with any other occupational diseases?
6. *Employee fitness programs:* Does the university have an employee fitness program? What level of commitment by the institution is involved? What is the level of participation?

Exercise 14.3
Preventing Violence on the Job

Option 1:

1. Divide into groups of four or five.
2. Each group is to visit a different site on campus where staff or faculty work.
3. Identify aspects of those worksites that either reduce or increase the likelihood that employees may become victims of violence.

Among the issues that will be of relevance in the analysis are the following:

- Does the physical design of the facilities ensure safe and secure conditions for employees; for example, are they designed so that employees can communicate with other staff in emergency situations via clear partitions, video cameras, speakers or alarms, and so forth, as appropriate to the workplace situation?
- Are work areas designed and furniture arranged to prevent entrapment of the employees and minimize potential for assault incidents?
- Is access to employee work areas controlled through the use of locked doors, buzzers, card access, and the like?
- Is adequate lighting provided for all indoor and outdoor facilities?
- What electronic or other security systems are used?
- Is there evidence that these systems are properly maintained?
- Are there written policies evident that instruct employees in how to deal with emergency situations?
- In talking with employees, is it clear that they have been trained to be aware of, avoid, and take actions to prevent mugging, robbery, rape, and other assaults?

Option 2: Do this same analysis but in cooperation with local businesses with which you have contacts.

Exercise 14.4
Safety on the Web

1. Rumor has it that the job of elephant keeper has the highest rate of occupational fatalities. However, there are so few elephant keepers that national statistics are not kept on the job as a separate entity. Find out which occupations and which industries are the most dangerous in terms of (1) the number of accidents and (2) the number of fatalities per year. *Hint:* Data are available at OSHA sites, Bureau of Labor Statistics sites, and National Safety Council sites.
2. Your small company is about to develop its first written safety policy. Locate some safety policies from other companies and assess their likely usefulness for your organization.
3. Your firm is thinking about joining OSHA's Voluntary Protection Program. Find out about the requirements and procedures for membership.

Notes and References

1. U.S. Bureau of Labor Statistics, "Fatal Work Injury Counts 1992–2002." (Available at: http://www.bls.gov/iif/oshwc/cfoi/cfch0001.pdf, accessed March 24, 2004)

2. Karl Jacobson, "Workplace Injuries: The Real Financial Impact," *Job Safety and Health Quarterly,* Vol 14 (4), 2003, pp. 13–14. (Available at: http://www.osha.gov/Publications/JSHQ/jshq-v14-4-summer_fall2003.pdf, accessed February 17, 2004); The Liberty Mutual Research Institute for Safety, "2003 Liberty Mutual Workplace Safety Index." (Available at: http://www.eorm.com/ezine/pp5/WorkPlaceSafetyIndex2003.pdf, accessed April 5, 2004); and U.S. Department of Energy's Voluntary Protection Program Information Portal, "Businesses Pay $1 Billion per Week for Workplace

Injuries: New Study Reveals Financial Burden of Workplace Injuries Growing Faster Than Inflation," October 23, 2003 (Available at: http://tis.eh.doe.gov/vpp_old/articles/injuries.html)

3. U.S. Department of Labor, Occupational Safety and Health Administration, *All About OSHA,* Report Number OSHA 2056-07R (Washington D.C.: U.S. Department of Labor, Occupational Safety and Health Administration, 2003); and U.S. Department of Labor, Occupational Safety and Health Administration, "Milwaukee Company Penalized $193,500 for Failing to Protect Workers from Electrical Hazards," Region 5 News Release 04-479-CHI, March 24, 2004. (Available at: http://www.osha.gov/pls/oshaweb/owadisp.show_document?p_table=NEWS_RELEASES&p_id=10751)

4. James Ledvinka and Vida Gulbinas Scarpello, *Federal Regulation of Personnel and Human Resource Management* (Boston: PWS-Kent, 1991); and Occupational Safety and Health Act of 1970, Public Law 91–596, 91st Congress, S.2193, December 29, 1970.

5. Occupational Safety and Health Act of 1970.

6. U.S. Department of Labor, Occupational Safety and Health Administration, *All About OSHA.*

7. Ibid.; and Occupational Safety and Health Act of 1970.

8. Quoted from the home page of the Occupational Safety and Health Review Commission. (Available at: http://www.oshrc.gov/, accessed April 5, 2004)

9. Susan Fleming and Monte Lutz, "Charting the Course to Workplace Safety & Health: OSHA's Strategic Management Plan for 2003 to 2008 Maps Out the Agency's Direction in Its Ongoing Mission to Protect America's Workers," *Job Safety and Health Quarterly,* Vol. 14 (3), 2003. (Available at: http://www.osha.gov/Publications/JSHQ/spring2003/safework.htm, accessed February 17, 2004)

10. U.S. Department of Labor, Occupational Safety and Health Administration, *All About OSHA.*

11. *Marshall v. Barlow's, Inc.,* 436 U.S. 307 (1978); and William Atkinson, "When OSHA Comes Knocking," *HR Magazine,* Vol. 44 (10), 1999, pp. 35–38.

12. U.S. Department of Labor, Occupational Safety and Health Administration, *All About OSHA,* p. 22.

13. Ibid., pp. 22–23.

14. U.S. Department of Labor, Occupational Safety and Health Administration, *OSHA Field Inspection Reference Manual CPL 2.103, Section 6, Chapter II. Inspection Procedures.* (Available at: http://www.osha.gov/Firm_osha_data/100006.html, accessed April 6, 2004)

15. Ibid.; William Atkinson, "When OSHA Comes Knocking," *HR Magazine,* Vol. 44 (10), 1999, pp. 35–38; Robert Grossman, "Handling Inspections: Tips from Insiders," *HR Magazine,* Vol. 44 (10), 1999, pp. 41–45; and U.S. Department of Labor, Occupational Safety and Health Administration, *All About OSHA,* pp. 22–23, 27

16. U.S. Department of Labor, Occupational Safety and Health Administration, *All About OSHA,* p. 35; Occupational Safety and Health Administration, "Revisions to the Voluntary Protection Programs to Provide Safe and Healthful Working Conditions," *Federal Register,* 65, July 24, 2000, pp. 45649–45663; and Judy Weinberg, "Happy Birthday VPP! OSHA's Voluntary Protection Programs Celebrate 20 Years of Success in Working with Companies to Promote Workplace Safety and Health," *Job Safety and Health Quarterly,* Vol. 13 (4), 2002. (Available at: http://www.osha.gov/Publications/JSHQ/summer2002/vpp.htm, accessed February 17, 2002)

17. Dov Zohar, "The Influence of Leadership and Climate on Occupational Health and Safety," in *Health and Safety in Organizations: A Multilevel Perspective,* eds. David Hofmann and Lois Tetrick (San Francisco: Jossey-Bass, 2003), pp. 201–230.

18. International Labour Office, *Guidelines on Occupational Safety and Health Management Systems,* International Labour Organization, CH-1211 Geneva 22, Switzerland, Report Number, ILO-OSH 2001.

19. Michelle Martinez, "Using Data to Create Wellness Programs That Work," *HR Magazine,* Vol. 44 (2), 1999, pp. 106–113.

20. William Atkinson, "Safety—At a Price," *HR Magazine,* Vol. 44 (11), 1999, pp. 52–59.

21. Ibid.

22. Donna Miles, "Denark Named 'Best of the Best': A Tennessee Construction Company Wins Top Honors in the Associated General Contractors of America's Annual Safety Awards Program," *Job Safety and Health Quarterly,* Vol. 14 (4) 2003. (Available at: http://www.osha.gov/Publications/JSHQ/jshq-v14-4-summer_fall2003.pdf, accessed February 17, 2004)

23. New Zealand Land Transport Safety Authority, "News Release—Winners of First Ever New

Zealand Road Safety Innovation Awards Announced Today," February 24, 2004. (Available at: http://www.ltsa.govt.nz/media/2004/040224.html)
24. Health and Safety Executive, *Reducing Error and Influencing Behaviour: Guidance Booklets* (London: Health and Safety Executive. June 1999); and Robert F. Scherer, James D. Brodzinski, and Elaine A. Crable, "The Human Factor," *HR Magazine,* Vol. 38 (4), 1993, p. 93.
25. Anonymous, "Rotating Shift Work Causes Many Problems," *Occupational Health and Safety,* September 1978, p. 21.
26. Layne Lathram, U.S. Department of Labor, Occupational Safety and Health Administration, "OSHA Launches Hazard Communication Initiative Compliance Assistance, Enforcement Will Improve Workplace Hazard Communication," OSHA Trade Release, March 16, 2004. (Available at: http://www.osha.gov/pls/oshaweb/owadisp.show_document?p_table=NEWS_RELEASES&p_id=10734)
27. U.S. Department of Labor, Occupational Safety and Health Administration, "Guidelines for Employer Compliance (Advisory) - 1910.1200 App E." (Available at: http://www.osha.gov/pls/oshaweb/owadisp.show_document?p_table=STANDARDS&p_id=10104); and J. M. Patterson, "VPP Companies' Best Practices," *Occupational Health and Safety,* January 1997, pp. 60–61.
28. N. A. Ashford, "The Nature and Dimension of Occupational Health and Safety Problems," *Personnel Administrator,* August 1977, p. 45.
29. R. Lewy, "The Healthy Workplace," in *The Columbia University College of Physicians & Surgeons Complete Home Medical Guide,* 3rd ed., (New York: Crown Publishers, 1997).
30. H. M. Sandler, "The Challenge of Low-Level Workplace Exposures," *Occupational Hazards,* January 1997, pp. 83–85.
31. U.S. Department of Labor, Occupational Safety and Health Administration, "Reiteration of Existing OSHA Policy on Indoor Air Quality: Office Temperature/Humidity and Environmental Tobacco Smoke," February 24, 2003. (Available at: http://www.osha.gov/pls/oshaweb/owadisp.show_document?p_table=INTERPRETATIONS&p_id=24602, accessed April 9, 2004); and U.S. Department of Labor, Occupational Safety and Health Administration, Regulations (Standards–29 CFR), Air contaminants. - 1910.1000. (Available at: http://www.osha.gov/pls/oshaweb/owadisp.show_document?p_table=STANDARDS&p_id=9991, accessed April 9, 2004)
32. Danny Lee, "If the Irish Can Ban a Great Pub Tradition, Anyone Can," *Times Online,* April 6, 2004. (Available at: http://www.timesonline.co.uk/article/0,,8128-1064981,00.html, accessed April 9, 2004)
33. Mike Maier and Juli Ross-Mota, "Work-Related Musculoskeletal Disorders, Oregon, 1990–2000," Oregon Department of Consumer and Business Services. (Available at: http://www.cbs.state.or.us/external/imd/rasums/resalert/msd.html, accessed April 9, 2004); and U.S. Department of Labor, Bureau of Labor Statistics, "Lost-Worktime Injuries and Illnesses: Characteristics and Resulting Days Away from Work, 2002," Report Number USDL 04-460. (Available at: http://www.bls.gov/news.release/osh2.nr0.htm, accessed April 9, 2004)
34. Safety Information Consultants, Inc. "Ergonomics and Cumulative Trauma Diseases." (Available at: http://www.safetyinfocur.com/safetytopics/sic02.html, accessed April 9, 2004); and Kathryn Tyler, "Sit Up Straight," *HR Magazine,* Vol. 43 (10), 1998, pp. 122–128.
35. Sara Kiesler and Tom Finholt, "The Mystery of RSI," *American Psychologist,* Vol. 43, December 1988, pp. 1004–1015; P. A. Nathan and R. C. Keniston, "Carpal Tunnel Syndrome and Its Relation to General Physical Condition," *Hand Clinics,* Vol. 9, 1993, pp. 253–261; P. Harber, L. Pena, G. Bland, and J. Beck, "Upper Extremity Symptoms in Supermarket Workers," *American Journal of Industrial Medicine,* Vol. 22, 1992, pp. 873–884; and E. F. Pascarelli and J. J. Kella, "Soft-Tissue Injuries Related to Use of the Computer Keyboard," *Journal of Occupational Medicine,* Vol. 35, 1993, pp. 522–532.
36. Department of Labor, Occupational Safety and Health Administration, "Ergonomics Program," 29 CFR 1910. 900, November 14, 2000.
37. U.S. Department of Labor, Occupational Safety and Health Administration, "Safety and Health Topics: Ergonomics." (Available at: http://www.osha.gov/SLTC/ergonomics/index.html, accessed April 9, 2004)
38. G. LaBar, "Can Ergonomics Cure 'Human Error'?" *Occupational Hazards,* April 1996, pp. 48–51.
39. U.S. Department of Labor, Occupational Safety and Health Administration, "Success with Ergonomics: Duracell," April 2003. (Available at: http://www.osha.gov/SLTC/ergonomics/duracell.html, accessed April 9, 2004)

40. U.S. Department of Justice, Civil Rights Division, Disability Rights Section, "The Americans with Disabilities Act and Persons with HIV/AIDS," March 10, 2002. (Available at: http://www.omhrc.gov/omh/aids/faq_ada_hiv_01.htm, accessed April 9, 2004)

41. Ibid.; and U.S. Department of Labor, Occupational Safety and Health Administration, "Bloodborne Pathogens Final Standards: Summary of Key Provisions," OSHA Fact Sheet No. OSHA 92-46. (Available at: http://www.osha-slc.gov/OshDoc/Fact_data/ FSNO92-46.html)

42. National Drug-Free Workplace Alliance, "Drug-Free Workplace Statistics: Summary." (Available at: http://www.ndfwa.org/statistics.htm, accessed April 9, 2004)

43. Janet Deming, "Drug-Free Workplace Is Good Business," *HR Magazine,* Vol. 35, April 1990, pp. 61–62.

44. Diane Cadrain, "Are Your Employee Drug Tests Accurate?" *HR Magazine,* Vol. 48 (1), 2003. (Available at: http://www.shrm.org/hrmagazine/articles/0103/0103cadrain.asp, accessed March 24, 2004)

45. *City Market, Inc. v. Industrial Claim Appeals Office,* No. 89CA1004, Court of Appeals of Colorado, Division Three, 800 P.2d 1335; 1990 Colo. App., December 13, 1990.

46. *Brickner v. N.Y. State DOT,* 88279, Supreme Court of New York, Appellate Division, Third Department, 284 A.D.2d 829; 727 N.Y.S.2d 523; 2001 N.Y. App. Div. June 28, 2001; and *Spencer v. Time Warner Cable,* 87057, Supreme Court of New York, Appellate Division, Third Department, 278 A.D.2d 622; 717 N.Y.S.2d 711; 2000 N.Y. App. Div., December 14, 2000.

47. Joanne Cole, "Destressing the Workplace: Hewlett-Packard Pushes the Envelope," *HR Focus,* Vol. 76 (10), 1999, p. 10.

48. Ibid.

49. Susan McCulloch, "Take the Bite Out of the Lunch Crunch," *HR Magazine,* Vol. 43 (8), 1998, pp. 55–62.

50. National Institute for Occupational Safety and Health, "Workplace Violence Awareness and Prevention: Facts and Information." (Available at: www.osha-slc.gov/workplace_violence/wrkplaceViolence.PartI.html, accessed October 7, 2003)

51. U.S. Department of Justice, Office of Justice Programs, Bureau of Justice Statistics, National Crime Victimization Survey, "Criminal Victimization in the United States: Table 64: Percent Distribution of Incidents, by Victim's Activity at Time of Incident and Type of Crime." (Available at: http://www.ojp.usdoj.gov/bjs/pub/pdf/cvus/current/cv0264.pdf)

52. Definitions and example incidents taken from Gregory Moffatt, "Subjective Fear: Preventing Workplace Homicide," *HR Focus,* Vol. 75 (8), 1998, pp. 11–12; and James Merchant and John Lundell, *Workplace Violence: A Report to the Nation,* University of Iowa Injury Prevention Research Center, pp. 5–11. (Available at: http://www.public-health.uiowa.edu/iprc/nation.pdf, accessed February 17, 2004)

53. National Institute for Occupational Safety and Health, "Violence in the Workplace: Risk Factors and Prevention Strategies," May 1998. (Available at: http://www.cdc.gov/niosh/violcont.html, accessed April 6, 2004)

54. Gregory Moffatt, "Subjective Fear: Preventing Workplace Homicide," *HR Focus,* Vol. 75 (8), 1998, pp. 11–12.

55. Steve Kaufer and Jurg W. Mattman, "Workplace Violence: An Employer's Guide," Workplace Violence Research Institute. (Available at: http://noworkviolence.com/articles/employers_guide.htm, accessed April 6, 2004)

56. U.S. Department of Labor, Occupational Safety and Health Administration, "Elements of a Workplace Violence Prevention Program," Part II. (Available at: http://www.osha.gov/workplace_violence/wrkplaceViolence.PartII.html),Part III (Available at: http://www.osha.gov/workplace_violence/wrkplaceViolence.PartIII.html, accessed February 17, 2004)

57. Long Island Coalition for Workplace Violence Awareness and Prevention, *Workplace Violence Awareness & Prevention: An Information and Instructional Package for Use by Employers and Employees* (New York: U.S. Department of Labor–OSHA, 1996).

58. U.S. Department of Labor, Occupational Safety and Health Administration, "Elements of a Workplace Violence Prevention Program," Part II and Part III.

59. The OSHA Web site links to a risk assessment list developed as part of a report to the South Carolina Governor's Workplace Security Advisory Committee, *Prepare, Prevent, Protect South Car-*

olina: Best Practices Workplace Security—A Report from the Governor's Workplace Security Advisory Committee, May 23, 2002. (Available at: http://www.llr.state.sc.us/workplace/Full%20Report.pdf)

60. U.S. Department of Labor, Occupational Safety and Health Administration, "Evacuation Planning Matrix." (Available at: http://www.osha.gov/dep/evacmatrix/index.html, accessed March 30, 2004); and U.S. Department of Labor, Occupational Safety and Health Administration, "Planning for Emergencies: OSHA's New Evacuation Planning Matrix Helps Employers Assess Their Risk and Plan for Emergency Evacuations," *Job Safety and Health Quarterly,* Vol. 14 (4), 2003, pp. 12. (Available at: http://www.osha.gov/Publications/JSHQ/jshq-v14-4-summer_fall2003.pdf, accessed March 30, 2004)

61. University of Calgary, Haskayne School of Business, Risk Management and Insurance, "Employee Health and Wellness Programs: Costs and Benefits." (Available at: http://www.ucalgary.ca/MG/inrm/industry/wellness/costsandb.htm), and "Employee Health and Wellness Programs: Nova Chemicals." (Available at: http://www.ucalgary.ca/MG/inrm/industry/wellness/nova.htm, accessed April 9, 2004)

62. Preventdisease.com, "Why Should Your Company Offer Worksite Wellness Programs?" (Available at: http://preventdisease.com/worksite_wellness/worksite_wellness.html, accessed April 9, 2004)

63. Lou Marano, "Wellness Programs Good for Bottom Line," *United Press International,* August 27, 2003. (Available at: http://web.lexis-nexis.com/universe/document?_m=f7c26c025cae232b179151bf78c9c76c&_docnum=35&wchp=dGLbVzz-zSkVb&_md5=c6ad64cfdf3ec23aa96475138221eeb0, accessed February 18, 2004); Jennifer Plotnick, "Kern County, California Wellness Programs Help Employees Stay Healthy, Productive," *The Bakersfield Californian,* February 1, 2004. (Available at: http://web.lexis-nexis.com/universe/document?_m=745b1bdcff4a585ddad260d7be3e9684&_docnum=18&wchp=dGLbVzz-zSkVb&_md5=712457a084060f2cea6dcb897d84fab7, accessed February 18, 2004); and Preventdisease.com, "Why Should Your Company Offer Worksite Wellness Programs?"

64. John C. Erfurt, Andrea Foote, and Max A. Heirich, "The Cost-Effectiveness of Worksite Wellness Programs for Hypertension Control, Weight Loss, Smoking Cessation, and Exercise," *Personnel Psychology,* Vol. 45, 1992, pp. 5–27; and David A. Harrison and Laurie Z. Liska, "Promoting Regular Exercise in Organizational Fitness Programs: Health-Related Differences in Motivational Building Blocks," *Personnel Psychology,* Vol. 47, 1994, pp. 47–71.

CHAPTER 15

Labor Relations and Collective Bargaining

- Collective Bargaining and Labor Relations in Context
- How Unions Are Formed: Organizing
- What Unions Do When They Are Formed: Collective Bargaining
- When Collective Bargaining Breaks Down: Impasse
- When the Meaning of the Contract Is in Dispute: The Grievance Procedure
- The Role of Labor Relations in Human Resource Management

HR Challenge

You are the HR director of Southern Poultry, a large nonunion poultry producer in the southeastern United States. Your company operates six major growout complexes, each with its own processing plant, feed mill, and array of contract growers. Altogether Southern Poultry directly employs more than 15,000 workers and indirectly employs another 6,000 to 8,000 grower-contractors. The vast majority of the workers are in the processing plants. Currently they are paid at or above average wages, and they have a small health benefits package.

Just as it happens every few years, you are facing union organizing campaigns at two of your processing plants. This year, however, the plants in question seem more vulnerable than in the past to a pro-union vote. A combination of relentless competition and economic recession has brought major changes in work force composition. Although wages remain at or above area averages, they haven't grown substantially in recent years. Under the best circumstances, poultry processing is hard work, and the plants have had difficulty attracting workers. A decade ago, nearly all of the workers were drawn from communities surrounding the plant. Today, 60 percent of the workers have migrated to the area from communities in Mexico and Guatemala. So many workers have arrived from Central America that, in a few locations, the company opened mobile-home parks to provide housing. Overtly hostile acts have been rare, but there is clearly an underlying tension in the relationship between native and immigrant workers. It is not entirely clear, but it appears to you that the union has at least some support among both groups.

Your CEO would like you to put together a report on the unionization challenge. He really wants you to let him know what can be done to keep the union out. But there are some unresolved issues in your mind. What will be your campaign strategy? What is in the best long-term interest of the company? What are the issues that made employees feel a need to unionize? Could their needs have been addressed without resorting to a union? Is it too late? What are the ethical issues at stake? Will race and ethnicity be a factor in the campaign? Can you use it to your advantage? Should you? Why are your CEO and other senior managers so adamantly opposed to the union?

COLLECTIVE BARGAINING AND LABOR RELATIONS IN CONTEXT

This chapter begins with an overview of the labor relations context in the United States. This includes some history of unionization and a discussion of the legal system that protects certain union activities in the private and public sectors. In addition, there is a discussion of the increasingly global context of labor–management relations. From there, the chapter goes on to describe consecutive phases of the **labor relations process.** These include the process of forming a union, collective bargaining after the union has been formed, and the various dispute-resolution processes used when agreement cannot be reached.

Employees have the right to form organizations for the purpose of seeking to influence their working conditions, wages, hours, and benefits. These employee-created organizations, called unions, seek to manage their working environment primarily through a process called **collective bargaining.** When unions are not present, employers usually set employment terms and conditions unilaterally (i.e., without consulting employees) within constraints imposed by market conditions and the law. Collective bargaining allows employees to participate in setting terms and conditions of employment through their unions. Through collective bargaining, the company and the union bilaterally address many of the HRM policies discussed in this text. Although this process puts additional constraints on employers, it also creates a more participative system of employee involvement.

Historical Context

Developments that have affected organized labor are closely related to changes in the political, social, and economic environments. Organized labor has, in turn, affected the development of society at large and is responsible for securing many of the workplace protections and privileges that Americans now enjoy.

The first American unions, formed in the 1700s, were primarily craft guilds in occupations such as shoemaking and carpentry. Their goal was to control the price of the skilled labor they provided by limiting apprenticeships, demanding uniform rates, and setting quality standards.[1] Later, in the 1850s and 1860s, the Industrial Revolution saw the rise of new unions in industries such as railroads and printing. The **American Federation of Labor (AFL)** was organized in 1886 by the leaders of a group of craft unions. **Craft unions,** sometimes called trade unions, organize workers on the basis of skill, trade, or occupation. Examples of early craft unions were the cigar makers, printers, and carpenters. The AFL emphasized collective bargaining about bread-and-butter issues as a means of improving working conditions for skilled workers[2] and set the stage for contemporary unionism.

The continued expansion of mass production created entirely new industries that employed large numbers of workers in large industrial facilities. The AFL found it difficult to organize the skilled workers in these facilities but was opposed to organizing the masses because doing so violated the principles of craft unionism. The **Congress of Industrial Organizations (CIO)** was formed in 1935 to fill this void. **Industrial unions** organize on the basis of industry, regardless of skill. The CIO sought to create one major union for each major industry and to include all workers, from the most highly skilled to the unskilled. Within a couple of years the CIO helped create the United Auto Workers, the United Steel Workers, and several other major unions.[3]

Unions grew dramatically alongside the economic expansion associated with World War II and its aftermath. Membership swelled to 35 percent of the labor force in 1946 and remained at roughly that level through 1955. Unions helped establish the basic contours of the American social compact. A forty-hour week became the norm, child labor was abolished, employers became liable for work-related accidents and injuries, minimum wages were enacted into law, and workers were insured against the risk of lost income because of unemployment or old age. More subtly, through contract negotiations, unions created pensions, health insurance, and grievance-arbitration procedures, as well as establishing the principle that wages should move as a function of (1) inflation (to keep purchasing power whole) and (2) productivity (a gain-sharing program). In combination, these and other factors helped the United States create the largest, wealthiest middle-class the world has ever known.

The American labor movement was united under the leadership umbrella of the **AFL-CIO** (http://www.aflcio.org) when the AFL and the CIO merged in 1955.[4] Unions were at the height of their strength in the U.S. economy, with one-third of the nation's nonagricultural work force belonging to them. As a percentage of the labor force, union membership began declining slowly but steadily thereafter (see Figure 15.1). In absolute numbers, union membership continued to grow slowly, reaching a peak in the late 1970s at around 24 million members. Finally, absolute membership declined through the 1980s and 1990s, accelerating the decline in membership as a proportion of the work force. By 2003 only 12.9 percent of the nonagricultural work force was unionized. A distinction should be noted however, between *unionized* workers and *organized* workers; many employees belong to professional associations that bear a number of similarities to unions.

In contrast to the private sector, which has experienced a half-century of declining unionization, the public sector experienced a dramatic surge in unionization in the 1960s and 1970s. By the 1980s public-sector unionization had grown to 35 to 40 percent and has remained at that level ever since.[5] The National Education Association, the American Federation of State, County, and Municipal Employees, and the International Association of Fire Fighters represent some of the largest and most powerful employee organizations in the country.

Union membership rates vary significantly across industries (see Table 15.1). Membership is relatively high in the transportation, communications, and public utilities industries, as well as in the public sector. It is quite low in the services, finance, insurance, and real estate industries. Membership also varies greatly from state to state, from New York, with 24.6 percent of its work force unionized, to North Carolina, with a unionization rate of only 3.1 percent. Although unions now

FIGURE 15.1

Union Membership as a Percentage of the Nonagricultural Labor Force, 1940–2003

Source: Data points 1980 and earlier compiled from Bureau of Labor Statistics, *Handbook of Labor Statistics,* 1980, table 165. Data points for 1985 and later compiled from Bureau of Labor Statistics, *Employment and Earnings,* January 1986, 1991, 1996, 2001, and 2003.

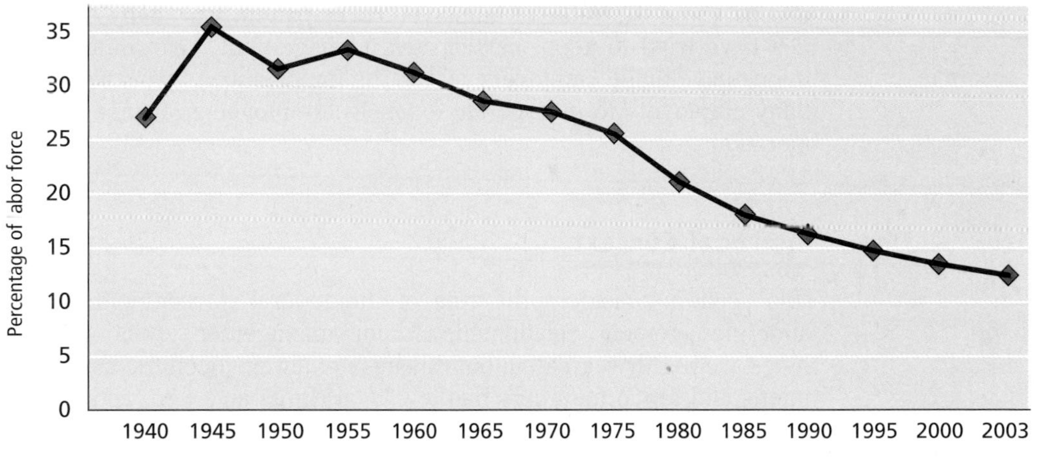

TABLE 15.1

Demographics of Union Membership

	Percentage of Work Force Unionized				
	1985	1990	1995	2000	2003
Total work force	18.0	16.1	14.9	13.5	12.9
Industry					
Manufacturing	24.8	20.6	17.6	14.8	13.5
Mining	17.3	18.0	13.8	10.9	9.1
Construction	22.3	21.0	17.7	18.3	16.0
Transportation, communication, and utilities	37.0	30.5	27.0	24.0	26.2
Trade	7.2	6.3	6.1	4.7	6.2
Finance, insurance, and real estate	2.9	2.5	2.1	1.6	2.1
Government	35.8	36.5	37.8	37.5	37.2
Other Characteristics					
Race					
Black	24.3	21.1	19.9	17.1	16.5
Hispanic	18.9	14.8	13.0	11.4	10.7
White	17.3	15.5	14.2	13.0	12.5
Sex					
Female	13.2	12.6	12.3	11.5	11.4
Male	22.1	19.3	17.2	15.2	14.3

Source: U.S. Department of Labor, Bureau of Labor Statistics, *Employment and Earnings,* January issues, 1986, 1991, 1996, 2001, and 2004.

constitute less than 15 percent of the nonagricultural work force, their impact on employers remains quite substantial. Many wholly or partially nonunionized employers copy the practices of unionized firms with regard to wages and benefits, both to discourage the further unionization of their work forces and to continue to be able to attract top employees. Unions also have taught management important lessons about the value of employee participation, and many progressive companies have tried to adopt participative management environments. Furthermore, unions have made employers realize the importance of workplace justice, leading many employers to incorporate extensive employee-grievance systems into their operations.[6]

The Legal Context

This section considers the role of the federal government in regulating the labor–management relationship. Union–management relations in the United States are highly regulated, but this has not always been the case. For many years unions and union members had few legal rights and were actively persecuted by employers and the courts. This began to change about eighty years ago. Table 15.2 lists major U.S. labor laws. At present, the two main laws that regulate the relationships between unions and employers are the **Railway Labor Act of 1926** and the **National Labor Relations Act.** The National Labor Relations Act is comprised of two main laws, the **Wagner Act of 1935** and the **Taft-Hartley Act of 1947** (also known as the **Labor-Management Relations Act**). The Railway Labor Act regulates labor–management relations in the railroad and airlines indus-

TABLE 15.2

Major U.S. Labor Laws

1926	Railway Labor Act	Railway workers are permitted to organize and bargain collectively. Airline workers were added in 1934.
1935	National Labor Relations Act (Wagner Act)	Establishes right to organize, to bargain collectively, and to engage in concerted activities; creates the National Labor Relations Board to implement and enforce the act.
1947	Labor Management Relations Act (Taft-Hartley Act)	Amends the NLRA. Adds union unfair labor practices (Section 8b). Weakens rights of workers and unions.
1962	Executive Order 10988	Encourages bargaining in federal sector. Followed by state laws encouraging bargaining by state and local government employees.
1978	Civil Service Reform Act	Establishes the current system for regulating labor–management relationships in the federal government.

Source: Thomas A. Kochan and Harry C. Katz, *Collective Bargaining and Industrial Relations* (Homewood, Ill.: Irwin, 1988), pp. 74–75. Reprinted by permission.

tries; the National Labor Relations Act regulates labor–management relations in the rest of the private sector. There are important differences between the Railway Labor Act and the National Labor Relations Act, but they are similar in their basic features. Both laws recognize workers' rights to organize into unions, to bargain collectively with employers, and, under appropriate circumstances, to strike.

The Railway Labor Act became law in 1926. The railroads comprised a large industry themselves, but they were also critically important to the operation of other industries. There was also a long history of labor strife in the railroads, so it is no surprise that it was the first industry to be regulated. In 1935 the Wagner Act, the first major portion of the National Labor Relations Act, extended the principles of the Railway Labor Act to most of the rest of the private sector. Because the National Labor Relations Act covers more of the economy and is viewed as the bedrock of U.S. labor policy, its provisions are summarized here.

The Wagner Act of 1935 affirms the principle that employees have the right to join, form, or assist unions free from the interference, restraint, or coercion of employers, to bargain collectively, and to engage in concerted activities in support of their aims (e.g., to strike). "It is hereby declared to be the policy of the United States," said Congress in Section 1 of the Wagner Act, to encourage unionization by "encouraging the practice and procedure of collective bargaining and by protecting the exercise by workers of full freedom of association, self-organization, and designation of representatives of their own choosing." But the Wagner Act went beyond a mere declaration of rights; it also created important implementation and enforcement mechanisms that were not included in the earlier laws. The Wagner Act was clearly a pro-employee and pro-union statute.

In contrast to the Wagner Act, the Taft-Hartley Act of 1947 was a pro-employer law, intended to weaken many of the employee and union rights established by the Wagner Act. Early sections of the National Labor Relations Act sketch the broad contours of American labor policy; later sections specify the details of implementation and enforcement:

- Section 2 defines various terms, such as "employers" and "employees," and spells out who is covered under the law and who is not. Basically, the National Labor Relations Act covers nearly all employees in the private sector. It does not cover very small firms that do not engage in interstate commerce; employees covered under the Railway Labor Act; public employees in federal, state, or local government; or agricultural workers. The Taft-Hartley Act excluded managerial and supervisory employees from coverage.
- Section 3 establishes the **National Labor Relations Board (NLRB)** (http://www.nlrb.gov) to administer the act.
- Section 7 is the heart of the act, articulating employee rights. "Employees shall have the right to self-organization, to join, form or assist labor organizations, to bargain collectively through representatives of their own choosing, and to engage in other concerted activities for the purpose of collective bargaining or other mutual aid or protection."
- The new rights given to employees in Section 7 implied that certain management behaviors could no longer be considered acceptable. Section 8 of the Wagner Act established a set of employer **unfair labor practices.** Taft-Hartley established a set of union unfair labor practices. Compare these lists of unfair labor practices in Table 15.3.

TABLE 15.3
Unfair Labor Practices

Management Unfair Labor Practices Wagner Act—Section 8a	Union Unfair Labor Practices Taft-Hartley Act—Section 8b
• Interfere with, restrain, or coerce employees in the exercise of their rights to organize, bargain collectively, or engage in other concerted activities for mutual aid or protection. • Dominate, interfere with, or contribute financial assistance to a labor organization. • Discriminate against employees on the basis of their union activities or sentiments. • Discriminate or retaliate for filing charges or giving testimony under the act. • Refuse to bargain (in good faith) with the exclusive representative of the employees.	• Interfere with, restrain, or coerce employees in the exercise of their rights under the act. • Cause or attempt to cause an employer to discriminate on the basis of union activities or sentiments. • Refuse to bargain (in good faith) with the employer. • Induce or encourage a work stoppage for the object of forcing an employer to stop doing business with another employer (secondary boycott) or forcing an employer to assign work to members of a particular union (jurisdictional strike). • Charging excessive dues or discriminatory initiation fees. • Cause or attempt to cause an employer to pay for work not performed or not to be performed (featherbedding). • Engaging in organizational or recognition picketing.

Source: Adapted with permission from *Primer of Labor Relations,* 24th ed., by John J. Kenny and Linda G. Kahn, pp. 1–3. Copyright 1989 by The Bureau of National Affairs, Inc. Washington, D.C.

Most of the remaining sections of the act specify in detail the administrative processes of the National Labor Relations Board. The NLRB has two basic functions: an implementation function to resolve **questions concerning representation,** and an enforcement function to adjudicate unfair labor practice charges. Questions concerning representation are most commonly settled by holding secret-ballot elections, which is discussed more fully later in the chapter. Adjudication of unfair labor practices involves a process for receiving and investigating complaints. It also involves, when necessary, attempting conciliation, holding formal hearings, issuing rulings, determining remedies for wrongdoing, and handling appeals.

In contrast to the private sector, public employees were exempted from the National Labor Relations Act and did not participate in the growth of unionization following its passage. Labor–management relations in the public sector remained largely unregulated into the 1960s. Beginning in the 1960s and continuing through the 1970s, many states, along with the federal government, passed laws creating a statutory framework for regulating labor–management relations between governments and their employees. Forty-one states have enacted laws regulating at least some aspect of labor–management relations in state and local governments.[7]

Many of these state laws contain union certification provisions modeled after the National Labor Relations Act whereby a union that wins an election majority is certified as the exclusive bargaining representative, which, in turn triggers the employer's duty to bargain with the union. Thirteen states now permit strikes by some public employees, but no state permits strikes by its safety forces (e.g., police and firefighters). In an effort to balance a policy encouraging collective bargaining against a desire to avoid disruption of public services by strikes, states have experimented with and developed an elaborate array of advanced dispute-resolution techniques combining mediation, fact finding, and various forms of interest arbitration.

In the federal government, a series of executive orders issued by Presidents Kennedy, Nixon, and Ford expanded the rights of federal employees to organize and bargain. These rights and others were codified into law in the Civil Service Reform Act of 1978 that created the **Federal Labor Relations Authority (FLRA)** (http://www.flra.gov), which is responsible for overseeing certification elections and investigating charges of unfair labor practices. Federal employees now have the right to unionize and bargain collectively, but the scope of issues over which bargaining occurs is dramatically narrower in the federal sector. Most significantly, collective bargaining does not occur over wages and most benefits as these are set by Congress. Strikes by federal employees remain illegal, and negotiation impasses are resolved with the aid of the **Federal Mediation and Conciliation Service,** by arbitration, or by the Federal Services Impasse Panel.

Global Context: Labor Relations Around the World

As national economies merge with the global economy, multinational enterprises and their workers are increasingly participating in operations around the world in countries and regions that may have very different labor policies and practices from their own. Reconciling labor policy and practice of the home country with that of the host country is not always easy. The labor problems a multinational enterprise will have to address may be very different depending on whether it is doing business in an advanced economy or a developing economy.

There are a number of important contrasts between the United States and other advanced economic democracies. The first and most dramatic contrast is in level of unionization. As Table 15.4 indicates, the United States is, and has been, among the most lightly unionized of the advanced economies. Only France, among advanced nations, had a lower trade union density rate at 9.7 percent in 2003. But in France a high degree of centralization of bargaining and close coordination between unions, employer associations, and government effectively extends collective bargaining coverage to 92.5 percent of all workers. American firms operating in Europe or Japan are more likely to have to deal with unions there than here. European and Japanese firms operating on U.S. soil are pleasantly surprised to learn that remaining union-free is an option. Even if the U.S. firm is able to avoid direct dealing with unions in Europe and Japan, the unions have other ways to exert their influence. For example, bargaining tends to be more centralized, often on an industry-by-industry basis. Firms are expected and sometimes required by law to adopt the industry bargain. Unions are often more deeply involved in politics than they are in the United States. As a result, protective legislation is far more prevalent in many of the advanced economies than it is in

TABLE 15.4

Trade Union Density and Collective Bargaining Coverage in Selected OECD Nations, 1980–2003

	Trade Union Density				Bargaining Coverage			
	1980	1990	1994	2003	1980	1990	1994	2003
Australia	48	41	35	24.5	88	80	80	82.5
Austria	56	46	42	36.5	98	98	98	97.5
Belgium	56	51	54	55.6	90	90	90	92.5
Canada	36	36	38	28.1	37	38	36	32.0
Denmark	76	71	76	74.4	69	69	69	82.5
Finland	70	72	81	76.2	95	95	95	92.5
France	18	10	9	9.7	85	92	95	92.5
Germany	36	33	29	25.0	91	90	92	68.0
Italy	49	39	39	34.9	85	83	82	82.5
Japan	31	25	24	21.5	28	23	21	17.5
Netherlands	35	26	26	23.2	76	71	81	82.5
New Zealand	56	45	30	22.7	67	67	31	27.5
Norway	57	56	58	54.3	75	75	74	72.5
Portugal	61	32	32	24.3	70	79	71	82.5
Spain	9	13	19	14.9	76	76	78	82.5
Sweden	80	83	91	81.1	86	86	89	92.5
Switzerland	31	27	27	17.8	53	53	50	42.5
United Kingdom	50	39	34	31.2	70	47	47	32.5
United States	22	16	16	12.8	26	18	18	14.0

Source: Compiled from OECD Employment Outlook, 1997, table 3.3, and from *OECD Employment Outlook*, 2004, chap. 3.

the United States. For example, the United States is the only advanced economy that still recognizes employment-at-will (see Chapter 16) and the only one without universal health insurance. Finally, there are a greater variety of employee representation schemes in many economically advanced nations. Two are worth mentioning—works councils and codetermination.

Works councils are mandated by law in most European countries. Each workplace has its own council of elected workers that participates in the shared governance of the workplace.[8] These councils are often linked together by an elaborate network of corporate, industrial, or geographic councils. Although the specific role and authority of councils varies from country to country, they generally participate with management in local governance of the workplace. They provide advice and consultation on a wide array of issues. On some issues, such as safety and health, they may have investigatory authority.

Codetermination is the European term for worker representation on the company's board of directors.[9] Worker representation is required in some European countries (e.g., Germany). Even when not required by law, codetermination tends to be more common in Europe than in the United States. Worker representation on the corporate board means that worker interests must be considered at the strategic level of the firm (e.g., which plant will be closed, or where will the new plant be built?). In the United States, there is no comparable system of employee representation at the strategic level of the firm, though union representatives have sometimes been placed on the boards of financially distressed companies.

When corporations from economically advanced nations set up operations in other such nations, they typically have little difficulty adapting and conforming to the new legal and cultural norms. For example, when IBM, a staunchly nonunion American firm, operates in Germany, it readily adapts to dealing with industry-wide bargaining, works councils, and codetermination processes. On the other hand, when firms from other economically advanced nations operate in the United States, such as Honda in Ohio or BMW in South Carolina, they often adopt an anti-union posture that would not be considered acceptable in their home countries.

When corporations from economically advanced nations operate in less developed nations, however, they often find labor conditions and standards that are well below those of the economically advanced nations. Numerous scholars and policymakers have commented on the **global division of labor** that has developed in recent decades, whereby design, financing, and marketing are managed in economically advanced nations but production and assembly are increasingly shifted to poorer economies where unskilled labor can be bought cheaply. Long hours for poverty-level wages, primitive health and safety precautions, prevalent use of child labor, even outright slavery—all occur in parts of the developing world.[10] In these cultures unions are more likely to operate as part of a broader social reform movement, but in many countries they may be illegal or severely legally constrained. Some countries continue to persecute labor leaders through official political channels.

For many years corporations from economically advanced nations operating in developing nations adopted one of two approaches for dealing with the local labor problem. First, those corporations that relied on skilled labor to produce and assemble complex products, such as automobiles or petroleum refineries, simply set up operations based largely on the American model. Plants were either owned by the home corporation or operated as joint ventures with prominent local firms. Because they relied on skilled labor, firms found it necessary to invest heavily in worker training and therefore found it beneficial to put in place practices that would reduce labor turnover. As a result, local-country employees of these firms, although poorly paid by American standards, often had higher standards of living and greater income security than many of their neighbors. The second approach, more commonly used by firms that rely on less skilled labor, was to subcontract production or assembly work to independent firms located in the host country. This has been a common arrangement in agricultural commodities, such as coffee and sugar, and remains prevalent in many of the garment and needle trades, from clothing and footwear to carpeting and soccer balls. One factor in the prevalence of subcontracting for unskilled labor is that the disparities between home- and host-country labor standards and practices are just too great to be reconciled. The low-wage, low-skill sectors of developing nations often resembled throwbacks to a bygone era from which modern multinational corporations wish to distance themselves. By subcontracting production to host-country or even third-country firms, they could maintain the flow of goods without accepting responsibility for local labor conditions.

In recent years it has become increasingly clear that multinational corporations can no longer divorce themselves from the labor conditions under which their products are made. When consumers are made aware that their favorite products are produced by forced labor, child labor, or otherwise under sweatshop conditions, they react in ways that can affect bottom-line considerations such as market share and stock prices. Companies including Nike, Reebok, Adidas, the Gap, Levi-Strauss, Disney, Philips-Van Heusen, Liz Claiborne, General Electric, Starbucks, Sears, Wal-Mart, and many others have been so embarrassed (and some of these have a strong reputation for better-than-average labor standards).

Under traditional subcontracting arrangements, there was little role for the human resource management function. But now that companies are realizing they must assume responsibility for the labor conditions of their contractors, human resource management comes back into the picture. Many firms are adopting codes of conduct and incorporating these codes into their contracts with suppliers in de-

ETHICAL PERSPECTIVE

Universal Human Rights in Employment

Employment is more than a contractual relationship involving contractual rights. It is more than a legal relationship involving statutory and, perhaps, constitutional rights. Employment is a fundamental human relationship and, therefore, necessarily implicates fundamental human rights. But just what human rights are at stake in employment?

The International Labour Organization (ILO) has been struggling with this question since it was founded in 1919. Today the ILO is part of the United Nations and seeks to advance worker rights and conditions of work around the globe.

A major milestone in the movement for global human rights occurred just after World War II with the founding of the United Nations and the adoption of the Declaration of Universal Human Rights in 1948. The declaration was followed by other United Nations human rights accords, which recognize the concept of worker rights as a subset of human rights. Human rights are deemed acquired by virtue of one's humanity and ought not be dependent on, or comprised by, any act of government or anyone else. In turn, employment rights are those acquired by virtue of employment and ought to exist independently of employer whim, government effectiveness, or stage of political or economic development. Within the U.N. framework for human rights, the ILO has adopted nearly 200 conventions addressing standards for employment rights. Over the years, eight of these conventions have come to be seen as fundamental. They are:

- Forced Labour Convention (#29)
- Freedom of Association and Protection of the Right to Organize (#87)
- Right to Organize and Collective Bargaining Convention (#98)
- Equal Remuneration Convention (#100)
- Abolition of Forced Labour Convention (#105)
- Discrimination (Employment and Occupation) Convention (#111)
- Minimum Age Convention (#138)
- Convention on Elimination of the Worst Forms of Child Labour (#182)

In 1998 the ILO adopted a Declaration on Fundamental Principles and Rights at Work that declares that all member states, even if they have not ratified the conventions in question, have an obligation to respect the principles concerning the fundamental rights that are the subject of those conventions.

Ironically, the United States, which considers itself a bastion of human rights, has one of the worst records in the world in terms of ratification of the fundamental worker rights conventions. The United States has ratified only two of the eight. Only 4 of 177 member nations have ratified fewer. The United States has ratified only conventions 105 (on forced labour) and 182 (on elimination of the worst forms of child labour—and this will require amending the Fair Labor Standards Act to bring it into compliance in agriculture).

veloping countries. The codes often require adherence to international employment rights standards as well as compliance with local laws. Some companies, but not all, have established monitoring programs to assure contractor compliance with the codes. And a few companies have incorporated social provisions, including employment rights concerns, into their auditing programs[11] (see the Ethical Perspective box).

HOW UNIONS ARE FORMED: ORGANIZING

Why Employees Want Unions

Numerous theories attempt to explain why workers organize, join, and support unions. Karl Marx saw unions as essential to the radicalization of a revolutionary working class,[12] but others see unions as fundamentally conservative organizations that give workers a sense of community stability in a world of constant change.[13] Others adopt a more modest view that unions humanize the face of capitalism by introducing an element of industrial democracy or control over one's job.[14] Still others see unions as an innate sociobiological human response in the face of a threat.[15] In contrast, economic models of unionization suggest that employees engage in a rational calculus of the benefits and costs associated with unionization.[16] Perceived benefits of unionization might include improved pay, benefits, and job security. Perceived costs might include union dues (usually about the equivalent of two hours pay per month), the potential costs of a strike, or the fear of retaliation by the employer. When the anticipated benefits exceed the perceived costs, economically rational employees will support unionization.

One challenge to the economic models of unionization is the persistent finding in survey research of a "representation gap." That is, more workers desire representation than have it. The vast majority of workers indicate a desire for a greater voice and more influence in the workplace than they currently have. A clear majority express a desire for representation that is both collective in nature and independent of management. And, about 40 percent of nonunion workers indicate that they would vote for union representation if given the chance.[17] If such a high proportion of nonunion workers want union representation, why does union density in the United States remain at less than 15 percent of the work force? An examination of the organizing process, and of the difficulties associated with unionization, may shed some light on the representation gap.

The NLRB and the Organizing Process

The National Labor Relations Act establishes procedures by which employees may organize and unions may be formally recognized as the **exclusive representative** of the employees for the purpose of collective bargaining. Although the process is conceptually simple—do a majority of the employees want a union?—it has become highly legalistic and is usually hotly contested. Figure 15.2 provides a simple overview of the process.

The process starts when either a union representative contacts a potential target group of employees or the employees themselves contact the union and inquire about the possibility of organizing their workplace. At this point the union

FIGURE 15.2
The Organizing Process

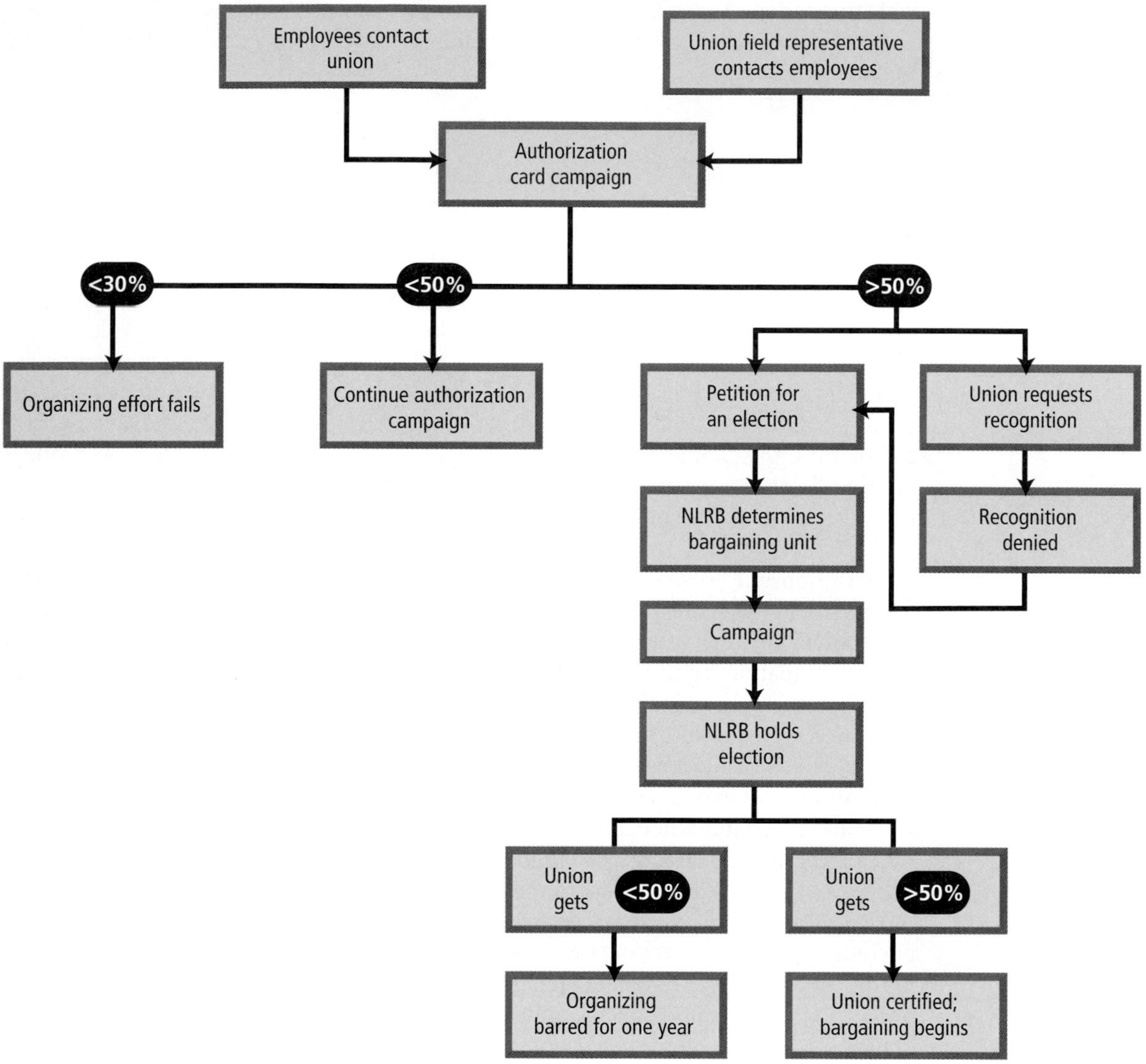

Employees contact union
Union field representative contacts employees
Authorization card campaign
<30%
<50%
>50%
Organizing effort fails
Continue authorization campaign
Petition for an election
Union requests recognition
NLRB determines bargaining unit
Recognition denied
Campaign
NLRB holds election
Union gets <50%
Union gets >50%
Organizing barred for one year
Union certified; bargaining begins

has to analyze the target plant, assess the possibility of success in organizing the workers, and, if it decides to proceed, start the initial advances to reach the employees. Usually an **organizing committee** is formed among the workers early in the process.

At some point, **authorization cards** are distributed and employees are asked to sign them if they want to be represented by the union in question. Under NLRB rules, at least 30 percent of the employees in a proposed bargaining unit must sign the cards for the board to proceed. However, most union organizers insist on having signatures of at least 50 percent of the employees before petitioning the NLRB.

They reason that, during the election campaign, employer opposition is likely to erode union support somewhat. Thus, if the union is not able to gain 50 percent of employee support, it may drop the organizing effort. On average, unions gather signatures of about 65 percent of the employees.

If support for the union during the authorization card campaign exceeds 50 percent, the union can approach management and request **voluntary recognition.** If management grants such a request, it will be legally required to bargain with the union, so voluntary recognition occurs only rarely. If management rebuffs the request, it triggers the NLRB election process that potentially leads to union **certification** as the exclusive representative.

The National Labor Relations Board must make several administrative determinations before it will hold a recognition election. When it receives a petition, the first step is to determine whether it has jurisdiction over the matter (i.e., whether the employees and employer are covered by the National Labor Relations Act). Second, the NLRB will investigate whether at least 30 percent of the employees in the unit have expressed interest in joining a specific union.

Perhaps the most difficult and important set of determinations involves the appropriateness of the proposed **bargaining unit.** The bargaining unit is made up of all employees who will be eligible to join the union and who will be covered by the union contract. The NLRB will first approach the parties (the union and employer) and seek an informal agreement on the proposed bargaining unit. If the parties cannot agree on the bargaining unit, then the NLRB will conduct a formal investigation and make the unit determination itself. In making unit determinations, the NLRB looks for a **community of interests** among employees with respect to wages, hours, skills, and working conditions. It may also consider history and traditions within the industry and the organization of the human resource management function within the firm.

Elections

Recognition elections are conducted by secret ballot by agents of the NLRB. The ballot will offer the voter at least two choices. One choice is always labeled "no representative." The other choice will be the name of the proposed union. To win, the union must obtain a majority of the valid votes cast. Sometimes there may be two or more unions listed on the ballot. In these cases, if no choice receives a majority on the first ballot, a runoff election is held between the two highest vote getters. Table 15.5 shows the percentage of union victories in certification elections.

The amended National Labor Relations Act also provides for the decertification of union representatives. Employees who are dissatisfied with their union may petition the NLRB to hold a **decertification election.** Decertification elections are held much less frequently than certification elections, and unions tend to lose most of them. In 2003, for example, a total of 423 decertification elections were held, and unions lost in 64 percent of them.[18]

Employer and Union Conduct During Organizing Campaigns

As noted previously, it is considered an unfair labor practice for either unions or employers to violate Section 7 of the National Labor Relations Act, which gives employees the right to form unions and to engage in collective activities. In numerous

TABLE 15.5

Results of Representation Elections, 1975–2003

Year	Total Elections	Union Victories	% Union Victories
1975	8,577	4,138	49.2%
1980	8,198	3,744	45.7
1985	4,614	1,956	42.4
1990	4,210	1,965	46.7
1995	3,399	1,611	47.4
2000	3,368	1,685	50.0
2003	2,937	1,579	53.8

Source: Adapted from the *Sixty-Eighth Annual Report of the National Labor Relations Board for the Fiscal Year Ended* September 30, 2003 (Washington, D.C.: U.S. Government Printing Office, 2004).

decisions, the National Labor Relations Board and federal courts have interpreted the meaning of these provisions with respect to the behavior of the parties during an organizing campaign. A helpful acronym to remember is *TIPS.* In simple terms, the employer may not *threaten* or *intimidate* employees in an attempt to convince them to vote against the union. The employer may not *promise* benefits to employees if the union is defeated or pre-emptively improve wages or conditions during an organizing campaign. Finally, the employer may not *spy* on employees at unionization meetings.

To what extent does someone arguing for unionization have the right to obtain access to employees to deliver that message? The answer depends on the employment status of the messenger. The Supreme Court has ruled that employers have the right to severely restrict nonemployees' access to employees. In other words, employers may bar nonemployees (such as professional union organizers) from their premises. Pro-union employees, however, have more extensive rights to approach their peers at work. They may carry the union message to employees during nonworking periods in nonworking areas—for instance, during lunchtime in the cafeteria.

To what extent are employers free to express their views regarding unionization during the course of a campaign to unionize? Section 8(c) of the amended National Labor Relations Act establishes a general principle that "the expressing of views, argument, or opinion, or the dissemination thereof, whether in written, printed, graphic, or visual form, shall not constitute or be evidence of an unfair labor practice . . . if such expression contains no threat of reprisal or force or promise of benefit." As Table 15.6 shows, most employers are willing to go to great lengths to avoid unionization. Management did not mount an active campaign in only 3 percent of elections, and unions almost always win these. In 75 percent of elections, management hired an outside consultant to help defeat the union. In 92 percent of elections, management held captive audience meetings (where employees are required to attend), averaging more than eleven such meetings per election. In 75 percent of elections, supervisors were directed to hold one-on-one sessions with employees. One-on-ones were conducted on a weekly basis 67 percent of the time. More than half of employers suggested that the workplace might close if the union won the election. Finally, in 25 percent of elections the employer

TABLE 15.6

Management Counterorganizing Campaign Tactics

Management Tactics	% of Campaigns
Active campaign against the union	97
Hired an outside consultant	75
Held captive audience meetings	92
Conducted supervisor one-on-one meetings with employees	78
Mailed anti-union letters	70
Distributed anti-union leaflets	75
Used anti-union videos	55
Suggested the workplace might close if the union won	51
Threatened to call the INS where undocumented workers were present	52
Assisted an anti-union employee committee	31
Discharged union activists	25

Source: Compiled from Kate Bronfenbrenner, *Uneasy Terrain: The Impact of Capital Mobility on Workers, Wages, and Union Organizing.* Report commissioned by the U.S. Trade Deficit Review Commission, 2000, table 8, p. 73, and pp. 18 and 44.

fired union activists, averaging just over four firings per campaign in which firings occurred.[19]

WHAT UNIONS DO WHEN THEY ARE FORMED: COLLECTIVE BARGAINING

The certification of a union as an exclusive bargaining representative simultaneously triggers the employees' right, and the employer's duty, to bargain collectively over "rates of pay, wages, hours of employment, or other conditions of employment." Employers and unions have a mutual obligation to bargain in **good faith** toward the settlement of a collective-bargaining contract. In the United States there are tens of thousands of agreements in place. With so many different employers and unions involved across the country, bargaining relationships are understandably highly varied. There are, however, some distinctive structures and types of bargaining that help to provide a frame of reference for understanding these diverse relationships. This section discusses the basic types of bargaining structures, the characteristics of the negotiation process, the types of bargaining that arise between and within parties, and the types of issues over which the parties typically negotiate.

Structure of Bargaining

The **bargaining structure** refers to the range of persons covered or affected by a current or planned collective-bargaining agreement. The formal structure consists of those employers and employees who are legally tied to the contract under negotiation. The informal structure includes those who may be materially affected by the negotiations. Often a settlement between two parties sets a pattern for subsequent settlements among many of the employers and unions in that industry.[20] For instance, **pattern bargaining** occurs in the automobile-manufacturing industry, where the United Auto Workers (UAW) typically focus on negotiating a settlement with one of the large domestic manufacturers, calling a strike against the target company if necessary. After a settlement is reached with the target company, the UAW expects and usually receives very similar agreements with the other large automakers. Historically, pattern bargaining has had the effect of taking such factors as wages out of the competitive matrix for employers in the same industry. Firms in an industry where all their competitors were unionized and under similar contracts did not have to consider the relative cost of labor in developing competitive strategies. With increasing globalization, pattern bargaining is now much less acceptable to U.S. firms because the "pattern" does not extend to primary competitors in Asia and Europe.

Another aspect of bargaining structure has to do with centralization within and among employers. A decentralized structure of bargaining is typified by a single-employer, single-plant arrangement, in which an employer negotiates with a union on a plant-by-plant basis. In a more centralized approach, an employer may negotiate on a multi-plant basis, bargaining with the same union for employees in multiple plants. Often the major **economic issues** (such as wages and benefits) are decided in the organization-wide multi-plant contract or industry-wide master contract. Further bargaining on **noneconomic issues** (such as work rules) is conducted at the plant level. A higher level of centralization occurs when several employers combine to negotiate a common agreement with a union. This is **multi-employer bargaining.** Multi-employer bargaining is often conducted in a geographically defined region or a single labor market. For instance, building contractors in a metropolitan area might form an employer association to negotiate master agreements with the unions representing carpenters, electricians, plumbers, and bricklayers.

Contract Negotiations

Before contract negotiations begin, both the union and management typically engage in considerable planning and research. Both sides assess the financial condition of the company and research patterns in competitor firms and among comparable workers. If there is an existing contract, it will be reviewed for areas where changes are needed. Both sides must select their bargaining teams and identify their chief negotiators. Finally, both sides need to develop a prioritized agenda of issues they intend to pursue. For the union, setting the bargaining agenda usually involves canvassing the membership in some way.

In the early stages of bargaining, important issues to be decided are the agenda and the ground rules for the remainder of the sessions. Decisions concerning these issues set the atmosphere for the bargaining process. For example, negotiating easy-to-resolve issues at the beginning of the session could create an atmosphere of trust and build good rapport between the parties, leading to a smoother resolution of difficult issues later on. Initial demands may have a strategic dimension. A seemingly unreasonable demand could provide future room for negotiation or serve as a tradeoff in return for concessions on other issues. After the initial demands are presented, more reasonable demands are expected to follow. Proposals and counterproposals are exchanged. Sometime thereafter, concessions are likely to follow. Concessions should be timed carefully. A hastily offered concession could convey a message of weakness or unpreparedness to the other side. More significant, however, is the possibility of having failed to consider all the ramifications of a concession. This mistake could have serious economic consequences for the conceding party. In this regard, cost estimates must be made on every proposal.

As negotiations approach their deadline, usually the expiration date of the existing contract, pressure builds. In addition to resolving the remaining substantive issues—and these are often the most difficult issues—the parties have several other important matters to address. What is the likelihood of reaching a settlement? Can a work stoppage be avoided? Is intervention by a third-party mediator needed? If a work stoppage appears likely, how will it be managed?

Types of Bargaining

Labor–management relations in the United States are commonly perceived as being highly adversarial in character. Press coverage of unions focuses attention on strikes, which, although rare, do represent an obvious manifestation of conflict. In practice, the negotiating parties can take a position anywhere along a broad spectrum of conflict to cooperation. Distributive bargaining and integrative bargaining differ with respect to the degree of conflict exhibited.[21]

Distributive bargaining, the most common type, has been defined as "the complex system of activities instrumental to the attainment of one party's goals when they are in basic conflict with those of another party."[22] This is zero-sum negotiation, in which one party's gain is the other party's loss. Wage issues typify distributive bargaining—every additional dollar paid to employees means a dollar less in profit for management.

Integrative bargaining, on the other hand, refers to activities "instrumental to the attainment of objectives which are not in fundamental conflict with those of the other party. Such objectives are said to define an area of common concern, a problem."[23] In this situation, one party's gain need not translate into another party's loss. Integrative bargaining can result in collaborative problem solving in which both parties come out ahead. Examples include gain-sharing programs or joint labor–management programs to improve the quality of work life, provide retraining for employees with obsolete skills, or improve plant safety.

Scope of Bargaining

The **scope of bargaining** is defined as the range of items over which the parties negotiate. Over time, the law has come to recognize three distinct categories of bargaining items—mandatory subjects, permissive subjects, and illegal subjects. These distinctions are not trivial, for they affect the rights of the parties in other areas, such as strikes. After examining these important legal distinctions, we will explore a more familiar dichotomy used to categorize the subject matter of collective bargaining. This is the distinction between economic and noneconomic issues.

Both parties have an obligation to negotiate over **mandatory subjects** in good faith if either party insists. This does not mean the parties are required to reach agreement; it only means they must try. **Permissive subjects** are matters over which the parties may negotiate if they both agree to, but neither is required to do so. Neither party may engage in a strike or lockout over a permissive issue or pursue a permissive issue to the point of impasse. Finally, neither party can legitimately bring **illegal**

TABLE 15.7
Subjects of Bargaining with Examples

Mandatory Subjects	Permissive Subjects	Illegal Subjects
Wages	Retiree benefits (changes in)	Featherbedding
Benefits	Product pricing and labeling	Discrimination in hiring
Incentive pay	Contract ratification procedures	Closed shop agreements
Overtime	Performance bonds	
Layoff and recall	Corporate investment policy	
Union security clause		
Management rights clause		
Grievance procedures		
Seniority rights		
Safety		

Source: Adapted from R. Allen and T. Keaveny, *Contemporary Labor Relations* © 1988 by Addison Wesley Publishing Company. Reprinted with permission of the publisher.

subjects to the bargaining table. Table 15.7 provides some examples to illustrate the distinctions among mandatory, permissive, and illegal subjects of bargaining.

Economic Issues

The economic matters commonly discussed in negotiations may be divided into two subgroups: wages and benefits. Several aspects of the wage system may be discussed. First, unions seek to raise the average wage level within the establishment to improve the standard of living among bargaining unit members. Unions typically raise pay by 10 to15 percent over comparable nonunion jobs (the raise is somewhat less in the public sector and in highly competitive sectors). Unions also attempt to influence how pay is structured. Unions tend to prefer more egalitarian pay structures and equal pay for equal work. As a result, unionized firms tend toward flatter pay structures from top to bottom and smaller differentials between jobs.[24] Competition may emerge within the union between highly skilled craft workers who would prefer sharp, skilled-based differentials and less-skilled workers who would prefer more egalitarian structures. Where there are pay differences among persons doing the same work, unions typically favor **seniority** as the basis rather than more subjective, management-controlled criteria, such as performance appraisal ratings.

If unions exert a substantial impact on wages, their impact on benefits is even greater. Union members receive 25 to 30 percent more in benefits than comparable nonunion workers.[25] The range of benefits negotiated in union contracts may include supplemental unemployment benefits, severance pay, death and disability insurance, legal aid, wellness programs, employee assistance programs, paid holidays, paid vacations, and sick days. Often where employer-provided benefits cannot be negotiated, the union provides the benefit itself. The union advantage is especially evident in two benefits of particular importance to many workers: health insurance and pensions.

Traditionally, two major concerns have exerted a profound influence on wage and benefits bargaining between labor and management: inflation and productivity. Many contracts specify a cost-of-living allowance, which provides for pay raises and benefit increases during the life of a contract, based on changes in some index of inflation. The basic purpose is to preserve whatever real wage gains the union secured in the original settlement. Second, unions have generally expected that their members would share in whatever productivity gains they produced. Productivity gain-sharing bonus plans were popular, but once productivity gains became permanent, unions sought to incorporate them into the base pay. This combination of inflation and productivity as the basic factors governing wage movement dominated in the post–World War II era up to the mid-1970s.

Since then two additional factors have assumed the dominant role: ability to pay and comparability. Ability to pay refers to the financial condition of the firm and suggests that wages should be closely tied to profitability. Through the 1980s, many unions granted wage and benefit concessions as corporate profits were squeezed. Unions strive to get back the give-backs when better times return, but concessions remain a common theme when companies can demonstrate a bona fide financial crisis. Comparability represents the ghost of pattern bargaining. No longer able to maintain strict industry patterns, both unions and management base their arguments on maintaining comparability with similarly situated others. For unions, this means maintaining a standard of living comparable to workers who have traditionally shared socioeconomic status. For companies, this means not being put at a cost disadvantage relative to competitors. See the Flexibility in the Workplace box for further information on how and why employers seek more flexibility in employment terms and conditions.

Noneconomic Issues

A number of issues may arise in the noneconomic area, including work rules, job security, quality of work life, management rights, and union security. The concept of *work rules* covers a great deal of ground, from crew size and the types of work that can (and cannot) be performed by members of various crafts to rest periods and dress codes. *Job security* refers to the protections from discharge or layoff afforded to employees. Unions typically attempt to negotiate just-cause provisions, which limit an employer's right to discharge or discipline employees to situations where there is *just cause* for such an action (e.g., incompetence, excessive absenteeism, or insubordination). Other provisions to enhance job security may specify that layoffs will be based on seniority and regulate the conditions under which more senior employees whose jobs are ending may "bump" (or displace) less senior employees out of their positions. Finally, unions usually negotiate a grievance procedure through which employees can protest managerial decisions involving contract administration. The *quality of work life* (QWL) area includes a host of issues ranging from occupational safety and health, job training or retraining, and educational opportunities, to social and recreational facilities and child care.

In negotiating a contract, both parties are understandably mindful of their institutional position and needs. In this context, management typically seeks a **management rights clause,** which explicitly reserves to management certain decision-making prerogatives. For instance, this clause may give management alone the right to decide on the types of products to produce or services to deliver, to supervise employees, to control production processes, and to control the introduction of new technologies into the production process. Table 15.8 shows two sample management rights clauses. The top one reserves to management all rights not specifically shared with the union in other provisions of the contract. The second clause enumerates the rights kept by management.

Flexibility and Industrial Relations

After World War II, unions took a standard approach to dealing with management that has been called "job control unionism." In this approach, unions saw their role as protecting workers against subjective and unfair treatment by management, largely by enshrining detailed work rules in labor contracts. These rules govern means of promotion and layoff (e.g., based on the objective criterion of seniority), discharge, assignment of work (via rules about demarcations between different jobs and crafts), and pay (based on job category rather than more subjective indicators such as individual skill or performance). Changes to terms and conditions could only be made via collective bargaining, usually every three years. The result of this approach was a stable, predictable, procedurally just, but quite inflexible workplace.

As global competition intensified and demands for speed, efficiency, and innovation grew, the inflexible job control approach made it more and more difficult for firms to succeed. There was little opportunity to vary the number of employees or hours employees worked, or to redeploy employees to different functions when demand changed or declined. Further, pay rates were locked in for years in advance, regardless of the company's ability to pay. The only way to reduce the wage bill was to lay off or retrench low seniority employees.

Over the past two decades, there has been a movement toward more flexible work practices, as detailed in the table. A much wider variety of employment arrangements are now common, including part-time and short-term contracts. A portion of pay is increasingly at risk, based on firm or unit performance through profit-sharing or gain-sharing systems. Demarcations between jobs are being reduced as individuals work in multiskilled teams.

Unions are justifiably worried about the loss of hard-won rights and job security that may accompany some flexible practices. While cooperating with some of these more flexible practices (e.g., profit-sharing provisions in UAW contracts), they resist others and may request greater employee involvement and empowerment in day-to-day decisions in return for cooperation.

Recent research suggests that the simultaneous use of several properly targeted employment strategies can enhance firm performance. For instance, the combination of short-term contracting that allows flexibility to meet peak needs together with the cultivation of a stable core of multiskilled and adaptable permanent employees that can be redeployed as needs change is positively associated with firm performance.

Comparison of Job Control and Flexible Approaches

	Employment Flexibility	**Job Control Unionism**
Wages	Individually based on merit, skills, or productivity, or pay-at-risk based on firm or unit performance	Based on job and seniority
Adaptability	Fast: readily changes with demands	Slow: contractually specified terms and conditions
Employment and hours of work	Full-time, part-time, temporary, subcontracting, outsourcing	Full-time, typically long-term employment
Job Structure	Mobile employees, work teams, job rotation, cross-training, employee involvement in decision making	Narrowly defined job, demarcations between crafts, unions influence management decisions only via collective bargaining

Source: John W. Budd, *Labor Relations: Striking a Balance* (Boston, Mass.: McGraw-Hill, 2004); D. P. Lepak, R. Takeuchi, and S. A. Snell, "Employment Flexibility and Firm Performance: Examining the Interaction Effects of Employment Mode, Environmental Dynamism, and Technological Intensity," *Journal of Management,* Vol. 29, 2003, pp. 681–703; AFL-CIO Committee on the Evolution of Work, *The New American Workplace: A Labor Perspective* (Washington, D.C.: American Federation of Labor–Congress of Industrial Organizations, 1994); and Nick Wiles and Russell D. Lansbury, "Collective Bargaining and Flexibility: Australia," LEG/REG Working Paper (Geneve: International Labour Office, 1999). (Available at: http://www.ilo.org/public/english/dialogue/govlab/legrel/papers/australia/index.htm)

TABLE 15.8

Examples of Management Rights Clauses

The Company retains the exclusive right to manage the business and direct the work force. In the exercise of its rights, the Company shall obey the provisions of this Agreement.
The right to hire, promote, discipline or discharge for cause, transfer, and lay off due to lack of work remain the sole responsibility of the Company. The Company also has the exclusive right to control the products to be manufactured, the subcontracting of work, plant locations and plant closings, and the introduction of new technology.

Unions also have an institutional status to protect. As recognized exclusive representatives, they have the obligation to negotiate for *all* members of the bargaining unit, whether or not they have joined the union. Thus nonmembers who work in the bargaining unit will benefit from union representation as much as union members, even though they do not have to bear any costs, such as dues. To prevent employees in these units from "free-riding," unions negotiate **union security clauses** of various kinds. These arrangements ensure that nonunion members of bargaining units will assume at least part of the cost of union representation. The union shop and the agency shop are two common union security arrangements. The **union shop** requires nonmembers to join the union within a certain time period (such as sixty days after hire) as a condition of continued employment. The **agency shop** requires that nonmembers pay a representational fee (usually equal to the dues paid by members) as a condition of continued employment. Both union and agency shop provisions are legal under the amended National Labor Relations Act. However, the act allows states to pass "right-to-work" laws that disallow these union security arrangements. As of 2004, twenty-two states had enacted such laws. Table 15.9 lists the states that currently have right-to-work statutes in force.

TABLE 15.9

Right-to-Work States

Alabama	Nevada
Arizona	North Carolina
Arkansas	North Dakota
Florida	Oklahoma
Georgia	South Carolina
Idaho	South Dakota
Iowa	Tennessee
Kansas	Texas
Louisiana	Utah
Mississippi	Virginia
Nebraska	Wyoming

Source: Adapted from *Labor Management Relations in a Changing World,* First ed., p. 69 by Michael Ballot. Copyright © 1992 by John Wiley & Sons, New York, N.Y. Reprinted by permission of John Wiley & Sons, Inc.

WHEN COLLECTIVE BARGAINING BREAKS DOWN: IMPASSE

Level of Strike Activity

Thousands of contract negotiations take place each year. Historically, most contract negotiations have resulted in a settlement without a strike. The estimate is that strikes occur in less than 2 or 3 percent of negotiations.[26] Strikes are more likely to occur in larger bargaining units.[27] Table 15.10 summarizes strike activity in the United States from 1952 to 2002. Several points can be made from an inspection of these data. The total percentage of work time lost to strikes has never been particularly large. In terms of lost work time, the economic impact of the common

TABLE 15.10

Major Work Stoppages in the United States, 1952–2002

Year	Number of Work Stoppages	Workers Involved (in thousands)	% of Work Time Lost
1952	470	2,746	.38%
1954	265	1,075	.13
1956	287	1,370	.20
1958	332	1,587	.13
1960	222	896	.09
1962	211	793	.08
1964	246	1,183	.11
1966	321	1,300	.10
1968	392	1,855	.20
1970	381	2,468	.29
1972	250	975	.09
1974	424	1,796	.16
1976	231	1,519	.12
1978	219	1,006	.11
1980	187	795	.09
1982	96	656	.04
1984	62	376	.04
1986	69	533	.05
1988	40	118	.02
1990	44	185	.02
1992	35	364	.01
1994	45	322	.02
1996	37	273	.02
1998	34	387	.02
2000	39	394	.06
2002	19	46	.00

Source: U.S. Department of Labor, Bureau of Labor Statistics, *Monthly Labor Review*, various issues. A major work stoppage is one involving at least 1,000 workers and lasting for at least a full shift.

cold is far larger than that of strikes. Second, the level of strike activity declined sharply and persistently in the 1980s. Some of the decline is attributable to the decline in union strength, but a large part is associated with a particular management practice—**permanent replacement of strikers**—that became prominent after a watershed event: President Reagan's firing of air traffic controllers in 1981 (see the Ethical Perspective box).

Before 1980, management attempted to continue operations during strikes through a variety of means. Managers and supervisors could often maintain some level of production, or production could be shifted to nonstruck facilities or temporarily contracted out. Some employers could stockpile prior to an anticipated strike and sell out of inventory. In some industries, employers created mutual protection strike pacts with their competitors to insure each other against permanent economic loss caused by strikes. Finally, management could hire temporary replacements who would do the work as best they could during the strike but would be let go when the strike was over. It was probably legal to hire permanent replacements, but it was just not done.[28]

When the Professional Air Traffic Controllers Organization (PATCO) struck in 1981, the Federal Labor Relations Authority ordered the union decertified, and, much to PATCO's surprise, President Reagan fired all the striking controllers and permanently replaced them. Reagan's example emboldened private employers to confront strikes more aggressively. The use of permanent replacements has since become fairly common in U.S. labor relations,[29] and the threat of permanent replacements plays a more frequent role in negotiations. It is important to remember that because the air traffic controllers were federal employees, their strike was illegal. In contrast, most private-sector workers who have been permanently replaced were engaged in a perfectly legal strike.

Types of Strikes and Rights of Strikers

There are many different types of strikes, and the rights of strikers and employers depend on the type. Three types discussed here are the economic strike, the unfair labor practice strike, and the wildcat strike.

Economic Strikes If the parties have negotiated in good faith but fail to reach an agreement, any strike that follows is called an **economic strike.**[30] This is the most common type of strike, and it is fully protected by Section 7 of the NLRA. In theory, economic strikers cannot be fired for engaging in protected concerted activity, and discrimination against employees for supporting a strike is illegal. But economic strikers can still lose their jobs if they are permanently replaced. They retain a right to return to their jobs after the strike only so long as the jobs still exist and the employer has not hired permanent replacements.[31]

Unfair Labor Practice Strikes As mentioned earlier, employers and unions have a duty to negotiate in good faith. Good faith may be breached by such actions as refusing to respond to a party's request to bargain, refusing to send bargaining representatives with sufficient authority to the negotiations, continually shifting bargaining positions in a clearly obstructionist manner, delaying and hampering negotiations, and refusing to make any counterproposals at all. If a strike is provoked or prolonged by an employer's unfair labor practice, such as the failure to bargain in good faith, the NLRA forbids the permanent replacement of strikers.

ETHICAL PERSPECTIVE

Permanent Replacement of Strikers

There is no management action that evokes greater condemnation by unions today than permanent replacement of strikers. Section 7 of the NLRA grants workers a legal right to strike, "to engage in other concerted activities for the purpose of collective bargaining or other mutual aid or protection." Unions claim the permanent replacement doctrine nullifies that right. As Professor James Atleson points out:

> Section 8(a)(1) protects concerted activity such as strikes against "interferences," and Sections 7 and 13 make doubly clear the critical role of the strike in the congressional scheme. One can conceive of few interferences greater than permanent replacement for striking. The replaced striker has joined the ranks of the unemployed because of the exercise of the statutory right to strike and the situation may well serve to deter protected activity by other employees. . . . Moreover, when the employer favors a replacement over a striker seeking reinstatement at the end of a strike, the employer literally "discriminates" on the basis of the exercise of a protected activity, a seemingly clear violation of Section 8(a)(3).

Workers may be justifiably confused over the fine legal distinction between having been fired and having been merely permanently replaced. In either case they have lost their jobs for engaging in a perfectly legal and protected strike. Under a threat of permanent replacement, striking can become the equivalent of committing mass occupational suicide. Therefore, strikes have become far less common since employers have begun to resort to the permanent replacement strategy. Some employers have become so emboldened as to deploy the "strike-decertification scenario," where the employer deliberately provokes a strike and then recruits a replacement work force that will vote the union out. In this way the employer is able to get rid of not only the strikers but also the union itself.

Can meaningful collective bargaining occur if workers are effectively barred from striking? What pressure can the union bring to bear to force management to take its concerns seriously? Trade unionists believe the permanent replacement doctrine not only nullifies the right to strike but is also inherently destructive of the bargaining process. The International Labour Organization agrees and has found that the permanent replacement doctrine violates ILO Convention #98 on collective bargaining.

Although a key source of their power may have been nullified, unions are not taking the matter lying down. Changing the law to outlaw permanent replacements is one of organized labor's highest political priorities. But the unions are doing more than that. They are devising new strategies that enable them to put pressure on employers in ways that better protect workers' jobs. Instead of the large, protracted, all-or-nothing strike, they may engage in intermittent strikes, rolling strikes, or demonstration and publicity strikes. These activities may be coordinated with campaigns directed at the consuming public, the corporation's board of directors, or other community organizations. Or the union might strike on the job. Instead of vacating the workplace and making it easier for the employer to bring in replacements, workers remain on the job (and continue collecting their pay) but put pressure on employers through slowdowns, work-to-rule campaigns, mass grievance filings, and any number of other creative and innovative tactics. Some of these tactics are controversial, and many are not considered protected concerted activities under the National Labor Relations Act, but unions often find them the only way to effectively pressure the employer while protecting workers' jobs.

Source: James B. Atleson, *Values and Assumptions in American Labor Law* (Amherst: University of Massachusetts Press, 1983); Lance Compa, *Unfair Advantage: Workers' Freedom of Association in the United States Under International Human Rights Standards* (Washington, D.C.: Human Rights Watch, 2000); and R. L. Lippke, "Government Support of Labor Unions and the Ban of Striker Replacements," *Business & Society Review,* Vol. 109, Summer 2004, pp. 127–151.

Employers found guilty of causing an **unfair labor practice strike** have a legal obligation to reinstate the strikers, even if they have hired permanent replacements in the interim.[32]

Wildcat Strikes Despite binding commitments to the contrary, some strikes occur in direct violation of a collective-bargaining agreement, usually without the official approval of union leaders. Contracts almost always contain no-strike clauses, through which the union pledges not to strike during the life of the contract but instead to use the grievance procedure to resolve any disagreements about the way the contract is applied. Employees who strike in defiance of such a clause are said to be on **wildcat strikes.** Generally, wildcat strikes lose the protection of Section 7 of the NLRA. Injunctions can be issued against the union, with damages or fines levied directly against union funds. In addition, striking employees may be discharged and have no right to return to their jobs. In practice, however, few employers find it feasible to terminate and replace their entire work force because of a wildcat strike.

Preventing Strikes

Strikes and lockouts have little impact on the economy as a whole, but they can have a dramatic impact on the parties involved. Workers go without pay, and this affects them, their families, and the merchants and banks with whom they trade. Companies experience diminished revenues, which may adversely affect shareholders, other workers, and the company's trading partners. Even though strikes and lockouts may sometimes be necessary, considerable resources have been invested in developing **alternative dispute resolution (ADR)** procedures to reduce the likelihood of strikes.

Mediation is a widely used alternative dispute resolution procedure. It occurs when a neutral third party who has no binding authority assists union and management in reaching agreement. Mediators help by scheduling meetings, keeping the parties engaged in negotiations, carrying messages between the parties, and making suggestions. This task is often performed by federal mediators who are full-time employees of the Federal Mediation and Conciliation Service (http://www.fmcs.gov/). Although mediation is credited with reducing the frequency of strikes, it cannot guarantee that disputes will be resolved because the mediator lacks binding authority.

Interest arbitration is an alternative dispute resolution procedure that can guarantee resolution of disputes and can therefore eliminate strikes altogether. Interest arbitrators are third-party neutrals authorized to make binding decisions to resolve interest disputes. Interest arbitration is rarely used in the private sector, but it is widely used in the public sector, where it is designed to compensate for the fact that public employees have no right to strike. Figure 15.3 traces the development of interest arbitration techniques.

The first forms of interest arbitration adopted in state laws were typically nonbinding forms of arbitration, sometimes called advisory arbitration or fact finding. Nonbinding arbitration, like mediation, may have reduced the frequency of strikes, but it could not eliminate them altogether. To eliminate strikes, states found they had to enact binding arbitration laws. To assure that arbitrators stayed within reasonable bounds, the law required that arbitrators base their awards on factors such as ability to pay and comparability.

FIGURE 15.3
Interest Arbitration

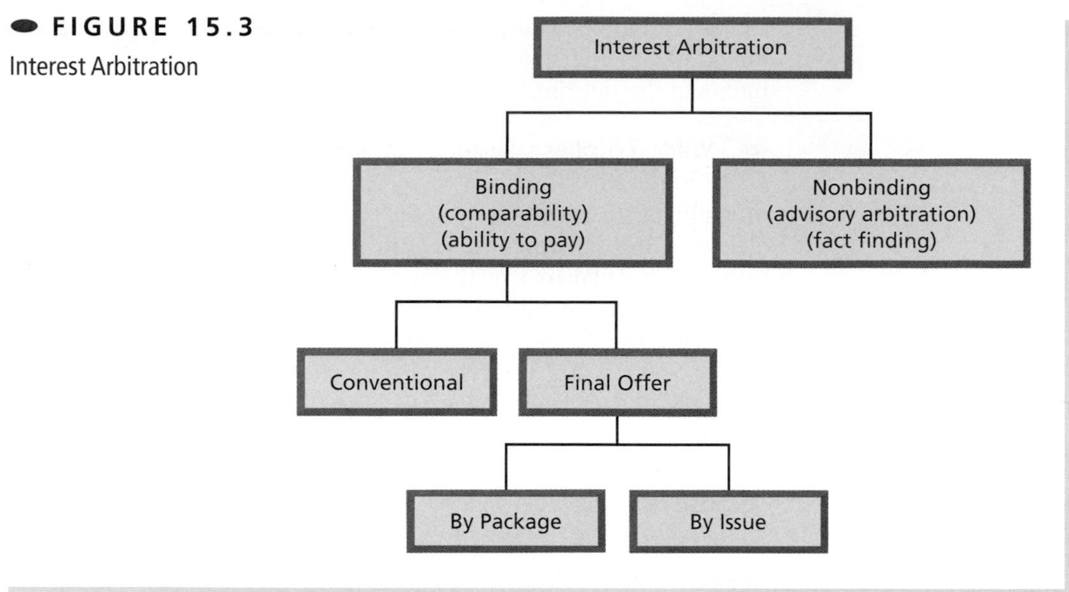

The first form of binding arbitration that was tried is called **conventional interest arbitration.** As with other forms of interest arbitration, the arbitrator is briefed on the positions of the parties, hears evidence from each side, and renders a decision. In conventional arbitration, the arbitrator is free to impose whatever settlement he or she deems reasonable. As a result, the tendency is to "split the difference" between the positions of the parties. Conventional interest arbitration solved the problem of strikes, but it had some unfortunate effects on the bargaining process. First, it produces a "chilling effect" on bargaining.[33] That is, parties introduce unrealistic initial offers and engage in surface bargaining until the arbitrator is called in to split the difference. It reduces the incentives to make meaningful concessions or engage in the give-and-take that is essential to real negotiations. Second, conventional interest arbitration produces a related "narcotic effect" whereby the parties become dependent on arbitration and unable to resolve conflicts on their own.[34]

To overcome some of the problems associated with conventional arbitration, more modern laws call for **final-offer arbitration.** In this approach, the arbitrator must choose between the final position of one party or the other. There is no opportunity to split the difference. This raises the risk to parties that fail to reach an agreement on their own. Final-offer arbitration forces labor and management to compete for the middle ground in negotiations. In other words, this approach encourages the parties to move toward reasonable final offers that will be attractive to the arbitrator; as a result, they may reach a settlement without resorting to arbitration at all.[35] Final-offer arbitration takes two forms. The first is final offer by issue, in which the arbitrator accepts one or the other final offer on each item remaining to be resolved. This form remains popular in many state laws. The second is final offer by package, in which the arbitrator accepts the final position of one party or the other on all issues submitted to arbitration. This is the state-of-the-art in arbitration techniques. It eliminates strikes but does so in a way that maximizes the incentives on the parties to resolve their own disputes in a mutually satisfactory way. Ironically, where final offer by package arbitration is required by law, it is seldom used.

National Emergency Dispute Procedures

The Taft-Hartley Act provides a set of procedures to help resolve strikes that constitute a national emergency because they threaten the health or safety of the general public. The act allows the president to seek an injunction to prohibit the strike for eighty days. During this so-called **cooling-off period,** the parties continue to bargain with the aid of the Federal Mediation and Conciliation Service. Meanwhile, fact finding and the force of public opinion are brought to bear on the parties. If no settlement is reached within the cooling-off period, the union is free to resume the strike. Since the late 1940s, these procedures have been invoked only forty times, most frequently in the coal mining, atomic energy, maritime, and longshoring industries.[36]

WHEN THE MEANING OF THE CONTRACT IS IN DISPUTE: THE GRIEVANCE PROCEDURE

Administering the Contract

Once a collective-bargaining agreement is in place, it is a legally binding contract. In the normal course of events, there may be very little conflict in the day-to-day administration of the agreement. In fact, most union contracts are printed as shirt-pocket-sized booklets so that minor disputes over "what the contract says" can be resolved on the spot. However, over time, difficult disputes over the meaning of the contract are bound to arise. These are referred to as **rights disputes** (as distinct from interest disputes) because they involve legally enforceable rights under the contract. Although both parties have agreed to live by the provisions of the contract, there is always room for disagreement about how the agreement should be interpreted and applied in specific cases. An employee who believes that his or her rights under the contract have been violated may file a **grievance.** Virtually all contracts provide a grievance procedure for resolving disagreements about contract administration.[37] The overwhelming majority of grievance procedures culminate in arbitration, and they are particularly important in maintaining workplace justice.

Steps in the Grievance Procedure

A typical grievance procedure clause is shown in Table 15.11. The procedure starts when an employee believes that he or she has been treated unfairly with respect to some right spelled out in the contract. For instance, the contract may specify that the "most senior qualified employee" be chosen for promotion. If someone else is promoted, the most senior employee may then file a grievance claiming that he or she was qualified and should have been selected. In the first step of a typical grievance procedure, the employee or his or her shop steward presents the complaint, usually orally, to the grievant's immediate superior. The superior must respond within a fixed time period, either agreeing that the employee has a valid point and suggesting a remedy or denying that the grievance has merit. If the answer received does not satisfy the grievant, the union puts the grievance in writing and appeals to the next level of management—perhaps to the foreman or a representative of the human resource management department. If the decision received at this level is not satisfactory, the grievance may be appealed yet again, to upper management. At this point, a representative from the national union may be present to help represent the grievant.

Grievance Arbitration

Most grievances are settled through the early steps, but when no mutually acceptable resolution is reached between the parties themselves, 96 percent of contracts specify binding **grievance arbitration** as the final step.[38] Nearly all contracts limit the arbitrator to interpreting the existing contract. The arbitrator is not allowed to change or amend the contract in any way but merely to clarify and apply its provi-

TABLE 15.11

A Grievance Procedure Clause

Step 1 The employee and the department steward, if the employee desires, shall take the matter up with his [or her] foreman. If no settlement is reached in Step 1 within two working days, the grievance shall be reduced to writing on the form provided for that purpose.

Step 2 The written grievance shall be presented to the foreman or the general foreman and a copy sent to the personnel office. Within two working days after receipt of the grievance, the general foreman shall hold a meeting, unless mutually agreed otherwise, with the foreman, the employee, the departmental steward, and the chief steward.

Step 3 If no settlement is reached in Step 2, the written grievance shall be presented to the departmental superintendent, who shall hold a meeting within five working days of the original receipt of the grievance in Step 2 unless mutually agreed otherwise. Those in attendance shall normally be the departmental superintendent, the general foreman, the foreman, the employee, the chief steward, departmental steward, a member of the personnel department, the president of the UNION or his representative, and the divisional committeeman.

Step 4 If no settlement is reached in Step 3, the UNION COMMITTEE and an international representative of the UNION shall meet with the MANAGEMENT COMMITTEE for the purpose of settling the matter.

Step 5 If no settlement is reached in Step 4, the matter shall be referred to an arbitrator. A representative of the UNION shall meet within five working days with a representative of the COMPANY for the purpose of selecting an arbitrator. If an arbitrator cannot be agreed upon within five working days after Step 4, a request for a list of arbitrators shall be sent to the Federal Mediation and Conciliation Service. Upon obtaining the list, an arbitrator shall be selected within five working days. Prior to arbitration, a representative of the UNION shall meet with a representative of the COMPANY to reduce to writing wherever possible the actual issue to be arbitrated. The decision of the arbitrator shall be final and binding on all parties. The salary, if any, of the arbitrator and any necessary expense incident to the arbitration shall be paid jointly by the COMPANY and the UNION.

Source: From *Labor Relations: Development, Structure, and Process*, 6th ed., p. 430 by John A. Fossum. Copyright © 1995 by Richard D. Irwin. Reproduced with permission of The McGraw-Hill Companies.

sions. Even though most grievances are resolved without resorting to arbitration, arbitration has a strong influence on how labor and management resolve their grievances. If the parties understand how an arbitrator is likely to rule on a given case, they are likely to adjust their position in lower steps of the grievance procedure accordingly. In cases involving employee discipline and discharge, arbitrators generally place the burden on management to prove just cause—that is, to prove the employee deserves discipline. In cases involving contract interpretation, arbitrators generally place the burden of proof on the union to show that management's interpretation violates the contract.

THE ROLE OF LABOR RELATIONS IN HUMAN RESOURCE MANAGEMENT

Clearly, there is a great deal to know about labor law and labor relations. Although unions today have a smaller role in many organizations, every HR manager needs to be conversant with labor law and highly attuned to preventing employee discontent that could grow into active conflict with a union. Unionized firms need someone with expertise in this area to guide their practices. In most organizations, the HR function provides labor relations expertise. Larger establishments will have industrial or labor relations specialists within the HR department, whereas in smaller firms the HR generalist may do most of the work.

When a union is present, HR and labor relations (LR) experts are responsible for educating management and supervisors on the details of the contract and how to comply with it. They also liaise with the union if changes in work procedures are envisioned, such as re-engineering or implementing joint employee–management committees. Prior to contract negotiations, HR/LR experts will have a large role in helping to develop the bargaining position of the company. This may involve holding meetings with supervisors to discover problems under the present contract and suggestions for modifying work rules. It will also include research and meetings with top management to develop a position on pay and other expensive benefits. HR/LR experts are also often involved in face-to-face negotiations and in advising management on proposed settlements.

In firms without unions, the HR function of managing the relationship between managers and workers is often called **employee relations.** Firms in which only some of the employees are unionized may have both employee relations and labor relations functions for dealing with the two types of employees. When operating without a union, HR experts and all other managers need to be aware of the law so that they do not accidentally commit an unfair labor practice such as threatening or firing an employee who starts to discuss the possibility of unionizing. HR experts also need to ensure that wages are fairly administered and competitive with other employers. In all areas, employer practices should be scrupulously fair and consistent and in line with written policies. Employees should have "voice mechanisms" to bring their complaints forward. These mechanisms should include a formal grievance procedure that can be modeled after the traditional union grievance procedure, with or without binding arbitration as the final step. Alternatively, a nonunion grievance procedure can use panels of peers (coworkers) to make recommendations to management on disposition of grievances, or it can use an HR ombudsman to respond to employee concerns. These voice mechanisms can be supplemented by a management open-door policy, regular employee question-and-answer sessions with management, employee surveys, and the like.

It has been said that organizations "get the union they deserve." This means that good, fair, conscientious human resource management can either prevent employees from feeling the need for a union to protect them or result in smooth and cooperative relations with an existing union because there are few issues on which employees feel mistreated. Employment practices seen as arbitrary, unfair, or exploitative are likely to lead to the formation of a more militant union.

Summary of Key Points

Unions have had a long and uneven history in the United States. Craft unions were formed first, and later workers began to organize by industry. Union membership as a percentage of the work force peaked in the late 1940s and has been declining since the late 1950s, despite a rise in unionization among public-sector employees.

In 1935 the Wagner Act opened the door to widespread unionization by establishing election procedures for unions to become certified bargaining agents for groups of employees, requiring management to bargain in good faith with a properly certified representative of its employees, and preventing discrimination against employees regarding their right to unionize. In 1947 the Taft-Hartley Act placed some limits on union behavior, shifting the balance of power back toward management. In the 1960s and 1970s, federal, state, and local governments began to extend limited collective bargaining rights to public-sector employees.

Once a union has been certified as representing a group of employees, it can begin negotiations with management in an attempt to secure a contract. Bargaining can be conducted in several different structural arrangements. Mandatory bargaining issues include wages, hours, and conditions of employment. Permissive items may be discussed, but neither party may insist on them to the point of impasse, and illegal items may not be bargained over. If an impasse is reached, private-sector employees may choose to strike. Economic strikers have some right to return to their jobs after a strike, whereas unfair labor practice strikers have unconditional rights, and wildcat or illegal strikers have no rights to return to their jobs. As an alternative to strikes, mediation or various forms of arbitration may be used. To settle disagreements over contract administration during the life of a contract, the grievance system is used.

The Manager's Vocabulary

AFL-CIO
agency shop
alternative dispute resolution (ADR)
American Federation of Labor (AFL)
authorization card
bargaining structure
bargaining unit
certification
codetermination
collective bargaining
community of interests
Congress of Industrial Organizations (CIO)
conventional interest arbitration
cooling-off period
craft unions
decertification election
distributive bargaining
economic issues
economic strike
employee relations
exclusive representative
Federal Labor Relations Authority (FLRA)
Federal Mediation and Conciliation Service
final-offer arbitration
global division of labor
good faith
grievance
grievance arbitration
illegal subjects of bargaining
industrial union
integrative bargaining
interest arbitration
Labor-Management Relations Act
labor relations process
management rights clause

mandatory subjects of bargaining
mediation
multi-employer bargaining
National Labor Relations Act
National Labor Relations Board (NLRB)
noneconomic issues
organizing committee
pattern bargaining
permanent replacement of strikers
permissive subjects of bargaining
questions concerning representation
Railway Labor Act of 1926
rights dispute
scope of bargaining
seniority
Taft-Hartley Act of 1947
unfair labor practices
unfair labor practice strike
union security clauses
union shop
voluntary recognition
Wagner Act of 1935
wildcat strike
works councils

Questions for Discussion

1. Why study unions and collective bargaining?
2. Compare and contrast craft unions and industrial unions.
3. How do multinational companies adapt to the different labor conditions they encounter in other parts of the world?
4. What are the major provisions of the Wagner Act? The Taft-Hartley Act?
5. What factors explain the high unionization rate among public-sector workers as compared with private-sector workers? What problems might be associated with a highly unionized public sector?
6. What factors explain the decline in unionization for the last half-century? Have unions outlived their usefulness to society? Will they die out? Should they?
7. What factors do individuals consider in choosing whether or not to support a union? What arguments does management commonly use in trying to persuade employees not to support a union?
8. Describe the certification process by which a union can become recognized as the sole bargaining agent for a group of employees. Does the process seem overly cumbersome to you? What can management do to discourage union activity?
9. What is a bargaining unit? Does the collective-bargaining contract apply to employees in the bargaining unit who have chosen not to join the union?
10. Scholars and practitioners continue to debate whether the Taft-Hartley Act restored a balance of power between labor and management that had been distorted by the Wagner Act, or whether it tilted the balance of power back in management's favor. Examine the list of union unfair labor practices created by Taft-Hartley and compare them to the employer unfair labor practices from the Wagner Act (Table 15.3). Which ones seem to reflect a balancing of power? Which ones seem designed to tilt the balance of power toward management?
11. How can procedural issues during negotiations be used strategically by the parties?
12. What is meant by the term "bargaining structure"? What might be the advantages and disadvantages to management of joining a multi-employer association for the purpose of negotiating a master agreement?
13. Compare and contrast distributive and integrative bargaining. Which of the two is preferred? Even though preferred, why might it be difficult to achieve?
14. What is meant by the phrase "bargaining in good faith"?
15. Suppose the union wants a cost-of-living adjustment in the pensions being paid to current retirees. May the union press this issue to the point of impasse and then strike because of it? Why or why not?
16. Distinguish between three major classes of strikes. Describe what rights (if any) strikers have to return to their jobs after each type of strike.
17. What methods may be used to resolve a bargaining impasse short of a strike?
18. Explain how the grievance procedure is used to enforce a contract.

Case 15.1
The Southern California Supermarket Strike

When Steven A. Burd, Safeway's tough CEO, called a meeting of industry executives and union leaders more than a year before the labor agreement covering Southern California was to expire, leaders of the United Food and Commercial Workers Union (UFCW) knew it was not a good sign. Burd pointed to the encroachment of major discount retailers such as Wal-Mart into the industry's market share. Wal-Mart was already the nation's largest retail grocer and could sell a typical shopping cart of groceries for 17 to 39 percent less than a traditional union supermarket. A major factor was labor cost. If the traditional supermarkets were to remain competitive over the next ten to fifteen years, the UFCW would have to accept major wage and benefit concessions on behalf of its members.

Leadership of the UFCW was not convinced. True, Wal-Mart had announced plans to build forty SuperCenters in Southern California, but none were in operation yet. Instead, the union blamed Safeway's woes on Burd's own mismanagement. At Safeway, which had 293 stores in Southern California and 1,702 stores nationwide, same-store sales were down 2.2 percent and the company had lost $828 million net income in 2002, figures that were far worse than competitors Kroger or Albertsons. The union pointed to botched acquisitions—Burd's specialty—in other parts of the country where Safeway cut customer service, cut staffing levels, and replaced popular regional brands with its own private label goods. They knew Burd was not bluffing—he had just closed three stores in Ontario rather than reach agreement with striking workers—but rather than confront the issue of concessions, the UFCW enacted a $2 per week tax on its members to build a strike fund.

Negotiations were already complicated enough, even without the specter of Wal-Mart hovering over the bargaining table. Seven UFCW local unions, representing 59,000 workers, were negotiating with three major corporations—Safeway, Kroger, and Albertsons. An additional 11,000 workers at Gelsons and Stater Bros. would be covered under any agreement that was reached. Few insiders were surprised, then, when contract negotiations failed to produce a new agreement. Ninety-seven percent of UFCW members voted to support a strike. The union's strike target was Safeway, not only because Safeway's Burd was the mastermind of the companies' bargaining demands, but also because the union was particularly galled that Burd had cashed out 150,000 of his stock option shares in the weeks leading up to the strike, netting himself a tidy $2.7 million. On October 11, 2003, the UFCW struck Safeway. On October 12, Kroger and Albertsons locked their workers out. This was the first indication of a remarkable level of solidarity among the three corporate competitors; as a Kroger spokesperson noted, "A strike against one will be considered a strike against all."

The strike itself was not a surprise, but few anticipated that it would drag on for 141 long days, making it the longest strike in Southern California since World War II. Early on, the union seemed to gain the upper hand. While management and newly hired replacement workers attempted to run the 859 affected stores, union picket lines cut business by 75 percent. Many strikers had saved up for the strike, many others took a second job during the strike, and all who served on the picket lines received $200 in weekly strike benefits. Public support for the strike was strong. After twenty days, the UFCW lifted its pickets from Kroger. The union stated it was to reward consumers for honoring their picket lines, but it was also a tactical move intended to divide the companies. Unlike Safeway's Burd, the UFCW felt it could deal with Kroger CEO David Dillon who had come up in the industry and had maintained better relations with the UFCW. But the move backfired when it was revealed that the companies had entered into a mutual aid pact before the strike. Kroger would reap a windfall when the pickets were lifted. The pact required Kroger to share that windfall with Safeway and Albertsons. At the conclusion of the strike, Kroger paid Safeway and Albertsons $147 million under the mutual aid pact. The pact not only undermined the effectiveness of the UFCW's picket-line strategy, it also served as a forceful indicator of the solidarity among the companies. It was now clear that all three were in for the long haul.

As the strike wore on into the holiday season, pressure began to mount on the union. The companies made a revised proposal and were able to score public relations points by portraying the strike as a tussle over $5 per week—the amount they said they were asking workers to pay for their health benefits. Meanwhile, current health care benefits for striking workers were scheduled to run out at the end of the year, and the union strike fund, which was being depleted at the rate of $10 million per week, would not last long into 2004. The UFCW offered a counterproposal it said would save the companies $350 million per year in health care costs, but the proposal was quickly rejected.

Finally, a series of secret meetings held in Denver during the second week of January 2004 set the stage for final settlement talks. On February 11, 2004, negotiators returned to the bargaining table with a resolve to get the deal done. Marathon bargaining sessions went on for sixteen straight days, often lasting into the wee hours of the morning. On February 26 the settlement was announced. When the proposed contract was presented to UFCW members for ratification, many expressed their dissatisfaction with the deal. Nevertheless, 86 percent voted to accept it and end the strike.

So, what was this strike about? Two issues really—wages and health care benefits. First, the wage issue. Under their previous contract, a UFCW bagger could top out at $7.40 per hour, a cashier could top out at $17.90 per hour, and a meat-cutter could top out at $18.19 per hour. Many employees work full time, but most are part-timers. Average hourly pay was between $12 and $13 per hour with an average workweek of 32 hours. Thus the companies incurred hourly wage rates that were 50 percent higher than the $8 per hour average for a Wal-Mart clerk. They wanted concessions. But UFCW members understandably did not want to take a pay cut. The solution was a two-tiered wage structure. Current employees would be in the first tier, new hires in the second. Current employees did not take a pay cut, but they also did not receive a pay increase. Instead of an increase, current workers got a lump-sum bonus, averaging $500 per employee, in each of the first two years of the contract. The bonus will cost the three companies $29.5 million per year, but the cost of their basic wage structure remains fixed. The companies will save money by hiring in new workers at lower rates than the current employees. For example, a current cashier can top out at $17.90 per hour after two years, but a newly hired cashier would top out at $15.10 per hour, and it would take six years to get up to that rate. This represents a savings of 16 percent in hourly wage costs. Turnover is relatively high in grocery stores, so company savings would compound as newly hired workers began to constitute larger and larger proportions of the total work force. Thus current workers were able to retain their existing wage rates, but the companies were able to capture the savings they needed by paying new hires less.

The health care issue is a bit more complex. Under the previous contract, all workers were enrolled in the health insurance plan at no expense to the employee. They paid nothing for their premiums, and there were no co-pays. The companies were now paying $4.30 into the health plan for every hour worked. They claimed their costs had escalated 50 percent over the last four years and that they could no longer afford such a generous plan, especially in competition with Wal-Mart where most employees do not even participate in the modest plan that is offered. The UFCW was willing to accept modest employee contributions toward premiums and modest co-pays but claimed that the companies' proposals would shift a billion dollars in yearly health care costs onto the workers and their families. Perhaps more importantly, the UFCW and the companies had very different ideas about how the health plan should be structured. The union sought a "maintenance of benefits" plan whereas the companies wanted a "capped contribution" plan. Under a maintenance of benefits plan, the union and the companies would negotiate coverage levels along with reasonable employee premiums and co-pays, and the companies would pay the rest. If costs escalated in the future, it would be the companies' responsibility to pay whatever it takes to maintain the level of benefits bargained for. A capped contribution plan would put a ceiling on company payments for health benefits. A board of trustees comprised of company and union officials would be established to administer the benefits. If costs escalated in the future, the trustees could take one of two actions: reduce benefit levels or charge employees more for participation.

The final settlement of the health insurance issue again called for a two-tiered plan. For current employees, the deal blends elements of maintenance of benefits and capped contributions. For the first two years of the contract, benefit levels remain unchanged, and employees are not required to contribute to premiums or co-pays. In the third year of the contract, however, if the companies' contribution exceeds $4.60 per hour, employees will be required to contribute premiums of $5 per week, $15 for family coverage, with modest co-pays, but benefit levels will remain intact. Second-tier new hires will be placed under a separate "capped contribution" health care plan with the company contribution capped at a stark $1.35 per hour—a savings of $2.95 per hour over the previous plan.

1. Safeway, Kroger, and Albertsons lost more than $1.5 billion in sales and at least a half billion in profits due to the strike. Was it worth it? The settlement reached at the end of February was very close to the proposals that had been on the table since early December. Why did it take so long?
2. On the surface, a two-tiered wage and benefit plan might seem like a win-win. Workers keep their pay and benefits, but management gets the savings it needs. Are there downsides to a two-tiered plan? Two-tiered plans were popular for a few years in the 1980s, but most of the plans that were adopted then were abandoned a few years later. Why? If workers are adamant about keeping their pay and benefits and management is adamant about cutting pay and benefits, what alternatives are there to two-tiered plans?
3. Some veteran workers have expressed concern that the two-tiered plan paints a target on their back. That is, management will have an incentive to buy them out or move them out so they can be replaced by cheaper second-tier workers. Do you think their concerns are warranted?
4. Peter Hurtgen, Director of the Federal Mediation and Conciliation Service, said this was the most difficult settlement he had ever mediated. He also points out that health care is the single most vexing issue on today's bargaining agenda throughout the United States, even more than wages or job security. He also suggests that in the health care issue labor and management are being asked to address a problem they did not create and that they cannot possibly solve. Do you agree? What solutions do you recommend?
5. Evaluate the competitive threat posed by Wal-Mart to both the supermarket chains and to the wages and benefits of UFCW members? How serious is the threat? What, if anything, should the supermarkets do about it? The unions?
6. California Attorney General Bill Lockyer sued the supermarkets for violation of state and federal antitrust laws over their mutual-aid strike pact. Do you see this kind of mutual aid pact as a conspiracy in restraint of trade? Should such pacts be legal? Or was Lockyer simply taking the union's side in the strike?

Source: Compiled from the *Los Angeles Times*, various issues from September 29, 2003, through June 23, 2004.

Case 15.2
The Arbitration Process

Mike is a forklift operator at a large industrial warehouse. During a particularly busy shift, Mike tipped over a very large load of television sets. Although no one was injured in the accident, about $10,000 worth of merchandise was damaged. Mike's supervisor (who had said on several occasions that Mike was a poor worker) insisted that Mike be given drug and alcohol tests. Mike tested positive for marijuana and was dismissed. He immediately filed a grievance, claiming that he had smoked marijuana the previous weekend, that he was not incapacitated at the time of the accident, and that he had never been high at work. The company refused to reverse its decision, and the matter will now be brought before an arbitrator.

Company policy regarding drug testing reads as follows: "Employees may be tested at the discretion of the supervisor following any accident in which another employee is injured or where there is significant damage to the employer's property." No employee had ever been tested in a property-damage accident before, although accidents involving many thousands of dollars of merchandise had occurred. Regarding the outcome of drug and alcohol testing, the company manual states, "Employees found to be incapacitated shall be summarily dismissed."

1. What strategy would you follow if you were preparing Mike's grievance? What kind of information would you want the arbitrator to be aware of?
2. Given what you have read here, how would you rule in this case if you were arbitrating it? What factors would lead you to your conclusion?
3. Do you think that the language of the company policy is properly worded? Would you have decided the case differently if Mike had passed a pre-employment urinalysis and then tested positive after the accident?

Case 15.3
Firing the Organizer

Dunlop Associates is a major third-party administrator in both workers' compensation and employee health insurance, handling claims processing for a number of large, self-insured employers and even a few insurance companies. It was now facing an unusual problem—a union organizing campaign in its major claims-processing center. Dunlop had never encountered a union organizing drive before and was caught by surprise. To management's chagrin, it looked as though the union might have a good chance of success. None of Dunlop's competitors in the industry were unionized, and Dunlop did not relish the idea of becoming the first.

Kay Harrison was leading the charge for the union in the claims-processing center. In addition to distributing union information pamphlets and talking up the union to her coworkers, she began to wear "Say Union Yes" T-shirts, hats, and buttons regularly to work. Supervisors began to notice that Kay was frequently away from her work area and seemed to be involved in animated conversations with other workers. Upon being questioned by the supervisors, some of the employees who had been seen talking with Kay at their workstations verified that she was trying to "sell them" on the union. After three weeks of this activity, Kay was called into her supervisor's office and advised that her behavior was disruptive and that she must refrain from any activity that interfered with other employees' work. She was also told that her own work had been observed to be below the acceptable standard for the past three weeks, and she was warned that she would be dismissed if it did not return to standard and remain there for at least three consecutive weeks.

Kay continued to wear the union paraphernalia, although she confined her conversations with other workers to break rooms and the cafeteria. Her work barely met the acceptable standard the following week. When it dropped below standard the week after that, Kay's employment was terminated. Immediately following the termination, Kay filed a complaint with the National Labor Relations Board, claiming that her dismissal was an unfair labor practice under Section 8 of the NLRA. At the board hearing on the matter, Dunlop insisted that it had terminated Kay because of her failure to meet performance standards.

1. How do you think this case should be resolved? Was Kay protected under the NLRA? What factors will the NLRB weigh in deciding the case?
2. What effect do you think Kay's dismissal will have on the union organizing attempt?
3. If the NLRB ordered that Kay be reinstated to her job, what effect do you think that would have on the union organizing effort?
4. Why did Dunlop fire Kay, really? Was it her performance? Or was it her union activities? Would they have fired her for her performance if she had not also been engaged in pro-union activities?

Exercise 15.1
Unions on the Web

Visit the AFL-CIO site: http://www.aflcio.org/

1. What is the general "feel" of the site? How does organized labor seem to view itself? Is this different from your personal view of unions and their role in society?
2. What seem to be the hot issues for organized labor today?
3. Suppose you are the HR manager of a small city. You have heard that the American Federation of State, County, and Municipal Workers is likely to start an organizing drive among city employees. Find as much information about this union as you can. What are their current interests? What kinds of issues do you think they are likely to raise in an organizing campaign? How can you counter these arguments?

Notes and References

1. John R. Commons et al., *History of Labour in the United States,* 2 Vols. (New York: Macmillan, 1918).
2. Foster Rhea Dulles and Melvyn Dubofsky, *Labor in America: A History of the International Workers of the World* (Arlington Heights, Ill.: Harlan Davidson, 1984), chap. 9.
3. Ibid., chap. 16.
4. Ibid., chap. 19.
5. Hugh D. Hindman and David B. Patton, "Unionism in State and Local Governments: Ohio and Illinois, 1982–1987," *Industrial Relations,* Vol. 33, 1994, pp. 106–120; and "Union Members by Selected Characteristics: 1999," *Statistical Abstract of the United States, 2000,* U.S. Census Bureau, table 713. (Available at: www.census.gov/prod.www/statistical-abstract-us.html)
6. John W. Budd, *Employment with a Human Face: Balancing Efficiency, Equity, and Voice.* (Ithaca, N.Y.: Cornell University Press, 2004); Alexander J. S. Colvin, "Institutional Pressures, Human Resource Strategies, and the Rise of Nonunion Dispute Resolution Procedures," *Industrial and Labor Relations Review* 56, April 2003, pp. 375–392.
7. B. V. H. Schneider, "Public-Sector Labor Legislation—An Evolutionary Analysis," in *Public-Sector Bargaining,* 2nd ed., eds. Benjamin Aaron, Joyce M. Najita, and James L. Stern (Washington, D.C.: Bureau of National Affairs, 1988), chap. 6; and John Lund and Cheryl L. Maranto, "Public Sector Labor Law: An Update," in *Public Sector Employment in a Time of Transition,* eds. Dale Belman, Morley Gunderson, and Douglas Hyatt (Madison, Wis.: Industrial Relations Research Association, 1996), chap. 1.
8. Joel Rogers and Wolfgang Streeck (eds.), *Works Councils, Consultation, Representation, and Cooperation in Industrial Relations* (Chicago: University of Chicago Press, 1995).
9. Kirsten S. Wever, *Negotiating Competitiveness: Employment Relations and Organizational Innovation in Germany and the United States* (Boston: Harvard Business School Press, 1995).
10. Drusilla K. Brown, "Labor Standards: Where Do They Belong on the International Trade Agenda?" *Journal of Economic Perspectives,* 15, Summer 2001, pp. 89–112; and Dani Rodrik, *Has Globalization Gone Too Far?* (Washington, D.C.: Institute for International Economics, 1997).
11. Lance A. Compa and Stephen F. Diamond (eds.), *Human Rights, Labor Rights, and International Trade* (Philadelphia: University of Pennsylvania Press, 1996); and Bob Hepple, "A Race to the Top? International Investment Guidelines and Corporate Codes of Conduct," *Comparative Labor Law and Policy Journal,* 20, Spring 1999, pp. 347–363.
12. Karl Marx and Friedrich Engels, *Manifesto of the Communist Party* (Moscow: Foreign Languages Publishing House, 1948).
13. Frank Tannenbaum, *A Philosophy of Labor* (New York: Knopf, 1951).
14. Sidney Webb and Beatrice Webb, *Industrial Democracy* (London: Longmans, 1897); and Selig Perlman, *A Theory of the Labor Movement* (New York: Macmillan, 1928).

15. Hoyt N. Wheeler, *Industrial Conflict: An Integrative Theory* (Columbia: University of South Carolina Press, 1985).
16. Arthur A. Sloane and Fred Witney, *Labor Relations,* 8th ed. (Englewood Cliffs, N.J.: Prentice-Hall, 1993), pp. 190–193.
17. Richard B. Freeman and Joel Rogers, *What Workers Want* (Ithaca, N.Y.: ILR Press, 1999).
18. "Sixty-Eighth Annual Report of the National Labor Relations Board for the Fiscal Year Ended September 30, 2003" (Washington, D.C.: U.S. Government Printing Office, 2004).
19. Kate Bronfenbrenner, *Uneasy Terrain: The Impact of Capital Mobility on Workers, Wages, and Union Organizing.* Report commissioned by the U.S. Trade Deficit Review Commission, 2000.
20. Thomas A. Kochan and Harry C. Katz, *Collective Bargaining and Industrial Relations,* 2nd ed. (Chicago: Irwin, 1988), pp. 136–140.
21. Ibid, chap. 1.
22. Ibid., chap. 4.
23. Ibid, chap. 5. See also Edward Cohen-Rosenthal and Cynthia E. Burton, *Mutual Gains: A Guide to Union-Management Cooperation* (New York: Praeger, 1987).
24. Richard B. Freeman and Medoff, *What Do Unions Do?* (New York: Basic Books, 1984), chaps. 3, 5.
25. Ibid, chap. 4.
26. Kochan and Katz, *Collective Bargaining and Industrial Relations,* chap. 8.
27. Cynthia L. Gramm, "The Determinants of Strike Incidence and Severity," *Industrial and Labor Relations Review,* April 1986, pp. 361–376.
28. *NLRB v. MacKay Radio & Telegraph Co.,* 304 U.S. 333 (1938).
29. *Replacement Workers: Evidence from the Popular and Labor Press, 1989 and 1990* (Washington, D.C.: Bureau of National Affairs, 1991).
30. Benjamin J. Taylor and Fred Witney, *Labor Relations Law,* 7th ed. (Englewood Cliffs, N.J.: Prentice-Hall, 1987).
31. *Primer of Labor Relations,* 25th ed. (Washington, D.C.: Bureau of National Affairs, 1994), chap. 7.
32. Taylor and Witney, *Labor Relations Law.*
33. Carl M. Stevens, "Is Compulsory Arbitration Compatible with Bargaining?" *Industrial Relations,* Vol. 5, 1966, pp. 38–50.
34. Hoyt N. Wheeler, "Compulsory Arbitration: A Narcotic Effect?" *Industrial Relations,* Vol. 14, 1975, pp. 117–120.
35. Peter Feuille, *Final Offer Arbitration* (Chicago: International Personnel Management Association, 1975), pp. 35–48.
36. Taylor and Witney, *Labor Relations Law.*
37. Bureau of National Affairs, *Collective Bargaining Negotiations and Contracts,* (Washington, D.C.: 1989) pp. 51.5–51.8.
38. Ibid., p. 51.6.

CHAPTER 16

Employment Transitions

- Career Paths and Career Planning
- Retirement
- Voluntary Turnover
- Involuntary Turnover
- Employment-at-Will
- Discipline Systems and Termination for Cause
- Retrenchment and Layoff

HR Challenge

It is estimated that 3 to 5 percent of the U.S. labor force now works in call centers. Employee turnover in call centers has always been high. In 2001 turnover rates varied from 22 percent in the Central states to 31 percent in the Northeast region, with some individual call centers experiencing turnover as high as 150 percent. To help attract and keep employees, wages have risen quickly, with average agent salaries increasing from $14,826 in 1996 to $25,575 in 2001.[1] It is hard for companies to deliver high-quality customer service with such high turnover of front-line staff, and even harder to service growth. Replacing agents who leave in addition to hiring for growth is a constant battle fought by most call-center managers.

Some call-center positions require advanced technical expertise and strong troubleshooting ability, such as providing telephone assistance from a computer help desk, but most feature much simpler transaction-processing, order-taking, sales, or information-giving activities. Jobs in call centers are often seen as just jobs, not as stepping stones to a career, and very few people aspire to become call-center agents. Call centers are sometimes less than ideal working environments; in fact, they have been likened to sweatshops and called "the factories of the future." Some work is highly routinized, with agents following precise scripts, having little leeway to respond to unusual customer needs, and being closely monitored by both electronic systems and supervisors. Shiftwork is common, with some centers operating on a 24/7 schedule. The work is often considered stressful, and burnout is common after several months or a year of work. Employees may feel caught between conflicting demands. On the one hand, they are required to appear polite and helpful to customers; on the other, they must handle calls very quickly and continuously in a highly controlling and almost dehumanized environment.[2]

The Royal Automobile Club (RAC) Customer Service Center in Bristol, England, provides an example of issues and potential solutions in managing employee turnover in a call center. The RAC consolidated seventeen separate units that took calls from existing and potential customers into a single call center located in Bristol. This location may have been a poor choice for a labor-intensive operation because the area has traditionally had low unemployment and a number of other large call centers had recently moved in. Competition to attract and retain agents was fierce. In the three years leading up to the consolidation, employee turnover in the RAC's call-center units had averaged 27 to 35 percent annually. Each unit had specialized in one type of transaction, such as membership renewals, telesales, travel insurance, and so forth, meaning that customers often had to be transferred from agent to agent to have a range of issues addressed. Because agents had to master only one type of work, training was very limited and the work was highly repetitive. Two wage systems were in place—an hourly salary plus overtime for those who answered customer questions and recorded simple information, and a commission-based system for agents selling products or memberships. On the whole, pay was below the market average. There were no progression routes between jobs.

Shortly after the consolidation, a number of innovative HR policies were developed to simultaneously improve customer service and employee retention. They were successful, with employee turnover reduced to 8 percent in the first year and an astonishing 2 percent the following year.[3] How did RAC do it? Where would you start if you wished to attract, retain, and motivate call-center staff in a competitive environment?

This chapter is about transitions made by employees after they enter an organization. Individuals may transition from one job or location to another within the organization. These moves may be relatively unplanned and ad hoc or the result of careful career planning and preparation with a long time horizon. Movements can be upward (promotion), lateral (to a different set of responsibilities or different function at the same level), or even downward (demotion). Many organizations recognize the importance of careers to their employees and provide career planning to encourage employees to stay and continuously upgrade their skills in anticipation of future opportunities. Such planning also assures that suitably skilled employees will be available to meet the organization's future human resource needs.

Another type of transition is exit from the organization. Departures from the organization can be classified as voluntary, in which the employee makes a decision to leave, or involuntary, in which the employer terminates the employee. Voluntary turnover is a huge concern for many organizations, especially when labor markets are tight. When the basis for competition is intellectual capital and skilled employees, organizations with a high rate of employee turnover are severely handicapped. Another form of (usually) voluntary turnover is retirement. With the aging of the large baby-boom cohort, this is an increasingly important issue for organizations to plan and manage.

Involuntary exit may occur when employees are discharged for inappropriate behavior or substandard performance. There are legal issues to be considered in disciplining and discharging employees for cause, and employers must assure that their processes minimize the risk of litigation as well as nurture the perception of fair treatment among all employees. Another form of involuntary exit occurs when employees are retrenched or laid off because the employer no longer needs their services. Although this can happen at any time when a business reorganizes or experiences a setback, it is a widespread concern in periods of slower economic growth. The high rate of mergers over the past decade has also been accompanied by large-scale retrenchments of surplus employees.

Distinctions among the different types of organizational exits have important practical implications. For example, a common concern of HR managers is whether or not a departing employee is eligible for unemployment compensation. When an employee voluntarily leaves a job or is fired for some good reason, he or she is not eligible to receive unemployment benefits. Only employees who lose their jobs through no fault of their own (as in layoffs) are entitled to unemployment compensation in most states.[4]

CAREER PATHS AND CAREER PLANNING

Most employees make a number of transitions between jobs during their working lives. These may include both job changes within a single employer and leaving one firm to take a job at another firm. In either case, the intention usually is to grow and increase in skills, responsibility, and remuneration, or to improve the "fit" between employee skills and desires and job requirements. A sequence of jobs that build on one another is called a career path, and a career path is likely to be more satisfying and successful if both the individual and the organization spend some time planning and preparing for these future transitions. The section that follows first explores trends and options in career paths, then considers how individuals and employers might engage in career planning to maximize outcomes for both parties.

New Organizational Structures and Changing Career Patterns

A number of economic and demographic trends have affected career patterns and expectations in the past two decades. A strong trend has been called **restructuring, downsizing,** or, more euphemistically, **rightsizing.** Organizations cut their labor costs by reducing the size of their permanent full-time staff. Some organizations abolished multiple levels of management to become "flatter," quicker to respond, and closer to the customer. To meet varying labor needs, rightsized firms may hire temporary workers or outsource work to smaller firms and consultants. There has been a rise in part-time employment both because part-timers are less expensive and receive fewer benefits, and because they provide greater flexibility in scheduling employees for peak demand periods.[5] In general, it is safe to say that the "psychological contract" employees have had with their employer has changed from "If you do your job well, we'll employ you until you retire" to "We'll employ you as long as we need your contribution to help us succeed in business."[6]

Consequently, career patterns for individual employees are changing. The left side of Figure 16.1 shows a traditional **linear career path,** in which one enters an organization near the bottom, works in the same firm for many years, and gradually and predictably moves up, retiring from a fairly high-level position in the same firm. This career pattern has become the exception rather than the rule.[7] The bulge of

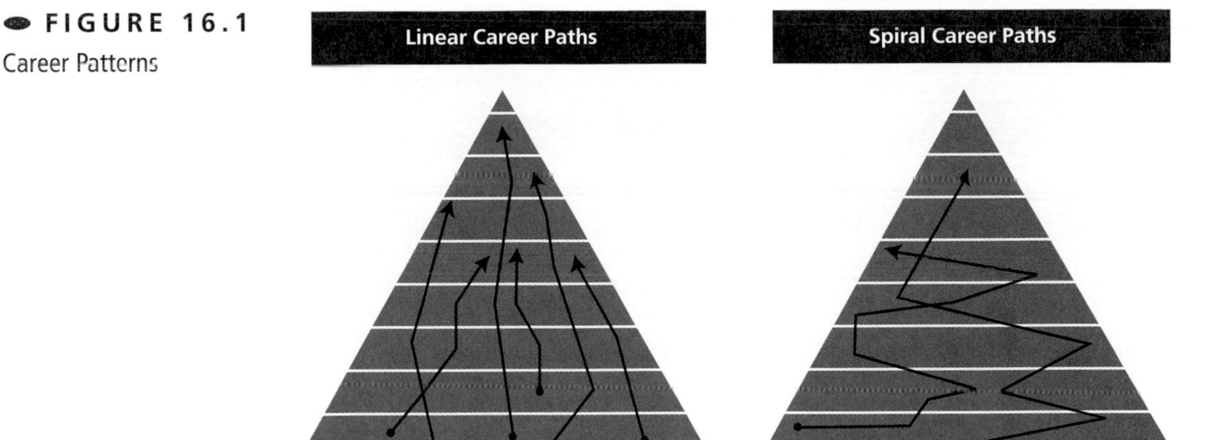

FIGURE 16.1
Career Patterns

baby boomers has made climbing the hierarchy much more competitive, the flattening of organizational structures has reduced the number of management positions just as the number of candidates has increased, and massive layoffs have destroyed faith in the employer as a long-term source of security. These changes have caused a great deal of frustration as middle-aged employees fail to advance as they had expected.[8] Even greater frustration and career blocking are afflicting baby busters as boomers monopolize middle- and upper-management positions.[9]

Organizations are trying to maintain the motivation and creativity of **career-plateaued** employees by developing alternatives to the traditional linear career success model. To some extent, the meaning of career success is changing. Some feel that career success now has more to do with self-actualization, skill growth, and self-satisfaction than with climbing a fixed ladder of jobs. Balancing family and life commitments with work has also taken on more importance for many employees.[10] Table 16.1 shows four possible career paths that an employee could follow. An **expert, or professional, career ladder** rewards growing expertise in a single technical specialty without the need to move into management. Professional ladders allow for career advancement within a single employer, even a "flat" one. In academics, an example is the move from assistant to associate to full professor, without the need to take on a management role such as department head or dean. Scientists and engineers also can follow similar ladders of increasing technical competence and status (junior engineer, engineer, senior engineer, etc.) without managerial responsibilities.

RAC found that part of the solution to high turnover in the perceived dead-end job of call-center agent was to build a career progression system. First, the job was retitled "customer adviser," and incumbents were trained to provide a much wider range of services to customers, including both providing information and selling. They were empowered and encouraged to solve problems and to remedy complaints rather than passing them on to another agent or supervisor. An expert career ladder with five steps was installed for customer advisers. Each level has higher performance requirements and, when achieved, provides a higher wage rate as well as the possibility of greater bonuses for above-target performance.[11] Though not used at RAC, there is a movement in the United States toward certifying call-center staff in basic skills such as "controlling the call, showing empathy,

TABLE 16.1
Characteristics of Four Career Paths

	Linear	Expert	Spiral	Transitory
Direction of movement	Upward	Little movement	Lateral	Lateral
Duration of stay in one field	Variable	Life	7–10 years	3–5 years
Incumbent motives	Power	Expertise	Personal growth	Variety
	Achievement	Security	Creativity	Independence
Organizational structure	Tall pyramid	Flat	Matrix	Loose, flexible structure
		Strong functional departments	Self-directed interdisciplinary teams	Temporary teams
Organizationally valued performance factors	Leadership	Quality	Creativity	Speed
	Efficiency	Reliability	Teamwork	Adaptability
	Logistics management	Stability	People development	Innovation
		Technical competence		
Organizational rewards	Promotions	Fringe benefits	Lateral assignments	Immediate cash bonuses
	Management perquisites	Recognition awards	Cross-training	Independence and autonomy
	Executive bonuses	Continuing technical training	Creative latitude	Special temporary assignments
				Job rotation

Source: Adapted from K. R. Brousseau, M. J. Driver, K. Eneroth, and R. Larsson, "Career Pandemonium: Realigning Organizations and Individuals," *Academy of Management Executive,* November 1996, Table 1 (p. 56) and Table 3 (p. 59).

identifying and solving problems, and acting on sales opportunities." This is another effort to raise the status of the occupation, and thus perhaps attract more people to enter and remain in the field.[12]

Another widely touted alternative career structure is the **spiral career path** (right side of Figure 16.1), which involves a number of moves, some lateral, between functional areas within the same organization. This combines broadening experience and the continuous challenge of new tasks with slower hierarchical progress.[13] As an example, one might begin a career in sales, move to operations after several years, move to a different operations job, and then move into the finance area by midcareer. To make these complex spiral career paths work, organizations need to design sophisticated career planning and career information systems to generate and disseminate information about lateral career opportunities throughout the organization.[14]

Organizational pay and job structures are changing to accommodate multiple forms of career movement. **Broadbanding** is the increasingly common practice of combining many previously discrete job titles, ranks, and pay grades into much wider categories. Northern Telecom has collapsed 19,000 job titles and more than thirty-two salary grades into just 200 titles and thirteen salary bands. This system encourages lateral job movement by de-emphasizing progress through a myriad of vertical job grades and by rewarding both performance excellence and in-band job changes.[15]

Another increasingly common path is the **transitory career path.** In this approach, the career occurs virtually independent of any single organization. The individual may move into and out of organizations and even occupations on a regular basis, either in search of better jobs and more satisfying challenges or because there is little choice when secure permanent jobs are rare. Some or even most of a transitory career may be spent as a consultant or independent contractor, short-term contract employee, part-timer, or entrepreneur. Individuals on this career path think of themselves as possessing and maintaining a portfolio of competencies that give them security and employability rather than assuming that security and employment are provided by a single organization. Career and development planning is critical for individuals on a transitory career path, but they are more likely to become their own career strategists than to rely on input from formal employer-provided career-planning systems.[16]

Spiral or transitory career paths may offer another attraction to today's employees: the possibility of staying in one location much longer. With the increasing number of dual-career couples, individuals may prefer to remain in the same community for a longer period, moving between different types of jobs within the same establishment or moving between local employers.

Unfortunately, HR specialists are finding that it is difficult to change the prevailing "up-or-out" culture of most organizations, which defines lack of upward progress as failure. Traditional linear careers are less feasible than before, and employer-initiated creative career planning is even more important to effectively utilize talent and provide satisfying careers for today's employees. It has been suggested that the most effective organizations of the future will provide all four types of career paths (linear, expert, spiral, and transitory) in varying proportions to meet the needs of their work force and to provide the combination of stable and flexible staffing necessary to carry out their business plans.[17] The lower two rows of Table 16.1 suggest the way in which performance appraisal criteria and reward systems might need to be tailored to meet the needs of employees on different types of career paths.

Career Planning

Ultimately, individuals are responsible for their own careers, though many organizations provide assistance with career planning. Organizational efforts to plan career moves for top managers were discussed in Chapter 3 under the rubrics of replacement charting and succession planning, but top management candidates are not the only employees in need of career-planning attention from the organization. Lower level managers, professionals, and nonexempt employees also desire satisfying careers and may leave organizations that are not seen as offering appropriate opportunities. Having defined career goals and being aware of other job opportunities within the firm also may motivate employees to work harder at developing their skills because they understand how effort now will pay off later. Career and development planning also helps ensure that skilled employees will be available internally when they are needed. Realizing this, many organizations engage in formal career-planning activities with their employees.[18]

Career planning typically involves several steps. The first is self-assessment by the employee—that is, coming to understand who one is, what one values, what one is good at and enjoys, and what one wants to accomplish over the longer term. Individuals are not always aware of what they are good at or what they most enjoy doing.[19] The process of self-assessment should include structured thinking about oneself in terms of skills, values, and life interests. Sometimes testing is helpful in this regard. After completing a self-assessment, employees should solicit feedback from others who know them well or who have worked with them or supervised them. At the end of this process, employees should have formed a clear picture of what they need or want and what they can offer to an employer.

The second step is gathering information about different job opportunities and potential career paths inside or outside the present organization. This is information on what employers need and want from incumbents and what they can offer to employees. Figure 16.2 shows these two sets of needs and offers; both

FIGURE 16.2

Aligning Personal Needs and Offers with Employer Needs and Offers

Source: Mike Broscio and Jay Scherer, Scherer Schneider Paulick, Chicago, www.sspcorp.net, "Taking Charge: Charting Your Way to Career Success," *Healthcare Executive*, Nov./Dec. 2000, pp. 18–22. © Scherer Schneider Paulick 2001.

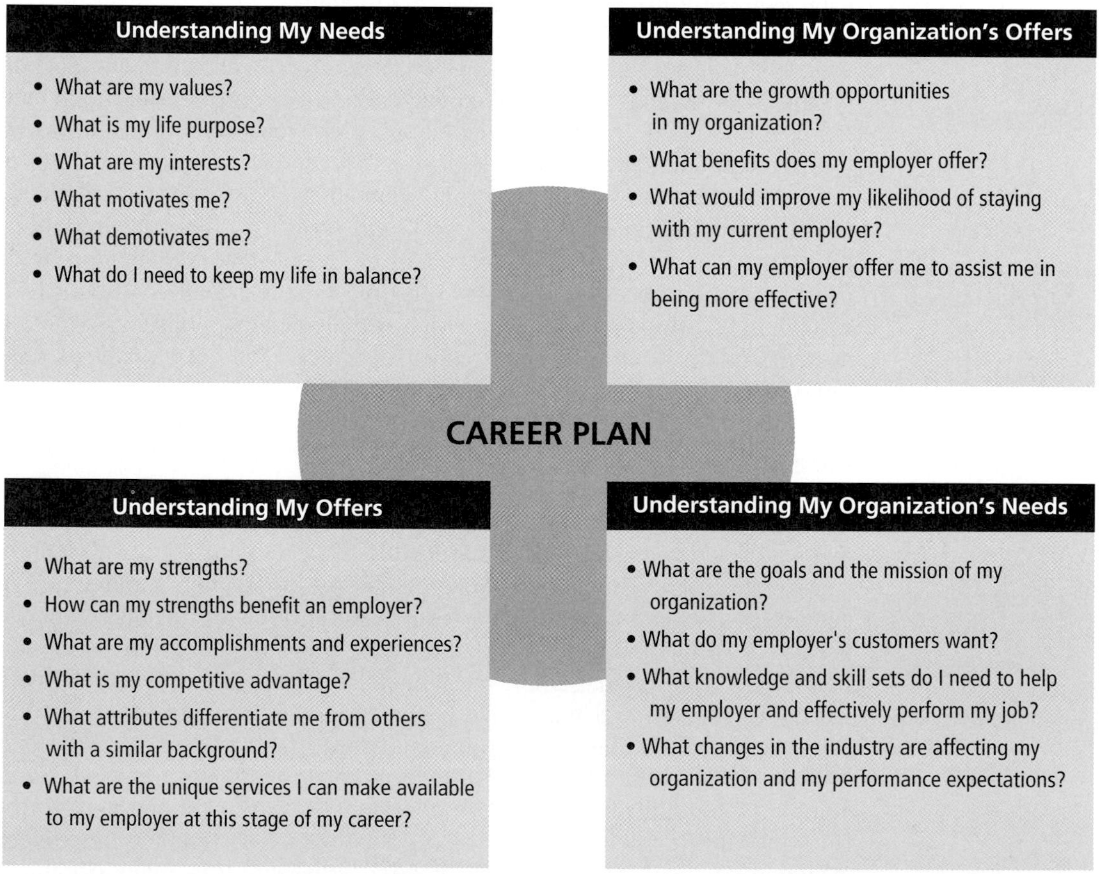

Understanding My Needs

- What are my values?
- What is my life purpose?
- What are my interests?
- What motivates me?
- What demotivates me?
- What do I need to keep my life in balance?

Understanding My Organization's Offers

- What are the growth opportunities in my organization?
- What benefits does my employer offer?
- What would improve my likelihood of staying with my current employer?
- What can my employer offer me to assist me in being more effective?

CAREER PLAN

Understanding My Offers

- What are my strengths?
- How can my strengths benefit an employer?
- What are my accomplishments and experiences?
- What is my competitive advantage?
- What attributes differentiate me from others with a similar background?
- What are the unique services I can make available to my employer at this stage of my career?

Understanding My Organization's Needs

- What are the goals and the mission of my organization?
- What do my employer's customers want?
- What knowledge and skill sets do I need to help my employer and effectively perform my job?
- What changes in the industry are affecting my organization and my performance expectations?

employer and employee must get a good exchange in terms of what the other offers that meets their needs for the relationship to work over the long run. Individuals can engage in this step of career planning on their own, with little assistance from their employer. However, employer involvement is desirable because better information on internal career paths can be made available, a larger percentage of employees can be induced to consider options within the organization, and plans can be more realistic in view of future organizational needs and development opportunities. Employers may offer to help employees learn about career opportunities and job requirements elsewhere in the organization through a variety of means. These include individual meetings with a career counselor in the organization, discussions with superiors, videos, electronic career resources, booklets detailing job requirements and competencies throughout the organization, job rotations, and so on.

The third step is formulating career goals and a plan for achieving them. Plans may include on- or off-the-job training; special assignments; and changes in job, occupation, or employer. A discussion of the plan at least annually with one's supervisor is recommended.

First USA Bank recently implemented a program of career planning and management for its nonexempt employees. Job satisfaction surveys showed that these employees were unhappy and unclear about their future prospects within the organization. The company responded by developing a careers program designed to increase job satisfaction, reduce voluntary turnover, and increase the rate of internal promotions. The idea was for employees to be more proactive in planning their own careers and to consider lateral as well as vertical movements. A consulting firm was hired to run a series of workshops on career planning. These first helped employees to assess themselves; then to seek feedback and confirmation of their self-assessment; then to understand more about the company, industry, and likely future needs in their profession; then to explore job alternatives and paths within the organization; and finally to create a blueprint for personal growth and job movement. The workshops were so eagerly received by employees that First USA Bank added two more components to the program, which was eventually called "Opportunity Knocks." The second component was career resource centers at each worksite. Employees can sign up to spend paid time in the room reading about careers, researching opportunities, and writing résumés. The third component was hiring "employment development advisers" to work with employees on their plans following the workshops. After pilot testing, the program was rolled out to multiple sites. In the first year, the rate of internal job changes increased by 50 percent and employee satisfaction with career development increased by 25 percent. Further, participants in the program were much more likely to stay with the organization than were nonparticipants. In the first three years of the program, First USA estimated that it saved $2.2 million in replacement costs as a consequence of better career development of employees.[20]

Dual-Career and Family Issues in Career Planning

Career planning historically has targeted one employee at a time. Now, however, an increasing number of employees have spouses who are active in the work force and whose career and employment prospects must also be factored into career decisions. Some authors distinguish **dual-income families** from **dual-career families.**

In the former, one or both spouses work at a non-career-oriented job, perhaps a less skilled position in retail, health care, food services, and so forth. The non-career-oriented partner's flexibility as to employer makes career planning relatively straightforward. This partner can seek employment wherever the other partner's career takes them. In dual-career families, each partner has a strong commitment to building a continuing and challenging career, and the needs of each must be carefully balanced in career-planning activities. The need to consider a spouse's employment prospects has made many employees less willing to accept relocation offers from their employers, and it has necessitated changes in the way organizations deploy and develop human resources. Organizations are paying more attention to the career needs of spouses employed by other firms when geographic transfers are necessary, and they are becoming more open to employing both partners in a dual-career marriage. Accommodating spousal career issues is one way to retain valued professionals.

A related trend is for many mothers to work.[21] The needs of working parents are somewhat different from those of the traditional husband-employee, mother-homemaker family. Working parents of either sex usually appreciate "family friendly" organizational policies, including some form of assistance with child care, flexible working hours, job sharing, part-time options, and generous family leave.[22] In terms of career planning, one or both parents may wish to cease work temporarily, enter a slower, low-pressure career track, or reduce working hours while family responsibilities are at their peak. Innovative career systems that allow these arrangements without permanently stereotyping such employees as low-commitment, low-potential can be effective, even for managers and professionals.[23]

RETIREMENT

The last transition in most employees' careers is retirement. Daniel Feldman defines **retirement** as "the exit from an organizational position or career path of considerable duration, taken by individuals after middle age, and with the intention of reduced psychological commitment to work thereafter."[24] As Feldman's definition indicates, retirement is not a homogeneous phenomenon, and it is useful to recognize differences in voluntariness, completeness, and timing. The Age Discrimination in Employment Act has essentially eliminated mandatory retirement, but other forms of involuntary retirement exist, such as when health problems force an employee to stop working. Retirement may or may not take place at the age considered "normal" and may be either complete (the individual withdraws from all forms of employment) or partial (he or she continues to work part time for the same or a different employer).

For many years, retirement was seen as a relatively unimportant but quite predictable aspect of organizational functioning. As workers neared the mandatory retirement age, retirement-planning workshops may have been held, and, on reaching the magical age of sixty-five, employees were presented with a gold watch and shown the door. With the abolition of a mandatory retirement age, predictability decreased and employees now have many more choices. Because some benefit plans allow for partial benefits to be paid before age sixty-five, a larger share of employees are taking early retirement now than in the past. For instance, in 1963, 76 percent of males were in the work force between ages sixty-two and sixty-four. By 1997, that number had fallen to 46 percent. At the same time, others are choosing to work well beyond the traditional retirement age.[25] Many individuals retire from a career-oriented job and then accept a **bridge job**—possibly part time, possibly in another field, and often with another employer.[26] Some interesting facts relevant to retirement are shown in Table 16.2.

Retirement is becoming an increasingly important issue as the large baby-boom generation begins to leave the labor force. The leading edge of the baby boom reached age fifty-five in 2001. There are concerns about how the relatively smaller generations behind them will support such a potentially large number of retirees. In times of low unemployement, there is concern among employers about how they will replace large numbers of highly skilled and experienced employees. Employees may worry about what they will do with themselves if they retire completely, given a life expectancy of eighteen years beyond the traditional retirement age of sixty-five. Another concern to many older employees is health insurance—they may be more willing to retire or retire early if their employer provides retiree medical benefits.[27]

Phased retirement is getting a lot of attention lately.[28] Phased retirement means remaining in some sort of employment relationship with the same employer after retiring. This can include being rehired as a consultant, part-timer, or seasonal employee. For instance, Avaya Technologies has about 1,500 "variable" technicians who work on an as-needed basis as part of their phased-retirement program. Phased retirement can also include gradually reducing hours worked or allowing extended leaves of absence between periods of full-time work. Job sharing is another possibility, as is a transfer to a job that is less demanding and perhaps less time consuming. Phased-retirement programs benefit the organization by retaining access to valuable skills usually at a lower cost than having a full-time permanent employee. Phased retirement allows retirees a chance to augment

TABLE 16.2

Some Facts Relevant to Retirement

- A child born today can be expected to live until age seventy-six.
- Someone who turns age sixty-five today can expect to live until age eighty-three.
- The fastest-growing segment of the population is those aged eighty-five and older.
- The age at which full Social Security retirement benefits can be received has been increasing gradually to age sixty-seven.
- Many defined benefit pension plans allow retirement with full benefits at age sixty or sixty-two.
- Most defined benefit pension plans allow early retirement at age fifty-five or earlier.
- The fastest-growing types of retirement plans allow participants to leave their employer and take their benefits at any time, regardless of age.
- Certain retirement accounts can be accessed without penalty once an individual reaches age fifty-nine and a half.
- Some accounts require distributions beginning no later than age seventy and a half.
- There is no longer a mandatory retirement age for most workers, and federal law protects older workers against discrimination regardless of their age.

Source: William J. Wiatrowski, "Changing Retirement Age: Ups and Downs," *Monthly Labor Review,* April 2001, p. 3.

their income, stay active and feel useful, and gradually become accustomed to not working (or working less). Many older workers now need to work at least some, because the stock portfolios that were to fund their retirement lost a great deal of value in recent market downturns. There are some legal disincentives to widespread phased-retirement programs, but moves to address problematic pension plan rules are being considered.[29]

Impact of Retirement on the Organization

From the organization's perspective, retirement can be a very positive process. It allows new employees with up-to-date skills to enter the organization and replace older workers whose skills may have become obsolete. Retirement also motivates remaining employees because older workers tend to be higher in the organizational hierarchy and their departure provides opportunities for promotion. New employees also typically cost less than older workers because their salaries are lower. When head count must be reduced, providing incentives for early retirement is among the less painful alternatives.

Not all effects of retirement are positive, however. The loss of older workers may increase the level of uncertainty with which the organization must contend. In an increasing number of cases, well-qualified replacements for retiring workers are extremely difficult to find. When older workers leave, they take with them a wealth of knowledge about the organization's processes, operations, and technology; the contacts and influence they have built up in dealing with the environment are also lost. The chemical, utilities, oil and gas, health care, automotive, and aerospace industries are among those with older work forces that face a "brain drain" as many highly skilled individuals retire over the next decade.[30]

Another example is the Defense Acquisitions work force. People in Acquisitions play a pivotal role in the development and purchase of new weapons systems. Acquisitions had about 124,000 civilian employees in 2000, with 60,000 of them eligible to retire by 2005. Funding cuts after the end of the Cold War meant that no new staff had been hired for eleven years, pushing up the average age of the work force. A major program to deal with the predicted shortfall was put in place. This included encouraging phased rather than complete retirements, increased recruitment, easier transfer of employees from other arms of government and from the defense industry, rehiring retirees without financial penalties, and higher wages for high-demand occupations.[31]

The next sections of this chapter consider earlier departures from the organization, those initiated by employees themselves in the form of voluntary turnover.

VOLUNTARY TURNOVER

The Bureau of Labor Statistics reports monthly quit rates for the whole of the labor force and by industry. The monthly rate for all industries was just under 2 percent between May 2003 and May 2004, or in the neighborhood of 25 percent per year. However, the monthly rate was over 3.5 percent in the leisure and hospitality industry, and a low .6 percent in the government sector.[32] Turnover among fast-food employees often tops 100 percent per year. Rates of **voluntary turnover** generally rise when unemployment falls, and vice versa. Regardless of the prevailing unemployment rate, highly skilled employees can always find new jobs and are at risk of departing. The next section of this chapter explores the reasons employees stay in or leave jobs and the processes by which they make the decision to depart. Then a strategic approach to thinking about turnover is described. Finally, employee retention and knowledge retention programs are discussed.

Causes of Voluntary Turnover

Turnover has been intensively studied for decades, and there are hundreds of studies of variables that help predict quitting. Traditionally, most research on why employees quit has considered two classes of variables: those external to the organization and those internal to the organization. External factors include the unemployment rate and employees' perceptions of the external job opportunities available to them. Turnover is higher when unemployment in the labor market is low, so that alternative employment appears readily available to job leavers. Clearly, RAC employees in Bristol felt they could readily find employment in another call center or one of the new office parks that had recently sprung up nearby. Even in a poor labor market, if employees believe they can easily find superior alternative employment, the propensity for turnover will be higher.[33]

Internal factors are usually based on employees' attitudes or perceptions with respect to the current job. Job satisfaction and organizational commitment are significant predictors of a decision to quit, with leavers being less satisfied and less committed than stayers. Employees are also more likely to leave if they believe the organization treats them unfairly; if they have a poor relationship with their manager; if job requirements are conflicting, unclear, or stressful; or if opportunities for growth, skill development, and promotion are lacking.[34] This sounds like a description of a typical call-center environment—perhaps it is not surprising that turnover in this sector tends to be high.

A great deal of research has confirmed that these attitudes and perceptions are correlated with turnover, but the relationships are not especially strong. Recently, a new predictor of staying versus quitting has been proposed that shows some promise—the **embeddedness** of the employee in the job setting. This approach considers that employees have a web of links and relationships between their family lives, work lives, and community. When these links are numerous and tight, employees are less likely to quit. Leaving a job means leaving the work itself, work friends, employer-provided development programs, and other work-related activities such as a company softball team. Further, leaving a job often means moving out of the community—leaving a spouse's job, a house, a school district, a church, hobby clubs, and nonwork friends. If the individual fits the job and community well and has developed many links, it is a substantial sacrifice to sever these links by quitting the job. Other sacrifices may occur if the employee must forgo unvested pension benefits, a company car, or other benefits based on seniority such as eligibility for sabbaticals. Research has shown that embeddedness contributes to the prediction of turnover above and beyond measures such as job satisfaction, organizational commitment, and the perception of viable employment alternatives.[35]

How Do Employees Decide to Quit?

In addition to identifying predictors of turnover, some researchers have investigated the *process* of deciding to quit a job. It turns out that the decision to quit can be made in different ways and in response to different stimuli. The **traditional**

model of turnover suggests that the decision to quit is made in a logical and step-by-step fashion, largely in response to dissatisfaction with the present job (see Figure 16.3). Individuals begin by evaluating the current job and level of satisfaction or dissatisfaction. If they are dissatisfied, they may begin to think of quitting, then assess the costs of quitting and the costs and likely success of searching for an alternative job. If they believe they have a reasonable chance of finding another job, they may begin a search. After the search, they compare the job alternatives they have discovered to the present job and decide whether it is better to quit or stay.[36] This model suggests that the process of deciding to quit is gradual and that an alternative job is located before the current job is left.

Other research finds that sometimes—about 25 percent of the time—individuals leave one job before beginning to search for another job. This may occur because they are suddenly and extremely unhappy in the old job or because they are highly confident of locating a new job with ease. Further, many people leave jobs not because of growing dissatisfaction but because of a single precipitating incident or "shock to the system." The incident can be negative and job related, such as being passed over for a promotion, receiving a bad performance review, or having a fight with a boss or peer. These negative work events can be relatively minor but still serve as "the last straw" that causes a sudden decision to leave. Not all shocks are negative events on the current job. A shock can also be positive and external, such as receiving an unsolicited job offer or being approached by a headhunter. Finally, the shock that initiates quitting could be an off-the-job event such as becoming pregnant, a spouse being transferred, or being accepted to graduate school.[37]

The Strategic Management of Voluntary Turnover

Research has provided information on why and how individuals choose to quit. The next question is how organizations should respond. Is all voluntary turnover bad, and should achieving a low turnover rate be a priority in all cases? As with so many decisions in strategic human resource management, it depends. Several recent studies have shown that turnover is generally harmful to organizational performance.[38] Another piece of research slightly qualified these findings. In a study of driver turnover in the trucking industry, the firms with the best financial perfor-

FIGURE 16.3
Traditional Model of Deciding to Quit

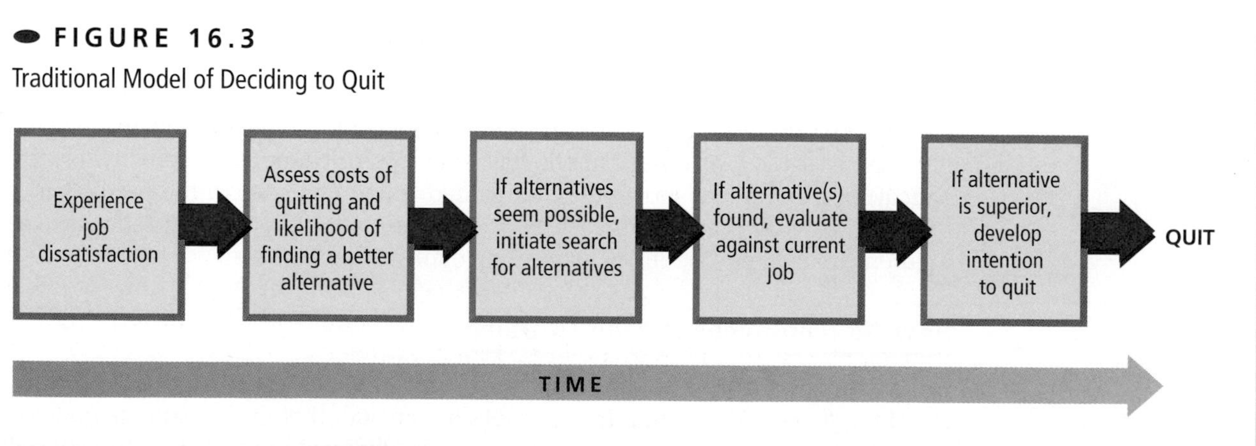

mance had low turnover rates and high investment in their drivers in the form of extensive training and high wages. However, the next best performing firms had high turnover rates paired with a strategy of little investment in drivers. These firms had become skilled at locating replacements and had simplified jobs such that little training was necessary. The worst performing firms invested a great deal in drivers but had high turnover, suggesting that organizational performance depends in part upon a match between the turnover rate and the amount organizations invest in employees.[39] Organizations must consider the costs and benefits of turnover in a particular situation and balance these against the costs of retention.

Costs and Benefits of Turnover to the Organization The departure of an employee can have considerable costs, as outlined in the left side of Table 16.3.[40] It is possible, though not easy, to put figures on these costs, to estimate the actual dollar loss from the departure of an employee.[41] Estimated costs of replacement for different job categories based on a number of studies are shown in Table 16.4. Note that costs vary substantially depending on the job. The cost to replace an Air Force pilot is about $6 million!

These high costs might lead one to believe that all turnover is dysfunctional and that the lowest possible rate of voluntary turnover would be the best. However, this is not necessarily true. Turnover may have benefits, as shown in the right side of Table 16.3. An organization with a turnover rate that is too low may become stagnant and hidebound, lack opportunities for employees to move up, and retain poor performers it would be better off without.[42]

Organizations should aim for an **optimal rate of turnover** rather than the lowest possible rate. One scholar suggests that the optimal rate occurs where the curve of **turnover costs** crosses the curve of **retention costs,** as shown in Figure 16.4. As the turnover rate increases, so do the costs of replacement and lost productivity. The organization can reduce turnover, but only by incurring retention costs, such as higher wages, better benefits, quality-of-work-life and development programs, and so on. The point at which these two curves cross represents the lowest total cost and thus the optimal turnover rate for the organization. This type of analysis suggests that a relatively high turnover rate may sometimes be less costly than a lower one. Consider the case of fast-food preparation employees. Turnover tends to be quite high, and wages are quite low. If wages were doubled or tripled, turnover would surely drop, but this strategy would not be cost-effective because replacing fast-food workers is fairly inexpensive.

Looking at the overall turnover rate may be misleading. It is important to consider what types of employees are choosing to leave. Whether a given turnover event hurts or helps the organization depends in part on the performance of the person leaving: Is he or she someone the organization would prefer to retain? A number of studies have explored the relationship between performance and turnover, and there appears to be a tendency for poor performers to be more likely to quit than good performers.[43] However, this may not be true for all organizations or at the extremes of the performance continuum. For instance, the very worst performers may not leave because no one else will hire them, and the very best may be repeatedly approached by other firms intent on luring them away.[44] Thus, it is not safe to assume that the organization is better off without the people who choose to leave.

A more sophisticated model for evaluating turnover functionality is shown in Figure 16.5. This model suggests that it is necessary to distinguish among

TABLE 16.3

Costs and Benefits of Voluntary Turnover

Costs of Turnover	Possible Benefits of Turnover
Exit costs	Poor performers may choose to leave and can be replaced with better employees.
Exit interviews	Leavers are replaced with more junior employees who cost less.
Farewell parties on work time	Morale improves following departure of problematic employees.
Administrative time to process final pay, close retirement accounts, etc.	Leavers are replaced with people having more up-to-date technical skill.
Replacement costs	Vacancies are created to allow for internal promotions of other employees, thus increasing their career satisfaction and motivation.
Recruitment advertising	Receptiveness to innovation and change may increase.
Selection testing, interviewing, reference checking, medical exams, etc.	Voluntary turnover is less painful than retrenchments.
Hiring bonuses, relocation costs	
New employee orientation	
Administrative costs to add to payroll, enroll in benefits, etc.	
Formal training	
Informal mentoring and coaching of new employees by supervisors and peers	
Other costs	
Lost business due to client loyalty to departing employees	
Lost business or poor quality due to short staffing before replacement, or lower skills before new hires are up to speed	
Expenses of hiring temporaries or paying overtime while awaiting replacements	
Reduced morale of those remaining, increased stress on those remaining while short staffed or breaking in replacements	
Reduction in company's reputation as an employer when many staff choose to leave; reduced ability to recruit in the labor market	
Inability to pursue growth or other business opportunities due to lack of staff	
Loss of training dollars invested in departing employee	
Loss of explicit and tacit organization-specific knowledge held by departing employee	

TABLE 16.4

Turnover Costs as a Percentage of Annual Salary

Job Type/Category	Turnover Cost Ranges (% of Annual Wage/Salary)*
Entry level—hourly, nonskilled (e.g., fast-food worker)	30–50
Service/production workers—hourly (e.g., courier)	40–70
Skilled hourly (e.g., machinist)	75–100
Clerical/administrative (e.g., scheduler)	50–80
Professional (e.g., sales representative, nurse, accountant)	75–125
Technical (e.g., computer technician)	100–150
Engineers (e.g., chemical engineer)	200–300
Specialists (e.g., computer software designer)	200–400
Supervisors/team leaders (e.g., section supervisor)	100–150
Middle managers (e.g., department manager)	125–200

*Percentages are rounded to reflect the general range of costs from studies. Costs are fully loaded to include all of the costs of replacing an employee and bringing him or her to the level of productivity and efficiency of the former employee.

Source: J. J. Phillips and A. O. Connell, *Managing Employee Retention: A Strategic Accountability Approach*. (Amsterdam: Elsevier Butterworth Heinemann, 2003), p. 69.

turnover events in terms of both employee performance level (high, acceptable, and low) and replaceability (easy, difficult). To maximize benefits to the organization, quite different techniques should be applied in each cell of the matrix in Figure 16.5 to discourage or encourage turnover.

In cell A, turnover is highly dysfunctional because incumbents are excellent performers who are difficult to replace, either because the skill is in short supply

FIGURE 16.4

Optimal Organizational Turnover

Source: Adapted from Michael A. Abelson and Barry D. Baysinger, "Optimal and Dysfunctional Turnover: Toward an Organizational Level Model," *Academy of Management Review,* Vol. 9, 1984, p. 333. Reprinted by permission.

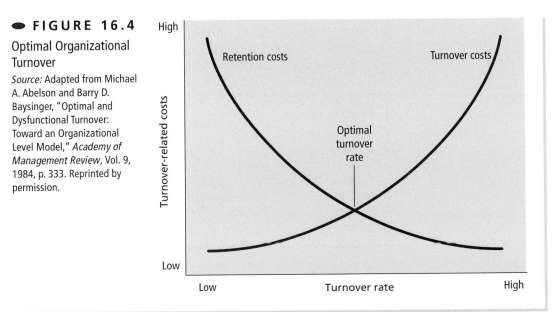

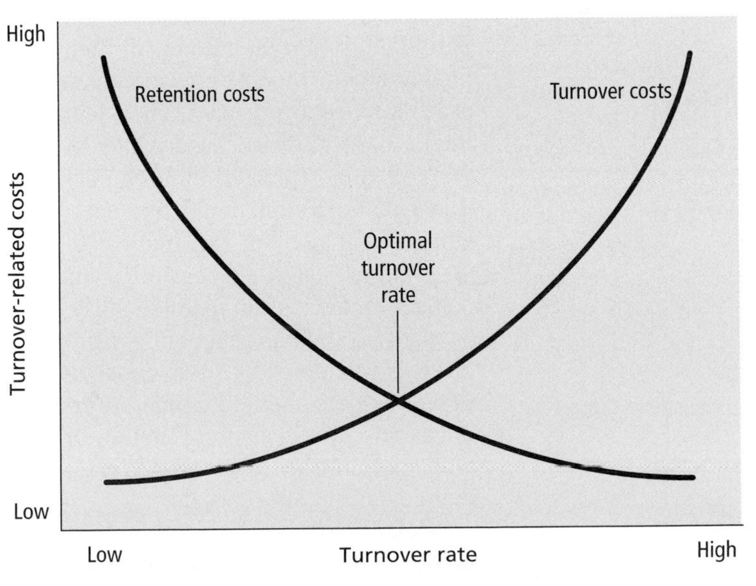

FIGURE 16.5
Performance Replaceability Strategy Matrix

Source: D. C. Martin and K. M. Bartol, "Managing Turnover Strategically." Reprinted with permission from the November 1985 issue of *Personnel Administrator,* copyright 1985, The American Society for Personnel Administration, Alexandria, Va.

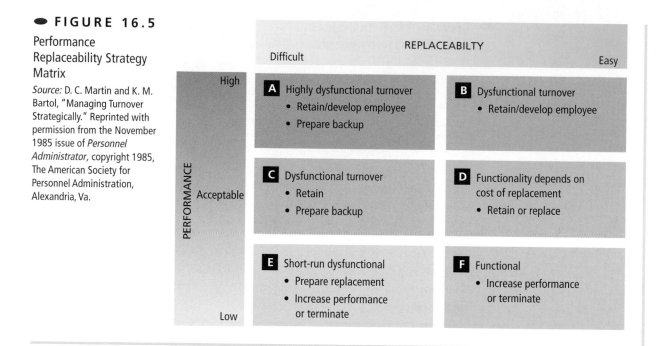

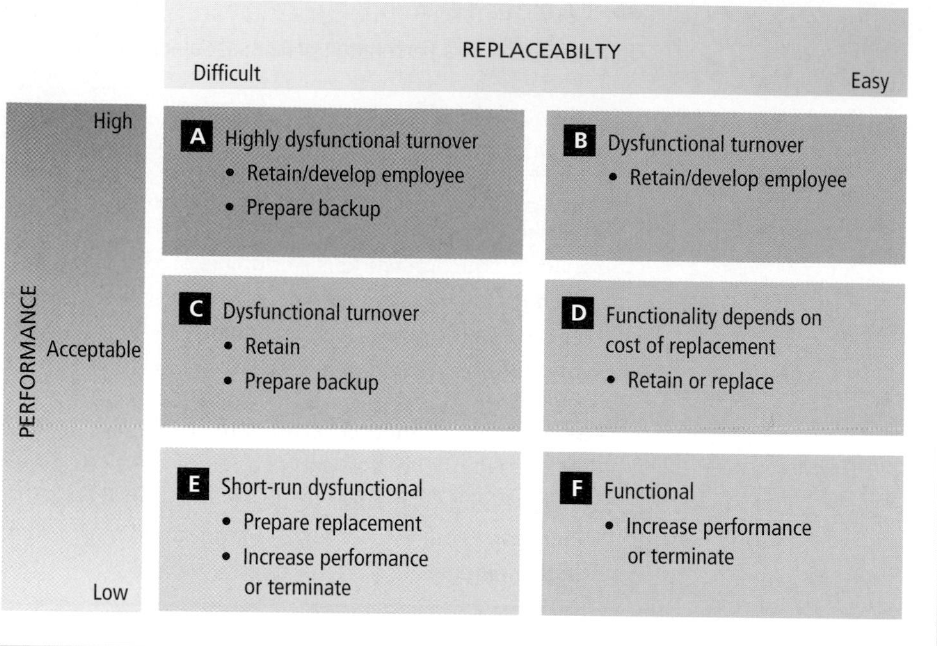

in the marketplace or the position requires a great deal of organization-specific skill, experience, or relationship building with clients that takes time to develop. Employers whose competitive strategy relies heavily on personal relationships between employees and customers, such as some high-service brokerage houses, law firms, or medical practices, might find that they have a large percentage of employees in this cell. Employers should make every effort to retain high performers who are difficult to replace, both by providing an excellent work environment and by meeting their unique needs. An example of the latter is provided by the second author of this textbook, who owns a rural resort. When his talented young chef got married and then couldn't find a place to rent because of their family dogs, Schoenfeldt bought a house of their mutual choice and contracted to rent it to the chef at a very modest rate in exchange for assurances that the chef would stay for at least two more years! When feasible, employers may also wish to identify and begin to develop successors in case staff members in this cell do leave.

Cell B is populated by high performers who are easier to replace. Turnover in this cell is dysfunctional but not disastrous. Efforts to retain these employees should be made, but extremely costly retention strategies are probably inappropriate. Sophisticated succession planning systems will also be unnecessary in this cell, as vacancies can be filled fairly easily.

Cell C contains acceptable performers who are hard to replace. Because of the disruption caused by their departure, turnover in this cell is considered dysfunctional. Efforts should be made to retain these employees and plan for replacement in case turnover occurs. Further, organizations should attempt to move cell C employees to higher levels of performance through training, goal setting, and performance-contingent rewards.

Cell D consists of acceptable performers who are easy to replace. Whether turnover in this cell is functional depends on the cost of finding and training a replacement and on the probability that the replacement will perform better than the current incumbent. If replacements are inexpensive and likely to possess better or more current skills than present employees, then special efforts to retain cell D employees will not be needed. However, any acceptable performers with potential should be trained, coached, and given incentives to improve their performance. In the case of some call centers, if the work is sufficiently simple and routine that training costs are low, new employees are easily found, and incumbents burn out after a year or so, it may make sense to tolerate a high turnover rate because new hires are likely to be more motivated and enthusiastic than their longer tenure peers.

The final two cells contain poor performers. The organization's appraisal and reward system should encourage these employees to improve their performance to acceptable levels. If this effort fails, then turnover will probably be functional. Employees in cell F, who are easily replaced, may be discharged following a fair disciplinary procedure (discussed later in this chapter) or encouraged to leave with accurate negative feedback on performance and minimal rewards under a merit or bonus system. Hard-to-replace employees (cell E) whose performance does not improve to acceptable levels should be retained until replacements can be located or developed, then encouraged to seek more suitable employment elsewhere.

Retention Management Programs

Having identified employees or job categories where turnover would be especially dysfunctional, organizations should be proactive in working to retain these people. Many employers adopted retention management programs in the late 1990s when turnover was very high.[45] However, retaining top performing employees with unique and hard to replace knowledge and skills is important in any labor market.[46]A comprehensive **retention management program** must be built on accurate information about why people are leaving a particular organization.[47] In the absence of such information, wrong conclusions may be drawn about the causes of departure and ineffective means to combat it adopted.[48] Table 16.5 shows the opinions of 1,148 employees in twenty companies and 273 human resource managers about the relative importance of some external and internal causes for turnover.[49] Clearly, the perceptions of the HR managers differ in some important ways from those of the employees who may actually do the quitting. Employees say that the least important factor in motivating them to quit is the availability of jobs that pay more. HR managers believe that this external factor, which is largely beyond their control, is the most important driver of turnover. In fact, employees say the most important reason they leave is because their work is underappreciated and not recognized. Any organization can improve in this area, regardless of the external labor market. Opportunities to move up and develop skills are also important to employees, and with proper career planning, innovative career ladders, mentoring, and employer-provided training or tuition reimbursement programs, much can be done in these areas as well.

The RAC call center used a number of approaches to reducing turnover. Because pay was substandard, it increased the amount by 10 to 30 percent, but it also made some of it contingent on performance. This focused employee attention on doing the job well, made performance feedback more meaningful, and provided recognition of high-quality work as well as bringing total compensation for employees

TABLE 16.5

Employee and HR Manager Beliefs about Why Employees Leave

Importance of Reasons for Leaving a Job	Employee Ranks	HR Manager Ranks
Reasons internal to firm		
Work goes unrecognized/unappreciated	1	7
Little chance to move ahead	3	4
Unhappiness with job demands/ requirements	5	3
Friction with supervisor or coworker	6	6
Disliked management or supervisory style	7	8
Dissatisfaction with company policies	8	10
Attractions outside firm		
Availability of better training/career opportunities	2	5
Easy availability of more interesting work	4	2
Desire to return to school	9	9
Easy availability of equal or better paying jobs	10	1

Source: Data are reported in D. J. Campbell and K. M. Campbell, "Why Individuals Voluntarily Leave: Perceptions of Human Resource Managers versus Employees," *Asia Pacific Journal of Human Resources,* Vol. 39 (1), 2001, pp. 23–41.

into the top quartile in the local labor market. Employee training was greatly increased to prepare agents to handle a much wider range of customer needs. A buddy system was adopted for new hires after their formal training was completed. Teams were created, and the team leader's role was changed from supervising to motivating and coaching employees and figuring out how to make the workplace "fun." A number of employee involvement programs were implemented. The "Bright Ideas" suggestion program generated 2,400 ideas on how to improve business in a single year, each rewarded with a raffle ticket in the monthly prize drawing. Daily team meetings were conducted with plenty of feedback on performance measures. Social events were held frequently, teams had special themed dress-up days, and prizes such as chocolates and wine were given spontaneously for especially noteworthy performances. Special cash bonuses were sometimes given to a team for surpassing performance standards. Taken together, these measures made the work more enjoyable, challenging, and rewarding.[50] The additional friendship bonds built with teammates increased embeddedness and made employees reluctant to leave.

Information about why employees quit or would think about quitting should be collected regularly by organizations. Two common methods for accessing this information are **exit interviews** and **organizational surveys.** Most major organizations conduct exit interviews with employees who quit. The exit interview is generally conducted by a human resource professional, not by the employee's immediate superior. Table 16.6 lists sample questions that may be asked in an exit interview. Tactful probing may be needed to determine the real reason for quitting, as departing employees may not want to burn their bridges with complete candor. A small percentage of organizations use a consultant rather than an organization

TABLE 16.6

Sample Exit Interview Questions

What is your primary reason for leaving?
Did anything trigger your decision to leave?
What was most satisfying about your job?
What was least satisfying about your job?
What would you change about your job?
Did your job duties turn out to be as you expected?
Did you receive enough training to do your job effectively?
Did you receive adequate support to do your job?
Did you receive sufficient feedback about your performance between merit reviews?
Were you satisfied with this company's merit review process?
Did this company help you to fulfill your career goals?
Do you have any tips to help us find your replacement?
What would you improve to make our workplace better?
Were you happy with your pay, benefits, and other incentives?
What was the quality of the supervision you received?
What could your immediate supervisor do to improve his or her management style?
Based on your experience with us, what do you think it takes to succeed at this company?
Did any company policies or procedures (or any other obstacles) make your job more difficult?
Would you consider working again for this company in the future?
Would you recommend working for this company to your family and friends?
What did you like most about this company?
What did you like least about this company?
What does your new company offer that this company doesn't?
Can this company do anything to encourage you to stay?
Did anyone in this company discriminate against you, harass you, or cause hostile working conditions?
Any other comments?

Source: J. S. Niznik, "Exit Interview Questions," at http://jobsearchtech.about.com/cs/interviewtips/a/exit_interview_2.htm. (accessed July 15, 2004)

member as the interviewer to encourage the employee to speak more freely. Other firms use a self-administered Web-based exit questionnaire, but this method lacks the rapport and depth that can be cultivated in a face-to-face interview, and it also misses the opportunity to re-recruit departing candidates. Finally, some firms conduct the exit interview by phone several weeks or months after the employee has left, again in the hope of gaining accurate information about the true cause of departure.[51] Exit interview data should be segmented for analysis. For instance, one may find that good performers leave for different reasons than poor performers, or men may leave for different reasons than women do. Understanding exactly what is going on is important in appropriately targeting retention initiatives.[52]

Many medium-sized and large companies use regular employee opinion surveys.[53] Anonymous employee surveys can be used for many purposes, depending on what questions are asked. For instance, organizations may use surveys to track employee acceptance of culture-change efforts such as team-based work systems. Another common use is to monitor employee satisfaction with such aspects of their jobs as pay, training and development, and supervision. Decreases in satisfaction may predict subsequent increases in turnover. If retention is a particular concern, surveys can be designed as written "pre-exit interviews," asking questions about why employees would consider leaving, what parts of their job are most frustrating or disappointing, or, more positively, why they stay.[54] Accurate information about why employees in different categories of jobs stay or leave the organization is useful in designing the specific features of a retention program. The following are some essential generic features of retention programs:[55]

- Benchmarking data on retention performance, retention programs, and other HR practices in the organization and successful firms in the same industry or labor market.
- Goal setting for retention—what is the target rate for each job or department? Remember that not all departures are preventable by the organization. Some flow from external events such as the transfer of a spouse, illness, an opportunity too good to pass up, or a decision to change lifestyle.
- A means of holding managers accountable for the retention of their staff. In addition to goals, this may include adding retention measures to their performance appraisal criteria and bonus formula.

Specific components in the race to keep talent might include the following:

- Many opportunities for challenging work, learning, and growth. These can be provided through job enrichment, job rotation, secondments, special projects, lateral transfers, mentoring, career planning, promotions, training, tuition reimbursement programs, and so forth.
- Effective performance-contingent rewards and recognition and frequent and honest performance feedback to satisfy employees' desire for information and appreciation.
- An innovative and competitive compensation system. Both fairness and amount of pay are important, though bear in mind that pay is not usually the only reason people leave.
- Flexibility in addressing special employee requests for job characteristics as well as work time and mode. See the Flexibility in the Workplace box for more detail on how some organizations might be flexible or inflexible to employee requests.
- Family-friendly policies such as emergency child care, flextime, leaves of absence, and so on if family responsibilities are a salient cause of departures.[56]

It is also helpful to *tell* particularly valuable employees that the firm is eager to keep them and ask what can be done to further this end. Some employees only find out after resigning that the firm really did value their work.[57] Following from the embeddedness concept, it may also be helpful for firms to enhance the number of formal and informal links among the employee, the firm, and the community. This might be done by encouraging teamwork and mentoring, enrolling employees in long-term education/development programs, using employee share-ownership plans, cultivating company volunteer or sporting activities, considering hiring spouses when qualified, providing child care, and perhaps providing home-purchase assistance.[58] As mentioned in Chapter 6, employees sometimes quit jobs that fail to meet the expectations they had when first hired. Both realistic job

FLEXIBILITY IN THE WORKPLACE

Are You Flexible Enough for Today's Employees?

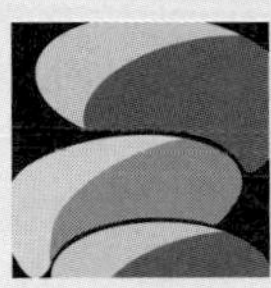

Today's employees may want more idiosyncratic contracts with their organization to allow for greater quality of life choices. They may also want more autonomy to choose their own means of accomplishing tasks. Retaining these employees may require flexibility on the part of the employer to accommodate employees' varied needs and desires. Read the following scenarios, imagining that you are the boss of the person making the request. Think about your responses to the requests. Decide when you would say yes or no and why. Consider the likely impact of your decision on other employees aside from just the one making the request. Use the scoring box below.

Count your scores across the columns, then think over those that fall in the "no way" box. Could you be more flexible, or are there very good reasons for your response?

Source: Kaye and Jordan-Evans, "Retention: Tag, You're It!" *Training and Development,* April 2000, p. 34. Reprinted by permission.

1. I want to adjust my work schedule (for personal reasons) three days a week, to come in half an hour earlier and leave half an hour earlier.
2. I want to get this task done in a brand-new way, not like you have ever seen it done before.
3. I want to complete the first five steps of this project before I have you review it with me.
4. I want to try a new technique, one that I'm more comfortable with, to increase sales.
5. Instead of taking that class you recommended, I found a mentor from whom I want to learn that skill.
6. I just took some great pictures on my vacation and want to put them on my cubicle walls.
7. I want to work from home two days a week.
8. I plan to work on Saturdays for a few weeks in order to get a project done on time, and I want to bring my well-trained dog to work with me.
9. I want to wear casual clothes to work rather than a business suit. I'm more comfortable and creative in my jeans and tennis shoes.
10. I know we've always done these projects solo, but I want to put together a team this time because I believe we will do a better job, more quickly.
11. I want six weeks off without pay to begin building my new home.
12. I want to bring my new baby to work for the first six weeks.

SCORING

Your response	1	2	3	4	5	6	7	8	9	10	10	12
"Sure, no problem."												
"No way."												
"Let me see what I can do."												

previews and a career-planning session in the first few months after hiring may help to cultivate realistic expectations that the company can meet.

Knowledge Retention Programs

When employees leave, either due to retirement or to turnover, they may take with them valuable knowledge. As intellectual capital is increasingly important to firm performance, some organizations have begun to work systematically to retain important knowledge even if employees themselves depart. A **knowledge retention program** might target both explicit and tacit knowledge. **Explicit knowledge** is readily codified and passed on in written form. Examples include passwords, details of contacts at supplier or buyer firms, locations of important files, and even suggestions about how to improve business processes based on the employee's long experience. However, this knowledge may be lost if there is no formal mechanism for eliciting and recording it before the employee leaves. A predeparture briefing or a modified traditional exit interview are ways to try to capture this knowledge. Better yet might be an ongoing system to record and store important information.

Other types of information are considered **tacit knowledge**—harder to quantify expertise or "feel" that comes from long experience with a job and memory of a vast number of past events and how they were dealt with successfully or unsuccessfully. Often this knowledge is best transmitted in person by active mentoring of younger staff. When departures are planned well in advance, as in retirement, there may be opportunities for the transmission of this tacit knowledge to nominated successors through day-to-day work. Other alternatives to capture tacit knowledge might include videotaping employees explaining a complex task while demonstrating how to perform it, or using expert systems software to capture and model the decision making of highly experienced incumbents. Yet another mechanism is to retain access to the person holding the knowledge, through phased retirement or postdeparture consulting roles. Continuous transfer of tacit knowledge among employees is facilitated by nurturing communities of practice, as described in Chapter 9.[59]

Thus far we have focused on employee-initiated transitions such as retirement and voluntary turnover. The next sections consider **involuntary turnover**—instances in which individuals are forced to leave because the organization no longer wants or needs them.

INVOLUNTARY TURNOVER

Involuntary turnover has important strategic implications for the organization. First, it affects the perception of the organization by the community, the media, and current and former employees. For example, a firm that effectively and humanely manages a reduction in its work force may maintain or even enhance its image among employees and the public, which could result in a variety of long-term benefits. In contrast, one that develops a reputation for treating employees badly, either through frequent layoffs or arbitrary and unfair firing, will have a harder time drawing a qualified applicant pool in the future.

Second, involuntary turnover helps the organization achieve its strategic goals. Poor performers are terminated, and the productivity of a firm can be improved.

Layoffs may allow an organization to reduce costs when market demand slumps. However, reductions in force are not always successful in improving organizational performance.

Third, involuntary turnover can aid coordination and integration within the organization by removing employees who cannot get along with others and therefore disrupt the smooth operation of the firm. Finally, involuntary turnover serves as a strategic influence on the culture of the organization. Removal of key executives can allow an organization to change its strategic focus. The reason for termination can send a message to other employees about important cultural norms and values, for example, a "no-exceptions" rule for using drugs while working or for violating safety rules.[60]

The sections that follow first consider the discharge of individuals, usually for reasons of unacceptable behavior or poor performance, then turn to larger scale layoffs, usually motivated by economic or strategic concerns rather than the behavior of the workers themselves.

EMPLOYMENT-AT-WILL

Can employers fire any employee at any time, for any reason at all? In the United States, the doctrine of **employment-at-will** says they can. This section presents a definition and brief history of the concept of employment-at-will and discusses the factors that limit an employer's ability to terminate employees. Finally, some suggestions for how management should deal with the employment-at-will issue are given.

What Is Employment-at-Will?

The employment-at-will doctrine stems from a nineteenth-century view that an employment contract is a private matter between free agents. A person is hired for an indefinite duration, and either employer or employee may end the relationship for any reason and at any time. In 1884 this doctrine found support in the case of *Payne v. Western and Atlantic RA Company,* when the court confirmed the right of an employer to hire or fire any individual for good cause, bad cause, or no cause at all.[61] Discussion of the employment-at-will issue has generally centered on the employer's right to fire a worker rather than on the employee's right to leave a job. With the Wagner Act of 1935, unions were able, through collective bargaining, to introduce the idea that employees should be fired only for just cause. Many public employees have also received statutory protection from arbitrary termination. The tenure system among university teachers, for example, protects teachers from arbitrary firing. However, between 70 and 75 percent of employees in the United States have no explicit protection.[62] Nevertheless, an employer's right to fire employees at will is limited by several factors, including civil rights legislation, union contracts, whistleblower statutes, and employees' limited right to sue on the grounds of wrongful discharge.[63]

Civil Rights Legislation

Federal civil rights legislation provides protection against employment discrimination for minority-group members, women, people with disabilities, older workers, and other protected groups. Organizations have learned to be careful about the fairness of their selection systems but frequently neglect to apply the same safeguards to their organizational exit procedures. The dismissal without cause of employees who are members of a protected class can be a dangerous affair, even when termination is part of a legitimate company-wide layoff. A worker who is discharged for *any* reason might claim that age, sex, or race was the *real* cause of the termination. If prima facie evidence of discrimination is found, the organization must spend considerable time, effort, and money to defend itself against the charge, or it must make a settlement with the plaintiff (possibly including back pay or reinstatement of the employee).

The issues of employment-at-will and employment discrimination have become closely linked in the matter of firing older employees. Chapter 5 describes the Age Discrimination in Employment Act, which prohibits employers from using age as a basis for hiring or firing people aged forty or above. Age discrimination suits are a common type of workplace bias charge. The typical litigant is a white male supervisor or professional between the ages of fifty and fifty-nine, discharged during corporate layoffs. Such employees have no unions to represent them but are sufficiently aware of the law to challenge their dismissal. As is shown in *Murphy v. American Home Products Corporation,* age discrimination can be used successfully to challenge at-will terminations when other, more traditional means of challenge are unsuccessful.[64]

Union Contracts

Collective-bargaining agreements also limit an organization's application of the employment-at-will doctrine. Typically, these agreements between unions and management specify the reasons for which an employee may be discharged and the procedures that should be followed in such a discharge. Unions often negotiate seniority provisions that determine who is to be discharged in the event of a company-wide layoff. If an organization takes care to follow the terms of the contract and appropriately documents all cases of termination for cause or layoffs, the constraints imposed by unionization should not be a major difficulty. However, if proper discharge processes are not followed, the employee may file a grievance. A formal grievance procedure then begins. The complaint is discussed at a series of meetings between representatives of the union and management at successively higher levels if agreement cannot be reached at lower levels. If the grievance procedure does not resolve the complaint, arbitration may follow.[65]

The Concept of Wrongful Discharge

Many employees cannot rely on federal or state legislation, labor contracts, or individually negotiated contracts in dealing with employment discharge situations. For most U.S. workers, a lawsuit claiming **wrongful discharge** is the only protection against the employment-at-will doctrine.[66] The number and payouts of such lawsuits have increased in recent years.[67] Court decisions associated with the wrongful discharge concept have delineated five types of situations under which the employment-at-will doctrine does not apply: (1) violations of public policy, (2) whistleblowing, (3) an expressed or implied guarantee of continued employment, (4) employer conduct that violates the concepts of "good faith and fair dealing," and (5) other tortious conduct by the employer.[68] These exceptions are summarized in Table 16.7.

TABLE 16.7

Exceptions to Employment-at-Will

Exception	Example	Important Cases/Laws
Employment discrimination	Termination based on sex or age	Title VII, Civil Rights Act
		Age Discrimination in Employment Act
Union contracts	Seniority-based terminations	Wagner Act
Public policy violations	Whistleblowers	*Palmateer v. International Harvester*
		Sheets v. Teddy's Frosted Foods
Expressed or implied guarantee of employment	Verbal contracts	*Touissant v. Blue Cross & Blue Shield*
	Written policies in employee manuals	
Good faith and fair dealing	Firing to prevent receiving benefits	*Fortune v. National Cash Register Co.*
Tortious conduct	Interfere with legitimate contract	*Monge v. Beebe Rubber Co.*

Violations of Public Policy Employees may not be fired for exercising rights protected by law—for instance, filing workers' compensation claims, refusing to commit perjury, or taking time off to serve on a jury. Employees are also protected when they exercise the "rights of shareholders." Employees who are shareholders in a company may, for example, exercise their rights by voting for or against a merger or stock float without fear of firing by management.[69] Most states have accepted the concept of wrongful discharge as a result of violations of public policy, though the situation is usually defined very narrowly. The critical issue is not whether the employee's behavior is of *benefit* to the public but whether a *clear and legal mandate* of public policy is involved.[70]

Whistleblowing Various forms of **whistleblowing** are also protected. For example, in *Palmateer v. International Harvester,* an employee was subjected to wrongful discharge after he reported coworkers who were involved in criminal activity. In *Sheets v. Teddy's Frosted Foods,* an employee who insisted that the company comply with the Food, Drug, and Cosmetic Act was found to have been wrongfully discharged.[71]

Expressed or Implied Guarantee of Continued Employment Although violation of public policy is the most recognized exception to the employment-at-will doctrine, an **expressed or implied contract** between the employer and the employee is also held to limit arbitrary firing in thirty-eight states.[72] Implied contracts are created in several ways. In one case, *Touissant v. Blue Cross and Blue Shield of Michigan,* employees had been fired for no apparent reason, even though there had been statements by the employer to the effect that "you can have your job as long as you do your job." These statements were deemed to form a contract between employee and employer.[73] In the same case, there were also written personnel policies stating that good cause was required before any nonprobationary employee would be fired and that employees could be fired only after receiving a series of warnings and a disciplinary hearing. The employees had been fired without the benefit of these procedures. They filed suit against the company and won the case.

Good Faith and Fair Dealing Judicial tradition also holds that a contract contains an implied promise of **good faith and fair dealing.** A violation of good faith on the employer's part may provide the basis for a suit claiming an exception to the employment-at-will doctrine. In *Fortune v. National Cash Register Company,* Fortune, a salesman, had worked for the company for twenty-five years under a contract that specifically stated that he had been hired on an at-will basis.[74] He was fired after having made a large sale—because, he charged, the company wanted to avoid paying him the commission it owed him. Although his contract included an at-will clause, the court ruled that National Cash Register had not acted in good faith and thus had violated the employment contract. Only eleven states recognize the covenant-of-good-faith exception to the employment-at-will doctrine.[75]

Tortious Conduct Some discharged employees have argued successfully that they were victims of **tortious conduct.** In law, a *tort* is the violation of a duty owed another person (aside from breach of specific contracts). "A termination by the employer of a contract of employment at will which is motivated by bad faith or malice or is based on retaliation is not in the best interest of the economic system or the public good and constitutes a breach of the employment contract."[76] An employer who acts with malicious intent in terminating employees, intentionally inflicting emotional distress on them or defaming their character, can be found guilty of wrongful discharge.[77]

Management's Response

Dealing effectively with the issue of employment-at-will and avoiding charges of wrongful discharge are important practical considerations for organizations. For example, the average award for a successful wrongful discharge suit reached $200,000 by the late 1990s.[78] Organizations may approach the issue of employment-at-will in several ways. Many companies have taken actions such as including explicit at-will statements on job application forms and in employee handbooks.[79] Some require employees to sign statements acknowledging that they can be fired at any time for any reason. Firms also carefully train recruiters and supervisors to avoid making any promises of job security that might be construed as an implicit contract. These actions may not completely protect firms from wrongful discharge litigation, but they reduce the likelihood of being taken to court.[80] A potential downside of repeating the at-will message frequently in employee communications is that it sends a very negative message to employees. Another approach has been to encourage specific labor contracts.[81] In the case of union contracts, discharge cases are handled within the framework of a collectively bargained grievance and arbitration procedure rather than in the courts. Individual employment contracts are commonly used with executive, professional, and sales employees. As well as specifying an at-will discharge policy, these contracts may include noncompete agreements and protect the employer's trade secrets or proprietary information should an employee leave or be fired. Some contracts also include a compulsory arbitration clause should the application of the contract be in dispute. Arbitration is likely to be much quicker and less costly than court proceedings for both the employee and the employer.[82]

Firms also take measures to reduce the need for discharges.[83] Management can improve employee selection procedures. Companies can provide realistic orientation programs, where employees both learn what level of performance is expected and receive the training that can help them achieve this level. Management may also develop accurate performance appraisal, performance feedback, and disciplinary systems, in which sanctions for poor performance are clearly specified and a paper trail of performance is maintained. Performance feedback provided by the system may help employees improve enough to avoid termination. If termination is necessary, everyone understands why. The next section examines the situation in which employees are fired for "just cause," such as poor performance or violation of important organizational rules.

DISCIPLINE SYSTEMS AND TERMINATION FOR CAUSE

For most managers, dealing with problem employees and firing an employee are very difficult and unpleasant things to do and more often than not are done awkwardly.[84] Managers are afraid they may jeopardize friendships or make the situation worse. Taking disciplinary action or firing a member of a work group may also damage the image of the manager with other employees.[85] As a result, many managers try to avoid dealing with problem employees. They are often unsure about how to deal effectively with the situation and assume that "if you ignore it, it will go away." They confront problem employees only after the situation becomes so bad that they have no other choice.[86] Even when a just cause for termination exists, it is important that actions leading to termination be effective and well documented so as to avoid wrongful discharge litigation or even more serious consequences. For example, the incidence of employees' killing their supervisors or coworkers, often after having been fired, has escalated in recent years.[87] The next section focuses on the use of discipline in organizations and the development of disciplinary systems, which should form an important part of the overall process leading to employees' **termination for cause.**

The Use of Discipline in Organizations

Considerable attention has been paid to whether disciplinary punishment is an appropriate part of organizational life. Discipline helps provide cues or signals as to what behavior is or is not acceptable. It serves as a form of role clarification and identifies important organizational norms and values for the employee. Even if punishment does not change the behavior of the offender, other members of the work group may be deterred from engaging in inappropriate behavior. Arguments against the use of disciplinary punishment are that it is unethical or inhumane and that it never really eliminates the undesired behavior. Undesirable behavior is suppressed only until the threat of punishment is gone or the behavior "goes underground," where the possibility of detection is reduced.[88]

Organizations can take several different approaches to discipline.[89] One is largely punitive, imposing punishments as retribution to get even for past wrongdoings. Supervisors are seen as police, and employees committing violations are treated like children who must be spanked with increasing vigor for each additional infraction. At the opposite end of the scale is a future-oriented developmental approach that treats the employee as an adult. The latter approach is called **positive discipline** or **discipline without punishment.**[90] In this model, oral and written coaching for the first few violations is followed by a one-day suspension *with pay.* During the day off, the employee is to think about whether he or she is willing and able to abide by the company's rules. The next day, the employee tells the supervisor that he or she has decided to comply, or voluntarily resigns. The onus of controlling subsequent behavior falls squarely on the employee. A further similar violation results in discharge because the employee has chosen not to honor his or her pledge to the employer.

Research on the effective use of disciplinary punishment in organizations suggests that punishment must:

- Be in proportion to the nature of the undesirable behavior exhibited
- Be applied before the undesired behavior has time to become a habit or a typical behavior pattern of the employee
- Be focused on a specific behavior, not a general pattern of behavior
- Be applied consistently across people and time
- Be administered by someone the employee trusts and respects[91]

The goal of fair and effective discipline is more likely to be achieved when there is a detailed written discipline policy that is clearly communicated to all employees. Often such policies specify a **progressive disciplinary system.** Such a system is shown in Table 16.8, although the nature of offenses should be defined

TABLE 16.8

An Example of a Progressive Disciplinary System

	Number of Offenses				
Nature of Offenses	**1st**	**2nd**	**3rd**	**4th**	**5th**
Excessive or habitual absenteeism	V	W	5	D	
Absence from overtime assignment	W	5	D		
Excessive or habitual tardiness	V	W	3	5	D
Leaving without permission	W	5	D		
Loafing, loitering, etc.	W	5	D		
Disorderly conduct	5	D			
Acts intending to harm persons or property	D				
Possessing alcohol at work	5	D			
Gambling	5	D			
Possession of narcotics	D				
Appearing for work under the influence of narcotics	D				
Possession of firearms at work	D				
Violating clearly marked safety rules	W	3	5	D	
Negligent acts during work that cause harm or damage to persons or property	5	D			
Stealing	D				
Unauthorized possession of company property	D				
Refusal to accept work or perform work in accordance with instructions	D				
Threats to or intimidation of management	D				
Slowdown, willful holding back of work	W	D			

Key to symbols: V = verbal warning; W = written warning; 3, 5 = suspension days; D = discharge

Source: Adapted from Louis Imundo, *Employee Discipline: How to Do It Right* (Belmont, Calif.: Wadsworth, 1985), pp. 34–41.

in more detail than is shown in the table. For instance, "excessive or habitual absenteeism" might be defined as missing more than four days of work, without a medical excuse or approval by the supervisor, during any sixty-day period.[92]

A few offenses—such as bringing a gun to work or striking a superior—warrant discharge the first time they are committed; others attract a graduated (progressive) series of penalties. For minor offenses, an oral warning is the first step. This assures that the employee understands that a rule or expectation has been violated, that he or she should not do it again, and that more severe consequences will follow for persisting in the violation. A second similar offense attracts a written warning and starts to lay the paper trail documenting the organization's efforts to reform the employee. Further offenses may result in suspension without pay, and a further repetition of the same offense results in discharge. Although the process of discharging individuals for violation of rules, excessive absenteeism, or other discrete on-the-job behaviors is fairly clear-cut, other situations may be more problematic. For instance, should an employer discharge an employee for objectionable off-duty conduct? This is discussed in the Ethical Perspective box.

Another difficult situation is termination for poor work performance. Superiors may tolerate poor performance for a long period of time before deciding to take action. They may write acceptable performance appraisals for poor performers to avoid unpleasantness or in the hope that the employee will improve with time. These actions may come back to haunt them if there is a subsequent attempt to discharge the employee for sustained poor performance. When there is a problem with poor job performance, employees need to be told very clearly (orally and in writing) exactly what the problem is, what they must do to fix the problem, how much their performance has to improve, by what date, and what will happen to them if improvement is not forthcoming.[93] Coaching during the designated period is helpful in showing that the employer has made a genuine effort to remedy the problem.

As part of an overall disciplinary procedure, the organization may want to provide access to counseling for problem employees. **Employee assistance programs** help employees with personal problems that affect performance, such as drug or alcohol abuse, and may help prevent an otherwise valuable employee from being fired.[94] Even if termination does occur, employees may feel less hostile if they recognize that the organization has done its best to help them stay employed. Supervisors may also feel less troubled about firing employees who have been given ample opportunity to correct their behavior.

Managing Termination for Cause

Despite rehabilitation efforts, firing is sometimes necessary. It is important to manage the termination process fairly and properly to reduce the likelihood of legal action against the company by the terminated employee. In the case of repeated violations, it is important to document the occurrence of each act and the feedback that was subsequently given to the employee. When a severe violation is suspected (e.g., violence, theft, sexual harassment, or extremely poor performance), a thorough investigation should be conducted to ascertain the true situation. Guidelines for ensuring that investigations will meet court scrutiny include the following:

- Take notes during interviews with the employee and any witnesses.
- Emphasize confidentiality, and proceed discreetly throughout the investigation.

ETHICAL PERSPECTIVE

Firing for Off-Duty Behavior—Legal? Ethical?

Can or should an employer discipline or discharge an employee for off-duty behavior such as:

- Smoking tobacco
- Smoking marijuana
- Drinking alcohol to excess
- Dating someone who works for a competitor
- Being arrested for a crime such as domestic abuse or shoplifting
- Moonlighting at an unrelated job
- Setting up a part-time business in competition with the employer
- Cross-dressing
- Having an adulterous relationship
- Being active in an extremist political group

Is it wrong for an employer who pays for eight hours per day of a person's time to attempt to dictate their behavior twenty-four hours per day? At present, there is no blanket legal right to privacy that protects employees of private companies against employer intrusion and action on the basis of their off-duty behavior. In some jurisdictions, however, there are protections for specific legal off-duty acts. For instance, twenty-eight states protect the rights of employees to use tobacco products off the job; in the remaining states the employer may ban all tobacco use. Many of the other "offenses" listed here may legally be used as grounds for terminating at-will employees in the vast majority of states.

Employers have a legitimate interest in prohibiting off-duty acts by employees that reflect badly on the company, undermine its competitive position, or impair the worker in the performance of on-the-job duties. For instance, an accountant accused of embezzling from a volunteer community group may seriously damage the reputation of the accounting firm for which he works. An employee with access to vital business intelligence who is in a romantic relationship with a competitor's employee may present a real risk to the company. Smokers and heavy drinkers have been found to have more absenteeism and to incur greater health care costs.

In other cases, employee behavior off the job may not influence the company at all. The Winn-Dixie grocery chain terminated a high-performing truck driver because he engaged in cross-dressing off the job. The employee sued for sex discrimination. The company won because the sex discrimination laws do not apply to "transgendered" people. Although the company had the legal right to fire the employee, was it wise to do so? Winn-Dixie experienced considerable bad publicity over the case and probably lost the trust of many current employees who saw the termination as unfair.

Companies should weigh both the legality and the merits of each particular off-duty behavior case before deciding how to proceed. Extensively regulating the off-duty behavior of employees is inappropriate, but a company can have some up-front policies on the issue. One HR consultant suggests the following wording for employee handbooks:

> Ordinarily we do not intervene in the private lives of our employees. However, should a conflict with a client or an activity on an employee's part be of a nature that it could tarnish the image of our company or hurt our business position in the community, management reserves the right to enforce proper disciplinary actions.

Source: J. A. Pearce II and D. R. Kuhn, "The Legal Limits of Employees' Off-Duty Privacy Rights," *Organizational Dynamics,* Vol. 32, 2003, pp. 372–383; and C. Hirschman, "Off Duty, Out of Work," *HR Magazine,* February 2003, pp. 51–56, quote at p. 56.

- Maintain a file of information resources, including a time line of occurrences, interview notes, and so forth.
- Conduct interviews in a private place in nonintimidating circumstances.
- Do not conduct group interviews.
- Avoid accusatory questions and police-style tactics.
- Do not question the employee for an unreasonable amount of time.

- Avoid any appearance of force or the suggestion that an employee may not leave the room.
- Explain that the purpose of the investigation is to provide a factual basis for any disciplinary action.
- Allow the person being interviewed to review any written statements and make changes to them.
- Consider having a witness present during the interview.
- Interview only people who have reason to know about the actions under investigation.[95]

Regardless of how thorough the investigation, a single person should rarely make the decision to terminate an employee. The decision should either be reviewed by a higher level manager or be made by a group of several managers.[96] This will help to prevent biased or spur-of-the-moment terminations.

In the preceding section on termination for cause, the focus has been on the termination of an individual employee. Another form of termination is layoff, whereby employees are terminated due to their jobs having become redundant or because of the need to reduce operating costs. The next section examines the issue of layoffs.

RETRENCHMENT AND LAYOFF

The term **retrenchment** is usually used to refer to permanently discharging an employee because he or she will not be needed for the foreseeable future. **Layoff** is sometimes used as a synonym for retrenchment, but it may also mean that an employee is temporarily put off work with the likelihood of being recalled once business picks up.

The need for firms to become leaner, more efficient, and more productive to meet the challenge of international competition has been one stimulus to reducing employee head count in recent times. Economic downturns are another, and over the past two decades many U.S. businesses have cut costs by reducing their work forces. Although a boom in the late 1990s reduced retrenchments for a while, a downturn in 2001 increased numbers again. The terrorist attacks of September 11, 2001, triggered further job cuts. In the ten weeks following September 11, mass layoffs at 350 establishments affecting 103,781 employees were attributed to the attacks. More than 70 percent of these job losses were in the air transport and hotel and motel industries.[97]

Although retrenching employees (also called a **reduction in force**) is not a new idea, historically it happened mainly to blue-collar workers, such as those in the auto industry. In contrast, layoffs during the 1980s and 1990s were felt throughout the hierarchy and among professional ranks in an unprecedented number of organizations.[98] High-tech firms and dot.coms were hit particularly hard in a recent downturn, with highly skilled information technology workers finding themselves suddenly jobless. The export of IT jobs to locations such as India has resulted in further domestic downsizing in some technical job categories. An unprecedented wave of mergers and acquisitions has also meant that many employees found themselves to be unnecessary.

How Effective Have Mass Layoffs Been?

Proponents of layoffs claim that reducing the number of employees in a firm will result in a variety of positive outcomes. Table 16.9 shows the percentage of firms that have actually realized these supposed benefits of layoff. These data indicate that the positive benefits expected from downsizing do not materialize for many organizations. As many as two-thirds of the firms that laid off employees ended up having to lay off more workers the next year.[99] In another study, more than 70 percent of companies surveyed reported grappling with serious problems of low morale and mistrust of management caused by multiple efforts to restructure.[100] One expert suggests that the cost savings expected from work force reductions often do not occur for the following reasons:

- Functions of those laid off are replaced by those of expensive outside consultants.
- Subsidiary units end up having to re-create the functions once carried out by corporate headquarters staff who have been laid off and so end up hiring new employees.
- When line staff are asked to perform duties formerly done by headquarters staff, the training needed to enable the line personnel to perform the functions is expensive and reduces the cost savings associated with the layoffs.[101]

In addition to employers not receiving the benefits associated with layoffs, there are numerous other negative results of work force reductions. Many organizations find that laid-off employees are needed later when market demand im-

TABLE 16.9

Outcomes of Using Layoffs to Increase Organizational Competitiveness

Outcome	% of Firms Reporting Layoff Outcomes
Reduced expenses	46
Increased profits	32
Improved cash flow	24
Increased productivity	22
Increased return on investment	21
Increased competitive advantage	19
Reduced bureaucracy	17
Improved decision making	14
Increased customer satisfaction	14
Increased sales	13
Increased market share	12
Improved product quality	9
Technological advances	9
Increased innovation	7
Avoidance of takeover	6

Source: A. Bennett, "Downsizing Doesn't Necessarily Bring an Upswing in Corporate Profitability," *Wall Street Journal*, June 6, 1991, p. B1; and Kim S. Cameron, "Guest Editor's Note: Investigating Organizational Downsizing—Fundamental Issues," *Human Resource Management*, Vol. 33 (2), 1994, pp. 183–186.

proves.[102] Employee morale often plummets, resulting in lower organizational commitment, lower job satisfaction, increased anxiety and feelings of job insecurity, increased job stress, voluntary turnover of high performers (who can find work elsewhere), and lower overall productivity. There is also research that indicates a negative effect of layoffs on a firm's stock price (at least in the short term).[103] Given the lack of positive outcomes from many layoff situations, along with the prevalence of negative outcomes, the question becomes how and when to use layoffs effectively. "Golden rules for effectively managing layoffs" are presented in Table 16.10.

Outplacement

Many organizations provide **outplacement** assistance to help laid-off employees find new jobs. Outplacement services may include personal counseling, career assessment and counseling, advice and aid in job search activities, and assistance with résumé preparation.[104] The services may be provided by HR staff or by outplacement consultants hired by the firm. Outplacement serves several functions. First, if an organization helps discharged employees find new jobs, reductions in force are likely to be less stressful and traumatic. Second, knowing that an organization is willing to look after its departing employees enhances the morale of those who remain behind. Third, outplacement seems to help employees find new jobs faster than would otherwise be possible. Over the long run, helping people become re-employed reduces the organization's unemployment insurance benefit costs. Fourth, some experts feel that outplacement tends to reduce the threat of litigation about the discharge.[105] Finally, more and more business organizations are simply recognizing that they have a moral and ethical responsibility toward their employees. Some 90 percent of all major companies now provide outplacement services for employees being laid off.[106]

Taking Care of Survivors

Often those who remain after a reduction in force are considered the lucky ones and are ignored by management. However, research has shown that survivors of a layoff suffer significant problems, which may have a dramatic impact on the organization. Survivors frequently show decreased productivity and satisfaction. They lose their motivation to work, and they worry about the future of their own jobs. After a reduction in force, many survivors seek new jobs elsewhere.[107]

Dealing effectively with survivors is essential for the long-term health of the organization. Practitioners and researchers have suggested several ways to minimize the negative effects of layoffs on survivors. When organizations provide generous outplacement and severance benefits, survivors feel more positive toward the firm, more comfortable, and less stressed by the layoffs.[108] Survivors should be told why the terminations are occurring and who will be affected. Trust and honest communication between management and employees during layoff episodes is very important. Any discrepancies will be discovered as employees compare notes, reducing the organization's ability to inspire confidence and commitment in its remaining employees.[109] Above all, survivors must perceive the layoff process as having been conducted fairly.[110] Increased training for survivors may also be essential. Survivors may be asked to add new tasks to their job

TABLE 16.10

The Golden Rules for Effectively Managing Layoffs

Plan

- Prepare ahead of time for downsizing.
- View human resources as assets rather than liabilities.
- Assess skills, abilities, and knowledge of all employees to help improve HR decisions.
- Identify the firm's future strategy and strategic imperatives; treat downsizing as providing a clear vision for the future, not just an escape from the past.
- Use HR planning practices that consider alternatives to layoffs.
- Set targets, deadlines, and objectives for downsizing.
- Implement downsizing by starting with small wins; i.e., things that can be changed quickly and easily and that achieve the desired results.

Focus on productivity improvement

- Approach downsizing as an opportunity for overall improvement.
- Focus on attacking sources of organizational fat.
- Map and analyze all processes in the organization to eliminate inefficiencies, redundancies, and non-value-added activities.
- Measure all activities and processes, not just output, to identify how improvements can be made.
- Institute a variety of cost-cutting procedures, not just head-count reduction.

Involve

- Involve employees, which includes the use of cross-level and cross-functional teams, to identify what needs to change and how.
- Hold everyone, not just top management, responsible for achieving targets and goals.
- Involve customers and suppliers.

Communicate

- Ensure that leaders are visible, accessible, and interactive.
- Project positive energy and initiative from leaders.
- Ensure that every employee is informed about what is happening.
- Make clear, direct, and emphatic announcements of layoff decisions.
- Explain why retrenchments must occur; if a clearly visible scapegoat exists that does not implicate management and is easy to understand, use it.
- Overcommunicate as layoffs proceed.

Take care of those laid off

- Give advance notification of layoffs.
- Provide safety nets for those who must leave, including severance pay, extended benefits, and outplacement assistance.
- Arrange collaboration between private- and public-sector organizations in providing services for those laid off.

Take care of survivors

- Implement layoffs in a fair and humane manner.
- Develop trust between management and surviving employees.
- Manage the rumor mill effectively.
- Provide training, cross-training, and retraining in advance for survivors, so that they will be able to handle the new demands.
- Do everything possible to maximize the retention of high performers.
- Change appraisal, reward, and pay systems to match new goals and objectives.

Source: Kim S. Cameron, "Strategies for Successful Organizational Downsizing," *Human Resource Management,* Vol. 33 (2), 1994, pp. 189–211; Daniel Feldman and Carrie Leana, "Better Practices in Managing Layoffs," *Human Resource Management,* Vol. 33 (2), 1994, pp. 239–260; Cynthia Hardy, *Strategies for Retrenchment and Turnaround: The Politics of Survival* (Berlin: Walter de Gruyter, 1990); and Mark Mone, "Relationships between Self-Concepts, Aspirations, Emotional Responses, Intent to Leave a Downsizing Organization," *Human Resource Management,* Vol. 33 (2), 1994, pp. 281–298.

duties—tasks that they may not have done before. Without adequate training, survivors may not only feel guilty about those laid off but also experience a sense of inadequacy and even failure in their newly defined jobs. A survey of HR executives indicated that at 80 percent of firms' employees experienced significant stress in trying to manage their post-layoff workload.[111]

Legal Constraints on Layoffs

In planning layoffs, organizations must consider legal constraints as well as their own needs and those of employees. Courts generally support management decisions in which seniority is used as the basis for layoffs. In a 1984 case, *Firefighters Local Union 1784 v. Stotts,* the Supreme Court ruled that it was illegal to lay off white employees with greater seniority to protect black workers who had less seniority but had been hired as part of an affirmative action plan.[112]

The **Worker Adjustment and Retraining Notification Act (WARN),** commonly known as the "Plant Closing Bill," requires employers covered by the law to give affected employees sixty days' written notice of anticipated plant closings or other mass layoffs.[113] WARN covers private and not-for-profit employers that have 100 or more full-time employees.[114]

According to WARN, a plant closing is defined as any temporary or permanent shutdown of an entire facility or significant part of a facility if the closing results in employment loss during a thirty-day period for fifty or more employees. A mass layoff occurs when a facility is not closed but there is a reduction in force affecting at least 500 employees, or as few as fifty employees if these fifty employees constitute at least one-third of the work force. Employers violating the law may be required to provide back pay and benefits for up to sixty days to workers laid off without proper notification. In some cases, employers may be required to pay fines of $500 per day, up to $30,000.

There are some exceptions to WARN. A "faltering company" is exempt if it was actively seeking capital to prevent the plant closing or layoff and reasonably believed that giving notice to employees would have prevented the company from receiving financing. An "unforeseeable business circumstance" may also exempt a company, such as when employees at a major supplier suddenly and unexpectedly go on strike and the company cannot operate without the supplies. Closings due to natural disasters such as floods and earthquakes likewise exempt a company from the sixty-day-notice requirement. A final exemption covers closings of plants that were originally established as "temporary facilities," if employees were hired with the understanding that their employment was not permanent.[115]

Summary of Key Points

Much attention has been given to selecting, training, and motivating employees. Equally important, however, is understanding the circumstances in which employees transition within organizations or leave them altogether. Most employees want to have a feeling of growth and progress through a series of jobs. Although career paths that take employees from one organization to the next fairly quickly seem to be increasingly common, organizations can and should assist employees to explore options and plot potential progress through a sequence of jobs within the firm. Lateral job moves across functions are becoming more common as a means of developing a breadth of skills, particularly since opportunities for hierarchical movement have declined. Career planning involves self-assessment of skills, values, and interests; exploration of alternative job movements; and planning for future development to enable desired transitions.

Another transition eventually made by most employees is retirement. Retirement has become an important issue as the population grows older. In most occupations, employees may no longer be forced to retire upon reaching a designated age. Some employers offer enhanced retirement packages to reduce head count in a company with too many employees. Others offer incentives for older employees to continue working, either full or part time, to retain valued skills or to enhance work force flexibility. Phased retirement seems to be the wave of the future.

Voluntary turnover occurs when employees quit their jobs. Many employers realize that the direct and indirect costs of employee turnover can be very high, and they have begun to work hard to retain valued employees. Employees are more likely to quit if they believe they have good alternatives and if they are dissatisfied with their jobs. When employees are embedded in their jobs with a multitude of links among family, employer, and community, they are less likely to quit. Employees may contemplate quitting for a long period of time as their job satisfaction gradually falls and they eventually decide to search for alternatives, or they may decide to quit suddenly on the basis of a single event. Retention management programs attempt to discover why employees quit or stay, then act to keep the most valuable employees by addressing their concerns. Recently, knowledge retention programs have also been implemented to capture valuable information held by departing employees.

Effectively managing nonvoluntary turnover is important. State legislation, court decisions, and labor contracts place some limitations on the right of organizations to terminate employees-at-will. Termination for unionized workers must follow the procedures spelled out in the contract. Nonunionized employees may challenge their firing using legal arguments that limit employment-at-will, such as violation of public policy, whistleblowing, implied contracts, good faith and fair dealing, or tortious acts. Organizations should always have proper written documentation to support their reasons for terminating an employee. In dealing with poor performers, it is important to use performance appraisal and corrective feedback, accompanied by an escalating series of punishments, for employees who are unable or unwilling to improve their behavior. A thorough investigation should be conducted before terminating an individual for alleged misconduct.

Organizations may also need to carry out large-scale layoffs or retrenchments. Thorough advance planning for reducing the work force is critical. It is vital to treat employees who are laid off humanely and to provide sufficient "outplacement" assistance. It is equally important for the organization to manage the survivors of a company-wide layoff. Proper counseling and training for survivors can help ensure a motivated and stable work force following retrenchment.

The Manager's Vocabulary

bridge job
broadbanding
career planning
career-plateaued
discipline without punishment
downsizing
dual-career family
dual-income family
embeddedness
employee assistance program
employment-at-will
exit interview
expert, or professional, career ladder
explicit knowledge
expressed or implied contract
good faith and fair dealing
involuntary turnover
knowledge retention program
layoff
linear career path
optimal rate of turnover
organizational survey
outplacement
phased retirement
positive discipline
progressive disciplinary system
reduction in force

restructuring
retention costs
retention management program
retirement
retrenchment
rightsizing
spiral career path
tacit knowledge
termination for cause
tortious conduct
traditional model of turnover
transitory career path
turnover costs
voluntary turnover
whistleblowing
Worker Adjustment and Retraining Notification Act (WARN)
wrongful discharge

Questions for Discussion

1. How are traditional career paths changing, and why? Do your career aspirations fit in with the changes that are occurring? Which type of career pattern appeals to you most?
2. Why should organizations become involved in career planning with their employees? What components might a career-planning system have?
3. Why is retirement an increasingly important issue, and how can it affect organizations?
4. Why and how do individuals decide to quit a job?
5. Explain some of the costs associated with voluntary employee turnover.
6. What can organizations do to strategically manage voluntary turnover?
7. How can an organization retain important knowledge held by departing employees?
8. What is the difference between voluntary and involuntary turnover? Between termination for cause and layoff?
9. What is employment-at-will? How does civil rights legislation restrict a company's ability to terminate employees-at-will?
10. Describe the difference between wrongful discharge as the result of an implied contract and as the result of a tortious act.
11. What are potential problems in the use of punishment in organizations?
12. Why is a progressive disciplinary system important when an organization is terminating an employee for cause? What should such a system involve?
13. How would you manage a disciplinary investigation into an employee you suspect may have been stealing from the company?
14. What are the "golden rules" of managing layoffs effectively?
15. Managing the survivors of layoffs is important. How would you help survivors deal with not having been laid off?
16. Why is the Worker Adjustment and Retraining Notification Act important for organizations planning a reduction in force? Who is covered by the law, and what does it require organizations to do?
17. Defend or refute the following statement: "Organizations should routinely provide outplacement programs for workers laid off in a work force reduction."

Case 16.1
Layoffs at Your University

Assume that you are the HR director at your university. For reasons beyond the university's control (a sudden drop in the enrollment of foreign students due to weakness in the international economy), the total budget for the coming year must be slashed by 6 percent. The president of the university has come to talk to you about retrenching staff as one way to reduce expenditures.

1. What issues would you discuss when considering using staff cuts as a means of dealing with a budget shortfall?

After much discussion and exploration of options, a decision is made to reduce employee headcount by sixty-five people within six months. One option is to impose the cuts equally across departments, another is to be more selective.

2. Comment on the choice of a specific number by which to reduce head count.
3. What means are potentially available to reduce employment by the target date?
4. How should decisions about who goes and who stays be made? Use your knowledge of your university and its programs in constructing your answer. You may wish to do some research to inform your answer.
5. What notice must be given to employees if any are retrenched?
6. What kind of outplacement program should be offered to employees, and will the same program be equally suitable to all those retrenched?
7. What else should management do during the layoffs?

Exercise 16.1

Planning Your Career: A Consideration of Alternate Paths

Divide into groups of three students with the same major.

1. Each individual should fill in the ideal job column of the accompanying grid, indicating his or her ideal job situation at intervals in the future. If you have difficulty with this assignment, perhaps you should spend more time in the self-analysis stage: What kinds of activities and tasks do you enjoy most? What do you want out of your life and career? What are your strengths and weaknesses? It also might be wise to spend more time gathering data about career options and patterns within your occupation. One starting point is the Department of Labor Web site. Check the Occupational Outlook Handbook (http://www.bls.gov/oco) and the Career Guide to Industries (http://www.bls.gov/oco/cg/home.htm).
2. Discuss the various career paths outlined by each individual. What accounts for differences in preferences? How likely is it that each career path will be achievable? How likely is it that your preferences will change with time and varying nonwork responsibilities? Have you included additional formal education in your plan? To what extent are you relying on a single stable employer to provide your career? How important are variety and geographic location to you? Do you expect your spouse to have a career?
3. With advice from the group, each person should use the right column of the table to sketch out an alternative career path that might be equally satisfying.

Years Since Graduation	Ideal Job Situation	Alternative Job Situation
1		
2		
5		
10		
15		
20		
30		
40		

Exercise 16.2

Conducting Exit Interviews

In class: Form into groups of four, with each group including at least two experiences of quitting a job. (A single person may have quit more than one job.)

Out of class: Each individual or group is to locate and interview people who have quit at least four full-time jobs between them.

1. Prepare to conduct a structured exit interview.
2. Interview each person about his or her decision to leave the job.
3. How did he or she make the decision to leave? Does the process resemble the traditional

model, or was it more of a sudden decision based on a specific event?

4. Was this turnover functional or dysfunctional for the employer? Why?

5. Could the employer have prevented this turnover from occurring? How? Why didn't it?

Notes and References

1. H. D. Hunt, "Information Please: The Scoop on Call Centers," at http://recenter.tamu.edu/pdf/1623.pdf. (accessed July 16, 2004)

2. J. Purcell and N. Kinnie, "Employment Regimes for the Factories of the Future: Human Resource Management in Telephone Call Centres." Paper presented at the Annual Meeting of the Academy of Management, Toronto, August 2000; A. Throne, "Capital One's Call Center Soars to New Heights," *Call Center Magazine,* March 2001, pp. 84–86; and B. R. Read, "Recipes for Effective Staffing," *Call Center Magazine,* April 2001, pp. 58–63.

3. S. Hutchinson, J. Purcell, and N. Kinnie, "Evolving High Commitment Management and the Experience of the RAC Call Centre," *Human Resource Management Journal,* Vol. 10 (1), 2000, pp. 63–78.

4. George T. Milkovich, Jerry M. Newman, and Carolyn Milkovich, *Compensation,* 5th ed. (Chicago: Irwin, 1995).

5. Chris Tilly, "Reasons for the Continuing Growth of Part-Time Employment," *Monthly Labor Review,* March 1991, pp. 10–18; and S. Hipple, "Contingent Work: Results from the Second Survey," *Monthly Labor Review,* November 1998, pp. 22–35.

6. Denise M. Rousseau, *Psychological Contracts in Organizations: Understanding Written and Unwritten Agreements* (New York: Sage, 1995).

7. The entire *Academy of Management Executive* issue for November 1996 and much of the issue for February 1997 are devoted to articles about careers in the twenty-first century. See also Michael B. Arthur and Denise M. Rousseau (eds.), *The Boundaryless Career: A New Employment Principle for a New Organizational Era* (Oxford: Oxford University Press, 1997).

8. Douglas T. Hall and Judith Richter, "Career Gridlock: Baby Boomers Hit the Wall," *The Executive,* August 1990, pp. 7–22.

9. Laura Zinn, "Move Over, Boomers: The Busters are Here—and They're Angry," *Business Week,* December 14, 1992, pp. 34–40.

10. F. L. Otte and W. M. Kahnweiler, "Long-Range Career Planning during Turbulent Times," *Business Horizons,* January–February 1995, pp. 2–7; E. H. Schein, "Career Anchors Revisited: Implications for Career Development in the 21st Century," *Academy of Management Executive,* November 1996, pp. 80–88; and D. T. Hall, *Careers In and Out of Organizations.* (Thousand Oaks, Calif.: Sage, 2002).

11. Hutchinson, Purcell, and Kinnie, "Evolving High Commitment Management and the Experience of the RAC Call Centre."

12. B. B. Read, "Certifying Your Call Center Staff," *Call Center Magazine,* April 2001, pp. 30–49; and W. S. Hersch, "Marking Progress," *Call Centre Magazine,* April 2003, p. 6.

13. Joel R. DeLuca, "Strategic Career Management in Non-Growing Volatile Business Environments," *Human Resource Planning,* Vol. 11 (1), 1988, pp. 49–61.

14. R. H. Vaughn and M. C. Wilson, "Career Management Using Job Trees: Charting a Path Through the Changing Organization," *Human Resource Planning,* Vol. 17 (4), 1994, pp. 43–55.

15. Kate Donnelly, Peter V. LeBlanc, R. Dale Torrence, and Margaret A. Lyon, "Career Banding," *Human Resource Management,* Spring–Summer 1992, pp. 35–43.

16. K. R. Brousseau, M. J. Driver, K. Eneroth, and R. Larsson, "Career Pandemonium: Realigning Organizations and Individuals," *Academy of Management Executive,* November 1996, pp. 52–66; M. Peiperl and Y. Baruch, "The Post-Corporate Career," *Organizational Dynamics,* Spring 1997, pp. 7–22; and Hall, *Careers In and Out of Organizations.*

17. Brousseau, Driver, Eneroth, and Larsson, "Career Pandemonium: Realigning Organizations and Individuals."

18. Zandy B. Leibowitz, Caela Farren, and Beverly L. Kaye, *Designing Career Development Systems* (San Francisco: Jossey-Bass, 1988).

19. Peter F. Drucker, "Managing Oneself," *Harvard Business Review,* March–April 1999, pp. 65–74.

20. Patrick J. Kiger, "At First USA Bank, Promotions and Job Satisfaction Are Up," *Workforce,* February 28, 2001. (Available at: www.workforce.com/archive/article/001/45/36.xci)

21. Howard V. Hayghe and Suzanne M. Bianchi, "Married Mothers' Work Patterns: The Job–Family Compromise," *Monthly Labor Review,* June 1994, pp. 24–30.

22. S. L. Grover and K. J. Crooker, "Who Appreciates Family-Responsive Human Resource Policies: The Impact of Family-Friendly Policies on the Organizational Attachment of Parents and Non-Parents," *Personnel Psychology,* Vol. 48, 1995, pp. 271–288.

23. Catherine R. Smith, "Dual Careers, Dual Loyalties: Management Implications of the Work/Home Interface," *Asia Pacific Journal of Human Resources,* Summer 1992, pp. 19–29; M. D. Lee, S. M. MacDermid, M. L. Williams, M. L. Buck, and S. Leiba-O'Sullivan, "Contextual Factors in the Success of Reduced-Load Work Arrangements among Managers and Professionals," *Human Resource Management,* Vol. 41, 2002, pp. 209–223.

24. Daniel Feldman, "The Decision to Retire Early: A Review and Conceptualization," *Academy of Management Review,* Vol. 19, 1994, pp. 285–311; quote at p. 287.

25. William J. Wiatrowski, "Changing Retirement Age: Ups and Downs," *Monthly Labor Review,* April 2001, pp. 3–12.

26. D. C. Feldman and S. Kim, "Bridge Employment during Retirement: A Field Study of Individual and Organizational Experiences with Post-Retirement Employment," *Human Resource Planning,* Vol. 23 (1), 2000, pp. 14–25.

27. A. M. Rappaport, "Postemployment Benefits," *Compensation and Benefits Management,* Autumn 2000, pp. 59–62.

28. Judy Greenwald, "Phased Retirement Begins to Catch On," *Business Insurance,* May 28, 2001, pp. 10–12; S. F. Gale, "Phased Retirement Keeps Employees—and Keeps Them Happy," *Workforce,* Vol. 82 (7), July 2003, pp. 92–95.

29. Patrick J. Purcell, "Older Workers: Employment and Retirement Trends," *Monthly Labor Review,* October 2000, pp. 19–30.

30. D. W. De Long and T. O. Mann, "Stemming the Brain Drain," *Outlook,* November 2003, pp. 38–43.

31. S. I. Erwin, "Pentagon Lays Out Game Plan to Address Workforce Losses," *National Defense,* January 2001, pp. 16–17.

32. "Technical Note," www.bls.gov/jlt/. (accessed July 14, 2004)

33. Barry Gerhart, "Voluntary Turnover and Alternate Job Opportunities," *Journal of Applied Psychology,* Vol. 75 (5), 1990, pp. 467–476; and R. W. Griffith, P. W. Hom, and S. Gaertner, "A Meta-Analysis of Antecedents and Correlates of Employee Turnover: Update, Moderator Tests, and Research Implications for the Next Millennium," *Journal of Management,* Vol. 26 (3), 2000, pp. 463–488; and P. W. Hom and R. W. Griffeth, *Employee Turnover* (Cincinnati, Ohio: South-Western College Publishing, 1995).

34. Griffith, Hom, and Gaertner, "A Meta-Analysis of Antecedents and Correlates of Employee Turnover;" D. G. Allen, L. M. Shore, and R. W. Griffeth, "The Role of Perceived Support and Supportive Human Resource Practices in the Turnover Process," *Journal of Management,* Vol. 29 (1), 2003, pp. 99–118.

35. T. R. Mitchell, B. C. Holtom, T. W. Lee, C. J. Sablynski, and M. Erez, "Why People Stay: Using Job Embeddedness to Predict Voluntary Turnover," *Academy of Management Journal,* Vol. 44 (6), 2001, pp. 1102–1121; and T. R. Mitchell, B. C. Holtom, and T. W. Lee, "How to Keep Your Best Employees: The Development of an Effective Retention Policy," *Academy of Management Executive,* Vol. 15 (4), 2001, p. 96.

36. P. W. Hom, F. Caranikas-Walker, G. E. Prussia, and R. W. Griffeth, "A Meta-Analytical Structural Equations Analysis of a Model of Employee Turnover," *Journal of Applied Psychology,* Vol. 77, 1992, pp. 890–909; W. H. Mobley, "Intermediate Linkages in the Relationship between Job Satisfaction and Employee Turnover," *Journal of Applied Psychology,* Vol. 62, 1977, pp. 237–240; and W. H. Mobley, *Employee Turnover: Causes, Consequences, and Control* (Reading, Mass.: Addison-Wesley, 1982).

37. Mitchell, Holtom, and Lee, "How to Keep Your Best Employees"; T. W. Lee and T. R. Mitchell, "An Alternative Approach: The Unfolding Model of Voluntary Turnover." *Academy of Management Review,* Vol. 19, 1994, pp. 51–89; and J. E. Sheridan, "A Catastrophe Model of Employee Withdrawal Leading to Low Job Performance, High Absenteeism, and Job Turnover during the First Year of Employment," *Academy of Management Journal,* Vol. 28, 1985, pp. 88–109.

38. J. C. McElroy, P. C. Morrow, and S. N. Rude, "Turnover and Organizational Performance: A

Comparative Analysis of the Effects of Voluntary, Involuntary, and Reduction-in-Force Turnover," *Journal of Applied Psychology,* Vol. 86 (6), 2001, pp. 1294–1299; and A. C. Glebbeek and E. H. Bax, "Is High Employee Turnover Really Harmful? An Empirical Test Using Company Records," *Academy of Management Journal,* Vol. 47, 2004, pp. 277–286.

39. J. D. Shaw, N. Gupta, and J. E. Delery, "Voluntary Turnover and Organizational Performance," Proceedings of the 62nd Annual Meeting of the Academy of Management, Denver, CO, U.S.A., 2002.

40. Beverly Kaye and Sharon Jordan-Evans, "Retention: Tag, You're It!" *Training and Development,* April 2000, pp. 29–34; and Suzanne Dibble, *Keeping Your Valuable Employees* (New York: Wiley, 1999).

41. For more detail on costing turnover, see W. F. Cascio, *Costing Human Resources: The Financial Impact of Behavior in Organizations* (Cincinnati: South-Western College Publishing, 2000). For an example of calculating costs for a specific job, see T. R. Hinkin and J. B. Tracey, "The Cost of Turnover," *Cornell Hotel and Restaurant Administration Quarterly,* June 2000, pp. 14–21.

42. Note however, that empirical evidence that turnover can be too low is very scarce.

43. Griffith, Hom, and Gaertner, "A Meta-Analysis of Antecedents and Correlates of Employee Turnover"; C. Williams and L. Livingstone, "Another Look at the Relationship between Performance and Voluntary Turnover," *Academy of Management Journal,* Vol. 37, 1994, pp. 269–298; and D. Schwab, "Contextual Variables in Employee Performance-Turnover Relationships," *Academy of Management Journal,* Vol. 34, 1991, pp. 966–975.

44. C. Trevor, B. Gerhart, and J. Boudreau, "Voluntary Turnover and Job Performance: Curvilinearity and the Moderating Influences of Salary Growth and Promotions," *Journal of Applied Psychology,* Vol. 82, 1997, pp. 44–61.

45. Saratoga Institute, *Retention Management: Strategies, Practices, Trends* (New York: American Management Association, 1997).

46. B. Kaye and J. Jordan-Evans, "Retention in Tough Times: Here's What 25 Global Talent Leaders Say about Keeping Good People—Especially Now," *Training & Development,* January 2002, pp. 32–37.

47. See Steel, Griffeth, and Hom, "Practical Retention Policy for the Practical Manager," for more advice.

48. J. J. Phillips and A. O. Connell, *Managing Employee Retention: A Strategic Accountability Approach.* (Amsterdam: Elsevier Butterworth Heinemann, 2003).

49. These data were collected in Singapore but parallel results for why U.S. employees say they leave. See Beverly Kaye and Sharon Jordan-Evans, *Love 'Em or Lose 'Em: Getting Good People to Stay* (San Francisco: Berrett-Koehler, 1999) for more on why U.S. employees stay.

50. Hutchinson, Purcell, and Kinnie, "Evolving High Commitment Management and the Experience of the RAC Call Centre."

51. Saratoga Institute, *Retention Management.*

52. Steel, Griffeth, and Hom, "Practical Retention Policy for the Practical Manager."

53. A. I. Kraut and L. M. Saari, "Organizational Surveys: Coming of Age in a New Era," in *Evolving Practices in Human Resource Management,* eds. A. I. Kraut and A. K. Korman (San Francisco: Jossey-Bass, 1999), pp. 302–327.

54. Kaye and Jordan-Evans, *Love 'Em or Lose 'Em.*

55. See Rita E. Numerof and Michael N. Abrams, *Employee Retention: Solving the Healthcare Crisis* (Chicago: Health Administration Press, 2003), for more advice on retaining staff in the health care industry.

56. Saratoga Institute, *Retention Management.*

57. Dick Sethi and Beverly Pinzon, "A Seven-Step Strategy to Help Retain Your Company's High-Impact Performers," *Human Resource Planning,* Vol. 21 (4), 1998, p. 16.

58. Mitchell, Holtom, and Lee, "How to Keep Your Best Employees."

59. D. W. De Long and T. O. Mann, "Stemming the Brain Drain," *Outlook,* November 2003, pp. 38–43; American Productivity and Quality Center, "Retaining Valuable Knowledge: Proactive Strategies to Deal with a Shifting Work Force," April 2002. American Productivity & Quality Center, Houston, Texas

60. Stephen Collarelli and Terry Beehr, "Organizational Exit: Firings, Layoffs, and Retirement," in *Personnel Selection in Organizations,* eds. Neal Schmitt, Walter Borman, et al. (San Francisco: Jossey-Bass, 1993), p. 343.

61. *Payne v. Western and Atlantic RA Company* (82 Tenn 507, 1884).

62. D. P. Twomey, *Equal Employment Opportunity,* 2nd ed. (Cincinnati, Ohio: South-Western, 1990), p. 132.

63. Stuart Youngblood and Leonard Bierman, "Due Process and Employment-at-Will: A Legal and Behavioral Analysis," in *Research in Personnel and Human Resources Management,* Vol. 3, eds. Kendrith Rowland and Gerald Ferris (Greenwich, Conn.: JAI Press, 1985), pp. 185–230; Charles J. Muhl, "The Employment-at-Will Doctrine: Three Major Exceptions," *Monthly Labor Review,* January 2001, pp. 3–11; and D. A. Ballam, "Employment-at-Will: The Impending Death of a Doctrine," *American Business Law Journal,* Summer 2000, pp. 653–687.

64. *Murphy v. American Home Products Corporation* (461 N.Y.2d 232 N.Y. State Ct. of Appeals, 1983).

65. Robert Coulson, *Labor Arbitration: What You Need to Know* (New York: American Arbitration Association, 1981).

66. Daniel Koys, Steven Briggs, and Jay Grenig, "State Court Disparity on Employment-at-Will," *Personnel Psychology,* Vol. 40, 1987, pp. 565–576; Youngblood and Bierman, "Due Process and Employment-at-Will."

67. Susan Gardner, Glenn M. Gomes, and James F. Morgan, "Wrongful Termination and the Expanding Public Policy Exception: Implications and Advice," *S.A.M. Advanced Management Journal,* Winter 2000, pp. 38–44.

68. William Fulmer and Ann W. Casey, "Employment at Will: Options for Managers," *Academy of Management Executive,* Vol. 4 (2), 1990, pp. 102–107; and Benjamin W. Wolkinson and Richard N. Block, *Employment Law: The Workplace Rights of Employees and Employers* (Cambridge, Mass.: Blackwell, 1996).

69. Fulmer and Casey, "Employment at Will."

70. A recent precedent in California suggests a broader interpretation of public policy. See Gardner, Gomes, and Morgan, "Wrongful Termination and the Expanding Public Policy Exception."

71. *Palmateer v. International Harvester* (85 Ill.2d 124, 421 N.E.2d 876, 1981); *Sheets v. Teddy's Frosted Foods, Inc.* (179 Conn. 471 A. 2d 385,1980).

72. Muhl, "The Employment-at-Will Doctrine."

73. *Touissant v. Blue Cross and Blue Shield of Michigan* (408 Mich. 579, 292 N.W.2d 880, 1980).

74. *Fortune v. National Cash Register Company* (373 Mass. 96, 36 N.E.2d 1251, 1977).

75. Muhl, "The Employment-at-Will Doctrine."

76. *Monge v. Beebe Rubber Company* (114 N.H. 130, 316, A.2d 549, 1974).

77. This exception to the employment-at-will doctrine is sometimes referred to as "abusive discharge." The court case most closely linked to this concept is *Monge v. Beebe Rubber Co.* (114 N.H. 130, 316 A.2d 549, 1974), in which a female employee was fired for not agreeing to date her supervisor. This was deemed abusive discharge. A case like *Monge v. Beebe Rubber* today most likely would be handled as a case of sex discrimination; however, other instances of abusive discharge may occur that would be considered a tortious act.

78. A. C. Goldberg, "Top 8 Legal Issues Affecting HR," *HR Focus,* December 1997, pp. 51–53.

79. Twomey, *Equal Employment Opportunity,* pp. 133–134.

80. Raymond Hilgert, "Employers Protected by at-Will Statements," *HR Magazine,* March 1991, pp. 57–60; and Sydney P. Freedberg, "Forced Exits? Companies Confront Wave of Age Discrimination Suits," *Wall Street Journal,* November 13, 1987.

81. Walt Baer, "Most U.S. Workers Still May Be Fired Under the Employment-at-Will Doctrine," *Supervision,* December 1987, p. 6.

82. C. M. Koen Jr. and W. H. Reinhardt Jr., "Employment Contracts: Preventative Medicine for Post-Termination Disputes," *Supervision,* July 2000, pp. 5–9.

83. Fulmer and Casey, "Employment at Will."

84. Kenneth Labich, "How to Fire People and Still Sleep at Night," *Fortune,* June 10, 1996, pp. 64–72.

85. Beth Tognetti, "How to Fire Someone Without Destroying Your Self-Esteem," *Supervision,* August 1987, p. 6.

86. Steven Brown, "The Case of the Incompetent Employee," *Supervisory Management,* Vol. 37 (1), 1992, pp. 1–2; Dave Day, "Training 101: Help for Discipline Dodgers," *Training & Development,* May 1993, pp. 19–21; and John Veiga, "Face Your Problem Employee Now!" *Academy of Management Executive,* Vol. 2 (2), 1988, pp. 145–152.

87. James Fox and Jack Levin, "The Workplace: Termination Can Be Murder," *Boston Globe,* May 2, 1993, p. 71.

88. Richard Arvey and Allen Jones, "The Use of Discipline in Organizational Settings: A Framework for Future Research," in *Research in Organizational Behavior,* Vol. 7, eds. L. Cummings and B. Staw (Greenwich, Conn.: JAI Press, 1985), pp. 367–408; Linda Trevino, "The Social Effects of Punishment in Organizations: A Justice Perspective," *Academy of*

Management Review, Vol. 17 (4), 1992, pp. 647–676; and Gail Ball, Linda Trevino, and Henry Sims Jr., "Just and Unjust Punishment: Influence on Subordinate Performance and Citizenship," *Academy of Management Journal,* Vol. 37 (2), 1994, pp. 299–322.

89. Louis Imundo, *Employee Discipline: How to Do It Right* (Belmont, Calif.: Wadsworth, 1985); Brian Klaas and Daniel Feldman, "The Evaluation of Disciplinary Appeals in Non-Union Organizations," *Human Resource Management Review,* Vol. 3 (1), 1993, pp. 49–81; and Jonathan Segal, "Firing Without Fear," *HR Magazine,* June, 1992, pp. 125–130.

90. C. J. Guffey and M. M. Helms, "Effective Employee Discipline: A Case of the Internal Revenue Service," *Public Personnel Management,* Spring 2001, pp. 111–127; and C. Osigweh and W. Hutchinson, "Positive Discipline," *Human Resource Management,* Vol. 28, 1991, pp. 367–383.

91. Arvey and Jones, "The Use of Discipline in Organizational Settings"; W. C. Hamner and D. W. Organ, *Organizational Behavior: An Applied Psychological Approach* (Dallas: BPI, 1978); and Terence Mitchell and Charles O'Reilly III, "Managing Poor Performance and Productivity in Organizations," *Research in Organizational Behavior,* Vol. 1, 1983, pp. 201–234.

92. Imundo, *Employee Discipline.*

93. Paul Falcone, "A Blueprint for Progressive Discipline and Terminations," *HR Focus,* August 2000, pp. 3–5.

94. D. W. Myers, *Employee Assistance Programs* (Chicago: Commerce Clearing House, 1986).

95. Adapted from CCH Business Law Editors, *Employee Termination Manual for Managers and Supervisors* (Chicago: Commerce Clearing House, 1991); and Cecily Waterman and Teresa Maginn, "Investigating Suspect Employees," *HR Magazine,* January 1993, pp. 85–87.

96. Kristin Kane, "Best Practices for Employee Termination," at www.wetfeet.com/employer/articles/article.asp?aid=389).

97. Kim Clark, "You're Laid Off! Kind of. Firms Look Beyond Pink Slips," *U.S. News & World Report,* July 2, 2001, pp. 50–53; Bureau of Labor Statistics, "Mass Layoffs in November 2001," December 28, 2001. (Available at: http://www.bls.gov/news.release/pdf/mmls.pdf.)

98. Pascal Zachary and Bob Ortega, "Workplace Revolution Boosts Productivity at Cost of Job Security," *Wall Street Journal,* March 10, 1993, pp. A1, A11.

99. S. Pearlstein, "Corporate Cutbacks Yet to Pay Off," *Washington Post,* January 1994, p. B6.

100. Gene Koretz, "The Downside of Downsizing," *Business Week,* April 28, 1997, p. 26.

101. Wayne Cascio, "Downsizing: What Do We Know? What Have We Learned?" *Academy of Management Executive,* Vol. 7 (1), 1993, pp. 95–104.

102. Samuel Greengard, "Don't Rush Downsizing: Plan, Plan, Plan," *Personnel Journal,* November 1993, pp. 64–76.

103. Mark Mone, "Relationships between Self-Concepts, Aspirations, Emotional Responses, and Intent to Leave a Downsizing Organization," *Human Resource Management,* Vol. 33 (2), 1994, pp. 281–298; and Dan Worrell, Wallace Davidson III, and Varinder Sharma, "Layoff Announcements and Stockholder Wealth," *Academy of Management Journal,* Vol. 34 (3), 1991, pp. 662–678.

104. Mark L. Lengnick-Hall, "Outplacement," in *The Blackwell Encyclopedic Dictionary of Human Resource Management,* eds. Lawrence H. Peters, Charles R. Greer, and Stuart A. Youngblood (Malden, Mass.: Blackwell, 1997).

105. Kenneth Dawson and Sheryl Dawson, "Immediate Outplacement Can Help Everyone Through the Transition," *HR Focus,* Vol. 71 (2), 1994, p. 4; and Robert J. Nobile, "Outplacement Counseling: Minimizing Legal Liability," *Personnel,* Vol. 68 (10), 1991, p. 10.

106. R. J. Lee, "Outplacement Counseling for the Terminated Manager," in *Applying Psychology in Business: The Handbook for Managers and Human Resource Professionals,* eds. J. W. Jones, B. D. Steffy, and D. W. Bray (Lexington, Mass.: Lexington Books, 1991).

107. Joel Brockner, "Layoffs, Self-Esteem and Survivor Guilt: Motivational, Affective, and Attitudinal Consequences," *Organizational Behavior and Human Decision Processes,* Vol. 36, June 1985, pp. 229–244; and Joel Brockner, Steven L. Grover, and Mauritz D. Blonder, "Predictors of Job Survivors' Job Involvement Following Layoffs: A Field Study," *Journal of Applied Psychology,* Vol. 73 (3), 1988, pp. 436–442.

108. Joel Brockner, "The Effects of Work Layoffs on Survivors: Research, Theory, and Practice," *Research in Organizational Behavior,* Vol. 10, 1988, pp. 213–255; and Frank Strasbourg, "Corporate Outplacement," *Business and Economic Review,* Vol. 38 (1), 1991, pp. 11–13.

109. Aneil Mishra and Karen Mishra, "The Role of Mutual Trust in Effective Downsizing Strategies," *Human Resource Management,* Vol. 33 (2), 1994, pp. 261–279.
110. Joel Brockner, Steven Grover, Thomas Reed, and Rocki Dewitt, "Layoffs, Job Insecurity, and Survivor's Work Effort: Evidence of an Inverted-U Relationship," *Academy of Management Journal,* Vol. 35 (2), 1992, pp. 413–425; G. M. Spreitzer and A. K. Mishra, "To Stay or to Go: Voluntary Survivor Turnover Following an Organizational Downsizing," *Journal of Organizational Behavior,* Vol. 23, 2002, pp. 707–729.
111. Jolene Sugarman, "The Survivor Syndrome," *Human Resource Executive,* January 1993, pp. 45–46.
112. *Firefighters Local Union 1784 v. Stotts* (U.S. Sup.Ct. 34 FEP 1702, 1984).
113. David Israel and Stephen Beiser, "Plant Closings and Layoffs Follow Special Rules," *HR Magazine,* July 1991, pp. 71–72.
114. Vida Scarpello, "Worker Adjustment and Retraining Notification Act, 1988," in Peters, Greer, and Youngbood (eds.), *The Backwell Encyclopedic Dictionary of Human Resource Management.*
115. Scarpello, "Worker Adjustment and Retraining Notification Act, 1988."

PART 6

Multinational Human Resource Management

CHAPTER 17

Managing Human Resources in Multinational Organizations

- What Is IHRM?
- Managing Human Resources in a Foreign Subsidiary
- Expatriate Managers
- Training Expatriates
- Appraising the Performance of Expatriates
- Paying Expatriates
- Expatriate Reentry
- IHRM: Adding Value in the Global Business Environment

HR Challenge

The Bonne Mare Group's CEO, Pierre Trollop, sits at his desk one afternoon reading his firm's most recent press release in the local paper.

> *The Bonne Mare Group has posted a 20 percent increase in its 2004 earnings to a record $37 million USD, the company announced today. The Bonne Mare Group, based in Provence, southern France, sold 502 new boats during 2004, up 18.1 percent from 425 the previous year. The company exports to more than 40 countries. Total revenue for 2004 was $305 million USD, up 21.6 percent from the 2005 revenue of $239 million USD.*

Pierre Trollop has a lot to be happy about. Bonne Mare's recent performance shows that its market position is firmly established throughout the world and its products are known for their innovative design, quality, and stability in even the roughest seas.

The Bonne Mare Group prides itself on combining personal craftsmanship with the latest twenty-first century technology. Its range of products is exported to boat enthusiasts in more than forty countries. Currently, all boats are manufactured at the firm's Aix en Provence manufacturing plant. Bonne Mare's five-year growth plan includes steps to further increase overseas markets while maintaining the flow of new high-quality boats for its customers.[1]

Despite this excellent news, Pierre Trollop is a little troubled. During a recent visit to clients in Germany, Pierre had been approached by two "friends-of-a-friend," one from Russia and the other from Poland, who pointed out that the economies of Poland and Russia were making significant gains. A growing number of individuals are rich, or at least comfortably wealthy. The Russian and his Polish colleague argued quite persuasively that Bonne Mare should consider opening export offices in St. Petersburg and Warsaw. The high-quality luxury items produced by Bonne Mare would be very attractive to those in the upper economic strata of Russia and Poland. Upon his return to Provence, Pierre asked his staff to look at the potential for the Russian and Polish luxury cruiser market, and somewhat to his surprise, he received very favorable feedback. As a result of this market analysis, Pierre is considering St. Petersburg and Warsaw as potential expansion sites for Bonne Mare.

One problem facing Pierre is how to staff these offices. Given the characteristics of Bonne Mare's product, and the unfamiliar nature of the Russian and Polish markets, Pierre thinks it would be important to have one of his own people head up each of these new offices—at least in the beginning. Unfortunately, no one in Bonne Mare has any real knowledge about Russia or Poland. It would be vitally important that the managers of the St. Petersburg and Warsaw offices have extensive knowledge of Bonne Mare's custom cruisers, including the technical manufacturing aspects. These managers must also be able to "mix, mingle, and network" with wealthy political and business figures in the two locations. Bonne Mare cruisers sell for an average of $610,000 USD, so potential buyers will represent a very special segment of Russian and Polish societies. All of Bonne Mare's current sales managers are experts in the technical and performance features of the cruisers, but none of them has ever worked in Russia or Poland, and none speak either language. Many of the managers have spouses, and many of those spouses have jobs—the typical dual-career situation of couples in the twenty-first century. If he were to send two of his managers to Russia and Poland for a year or two, it could be difficult.

After discussing the issue individually with members of his management team, Pierre has called a meeting of his managers to discuss this potential venture. He outlines the basic issue and then asks: "So what do think about Russia and Poland as potential markets? Does it make sense for us to go there? If we did, what would we do about staffing the St. Petersburg and Warsaw offices?"

In 1978 Arvind Phatak defined a *multinational corporation* as "an enterprise that has an interlocking network of subsidiaries in several countries, whose executives view the whole world as its theater of operations, and who therefore obtain and allocate financial, material, technical, and managerial resources in a manner conducive to the achievement of total enterprise objectives."[2] Today, organizations that fit Phatak's definition are often referred to as global or transnational corporations, with their key feature being that executives see all operations within the corporation as part of a *highly integrated* set of business activities that must be managed collectively to ensure global competitiveness. In this chapter, the term **multinational corporation (MNC)** will be used to describe *any* organization that has international operations and attempts to achieve some moderate level of integration among its foreign units. The term **global corporation** will be reserved for firms that fit Phatak's definition of organizations with highly integrated operations across several foreign locations.

In the 1950s and 1960s, most large multinational companies were American and operated in a world economy relatively safe from competition. In the 1970s and particularly in the 1980s, the world of international business became far more complex and competitive. In the 1990s MNCs were competing in a truly global marketplace, with it being possible for a French firm to manufacture a product in Germany in a plant partially staffed by U.S. and Belgian expatriates and sell most of its product in Britain. In the twenty-first century, global economic integration continues at a rapid pace. The World Wide Web and e-commerce are becoming increasingly important aspects of this new global economy. MNCs are now competing not only with other MNCs but also with e-commerce firms that can penetrate international markets without having a physical presence. The competition has become increasingly fierce, and the stakes are very high. For example, the average *monthly* value of goods imported by the thirty countries of the Organization for Economic Cooperation and Development grew from $387.5 billion in 2001 to $460.2 billion in 2003. Average monthly exports in the OECD countries grew from $362.2 billion in 2001 to $428.9 billion in 2003.[3] The amount of international trade is enormous, and competition for a slice of this "trade pie" is intense.

As we indicated in Chapter 2, an important source of competitive advantage for an organization is its human resources. The competitive value of effective human resource management in multinational firms is certainly as great as, if not greater than, its value in purely domestic organizations. In *The New Expatriates: Managing Human Resources Abroad,* Rosalie Tung stated that "human resource planning is pivotal to the successful operation of a multinational corporation (MNC) because technology, capital, and know-how cannot be effectively and efficiently utilized nor transferred from corporate headquarters without using human power."[4] Although many factors contribute to or detract from international competitiveness, the efficient use of human resources is essential and will remain so for the foreseeable future.

This chapter examines issues involved in managing human resources in multinational corporations. The process is referred to as *international human resource management (IHRM).* We begin with a discussion of the differences between human resource management in domestic and international environments and then look at the approaches to international human resource management that MNCs can take and the factors that affect the choice of approach. Finally, we consider specific HR functions within an MNC, such as staffing, training, performance appraisal, and compensation, examining them from two perspectives. The first perspective is that of the HR manager operating within a foreign subsidiary, and the second is that of an HR manager based in the MNC's headquarters.

WHAT IS IHRM?

It is not easy to provide a precise definition of international human resource management. What an HR manager does in a multinational corporation varies from firm to firm. It also depends on whether the manager is located in a global corporation's headquarters or on-site in a foreign subsidiary.

A Definition

Broadly defined, **international human resource management (IHRM)** is the process of procuring, allocating, and effectively utilizing human resources in a multinational corporation. If the MNC is simply exporting its products, with only a few small sales offices in foreign locations, then the task of the international HR manager is relatively straightforward. However, in global firms, human resource managers must achieve two somewhat conflicting strategic objectives. First, they must integrate human resource policies and practices across a number of subsidiaries in different countries so that overall corporate objectives can be achieved. At the same time, the approach to HRM must be sufficiently flexible to allow for significant differences in the types of HR policies and practices that are most effective in different business and cultural settings. This problem of balancing **integration** (control and coordination from HQ) and **differentiation** (flexibility in policies and practices at the local subsidiary level) is a common dilemma facing HR and other functional managers in global corporations.[5] Although some argue that IHRM is not unlike HRM in domestic settings, others point out that there are significant differences. Specifically, compared with domestic HRM, IHRM (1) encompasses more functions, (2) has more heterogeneous functions, (3) involves constantly changing perspectives, (4) requires more involvement in employees' personal lives, (5) is influenced by more external sources, and (6) involves a greater level of risk than typical domestic HRM.[6]

When compared with domestic human resource management, IHRM requires a much broader perspective on even the most common HR activities. This is particularly so for HR managers operating from an MNC's headquarters (HQ) location. The number and variety of IHRM activities are daunting. International HR managers must deal with issues as varied as international taxation; international relocation and orientation; various other administrative services for expatriates; selecting, training, and appraising local and international employees; and managing host-government relations in a number of countries around the world. Even when dealing with one particular HR functional area such as compensation, the international HR manager is faced with a great variety of national and international pay issues. For example, the HQ-based HR manager must coordinate pay systems in different countries with different currencies that may change in relative value to one another over time. An American expatriate in Tokyo who receives a salary of U.S. $200,000 may suddenly find the buying power of that salary dramatically diminished if the Japanese yen strengthens in value relative to the U.S. dollar. A U.S. dollar purchased 248 yen in 1985 but less than 115 yen in 2004. In the case of fringe benefits provided to host-country employees, some interesting complications might arise. For example, it is common in the United States for companies to provide health insurance benefits to the employee and the employee's family, which usually means spouse and children. In some countries, however, the term "family" may encompass a more extended group of relatives—multiple spouses, aunts, uncles, grandparents, nephews, and nieces. How does the firm's benefit plan deal with these different definitions of family?[7]

A final aspect of the broader scope of IHRM is that HQ-based managers deal with employee groups that have very different cultural backgrounds. The HQ manager must coordinate policies and procedures to manage expatriates from the firm's home country **(parent-country nationals, PCNs), host-country nationals (HCNs),** as well as **third-country nationals (TCNs,** e.g., a French manager working for an American MNC in the firm's Nigerian subsidiary) in subsidiaries around the world. Although such issues are important for the HQ-based manager, they are also relevant to the HR manager located in a subsidiary. This manager must develop HR systems that are not only acceptable in the host country but also compatible with the company-wide systems being developed by his or her HQ-based counterpart. These policies and practices must effectively balance the needs and desires of local employees, PCNs, and TCNs.

It is at the subsidiary level that the increased involvement of IHRM in the personal lives of employees becomes particularly apparent. It is not unusual for subsidiary HR managers to be involved in arranging housing, health care, transportation, education, and recreational activities for expatriate and local staff. For example, foreign firms operating in Taiwan often provide dormitory housing for local assembly workers; this housing is managed by the MNC's local HR staff. Subsidiary managers may even find themselves dealing with expatriates who have marital or alcohol problems, acting as counselor and legal adviser.[8]

IHRM activities are also influenced by a greater number of external forces than are domestic HRM activities. The HQ-based manager may have to set equal employment opportunity (EEO) policies that meet the legal requirements of both the home country and a number of host countries. Because of the visibility foreign firms tend to have in host countries (especially in developing countries), subsidiary HR managers may have to deal with government ministers, other political figures, and a greater variety of social and economic interest groups than would normally be encountered in purely domestic HRM.

The final difference between domestic and international HRM relates to the level of risks and consequences associated with HR decisions. There certainly are major risks associated with HRM in domestic situations. Unfair hiring practices may result in a firm being charged with a violation of EEO laws and subjected to financial penalties. The failure to establish constructive relationships with domestic unions can lead to strikes and other forms of labor actions. However, international HR managers face these same risks, as well as some additional ones that are unique and more threatening. Depending on the countries where the MNC operates, HQ and subsidiary HR managers may have to worry about the physical safety of employees. The threat of terrorism and its effect on both expatriate and local employees of a multinational firm have become increasingly important aspects of the international HR manager's responsibilities.[9] A 2003 article in the *The Times* newspaper is indicative of the new world faced by international HR managers. *The Times* reported that "British expatriates celebrating Christmas in Bahrain are being told that Islamic militants have been scouting the island's bars and restaurants for a holiday attack. . . . The U.S. Embassy in Bahrain said last night that it had received a specific threat of an al-Qaeda strike and told Americans to avoid places such as clubs frequented by Westerners."[10] In all too many countries, kidnapping and terrorism are of concern to international HR managers.[11]

Besides these risks, it has been estimated that maintaining an average expatriate manager, with family, overseas costs between U.S. $300,000 and $1 million per year. Over the past decade, as found in studies of 750 firms, 10 to 20 percent of U.S. expatriates return early from foreign assignments.[12] If managers do not perform well and must be recalled to the home country, their failure represents a huge financial loss for the firm.

The final risk is that of expropriation or seizure of the MNC's assets by a host country's government. If HR policies antagonize host-country unions or important political groups, the MNC may be asked to leave the country, have its assets seized, or find the local government taking majority control of its operation. Again, this is not the sort of risk that most domestic HR managers face.

Approaches to IHRM

MNCs can approach the management of international human resources in a number of ways. Four of these are presented in Table 17.1.[13] In the **ethnocentric approach,** the MNC simply exports HR practices and policies used in the home country to subsidiaries in foreign locations. Expatriates from the MNC's home country manage the foreign subsidiaries, and the MNC's headquarters maintains tight control over the subsidiaries' policies. This approach emphasizes consistency and integration across all subsidiaries. However, this approach is often viewed as

TABLE 17.1

Four Approaches to IHRM

	Orientation			
Aspect of the Enterprise	Ethnocentric	Polycentric	Regiocentric	Geocentric
HR strategy	Uniform strategy across units	Diverse strategies across units	Regional integration of strategy, but differentiation across regions	Global overarching strategy on key corporate issues but differentiated policies on more local issues
Performance criteria evaluation and control	By home-country HQ	By local subsidiary management	Coordination across countries in the region	Global as well as local standards and control
Information and resource flows	Mainly from HQ to local subsidiary	Little among subsidiaries, little between subsidiary and HQ	Little between subsidiary and HQ, medium to high among subsidiaries in region	Inflows and outflows between and among HQ and subsidiaries
Staffing mix	Home-country managers	Host-country managers	Host-country and third-country nationals from within the region	Best people where they can be best used
Career development	Home-country managers developed to work anywhere	Totally within subsidiary career paths and development	Regional career paths and development	Managers anywhere developed to work anywhere
Purpose of socialization process	Gain loyalty, commitment, and understanding of HQ	Gain loyalty and commitment to the subsidiary	Gain loyalty and commitment to the region	Gain loyalty, commitment, and understanding of the total firm and its diverse units

Sources: Adapted from D. A. Heenan and Howard V. Perlmutter, *Multinational Organization Development* (Reading, Mass.: Addison-Wesley, 1979), pp. 18–19; Ken Kamoche, "The Integration-Differentiation Puzzle: A Resource-Capability Perspective in International Human Resource Management," *The International Journal of Human Resource Management,* Vol. 7 (1), 1996, pp. 230–244.

inflexible. It ignores potentially critical local differences and may overlook opportunities with respect to HQ-subsidiary and cross-subsidiary learning. This may result in foreign subsidiaries resisting HR practices that they feel are inappropriately imposed on them by HQ.

In the **polycentric approach,** the subsidiaries are basically independent from headquarters. HR policies are adapted to meet the circumstances in each foreign location. Local managers in the foreign sites are hired to manage HRM activities. One obvious advantage of the polycentric approach is that each subsidiary's HRM system is in tune with its local context and should be more readily accepted by local employees and managers. Disadvantages also occur, however. It is likely that a lack of coherence within the MNC will develop on a number of important HR-related issues. For example, foreign subsidiaries may use different performance criteria to assess employees. These criteria are focused on the most important local performance objectives. Unfortunately, such objectives may not be consistent with the overall business objectives within the MNC as a whole. Because each subsidiary has its own HR system, duplication of effort occurs, and opportunities for economies of scale or synergies in terms of cross-subsidiary learning are ignored.

The **closed hybrid model** can be described as a compromise between the ethnocentric and polycentric approaches. In this approach to HR, a subsidiary uses a parent-country "template" for HR but adapts practices within the template to local conditions.[14]

The **regiocentric approach** represents a regional grouping of subsidiaries. HR policies are coordinated within the region to as great an extent as possible. Subsidiaries may be staffed by managers from any of the countries within the region. Relative to a purely polycentric approach, the regiocentric approach enhances coordination and communication among subsidiaries within a region. However, the approach is quite limited in its ability to encourage coordination, economies of scale, and learning between subsidiaries in different regions or between a region and the MNC's headquarters.

In the **geocentric approach,** HR policies are developed to meet the goals of the global network of home-country locations and foreign subsidiaries. This may include policies that are applied across all subsidiaries as well as policies adapted to the needs of individual locations—depending on what is best to maximize global results. This approach has also been referred to as an **open hybrid model** because subsidiary practices are a hybrid of activities to meet both global and local demands, with extensive sharing among subsidiaries of effective practices.[15] An attempt is made to identify the best HR practices from both the home and host countries and to apply them in an integrative manner where most appropriate around the world. The firm is viewed as a single international business entity rather than a collection of individual home-country and foreign business units. HRM and other activities throughout the MNC are managed by the individuals most appropriate for the job, regardless of their nationality. Thus you might find a British manager handling HRM activities in the New York office of a Dutch MNC.

Factors Affecting the Approach to IHRM

A number of factors may influence the IHRM approach taken by an MNC. Included among these are external factors such as the political policies and legal regulations within the host countries; the state of managerial, educational, and technological development in the host countries; and the national cultures of both the home and host countries. Factors internal to the firm also affect the IHRM approach. These include the level of international experience in the firm, the method by which worldwide subsidiaries are founded, the technology and nature of the product or products of the MNC, the strategic importance of particular groups of employees, the MNC's internal organizational culture including the beliefs and values of top management, and the life cycle of the organization.[16]

Political Policies and Legal Regulations The nature of IHRM may be restricted by government policies and legal regulations in the host country. For example, policies limiting the number of expatriates and requiring extensive employment of host-country nationals may be in place to encourage MNCs to hire, train, and develop local employees, particularly managerial and technical staff. This is especially likely in developing countries, where management and technical training within the host country's educational system is rudimentary and the local government views the presence of MNCs in the country as a means of developing local expertise.

Managerial, Educational, and Technological Development in the Host Country An MNC opening subsidiaries in Europe faces a much different IHRM challenge than one opening subsidiaries in, say, western Africa. In Europe, the available work force is likely to be well educated and have considerable technical and management experience. Therefore, the opportunity to develop polycentric, regiocentric, or geocentric IHRM strategies is available. In western African countries, management and technical education is likely to be limited, and the bulk of the work force may lack basic skills needed to deal with modern production processes or service activities. A more centralized IHRM strategy is necessary, with careful on-site monitoring by home-country personnel.

Home- and Host-Country Cultures Culture, particularly national culture at the headquarters level, plays a role in determining IHRM practices.[17] Culture may affect HQ decisions in at least two ways. First, some cultures are simply more comfortable than others in taking an ethnocentric approach to management. For example, Japanese MNCs more frequently staff management positions in their foreign subsidiaries with home-country managers than do American or European MNCs. There are, of course, exceptions to this, but worldwide this tendency toward ethnocentric staffing is greater in Japanese MNCs.[18]

Second, the mix of cultures in the subsidiaries of an MNC and the level of cultural difference among the subsidiaries will restrict the IHRM approach taken. As the number and level of cultural differences among subsidiaries increase, it becomes much more difficult for HR staff at the MNC's headquarters to formulate and implement consistent HR practices worldwide. Thus, even though an MNC might prefer an ethnocentric approach to managing human resources, the policies and practices formulated at HQ may be totally inappropriate and unacceptable in particular subsidiary locations. A more polycentric or regiocentric approach may be necessary.

International Experience of the Firm Firms with extensive international experience have had the opportunity to develop more diverse methods of maintaining coordination and control over their foreign operation. Thus they may focus less on centralized control of HR functions than do firms with little international experience. Newcomers to the global marketplace may view the international business environment as more unpredictable, higher in ambiguity and uncertainty, and perhaps more threatening than more experienced global players. Not only the experience of the MNC as a whole but also that of specific subsidiaries will affect the IHRM approach used. Although the MNC may be very experienced internationally and emphasize more decentralized control of foreign subsidiaries, top management may decide that very new subsidiaries need to be more closely monitored and controlled by HQ, resulting in a more ethnocentric approach to IHRM.[19]

Method of Subsidiary Founding The method used to establish operations in foreign locations also may affect HR policies. At new sites, it may be more likely that HR practices and policies from the home country will be implemented. In the case of foreign operations that are acquired by merger or acquisition, the presence of existing HR practices in the acquired/merged operation likely will reduce the wholesale exportation of home-country HR systems into the subsidiary.

Technology and the Nature of the Product For technologically sophisticated products or services, the need to maintain specific production standards and quality control necessitates a greater degree of centralization of IHRM functions at the MNC's headquarters location and the use of home-country managers and technical personnel to monitor these standards. This is the case particularly when the subsidiaries involved are located in host countries with low levels of technological and managerial expertise. Other products must be adapted to host-country tastes to succeed in the local market. For example, some food items highly popular in the United States would be viewed as quite repulsive in other countries. In this case, the reliance on local talent to adapt the product to suit the host-country market may require a very different approach to managing the subsidiary's recruiting activities.

Strategic Importance of Particular Employee Groups Another factor to consider is the strategic role of particular employee groups. A higher level of centralized control may be adopted for those groups of employees who are most critical to the MNC's strategic performance. For example, although its overall approach to IHRM is quite decentralized, the firm Interbrew adopts a highly ethnocentric mode for training employees in technical brewer functions. The skills and knowledge related to the brewing process are considered to be core competencies of this brewery founded in the fourteenth century. As a result, HQ closely controls brewer training in all subsidiaries, whereas training programs for other functions such as marketing and sales are developed locally.[20]

Organizational Culture Regardless of the national culture of a firm, each organization develops its own internal work culture. Although national culture has an impact on organizational culture, there is considerable room for variation across firms within the same country. Competitive orientation and profit focus, the level of employee involvement in decision making, and basic assumptions about employee proactivity, malleability, and responsibility seeking will affect how an MNC's headquarters approaches human resource management in foreign subsidiaries. Ethnocentric approaches to IHRM are more likely in firms where employees are generally viewed as malleable, not very proactive, and not likely to desire and seek responsibility. In such organizational cultures, the more controlling nature of ethnocentric IHRM would likely seem most appropriate for HQ managers.[21]

Organizational Life Cycle Some researchers argue that the appropriate IHRM approach will depend on the life cycle of the organization and the life cycle of the firm's products within various international markets.[22] During the initiation stage, the organization is concentrating on getting itself started and establishing itself within domestic and limited foreign markets. International involvement may be restricted to exporting or very limited international sales operations. During this phase, the organization tends toward an ethnocentric approach to IHRM. In the functional growth stage, international operations become a significant part of this growth, with foreign product divisions established within the firm. The firm views foreign operations as "add-ons" to its organizational growth but not necessarily integral parts of its overall strategic development. A polycentric approach to IHRM is likely, with the firm's headquarters relying on local management to run each foreign location.[23] During controlled growth, the firm attempts to increase productivity and control costs by identifying economies of scale and functional integration across major overseas and domestic units. A more regiocentric approach to IHRM may evolve, and trends toward a geocentric approach may develop. Finally, in the strategic growth stage, domestic and international competition force the firm to view its operations as a truly global unit. Global networks, alliances, and joint ventures are formed. Functional areas within the organization (both domestic and international) must be integrated to maximize competitive advantage. A global, geocentric approach to IHRM is needed to match the integration of research and development, marketing, production, and distribution worldwide.

MANAGING HUMAN RESOURCES IN A FOREIGN SUBSIDIARY

Culture not only influences an MNC's overall approach to IHRM but also plays a critical role in determining the activities of HR managers within foreign subsidiaries. In fact, culture has a potential impact on every HR function.

Culture and HR Functions in a Foreign Subsidiary

The role of a subsidiary HR manager is to develop HR practices that are (1) acceptable within the local culture and (2) acceptable to management at the MNC's headquarters. Balancing these two requirements is a difficult task. Whether subsidiary HR managers are home-, host-, or third-country nationals, they bring their own "cultural baggage," which may affect their ability to accommodate cultural differences in the host work force. Employees in a subsidiary may consist of a mixture of home-, host-, and third-country nationals—all with their own distinct cultural backgrounds and preferences. The subsidiary's HR manager must help all employees adapt to the HR practices operating in the subsidiary, even though these practices may be derived from cultures very different from their own. (See the Ethical Perspective box for more on this issue.)

Numerous studies indicate that cultural differences do affect how managers manage and how subordinates react to different management styles. To relate differences in culture to differences in IHRM practices, it is first necessary to identify

ETHICAL PERSPECTIVE

Ethical Relativity versus Ethical Absolutism: HR Decision Making in Overseas Operations

What should an international human resource manager do when an employment practice that is illegal and morally repugnant in the home country is commonplace and legal in the host country? Examples might include blatant sex discrimination or racist practices in hiring, job assignment, or compensation; use of child labor; or provision of unsafe working conditions.

Ethicists discuss two opposite approaches to questions of this type. One approach is *ethical relativism*, which suggests that what is good is what a society defines as good. If a society says that virgins shall be sacrificed at every full moon or that women shall not be paid the same as men for the same work, those rules are right for that society at that point in time. There can be no external frame of reference for judging that one society's set of rules is "better" than another's. The IHR manager who attempts to impose his or her values on personnel practices in the host country is guilty of ethical imperialism. Under the doctrine of ethical relativism, it is entirely appropriate to follow local practices relating to the treatment of employees. Although appearing on the surface to be a liberal, open-minded approach, this view may result in actions that most home-country constituencies would find entirely unacceptable, such as child labor or slavery.

The opposite position is called *ethical absolutism*. This is the view that there is a single set of universal ethical principles that apply at all times and to all cultures. This approach would be very useful because it would suggest which local practices, while different from those of the home country, are morally acceptable because they do not violate universal principles and which ones are not morally acceptable and must not be followed. The problem with this view is in specifying what the universal principles are and developing a logical case for why these, and only these, principles are truly universal. Adopting the values of a single culture or religion as universal again runs the risk of ethical imperialism.

Ethicists can marshal impressive arguments against both preceding views. So where does an expatriate decision maker turn for guidance? Thomas Donaldson has attempted to provide a framework for multinational decision making involving an ethical dimension. He states that the task is to "tolerate cultural diversity while drawing the line at moral recklessness."* In some ways his approach is absolutist because it relies on a statement of ten fundamental international rights: freedom

the aspects, or dimensions, on which cultures vary. Any discussion of the effect of culture on organizations would be incomplete without mentioning the groundbreaking research of Gerte Hofstede and Fons Trompenaars. More recent research conducted as part of the GLOBE (Global Leadership and Organizational Behavior Effectiveness) program has utilized some of Hofstede and Trompenaars' research to study cross-cultural differences in leader and organizational behavior. The GLOBE research has also identified a number of additional dimensions along which cultures may vary. A list of the Hofstede, Trompenaars, and GLOBE dimensions, along with their definitions, is presented in Table 17.2.

Differences in culture based on these cultural dimensions may significantly affect HR practices. The following subsections on subsidiary HR planning, staffing, training, performance appraisal, and compensation describe the difficulties faced by the subsidiary HR manager in developing effective HR systems. Many of these difficulties stem from cultural differences. They are discussed along with other problems facing the HR manager that are not exclusively cultural in nature.

of physical movement; the right to own property; freedom from torture; the right to a fair trial, nondiscriminatory treatment, physical security, freedom of speech and association; and the right to minimal education, political participation, and subsistence. Organizations, wherever they may do business, need to avoid depriving individuals of these rights.

However, these rights alone are not sufficient guidelines. When IHR managers are attempting to decide whether a practice is permissible for a multinational corporation, when it is not legal or morally acceptable in the home country but is legal and acceptable in the host country, Donaldson suggests that they ask themselves a series of questions. First, ask why the practice is acceptable in the host country but not at home. Answers to this question fall into two categories: (1) because of the host country's relative level of economic development or (2) for reasons unrelated to economic development. If the answer is (1), the next question is whether the home country would have accepted the practice when it was or if it were at the same level of economic development. If it would have, the practice is permissible. An example would be building a fertilizer plant that provides a product absolutely crucial to feeding the starving population of a nation despite the fact that there is some slight risk of occupational disease for individuals working in the plant. If the home country itself were starving, it would accept the risk to workers in the interest of the greater good.

The second answer—that the difference is not based on economic considerations—requires a more complicated decision-making process. The manager must ask two additional questions: "Is it possible to conduct business successfully in the host country without undertaking the practice?" and "Is the practice a clear violation of a fundamental international right?"[†] The practice is permissible only if the answer to both questions is no. That is, the practice is acceptable if it is critical to doing business in the country and does not violate a fundamental right. Otherwise, the organization should refuse to follow the local practice.

*Donaldson, *The Ethics of International Business,* p. 103.
[†]Donaldson, *The Ethics of International Business,* p. 104.
Sources: Walter T. Stace, "Ethical Relativity and Ethical Absolutism," in *Ethical Issues in Business,* eds. Thomas Donaldson and Patricia H. Werhane (Englewood Cliffs, N.J.: Prentice-Hall, 1988), pp. 27–34; William Shaw and Vincent Barry, *Moral Issues in Business* (Belmont, Calif.: Wadsworth, 1989), pp. 11–13; and Thomas Donaldson, *The Ethics of International Business* (New York: Oxford University Press, 1989).

TABLE 17.2
Dimensions of Culture

Dimension	Source	Definition
Power distance	Hofstede, GLOBE	The degree to which power is unequally distributed in a society or organization.
Uncertainty avoidance	Hofstede, GLOBE	The degree to which a society considers itself threatened by uncertain events and ambiguous situations and tends to avoid these types of situations or tries to control them through formal means.
Individualism–collectivism/communitarianism	Hofstede, Trompenaars	The extent to which society emphasizes the importance of the individual versus the group.
Societal collectivism	GLOBE	The degree to which organizational and societal institutional practices encourage and reward collective distribution of resources and collective action.

(continued)

TABLE 17.2
Continued

Dimension	Source	Definition
In-group collectivism	GLOBE	The degree to which individuals express pride, loyalty, and cohesiveness in their organizations or families.
Masculinity–femininity	Hofstede	The extent to which society values masculine characteristics of aggressiveness, assertiveness, and not caring for others; also, the extent to which male and female roles are clearly defined.
Long-term orientation	Hofstede	The degree to which a society embraces, or does not embrace, long-term devotion to traditional, forward thinking values. A long-term orientation is thought to support a strong work ethic where long-term rewards are expected as a result of today's hard work.
Gender egalitarianism	GLOBE	The extent to which an organization or a society minimizes gender role differences and gender discrimination.
Universalism vs. particularism	Trompenaars	Rules are more important than relationships; legal contracts are drawn up, and to be seen as trustworthy you must honor them; a deal is a deal. Or whether a rule applies "depends"; attention is given to the particular relationships, obligations, and unique circumstances involved; relationships evolve.
Neutral vs. affective	Trompenaars	Thoughts and feelings are hidden; there is a cool self-control; don't touch; monotone expression. Or people express their thoughts openly; there is a heated vitality to discussions; people touch, use gestures, and can be dramatic in their expressions.
Specific vs. diffuse	Trompenaars	Direct and to the point; precise, blunt, clear; looks at the facts, not the person involved. Or indirect and tactful; ambiguous; considers the situation.
Achieved vs. ascribed status	Trompenaars	Little focus on titles; titles used only when they reflect competence; judged on what you do and know. Or many titles; the boss is boss; generally older male authority.
Past vs. present vs. future	Trompenaars	History is important in determining our present actions. Or our actions should focus on the present, and the current situation should determine what we do. Or our actions should focus on the future and the attainment of future goals.
Sequential vs. synchronic time orientation	Trompenaars	One thing at a time; schedule is more important than relationships; follow original plan. Or many things at once; appointments are flexible; relationships are more important than schedules; like to "see what happens" to determine actions.
Internal vs. external control	Trompenaars	The extent to which people have a sense of being able to control what happens in their lives. Or whether they are controlled by external forces and the environment.
Assertiveness	GLOBE	The degree to which individuals in organizations or societies are assertive, confrontational, and aggressive in social relationships.
Future orientation	GLOBE	The degree to which individuals in organizations or societies engage in future-oriented behaviors such as planning, investing in the future, and delaying gratification.
Performance orientation	GLOBE	The extent to which an organization or society encourages and rewards group members for performance improvement and excellence.
Humane orientation	GLOBE	The degree to which individuals in organizations or societies encourage and reward individuals for being fair, altruistic, friendly, generous, caring, and kind to others.

Sources: Adapted from "Gerte Hofstede Analysis," at http://www.cyborlink.com/besite/hofstede.htm (accessed May 25, 2004); Fons Trompenaars and Charles Hampden-Turner, *Riding the Waves of Culture: Understanding Diversity in Global Business* (New York: McGraw-Hill, 1998); and Robert House, Mansour Javidan, Paul Hanges, and Peter Dorfman, "Understanding Cultures and Implicit Leadership Theories across the Globe: An Introduction to Project GLOBE," *Journal of World Business*, Vol. 37 (1), 2002, pp. 3–10.

Staffing in the Subsidiary

A subsidiary HR manager ought to use a hiring process that fits the local labor market, and local employment laws must be followed. In some countries, hiring may require using a government-controlled labor bureau. In Vietnam, for example, the Law on Foreign Investment permits overseas businesses to employ local Vietnamese as well as foreign employees. However, businesses usually have to use an employment agency to recruit local staff. Only with special permission can foreign enterprises recruit staff directly.[24] When local labor bureaus are involved in the hiring process, they sometimes supply a foreign subsidiary with employees not adequately skilled for the job, and it may be difficult for the subsidiary to refuse to employ them.

In particularistic cultures, nepotism may be a problem in hiring. As defined in Table 17.2, personal relationships are important in particularlistic cultures. Pressure may come from local managers or other employees to hire a close personal friend or relative who is having financial problems and desperately needs a job. This person may not be the best individual to hire in terms of technical competency. If the HR manager hires the individual, a potentially unqualified employee has been placed in the work setting. If the HR manager does not hire the individual, important cultural values have been violated, and the HR manager may be viewed as cold and unfeeling by local employees.

The development of a selection system may be complicated by the fact that selection tests used in the home country of the MNC may be culturally biased and inappropriate elsewhere. For example, many personality tests were developed using Western samples. Assertive individuals who take initiative and stand out from the crowd may appear well adjusted according to the norms of Western personality tests. However, a Japanese job applicant with a similar score might be a disaster if hired to work in the MNC's subsidiary in Tokyo because "standing out" as an individual is inconsistent with the more collectivist Japanese culture. Even if the concepts measured by the tests are applicable, there are difficulties in getting many tests adequately translated into the host-country language.

Issues of race, age, and sex discrimination can cause considerable difficulties for the subsidiary HR manager. In some countries it is acceptable and legal to place job advertisements that specifically state the race, age range, and sex of employees being sought. This would blatantly violate American EEO laws. An American working as an HR manager in one of those countries could experience a moral dilemma in following practices that are in line with local laws and culture but conflict with home-country laws and home-country organizational culture.

There also can be unexpected disadvantages associated with hiring particular types of local employees. For example, in a multicultural society, the use of an employee from one ethnic group in a managerial position may not be acceptable to members of other ethnic groups. The caste system, which historically has played a prominent role in Indian society, could make it inappropriate to hire someone from a lower caste to supervise employees of a higher caste. In some countries (Japan, for example), it may be inappropriate to hire a younger person for a job that has supervisory responsibilities over older employees.

Training in the Subsidiary

One of the major problems associated with hiring in less developed countries is that the skill level of individuals may be less than desired. In such circumstances, it is important to invest considerable time and effort in the selection process and to provide increased training to local employees when they arrive on the job. However, much like the problem of transferring HQ-based selection procedures to subsidiaries, training programs designed in the home country to teach employees the skills needed to perform their jobs may be inappropriate for use in other cultures. Translating training materials may be difficult. In addition, how people learn and the methods of training with which they are comfortable vary across cultures. For example, the Chinese, whose culture is very hierarchical, are taught respect and deference for teachers. As a result, Chinese students see themselves as the "receivers" and the teachers as the "givers" of knowledge.[25] Chinese students rarely ask questions or challenge a teacher's statements. To do so would be disrespectful. Consequently, Chinese students take a passive role in learning, and the very active, high-participation methods often used in Western training programs would perhaps be inappropriate for them.

An alternative to training local employees in the subsidiary's foreign location is to train them in the MNC's home headquarters or in a training facility in some other country. When ANZ Bank prepared to open operations in Vietnam, it needed twenty-eight people to staff its facility. No one was available locally with the appropriate financial expertise, so ANZ could not simply hire fully qualified Vietnamese bankers. Instead, it looked for locals with English-language skills and the ability to be trained. Once selected, these employees participated in training in Australia for three months with Australian financial experts.[26] Although this approach to training host-country employees has many advantages, it is not without its difficulties. MNCs must get visas and work permits for their employees to allow them to enter the home country for such training. Immigration laws and quotas placed on immigration by certain nations may make it difficult or even impossible to obtain the necessary visas and permits. Special agreements between the MNC and its home (or third-country) government may be needed.

Appraising the Performance of Subsidiary Staff

Culture helps determine the *importance* of performance appraisal, the *purposes* for which performance appraisal data are used, *what* aspects of performance should be appraised, and *how* that appraisal should be conducted. In cultures that value ascribed status, such as Austria or Saudi Arabia, your rank, title, family, or social background may be more important than how well you perform. Thus less importance is given to performance appraisal information than in achieved-status cultures such as the United States, Ireland, or Norway.

The purposes for which performance appraisals are used may vary from one culture to another. The results of a cross-national study on the purposes of performance appraisal are shown in Table 17.3.[27] In all but one country studied, there is a high level of focus on using appraisal information to aid in the development of employees (in Mexico there was insufficient data available to draw any conclusions). In the United States and Canada, one of the key purposes of appraisals is to document employee performance in relation to decisions made (e.g., termination) that might have legal implications. Both the United States and Canada are fairly "universalistic" countries where even-handed application of rules is important. Thus evidence of this fairness through documentation would be expected. Appraisals do not play this role in Japan, which is a more particularistic culture. In some countries the appraisal interview is used to allow subordinate expressions; that is, to provide feedback to management about how employees perceive the or-

TABLE 17.3

Purposes of Performance Appraisal in Different Countries

Country	Development	Documentation	Subordinate Expression	Pay	Promotion
Australia	High	?	?	Low	High
Canada	High	High	High	Low	High
Japan	High	Low	High	Low	Moderate
Korea	High	?	Low	Low	High
Mexico	?	?	Low	Low	Low to Moderate
PRC	High	?	Low	Low	Low to Moderate
Taiwan	High	?	Low	Low	Low
United States	High	High	Moderate to High	Moderate to High	High

Source: John Milliman, Stephen Nason, Cherrie Zhu, and Helen De Cieri, "An Exploratory Assessment of the Purposes of Performance Appraisals in North and Central America and The Pacific Rim," *Human Resource Management,* Vol. 41 (1), 2002, pp. 87–102, table 1, p. 89.

ganization and their role in the firm. In Korea and Mexico, where there is a high level of power distance, appraisals do not play this sort of role. Many of the performance appraisal methods discussed earlier in this text were developed in the United States—a very individualistic culture—and therefore tend to focus on the assessment of individual performance (e.g., behaviorally anchored rating scales, behavioral observation scales). By contrast, in collective cultures such as Japan or China, group performance is critical, and appraisals that focus on individual performance are highly threatening. This is consistent with the finding that appraisals play a key role in determining individual pay and promotion in the United States but much less of a role in Japan and China.

Culture also affects what aspects of an employee's behavior are likely to be appraised. In Japan, behaviors directed toward maintaining group harmony and cohesiveness (e.g., helping resolve conflicts among group members) may be valued as much as, if not more than, behaviors focused on more objective performance activities (e.g., producing more widgets). A similar situation may exist in feminine cultures, in which maintenance of good personal relationships is valued. Managers who maintain good personal networks and develop warm, trusting relationships with their subordinates may be viewed as better managers than those with higher levels of objective task performance. One study found marked differences in the criteria used by British and Chinese firms in determining whether employees were ready for promotion. In British firms the focus was on bottom-line delivery, evidence of experience in more than one business area, and experience in another country. In Chinese firms criteria included loyalty to the Communist party, good quality of relationships, evidence of being a hard worker, and good "moral" practices.[28]

In addition to *what* aspects of performance are measured, organizations vary in *how* they assess employee performance. Management by objectives (MBO) or other forms of goal setting are widely accepted in managing and appraising performance. In MBO, subordinates and supervisors agree on moderately difficult and challenging goals that the subordinates must achieve. At least four assumptions underlie the use of MBO programs. First, subordinates are assumed to be capable and have the right to negotiate with their boss about performance objectives.

Second, managers accept the need to allocate responsibility and delegate authority to the subordinates. Third, both supervisors and employees accept the risk associated with employee involvement in setting and achieving challenging objectives. Finally, both parties believe performance is an important element.

These assumptions are less true in countries in which a large power distance exists between the leaders and the led. Hierarchy and the chain of command are very important to both supervisors and subordinates. One example of culture affecting *how* appraisals should be done is found in Japan and relates to Trompenaars's neutral/affective and diffuse/direct cultural dimensions. Japan is a very neutral and diffuse culture. Thoughts and feelings are hidden, and communication is indirect and tactful in nature. Americans and Australians might appreciate a direct and "to the point" discussion with a supervisor about their performance, but a Japanese employee would likely see such a session as aggressive and harsh. Another example relates to Hofstede's dimensions of power distance and uncertainty avoidance. The role of managers in French firms is to eliminate risk and uncertainty and to devise ways to achieve the firm's objectives. The negotiation of objectives that makes up part of the MBO process is inconsistent with the French manager's role as "the boss." The manager has high personal status and power and is assumed to be qualified for this role; otherwise he or she would not have been made a manager. To further complicate the use of MBO in France, the role of an average French employee is also to reduce risk—for him- or herself. MBO increases personal risk; MBO does not work in France.[29]

Subsidiary Compensation Systems

The task facing the international compensation manager is pictured in Figure 17.1. Compensation policies within each subsidiary must be consistent with the local wage market, wage legislation and regulations (e.g., minimum wage), union influences, other legal restrictions (e.g., prohibitions against sex-based wage discrimination), and cultural preferences.[30] At the same time, the subsidiary's compensation system must provide an adequate level of strategic consistency within the MNC's overall business strategy. Much has been written about compensation for expatriates, but much less is known about how MNCs should determine the most effective compensation system within local subsidiaries. Some researchers suggest that it is important to first identify the compensation practices that are needed and desired by employees in each subsidiary rather than simply imposing some standard approach used within an MNC. Once these needs and desires are identified, the MNC can make more intelligent choices about which local compensation practices to adopt as is, which to adapt, and which practices might be exported directly from the MNC's headquarters operations.[31]

In addition to dealing with a pay system developed for host-country employees, the subsidiary HR manager must also deal with a separate system applicable to home-country expatriates and third-country nationals working for the subsidiary. Expatriate pay systems, which are discussed later in this chapter, are often very different from those used for host-country employees within a subsidiary. In some cases, expatriate employees make more money than host-country nationals who have jobs of equal or greater importance and complexity. These differences can result in host-country employees feeling that they are being treated unfairly.[32] However, research has shown that some situations may reduce the likelihood that

FIGURE 17.1
Multinational Compensation Systems

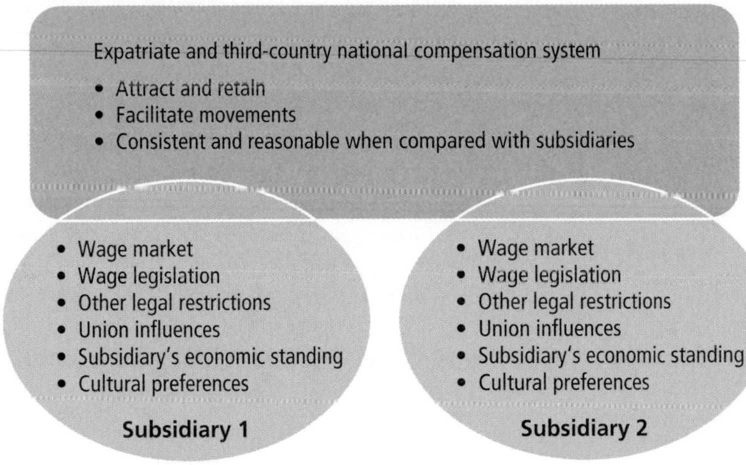

locals will perceive the pay system as unfair. In one study, local employees were less likely to view expatriate pay (which was significantly higher than that of locals) as unfair if their own pay was higher than locals employed in other firms. It was also found that providing locals with explanations as to why expatriate pay was higher (e.g., higher living costs for expats, higher levels of managerial experience among expats) helped alleviate perceptions of pay unfairness. Finally, the level of interpersonal sensitivity that expatriate managers showed local employees (i.e., being kind, considerate, and respectful) also affected pay fairness perceptions.[33]

Factors Affecting Compensation Systems

A variety of factors affect compensation systems within MNCs, including internal business factors such as varying wage costs, levels of job security, and differing business strategies. Compensation is affected by differences in prosperity and spending power related to the strength of national economies and currencies. Social factors such as the extent to which pay differences are considered acceptable, the appreciation of different forms of pay, and the acceptance of different forms of compensation and appraisal (e.g., stock options, incentive pay based on performance) also affect MNC compensation systems in a particular country. Wage and other legislation, along with the influence of unions, has an impact on compensation systems as well.

It is beyond the limits of this chapter to discuss the myriad influences on MNC compensation practices around the world. Suffice it to say that the subsidiary HR manager must know or have access to information about these issues. Regulations concerning pensions, medical insurance, and other benefits are critically important and vary greatly. In some countries, benefits such as housing, transportation, and year-end bonuses are common; in others, they are not.

Issues relating to sex-based or racially based wage differentials are of particular concern for subsidiaries of U.S. firms. Even though such differentials may be acceptable in countries where American MNCs operate, they are certainly not consistent with U.S. HR philosophies. An American HR manager in a foreign subsidiary must make decisions as to whether it is ethical to have discrimination in one part of the MNC but not in another. Union influences may play an important role in determining wage policies in some countries but not in others. For example, Australia has had for some years now a national wage-setting system in which the government and unions negotiate pay rates for workers, which apply countrywide. In Hong Kong, by contrast, labor unions are extremely weak, and wage rates are determined by the free market.

As with performance appraisal systems, cultural preferences may influence the type of compensation system that is appropriate. For example, Lincoln Electric, one of the first companies to successfully implement a productivity-based incentive system in the United States, has attempted to transfer that system of piecework, end-of-year bonus, and continuous employment to its operations in other countries. The entire incentive package was implemented in its Australian operation, part of the package operated in Mexico, but its European operations were highly resistant to the incentive plan.[34] If we relate specific cultural dimensions to pay systems, in high power distance cultures compensation systems should reflect hierarchical divisions within the firm with large differences in the pay levels of the highest and lowest level workers. In contrast, compensation systems in low power distance cultures should be more egalitarian, with relatively small differences between the top and bottom earners. In individualistic cultures, compensation systems should reward individual achievement, and in collective cultures, pay should be group or seniority based.[35] The highly individualistic incentive system of Lincoln Electric works wonderfully well in the United States, but it was less well received in more collectivist Europe.

The job of the HR manager in a foreign subsidiary is a difficult one. The procedures and policies developed must be consistent with the host country's legal requirements and cultural traditions. Overlaying this HR system are the policies and procedures of the home-country MNC. If the overall HR approach of the MNC is polycentric, the HR manager's job is much simpler because subsidiaries are given substantial autonomy in developing their own HR policies. Where the MNC takes a more ethnocentric approach, inevitable conflict occurs as the subsidiary HR manager attempts to work within HQ's guidelines while providing procedures that are acceptable to the host country's work force. With regiocentric or geocentric IHRM approaches, the subsidiary HR manager's job becomes a delicate balancing act of local adaptation and strategic consistency to ensure that HR policies and procedures result in efficient use of subsidiary human resources to the maximum benefit of both the subsidiary and global MNC.

EXPATRIATE MANAGERS

The increasingly complex nature of global markets and the existence of global competitors have made it necessary for MNCs to exert centralized, strategic control over their worldwide operations. At the same time, intensified competition in local markets, specific cultural conditions, and unique regulatory systems put pressure on MNCs to be locally responsive. For most MNCs, the person assigned to carry out this balancing act between global and local demands has been the expatriate manager. Vladimir Pucik and Tania Saba have defined an **expatriate manager** as "an executive who is able to assume a leadership position fulfilling international assignments across countries and cultures."[36] Traditionally, expatriates were employees from the home country of the MNC. However, during the 1980s and 1990s, as MNC operations became more diverse, managers from any country in which the MNC operated were selected to manage its foreign subsidiaries around the world. These third-country nationals are also considered as expatriate managers for the purposes of our discussions in this chapter. More recently, the selection and effective utilization of *inpatriates* (foreign-country managers brought to an MNC's home country) has become an important issue for many multinational firms.[37]

Much of what has been written about IHRM has focused on the problems of selecting and training managers for international assignments and then successfully repatriating them when their foreign tours of duty end. However, the task faced by HR specialists in the MNC's home headquarters in effectively managing expatriate assignments is an extremely complex one. The remaining sections of this chapter examine many of the important processes involved in effectively managing expatriates. We begin with two basic questions. First, "What is an expatriate assignment?" Second, "Why is it so important to manage expatriates effectively?"

Types of Expatriate Assignments

Multinational companies use expatriate assignments to accomplish three major roles.[38] The first is to fill specific positions. **Project assignments** occur when project work specialists develop and implement plans in a foreign location and then return home or go on to other expatriate assignments. These assignments may involve any type of task or activity. **Technology transfer assignments** may be either short or long in duration and are carried out by technical specialists whose specific task is to transfer technologies from one part of the organization to another. Technology transfer assignments are, for the most part, simply a special class of project assignment.

The second major role of expatriate assignments is management development. **Developmental assignments** occur when managers are sent to work in foreign locations primarily to develop specific "global competencies" that are believed of long-term value to the firm. For example, learning a foreign language or developing better cross-cultural interpersonal skills are among the types of competencies that may have extended value to an MNC.

The third reason for expatriate assignments is not individual development but organizational development, coordination, and control. These assignments consist of two elements: the socialization of expatriate and local managers into a common corporate culture, and the creation of a verbal information network that provides links between subsidiaries and headquarters. In these **coordination and control assignments,** a manager may be sent to oversee the operations of a single subsidiary, a geographic region, or even the worldwide operations of the MNC in a particular functional or product area.

Although the expatriate assignments described here cover a wide range of activities, other, often more short-term assignments are also "expatriate" in nature. For example, employees in exporting firms often make brief visits to various foreign markets to check on distributors and customers or to provide information about the nature and use of their product. The establishment of foreign franchises also involves important "expatriate assignments" that may require an initial lengthy setup stay and then multiple short-term follow-up visits for monitoring and control. Similarly, the establishment of joint ventures often requires a combination of brief visits for "flag waving," extended visits for, perhaps, training purposes, and then full, more traditional expatriate assignments as well. Most of the research on expatriation has focused on situations in which individuals go and live for an extended period of time in a foreign country. Although the depth of the expatriate experience may be greater in these traditional assignments, many of the problems of cultural adaptation, communication, and adjustment to a foreign business environment are also present in assignments of far shorter duration. Furthermore, short-term assignments, such as might be given to a sales representative of an exporting firm, can have significant negative consequences for the firm if they are not handled effectively.[39] The following brief story illustrates the point quite well:

> Once upon a time there came a Texan to Shanghai to do some business. In his first meeting with his Chinese hosts, he put his feet up on a table. Then he used his business card to pick his teeth. The Chinese hosts abruptly left the room. Meeting adjourned.[40]

The Cost of Expatriate Failures

The failure of an expatriate can have disastrous results. There are substantial monetary costs associated with sending expatriates abroad, bringing them back to the home country, and finding replacements (between $300,000 and $1 million per expatriate per year). One estimate is that U.S. companies lose $2 billion a year as a result of expatriate failure with one-third of expatriate managers not performing up to the expectations of their superiors.[41] In addition to monetary costs, the poor performance of an expatriate may damage the firm's image in the host country. There are also the personal tragedies of employees who fail even though they had been viewed as competent managers within the domestic organization. These individuals may have sold their homes, left jobs they liked, and uprooted their families to take a foreign assignment—only to find themselves back in the home country branded as failures. Their early return may also affect their future career prospects in the firm.[42]

The common definition of an expatriate failure is when an expatriate is forced or chooses to return to his or her home organization before the expected duration of a foreign assignment is complete. These "early returns," however, are only one type of expatriate failure. Those expatriates who perform poorly but remain in their foreign assignment must also be considered failures. They may cause damage to the firm's reputation, reduce employee morale, and disrupt relationships with local nationals.

Determining the Need for an Expatriate

A model of the life cycle of an expatriate assignment is given in Figure 17.2. It involves a process of determining the need for an expatriate assignment, identifying and selecting likely candidates, preassignment training, departure, postarrival orientation and training, crisis and adjustment or crisis and failure, reassignment abroad, and repatriation and adjustment.

Although cost considerations and improvements in communication technology persuaded many companies to reduce their use of expatriate managers in the early 1990s, recent surveys indicate that expatriate assignments are increasing, al-

FIGURE 17.2

The Expatriate Assignment Life Cycle

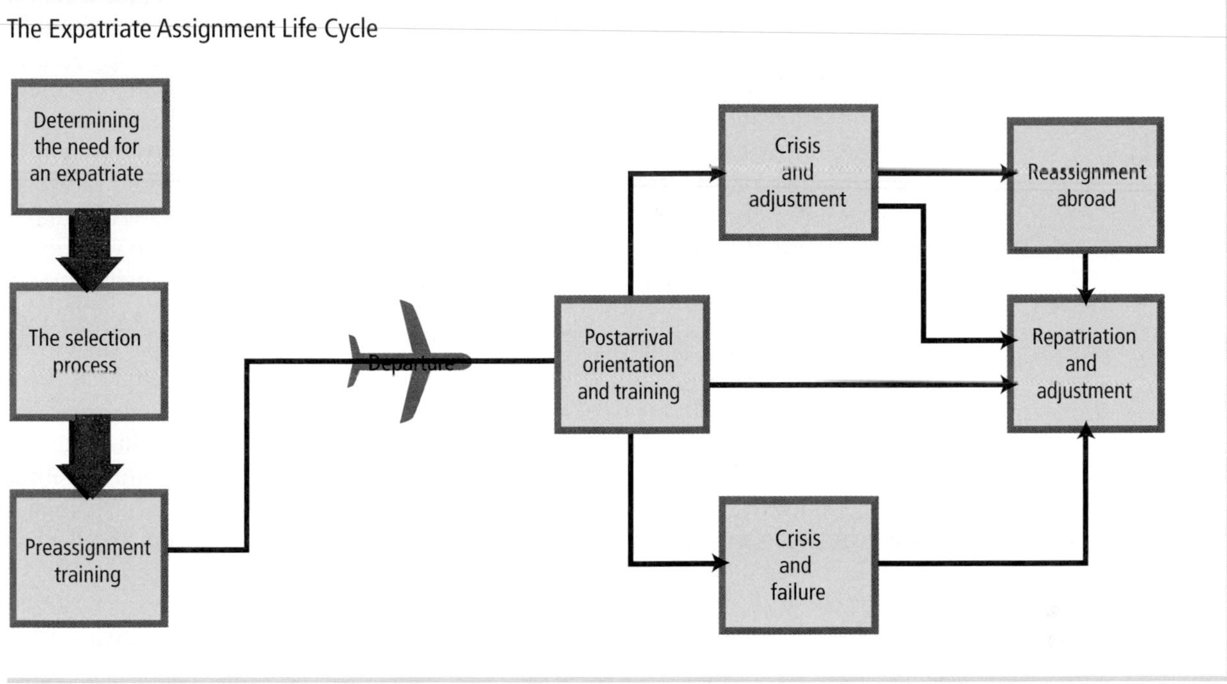

though the rate of increase and the nature of assignments may be changing. In a survey conducted in 2003, 31 percent of firms indicated that the number of expatriates had increased in 2003, and 39 percent expected the number to increase further in 2004. However, both of these percentages were lower than the average that had been found in previous surveys on the same issue. More than half of respondents (56 percent) indicated that they were seeking to reduce the number of long-term expatriate assignments, primarily due to cost considerations. For example, in past surveys, assignments of one year or less in duration had represented, on average, 13 percent of all expatriate assignments. In the 2003 survey, 70 percent of international assignments were scheduled for one year or less. In addition, 52 percent of the respondents indicated that they were using more local employees rather than relying on expatriates.[43]

The decision as to whether a particular foreign assignment is filled with a home-country national, host-country national, or third-country national may derive partly from the overall IHRM approach taken by the MNC. As noted previously, cost factors play an important role, but other factors also are taken into account.

The level of the position in the foreign subsidiary is one such factor. One survey of U.S., European, and Japanese MNCs indicated that expatriates were more likely to be found at the senior management level than at the middle or lower management level. On average, home-country expatriates filled 53 percent of top management positions but less than 30 percent of lower management positions. There were national differences, however, with Japanese firms filling 74 percent of their top foreign subsidiary management positions with PCNs, whereas European and U.S. firms used PCNs to fill only 48 percent and 31 percent of their top management positions, respectively.[44]

The degree of interaction between host-country nationals and the person in the position is also an important issue in deciding whether an expatriate should be used. If the position requires a high level of interaction, which in turn requires a high level of knowledge about the local culture, it may be best to use a host-country national. Such individuals often have political connections and influence networks that are of great value to the firm, and these connections and networks would be very difficult for an expatriate to develop. The similarity of the home and host cultures must be considered as well. If the cultures are very different, it may be difficult to identify an expatriate able to adapt and perform well in the foreign subsidiary. The MNC must then weigh any advantages associated with using an expatriate against the increased probability of the expatriate's failing to adjust and perform well in the assignment. The cost of the training needed to prepare the expatriate for the assignment in a very different culture also must be taken into account in this cost-benefit analysis.

Political factors, too, may determine whether an expatriate should be used to fill a foreign position. As noted earlier, policies or regulations may limit the number of expatriates that can be used to fill positions in a foreign subsidiary. In situations where no such policies exist, it still may be good public relations to fill a large number of positions in a subsidiary with host-country nationals. In other cases, local people may have political or social disadvantages that would warrant the use of an expatriate. For example, in a country with many ethnic groups, giving a local person a prominent position in the subsidiary may alienate local employees from other ethnic groups. The perceived neutrality of an expatriate might be extremely important in such instances.

Firms such as Mitsui & Co. USA and 3M make international assignments part of managers' overall career development plans. Whirlpool, Westinghouse Electric, and 3M make foreign assignments a prerequisite for promotion to senior management positions.[45] Thus, even though local nationals could do the job, some positions may be filled by expatriates because the positions give home-country managers the opportunity to develop skills in international dealings.

Practical issues also may affect the use of PCN or TCN expatriates. The level of personal risk in the host country may make it difficult to send home- or third-country personnel to a particular location. Imagine the dangers involved in an American MNC sending a U.S. citizen to work in an operation in Palestinian-controlled Gaza or in Iraq! The availability of appropriate job applicant pools both inside the firm and in the host country will determine what type of person is selected. This is often a problem for firms that are new to international business and would like to send a PCN to manage a foreign operation but simply do not have anyone in the home firm who has the experience, expertise, or willingness to manage its foreign activities.[46]

Factors Associated with Expatriate Success and Adjustment

The factors that affect the success and adjustment of expatriate managers are probably one of the most highly researched areas in the field of international human resource management. One study identified eighteen variables that affected success and grouped them into four general categories: job competence, personality traits and relational abilities, environmental variables, and family variables. In particular, this study highlighted the importance of family considerations, such as the stability of expatriate marriages and circumstances related to the interest and willingness of the spouse and children to move to a foreign location.[47] Another study pointed to the importance of expatriate career path issues (i.e., the impact of the foreign assignment on the person's career) and the expatriates' overall belief in the mission that they would be carrying out in the foreign location in determining assignment adjustment.

A 1999 study identified another factor, referred to as **learning orientation,** that may determine an expatriate's ability to adjust to a foreign assignment. People with high learning orientation "believe that incremental change is possible. They do *not* see each attempt as something that culminates either in success or failure. If the outcome is less than their goal, that is merely a signal that some adaptation or change in strategy is needed for the next try."[48] Individuals with high levels of learning orientation make use of their experiences and attempt to learn from them and adjust their behavior accordingly. Complete preparation for an expatriate assignment is impossible, and significant learning must occur after arrival in the foreign location. Individuals high in learning orientation may be more successful at postarrival adjustment than those with lower levels of learning orientation.

Another study identified four major dimensions that influenced whether an expatriate could adapt successfully to a foreign assignment.[49] The first, **self-oriented dimension,** concerns activities that contribute to the expatriate's self-esteem and self-confidence. There are three subfactors in this dimension: (1) **reinforcement substitution,** (2) **stress reduction,** and (3) **technical competence.** Expatriates who are high on the reinforcement substitution factor are able to readily substitute activities in the new culture for those that they liked to do in their home culture. For example, an American manager in Australia would find it difficult to attend American football games. Instead, the manager might develop an interest in rugby, thus substituting a local sport for one that he or she enjoyed in the United States. Expatriate managers also tend to acculturate more readily if they engage in activities that help them reduce stress. Individuals who can reduce stress by reading, jogging, sailing, watching television, meditating, or whatever tend to acculturate more readily than those without such means of relief. Technical competence also has a strong bearing on the acculturation process. Expatriates who are technically competent and feel confident in their ability to handle their international assignments acculturate more easily than those who are less qualified.

The second major dimension of acculturation, the **others-oriented dimension,** consists of two subfactors: (1) **relationship development** and (2) **willingness to communicate.** Expatriates who are able to develop lasting friendships and close relationships with people different from themselves acculturate more easily in overseas assignments. In addition, individuals who are willing to communicate in the host country's language also adapt more readily. It is interesting to note that this second subfactor suggests that simply being able to speak a host country's language is unimportant unless one is willing to do so. A person who is less proficient in the host language but willing to use it even at the risk of making mistakes and looking foolish may adapt more easily than someone with excellent knowledge of the language but a reluctance to try it out in daily conversation.

The third dimension of acculturation, the **perceptual dimension,** concerns the ability of expatriates to understand why foreign nationals behave the way they do. Expatriates who do not jump to conclusions about the causes of a local employee's behavior have an easier time of adjusting than those who make judgments more quickly. A large body of research in social psychology indicates that people are motivated to attribute causes to other people's behavior. Thus, if an employee is performing poorly or acts in a dour, uncommunicative manner, the typical manager will attribute some cause to those actions—the employee is lazy or stupid or has a sullen personality. Social psychological research indicates that we are not very good at accurately assessing the causes of the behavior of people from our own culture. Imagine how poorly we do in explaining the behavior of persons from cultures very different from our own. It is likely that expatriates who are able to reserve judgment and gather more facts before assigning causes to behavior are able to adjust more readily to foreign assignments.

The final dimension characterizes situations rather than people and is called **cultural toughness.** Some foreign assignments are tougher than others. American expatriates sent to a small village of yak herders in Mongolia would have a much harder time adjusting than if they had been assigned to Sydney, Australia—a modern city with friendly people and the same basic language.

Taken collectively, the many studies on expatriate adjustment and success seem to indicate that persons selected for an international assignment must (1) be willing and motivated to go overseas, (2) be technically able to do the job, including having relevant managerial, administrative, and strategic skills, (3) be adaptable, (4) have good interpersonal and team-building skills and be able to form relationships, (5) have good communication ability, and (6) have a supportive family situation. An overall model of the factors important in selecting the right person for an expatriate assignment is presented in Figure 17.3.

FIGURE 17.3
A Model for Selecting Expatriates

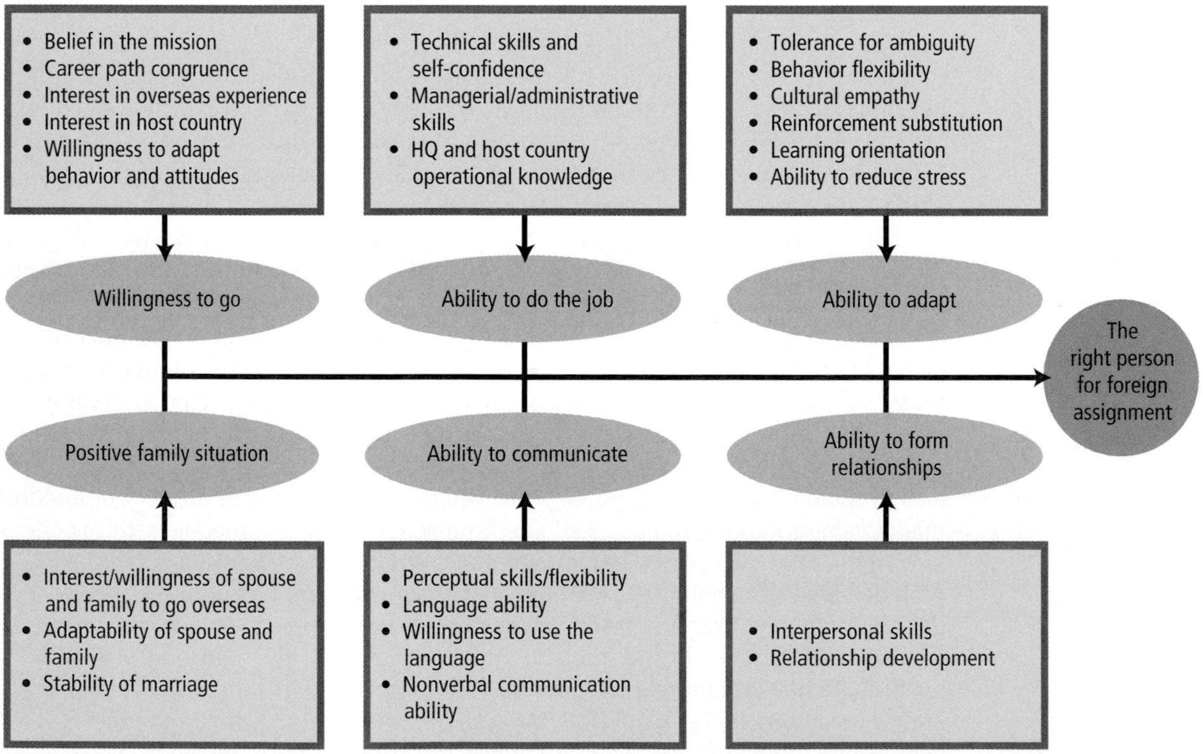

Procedures for Selecting Expatriates

Because there is a good deal of knowledge about the factors linked to the success or failure of individuals in foreign assignments, and because expatriate failures are expensive, one might assume that MNCs spend considerable time and effort screening employees and their families before sending them abroad. A 1995 survey by the National Foreign Trade Council and Survey Research International shed some light on common practices in expatriate selection.[50] Among the survey's findings were the following:

- Just over 50 percent of the firms had identified technical, managerial, and interpersonal skills that contribute to international success.
- Thirty-two percent had linked these international competencies criteria to the development of personnel and succession planning systems.
- Ninety-four percent held line management responsible for assessing the suitability of international assignees.
- Seventy-six percent said possible expatriates were interviewed by HR staff as well.
- Eighteen percent used structured interviews to assess expatriate candidates.
- Twelve percent used candidate/spouse self-assessment.
- Six percent used psychological and cognitive testing.
- Two percent had a formal assessment center.
- Fifty-six percent said that managers relied heavily on their own judgment when making final expatriate selection decisions.
- Ninety-six percent rated the technical requirements of the job as the most important selection criterion for international assignments.

These results indicate that many firms do not use sophisticated procedures to measure such attributes as relational skills and adaptability. The 1995 results were confirmed by a 2002 survey conducted in the United Kingdom. This survey of twenty-three multinational firms found that when assessing potential expatriate candidates, the two most important criteria for selection were technical expertise followed by leadership qualities. However, the survey also revealed that fewer than half (48 percent) of the participants had a formal selection process for expatriate placements. Of those that did, the majority used interviews as the main selection tool.[51] These surveys do not indicate that multinational firms lack interest in the expatriate selection process. Rather, they often assess expatriate candidates using informal methods. For example, a method used by Jon Huntsman of the Huntsman Corporation in Salt Lake City, Utah—a private chemical company with $4.75 billion in sales is as follows:

> [Huntsman] asks employees he believes have global leadership potential to accompany him on international trips, even if immediate business needs don't justify the expense. During such trips, he takes the managers to local restaurants, shopping areas, and side streets and observes their behavior. Do they approach the strange and unusual sights, sounds, smells, and tastes with curiosity or do they look for the nearest Pizza Hut? Do they try to communicate with local shopkeepers or do they hustle back to the Hilton? Huntsman also observes how managers act among foreigners at home. In social settings, he watches to see if they

> seek out the foreign guests or talk only with people they already know. During negotiations with foreigners, he gauges his managers' ability to take a collaborative rather than a combative approach.[52]

Whether informal approaches such as Jon Huntsman's or more formal means are used to assess foreign assignment capabilities, it is important to develop selection procedures specifically for international assignments. An organization should not rely on selection methods used for domestic hiring or on information about candidates collected with purely domestic purposes in mind. It is possible, for example, that an individual who is an excellent manager in a domestic situation does not have the ability to take on the additional responsibilities usually attached to international assignments. An American manager who is considered an excellent communicator by his U.S. colleagues because of his direct, face-to-face, to-the-point style may be a total disaster when required to communicate with Chinese or Japanese subordinates who value subtle, indirect forms of communication. Examples of methods that might be used to identify individuals with the important attributes for international success are given in Table 17.4.

Additionally, a number of "yellow flags" and "red flags" that firms should be aware of in determining who might not make good expatriates have been identified. Among these yellow flags (i.e., things that might indicate possible difficulties in adjusting to a foreign assignment) are overblown expectations of career or financial rewards from the assignment, a resentful spouse, aging parents for whom the expatriate is mainly responsible, teenagers who must remain behind to finish school, imminent birth of a child, health problems, special schooling requirements, and denial by the expatriate and his or her family that any concerns or potential problems exist. None of these yellow flag issues will necessarily cause an expatriate to fail in an assignment. What they do indicate, however, is the need for careful thought and preparation by the expatriate, his or her family, and the company as to how these issues will be dealt with effectively. Among the red flags (i.e., things that research and past experience have shown to make expatriate failure likely) are alcohol or drug dependency, obvious marital discord, evidence of marginal social functioning (e.g., excessive shyness, inability to interact with people in common social situations), serious health problems, mental illness, and obvious racism/ethnocentrism.[53]

Selecting Global versus Expatriate Managers

As noted earlier, one of the types of assignments that an expatriate manager may be given is that of *worldwide oversight.* This type of assignment requires the manager to integrate the activities of the MNC's subsidiaries in several geographic regions. Several authors have suggested that this role requires something more than what one normally expects of an expatriate.[54] A **global manager** "refers to an executive assigned to a position with a cross-border responsibility, who has a flexible and open mind, with a well-rounded understanding of international business and an ability to work across cross-cultural and cross-functional boundaries, who perceives global competition as an opportunity, and who is able to balance the simultaneous demands of global integration and national responsiveness."[55] The key differences between expatriate and global managers are presented in Table 17.5 along with the different skills required of the two types of managers. Multinational firms are placing considerable emphasis on developing global as well as expatriate

TABLE 17.4

Some Methods for Selecting Successful Expatriates

Willingness to go

- Interview questions to assess the person's understanding of the mission and why the person thinks that he or she has the characteristics that will help accomplish that mission.
- Discussion of the career implications of the foreign assignment. What skills and experiences, in the individual's view, will the foreign position provide for advancement in the chosen career path? What position would the individual expect to receive upon return from the foreign assignment?
- Biodata that might indicate the level of the individual's interest in and knowledge of the host country—for example, history of holiday trips overseas, family connections to the country, and so forth.

Ability to do the job

- For individuals who may have made short-term (one to two weeks) troubleshooting trips overseas, assessments of their performance during those assignments collected from individuals with whom they worked.
- Technical knowledge tests related to particularly important or unusual aspects of the job that will occur in the foreign assignment; for example, technical standards required by the host country, or knowledge of labor relations laws relevant to operation in the host country. Obviously, what is tested is determined by the exact nature of the foreign job assignment and what can be learned readily on the job.
- Assessment by domestic colleagues of the individual's managerial and administrative abilities. Current performance appraisals.
- Situational exercises, role plays, or simulations in which the individual must deal with situations likely to arise in the foreign location. For example, the candidate might have to explain a relatively complicated technical procedure to a host-country national and also might be asked to role play a performance feedback session with the person.

Ability to adapt

- Situational exercises characterized by high levels of ambiguity and time pressure to examine how well the candidate performs under such conditions.
- Behavior description interviews focused on previous examples of behavioral flexibility or situations where the individual has made mistakes, then used what he or she learned from the experience to perform better in a later, similar situation.
- Biodata concerning the nature and breadth of hobbies and other leisure activities and a check of the availability of those activities in the foreign location. For example, an individual whose sole hobby is horse jumping may have a difficult time finding an adequate substitute for that hobby in a country where practically no one has ever seen a horse and the few horses that do exist are used for food or as pack animals.

Ability to form relationships

- Psychological tests of traits typically associated with relationship development.
- Assessment of how the individual typically deals with conflict and how that compares with the conflict management norms in the host country.
- Situational exercises where the individual must meet, greet, and establish initial positive social interactions with people from different cultures.
- Biodata relating to the person's ability to establish friendships with people from other cultures.

Ability to communicate

- Traditional written and oral tests of language ability.
- Situational exercises in which the language ability must be used, for example, explaining a technical procedure to individuals from the host culture using the host language.
- Videos of host-country nationals in which the candidate is asked to interpret the nonverbal communication taking place in the situation on the video.
- "Diplomacy exercises"—asking that the candidate, without saying "Your performance is lousy and I am going to have to fire you if you do not improve," to express this same sentiment tactfully to a Japanese subordinate.

Family situation

- Interviews with spouse and family members to determine interest and willingness to go overseas.
- Family biodata to identify possible predictors of adjustment, for example, previous experiences abroad.
- In addition, most of the preceding selection procedures also may be used to assess the spouse's ability to adapt and communicate in a foreign environment.

TABLE 17.5

Expatriate versus Global Managers

	Expatriate Manager	Global Manager
Global perspective	• Focuses on a single foreign country and on managing relationships between headquarters and that country	• Understands worldwide business environment from a global perspective
Local responsiveness	• Becomes an expert on one culture	• Must learn about many foreign cultures' perspectives, tastes, trends, technologies, and approaches to conducting business
Synergistic learning	• Works with and coaches people in each foreign culture separately or sequentially	• Works with and learns from people from many cultures simultaneously
	• Integrates foreigners into the headquarters' national organizational culture	• Creates a culturally synergistic organizational environment
Transition and adaptation	• Adapts to living in a foreign culture	• Adapts to living in many foreign cultures
Cross-cultural interaction	• Uses cross-cultural interaction skills primarily on foreign assignments	• Uses cross-cultural skills on a daily basis throughout career
Collaboration	• Interacts with colleagues from within clearly defined hierarchies of structural and cultural dominance and subordination	• Interacts with foreign colleagues as equals
Foreign experience	• Expatriation or inpatriation primarily to get the job done	• Transpatriation for career and organizational development

Sources: N. J. Adler and S. Bartholomew, "Managing Globally Competent People," *Academy of Management Executive*, Vol. 6 (3), 1992, pp. 52–65; and Vladimir Pucik and Tania Saba, "Selecting and Developing the Global vs. the Expatriate Manager: A Review of the State-of-the-Art," *Human Resource Planning*, Vol. 21 (4), 1998, p. 44.

managers. For example, TRW conducts a global leadership program that combines U.S.-based classroom teaching with real-life learning experiences from a variety of locations around the world.[56]

Two Other Special Expatriate Selection Issues

Female Expatriates In domestic U.S. firms, there has been a significant increase in the ability of women to move into senior positions. However, when it comes to overseas assignments, women fall far behind their male counterparts. This may be changing. A 2003 survey of global relocation trends indicated that 18 percent of expatriates were women.[57] Two questions arise regarding the assignment of females to expatriate positions. The first is whether female managers want to go on foreign assignments. A study of 261 female expatriates indicates that the answer to this question is yes. However, women with children did express less interest in foreign assignments than did those without children.[58]

The second question is whether female expatriates have a more difficult time handling international assignments and are likely, therefore, to be less successful. There is anthropological evidence that suggests women possess many characteristics that would make them well adapted to expatriate positions. One anthropologist suggests that women have "a broad contextual view of any issue, a penchant for long-term planning, a gift for networking and negotiating . . . a preference for cooperating, reaching consensus, and leading via egalitarian teams . . . an ability to do and think several things simultaneously . . . emotional sensitivity . . . and a talent with words.[59] If these characteristics are compared to the important criteria for selecting expatriates that were discussed earlier, there are many obvious parallels, particularly in the abilities to communicate and adapt, as well as interpersonal and relationship skills. Another author suggests that many of these characteristics "reflect not only the style of many American women managers, but also those of successful men and women in most parts of the world."[60]

Further evidence of the success of female expatriates exists. In one study conducted in the late 1980s, fifty-two female expatriates were interviewed during their assignments in Asia or shortly after their return from an Asian assignment. Ninety-seven percent of these women described their assignments as successful, and many of the women suggested that the most difficult part of their assignment had been getting their firm to send them abroad. Others suggested that they were discriminated against more by Western expatriates than by local Asian businessmen. Surveys of female expatriates conducted in 1992–1993 and in 2000 supported these earlier findings. The women in these studies indicated that, although some early difficulties in adjustment had occurred, as time went by they had been able to adjust very successfully to their work environment and that their performance had been very high.[61] In both studies many of the women cited their sex as an advantage. Their distinctiveness caused their clients and associates to remember them more readily—an asset in any sales position. Many of their male clients found it easier to talk with a woman, particularly in cultures where the aggressive American male approach is overly threatening. In the 1980s study, a common theme appeared: Female expatriates were regarded, first and foremost, as foreigners, and the normal expectations for the behavior of local females were not applied to them. Women in the 1992–1993 study also indicated that having often been discriminated against in their home country because of their gender, they had developed skills that allowed them to deal effectively with any discrimination they encountered in their foreign assignments.

To summarize, what these research studies imply is that even in very masculine societies such as Japan and Korea, female expatriates provide important skills and competitive advantages. In selecting individuals for foreign positions, it seems most rational to look for the kinds of attributes associated with success in foreign assignments, regardless of the gender of the candidate.

Inpatriates Like female expatriates, inpatriates are an increasingly frequent phenomenon in global organizations. **Inpatriates** are foreign nationals who are hired by an MNC and stationed for some length of time (often one to three years) in the MNC's corporate operations before returning to their home locations. Inpatriate managers are seen as a viable alternative to high-cost expatriate managers by many firms. Several reasons have been identified as to why the use of inpatriates is rising. Emerging markets are becoming more difficult to serve in, and these countries often present greater adjustment problems for expatriates due to differences in culture and level of economic development. Inpatriate managers have the cultural and economic background to more effectively address the problems in emerging markets. Particularly while located at corporate headquarters, they provide a diversity of perspectives to corporate management for developing global strategies and policies, and they are effective boundary spanners between headquarters and managers at subsidiary locations.[62]

Japanese firms have been involved in hiring inpatriates, usually fresh from a university, for some time. Typically, the inpatriates spend two to three years in the firm's headquarters in Japan before returning to their home country. Japanese firms have found a number of advantages associated with the use of inpatriates. They are uncontaminated by their home-country work practices because they usually come fresh from a university. They are young and willing to work in the Japanese system of slow promotions but high job security. They typically are very interested in international assignments as part of their careers. They are fluent in their home-country language when assigned back home, thus avoiding a common problem with typical expatriates.

However, there are some disadvantages associated with inpatriates. They often have less formal business education, do not have language or written communication skills as good as those of native speakers, and are more likely to be plagued by social class and status problems. They may also have different motivation and reward orientations, as well as different time perspectives on how long it should take to get things done. There may be legal restrictions that complicate the use of inpatriates in the home country. Jealousy may be felt by the inpatriate's home-country staff when he or she returns home but is treated by the firm as if he or she is an expatriate manager in terms of pay and other working conditions.

For the most part, the criteria for effective selection and management of inpatriates are similar to those for any expatriate manager. International competencies are important. Family issues must be dealt with effectively. Inpatriates may need assistance in dealing with their new work role, as well as with basic aspects of life such as housing, transportation, or establishing a line of credit in the new home. Perhaps the greatest difference between inpatriates and expatriates is that expatriate assignments are often high in visibility, power, and responsibility, whereas inpatriates are brought to the MNC's home operations as "learners" rather than primarily as managers and controllers. To ensure the successful adjustment of inpatriates to their new role within the organization, the firm must provide the inpatriate with a clear understanding of (1) the core values and global vision of the organization; (2) the home organization's culture; (3) the differences in human resource management practices between headquarters and the inpatriate's home location, as well as how these differences may affect the inpatriate; and (4) the career opportunities for the inpatriate manager in the parent country organization.[63] Many of the recommendations about training expatriates found in the next section of this text apply equally well to inpatriate managers. By adequately preparing and supporting inpatriate managers, multinational firms may significantly increase their available cadre of competent managers to oversee an increasingly complex array of global business opportunities.

TRAINING EXPATRIATES

The goal of good expatriate selection procedures is to identify individuals who will have the skills necessary to adjust to and perform well in an international assignment. However, selection is only one of many factors that determine adjustment to an international assignment.[64] Among the other important factors affecting adjustment is the degree of training, both predeparture and postarrival, that the expatriate receives. Despite this, a 2003 survey indicated that only 60 percent of multinationals in the sample provided formal cross-cultural preparation to expatriates. Twenty-eight percent provided training for the entire family, 27 percent for expatriate and spouse, and 5 percent for expatriates alone. Only 26 precent of respondents indicated that this training was mandatory, and 74 percent responded that it was optional. An earlier survey of expatriate training indicated that among the reasons given for the relatively low level of expatriate training are that training is not seen as effective, the time between selection for an assignment and departure is so short that there is no time to train, what training is needed is not clear, and there is a belief that technical skills alone are sufficient for success.[65]

Is Training Effective?

It is unfortunate that the use of formal cross-cultural training programs for expatriates is not more widespread. A number of studies over the years have examined the effectiveness of cross-cultural training (CCT) of expatriates. CCT has been associated with increases in general cross-cultural skill development, job performance, the psychological well being of expatriates, their social skills with host country nationals, the ability of expatriates to adjust, and the development by expatriates of accurate perceptions of the host culture and its people. In general, the research on CCT indicates it is effective, although the level of effectiveness may depend on a variety of individual, environmental, and organizational factors.[66] In a 2003 survey of multinational firms, of those with formal expatriate training programs (60 percent), 73 percent indicated that their formal programs had great or high value, 21 percent rated them as having some value, and 6 percent rated them as having little value.[67]

Training Approaches

Two convenient ways to categorize approaches to training expatriates are by the content of the program and by the specific technique used. Within the content category, some programs focus primarily on the job or organization, whereas others concentrate on aspects of the culture in the foreign location. Job training may stress the new operational or supervisory skills that will be needed in the foreign assignment. Another form of job training can be referred to as "strategic training," where expatriates are given the "big picture" of the global business strategy of the MNC, with emphasis placed both on the global strategy and on how the particular subsidiary to which the expatriate will be assigned fits into that strategy. Strategic training also might include the enhancement of strategic skills, such as the development and use of global information management systems or interpersonal communication skills that could aid in the transmission of critical information to and from headquarters and units around the world.

Cultural training may offer basic information on topics such as geography, politics, cost of living, and social and business customs. Other types of cultural training may aim at increasing the expatriate's attributional and perceptual skills—that is, helping the expatriate accurately perceive and understand the behavior of persons from a foreign culture. Special issues such as partners and families abroad, daily living, and repatriation should be covered prior to departure.[68] Regardless of the specific topics covered in any expatriate training program, the program should be devised to ensure that the expatriate can (1) manage the personal and professional changes necessary in the new assignment, (2) understand and manage cultural differences, and (3) effectively manage their professional responsibilities in the foreign assignment.[69] See Table 17.6 for a detailed analysis of these important expatriate training outcomes.

Cultural and job training can be accomplished through a variety of techniques. Lectures, briefings, and assigned readings can convey factual information to trainees. Role playing, case analyses, and simulations constitute more active learning methods. In **cultural assimilator** training, the employee must consider 75 to 100 cultural incidents selected by a panel of experts as representative of situations that the person may confront in the host culture. The trainee has to analyze what is happening in the situation and why it is happening; then the trainee receives feedback on the correctness of their analysis. Trainees may undergo field experiences as well, by visiting either the host country or enclaves of the host culture within the home country (e.g., they may visit a predominantly Chinese part of a city within the home country).[70]

Expatriate training using CD-ROM and Internet-based training is also increasing and may incorporate standard lecture-type material as well as cases, simula-

TABLE 17.6

Essential Outcomes of Expatriate Training Programs

An expatriate training program can be considered effective to the extent that when the expatriate completes the program, he or she will have gained skill and knowledge in the following areas.

1. Managing the Personal and Professional Transition to the Foreign Assignment—which includes:
   1.1. Understanding and being ready to manage the impact of the change on the employee, family, and friends
   1.2. Understanding the cultural adaptation process and identifying effective coping strategies
   1.3. Creating a personal and professional action plan for managing change, achieving goals, and maintaining key relationships during the assignment and post assignment
   1.4. Recognizing that repatriation planning is an integral part of managing their assignment and developing an approach for preparing for repatriation
2. Managing Cultural Differences—which includes:
   2.1. Understanding the meaning of culture and how it shapes people's beliefs, values, assumptions, expectations, and behaviors
   2.2. Understanding and being able to apply frameworks for analyzing cross-cultural interactions and developing skills to reconcile differences that may occur in the new assignment
   2.3. Developing intercultural communication skills
   2.4. Acquiring important information about the host country and recognizing cultural differences between home and host cultures
   2.5. Gaining practical information about daily life in the host country
3. Managing Professional Responsibilities—which includes:
   3.1. Being able to apply information and insights acquired in the program to accomplish the job objectives
   3.2. Understanding how business and specific job responsibilities are handled in the countries or regions in which employees will work
   3.3. Determining how to adapt individual style and approach to be effective with local nationals

tions, and assimilators. In addition to consulting firms offering their services for a fee on the Internet, many free Web sites contain useful information for expatriates. The Web sites constructed by expatriates themselves are particularly useful. For example, www.hostetler.net (an American family living in Italy), http://www.outpostexpat.nl/archivecentre/ (an archive Web site for Shell Oil expatriate families where the families contribute stories about their expatriate experiences), and http://www.familylifeabroad.com/articles.html (an archive for stories about family life abroad). Some other Web sites with links that might be of benefit to expatriates are Australians International (http://www.ausint.com.au/subs/index.htm), CIA World Fact Book (http://www.cia.gov/cia/publications/factbook/), the Expat Forum (www.expatforum.com), Living in Indonesia (http://www.expat.or.id/), and ExpatFocus (http://www.expatfocus.com/).

Training programs may also be differentiated according to how long and rigorous they are. Researchers have suggested three basic levels of training "rigor" on the basis of the amount of time spent in training and the mental involvement and effort required of both trainer and trainee. A program of low training rigor would last from 4 to 20 hours and involve such methods as lectures, films, books, and simple area briefings. Programs of moderate rigor would take 20 to 60 hours and include all the methods involved in low-rigor programs plus role plays, cases, cultural assimilators, and "survival-level" language training. High-rigor programs would last from 60 to 180 hours, include all the previous methods, and also include assessment center activities, simulations, field trips, and in-depth language training.[71]

A Contingency Approach to Expatriate Training

Multinational firms are increasingly cost-conscious when dealing with expatriate assignments. In training expatriates, the international HR manager must maximize efficiency by selecting and developing programs that best fit the particular assignment and individual. A number of authors have identified factors that can be used in making these decisions.[72]

Four factors are important in selecting the type of training program needed: (1) business strategy, (2) job toughness, (3) cultural toughness, and (4) communication toughness. The first factor is important only for training expatriates in managerial and control-level positions, but the remaining three apply to the training for any type of expatriate position (e.g., an expatriate on assignment to fix specific technical problems in manufacturing).

Business Strategy Business strategy partly determines the nature of training needed. The international involvement of some MNCs is limited primarily to a group of international sales offices or subsidiaries in various countries. In such cases, expatriate training should focus on operational and cultural aspects of the subsidiary and the expectations that the domestic organization has of this particular foreign business unit. In contrast, some MNCs are truly global businesses with a worldwide business strategy, the nature of which must be clearly understood by expatriate managers.

Job Toughness **Job toughness** refers to whether the job in the foreign location is similar to other jobs that the expatriate has held. Although the basic functions of the domestic and foreign jobs may seem alike, often the scope and responsibility levels associated with the expatriate position are considerably greater. For example, an individual may be transferred to a foreign assignment from a managerial position in the domestic organization that involved supervising fifty employees. In that position, when issues involving equal employment opportunity, government regulations, or labor relations arose, the manager had specialist staff within the organization to call on for advice. In the foreign assignment, the manager may once again be supervising fifty employees carrying out the same basic task as in the domestic situation—for example, selling insurance to local businesses. However, in the foreign location the manager may have to deal with all the issues that other departmental specialists took care of at the home office. Differences in performance standards, material resources, technology, bureaucratic procedures, and legal restrictions will affect the "toughness" of the foreign job assignment.

To the extent that the foreign assignment requires new and different job skills compared with the domestic position, job content training becomes a more critical component of predeparture training. As noted in the section on expatriate selection, MNCs tend to choose individuals for foreign assignments on the basis of their competence in a domestic position. This approach often means that a person who has been an effective performer is assumed to have all the skills needed in the new assignment. The failure of many expatriates may stem from this assumption. Good international HR managers do not make such assumptions but instead carefully evaluate the novelty of the foreign position relative to the person's job history.

Cultural Toughness Expatriates may find themselves transferred from a domestic culture that is fairly high on individualism, low on power distance, and feminine to a foreign culture that is highly collective, has high power distance, and is extremely masculine. The values, attitudes, and behaviors in the two cultures would be quite different. In such a situation cross-cultural training can help the expatriate understand the attitudes and values of the new culture and learn appropriate behavior patterns. When the home- and host-country cultures are relatively similar (e.g., the United States and Australia), the need for cross-cultural training decreases but does not disappear.

Communication Toughness **Communication toughness** concerns the level of difficulty and the amount of communication with local nationals. Communication toughness must also be considered in deciding the necessary level of cross-cultural training. Aspects of communication toughness include the following:

- Differences in the norms and rules for communication
- Frequency of communication
- Difficulty in learning the host language
- Length of the foreign assignment
- Mode of communication—face to face or by phone or memo only
- Formality of communication required [73]

Determining the level and nature of communication is critical. Even though the home and host cultures are quite different, if the expatriate is not expected to interact with local nationals to any great extent or if the interactions are of little importance, then limited cross-cultural training in the form of general cultural information might suffice. For example, some American expatriates in Jakarta, Indonesia, hold positions that require them to interact mainly with other expatriates from MNCs in the region—not local Indonesians. These Americans live in expensive expatriate neighborhoods outside the city. Houses are surrounded by high walls, protected by security personnel, and represent little replicas of Western society in an Asian land. Interaction with local nationals is confined to a few key Indonesian government officials and businessmen (who may have been educated in the West, possibly in the United States) and servants are hired to clean, cook, wash, take care of the children, and drive the expatriates to work.

Even when the cultures are relatively similar, if extensive interaction and communication with local nationals are required, cross-cultural training becomes vital. An American sent to Australia to set up a new subsidiary would have to interact with many different types of local Australians: union leaders, managers, government officials, and so on. Even though Australia and the United States are relatively similar in culture, there are differences. The American expatriate who arrives to establish a new business in Australia and exhibits inappropriate behavior and attitudes would probably return home a failure because establishing the new business would require the American to gain acceptance by local Aussies. Some moderate level of cross-cultural training in this situation would be warranted.

The contingency model of cross-cultural training suggests that the content and rigor of cross-cultural training are contingent on the four factors just discussed. As job, cultural, and communication toughness increase, the training rigor needed to prepare an expatriate for an assignment increases. The content of the training will also depend on the relative toughness of the three areas as well as the overall business strategy of the firm. Thus, if communication toughness is very high but job toughness is only moderate, training should focus more on communication issues than on job issues. To the extent that the firm's business strategy is moving toward a truly global enterprise, the content of training programs must stress strategic issues such as global production and efficiency systems, corporate culture, international strategy, and multicultural business systems.[74]

Postarrival Training and Training for the Expatriate Family

The training of expatriates involves two additional issues: (1) postarrival training and support and (2) training and support for the expatriate family. In a sense, the term **postarrival training** is somewhat inappropriate. What it actually refers to is the initial socialization of the expatriate into the work setting and practical assistance in getting settled into a new home and environment.

Postarrival Training and Support Predeparture training may have accomplished what has been called "anticipatory adjustment," but the shock of arriving at the foreign assignment may warrant additional fine-tuning of cross-cultural or job skills.[75] As with any training program, the problem of transferring the training from the training site to the job is always present. Thus resources need to be available to help expatriates use what they learned before departure. For example, if knowing the host country's language is important in the expatriate's position, additional language training once the individual has arrived in the foreign location would be helpful. Providing a more experienced expatriate mentor or a reliable local contact is also a good idea. Large MNCs with significant numbers of expatriates in any one location also have informal networks of expatriates who help new arrivals adjust and learn the lay of the land. Support from others is especially crucial during the first few months when everything is unfamiliar and many questions need answers. This aspect of postarrival training is referred to as **culture shock,** and help should be provided in developing specific methods to cope with the wide range of new experiences and impressions the expatriate has been experiencing.[76]

Training and Support for the Spouse and Family

In many ways, the adjustment of the spouse and family to an expatriate assignment may be more difficult than that of the expatriate. After all, the expatriate arrives at the foreign assignment with an already structured environment (the job) that has many similarities to the old environment. The expatriate is still working for the same company and using many of the same work procedures and practices. The expatriate's work helps insulate him or her from the foreign world outside the office, and there is a readily available source of friends and colleagues at work. The job provides structure and consistency—a sense of familiarity and comfort.

This is not the case for the spouse and family. Many of the adjustments required to accommodate daily life in a foreign country fall more heavily on the children and spouse than on the expatriate. The children find themselves in a strange school and must cope with all the social traumas this can cause. The spouse must cope with local tradespersons and shopping in an unfamiliar language, make new friends, and may be prohibited from seeking employment. In many cases, the expatriate family is a **dual-career couple** in which the spouse has left a good job in the home country.

This increased prevalence of dual-career couples has required MNCs to broaden their view of what the expatriation process must involve. For dual-career couples that broader view must include adequate consideration and management of the **trailing spouse,** who follows the partner to the foreign location, often having to quit his or her own job in the process. In addition to reducing the likelihood that a foreign assignment will be accepted, research indicates that dual-career couples in foreign assignments tend to take longer to adjust, often suffer decreases in overall family income, have heightened dysfunctional family consequences (e.g., drastically changed roles of the spouses within the marriage), and experience greater problems in repatriating to the home country.[77] Interviews with expatriate spouses have shown that their successful adjustment to a foreign assignment depends on (1) how well they can build relationships with host-country nationals, (2) how well they adjust to local customs and the culture in general, and (3) the extent to which they develop a sense of being part of or feeling at home in the foreign country.[78] Some examples of innovative dual-career programs that have been developed by multinational companies are shown in Table 17.7.

TABLE 17.7
Innovative Dual-Career Expatriation Programs

Firms	Nature of Programs
Motorola, Monsanto, Hewlett-Packard, Royal Dutch Shell, and GE	Allowances provided for accompanying spouses for career-enhancing activities such as education, attending conferences and seminars, purchasing computers, subscribing to trade publications, and paying attorney's fees for obtaining work permits.
Royal Dutch Shell	Full-time career counselors available at HQ and unmarried partners included in its spousal services.
Shell Oil	Created "Outpost," a network of forty-four information network centers around the world that identifies employment opportunities for spouses abroad.
Deloitte & Touche	Established a Lotus Notes Web-based data system that helps expatriate spouses find work.
Eastman Chemicals	Spouses provided with a dislocation allowance while unemployed overseas, and this can last for three years.
Sara Lee and Quaker Oats	"Lifestyle assistance" policies established along with services for single-parent families on expatriate assignments, or expatriates with elder-care requirements, or those caring for the disabled.
Colgate Palmolive	Reimbursement program for spouses during the assignment as well as help in finding employment, career counseling, trips home to meet business contacts, seed money for setting up businesses, and tuition reimbursement for career- and non-career-related courses.
Ingersoll Rand	Mentoring/matching program established between former expatriate couples and new arrivals.

Source: Reprinted with permission from Ruth Thaler-Carter, "Vowing to Go Abroad," *HR Magazine*, Vol. 44, No. 12, 1999, pp. 91–96 published by the Society for Human Resource Management, Alexandria, Va. Permission conveyed through Copyright Clearance Center, Inc.

APPRAISING THE PERFORMANCE OF EXPATRIATES

Along with problems common to the development of any appraisal method, significant environmental and task factors affect how MNCs appraise expatriate performance in foreign subsidiaries.[79] The physical distance that usually separates expatriate managers and their HQ superiors makes it difficult for HQ-based personnel to adequately observe and record expatriates' behavior. Environmental conditions vary considerably across different countries. Political upheavals may reduce the capacity of expatriates to perform. The conditions in some countries may be so difficult that expatriates and third-country nationals must expend considerable effort simply adapting to daily living. The education and skill level of the local work force may also affect performance. Managers of relatively unskilled employees may spend much of their time training workers and supervising the most basic activities in their subsidiary. Objective indicators of subsidiary performance may be low, even though the manager is doing a great job given what he or she has to work with.

The nature of an expatriate's specific task affects the performance dimensions that are appropriate for use in appraisal.[80] For example, consider the criteria that would be used to assess the success of a developmental assignment. In addition to measures of typical job performance, success criteria would focus on the acquisition by the expatriate manager of skills and abilities needed by international managers and then the use of those skills in subsequent management positions. In contrast, for an expatriate in a technology transfer assignment, criteria of success would focus more on the speed and technical efficiency of the transfer as well as the transfer of skills to host-country employees who will use the technology.

For managers in managerial oversight assignments, performance in terms of both the operational performance of the subsidiary and its strategic performance level must be assessed. **Operational performance** is the performance of a subsidiary as a single business unit within the MNC. **Strategic performance** refers to how the performance of the subsidiary fits into the overall strategic objectives of the MNC. A subsidiary may perform well at an operational level yet not contribute significantly to strategic performance. For example, a subsidiary may have done well because of a large infusion of capital from the MNC parent organization. However, this capital might have contributed more to the overall strategic objectives of the MNC if it had been used in another subsidiary. A number of factors must be considered in developing operational and strategic measures of subsidiary performance; they are summarized in Table 17.8.

TABLE 17.8

Factors Affecting Operational and Strategic Appraisal

Factor	Implication
Currency conversions	A 10 percent profit of the subsidiary may be wiped out if the local currency is suddenly devalued relative to the home-country's currency. This lack of results is not under the control of the subsidiary management.
Accounting methods	Different countries have different accounting practices, which makes it difficult to compare results across subsidiaries.
Ethical and legal issues	Many MNCs assess performance using results-oriented measures. It may be important, however, to assess how the subsidiary management is achieving the results. For example, the Foreign Corrupt Practices Act makes it illegal for U.S. managers operating overseas to use bribes and payoffs to achieve business advantages.
Strategic role	A subsidiary may be opened in a market primarily to counter a competitor that has a dominant position in that market. Subsidiary performance may be limited, but the existence of the subsidiary has a strategic benefit.
Time and distance	Time and distance make it difficult for headquarters to understand the problems and situation of subsidiaries. Higher level managers may have little real opportunity to observe the performance of subsidiary managers unless considerable time, effort, and money are expended in traveling to visit subsidiary locations.
International volatility	Economic, social, and political changes may occur very rapidly in the world. These changes may directly affect subsidiary performance yet are often very difficult to monitor and predict.
HQ–subsidiary interdependence	How the subsidiary performs depends, to some extent, on how well the MNC as a whole performs.
Market maturity	Some markets are simply less well developed than others. Subsidiaries in these markets may perform much less well in terms of sales volume than subsidiaries in more established markets. This makes any purely bottom-line assessment of performance inappropriate.

Source: Based on information from Peter J. Dowling and Randall S. Schuler, *International Dimensions of Human Resource Management* (Boston: PWS-Kent, 1990), pp. 83–88.

The development of performance appraisal systems for use with expatriates requires extreme care. A variety of hard, soft, and contextual performance criteria should be used. **Hard performance criteria** are results or outcome-based, for example, sales volume or profit level. **Soft performance criteria** focus on interpersonal abilities or personality factors such as being able to develop good relations with employees or local business leaders, or behaving in a stable, calm fashion during crises. **Contextual criteria** are factors mainly outside of the expatriate's control that affect his or her performance, for example, currency fluctuations, political restrictions on the firm's operations, the traditional role of unions in the foreign locations (i.e., adversarial or cooperative), or other situational factors that might affect the expatriate's performance.[81]

In developing an effective expatriate appraisal process, active involvement by the expatriate, the home-country supervisor, and the host-country supervisor is essential. Evaluations of an expatriate's performance may differ greatly between the home and host country organizations due to differences in the criteria considered to be important, or differences in the amount of knowledge the home and host country supervisors have about the behavior of the expatriate and the circumstances under which the expatriate has had to operate. For example, an expatriate stationed in Chile almost single-handedly stopped a strike that would have disrupted operations for months. At the time, strikes were common in Chile and labor negotiations were complex, involving labor, government, and local management representatives. Although the expatriate had shown a high level of local knowledge and exemplary behavior in preventing the strike, home-country management did not see the expatriate's performance as being of a high level. Due to exchange rate fluctuations in South America, the demand for the firm's product (iron ore) had dropped 30 percent. As a result, the parent company regarded the expatriate's performance as only somewhat better than mediocre (due to lower sales), instead of recognizing the expatriate for exceptional negotiation skills (which was recognized in the local firm).[82]

In addition to the question of what the performance criteria should be, the question of who should assess the expatriate's performance is also complex. It is common for an employee's immediate superior to serve as the primary rater of that individual's performance. However, in the case of expatriate managers, the direct superior is often someone at the company's home office—several thousand miles away. Because the immediate superior may have little opportunity to observe the expatriate's performance, information must be provided by those in a position to evaluate the expatriate's activities. As with performance evaluations handled in domestic situations, many different individuals may be able to provide useful information about the performance of a particular employee.

A 2003 study of expatriate performance appraisals recommends five ways to enhance the overall success of expatriate appraisal systems: (1) clarify performance expectations (make sure expatriates clearly understand the criteria upon which their performance will be assessed), (2) consider contextual criteria (the system must take into account special circumstances within the local and international environment that will affect expatriates' ability to perform), (3) plan frequent appraisals (once-a-year appraisals are usually not enough, and expatriates should receive appraisal information more frequently throughout the year), (4) demonstrate fairness (it is important for expatriates to be able to appeal or challenge appraisals made of them), and (5) stress career development (the appraisal system must be clearly linked to the overall career development of expatriates within the multinational firm).[83] By paying attention to these issues, multinational firms can enhance the overall success of expatriate appraisal systems.

PAYING EXPATRIATES

Most expatriate compensation plans are designed to achieve four major objectives: (1) attract employees who are qualified and interested in international assignments; (2) facilitate the movement of expatriates from one subsidiary to another, from home to subsidiaries, and from subsidiaries back home; (3) provide a consistent and reasonable relationship between the pay levels of employees at headquarters, domestic affiliates, and foreign subsidiaries; and (4) be cost-effective by reducing unnecessary expenses. Specific policies vary across companies. In surveys of expatriate compensation approaches in Australia, Canada, Europe, and the United States, four basic approaches to compensation were identified:[84]

HQ-based model: Expatriates are paid according to the headquarters' compensation structure.

Modified home-country model: Expatriates are paid according to their home-country salary structures, and their living standard is protected so it is comparable to the home country or some other chosen standard.

Better of home or host model: Expatriates receive the higher of the home-country system or the host-country system.

Host-country/local-market package: Expatriates are paid according to the host-country compensation structure.

Approximately 85 percent of U.S. multinationals used the modified home-country approach, more widely known as the *balance sheet approach,* to determine expatriate pay.[85]

Balance Sheet Approach

The **balance sheet approach** ensures that an expatriate has enough money to buy exactly the same basket of goods in the host country that he or she could buy in the home country. A **standard index** is derived for this basket of goods by calculating the total price of these goods in both the home and host countries. The difference between the two prices then serves as an index for adjusting the expatriate's compensation package. The expatriate's compensation package would include a group of allowances provided to cover differences between the home and host countries in the price of the goods included in the standard index and to cover additional expenses associated with setting up home in a new location. For example, public schools in foreign locations are sometimes not suitable for the children of expatriates, and companies may provide funds to allow expatriates to send their children to private schools. Shipping and storage costs are paid by the firm, and there is usually some allowance for home visits by all members of the expatriate's family at least once a year. Table 17.9 provides an example of a balance sheet compensation plan.

In addition to these components of a balance sheet-based compensation package, a number of premiums may be paid to encourage and reward employees for going abroad and to compensate them for any hardships that may exist in the new

TABLE 17.9

Example of the Balance Sheet Approach to Expatriate Compensation

Home country: the Netherlands (Cost of living index = 118)	
Expatriate assignment is in Denmark (Cost of living index = 133)	
Currency exchange rate is 1 Euro (EUR) = 7.43 Danish kroner (DKK)	
Gross income in the Netherlands (EUR)	80,000
• Less pension payments	2,800
• Less social security payments	16,640
• Less income tax	20,000
• Less health insurance premiums	2,240
• Less housing costs	8,000
• Less car expenses	10,640
Total Expenses	60,320
Net income in Euros in the Netherlands	19,680
Net income in the Netherlands in Danish Kroners (DKK)	146,220
Suppose that the following are typical expenses of living in Denmark (in DKK):	
• Car expenses	12,000
• Housing costs	10,000
• Health insurance payments	8,500
• Pension payments	12,000
Total income needed in Denmark to maintain previous net income and pay these Danish expenses	188,720
• Add income tax on 188,720 DKK (paid by company)	79,830
• Add social security payments on 188,720 DKK (paid by company)	1,135
Gross cost to company to allow expatriate to achieve equivalent net income as in the Netherlands	269,685

Source: Housing and car expenses in Denmark were adjusted using the cost of living index differential found at Expat Forum, *International Cost of Living Indices*, http://www.expatforum.com/Resources/icol.htm (data last updated January 2004; site accessed June 22, 2004). Other expenses were adapted from an example on pp. 257–258 in Ed Logger and Rob Vinke, "Compensation and Appraisal of International Staff," in *International Human Resource Management: An Integrated Approach*, eds. Anne-Wil Harzing and Joris Van Ruysseveldt, (London: Sage, 1995), pp. 252–269; Currency rate Euro to Danish Kroner found at http://www.xe.com/ucc/ (Accessed June 22, 2004).

assignment. These premiums may be paid in several ways. In some cases, a one-time payment of 10 to 20 percent of salary is made to encourage the employee to move abroad. In other cases, a constant premium is paid each year the employee is on a foreign assignment. A final variation is a "phase-out" method; a premium is paid in decreasing amounts until it is phased out after a certain number of years. Continuous premiums encourage the expatriate to remain abroad, whereas phased-out payments tend to encourage the person to return home or move to another foreign location, where the premiums will start again.

When an employee takes an assignment in an undesirable location, a **hardship premium** is often paid, with the amount varying according to the level of hardship. Factors used in determining the level of hardship might include distance from the home country, difficulty of learning the host-country language, climate, quality of medical facilities, and risks such as terrorism or crime. Hardship premiums may be given in the form of direct cash payments or in more innovative forms such as company-paid holidays or additional annual trips home.

International Citizen's Approach

Recent alternatives to the balance sheet have been suggested, including the **international citizen's approach.**[86] In this approach to expatriate compensation, an international basket of goods is used for all expatriates regardless of country of origin. The basket of goods includes food, clothing, housing, and so forth. However, expatriates are not provided pay adjustments that would allow them to purchase exactly the same item in the host country as in the home country. Rather, they receive adjustments that would allow them to purchase a comparable local product of the same nature; for example, rather than a Mercedes (which they had in the home country), they could buy a local luxury car. There are a number of advantages to using the international citizen's (IC) approach.[87]

In terms of its cost-effectiveness, an IC approach is about 30 percent lower than a standard index based on the balance sheet approach. The IC approach may also have advantages in terms of its consistency and fairness. Traditionally, cost-of-living allowances (COLAs) were determined through a comparison of a specific pair of countries (home–host for each expatriate). Such pairing could result in situations wherein an American might get a 60 percent bonus for going to Brazil, but an Italian might get only a 20 percent bonus for going to Brazil. The international citizen's basket of goods is the same for all expatriates, and so the comparison is between the international basket and the host country for everyone. The IC approach might also aid in attracting and retaining good international managers. The traditional balance sheet approach has tended to result in favorite assignment locations due to the high COLAs given for those sites. The IC approach reduces the luxury aspects of most foreign assignments and these favorite sites in particular. This makes it easier for MNCs to move staff from one location to another. The reduction of luxury compensation packages also helps reduce repatriation problems that occur when expatriates are reluctant to return home due to reduced compensation packages in the home location relative to their foreign assignment. The IC approach also may be more in keeping with the desire of global firms to have managers take a global view of the firm's operations. Finally, this international basket is also more likely to require expatriates to interact with locals in order to purchase local substitutes for desired home items, thus increasing their cross-cultural skills and adaptability.

Issues Common to Most Compensation Packages

Taxes can be a very large cost associated with overseas assignments.[88] Because of the potential for their having a highly negative impact on expatriates, most compensation packages, regardless of the particular approach taken, must deal effectively with tax and social security issues. There are many ways in which companies provide tax protection or equalization so that employees do not incur an increased tax liability in foreign countries. A perquisite, such as the use of a company car, might not be taxable, whereas an increase in salary sufficient for buying or leasing a car would be. Companies usually deduct income taxes from the employee's pay at the rate that would be paid in the home country. The company then pays any additional tax owed because of higher tax rates in the foreign location. For U.S. expatriates, the taxation problems are particularly troublesome, for they are taxed by both the foreign country where they earn their salary and by the U.S. government. U.S. expatriates can shelter from U.S. taxes up to U.S. $80,000 of their salary earned abroad provided they live abroad 330 days during a twelve-month period. Income above this level is taxed at applicable U.S. rates.[89]

Issues related to national social security or pension systems may affect expatriates. Reciprocal agreements between some countries may allow an expatriate to remain in the home-country system, at least for a while, before having to pay the host country's social security tax. This may simplify the problem if the assignment is of a duration that falls within this grace period. However, if the expatriate is required to pay host-country social security taxes, then a variety of difficulties can arise. The pension earned in a host country may be significantly less than that in the home country (which may be important if the host-country assignment is for a substantial number of years). The host-country pension may be payable in host-country currency, which might fluctuate dramatically or decrease in value relative to the home country's currency over the years. Finally, it may be difficult for an expatriate to collect the social security benefits to which he or she is entitled from the host country. This is particularly so if many years pass between the assignment and retirement.[90]

Clearly, developing and monitoring an expatriate pay system constitute a complex task. Expatriates may work in a number of different countries, each with a pay system based on its own cultural preferences, traditions, and legal precedents. Expatriate compensation systems must be flexible enough to take into account this variability and not create unacceptable levels of perceived inequity on the part of local employees when they compare their wages and benefits with those of their expatriate colleagues.

EXPATRIATE REENTRY

One aspect of the HQ-based HR manager's job often overlooked is the task of effectively repatriating employees after their foreign assignments. All too often the story of the returning expatriate is similar to this example:

> A senior manager worked for a large multinational firm in Australia. After nearly 10 years running a major operation for the firm in southeast Asia, the manager returned home. Upon arrival, the firm had no real position for him. He said, "I was given an office, a desk, and a telephone—but nothing to do. I literally sat in my office and read the newspaper." Not surprisingly, the manager left to join a direct competitor a few months later and ended up using the knowledge and skills he had acquired in the foreign assignment against his former employer.[91]

The Problems and Impact of Reentry

Some studies have estimated that 20 to 48 percent of expatriates intend to leave their firm within a year after they return home, and many returnees suggest that returning home results in a greater "culture shock" than moving abroad. A recent survey of multinational firms found that 13 percent of expatriates left their company within one year of returning from an assignment, and an *additional* 10 percent left within two years. The loss of a "repatriated" manager is costly, with some estimates as high as $1.2 million.[92] It seems clear that multinational firms need to improve their management of returning expatriates to enhance repatriates' general cultural readjustment and readjustment to the job.

General Cultural Readjustment There is often a cultural and social loss associated with reentry into the home culture. The international assignment may have been an exciting, interesting, and fulfilling experience. The lifestyles of many expatriates may have been of a considerably higher standard (servants to take care of the cooking, cleaning, and children) abroad than it can be on return to the home culture. Children may have a difficult time readjusting to school. Marital problems may develop as each spouse faces the problems of returning to the domestic lifestyle, and there may be unexpected financial pressures as salaries revert to domestic levels and allowances disappear.

Job Readjustment Research indicates that less that 15 percent of returning expatriates receive a promotion when they get home. In fact, more than 75 percent report receiving a demotion, and 70 percent indicate that they did not know their specific job assignment when they returned.[93] No wonder so many expatriates leave their firms soon after their return.

Returning expatriates face relatively bleak job prospects for several reasons.[94] First, employees who are sent overseas have too often been mediocre performers because overseas assignments are given secondary importance. High-potential employees stay home and occupy the best jobs, thus limiting the positions available to returning expatriates. Foreign assignments often result in an "out of sight, out of mind" situation for expatriates due to the foreign assignment's physical remoteness from HQ. Job opportunities are further limited for repatriates because organizations require expatriates to return to the same division they were in when they left. Going overseas may also cause a "burnt bridges" situation between the expatriate and his or her potential future bosses. When the expatriate returns home, none of these managers want the expatriate in their division. Finally, returning expatriates often receive a hostile reception from their home-country colleagues simply due to a "fear of anything foreign."

Another significant problem arises when supposedly equivalent positions in the domestic organization have a level of responsibility and authority much lower than the expatriate had in the foreign assignment. Expatriates often have considerable autonomy and decision-making power abroad, but much of that disappears once they are back in the home office. This transition is very difficult to make.

Enhancing the Likelihood of Reentry Adjustment

A study found that 77 percent of international transferees received no career counseling from their employers on their return from abroad and only 6 percent were offered reentry training.[95] Several key components of organizational and individual strategies for effective repatriation have been suggested and are described in the following sections.

Organizational Strategies for Effective Repatriation As suggested earlier, it is advisable to discuss repatriation issues during predeparture training. Firms should assign a formal sponsor for each expatriate to prevent the "out of sight, out of mind" phenomenon—and train the sponsor in that role. The sponsor should have had personal international experience and have sufficient clout in the organization to provide support for the expatriate while overseas and after returning. The organization should create a repatriate directory so that newly repatriated employees can seek advice from "old hands" as well as their sponsor. Companies should also leverage technology. Sending periodic e-mails about changes and career opportunities, having a special Web site, and publishing quarterly newsletters can help companies remain in constant touch with expatriates.[96]

It is also suggested that expatriates be retained in the home-country HR planning system. Overseas assignments must be linked to long-term career plans. The length and flexibility of the time period during which an expatriate can return home may need to be increased. This provides a greater likelihood of having the person come into a job when he or she is needed. Divisional boundaries must also be transcended; that is, an expatriate should be able to return to any division within the firm, not just the one he or she left. One of the main reasons repatriated employees grow dissatisfied with their jobs after they return is that they feel their new skills and experience are not being put to use. Upon his return home, one expatriate manager who had been stationed in Turkey for two years said, "I think that our corporation can benefit from the experience I gained abroad, but no one asked me for any information. It is as if I never went. It is too bad the company spent all this money and effort for me for 2 years and failed to capitalize on its investment."[97]

One possible use for repatriates is as trainers for managers who are getting ready to take on an expatriate position. This provides a very direct way of making use of the skills gained by repatriates while in their own foreign assignments. It is also important for top managers to foster an appreciation in the home-country environment of the value of international assignments. This may mean sending home-country managers overseas for short-term projects. These sorts of actions, if undertaken by an organization, should significantly enhance the probability that returning expatriates will adapt well and become valuable human assets to the firm.

Although many firms do a poor job of managing repatriation, there are notable exceptions. For example, at the Monsanto head office, planning started three to six months in advance of an expatriate's return. An HR manager and the expatriate's senior line officer looked at the skills gained by the expatriate during the foreign assignment. The HR manager and senior line officer reviewed potential job openings within Monsanto for the expatriate upon his or her return. At the same time, the expatriate wrote a report that self-assessed skills and identified career goals. The expatriate, HR manager, and senior line officer met and decided which of the available jobs best fit. As a result of this process, turnover rates among repatriates dropped significantly.[98]

Individual Strategies for Effective Repatriation In addition to actions taken by the organization, the expatriate manager must play a critical role in ensuring that the repatriation process is effective. Among the actions that the expatriate should take are the following:

1. Remain in close contact with the sponsor at home.
2. In addition to the formal sponsor, develop close relationships with several informal sponsors at home to gain a broader view of the home environment.

3. Develop rapport with several managers who supervise positions considered to be attractive target repatriation positions.
4. Maintain visibility through e-mail, regular phone calls, and the like.
5. Visit HQ frequently during the overseas assignment to renew contacts.
6. Be aware of the dangers of leaving your fate in the hands of the HR system alone; actively manage your own career while on expatriate assignment.

Support and Coping In addition to these job-related strategies, other components of a good repatriation system focus more on social and emotional support to expatriates and their families. The more social support available to an expatriate on return, the easier the reentry will be. They should talk with former expatriates who have made the transition back home successfully to identify likely problems that will arise and get ideas for dealing with these problems. Unocal provides a day-long debriefing session for expatriates and their families. The returnees watch videos of other repatriates and their families discussing their experiences. These taped discussions lead to a live discussion with repatriates, which usually ends with the "old hands" sharing tips that have been helpful to them in making the adjustment back home.[99]

IHRM: ADDING VALUE IN THE GLOBAL BUSINESS ENVIRONMENT

In each chapter of this text we have provided ideas about how to assess whether HRM activities add value to the organization, either by measuring the dollar costs and benefits of those activities or by assessing other nonfinancial inputs and outcomes. To a significant extent, assessing the value added by international HRM activities can be accomplished using indices similar to those used in domestic situations. The process of determining the costs and benefits of cross-cultural training programs is essentially the same as that used to assess training for domestic managers. Measures used in assessing stakeholder perceptions of changes in domestic pay packages may be equally applicable to determining reactions to expatriate pay policies.

There are, however, some HR activities unique to IHRM that should be assessed on a "value-added" basis. Examples of these include the following:[100]

- The costs and benefits of repatriation programs
- The ability of IHRM policies to provide an appropriate mix of PCN, HCN, and TCN managers for optimal organizational efficiency and effectiveness
- The costs and subsequent benefits of localization programs (reducing expatriate and increasing local employees) in foreign subsidiaries
- The costs and benefits of customizing HR activities to suit particular national cultures and legal systems
- The costs and benefits of HR programs developed to deal with the special problems of foreign taxation and social security systems

This list is not intended to be exhaustive. It does, however, exemplify the need for international human resource managers to be vigilant in identifying the unique aspects of HR programs in an international business environment that may add to the costs and benefits of such programs.

Summary of Key Points

International human resource management is distinct from domestic human resource management because of its broader perspective, greater scope of activities, and higher level of risk. Multinational corporations may take any one of a number of different approaches to HRM, with the choice of approach depending on political issues and legal regulations; the level of managerial, educational, and technological development in the host country; technology and the nature of the product; the stage of the organization's life cycle; and differences between the home and host cultures.

HR managers located in an MNC's foreign subsidiaries have many tasks. Often they must deal with labor markets that lack the level of skill needed for technical and managerial positions in their subsidiaries. Selection, training, and appraisal systems used at the headquarters of the MNC may be inappropriate for local use. Pay systems must conform to local laws and customs while fitting into global MNC policies.

The HQ-based manager must coordinate IHRM operations in a variety of countries, each with its own local cultural, legal, and traditional influences. Headquarters' policies must be flexible enough to allow for these local variations. However, policies also must be developed to help achieve the overall strategic global objectives of the MNC.

One important IHRM activity is the management of expatriate and inpatriate managers. MNCs often select expatriates based primarily on technical competence, although research shows that many other factors are important in determining expatriate success. The ability of an expatriate's spouse and family to adapt to the new location is a significant determinant of expatriate success or failure. The expatriate's ability to establish personal relationships and understand the behavior of people from a foreign culture is a critical factor. Training, both before and after the foreign assignment begins, plays a crucial role in determining how expatriates perform. Extensive training is required when the job and culture to which the individual is being sent are very different from the person's current job and cultural background. In addition, programs to help dual-career couples deal with the special problems associated with the "trailing spouse" should be part of any effective program for preparing and managing expatriates abroad.

MNCs often underestimate the desirability of sending female employees to foreign assignments. They believe women will not be accepted by businesspersons in many cultures. However, research contradicts this view and indicates that female expatriates can perform extremely well.

Care must be taken in developing performance appraisal systems for expatriates. Physical distance, the nature of the expatriate's tasks, and a variety of environmental factors make accurate assessment of expatriate performance very difficult. The development and coordination of compensation systems for expatriates also constitute a complex task. Expatriate pay systems that attempt to balance the living costs of home and foreign assignments also must be integrated into the overall MNC compensation system. In addition to managing expatriates while they are abroad, the company also must design programs to effectively reintegrate the expatriates on their return so that it can make maximum use of the skills and experience these employees have gained in their international assignments.

In assessing the costs and benefits of international HR programs, the basic natures of the factors that contribute to the value added are the same as for domestic HR activities. However, the magnitude of these costs and potential benefits may be considerably different in the international context. In addition, some HR activities not typically found in domestic HR operations should be assessed for value added.

The Manager's Vocabulary

balance sheet approach
better of home or host model
closed hybrid model
communication toughness
contextual criteria
coordination and control assignments
cultural assimilator
cultural toughness
culture shock
developmental assignments
differentiation
dual-career couple
ethnocentric approach

expatriate managers
geocentric approach
global corporation
global manager
hard performance criteria
hardship premium
host-country/local-market package
host-country national (HCN)
HQ-based model
inpatriate
integration
international citizen's approach
international human resource management (IHRM)
job toughness
learning orientation
modified home-country model
multinational corporation (MNC)
open hybrid model
operational performance
others-oriented dimension
parent-country national (PCN)
perceptual dimension
polycentric approach
postarrival training
project assignments
regiocentric approach
reinforcement substitution
relationship development
self-oriented dimension
soft performance criteria
standard index
strategic performance
stress reduction
technical competence
technology transfer assignments
third-country national (TCN)
trailing spouse
willingness to communicate

Questions for Discussion

1. What are the differences between international and domestic human resource management?
2. What are some of the different approaches MNCs take to managing human resources? What factors determine which approach an MNC is likely to take?
3. How can culture affect HR planning, staffing, training, and performance appraisal in a subsidiary?
4. Suppose your firm was about to set up a subsidiary in Thailand. What factors would be important in determining the type of compensation system the firm set up for local Thai workers?
5. You are planning to set up a subsidiary in India and are trying to decide whether the managing director of the new facility should be a local Indian manager, an expatriate manager from your firm's home country, or a third-country manager from elsewhere in your worldwide operations. On what basis would you make the decision?
6. Several researchers have identified the factors that seem to make it easier or more difficult for expatriates to adjust to foreign assignments. What are these factors, and which of them do you think are the most important?
7. Defend or refute this statement: "It is appropriate that most MNCs send males instead of females on expatriate assignments."
8. What is an inpatriate? What are the advantages and disadvantages of using inpatriate managers in an MNC?
9. What methods of cross-cultural training would you use to prepare an American manager for a foreign assignment in China? Why?
10. What is a "trailing spouse"? Why should MNCs be concerned about trailing spouses? How have some firms attempted to deal effectively with dual-career couples and the trailing spouse issue?
11. What is the difference between hard, soft, and contextual performance criteria?
12. What are the components of an expatriate compensation system? What purposes do these components serve?
13. Suppose you were an expatriate about to complete a foreign assignment in France. What steps would you take to get ready to return to a position in your home country? What would you have done before you left for the French assignment?
14. You are the IHRM director of an MNC. Your boss has just asked you to prepare a program for repatriating a manager who has been on a foreign assignment. Describe that program.

Case 17.1
The Office Equipment Company

The Office Equipment Company (OEC) must identify a manager to help set up and run a new manufacturing facility located in India. The position will have a minimum duration of three years. OEC manufactures office equipment such as copying machines, recording machines, mail scales, and paper shredders in eight different countries. OEC's products are distributed and sold worldwide.

Currently, OEC has no manufacturing facilities in India but has been selling and servicing products in Thailand, the Philippines, and several European and Latin American countries since the early 1970s. OEC sells its products in Thailand and the Philippines through independent importers but is now convinced that it needs to expand its operations into the rapidly growing Indian economy. OEC believes it must have a local manufacturing facility in India to enhance its competitive advantage in relation to both foreign and local competitors.

OEC hopes to begin constructing a factory in India within the next six months. This factory would import product components and assemble them. The construction of the assembly plant would be supervised by a U.S. technical team, and a U.S. expatriate would be assigned to direct the production. This expatriate manager would report directly to the U.S. headquarters of OEC.

The option of filling the managing director position with someone from outside the firm is alien to OEC's policy. Otherwise, the options are fairly open. OEC uses a combination of home-country, host-country, and third-country nationals in top positions in foreign countries. It is not uncommon for managers to rotate among foreign and U.S. domestic locations. In fact, it is increasingly evident that international experience is an important factor in deciding who will be appointed to top corporate positions. The sales and service operations in Thailand and the Philippines have been controlled through OEC's Asian regional office located in Manila. A committee at the Asian regional office has quickly narrowed its choice to the following five candidates.

Tom Zimmerman Zimmerman joined the firm thirty years ago and is well versed in all the technical aspects required by the job. Zimmerman is a specialist in start-up projects and has supervised the construction of new manufacturing facilities in four countries. He has never been assigned to work abroad permanently. His assignments usually have been in European countries and for periods of less than six months. He is considered to be extremely competent in the duties he has performed during the years and will retire in about four and a half years. Neither he nor his wife speaks any language other than English; their children are grown and living with their own children in the United States. Zimmerman is currently in charge of an operation about the size that the one in India will be after the factory begins operating. However, that operation is being merged with another, so his present position will become redundant.

Brett Harrison At age forty, Brett has spent fifteen years with OEC. He is considered highly competent and capable of moving into upper level management within the next few years. He has never been based abroad but has traveled frequently to Latin America. Both he and his wife speak Spanish adequately. Their two children, ages fourteen and fifteen, are just beginning to study Spanish. His wife is a professional as well, holding a responsible marketing position with a pharmaceutical company.

Carolyn Moyer Carolyn joined OEC after getting her B.S. in engineering from Purdue University and an M.B.A. from the prestigious Bond University in Australia. At age thirty-seven she has already moved between staff and line positions of growing responsibility. For two years she was second-in-command of a manufacturing plant in Texas about the size of the new operation in India. Her performance in that post was considered excellent. Currently she works as a member of a staff production planning team. When she joined OEC, she had indicated her eventual interest in international responsibilities because of a belief that it would help her advancement. She speaks French well and is not married.

Francis Abrams Francis is currently one of the assistant managing directors in a large Argentinian operation, which produces and sells for the Argentinian market. He is a New Yorker who has worked for OEC in Argentina for five years. He holds an M.B.A. from New York University and is considered to be one of the likely candidates to head OEC's operation in Chile when the present managing director retires in four years. He is thirty-five and married with four children (ages two to seven). He speaks Spanish adequately. His wife does not work outside the home and speaks only English.

Leon Smith At thirty, Leon is assistant to the managing director at the Athens manufacturing facility, a position he assumed when he joined OEC after completing his undergraduate studies in the United States seven years ago. He is considered competent, especially in production operations, but lacking in managerial experience. He was successful in increasing OEC's production output in Athens. During his tenure in Athens, Leon traveled extensively in Pakistan and India. He went to college with a number of students from Pakistan and India. These individuals came from prominent political and business families in their countries, and Leon has visited them during his travels. He thus has the advantage of being reasonably well connected with influential families in the region. He is not married.

1. Whom should the committee choose for the assignment and why?
2. What problems might each individual encounter in the position?
3. How might OEC go about minimizing the problems that the chosen person would have in managing the Indian operations?

Source: International Business: Environments and Operations, 7th ed., by Daniels/Radeburgh, © 1995. Reprinted by permission of Pearson Education, Inc., Upper Saddle River, N.J.

Exercise 17.1
Bicycles to New Zealand—Help from the World Wide Web

You are the assistant human resource director of a medium-sized firm that has been exporting bicycles to New Zealand. The bicycle market in New Zealand has expanded significantly in the past three years, and your firm is planning to open a small manufacturing facility in Wellington. Although you have hired a New Zealand national to run your facility, the initial construction and operation of the plant will be co-managed by both the New Zealand manager and one of your home-country executives.

Your firm has not manufactured in New Zealand before, and your home-country managers have no knowledge of many common human resource issues such as occupational safety and health laws, union practices and legislation, and pay rates and systems. Although the New Zealand manager will handle most of these issues, you have been asked to develop a briefing paper for the home-country manager on health and safety, unions, and pay systems in New Zealand. This paper will not make the manager an expert but will at least give the individual a general knowledge of the HR environment in which the plant will operate. Rather than "reinventing the wheel," you decide that the best way for the manager to get acquainted with these issues is through the World Wide Web.

Your task is to search the Internet for Web sites that will provide the home country manager with useful information about occupational health and safety, unions, and pay systems in New Zealand.

Note: You may focus on another country rather than New Zealand if you wish.

Exercise 17.2

Managing Human Resources in a Foreign Country: How Well Would You Do?

You are really interested in a career in international human resource management. You want to work with a big global corporation, travel the world working with people from many different cultures—and make a nice fat salary while you are at it. You are sure you have the "right stuff." You took French in high school. You traveled for three weeks in Europe last summer. You even spent a week in Japan three years ago when your mother went there on a business trip and you tagged along. You are sure you have the right kind of "international perspective" to do well as an international HRM specialist.

Well, here is your chance to show your innate cross-cultural management skills. Answer the following eight questions dealing with meeting, motivating, training, and appraising people from several cultures.

1. In talking with Americans, you should:
   a. keep two arms' lengths away.
   b. keep half an arm's length away.
   c. keep one arm's length away.
   d. put your left hand in your pocket.
2. At the end of a discussion with a Japanese colleague, you ask him if the sales proposal you have offered is acceptable. He answers "yes, yes"—meaning that:
   a. he is confirming his acceptance of your price.
   b. he has heard and understood your offer.
   c. you should give a deeper discount.
   d. he is politely saying no.
3. You are HR director in a manufacturing facility in China. One of the expatriate managers from Australia approaches you one day and asks your advice on how to best motivate his production supervisor. The expatriate manager asks, "What should I tell Lee Chow Hou to really get him motivated to meet or exceed our production quotas?" Your advice is to tell him:
   a. "If our department increases output by 10 percent, you will get a 1 percent bonus next month."
   b. "I'm planning to reorganize the department, and I am thinking of promoting you if production increases."
   c. "If your team does not meet the production quotas we have set for next month, you are fired."
   d. "Why don't you put in some overtime to finish the production quotas for next month?"
4. Your Japanese team has just finished putting on a management development program for top executives in your firm. The CEO has told you that the program was exceptionally well done and of great value. Your team did a fantastic job. How should you acknowledge your team's achievements?
   a. Treat the group to a sushi dinner, where you give special recognition to the group leader.
   b. Don't mention it, because doing a good job is what they are supposed to do.
   c. Call the oldest person in the group aside and thank him.
   d. Thank the group at your next meeting and ask them to increase their efforts toward excellence in the future.
5. The plan for a new compensation system for your local work force in Saudi Arabia is due in two days. The CEO, an English expatriate manager, is waiting eagerly to see what the plan will look like. You are behind schedule and may not be able to meet the CEO's deadline. You approach one of your Arab colleagues and ask her to help you finish the project. You are most likely to get her to help you by saying:
   a. "In the name of God, please help me."
   b. "If you help me, I'll buy you dinner."
   c. "My friend, I need your help."
   d. "Let's try to finish this project ahead of schedule."
6. Betty Hu, in Taiwan, is new on the assembly line and is having difficulty putting the units together properly. You want to train her. You should:
   a. say, "Betty, you should pay closer attention to what you are doing!"
   b. shout across the room, "Betty, do you need help?"
   c. tell her, "Betty Hu, you are learning very fast," then show her how to put the units together.
   d. take her aside and show her how to put the units together.

7. You are conducting a performance appraisal with a Vietnamese employee. You ask, "Where would you like to be in two years?" He looks surprised. The reason may be that:
   a. he thinks you, the manager, should know that.
   b. he thinks you are suggesting he should leave the firm.
   c. he thinks you want him to change jobs in the firm.
   d. he thinks you are not giving him a good evaluation.

8. During a performance appraisal with her boss (a Singaporean manager), an American employee would probably:
   a. agree with the manager because he is the boss.
   b. point out how the company stock is rising and ask for a share in the profits.
   c. openly discuss and defend her point of view.
   d. point out her good relationship with other employees.

Source: Questions are adapted from tests of intercultural skills found in Farid Elashmawi and Philip Harris, *Multicultural Management: New Skills for Global Success* (Houston: Gulf Publishing Company, 1993), pp. 98–160.

Notes and References

1. Although this HR Challenge is a hypothetical situation, it is based somewhat on a real luxury cruiser manufacturer, The Riviera Group, located on the Gold Coast, Australia. You can get a feel for what the products of a company like Bonne Mare would look like by visiting the Web site of The Riviera Group at http://www.riviera.com.au/main.cfm?page=about_riviera. Check out their product videos to learn even more about this type of product.
2. Arvind V. Phatak, *Managing Multinational Corporations* (New York: Praeger, 1978), pp. 21–22.
3. Organization for Economic Cooperation and Development, "International Trade for OECD Countries," at: http://www.oecd.org/dataoecd/55/28/18628003.pdf (accessed May 24, 2004).
4. Rosalie L. Tung, *The New Expatriates: Managing Human Resources Abroad* (Cambridge, Mass.: Ballinger, 1988), p. 1.
5. Randall S. Schuler, Pawan S. Budhwar and Gary W. Florkowski, "International Human Resource Management: Review and Critique," *International Journal of Management Reviews,* Vol. 4 (1), pp. 41–70.
6. Randall Schuler, Peter Dowling, and Helen DeCieri, "An Integrative Framework of Strategic International Human Resource Management," *Journal of Management,* Vol. 19 (2), 1991, p. 430; Patrick V. Morgan, "International HRM: Fact or Fiction," *Personnel Administrator,* Vol. 31 (9), 1986, pp. 43–47; Peter Dowling and Denise E. Welch, "The Strategic Adaptation Process in International Human Resource Management: A Case Study," *Human Resource Planning,* Vol. 14 (1), 1991, pp. 61–69; and Jaap Paauwe and Philip Dewe, "Human Resource Management in Multinational Corporations: Theories and Models," in *International Human Resource Management: An Integrated Approach,* eds. Anne-Wil Harzing and Joris Van Ruysseveldt (London: Sage, 1995), pp. 75–98.
7. Patrick V. Morgan, "International HRM: Fact or Fiction," *Personnel Administrator,* Vol. 31 (9), 1986, pp. 43–47
8. Charlene Solomon, "Danger Below! Spot Failing Global Assignments," *Personnel Journal,* Vol. 75 (11), 1996, pp. 78–85.
9. Anonymous, "Terrorism Worries U.S. Execs More Than War," *USA Today,* Section: Money, December 24, 2002, p. 3b.
10. Anonymous, "Killers Are Looking for Targets, Gulf Britons Told," *The Times* (United Kingdom), Section: Overseas News, December 24, 2003, p. 13.
11. Insurecast, "Kidnap/Ransom and Extortion Insurance," at http://www.insurecast.com/html/kidnapransom_insurance.asp (accessed May 24, 2004).
12. J. Stewart Black and Hal Gregersen, "The Right Way to Manage Expats," *Harvard Business Review,* March–April, 1999, pp. 52–63.
13. Material in the following paragraphs is based on work by D. A. Heenan and Howard V. Perlmutter, *Multinational Organization Development* (Reading, Mass.: Addison-Wesley, 1979), pp. 18–19; Maddy Janssens, "Developing a Culturally Synergistic Approach to International Human Resource Management," *Journal of World Business,* Vol. 36 (4), 2001, pp.429–450; Ken Kamoche, "The Integra-

tion-Differentiation Puzzle: A Resource-Capability Perspective in International Human Resource Management," *The International Journal of Human Resource Management,* Vol. 7 (1), 1996, pp. 230–244; and Sully Taylor, Schon Beechler, and Nancy Napier, "Toward an Integrative Model of Strategic International Human Resource Management," *Academy of Management Review,* 21 (4), 1996, pp. 959–985.

14. Allan Bird, Sull Taylor, and Schon Beechler, "A Typology of International Human Resource Management in Japanese Multinational Corporations: Organizational Implications," *Human Resource Management,* Vol. 37 (2), 1998, pp. 152–172.

15. Ibid.

16. Zeynep Aycan, Rabindra Kanungo, Manuel Mendonca, Kaicheng Yu, Jurgen Deller, Gunter Stahl, and Anwar Kurshid, "Impact of Culture on Human Resource Management Practices: A 10-Country Comparison," *Applied Psychology: An International Review,* Vol. 49 (1), 2000, pp. 192–221; Maddy Janssens, "Developing a Culturally Synergistic Approach to International Human Resource Management," *Journal of World Business,* Vol. 36 (4), 2001, pp. 429–450; Philip Rosenzweig and Nitin Nohria, "Influence on Human Resource Management Practices in Multinational Corporations," *Journal of International Business Studies,* Vol. 25 (2), 1994, pp. 229–251; Randall Schuler, Peter Dowling, and Helen De Cieri, "An Integrative Framework of Strategic International Human Resource Management," *The International Journal of Human Resource Management,* Vol. 4 (4), 1993, pp. 717–764; and Sully Taylor, Schon Beechler, and Nancy Napier, "Toward An Integrative Model of Strategic International Human Resource Management," *Academy of Management Review,* 21 (4), 1996, pp. 959–985.

17. Philip Rosenzweig and Nitin Nohria, "Influence on Human Resource Management Practices in Multinational Corporations," *Journal of International Business Studies,* Vol. 25 (2), 1994, pp. 229–251.

18. Jochen Legewie, "Control and Co-Ordination of Japanese Subsidiaries in China: Problems of An Expatriate-Based Management System," *International Journal of Human Resource Management,* Vol. 13 (6), 2002, pp. 901–919; and Won Shul Shim, "Expatriate Management— The Differential Role of National Multinational Corporation Ownership," *The International Executive,* Vol. 38 (4), 1996, pp. 543–562.

19. Maddy Janssens, "Developing a Culturally Synergistic Approach to International Human Resource Management," *Journal of World Business,* Vol. 36 (4), 2001, pp. 429–450.

20. Ibid.

21. Aycan, Kanungo, Mendonca, Yu, Deller, Stahl, and Kurshid, "Impact of Culture on Human Resource Management Practices."

22. Janssens, "Developing a Culturally Synergistic Approach to International Human Resource Management"; and John F. Milliman and Mary Ann Von Glinow, "A Life Cycle Approach to Strategic International Human Resource Management in MNCs," in *Research in Personnel and Human Resource Management: Supplement 2,* eds. James B. Shaw, John E. Beck, Gerald R. Ferris, and Kendrith M. Rowland (Greenwich, Conn.: JAI Press, 1990), pp. 21–36.

23. N. Adler and F. Ghadar, "Globalization and Human Resource Management," in *Research in Global Strategic Management: A Canadian Perspective,* ed. A. Rugman (Greenwich, Conn.: JAI Press, 1990), pp. 179–205.

24. LautViet Legal Consultants, at http://www.luatviet.com/html/doingbizinvn_labor.html (accessed May 25, 2004).

25. Swee Noi Smith, "Implications of Chinese Learning Styles for Off-Shore Education," at http://www.vtpu.org.au/resources/publications/internetpubs/crc/sweenoismith.pdf, 1999 (accessed May 25, 2004).

26. Charlene Solomon, "Learning to Manage Host-Country Nationals," *Personnel Journal,* Vol. 74 (3), 1995, pp. 60–67.

27. John Milliman, Stephen Nason, Cherrie Zhu, and Helen De Cieri, "An Exploratory Assessment of the Purposes of Performance Appraisals in North and Central America and the Pacific Rim," *Human Resource Management,* Vol. 41 (1), 2002, pp. 87–102.

28. Mark Easterby-Smith, Danusia Malina, and Lu Yuan, "How Culture-Sensitive Is HRM? A Comparative Analysis of Practice in Chinese and UK Companies," *The International Journal of Human Resource Management,* Vol. 6 (1), 1994, pp. 32–59.

29. Tony Morden, "International Culture and Management," *Management Decision,* Vol. 33 (2), 1995, pp. 16–21.

30. P. J. Dowling, D. E. Welch, and R. S. Schuler, *International Human Resource Management: Managing People in a Multinational Context,* 3rd ed. (Cincinnati, Ohio: South-West, 1999).

31. Kevin B. Lowe, John Milliman, Helen De Cieri, and Peter J. Dowling, "International Compensation Practices: A Ten-Country Comparative Analysis," *Human Resource Management,* Vol. 41 (1), 2002, pp. 45–66.

32. Soo Min Toh and Angelo DeNisi, " Host Country Nationals Reactions to Expatriate Pay Policies: A Model and Implications," *Academy of Management Review,* Vol. 28 (4), 2003, pp. 606–621.

33. Chao Chen, Jaepil Choi and Shu-Cheng Chi, "Making Justice Sense of Local-Expatriate Compensation Disparity: Mitigation by Local References, Ideological Explanations, and Interpersonal Sensitivity in China Foreign Joint Ventures," *Academy of Management Journal,* Vol. 45 (4), 2002, pp. 807–817.

34. Kenneth Chilton, "Lincoln Electric's Incentive System: Can It Be Transferred Overseas?" *Compensation & Benefits Review,* November–December 1993, pp. 21–30; and Donald F. Hastings, "Lincoln Electric's Harsh Lessons from International Expansion," *Harvard Business Review,* Vol. 77 (3), May–June 1999, pp. 163–174.

35. Luis Gomez-Mejia and Theresa Wellbourne, "Compensation Strategies in a Global Context," *Human Resource Planning,* Vol. 14 (1), 1991, pp. 29–41.

36. Vladimir Pucik and Tania Saba, "Selecting and Developing the Global vs. the Expatriate Manager: A Review of the State-of-the-Art," *Human Resource Planning,* Vol. 21 (4), 1998, pp. 40–55; quote at p. 41.

37. Michael Harvey, Timothy Kiessling, and Milorad Novicevic, "Staffing Marketing Positions During Global Hyper-Competitiveness: A Market-Based Perspective," *International Journal of Human Resource Management,* Vol. 14 (2), 2003, pp. 223–245; and Richard Peterson, "The Use of Expatriates and Inpatriates in Central and Eastern Europe Since the Wall Came Down," *Journal of World Business,* Vol. 38 (1), 2003, pp. 55–69.

38. Anne-Wil Harzing, "Of Bears, Bumble-Bees and Spiders: The Role of Expatriates in Controlling Foreign Subsidiaries," *Journal of World Business,* Vol. 36 (4), 2001, pp. 366–379; and Reyer Swaak, "Expatriate Management: The Search for Best Practices," *Compensation & Benefits Review,* Vol. 27 (2), 1995, pp. 21–29.

39. Denise Welch and Lawrence Welch, "Linking Operation Mode Diversity and IHRM," *The International Journal of Human Resource Management,* Vol. 5 (4), 1994, pp. 911–926.

40. Clifford Hebard, "Managing Effectively in Asia," *Training & Development,* April 1996, p. 35.

41. J. Stewart Black, and Hal B. Gregersen, "The Right Way to Manage Expats," *Harvard Business Review,* March–April, 1999, pp. 52–62; and Michael Harvey, "The Selection of Managers for Foreign Assignments: A Planning Perspective," *Columbia Journal of World Business,* Vol. 31 (4), 1996, pp. 102–118.

42. Aaron W. Andreason, "Expatriate Adjustment to Foreign Assignments," *International Journal of Commerce and Management,* Vol. 13 (1), 2003, pp. 42–60.

43. GMAC Global Relocation Services, National Foreign Trade Council (NFTC) and SHRM Global Forum, *Global Relocation Trends 2003/2004 Survey Report,* at http://www.gmacglobalrelocation.com/Surveys.html (accessed May 26, 2004).

44. Rochelle Kopp, "International Human Resource Policies and Practices in Japanese, European, and United States Multinationals," *Human Resource Management,* Vol. 33 (4), 1994, pp. 581–599.

45. Pucik and Saba, "Selecting and Developing the Global vs. the Expatriate Manager."

46. Harvey, "The Selection of Managers for Foreign Assignments."

47. Rosalie Tung, "Selection and Training of Personnel for Overseas Assignments," *Columbia Journal of World Business,* Vol. 16 (1), 1981, pp. 68–78.

48. Gayle Porter and Judith W. Tansky, "Expatriate Success May Depend on a 'Learning Orientation': Considerations for Selection and Training," *Human Resource Management,* Vol. 38 (1), 1999, pp. 47–60; quote at p. 49.

49. Mark Mendenhall and Gary Oddou, "The Dimensions of Expatriate Acculturation: A Review," *Academy of Management Review,* Vol. 10 (1), 1985, pp. 39–47.

50. Reyer Swaak, "Expatriate Failures: Too Many, Too Much Cost, Too Little Planning," *Compensation & Benefits Review,* Vol. 27 (6), 1995, pp. 47–55.

51. Mercer Human Resource Consulting, "Expatriate Risk Management Survey," at http://www.mercerhr.com/pressrelease/details.jhtml/dynamic/idContent/1065135, 2002 (accessed May 27, 2004).

52. J. Stewart Black and Hal Gregersen, "The Right Way to Manage Expats," *Harvard Business Review,* March–April, 1999, pp. 52–63.

53. Kreicker's comments are found in Charlene Solomon, "Staff Selection Impacts Global Success,"

Personnel Journal, Vol. 73 (1), 1994, pp. 88–101, at p. 91.

54. Mansour Javidan and Robert House, "Cultural Acumen for the Global Manager: Lessons from Project GLOBE," *Organizational Dynamics,* Vol. 29 (4), 2001, pp. 289–305; Pucik and Saba, "Selecting and Developing the Global vs. the Expatriate Manager"; and Mary Beth Stanak, "The Need for Global Managers: A Business Necessity," *Management Decisions,* Vol. 38 (4), 2000, pp. 232–242.

55. Pucik and Saba, "Selecting and Developing the Global vs. the Expatriate Manager."

56. Bradford Neary and Don O'Grady, "The Role of Training in Developing Global Leaders: A Case Study at TRW, Inc.," *Human Resource Management,* Vol. 39 (2&3), 2000, pp. 185–193.

57. Nancy J. Adler, "Global Managers: No Longer Men Alone," *International Journal of Human Resource Management,* Vol. 13 (5), 2002, pp. 743–760; GMAC Global Relocation Services, National Foreign Trade Council (NFTC) and SHRM Global Forum, *Global Relocation Trends 2003/2004 Survey Report;* and Linda Stroh, Arup Varma, and Stacey Valy-Durbin, "Why Are Women Left at Home: Are They Unwilling to Go on International Assignments?" *Journal of World Business,* Vol. 35 (3), 2000, pp. 241–255.

58. Stroh, Varma, and Valy-Durbin, "Why Are Women Left at Home."

59. H. Fisher, *The First Sex: The Natural Talents of Women and How They Are Changing the World* (New York: Random House, 1999), p. xvii.

60. Quote from Adler, "Global Managers: No Longer Men Alone," p. 749.

61. Nancy J. Adler, "Pacific-Basin Managers: A Gaijin, Not a Woman," *Human Resource Management,* Vol. 26 (2), 1987, pp. 169–192; Stroh, Varma, and Valy-Durbin, "Why Are Women Left at Home"; and Sully Taylor and Nancy Napier, "Working in Japan: Lessons from Women Expatriates," *Sloan Management Review,* Vol. 37 (3), 1996, pp. 76–84.

62. Michael G. Harvey, Milorad M. Novicevic, and Cheri Speier, "An Innovative Global Management Staffing System: A Competency-Based Perspective," *Human Resource Management,* Vol. 39 (4), 2000, pp. 381–394; and Michael G. Harvey, Tomothy Kiessling, and Milorad M. Novicevic, "Staffing Marketing Positions during Global Hyper-Competitiveness: A Market-Based Perspecitive," *Journal of International Human Resource Management,* Vol. 14 (2), 2003, pp. 223–245.

63. Michael Harvey, Milorad Novicevic, and Cheri Speier, "Inpatriate Managers: How to Increase the Probability of Success," *Human Resource Management Review,* Vol. 9 (1), 1999, pp. 51–81; and Michael Harvey, Cheri Speier, and Milorad Novicevic, "The Role of Inpatriates in Globalization Strategy and Challenges Associated with the Inpatriation Process," *Human Resource Planning,* Vol. 22 (1), 1999, pp. 39–50.

64. J. Stewart Black, Mark Mendenhall, and Gary Oddou, "Toward a Comprehensive Model of International Adjustment: An Integration of Multiple Theoretical Perspectives," *Academy of Management Review,* Vol. 16 (2), 1991, pp. 291–317; and Jeffrey Shay and Sally Baack, "Expatriate Assignment, Adjustment, and Effectiveness: An Empirical Examination of the Big Picture," *Journal of International Business Studies,* Vol. 35 (3), 2004, pp. 216–232.

65. Kerstin Baumgarten, "Training and Development of International Staff," in *International Human Resource Management,* eds. Anne-Will Harzing and Joris Van Ruysseveldt (London: Sage, 1995) pp. 205–228; and GMAC Global Relocation Services, National Foreign Trade Council (NFTC) and SHRM Global Forum, *Global Relocation Trends 2003/2004 Survey Report.*

66. J. Stewart Black and Mark Mendenhall, "Cross-Cultural Training Effectiveness: A Review and a Theoretical Framework for Future Research," *Academy of Management Review,* Vol. 15 (1), 1990, pp. 113–36; S. P. Deshpande and C. Viswesvaran, "Is Cross-Cultural Training of Expatriate Managers Effective?: A Meta Analysis," *International Journal of Intercultural Relations,* Vol. 16, 1992, pp. 295–310; Doris M. Eschbach, Gerald E. Parker, and Philipp A. Stoeberl, "American Repatriate Employees' Retrospective Assessments of the Effects of Cross-Cultural Training on Their Adaptation to International Assignments," *International Journal of Human Resource Management,* Vol. 12 (2), 2001, pp. 270–287; and Mark A. Morris and Chet Robie, "A Meta-Analysis of the Effects of Cross-Cultural Training on Expatriate Performance and Adjustment," *International Journal of Training and Development,* Vol. 5 (2), 2001, pp. 112–125.

67. GMAC Global Relocation Services, National Foreign Trade Council (NFTC) and SHRM Global Forum, *Global Relocation Trends 2003/2004 Survey Report;* Mark E. Mendenhall and Günter K. Stahl, "Expatriate Training: Where Do We Go from Here?"

Human Resource Management, Vol. 39 (2&3), 2000, pp. 251–265; and Morris and Robie, "A Meta-Analysis of the Effects of Cross-Cultural Training on Expatriate Performance and Adjustment."

68. Rita Bennett, Anne Aston, and Tracy Colquhon, "Cross-Cultural Training: A Critical Step in Ensuring the Success of Interntional Assignments," *Human Resource Management,* Vol. 39 (2&3), 2000, pp. 239–250.

69. Ibid.

70. J. Kline Harrison, "Developing Successful Expatriate Managers: A Framework for the Structural Design and Strategic Alignment of Cross-Cultural Training Programs," *Human Resource Planning,* Vol. 17 (3), 1994, pp. 17–34; and Gary Oddou, Mark E. Mendenhall, and J. Bonner Ritchie, "Leveraging Travel as a Tool for Global Leadership Development," *Human Resource Management,* Vol. 39 (2&3), 2000, pp. 159–172.

71. J. Stewart Black, Hal Gregersen, and Mark Mendenhall, *Global Assignments: Successfully Expatriating and Repatriating International Managers* (San Francisco: Jossey-Bass, 1992); and Mendenhall and Stahl, "Expatriate Training."

72. The following discussion is based on information on contingency training models described in Peter J. Dowling and Randall S. Schuler, *International Dimensions of Human Resource Management* (Boston: PWS-Kent, 1990), pp. 83–88; J. Stewart Black and Mark Mendenhall, "A Practical But Theory-Based Framework for Selecting Cross-Cultural Training Methods," *Human Resource Management,* Vol. 28 (4), 1989, pp. 511–539; Black, Gregersen, and Mendenhall, *Global Assignments;* and Rosalie L. Tung, *The New Expatriates: Managing Human Resources Abroad* (Cambridge, Mass.: Ballinger, 1988), p. 25.

73. Black, Gregersen, and Mendenhall, *Global Assignments,* p. 100.

74. Ibid., p. 109.

75. Ibid.

76. Jan Selmer, Ingemar Torbiorn, and Corrina T. de Leon, "Sequential Cross-Cultural Training for Expatriate Business Managers: Pre-Departure and Post-Arrival," *The International Journal of Human Resource Management,* Vol. 9 (5), 1998, pp. 831–840.

77. Michael Harvey and Ronald Buckley, "The Process for Developing an International Program for Dual-Career Couples," *Human Resource Management Review,* Vol. 8 (1), 1998, pp. 99–123; and Talya Bauer and Sully Taylor, "When Managing Expatriate Adjustment, Don't Forget the Spouse," *Academy of Management Executive,* Vol. 15 (4), 2001, pp. 135–137.

78. M. A. Shaffer and D. A. Harrison, "Forgotten Partners of International Assignments: Development and Test of a Model of Spouse Adjustment," *Journal of Applied Psychology,* Vol. 86 (2), 2001, pp. 238–254.

79. David Martin and Kathryn Bartol, "Factors Influencing Expatriate Performance Appraisal System Success: An Organizational Perspective," *Journal of International Management,* Vol. 9 (2), 2003, pp. 115–132; Mark Mendenhall and Gary Oddou, *Readings and Cases in International Human Resource Management* (Cincinnati: South-Western College Publishing, 2000); and Wayne Mondy, Robert Noe, and Shane Premeaux, *Human Resource Management* (Upper Saddle River, N.J.: Prentice Hall, 1999).

80. Vesa Suutari and Marja Tahvanainen, "The Antecedents of Performance Management among Finnish Expatriates," *International Journal of Human Resource Management,* Vol. 13 (1), 2002, pp. 55–75.

81. Hal Gregersen, Julie Hite and J. Stewart Black, "Expatriate Performance Appraisal in U.S. Multinational Firms," *Journal of International Business Studies,* Vol. 27 (4), 1996, pp. 711–738.

82. Mendenhall and Oddou, *Readings and Cases in International Human Resource Management,* p. 215; described in Martin and Bartol, "Factors Influencing Expatriate Performance Appraisal System Success."

83. Martin and Bartol, "Factors Influencing Expatriate Performance Appraisal System Success."

84. Carolyn Gould, "The Impact of Headquarters Location on Expatriate Policy," *HR Magazine,* Vol. 43 (5), 1998, pp. 8–12.

85. Stephanie Overman, "In Sync," *HR Magazine,* Vol. 45 (3), 2000, pp. 86–92.

86. Kimberly Freeman and Jeffrey Kane, "An Alternative Approach to Expatriate Allowances: An 'International Citizen,'" *The International Executive,* Vol. 37 (3), 1995, pp. 245–259.

87. Ibid.

88. Sarah Gale, "Taxing Situations for Expatriates," *Workforce Management—Vendor Directory,* Vol. 82 (11), 2004, p. 33.

89. U.S. Internal Revenue Service, *Tax Guide for U.S. Citizens and Resident Aliens Abroad: Section 4.*

Foreign Earned Income and Housing: Exclusion—Deduction, Publication 54, at http://www.irs.gov/publications/p54/ch04.html#d0e2584, 2003 (accessed May 31, 2004).

90. Leigh Ann Collins Allard, "Managing Globe Trotting Expats," *Management Review,* Vol. 85 (5), 1996, pp. 38–43.

91. Personal story related to the third author of this textbook from a participant in one of his executive development programs.

92. J. Stewart Black, Hal Gregersen, and Mark Mendenhall, "Toward a Theoretical Framework of Repatriation Adjustment," *Journal of International Business Studies,* Vol. 23 (4), 1992, pp. 737–760; GMAC Global Relocation Services, National Foreign Trade Council (NFTC) and SHRM Global Forum, *Global Relocation Trends 2003/2004 Survey Report;* and Mila Lazarova and Paula Caligiuri, "Retaining Repatriates: The Role of Organizational Support Practices," *Journal of World Business,* Vol. 36 (4), 2001, pp. 389–401.

93. Patricia Borstorff, Stanley Harris, Hubert Field, and William Giles, "Who'll Go? A Review of Factors Associated with Employee Willingness to Work Overseas," *Human Resource Planning,* Vol. 20 (3), 1997, pp. 29–41.

94. Douglas Allen and Sharon Alvarez, "Empowering Expatriates and Organizations to Improve Repatriation Effectiveness," *Human Resource Planning,* Vol. 21 (4), 1998, pp. 29–39.

95. Andrea C. Poe "Welcome Back," *HR Magazine,* Vol. 45 (3), 2000, pp. 94–102.

96. Allen and Alvarez, "Empowering Expatriates and Organizations to Improve Repatriation Effectiveness"; and Lazarova and Caligiuri, "Retaining Repatriates."

97. Lazarova and Caligiuri, "Retaining Repatriates," p. 395.

98. J. Stewart Black and Hal Gregersen, "The Right Way to Manage Expats," *Harvard Business Review,* March–April, 1999, pp. 52–63.

99. Ibid.

100. Gary Florkowski and Randall Schuler, "Auditing Human Resource Management in the Global Environment," *The International Journal of Human Resource Management,* Vol. 5 (4), 1994, pp. 827–851.

Company Index

Name Index

Subject Index

FOR STUDENTS

Student Website. This site provides study aids that promote a hands-on approach to solving HR problems and making HR decisions. These resources include:

- Chapter learning objectives
- Chapter outlines
- ACE self-assessment quizzes

FOR INSTRUCTORS

Instructor's Resource Manual. For each chapter in the textbook, the resource manual includes a chapter synopsis, chapter objectives, an overview of the HR Challenge, an extensive lecture outline, suggested answers to the end-of-chapter discussion questions, teaching notes for the end-of-chapter cases and exercises, summaries of the boxed text features, additional lecture topics, sources for further reading, and suggested research paper topics. For users of previous editions, the *Instructor's Resource Manual* also includes a detailed transition guide describing changes in the text.

HMTesting. This Computerized Test Bank allows instructors to administer tests via a network system, modem or personal computer, and includes a grading function that lets them set up a new class, record grades from tests or assignments, and analyze grades and produce class and individual statistics.

Video. A video program with author-chosen segments highlights real companies and key themes in human resource management. The video has been updated to represent the current themes and concepts of the text.

PowerPoint Presentation. Has been professionally prepared for instructors who wish to use computer projection and/or customize our slides to fit their own lectures.

Instructor Website. This password-protected site features the electronic Instructor's Manual and lecture outlines that can be downloaded for customization. PowerPoint slides are available for previewing and downloading.